THE WORLD IN 1997

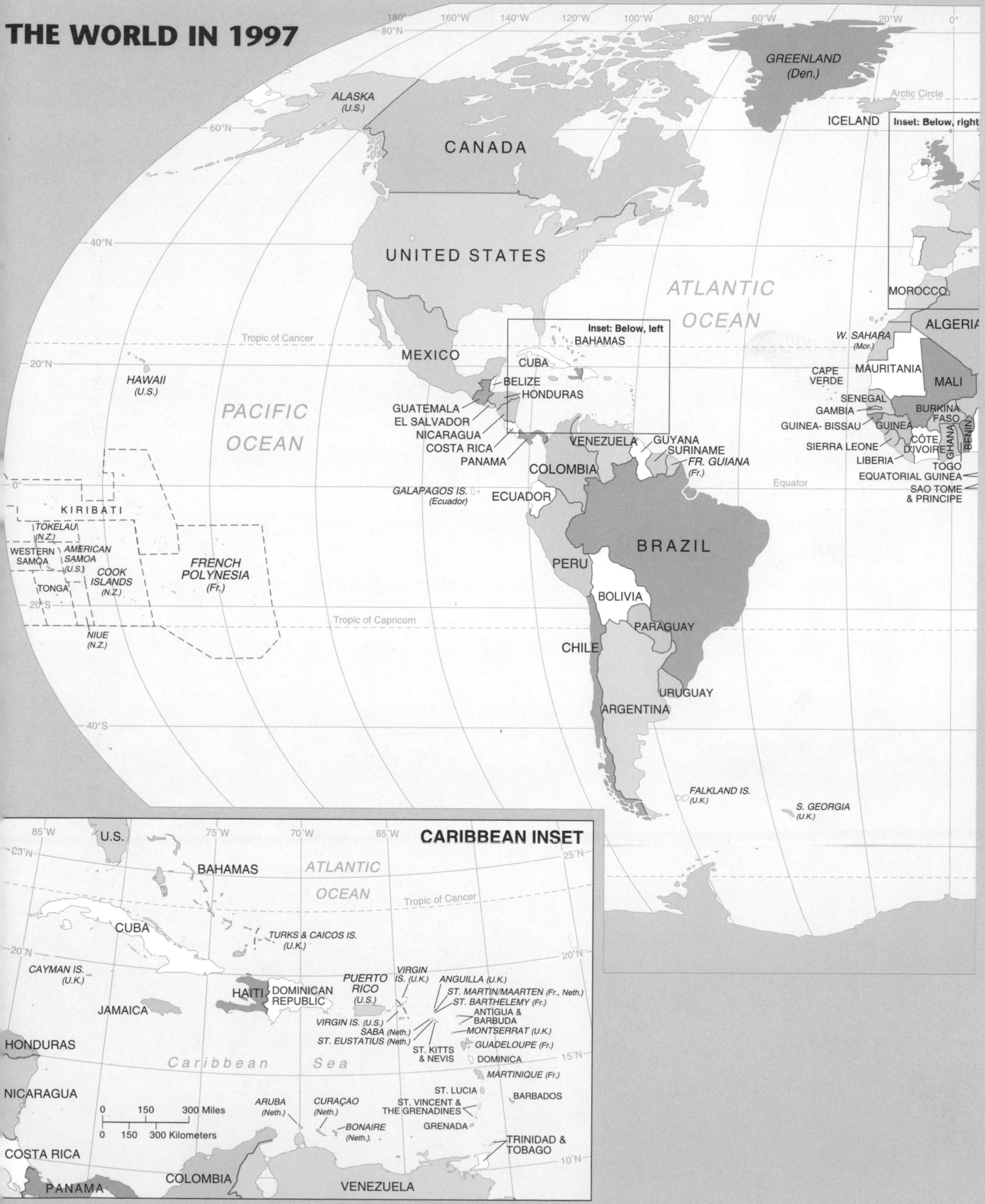
180°
160°W
140°W
120°W
100°W
80°W
60°W
20°W
0°
80°N
60°N
40°N
20°N
0°
20°S
40°S
Arctic Circle
Tropic of Cancer
Equator
Tropic of Capricorn
GREENLAND
(Den.)
ALASKA
(U.S.)
ICELAND
Inset: Below, right
CANADA
UNITED STATES
ATLANTIC
OCEAN
MOROCCO
ALGERIA
Inset: Below, left
BAHAMAS
W. SAHARA
(Mor.)
MEXICO
CUBA
MAURITANIA
HAWAII
(U.S.)
BELIZE
HONDURAS
CAPE
VERDE
MALI
PACIFIC
OCEAN
GUATEMALA
EL SALVADOR
NICARAGUA
COSTA RICA
PANAMA
SENEGAL
GAMBIA
GUINEA- BISSAU
GUINEA
SIERRA LEONE
LIBERIA
BURKINA
FASO
CÔTE
D'IVOIRE
GHANA
BENIN
TOGO
EQUATORIAL GUINEA
SAO TOME
& PRINCIPE
VENEZUELA
GUYANA
SURINAME
FR. GUIANA
(Fr.)
COLOMBIA
GALAPAGOS IS.
(Ecuador)
ECUADOR
KIRIBATI
TOKELAU
(N.Z.)
WESTERN
SAMOA
AMERICAN
SAMOA
(U.S.)
COOK
ISLANDS
(N.Z.)
TONGA
NIUE
(N.Z.)
FRENCH
POLYNESIA
(Fr.)
BRAZIL
PERU
BOLIVIA
PARAGUAY
CHILE
URUGUAY
ARGENTINA
FALKLAND IS.
(U.K.)
S. GEORGIA
(U.K.)
CARIBBEAN INSET
85°W
75°W
70°W
65°W
25°N
20°N
15°N
10°N
U.S.
BAHAMAS
ATLANTIC
OCEAN
Tropic of Cancer
CUBA
TURKS & CAICOS IS.
(U.K.)
CAYMAN IS.
(U.K.)
HAITI
DOMINICAN
REPUBLIC
PUERTO
RICO
(U.S.)
VIRGIN
IS. (U.K.)
ANGUILLA (U.K.)
ST. MARTIN/MAARTEN (Fr., Neth.)
ST. BARTHELEMY (Fr.)
ANTIGUA &
BARBUDA
JAMAICA
VIRGIN IS. (U.S.)
SABA (Neth.)
ST. EUSTATIUS (Neth.)
MONTSERRAT (U.K.)
GUADELOUPE (Fr.)
ST. KITTS
& NEVIS
DOMINICA
HONDURAS
Caribbean Sea
MARTINIQUE (Fr.)
ST. LUCIA
BARBADOS
NICARAGUA
ARUBA
(Neth.)
CURAÇAO
(Neth.)
ST. VINCENT &
THE GRENADINES
BONAIRE
(Neth.)
GRENADA
0 150 300 Miles
0 150 300 Kilometers
TRINIDAD &
TOBAGO
COSTA RICA
COLOMBIA
VENEZUELA
PANAMA

MARKETING

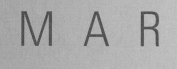

Contents

Brief Contents

To

Linda, Stacey, and Jennifer

Linda, Glenna, and Lisa

Library of Congress Cataloging-in-Publication Data

Evans, Joel R.
Marketing / Joel R. Evans, Barry Berman.—7th ed.
784 p. cm.
Includes bibliographic references and indexes.
ISBN 0-13-242611-0
1. Marketing. I. Berman, Barry. II. Title.
HF5415.E86 1997
658.8—dc20 96-8720
CIP

Acquisitions Editor: **David Borkowsky**
Production Editor: **Anne Graydon**
Managing Editor: **Valerie Lentz**
Design Director: **Patricia Wosczyk**
Senior Designer: **Ann France**
Interior Designer: **BBD&K**
Cover Designer: **Maureen Eide**
Cover Illustrator: **Theo Rudnak**
Marketing Manager: **John Chillingworth**
Buyer: **Arnold Vila**
Assistant Editor: **John Larkin**
Editorial Assistant: **Theresa Festa**
Production Coordinator: **David Cotugno**
Production House: **York Production Svcs.**

Printed in the United States of America.
10 9 8 7 6 5 4 3 2 1

ISBN 0-13-242611-0

Prentice-Hall International (UK) Limited, London
Prentice-Hall of Australia Pty. Limited, Sydney
Prentice-Hall Canada Inc., Toronto
Prentice-Hall Hispanoamericana, S.A., Mexico
Prentice-Hall of India Private Limited, New Delhi
Prentice-Hall of Japan, Inc., Tokyo
Simon & Schuster Asia Pte. Ltd., Singapore
Editora Prentice-Hall do Brasil, Ltda., Rio de Janeiro

SEVENTH EDITION

MARKETING

Joel R. Evans
Hofstra University

Barry Berman
Hofstra University

PRENTICE HALL
Upper Saddle River, NJ 07458

Preface

These are very exciting times for all of us. During recent years, we have seen the true arrival of the PC age and the World Wide Web, the steady global movement toward service- rather than production-driven economies, a growing understanding and interest in customer service and customer satisfaction, greater focus on consumer diversity in the marketplace, the emergence of free-market economies in Eastern Europe, business and government grappling with such ethical issues as the consumer's right to privacy, the impact of deregulation on society, and many similar events.

The years ahead promise to be even more intriguing—as the European Union becomes more strongly unified; North American countries make their markets further accessible to one another; opportunities in other foreign countries grow; technological advances continue; and we try to cope with slow-growth economies in various parts of the globe. As we prepare for the rest of this decade and beyond, a thorough understanding and appreciation of marketing becomes critical.

We believe that a good marketing textbook must do several things in order to provide this critical understanding: It should incorporate both traditional and contemporary aspects of marketing, including the careful consideration of environmental factors; address the roles of marketing and marketing managers; and show the relevance of marketing for those who interact with or who are affected by marketing activities (such as consumers). We also believe that presentation is important: A textbook must describe marketing concepts to readers in an interesting, comprehensive, and balanced manner. As we indicate at the beginning of Chapter 1, marketing is truly "an exciting, fast-paced, and contemporary business discipline."

Although the basic, or traditional, components of marketing (such as consumer behavior, marketing research and informations systems, and product, distribution, promotion, and price planning) form the foundation of any introductory-level marketing textbook, contemporary techniques and topics also need to be covered in depth. Among the contemporary topics that are examined in full chapter length in *Marketing* are strategic planning and marketing; societal, ethical, and consumer issues; global marketing; final consumer demographics; final consumer life-styles and decision making; organizational consumers (including manufacturers, wholesalers, retailers, government, and nonprofit institutions); goods versus services marketing (including nonprofit marketing); and integrating and analyzing the marketing plan. Environmental effects are noted throughout the book.

Marketing explains all major principles, defines key terms, integrates topics, and demonstrates how marketers make everyday and long-run decisions. Examples based on such diverse organizations as Andersen Consulting, Black & Decker, BMW, British Airways, Coca-Cola, Hyatt, Kodak, Lands' End, MCI, Metropolitan Life, Perrier, Pizza Hut, Radio Shack, Swatch, Toyota, United Parcel Service (UPS), Visa, and Wrigley appear in each chapter. The illustrations build on the conceptual material, reveal the exciting and dynamic nature of marketing, cover a wide variety of firms, and involve students in real-life applications of marketing.

The Tradition Continues

These general features have been retained from prior editions of *Marketing*:

- A lively, easy-to-read writing style.
- A balanced treatment of topics (by size of firm, goods- and service-based firms, profit-oriented and nonprofit firms, final and organizational consumers, etc.).

- Comprehensive coverage of all important marketing concepts, including twelve chapters on the marketing mix (product, distribution, promotion, and price planning).
- A full-color design throughout the book, including about 145 photos and 140 figures. These visually attractive illustrations are all keyed to the text.
- Part openers that provide integrated overviews of the chapters they contain. These openers each emphasize a different piece of the marketing "puzzle," which ties the various parts of the book together.
- Many definitions from the American Marketing Association's new 1995 *Dictionary of Marketing Terms*.
- Early coverage of societal, ethical, and consumer issues, and global marketing (Chapters 5 and 6 respectively).
- Service marketing coverage in the section on product planning (Chapter 12).
- Detailed part-ending cases.
- An appendix on careers in marketing.
- An appendix on marketing mathematics.
- An appendix on computerized exercises that accompany the text. A computer symbol in the relevant chapters keys the exercises to the concepts involved.
- A detailed glossary.
- Separate company, name, and subject indexes.

These features have also been retained from the sixth edition and are contained in each chapter:

- Chapter objectives that outline the major areas to be investigated.
- An opening vignette that introduces the material through a real-world situation.
- An introductory overview to set the tone for the chapter.
- Thought-provoking boxed extracts on key marketing topics.
- Descriptive margin notes that highlight major concepts.
- Boldface key terms that identify important definitions.
- Many flowcharts that demonstrate marketing concepts; and current figures and tables that provide up-to-date information.
- Numerous footnotes to enable the reader to do further research.
- Chapter summaries keyed to chapter objectives. These summaries are followed by a listing of key terms with text page references.
- End-of-chapter questions divided into separate "review" and "discussion" categories.
- Two cases (except Chapter 1, which has an appendix on hints for analyzing cases) that deal with real companies or situations. There are 44 end-of-chapter cases in all, involving all types of companies. One case per chapter has a video component.

New to the Seventh Edition

We are as dedicated today as in the first edition of *Marketing* to having **the** state-of-the-art introductory-level marketing text. Thus, we have listened very carefully to the feedback from our colleagues, students, and Prentice Hall sales representatives. And we have acted on this feedback. The world is evolving and so are we. In the seventh edition, there are some subtle changes—such as the revamped design of the book—and some major changes—such as the way we have revised certain chapters.

Here is a synopsis of the changes we have made for the seventh edition of *Marketing*. We hope you are pleased with them:

1. The book is considerably shorter, without any dilution of coverage.
2. There is now a vignette at the beginning of each of the eight parts in the book. This new feature is very reader friendly and linked to videos produced expressly for *Marketing*, Seventh Edition.
3. These substantive chapter changes have been made:
   a. *Chapter 1* (Marketing in Contemporary Society)—There are now two student-oriented examples of real-world marketing, one from a business perspective and one from a consumer perspective. Coverage of the marketing concept has been expanded. New coverage on customer service and relationship marketing has been added. There are illustrations of marketing decisions by professionals.
   b. *Chapter 2* (The Environment in Which Marketing Operates)—There is now coverage of both the macroenvironment and the microenvironment within which marketing operates. The discussion of corporate culture is expanded, as is the role of suppliers and distributors as an uncontrollable factor. The material on marketing myopia has also been enlarged.
   c. *Chapter 3* (Strategic Planning: A Marketing Perspective)—There is now coverage of strategic planning through a total-quality approach. The material on devising a strategic plan has also been revised.
   d. *Chapter 4* (Information for Marketing Decisions)—There is now updated material from the AMA's *Survey of Marketing Research*, enhanced coverage of data-base marketing, and discussion of ethical questions relating to marketing research.
   e. *Chapter 5* (Societal, Ethical, and Consumer Issues)—There is now a discussion of ethical theories (egoism, utilitarianism, duty-based, and virtue ethics).
   f. *Chapter 6* (Global Aspects of Marketing)—There is now enhanced coverage of global marketing, the World Trade Organization (WTO), and the North American Free Trade Agreement (NAFTA).
   g. *Chapters 7–10* (Part 3: Consumer Analysis)—All data and examples are new or have been updated.
   h. *Chapters 11–14* (Part 4: Product Planning)—All examples and data are new or have been updated. Chapter 12 now discusses the service gap. Chapter 14 includes material on color receiving trademark protection.
   i. *Chapters 15–17* (Part 5: Distribution Planning)—Chapter 15 now has expanded coverage of relationship marketing and potential causes of channel cooperation. In Chapters 16 and 17, the sections on recent trends have been completely revised.
   j. *Chapters 18–20* (Part 6: Promotion Planning)—Chapter 18 now has more coverage of integrated marketing communications.
   k. *Chapters 21–22* (Part 7: Price Planning)—All data and examples are new or have been updated.
   l. *Chapter 23* (Pulling It All Together: Integrating and Analyzing the Marketing Plan)—There is now greater emphasis on the value of integrated marketing plans and new coverage of benchmarking and customer satisfaction research, including the American Consumer Satisfaction Index (ACSI).
4. Comprehensive discussions on ethical and societal issues, global marketing, service and nonprofit marketing, industrial marketing, and marketing by small firms have been better integrated throughout the text.
5. All of the opening vignettes are new. As in the sixth edition, there is an international aspect in many of the vignettes. The vignettes deal with major events that are connected to the chapter, such as how companies are relating better to customers, the cutthroat nature of competition today, the social values of Ben & Jerry's, Avon in the Amazon, the changing demographics of women around the world, opportunities in services, counterfeit products and what to do about them, getting people to visit the mall, infomercials, a charm school for salespeople, the pricing of CDs, and management "meccas."

6. All the in-chapter boxes are new. Two of the boxes have a similar theme as the sixth edition: "Ethics in Today's Society" and "International Marketing in Action." The theme of the third box is completely new: "Technology & Marketing." The interactive nature of the boxes has been retained, as can be seen by the following sampling of box titles:.
   a. Ethics boxes: "What Practices Do YOU Believe Are Ethical?"; "How Much Should Regulations Be Regulated?"; "When Selling a PC, What Does 'New' Mean?"; and "Is It Getting Harder to Tell the TV Programs from the Ads?"
   b. International boxes: "Can Small Firms Be Successful Internationally in the Long Run?"; "Is India the Next Big Marketing Opportunity?"; "Which Soft Drink Is the Real Thing in Brazil?"; and "Will the Euro Ever Come to Pass?"
   c. Technology boxes: "Will Computers Ever Be Truly 'User-Friendly'?"; "How Can You 'Net' College Students?"; "Self-Scanning: Will Consumers Pass the Honesty Test?"; and "Will Consumers Fly Toward Ticketless Travel?"
7. "Marketing in a Changing World" is a new, very accessible in-text feature. Just before the summary in every chapter is a discussion of a key issue facing marketers. The issues range from trends that will affect America's future, to Boomers and Xers, to competing in the age of Wal-Mart, to dos and don'ts for using the Web.
8. All chapter cases are new or revised, with half having a video component. The video cases may be used in conjunction with the appropriate videos or as stand-alone cases. Among the organizations included in chapter cases are Arm & Hammer, General Electric, Incredible Universe, Intel, Levi Strauss, Mercedes, Reebok, Roadway Express, Charles Schwab, and Starbucks.
9. All the part-ending cases are new. The titles indicate their content: "Preparing for a High-Tech Future," "Should International Firms Go Multilingual?," "Digging into the Personalities of Organizational Consumers," "Using Packaged-Goods Strategies in Service Marketing," "Relationship Marketing and Distribution Networks," "The Changing Role of Salespeople," "Yield Management Pricing: Improving Capacity-Allocation Guesswork," and "Marketing Under Fire: The Heat Is On."
10. All data and examples are as current as possible.
11. The computer exercises, keyed to the text, have been revised and are included in Appendix C.
12. The end papers have an international flavor and have been updated.

The Marketing, Seventh Edition Package

A complete package accompanies *Marketing*, Seventh Edition. For students, there are a computerized exercises disk, a softcover study guide, and a softcover career guide. To aid the classroom learning experience, there are numerous videos and transparency acetates. For professors, there are separate lecture and resource manuals, testing materials, and a multimedia teaching guide. To obtain further information, please access the Prentice Hall web site at http://www.prenhall.com and then click on the FTP site button for Evans and Berman, *Marketing*, 7E.

How Marketing Is Organized

Marketing is divided into eight parts. Part 1 presents marketing in a contemporary society, describes the environment within which it operates, presents strategic planning from a marketing perspective, and discusses marketing information systems and the marketing research process. Part 2 covers the broad scope of marketing: societal, ethical, and consumer issues; and international marketing. Part 3 deals with marketing's central thrust: understanding final and organizational consumers in the diverse marketplace. It examines demographics, life-style factors, consumer decision making, target market strategies, and sales forecasting.

Part 4 encompasses product planning, the product life cycle, goods versus services marketing, new products, mature products, branding, and packaging. Part 5 deals with distribution planning, channel relations, physical distribution, wholesaling, and retailing. Part 6 examines promotion planning, the channel of communication, advertising, public relations, personal selling, and sales promotion. Part 7 covers price planning, price strategies, and applications of pricing. Part 8 integrates marketing planning—including benchmarking and customer satisfaction measurement—and looks to the future.

We are pleased that previous editions of *Marketing* were adopted at hundreds of colleges and universities nationwide and around the world. We hope the seventh edition will be satisfying to continuing adopters and meet the needs of new ones. Thanks for your support and encouragement.

Please feel free to communicate with us. We welcome comments regarding any aspect of *Marketing*, Seventh Edition, or its package: Joel R. Evans or Barry Berman, Department of Marketing and International Business, Hofstra University, Hempstead, N.Y., 11550-11725. You can also E-mail us at MKTJRE@HOFSTRA.EDU or MKTBXB@HOFSTRA.EDU. We promise to reply to any correspondence we receive.

Joel R. Evans
Barry Berman
Hofstra University

A Brief Walk Through *MARKETING*, Seventh Edition

On the following pages, you will find an overview of several distinctive features we have included in Marketing, *Seventh Edition. These features enable us to present the most complete coverage possible of the field of marketing—and to do so in an interesting, interactive, and contemporary way.*

It's all covered—from absolute product failure to yield management pricing.

In Marketing, *we introduce and integrate key marketing concepts, many of which have grown in importance in recent years. For this edition, benchmarking, customer satisfaction, ethical theories, the global firm, and integrated marketing communications are just a few of the concepts with expanded coverage.*

We look at how "success" may be defined

Benchmarking

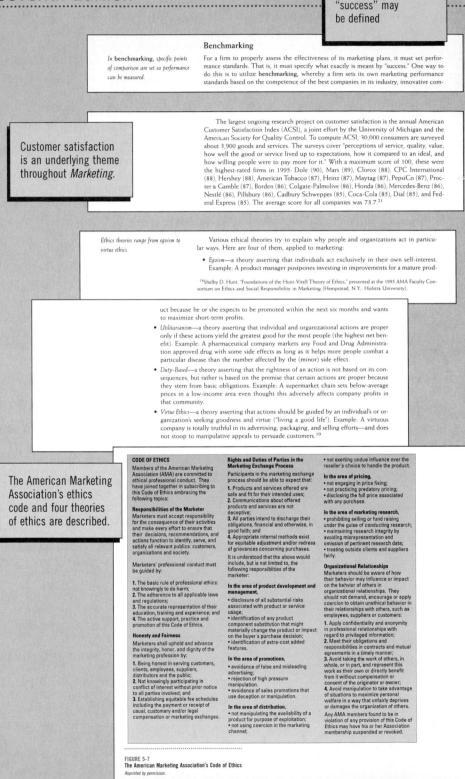

In **benchmarking,** *specific points of comparison are set so performance can be measured.*

For a firm to properly assess the effectiveness of its marketing plans, it must set performance standards. That is, it must specify what exactly is meant by "success." One way to do this is to utilize **benchmarking,** whereby a firm sets its own marketing performance standards based on the competence of the best companies in its industry, innovative com-

Customer satisfaction is an underlying theme throughout *Marketing.*

The largest ongoing research project on customer satisfaction is the annual American Customer Satisfaction Index (ACSI), a joint effort by the University of Michigan and the American Society for Quality Control. To compute ACSI, 30,000 consumers are surveyed about 3,900 goods and services. The surveys cover "perceptions of service, quality, value, how well the good or service lived up to expectations, how it compared to an ideal, and how willing people were to pay more for it." With a maximum score of 100, these were the highest-rated firms in 1995: Dole (90), Mars (89), Clorox (88), CPC International (88), Hershey (88), American Tobacco (87), Heinz (87), Maytag (87), PepsiCo (87), Procter & Gamble (87), Borden (86), Colgate-Palmolive (86), Honda (86), Mercedes-Benz (86), Nestlé (86), Pillsbury (86), Cadbury Schweppes (85), Coca-Cola (85), Dial (85), and Federal Express (85). The average score for all companies was 73.7.[21]

Ethics theories range from egoism to virtue ethics.

Various ethical theories try to explain why people and organizations act in particular ways. Here are four of them, applied to marketing:

- *Egoism*—a theory asserting that individuals act exclusively in their own self-interest. Example: A product manager postpones investing in improvements for a mature prod-

[18]Shelby D. Hunt, "Foundations of the Hunt-Vitell Theory of Ethics," presented at the 1995 AMA Faculty Consortium on Ethics and Social Responsibility in Marketing (Hempstead, N.Y.: Hofstra University).

uct because he or she expects to be promoted within the next six months and wants to maximize short-term profits.

- *Utilitarianism*—a theory asserting that individual and organizational actions are proper only if these actions yield the greatest good for the most people (the highest net benefit). Example: A pharmaceutical company markets any Food and Drug Administration approved drug with some side effects as long as it helps more people combat a particular disease than the number affected by the (minor) side effect.
- *Duty-Based*—a theory asserting that the rightness of an action is not based on its consequences, but rather is based on the premise that certain actions are proper because they stem from basic obligations. Example: A supermarket chain sets below-average prices in a low-income area even thought this adversely affects company profits in that community.
- *Virtue Ethics*—a theory asserting that actions should be guided by an individual's or organization's seeking goodness and virtue ("living a good life"). Example: A virtuous company is totally truthful in its advertising, packaging, and selling efforts—and does not stoop to manipulative appeals to persuade customers.[19]

The American Marketing Association's ethics code and four theories of ethics are described.

CODE OF ETHICS

Members of the American Marketing Association (AMA) are committed to ethical professional conduct. They have joined together in subscribing to this Code of Ethics embracing the following topics:

Responsibilities of the Marketer

Marketers must accept responsibility for the consequence of their activities and make every effort to ensure that their decisions, recommendations, and actions function to identify, serve, and satisfy all relevant publics: customers, organizations and society.

Marketers' professional conduct must be guided by:

1. The basic rule of professional ethics: not knowingly to do harm;
2. The adherence to all applicable laws and regulations;
3. The accurate representation of their education, training and experience; and
4. The active support, practice and promotion of this Code of Ethics.

Honesty and Fairness

Marketers shall uphold and advance the integrity, honor, and dignity of the marketing profession by:

1. Being honest in serving customers, clients, employees, suppliers, distributors and the public;
2. Not knowingly participating in conflict of interest without prior notice to all parties involved; and
3. Establishing equitable fee schedules including the payment or receipt of usual, customary and/or legal compensation or marketing exchanges.

Rights and Duties of Parties in the Marketing Exchange Process

Participants in the marketing exchange process should be able to expect that:

1. Products and services offered are safe and fit for their intended uses;
2. Communications about offered products and services are not deceptive;
3. All parties intend to discharge their obligations, financial and otherwise, in good faith; and
4. Appropriate internal methods exist for equitable adjustment and/or redress of grievances concerning purchases.

It is understood that the above would include, but is not limited to, the following responsiblities of the marketer:

In the area of product development and management,

- disclosure of all substantial risks associated with product or service usage;
- identification of any product component substitution that might materially change the product or impact on the buyer's purchase decision;
- identification of extra-cost added features.

In the area of promotions,

- avoidance of false and misleading advertising;
- rejection of high pressure manipulation.
- avoidance of sales promotions that use deception or manipulation.

In the area of distribution,

- not manipulating the availability of a product for purpose of exploitation;
- not using coercion in the marketing channel;
- not exerting undue influence over the reseller's choice to handle the product.

In the area of pricing,

- not engaging in price fixing;
- not practicing predatory pricing;
- disclosing the full price associated with any purchase.

In the area of marketing research,

- prohibiting selling or fund raising under the guise of conducting research;
- maintaining research integrity by avoiding misrepresentation and omission of pertinent research data;
- treating outside clients and suppliers fairly.

Organizational Relationships

Marketers should be aware of how their behavior may influence or impact on the behvior of others in organizational relationships. They should not demand, encourage or apply coercion to obtain unethical behavior in their relationships with others, such as employees, suppliers or customers:

1. Apply confidentiality and anonymity in professional relationships with regard to privileged information;
2. Meet their obligations and responsibilities in contracts and mutual agreements in a timely manner;
3. Avoid taking the work of others, in whole, or in part, and represent this work as their own or directly benefit from it without compensation or consent of the originator or owner;
4. Avoid manipulation to take advantage of situations to maximize personal welfare in a way that unfairly deprives or damages the organization of others.

Any AMA members found to be in violation of any provision of this Code of Ethics may have his or her Association membership suspended or revoked.

FIGURE 5-7
The American Marketing Association's Code of Ethics
Reprinted by permission.

- A **multinational firm** is a worldwide player. Although corporate headquarters are in the home nation, the domestic market often accounts for less than 50 percent of sales and profits—and the firm operates in dozens of nations or more. The business scope and search for opportunities are quite broad with regard to geography. Many leading U.S. players (like Boeing, Citicorp, and McDonald's) tend to fall into this category; they market items around the world, but have an American business culture.
- A **global firm** is also a worldwide player. Yet, because its domestic sales are low, it places even more reliance on foreign transactions. It has the greatest geographic business scope. Such firms have been more apt to emerge in smaller nations, where the firms have historically needed foreign markets to survive (in contrast to U.S. firms). The quintessential global firm is Switzerland's Nestlé, which for decades has derived less than 2 per cent of total sales from its home market, makes products in hundreds of plants all over the world, and has employees from 50 nations at headquarters. As illustrated in Figure 6-1, its brands are among the world's most popular. In 1996, Coca-Cola announced that it was converting from a U.S.-based multinational to a global company.[3] See Figure 6-2 on page 148.

The range of international marketing options from domestic firm to global firm are discussed and illustrated.

FIGURE 6-2
Coca-Cola: From U.S. Multinational to Global Firm
Due to the enormous size of its home market in the United States, until recently Coca-Cola was a U.S.-based multinational. Then, in 1996, Coca-Cola decided to eliminate the concepts of "domestic" and "international." Its U.S. business was downgraded to be just one of six global units. Why the change? U.S. sales are now only one-fifth of total company revenues.
Reprinted by permission.

When a well-coordinated promotion mix is involved, a firm is undertaking **integrated marketing communications (IMC)**. As defined by the American Association of Advertising Agencies, IMC "recognizes the value of a comprehensive plan that evaluates the strategic roles of a variety of communication disciplines—advertising, public relations, personal selling, and sales promotion—and combines them to provide clarity, consistency, and maximum communication impact."[12] For example, Frito-Lay has a sales force that visits every store stocking its products, advertises in papers and magazines and on TV, and distributes cents-off coupons. Hitachi has a large technical sales force, advertises in business and trade publications, and sends representatives to trade shows.

Each type of promotion has a distinct function and complements the other types. Ads appeal to big audiences and create awareness; without them, selling is more difficult, time consuming, and costly. The publicity aspect of public relations provides credible information to a wide audience, but content and timing cannot be controlled. Selling has one-to-one contact, flexibility, and the ability to close sales; without it, the interest caused by ads might be wasted. Sales promotion spurs short-run sales and supplements ads and selling.

The selection of a promotion mix depends on company attributes, the product life cycle, media access, and channel members. A small firm is limited in the kinds of ads it can afford or use efficiently; it may have to stress personal selling and a few sales promotions. A large firm covering a sizable geographic area could combine many ads, personal selling, and frequent sales promotions. As products move through the life cycle, promotion emphasis goes from information to persuasion to reinforcement; different media and messages are needed at each stage. Some media may not be accessible (no cigarette ads on TV) or require lengthy lead time (Yellow Pages). Channel members may demand special promotions, sales support, and/or cooperative advertising allowances.

[12]Adapted by the authors from Janet Smith, "Integrated Marketing," *Marketing Tools* (November–December 1995), p. 64.

The role of integrated marketing communications is amplified.

Because we believe marketing's vital role should be shown in varied situations, we have worked especially hard to present a balance of examples on domestic and international marketing, large and small firms, goods and services, and final consumers and organizational consumers.

Omaha Steaks International sells gourmet foods such as seafood, pasta, veal, steak, and desserts through the mail and at retail stores. In 1994, it was honored with the Direct Marketing Association's Award for Customer Service Excellence. The firm's customer service representatives receive extensive and continuous training, including 80 classroom hours and on-the-job training. They sample every menu item, get weekly evaluations, and participate in monthly retraining programs. AMP, an electrical connector supplier, requires

Nonstop to London.
Showers expected upon arrival.
British Airways' new arrival facilities at London's Heathrow and Gatwick airports are making quite a splash. Now, ClubWorld℠ and First Class passengers can enjoy a hot shower and breakfast or even catch up on business in our private lounge. You'll be off to a flying start. *It's the way we make you feel* that makes us the world's favourite airline.
BRITISH AIRWAYS
The world's favourite airline

FIGURE 1-7
Customer Service and British Airways
Reprinted by permission.

This highlights our extensive coverage of domestic and international marketing.

Small firms, as well as large ones, are involved with marketing and strategic planning.

American Images: Great Planning by a Small Aerial-Photography Firm[31]

Although a small company, American Images has a detailed strategic plan.

In 1980, Harlan Accola and his brother Conrad started an aerial-photography business, Skypix. They took aerial shots of farms and homes, and then sold them. The brothers did well for a while, but eventually ran into trouble—and nearly went out of business. As Harlan Accola said, "I didn't know anything about business. And worse. I didn't think it was important." At that time, Skypix's plan was simple: "Always have enough cash to pay next week's bills."

Chapter 12, "Goods Versus Services Planning," integrates services marketing into product planning.

Overview

When devising and enacting product plans, a firm must fully comprehend the distinctions between goods and services—beyond the brief coverage in Chapter 11. Although the planning process is the same for goods and services, their differences need to be reflected by the decisions made in the process.

Both final and organizational consumers are important to marketers.

In Chapters 7 to 10, the concepts needed to understand consumers in the United States and other nations worldwide, select target markets, and relate marketing strategy to consumer behavior are detailed. Chapters 7 and 8 examine final consumer demographics, life-styles, and decision making. **Final consumers** buy goods and services for personal, family, or household use. Chapter 9 centers on the characteristics and behavior of **organizational consumers**, those buying goods and services for further production, usage in operating the organization, or resale to other consumers. Chapter 10 explains how to devise a target market strategy and use sales forecasts.

Final consumers *buy for personal, family, or household use,* **organizational consumers** *buy for production, operations, or resale.*

Ethics IN TODAY'S SOCIETY

For Marketing, Seventh Edition, we have all-new interactive boxes in each chapter. Each one presents a real-life situation and asks readers to be decision makers and state positions/suggestions.

The ethics boxes deal with current dilemmas facing marketing managers.

International Marketing in *Action*

The international boxes highlight marketing activities around the world.

TECHNOLOGY & MARKETING

Because of the growing importance and use of technology by marketers, a full range of technology issues are addressed in these boxes.

Please note: Besides these interactive boxes, ethical, international, and technological concepts are integrated into and covered throughout the text.

CASE 2

The Marketing Research Association: Hearing from Survey Respondents[†]

Consumer survey refusal rates have been rather high in recent years. According to Walker Industry Image studies, one in three respondents refuse to participate in a survey or poll. This leads to higher survey costs, questions about the representativeness of the data obtained, and larger sampling errors.

As a way to improve consumer participation rates in marketing research surveys, the Marketing Research Association (MRA)—the leading U.S. trade association for market researchers—formed a Consumer Advocacy Council (CAC) in 1992. The CAC's role is to raise respondent participation by (1) educating consumers about the goals of marketing research and (2) better informing market researchers about consumer perceptions of the industry.

By conducting small-group research sessions, the CAC learned a lot about why people refuse to participate in surveys. It then proposed three tactics to help increase survey participation rates:

- Educate consumers about the benefits of marketing research.
- Educate market researchers about the impact of research on consumers.
- Reduce the negative accusations in the industry (such as data collectors saying research firms have poorly designed questionnaires and research firms blaming interviewers for faulty data collection).

The CAC decided to first concentrate its efforts on educating market researchers about the impact that research practices have on consumers. CAC devised special programs that were pre-tested in MRA's Great Lakes and Florida chapters. For these programs, interviewers and their supervisors were divided into small groups, each asked to suggest solutions to some common consumer problems. These were among the issues discussed:

- Questionnaire design: What happens when a survey is hard to understand by respondents? What are the proper channels of communication for a buyer of research to contact a data collection firm?
- Interviewer training: What should be the minimum amount of training for interviewers? What skills should be taught? How can performance on specific skills be evaluated?
- Just do the job, or do it right? Should field personnel have input in design of a questionnaire? When are respondent incentives appropriate?
- Responsibilities of the research industry: Should the industry develop a system to detect and monitor respondent abuse? Who would be responsible for developing and implementing such a system?

CAC also looked at the interviewing process. It then produced consumer education brochures, a handbook entitled *Guidelines and Practices to Promote Respondent Cooperation*, a *We Can Make a Difference* video, and other materials.

In analyzing the data-collection process, CAC concluded that the industry's basic methods of collecting data were unchanged from 20 years ago. It also believed that technology development in the industry benefitted the researchers, but not necessarily the respondents. CAC's qualitative research also found that researchers must re-engineer their interviewing process to better meet the expectations a[...] today's respondents. Among the concerns me[...] ple were their being called at inconvenient [...] quent use of incentives, the abundance of le[...] naires, and interviewers not indicating the r[...] in the data-collection process at the beginn[...] view.

CAC strongly recommends that intervi[...] spondents more as individuals, that they b[...] move interviews along at a good pace, and t[...] make better use of computers. It is also imp[...] confidentiality of respondent comments be [...] at the beginning of and during the interview[...]

QUESTIONS

1. Comment on the problems caused by low respondent participation in market research surveys.
2. What are the potential biases of using interviewers to collect survey information? Of having respondents fill out their own questionnaire forms?
3. Develop a program for educating interviewers about consumer perceptions of the interviewing process.
4. Discuss how *you* would try to further increase survey response rates.

VIDEO QUESTIONS ON THE MARKETING RESEARCH ASSOCIATION

1. Evaluate the research design for the Market Research Association study.
2. List and discuss consumer likes and dislikes concerning the marketing research process.

[†]The data in this case are drawn from Betsy Peterson, "Insight into Consumer Cooperation," *Marketing Research*, Vol. 6 (Fall 1994), pp. 52–53.

104

Each chapter (beginning with Chapter 2) ends with two cases, one of which has an accompanying video and separate video questions—as shown here.

Marketing, Seventh Edition, has 44 chapter-ending cases and 8 longer, part-ending cases. These cases cover a wide range of companies and scenarios. All are new to this edition and extremely current. One case in every chapter has an optional video component.

PART 7 CASE

Yield Management Pricing: Improving Capacity-Allocation Guesswork

End-of-part cases integrate the material discussed in the group of chapters immediately preceding each case.

Introduction

Yield management (YM) is an integrated demand-management, capacity-planning process that focuses on two aspects of service quality: order-change responsiveness and delivery reliability. Unlike service design, advertised image, or positioning, these two traits of service quality are process-based and difficult for competitors to imitate. Thus, a corporate strategy expressed using yield management can provide a source of sustainable price premiums.

For the individual service firm, segmenting markets and setting pricing differentials are complicated by the perishability of service capacity, the inability to change prices easily and quickly in response to unexpected demand shifts, and the need to make capacity choices before demand is known.

A hospital or an airline must acquire and schedule capacity before demand for elective surgeries or an 11 A.M. flight. Careful scheduling and creative adjustment of a marketing mix can affect the order flow of these businesses, but they can never remove entirely the impact of random demand. And service flows are nonstorable—no revenue can be realized tomorrow from empty airline seats or unused surgical rooms.

Unsold seats and unused operating tables—not to mention the revenue lost from denying service to high-margin, repeat-purchase customers when capacity is sold out—are serious problems critical to the success of many service firms. American Airlines recently calculated the added revenues it has gained from attending to these problems (mostly by employing yield management) to be about $470 million per year. by hotels, auto rental firms, printing and publishing firms, hospital outpatient services, and broadcast advertising. Future generations of applications can be expected to involve services such as accounting partnerships, entertainment facilities such as Broadway theaters and movies, and flexible manufacturing systems.

Yield Management in Use

A simplified airline-industry example shows how fares are set and seating capacity is allocated for two classes of airline passengers: business and leisure. We make these assumptions:

- The airline has a single 170-seat plane flying between Atlanta and Chicago.
- It has two passenger classes, business and leisure.
- Expected demand (the initial "demand function") for each class is based on past experience and is reasonably stable.
- Past experience tells how reservations come in over time for both passenger classes, so actual reservations can be mapped against expected ones for this flight during the months and weeks prior to departure.
- Fares for the two classes are based on their expected demand functions and expected marginal operating costs, are set months ahead of the flight date, and will not change.

To minimize complexity, we have held fares constant—but in actuality, they will often be adjusted to reflect the changes in market conditions.

Our goal is to reinforce the principles in Marketing, Seventh Edition, in a useful and energetic way. So, we've got all the in-text pedagogy you could want: part vignettes, part openers, chapter objectives, chapter vignettes, highlighted key terms and margin notes, photos and line art, bottom-of-page footnotes, the integrated Changing World of Marketing features, summaries linked to chapter objectives, review and discussion questions—appendixes, and more!

Part-opening vignettes now engage students in marketing in a very reader-friendly manner. These vignettes cover four diverse firms and are linked to the On Location video program, prepared exclusively for *Marketing*, Seventh Edition.

Part 1 Video Vignette

FD&B Inc.

ON LOCATION!

As we will show throughout *Marketing*, organizations involved with "marketing" practices come in all sizes and orientations. And those who work in marketing have a variety of backgrounds—sometimes very far removed from formal business education.

To demonstrate the diversity of organizations engaged in marketing, consider that FD&B Inc. (founded in 1991) is an integrated marketing communications agency with $24 million in annual billings and 20 employees. In contrast, FD&B's client MasterCard International (founded as the Interbank Card Association in 1966) serves thousands of member banks, which account for several hundred billion dollars in yearly MasterCard volume in the United States alone. There are millions of MasterCard locations in well over 200 countries and territories around the world.

Organizations involved with "marketing" practices come in all sizes and orientations. And those who work in marketing have a variety of backgrounds.

Besides MasterCard International, FD&B's client roster has included Citicorp Financial Services, Eight O'Clock Coffee, the Hain Food Group, Olsten Corporation (temporary employment), United States Luggage, and Watson Pharmaceuticals. The agency has also done pro bono (no fee) work for the Boys & Girls Club of Oyster Bay and the Make a Wish Foundation.

Why do clients hire FD&B when there are literally thousands of agencies from which to choose? In large part, they do so because of FD&B's personal attention—a willingness to go the extra mile—and tailored approach to each client's needs, as well as the expertise of FD&B personnel. According to FD&B's mission statement, "We do not choose to be a common Advertising Agency. From the initial defining of [client] goals and objectives, through the proper positioning of the goods or services, to the identification of challenges and opportunities and the development of creative and media strategies, every step is planned and based on in-depth research and proven strategic marketing principles."

FD&B is headed by four partners, with wide-ranging backgrounds: Phil Franznick is a 25-year veteran of the advertising industry and the chief executive officer of the company. He has a bachelor's degree (BFA) in Fine Arts from Ohio University. Kevin Franznick oversees the day-to-day business and finances of the company. He has a bachelor's degree (BFA) in Theater from Ohio University. Ellen Deutsch has directed campaigns and worked on the marketing strategies for a number of accounts. She has a bachelor's degree (BBA) and a master's degree (MBA) in Marketing, both from Hofstra University. Todd Brenard is most involved with client services (customer relations). He has a bachelor's degree (BS) in Communications and Psychology from the University of Wisconsin, Stevens Point.

In the part-opening vignettes for *Marketing*, FD&B and three of its clients (Hain, MasterCard, and Watson) will be featured. Enjoy these vignettes and the videos that accompany them.

2

In each chapter, there is a NEW feature entitled "Marketing in a Changing World." This feature demonstrates the kinds of marketing issues that occur in today's tough business environment.

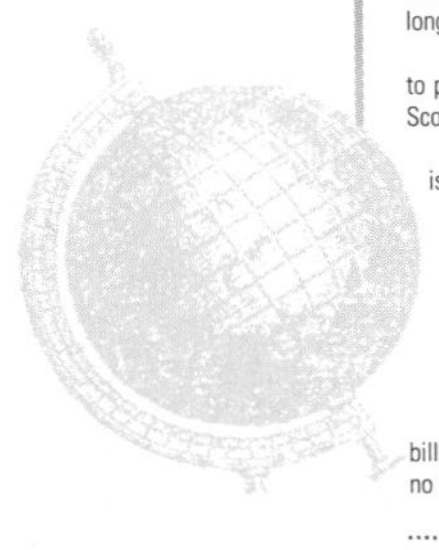

MARKETING IN A CHANGING WORLD

Dealing with Slow-Paying Customers[9]

One of the problems facing many firms today is that more customers seem to be paying late (or sometimes not paying at all). When customers buy goods and services through their revolving credit accounts, there is usually a simple remedy: interest charges accrue. And since some revolving credit costs more than 20 per cent in annual interest rates, late payments can be quite profitable—as long as customers do not default.

A company may encounter real trouble when a customer requests a service and then decides to pay late or not at all. What do you do then? You cannot repossess the service. Rural Metro, a Scottsdale, Arizona-based ambulance service, is asking itself that very question.

Rural Metro operates a fleet of 650 ambulances in 80 communities covering ten states. This is what it has encountered:

> Ambulance service is a tough product to make money on. True, demand is—as economists say—price inelastic: Anyone who needs the service is unlikely to haggle over its price. On the other hand, costs in the business are high and fixed: An ambulance costs $70,000 to buy and around $450,000 a year to operate. And revenues are variable: Once a customer has used the service, there's not much a provider can do to make the person pay the bill. Ambulance companies' average bill for emergency transports runs from $250 to $550 a patient, but the companies collect only 60 to 70 per cent of their bills.

As a result, Rural Metro is forced to use "account collectors" to call customers with past-due bills, send frequent computerized bills and rebills, and engage in other aggressive tactics—through no fault of its own.

[9] The material in this section is based on Nina Munk, "Making the Customer Pay," *Forbes* (February 13, 1995), pp. 74–75.

About the Corporate Videos that Accompany MARKETING, Seventh Edition

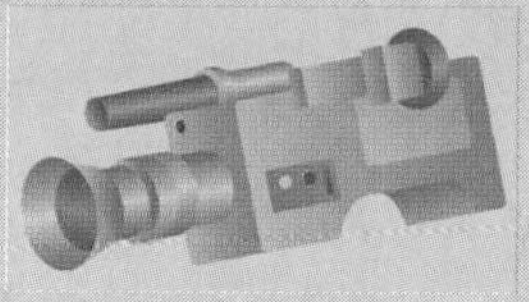

Marketing has an extensive video supplement available for adopters. It consists of four components: text part-opening video vignettes, text video cases, videos on special topics, and teaching videos. In total, there are nearly 70 different video segments, equal to about ten hours of viewing time.

1. Every part in the book has an opening vignette that is accompanied by a video clip showing the exciting and dynamic nature of real-world marketing. These videos, produced especially for *Marketing*, Seventh Edition, feature four highly diverse companies (both in size and orientation): FD&B Inc., a full-service advertising agency; Hain Food Group, a food manufacturer; MasterCard International, a consumer-payment services firm; and Watson Pharmaceuticals, a pharmaceutical manufacturer.

2. Each chapter (except Chapter 1) has two end-of-chapter cases, one of which is a video case. A career-oriented video clip, corresponding to Appendix A, is also provided. These are the firms represented in the chapter video cases (and Appendix A), with their chapter number, topic, and text page noted:

3. Besides the video cases, a number of video clips are available so that the professor can augment his or her coverage of these special marketing topics: societal, ethical, and consumer issues; global marketing; industrial marketing; and service marketing. Among the organizations featured in the special topics video collection are the Advertising Council, Banc One, H&R Block, Cross Pointe Paper, H.J. Heinz, Mobil, Safety-Kleen, Sunkist, and Warner Lambert.

4. There are also eight teaching videos, each geared to a part in *Marketing*. These teaching videos are broader, more conceptual, and cover more topics than the other videos. Thus, full class lectures can be built around these videos. The video titles are "An Introduction to Marketing," "European Union," "Psychology of Advertising" (a consumer-behavior video), "Branding, Packaging, and Labeling," "Channels of Distribution," "Print Media," "Markup," and "Relationship Marketing."

Please note: Both the part-opening video vignettes and the chapter-ending video cases are indicated in the text by video camera symbols.

CHAPTER	COMPANY	TOPIC	PAGE REFERENCE
2	Louisiana Pacific	The marketing environment	48
3	Schering-Plough	Marketing strategy	76
4	Marketing Research Association	Hearing from survey respondents	104
5	Herman Miller	Concern for the environment	142
6	Roadway Express	International distribution	174
7	Wellcome	Demographics in Taiwan	203
8	Greeting cards	Shopping behavior in supermarkets	231
9	Parker Hannifin	Relationship marketing	258
10	Gannett	Marketing newspapers to women	291
11	Raychem	The generic product concept	323
12	Olsten	Differential advantages for a service business	353
13	Allegheny Ludlum	Managing mature products	380
14	Roadway Package Systems	Using package bar codes	406
15	CSX	Intermodal shipping	443
16	Nash Finch	Food wholesaling	464
17	Incredible Universe	Power retailing	491
18	Advertising Council	Public service communications	523
19	Acuvue	Developing an advertising campaign	551
20	Rhodes Furniture	Personal selling	577
21	Charles Schwab	Assessing a pricing strategy	607
22	Supermarkets	Pricing of beef	636
23	General Electric	Integrated marketing strategy	676
App. A	Canadian Imperial Bank	Pursuing a career in marketing	A-1

About the Computer Supplement that Accompanies MARKETING, Seventh Edition

As noted in the preface, *Marketing*, Seventh Edition, has a computer supplement available for students: *Computer-Based Marketing Exercises*. It is microcomputer-based and geared to IBM PCs and compatibles. It is also extremely user-friendly, does not require prior computer experience, operates in the Windows environment, and is not dependent on knowledge of such software as Lotus 1-2-3. All directions are contained on computer screens and are self-prompting.

Computer-Based Marketing Exercises is designed to apply and reinforce specific individual concepts in *Marketing*, Seventh Edition, in an interactive manner. The exercises are explained in Appendix C at the end of this text; throughout *Marketing*, a computer symbol is used to signify which concepts are related to the exercises. An accompanying master computer diskette (which may be ordered by the instructor) can be used to reproduce student exercise disks. The 18 exercises are as realistic as possible; relate to important marketing concepts; allow students to manipulate marketing factors and see their impact on costs, sales, and profits; are relatively independent of one another; and encourage students to improve computer skills.

The exercises may be handed in as class assignments or used for student self-review/self-learning. Page references to the relevant concepts in *Marketing*, Seventh Edition, are provided for each exercise, both on the computer diskette and in Appendix C at the end of this text. Students get to experiment with cross-tabulation tables, bar charts, spreadsheets, graphic scales, data bases, positioning maps, and other learning tools. Graphics quality is high. Here are the exercises:

1. Marketing Orientation.
2. Boston Consulting Group Matrix
3. Questionnaire Analysis
4. Ethics in Action
5. Standardization in International Marketing Strategy
6. Vendor Analysis
7. Segmentation Analysis
8. Product Positioning
9. Services Strategy
10. Product Screening Checklist
11. Economic Order Quantity
12. Wholesaler Cost Analysis
13. Advertising Budget
14. Salesperson Deployment
15. Price Elasticity
16. Key Cost Concepts
17. Performance Ratios
18. Optimal Marketing Mix

We believe this computer supplement greatly enhances text material, further demonstrates the dynamic and exciting nature of marketing, and is an important learning tool in the emerging age of the computer. We welcome your feedback on *Computer-Based Marketing Exercises*.

Acknowledgments

Throughout our professional lives and during the period of time that the various editions of this book have been researched and written, a number of people have provided us with support, encouragement, and constructive criticism. We would like publicly to acknowledge and thank many of them.

In our years as graduate students, we benefited greatly from the knowledge transmitted from professors Conrad Berenson, Henry Eilbirt, and David Rachman, and colleagues Elaine Bernay, William Dillon, Stanley Garfunkel, Leslie Kanuk, Michael Laric, Kevin McCrohan, Leon Schiffman, and Elmer Waters. We learned a great deal at the American Marketing Association's annual consortium for doctoral students, the capstone of any marketing student's education.

At Hofstra University, colleagues Benny Barak, Herman Berliner, Dorothy Cohen, Andrew Forman, Joel Greene, William James, Keun Lee, Anil Mathur, William McDonald, Rusty Moore, James Neelankavil, Ralph Polimeni, Elaine Sherman, and Yong Zhang have stimulated us by providing the environment needed for a book of this type.

We would especially like to thank the following colleagues for reviewing *Marketing* during preparation of this edition. These reviewers made many helpful comments and significant contributions to revisions in the book:

Wayne Alexander (Moorhead State University)
John Cronin (Western Connecticut State University)
Mort Ettinger (Salem State University)
Charles Gulas (Wright State University)
Rajshekhar Javalgi (Cleveland State University)
Gail Kirby (Santa Clara University)
Kenneth Lord (Niagra University)
Yusen Liu (University of St. Thomas)
Jacob Manakkalathil (University of North Dakota)
Scott Roberts (Old Dominion University)
Peter Sanchez (Villanova University)
Reshma Shah (University of Pittsburgh)
Anthony Urbaniak (Northern State University)
Colleen Wheeler (St. Cloud University)

We would also like to thank these colleagues for their insightful reviews for prior editions of *Marketing* and *Principles of Marketing*:

Rolph Anderson (Drexel University)
Julian Andorka (DePaul University)
Kenneth Anglin (Mankato State University)
Thomas Antonielli, Sr. (Strayer College)
Harold Babson (Columbus State Community College)
Ken Baker (University of New Mexico)
John Bates (Georgia Southwestern College)
Stephen Batory (Bloomsburg University)
Richard Behr (Broome Community College)
Kurt Beran (Oregon State University)
Wanda Blockhus (San Jose State University)
John Boos (Ohio Wesleyan University)
Jeff Bradford (Bowling Green State University)
Donald Bradley, III (University of Central Arkansas)
James Brock (Montana State University)
Harvey Bronstein (Oakland Community College)
Sharon Browning (Northwest Missouri State University)
John Bunnell (Broome Community College)
Jim Burrow (North Carolina State)
Gul Butaney (Bentley College)
Steven Calcich (Norfolk State University)
Robert Chapman (Orlando College)
Yusef Choudhry (University of Baltimore)
Gloria Cockerell (Collin County College)
Barbara Coe (University of North Texas)
Linda Jane Coleman (Salem State College)
Kenneth Crocker (Bowling Green State University)
James Cronin, Jr. (Cape Cod Community College)
Richard Cummings (College of Lake County)
Benjamin Cutler (Bronx Community College)
Homer Dalbey (San Francisco State University)
Betty Diener (University of Massachusetts at Boston)
Peter Doukas (Westchester Community College)
Rebecca Elmore-Yalch (University of Washington)
Roland Eyears (Central Ohio Technical College)
Frank Falcetta (Middlesex Community College)
Lawrence Feick (University of Pittsburgh)
Benjamin Findley, Jr. (University of West Florida)
Frank Franzak (Virginia Commonwealth University)
Stanley Garfunkel (Queensborough Community College)
Betsy Gelb (University of Houston)
Donald Gordon (Illinois Central College)
Jill Grace (University of Southern California)
Harrison Grathwohl (California State University at Chico)
Blaine Greenfield (Bucks County Community College)
Thomas Greer (University of Maryland)
Gregory Gundlach (University of Notre Dame)
Robert Gwinner (Arizona State University)
Rita Hall (Sullivan Junior College)

Robert Hammond (Lexington Community College)
G. E. Hannem (Mankato State University)
Nancy Hansen (University of New Hampshire)
William Harris, III (Ohio University)
Douglas Hawes (University of Wyoming)
Jon Hawes (University of Akron)
Dean Headley (Wichita State University)
Allen Heffner (Lebanon Valley College)
Thomas Hickey (State University of New York at Oswego)
Nathan Himmelstein (Essex County College)
Patricia Hopkins (California State Polytechnic University at Pomona)
Jerry Ingram (Auburn University at Montgomery)
Laurence Jacobs (University of Hawaii)
Norma Johansen (Scottsdale Community College)
Edna Johnson (North Carolina Agricultural and Technical State University)
Paul Joice, Sr. (Walla Walla College)
Mary Joyce (Emerson College)
Albert Kagan (University of Northern Iowa)
Ruel Kahler (University of Cincinnati)
Bernard Katz (Oakton Community College)
J. Steven Kelly (DePaul University)
John Kerr (Florida State University)
Bettie King (Central Piedmont Community College)
Charles Knapp (Waubonsee Community College)
John Krane (Community College of Denver)
R. Krishnan (California Polytechnic State University)
Darwin Krumrey (Kirkwood Community College)
J. Ford Laumer (Auburn University)
William Layden (Golden West College)
Marilyn Liebrenz-Himes (George Washington University)
Robert Listman (Valparaiso University)
James Littlefield (Virginia Polytechnic Institute and State University)
John Lloyd (Monroe Community College)
William Locander (University of South Florida)
Robert Lorentz (Florida Institute of Technology)
William Lovell (Cayuga Community College)
Keith Lucas (Ferris State College)
Scott Marzluf (National College)
Michael Mayo (Kent State University)
Ken McCleary (Virginia Polytechnic Institute and State University)
Elaine McGivern (Bucknell University)
James McMillan (University of Tennessee)
H. Lee Meadow (Northern Illinois University)
John Mentzer (University of Tennessee)
Jim Merrill (Indiana University)
James Meszaros (County College of Morris)
Ronald Michael (University of Kansas)
Ronald Michman (Shippensburg State University)
John Milewicz (Jacksonville State University)
Howard Mills (Ulster City Community College)
Edward Moore (State University of New York College at Plattsburgh)
Linda Morable (Richland College)
John Morgan (West Chester University)
Linda Morris (University of Idaho)
Ed Mosher (Laramie County Community College)
Carol Stewart Mueller (Nassau Community College)
Paul Murphy (John Carroll University)
Margaret Myers (Northern Kentucky University)
Donald Nagourney (New York Institute of Technology)
Peter Nye (Northeastern University)
Kenneth Papenfuss (Ricks College)
Dennis Pappas (Columbus State Community College)
Terry Paul (Ohio State University)
William Perttula (San Francisco State University)
Michael Peters (Boston College)
Ann Pipinski (Northeast Institute of Education)
Robert Pollero (Anne Arundel Community College)
Edward Popper (Aurora University)
William Qualls (Massachusetts Institute of Technology)
S. R. Rao (Cleveland State University)
Lloyd Rinehart (Michigan State University)
Edward Riordan (Wayne State University)
David Roberts (Virginia Polytechnic Institute and State University)
Mary Lou Roberts (University of Massachusetts at Boston)
Donald Robin (University of Southern Mississippi)
John Rogers (California Polytechnic State University at San Luis Obispo)
Randall Rose (University of South Carolina)
Barbara Rosenthal (Miami Dade Community College)
Thomas Rossi (Broome Community College)
Nancy Ryan-McClure (Texas Tech University)
Barbara Samuel (University of Scranton)
Alan Sawyer (University of Florida)
Robert Schaffer (California State Polytechnic University at Pomona)
Martin Schlissel (St. John's University)
Stanley Scott (University of Alaska at Anchorage)
Donald Self (Auburn University at Montgomery)
Mohamad Sepehri (Sheperd College)
Raj Sethuraman (University of Iowa)
Richard Sielaff (University of Minnesota at Duluth)
M. Joseph Sirgy (Virginia Polytechnic Institute and State University)
Richard Skinner (Ashland University)
Michael Smith (Temple University)
Norman Smothers (California State University at Hayward)
Gregory Snere (Ellsworth Community College)
Michael Solomon (Rutgers University at New Brunswick)
Patricia Sorce (Rochester Institute of Technology)
A. Edward Spitz (Eastern Michigan University)
Tom Stafford (Cameron University)
Gary Stanton (Erie Community College)
Margery Steinberg (University of Hartford)
Jeffrey Stoltman (Wayne State University)
Robert Swerdlow (Lamar University)
Richard Szecsy (St. Mary's University)
Donna Tillman (California State Polytechnic University at Pomona)
Ed Timmerman (Abilene Christian University)
Frank Titlow (St. Petersburg Junior College)
Charles Treas (University of Mississippi)
David Urban (Virginia Commonwealth University)
Richard Utecht (University of Texas at San Antonio)
William Vincent (Santa Barbara City College)
Gerald Waddle (Clemson University)
Donald Walli (Greenville Technical College)
John Walton (Miami University)
J. Donald Weinrauch (Tennessee Technological University)
Mildred Whitted (St. Louis Community College at Forest Park)
Jack Wichert (Orange Coast College)
David Wills (Sussex County Community College)
George Winn (James Madison University)
Martin Wise (Harrisburg Area Community College)
Joyce Wood (Northern Virginia Community College)
Gene Wunder (Ball State University)
Richard Yalch (University of Washington)
Anthony Zahorik (Vanderbilt University)
William Ziegler (Seton Hall University)

To the many students at Hofstra who have reacted to the material in *Marketing*, we owe a special thanks, because they represent the true constituency of any textbook authors.

Our appreciation is extended to the fine people at Prentice Hall. We expressly thank the team for *Marketing*, Seventh Edition: Dave Borkowsky, Theresa Festa, Anne Graydon, Kirsten Kauffman (from York Production), Jim Boyd, and Joanne Jay.

We are pleased to recognize the contributions of Diane Schoenberg, our editorial associate; Linda Berman, for comprehensive indexes; Linda Evans, for editorial work; and Marni Shapiro and Andreas Kouroumalis, our graduate research assistants. Our appreciation and a special thanks are due to Chip Galloway for his continued *outstanding* work on the computer supplement.

To our wives and children, this book is dedicated—out of respect and love.

Joel R. Evans
Barry Berman

About the Authors

Joel R. Evans (Ph.D. in Business with majors in Marketing and Public Policy) is the RMI Distinguished Professor of Business and Professor of Marketing and International Business at Hofstra University. Previously, Dr. Evans was department chairperson for seven years. Before joining Hofstra, he worked for United Merchants and Manufacturers, owned a retail mail-order business, and taught at Bernard M. Baruch College and New York University. He has also served as a consultant for such diverse companies as PepsiCo, Nynex, and McCrory.

Dr. Evans is author or editor of numerous books and articles and is active in various professional associations. At Hofstra, he has been honored as a faculty inductee in Beta Gamma Sigma and received two Dean's Awards and the School of Business Faculty Distinguished Service Award. Dr. Evans has also been honored as Teacher of the Year by the Hofstra M.B.A. Association.

Barry Berman (Ph.D. in Business with majors in Marketing and Behavioral Science) is the Walter H. "Bud" Miller Distinguished Professor of Business and Professor of Marketing and International Business at Hofstra University. Previously, Dr. Berman was associate dean of the Hofstra School of Business for seven years. He has served as a consultant to such organizations as the Singer Company, Associated Dry Goods, the State Education Department of New York, and professional and trade groups.

Dr. Berman is author or editor of numerous books and articles and is active in various professional associations. He served as associate editor of the *Marketing Review* for many years. At Hofstra, he has been honored as a faculty inductee in Beta Gamma Sigma and received two Dean's Awards. Dr. Berman has also been honored as Teacher of the Year by the Hofstra M.B.A. Association.

Joel R. Evans and Barry Berman are co-authors of several best-selling texts, including *Marketing*, a Russian-language version of *Marketing, Principles of Marketing*, and *Retail Management: A Strategic Approach*. They were two of the co-chairpersons for the 1990 American Marketing Association Microcomputers in Marketing Education Conference in New Orleans and co-edited the conference proceedings. They were co-chairpersons for the 1995 American Marketing Association Faculty Consortium on the topic of "Ethics and Social Responsibility in Marketing." Drs. Evans and Berman co-founded the American Marketing Association Special Interest Group in Retailing and Retail Management. Each has a chapter in the most recent edition of Dartnell's *Marketing Manager's Handbook*. For several years, they were co-directors of the Business Research Institute and the Retail Management Institute at Hofstra University. Both regularly teach undergraduate and graduate marketing courses to a wide range of students.

AN INTRODUCTION TO

PART 1

MARKETING

In Part 1, we begin our study of marketing and discuss concepts that form the foundation for the rest of the text.

1 Marketing in Contemporary Society

Here, we show the dynamic nature of marketing, broadly define the term "marketing," and trace its evolution. We pay special attention to the marketing concept, a marketing philosophy, customer service, and customer satisfaction and relationship marketing. And we examine the importance of marketing, as well as marketing functions and performers.

2 The Environment in Which Marketing Operates

In this chapter, we look at the complex environment within which marketing functions, with an emphasis on both the factors that can be controlled and those that cannot be controlled by an organization and its marketers. We demonstrate that without adequate environmental analysis, a firm may function haphazardly or be shortsighted.

3 Strategic Planning: A Marketing Perspective

Here, we first distinguish between strategic business plans and strategic marketing plans, and describe the total quality approach to strategic planning. Next, we look at the different kinds of strategic plans and the relationships between marketing and other functional areas. We then present the steps in the strategic planning process in considerable detail. A sample outline for a strategic plan is presented and the actual strategic plan of a small firm is highlighted.

4 Information for Marketing Decisions

In this chapter, we explain why marketing decisions should be based on sound information. We explain the role and importance of the marketing information system—which coordinates marketing research, continuous monitoring, and data storage and provides the basis for decision making. We also describe marketing research and the process for undertaking it. We show that research may involve surveys, observation, experiments, and/or simulation.

Part 1 Video Vignette

FD&B Inc.

As we will show throughout *Marketing*, organizations involved with "marketing" practices come in all sizes and orientations. And those who work in marketing have a variety of backgrounds—sometimes very far removed from formal business education.

To demonstrate the diversity of organizations engaged in marketing, consider that FD&B Inc. (founded in 1991) is an integrated marketing communications agency with $24 million in annual billings and 20 employees. In contrast, FD&B's client MasterCard International (founded as the Interbank Card Association in 1966) serves thousands of member banks, which account for several hundred billion dollars in yearly MasterCard volume in the United States alone. There are millions of MasterCard locations in well over 200 countries and territories around the world.

Organizations involved with "marketing" practices come in all sizes and orientations. And those who work in marketing have a variety of backgrounds.

Besides MasterCard International, FD&B's client roster has included Citicorp Financial Services, Eight O'Clock Coffee, the Hain Food Group, Olsten Corporation (temporary employment), United States Luggage, and Watson Pharmaceuticals. The agency has also done pro bono (no fee) work for the Boys & Girls Club of Oyster Bay and the Make a Wish Foundation.

Why do clients hire FD&B when there are literally thousands of agencies from which to choose? In large part, they do so because of FD&B's personal attention—a willingness to go the extra mile—and tailored approach to each client's needs, as well as the expertise of FD&B personnel. According to FD&B's mission statement, "We do not choose to be a common Advertising Agency. From the initial defining of [client] goals and objectives, through the proper positioning of the goods or services, to the identification of challenges and opportunities and the development of creative and media strategies, every step is planned and based on in-depth research and proven strategic marketing principles."

FD&B is headed by four partners, with wide-ranging backgrounds: Phil Franznick is a 25-year veteran of the advertising industry and the chief executive officer of the company. He has a bachelor's degree (BFA) in Fine Arts from Ohio University. Kevin Franznick oversees the day-to-day business and finances of the company. He has a bachelor's degree (BFA) in Theater from Ohio University. Ellen Deutsch has directed campaigns and worked on the marketing strategies for a number of accounts. She has a bachelor's degree (BBA) and a master's degree (MBA) in Marketing, both from Hofstra University. Todd Brenard is most involved with client services (customer relations). He has a bachelor's degree (BS) in Communications and Psychology from the University of Wisconsin, Stevens Point.

In the part-opening vignettes for *Marketing*, FD&B and three of its clients (Hain, MasterCard, and Watson) will be featured. Enjoy these vignettes and the videos that accompany them.

CHAPTER 1

Marketing in Contemporary Society

Chapter Objectives

1. To illustrate the exciting, dynamic, and influential nature of marketing
2. To define marketing and trace its evolution—with emphasis on the marketing concept, a marketing philosophy, customer service, and customer satisfaction and relationship marketing
3. To show the importance of marketing as a field of study
4. To describe the basic functions of marketing and those that perform these functions

Marketers used to target customers; now they must learn to invite them in. Consumers have more information about products and more products to choose from than ever before. They have more ways to shop: at malls, specialty shops, and superstores; through mail-order, home shopping networks, and virtual stores on the Internet. And they are bombarded with messages from television, radio, online computer networks, the Internet, fax machines and telemarketing, and magazines and other print media.

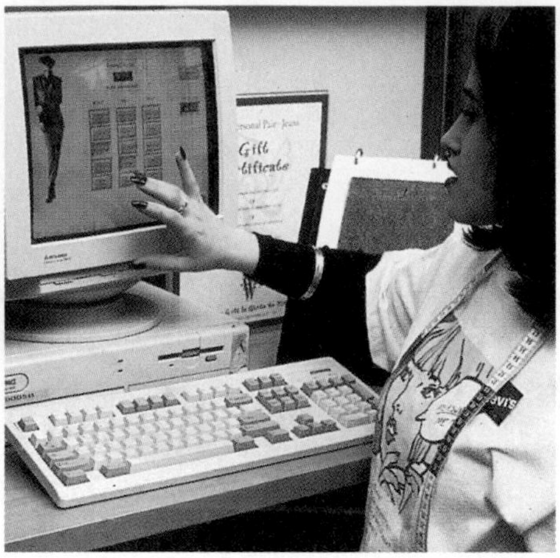

Reprinted by permission.

For marketing-oriented firms, "inviting customers in" is a fundamental part of their business strategies. After all, one of the underpinnings of marketing is a strong interest in consumers—based on a belief that companies cannot succeed unless they understand and satisfy their clientele. How can firms do this in today's high-tech world? They can use information technology such as the Internet and toll-free 800 numbers to keep customers engaged in an ongoing dialog.

In contrast to traditional consumer surveys, "real-time" marketing provides continuous consumer contacts and uses consumer feedback as a critical element in developing and improving products, focuses on customer satisfaction, and refocuses the role of marketing within a firm. Let us look at how Levi Strauss, Federal Express, and Philips NV utilize real-time marketing.

Levi Strauss & Co. uses real-time marketing through its Personal Pair Jeans for Women Program offered at Original Levi's Stores. Trained sales associates take customer measurements and enter them into PCs to determine prototype trial jeans. Customers try on the prototype jeans and modifications can be made. Sales associates input the new measurements into the computer. When customers are totally satisfied, personal orders are sent via modem to the Levi Strauss & Co. factory in Tennessee. In approximately three weeks, customers can either pick up their Personal Pair Jeans at the Original Levi's Store or, for a small fee, have them sent directly to them. Levi's Personal Pair Jeans cost just $10 more than a regular pair of Levi's Jeans for Women.

Federal Express provides its larger customers with software and computer terminals to let them track their shipments. National Semiconductor, for instance, can determine if each of its customers worldwide has received the parts ordered by using the software. And a computer company seeking to order parts from National Semiconductor can look at the firm's online catalog, order parts from Federal Express, and track parts shipping. Federal Express plans to communicate with most customers via real-time systems by the year 2000.

Philips NV, the Dutch electronics firm, recently introduced a new online product for children based on detailed marketplace analysis. Before designing the product, it sent cognitive psychologists, anthropologists, sociologists, and industrial designers into Italy, France, and the Netherlands via mobile vans. These researchers asked both children and adults to brainstorm with them for ideas on new electronics products to meet changing consumer needs. Thus, the researchers and potential customers interactively came up with new ideas. Philips then picked one of those ideas (in this case, a new online service) and sent its researchers back to test the concept further with the same adults and children.[1]

In this chapter, we will learn more about the roles of marketing, see how marketing has evolved over the years, and look at its scope.

Overview

Marketing is a dynamic field, encompassing many activities.

Marketing is an exciting, fast-paced, and contemporary business discipline. We engage in marketing activities or are affected by them on a daily basis, both in our business-related roles and as consumers. Okay, but what exactly does "marketing" mean? Well, it is not just advertising or selling goods and services, although these are aspects of marketing. And it is not just what we do as supermarket shoppers every week, although this too is part of marketing.

As formally defined in the next section, "marketing" encompasses the activities involved in anticipating, managing, and satisfying demand via the exchange process. As

[1]Regis McKenna, "Real-Time Marketing," *Harvard Business Review*, Vol. 73 (July–August 1995), pp. 87–95; and 1996 Levi Strauss correspondence.

such, marketing encompasses all facets of buyer/seller relationships. Specific marketing activities (all discussed later in this chapter) include environmental analysis and marketing research, broadening an organization's scope, consumer analysis, product planning, distribution planning, promotion planning, price planning, and marketing management.

In a less abstract way, here are two examples of real-world marketing—one from a business perspective and one from a consumer perspective:

BUSINESS PERSPECTIVE: Marie Jackson, a 1992 BBA with an accounting major and a CPA certification, has worked for a large accounting firm since graduating from college. She is now ready to open her own practice, but must make a number of decisions: Who should her clients be? What accounting services should she offer? Where should she open her office? How will she attract her clients? What fee schedule should she set? Is it ethical to try to attract clients that she worked with from her old firm? *Each of these questions entails a business-related marketing decision.*

Let's look at some of Marie Jackson's marketing options:

- *Clients*—Marie could target small or medium businesses, such nonprofit organizations as local libraries, and/or individuals (for personal tax and estate planning).
- *Accounting services*—Marie could be a full-service accountant for her clients or specialize in a particular accounting task (such as developing customized accounting software).
- *Office location*—Marie could open an office in a professional building, a small shopping center, or her home. She could also go on on-site visits to clients, thus making the choice of her office location less important.
- *Attracting clients*—Marie must determine if she is from the "new" school—where it is acceptable to run ads in local newspapers, send out direct mail pieces to prospective clients, etc.—or from the "old" school—where most forms of promotion are viewed as being unprofessional.
- *Fee schedule*—Marie must rely on her own experience with her previous firm and look at what competitors are doing. Then, she could price similar to others or lower/higher than them (depending on her desired image and a realistic reading of the marketplace).
- *Ethics*—Marie must weigh the personal dilemma of "stealing" clients from her old firm against the difficulty of starting a business from scratch without any client base.

CONSUMER PERSPECTIVE: At the same time that Marie Jackson is making decisions about her new accounting practice, Albert Sampson is reappraising his status as an accounting client. He owns a small furniture repair store and has been a client of a mid-sized accounting firm for ten years. That firm has been responsible for Albert Sampson's store and personal accounts. Yet, he is now unhappy. He feels the accounting firm takes him for granted. But before switching accountants, these questions must be answered: What kind of firm should he select? What accounting services should he seek? Where should the accounting firm be located? How will he learn more about possible firms? What fees should he be willing to pay? Is it ethical to show prospective firms samples of the work from his present accountant? *Each of these questions addresses a consumer-related marketing decision.*

Let's look at some of Albert Sampson's marketing options:

- *Kind of firm*—Albert could select a small, medium, or large accounting firm. Given his current dissatisfaction, he would probably avoid medium and large firms.
- *Accounting services*—Albert could continue having his accountant perform all accounting tasks for him, or he could take on some of the tasks himself (such as maintaining ledger books and paying bills).
- *Office location*—Albert could look for an accountant that makes on-site visits (as his accountant does now) or seek a firm that has an office near to his store or residence.
- *Learning about firms*—Albert could ask prospective firms for references, check out accountants' credentials, interview candidates, and/or require firms to perform a sample task.

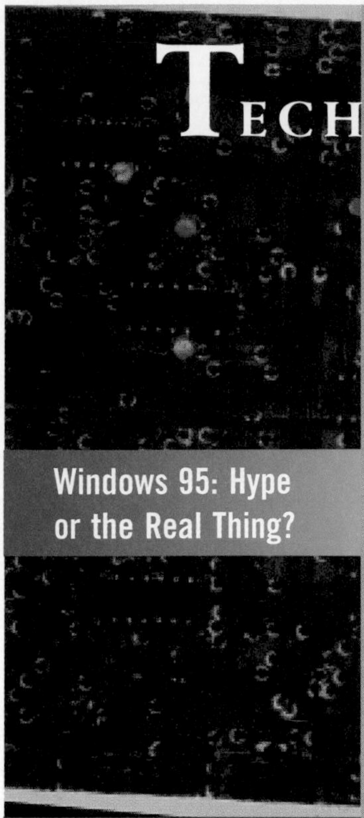

TECHNOLOGY & MARKETING

Windows 95: Hype or the Real Thing?

Microsoft introduced Windows 95 in August 1995. The launch was accompanied by demonstrations at convention centers, testing by 400,000 trial users, and special promotions by retailers. At its Washington headquarters, Microsoft sponsored a carnival and trade show for 2,500. In total, Microsoft spent $150 million on the kickoff.

These are some of Windows 95's heralded benefits: (1) Under DOS and older Windows versions, file names were limited to eight letters, with three more after a period—like "MKTGTEXT.DOX". In Windows 95, the same file could be "MARKETING, 7th Edition," a more identifiable title. (2) Windows 95 can run up to a dozen or more programs at the same time, versus a maximum of six for the older Windows version. (3) Windows 95-compatible CD-ROMs begin playing as soon as they are inserted in a drive, without entering special commands.

However, some critics say Windows 95's benefits are overstated, and that most benefits will not occur unless a person buys new 32-bit versions of existing programs. Even Microsoft acknowledged that much of this software took months to be available and that consumers would have to buy software upgrades. Critics also feel that Microsoft has understated the PC hardware needed to properly run Windows 95, which requires more memory and a larger hard drive than most existing systems have. The cost of such hardware upgrades can easily exceed $900 per computer. And although Windows 95 is the most tested piece of software ever, defects and incompatibilities are still common. Furthermore, Apple has run ads commenting on how hard Windows 95 is to install, compared to easy-to-run Macintosh computers.

As a Microsoft marketing manager, how would you explain Windows 95's benefits and answer the criticisms for a cynical newspaper columnist?

Sources: Based on material in Don Clark, "Amid Hype and Fear, Microsoft Windows 95 Gets Ready to Roll," *Wall Street Journal* (July 14, 1995), pp. A1, A9; Walter S. Mossberg, "Most PC Users Should Take Their Time Moving to Windows 95," *Wall Street Journal* (August 10, 1995), p. B1; and Steve Lohr, "It's Been an Uphill Battle to Sell Windows 95," *New York Times* (January 18, 1996), pp. A1, D7.

- *Fee schedule*—Albert knows he must get "fair" quotes, not "low ball" ones. He recognizes that you get what you pay for, and he wants better service.
- *Ethics*—Albert must determine whether he, as the client, has the right to show any old work to prospective firms—or whether there is a client/accountant relationship that he should not violate.

A MARKETING MATCH? For "marketing" to operate properly, buyers and sellers need to find and satisfy each other (conduct exchanges). Do you think that Marie Jackson and Albert Sampson would make a good marketing match? We do—but only if their strategy (Marie) and expectations (Albert) are in sync.

In some way, we are all involved with or affected by marketing.

As these examples show, goods and service providers ("sellers") make marketing-related decisions like choosing who customers are, what goods and services to offer, where to sell these goods and services, the features to stress in ads, and the prices to charge. They also determine how to be ethical and socially responsible, and whether to sell products internationally in addition to domestically. Marketing-related activities are not limited to industrial firms, large corporations, or people called "marketers." They are taken on by all types of companies and people.

As consumers ("buyers"), the marketing practices of goods and service providers impact on many of the choices made by our parents, spouses, other family members, friends and associates, and/or us. For virtually every good and service we purchase, the marketing process affects whom we patronize, the assortment of models and styles offered in the marketplace, where we shop, the availability of knowledgeable sales personnel, the prices we pay, and other factors. Marketing practices are in play when we are born (which doctor our parents select, the style of baby furniture they buy), while we grow (our parents' purchase of a domestic or foreign family car or minivan, our choice of a college), while we conduct our everyday lives (the use of a particular brand of toothpaste, the purchase of status-related items), and when we retire (our consideration of travel options, a change in living accommodations).

The formal study of marketing requires an understanding of its definition, evolution (including the marketing concept, a marketing philosophy, and customer service), importance and scope, and functions. These principles are discussed throughout Chapter 1.

Marketing Defined

A broad, integrated definition of marketing forms the basis of this text:

> **Marketing** is the anticipation, management, and satisfaction of demand through the exchange process.

Marketing *includes anticipating demand, managing demand, and satisfying demand.*

It involves goods, services, organizations, people, places, and ideas.

Anticipation of demand requires a firm to do consumer research on a regular basis so it can develop and introduce offerings desired by consumers. Management of demand includes stimulation, facilitation, and regulation tasks. Stimulation motivates consumers to want a firm's offerings due to attractive product designs, distinctive promotion, fair prices, and other strategies. Facilitation is the process whereby the firm makes it easy to buy its offering by having convenient locations, accepting credit cards, using well-informed salespeople, and implementing other strategies. Regulation is needed when there are peak demand periods rather than balanced demand throughout the year or when demand is greater than the supply of the offering. Then, the goal is to spread demand throughout the year or to demarket a good or service (reduce overall demand). Satisfaction of demand involves product availability, actual performance upon purchase, safety perceptions, after-sale service, and other factors. For consumers to be satisfied, goods, services, organizations, people, places, and ideas must fulfill their expectations. See Figure 1-1.

FIGURE 1-1
Nash Finch's Customer Service Philosophy
Reprinted by permission.

Jenny Hubbs, Special Olympics Runner
THAT POUNDING
IN YOUR HEART. IT'S PRIDE.
BE PART OF THE LARGEST SPORTS EVENT ON EARTH IN 1995, THE SPECIAL OLYMPICS WORLD GAMES IN CONNECTICUT. YOUR LOCAL PROGRAM NEEDS ATHLETES, COACHES, VOLUNTEERS AND SPONSORS TO PREPARE FOR THE GAMES. JOIN NOW AND GET READY TO BELIEVE.
Special Olympics
World Games
Connecticut 1995
TO LEARN MORE ABOUT THE WORLD GAMES, CALL 1-800-700-8585

FIGURE 1-2
Marketing and the Special Olympics
Marketing not only encompasses goods and services, but also organizations, people, and places.
Reprinted by permission.

Demand *is affected by both* **consumers** *and* **publics**.

Marketing can be aimed at consumers or at publics. **Consumer demand** refers to the attributes and needs of final consumers, industrial consumers, wholesalers and retailers, government institutions, international markets, and nonprofit institutions. A firm may appeal to one or a combination of these. **Publics' demand** refers to the attributes and needs of employees, unions, stockholders, the general public, government agencies, consumer groups, and other internal and external forces that affect company operations.

Exchange *completes the process.*

The marketing process is not concluded until consumers and publics **exchange** their money, their promise to pay, or their support for the offering of a firm, institution, person, place, or idea. Exchanges must be done in a socially responsible way, with both the buyer and the seller being ethical and honest—and considering the impact on society and the environment.

A proper marketing definition should not be confined to economic goods and services. It should cover organizations (Red Cross), people (politicians), places (Hawaii), and ideas (the value of seat belts). See Figures 1-2 and 1-3. A consumer orientation must be central to any definition. And from a societal perspective, a firm needs to ask whether a good or service should be sold, besides whether it can be sold.

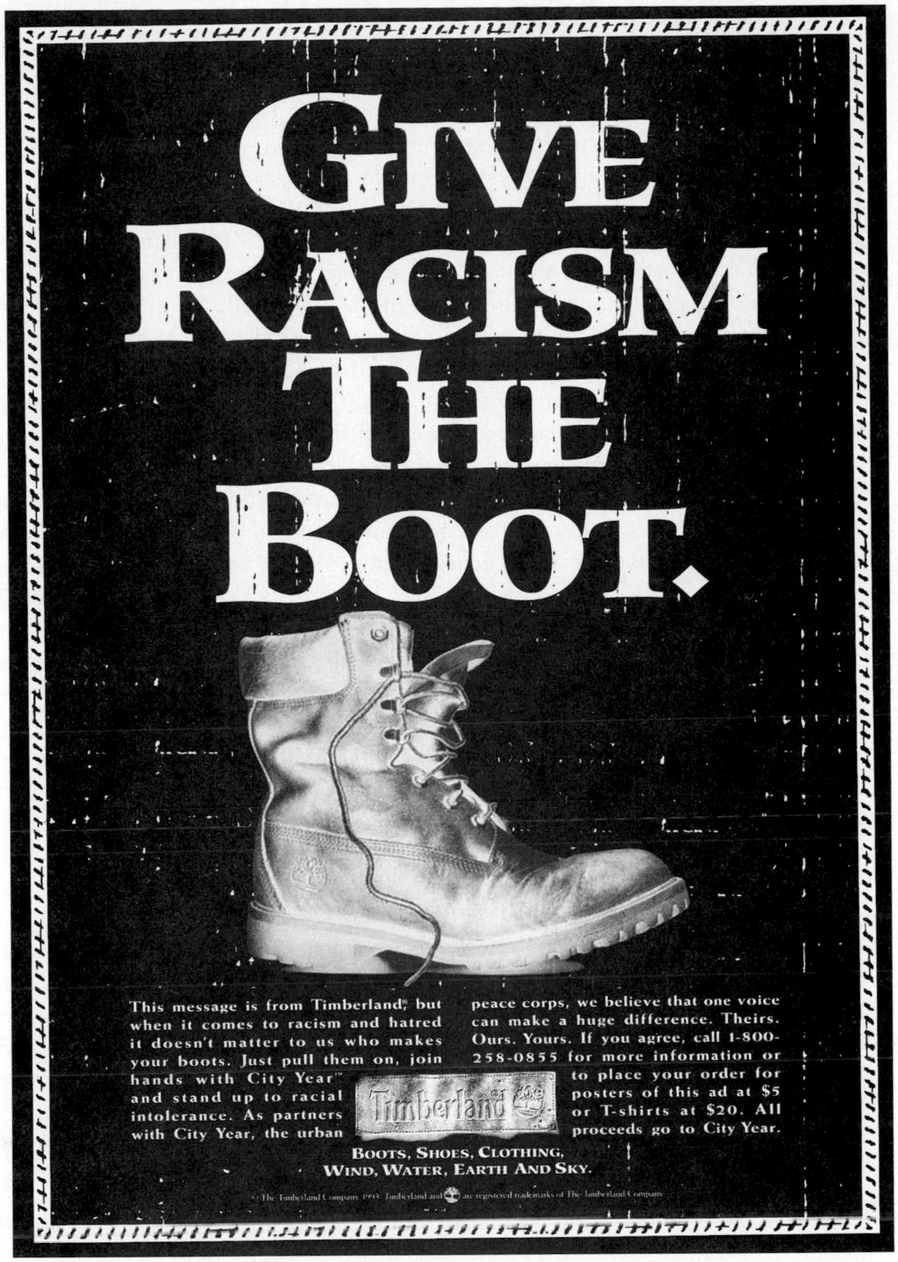

FIGURE 1-3
Timberland on Racism
Marketing can be used to make powerful statements about the social issues of the day (ideas).
Reprinted by permission.

The Evolution of Marketing

Marketing's evolution in an industry, country, or region of the world may be viewed as a sequence of stages: barter era → production era → sales era → marketing department era → marketing company era. In some industries, nations, and regions, marketing practices have moved through each stage and involve a good consumer orientation and high efficiency; in others, marketing practices are still in infancy.

Marketing can be traced to the **barter era**.

Marketing's origins can be traced to people's earliest use of the exchange process: the **barter era**. With barter, people trade one resource for another—like food for animal pelts. To accommodate exchanges, trading posts, traveling salespeople, general stores, and cities evolved along with a standardized monetary system. In the least developed nations of the world, barter is still widely practiced.

In the **production era**, *output increases to meet demand.*

The modern system of marketing begins with the industrialization of an industry, country, or region. For the world's most developed nations, this occurred with the Industrial Revolution of the late 1800s. For developing nations, efforts to industrialize are now under way. Why is industrialization so important in marketing's evolution? Unless industrialization takes place, exchanges are limited since people do not have surplus items to trade. With the onset of mass production, better transportation, and more efficient technology, products can be made in greater volume and sold at lower prices. Improved mobility, densely populated cities, and specialization also let more people share in the exchange process: They can turn from self-sufficiency (such as making their own clothes) to purchases (such as buying clothes). In the initial stages of industrialization, output is limited and marketing is devoted to products' physical distribution. Because demand is high and competition is low, firms typically do not have to conduct consumer research, modify products, or otherwise adapt to consumer needs. The goal is to lift production to meet demand. This is the **production era** of marketing.

In the **sales era**, *firms sell products without first determining consumer desires.*

The next stage takes place as companies expand production capabilities to keep up with consumer demand. At this point, many firms hire a sales force and some use advertising to sell their inventory. Yet, since competition is still rather low, when firms develop new products, consumer tastes or needs receive little consideration. The role of the sales force and advertising is to make consumer desires fit the features of the products offered. For example, a shoe manufacturer might make brown wingtip shoes and use ads and personal selling to convince consumers to buy them. That firm would rarely determine consumer tastes before making shoes or adjust output to those tastes. This is the **sales era** of marketing. It still exists where competition is limited, such as in nations recently converting to free-market economies.

The **marketing department era** *occurs when research is used to determine consumer needs.*

As competition grows, supply begins to exceed demand. Firms cannot prosper without marketing input. They create marketing departments to conduct consumer research and advise management on how to better design, distribute, promote, and price products. Unless firms react to consumer needs, competitors might better satisfy demand and leave the firms with surplus inventory and falling sales. Yet, although marketing departments share in decisions, they may be in a subordinate position to production, engineering, and sales departments. This is the **marketing department era**. It still exists where marketing has been embraced, but not as the driving force in an industry or company.

The **marketing company era** *integrates consumer research and analysis into all company efforts.*

Over the past 40 years, firms in a growing number of industries, nations, and regions have recognized marketing's central role; marketing departments at those firms are now the equal of others. The firms make virtually all key decisions after thorough consumer analysis: Since competition is intense and sophisticated, consumers must be aggressively drawn and kept loyal to a firm's brands. Company efforts are well integrated and regularly reviewed. This is the **marketing company era**. Figure 1-4 indicates the key aspects of each era in marketing's evolution.

The marketing concept, a marketing philosophy, customer service, and customer satisfaction and relationship marketing are the linchpins of the marketing company era. They are examined here.

FIGURE 1-4
How Marketing Evolves

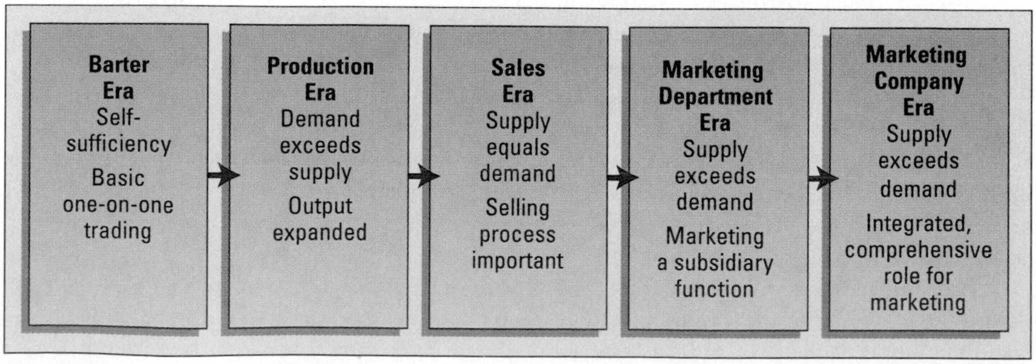

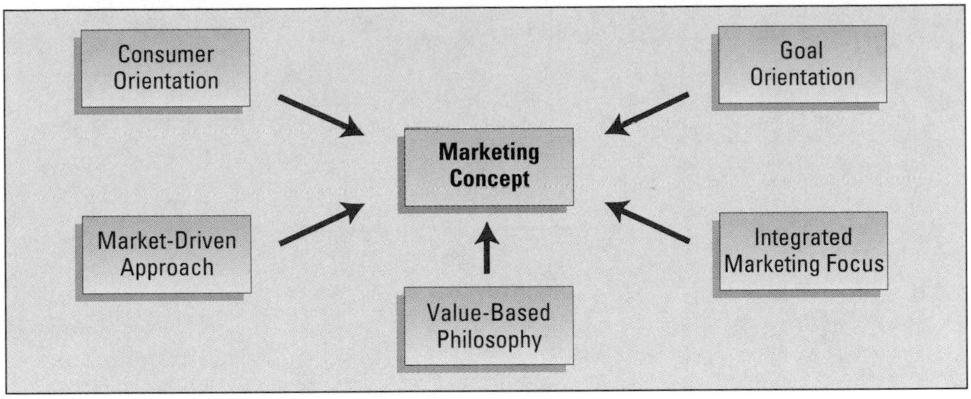

FIGURE 1-5
The Marketing Concept

The Marketing Concept

The **marketing concept** *is consumer-oriented, market-driven, value-driven, integrated, and goal-oriented.*

As Figure 1-5 shows, the **marketing concept** is a consumer-oriented, market-driven, value-based, integrated, goal-oriented philosophy for a firm, institution, or person.[2] Here is an illustration of it in action:

> How does a $35 million manufacturer compete with the global giant Sony? By giving dealers (its customers) what they want. Koss Corporation has been dominant in headphones since it invented "stereophones" in 1958. Even when Sony came on the scene in the 1980s with its Walkman, which created a market for low-end headphones, Koss was able to triple its sales and stay competitive.
>
> The simple philosophy "anything for the customer" has kept Koss in the game. In 1982, dealers requested that Koss change packaging so the headphones would be visible when hung on display. Koss responded by switching to clear packing. In 1987, after dealers requested a bigger share of Koss' advertising dollars, the firm, which was spending the bulk of its budget on national print ads, converted most of its ad dollars to cooperative advertising. To meet dealer inventory demand, Koss began electronic data interchange (EDI) in 1989.
>
> On a number of occasions, Koss has even gone so far as to alter product features based on one dealer's request. In 1994, Koss built a beefed-up headphone that could take customer abuse to use on store displays for one national record store chain. The store liked the headphones so much it asked Koss to also package them for sale. "We make small changes every day," says CEO Michael Koss. "Even small enhancements like changing the color or size of packaging help keep us close to our dealers."[3]

The marketing concept's five elements are crucial to the long-term success of a good, service, organization, person, place, or idea: A *customer orientation* means examining consumer needs, not production capability, and devising a plan to satisfy them. Goods and services are seen as means to accomplish ends, not the ends themselves. A *market-driven approach* means being aware of the structure of the marketplace, especially the attributes and strategies of competing firms. A *value-based philosophy* means offering goods and services that consumers perceive to have superior value relative to their costs and the offerings of competitors. With an *integrated marketing focus,* all the activities relating to goods and services are coordinated, including finance, production, engineering, inventory control, research and development, and marketing. A *goal-oriented firm* employs marketing to achieve both short- and long-term goals—which may be profit, funding to find a cure for a disease, increased tourism, election of a political candidate, a better company image, and so on. Marketing helps attain goals by orienting a firm toward pleasing consumers and offering desired goods, services, or ideas.

These are fifteen things that managers can do to ensure that they adhere to the spirit of the marketing concept:

[2]For a comprehensive analysis of the marketing concept, see Frederick E. Webster, Jr., "Defining the New Marketing Concept," *Marketing Management*, Vol. 2 (Number 2, 1994), pp. 23–31.
[3]Ginger Trumfio, "Anything for a Customer," *Sales & Marketing Management* (November 1995), p. 25.

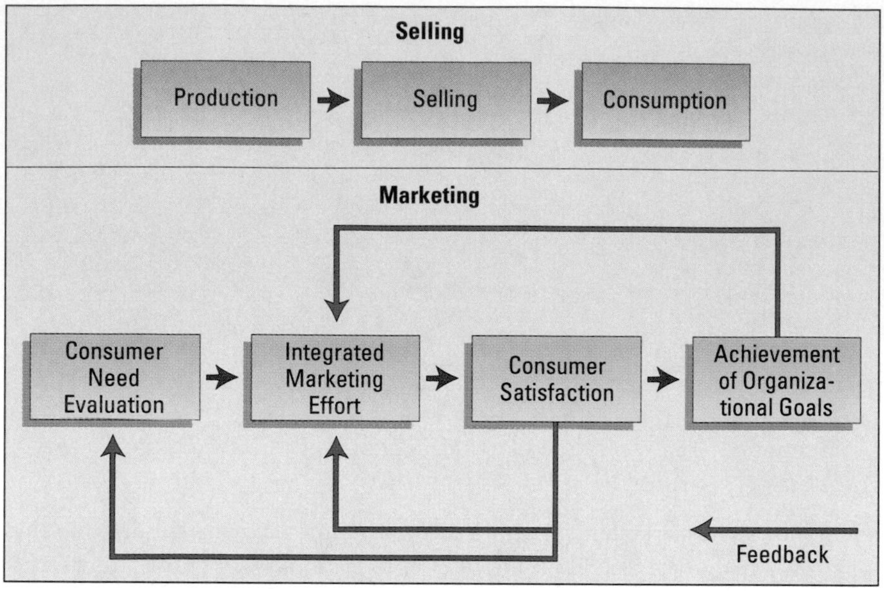

FIGURE 1-6
The Focus of Selling and Marketing Philosophies

1. Create customer focus throughout the firm.
2. Listen to the customer.
3. Define and cultivate distinctive competences.
4. Define marketing as market intelligence.
5. Target customers precisely.
6. Manage for profitability, not sales volume.
7. Make customer value the guiding star.
8. Let the customer define quality.
9. Measure and manage customer expectations.
10. Build customer relationships and loyalty.
11. Define the business as a service business.
12. Commit to continuous improvement and innovation.
13. Manage the company culture along with strategy and structure.
14. Grow with partners and alliances.
15. Destroy marketing bureaucracy.[4]

Although the marketing concept lets a firm analyze, maximize, and satisfy consumer demand, it is only a guide to planning. A firm must also consider its strengths and weaknesses in production, engineering, and finance. Marketing plans need to balance goals, customer needs, and resource capabilities. The impact of competition, government regulations, and other external forces must also be evaluated. These factors are discussed in Chapters 2 and 3.

Selling Versus Marketing Philosophies

With a marketing orientation, selling is used to communicate with and understand consumers.

Figure 1-6 highlights the differences between selling and marketing philosophies. The benefits of a marketing, rather than a sales, orientation are many. Marketing stresses consumer analysis and satisfaction, directs the resources of a firm to making the goods and services consumers want, and adapts to changes in consumer traits and needs. Under a marketing philosophy, selling is used to communicate with and understand consumers; consumer dissatisfaction leads to changes in policy, not a stronger or different sales pitch. Marketing looks for real differences in consumer tastes and devises offerings to satisfy

[4]Frederick E. Webster, Jr., "Executing the New Marketing Concept," *Marketing Management*, Vol. 3 (Number 1, 1994), pp. 9–16.

them. Marketing is geared to the long run, and marketing goals reflect overall company goals. Finally, marketing views customer needs broadly (for example, heating) rather than narrowly (for example, fuel oil).

As an example, at Wahl Clipper Corporation—which makes electric shavers and hair trimmers—sales have grown at a 16 per cent annual compounded rate for 20 years. Why? According to company president Jack Wahl, "I realized the difference between sales and marketing. That's a big thing for a small company. Sales means simply presenting the product and collecting money. Marketing means stepping back and looking for the needs of the customer, and for the best way to get through to that user."[5]

Customer Service

Customer service involves the identifiable, but rather intangible, activities undertaken by a seller in conjunction with the basic goods and/or services it offers.[6] In today's highly competitive marketplace, the level of customer service a firm provides can affect its ability to attract and retain customers more than ever before.

Customer service *tends to be intangible, but quite meaningful, to many consumers.*

Unless a consumer is happy with *both* the basic good (such as a new auto) or service (such as an auto tune-up) offered by a seller *and* the quality of customer service (like polite, expert sales personnel and on-time appointments), he or she is unlikely to patronize the seller—certainly not in the long run. Imagine your reaction to these situations:

> Stores often tell customers that home deliveries and repairs will be made any time between 8 A.M. and 5 P.M., often effectively killing a workday. Doctors and other health professionals frequently overbook appointments, so patients waste hours waiting to be seen. The Internal Revenue Service and other public agencies are often unreachable on the telephone.[7]
>
> With millions of new buyers, many of them individuals and small businesses clueless about computers, some manufacturers can't keep up with service complaints and requests for help. The result: hordes of confused and resentful—even outraged—customers.[8]

Yet, firms often have to make customer service trade-offs. For instance, supermarkets must weigh the potential loss of business if waiting lines are too long versus the cost of opening additional lines.[9]

According to one survey, most people rate the overall level of customer service of U.S. businesses as excellent or pretty good, but over 40 per cent rate service as only fair or poor. More than one-third of people say they usually purchase from a business having excellent service but higher prices, rather than a lower-priced competitor with lesser service.[10]

This is how several firms are addressing the issue of customer service: Such companies as Kroger, Federal Express, Avis, and Phelps County Bank (of Rolla, Missouri) are **empowering employees**—whereby, workers are given broad leeway to satisfy customer requests. With empowerment, employees are encouraged and rewarded for showing initiative and imagination. They can "break the rules" if in their judgment customer requests should be honored: Kroger employees can "do whatever it takes to make our customers happy. That doesn't mean a bagger can cash a check. But he or she can bring a customer to the person who can cash it and stay with him or her until it's done." Similarly, Federal Express drivers can help customers pack breakable items, Avis airport rental agents can keep their counters open if flights are delayed, and Phelps employees can look for a person's lost Veterans' Administration check.[11]

To offer better customer service, some firms are **empowering employees**.

[5]Jerry Flint, "Father Says, 'Jump,'" *Forbes* (August 14, 1995), p. 144.

[6]Peter D. Bennett (Editor), *Dictionary of Marketing Terms*, Second Edition (Chicago: American Marketing Association, 1995), p. 73.

[7]Theodore D. Kemper, "Good Service Serves the Economy, Too," *New York Times* (January 9, 1994), Section 3, p. 13.

[8]Jim Carlton, "Support Lines' Busy Signals Hurt PC Makers," *Wall Street Journal* (July 6, 1995), p. B1.

[9]Steve Weinstein, "Rethinking Customer Service," *Progressive Grocer* (May 1995), pp. 63–68.

[10]"Many Consumers Expect Better Service—And Say They Are Willing to Pay for It," *Wall Street Journal* (November 12, 1990), pp. B1, B4.

[11]Steve Weinstein, "Empowerment Pays," *Progressive Grocer* (April 1995), pp. 53–62; Dallas Gatewood, "Empowering Employees, Improving Service," *Newsday* (May 28, 1995), Money & Careers, p. 7; and John Case, "Total Customer Service," *Inc.* (January 1994), pp. 52–61.

International Marketing in Action

Why Is Customer Service at Germany's Deutsche Telekom Lagging Behind?

Customer service at Deutsche Telekom, Germany's phone monopoly, has been generally considered to be poor. Thus, the German government hoped to privatize the company in 1996 and to let international competitors (such as AT&T and BellSouth) offer phone service in Germany as of 1998.

Experts say Deutsche Telekom has a number of customer service problems:

- It is relatively easy to tap into someone's telephone. This encourages fraud and misbilling problems.
- There are only one-quarter the number of pay phones per capita in Germany as compared to the U.S. market.
- Although most telephone traffic in industrialized nations is switched by computer, one-half of Telekom's calls use outdated analog systems. Not only is its equipment inefficient and trouble-prone, but also it is incompatible with modern services such as call waiting.
- Deutsche Telekom is often ridiculed with regard to its customer service policies. A popular German television comedy routine, for example, shows Deutsche Telekom employees throwing complaint letters in the garbage.

Even though Deutsche Telekom executives know the firm's problems, they feel that they are due to legal factors beyond their control. For instance, German laws require phone lines to be buried underground rather than strung from poles. This increases the costs and time to service customers. German laws also require German long-distance users to subsidize local rates. Lastly, Deutsche Telekom workers are considered to be government employees; they are, thus, entitled to such benefits as annual five- to six-week paid vacations.

Despite the best intentions, some observers believe that Telekom's new competitors will direct their efforts at large industrial and commercial accounts and have little impact on small residential customers.

As a Deutsche Telekom executive, what would you do to increase the quality of your customer service?

Source: Based on material in Greg Steinmetz, "Customer-Service Era Is Reaching Germany Late, Hurting Business," *Wall Street Journal* (June 1, 1995), pp. A1, A8.

Omaha Steaks International sells gourmet foods such as seafood, pasta, veal, steak, and desserts through the mail and at retail stores. In 1994, it was honored with the Direct Marketing Association's Award for Customer Service Excellence. The firm's customer service representatives receive extensive and continuous training, including 80 classroom hours and on-the-job training. They sample every menu item, get weekly evaluations, and participate in monthly retraining programs. AMP, an electrical connector supplier, requires salespeople to "get to know customers from the president to the janitor. They get involved in customers' research and development projects to save them weight, space, or money in their manufacturing processes." Xerox, Ameritech, BMW, and Domino's link some employee pay to customer satisfaction. At Metamor Technologies, a small Chicago-area com-

Nonstop to London.
Showers expected upon arrival.
British Airways' new arrival facilities at London's Heathrow and Gatwick airports are making quite a splash. Now, ClubWorld℠ and First Class passengers can enjoy a hot shower and breakfast or even catch up on business in our private lounge. You'll be off to a flying start. *It's the way we make you feel* that makes us the world's favourite airline.
BRITISH AIRWAYS
The world's favourite airline

FIGURE 1-7
Customer Service and British Airways
Reprinted by permission.

puter consulting firm, 40 per cent of employees' potential bonuses are tied to customer feedback.[12]

As Figure 1-7 illustrates, no company is more comprehensive in its approach to customer service than airline giant British Airways:

> The firm tracks some 350 measures of performance, including aircraft cleanliness, punctuality, customer opinions on check-in experiences, the time it takes for a customer to get through when phoning a reservations agent, and customer satisfaction with in-flight and ground services. A monthly report goes to the chief executive officer, the managing director, the chief financial officer, and the top management team responsible for service and performance. The report usually has a section focusing on a particular problem or issue. For example, it might address in-flight food service.[13]

[12]"Rare Philosophy," *Marketing Management* (Summer 1995), pp. 4–6; Ernest F. Cooke, "It's Basic But Necessary: Listen to the Customer," *Marketing News* (March 5, 1990), pp. 22–23; Laura Loro, "Customer Is Always Right," *Advertising Age* (February 10, 1992), p. 26; and Stephanie Gruner, "The Customer-Driven Bonus Plan," *Inc.* (November 1995), p. 89.

[13]Steven E. Prokesch, "Competing on Service: An Interview with British Airways' Sir Colin Marshall," *Harvard Business Review*, Vol. 73 (November–December 1995), p. 108.

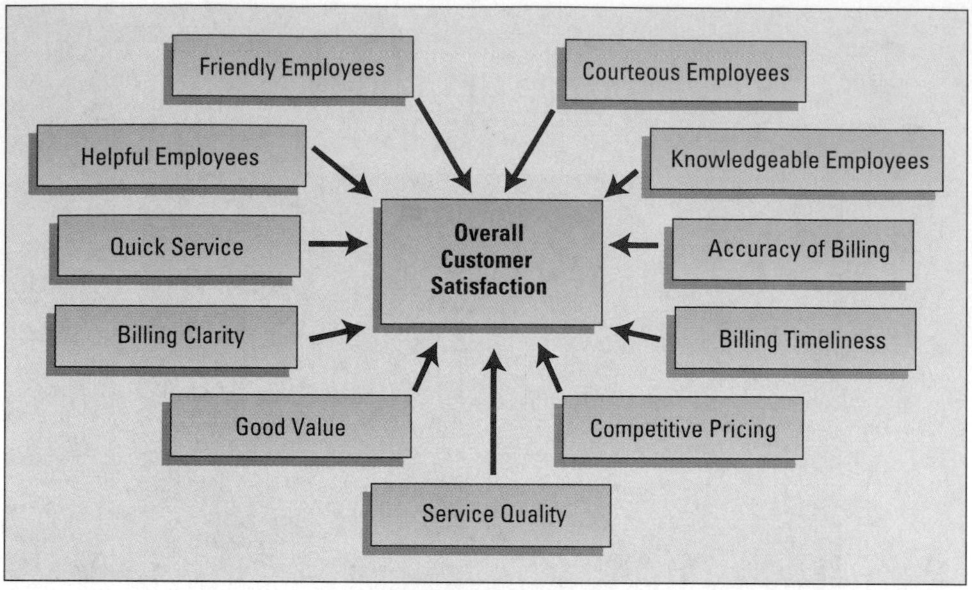

FIGURE 1-8
Factors That Affect Customer Satisfaction

Source: Steven Hokanson, "The Deeper You Analyze, the More You Satisfy Customers," *Marketing News* (January 2, 1995), p. 16. *Reprinted by permission of the American Marketing Association.*

Customer Satisfaction and Relationship Marketing

Firms cannot usually prosper without a high level of **customer satisfaction**.

As previously noted, **customer satisfaction** is a crucial element in successful marketing. It is the degree to which there is a match between a customer's expectations of a good or service and the actual performance of that good or service, including customer service.[14] As one expert says: "Firms that satisfy customers are ones that do their homework. They know a customer satisfaction commitment must be backed up by a complete understanding of the customer, the competition, and the marketplace—and an ability to identify and respond to areas where change is needed."[15] Figure 1-8 shows eleven representative factors that affect overall customer satisfaction.

This is how formidable it can be to keep customers satisfied:

> Do smaller companies give better customer service? The clients of Roberts Express Inc. thought so. In 1983, when sales were $3 million at the Akron, Ohio-based freight company specializing in emergency shipments, customers were spoiled and they enjoyed it. They spoke to service representatives on a first-name basis. Calling in, clients expected to reach a shipping agent who knew their business, even what truck size would best suit their company's products. Roberts Express rarely disappointed its small group of customers.
>
> But as sales doubled annually, that service started to change. Customer service reps and shipping agents who once sat side by side and solved problems by talking over a cubicle wall, now worked in separate buildings. In monthly satisfaction surveys, clients complained that the company had become too large. Customers weren't recognized anymore. "They were saying, 'I'm calling a customer service organization and one of 100 people could pick up the phone,'" recalls Bruce Simpson, president of Roberts Express.
>
> To get back to its small-company roots, Roberts started to reorganize six years ago into teams. It now has 18 teams that give Roberts a small company feel while allowing it to grow sales. When a customer calls, the team member who picks up the phone owns the service from start to finish. The firm can give personal, immediate service because each team works as a small business for its geographic area. Today, sales are about $150 million.[16]

Through **relationship marketing**, *companies try to increase long-term customer loyalty.*

Companies with satisfied customers have a good opportunity to convert them into loyal customers—who purchase from those firms over an extended period. From a consumer-oriented perspective, when marketing activities are performed with the conscious intention of developing and managing long-term, trusting relationships with customers, **relationship marketing** is involved.[17] Why is this so important? According to one ob-

[14]Bennett, *Dictionary of Marketing Terms*, p. 73.
[15]Stanley Brown, "You Can Get Satisfaction," *Sales & Marketing Management* (July 1995), p. 106.
[16]Weld F. Royal, "Keep Them Coming Back," *Inc.* (September 1995), p. 51.
[17]Bennett, *Dictionary of Marketing Terms*, p. 242.

server, "Are you keeping your customers? You'd better be because it's far cheaper to hold on to the ones you have than to acquire new ones. A happy contingent inside your tent lessens your need to beat the street for business. Loyalists may even drum up fresh prospects for you."[18]

Great Plains Software, the biggest U.S. provider of high-end programs for accountants, is one of many firms that has mastered relationship marketing:

> How's this for getting close to the customer? Great Plains codes every program in a way that blocks its use after 50 transactions. The customer must call the firm for the code that gets the program running again. At this point, the folks who answer the phones ask questions about the customer's business, computer system, and software requirements. Sound annoying? "Customers don't seem to mind a simple phone call," insists CEO Doug Bergum. Today, Great Plains has some 45,000 buyer profiles in its data bank and personally solicits those likely to upgrade. In 1993, the firm persuaded a phenomenal 42 per cent of the owners of Great Plains Accounting Version 6 to buy new Version 7.
>
> These retention skills got dearly tested when Version 7 turned out to contain bugs. Concerned that his reputation for bug-free products would be ruined, Bergum spent $250,000 to mail new disks to every Version 7 buyer. He also wrote all 2,700 Great Plains dealers, admitting that he failed to test Version 7 properly and offering cash compensation to anyone whose business suffered from the glitch. Great Plains' goof may have *enhanced* customer loyalty. More dealers wrote to praise Bergum's response than to claim redress—which amounted to $25,000, less than 0.5 per cent of the sales from Version 7 sales. *Accounting Today* commended Great Plains for being "a model of how problems should be handled." At "Stampede to Fargo," the firm's annual dealer conference, Bergum won the crowd by standing onstage, explaining his mistakes at length, and smashing three fresh eggs on his head.[19]

The Importance of Marketing

Marketing stimulates consumers, costs a large part of sales, employs people, supports industries, affects all consumers, and plays a major role in our lives.

Here are several reasons why the field of marketing should be studied: Because marketing stimulates demand, a basic task for it is to generate consumer enthusiasm for goods and services. Worldwide, about $26 trillion of goods and services are produced annually, with the United States accounting for over $7 trillion of that sum.

A large amount of each sales dollar goes to cover the costs related to such marketing activities as product development, packaging, distribution, advertising and personal selling, price marking, and administering consumer credit programs. Some estimates place the costs of marketing as high as 50 per cent or more of sales in certain industries. Yet, it should not be assumed that the performance of some marketing tasks by consumers would automatically lead to lower prices. For example, could a small business really save money by having the owner fly to Detroit to buy a new truck directly from the maker rather than from a local dealer? Would a family be willing to buy clothing in bulk to reduce a retailer's transportation and storage costs?

Tens of millions of people work in marketing-related jobs in the United States alone. They include those employed in the retailing, wholesaling, transportation, warehousing, and communications industries and those involved with marketing jobs for manufacturing, service, agricultural, mining, and other industries. About 20 million people work in retailing, 6 million in wholesaling, and 4 million in transportation. Projections indicate future employment in marketing will remain strong.

Marketing activities also involve entire industries, such as advertising and marketing research. Total annual worldwide advertising expenditures exceed $350 billion. Many agencies, such as WPP Group and Cordiant of Great Britain, Interpublic Group and Omnicom Group of the United States, and Dentsu of Japan have worldwide billings of several billion dollars each. Around $8 billion worldwide is spent yearly on various types of commercial marketing research. Firms such as Nielsen, Information Resources Inc., Research International (Great Britain), and GfK (Germany) generate yearly revenues of more than $100 million each.

[18]Patricia Sellers, "Keeping the Buyer You Already Have," *Fortune* (Autumn–Winter 1993), p. 56.
[19]Ibid., p. 57.

All people and organizations serve as consumers for various goods and services. By understanding the role of marketing, consumers can become better informed, more selective, and more efficient. Effective channels of communication with sellers can also be established and complaints resolved more easily and favorably. Consumer groups have a major impact on sellers.

Because resources are scarce, marketing programs and systems must function at their peak. Thus, by optimizing customer service, inventory movement, advertising expenditures, product assortments, and other areas of marketing, firms will better use resources. Some industries may even require demarketing (lowering the demand for goods and services). The latter often include energy consumption.

Marketing impacts strongly on people's beliefs and life-styles. In fact, it has been criticized as developing materialistic attitudes, fads, product obsolescence, a reliance on gadgets, status consciousness, and superficial product differences—and for wasting resources. Marketers reply that they merely address the desires of people and make the best goods and services they can at the prices people will pay.

Marketing has a role to play in improving our quality of life. For example, marketing personnel often encourage firms to make safer products, such as child-proof bottle caps. They create public service messages on energy conservation, AIDS prevention, driver safety, alcohol abuse, and other topics. They help new goods, ideas, and services (such as cellular phones, improved nutrition, and ATMs) to be accepted by people and organizations.

Marketing awareness is invaluable for those in nonmarketing jobs.

A knowledge of marketing is extremely valuable for those not directly involved in a marketing job. For example, marketing decisions must be made by

- *Doctors*—What hours are most desirable to patients?
- *Lawyers*—How can new clients be attracted?
- *Management consultants*—Should fees be higher, lower, or the same as competitors' fees?
- *Financial analysts*—What investments should be recommended to clients?
- *Research and development personnel*—Is there consumer demand for a potential "breakthrough" product?
- *Economists*—What impact will the economy have on the way various industries market their offerings?
- *Statisticians*—How should firms react to predicted demographic shifts?
- *Teachers*—How can students become better consumers?
- *City planners*—How can businesses be persuaded to relocate to the city?
- *Nonprofit institutions*—How can donor contributions be raised?

Each of these professions and organizations needs to understand and satisfy patient, client, consumer, student, taxpayer, or contributor needs. And more of them than ever before are now undertaking marketing activities such as research, advertising, and so on.

Marketing Functions and Performers

Basic **marketing functions** *range from environmental analysis to marketing management.*

There are eight basic **marketing functions**: environmental analysis and marketing research, broadening an organization's/individual's scope, consumer analysis, product planning, distribution planning, promotion planning, price planning, and marketing management. They are shown in Figure 1-9, which also notes where they are discussed in the text.

Here are brief descriptions of the functions:

- *Environmental analysis and marketing research*—Monitoring and adapting to external factors that affect success or failure, such as the economy and competition; and collecting data to resolve specific marketing issues.
- *Broadening an organization's/individual's scope*—Deciding on the emphasis to place, as well as the approach to take, on societal issues and international marketing.

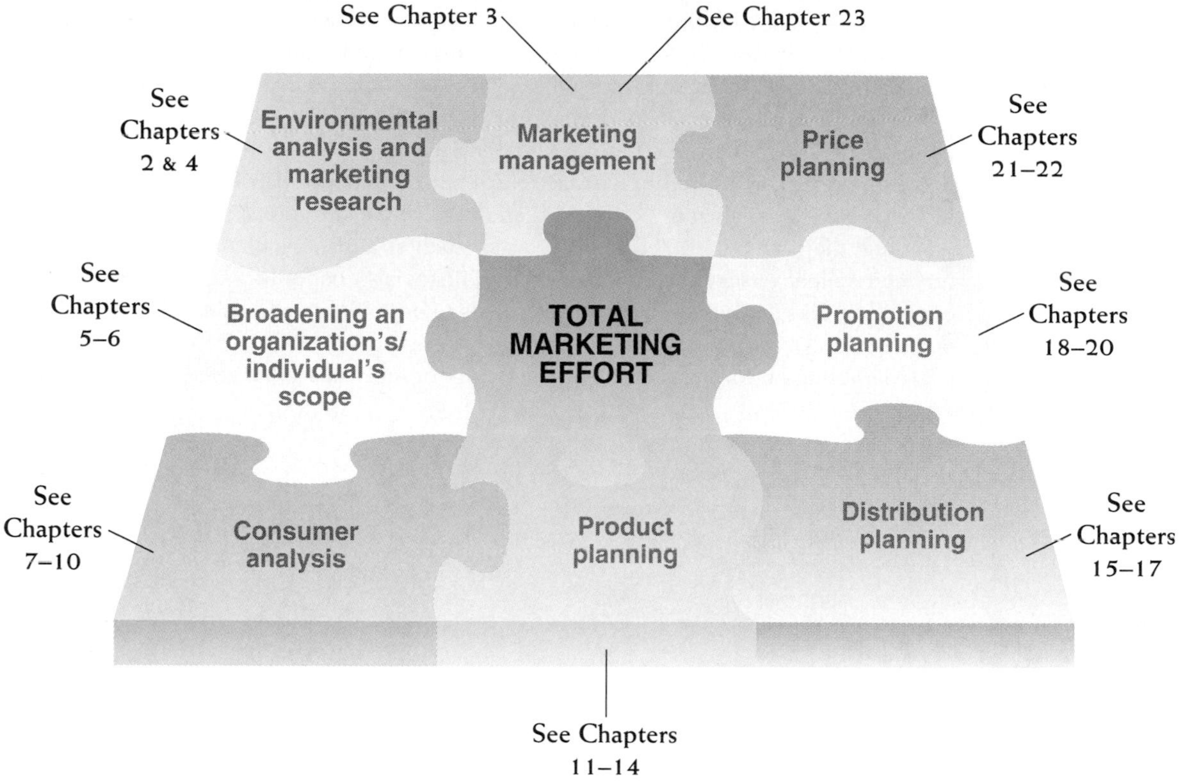

FIGURE 1-9
The Basic Functions of Marketing

- *Consumer analysis*—Examining and evaluating consumer characteristics, needs, and purchase processes; and selecting the group(s) of consumers at which to aim marketing efforts.
- *Product planning* (including goods, services, organizations, people, places, and ideas)—Developing and maintaining products, product assortments, product images, brands, packaging, and optional features; and deleting faltering products.
- *Distribution planning*—Forming relations with distribution intermediaries, physical distribution, inventory management, warehousing, transportation, the allocation of goods and services, wholesaling, and retailing.
- *Promotion planning*—Communicating with customers, the general public, and others through some form of advertising, public relations, personal selling, and/or sales promotion.
- *Price planning*—Determining price levels and ranges, pricing techniques, terms of purchase, price adjustments, and the use of price as an active or passive factor.
- *Marketing management*—Planning, implementing, and controlling the marketing program (strategy) and individual marketing functions; appraising the risks and benefits in decision making; and focusing on total quality.

Generally, a firm should first study its environment and gather relevant marketing information. The firm should determine how to act in a socially responsible and ethical manner and consider whether to be domestic and/or international. At the same time, the firm should analyze potential customers to learn their needs and select the group(s) on which to focus. It should next plan product offerings, make distribution decisions, choose how to communicate with customers and others, and set proper prices. These four functions (in combination, known as the *marketing mix*) should be done in a coordinated manner, based on environmental, societal, and consumer analysis. Through marketing management, the firm's overall marketing program would be planned and carried out in an integrated manner, with fine-tuning as necessary.

Although many marketing transactions require the performance of similar tasks, such as being ethical, analyzing consumers, and product, distribution, promotion, and price planning, they can be enacted in many ways (such as a manufacturer distributing via full-service retailers versus self-service ones, or a financial-services firm relying on telephone contacts by its sales force versus in-office visits to potential small-business clients by salespeople).

Marketing performers are the organizations or individuals that undertake one or more

Ethics IN TODAY'S SOCIETY

What Practices Do YOU Believe are Ethical?

Ethical values in marketing can be determined by using a checklist. So, here is an opportunity for YOU to assess your level of marketing ethics.

Respond to these statements on a 1 to 9 scale. For items 1–4, let "1" mean that you completely disagree and "9" mean that you completely agree. For items 5–10, use a "1" for complete agreement and a "9" for complete disagreement.

1. Business ethics and social responsibility are critical to the survival of a business enterprise.
2. Business has a social responsibility beyond making a profit.
3. Good ethics is often good business.
4. Social responsibility and profitability can be compatible.
5. If stockholders are unhappy, nothing else matters.
6. The most important concern for a firm is making a profit, even if it means bending or breaking the rules.
7. To remain competitive in a global environment, business firms will have to disregard ethics and social responsibility.
8. Efficiency is much more important to a firm than whether or not the firm is seen as ethical or socially responsible.
9. Although output quality is essential to corporate success, ethics and social responsibility are not.
10. Communication is more important to the overall effectiveness of a firm than whether it is concerned with ethics and social responsibility.

Items 1–4 measure a "good ethics is good business" orientation, items 5–8 measure a "profits are not paramount" orientation, and items 9–10 measure a "quality and communication" orientation. Summarize and describe your ethical nature by determining your total score, as well as your score on the three individual scales.

Source: Based on material in Anusorn Singhapakdi, Kenneth L. Kraft, Scott J. Vitell, and Kumar C. Rallapalli, "The Perceived Importance of Ethics and Social Responsibility on Organizational Effectiveness: A Survey of Marketers," *Journal of the Academy of Marketing Science,* Vol. 23 (Winter 1995), pp. 49–56.

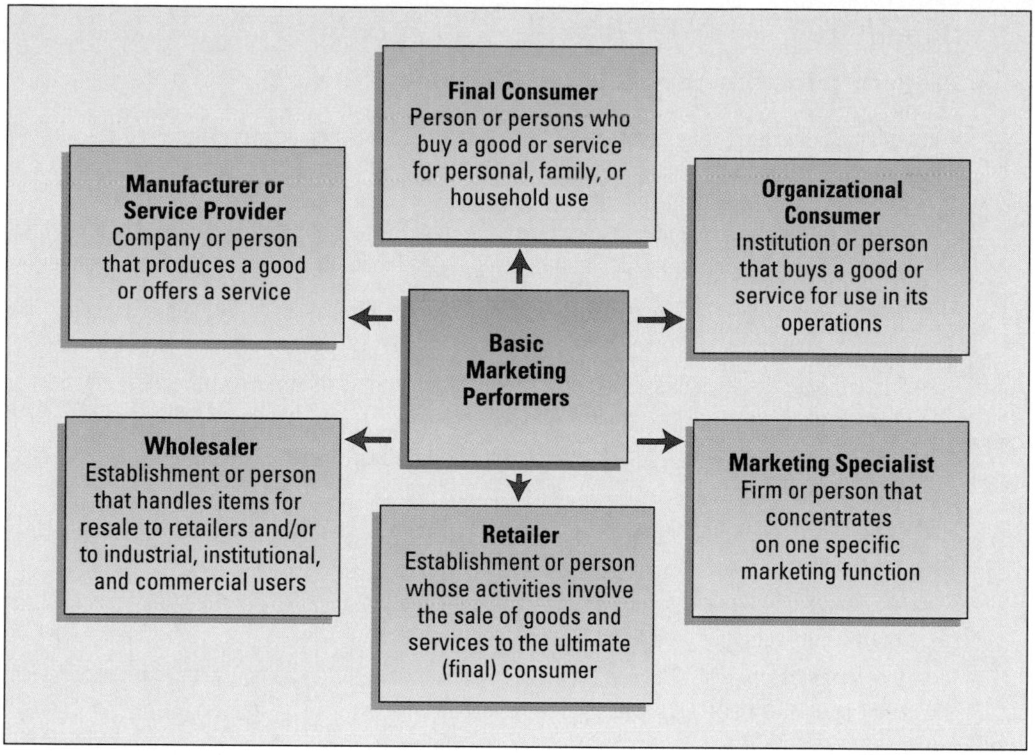

FIGURE 1-10
Who Performs Marketing Functions

marketing functions. They include manufacturers and service providers, wholesalers, retailers, marketing specialists, and organizational and final consumers. As Figure 1-10 shows, each performer has a different role. Even though the responsibility for marketing tasks can be shifted and shared in various ways, basic marketing functions usually must be done by one performer or another. They cannot be omitted in many situations.

Usually at least one **marketing performer** *must undertake each of the basic marketing functions.*

Sometimes, one marketing performer decides to carry out all—or virtually all—marketing functions (such as Boeing analyzing the marketplace, acting ethically, operating domestically and internationally, seeking various types of customers, developing aerospace and related products, distributing products directly to customers, using its own sales force and placing ads in select media, and setting prices). Yet, for these reasons, one performer often does not undertake all marketing functions:

- Many firms do not have the financial resources to sell products directly to consumers. They need intermediaries to share in the distribution process.
- Marketing directly to customers may require goods and services producers to offer complementary products or sell the complementary products of other firms so the distribution process is carried out efficiently.
- A performer may be unable or unwilling to complete certain functions and may seek a marketing specialist to fulfill them.
- Many performers are too small to do certain functions efficiently.
- For many goods and services, established distribution methods are in force and it is difficult to set up other methods (such as bypassing independent soda distributors to sell directly to retail stores).
- Some consumers may want to buy in quantity, visit self-service outlets, pay cash, and so on, to save money.

MARKETING IN A CHANGING WORLD

Preparing for the Year 2000 and Beyond

A daunting challenge for any organization is to examine the changing world so as to plan for the future. Thus, in each text chapter (including this one), we will look at some of the key events that are affecting or will affect marketing decision making.

Experts at Batelle, a leading research institute, feel these technologies are most apt to "bring rich rewards" to firms that are capable of developing and marketing them in the next decade:

- *Genetic mapping*—New treatments for ailments ranging from AIDS to Alzheimer's disease may be on the way.
- *Super materials*—Scientists will increasingly produce new materials with almost any desired characteristic.
- *High-density energy sources*—Batteries the size of sugar packets will bring many new, revolutionary products to life.
- *Digital HDTV*—Digital high-definition television could be the next "hot" item in the entertainment industry.
- *Miniaturization*—It will be possible to carry around a laptop computer the size of a pocket calculator. This computer will be interactive and wireless.
- *Smart manufacturing*—Factory assembly lines will more often be controlled by smart devices and systems rather than people.
- *Anti-aging goods and services*—New developments will range from aging creams that may actually work to an effective cure for baldness.
- *Medical treatments*—There will be new diagnostic tools that use extremely accurate sensors to detect diseases at very early stages.
- *Hybrid-fuel vehicles*—Research on alternative fuels will be stepped up.
- *Edutainment*—Computer software and other products will increasingly meld education and entertainment features.[20]

Format of the Text

This book is divided into eight parts. The balance of Part 1 focuses on the marketing environment, developing marketing plans, and the information needed for marketing decisions. Part 2 covers the key topics related to the broadened scope of marketing: societal, ethical, and consumer issues; and international marketing. The discussion in Parts 1 and 2 sets the foundation for studying the specific components of marketing.

Part 3 deals with marketing's central orientation: understanding consumers. It looks at demographics, social and psychological traits, and the decision process of final consumers; organizational consumer attributes and decision making; and developing a target market and sales forecasting. Parts 4 to 7 discuss the elements of the marketing mix (product, distribution, promotion, and price planning) and the actions needed to carry out a marketing program in depth. Part 8 considers the marketing management implications of the topics raised throughout *Marketing* and discusses how to integrate and analyze an overall marketing plan.

Numerous examples and illustrations of actual marketing practices by a variety of organizations and individuals are woven into our discussions. And although such topics as marketing and society, international marketing, organizational consumers, and goods versus service marketing get separate chapter coverage to highlight certain points, applications in these areas are presented throughout the text.

[20]Douglas E. Olesen, "The Top 10 Technologies for the Next 10 Years," *Futurist* (September–October 1995), pp. 9–13.

SUMMARY

In this and every chapter in the text, the summary is linked to the objectives stated at the beginning of the chapter.

1. *To illustrate the exciting, dynamic, and influential nature of marketing* Marketing may be viewed from both business and consumer perspectives; and it influences us daily. As goods and service providers, we make such marketing-related decisions as choosing who customers are, what goods and services to offer, where to sell them, what to stress in promotion, what prices to charge, how to be ethical and responsible, and whether to operate internationally. As consumers, the marketing process affects whom we patronize, choices in the marketplace, where we shop, the availability of sales personnel, the prices we pay, and other factors.

2. *To define marketing and trace its evolution—with emphasis on the marketing concept, a marketing philosophy, customer service, and customer satisfaction and relationship marketing* Marketing involves anticipating, managing, and satisfying demand via the exchange process. It includes goods, services, organizations, people, places, and ideas.

The evolution of marketing can be traced to people's earliest use of barter in the exchange process (the barter era); but, it has truly developed since the Industrial Revolution, as mass production and improved transportation have enabled more transactions to occur. For many firms, modern marketing has evolved via these eras: production, sales, marketing department, and marketing company. Yet, in less-developed and developing countries, marketing practices are in the early stages of development.

The marketing concept requires an organization or individual to be consumer-oriented, market-driven, value-based, have an integrated effort, and be goal-oriented. A marketing philosophy means assessing and responding to consumer wants, to real differences in consumer tastes, and to long-run opportunities and threats, and to engage in coordinated decision making.

To prosper today, emphasis must be placed on customer service: the identifiable, rather intangible, acts performed by a seller in conjunction with the basic goods and/or services it offers. A number of firms now empower employees so as to improve the level of customer service. Customer satisfaction occurs when consumer expectations are met or exceeded; then, there are opportunities for firms to attract loyal customers by paying attention to relationship marketing.

3. *To show the importance of marketing as a field of study* Marketing is a crucial field for several reasons: it stimulates demand; marketing costs can be high; a large number of people work in marketing positions; it involves entire industries, such as advertising and marketing research; all organizations and people are consumers in some situations; it is necessary to use scarce resources efficiently; marketing impacts on people's beliefs and life-styles; and marketing influences the quality of our lives. Some marketing knowledge is valuable to all of us, regardless of occupation.

4. *To describe the basic functions of marketing and those that perform these functions* The major marketing functions are environmental analysis and marketing research; broadening an organization's/individual's scope; consumer analysis; product, distribution, promotion, and price planning; and marketing management. Responsibility for performing these tasks can be shifted and shared in several ways among manufacturers and service providers, wholesalers, retailers, marketing specialists, and consumers. Due to costs, assortment requirements, specialized abilities, company size, established distribution methods, and consumer interests, one party usually does not perform all functions.

KEY TERMS

marketing (p. 7)
consumer demand (p. 8)
publics' demand (p. 8)
exchange (p. 8)
barter era (p. 9)
production era (pp. 9–10)
sales era (p. 10)
marketing department era (p. 10)
marketing company era (p. 10)
marketing concept (p. 11)
customer service (p. 13)
empowering employees (p. 13)
customer satisfaction (p. 16)
relationship marketing (p. 16)
marketing functions (p. 18)
marketing performers (p. 21)

Review Questions

1. How does marketing influence us daily in both our business roles and as consumers?

2. Explain the

a. Anticipation of demand.
b. Management of demand.
c. Satisfaction of demand.
d. Exchange process.

3. Distinguish between consumer and publics' demand.

4. Give an example of a good, service, organization, person, place, and idea that may be marketed.

5. Describe the five eras of marketing.

6. What are the five components of the marketing concept? Give an example of each component.

7. What is customer service? Why is it so important to any firm?

8. What is customer satisfaction? Why is it so important to any firm?

9. What are the basic functions performed by marketing?

10. Why do most consumers *not* buy products directly from manufacturers?

Discussion Questions

1. **a.** As Marie Jackson, CPA, what business-related marketing decisions would you make? Why?

b. As Albert Sampson, accounting client, what consumer-related marketing decisions would you make? Why?

c. Develop a plan for Marie Jackson to attract Albert Sampson as a client.

2. Does the presence of a marketing department mean a firm is following the marketing concept? Explain your answer.

3. As the manager of a full-service hotel chain, how would your customer services differ from those offered by a limited-service hotel chain? Why?

4. Develop a seven-item questionnaire to assess the quality of a firm's customer satisfaction efforts.

5. What would a nonmarketing major learn by studying marketing? Give examples for three distinct majors (including at least two nonbusiness majors).

Hints for Solving Cases

At the end of each chapter, from 2 through 23, there are two short cases— a total of 44. In addition, there is one longer, more provocative case at the end of each part—a total of 8. All cases are intended to build on text discussions, improve your reasoning skills, and stimulate class discussions.

The cases in *Marketing* describe actual marketing scenarios faced by a variety of organizations and individuals. The facts, situations, and people are all real. The questions following each case are designed to help you pinpoint major issues, foster your analysis, have you cite alternative courses of future action, and have you develop appropriate marketing strategies. The information necessary to answer the questions may be drawn from the case and the text chapter(s) to which the case relates.

One case per chapter also has a video component, which your professor may or may not assign. The material in the text is sufficient to answer the first four questions regarding a case; there are two other questions for the case that pertain to its video.

These hints should be kept in mind when solving a case:

- Read (observe) all material carefully. Underline or take notes on important data and statements.
- List the key issues and company actions detailed in the case.
- Do not make unrealistic or unsupported assumptions.
- Read each question following the case. Be sure you understand the thrust of every question. Do not give similar answers for two distinct questions.
- Write up tentative answers in outline form. Cover as many aspects of each question as possible.
- Review relevant material in the appropriate chapter of the text. In particular, look for information pertaining to the case questions.
- Expand your tentative answers, substantiating them with data from the case and the chapter(s).
- Reread the case and your notes to be sure you have not omitted any important concepts in your answers.
- Make sure your answers are clear and well written, and that you have considered their ramifications for the organization.
- Reread your solutions at least one day after developing your answers. This ensures a more objective review of your work.
- Make any necessary revisions.
- Be sure your answers are not a summary ("rehash") of the case, but that you have presented a real analysis and recommendations.

CHAPTER 2

The Environment in Which Marketing Operates

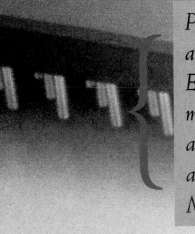

Chapter Objectives

1. To examine the environment within which marketing decisions are made and marketing activities are undertaken

2. To differentiate between those elements controlled by a firm's top management and those controlled by marketing, and to enumerate the controllable elements of a marketing plan

3. To enumerate the uncontrollable environmental elements that can affect a marketing plan and study their potential ramifications

4. To explain why feedback about company performance and the uncontrollable aspects of its environment and the subsequent adaptation of the marketing plan are essential for a firm to attain its objectives

Pitches by AT&T, MCI, and Sprint, as merciless as they are amusing, pose a challenge worthy of biblical scholars: Each claims to have the best deal. Sorting through the many offers could easily cost more time than most people actually spend on the phone. But one thing rings clear to almost every viewer: That staid bastion of bureaucracy, Ma Bell, has turned into one mean mother.

Reprinted by permission.

At one time, competitors were more genteel. They would not mention a direct competitor in an ad—or even think about saying something disparaging in public. Now, the rules of conduct have changed. Let's look at the new competitive tactics.

Perhaps the most ferocious battle is the rivalry between AT&T and MCI. For example, one recent AT&T advertising campaign took direct aim at MCI's Friends & Family program, which offered lower rates if both the caller and the called party were MCI customers. AT&T's ad said that asking MCI subscribers for the names of their friends and family members could be viewed as violating a customer's right to privacy. And AT&T does not limit its competitive tactics to advertising. It also offers customers who have switched to competing firms up to $100 if they return to AT&T. According to one estimate, during one month alone, AT&T has mailed out as much as $55 million in checks to MCI customers.

And it's not just larger firms that are picking the fights with their smaller rivals. In a television ad broadcast in New England, Boston-based U.S. Trust (with assets of $1.8 billion) took aim at Fleet Financial and Shawmut National (with combined assets of $81 billion) during their merger talks. U.S. Trust's ad showed two overweight and balding bankers seated on a bench and asked: "Now that they have twice the assets, will they sit on your loan twice as long?"

Other firms have resorted to using litigation as a competitive tactic. Take Cyrix's feud with Intel. Although Cyrix's sales are a small fraction of Intel's (Cyrix's 1994 sales were $250 million versus Intel's sales of $11.5 billion), nevertheless, Cyrix was forced to expend more than $20 million in legal bills—responding to law suits filed by Intel (all of which were won or settled favorably by Cyrix). According to Cyrix's top marketing executive, "I can't say we encourage our people to think ill of Andy Grove [Intel's chief executive], but we did put Intel's tombstone in our lobby atrium, and we make sure the flowers stay fresh."

Fierce competition is not limited to the United States. For example, Sony has engaged in combat with long-time rival Matsushita in Thailand. In 1988, when Sony first entered Thailand, it had no market presence and Matsushita controlled one-third of the market. Today, each brand has the same market share there. Kazunori Somaya, manager of Sony's consumer electronic business in Thailand, used a strategy that combined elements of both pricing and advertising. He quickly established the Sony brand as a status symbol by selling only high-end products and promoting them on the basis of image, not technical attributes. Sony also waged a price war by attacking Matsushita's market where its rival was strongest and had the most to lose.[1]

In this chapter, we will study the complex environment in which marketing decisions are made. We will see that an organization's level of success (or failure) is related not only to its marketing efforts, but also to the external environment in which it operates and its ability to adapt to environmental changes.

Overview

The environment within which marketing decisions are made and enacted is depicted in Figure 2-1. The **marketing environment** consists of these five parts: controllable factors, uncontrollable factors, the organization's level of success or failure in reaching objectives, feedback, and adaptation.

The **marketing environment** *consists of controllable factors, uncontrollable factors, organizational performance, feedback, and adaptation.*

[1]Jaclyn Fierman, "When Genteel Rivals Become Mortal Enemies," *Fortune* (May 15, 1995), pp. 90–100; and 1996 Cyrix correspondence.

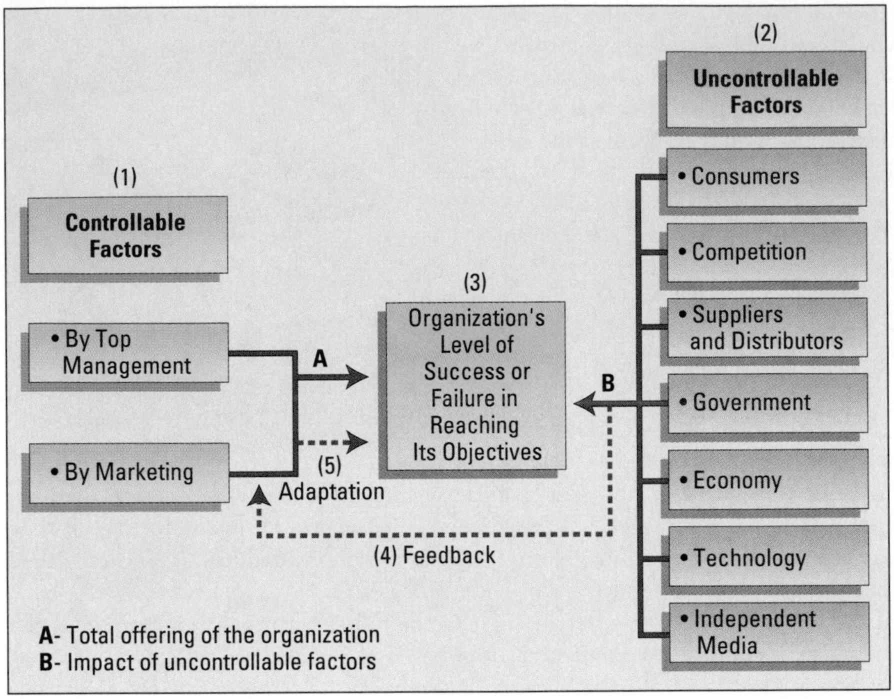

FIGURE 2-1
The Environment Within Which Marketing Operates

Controllable factors are those directed by an organization and its marketers. First, several broad, fundamental decisions are made by top management. Then, marketing managers make specific decisions based on the guidelines. In combination, these factors result in an overall strategy or offering (*A* in Figure 2-1). The major uncontrollable factors are beyond the control of an individual organization, but they have an impact on how well an organization does (*B* in Figure 2-1).

The interaction of controllable factors and uncontrollable factors determines an organization's level of success or failure in reaching its goals. Feedback occurs when a firm makes an effort to monitor uncontrollable factors and assess its strengths and weaknesses. Adaptation refers to the changes in a marketing plan that an organization makes to comply with the uncontrollable environment. If a firm is unwilling to consider the entire environment in a systematic manner, it increases the likelihood that it will have a lack of direction and not attain proper results.

Both the **macroenvironment** *and the* **microenvironment** *must be understood.*

When analyzing the environment, an organization should consider it from two perspectives: the macroenvironment and the microenvironment. The **macroenvironment** refers to the broad demographic, societal, economic, political, technological, and other forces that an organization faces. The **microenvironment** refers to the forces close to an organization that have a direct impact on its ability to serve customers, including distribution intermediaries, competitors, consumer markets, and the capabilities of the organization itself.[2]

Throughout this chapter, the various parts of Figure 2-1 are described and drawn together so the complex environment of marketing can be understood. In Chapter 3, the concept of strategic planning is presented. Such planning establishes a formal process for developing, implementing, and evaluating marketing programs in conjunction with the goals of top management.

Controllable Factors

The organization and its marketers can manage **controllable factors**.

Controllable factors are internally directed by an organization and its marketers. Some of these factors are directed by top management; these are not controllable by marketers, who must develop plans to satisfy overall organizational goals. In situations involving small

[2]Peter D. Bennett (Editor), *Dictionary of Marketing Terms*, Second Edition (Chicago: American Marketing Association, 1995), pp. 159, 177.

or medium-sized institutions, both broad policy and marketing decisions are often made by one person, usually the owner. Even in those cases, broad policies are typically set first and marketing plans must adjust to them. For example, a person could decide to open an office-supply store selling products to small businesses (broad policy) and stress convenient hours, a good selection of items, quantity discounts, and superior customer service (marketing plan).

Factors Directed by Top Management

Although top management is responsible for numerous decisions, five are of extreme importance to marketers: line of business, overall objectives, role of marketing, role of other business functions, and corporate culture. They have an impact on all aspects of marketing. Figure 2-2 shows the types of decisions in these areas.

A firm's **line of business** *refers to its business category.*

The **line of business** refers to the general goods/service category, functions, geographic coverage, type of ownership, and specific business of a firm. The general goods/service category is a broad definition of the industry in which a firm seeks to be involved. It may be energy, transportation, computing, or any number of others. The functions of the business outline a firm's position in the marketing system—from supplier to manufacturer to wholesaler to retailer—and the tasks it seeks to do. A firm may want to be in more than one of these positions. Geographic coverage can be neighborhood, city, county, state, regional, national, or international. The type of ownership ranges from a sole proprietorship, partnership, or franchise to a multiunit corporation. The specific business is a narrow definition of the firm, its functions, and its operations, such as Elaine's Dry Cleaners (a local full-service dry cleaner specializing in outerwear).

Overall objectives are the broad, measurable goals set by top management. A firm's success or failure may be determined by comparing objectives with actual performance. Usually, a combination of sales, profit, and other goals is stated by management for short-run (one year or less) and long-run (several years) periods. Most firms cite customer acceptance as a key goal with a strong effect on sales, profit, and long-run existence.

Top management determines the role of marketing by noting its importance, outlining its activities, and integrating it into a firm's overall operation. Marketing's importance is evident when marketing people have decision making authority, the rank of the chief

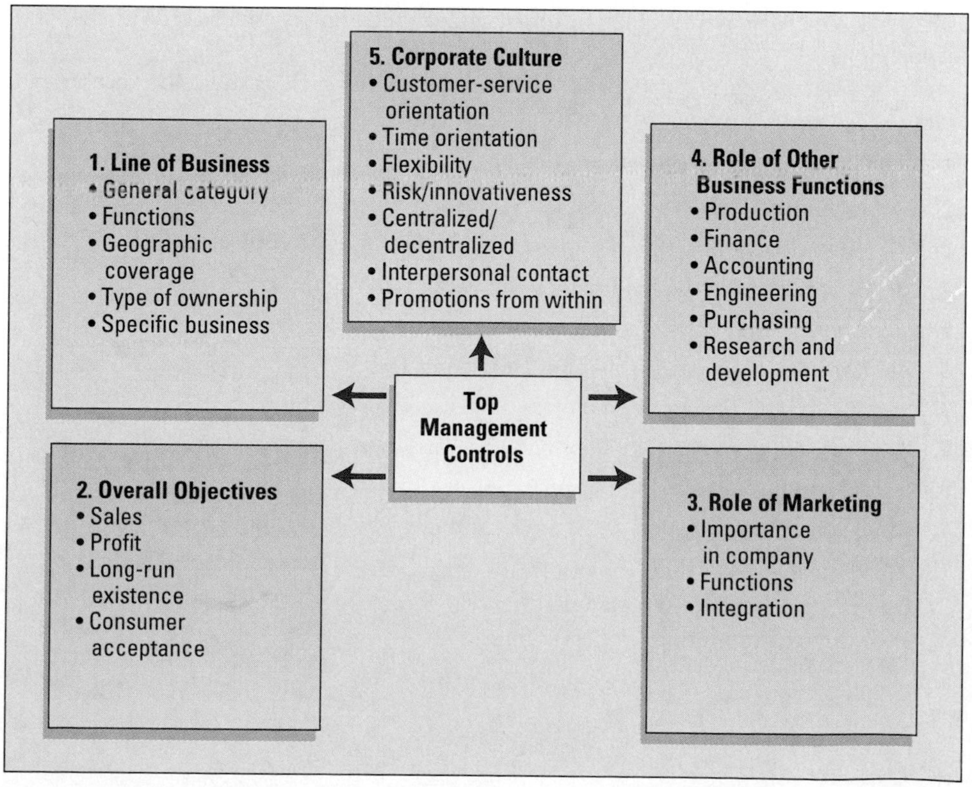

FIGURE 2-2
Factors Controlled by Top Management

marketing officer is equal to that of other areas (usually vice-president), and proper resources are given. It is not considered important by a firm that gives marketing people advisory status, places marketing personnel in a subordinate position (like reporting to the production vice-president), equates marketing with sales, and withholds the funds needed for research, promotion, and other marketing tasks. The larger marketing's role, the greater the likelihood that a firm has an integrated marketing organization. The smaller its role, the greater the possibility that a firm undertakes marketing tasks on a project, crisis, or fragmented basis.

The roles of other business functions and their interrelationships with marketing need to be defined clearly to avoid overlaps, jealousy, and conflict. Production, finance, accounting, engineering, purchasing, and research and development departments each have different perspectives, orientations, and goals. This is discussed further in Chapter 3.

Corporate culture *involves shared values, norms, and practices.*

Top management strongly influences a firm's **corporate culture**: the shared values, norms, and practices communicated to and followed by those working for the firm. It may be described in terms of:

- *A customer-service orientation*—Is the commitment to customer service clearly transmitted to employees?
- *A time orientation*—Is a firm short- or long-run oriented?
- *The flexibility of the job environment*—Can employees deviate from rules? How formal are relations with subordinates? Is there a dress code?
- *The level of risk/innovation pursued*—Is risk taking fostered?
- *The use of a centralized/decentralized management structure*—How much input into decisions do middle managers have?
- *The level of interpersonal contact*—Do employees freely communicate with one another?
- *The use of promotions from within*—Are internal personnel given preference as positions open?

For example, Maryland-based PHH Corporation markets vehicle management services, relocation and real-estate services, and mortgage banking services to more than 2,000 corporate clients. It communicates its corporate culture through written materials, as well as face-to-face conversations. It lists these values as essential: moral integrity, openness and trust, dedication to quality, respect for the individual, team spirit, efficiency, initiative, and adaptability.[3]

Today, many experts recommend "10 commandments" such as these to executives in order to foster a nurturing corporate culture:

1. Seek consensus—don't bark orders.
2. Set broad visions, then give people the freedom needed to carry them out.
3. Make sure people have the resources and support they need to succeed.
4. Spend more time in the field with employees than in your office.
5. Spend some time with employees off the job, too.
6. Monitor progress on projects—don't micromanage.
7. Be quick to give ambitious employees increased responsibilities.
8. Make sure all employees are continuously learning and growing.
9. Reward people for reaching personal, not just financial, goals.
10. Before criticizing someone for "failing," find out why he or she fell short of expectations.[4]

After top management sets company guidelines, the marketing area begins to develop the factors under its control.

[3] *PHH Corporation 1995 Annual Report*, p. 16.
[4] Geoffrey Brewer, "The New Managers," *Performance* (March 1995), p. 32.

Ethics IN TODAY'S SOCIETY

How Does Corporate Culture Influence Ethical Behavior?

A study of thirty recent Harvard MBAs found that, in many cases, they now feel pressure from their companies to engage in unethical and sometimes illegal behavior. For example, a management trainee at a consumer products company was told to make up the data to support a new-product introduction. In another situation, a person was asked to overlook a safety defect in a product and to ship items that did not meet published specifications.

According to ethics experts, these new managers are subjected to four commandments: (1) Performance is what really counts, so make your numbers. (2) Be loyal, and show us that you are a team player. (3) Don't break the law. (4) Don't overinvest in ethical behavior. The first three of these commandments become troublesome when combined with the fourth.

Here is how the managers responded to a series of questions involving ethical and unethical behavior:

- Only a few believe that "sleazy" behavior will be a drag on their career.
- Less than a third believe their firms respect or encourage "whistle blowing."
- When asked what offenses would result in punishment, they rarely mention unethical behavior. Instead, such infractions as poor performance, failure at being a team player, stealing, or drinking at the job were noted.
- More than half of the 30 executives fear repercussions from doing what they see as "the right thing."

Although half of the managers worked in firms with formal ethics programs, in general, these programs had little effect on their behavior or attitudes.

As an ethical compliance manager for a bank, how would you help institute a corporate culture that values high moral principles?

Source: Based on material in Joseph L. Badaracco, Jr., and Allen P. Webb, "Business Ethics: A View From the Trenches," *California Management Review,* Vol. 37 (Winter 1995), pp. 8–28.

Factors Directed by Marketing

The major factors controlled by marketing personnel are the selection of a target market, marketing objectives, the marketing organization, the marketing mix, and assessment of the marketing plan. See Figure 2-3.

A **target market** *is the customer group to which an organization appeals.* **Market segmentation** *is often used in choosing a target market.*

One of the most crucial marketing-related decisions involves selecting a **target market**, which is the particular group(s) of customers a firm proposes to serve, or whose needs it proposes to satisfy, with a particular marketing program. When selecting a target market, a company usually engages in some form of **market segmentation**, which involves subdividing a market into clear subsets of customers that act in the same way or that have comparable needs.[5] A company can choose a large target market or concentrate on a small one, or try to appeal to both with separate marketing programs for each. Generally, these questions must be addressed before devising a marketing approach: Who are our customers? What kinds of goods and services do they want? How can we attract them to our company?

[5]Bennett, *Dictionary of Marketing Terms*, pp. 165–166.

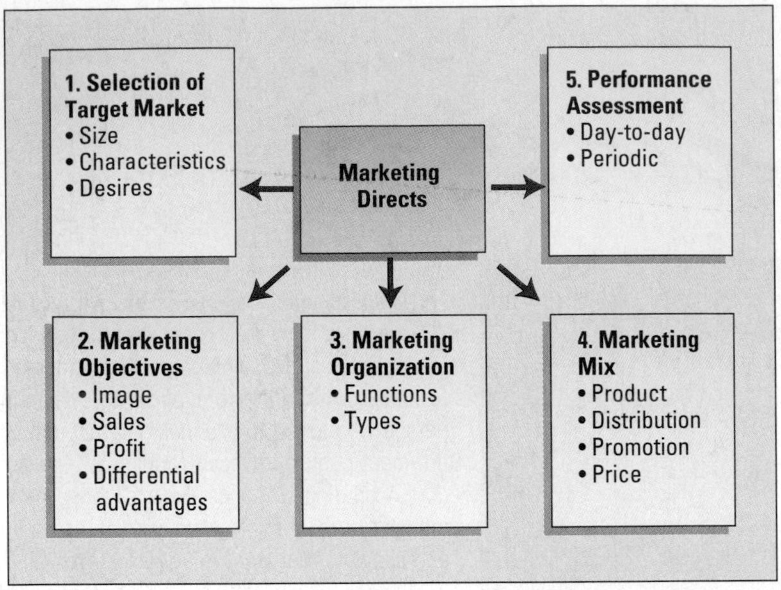

FIGURE 2-3
Factors Controlled by Marketing

At marketing-oriented firms, the choice of a target market has an impact on all other marketing decisions. For example, a book publisher appealing to the high school science market would have a different marketing approach than one appealing to the adult fiction market. The first firm would seek an image as a prestigious, well-established publisher; specialize product offerings; make presentations to high school book-selection committees; sell in large quantities; offer durable books with many photos and line drawings that could be used for several years; and so on. The second firm would capitalize on well-known authors or publish books on hot topics to establish an image; have books on a variety of subjects; use newspaper ads and seek favorable reviews; distribute via bookstores; sell in small quantities (except if large bookstore chains are involved); de-emphasize durability, photos, and line drawings and produce books as efficiently as possible; and so on.

Differential advantages *consist of the firm's unique features that attract consumers.*

Marketing objectives are more customer-oriented than those set by top management. Marketers are quite interested in the image consumers hold of a firm and its products. Sales goals reflect a concern for brand loyalty (repeat purchases), growth via new-product introductions, and appeal to unsatisfied market segments. Profit goals can be related to long-term customer loyalty. Most importantly, marketers seek to create **differential advantages**, the unique features in a firm's marketing program that cause consumers to patronize that firm and not its competitors. Without differential advantages, a firm would have a "me-too" philosophy and offer the consumer no reasons to select its offerings over competitors' products. Differential advantages can be based on a distinctive image, new products or features, product quality, customer service, low prices, availability, and other factors. For example, Snapple is known for its offbeat beverages, Levi's Dockers for their comfortable fit, Sony for its portable audio and video products, Tiffany for its high-quality jewelry, Nordstrom for its courteous store employees, and Wal-Mart for its low prices. Figure 2-4 shows how GTE markets its differential advantages.

A **marketing organization** *may be functional, product-oriented, or market-oriented.*

A **marketing organization** is the structural arrangement that directs marketing functions. It outlines authority, responsibility, and tasks to be done. With it, functions are assigned and coordinated. As illustrated in Figure 2-5, an organization may be functional, with jobs assigned in terms of buying, selling, promotion, distribution, and other tasks; product-oriented, with product managers for each product category and brand managers for each brand, in addition to functional categories; or market-oriented, with jobs assigned by geographic market and customer type, in addition to functional categories. A single firm may use a mixture of forms.

The **marketing mix** *consists of four elements: product, distribution, promotion, and price.*

A **marketing mix** is the specific combination of marketing elements used to achieve objectives and satisfy the target market. It encompasses decisions regarding four major variables: *Product* decisions involve determining what goods, services, organizations, people, places, and/or ideas to market, the number of items to sell and their quality, the innovativeness pursued, packaging, product features, warranties, when to drop existing of-

HOW WELL DOES YOUR CELLULAR SERVICE
PERFORM AT 1,000 DEGREES?
GTE Cellular Service has helped our customers get through firestorms, floods, hurricanes and earthquakes, not to mention
the millions of much smaller crises that happen every day. It's amazing what we can do together.™
GTE

FIGURE 2-4
The Marketing of Differential Advantages
Reprinted by permission.

ferings, and so on. *Distribution* decisions include determining whether to sell via intermediaries or directly to consumers, how many outlets to sell through, how to interact with other channel members, what terms to negotiate, the functions to assign to others, supplier choice, and so on. *Promotion* decisions include selecting a combination of tools (ads, public relations, personal selling, and sales promotion), whether to share promotions with others, the image to pursue, the level of personal service, media choice, message content, promotion timing, and so on. *Price* decisions include choosing overall price levels, the range of prices, the relation between price and quality, the emphasis on price, how to react to competitors, when to offer discounts, how prices are computed, what billing terms to use, and so on.

When devising a marketing mix, these questions should all be considered:

- Is the target market precisely defined?
- Does the total marketing program, as well as each element of the mix, meet the target market's needs?
- Are marketing-mix elements consistent with one another?
- Do the elements add up to form a harmonious, integrated whole?
- Is each marketing-mix element being given its best use?
- Does the marketing mix build on the firm's cultural and tangible strengths? Does the marketing mix imply a way to correct any weaknesses?
- Is a distinctive personality in the competitive marketplace created?
- Is the company protected from the most obvious competitive threats?[6]

[6]Benson P. Shapiro, "Rejuvenating the Marketing Mix," *Harvard Business Review*, Vol. 63 (September–October 1985), p. 34. See also Walter van Waterschoot and Christophe Van den Bulte, "The 4P Classification of the Marketing Mix Revisited," *Journal of Marketing*, Vol. 56 (October 1992), pp. 83–93.

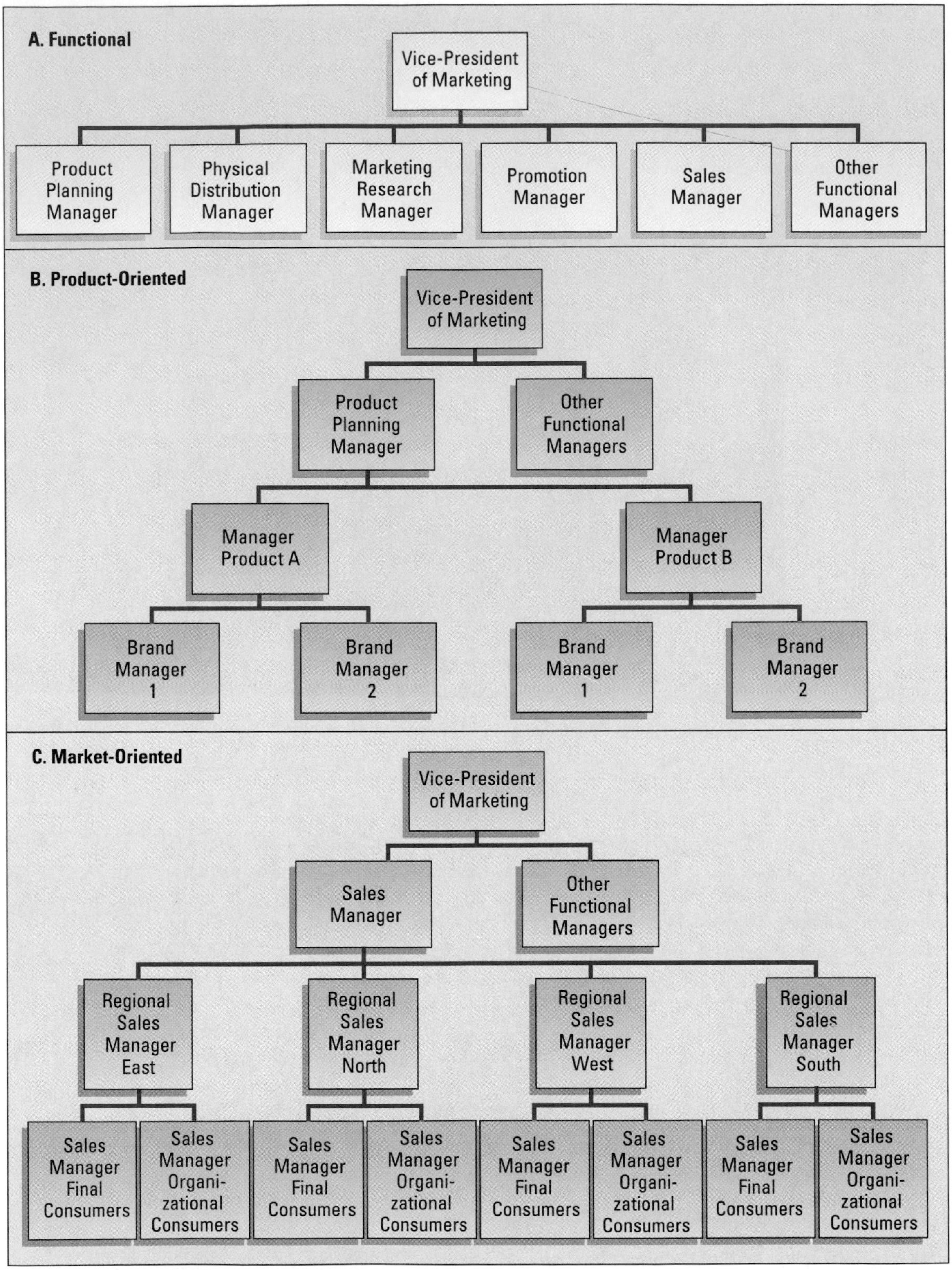

FIGURE 2-5
Illustrations of Marketing Organizations

Olympus, a leading maker of cameras and other products, is an example of a firm applying the marketing-mix concept well. It has distinct marketing mixes for different target markets, such as beginners, serious amateurs, and professional photographers. For beginners, it offers very simple cameras with automatic focus and a built-in flash. The cameras are sold in all types of stores, such as discount and department stores. Ads appear on TV and in general magazines. The cameras retail for well under $100. For serious amateur photographers, Olympus has more advanced cameras with superior features and many attachments. The cameras are sold in camera stores and finer department stores. Ads are in specialty magazines. The cameras sell for several hundred dollars. For professional photographers, Olympus has even more advanced cameras with top-of-the-line features and attachments. The cameras are sold via select camera stores. Ads are in trade magazines. These cameras are quite expensive. In sum, Olympus markets the right products in the right stores, promotes them in the right media, and has the right prices for its various target markets. See Figure 2-6.

The last, but extremely important, factor directed by marketers involves performance assessment: monitoring and evaluating overall and specific marketing effectiveness. Evaluations need to be done regularly, with both the external environment and internal company data being reviewed. In-depth analysis of performance should be completed at least once or twice each year. Strategy revisions need to be enacted when the external environment changes or the company encounters difficulties.

Performance assessment involves monitoring and evaluating marketing activities.

Uncontrollable Factors

Uncontrollable factors are the external elements affecting an organization's performance that cannot be fully directed by that organization and its marketers. A marketing plan, no matter how well conceived, may fail if uncontrollable factors have too adverse an impact. Thus, the external environment must be regularly observed and its effects considered in

Uncontrollable factors *influence an organization and its marketers but are not fully directed by them.*

FIGURE 2-6
Focused Marketing Mixes
The Olympus Stylus camera is a simple device for beginners, while the Olympus IS-3 is a sophisticated device for advanced camera buffs. A distinct marketing mix is used with each camera.
Reprinted by permission.

any marketing plan. Contingency plans relating to uncontrollable variables should also be a key part of a marketing plan. Uncontrollable factors that especially bear studying are consumers, competition, suppliers and distributors, government, the economy, technology, and independent media. See Figure 2-7.

Consumers

Organizations need to understand consumer trends, interpersonal influences, the decision process, and consumer groups.

Although a firm has control over its selection of a target market, it cannot control the changing characteristics of its final or organizational consumers. A firm can react to, but not control, consumer trends related to age, income, marital status, occupation, race, education, place and type of residence, and the size of organizational customers. For example, health insurers must deal with the fact that many of their largest business customers are downsizing; thus, there are fewer employees to be insured there.

Interpersonal influences on consumer behavior need to be understood. People's purchases are affected by the corporate culture at their jobs as purchasing agents; their family, friends, and other social contacts; and the customs and taboos shaping culture and society. For instance, in some parts of the United States, liquor sales are more regulated (as to outlets, prices, other goods that can be sold, and days open) than they are in other parts.

Because people act differently in buying various types of goods and services, the consumer decision process—the steps people go through when buying products—affects the way that products are marketed. In the case of company cars, a purchasing agent carefully searches for information on a number of models, ranks several alternatives, selects a favorite, negotiates terms, and finally completes the purchase. On the other hand, with an inexpensive meal, a person looks at a watch, sees it is lunch time, and goes to a nearby fast-food outlet.

Today, consumer-rights groups speak out on behalf of consumers at public hearings, at stockholder meetings, and before the media. To avoid negative consequences brought on by active consumer groups, a firm must communicate with customers on relevant issues (such as a product recall), anticipate problems (such as delays in filling orders), respond to complaints (such as unsatisfactory customer service), and be sure it has good community relations (such as sponsoring neighborhood projects).

FIGURE 2-7
Uncontrollable Factors

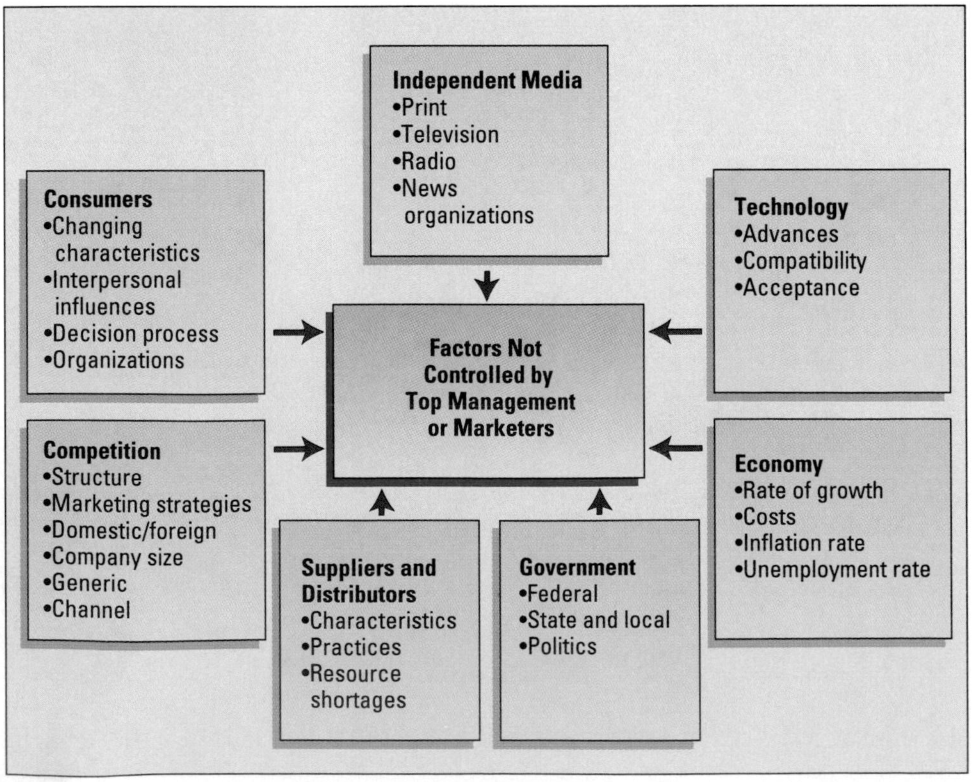

International Marketing in *Action*

Can Small Firms Be Successful Internationally in the Long Run?

A survey of almost 750 companies, conducted by Arthur Andersen and National Small Business United, found that 20 per cent of U.S. firms with less than 500 employees now export goods and services (up from 11 per cent in 1992). One of the key factors behind the growth in exporting is that more small firms are being provided with market information by federal and state agencies. As an example, the U.S. Commerce Department has a data base with research reports on 117 industries in 228 countries.

For the average small U.S. company, using a foreign partner or distributor is the ideal way to enter a foreign market. And small firms with larger budgets can even participate in trade shows sponsored by state and federal agencies.

One common problem for small firms is obtaining financing for international business or for extending trade credit to foreign customers. Many U.S. banks stopped such financing in the 1980s. And together, the Small Business Administration and the Export-Import Bank guaranteed only $253 million in export-related lending in 1994.

Other difficulties also abound for small firms seeking foreign expansion. They have to avoid choosing foreign partners that are either financially weak or lazy. Small companies often underestimate the amount of red tape associated with international marketing: Importers may insist that exported goods meet all guidelines established by the International Organization for Standardization. Adhering to these guidelines is especially costly and time-consuming for a small firm. Finally, small firms need to be careful in foreign transactions. For instance, one small exporter forgot to add in the French value-added tax (which amounted to $2,500) to the price of its $10,000 computer component.

As the sales manager for a small office furniture manufacturer, what would you do to increase your chances for success in international markets?

Source: Based on material in Amy Barrett, "It's A Small (Business) World," *Business Week* (April 17, 1995), pp. 96–101.

Competition

The competitive environment often affects a company's marketing efforts and its success in reaching a target market. Thus, a firm should assess its industry structure and examine competitors in terms of marketing strategies, domestic/foreign firms, size, generic competition, and channel competition.

Monopoly, **oligopoly**, **monopolistic competition**, *and* **pure competition** *are the main types of competitive structure.*

A company could operate under one of four possible competitive structures: With a **monopoly**, just one firm sells a given good or service and has a lot of control over its marketing plan. This occurs in the United States when a firm has a patent (exclusive rights to sell a product it invented for a fixed number of years) or is a public utility, such as a local power company. In an **oligopoly**, a few firms—usually large ones—account for most industry sales and would like to engage in nonprice competition. The auto industry is a good example of this. General Motors, Ford, Honda, Toyota, Chrysler, and Nissan account for about 90 per cent of U.S. auto sales. In **monopolistic competition**, there are several firms in an industry, each trying to offer a unique marketing mix—based on price or nonprice factors. It is the most common U.S. industry structure, followed by oligopoly. Service stations, beauty salons, stores, garment makers, computer-clone makers, and furniture makers are some firms facing monopolistic competition. In **pure competition**, many firms sell virtually identical goods or services and they are unable to create differential advantages. This occurs rarely in the United States and is most common for selected food items and commodities (and happens if numerous small firms compete with each other).

After analyzing its industry's competitive structure, a firm should study the strategies of competitors. Specifically, it should look at their target markets and marketing mixes, their images, their differential advantages, which markets are saturated and which are unfulfilled, and the extent to which consumers are content with the service and quality provided by competitors.

Foreign competition is intensifying.

Both domestic and foreign competition should be examined. For instance, in the United States, Merrill Lynch competes with Citicorp, American Express, and others—besides traditional brokerage firms—for financial-services business. Many U.S. and West European industries are mature; the amount of domestic competition there is rather stable. In some industries, competition is rising due to the popularity of innovations like notebook PCs. In others, domestic competition is intensifying as a result of government deregulation. For instance, by 1998 there will be about 900 companies offering long-distance telephone service in the United States alone.[7]

Foreign competitors now play a major role in many industries. In the United States, foreign-based firms are capturing large market shares—50 per cent for steel, 65 per cent for clothing, 75 per cent for shoes, and up to 98 per cent for some consumer electronics. At the same time, competition in foreign markets is more intense for U.S.-based firms than before as rivals stress innovations, cost cutting, good distribution and promotion, and other factors. Nonetheless, U.S.-based firms remain internationally dominant in such areas as aerospace, paper products, pharmaceuticals, and food and beverages.

For many industries, there has been a trend toward larger firms because of mergers and acquisitions, as well as company sales growth. Over the last decade, mergers and acquisitions have involved telecommunications firms (AT&T acquiring McCaw, a cellular phone service), food firms (Nestlé acquiring Perrier), pharmaceuticals firms (Bristol-Myers merging with Squibb), media firms (Time merging with Warner), consumer-products firms (Sony buying CBS Records), retailers (Federated Department Stores acquiring R.H. Macy), and numerous others. Internal sales growth has been great for such firms as Boeing, Wal-Mart, Microsoft, Toyota, and Federal Express—each with annual sales of several billion dollars.

From the vantage point of small firms, personal service, a focus on underserved market segments, an entrepreneurial drive, and flexibility are major differential advantages; cooperative ventures and franchising allow such firms to buy in quantity and operate more efficiently. To large firms, widespread distribution, economies of scale, well-known brands, mass-media ads, and low-to-moderate prices are competitive tactics.

Competition should be defined generically—as widely as possible.

Every organization should define its competition generically, meaning as broadly as possible. Direct competitors are similar to the firm with regard to the line of business and marketing approach. Indirect competitors are different from the firm, but still compete with it for customers. Both types of competitors should be studied and accounted for in a firm's marketing plan. For instance, a movie theater not only competes with other theaters (direct competitors), but with video stores, TV and radio shows, video games, sporting events, operas, plays, amusement parks, bookstores, restaurants, and schools (indirect competitors all). A theater owner should ask, "What can I do to compete with a variety of entertainment and recreation forms, in terms of movie selection, prices, hours, customer service, refreshments, and parking?"

A company should also study the competition from its channel members (resellers). Each party in the distribution process has different goals and would like to maximize its control over the marketing mix. Some wholesalers and retailers carry their own brands besides those of manufacturers.

[7]Emory Thomas, Jr., "Nibbling at the Edges," *Wall Street Journal* (March 20, 1995), p. R14.

Suppliers and Distributors

Suppliers and distributors can have a dramatic impact on an organization.

Many firms rely on their suppliers and distributors (wholesalers and retailers) to properly run their own businesses. Without their ongoing support, it would be difficult, if not impossible, for a company to succeed.

Suppliers provide the goods and services that firms need to operate, as well as those that they resell to their own customers. In general, a firm is most vulnerable when there are relatively few suppliers, specific goods and services are needed to run a business or satisfy customer demand, competitors would gain if the firm has a falling-out with a supplier, suppliers are better attuned to the desires of the marketplace, suppliers informally take care of maintenance and repair services, the turnaround time to switch suppliers is lengthy, and suppliers have exclusive access to scarce resources.

For firms that cannot market their products directly to consumers, distributors (be they wholesalers or retailers) are needed. In general, a firm is most vulnerable when there are relatively few distributors in an area, the distributors carry many brands, shelf space is tight, the firm is unknown in the marketplace, particular distributors account for a large portion of the firm's revenues, distributors help finance the firm, distributors are better attuned to the marketplace, and other competitors are waiting in the wings to stock the distributors.

These are among the supplier/distributor practices that a firm should regularly study: delivery time or requests, product availability, prices, flexibility in handling special requests, marketing support, consistency of treatment, returns policies, and other services. Unsatisfactory performance in one or more of these areas could have a lasting impact on a firm and its competence to enact marketing plans.

Regardless of suppliers' good intentions, a firm's ability to carry out its plans can be affected by the availability of scarce resources. Over the past 25 years, sporadic shortages and volatile price changes have occurred for a variety of basic commodities, such as home heating oil, other petroleum-based products, plastics, synthetic fibers, aluminum, chrome, silver, tungsten, nickel, steel, glass, grain, fertilizer, cotton, and wool. And despite efforts at conservation, some raw materials, processed materials, and component parts may remain or become scarce over the next decade.[8]

Resource shortages and/or rapid cost increases would require one of three actions. First, substitute materials could be used in constructing products, requiring intensified research and product testing. Second, prices could be raised for products that cannot incorporate substitute materials. Third, firms could abandon products where resources are unavailable and demarket others where demand is greater than they are able to satisfy.

Government

U.S. federal legislation involves interstate commerce. And each state and local government has its own regulations, as well.

Worldwide, governmental bodies have a great impact on marketing practices by placing (or removing) restrictions on specified activities. In any country, government rulings can be on a national, state, and/or local level.

In the United States, for over 100 years, the Congress has enacted federal legislation affecting marketing practices, as highlighted in Table 2-1. This legislation can be divided into three groups: antitrust, discriminatory pricing, and unfair trade practices; consumer protection; and deregulation.

Laws in the first group protect smaller firms from anticompetitive acts by larger ones. These laws seek a "level playing field" for all by barring firms from using marketing practices that unfairly harm competitors. Laws in the second group help consumers deal with deceptive and unsafe business practices. These laws protect consumer rights and restrict certain marketing activities (like banning cigarette ads from TV and radio). Laws in the third group have deregulated various industries to create a more competitive marketplace. They allow firms greater flexibility in enacting marketing plans. The Federal Trade Com-

[8]William B. Wagner, "Establishing Supply Service Strategy for Shortage Situations," *Industrial Marketing Management*, Vol. 23 (1994), pp. 393–401.

Table 2-1

Key U.S. Legislation Affecting Marketers

YEAR	LEGISLATION	MAJOR PURPOSE
A. Antitrust, Discriminatory Pricing, and Unfair Trade Practices		
1890	Sherman Act	To eliminate monopolies
1914	Clayton Act	To ban anticompetitive acts
1914	FTC Act	To establish the Federal Trade Commission to enforce rules against restraints of trade
1936	Robinson-Patman Act	To prohibit price discrimination toward small distributors or retailers
1938	Wheeler-Lea Amendment	To amend the FTC Act to include more unfair or deceptive practices
1946	Lanham Trademark Act	To protect and regulate trademarks and brands
1989	Trademark Revision Act	To revise the Lanham Trademark Act to include products not yet introduced on the market
1990	Antitrust Amendments Act	To raise the maximum penalties for price fixing
B. Consumer Protection		
1906 1906	Food and Drug Act Meat Inspection Act	To ban adulterated and misbranded food and drugs, and form the Food and Drug Administration (FDA)
1914 1938	FTC Act Wheeler-Lea Amendment	To establish a commission and provisions for protecting consumer rights
1939 1951 1953 1958	Wool Products Labeling Act Fur Products Labeling Act Flammable Fabrics Act Textile Fiber Identification Act	To require wool, fur, and textile products to show contents and to prohibit dangerous flammables
1958 1960 1962	Food Additives Amendment Federal Hazardous Substances Labeling Act Kefauver-Harris Amendment	To prohibit food additives causing cancer, require labels on hazardous household products, and require drug makers to demonstrate effectiveness and safety
1966	Fair Packaging and Labeling Act	To require honest package labeling and reduce package-size proliferation
1966	National Traffic and Motor Vehicle Safety Act	To set safety standards for autos and tires
1966 1969 1970 1972	Child Protection Act Child Toy Safety Act Poison Prevention Labeling Act Drug Listing Act	To ban hazardous products used by children, create standards for child resistant packages, and provide drug information
1966 1970	Cigarette Labeling Act Public Health Smoking Act	To require warnings on cigarette packages and ban radio and TV cigarette ads
1967 1968	Wholesome Meat Act Wholesome Poultry Act	To mandate federal inspection standards
1968 1970	Consumer Credit Protection Act Fair Credit Reporting Act	To have full disclosure of credit terms and regulate the use of credit information
1970	Clean Air Act	To protect the environment
1972	Consumer Product Safety Act	To create the Consumer Product Safety Commission (CPSC) and set safety standards

Table 2-1 (Cont.)

YEAR	LEGISLATION	MAJOR PURPOSE
1975	Magnuson-Moss Consumer Product Warranty Act	To regulate warranties and set disclosure requirements
1975	Consumer Goods Pricing Act	To disallow retail price maintenance
1980	Fair Debt Collection Act	To eliminate the harassment of debtors and ban false statements to collect debts
1980	FTC Improvement Act	To reduce the power of the FTC to implement industrywide trade regulations
1990	Clean Air Act	To expand the 1970 Clean Air Act
1990	Children's Television Act	To reduce the amount of commercials shown during children's programming
1990	Nutrition Labeling and Education Act	To have the FDA develop a new system of food labeling
1991	Telephone Consumer Protection Act	To safeguard consumers against undesirable telemarketing practices
1992	Cable Television Consumer Protection and Competition Act	To better protect consumer rights with regard to cable television services

C. Industry Deregulation

Over the last 20 years, a host of laws have been enacted to make the natural gas, airline, trucking, railroad, banking, telecommunications, and other industries more competitive.

mission (FTC) is the major U.S. regulatory agency monitoring restraint of trade and enforcing rules against unfair methods of competition and deceptive business practices.

In addition to federal regulation and agencies, each state and local government in the United States has its own legal environment. State and local laws may regulate where a firm is allowed to locate, the hours open, the types of items sold, if prices must be marked on every item sold, how goods must be labeled or dated, and so on. State and local governments may also provide incentives, such as small business assistance, for firms to operate there.

The political environment often affects legislation. Marketing issues such as these are typically discussed via the political process prior to laws being enacted (or not enacted): Should certain goods and services be stopped from advertising on TV? Should mail-order sales to out of state customers be taxed? Should state governments become more active in handling consumer complaints? Both firms and consumer groups can have input into the process. The goal is to market their positions to government officials. A strength of the U.S. political system is its continuity, which lets organizations and individuals develop strategies for long periods of time.

Privatization is changing the number of businesses in foreign countries.

Outside the United States, one of the biggest legal and political challenges facing countries is how to "privatize" organizations that were formerly run by the government:

> The obstacles to privatization are numerous. They include lack of a free-market culture; confusion over who owns the enterprises and what they're worth; poor physical infrastructure, which discourages foreign investment; the absence of a legal framework governing the conduct of business; and shortage of investment capital. After privatization, consequences can include higher prices for basic goods and services, large-scale layoffs, loss of national assets to foreign buyers, and the possible closure of vital industries.[9]

[9]Christopher McIntosh, "To Market, to Market," *Futurist* (January–February 1994), p. 24.

FIGURE 2-8
Marketing Flexibility to Organizational Consumers
Reprinted by permission.

The Economy

The rate of growth in a nation's or region's economy can have a big impact on a firm's marketing efforts. A high growth rate means the economy is strong and the marketing potential large. Quite important to marketers are consumer perceptions—both in the business and final consumer sectors—regarding the economy. For instance, if people believe the economy will be favorable, they may increase spending; if they believe the economy will be poor, they may cut back. To measure consumer perceptions, the U.S. government, the Conference Board, and the University of Michigan (among others) conduct monthly "consumer confidence" surveys to see if Americans are optimistic, pessimistic, or neutral about the economy. In uncertain times, many organizational consumers are interested in preserving their flexibility. See Figure 2-8.

Economic growth is measured by the **Gross Domestic Product**.

A country's economic growth is reflected by changes in its **Gross Domestic Product (GDP)**, which is the total annual value of goods and services produced in a country less net foreign investment. These are the estimated 1996 GDPs (in U.S. dollars) for ten selected nations: United States, $7.4 trillion; Japan, $5.3 trillion; Germany, $2.3 trillion; France, $1.5 trillion; Italy, $1.2 trillion; Brazil, $950 billion; Canada, $630 billion; Mexico, $375 billion; India, $370 billion; and Thailand, $175 billion.[10] In recent years, the yearly growth in most of these nations has been three per cent or less; and when certain

[10]Louis Richmond, "Global Growth Is on a Tear," *Fortune* (March 20, 1995), p. 108.

industries, such as autos and housing, slow down, repercussions are felt in other areas, such as insurance and home furnishings. The United States is expected to have real GDP growth averaging about 2 to 4 per cent annually during the rest of the 1990s—but the rate could be lower if budget and trade deficits are not reduced.

Several business costs—like raw materials, unionized labor wages, taxes, interest rates, and office (factory) rental—are generally beyond any firm's control. If costs rise by a large amount, marketing flexibility may be limited because a firm often cannot pass along all of the increase; it might have to cut back on marketing activities or accept lower profit margins. If costs are stable, marketers are better able to differentiate products and expand sales because their companies are more apt to invest in marketing activities.

Real income *describes earnings adjusted for inflation. Both inflation and unemployment affect purchases.*

From a marketing perspective, what happens to a consumer's real income is critical. While actual income is the amount earned by a consumer (or his/her family or household) in a given year, **real income** is the amount earned in a year adjusted by the rate of inflation. For example, if a person's actual income goes up by 4 per cent in a year (from $40,000 to $41,600) and the rate of inflation (which measures price changes for the same goods and services over time) is 4 per cent for the year, real income remains constant [($41,600) − ($41,600/1.04) = $40,000]. If actual income increases exceed the inflation rate, real income rises and people can buy more goods and services. If actual income increases are less than the inflation rate, real income falls and people must buy fewer goods and services.

A high rate of unemployment can adversely affect many firms because people who are unemployed are likely to cut back on nonessentials wherever possible. Low unemployment often means substantial sales of large-ticket items, as consumers are better off, more optimistic, and more apt to spend earnings.

Technology

Technology *includes machinery, products, and processes.*

Technology refers to developing and using machinery, products, and processes. Individual firms, especially smaller ones with limited capital, must usually adapt to technological advances (rather than control them).

Many firms depend on others to develop and perfect new technology, such as computer microchips; only then can they use the new technology in products, such as automated gas pumps at service stations, talking toys, or electronic sensors in smoke detectors for office buildings. With new technology, the inventor often secures patent protection, which excludes competitors from using that technology (unless the inventor licenses rights for a fee).

In a number of areas, companies have been unable to achieve practical technological breakthroughs. For example, no firm has been able to develop and market a cure for the common cold, a good-tasting nontobacco cigarette, a commercially acceptable electric car, or a truly effective and safe diet pill.

When new technology first emerges, it may be expensive and in short supply, both for firms using the technology in their products and for final consumers. The challenge is to mass produce and mass market the technology efficiently. In addition, some technological advances require employee training and consumer education before they can succeed. Thus, an emphasis on user-friendliness can speed up the acceptance of new technology.

Certain advances may not be compatible with goods and services already on the market and/or require retooling by firms wanting to use them in products or operations. Every time an auto maker introduces a significantly new car model, it must invest hundreds of millions of dollars to retool facilities. Each time a firm buys new computer equipment to supplement existing hardware, it must see if the new equipment is compatible. (Can it run all the computer programs used by the firm and "talk" to the firm's existing machines?)

To flourish, technological advances must be accepted by each firm in the distribution process (manufacturer/service provider, wholesaler, retailer). Should any of the firms not use a new technology, its benefits may be lost. If small retailers do not use electronic scanning equipment, cashiers must ring up prices by hand even though packages are computer-coded by manufacturers.

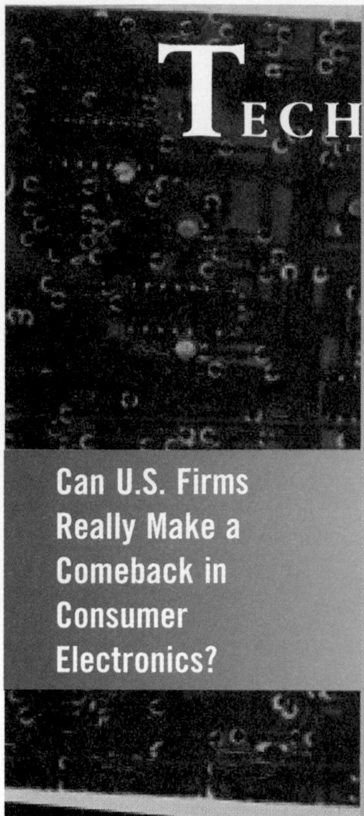

TECHNOLOGY & MARKETING

Can U.S. Firms Really Make a Comeback in Consumer Electronics?

Although Japanese companies have dominated consumer electronics for years, American firms now see vast opportunities there. Why? More U.S. and other households are purchasing computer accessories, telephone equipment, and other electronic gear. Americans now spend more on home PCs and software than on color TV sets. And these expanding product categories are dominated by U.S. firms with reputations for high-quality products.

Much of the success in PC accessories is because U.S. firms such as Intel, Microsoft, Hewlett-Packard, and Iomega are selling more equipment to final consumers. Thus, while in the past, Iomega sold its PC backup equipment mostly to technicians, more than half its sales are now to final consumers.

The growth in telephone and accessories sales is due to several strong product categories targeted to final consumers: cordless telephones, cellular phones, pagers, and answering machines. Among the strong U.S. firms in these categories are AT&T and Motorola (which has a 65+ per cent market share in the United States for both cellular phones and pagers).

In many cases, the strength of U.S. firms in consumer markets is due to the investments made in industrial markets. For instance, Hewlett-Packard's prowess with home printers can be traced to its investment in inkjet technology in the 1980s. At that time, Japanese competitors ignored the technology, viewing the market as too small. Today, Hewlett-Packard dominates the low-end color printer market with its inkjet machines—which now retail for less than $300, down from over $1,000 not long ago.

Despite these successes, U.S. firms remain weak in stereos, TVs, VCRs, CD players, and other consumer electronics categories. Foreign products are often perceived as more innovative, better built, and of higher quality. The United States exports $3 billion in consumer electronics—and imports $15 billion.

As a product manager for a U.S. stereo manufacturer, devise a strategy to compete with Japanese competitors.

Source: Based on material in Stephen Kreider Yoder, "Back in the Running," *Wall Street Journal* (June 19, 1995), pp. R22, R26.

Independent Media

Independent media *affect perceptions of products and company image.*

Independent media are communication vehicles not controlled by a firm; yet, they influence government, consumer, and publics' perceptions of that firm's products and overall image. Media can provide positive or negative coverage when a firm produces a new product, pollutes the air, mislabels products, contributes to charity, or otherwise performs a newsworthy activity. Coverage may be by print media, TV, radio, or news organizations. To receive good coverage, a firm should willingly offer information to independent media and always try to get its position written or spoken about.

Although the media's coverage of information about a firm or information released by a firm is uncontrollable, paid advertising is controllable by the firm. Ads may be rejected by the media; but, if they are accepted, they must be presented in the time interval and form stipulated by the firm.

Attainment of Objectives, Feedback, and Adaptation

An organization's success or failure in reaching objectives depends on how well it directs its controllable factors and the impact of uncontrollable factors. As shown in Figure 2-1, it is the interaction of an organization's total offering and the uncontrollable environment that determines how it does.

To optimize marketing efforts and secure its long-run existence, a firm must get **feedback**—information about the uncontrollable environment, the organization's performance, and how well the marketing plan is received. Feedback is gained by measuring consumer satisfaction, looking at competitive trends, evaluating relationships with government agencies, studying the economy and potential resource shortages, monitoring the independent media, analyzing sales and profit trends, talking with suppliers and distributors, and utilizing other methods of acquiring and assessing information.

Feedback *provides information that lets a firm* **adapt** *to its environment.*

After evaluating feedback, a company—when necessary—needs to engage in **adaptation**, thereby fine-tuning its marketing plan to be responsive to the surrounding environment, while continuing to capitalize on differential advantages. The firm should look continually for new opportunities that fit its overall marketing plan and are attainable by it, and respond to potential threats by revising marketing policies.

For instance, small optical shops are struggling to succeed because of the growing strength of LensCrafter, Pearle, Sterling Optical, and other chains. The latter advertise extensively, buy in quantity to get special deals, and offer fast service and good prices. Thus, they now account for 40+ per cent of industry sales, a big increase from a decade ago. To last in this environment, small optical shops use such adaptation strategies as these: Eyetique in Pittsburgh has local celebrities appear in newspaper ads; they are not paid, but keep the glasses with which they pose. Robin Kelly, a Spokane, Washington, optometrist, gives out gifts such as a box of peanut brittle or a dinner at a nearby restaurant to clients who refer others to her. Thomas Appler, a Towson, Maryland, optometrist, offers color-coordination consultations so female clients can match eyewear, makeup, and clothing. The San Francisco Bay Area Optometric Council, comprised of 400 local businesses, has sponsored radio ads saying "all eye doctors and all eye exams are not equal."[11]

In gearing up for the future, a firm must strive to avoid **marketing myopia**—a short-sighted, narrow-minded view of marketing and its environment. It is a "self-inflicted and avoidable harm caused to an organization due to a lack of attention to and poor implementation of marketing concepts and principles." These are some major warning signs:

Marketing myopia *is an ineffective marketing approach.*

- *We-know syndrome*—This is an ongoing assumption that the correct answers are always known to crucial questions.
- *Me-tooism*—This occurs when goods and services are too similar to those of competitors and there is no competitive advantage.
- *Monopricis*—This occurs when a firm's primary (or only) marketing/competitive tool is changing prices.
- *Customerphobia*—This is the fear of having a close relationship with and really caring about consumers and their wants.
- *Fax-me complex*—This occurs when the firm is completely dominated by tasks that require immediate attention (crises).
- *Hypermentis*—This occurs when executives devote too much of their time to thinking, studying, and planning while they take little action.
- *Global idiosis*—This is the lack of ability or willingness to compete in the international marketplace.
- *If it works, don't fix it*—This occurs when business is very good; but no one knows why and everyone is hesitant to make changes.
- *Interfunctionalphobia*—This is a lack of mutual understanding, integration, and cooperation among a firm's various functional areas.
- *Short-run fetish*—This occurs when decisions are too biased toward the short-run, thus sacrificing long-run performance.[12]

[11]Barbara Marsh, "Small Eyeglass Shops' Comeback Is No Optical Illusion," *Wall Street Journal* (May 13, 1992), p. B2.

[12]John H. Antil, "Are You Committing Marketcide?" *Journal of Services Marketing*, Vol. 6 (Spring 1992), pp. 45–53.

MARKETING IN A CHANGING WORLD

Trends That Will Affect America's Future

Futurist Marvin Cetron recently identified 74 environmental trends that will greatly influence life and business in the United States during the next several years. Here are several of them. Are we ready? Do you agree with all of these predictions?

- Economic prosperity will continue through the foreseeable future.
- The growth of the information industry is creating a knowledge-dependent society.
- The very poor and very wealthy will decline in American society. The middle class will prevail.
- The growing acceptance of cultural diversity will promote a truly integrated national society.
- Americans will be increasingly mobile in personal life, residence locations, and occupations.
- The U.S. economy will become more integrated with the international economy.
- Demand for lifelong education and training will heat up throughout society.
- Education costs will continue to rise.
- The work ethic will keep vanishing from American society.
- Societal values will change rapidly.
- Tourism, vacationing, and travel (particularly international) will grow.
- The do-it-yourself movement will continue to expand.
- American consumers will increasingly demand socially responsible acts from companies and each other.[13]

SUMMARY

1. *To examine the environment within which marketing decisions are made and marketing activities are undertaken* The marketing environment consists of controllable factors, uncontrollable factors, the organization's level of success or failure in reaching its objectives, feedback, and adaptation. The macroenvironment includes the broad societal and economic forces that a firm faces, while the microenvironment refers to the forces that more directly affect a firm's ability to serve its customers.

2. *To differentiate between those elements controlled by a firm's top management and those controlled by marketing, and to enumerate the controllable elements of a marketing plan* Controllable factors are the internal strategy elements directed by a firm and its marketers. Top management decides on the line of business, overall objectives, the role of marketing and other business functions, and the corporate culture. These decisions have an impact on all aspects of marketing.

The major factors directed by marketing personnel are the selection of a target market, which is the group(s) of customers a firm proposes to serve; marketing objectives, which are more customer-oriented than those set by top management; the marketing organization; the marketing mix, which is a specific combination of product, distribution, promotion, and price decisions; and performance assessment, which involves monitoring and evaluating marketing outcomes. It is important for marketing personnel to strive to create differential advantages—the unique features that cause consumers to patronize a firm and not its competitors.

3. *To enumerate the uncontrollable environmental elements that can affect a marketing plan and study their potential ramifications* Uncontrollable factors are the external elements affecting a company's performance that cannot be fully directed by the top management and marketers of a firm. Any marketing plan, no matter how well conceived, may fail if uncontrollable factors influence it too much.

Among the key uncontrollable variables are changing consumer traits, interpersonal influences on consumer behavior, the consumer decision process, and consumer groups; the competitive structure of the industry in which a firm operates (monopoly, oligopoly, monopolistic competition, or pure competition) and such competitor attributes as marketing strategies, country of origin, size, generic competition, and channel competition; suppliers and distributors, their traits and practices, and resource shortages; government legislation and the political environment; the rate of economic growth (as measured by the GDP and real income), the costs of doing business, and other economic factors; technology, which refers to the development and use of machinery, products, and processes; and independent me-

[13]Marvin J. Cetron, *An American Renaissance in the Year 2000* (New York: St. Martin's Press, 1994).

dia, the communication vehicles not controlled by the firm. 4. *To explain why feedback about company performance and the uncontrollable aspects of its environment and the subsequent adaptation of the marketing plan are essential for a firm to attain its objectives* A firm's level of success or failure in reaching its goals depends on how well it directs and implements its controllable factors and the impact of uncontrollable factors on the marketing plan. When enacting a marketing strategy, a firm should obtain feedback (information about both its overall and marketing performance and the uncontrollable environment) and adapt the strategy to be responsive to the surrounding environment while continuing to exploit its differential advantages. Marketing myopia, a shortsighted view of marketing and its environment, must be avoided.

KEY TERMS

marketing environment (p. 27)
macroenvironment (p. 28)
microenvironment (p. 28)
controllable factors (p. 28)
line of business (p. 29)
corporate culture (p. 30)
target market (p. 31)
market segmentation (p. 31)
differential advantages (p. 32)
marketing organization (p. 32)
marketing mix (p. 32)
uncontrollable factors (p. 35)
monopoly (p. 37)
oligopoly (p. 37)
monopolistic competition (p. 37)
pure competition (pp. 37–38)
Gross Domestic Product (GDP) (p. 42)
real income (p. 43)
technology (p. 43)
independent media (p. 44)
feedback (p. 45)
adaptation (p. 45)
marketing myopia (p. 45)

Review Questions

1. Explain the environment within which marketing operates.
2. Differentiate between the "macroenvironment" and the "microenvironment."
3. Why are the factors controlled by top management usually considered uncontrollable by marketing personnel?
4. What criteria would you use to assess the role of marketing in a company?
5. Why should a firm select a target market before developing a specific marketing mix?
6. What is the most important marketing objective for an organization? Why?
7. Describe the four components of the marketing mix.
8. Why are suppliers an important uncontrollable factor for many companies?
9. What is the intent of each of these categories of federal legislation?
   a. Antitrust, discriminatory pricing, and unfair trade practices.
   b. Deregulation.
   c. Consumer protection.
10. How do the independent media affect a firm's marketing practices?

Discussion Questions

1. How does a firm's corporate culture influence the performance of its personnel? Relate your answer to a small taxi service that caters to corporate accounts.
2. What are the differential advantages for each of these? Explain your answers.
   a. Your college or university.
   b. *People* magazine.
   c. A local printing service.
3. Distinguish between the marketing mixes used by Cadillac and Saturn, two car lines of General Motors.
4. Deregulation represents both opportunities and potential problems for companies. Offer several examples of both for the cable TV industry.
5. Comment on this statement: "By defining competition in generic terms, acquiring information about the uncontrollable environment, and modifying strategy when necessary, an organization will avoid marketing myopia and guarantee its long-term success."

CASE 1

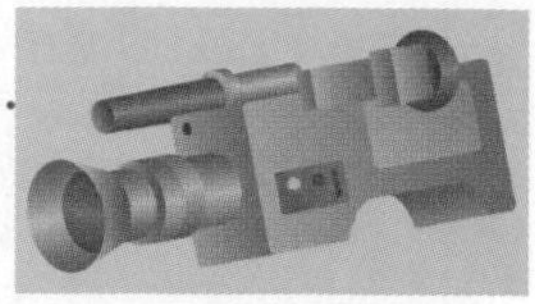

*Louisiana-Pacific: A Marketing Environment Analysis**

Louisiana-Pacific (LP) is one of the world's largest lumber producers with annual revenues of over $3 billion; net profits average about 11 per cent of sales. Unlike other forest-products firms that produce mostly paper and packaging materials, over 90 per cent of LP's businesses are related to the building-products industry. Its sales by product line are: structural panel products (such as plywood used for flooring and roofing)—40 per cent; lumber— 28 per cent; other building products (such as I-Beams and vinyl windows and doors)—17 per cent; other panel products (such as particleboard and hardboard)—8 per cent; and pulp—7 per cent.

LP's building-products emphasis makes it a specialist, as well as the single source for many of its builder-customers' lumber needs. This also ties LP's financial success to the level of new home construction. In 1994, demand for LP's products was excellent due to strong housing starts of 1.45 million homes, the highest level in six years. In contrast, only 840,000 single-family homes were built in 1990.

The U.S. lumber industry is heavily regulated with regard to the physical environment. Firms must reduce harvesting of timberland to protect certain wildlife (such as the grizzly bear and certain species of salmon) from extinction, as well as provide land set-asides for wildlife protection and for recreational uses.

LP has two major differential advantages. The first relates to the location of much of its timberland; the second involves its technological advances. In contrast to many competitors, LP produces much of its lumber from small-diameter trees located in the Southeast. While the Endangered Species Act and legal suits by environmentalists caused National Forest timber production in Oregon and Washington to fall from almost 5 billion feet in 1987 to less than 1 billion feet in 1994, state-based environmental restrictions are less stringent in the Southeast.

LP is also a technological innovator in terms of developing products from quick-growing kinds of lumber and from wood fibers. In many cases, these products have significant performance advantages over traditional building materials they compete against. One innovative LP product is finger-pointed studs that are made by joining shorter sections of 2 × 4s and 2 × 6s. Builders prefer finger-pointed studs to regular lumber because these studs are less prone to warping and twisting. Finger-pointed studs are also highly profitable to LP since they are made from trim ends that would otherwise be discarded or sold as low-grade wood. LP's innovations enable it to get the most value from its timberland and to use fast-growing varieties of lumber.

LP is viewed as an environmental leader in the forest products industry. It has voluntarily stopped clearcutting on company-owned timberlands. With clearcutting, all the trees in a given area (regardless of size, age, or type) are cut down at the same time. While clearcutting is efficient, the clearcut area usually resembles a war zone. LP's pulp mill in British Columbia was also among the first to recycle 100 per cent of the water used in the pulp-making process.

Despite its good overall reputation, LP has been required to pay fines for noncompliance with current environmental laws. It also had a major problem with an engineered wood product, oriented strand board (OSB). Although the product performed well when used for floor and roof sheeting, it quickly deteriorated when used as an exterior siding material in humid climates. Poor performance by this product led LP to spend $46 million for legal fees and product-settlement costs.

QUESTIONS

1. Define and evaluate Louisiana-Pacific's line of business.
2. Explain the impact of the role of government on Louisiana-Pacific's marketing strategy.
3. Assess Louisiana-Pacific's differential advantages.
4. Discuss Louisiana-Pacific's decision to recycle water in the pulp-making process in advance of its being legally required to do so.

VIDEO QUESTIONS ON LOUISIANA-PACIFIC

1. Comment on Louisiana-Pacific's predictions for the year 2000.
2. Analyze Louisiana-Pacific's changing target-market strategy.

*The data in this case are drawn from *Louisiana-Pacific Corporation 1994 Annual Report*; Michael K. Ozanian, "Louisiana-Pacific: Thank You Environmentalists Part II," *Financial World* (February 1, 1994), p. 18; and Eric Shine and Anita Marks, "The Fall of a Timber Baron," *Business Week* (October 2, 1995), pp. 85–92.

CASE 2

Are Good Times Ahead for Planet Reebok?[†]

American Paul Fireman became aware of Reebok (then a small British shoe maker) at a 1979 Chicago trade show and quickly purchased the exclusive rights to sell Reebok running shoes in North America. Fireman acquired Reebok in 1984 and later renamed it Reebok International.

After Fireman's acquisition, Reebok's first major new-product success was its Freestyle line of aerobic shoes. To avoid directly competing against Nike, Reebok targeted Freestyle shoes at the female market; and Freestyle became one of the best-selling shoes in history. It was instrumental in pushing Reebok's sales from $3.5 million in 1982 to $919 million in 1986—and in giving Reebok a sales edge over Nike. Reebok kept this sales advantage over Nike until 1990.

Since Nike has surged ahead, Reebok is now the world's second-largest athletic shoe maker (with a global market share of 24 per cent versus Nike's 33 per cent). In 1995, Reebok total sales were $3.5 billion and net profit was 4.7 per cent of sales; Nike had $4.8 billion in sales and a net profit of 8.4 per cent of sales. The only other true global competitor is Adidas, with a 10 per cent market share. Let's now look at Reebok's and Nike's marketing strategies.

There are several similarities in the marketing strategies of the two firms: Each has a similar philosophy in terms of product design, marketing, and production. Both Reebok and Nike design and market their products, but use subcontractors (located in low-cost countries) to produce their footwear and apparel items. This approach lowers plant investment costs and lets the companies reduce the risks associated with wide variations in demand. Both Reebok and Nike also make extensive use of athletes to endorse their products. Reebok features Michael Chang (tennis), Frank Thomas (baseball), Emmitt Smith (football), and Shaquille O'Neal (basketball), while Nike features Andre Agassi and Pete Sampras (tennis); Ken Griffey, Jr. (baseball); Troy Aikman (football); and Michael Jordan, Charles Barkley, and Shawn Kemp (basketball). Reebok's signing of Shaquille O'Neal was quite important due to his appeal to males aged 18 and under, a group accounting for one-quarter of total U.S. athletic footwear sales.

There are also some key differences between Reebok's and Nike's marketing strategies: Although the firms are in the same general industry, they often appeal to different market segments. Reebok's major market is still women's fitness shoes and apparel; and its product line includes lower-priced casual shoes. In contrast, Nike places greater attention on higher-priced shoes for males. And until recently, Nike had a much stronger group of endorsers in the basketball market than Reebok.

Even though Reebok's overall performance is generally strong, it has had some problems: Nike's market share is much higher than Reebok's. Nike has entered Reebok's core market—women's fitness footwear. And despite the signing of Shaquille O'Neal, Reebok has not yet been as successful in the basketball shoe and apparel segment. Lastly, Reebok has been unable to move quickly into such fast-growing markets as hiking and outdoor gear.

Reebok made extensive use of the 1996 Summer Olympics to boost its image. More than 3,000 Olympic athletes wore Reebok footwear and apparel, and it had advertising exclusivity in the athletic footwear category on NBC's Olympics telecasts. Reebok also used the Olympics to introduce a new advertising slogan, "This is my planet, Planet Reebok."

During March 1996, Reebok introduced Mobius, a new line of footwear and apparel products that cuts across all performance categories. The Mobius line was devised to give Reebok a more integrated presence across all sports areas.

QUESTIONS

1. Develop appropriate marketing objectives for Reebok.
2. Describe the competitive environment for the athletic shoe and apparel business. What are the implications of this for Reebok?
3. What would you do to take market share away from Nike?
4. Reebok plans to enter the soccer shoe market that is currently dominated by Adidas. Present a marketing mix for Reebok to do so.

[†]The data in this case are drawn from Patrick J. Spain and James R. Talbot (Editors), *Hoover's Handbook of American Business 1996* (Austin, Texas: Reference Press, 1995), pp. 1224–1225; Geoffrey Smith, "Reebok Is Tripping Over Its Own Laces," *Business Week* (February 26, 1996), pp. 62–66; and Kenneth Labich, "Nike Vs. Reebok: A Battle for Hearts, Minds, and Feet," *Fortune* (September 18, 1995), pp. 90–106.

CHAPTER 3

Strategic Planning: A Marketing Perspective

Chapter Objectives

1. To define strategic planning and consider its importance for marketing

2. To describe the total quality approach to strategic planning and show its relevance to marketing

3. To look at the different kinds of strategic plans and the relationships between marketing and the other functional areas in an organization

4. To describe thoroughly each of the steps in the strategic planning process: defining organizational mission, establishing strategic business units, setting marketing objectives, performing situation analysis, developing marketing strategy, implementing tactics, and monitoring results

5. To show how a strategic plan may be devised and applied

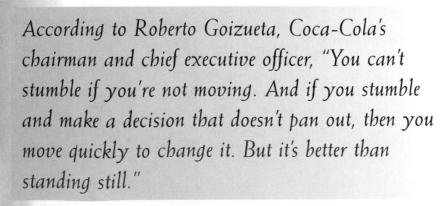

According to Roberto Goizueta, Coca-Cola's chairman and chief executive officer, "You can't stumble if you're not moving. And if you stumble and make a decision that doesn't pan out, then you move quickly to change it. But it's better than standing still."

Although Coca-Cola has always had a reputation as a successful marketer, until recently its strategic planning efforts were slow in responding to changes in the marketplace. Thus, the firm did not enter India until the late 1980s; at the same time, it was sluggish in dealing with the popularity of private-label soda in Great Britain; and in the early 1990s, it virtually ignored iced teas, new-age juices, and flavored waters. By the time Coca-Cola responded in each of these instances, its competitors were able to garner a sizable market share.

Reprinted by permission.

Today, Coca-Cola utilizes a much more aggressive and quicker approach in its market-planning activities. For example, the firm now markets such new drinks as Mountain Blast Powerade sports drink and Strawberry Passion Awareness Fruitopia fruit drink; and it has developed and introduced new packaging and promotions. As a result, in 1995, Coca-Cola accounted for more than 80 per cent of the growth in the U.S. soft-drink market, almost twice the prior year's growth. Says Roberto Goizueta, "Nothing energizes an organization like speed."

In the not-too-distant past, some marketing analysts saw PepsiCo as the "hot" soft-drink company most likely to come out with new products and the best advertising campaigns. Now, they credit Coca-Cola with these qualities. Even archrival PepsiCo acknowledges Coca-Cola's new-found strength. PepsiCo's head of marketing states that "Coke has definitely raised the bar."

One good example of Coca-Cola's peppy approach to planning involves Japan, the firm's most profitable market. Japanese consumers are noted for demanding new products at break-neck speed; and while soda companies typically launch a total of 700 to 800 new drinks per year, few last for more than a month. Until 1993, Coca-Cola did not keep pace with its competitors. Then, it set up a product development center that reduced the launch time for new drinks from 90 days to 30 days. Because of this, Coca-Cola now releases 50 new products per year in Japan—and its Japanese development center serves all of Asia. A similar strategy is also being used for the United States and Europe.

Coca-Cola's increased planning savvy applies equally to the withdrawal of slow-selling products. Formerly, the firm would take its time in discontinuing poor-selling products. Thus, ViProMin, a fortified tomato juice launched in the 1960s, was distributed by Coca-Cola for several years despite poor sales. Some analysts feel the slow-withdrawal strategy was caused by Coca-Cola's unwillingness to publicly acknowledge defeat. Now, Coca-Cola is better able to shrug off failure. That is why the firm's Japanese "lactic-based" drink was quickly pulled after the product's initial sales growth slowed.

Coca-Cola's superior planning is quite evident in Eastern Europe. When the Soviet Union collapsed, Coca-Cola rapidly built manufacturing, distribution, and marketing facilities from scratch. In contrast, PepsiCo kept using its old network of inefficient state-run bottlers. Furthermore, Coca-Cola's aggressive strategy has given its products the image as the "milk of capitalism," especially among the young. Not surprisingly, Coca-Cola's current sales in Eastern Europe greatly exceed those of Pepsi.[1]

In this chapter, we will consider strategic planning from a marketing perspective and review, in depth, each of the steps in the strategic planning process. We will also examine the use of strategic planning by both small and large firms.

Overview

As described in Chapter 2, the environment within which marketing operates includes a number of factors directed by top management and others directed by marketing. To coordinate these factors and provide guidance for decision making, it is helpful to employ

[1]Robert Frank, "Coca-Cola Is Shedding Its Once-Stodgy Image with Swift Expansion," *Wall Street Journal* (August 22, 1995), pp. A1, A5.

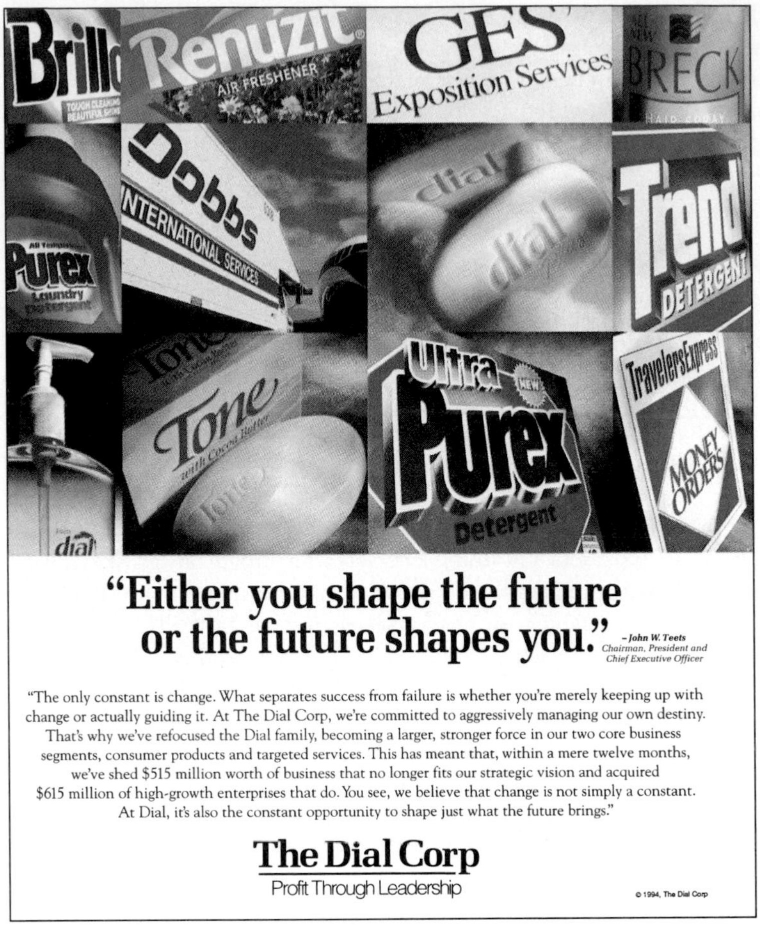

FIGURE 3-1
The Benefits of Strategic Planning
The Dial Corp practices what it preaches. As a result, in 1996, it announced plans to split into separate consumer products and services firms. According to John Teets, Dial's chief executive, "We believe this plan will help unlock the intrinsic value of Dial and place both companies on an aggressive, new growth track."
Reprinted by permission of the Dial Corp.

a formal strategic planning process. To marketers, such a process consists of two main components: a strategic business plan and a strategic marketing plan.

A **strategic business plan** "describes the overall direction an organization will pursue within its chosen environment and guides the allocation of resources and effort. It also provides the logic that integrates the perspectives of functional departments and operating units, and points them all in the same direction." It has (1) an external orientation; (2) a process for formulating strategies; (3) methods for analyzing strategic situations and alternatives; and (4) a commitment to action.[2]

Strategic planning involves both **strategic business plans** *and* **strategic marketing plans**.

A **strategic marketing plan** outlines the marketing actions to undertake, why those actions are needed, who is responsible for carrying them out, when and where they will be completed, and how they will be coordinated. Thus, a marketing plan is carried out within the context of a firm's broader strategic plan.

Our discussion of strategic planning and marketing is presented early in this book for several reasons. One, strategic planning gives direction to a firm's efforts and better enables it to understand the dimensions of marketing research, consumer analysis, and product, distribution, promotion, and price planning. It is a hierarchal process, moving from companywide guidelines down to specific marketing decisions. Two, a strategic plan makes sure each company division has clear goals that are integrated with firmwide goals. Three, different functional areas are encouraged to coordinate efforts. Four, as illustrated in Figure 3-1, strategic planning forces a firm to assess its strengths and weaknesses and to consider environmental opportunities and threats. Five, the alternative actions or combina-

[2]Peter D. Bennett (Editor), *Dictionary of Marketing Terms*, Second Edition (Chicago: American Marketing Association, 1995), p. 276.

tions of actions a firm can take are outlined. Six, a basis for allotting resources is set. Seven, the value of having a procedure for assessing performance can be shown.

Marketing's role in strategic planning is indeed a crucial one:

Marketing should have a key role in strategic planning.

> In industry after industry, the opportunity today is clear. It is now possible for companies to focus directly on achieving the full potential of customer relationships. Doing so will require executives to abandon outdated management models. But, as with prior shifts in management thinking, those who act early will reap disproportionate rewards.[3]

> Strategic planning should stress market information, market-segment definition, and market targeting. All company activities should be built around the goal of creating the desired position with a well-defined set of customers. Separate market segments should be the subject of separate plans that focus on developing customer relationships that emphasize the firm's distinctive competence. Marketing's contribution to strategic planning and implementation begins with the analysis of market segments and an assessment of a firm's ability to satisfy customer needs. This includes analyzing demand trends, competition, and in industrial markets, competitive conditions. Marketing also plays a key role by working with top management to define business purpose in terms of customer-need satisfaction. In a market-oriented view of the strategic planning process, financial goals are seen as results and rewards, not the fundamental purpose of business.[4]

In Chapter 3, we discuss a total quality approach to strategic planning, various kinds of strategic plans, relationships between marketing and other functional areas, and the strategic planning process—and show how strategic planning may be applied. Chapter 23, which concludes the text, deals with how marketing plans are integrated and analyzed in a total quality framework.

A Total Quality Approach to Strategic Planning

When devising strategic plans, any firm—small or large, domestic or international, manufacturing or services driven—should adopt a total quality perspective. **Total quality** is a process- and output-related philosophy, whereby a firm strives to fully satisfy customers in an effective and efficient manner. To flourish, a total quality program needs a customer focus; top management commitment; an emphasis on continuous improvement; and support from employees, suppliers, and distribution intermediaries:

All firms should adopt a **total quality** *approach, thereby becoming more process- and output-related in satisfying consumers.*

- *Process-related philosophy*—Total quality is based on all the activities undertaken to create, develop, market, and deliver a good or service to the customer. A firm gains a competitive advantage if it can offer the same quality good or service at a lower cost or if it can offer a better-quality good or service than other companies.
- *Output-related philosophy*—Although process-related activities give a good or service its value, the consumer usually can only judge the total quality of the finished product that he or she purchases. Many consumers care about what they buy, rather than how it was made.
- *Customer satisfaction*—To the consumer, total quality refers to how well a good or service performs. Thus, customer service is a key element in a person's ultimate satisfaction, which is affected by the gap between that person's expectations of product performance and actual performance.
- *Effectiveness*—To a marketer, this involves how well various marketing activities (such as adding new product features) are received by consumers.
- *Efficiency*—To a marketer, this involves the costs of various marketing activities. A firm is efficient when it holds down costs while offering consumers the appropriate level of quality.

[3]Alan W. H. Grant and Leonard A. Schlesinger, "Realize Your Customers' Full Profit Potential," *Harvard Business Review*, Vol. 59 (September–October 1995), p. 72.

[4]Frederick E. Webster, Jr., "The Rediscovery of the Marketing Concept," *Business Horizons*, Vol. 31 (May–June 1988), pp. 37–38.

- *Customer focus*—With a total quality perspective, a firm views the consumer as a partner and seeks input from that partner as it creates, develops, markets, and delivers a good or service.
- *Top management commitment*—Because a total quality program must be believed in by everyone who works for and comes into contact with a firm, senior executives must be dedicated to making it work and make sure corners are not cut in an attempt to be more efficient. In the best firms, "total quality" becomes ingrained as part of the corporate culture.
- *Continuous improvement*—In most cases, today's total quality will become tomorrow's suboptimal quality; so, a firm must continuously improve its quality. A complacent firm will be hurt by the dynamics of the marketplace and fast-paced technological and global marketplace trends.
- *Employee support and involvement*—For a total quality program to work, employees must "buy into" it. Empowering employees not only gets them involved in the total quality process, but it also assures that customer problems are promptly addressed and resolved in the customer's favor.
- *Supplier and distributor support and involvement*—Due to their involvement in creating total quality, both suppliers and resellers can have a dramatic effect on it. They too must "buy into" a firm's efforts at total quality.

For a total quality program to work, every party in the process must participate.

Figure 3-2 shows how a successful total quality program works. At the left are the participants in a total quality program, who together engage in the process of creating total quality. There is an interchange among the parties and between the parties and the process. Through the total quality process, a good's or service's effectiveness and efficiency are influenced; likewise, these factors are considered during the process. Total quality is the output of the process. The process and total quality itself are regularly improved. If a consumer feels a good or service has superior total quality, a purchase is made. When the experience with a good or service is pleasing, customer satisfaction occurs. Since one effectiveness measure is customer satisfaction, there is an impact arrow. Finally, the level of customer satisfaction is a feedback loop that affects the consumer's future input into the

FIGURE 3-2
The Keys to a Successful Total Quality Program

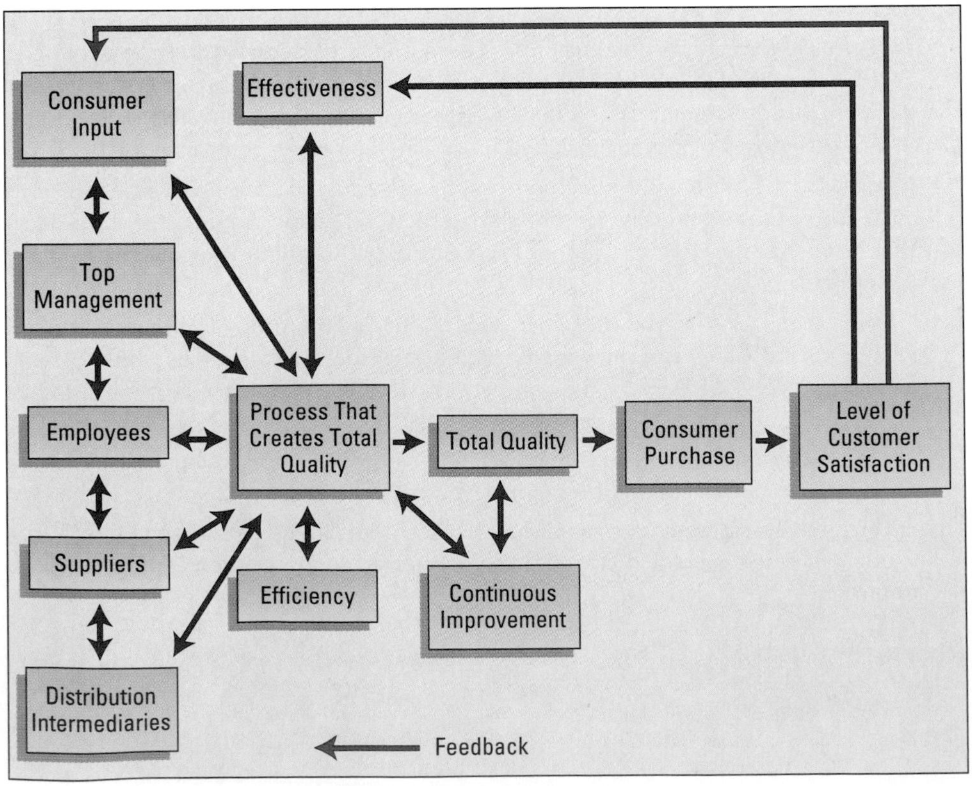

total quality process. The consumer's central focus is evident because the consumer appears three times: consumer input, consumer purchase, and customer satisfaction.

As one expert notes, "To see things truly from the customer's perspective is to stand at the end of a long sequence of events, all of which have to mesh smoothly. Hotel clerks may be charming and attentive, but if the computer system is down, their courtesy isn't going to help much. Within any company, TQM theory holds, is a whole chain of 'internal customers' like the hotel clerk, ending with the person at the cash register, credit card in hand. The trick is to get everyone working together while keeping the ultimate customer in focus." To Siemens (the German-based industrial firm), "Quality is when your customers come back and your products don't."[5]

Kinds of Strategic Plans

Strategic plans can be categorized by their duration, scope, and method of development. They range from short run, specific, and department generated to long run, broad, and management generated.

Plans may be short run (typically one year), moderate in length (two to five years), or long run (5 to 10 or even 15 years). Many firms rely on a combination: Short-run and moderate-length plans are more detailed and operational in nature than long-run plans.

Short-run plans are precise; long-run plans outline needs.

At Japan's Canon Corporation (which makes cameras, business machines, and optical products), short-run plans show a "numerical expression of management activities during defined operating periods"; moderate-length plans "develop strategies to achieve the direction and goals defined by long-range plans, to provide guidelines for short-range plans, and to ensure optimum resource procurement and allocation"; and long-run plans are "more a vision or concept rather than plans, in the sense that they provide the direction and goals for a firm to pursue in a rapidly changing environment, and they lead to the achievement of qualitative innovations in every aspect of operations."[6]

The scope of strategic marketing plans also varies. There may be separate marketing plans for each of a firm's major products; a single, integrated marketing plan encompassing all products; or a broad business plan with a section devoted to marketing. Separate marketing plans by product line are often used by consumer-goods manufacturers; a single, integrated marketing plan is often employed by service firms; and a broad business plan is often utilized by industrial-goods manufacturers. A firm's diversity and the number of distinct market segments it seeks both have a strong influence here.

Consumer-products firms often have plans for each line.

Last, strategic plans may be developed via a bottom-up, top-down, or combination approach. In bottom-up marketing planning, input from salespeople, product managers, advertising personnel, and other marketing areas is used to set objectives, budgets, forecasts, timetables, and marketing mixes. Bottom-up plans are realistic and good for morale. Yet, it may be hard to coordinate each bottom-up plan and to include different assumptions about the same concept when setting an integrated companywide marketing plan.

The shortcomings of bottom-up plans are resolved in the top-down approach, whereby senior managers centrally direct and control planning activities. A top-down plan can use complex assumptions about competition or other external factors and provide a uniform direction for the marketing effort. Yet, input from lower-level managers is not actively sought and morale may be diminished.

Bottom-up plans foster employee input; top-down plans are set by top management.

A combination of the two approaches could be used if senior executives set overall goals and policy and marketing personnel form plans for carrying out marketing policies. As the chief executive of one firm remarked: "You can't have a workable strategy forced down from the top. Empowering middle managers is a necessity. They manage what we

[5]Frank Rose, "Now Quality Means Service Too," *Fortune* (April 22, 1991), pp. 97–108; and Earl Naumann and Patrick Shannon, "What Is Customer-Driven Marketing?" *Business Horizons*, Vol. 35 (November–December 1992), p. 44. See also John Shea and David Gobeli, "TQM: The Experience of Ten Small Businesses," *Business Horizons*, Vol. 38 (January–February 1995), pp. 71–77.

[6]Toshio Nakahara and Yutaka Isono, "Strategic Planning for Canon; The Crisis and the New Vision," *Long Range Planning*, Vol. 25 (February 1992), p. 67.

Table 3-1
The Orientations of Different Functional Areas

FUNCTIONAL AREA	MAJOR STRATEGIC ORIENTATION
Marketing	To attract and retain a loyal group of consumers through a unique combination of product, distribution, promotion, and price factors
Production	To utilize full plant capacity, hold down per-unit production costs, and maximize quality control
Finance	To operate within established budgets, focus on profitable items, control customer credit, and minimize loan costs for the company
Accounting	To standardize reports, detail costs fully, and routinize transactions
Engineering	To develop and adhere to exact product specifications, limit models and options, and concentrate on quality improvements
Purchasing	To acquire items via large, uniform orders at low prices and maintain low inventories
Research and Development	To seek technological breakthroughs, improvements in product quality, and recognition for innovations
Personnel	To hire, motivate, supervise, and compensate employees in an efficient manner
Legal	To ensure that a strategy is defensible against challenges from the government, competitors, channel members, and consumers

as a corporation want to accomplish. To make them think strategically comes from sharing the direction and from having a set of supportive organizational systems. So it's real work, not sermons, that makes us and our middle managers strategic thinkers."[7]

Strengthening Relationships Between Marketing and Other Functional Areas in an Organization

The perspectives of marketing and other functional areas need to be reconciled.

An organization's strategic planning must accommodate the distinct needs of marketing and other functional areas. This is not always simple, due to the different orientations of each area, as shown in Table 3-1. Marketing people may seek tailor-made products, flexible budgets, nonroutine transactions, many product versions, frequent purchases, customer-driven new products, employee compensation incentives, and aggressive actions against competitors. This may conflict with the goals of other functional areas to seek mass production (production), well-established budgets (finance), routinized transactions (accounting), limited models (engineering), infrequent orders (purchasing), technology-driven new products (research and development), fixed employee compensation (personnel), and passive actions against competitors (legal).

Top management's job is to make sure every functional area sees the need for a balanced view in company decision making and has input on decisions. Although some degree of tension among departments is inevitable, conflict can be lessened by encouraging interfunctional contact; seeking employees with both technical and marketing expertise; forming multifunctional task forces, committees, and management-development programs; and setting goals for each department that take the other departments into account.[8]

[7]Manab Thakur and Luis Ma. R. Calingo, "Strategic Thinking Is Hip, But Does It Make a Difference?" *Business Horizons*, Vol. 35 (September–October 1992), p. 47.

[8]See Jeen-Su Lim, "Vital Cross-Functional Linkages with Marketing," *Industrial Marketing Management*, Vol. 21 (May 1992), pp. 159–165; Victoria L. Crittenden, "Close the Marketing/Manufacturing Gap," *Sloan Management Review*, Vol. 33 (Spring 1992), pp. 41–51; and Michael D. Hutt, Beth A. Walker, and Gary L. Frankwick, "Hurdle the Cross-Functional Barriers to Strategic Change," *Sloan Management Review*, Vol. 36 (Spring 1995), pp. 22–30.

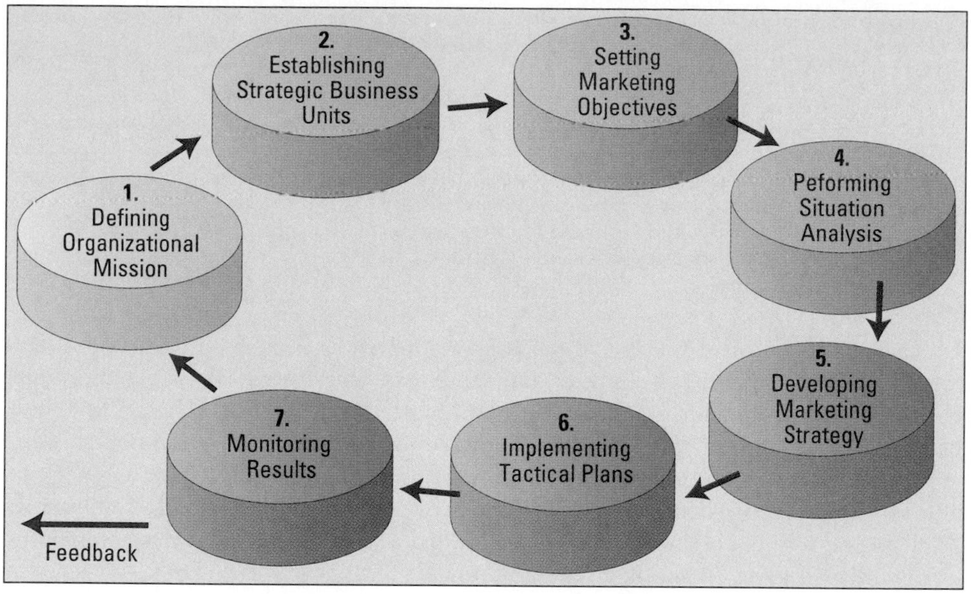

FIGURE 3-3
The Strategic Planning Process

The Strategic Planning Process

The **strategic planning process** *includes steps from defining a mission to monitoring results.*

The **strategic planning process** has seven interrelated steps: defining organizational mission, establishing strategic business units, setting marketing objectives, performing situation analysis, developing marketing strategy, implementing tactics, and monitoring results. Because the process encompasses both strategic business planning and strategic marketing planning, it should be conducted by a combination of senior company executives and marketers. It is depicted in Figure 3-3.

This process is applicable for small and large firms, consumer-products and industrial-products firms, goods- and services-based firms, domestic and international firms, and profit-oriented and nonprofit-oriented institutions. While planning at each step in the process may differ by type of organization, using a thorough strategic plan is beneficial for any organization.

The steps in strategic planning are discussed in the following sections.

Defining Organizational Mission

A firm sets its direction in an **organizational mission**.

Organizational mission refers to a long-term commitment to a type of business and a place in the market. It "describes the scope of the firm and its dominant emphasis and values," based on that firm's history, current management preferences, resources, and distinctive competences, and on environmental factors.[9]

An organizational mission can be expressed in terms of the customer group(s) served, the goods and services offered, the functions performed, and/or the technologies utilized. It is more comprehensive than the line of business concept noted in Chapter 2. And it is considered implicitly whenever a firm seeks a new customer group or abandons an existing one, introduces a new product (good or service) category or deletes an old one, acquires another company or sells one of its own businesses, engages in more marketing functions (a wholesaler opening retail stores) or in fewer marketing functions (a small innovative toy maker licensing its inventions to an outside company that produces, distributes, and promotes them), or shifts its technological focus (a phone manufacturer placing more emphasis on cellular phones).

Here are two diverse illustrations of clear organizational missions:

> Lands' End is a leading international direct merchant of traditionally styled, casual clothing for men, women, and children; accessories; domestics; shoes; and soft luggage. Its products are offered through regular mailings of a monthly catalog and four specialty catalogs. Lands' End is

[9]Bennett, *Dictionary of Marketing Terms*, p. 67. See also James Krobe, Jr., "Do You Really Need a Mission Statement?" *Across the Board* (July–August 1995), pp. 17–21.

known for providing products of exceptional quality at prices representing honest value, enhanced by a commitment to excellence in customer service.[10]

When it comes to food, it's hard to get more obscure than an Atlanta-made delicacy called Larder of Lady Bustle Lemon Sauce. The name itself is a mouthful, and the product, used as a biscuit spread and cake filling, is hardly a kitchen staple. But for Joan and Donald Moore, the quaintly named dressing has launched a small, but thriving, home-based specialty-food company. Larder of Lady Bustle Ltd. has annual sales of $100,000 and makes six sauces and condiments. That's less than a drop in the kettle for a typical food company. But it's about right for the Moores, who are sticklers for quality: "There's no way you can mass produce these things. We have to stay small."[11]

Organizations that diversify too much may not have a clear sense of direction. For example, Jostens—the maker of class rings, yearbooks, and other items targeted to high school and college students—was extremely profitable for four decades. Then, it launched Jostens Learning Corporation in 1989, even though its senior executives did not have expertise in educational software. Jostens' software business flopped largely because of the high startup costs for clients and intense competition; and the firm lost $16 million in 1994. As one analyst observed, "Nobody was taking a hard look at what was going on—nobody seemed to be asking the right questions."[12]

Establishing Strategic Business Units

Strategic business units (SBUs) *are separate operating units in an organization.*

After defining its mission, a firm can form strategic business units. Each **strategic business unit (SBU)** is a self-contained division, product line, or product department in an organization with a specific market focus and a manager with complete responsibility for integrating all functions into a strategy.[13] An SBU may include all products with the same physical features or products bought for the same use by customers, depending on the mission of the organization. Each SBU has these general attributes:

- A specific target market.
- Its own senior marketing executive.
- Control over its resources.
- Its own marketing strategy.
- Clear-cut competitors.
- Distinct differential advantages.

The SBU concept lets companies identify those business units with the greatest earnings potential and allocate to them the resources needed for their growth. For instance, at General Electric, every SBU must have a unique purpose, identifiable competitors, and all its major business functions (manufacturing, finance, and marketing) within the control of that SBU's manager. Units not performing up to expectations are constantly reviewed and, if necessary, consolidated with other units, sold, or closed down.[14]

The proper number of SBUs depends on a firm's organizational mission, its resources, and the willingness of top management to delegate authority. A small or specialized firm can have as few as one SBU, a diversified one up to 100 or more. Thus, Johnson Controls has the four SBUs depicted in Figure 3-4; General Electric has 12 SBUs—ranging from aircraft engines to lighting to information services; Dover has 70 SBUs—ranging from elevators to garbage trucks to welding torches; and Johnson & Johnson has 165+ SBUs—related to consumer, pharmaceutical, and professional products.[15]

[10] *Lands' End 1995 Annual Report.*

[11] Eugene Carlson, "Small-Time Food Producers Find Growth Doesn't Pay," *Wall Street Journal* (January 4, 1993), p. B2.

[12] Kenneth Labich, "Why Companies Fail," *Fortune* (November 14, 1994), pp. 52–54.

[13] Subhash C. Jain, *Marketing Planning & Strategy*, Fourth Edition (Cincinnati: South-Western, 1993), pp. 15–19.

[14] Noel M. Tichy and Stratford Sherman, *Control Your Destiny or Someone Else Will* (New York: Doubleday, 1993).

[15] *General Electric 1995 Annual Report*; Phillip L. Zweig, "Who Says the Conglomerate Is Dead?" *Business Week* (January 23, 1995), pp. 92–93; and Brian O'Reilly, "J&J Is on a Roll," *Fortune* (December 26, 1994), pp. 178–192.

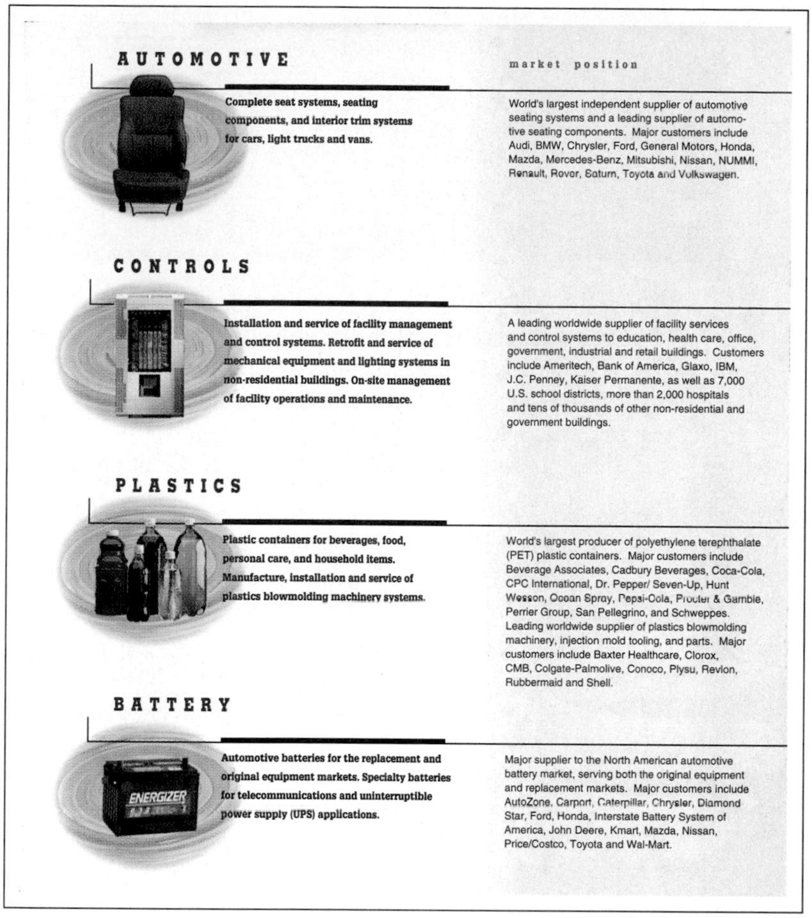

FIGURE 3-4
The SBUs of Johnson Controls
Reprinted by permission.

Setting Marketing Objectives

Marketing objectives may include quantitative and qualitative measures.

A firm needs overall marketing objectives, as well as goals for each SBU. Objectives are often described in both quantitative terms (dollar sales, percentage profit growth, market share, etc.) and qualitative terms (image, level of innovativeness, industry leadership role, etc.).

For example, Quaker Oats Company's eight key goals are: (1) "Provide total shareholder returns that exceed the cost of equity and the S&P 500 stock index over time." (2) "Maintain a robust financial position from strong operating cash flows, while generating economic value via the use of leverage." (3) "Aggressively market brands for leadership positions. We assess our strength by our ability to grow, acquire, or maintain brands that are number one or two in their categories." (4) "Profitably grow the volume of key brands at better-than-industry-average rates by offering greater value to the customer." (5) "Enhance productivity and efficiency in every element of our business." (6) "Develop mutually beneficial, interdependent relationships with our trade customers to improve the economic return of both parties." (7) "Build high-performance teams of resourceful, motivated, and productive employees." (8) "Raise the productivity of low-return businesses or divest them."[16]

Small firms' goals are often less ambitious, but no less important:

> Mom-and-pop kitchen operations such as Larder of Lady Bustle like to take things slow. In an industry dominated by giant processors, they stay small by design. Says Margaret Engel, co-author of *Food Finds*, a compendium of local food manufacturers, "There's a margin of profitability if you stay local and stay small. These firms have thought long and hard about where they want to be. For most of them, it's not worth it to get to the next level."[17]

[16]*Quaker Oats Company 1995 Annual Report.*

[17]Carlson, "Small-Time Food Producers Find Growth Doesn't Pay," p. B2.

International Marketing in Action

How Do the Marketing Strategies of U.S. and South African Firms Differ?

To study and compare the marketing strategies of U.S. and South African firms, a survey was recently sent to senior marketing executives in those two countries. Usable responses were received from 94 U.S. executives and 87 South African executives. In many areas, there were strong similarities between the strategies used by the executives in each country.

These are some of the differences in the marketing strategies of U.S. and South African firms:

- U.S. firms focus more on competitive advantage and identifying target markets as key components in their strategies. In contrast, South African firms place more emphasis on company positioning and taking advantage of trends and opportunities as market strategy components.
- With regard to target marketing approaches, South African firms have a greater tendency to focus on the entire market (rather than individual customers or multiple segments).
- In terms of demand-based strategies, U.S. firms are more apt to try to take customers from competitors and attract new users to the market.
- In terms of pricing, U.S. firms engage in more penetration pricing (aimed at charging a lower price to capture the mass market) than South African firms.
- U.S. firms use market research and on-line data bases more than their South African counterparts, while South African firms make greater use of product portfolio analysis and formal planning procedures.
- South African firms use more financial managers and external consultants.

As a marketing manager for a small U.S. firm manufacturer, what could you learn from the above findings?

Source: Based on material in Michael H. Morris and Leyland F. Pitt, "Implementing Marketing Strategies in the U.S. and South Africa," *Long Range Planning,* Vol. 27 (February 1994), pp. 56–71.

Performing Situation Analysis

Situation analysis *investigates a firm's strengths, weaknesses, opportunities, and threats.*

In **situation analysis**, also known as SWOT analysis, an organization identifies its internal strengths (*S*) and weaknesses (*W*), as well as external opportunities (*O*) and threats (*T*). Situation analysis seeks to answer: Where is a firm now? In what direction is it headed? Answers are derived by recognizing both company strengths and weaknesses relative to competitors, studying the environment for opportunities and threats, assessing the firm's ability to capitalize on opportunities and to minimize or avoid threats, and anticipating competitors' responses to company strategies.

Situation analysis can, and should be, conducted at any point in a firm's life. For instance, when college classmates Joshua Baker and Larry Weinberg decided to start a home-remodeling firm (after scraping together $5,000), they conducted a situation analysis—which steered them to using a professional approach to job costing and accounting. Their first purchase was a PC. As Baker recently noted, "While the competition was doing hand-written proposals, we gave customers something nice in print, on letterhead, in a folder with our logo on it." Today, BOWA Builders' annual revenues are $3+ million.[18]

[18]Jay Finegan, "(Re)Model Startup," *Inc.* (August 1995), p. 29.

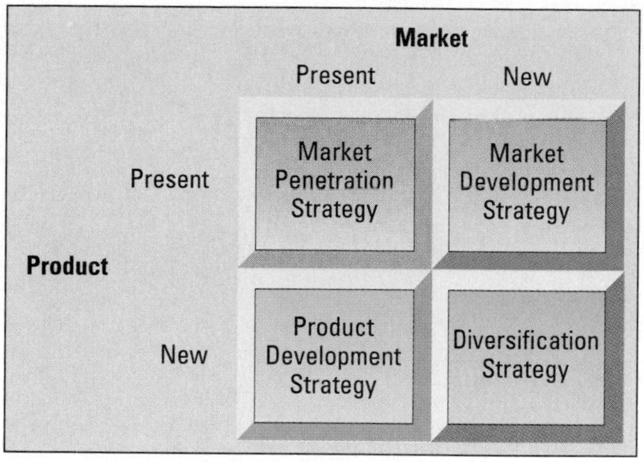

FIGURE 3-5
The Product/Market Opportunity Matrix

Source: Adapted from H. Igor Ansoff, "Strategies for Diversification," *Harvard Business Review,* Vol. 35 (September–October 1957), pp. 113–124.

Likewise, here is what 60-year-old Avery Dennison learned from a situation analysis and how its future plans reflect the conclusions reached. Avery makes self-adhesive labels and other materials; its yearly sales are $3 billion.

> Avery's biggest weakness is in Asia and Latin America, which provide five per cent of its sales. Avery has progressed in Europe, which yields nearly $1 billion in foreign sales, but has a small Japanese presence. The sticky-paper business typically grows at a rate of three times the rate of a nation's gross domestic product. So, the potential in Asia and Latin America is tantalizing. To catch up to and beat Japanese competitors in these growth markets, Avery will do a lot of spending there—building factories in China, expanding in Singapore and Korea, and putting up warehouses in Latin America.[19]

Sometimes, situation analysis reveals weaknesses or threats that cannot be overcome, and a company opts to drop or sell a product line or division. Thus, in 1995, General Mills sold its restaurant division—comprised of the Red Lobster, Olive Garden, and China Coast chains. Why? Fifty-five per cent of General Mills' food profits were being used to fund the restaurant business; and the firm decided to focus instead on its leading food brands: Wheaties, Cheerios, Betty Crocker baking products, Yoplait yogurt, and others.[20]

Developing Marketing Strategy

A good **marketing strategy** *provides a framework for marketing activities.*

A **marketing strategy** outlines the way in which the marketing mix is used to attract and satisfy the target market(s) and achieve an organization's goals. Marketing-mix decisions center on product, distribution, promotion, and price plans. A separate strategy is necessary for each SBU in an organization; these strategies must be coordinated.

A marketing strategy should be explicit to provide proper guidance. It should take into account a firm's mission, resources, abilities, and standing in the marketplace; the status of the firm's industry and the product groups in it (such as light versus ice beer); domestic and international competitive forces; such environmental factors as the economy and population growth; and the best opportunities for growth—and the threats that could dampen it.

Four strategic planning approaches are presented next: the product/market opportunity matrix, the Boston Consulting Group matrix, the General Electric business screen, and the Porter generic strategy model.

The **product/market opportunity matrix** *involves* **market penetration, market development, product development,** *and* **diversification** *options.*

The Product/Market Opportunity Matrix The **product/market opportunity matrix** identifies four alternative marketing strategies to maintain and/or increase sales of business units and products: market penetration, market development, product development, and diversification.[21] See Figure 3-5. The choice of an alternative depends on the market

[19]Damon Darlin, "Thank You, 3M," *Forbes* (September 25, 1995), pp. 86, 88.

[20]Leah Rickard, "General Mills Gathers Rewards of Change," *Advertising Age* (July 10, 1995), p. 4; and Richard Gibson, "General Mills Gets in Shape for Turnaround," *Wall Street Journal* (September 26, 1995), pp. B1, B4.

[21]H. Igor Ansoff, "Strategies for Diversification," *Harvard Business Review*, Vol. 35 (September–October 1957), pp. 113–124.

FIGURE 3-6
UPS: The Leader in Package Delivery
Reprinted by permission.

saturation of an SBU or product and the firm's ability to introduce new products. Two or more alternatives may be combined.

Market penetration is effective when the market is growing or not yet saturated. A firm seeks to expand the sales of its present products in its present markets through more intensive distribution, aggressive promotion, and competitive pricing. Sales are increased by attracting nonusers and competitors' customers and raising the usage rate among current customers.

Market development is effective when a local or regional business looks to widen its market, new market segments are emerging due to changes in consumer life-styles and demographics, and innovative uses are discovered for a mature product. A firm seeks greater sales of present products from new markets or new product uses. It can enter new geographic markets, appeal to market segments it is not yet satisfying, and reposition existing products. New distribution methods may be tried; promotion efforts are more descriptive.

Product development is effective when an SBU has a core of strong brands and a sizable consumer following. A firm develops new or modified products to appeal to present markets. It stresses new models, better quality, and other minor innovations closely related to entrenched products—and markets them to loyal customers. Traditional distribution methods are used; promotion stresses that the new product is made by a well-established firm.

Diversification is used so a firm does not become too dependent on one SBU or product line. The firm becomes involved with new products aimed at new markets. These prod-

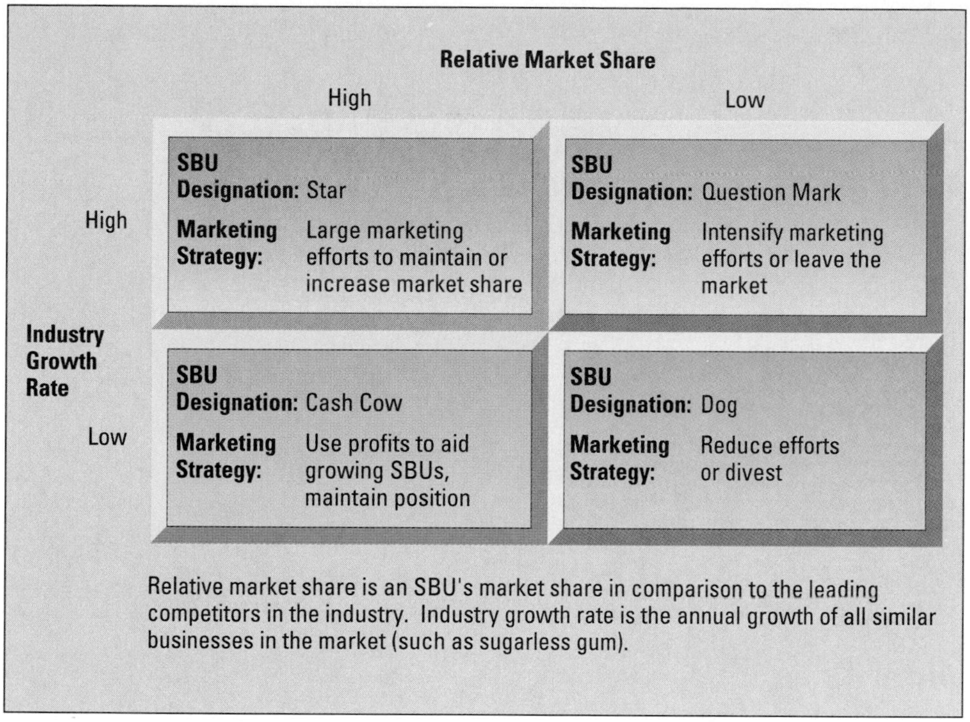

Relative Market Share
High
Low
High
Low
Industry Growth Rate
SBU Designation: Star
Marketing Strategy: Large marketing efforts to maintain or increase market share
SBU Designation: Question Mark
Marketing Strategy: Intensify marketing efforts or leave the market
SBU Designation: Cash Cow
Marketing Strategy: Use profits to aid growing SBUs, maintain position
SBU Designation: Dog
Marketing Strategy: Reduce efforts or divest
Relative market share is an SBU's market share in comparison to the leading competitors in the industry. Industry growth rate is the annual growth of all similar businesses in the market (such as sugarless gum).

FIGURE 3-7
The Boston Consulting Group Matrix
Source: Adapted from Bruce D. Henderson, "The Experience Curve Reviewed: IV. The Growth Share Matrix of the Product Portfolio" (Boston: Boston Consulting Group, 1973). *Perspectives,* No. 135.

ucts may be new to the industry or new only to the company. Distribution and promotion orientations are both different from those usually followed by the firm.

Here is how the product/market opportunity matrix can be applied to United Parcel Service (UPS):

- Market penetration—UPS is the world's largest package-delivery firm. It advertises extensively on TV and in magazines. The current slogan is "Moving at the Speed of Business." It handles more than 1.3 million customers through its automatic daily pickup service.
- Market development—It is stepping up efforts around the world, where client use of delivery services tends to be much less than in the United States. Ten years ago, UPS' International Air service operated in 40 nations; now, it is in more than 200 countries and territories—including a joint venture with Sovtransavto to serve Russia and many of its former republics.
- Product development—It now offers more shipping choices than ever before, including Next Day Air (delivered by 10:30 A.M. the next day), Early A.M. (delivered by 8:00 or 8:30 A.M. the next day), Same Day, 2nd Day Air, 3 Day Select, and Worldwide Express services. See Figure 3-6.
- Diversification—Although UPS' major focus is on package delivery, it also operates such subsidiaries as UPS Worldwide Logistics (which offers inventory management, facilities planning, site location, and other services), II Morrow (which manufactures navigational and communication equipment), and Roadnet Technologies (which develops software and systems for managing distribution fleets).[22]

The Boston Consulting Group Matrix The **Boston Consulting Group matrix** lets a firm classify each SBU in terms of market share relative to major competitors and annual industry growth. A firm can see which SBUs are dominant—compared to competitors—and whether the industries in which it operates are growing, stable, or declining. The matrix identifies four types of SBUs: star, cash cow, question mark, and dog, and offers strategies for them.[23] See Figure 3-7.

The **Boston Consulting Group matrix** *uses market share and industry growth to describe* **stars**, **cash cows**, **question marks**, *and* **dogs**.

[22]Patrick J. Spain and James R. Talbot (Editors), *Hoover's Handbook of American Business 1996* (Austin, Texas: Reference Press, 1995), pp. 1456–1457; and 1996 UPS correspondence.

[23]See *Perspectives on Experience* (Boston: Boston Consulting Group, 1972); and D. Sudharshan, *Marketing Strategy: Relationships, Offerings, Timing & Resource Allocation* (Englewood Cliffs, N.J.: Prentice Hall, 1995), pp. 244–253.

TECHNOLOGY & MARKETING

What's in the Chips for Intel?

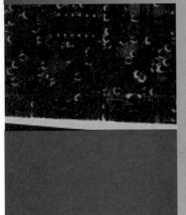

Due to its estimated 75 per cent of the microprocessor chip market, Intel Corporation has the advantage of economies of scale (lower per-unit costs than competitors) and high profits. As a result, the firm regularly generates all the cash it needs for new-product development. And because the investment required to develop new microprocessor chips is growing quite rapidly, this places a tough burden on Intel's competitors. According to industry experts, the capital spending needed to devise the Pentium chip was $5 billion. This was five times the amount needed for the 486 chip and 50 times that for the 386 chip. In general, plant and equipment costs double every four years.

Some analysts say that Intel will become the world's most profitable company by the year 2000. They estimate that Intel's annual earnings may hit $8 billion to $11 billion in that year. In fact, few large firms have been able to match Intel's recent five-year average earnings growth rate of 37 per cent. In addition, company executives suggest that microprocessor chips are less vulnerable than other products to the business cycle.

Much of Intel's strategy evolves around an observation made in 1965 by Intel's then chairman, Gordon E. Moore. This observation, now known as Moore's Law, states that the number of transistors that can be placed on a chip doubles every 18 months or so. Making smaller circuits also means that chips get faster, consume less energy, become more reliable, and cost less. For example, Intel's new P6 chip has 254 times the computing power per $100 in cost than the Intel 8086 chip used by IBM in its initial PC sold in 1981.

As a marketing analyst, what do you think that Intel must do to meet the year 2000 profit goals noted above?

Source: Based on material in Don Clark, "A Big Bet Made Intel What It Is Today: Now, It Wagers Again," *Wall Street Journal* (July 7, 1995), pp. A1, A6; and Brent Schlender, "Why Andy Grove Can't Stop," *Fortune* (July 10, 1995), pp. 88–98.

The assumption is that the higher an SBU's market share, the better its long-run marketplace position because of rather low per-unit costs and high profitability. This is due to economies of scale (larger firms can automate or standardize production, service tasks, distribution, promotion, and so on), experience (as operations are repeated, a firm becomes more effective), and better bargaining power. At the same time, the industry growth rate indicates a firm's need to invest. A high growth rate means a big investment will be needed to maintain or expand the firm's position in a growing market.

A **star** is a leading SBU (high market share) in an expanding industry (high growth). The main goal is to sustain differential advantages in the face of rising competition. A star can generate substantial profits but requires financing for continued growth. Market share can be kept or increased via intensive advertising, product introductions, greater distribution, and/or price reductions. As industry growth slows, a star becomes a cash cow.

A **cash cow** is a leading SBU (high market share) in a mature or declining industry (low growth). It often has loyal customers, making it hard for competitors to woo them. Since sales are rather steady, without high costs for product development and the like, a cash cow produces more cash (profit) than needed to keep its market share. Profits support the growth of other company SBUs. Marketing is oriented to reminder ads, periodic price discounts, keeping up distribution channels, and offering new styles or options to encourage repurchases.

A **question mark** is an SBU that has had little impact (low market share) in an expanding industry (high growth). There is low consumer support, differential advantages are weak, and competitors are leaders. To improve, a big marketing investment is needed in the face of strong competition. A firm must decide whether to beef up promotion, add distributors, improve product attributes, and cut prices—or to abandon the market. The

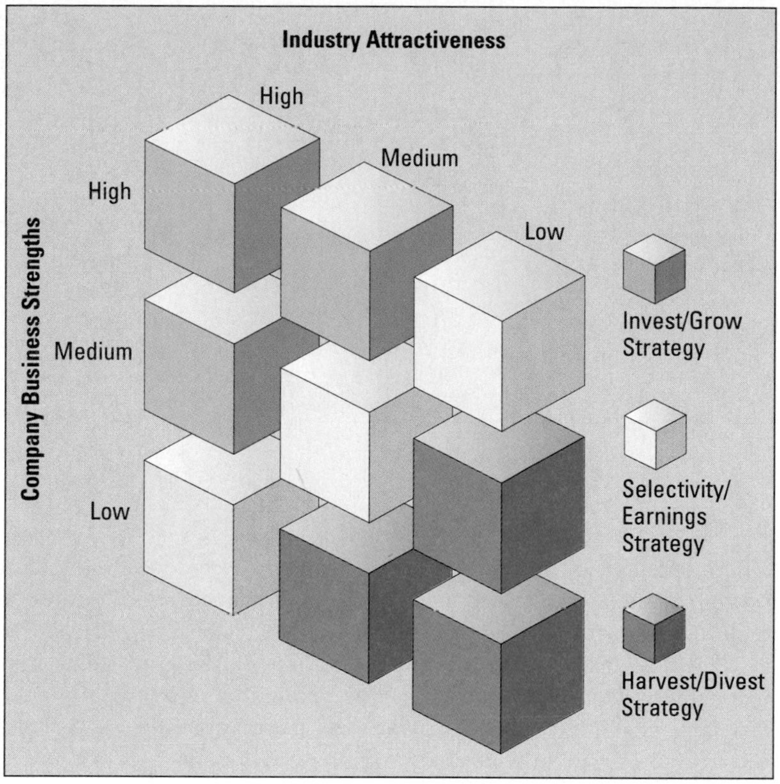

FIGURE 3-8
The General Electric Business Screen
Source: Maintaining Strategies for the Future Through Current Crises (Fairfield, Ct.: General Electric, 1975).

choice depends on whether a firm believes the SBU can compete successfully with more support and what that support will cost.

A **dog** is an SBU with limited sales (low market share) in a mature or declining industry (low growth). Despite time in the marketplace, a dog has a small customer following—and lags behind competitors in sales, image, and so on. A dog usually has cost disadvantages and few growth opportunities. A firm with such an SBU can appeal to a specialized market, harvest profits by cutting support services, or exit the market.

Pall Corporation, a maker of industrial fluid clarification equipment (which removes contaminants from liquids and gases), applies the principles suggested by the Boston Consulting Group matrix. Pall examines its business units in terms of expected industry growth and market position, and then sets marketing strategies. Over the past decade, there has been a shift away from Aeropower—which now contributes 26 per cent of overall Pall revenues (down from 40 per cent)—and to Health Care, which now accounts for 50 per cent of company sales (up from 28 per cent). The shift is due to a combination of declining aerospace sales, the culling out of unprofitable businesses, and the quintupling of Health Care sales.[24]

The **General Electric business screen** *measures industry attractiveness and company business strengths.*

The General Electric Business Screen The **General Electric business screen** categorizes SBUs and products in terms of industry attractiveness and company business strengths. It involves more variables than the product/market opportunity matrix or the Boston Consulting Group matrix. Industry attractiveness factors include market size and growth, competition, technological advances, and the social/legal environment. Company business strength factors embody differential advantages, market share, patent protection, marketing effectiveness, control over prices, and economies of scale. An SBU may have high, medium, or low industry attractiveness, as well as high, medium, or low company business strengths; it would be positioned accordingly on the business screen in Figure 3-8.[25]

[24]*Pall Corporation 1994 Annual Report.*

[25]See Derek F. Abell and John S. Hammond, *Strategic Market Planning* (Englewood Cliffs, N.J.: Prentice-Hall, 1979), pp. 211–227; and David A. Aaker, *Strategic Market Management* (New York: Wiley, 1995), pp. 164–167.

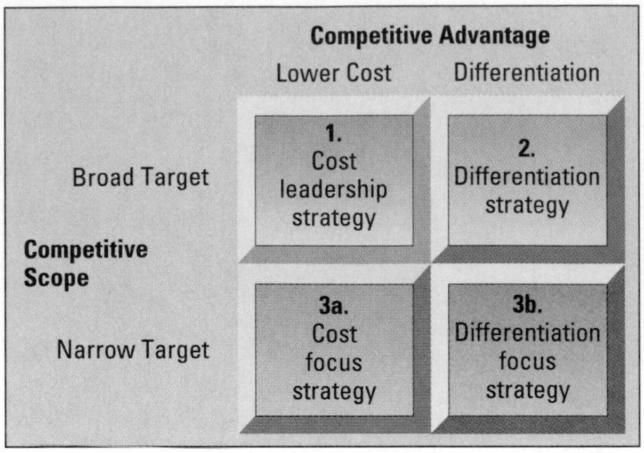

FIGURE 3-9
The Porter Generic Strategy Model

Source: Michael E. Porter, *Competitive Advantage: Creating and Sustaining Superior Performance* (New York: Free Press, 1985), p. 12. *Reprinted with the permission of The Free Press, a division of Simon & Schuster, Inc. Copyright © 1985 by Michael E. Porter.*

SBUs in green are investment/growth areas. They are in strong industries and performing well. They are similar to stars in the Boston Consulting Group matrix. Full marketing resources are proper, and high profits are expected. Innovations, product-line extensions, product and image ads, distribution intensity, and solid price margins are pursued.

SBUs in yellow are selectivity/earnings areas. They are not positioned as well as investment/growth ones. An SBU may be strong in a weak industry (as a cash cow), okay in a somewhat attractive industry, or weak in an attractive industry (as a question mark). A firm wants to hold the earnings and strength of cash cows, and use marketing to maintain customer loyalty and distribution support. For question marks, a firm must decide whether to raise its marketing investment, focus on a specialized market niche, acquire another business in the industry, or trim product lines. The medium/medium SBU is an opportunity to appeal to underserved segments and to invest selectively in marketing.

SBUs in red represent harvest/divest areas. They are similar to dogs in the Boston Consulting Group matrix. A firm can minimize its marketing effort, concentrate on a few products rather than a product line, divest, or close down the SBU. Profits are harvested because investments are minimal.

Bausch & Lomb applies the fundamentals of the business screen: It has "a heritage of technical achievement and product excellence dating to 1853. The company markets personal health, medical, biomedical, and optics products on the basis of quality and differentiated benefits. Its strategic focus is on selected segments of global health care and optical markets where it is advantaged with superior technology, low production costs, and established brand names. Products have earned worldwide consumer recognition and are frequently recommended by health-care professionals."[26]

The **Porter generic strategy model** *distinguishes among cost leadership, differentiation, and focus strategies.*

The Porter Generic Strategy Model The **Porter generic strategy model** identifies two key marketing planning concepts and the options available for each: competitive scope (broad or narrow target) and competitive advantage (lower cost or differentiation). The model pinpoints these basic strategies: cost leadership, differentiation, and focus.[27] See Figure 3-9.

With a cost-leadership strategy, an SBU aims at a broad market and offers goods or services in large quantities. Due to economies of scale, a firm can reduce per-unit costs and have low prices. This gives it higher profit margins than competitors, responds better to cost rises, and/or lures price-conscious consumers. Among those using cost leadership are UPS, DuPont, and Wal-Mart.

In a differentiation strategy, an SBU aims at a large market by offering goods or services viewed as quite distinctive. The goods or services have a broad appeal, yet are per-

[26]*Bausch & Lomb 1992 Annual Report*; and *Bausch & Lomb 1994 Annual Report*.

[27]Michael E. Porter, *Competitive Advantage: Creating and Sustaining Superior Performance* (New York: Free Press, 1985), pp. 11–26; and Michael E. Porter, *Competitive Strategy: Techniques for Analyzing Industries and Competitors* (New York: Free Press, 1980), pp. 34–46. See also Steven P. Schnaars, *Marketing Strategy: A Customer-Driven Approach* (New York: Free Press, 1991), pp. 112–131.

ceived by consumers as unique by virtue of features, availability, reliability, etc.; price is less important. Among those using differentiation are Federal Express, Seiko, and Caterpillar Tractor.

With a focus strategy, an SBU (which could be a small firm) seeks a narrow market segment via low prices or a unique offering. It can control costs by concentrating on a few key products aimed at specific consumers or by having a specialist reputation and serving a market unsatisfied by competitors. Samsung is a low-cost South Korean maker of inexpensive consumer electronics, while Safety 1st of Massachusetts makes novelties like "Baby on Board!" signs. A neighborhood hardware store typically provides a good combination of service, convenient location, and long hours; a local radio station may cater to an over-50 audience by playing mostly music from the "big band" era.

The Porter model shows that a small firm can profit by concentrating on one competitive niche, even though its total market share may be low. A firm does not have to be large to do well.

Strategic models have pros and cons, and should be only part of planning.

Evaluation of Strategic Planning Approaches The strategic planning approaches just discussed are widely utilized—at least informally. Many firms assess alternative market opportunities; know which products are stars, cash cows, question marks, and dogs; recognize what factors affect performance; understand their industries; and realize they can target broad or narrow customer bases. Formally, strategic planning models are most apt to be used by larger firms; and the models are adapted to the needs of the specific firms employing them.

The approaches' major strengths are that they let a firm analyze all SBUs and products, study various strategies' effects, learn the opportunities to pursue and the threats to avoid, compute marketing and other resource needs, focus on meaningful differential advantages, compare performance against designated goals, and discover principles for improving. Competitors' actions and long-term trends can also be followed.

The approaches' major weaknesses are that they may be hard to use (particularly by a small firm), may be too simplistic and omit key factors, are somewhat arbitrary in defining SBUs and evaluative criteria (like relative market share), may not be applicable to all companies and situations (a dog SBU may actually be profitable and generate cash), do not adequately account for environmental conditions (like the economy), may overvalue market share, and are often used by staff planners rather than line managers.

These techniques only aid planning. They do not replace the need for managers to engage in hands-on decisions by studying each situation and basing marketing strategies on the unique aspects of their industry, firm, and SBUs.

Implementing Tactical Plans

A marketing strategy is enacted via **tactical plans**.

A **tactical plan** specifies the short-run actions (tactics) that a firm undertakes in implementing a given marketing strategy. At this stage, a strategy is operationalized. A tactical plan has three basic elements: specific tasks, a time frame, and resource allocation.

The marketing mix (specific tasks) may range from a combination of high quality, high service, low distribution intensity, personal-selling emphasis, and above-average prices to a combination of low quality, low service, high distribution intensity, advertising emphasis, and low prices. There would be a distinct marketing mix for each SBU, based on its target market and strategic emphasis. The individual mix elements must be coordinated for each SBU and conflicts among SBUs minimized.

Proper timing (time horizon) may mean being the first to introduce a product, bringing out a product when the market is most receptive, or quickly reacting to a competitor's strategy to catch it off guard. A firm must balance its desire to be an industry leader with clear-cut competitive advantages against its concern for the risk of being innovative. Marketing opportunities exist for limited periods of time, and the firm needs to act accordingly.

Marketing investments (resource allocation) can be classed as order processing or order generating. Order-processing costs are associated with recording and handling orders, such as order entry, computer-data handling, and merchandise handling. The goal is to minimize those costs, subject to a given level of service. Order-generating costs, such as

Ethics IN TODAY'S SOCIETY

Is Genentech Too Aggressive with Its Marketing?

Genentech, a biotechnology company, has always been an aggressive marketer. Some observers feel that it may be too aggressive. One industry expert familiar with G. Kirk Raab, Genentech's chief executive officer, says "Within the law, Kirk will take it as close to the edge as he can." As a result, the Food and Drug Administration has been investigating Genentech's marketing practices, particularly its sale of approved drugs for nonapproved uses or at higher than approved dosage levels.

An example of a questionable Genentech strategy is its use of a data base of patients who have particular illnesses. Genentech pays nurses and doctors' assistants as much as $50 per patient for information on the person's illness, current treatment, and outcome. Its heart attack registry, for instance, includes detailed questions about Genentech's clot-buster for heart attack patients (TPA), but not about those patients who are receiving other medicines or treatments. According to sources critical of Genentech, the firm has used this data base to exaggerate the effectiveness of TPA and understate its drawbacks (which include the increased likelihood of a stroke and high drug costs). Genentech even promoted a seminar with a malpractice attorney to warn doctors of the liability associated with using an inferior substitute product.

Perhaps the greatest source of controversy concerns Genentech's marketing of Protropin, its growth hormone product. In an indictment, a Genentech executive was accused of providing a $224,000 research grant and consulting fee to a doctor who prescribed high doses of Protropin. And while Genentech has also funded charities that screen school-aged children who are very short, Genentech does not disclose its funding to either the schools or parents. Critics say Genentech is selling its growth hormone to about twice the number of children that would benefit from the product.

As a marketing manager for Protropin, where do you draw the line between ethical and unethical behavior?

Source: Based on material in Ralph T. King, "In Marketing of Drugs, Genentech Tests Limits of What Is Acceptable," *Wall Street Journal* (January 10, 1995), pp. A1, A6.

advertising and personal selling, produce revenues. Reducing them may have a harmful effect on sales and profits. Thus, a firm should estimate sales at various levels of costs and for various combinations of marketing functions. Maximum profit rarely occurs at the lowest level of expenditure on order-generating costs.

Tactical decisions differ from strategic decisions in several key ways:

- They are less complex and more structured.
- They have a much shorter time horizon.
- They require a considerably lower resource commitment.
- They are enacted and adjusted more often.

At Frito-Lay, tactical planning means preparing its deliverypeople and its retailers for new-product introductions, aggressively promoting its products, and maintaining its profit margins—while not giving competitors any opportunities to win market share through lower prices, and servicing its retail accounts very well. As Anheuser-Busch discovered, "Frito's a fortress," with leading market shares in salty snacks, potato chips, and tortilla chips—among others. So, Anheuser-Busch decided to sell its Eagle Snacks division. How do Frito-Lay personnel avoid complacency in light of such a strong position? As its chief executive says, "I wake up every morning thinking, I haven't sold one bag of Fritos yet. We're always raising the bar on ourselves and our future."[28]

Monitoring Results

Performance is evaluated by **monitoring results**.

Monitoring results involves comparing the actual performance of a firm, business unit, or product against planned performance for a specified period. Actual performance data are then fed back into the strategic planning process. Budgets, timetables, sales and profit statistics, cost analyses, and image studies are just some measures that can be used to assess results.

When actual performance lags behind plans, corrective action should be taken. For instance, "if implementation problems persist, it is not (in most instances) because employees mean to do the wrong thing. It is because they do not know the right thing to do. The first task in making strategy work, then, is to identify the right behavior—that is, behavior that reduces costs, improves quality, pleases customers, and adds to profitability."[29]

Some plans must be revised due to the impact of uncontrollable factors on sales and costs. Thus, many farsighted firms develop contingency plans to outline their responses in advance, should unfavorable conditions arise.

In Chapter 23, techniques for evaluating marketing effectiveness will be discussed in depth. The techniques are covered in Chapter 23, so the fundamental elements of marketing can be thoroughly explored first.

Devising a Strategic Plan

Written documents aid strategic planning and are useful for all sorts of firms.

Creating, implementing, and monitoring a strategic plan best occur when a firm has a written plan. This encourages executives to carefully think out and coordinate each step in the planning process, better pinpoint problem areas, be consistent, tie the plan to goals and resources, measure performance, and send a clear message to employees and others.

A sample outline for a written strategic plan and an application of strategic planning by a small firm are presented next.

A Sample Outline for a Written Strategic Plan

What are the ingredients of a good strategic plan? Here is a brief list:

- It should effect the consideration of strategic choices.
- It should force a long-range view.
- It should make the resource allocation system visible.
- It should provide methods to help strategic analysis and decision making.
- It should provide a basis for managing a firm or SBU strategically.
- It should provide a communication and coordination system both horizontally (between SBUs and departments) and vertically (from senior executives to front-line employees).
- It should help a firm and its SBUs cope with change.[30]

Table 3-2 presents a sample outline for a written strategic plan—from a marketing perspective. This outline may be used by firms of any size or type.

[28]Robert Frank, "Frito-Lay Devours Snack-Food Business," *New York Times* (October 27, 1995), pp. B1, B4.
[29]Steven J. Heyer and Reginald Van Lee, "Rewiring the Corporation," *Business Horizons*, Vol. 35 (May–June 1992), p. 21.
[30]Aaker, *Strategic Market Management*, pp. 17–18.

Table 3-2

A Sample Outline for a Written Strategic Plan—From a Marketing Perspective

Using as much detail as possible, please address each of these points for your firm:

1. Organizational Mission
   a. In 50 words or less, describe the current mission of your organization.
   b. In 50 words or less, describe how you would like your organizational mission to evolve over the next five years. The next ten years.
   c. Is your firm on track regarding the mission statements in (a) and (b)? Explain your answer.
   d. Discuss the organizational mission in terms of your target market(s), your functions performed, and your overall style of marketing.
   e. Discuss the organizational mission in terms of company diversification.
   f. How is the organizational mission communicated to employees?

2. Strategic Business Units
   a. State the present organizational structure of your firm.
   b. Assess the present organizational structure.
   c. How would you expect the organizational structure to evolve over the next five years? The next ten years?
   d. Does your firm have strategic business units? If yes, describe them. If no, why not?
   e. Does your firm have a separate marketing plan for each target market, major product, and so on? Explain your answer and relate it to (d).
   f. Does each product or business unit in your firm have a marketing manager, proper resources, and clear competitors? Explain your answer.

3. Marketing Objectives
   a. Cite your organization's overall marketing goals for the next one, three, five, and ten years.
   b. Cite your organization's specific marketing goals by target market and product for the next one, five, and ten years:
      *Sales.
      *Market share.
      *Profit.
      *Image.
      *Customer loyalty.
   c. What criteria will be used to determine whether goals have been fully, partially, or unsatisfactorily reached?

4. Situation Analysis
   a. Describe the present overall strengths, weaknesses, opportunities, and threats (SWOT) facing your organization.
   b. How do you expect the factors noted in your answer to (a) to change over the next five to ten years?

American Images: Great Planning by a Small Aerial-Photography Firm[31]

Although a small company, American Images has a detailed strategic plan.

In 1980, Harlan Accola and his brother Conrad started an aerial-photography business, Skypix. They took aerial shots of farms and homes, and then sold them. The brothers did well for a while, but eventually ran into trouble—and nearly went out of business. As Harlan Accola said, "I didn't know anything about business. And worse. I didn't think it was important." At that time, Skypix's plan was simple: "Always have enough cash to pay next week's bills."

Today, American Images (the current name of Skypix) is a successful firm with annual sales of $5 million and profits of $350,000. Why? It has created, implemented, and monitored detailed strategic plans. In 1993, it even devised its first written strategic plan. So, let's look at American Images' planning.

[31]The material in this section is based on Jay Finegan, "Everything According to Plan," *Inc.* (March 1995), pp. 78–85.

Table 3-2 (Cont.)

- c. For each of the key products or businesses of your firm, describe the present strengths, weaknesses, opportunities, and threats.
- d. How do you expect the factors noted in your answer to (c) to change over the next five to ten years?
- e. How will your firm respond to the factors mentioned in the answers for (a) to (d)?

5. Developing Strategy
- a. Describe the target market, marketing mix, and differential advantages for each of your products or businesses.
- b. Does your firm have sufficient resources and capabilities to carry out its marketing strategy? Explain your answer.
- c. Compare your firm's strategy with those of leading competitors.
- d. Describe your use of these strategic approaches: market penetration, market development, product development, and diversification.
- e. For each product or business, detail the characteristics of your firm's present customers, as well as those who should be sought in the future.
- f. Categorize each of your products or businesses as a star, cash cow, question mark, or dog. Explain your reasoning.
- g. What is the impact of the categorization cited in (f) on your strategy?
- h. For each product or business, which of these approaches is most apt: invest/grow, selectivity/earnings, or harvest/divest? Explain your reasoning.
- i. For each of your products or businesses, which of these approaches is most appropriate: cost leadership, differentiation, cost focus, or differentiation focus? Explain your reasoning.
- j. Describe how the plans for all of your firm's products or businesses are coordinated.

6. Implementation
- a. Describe the procedures to activate your firm's strategy.
- b. For each product or business, how does your firm ensure that the strategy is implemented as intended with regard to the target market and marketing mix?
- c. Do marketing personnel have appropriate authority (i.e., are they empowered) and resources to implement plans? Explain your answer.
- d. Are ongoing marketing budgets sufficient? Does your organization differentiate between order-generating and order-processing costs? Explain your answers.
- e. How do you expect competitors to react as you implement your strategy?
- f. Are there contingency plans in case of unexpected results?

7. Monitoring Results
- a. Describe the procedures used by your firm to monitor steps 1 to 6.
- b. For each company product or business, is planned performance compared with actual performance on a regular basis? Explain your answer.
- c. Is a SWOT analysis conducted regularly? Explain your answer.
- d. How are performance results communicated through the organization?
- e. What procedures do you use to respond to the findings of performance reviews?

Organizational Mission Skypix originally operated "on spec," meaning that the Acolas flew around and shot aerial photos that interested them—and then tried to sell them to owners of homes, farms, and businesses. This was an inefficient system and often resulted in the brothers being unable to sell some photos at all.

In contrast, American Images now does "custom aerial-photograhy work." It lines up customers in advance and then shoots photos. This makes it easier to schedule flight crews (each with a pilot and a photographer) and keeps the firm from shooting unwanted photos. Most competitors still act "on spec."

Establishing Strategic Business Units Due to its size and specialized nature, American Images has just one main SBU: customized aerial photography. However, it does have several departments, such as telemarketing, and it encourages each one of them to set specific goals and the plans to reach them. In company planning sessions, department heads jointly discuss everything from lead-generation costs to financing.

American Images employs more than 50 people and works with 22 independent sales reps. It owns three single-engine Cessnas and leases four others. The firm operates in 31 states, with headquarters in Marshfield, Wisconsin.

Setting Marketing Objectives American Images has several marketing goals, including these:

- To identify the best prospective customers.
- To have a high closing rate for sales calls (at least 85 per cent).
- To provide superior customer service.
- To increase sales, while keeping profit margins at 7 per cent of revenues.
- To keep a high level of customer loyalty.
- To expand in a controlled manner.
- To take full advantage of the company's marketing efforts.
- To empower employees and engender high morale.

Performing Situation Analysis For the last several years, American Images has been a big believer in SWOT analysis. It continuously studies the marketplace, the firm's status in it, competitors, the economy, and other factors. And the company is not hesitant to criticize its own shortcomings. In looking back at his firm's early years, Harlan Accola says, "We grew too fast, and it was simply from a lack of planning. We must have looked like a real comedy team to our suppliers."

In 1993, the Accolas acknowledged that their financial expertise was still weak and decided to bring in an outside expert. They recruited Dennis Kearns (who had been a cheese company's controller) and made him an equal partner. Kearns then recruited a data-processing manager and a telemarketing manager.

Developing Marketing Strategy American Images has a defined target market: homes, farms, and businesses interested in aerial photographs. The quality of the flight crews, extensive market coverage, superior customer service, and professional approach provided by the firm are differential advantages. The marketing mix is coordinated— state-of-the-art aerial photography, convenient delivery of photos, an emphasis on direct-mail solicitations and telemarketing, and fair prices.

The firm applies the precepts of the product/marketing opportunity matrix (market development—expansion into 31 states) and Porter's generic strategy model (differentiation focus—a narrow customer base with high service).

Implementing Tactical Plans American Images believes its strategic plan makes tactical implementation easier and fosters, rather than inhibits, flexibility. As Harlan Accola says, "We try to figure out what is realistic in sales and production. Then, we ask our people, 'Can you make these numbers work? How?'" He feels that if these questions are asked often during planning, they become second nature during implementation; and if the marketplace is shifting, employees can best respond by understanding the elements of the plan. Thus, the firm will not go off the track and try to act in a way that is not in keeping with its mission.

Monitoring Results The company is fanatical about monitoring performance and making proper strategy adjustments. There are regular meetings of executives, ongoing computer reports that are widely disseminated, and so on. All employees are encouraged to pass on their comments.

MARKETING IN A CHANGING WORLD

What Business Are We In?[32]

According to Peter Drucker, the long-time management guru, "What to do" (organizational mission) is the main challenge now facing top management:

> The story is a familiar one: a firm that was a superstar only yesterday finds it is stagnant, frustrated, and in trouble. This phenomenon is not confined to the United States. It is common in Japan and Germany, the Netherlands and France, Italy and Sweden. The root cause of nearly every one of these crises is not that things are being done poorly. It is not even that the wrong things are being done. Usually, the right things are being done—but fruitlessly.

This occurs when the assumptions that a firm makes about its mission no longer fit reality. These are assumptions that shape its behavior, dictate its decisions about what to do and what not to do, and define what a firm deems meaningful results. The assumptions relate to markets; customer and competitor values and behavior; technology and its dynamics; and company strengths and weaknesses. They are what Drucker calls a company's "theory of the business."

To remedy the situation, Drucker suggests that a company needs to assess its current business [organizational mission] regularly—and decide what it really should be. Here is how a firm can do this:

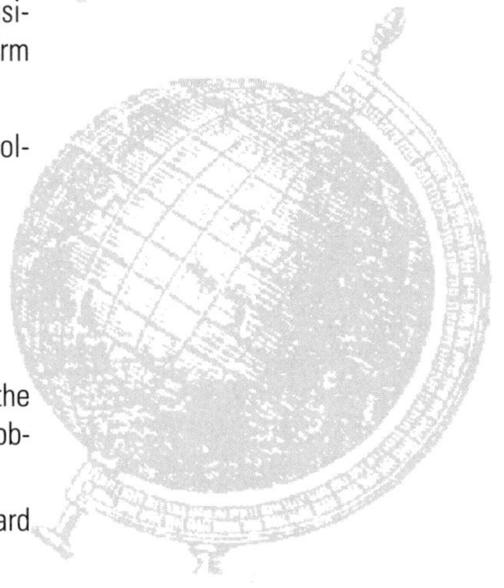

- "Every three years, an organization should challenge every product, every service, every policy, every distribution channel with the question, 'If we were not in it already, would we be going into it now?'"
- It should "study what goes on outside the business, especially with regard to noncustomers. The first signs of fundamental change rarely appear within one's own organization or among one's own customers. Almost always they show up first among one's noncustomers."
- "To diagnose problems early, managers must pay attention to warning signs. A theory of the business always becomes obsolete when a firm attains its original goals. Attaining one's objectives is not cause for celebration; it is cause for new thinking."
- To establish, maintain, or reorient an organizational mission does not require genius, but hard work. "It is not being clever; it is being conscientious. It is what CEOs are paid for."

SUMMARY

1. *To define strategic planning and consider its importance for marketing* Strategic planning encompasses both strategic business plans and strategic marketing plans. Strategic business plans describe the overall direction firms will pursue within their chosen environment and guide the allocation of resources and effort. Strategic marketing plans outline what marketing actions to undertake, why those actions are needed, who is responsible for carrying them out, when and where they will be completed, and how they will be coordinated.

Strategic planning provides guidance via a hierarchal process, clarifies goals, encourages cooperation among departments, focuses on strengths and weaknesses (as well as opportunities and threats), examines alternatives, helps allocate resources, and points up the value of monitoring results.

2. *To describe the total quality approach to strategic planning and its relevance to marketing* A total quality approach should be used while devising and enacting business and marketing plans. With this approach, a firm adopts a process- and output-related philosophy, by which it strives to fully satisfy consumers in an effective and efficient manner. There is a customer focus; a top management commitment; emphasis on continuous improvement; and support and involvement from employees, suppliers, and channel members.

3. *To look at the different kinds of strategic plans and the relationships between marketing and the other functional areas in an organization* A firm's strategic plans may be short run, moderate in length, or long run. Strategic marketing plans may be for each major product, presented as one companywide marketing plan,

[32]The material in this section is based on Peter F. Drucker, "The Theory of the Business," *Harvard Business Review*, Vol. 72 (September–October 1994), pp. 95–104.

or considered part of an overall business plan. A bottom-up, top-down, or combined management approach may be used.

The interests of marketing and the other key functional areas in a firm need to be accommodated in a strategic plan. Departmental conflict can be reduced by improving communications, employing personnel with broad backgrounds, establishing interdepartmental development programs, and blending departmental goals.

4. *To describe thoroughly each of the steps in the strategic planning process* First, a firm defines its organizational mission—the long-term commitment to a type of business and a place in the market. Second, it establishes strategic business units (SBUs), which are self-contained divisions, product lines, or product departments with specific market focuses and separate managers. Third, quantitative and qualitative marketing objectives are set. Fourth, through situation analysis, a firm identifies its internal strengths and weaknesses, as well as external opportunities and threats.

Fifth, a firm develops a marketing strategy—to outline the way in which the marketing mix is used to attract and satisfy the target market(s) and accomplish organizational goals. Every SBU has its own marketing mix. The approaches to strategy planning include the product/market opportunity matrix, the Boston Consulting Group matrix, the General Electric business screen, and the Porter generic strategy model. They should be viewed as planning tools that aid decision making; they do not replace the need for executives to engage in hands-on planning for each situation.

Sixth, a firm uses tactical plans to specify the short-run actions necessary to implement a given marketing strategy. At this stage, specific tasks, a time horizon, and resource allocation are operationalized. Seventh, a firm monitors results by comparing actual performance against planned performance; and this information is fed back into the strategic planning process. Adjustments in strategy are made as needed.

5. *To show how a strategic plan may be devised and applied* Strategic planning works best when it is done systematically and comprehensively. This is exemplified by American Images, a small aerial-photography firm.

KEY TERMS

strategic business plan (p. 52)
strategic marketing plan (p. 52)
total quality (p. 53)
strategic planning process (p. 57)
organizational mission (p. 57)
strategic business unit (SBU) (p. 58)
situation analysis (p. 60)
marketing strategy (p. 61)
product/market opportunity matrix (p. 61)
market penetration (p. 62)
market development (p. 62)
product development (p. 62)
diversification (p. 62)
Boston Consulting Group matrix (p. 63)
star (p. 64)
cash cow (p. 64)
question mark (p. 64)
dog (p. 65)
General Electric business screen (p. 65)
Porter generic strategy model (p. 66)
tactical plan (p. 67)
monitoring results (p. 69)

Review Questions

1. What are the benefits of strategic planning?
2. Explain Figure 3-2, which deals with the total quality approach.
3. Distinguish between bottom-up and top-down strategic plans. What are the pros and cons of each?
4. Why are conflicts between marketing and other functional areas inevitable? How can these conflicts be reduced or avoided?
5. Under what circumstances should a company consider reappraising its organizational mission?
6. What is a strategic business unit? Why is this concept so important for strategic planning?
7. In situation analysis, what is the distinction between strengths and opportunities and between weaknesses and threats? How should a firm react to each of these factors?
8. Describe the General Electric business screen and the Porter generic strategy model.
9. Explain how tactical decisions differ from strategic decisions.
10. What are the ingredients of a good strategic plan?

Discussion Questions

1. Do you think your college or university is following a total quality approach? Why or why not? What total quality recommendations would you make for your school?
2. Comment on this statement: "In the market-oriented view of the strategic planning process, financial goals are seen as results and rewards, not the fundamental purpose of business."
3. What issues should a small airline study during situation analysis? How could it react to them?
4. Give a current example of each of these strategic approaches: market development, product development, market penetration, and diversification. Evaluate the strategies.
5. Develop a rating scale to use in analyzing the industry attractiveness and company business strengths of a small stock brokerage firm, a medium-sized management consulting firm, or a large auto supplies manufacturer.

CASE 1

*Michael G. Rubin: How to Succeed at an Early Age**

In his twenties, Michael G. Rubin is a well-known and respected deal maker in the world of sporting goods. Some analysts even go so far as to compare his early business career with that of Bill Gates and Michael Dell. Gates started Microsoft at the age of 19 after dropping out of Harvard. Dell began selling stamps via mail order at the age of 13 and at 17 sold computer components from his home. Michael Dell dropped out of the University of Texas, after founding Dell Computer. Like Gates and Dell, Michael Rubin attended college, Villanova University, but quit after a semester and a half.

Rubin started his business career at the age of 13, when—with $2,500—he started repairing skis in the basement of his parent's home. Soon thereafter, he purchased ski equipment on a consignment basis, paying the manufacturer after its goods were resold to Rubin's retail customers. At the age of 14, he convinced an owner of commercial real estate to rent him a store in a local shopping center. Rubin then arranged to get out of classes early each day to work at his store as part of his school's cooperative education program. Soon thereafter, he opened four additional ski shops.

At the age of 17, Michael Rubin discovered the closeout business. In this business, distributors buy manufacturers' overruns, discontinued merchandise, and end-of-season stock at substantial discounts and resell the items to retailers. One of Rubin's early deals was the purchase of $200,000 worth of ski equipment for $17,000. He then formed Nationwide Liquidators Inc., to purchase and resell unwanted sporting goods equipment. Rubin eventually sold the ski stores to concentrate on the closeout business. Nationwide Liquidators was then renamed KPR, based on the first initials of Rubin's parents, Ken and Paulette.

Rubin's firm, KPR Sports International (KPR), specializes in the sale of discontinued sporting goods such as athletic equipment and ski equipment. KPR purchases these goods directly from manufacturers at closeout prices (sometimes even below a manufacturer's cost) and resells them to retailers. Manufacturers rely on firms such as KPR to reduce bloated inventories, raise cash in slow seasons, and dispose of unwanted colors, styles, and stocks with uneven size distributions. KPR had sales of $18 million in 1993 and $27 million in 1994; Rubin hoped that KPR would reach revenues of $50 million and profits of $5 million in 1995.

In 1995, KPR went on an expansion binge. In May, it purchased Trail Sports, a Dutch sporting goods retailer. The acquisition of Trail Sports enabled KPR to further expand its business in Europe; foreign sales now account for over one-half of KPR's total sales. In June 1995, KPR announced that it would lend Ryka, a financially-troubled athletic shoe manufacturer, $8 million in return for up to 40 per cent of Ryka's common stock. As part of this deal, Michael Rubin was named chairman of Ryka. And in summer 1995, KPR launched Yukon, its own brand of hiking shoes and boots.

Even after a decade of experience as an entrepreneur, many people feel uncomfortable conducting business with a twenty-something "whiz kid." As a result, Rubin prefers to conduct many of his deals on the phone. When they meet him, many of Rubin's new clients assume that he is working for his parents' business.

Rubin feels his athletic shoe business will offset the slow periods in his other businesses. So, instead of just stocking shoe leftovers, KPR can now sell its own shoe brand via a company-owned network of discount and sporting-goods stores. Yet, despite the increase in KPR's size and scope, Michael Rubin promises to keep his company agile and free of bureaucracy as it continues to grow: "I don't want to have meetings to discuss meetings. The day we lose that entrepreneurial spirit, I should pack my bags."

QUESTIONS

1. Present a long-run organizational mission for KPR. Explain your reasoning.
2. What are the advantages to KPR by virtue of its being a small firm? The disadvantages?
3. Discuss the value of strategic planning to KPR.
4. How will KPR's strategic planning process change as it matures?

*The data in this case are drawn from Stephanie N. Mehta, "Man in a Hurry: A Mogul in Sporting Goods at Age 22," *Wall Street Journal* (June 5, 1995), pp. B1, B7.

CASE 2

Schering-Plough: Devising a Marketing Strategy†

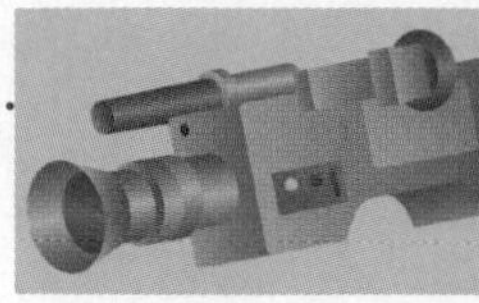

Schering-Plough (SP) is a diversified pharmaceutical manufacturer. It markets prescription and over-the-counter (OTC) drugs for a variety of illnesses—including asthma and allergies, cancer and infectious diseases, and skin disorders. SP also markets disposable contact lenses and foot-care and sun-care products. Among its best-known OTC brands are Coricidin, Afrin, Dr. Scholl's, Coppertone, and Solarcaine.

To get a picture of Schering-Plough, let's look at each of these facets of its marketing strategy: the new-product development process, cost containment, and the importance of the OTC drug segment.

SP is committed to research to discover innovative drugs that offer important cost-effective therapeutic advantages. Therefore, in 1994, it spent $620 million on research, about 13.3 per cent of its total revenues. SP is working hard to streamline the new-product discovery process. For example, SP now makes better decisions as to whether to go ahead with or drop a product at an early stage in the development process. SP recognizes that since it costs hundreds of million of dollars to develop a new pharmaceutical product, it can only back the most promising projects. As an alternative to developing and testing new products itself, SP also actively seeks to acquire and license drug products developed by other firms. SP's most successful new product ever is Claritin, an antihistamine. Worldwide sales of Claritin increased 71 per cent between 1993 and 1994 alone. This drug captured the number one position in its market after less than 18 months on the market (with close to a 40 per cent market share).

SP recognizes that any marketing strategy in the health care field must reflect government concerns about cost containment, the increasing use of pharmacy benefit management (involving firms that buy drugs for health maintenance organizations [HMOs], hospitals, and pharmacies at large discounts), the increased presence of HMOs (providers of medical care to employees of selected firms), and the expanding market share of low-cost generic brands. SP was one of the first drug firms to establish a separate marketing organization to serve the HMO sector. It is also working hard to profitably offer drugs at prices acceptable to HMOs and pharmacy benefit management organizations. These organizations typically negotiate for discounts that are as much as 40 per cent off prevailing drug prices. SP has been able to sustain its profitability by becoming more efficient as a manufacturer and as a marketer. Over the last several years, SP's cost of sales as a per cent of sales revenue has gone from 24 per cent to 20 per cent; and its selling, general, and administrative expenses have gone from 43 per cent to 39 per cent of sales revenues.

SP has leading market positions in several big OTC markets. These include drugs to alleviate allergy symptoms (Afrin), coughs and colds (Drixoral and Coricidin), and female health products (Gyne-Lotrimin). Unlike prescription drugs, these products are advertised directly to final consumers. Advertising for OTC drugs is regulated by the Food and Drug Administration (FDA), which requires that ads balance the pros and cons associated with use of the drug. The FDA also mandates that advertising provide information on drug side effects. A significant decision for SP is knowing when to switch a drug from prescription to OTC status. For example, two years after SP switched Gyne-Lotrimin to OTC status, its sales more than doubled.

QUESTIONS

1. Evaluate Schering-Plough's overall marketing strategy.
2. How could the Boston Consulting Group matrix be used in identifying possible strategies for Schering-Plough?
3. Apply the Porter generic strategy model to Schering-Plough.
4. Present several suggestions as to how Schering-Plough could evaluate its performance.

VIDEO QUESTIONS ON SCHERING-PLOUGH

1. Describe Schering-Plough's organizational mission.
2. Discuss Schering-Plough's marketing strategy for its health-care products.

†The data in this case are drawn from D. P. Hamacher, "Step Up to Better Foot Care Sales," *Drug Topics* (March 20, 1994), pp. 68–69; Cyndee Miller, "Drug Firms Boost Pitch Directly to Consumers," *Marketing News* (November 21, 1994), pp. 1, 16; Jennifer Reingold, "Schering-Plough: Great Expectations," *Financial World* (December 6, 1994), p. 20; and Edward A. Wyatt, "Counter Moves," *Barron's* (July 18, 1994), pp. 20–22.

CHAPTER 4
Information for Marketing Decisions

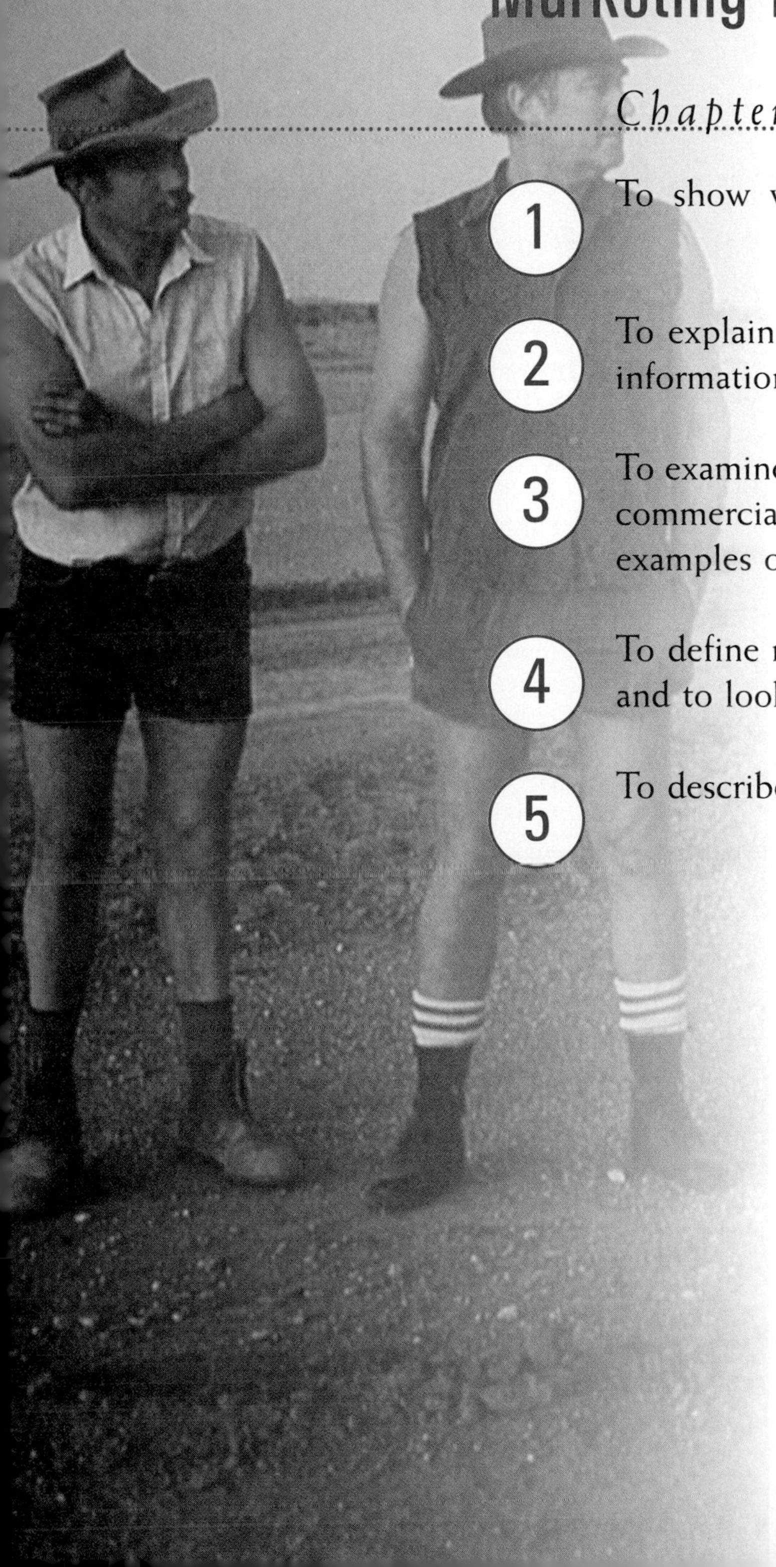

Chapter Objectives

1. To show why marketing information is needed
2. To explain the role and importance of marketing information systems
3. To examine a basic marketing information system, commercial data bases, data-base marketing, and examples of MIS in action
4. To define marketing research and its components and to look at its scope
5. To describe the marketing research process

At a time when growing numbers of publishing firms are racing to develop data bases to market their products better, Reader's Digest Association is years ahead. Its files, started 40 years ago in much simpler form, now hold data on an astounding 100 million households worldwide [half of which are in the United States]. Although the 72-year-old Reader's Digest magazine gives the company its identity, the data base is its lifeblood. Virtually all company operations are connected to it. And the Association, protecting the secrecy of the data base, neither rents nor sells its list of names.

Reprinted by permission of The Reader's Digest Association, Inc.

Reader's Digest Association has one of the largest private consumer data bases in the world. The files in its data base are updated continuously to reflect information about subscribers to the firm's magazines, books (both general interest and reference), interactive CDs (reference and cook books), recorded music cassettes, and videocassettes.

The main source of names for the Association's data base is *Reader's Digest*, with a monthly worldwide circulation of 28 million—including 16 million in the United States. Two-thirds of *Reader's Digest* readers renew their subscriptions annually; and 5 million new subscriptions are sold each year. *Reader's Digest* has the second-largest circulation among U.S. magazines, behind only *Modern Maturity*, a magazine mailed to all members of the American Association of Retired Persons.

Reader's Digest has been expanding its global circulation. In total, the magazine publishes 47 editions in 18 different languages; and it has the largest circulation of any magazine in Canada, Britain, Finland, Germany, Mexico, and Southeast Asia. The Association publishes its general interest books and CDs in 11 languages and its condensed books in 12 languages.

In 1989, the Association began to acquire special-interest magazines. It now publishes *American Health, Family Handyman, Moneywise* (in Great Britain), *New Choices: Living Even Better After 50*, and *Travel Holiday*. According to the company, its main goal in these acquisitions was to strengthen its data base. As of 1995, 3 million additional names were added to the firm's data base because of the acquisitions.

Although the Association's management of its data base is well respected, even this company has, on occasion, had difficulties in using it efficiently. Several years ago, for example, the firm had trouble coordinating offers from its various divisions. Thus, a *Reader's*

Digest subscriber with an interest in travel might receive offers for travel books, a video on a foreign country, and a subscription to *Travel Holiday*. At that time, many people in the data base felt so inundated with the direct mail offers that the firm's "hit rate" in getting new business fell off. After realizing the consumer discontent, the Association reduced its promotional mailings in the book and home entertainment business. It also became more selective in the use of its promotional mailings.[1]

In this chapter, we will look at the value of marketing information, explain the role of a marketing information system (which gathers, analyzes, disseminates, and stores relevant marketing data), and describe the marketing research process. We will also take another peek at data-base marketing.

Overview

Firms make better marketing decisions when they have good information.

It is essential for a firm to have appropriate information before, while, and after making (and enacting) marketing decisions if strengths, weaknesses, opportunities, and threats are to be assessed accurately; actions are to be proper for a given marketing environment; and performance is to be maximized.

Good information enables marketers to:

- Gain a competitive edge.
- Reduce financial and image risks.
- Determine consumer attitudes.
- Monitor the environment.
- Gather competitive intelligence.
- Coordinate strategy.
- Measure performance.
- Improve advertising credibility.
- Gain management support for decisions.
- Verify intuition.
- Improve effectiveness.

Relying on intuition, executive judgment, and past experience is not enough:

> In markets that are growing more slowly and are saturated with competition, businesses prosper by following two strategies. First, they learn more and more about the characteristics and location of their customers. Second, they use that knowledge to develop better goods or services and reduce unsuccessful marketing efforts.[2]

The **scientific method** *requires objectivity, accuracy, and thoroughness.*

When collecting and analyzing marketing information, the **scientific method**—incorporating objectivity, accuracy, and thoroughness—should be followed. Objectivity means information is gathered in an open-minded way. Judgments are not reached until all data are collected and analyzed. Accuracy refers to the use of carefully constructed research tools. Each aspect of information gathering, such as the study format, the sample, interviewer training, and tabulation of responses, must be well planned and executed. Thoroughness deals with the comprehensive nature of information gathering. Mistaken conclusions may be reached if probing is not intense enough.

In this chapter, two vital aspects of marketing information are covered: marketing information systems and marketing research. A marketing information system guides all of a firm's marketing-related information efforts—and stores and disseminates data—on a continuous basis. Marketing research involves gathering and analyzing information on specific marketing issues.

[1]Deirdre Carmody, "Lifeblood of Reader's Digest Is 40-Year-Old Data Base," *New York Times* (May 16, 1995), pp. D1, D7; and Patrick J. Spain and James R. Talbot (Editors), *Hoover's Handbook of American Business 1996* (Austin, Texas: Reference Press, 1995), pp. 1222–1223.

[2]Peter Francese, "Managing Market Information," *American Demographics* (September 1995), p. 59.

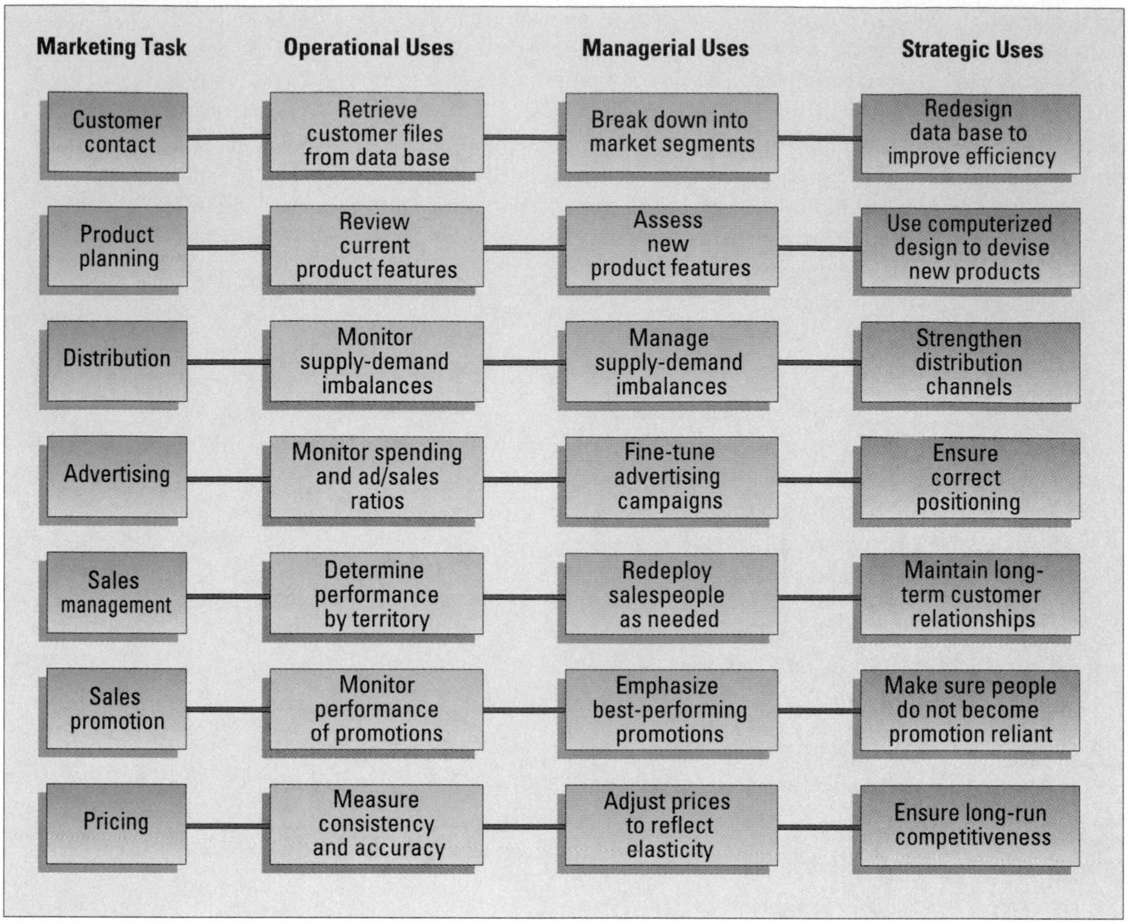
Marketing Task
Operational Uses
Managerial Uses
Strategic Uses
Customer contact
Retrieve customer files from data base
Break down into market segments
Redesign data base to improve efficiency
Product planning
Review current product features
Assess new product features
Use computerized design to devise new products
Distribution
Monitor supply-demand imbalances
Manage supply-demand imbalances
Strengthen distribution channels
Advertising
Monitor spending and ad/sales ratios
Fine-tune advertising campaigns
Ensure correct positioning
Sales management
Determine performance by territory
Redeploy salespeople as needed
Maintain long-term customer relationships
Sales promotion
Monitor performance of promotions
Emphasize best-performing promotions
Make sure people do not become promotion reliant
Pricing
Measure consistency and accuracy
Adjust prices to reflect elasticity
Ensure long-run competitiveness

FIGURE 4-1
How a Marketing Information System Can Be Utilized

Source: Adapted by the authors from Rajendra S. Sisodia, "Marketing Information and Decision Support Systems for Services," *Journal of Services Marketing*, Vol. 6 (Winter 1992), pp. 51–64.

Marketing Information Systems

The collection of marketing information should not be a rare event that occurs only when data are needed about a specific marketing topic. If research is done this way, a firm faces several risks. Opportunities may be missed. There may be a lack of awareness of environmental changes and competitors' actions. It may not be possible to analyze data over several periods. Marketing plans and decisions may not be properly reviewed. Data collection may be disjointed. Previous studies may not be stored in an easy-to-use format. Time lags may result whenever a new research study is required. Actions may be reactionary rather than anticipatory.

A **marketing information system** *regularly gathers, analyzes, disseminates, and stores data.*

Thus, it is essential for any firm, regardless of its size or type, to devise and employ some form of marketing information system to aid decision making. A **marketing information system (MIS)** is "a set of procedures and methods designed to generate, analyze, disseminate, and store anticipated marketing decision information on a regular, continuous basis."[3]

What this means is that a firm should:

- Aggressively amass data from internal company documents, existing external documents, and primary studies (when necessary).

[3]Adapted by the authors from Robert A. Peterson, *Marketing Research*, Second Edition (Dallas: Business Publications, 1988), p. 31; and Peter D. Bennett (Editor), *Dictionary of Marketing Terms*, Second Edition (Chicago: American Marketing Association, 1995), p. 167.

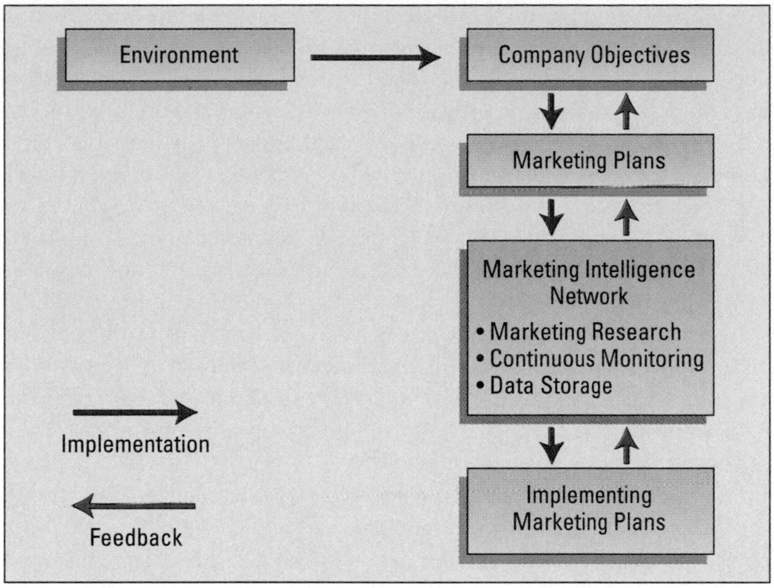

FIGURE 4-2
A Basic Marketing Information System

- Analyze the data and prepare appropriate reports—in terms of the company mission, strategy, and proposed tactics.
- Disseminate the analyzed data to the right marketing decision makers in the company. They will vary on the basis of the particular topics covered.
- Store data for future use and comparisons.
- Seek out all relevant data that have either current or future marketing ramifications—not just data with specific short-term implications.
- Undertake ongoing data collection, analysis, dissemination, and storage.

Figure 4-1 shows how an information system can be used operationally, managerially, and strategically for several aspects of marketing.

Next, the components of a basic marketing information system, commercial data bases, data-base marketing, and examples of MIS in action are presented.

A Basic Marketing Information System

Figure 4-2 presents a basic marketing information system. It begins with a statement of company objectives, which provide broad guidelines. These goals are affected by environmental factors, such as competition, government, and the economy. Marketing plans involve the choice of a target market, marketing goals, the marketing organization, the marketing mix (product, distribution, promotion, and price decisions), and performance measurement.

A **marketing intelligence network** *includes* **marketing research**, **continuous monitoring**, *and* **data storage**.

After marketing plans are outlined, a firm's total marketing information needs can be specified and satisfied via a **marketing intelligence network,** which consists of marketing research, continuous monitoring, and data storage. **Marketing research** is used to obtain information on particular marketing issues (problems). Information may be retrieved from storage (existing company data) or acquired by collecting external secondary data and/or primary data. **Continuous monitoring** is used to regularly study a firm's external and internal environment. It can entail subscribing to trade publications, observing news reports, getting constant feedback from employees and customers, attending industry meetings, watching competitors' actions (competitive intelligence), and compiling periodic company reports. **Data storage** involves retaining all types of relevant company records (such as sales, costs, personnel performance, etc.), as well as information collected through marketing research and continuous monitoring. These data aid decision making and are kept for future reference. Marketing research should be considered as just one part of an ongoing, integrated information system.

Depending on a firm's resources and the complexity of information needs, a marketing intelligence network may or may not be computerized. Small firms can do well without computerizing; they merely need to read industry publications, attend trade shows, observe competitors, talk with suppliers and customers, track performance, and store the results of these efforts. In any event, information needs must be stated and regularly reviewed, data sources must be identified, personnel must be given information tasks, storage and retrieval facilities must be set up, and data must be routed to decision makers. The keys to a successful MIS are consistency, completeness, and orderliness.

Marketing plans should be enacted based on information obtained from the intelligence network. For example, by continuous monitoring, a firm could ascertain that a leading competitor intends to cut prices by 7 per cent during the next month. This would give the firm time to explore its own marketing options (e.g., switch to cheaper materials, place larger orders with suppliers to get discounts, or ignore the cuts) and select one. If monitoring is not done, the firm might be caught by surprise and forced just to cut prices, without any other choice.

A basic MIS generally has many advantages: organized data collection, a broad perspective, the storage of important data, an avoidance of crises, coordinated marketing plans, speed in gathering enough data to make decisions, data amassed and kept over several time periods, and the ability to do cost-benefit analysis. Yet, forming an information system may not be easy. Initial time and labor costs may be high, and setting up a sophisticated system may be complex.

Commercial Data Bases

Commercial data bases *can provide useful ongoing information.*

Because companies need current, comprehensive, and relatively inexpensive information about the environment in which they operate, many specialized research firms offer ongoing **commercial data bases** with information on population traits, the business environment, economic forecasts, industry and individual companies' performance, and other items. Data bases may include newspaper and magazine articles, business and household addresses culled from Yellow Pages and other sources, industry and company news releases, government reports, conference proceedings, indexes, patent records, and so on. The research firms sell access to their data bases to clients, usually for a relatively low fee.

Data bases are typically available in printed form; on computer disks, CD-ROMs, or tapes; and "online" using a PC and a modem. There are commercial data-base firms that concentrate on tracking and clipping newspaper and magazine articles on an orderly basis; unlike with computerized data bases, these firms actually look for information on subjects specified by clients. They offer their services for a fee. The annual *Burwell Directory of Information Brokers* cites over 1,200 information brokers in the United States and about 45 other nations.

Firms such as American Business Information (ABI) provide business and household addresses in CD-ROM format. ABI gathers data from phone directories, annual reports, and government agencies; in addition, it makes 14 million calls per year and sends out more than 700,000 mail surveys to keep its data bases current. A $39.95 CD sold by ABI contains data on 70 million U.S. households, while a $2,500 CD has data on 10 million businesses. ABI has over 400,000 customers—from small single-person firms to giant corporations.[4]

Many companies and libraries subscribe to one or more online computerized data bases, whereby users are charged a fee based on the time involved. Among the best-known computerized data-base services are ABI/Inform, CompuServe, Dow Jones News Retrieval, and Nexis. With these services, the user can do a search on a particular topic or company, generate the names and abstracts of relevant articles or reports, and then print out the information. Full articles or reports may also be accessed and printed; but this could be expensive.

Figure 4-3 highlights the "power" of information and how it may be better harnessed by utilizing commercial data bases.

[4]Jacqueline M. Graves, "Building a Fortune on Free Data," *Fortune* (February 6, 1995); and American Business Information brochures.

The transfer of accurate, organized information. In every venue, it is the power to motivate essential action.
At GTE, we make sure that power is at hand. When you need it. Where you need it.
For example, GTE Directories Corporation publishes 1,100 different telephone information directories worldwide, in 7 languages, with a total circulation of over 52 million. Necessary information. Emergency information. Available information.
Information. It gives you the power you need to direct your own destiny.
And at GTE, the power is on.
ACCESSIBLE INFORMATION. THE POWER TO MOVE A SOCIETY.
GTE
THE POWER IS ON

FIGURE 4-3
The Power of Information
Reprinted by permission.

Data-Base Marketing

Through **data-base marketing**, *companies can better reach and interact with customers.*

In conjunction with their marketing information systems, growing numbers of firms are using data-base marketing to better identify target markets and more efficiently reach them. **Data-base marketing** is "an automated system to identify people—both customers and prospects—by name, and to use quantifiable information about them to define the best possible purchasers and prospects for a given offer at a given point in time."[5] Data-base marketing

> creates a bank of information about individual customers (taken from orders, inquiries, external lists), uses it to analyze buying and inquiry patterns, and creates the ability to target goods and services more accurately to specific customers. It may be used to promote the benefits of brand loyalty to customers at risk from competition. It can fuel sales growth by identifying customers most apt to buy new goods and services. It can increase sales effectiveness. It can support low-cost alternatives to traditional sales methods. These include telemarketing and direct mail, which can be important in markets where margins are eroding.[6]

[5]Susan K. Jones, *Creative Strategy in Direct Marketing* (Lincolnwood, Ill.: NTC Publishing, 1991), p. 5.

[6]Robert Shaw and Merlin Stone, *Data-Base Marketing: Strategy & Implementation* (New York: Wiley, 1990), p. 4. See also Mary Lou Roberts, "Expanding the Role of the Direct Marketing Data Base," *Journal of Direct Marketing*, Vol. 6 (Spring 1992), pp. 51–60; and Terry G. Vavra, "The Data-Base Marketing Imperative," *Marketing Management*, Vol. 2 (Number 1, 1993), pp. 47–57.

Ethics IN TODAY'S SOCIETY

Is There a Privacy Paradox for Marketers?

Until recently, much of the debate on consumer privacy regarding telephone directories centered around the way subscriber listings were used (or sold). Now, and in the future, publishers of Yellow Pages need to examine issues relating to interactive advertising.

Interactive media give firms a better ability to aim at target markets because the firms have very specific information on customer product usage, life-styles, and shopping behavior. And by allowing companies access to their data bases, interactive media receive hefty fees.

America Online generated national news headlines in 1994 when it made its customer list available to others. Although specific legislation did not result from this activity, some members of Congress began to suggest limits on marketer access to information.

The policy of the Direct Marketing Association (DMA) is clear in this area. According to the vice-president of consumer affairs for the DMA, "if the consumer thinks that the receipt of a telephone call or a piece of mail is a violation of his or her privacy, then it is a violation of his or her privacy and [a responsible business] should take the consumer's name off its list."

American Express is an example of a firm that carefully guards its customers' right to privacy. In 1974, it was the first company that offered customers the right not to be on a mailing list. And in 1978, American Express adopted a series of privacy principles requiring employees to collect only the data absolutely needed. The firm still reviews its data-collection activities each year; and everyone with access to customer information receives customer privacy training. American Express even distributes brochures to consumers explaining how they can refuse to provide the information requested on warranty cards.

Is there really a privacy paradox for marketers?

Source: Based on material in Jeffrey Casey, "The Privacy Paradox," *Link* (May 1995), pp. 19–22; and "Private Eyes," *Marketing Tools* (January–February 1996), pp. 31–32.

See Figure 4-4.

Data-base marketing is especially useful in the relationship marketing process. A company can identify those customers with whom it would most like to have long-term relationships, learn as much as possible about them (such as demographics and purchase behavior), tailor its marketing efforts toward them, and follow up to learn the level of customer satisfaction. A firm might even compute a "lifetime value" for specific customers, based on their purchase history with the company—and plan its marketing efforts accordingly.[7]

When setting up a data base, each actual or potential customer is given an identifying code. Then, contact information (name, address, phone number, industry code—if a business customer, and demographic data—when appropriate) and marketing information (source and date of contact(s) with firm, purchase history, product interests, and responses to offers) are entered and updated for each customer. The information should be distrib-

[7]See Timothy J. Keane and Paul Wang, "Applications for the Lifetime Value Model in Modern Newspaper Publishing," *Journal of Direct Marketing*, Vol. 9 (Spring 1995), pp. 59–66.

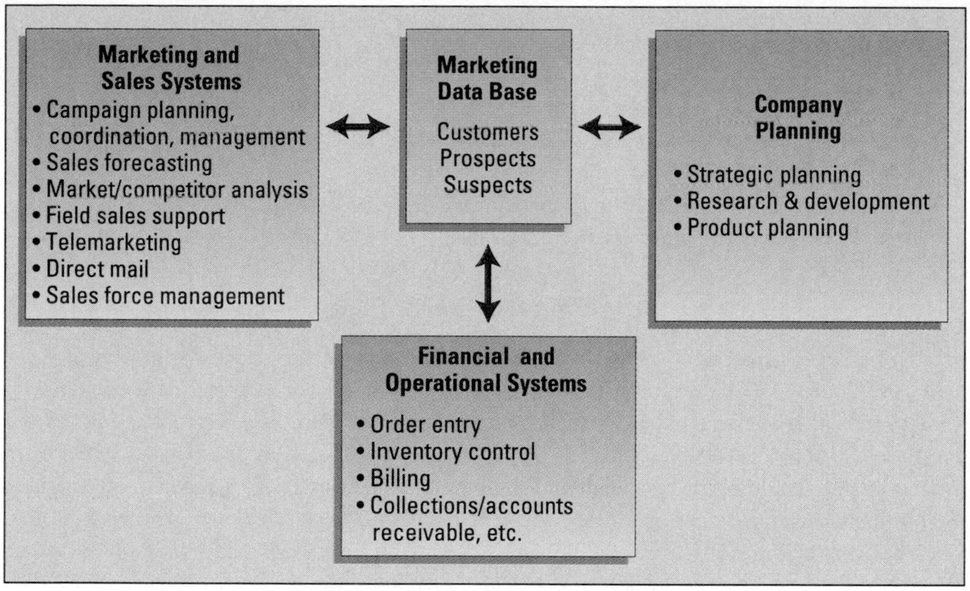

FIGURE 4-4
Fully Integrated Data-Base Marketing

Source: Robert Shaw and Merlin Stone, *Data-Base Marketing: Strategy & Implementation* (New York: Wiley, 1990). *Reprinted by permission of Gower Publishing Company, Limited.*

uted to marketing decision makers in the firm and kept in the MIS, and company efforts should be coordinated so customers are not bombarded with mailings and there is a consistent image.

In practice, data-base marketing actually works like this:

> [1] You may think you're just sending in a coupon, filling out a warranty card, or entering a sweepstakes. But to a marketer, you're also volunteering information about yourself—data that gets fed into a computer, where it's combined with more information from public records. [2] Using sophisticated statistical techniques, the computer merges different sets of data into a coherent, consolidated data base. Then, with powerful software, brand managers can "drill down" into the data to any level of detail they require. [3] The computer identifies a model consumer for a chosen product based on the common characteristics of high-volume users. Next, clusters of consumers who share those characteristics—interests, incomes, brand loyalties, for instance—can be identified as targets for marketing efforts. [4] The data can be used in many ways: to determine the values of coupons and who should get them; to develop new products and ensure that the appropriate consumers know about them; to tailor ad messages and aim them at the right audience. [5] Cash-register scanners provide reams of information about exactly what shoppers are buying at specific stores. Merged with the manufacturer's data, this intelligence helps to plan local promotional mailings, fine-tune shelf displays, and design store layouts. [6] The data base is continually updated with information collected from product-oriented clubs, responses to coupons, calls to 800 numbers, and sweepstakes entries, as well as with new lists from outside sources.[8]

Although often associated with a computerized MIS, data-base marketing may also be used by small noncomputerized firms: A company could ask potential and existing customers for their names, addresses, phone numbers, and product interests as they contact it; these data are entered on large index cards. Consumers could be enticed to provide data via a monthly raffle that awards a low-value prize to the winner. The firm would alphabetize the cards, keep them in a file cabinet, and update records from sales receipts. Separate mailings could be sent to regular customers and to noncustomers from the data base.

MIS in Action

Information systems are being applied today in various settings.

Worldwide, millions of organizations now use some form of MIS in their decision making, and the trend is expected to continue. In fact, as a result of computer networking, progressive firms (and divisions within the same firm) around the globe are transmitting and sharing their marketing information with each other—quickly and inexpensively.

[8] Coopers & Lybrand Consulting, "Data-Base Marketing: How It Works," *Business Week* (September 5, 1994), pp. 56–57.

One recent study on the use of MIS by large U.S. firms discovered that:

- More than three-quarters have a marketing information system. Of those that do, over 95 per cent are computer-based.
- Nearly 80 per cent use computers to produce reports; and two-thirds store marketing data in their computers.
- All gather customer data, three-quarters are involved with competitive intelligence, and 37 per cent track government actions.
- More than 70 per cent use annual reports, sales call reports, and purchased reports to amass competitive intelligence. Just over one-half hire clipping services.[9]

In Sweden, financial institutions have taken the lead in developing MIS: "During the late 1970s, the banking community took an innovative step by organizing a business intelligence (BI) research company called Upplysnigs Centralen (UC Research). It provides fee-based BI services for banks and their major customers, such as data-base services consisting of public and published information on firms and individuals; proactive intelligence gathering, using participating banks' overseas offices to answer specific and time-urgent requests; and the use of some 3,000 business agents around the world who can be tapped for specific expertise or information."[10]

In Japan today, almost all major firms engaged in international business have an internal intelligence unit: "Typically, it is located in the planning or research departments. Some 10 to 20 employees are assigned responsibilities at company headquarters; but intelligence gathering is companywide, with virtually every employee participating (from the president to salespeople). Intelligence collection and dissemination are well developed at most Japanese firms. However, it is the ability—almost culturally inherent—for sharing intelligence that makes MIS use in Japanese firms so effective."[11]

Among the specific firms with superior marketing information systems are NutraSweet, Great Plains Software, Johnson & Johnson, and Frank's Nursery & Crafts. Each devotes considerable time and resources to its system. Here are examples of how they apply MIS.[12]

Because NutraSweet's patent protection on its aspartame-based artificial sweeteners has expired in both Europe and the United States, the company is now vulnerable to the actions of competitors. Yet, it remains, by far, the industry leader. Why? It regularly gathers competitive intelligence—with regard to competitors' prices, expansion plans, and advertising campaigns—and then stores this information in a computer data bank. In response to its MIS findings, NutraSweet has cut costs and improved customer service.

Great Plains Software is a North Dakota-based producer and marketer of accounting software. Its annual sales are $35 million. The firm has a comprehensive file on each of its thousands of customers, garnered from phone surveys. All records are stored in a computer data bank and available to any company employee. The data aid in software development, lead tracking, and forecasting customer needs.

Johnson & Johnson, the maker and marketer of consumer, professional, and health-related products that are sold around the globe, employs a variety of marketing information systems to enhance its performance. For instance, when the Acuvue line of disposable contact lenses was launched, the firm developed and implemented the data-base marketing program shown in Figure 4-5. The success of that program was due to the company's recognizing that two data bases were necessary: potential customers and eye-care professionals (who had to be properly encouraged and supported).

Frank's Nursery & Crafts, the largest U.S. retail chain devoted to lawn and garden products and Christmas merchandise, has 265 stores in 16 states. Management informa-

[9]Eldon Y. Li, "Marketing Information Systems in the Top U.S. Companies: A Longitudinal Analysis," *Information & Management*, Vol. 28 (January 1995), pp. 13–31.

[10]Jan P. Herring, "Business Intelligence in Japan and Sweden: Lessons for the U.S.," *Journal of Business Strategy*, Vol. 13 (March–April 1992), p. 45.

[11]Ibid., p. 47.

[12]Michael Haddigan, "Competitor Intelligence Considered More Vital Now," *Marketing News* (October 9, 1995), p. 3; Jay Finegan, "Taking Names," *Inc.* (September 1992), pp. 121–130; Robert C. Blattberg and John Deighton, "Interactive Marketing: Exploiting the Age of Addressability," *Sloan Management Review*, Vol. 33 (Fall 1991), pp. 10–11; and *General Host Corporation 1994 Annual Report*.

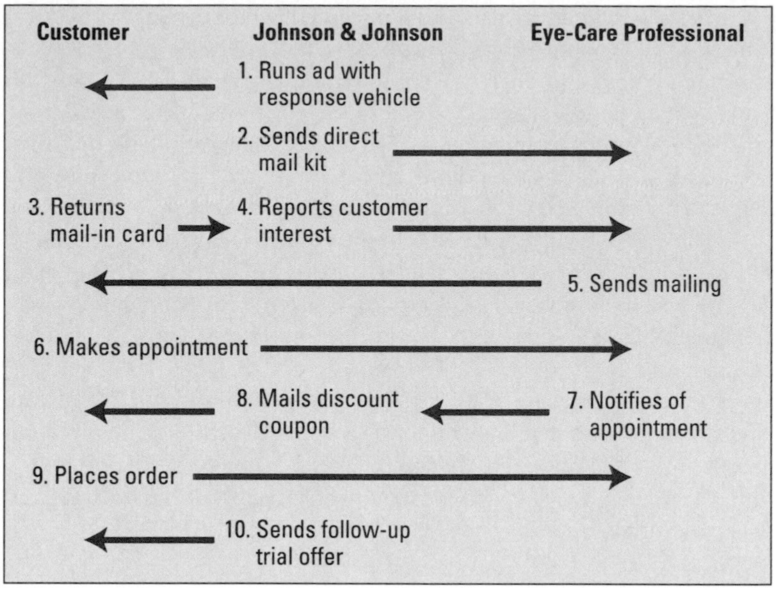

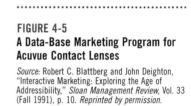

FIGURE 4-5
A Data-Base Marketing Program for Acuvue Contact Lenses

Source: Robert C. Blattberg and John Deighton, "Interactive Marketing: Exploring the Age of Addressibility," *Sloan Management Review,* Vol. 33 (Fall 1991), p. 10. *Reprinted by permission.*

tion systems in each store enable personnel to closely track sales and inventory. Thus, Frank's can better plan and adapt to market conditions. See Figure 4-6.

Marketing Research Defined

Marketing research involves systematically gathering, recording, and analyzing information about specific issues related to the marketing of goods, services, organizations, people, places, and ideas. It may be done by an outside party or by the firm itself. As indicated earlier, marketing research should be one component of a firm's marketing information efforts.

Marketing research *involves collecting, tabulating, and analyzing data about specific marketing issues.*

FIGURE 4-6
The Value of In-Store Information Systems
Through its in-store MIS network, Frank's can closely monitor data on a daily basis in each of its 300 outlets, and thereby make better marketing decisions.

Reprinted by permission of General Host Corporation, Ted Kawalerski photographer.

Several points about marketing research need to be emphasized. First, to be effective, it must not be conducted haphazardly. Second, it involves a sequence of tasks: data gathering, recording, and analysis. Third, data may be available from different sources: the firm itself, an impartial agency (such as the government), or a research specialist working for the firm. Fourth, it may be applied to any aspect of marketing that requires information to aid decision making. Fifth, research findings and their implications must be communicated to the proper decision maker(s) in the firm.

A firm's decision to use marketing research does not mean it must engage in expensive projects like test marketing and national consumer attitude surveys. It may get enough data by analyzing internal sales reports or from informal meetings with customer-service personnel. Marketing research does require an orderly approach and adherence to the scientific method.

For each marketing issue studied, the amount and cost of research depend on the kinds of data needed to make informed decisions, the risk involved in making those decisions, the potential consequences of the decisions, the importance of the issue to the firm, the availability of existing data, the complexity of the data-gathering process for the issue, and other factors.

The Scope of Marketing Research

Global marketing research expenditures total several billion dollars each year.

Companies annually spend about $8 billion worldwide (one-third in the United States) for data gathered by marketing research firms. The top 25 research firms (nearly half of which are U.S.-based) account for more than $4 billion of that amount, with over 1,000 firms responsible for the rest.[13] These amounts are in addition to research sponsored by government and other institutions and to internal research efforts of firms themselves—which also run into billions of dollars each year.

According to the American Marketing Association's most recent *Survey of Marketing Research*, these are the topical areas in which companies are most apt to engage in or sponsor research efforts: industry/market characteristics and trends, product satisfaction, market-share analyses, segmentation studies, brand awareness and preference, purchase intentions, and concept development and testing. And, on average, the surveyed companies spend 1 per cent of their revenues on marketing research.[14]

Five aspects of marketing research merit special discussion. These involve the rapid rise in customer satisfaction studies, the use of state-of-the-art technology, the application of single-source data collection, ethical considerations, and the complexities of international marketing research.

Companies now participate in more customer satisfaction research than ever before, in keeping with the customer focus noted in Chapter 1. This form of research has more than doubled in recent years, with some firms doing their own studies and others hiring outside specialists. For instance, Whirlpool sends surveys on appliance satisfaction to 180,000 households each year. It also pays hundreds of consumers per year to "fiddle" with computer-simulated products at its Usability Lab. Whirlpool's research also extends to its European marketplace. On the other hand, the Walker Group and Maritz Marketing Research, two U.S.-based research firms, each generate worldwide revenues of several million dollars by doing customer satisfaction studies for clients. As a Maritz executive remarked, this is "due to the quality movement in the country, global competitiveness, and a desire to get back to basics and make the marketing orientation more customer-driven."[15]

Over the last decade, significant technological innovations have been applied in a marketing research setting, as these examples indicate:

[13]Jack Honomichl, "The Honomichl 50," *Marketing News* (June 5, 1995), special section; and Stuart Elliott, "Advertising," *New York Times* (January 15, 1996), p. D5.

[14]Thomas C. Kinnear and Ann R. Root (Editors), *1994 Survey of Marketing Research* (Chicago: American Marketing Association, 1995), pp. 38, 49.

[15]Sally Solo, "How to Listen to Consumers," *Fortune* (January 11, 1993), pp. 77, 79; Laura Loro, "Customer Is Always Right," *Advertising Age* (February 10, 1992), p. 26; and "1995 Directory of Customer Satisfaction Measurement Firms," *Marketing News* (October 23, 1995), special section.

TECHNOLOGY & MARKETING

Who'll Win the Information Technology Battle?

Electronic data linkages between firms let them reduce their inventory levels and order-processing times. Companies joined by such data linkages can also eliminate duplicate functions that occur in billing and purchasing. According to the author of a book on customer-supplier alliances, 30 to 40 per cent of savings from these alliances come from improving joint processes.

With electronic linkages, firms can gather and study information as products go from raw materials to finished goods to retailer shelves. In many cases, the most influential companies in a value chain are those that have the best knowledge of the marketplace. In particular, managers need to ask three questions: What information drives our business? Who has that information? What is it worth?

MicroAge and W.W. Grainger are two examples of firms that understand the value of information. MicroAge shifted from being a wholesaler that stocked Apple, Compaq, Hewlett-Packard, and IBM computers to a producer of computers tailored to individual consumer needs. Instead of selling systems produced by single companies, MicroAge now assembles computers using parts from over 500 companies. MicroAge relies on its knowledge of customer needs, as well as the costs, features, and compatibilities of different manufacturers' products.

W.W. Grainger, a distributor of maintenance, repair, and operating supplies, has an average order size of $129. Unlike competitors, the firm is able to tailor its services to customer needs. Based on the desires of individual customers, Grainger might offer electronic ordering and payment capabilities or even perform a customer's inventory management functions. According to a Grainger vice-president, "On sales calls these days, we're seldom talking about why the motor we sell is better than someone else's motor; we talk about value-added services."

As a W.W. Grainger product manager, describe how a marketing information system can be used to maximize its value-added services.

Source: Based on material in Thomas A. Stewart, "The Information Wars: What You Don't Know Will Hurt You," *Fortune* (June 12, 1995), pp. 119–120.

- Strategy Decision Systems' QuestPlus enables hospital patients to answer survey questions by touching responses on a computer screen. Thus, they can easily "voice" opinions about the quality of care received.
- Advanced Neurotechnologies has designed MindTrack to detect emotional responses to ads and other forms of communication. MindTrack detects brainwaves via sensors attached to a headband; people are exposed to an ad campaign or a TV show and quantitative digital results appear.
- More companies are using facsimile machines to get responses to marketing surveys. In general, faxed responses are obtained quicker; response rates are higher due to the ease of return; and answer quality approximates that for other methods of transmission.[16]

Single-source data collection *is a result of high-tech advances.*

Due to technological advances, **single-source data collection**—whereby research firms track the activities of individual consumer households from the programs they watch on TV to the products they purchase at stores—has been gaining momentum. For instance, via its BehaviorScan service, Information Resources Inc. (IRI) monitors the view-

[16]"Hospitals to Patients: 'Where Does It Hurt?'" *Sales & Marketing Management* (August 1992), p. 31; Kelly Shermach, "Respondents Get Hooked Up and Show Their Emotions," *Marketing News* (August 28, 1995), p. 35; and John P. Dickson and Douglas L. MacLachlan, "Fax Surveys?" *Marketing Research*, Vol. 4 (September 1992), pp. 26–30.

ing habits and shopping behavior of thousands of households in various markets. Microcomputers are hooked to household TVs and note all programs and ads watched. Consumers shop in supermarkets and drugstores with scanning registers and present cashiers with Shoppers Hotline cards (resembling credit cards). Cashiers enter each consumer's identification code, which is electronically keyed to every item bought. Via computer analysis, viewing and shopping behavior are then matched with such information as age and income.

Due to the unethical practices of some firms, many potential respondents are "turned off" to participating in marketing research projects. In fact, nearly one-third of Americans say they will not answer a survey. To turn the situation around, researchers need to avoid such practices as these:

- Unrealized promises of anonymity.
- False sponsor identification.
- Selling or fund raising under the guise of research.
- Misrepresenting research procedures.
- Observational studies without informed consent.
- Asking overly personal questions.
- Selling consumer demographic information for data-base use without consent.
- Misportraying research findings in ads and other communications.[17]

With more and more firms striving to expand their foreign endeavors, international marketing research is taking on greater importance. This can be quite challenging. For instance, the language of the survey, respondent selection, and interviewer training are among the many areas that require special consideration. Consider this example.

Firms deciding how to market to the 350 million consumers in Eastern Europe and Central Asia increasingly do marketing research there. Yet, designing and conducting research is difficult. Many times, people have never been surveyed before. Communications systems, especially phone service, may be primitive by Western standards. Secondary data from government agencies and trade associations may be lacking or unavailable. Thus, companies must be adaptable. When it did research, Kodak could not find relevant consumer data, a photography trade association, or pictures of local cameras for use in a questionnaire. So, to gather data on camera usage and preferences, Kodak took part in a multiclient survey devised by SRG International Ltd., a research firm. The survey was conducted in nine former Soviet republics; since each had its own language, nine questionnaire versions were prepared.[18]

The Marketing Research Process

The **marketing research process** *consists of steps from issue definition to implementation of findings.*

The **marketing research process** consists of a series of activities: defining the issue or problem to be studied; examining secondary data (previously collected); generating primary data (new), if necessary; analyzing information; making recommendations; and implementing findings.

Figure 4-7 presents the complete process. Each step is completed in order. For example, secondary data are not examined until a firm states the issue or problem to be studied, and primary data are not generated until secondary data are thoroughly reviewed. The dashed line around primary data means these data do not always have to be collected. Many times, a firm can obtain enough information internally or from published sources to make a marketing decision without gathering new data. Only when secondary data are insufficient should a firm generate primary data. The research process is described next.

[17]Gene R. Laczniak and Patrick E. Murphy, *Ethical Marketing Decisions: The Higher Road* (Needham Heights, Mass.: Allyn and Bacon, 1993), pp. 53–68.

[18]Lourdes Lee Valeriano, "Western Firms Poll Eastern Europeans to Discern Tastes of Nascent Consumers," *Wall Street Journal* (April 27, 1992), pp. B1–B2; Richard W. Stevenson, "Teaching the Hard Sell of Soap to Eastern Europe," *New York Times* (February 18, 1993), pp. D1, D7; and R. Craig Endicott, "European Dream Captivates Researchers," *Advertising Age* (October 18, 1993), p. S–6.

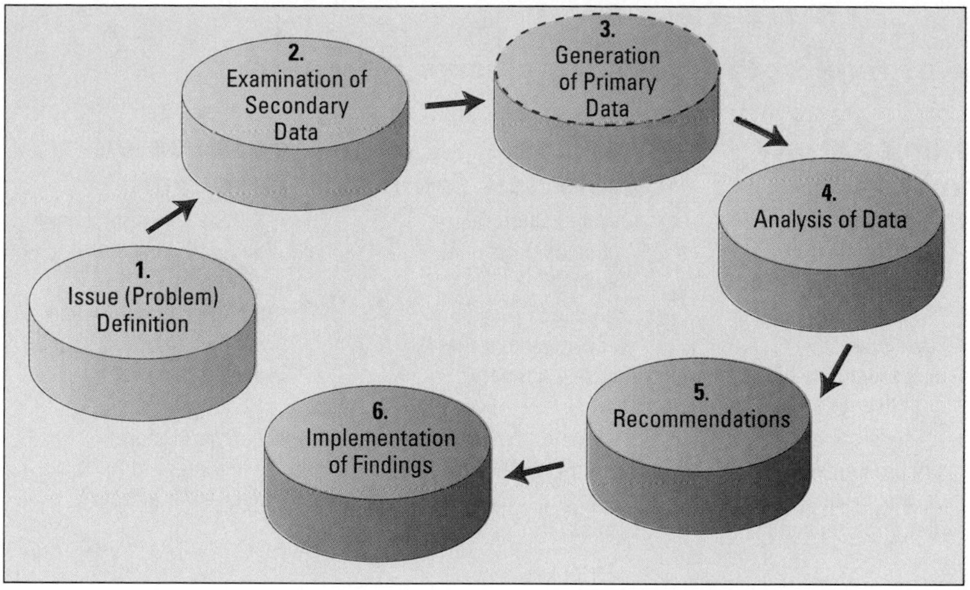

FIGURE 4-7
The Marketing Research Process

Issue (Problem) Definition

Research efforts are directed by the **issue definition**.

Issue (problem) definition is a statement of the topic to be looked into via marketing research. Without a focused definition, irrelevant and expensive data—which could confuse rather than illuminate—may be gathered. A good problem definition directs the research process to collect and analyze appropriate data for the purpose of decision making.

Exploratory research *looks at uncertain topics;* **conclusive research** *is better defined.*

When a firm is uncertain about the precise topic to be investigated or wants to informally study an issue, exploratory research is used. The aim of **exploratory research** is to gain ideas and insights, and to break broad, vague problem statements into smaller, more precise statements.[19] Exploratory research, also called "qualitative research," may involve in-depth probing, small group discussions, and understanding underlying trends.

Once an issue is clarified, conclusive research, also called "quantitative research," is used. **Conclusive research** is the structured collection and analysis of data pertaining to a specific issue or problem. It is more focused than exploratory research, and requires larger samples, more limited questions, and so on, in order to provide the quantitative data to make decisions. Table 4-1 contrasts exploratory and conclusive research.

Secondary Data

Secondary data *have been previously gathered for purposes other than the current research.*

Secondary data consist of information not collected for the issue or problem at hand but for some other purpose; this information is available within a firm or externally. Whether secondary data fully resolve an issue or problem or not, their low cost and rather fast availability mean that primary data should not be collected until a thorough secondary data search is done.

Advantages and Disadvantages Secondary data have these general advantages:

- Many types are inexpensive because primary data collection is not involved.
- Data assembly can be fast, especially for published or company materials.
- There may be several sources and perspectives available.
- A source (such as the government) may obtain data a firm could not get itself.
- There is high credibility for data assembled by independent sources.
- They are helpful when exploratory research is involved.

Secondary data also have these general disadvantages:

- Available data may not suit the current research purpose due to incompleteness and generalities.

[19]Bennett, *Dictionary of Marketing Terms*, p. 103.

Table 4-1
Examples of Exploratory and Conclusive Research

VAGUE RESEARCH TOPIC	EXPLORATORY RESEARCH	PRECISE RESEARCH TOPIC	CONCLUSIVE RESEARCH
1. Why are sales declining?	1. Discussions among key personnel to identify major cause	1. Why is the turnover of sales personnel so high?	1. Survey sales personnel and interview sales managers
2. Is advertising effective?	2. Discussions among key advertising personnel to define effectiveness	2. Do adults recall an advertisement the day after it appears?	2. Survey customers and noncustomers to gauge advertising recall
3. Will a price reduction increase revenues?	3. Discussions among key personnel to determine the level of a price reduction	3. Will a 10 per cent price reduction have a significant impact on sales?	3. Run an in-store experiment to determine effects

- Information may be dated or obsolete.
- The methodology used in collecting the data (such as the sample size, date of the research, etc.) may be unknown.
- All the findings of a research study may not be made public.
- Conflicting results may exist.
- Because many research projects are not repeated, the reliability of data may not be proven.

Sources There are two major sources of secondary data, internal and external. Internal secondary data are available within a firm. External secondary data are available outside a firm. Most companies use each source in some way.

A firm's records or past studies comprise internal secondary data.

Internal Secondary Data Before spending time and money searching for external secondary data or collecting primary data, the information contained inside a firm should be reviewed. Internal sources include budgets, sales figures, profit-and-loss statements, customer billings, inventory records, prior research reports, and written reports.

At the beginning of the business year, most firms set detailed budgets for the next 12 months. The budgets, based on sales forecasts, outline planned expenditures for every good and service during the year. By examining the sales of each division, product line, item, geographic area, salesperson, time of day, day of week, and so on—and comparing these sales with prior periods, performance can be measured. Through profit-and-loss statements, actual achievements can be measured against profit goals by department, salesperson, and product. Customer billings provide information on credit transactions, sales by region, peak selling seasons, sales volume, and sales by customer category. Inventory records show the levels of goods bought, manufactured, stored, shipped, and/or sold throughout the year.

Prior research reports, containing findings of past marketing research efforts, are often stored and retained for future use. When a report is used initially, it is primary data. Later reference to that report is secondary in nature because it is no longer employed for its basic purpose. Written reports (ongoing data stored by a firm) may be compiled by top management, marketing executives, sales personnel, and others. Among the information attainable from such reports are typical customer complaints.

Government and nongovernment sources make available external secondary data.

External Secondary Data If a research issue or problem is not resolved through internal secondary data, a firm should use external secondary data sources. There are government and nongovernment sources.

All levels of government distribute economic and business statistics. In addition, various U.S. government agencies publish pamphlets on such diverse topics as franchising and deceptive sales practices. These materials are usually distributed free of charge or sold for a nominal fee. The *Monthly Catalog of U.S. Government Publications* contains a listing of these items. When using government data, particularly census statistics, the research date must be noted. There may be a lag before government data are released.

There are three kinds of nongovernment secondary data: regular publications; books, monographs, and other nonregular publications; and commercial research houses. Regular publications contain articles on diverse aspects of marketing and are available in libraries or via subscriptions. Some are quite broad in scope (*Business Week*); others are more specialized (*Journal of Advertising*). Periodicals are published by conventional publishing companies, as well as by professional and trade associations.

Books, monographs, and other nonrecurring literature are also published by conventional publishing companies, as well as by professional and trade associations. These materials deal with special topics in depth and are compiled on the basis of interest by the target audience.

Various commercial research houses conduct periodic and ongoing studies and make results available to many clients for a fee. The fee can be rather low or range into the tens of thousands of dollars, depending on the extent of the data. That kind of research is secondary when a firm purchasing the data acts as a subscriber and does not request specific studies pertaining only to itself; in this way, commercial houses provide a number of research services more inexpensively than if data are collected for a firm's sole use. Among the research houses in this area are A.C. Nielsen and IMS International (both owned by Dun & Bradstreet), Information Resources Inc., Arbitron (owned by Ceridian), and Burke Marketing Services. Figure 4-8 shows one subscription service provided by commercial research houses. A great many others are also available.

American Demographics annually publishes a "Best 100" list of marketing information sources. This list includes both government and nongovernment organizations, and gives a brief description of the secondary data that each has available.

Primary Data

Primary data consist of information gathered to address a specific issue or problem at hand. Such data are needed when a thorough analysis of secondary data is insufficient for a proper marketing decision to be made.

Primary data *relate to a specific marketing issue.*

FIGURE 4-8
Retail Store Auditing by Burke Marketing Services
Burke auditors regularly visit a national sample of stores to provide clients with data about sales, inventories, brand distribution, prices, displays, and so on.
Reprinted by permission.

Advantages and Disadvantages Primary data have these general advantages:

- They are collected to fit the precise purpose of the current research topic.
- Information is current.
- The methodology of data collection is controlled and known by the firm.
- All findings are available to the firm, which can maintain their secrecy.
- There are no conflicting data from different sources.
- A study can be replicated (if desired).
- When secondary data do not resolve all questions, collecting and analyzing primary data are the only ways to acquire information.

Primary data also have these general disadvantages:

- Collection may be time consuming.
- Costs may be high.
- Some types of information cannot be collected (e.g., *Census* data).
- The company's perspective may be limited.
- The firm may be incapable of collecting primary data.

The **research design** *outlines data collection.*

Research Design If a firm decides primary data are needed, it must devise a **research design**—which outlines the procedures for collecting and analyzing data. A research design includes the following decisions.

Internal or outside personnel can be used.

Who Collects the Data? A company can collect data itself or hire an outside research firm for a specific project. The advantages of an internal research department are the knowledge of company operations, total access to company personnel, ongoing assembly and storage of data, and high commitment. The disadvantages of an internal department are the continuous costs, narrow perspective, possible lack of expertise on the latest research techniques, and potentially excessive support for the views of top management. The strengths and weaknesses of an outside research firm are the opposite of those for an inside department.

What Information Should Be Collected? The kinds and amounts of data to be collected should be keyed to the issue (problem) formulated by the firm. Exploratory research requires different data collection than conclusive research.

Who or What Should Be Studied? First, the people or objects to be studied must be stated; they comprise the population. People studies generally involve customers, company personnel, and/or distribution intermediaries. Object studies usually center on company and/or product performance.

Sampling *the population saves time and money.*

Second, the way in which people or objects are selected must be decided. Large and/or dispersed populations usually are examined by **sampling**, which requires the analysis of selected people or objects in the designated population, rather than all of them. It saves time and money; and when used properly, the accuracy and representativeness of sampling can be measured.

The two approaches to sampling are probability and nonprobability. With a probability (random) sample, every member of the designated population has an equal or known probability of being chosen for analysis. For example, a researcher may select every fiftieth person in a phone directory. With a nonprobability sample, members of the population are chosen on the basis of convenience or judgment. For instance, an interviewer may select the first 100 dormitory students entering a college cafeteria. A probability sample is more accurate; but it is more costly and difficult than a nonprobability sample.

Third, the sample size studied must be set. Generally, a large sample will yield greater accuracy and cost more than a small sample. There are methods for assessing sample size in terms of accuracy and costs, but a description of them is beyond the scope of this text.

What Technique of Data Collection Should Be Used? There are four basic primary-data collection methods: survey, observation, experiment, and simulation.

A **survey** gathers information from respondents by communicating with them. It can uncover data about attitudes, purchases, intentions, and consumer traits. Yet, it is subject to incorrect or biased answers. With a survey, a questionnaire is used to record responses. A survey can be conducted in person, by phone, or by mail.

A **survey** *communicates in person, over the phone, or by mail.*

A personal survey is face-to-face and flexible, can elicit lengthy replies, and reduces ambiguity. It is relatively expensive, however, and bias is possible because the interviewer may affect results by suggesting ideas to respondents or by creating a certain mood during the interview. A phone survey is fast and relatively inexpensive, especially with the growth of discount telephone services. Responses are usually brief, and nonresponse may be a problem. It must be verified that the desired respondent is the one contacted. Some people do not have a phone, or they have unlisted numbers. The latter problem is now overcome through computerized, random digit-dialing devices. A mail survey reaches dispersed respondents, has no interviewer bias, and is relatively inexpensive. Nonresponse, slowness of returns, and participation by incorrect respondents are the major problems. The technique chosen depends on the goals and needs of the specific research project. See Figure 4-9.

A survey may be nondisguised or disguised. With a nondisguised survey, the respondent is told a study's real purpose; in a disguised survey, the person is not. The latter may be used to indirectly probe attitudes and avoid a person's answering what he or she thinks the interviewer or researcher wants to hear or read. The left side of Figure 4-10 is a nondisguised survey showing the true intent of a study on sports car attitudes and behavior. The right side of the figure shows how the survey can be disguised: By asking about sports car owners in general, a firm may get more honest answers than with questions geared right at the respondent. The intent of the disguised study is to uncover the respondent's actual reasons for buying a sports car.

A nondisguised survey reveals its purpose, whereas a disguised one does not.

A **semantic differential** is a list of bipolar (opposite) adjective scales. It is a survey technique with rating scales instead of, or in addition to, traditional questions. It may be disguised or nondisguised, depending on whether the respondent is told a study's true purpose. Each adjective in a semantic differential is rated on a bipolar scale, and average

A **semantic differential** *uses bipolar adjectives.*

FIGURE 4-9
Consumer Surveys at Stanley Works
Roundtable discussions with consumers are used to spark reactions to company products, such as the Stanley Closet Organizer.
Reprinted by permission.

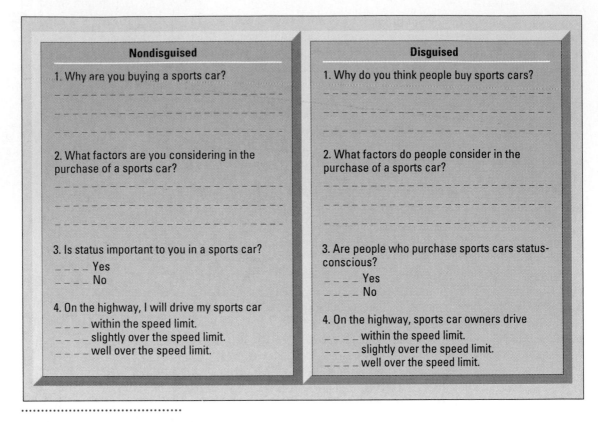

Nondisguised	Disguised
1. Why are you buying a sports car? _	1. Why do you think people buy sports cars? _
2. What factors are you considering in the purchase of a sports car? _	2. What factors do people consider in the purchase of a sports car? _
3. Is status important to you in a sports car? _ _ _ _ Yes _ _ _ _ No	3. Are people who purchase sports cars status-conscious? _ _ _ _ Yes _ _ _ _ No
4. On the highway, I will drive my sports car _ _ _ _ within the speed limit. _ _ _ _ slightly over the speed limit. _ _ _ _ well over the speed limit.	4. On the highway, sports car owners drive _ _ _ _ within the speed limit. _ _ _ _ slightly over the speed limit. _ _ _ _ well over the speed limit.

FIGURE 4-10
Nondisguised and Disguised Surveys

scores for all respondents are computed. An overall company or product profile is then devised. The profile may be compared with competitors' profiles and consumers' ideal ratings. Figure 4-11 shows a completed semantic differential.

In **observation**, *behavior is viewed.*

Observation is a research method whereby present behavior or the results of past behavior are observed and noted. People are not questioned and cooperation is unnecessary. Interviewer and question bias are minimized. Observation often is used in actual situations. The major disadvantages are that attitudes cannot be determined and observers may misinterpret behavior.

In disguised observation, a consumer is unaware he or she is being watched. A two-way mirror, hidden camera, or other device would be used. With nondisguised observation, a participant knows he or she is being observed. Human observation is carried out by people; mechanical observation records behavior through electronic or other means, such as a movie camera filming in-store customer behavior or reactions to a sales presentation.

An **experiment** *varies marketing factors under controlled conditions.*

An **experiment** is a type of research in which one or more factors are manipulated under controlled conditions. A factor may be any element of marketing from package design to advertising media. In an experiment, just the factor under study is varied; all other factors remain constant. For example, to evaluate a new package design for a product, a manufacturer could send new packages to five retail outlets and old packages to five similar outlets; all marketing factors other than packaging remain the same. After one month, sales of the new package at the test outlets are compared with sales of the old package at the similar outlets. A survey or observation is used to determine the reactions to an experiment.

An experiment's key advantage is that it can show cause and effect—like a new package lifting sales. It is also methodically structured and enacted. Key disadvantages are the rather high costs, frequent use of contrived settings, and inability to control all factors in or affecting a marketing plan.

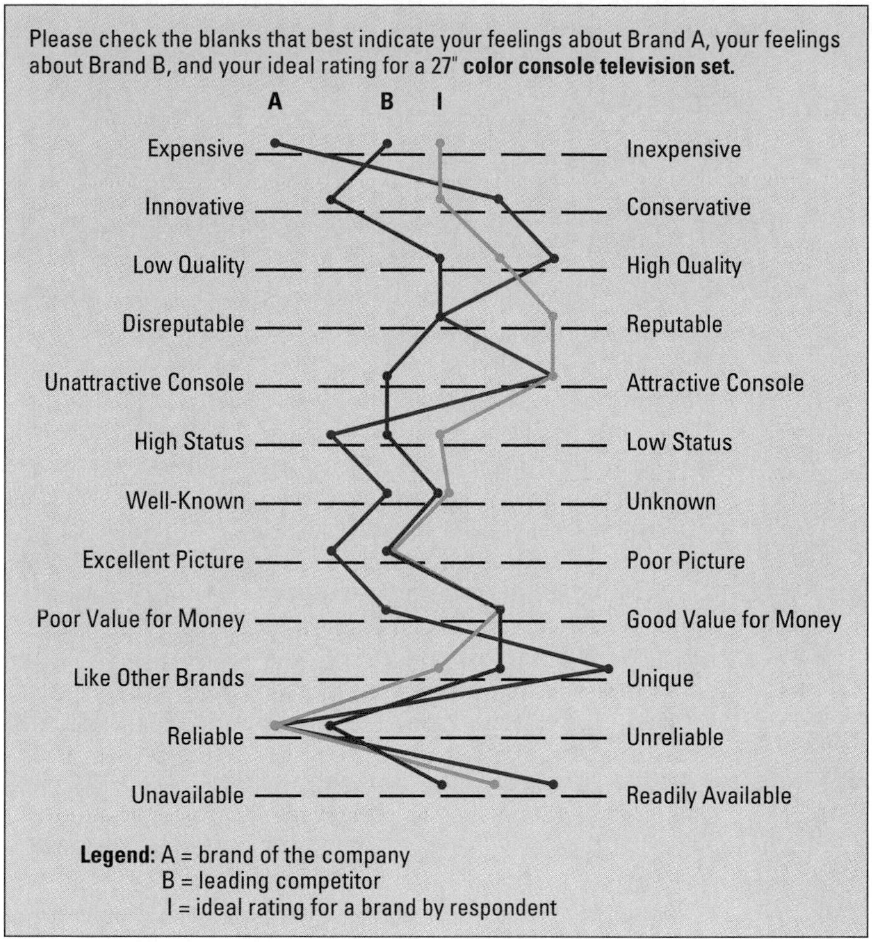

FIGURE 4-11
A Semantic Differential for a Color Television

Simulation *enables marketing factors to be analyzed via a computer model.*

Simulation is a computer-based method to test the potential effects of various marketing factors via a software program rather than real-world applications. A model of the controllable and uncontrollable factors facing the firm is first constructed. Different combinations of the factors are then fed into a computer to determine their possible impact on an overall marketing strategy. Simulation requires no consumer cooperation and can handle many interrelated factors. However, it may be complex and hard to use; does not measure actual attitudes, behavior, and intentions; and is subject to the accuracy of the assumptions made.

Table 4-2 (on page 99) shows the best uses for each kind of primary data collection.

Research costs range from personnel time to marketing costs.

How Much Will the Study Cost? The overall and specific costs of a study must be clearly outlined. These costs may include executive time, researcher time, support-staff time, pre-testing, computer usage, respondent incentives (if any), interviewers, supplies, printing, postage or phone expenses, special equipment, and marketing expenses (such as advertising).

A study's expected costs should be compared with the expected benefits to be derived. Suppose a consumer survey costing $10,000 would let a firm improve the package design of a new product. With the changes suggested by research, the firm would lift its first-year profit by $30,000. Thus, the net increase due to research is $20,000 ($30,000 profit less $10,000 in costs).

How Will the Data Be Collected? The people needed to collect the data outlined in the research design must be determined and the attributes, skills, and training of the data-collection force specified. Too often, this important phase is improperly planned, and data are collected by unqualified people.

International Marketing in Action

Is Rummaging Through Trash in Argentina "Marketing Research?"

After evaluating its garbage-digging research technique, the Dynamics Group consulting firm decided to expand its market-surveillance activities from 400 to 1,650 residences in greater metropolitan Buenos Aires, Argentina. The bulk (no pun intended) of the firm's research results come from studying disposable packaging.

As Dynamics Group's research director says, "By analyzing disposable containers, we can certify that this is real consumption and not what somebody felt like saying or what they 'thought' was right for a survey. The people in this study don't know that we are studying their garbage so the information is totally objective." Among the firm's clients are food and beverage marketers such as Coca-Cola, Argentina's largest dairy products marketer, a major pasta maker, and two big wine and meat marketers. Dynamics Group is now seeking to attract marketers of health and beauty aids, household cleaning products, and paper goods.

Dynamics Group provides clients with data on brand share gains and losses, key competitors, and customer loyalty. It can also furnish data on associated consumption (such as what food item was consumed with a specific type of beverage), the impact of advertising campaigns (measured by the amount of the advertised product in the trash), and product usage by day of week. Discarded newspapers, magazines, and cable television guides can also give marketers data on media availability by household.

As a Coca-Cola de Argentina spokesperson states, "We can get information about sales from Nielsen, but this shows us more about end consumption." For example, an analysis of garbage data suggested that people in poorer areas of Argentina consumed more expensive wines and champagnes on weekends, while the opposite pattern occurred in wealthier areas.

What types of data would you, as a brand manager for an Argentine pasta maker, want to obtain through the garbage-digging method? Why?

Source: Based on material in Mike Galetto, "Turning Trash to Research Treasure," *Advertising Age* (April 17, 1995), p. J-16.

Interviewers administer surveys or respondents fill them out.

Data collection can be administered by research personnel or it can be self-administered. With administered collection, interviewers ask questions or observers note behavior; they record answers or behavior and explain questions (if asked) to respondents. With self-administered collection, respondents read questions and write their answers. There is a trade-off between control and interviewer probing (administered) versus privacy and limited interviewer bias (self-administered).

How Long Will the Data-Collection Period Be? The time frame within which data are collected must be stipulated, or else a study can drag on. Too long a time frame may lead to inconsistent responses and secrecy violations. Short time frames are easy to set for personal and phone surveys. Mail surveys, observation, and experiments often require much more time to implement; nonetheless, time limits must be defined.

When and Where Should Information Be Collected? The day and time of data collection must be set. It must also be decided if a study is done on or off a firm's premises. The

Table 4-2

The Best Uses of Primary Data-Collection Techniques

TECHNIQUE	MOST APPROPRIATE USES
1. Survey	When determining consumer or distribution intermediary attitudes and motivations toward marketing-mix factors; measuring purchase intentions; relating consumer traits to attitudes
2. Observation	When examining actual responses to marketing factors under realistic conditions; interest in behavior and not in attitudes
3. Experiment	When controlling the research environment is essential and establishing a cause-and-effect relationship is important
4. Simulation	When deriving and analyzing many interrelationships among variables

desire for immediacy and convenience have to be weighed against the need to contact hard-to-reach respondents at the proper time.

Data Collection After the research design is thoroughly detailed, data are actually collected. Those engaged in data collection must be properly supervised and follow directions exactly. Responses or observations must be entered correctly.

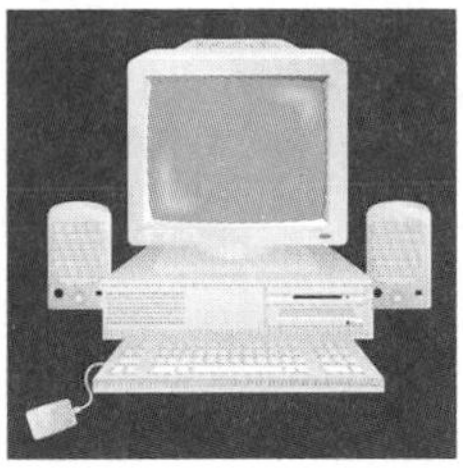

Data Analysis

In **data analysis**, the information on questionnaires or answer forms is first coded and tabulated and then analyzed. Coding is the process by which each completed data form is numbered and response categories are labeled. Tabulation is the calculation of summary data for each response category. Analysis is the evaluation of responses, usually by statistical techniques, as they pertain to the specific issue or problem under investigation. The relationship of coding, tabulation, and analysis is shown in Figure 4-12.

Data analysis *consists of coding, tabulation, and analysis.*

Recommendations

Recommendations are suggestions for a firm's future actions that are based on marketing research findings. They are typically presented in written (sometimes, oral) form to marketing decision makers. The report must be written for the audience that reads it. Thus, technical terminology must be defined. Figure 4-12 shows recommendations flowing from completed research.

After recommendations are passed on to the proper decision makers, the research report should be kept in the data storage part of a firm's marketing intelligence network. It may then be retrieved in the future, as needed.

Implementation of Findings

A research report represents feedback for marketing managers, who are responsible for using findings. If they ignore the findings, research has little value. If they base decisions on the results, then marketing research has great value and the organization benefits in the short and long run.

Marketing managers are most apt to implement research findings if they have input into the research design, broad control over marketing decisions, and confidence that results are accurate. Figure 4-12 provides an illustration of how a firm could implement research findings.

1. Do you drink coffee?	☐ Yes	01	300
	☐ No	02	200
2. In general, how frequently do you drink coffee? (Check only one answer.)	☐ Two or more times per day	03	142
	☐ Once per day	04	84
	☐ Several times per week	05	42
	☐ Once or twice per week	06	20
	☐ One to three times per month	07	12
	☐ Never	08	200
3. During what time of day do you drink coffee? (Check all answers that apply.)	☐ Morning	09	270
	☐ Lunch time	10	165
	☐ Afternoon	11	100
	☐ Dinner time	12	150
	☐ Evening	13	205
	☐ None	14	200

Coding: Questionnaires numbered A001 to A500. Each response is labeled 01 to 14 (e.g., Morning is 09. Evening is 13). Question 3 is a multiple-response question.

Tabulation: Total responses are shown above right.

Analysis: 60% drink coffee. About 28% drink coffee two or more times daily (representing 47% of all coffee drinkers); almost 25% of coffee drinkers (74 people) consume coffee less than once per day. 90% of coffee drinkers consume coffee in the morning; only one-third consume it in the afternoon.

Recommendations: The coffee industry and individual firms need to increase the advertising geared toward noncoffee drinkers, as well as infrequent coffee drinkers. Emphasis should also be placed on lifting coffee consumption during afternoon hours.

Implementation of findings: New, more aggressive advertising campaigns will be developed and the annual media budgets devoted to increasing overall coffee consumption will be expanded. One theme will stress coffee's value as an afternoon "pick-me-upper."

FIGURE 4-12
Data Analysis, Recommendations, and Implementation of Findings for a Study on Coffee

MARKETING IN A CHANGING WORLD

Talking to Former Customers

In today's competitive marketplace, it may not be enough for a firm to focus its efforts on current and prospective customers. It may also be a good idea to research and try to win back various former customers. To do that, a company needs to engage in the sometimes painful task of finding out why these are "former" customers:

> Yet, because most company owners hate to hear harsh words about their babies, they find the hardest part of tracking lost customers is picking up the phone. Bob Ottley, president of One Step Tree and Lawn Care, in North Chili, New York, hesitated for fear "the negative feedback would be impossible to deal with."

At the same time, Ottley was smart enough to know that he had to better track and talk to former customers if his firm was to survive. Today, One Step has a weekly "cancels" report; and Ottley knows what per cent of cancellations are due to people moving, deciding to mow their own lawns, or no longer being able to afford his service—and switching to a lower-priced competitor. One Step has cut its customer attrition rate in half since it began the "cancels" report. And its "leave-behind" survey of current customers "puts the idea into their heads that we want to know if there's a problem."

Bruce Grench, chief executive of HDIS (a small mail-order firm in Olivette, Missouri, that specializes in personal-care products), is another executive who has overcome his qualms. Grench uses six different approaches, from small-group gripe sessions to one-on-one telephone surveys, to gather comments from would be, current, and former customers. He says, "We kind of look forward to it [contacting former customers], even though it's tough medicine. The hope is that we can find something we're not doing right because it offers us an opportunity." He did; that's why HDIS now offers private-label products for price-conscious customers."[20]

SUMMARY

1. *To show why marketing information is needed* Marketing information lets a firm accurately assess its strengths, weaknesses, opportunities, and threats; operate properly in the marketing environment; and maximize performance. Reliance on intuition, judgment, and experience are not sufficient. The scientific method requires objectivity, accuracy, and thoroughness in research projects.

2. *To explain the role and importance of marketing information systems* Collecting marketing information should not be viewed as an infrequent occurrence. Acting in that way can have negative ramifications, especially with regard to misreading the competition and other external factors that can affect a firm's performance.

A marketing information system (MIS) is a set of procedures to generate, analyze, disseminate, and store anticipated marketing decision information on a regular, continuous basis. It can aid a company operationally, managerially, and strategically.

3. *To examine a basic marketing information system, commercial data bases, data-base marketing, and examples of MIS in action* The key aspect of a basic MIS is the marketing intelligence network, which consists of continuous monitoring, marketing research, and data storage. The intelligence network is influenced by the environment, company goals, and marketing plans; and it affects the implementation of marketing plans. Marketing research should be considered as just one part of an ongoing, integrated information system. An MIS can be used by both small and large firms, and does not have to be computerized.

Specialized research firms offer valuable information via commercial data bases that contain data on the population, the business environment, the economy, industry and company performance, and other factors. Data bases are available in printed form; on computer diskettes, CD-ROMs, or tapes; and via online hookups.

An increasing number of firms are looking to data-base marketing to improve their interactions with customers. Data-base marketing involves setting up an automated system to identify and characterize customers and prospects and then using quantifiable information to better reach them.

Marketing information systems are being used by firms of every size and type.

4. *To define marketing research and its components and to look at its scope* Marketing research entails systematically gathering, recording, and analyzing data about specific issues related to the marketing of goods, services, organizations, people, places, and ideas. It may be conducted internally or externally.

Expenditures on marketing research run into the billions of dollars annually. Five key aspects of marketing research are particularly noteworthy: customer satisfaction studies, the use of advanced technology, single-source data collection, ethical considerations, and the intricacies of international research.

5. *To describe the marketing research process* It has a series of activities: defining the issue or problem to be studied, examining secondary data, generating primary data (when needed), analyzing data, making recommendations, and implementing findings. Many considerations and decisions are needed in each stage of the process.

Exploratory (qualitative) research is used to develop a clear definition of the study topic. Conclusive (quantitative) research looks at a specific issue in a structured manner. Secondary data—not gathered for the study at hand but for some other purpose—are available from internal and external (government, nongovernment, commercial) sources. Primary data—collected specifically for the purpose of the investigation at hand—are available through surveys, observation, experiments, and simulation. Primary data col-

[20]"Where Did We Go Wrong?" *Inc.* (July 1995), p. 91.

lection requires a research design: the framework for guiding data collection and analysis. Primary data are gathered only if secondary data are inadequate. Costs must be weighed against the benefits of research. The final stages of marketing research are data analysis—consisting of coding, tabulating, and analysis stages; recommendations—suggestions for future actions based on research findings; and the implementation of findings by management.

KEY TERMS

scientific method (p. 79)
marketing information system (MIS) (p. 80)
marketing intelligence network (p. 81)
continuous monitoring (p. 81)
data storage (p. 81)
commercial data bases (p. 82)
data-base marketing (p. 83)
marketing research (p. 87)
single-source data collection (p. 89)
marketing research process (p. 90)
issue (problem) definition (p. 91)
exploratory research (p. 91)
conclusive research (p. 91)
secondary data (p. 91)
primary data (p. 93)
research design (p. 94)
sampling (p. 94)
survey (p. 95)
semantic differential (p. 95)
observation (p. 96)
experiment (p. 96)
simulation (p. 97)
data analysis (p. 99)

Review Questions

1. Why is marketing information necessary? What may result if managers rely exclusively on intuition?
2. What is the scientific method? Must it be used each time a firm does research? Explain your answer.
3. Describe the elements of a basic marketing information system.
4. Distinguish between commercial data bases and data-base marketing.
5. What is single-source data collection?
6. Differentiate between conclusive and exploratory research. Give an example of each.
7. What are the pros and cons of secondary data?
8. When is primary data collection necessary?
9. Outline the steps in a research design.
10. Under what circumstances should a firm use surveys to collect data? Observation? Explain your answers.

Discussion Questions

1. A small jeweler wants to get information on the average amounts that U.S. consumers spend on gold jewelry, the incomes and occupations of gold jewelry consumers, the time of year when gold jewelry purchases are heaviest and lightest, sales of the leading competitors, the criteria people use in choosing gold jewelry, and consumer satisfaction. Explain how the firm should set up and implement a marketing intelligence network. Include internal and external data sources in your answer.
2. How could a firm use a modified version of Johnson & Johnson's data-base marketing program as shown in Figure 4-6? Apply your answer to a firm marketing expensive attaché cases to business customers via office-supply stores.
3. Pizza Hut is an internationally oriented fast-food chain. Pierre's Pizza is an independent local European fast-food restaurant. If both gather data about their respective competitors' marketing practices, how would your research design differ for each?
4. Develop a five-question disguised survey to determine attitudes toward the reputations of colleges in your area. Why use a disguised survey for this topic?
5. Comment on the ethics of disguised surveys. When would you recommend that they *not* be used?

CASE 1

*Telogy, Inc.: Coordinating Company Data Bases**

Telogy is a manufacturer of electronic testing and measurement products. On an average day, it receives customer service calls from as many as 60 current or prospective customers. The typical caller requests data on price, product availability, or product specifications for one or more of Telogy's 3,000 products.

Prior to 1993, none of Telogy's data bases were integrated. Accordingly, customer service personnel had to query multiple data bases to get the necessary information. For example, information on pricing was contained in one data base, while customer information was in another. In some cases, it took customers at least 15 to 20 minutes to obtain essential data. If a sales representative had to be contacted, the process could take as long as a day. And in most cases, Telogy had no idea if the caller was an existing or a prospective customer unless it asked.

Telogy's old system also did not provide the firm with information deemed vital to running its business. The company had a hard time learning what types of products a client bought, whether these items were purchased or leased, and what types of problems, if any, were encountered. Telogy also missed many sales opportunities due to the poor level of integration of its old marketing information system. A particularly embarrassing problem was that in some cases an item was sold out between the time an order was placed with a salesperson and the time the order was transferred to the shipping department.

So, Telogy decided that it needed to centralize its data base. This would enable customer desires to be better matched with specific products, the firm's order-processing system could be simplified, and each of Telogy's salespeople could have access to data on customer leads, product availability, and pricing.

Telogy's new software now lets its order-processing and marketing departments have access to the same data at the same time. This eliminates the problem with orders "being sold out" during the time between a customer's ordering with a sales representative and the order-processing department receiving that order. And by centralizing information on product availability and pricing, sales reps can better service customers and process orders. Although the software conversion process took ten months (the delay was caused by having to change computer systems), sales training averaged only four hours per person.

Telogy's $500,000 system enables its customer-support personnel to look up any customer's file and quickly determine whether a caller is a prospective or past customer. And if the customer calls customer support and then decides to place an order, the customer-support representative can instantaneously send that information to the sales department without rekeying the order. This system also allows Telogy's telemarketing sales group to better profile their accounts based on past order histories, and to more easily pass along data to the firm's outside sales force.

Besides setting up a new data base, Telogy has automated its outside sales force. Each of the firm's sales reps now has a notebook PC equipped with word processing and spreadsheet software, an E-mail system, and a sales-tracking system with key customer profile data. As a result, sales reps can more quickly record orders and spend more time selling.

There are many ways to evaluate the success of Telogy's new data base. One is to see whether inventory is better utilized. Thus, in comparing sales and inventory levels under the old and new information systems, Telogy computed that its sales revenues increased by 15 per cent and inventory levels were reduced by 10 per cent.

QUESTIONS

1. List and discuss the benefits of an integrated data base beyond those discussed in this case.
2. Describe how Telogy's data base can be used in strategic planning. Refer to Figure 4-5 in your answer.
3. How can Telogy use its new data base as part of a data-base marketing system?
4. Discuss three other measures (beyond inventory utilization) that can be used to assess Telogy's new data-base system.

*The data in this case are drawn from Melissa Campanelli, "On the Right Track," *Sales & Marketing Management* (August 1995), pp. 47–51.

CASE 2

The Marketing Research Association: Hearing from Survey Respondents[†]

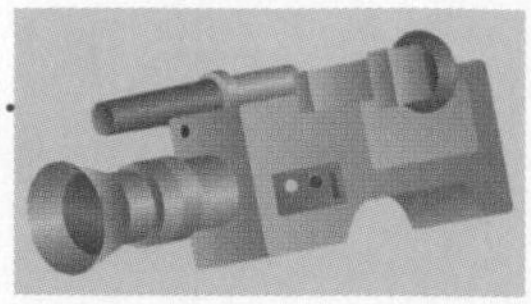

Consumer survey refusal rates have been rather high in recent years. According to Walker Industry Image studies, one in three respondents refuse to participate in a survey or poll. This leads to higher survey costs, questions about the representativeness of the data obtained, and larger sampling errors.

As a way to improve consumer participation rates in marketing research surveys, the Marketing Research Association (MRA)—the leading U.S. trade association for market researchers—formed a Consumer Advocacy Council (CAC) in 1992. The CAC's role is to raise respondent participation by (1) educating consumers about the goals of marketing research and (2) better informing market researchers about consumer perceptions of the industry.

By conducting small-group research sessions, the CAC learned a lot about why people refuse to participate in surveys. It then proposed three tactics to help increase survey participation rates:

- Educate consumers about the benefits of marketing research.
- Educate market researchers about the impact of research on consumers.
- Reduce the negative accusations in the industry (such as data collectors saying research firms have poorly designed questionnaires and research firms blaming interviewers for faulty data collection).

The CAC decided to first concentrate its efforts on educating market researchers about the impact that research practices have on consumers. CAC devised special programs that were pre-tested in MRA's Great Lakes and Florida chapters. For these programs, interviewers and their supervisors were divided into small groups, each asked to suggest solutions to some common consumer problems. These were among the issues discussed:

- Questionnaire design: What happens when a survey is hard to understand by respondents? What are the proper channels of communication for a buyer of research to contact a data collection firm?
- Interviewer training: What should be the minimum amount of training for interviewers? What skills should be taught? How can performance on specific skills be evaluated?
- Just do the job, or do it right? Should field personnel have input in design of a questionnaire? When are respondent incentives appropriate?
- Responsibilities of the research industry: Should the industry develop a system to detect and monitor respondent abuse? Who would be responsible for developing and implementing such a system?

CAC also looked at the interviewing process. It then produced consumer education brochures, a handbook entitled *Guidelines and Practices to Promote Respondent Cooperation*, a *We Can Make a Difference* video, and other materials.

In analyzing the data-collection process, CAC concluded that the industry's basic methods of collecting data were unchanged from 20 years ago. It also believed that technology development in the industry benefitted the researchers, but not necessarily the respondents. CAC's qualitative research also found that researchers must re-engineer their interviewing process to better meet the expectations and life-styles of today's respondents. Among the concerns mentioned by people were their being called at inconvenient times, the infrequent use of incentives, the abundance of lengthy questionnaires, and interviewers not indicating the respondent's role in the data-collection process at the beginning of an interview.

CAC strongly recommends that interviewers treat respondents more as individuals, that they better attempt to move interviews along at a good pace, and that interviewers make better use of computers. It is also imperative that the confidentiality of respondent comments be mentioned both at the beginning of and during the interview.

QUESTIONS

1. Comment on the problems caused by low respondent participation in market research surveys.
2. What are the potential biases of using interviewers to collect survey information? Of having respondents fill out their own questionnaire forms?
3. Develop a program for educating interviewers about consumer perceptions of the interviewing process.
4. Discuss how *you* would try to further increase survey response rates.

VIDEO QUESTIONS ON THE MARKETING RESEARCH ASSOCIATION

1. Evaluate the research design for the Market Research Association study.
2. List and discuss consumer likes and dislikes concerning the marketing research process.

†The data in this case are drawn from Betsy Peterson, "Insight into Consumer Cooperation," *Marketing Research*, Vol. 6 (Fall 1994), pp. 52–53.

PART 1 CASE

Preparing for a High-Tech Future

Introduction

The computer's increasing presence and power, corresponding advances in computer literacy, and the advent of global telecommunications are nudging industrial societies toward an information-based economy and the prospect of an electronic distribution system. Companies must re-engineer their marketing functions accordingly. With mass markets splintering into ever-finer segments, an important element of re-engineering will be the sophisticated use of information technologies to identify, reach, and retain customers.

Certainly, any attempt to predict the details of customer tastes or technological developments more than a few years ahead is doomed. Still, the broad outlines of the landscape of the next century can be glimpsed now.

The March of Technology

None of the so-called high-technology sectors existed commercially until halfway through this century. But their impact on industrialized society has already been huge, and the pace is accelerating. The sales of electronics goods worldwide are now one trillion dollars yearly, with Asia having a rising share of global production. And alliances among computer, telecommunications, entertainment, and information companies are fueling the development and deployment of online technology.

Evidence of high-tech's penetration is everywhere, from the ease with which you make theater reservations by punching the numbers of your credit card into a phone to the speed with which the supermarket checker flicks your groceries past a scanner. Increasingly powerful and inexpensive computer chips have not only made the PC a household item, but also ensured the spread of programmability across a wide array of household appliances, games and toys, cars, industrial tools, and, increasingly, televisions and telephones.

The marriage of telecommunications and computing power is generating new product classes—the hallmark of high-tech. Voice mail is taken for granted; personal communications devices and hand-held global-positioning system units, which pinpoint your location within 100 meters anywhere on earth, soon may be. A Pacific Bell/Intel alliance now permits videoconferencing via PCs connected by regular phone lines. By the beginning of the next century, high-definition TV, with its computer-friendly format, will be in place throughout the United States, enabling crisp displays and easy manipulation of images and data.

Source: Adapted by the authors from New Marketing Imperatives Roundtable, "Preparing for a Point-to-Point World," *Marketing Management* (Spring 1995), pp. 30–40. Reprinted by permission of the American Marketing Association.

Advances in fiber optics, satellite technology, and high-speed switching software will usher in an era of inexpensive, global, two-way, point-to-point telecommunications. Talk of national and global networks for instantaneous two-way transfer of voice, text, realistic video and graphic displays, and numeric data—dismissed as science fiction only a few short years ago—is now being backed up with huge corporate investments in infrastructure.

Collaborations featuring upstarts and established giants are announced almost daily. The number and cumulative size of the ventures initiated so far invite speculation about which ones will prove to be profitable—and when. In the United States, private satellite telecommunication system proposals—representing capital spending of \$15+ billion—have sought FCC approval.

Can these projects all be winners? Maybe not, but though hot competition and sudden shifts in political, regulatory, and financial environments may wreak havoc with specific deals, one thing is clear: In 10 or 15 years, many— perhaps most— homes, businesses, schools, and hospitals will be linked to interactive, network-based multimedia systems working at natural speeds. And object-oriented software may make the dream of real-time automatic translation among native languages a reality, greatly speeding the trend toward a truly global economic system.

Electronic Distribution

Today's adult consumer is yesterday's child, heavily influenced by the TV era and mass marketing. But the tastes, expectations, and tolerances of tomorrow's buyers will reflect their immersion since childhood in a high-tech, high-choice environment in which constant technological improvement and precisely targeted marketing messages are the norm.

Those people will receive an enormous barrage of electronic information. Signal compression promises to expand channel availability throughout this decade, even before fiber-optic cable opens the floodgates. We may see channels for computer hackers, dog lovers, stamp collectors, and speakers of the Farsi language—each with its own demographics.

With the TV evolving steadily into a two-way information appliance, marketers confront the possibility of a radical change: the electronic distribution of goods and services. In *Fast Forward: Where Technology, Demographics, and History Will Take America and the World in the Next 30 Years*, Richard Carlson and Bruce Goldman describe the culture shock today's generation may face during the next few decades. "A time traveler from the present, arriving in the year 2020, might ask: 'Where did all the shopping malls go?' Buyers will be able to electronically pre-screen homes for sale, walk down supermarket aisles, and watch models exhibiting the latest fashions, and then place orders through electronic catalogs."

Although it's more convenient, online shopping largely ignores some other reasons shoppers crowd malls today, such as social interaction and the ability to use the sense of touch in buying. Developers of online shopping services, therefore, may have to accommodate shoppers' social needs; otherwise, they will use these services merely to supplement malls.

We don't have to wait until 2020 for early versions of these options. Some companies have fast-tracked plans for cable TV channels targeted at computer users, with synchronized electronic-information services that allow viewers to make purchases electronically via their own PCs:

- AT&T has a nationwide network, called PersonaLink, into which users can dispatch programmable electronic "agents" that scan listings and report back when a desired item becomes available.
- Motorola has announced the introduction of just such an agent, which works even when the user's computer is turned off.
- A small Cupertino, California, company has an electronic bulletin board for used-car shoppers; if they have the right software, they can download photos of the vehicles.

Brokers, salespeople, retailers, and distributors, working on high volume for small commissions, will become paid information consultants supported by computer software. Rather than search through a newspaper, drive to the store, browse, stand in line for a purchase, and drive home, it will be simpler for you to "commission" an electronic agent, pay a small fee to the network, and, for an extra $4, get the item delivered to your door, just like a pizza.

The effect of this marketplace decentralization is not that brand names will lose their value, but rather that mass advertising will be less able to capture increasingly splintering markets. One likely result is that the cost of newspapers, magazines, and TV—today largely defrayed by ads—will climb.

Online services are a new vehicle for marketing to individuals rather than mass markets; getting into a customer's home will be more effective than an ad in a newspaper ever was. But that customer won't be easy to reach. Control is shifting to users, who will be reachable only when they signal an interest. According to Carlson and Goldman, "When, at the touch of a keyboard, any issue—or paragraph—of any paper or magazine can be summoned up on the screen or printed out in color on the spot, or any TV commercial zapped, how can mass-media advertisers cope? They can't."

A Real-Time World

Marketing shifts can occur with stunning speed. In recent years, Porsche has lost 85 per cent of its U.S. customers. Why? Competition changed, social and buying habits changed, and American tax laws changed. Porsche didn't change fast enough. There is no percentage in building a car that goes 500 miles an hour if the customer's real concern is safety and easy maintenance. It's as dangerous to be too far out in front as it is to be a step behind.

You can't predict a real-time world. A firm's main marketing goal must be to keep in touch with the market, reduce inventory to zero, create integrated systems such as flexible manufacturing lines and advanced inventory controls at both producer and distributor levels, and design for demand. As customers become more elusive and segmented, mass marketing—for decades so successful with products from packaged goods to computers—is becoming more irrelevant.

Bringing Customers Online Business and institutional use of online services is exploding. According to published reports, American companies pay more than 35 million invoices electronically. Internet traffic is growing at a phenomenal rate. This explosive growth is not confined to business users. Each year, millions of PCs are bought for home use in the United States—about 43 per cent of all domestic PC sales. Today, CompuServe, Prodigy, and America On-Line subscribers are rapidly growing in number.

Seeing this growth, Capital Cities/ABC and the parent of the *Washington Post* are working with Oracle to devise a service to let a viewer watching a standard TV newscast on China, say, or a business executive who has just read a feature about opportunities in South America, to call up related news footage, additional text, maps, or a reading list via a remote control device.

Not just data but full-fledged products can be ordered in this manner. An online order-processing system is quick, accurate, and streamlined; the order goes straight to the producer for immediate fulfillment. Such a system can keep a "memory" of each customer's previous specifications, thus reducing the need for alterations—a benefit that saves money and time for the customer.

Electronic shopping for existing products is just the first step. Online ordering, combined with its producer counterpart of flexible manufacturing, permits the customized conjuring of "virtual products"—goods and services that don't exist until the moment they are ordered (or not long after that).

Bringing Customers In-house The need to rush a new product to market means ever more rapid product development, the success of which depends on speedy incorporation of customer, vendor, and channel feedback into the development process.

Motorola, Apple, Pacific Bell, software developer Ungermann-Bass (U-B), and others whose product development has usually been driven by technologists are elevating their marketing functions and, in specific product lines, integrating them with other functions in a leadership role. Videogame maker Electronic Arts staffs its marketing department with "surrogate customers" who fit the profile of the typical product user, equipping each of them with a video game player, and encouraging them to use it.

Oracle hires experts from the pharmaceutical, oil and gas, financial, utilities, public-sector, and retail industries to help managers understand the issues and concerns of those specialized industries so they can tailor applications accordingly.

And a large portion of Intel's marketing staff is devoted to calling on corporate information technology (IT) managers who never order, and the firm sponsors two-day meetings three times a year with a "corporate advisory board" made up of IT managers in North America, Europe, and Asia. Intel incorporates its original-equipment manufacturer customers directly into the design of its chips.

Decentralizing Decision Making Numerous companies are reorganizing in a more responsive, less hierarchical fashion. High-tech distributor Ingram Micro has boosted the autonomy of its salespeople by shifting them from reliance on a mainframe system to their own PCs. Mitsubishi has pushed decision-making authority down from the board level to the division manager level. Each Motorola division is a stand-alone outfit; this may be, in a classical sense, "wasteful" because it permits functional redundancies, but it's faster—and, today, the race goes to the swift.

With margins shrinking as they are, the area of greatest profit potential is in follow-on business—retaining hard-won customers through better service and support. The blurring of product identity can be countered by warrantee protection, ease of delivery, responsive operations support, and other intangibles. The focus of high-tech companies today is no longer on educating customers about how the product was built but on helping them use it. Oracle, Ungermann-Bass, and DDI, a fast-growing Japanese telecommunications company, all have seven-day-a-week, 24-hour service and support centers.

Because their products are typically sold through third parties, software producers seldom know who customers are. For this reason, many of these firms are investing in up-to-date, centralized information systems. U-B, which has redirected much of its large direct-sales force into nonsales customer contact, uses a round-the-clock support center to capture information about users who have bought its products. When a customer is serviced, a single phone call or Lotus Notes message by U-B's service-providing partner at the user site relays the customer's name, phone number, product in question, and operating environment to a central system at U-B.

Taligent, a maker of object-oriented software, uses several methods—toll-free phone numbers for users and potential customers, direct sales, warrantee cards with software preloaded in hardware—to capture data about how customers want to buy, receive, pay for, and get support for products. Taligent also has information management systems to gain efficient data access and cross-referencing, as well as to break down markets into smaller sectors.

Sharing Information Intel's footloose employees are linked by E-mail and more sophisticated groupware. U-B has invested in a huge Lotus Notes groupware system to permit instant worldwide distribution of information on customer service, support, and requirements. All Frito-Lay salespeople use laptops to access the firm's main office computer each night and download all of that day's sales data.

Today, there's no reason why a big supplier can't have a list of its top 100 customers pop up on the CEO's screen every morning (instead of quarterly printouts), with the customers making important buying decisions each day displayed in red. The CEO can then call the president of each of those firms, and say, "I'd like to fly out and talk to you about your upcoming purchase decision." (Many such flights are being replaced by video conferences.)

A good information system might alert a firm to the fact that customers in Chicago prefer a particular cellular phone model, Los Angeles customers another. Follow-up marketing research might then reveal that Chicago users spend more time in their offices than Los Angeles users, who make and take a lot of calls outdoors and from restaurants and are more fashion-conscious; or that cold Chicago weather favors a particular plastic housing; or that because Chicago air is moister and electrical storms are more frequent, the city's cellular-phone users will pay a premium for static-free communication.

Outsider access to a superior data base not only provides feedback to suppliers but can be an excellent sales tool. Electronic Arts gets product sales breakdowns from a key retailer, Toys "R" Us. Blockbuster Video packages all the scanned data gathered in its outlets each day and not only uses the data to fine-tune its offerings, but passes it through to movie producers.

The laptops carried by biotech leader Genentech salespeople contain a constant update of test data on Genentech's and other firms' pharmaceutical products. When physicians want to see the latest testing information, they call in a Genentech salesperson. This is an outstanding example of relational technology: a focus on customer service translates directly into higher sales.

It's important for firms to find the right partners and learn how to work with them. Having identified their own core competencies, firms must identify, solicit, and engage partners with complementary skills. The boundaries that separate cooperation from competition are subtle, and ground rules for the partnership have to be established and enforced. Moreover, marketing and sales must be reoriented to systems integration—selling the customer on a company's product as an ideal component in a system tailored to the customer's needs.

Integrating Systems It used to be that installing a phone was as simple as plugging a jack into a wall; for data communications, you just connected a modem between a terminal and a phone jack. Now, a potential customer has an array of possibilities; and a regional Bell often has 500,000+ small-business users who lack the resources for determining their ideal choice, let alone mastering the support interface.

Small users need service and support as much as big users do, yet cannot afford the premiums big users pay value-added service providers, and they won't find support in the low-end channels. For these customers, the answer may be to package solutions—setup, failure diagnosis, and servicing—into a relatively standardized product.

Tomorrow's Corporation

Global customer feedback will be almost instantaneous. Those who choose to use that feedback will be market leaders. With huge amounts of raw data sloshing around, the slicing and dicing of data becomes as important as the data itself. The premium will be on maintaining and using huge, current, and accurate data bases on customers, competitors, regulations, and standards.

The corporation of tomorrow will be less a physical, localized entity than a network-based consortium, with an ad-hoc-oriented rather than hierarchical culture, constant redeployments of its professionals, and semi-permeable boundaries with its partner/competitors. And tomorrow's CEO will need to be a skillful delegator who understands the power of statistical analysis to filter and process data, who can and will market the technology that defines her or his firm, who welcomes innovation, and who can sustain relationships across daunting cultural and spacial abysses. She or he will also need a healthy measure of luck.

QUESTIONS

1. In the coming new era of marketing described in this case, how should customer service and relationship marketing be utilized?
2. What marketing functions will be most affected by high-tech trends? Why?
3. As a commercial banker, what are several differential advantages that you would pursue in the future?
4. As discussed in the case, would you say that technology is a controllable or an uncontrollable factor? Explain your answer.
5. Read AT&T's most recent annual report to determine its organizational mission. How would you modify it in preparation for the 21st century? Why?
6. What could a high-tech marketer learn by studying the Porter generic strategy model?
7. How would you accomplish this? "A firm's main marketing goal must be to keep in touch with the market, reduce inventory to zero, create integrated systems such as flexible manufacturing lines and advanced inventory controls at both producer and distributor levels, and design for demand."
8. How would you do an online marketing research study on deodorants?

PART 2

BROADENING THE SCOPE O

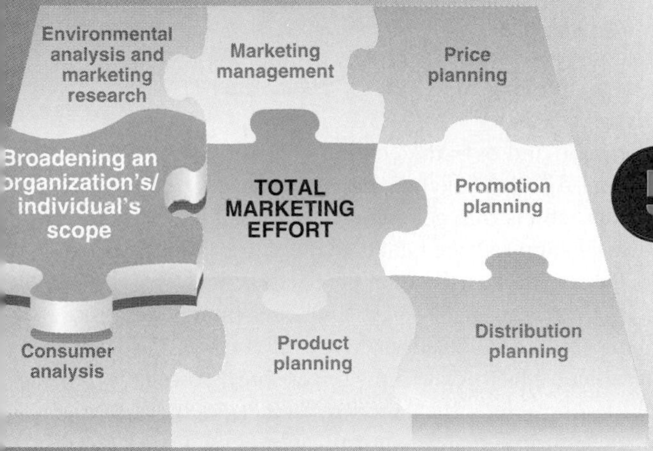

In Part 2, we present an expanded perspective of marketing—one that is necessary today.

5 Societal, Ethical, and Consumer Issues

In this chapter, we examine the interaction of marketing and society. We begin by exploring the concept of social responsibility and discussing the impact of company and consumer activities on natural resources, the landscape, environmental pollution, and planned obsolescence. Next, there is an in-depth discussion of ethics from several vantage points: business, consumer, international, and teachability. We then turn to consumerism and consider the basic rights of consumers: to information, to safety, to choice in product selection, and to be heard. We also note the current trends related to the role of consumerism.

6 Global Aspects of Marketing

Here, we place marketing into a global context—important for both domestic and international firms, as well as those large and small. First, we distinguish among domestic, international, and global marketing. Then, we see why international marketing takes place and how widespread it is. We assess cultural, economic, political and legal, and technological factors. We conclude by looking at the stages in the development of an international marketing strategy: company organization, market entry decisions, degree of standardization, and product, distribution, promotion, and price planning.

Part 2 Video Vignette

Watson Pharmaceuticals

Watson Pharmaceuticals develops, manufactures, and markets a comprehensive array of off-patent pharmaceuticals (often called "generics"), and also develops its own patented pharmaceutical products employing advanced drug delivery systems (such as a proprietary injection molding technique and a process for producing drugs in several different dosage forms). Watson's annual revenues are over $100 million, and it offers both prescription and over-the-counter products.

Watson's prescription drugs include Albuterol Sulfate asthma syrup that competes with Proventil, Furosemide cardiovascular tablets that compete with Lasix, Hydrocodone Bitartrate and Acetaminophen analgesic and anti-pyretic tablets that compete with Lorcet, and Glipizide anti-diabetic tablets that compete with Glucotrol. Watson's Circa products are marketed as a private label over-the-counter line that competes with such brands as Benadryl allergy relief tablets, Sudafed nasal decongestant tablets, and Micatin anti-fungal spray powder.

To be socially responsible, ethical, and consumer-oriented, Watson has superior manufacturing-quality control facilities. Watson's goal is to exceed basic FDA (Food and Drug Administration) guidelines. For example, most pharmaceutical companies its size have 50 to 60 people working in quality assurance. In contrast, Watson has approximately 100 people, many of whom have advanced graduate degrees. As a result, Watson has not had an FDA recall during the last several years. Most companies cannot make this statement.

To be socially responsible, ethical, and consumer-oriented, Watson has superior manufacturing-quality control facilities.

The FDA has separate approval processes for branded drugs (NDAs—New Drug Applications) and generic drugs (ANDAs—Abbreviated New Drug Applications). NDAs are for drug innovations. They entail full reviews of drug safety and efficacy (including animal and human testing). An NDA can cost $10 million to $30 million and take years to complete. In contrast, an ANDA for a generic drug (designed to test the bioequivalency to a branded drug that has already been approved) takes 12 months to two years and costs between $300,000 and $2 million, on average.

Based on its success in the United States, Watson has recently begun to expand internationally. However, marketing off-patent pharmaceuticals internationally is complex because each drug must be separately tested (through clinical trials) and then separately approved for each foreign market. As a consequence, off-patent pharmaceutical firms such as Watson have had little international involvement.

China is one foreign market that Watson is developing. The company has a Chinese manufacturing facility and 50 to 60 sales representatives in China. The off-patent pharmaceuticals that Watson produces in China are to be sold there (and not exported to other markets).

For its patented pharmaceuticals, Watson employs licensing agreements that enable foreign firms to sell or produce Watson products in selected foreign markets. The licensees need to get permission from Watson to sell these drugs in each foreign market.

CHAPTER 5

Societal, Ethical, and Consumer Issues

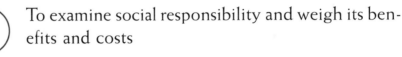

Chapter Objectives

1. To consider the impact of marketing on society
2. To examine social responsibility and weigh its benefits and costs
3. To look into the role of ethics in marketing
4. To explore consumerism and describe the consumer bill of rights
5. To discuss the responses of manufacturers, retailers, and trade associations to consumerism and study the current role of consumerism

In 1978, Ben Cohen and Jerry Greenfield opened an ice cream shop in an abandoned gas station in Burlington, Vermont. Their total investment: $12,000 and a $5, ten-day correspondence course from Penn State on "How to Make Ice Cream." Today, Ben & Jerry's has annual sales of more than $140 million. And Time *magazine says Ben & Jerry's makes "the best ice cream in the world." The company's own motto is, "If it's not fun, why do it?"*

Many organizations make it a practice to be both socially conscious and profitable, but at Ben & Jerry's, social responsibility is part of its very essence (organizational mission) as a firm. Ben & Jerry's buys milk from Vermont farms at above-market prices because "farmers need the money more than the dairy does." Part of company profits go to Ben & Jerry's Foundation (founded in 1985), which distributes 7.5 per cent of the firm's pre-tax profits to charities. During a typical year, the foundation contributes $800,000 to 150 or so organizations.

For example, to honor the late rock legend Jerry Garcia, for a 10-day period following Garcia's 1995 death, the firm donated 50 cents for each customer purchase of Cherry Garcia ice cream, frozen yogurt, and related products that was made at its 120 scoop shops. These funds went to the Rex Foundation, a charity set up by the Grateful Dead band to distribute funds to a wide range of social causes.

Ben & Jerry's seeks to use its business and the power of its business as a force for progressive social change. Thus, Ben & Jerry's worked with the Children's Defense Fund to set up a data base for social purposes. The data base contains citizen voters who can be contacted when laws or bills that relate to children's issues come before Congress. The joint goal is eventually to have a list of 100,000 people who are willing to work with the Children's Defense Fund. To help reach that goal, during 1995, the firm included a message about its *Call for Kids* program on its toll-free 800 phone number; and franchised scoop shops had special red phones so consumers could hear a recording from Ben and Jerry explaining the project.

Although some Ben & Jerry's customers buy its products for social reasons, others buy them for the flavors. Popular ones include Cherry Garcia, Heath Bar Crunch, and Chocolate Chip Cookie Dough (the firm's best-seller). Further evidence of the firm's popularity with customers is that its Vermont plant draws more tourists (225,000 per year) than any other destination in Vermont.

In the United States, Ben & Jerry's has a 36 per cent market share for its super-premium ice cream, up from less than 20 per cent in 1989. Its new line of frozen yogurt, introduced in cities nationwide, has so exceeded the firm's expectations that at one point in time, it could not produce enough of the product to meet market demand. Oh yes, its profits are very strong.[1]

In this chapter, we will study several issues relating to the interaction of marketing with overall society, as well as with consumers. We will also show how ethics and marketing are interwoven.

Overview

Marketing can have both a positive and a negative impact on society.

Individually (at the company level) and collectively (at the industry level), the activities involved with marketing goods, services, organizations, people, places, and ideas can strongly impact on society. They have the potential for both positive and negative consequences, regarding such factors as the following:

- The quality of life (standard of living).
- Natural resources, the landscape, and environmental pollution.
- Consumer expectations and satisfaction with goods, services, and so on.
- Consumer choice.
- Innovation.
- Product design and safety.
- Product durability.
- Product and distribution costs.
- Product availability.
- Communications with consumers.
- Final prices.
- Competition.
- Employment.
- Deceptive actions.

In the United States and many other highly industrialized nations, marketing practices have made a wide variety of goods and services available at relatively low prices and via convenient locations. These include food products, transportation goods and services, telecommunications services, clothing, entertainment, books, insurance, banking and other financial services, audio and video equipment, furniture, and PCs.

At the same time, the lesser use of modern marketing practices in Eastern Europe, Africa, and other parts of the world have often led to fewer product choices, higher prices, and less convenient shopping locations. For example,

> Developments in Russia, its former republics, and other Eastern European nations clearly indicate that the lack of basic possessions (appliances, electrical goods, autos, and so on) has contributed greatly to the high level of dissatisfaction among citizens. In many developing nations, citizens have been viewed as simply *producers* of infrastructure, heavy industry, and public housing, while citizens as *consumers* have been ignored.[2]

Yet, even in the United States and other nations where marketing is quite advanced, marketing acts can create unrealistic consumer expectations, result in costly minor product design changes, and adversely affect the environment. Thus, people's perceptions of

[1] "Ben & Jerry's Donations Set in Rock Star's Honor," *Wall Street Journal* (August 11, 1995), p. A5; Murray Raphel, "What's the Scoop on Ben & Jerry's?" *Direct Marketing* (August 1994), pp. 23–24; and 1996 correspondence from Ben & Jerry's.

[2] Orose Leelakulthanit, Ralph Day, and Rockney Walters, "Investigating the Relationship Between Marketing and Overall Satisfaction with Life in a Developing Country," *Journal of Macromarketing*, Vol. 11 (Spring 1991), p. 19.

marketing are mixed, at best. Over the years, studies have shown that many people feel cheated in their purchases due to deception, the lack of proper information, high-pressure sales pitches, and other tactics. Consumers may also believe they are being "ripped off" when prices are increased. And waiting on store lines and poor customer service are two more key areas of consumer unhappiness.

Firms need to realize that consumer displeasure is not always transmitted to them. People may just decide not to buy a product and privately complain to friends. Usually, only a small percentage of disgruntled consumers take time to voice complaints. The true level of dissatisfaction is hidden. However, few people who are displeased, but do not complain, buy a product again. In contrast, many who complain and have their complaints resolved do buy again:

> A gripe from a customer gives a firm the chance to retain that business. Solving a complaint can mean holding on not only to that customer, but also to the 11 or 12 others the customer will likely tell about a negative experience. "If we have a customer who's not happy, other prospective customers hear about it. Bad news is like gossip. It travels quickly because it's a little juicier and people seem to remember it more," says David Heppe, sales and marketing manager of California-based Eigen Inc., a medical-equipment maker.[3]

In this chapter, the discussion is broken into three broad areas: social responsibility—which deals with issues concerning the general public and the environment, employees, channel members, stockholders, and competitors; ethics—which entails firms deciding upon and doing what is morally correct, with regard to society in general and individual consumers; and consumerism—which focuses on the rights of consumers.

Social Responsibility

Social responsibility *aids society. The* **socioecological view of marketing** *considers voluntary and involuntary consumers.*

Social responsibility involves a concern for "the consequences of a person's or firm's acts as they might affect the interests of others."[4] Corporate social responsibility means weighing the impact of company actions and behaving in a way that balances short-term profit needs with long-term societal needs. This calls both for firms to be accountable to society and for consumers to act responsibly—such as disposing of trash properly, wearing seat belts, not driving after drinking, and not being abusive to salespeople. See Figure 5-1.

From a marketing perspective, social responsibility also encompasses the **socioecological view of marketing.** According to this view, firms, their customers, and others should consider all the stages in a product's life span in developing, selling, purchasing, using, and disposing of that product. And the interests of everyone affected by a good's or service's use, including the involuntary consumers who must share the consequences of someone else's behavior, should be weighed. For example, how much of a scarce resource should a firm use in making a product? What should be the rights and responsibilities of smokers and nonsmokers (as involuntary consumers) to one another?

As one observer noted:

> In marketing, much debate has centered on the role and scope of marketing in society, and particularly marketing's role in the quality of life. A basic premise of societal marketing, as a philosophy guiding marketing efforts, is the creation of consumer satisfaction of particular consumer segments in society with the minimal social cost to society. In other words, marketers guide the development of goods and services that meet certain needs of consumer groups in a manner that may not tax other publics through pollution, product hazards, environmental clutter, energy depletion, etc.[5]

To respond to the socioecological view of marketing, many firms are now applying a concept known as "design for disassembly" (DFD)—whereby their products are designed to be disassembled in a more environmentally friendly manner once these products out-

[3] Weld F. Royal, "Cashing in on Complaints," *Sales & Marketing Management* (May 1995), p. 88.

[4] Peter D. Bennett (Editor), *Dictionary of Marketing Terms*, Second Edition (Chicago: American Marketing Association, 1995), p. 267.

[5] M. Joseph Sirgy, "Can Business and Government Help Balance the Quality of Life of Workers and Consumers?" *Journal of Business Research*, Vol. 22 (June 1991), p. 332.

© 1993 Joseph E. Seagram & Sons, Inc., NY, NY
SOMETIMES DRINKING RESPONSIBLY MEANS NOT DRINKING AT ALL. DESIGNATE A DRIVER.
JOSEPH E. SEAGRAM & SONS, INC.

FIGURE 5-1
A Socially Responsible Ad
Reprinted by permission of Joseph E. Seagram & Sons, Inc.

live their usefulness. With DFD, firms use fewer parts, less materials, and more snap-fits instead of screws, and recycle more materials. The pioneer DFD product was BMW's Z1 limited-production, two-seat roadster. It had an all-plastic exterior that could be removed from the metal chassis in 20 minutes. All major "skin" components—doors, bumpers, and panels (front, rear, and side)—were made of recyclable plastic. Among the current worldwide crop of DFD products are Siemens coffee pots, Caterpillar tractors, Xerox copiers, Kodak cameras, Hewlett-Packard workstations, BMW 3 Series autos, IBM PCs, and Northern Telecom phones.[6] See Figure 5-2.

There are times when social responsibility poses dilemmas for firms and/or their customers because popular goods and services may have potential adverse effects on consumer or societal well-being. Examples of items that offer such dilemmas are tobacco products, no-return beverage containers, food with high taste appeal but low nutritional content, crash diet plans, and liquor.

Until the 1960s, it was generally felt that marketing's role was limited to satisfying customers and generating profits. Such resources as air, water, and energy were seen as limitless. Responsibility to the general public was rarely considered. Many firms now realize they should be responsive to the general public and the environment, employees, channel members, stockholders, and competitors—as well as customers. Table 5-1 shows how marketing can be socially responsible in these areas.

This is how Weyerhaeuser, the forest products' firm, views its societal role:

> *Our [business] customers expect:* Products that consistently satisfy their performance needs. Dependability. Quality assurance, responsive service, and timely delivery—every time. Innova-

[6]Gene Bylinsky, "Manufacturing for Reuse," *Fortune* (February 6, 1995), pp. 102–112.

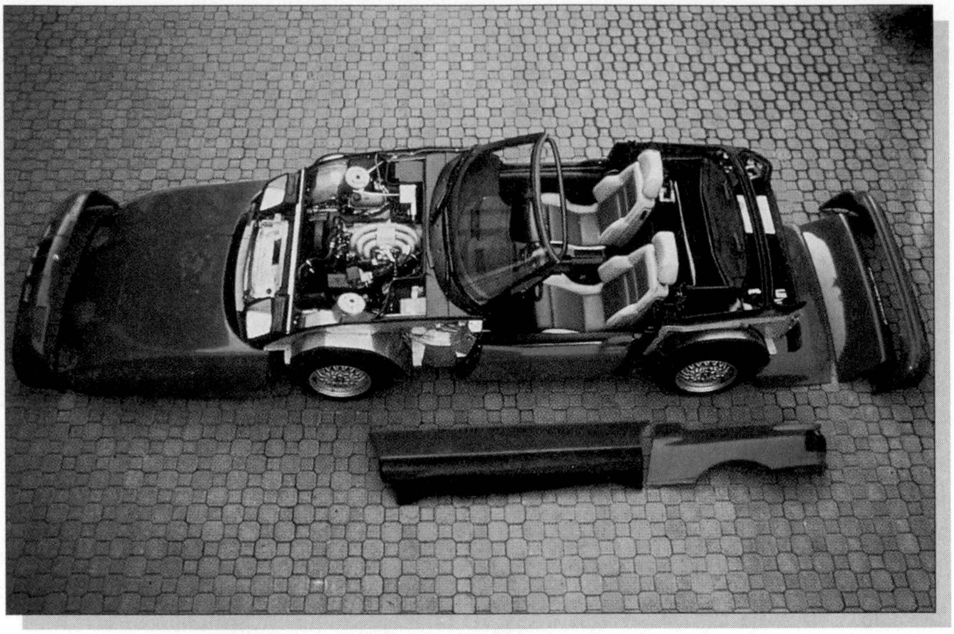

FIGURE 5-2
BMW's "Design for Disassembly"
Reprinted by permission.

tive, value-adding solutions. Suppliers that meet their own customers' standards of environmental responsibility and continuous improvement. *Our employees expect:* A safe work environment. To be respected, valued, rewarded, and listened to. To have the authority to set goals and use their skills to satisfy the customer. To be part of a winning team. To receive and give feedback. To work for a company that is ethical, well-managed, and competitive. *Our communities expect:* Forests to last forever. Clean air and water. Industry support for local jobs. Conservation of precious resources. Protection of fish, wildlife, and unique and special places. Economically viable communities. Affordable housing. Elimination of waste. Good corporate citizenship. *Our shareholders expect:* Continued management focus on creating shareholder value. Consistent improvement in operating performance. Prudent capital expenditures. A clear understanding of the company's plans and direction for the future. Clear, concise, meaningful information about the company.[7]

Company and consumer activities have a significant impact on natural resources, the landscape, pollution, and planned obsolescence. These areas are discussed next.

Natural Resources

Today, we are aware that our global supply of natural resources is not unlimited. Both consumer behavior and marketing practices have contributed to some resource shortages: "The 25 per cent of the world population in industrialized nations consumes 70 per cent of the world's resources that are used annually. As developing nations boost economic growth, demand will skyrocket."[8]

Nonetheless, resource waste goes on. Americans annually throw out 1,600 pounds of trash per person. This includes large amounts of paper, food, yard waste, aluminum, glass, plastic, tires, appliances, copper, furniture, and clothing. How do other nations compare? Canadians discard 1,400 pounds of trash per person, the Japanese 900 pounds, the Germans 825 pounds, the British 800 pounds, and the French 675 pounds. In the less-developed Ivory Coast, about 400 pounds per person are discarded.[9] The United States, with 5 per cent of the world's population, generates nearly one-half of all trash.

Although Americans spend over $30 billion each year on garbage collection and disposal—and there are 5,500 curbside recycling programs nationwide—only 20 per cent of U.S. trash is actually recycled. The most ambitious formal recycling program in the world

[7] *Weyerhaeuser 1994 Annual Report.*

[8] Emily T. Smith, "Growth Vs. Environment," *Business Week* (May 11, 1992), p. 66.

[9] Ferdinand Protzman, "Garbage," *New York Times* (July 12, 1992), Section 3, p. 1; and *Statistical Abstract of the United States 1995* (Washington, D.C.: U.S. Bureau of the Census, 1995).

Table 5-1

Illustrations of Socially Responsible Marketing Practices

Regarding the General Public and the Environment
Community involvement
Contributions to nonprofit organizations
Hiring hard-core unemployed
Product recycling
Eliminating offensive signs and billboards
Properly disposing of waste materials
Using goods and services requiring low levels of environmental resources

Regarding Employees
Ample internal communications
Employee input empowerment into decisions
Employee training about social issues and appropriate responses to them
No reprisals against employees who uncover questionable company policies
Recognizing socially responsible employees

Regarding Channel Members
Honoring both verbal and written commitments
Fairly distributing scarce goods and services
Accepting reasonable requests by channel members
Encouraging channel members to act responsibly
No coercion of channel members
Cooperative programs addressed to the general public and the environment

Regarding Stockholders
Honest reporting and financial disclosure
Publicity about company activities
Stockholder participation in setting socially responsible policy
Explaining social issues affecting the company
Earning a responsible profit

Regarding Competitors
Adhering to high standards of performance
No illegal or unethical acts to hinder competitors
Cooperative programs for the general public and environment
No actions that would lead competitors to waste resources

is in Germany, where 80 per cent of all packaging materials—from aluminum to paper—must be recycled.[10]

The depletion of natural resources can be reduced if the consumption of scarce materials is lessened and more efficient alternatives are chosen; fewer disposable items—such as soda cans, pens, and cigarette lighters—are bought; products are given longer life spans; and styles are changed less frequently. Convenient recycling and repair facilities, better

Resource depletion can be slowed by reducing consumption, improving efficiency, limiting disposables, and lengthening products' lives.

[10]David Fischer, "Turning Trash into Cash," *U.S. News & World Report* (July 17, 1995), p. 43; Jeff Bailey, "Curbside Recycling Comforts the Soul, But Benefits Are Scarce," *Wall Street Journal* (January 19, 1995), pp. A1, A8; "A Guilt-Free Guide to Garbage," *Consumer Reports* (February 1994), pp. 91–113; and Marilyn Stern, "Is This the Ultimate in Recycling?" *Across the Board* (May 1993), pp. 28–31.

trade-in arrangements, such common facilities as apartments (which share electricity, water, and so on), and simpler packaging can also contribute to more efficient resource use.

Progressive actions require cooperation among business, stockholders, government, employees, the general public, consumers, and others. They also involve changes in lifestyles and corporate ingenuity:

> This is perhaps the ultimate recycling system: a popcorn bag becomes a seat belt, a seat belt becomes a shirt, a shirt becomes a sheet of packaging film, the packaging film becomes a videotape, the videotape becomes an X-ray, and (after many more metamorphoses) may become a popcorn bag again.[11]

The Landscape

Garbage dumps and landfills, discarded beverage containers, and abandoned cars are examples of items marring the landscape.

In the United States, two-thirds of discarded materials are disposed of in dumps and landfills. But currently, many U.S. communities are not allowing new dumps and landfills, existing ones are closing for environmental reasons (there are now less than 6,000 landfills, down from 18,000 at their peak), and recycling efforts are being stepped up at existing dumps and landfills. In several areas of Europe and Japan, landfills are already at capacity—hence, a greater interest there in recycling and incineration.[12]

Dumps and littering have become major factors in marring the landscape. Various communities have enacted rules to lessen them.

At one time, virtually all beverage containers were recycled. Then, no-return bottles and cans were developed; and littering at roadsides and other areas became a major problem. To reduce litter, there are several state and local laws requiring beverage containers to have deposit fees that are refunded when consumers return empty containers. Many manufacturers and retailers feel the laws unfairly hold them responsible for container disposal, since littering is done by consumers—not them. Also, the labor and recycling costs associated with container returns have led to slightly higher beverage prices. Presently, container laws are just moderately effective;[13] and consumers must be better educated as to the value of proper disposal.

Cars are sometimes abandoned on streets, where they are then stripped of usable parts. One suggestion to cover the disposal of a car is to include an amount in its original price or in a transfer tax. For example, Maryland has a small fee on title transfers to aid in the removal of abandoned cars.

Other ways to reduce the marring of the landscape include limits or bans on billboards and roadside signs, fines for littering, and better trade-ins for autos and appliances. Neighborhood associations, merchant self-regulation, area planning and zoning, and consumer education can also improve appreciation for the landscape. Keeping the landscape attractive is a cooperative effort. A merchant cleanup patrol cannot overcome pedestrians who throw litter on the street rather than in waste baskets.

Here is what Nike is doing to help:

> Around the world, the company famous for making shoes to wear on basketball courts is now making courts out of shoes. And running tracks and playground mats, to boot. So far, Nike's "Reuse a Shoe" program has recycled more than one million used and defective shoes. And not just Nikes—all sneakers are equal in the great polymer melting pot. Nike's shoes-to-court formula was first concocted, appropriately, in the Michael Jordan Building at Nike's Beaverton, Oregon, headquarters when its scientists wondered if there was a better, and cheaper, alternative to dumping old shoes and factory rejects in the world's landfills. Nike, which preaches environmental kindness, was spending some $300,000 a year on landfill and getting a bad conscience, too—some shoe materials take 100 years to break down.[14]

[11]*DuPont 1994 Annual Report.*

[12]*Statistical Abstract of the United States 1995*; George C. Lodge and Jeffrey F. Rayport, "Knee-Deep and Rising: America's Recycling Costs," *Harvard Business Review*, Vol. 69 (September–October 1991), pp. 128–139; and Subrata N. Chakravarty, "Dean Buntrock's Green Machine," *Forbes* (August 2, 1993), pp. 96–100.

[13]See Stephanie Anderson Forest, "There's Gold in Those Hills of Soda Bottles," *Business Week* (September 11, 1995), p. 48.

[14]Roger Thurow, "Nike Makes Old Shoes Resurface as New Courts," *Wall Street Journal* (April 7, 1995), p. B12.

Environmental Pollution

Dangerous pollutants need to be eliminated and safe substitutes found. The Environmental Protection Agency (EPA) is the major U.S. government agency involved with pollution; a number of state agencies are also quite active in this area. Numerous other nations have their own government agencies to deal with this issue.

Environmental pollution can be generated by spray-can propellants, the ocean dumping of industrial waste, lead from gasoline and paint, pesticides, sulfur oxide and other factory emissions, improper disposal of garbage, and other pollutants. As one observer noted:

> To those doubting the wisdom of pollution control—those who believe there is a conflict between economic growth and environmental protection—let them see the Vistula River in Poland; over 80 per cent is so corrosive that it is useless for even cooling machinery. Let them see sulfur dioxide levels in Krakow, so high that 500-year-old monuments have crumbled in just 40 years. Pollution is not an economic shortcut. In the long run, it will only drain economies and make living conditions unproductive.[15]

Both government and business actions are needed to reduce dangerous environmental pollution.

While greater attention is being paid to it, environmental pollution will be a big challenge for the foreseeable future. That is why the U.S. Clean Air Act of 1990 has specific standards and goals to reduce the level of smog, toxic emissions, and acid rain. It is also why 30,000 people—from 180 nations—attended a 1992 United Nations' Earth Summit in Rio de Janeiro, Brazil. Here are examples of how the pollution challenge is being addressed.

Government and industry in the United States, Western Europe, and Japan spend a combined total of more than $300 billion annually on environmental protection. In addition, anti-pollution expenditures have gone up dramatically in several less-developed nations in Latin America, Asia, and Africa.

Among the voluntary activities of companies and associations are:

- New PCs, printers, monitors, and other devices automatically "power down" when not in use to reduce air pollution and conserve energy. See Figure 5-3.
- The Chemical Manufacturers Association has been working with the EPA to keep hazardous compounds out of the environment. See Figure 5-4.
- 3M devotes 15 per cent of its overall research-and-development budget to projects involving environmental protection.
- Japan's Ebara Corporation uses its own technology to remove harmful sulphur dioxides and nitrogen oxides from power plants more efficiently.
- A number of firms have joined together to form the Global Environmental Management Initiative (GEMI), with the goal of fostering an exchange of information about environmental protection programs.
- Sun Co., the parent of Sunoco, was the first big firm to sign the Coalition for Environmentally Responsible Economies (CERES) principles—which were drawn up by the National Wildlife Federation, among others.[16]

Planned Obsolescence

Planned obsolescence *can involve materials, styles, and functions.*

Planned obsolescence is a marketing practice that capitalizes on short-run material wearout, style changes, and functional product changes.

In material planned obsolescence, firms choose materials and components that are subject to comparatively early breakage, wear, rot, or corrosion. For example, the makers

[15]William K. Reilly, "Environment, Inc.," *Business Horizons*, Vol. 35 (March–April 1992), p. 9.

[16]Jerry J. Jasinowski, "Business Is America's Leading Environmentalist," *Christian Science Monitor* (April 21, 1995), p. 19; Richard A. Westin, "Global Climate Change," *Columbia Journal of World Business*, Vol. 27 (Spring 1992), p. 82; Lee M. Thomas, "The Business Community and the Environment: An Important Partnership," *Business Horizons*, Vol. 35 (March–April 1992), p. 24; and Faye Rice, "Who Scores Best on the Environment," *Fortune* (July 26, 1993), pp. 114–118.

FIGURE 5-3
"Powering Down"
Reprinted by permission.

of disposable lighters and razors use this form of planned obsolescence in a constructive manner by offering inexpensive, short-life convenient products. However, there is growing resistance to material planned obsolescence because of its effects on natural resources and the landscape.

In style planned obsolescence, a firm makes minor changes to differentiate this year's offering from last year's. Since some people are style-conscious, they are willing to discard old items while they are still functional so as to acquire new ones with more status. This is common with fashion items and cars.

With functional planned obsolescence, a firm introduces new product features or improvements to generate consumer dissatisfaction with currently owned products. Sometimes, features or improvements may have been withheld from an earlier model to gain faster repurchases. A style change may accompany a functional one to raise consumer awareness of a "new" product. This form of planned obsolescence occurs most often with high-tech items such as computers.

Marketers reply to criticisms thusly: Planned obsolescence is responsive to people's desires as to prices, styles, and features and is not coercive; without product turnover, people would be disenchanted by the lack of choices; consumers like disposable items and often discard them before they lose their effectiveness; firms use materials that hold down prices; competition requires firms to offer the best products possible and not hold back improvements; and, for such products as clothing, people desire continuous style changes.

A number of firms have enacted innovative strategies with regard to planned obsolescence. For example, Kodak and Fuji have programs for recycling their single-use disposable cameras, after people take them to photoprocessing labs. Canon has a factory in China that reconditions and refills used copier cartridges. SKF of Sweden is a worldwide bearings maker; to increase the life of its products, it has added more preventative maintenance services.

What's the **most important thing** to do after keeping **93%** of our toxic chemical waste out of the environment?
Work on the other 7%.
© 1994 CMA
CHEMICAL MANUFACTURERS ASSOCIATION
The EPA and the Chemical Manufacturers Association have targeted 311 compounds as top priorities for action. We kept 93% of these compounds out of the environment through treatment, recycling and energy conversion. While we feel our most recent report was good, we know there's more work to be done. Find out more about how our 180 members and partners are working for change. **Call 1-800-624-4321.**
RESPONSIBLE CARE

FIGURE 5-4
Eliminating Dangerous Pollutants
Copyright Chemical Manufacturers Association. Reprinted by permission.

The Benefits and Costs of Social Responsibility

Social responsibility has benefits as well as costs; these need to be balanced.

Socially responsible actions have both benefits and costs. Among the benefits are improved worker and public health, as reflected in fewer and less severe accidents, longer life spans, and less disease; cleaner air; better resource use; economic growth; a better business image; an educated public; government cooperation; an attractive, safe environment; an enhanced standard of living; and self-satisfaction for the firm. Many of these benefits cannot be quantified. Nonetheless, expectations are that the U.S. Clean Air Act and other nations' laws will ultimately save thousands and thousands of lives each year, protect food crops, reduce medical costs, and lead to clearer skies.

Although some social-responsibility expenditures are borne by a broad cross-section of firms and the general public (via taxes and higher product prices), the benefits of many environmental and other programs are enjoyed primarily by those living or working in affected areas. The costs of socially responsible actions can be high. For instance, U.S. environmental-protection spending is expected to amount to 2.5 per cent—$200 billion—of the annual Gross Domestic Product by the year 2000.[17] Various environmentally questionable products that are efficient have been greatly modified or removed from the marketplace, such as leaded gasoline. Because of various legal restrictions and fears of law suits, new-product planning tends to be more conservative; and resources are often allotted to prevention rather than invention. Furthermore, trade-offs have to be made in determining which programs are more deserving of funding. See Figure 5-5.

[17]Noah Walley and Bradley Whitehead, "It's Not Easy Being Green," *Harvard Business Review*, Vol. 72 (May–June 1994), p. 49.

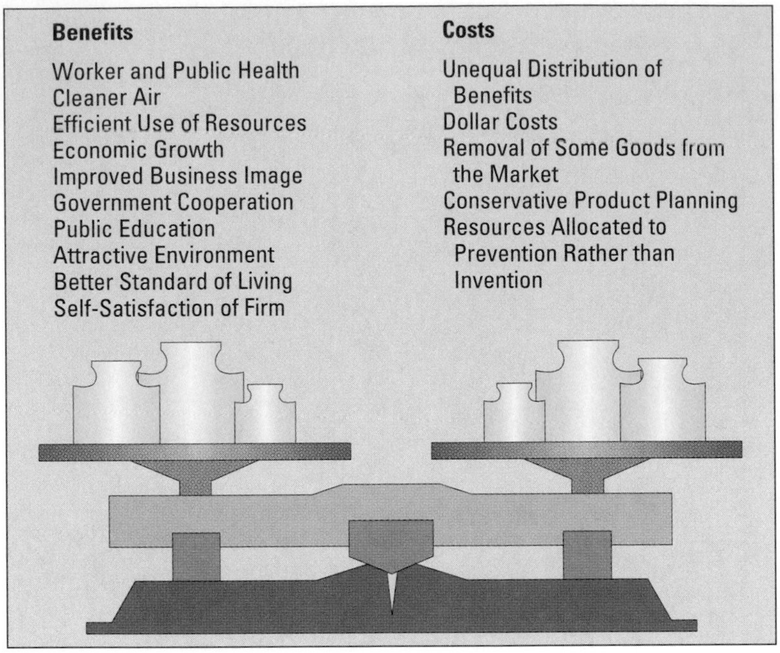
Benefits
Worker and Public Health
Cleaner Air
Efficient Use of Resources
Economic Growth
Improved Business Image
Government Cooperation
Public Education
Attractive Environment
Better Standard of Living
Self-Satisfaction of Firm
Costs
Unequal Distribution of Benefits
Dollar Costs
Removal of Some Goods from the Market
Conservative Product Planning
Resources Allocated to Prevention Rather than Invention

FIGURE 5-5
The Benefits and Costs of Social Responsibility

Green marketing *efforts will expand during this decade.*

For socially responsible efforts to be effective, all parties must partake in the process—sharing benefits and costs. This means business, consumers, government, channel members, and others. The rest of the 1990s promises to see the further emergence of **green marketing,** a form of socioecological marketing, whereby the goods and services sold, and the marketing practices involved in their sale, take into account environmental ramifications for society as a whole. To succeed in green marketing, firms must be sure not to mislead consumers or create unrealistic expectations about reformulated products' ability to be recycled, not to pollute, and so on.

Ethics

Ethical behavior *involves honest and proper conduct.*

In any marketing situation, **ethical behavior** based on honest and proper conduct ("what is right" and "what is wrong") should be followed. This applies both to situations involving company actions that affect the general public, employees, channel members, stockholders, and/or competitors and to situations involving company dealings with consumers.

Figure 5-6 (on page 124) outlines an ethical decision/action process—with a moral decision structure, decision maker traits, situational factors, and outcomes. Figure 5-7 (on page 125) shows the code of ethics of the American Marketing Association.

Of particular importance in the study of ethics are answers to these two questions: How do people determine whether an act is ethical or unethical? Why do they act ethically or unethically?[18] People *determine* (learn) whether given actions are ethical or not through their upbringing, education, job environment, and life-long experiences—and others' responses to their behavior. In addition, people may apply their own cognitive reasoning skills to decide what is morally acceptable. People *act* ethically or unethically based on their expectations of the rewards or punishments—financial, social, and so forth—flowing from their actions. They consider both the magnitude of the rewards or punishments (such as the size of a raise or the maximum fine that could be imposed on a company) and the likelihood of their occurrence (such as the probability of getting a large raise or having a large fine imposed on the firm).

Ethics theories range from egoism to virtue ethics.

Various ethical theories try to explain why people and organizations act in particular ways. Here are four of them, applied to marketing:

- *Egoism*—a theory asserting that individuals act exclusively in their own self-interest. Example: A product manager postpones investing in improvements for a mature prod-

[18]Shelby D. Hunt, "Foundations of the Hunt-Vitell Theory of Ethics," presented at the 1995 AMA Faculty Consortium on Ethics and Social Responsibility in Marketing (Hempstead, N.Y.: Hofstra University).

Ethics IN TODAY'S SOCIETY

How Much Should Regulations Be Regulated?

In recent years, this question has been asked repeatedly: "How much U.S. government regulation is enough?" And the status of Vernon Garner shows why:

> Vernon Garner, president of his family's $9.7 million trucking firm in Findlay, Ohio, trekked to Capitol Hill recently to relate a tale of regulatory woe. Appearing before a House subcommittee, Garner told legislators that compliance with two Environmental Protection Agency laws forced his firm to invest $352,000 in new facilities that require $68,500 yearly to maintain.
>
> Garner said neither the water nor the air is cleaner because of the pond Garner Trucking had to dig or the new fuel tanks it had to install. "Perhaps, I could understand the need for this if I'd been in violation of something," he told the subcommittee. "But, I've never been cited for an environmental offense. I've already put a lot of money into equipment, record keeping, and training to comply with environmental rules. I just want to know—when is it going to stop?"

Critics of government regulation feel that many rules are too costly, have little positive effect on society, inhibit firms from being innovative, and lead to more goods and services being produced in foreign markets. Some even suggest that a strict cost-benefit analysis be conducted before any new rules are enacted. This would ensure that "regulations do more good than harm."

On the other side, there are numerous strong advocates of government regulations. They are quite concerned that important regulations affecting deceptive business practices, marketplace competition, drinking-water purity, food safety, and worker health may be dropped as a result of anti-regulation forces. Such actions could have long-term detrimental affects on consumer and worker quality of life.

What do you think about limiting U.S. government regulations? Why?

Source: Based on material in Linda Grant, "Shutting Down the Regulatory Machine," *U.S. News & World Report* (February 13, 1995), pp. 70–72.

uct because he or she expects to be promoted within the next six months and wants to maximize short-term profits.

- *Utilitarianism*—a theory asserting that individual and organizational actions are proper only if these actions yield the greatest good for the most people (the highest net benefit). Example: A pharmaceutical company markets any Food and Drug Administration approved drug with some side effects as long as it helps more people combat a particular disease than the number affected by the (minor) side effect.
- *Duty-Based*—a theory asserting that the rightness of an action is not based on its consequences, but rather is based on the premise that certain actions are proper because they stem from basic obligations. Example: A supermarket chain sets below-average prices in a low-income area even thought this adversely affects company profits in that community.
- *Virtue Ethics*—a theory asserting that actions should be guided by an individual's or organization's seeking goodness and virtue ("living a good life"). Example: A virtuous company is totally truthful in its advertising, packaging, and selling efforts—and does not stoop to manipulative appeals to persuade customers.[19]

[19]Gene R. Laczniak and Patrick E. Murphy, *Ethical Marketing Decisions: The Higher Road* (Needham Heights, Mass.: Allyn & Bacon, 1993), pp. 28–42.

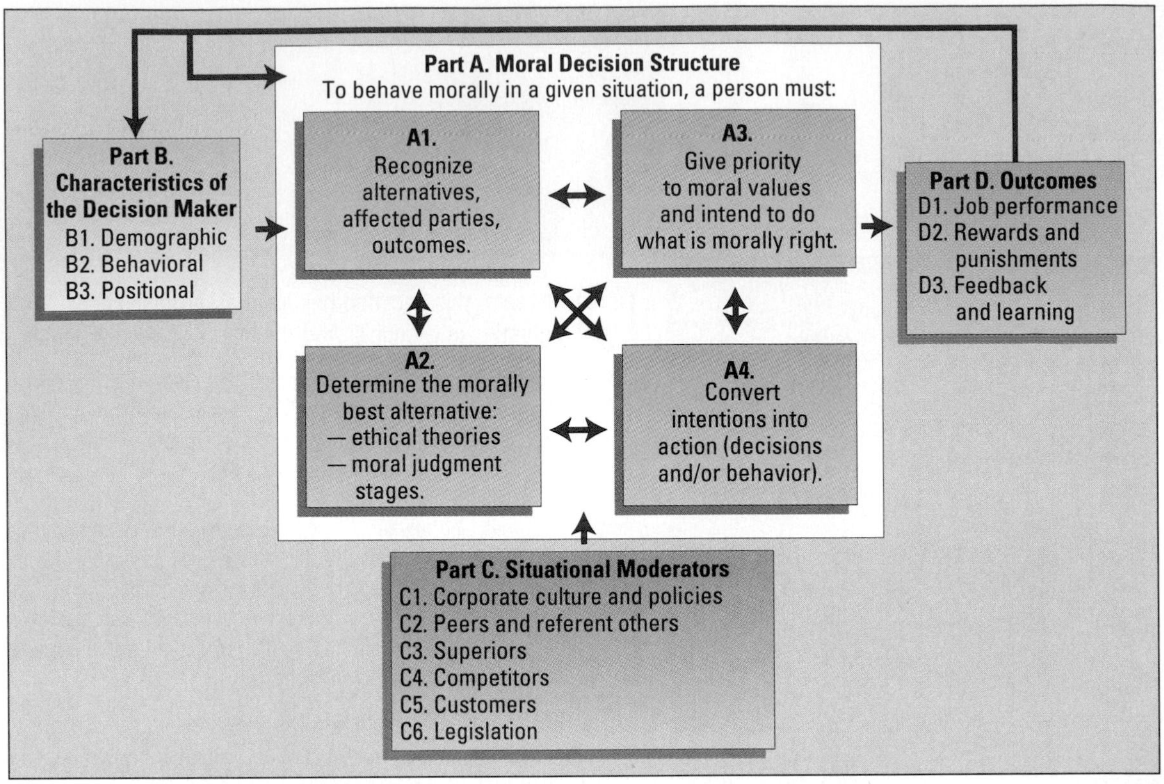

FIGURE 5-6
An Ethical Decision/Action Process
Source: Thomas R. Wotruba, "A Comprehensive Framework for the Analysis of Ethical Behavior, with a Focus on Sales Organizations," *Journal of Personal Selling & Sales Management*, Vol. 10 (Spring 1990), p. 31. *Reprinted by permission.*

Marketers need to consider **process-related** *and* **product-related ethical issues.**

Ethical issues in marketing can generally be divided into two categories: process-related and product-related.[20] **Process-related ethical issues** involve "the unethical use of marketing strategies or tactics." Examples include bait-and-switch advertising, price fixing, selling products overseas that have been found unsafe in the United States, and bribing purchasing agents of large customers. **Product-related ethical issues** involve "the ethical appropriateness of marketing certain products." For example, should tobacco products, sugar-coated cereals, and political candidates be marketed? More specifically, should cigarettes be sold? Should there be restrictions on their sales? Should cigarette ads be allowed? Should cigarette taxes be raised to discourage use? Should smoking be banned in offices, restaurants, and planes?

These comments sum up the complexity of many ethical issues:

> Some employees may believe unethical activity is in the company's best interest and is thus expected of them—or will at least be tolerated. Top management wants employees to be ethical and tells them so, but some people may not believe it, thinking instead that requests to be ethical are simply window dressing. Because of their loyalty to their company, they engage in unethical conduct. Some employees act unethically because they may believe this conduct is in their self-interest. Those who want to get ahead sometimes seek ways to distinguish themselves by outperforming others. Such employees may believe that unethical conduct is a way to improve their performance and is, thus, in their self-interest. Other employees may not always know they're doing something unethical. There certainly is a sense in which ethics is a matter of opinion—an art rather than a science. Where is the line between the sharp deal and the shady deal? Between profit maximization and social irresponsibility? Between clever advertising and fraud? These can sometimes be difficult questions for an employee to answer.[21]

[20]Gene R. Laczniak, Robert F. Lusch, and William A. Strang, "Ethical Marketing: Perceptions of Economic Goods and Social Problems," *Journal of Macromarketing*, Vol. 1 (Spring 1981), p. 49.

[21]John Collins, "Why Bad Things Happen to Good Companies—And What Can Be Done," *Business Horizons*, Vol. 33 (November–December 1990), p. 18. See also Donald P. Robin, R. Eric Reidenbach, and P. J. Forrest, "The Importance of an Ethical Issue as an Influence on the Ethical Decision-Making of Ad Managers," *Journal of Business Research*, Vol. 35 (January 1996), pp. 17–28.

CODE OF ETHICS

Members of the American Marketing Association (AMA) are committed to ethical professional conduct. They have joined together in subscribing to this Code of Ethics embracing the following topics:

Responsibilities of the Marketer

Marketers must accept responsibility for the consequence of their activities and make every effort to ensure that their decisions, recommendations, and actions function to identify, serve, and satisfy all relevant publics: customers, organizations and society.

Marketers' professional conduct must be guided by:

1. The basic rule of professional ethics: not knowingly to do harm;
2. The adherence to all applicable laws and regulations;
3. The accurate representation of their education, training and experience; and
4. The active support, practice and promotion of this Code of Ethics.

Honesty and Fairness

Marketers shall uphold and advance the integrity, honor, and dignity of the marketing profession by:

1. Being honest in serving customers, clients, employees, suppliers, distributors and the public;
2. Not knowingly participating in conflict of interest without prior notice to all parties involved; and
3. Establishing equitable fee schedules including the payment or receipt of usual, customary and/or legal compensation or marketing exchanges.

Rights and Duties of Parties in the Marketing Exchange Process

Participants in the marketing exchange process should be able to expect that:

1. Products and services offered are safe and fit for their intended uses;
2. Communications about offered products and services are not deceptive;
3. All parties intend to discharge their obligations, financial and otherwise, in good faith; and
4. Appropriate internal methods exist for equitable adjustment and/or redress of grievances concerning purchases.

It is understood that the above would include, but is not limited to, the following responsiblities of the marketer:

In the area of product development and management,

• disclosure of all substantial risks associated with product or service usage;
• identification of any product component substitution that might materially change the product or impact on the buyer's purchase decision;
• identification of extra-cost added features.

In the area of promotions,

• avoidance of false and misleading advertising;
• rejection of high pressure manipulation.
• avoidance of sales promotions that use deception or manipulation.

In the area of distribution,

• not manipulating the availability of a product for purpose of exploitation;
• not using coercion in the marketing channel;
• not exerting undue influence over the reseller's choice to handle the product.

In the area of pricing,

• not engaging in price fixing;
• not practicing predatory pricing;
• disclosing the full price associated with any purchase.

In the area of marketing research,

• prohibiting selling or fund raising under the guise of conducting research;
• maintaining research integrity by avoiding misrepresentation and omission of pertinent research data;
• treating outside clients and suppliers fairly.

Organizational Relationships

Marketers should be aware of how their behavior may influence or impact on the behior of others in organizational relationships. They should not demand, encourage or apply coercion to obtain unethical behavior in their relationships with others, such as employees, suppliers or customers:

1. Apply confidentiality and anonymity in professional relationships with regard to privileged information;
2. Meet their obligations and responsibilities in contracts and mutual agreements in a timely manner;
3. Avoid taking the work of others, in whole, or in part, and represent this work as their own or directly benefit from it without compensation or consent of the originator or owner;
4. Avoid manipulation to take advantage of situations to maximize personal welfare in a way that unfairly deprives or damages the organization of others.

Any AMA members found to be in violation of any provision of this Code of Ethics may have his or her Association membership suspended or revoked.

FIGURE 5-7
The American Marketing Association's Code of Ethics
Reprinted by permission.

Thus, to maintain the highest possible ethical conduct by employees, the senior executives in a firm must make a major commitment to ethics, communicate standards of conduct to every employee (perhaps via a written ethics code), reward ethical behavior, and discourage unethical behavior.

Next, ethics is examined from four vantage points: a business perspective, a consumer perspective, an international perspective, and the teachability of ethics.

A Business Perspective

Many companies have ethics codes; some have implicit standards.

Over three-quarters of the firms listed in the U.S. *Fortune 500* have formal ethics codes. Some codes are general and, thus, similar to organizational mission statements; others are specific and operational. In contrast, French, British, and German firms are less apt to have formal codes; acceptable standards of behavior are more implied. Why? According to one ethics expert: "American society guarantees people the right to determine their moral values and obligations, but it really doesn't offer guidelines on how to fulfill them. Thus, it depends less on roles and traditions and more on laws and formal statements of ethics."[22]

One of the most complex aspects of business ethics relates to setting the boundaries as to what is ethical. To address this, the following scale was devised and tested with a variety of marketing personnel. The scale suggests that businesspeople would make better decisions if they consider whether a specific marketing action (is):[23]

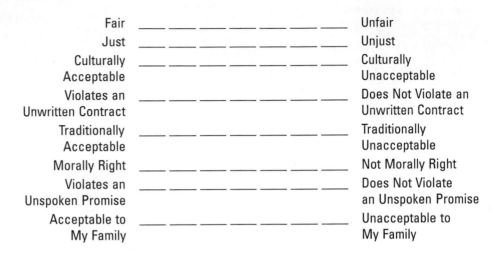

Fair	___	___	___	___	___	___	___	Unfair
Just	___	___	___	___	___	___	___	Unjust
Culturally Acceptable	___	___	___	___	___	___	___	Culturally Unacceptable
Violates an Unwritten Contract	___	___	___	___	___	___	___	Does Not Violate an Unwritten Contract
Traditionally Acceptable	___	___	___	___	___	___	___	Traditionally Unacceptable
Morally Right	___	___	___	___	___	___	___	Not Morally Right
Violates an Unspoken Promise	___	___	___	___	___	___	___	Does Not Violate an Unspoken Promise
Acceptable to My Family	___	___	___	___	___	___	___	Unacceptable to My Family

Here are examples showing varying business responses to ethical issues:

Cause-related marketing *has good and bad points.*

- **Cause-related marketing** is a somewhat controversial practice. With it, profit-oriented firms contribute specific amounts to given nonprofit organizations for each consumer purchase of certain goods and services during a special promotion (such as sponsorship of a sport for the 1998 Winter Olympics). It has been used by such firms as American Express and MasterCard, and such nonprofit groups as the Red Cross. Advocates feel cause-related marketing stimulates direct and indirect contributions and benefits the images of both the profit-oriented firms and the nonprofit institutions involved in it. Critics feel there is too much commercialism on the part of nonprofit groups and implicit endorsements for sponsor products.
- According to a recent survey, CEOs of large American firms overwhelmingly feel it is always wrong to use misleading advertising or labeling, sell goods and services that have poor safety, dump banned or flawed products in foreign markets, and cause environmental harm.
- Mary Kay Cosmetics was one of the first companies to halt product testing on animals. As its vice-chairman noted, "Our goal was to take the high ground. The decision meant putting a hold on new products for a while, which meant lost sales. Ethical decision making, by its very nature, is relative—what will be the effect of our decision on others? Is the decision right, not only for us, but also for society? Ethical corporate conduct is not easy and can be costly, but I believe ethics is good business."
- "Despite some recent reforms, U.S. hotels still have phone fees that are hard to detect and harder to believe. Even well-respected chains like Marriott and Hilton Hotels charge guests $4 or $5 for calls that cost them pennies in long-distance fees. Others charge guests for calls they never made or go to imaginative lengths to hide high fees. Each year, the lodging industry charges $1.8 billion in phone fees, which range from $1 for local calls to a 300 per cent "service charge" for long distance. In the past,

[22]Joanne B. Ciulla, "Why Is Business Talking About Ethics?: Reflections on Foreign Conversations," *California Management Review*, Vol. 34 (Fall 1991), pp. 73–76.

[23]R. Eric Reidenbach, Donald P. Robin, and Lyndon Dawson, "An Application and Extension of a Multidimensional Ethics Scale to Selected Marketing Practices and Marketing Groups," *Journal of the Academy of Marketing Science*, Vol. 19 (Spring 1991), p. 84.

hotels argued they were barely making money from their phones. But hotel profits have soared 50 per cent since 1990."[24]

A Consumer Perspective

Consumers should act as ethically to businesses as they expect to be treated.

Just as businesses have a responsibility to act in an ethical and a societally oriented way, so do consumers. Their actions impact on businesses, other consumers, the general public, the environment, and so on. In marketing transactions, ethical standards can truly be maintained only if both sellers and buyers act in a mutually respectful, honest, fair, and responsible manner.

Yet, especially with regard to broad societal issues, consumers may find it hard to decide what is acceptable. Daniel Yankelovich (an expert in the area) says a society goes through seven stages to form a consensus on major issues (such as how to deal with health care):

1. People begin to become aware of an issue.
2. They develop a sense of urgency about it.
3. They start exploring choices for dealing with the issue.
4. There is resistance to costs and trade-offs—leading to wishful thinking.
5. The pros and cons of alternatives are weighed.
6. People take a stand intellectually.
7. A responsible judgment is made morally and emotionally.[25]

In terms of consumer perceptions about whether specific activities on their part are proper, a large-scale study on ethical beliefs in the United States offers some interesting insights: First, people have a rather high level of ethical concern about some acts that could be done by consumers (with ethical concern measured as strongly agreeing—answer 1—or agreeing—answer 2—that given actions are wrong). See Table 5-2. Second, ethical perceptions are affected by how often consumers themselves engage in these actions, whether deceitful or fraudulent behavior is involved, and the degree to which sellers are harmed. Third, the strongest ethical concerns belong to older people with lower levels of education and income; younger, better educated, and more affluent people have less concern.[26]

An International Perspective

Ethical decisions can be complicated on an international level.

Ethical standards are more complex to assess in an international setting due to several factors. First, different societies have their own views of acceptable behavior regarding interpersonal conduct, communications, and business practices. Second, there may be misunderstandings due to language translations. Third, in less-developed nations, there may be less concern for social and consumer issues than for improving the level of industrialization. Fourth, in their self-interest, governments in some nations may devise questionable rules to protect domestic firms. Fifth, executives are usually more aware of ethical standards in their home nations than in foreign ones. Sixth, international ethical disputes may be hard to mediate; under whose jurisdiction are disputes involving firms from separate nations?

Here are some views of the ethical challenges on the international level:

- U.S. executives generally feel there are just minor differences in ethics as practiced in the United States, Canada, and Northern Europe. However, there are "some de-

[24]Daniel Shannon, "Doing Well by Doing Good," *Promo* (February 1996), pp. 29–33; Gene R. Laczniak, Marvin W. Berkowitz, Russell G. Booker, and James P. Hale, "The Ethics of Business: Improving or Deteriorating?" *Business Horizons*, Vol. 38 (January–February 1995), p. 43; Richard C. Bartlett, "Mary Kay's Foundation," *Journal of Business Strategy*, Vol. 16 (July–August 1995), p. 16; and Jonathan Dahl, "Before You Use the Hotel Phone, Read This," *Wall Street Journal* (August 2, 1994), pp. B1, B4.

[25]Daniel Yankelovich, "How Public Opinion Really Works," *Fortune* (October 5, 1992), p. 103.

[26]James A. Muncy and Scott J. Vitell, "Consumer Ethics: An Investigation of the Ethical Beliefs of the Final Consumer," *Journal of Business Research*, Vol. 24 (June 1992), pp. 297–311.

Table 5-2

Selected Consumer Beliefs About Ethical Behavior on Their Part

	STRONGLY BELIEVE IT IS WRONG 1	2	3	4	STRONGLY BELIEVE IT IS NOT WRONG 5
Changing price-tags on merchandise in a retail store	81%	16%	1%	0%	2%
Drinking a can of soda in a supermarket without paying for it	71%	28%	1%	0%	1%
Using a long-distance telephone access code that does not belong to you	65%	30%	3%	1%	1%
Reporting a lost item as "stolen" to an insurance company in order to collect the money	58%	34%	5%	2%	1%
Giving misleading price information to a clerk for an unpriced item	53%	42%	3%	1%	1%
Getting too much change and not saying anything	42%	45%	6%	5%	1%
Observing someone shoplifting and ignoring it	38%	43%	15%	4%	1%
Stretching the truth on an income-tax return	34%	41%	12%	10%	3%
Joining a record club just to get some free records without any intention of buying	29%	41%	13%	13%	4%
Using computer software or games you did not buy	12%	25%	39%	18%	6%
Returning merchandise after trying it and not liking it	8%	14%	15%	46%	16%
Taping a movie off the TV	4%	9%	20%	37%	30%

Note: There are some rounding errors in the above percentages.

Source: James A. Muncy and Scott J. Vitell, "Consumer Ethics: An Investigation of the Ethical Beliefs of the Final Consumer," *Journal of Business Research*, Vol. 24 (June 1992), p. 303. Reprinted by permission of Elsevier Science Publishing Company, Inc. Copyright (c) 1992.

partures" in ethical practices when doing business in Southern Europe—such as Italy and Spain—and a "tremendous" difference in the underdeveloped nations. With the latter, "it's difficult. You'll be tested constantly, and, at times, you'll think you've lost business."

- "The Japanese are a special case. Take gift giving. It is an important part of how they conduct themselves. There is little thought given to the idea: 'Give me the business and I'll give you a gift.'"
- "A kind of noblesse oblige (honor) still exists among the business classes in Canada, Great Britain, Australia, and perhaps Germany. Conversely, in the United States, where there is a less entrenched business group, the prevailing attitude is that you make it whatever way you can."
- "Whether U.S. standards are in fact higher [or lower] than those abroad is likely to remain a moot point. But, in one respect, the United States stands alone: It is the only nation that has sought legislation to legislate moral business conduct overseas [via the Foreign Corrupt Practices Act prohibiting improper sales tactics by U.S. firms in international markets]."[27]

Firms that market internationally need to keep three points in mind: One, *core business values* provide the foundation for worldwide ethics codes. Core values are company prin-

[27]Andrew W. Singer, "Ethics: Are Standards Lower Overseas?" *Across the Board* (September 1991), pp. 31–34.

International Marketing in Action

Is There a Common Ground Between Russian and American Ethics?

A four-quadrant matrix may be used to compare the ethical values of Russian and American businesspeople:

- Quadrant I—Consists of practices viewed as ethical by both Russians and Americans. These include keeping one's word, maintaining trust, competing fairly, and receiving rewards that are commensurate with performance.
- Quadrant II—Consists of practices viewed as unethical by businesspeople in both countries. These include gangsterism, racketeering and extortion; black market activity; price gouging; and refusing to pay bills.
- Quadrant III—Consists of practices viewed as ethical by Russians, but unethical by Americans. These include showing personal favoritism, making "grease" payments (to facilitate transactions), manipulating data, fixing prices, and ignoring "senseless" laws and regulations.
- Quadrant IV—Consists of practices viewed as ethical by Americans, but not by Russians. These include maximizing profits, high salary differentials between management and workers, employee layoffs, and whistleblowing (reporting poor company practices to others).

By understanding this matrix, Russian and American businesspeople can acquire a better appreciation for each other's behavior. Nonetheless, American firms doing business in Russia (and visa versa) must still decide whether Russian managers are accountable to Russian or American ethical standards.

The differences in Russian and American ethical standards are due to such factors as Russia's rapid transition to a free-market economy, Russia's lack of a strong legal structure, Russian experiences under Communism, and Russian notions about the social and economic inequality of capitalism. One way of developing ethical measures acceptable to both Russians and Americans is to jointly set standards. Americans should explain why some Russian standards are viewed as questionable and Russians should state their viewpoints.

As marketing manager for a U.S. firm selling U.S. cosmetics in Russia, use the above information to devise an ethical code for your Russian operations.

Source: Based on material in Sheila M. Puffer and Daniel J. McCarthy, "Finding the Common Ground in Russian and American Business Ethics," *California Management Review,* Vol. 37 (Winter 1995), pp. 29–46.

ciples "that are so fundamental they will not be compromised" in any foreign markets. These include nonmaleficence (to not knowingly do harm), promise keeping, nondeception, and protection of societal and consumer rights. Two, *peripheral business values* are less important to the firm and may be adjusted to foreign markets. These relate to local customs in such areas as buyer-seller exchanges, selling practices, and so forth. Three, when possible, *ethnocentrism*—perceiving other countries' moral standards in terms of one's own country—must be avoided.[28]

[28]Gene R. Laczniak, "Observations Concerning International Marketing Ethics," presented at the 1995 AMA Faculty Consortium on Ethics and Social Responsibility in Marketing (Hempstead, N.Y.: Hofstra University); and Laczniak and Murphy, *Ethical Marketing Decisions: The Higher Road,* p. 218.

The Teachability of Ethics

Ethical concepts can be communicated.

Given the impact of societal values, peer pressure, self-interests and personal ambitions (and fear of failure), and other factors on people's sense of ethically acceptable behavior, there has been considerable debate as to whether ethics can be taught—either in a classroom or business setting. For example, as reported in Table 5-2, none of the statements on questionable consumer activities had the study's respondents in full agreement.

Nonetheless, what can be transmitted to people are

- Clear ethics codes.
- Role models of ethical people.
- Wide-ranging examples of ethical and unethical behavior.
- Specified punishments if ethical behavior is not followed.
- How vigilant professors and top management are regarding such issues as cheating on tests, misleading customers, and other unethical practices.
- The notion that ethical behavior will never put a person in jeopardy (for instance, a salesperson should not be penalized for losing a customer if that salesperson is unwilling to exaggerate the effectiveness of a product).

These are two perspectives about ethics and business students:

> It appears that ethical priorities depend on where you sit. If you are responsible for promoting and protecting the company, you are likely to attach the highest priority to the organization's welfare. If you are an ambitious student aspiring to business leadership, you are most concerned that a company offer you opportunity and judge you according to your contribution.[29]

> We're not converting sinners. We're taking young people with integrity and trying to get them to connect ethics with business decisions.[30]

Consumerism

Consumerism *protects consumers from practices that infringe upon their rights.*

Whereas social responsibility involves firms' interfaces with all of their publics, consumerism focuses on the relations of firms and their customers. **Consumerism** encompasses "the wide range of activities of government, business, and independent organizations that are designed to protect people from practices that infringe upon their rights as consumers."[31]

Consumer interests are most apt to be served in industrialized nations, where people's rights are considered important, and governments and firms have the resources to address consumer issues. In less-developed nations and those just turning to free-market economies, consumer rights have not been as well honored due to fewer resources and to other commitments; the early stages of consumerism are just now emerging in many of these nations.

U.S. consumerism has evolved through four distinct eras, and is now in a fifth. The first era was in the 1900s and focused on the need for a banking system, product purity, postal rates, antitrust regulations, and product shortages. Emphasis was on business protection against unfair practices. The second era was from the 1930s to the 1950s. Issues were product safety, bank failures, labeling, misrepresentation, stock manipulation, deceptive ads, credit, and consumer refunds. Consumer groups, like Consumers Union and Consumers' Research, and legislation grew. Issues were initiated but seldom resolved.

President Kennedy declared a **consumer bill of rights:** *to information, to safety, to choice, and to be heard.*

The third era began in the early 1960s and lasted to 1980. It dealt with all marketing areas and had a great impact. Ushering in this era was President Kennedy's stating a **consumer bill of rights:** to information, to safety, to choice in product selection, and to be heard. These rights, cited in Figure 5-8, apply to people in any nation or economic system. Other events also contributed to the era's effectiveness. Birth defects from using the drug thalidomide occurred. Several books—on such topics as marketing's ability to in-

[29]Ronald E. Berenbeim, "Bad Judgment or Inexperience?" *Across the Board* (October 1992), p. 46.

[30]John A. Byrne, "Can Ethics Be Taught? Harvard Gives It the Old College Try," *Business Week* (April 6, 1992), p. 34.

[31]Bennett, *Dictionary of Marketing Terms*, p. 62.

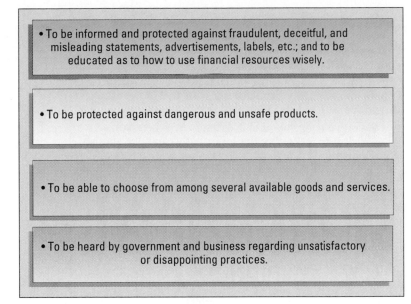

- To be informed and protected against fraudulent, deceitful, and misleading statements, advertisements, labels, etc.; and to be educated as to how to use financial resources wisely.
- To be protected against dangerous and unsafe products.
- To be able to choose from among several available goods and services.
- To be heard by government and business regarding unsatisfactory or disappointing practices.

FIGURE 5-8
Consumers' Basic Rights

fluence people, dangers from unsafe autos, and funeral industry tactics—were published. Consumers became more discontented with product performance, firms' complaint handling, and deceptive and unsafe practices; and they set higher—perhaps unrealistic—expectations. Product scarcity occurred for some items. Self-service shopping and more complex products caused uncertainty for some. The media publicized poor practices more often. Government intervention expanded; in particular, the FTC extended its activities on consumer issues.

The fourth era took place during the 1980s as consumerism entered a mature phase, due to the dramatic gains of the 1960s and 1970s—and an emphasis on business deregulation and self-regulation. Nationally, no major consumer laws were enacted and budgets of federal agencies concerned with consumer issues were cut. Yet, state and local governments became more active. In general, the federal government believed that most firms took consumer issues into account when devising and applying their marketing plans, and fewer firms did ignore consumer input or publicly confront consumer groups. Cooperation between business and consumers was better, and confrontations were less likely.

Since 1990, the federal government has been somewhat more involved with consumer issues. Its goal is to balance consumer and business rights. Some national laws have been enacted and U.S. agencies have stepped up enforcement practices. At the same time, many state and local governments are keeping a high level of commitment. Unfair business tactics, product safety, and health issues are the areas with the most current attention. Today, more firms are willing to address consumer issues and resolve complaints than ever before.

These key aspects of consumerism are examined next: consumer rights, the responses of business to consumer issues, and the current role of consumerism.

Consumer Rights

As noted, consumer rights fall into four categories: information and education, safety, choice, and the right to be heard. Each is discussed next.

Consumer Information and Education The right to be informed includes protection against fraudulent, deceitful, or grossly misleading information, advertising, labeling, pricing, packaging, and so on, and being given enough information to make good decisions. In the United States, there are many federal and state laws in this area.

A federal example is the Magnuson-Moss Consumer Product Warranty Act. A **warranty** is an assurance to consumers that a product meets certain standards. An express warranty is explicitly stated, such as a printed form showing the minimum mileage for truck tires. An implied warranty does not have to be stated to be in effect; a product is assumed to be fit for use and packaged properly, and to conform to promises on the label. The

A **warranty** *assures consumers that a product will meet certain standards.*

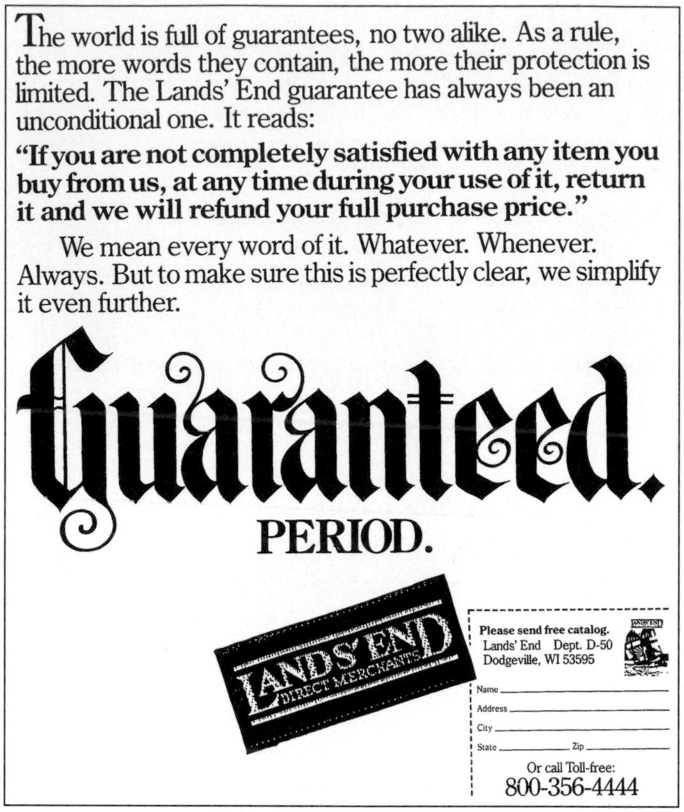

FIGURE 5-9
The Lands' End Full Warranty
Reprinted by permission.

Magnuson-Moss Act requires warranties to be properly stated and enforced. They must be available prior to purchases, so consumers may read them in advance. The FTC can monitor product-accompanying information as to the warrantor's identity and location, exceptions in warranty coverage, and how people may complain. A full warranty must cover all parts and labor for a given period. A limited warranty may have conditions and exceptions, as well as a provision for labor charges. Implied warranties may not be disclaimed. Figure 5-9 shows the full warranty provided by Lands' End, a direct marketer.

Many states have laws relating to consumer information. For instance, cooling-off laws (allowing people to reconsider and, if they desire, cancel purchase commitments made in their homes with salespeople) are now in force in about 40 states. Unit-pricing laws that let people compare the prices of products coming in many sizes (such as small, medium, large, and economy) are likewise on a state-by-state basis.

Government actions involving consumer information are also picking up internationally. For instance, in Hungary, an Eastern European nation with rapid growth in advertising, Home Shopping Budapest—a mail-order firm—was fined $1.25 million (U.S.) for misleading ads. Said one observer, "Until now, there was a feeling the government's attitude was laissez faire. But, they've shown they're ready to intervene and rather powerfully."[32]

Unfortunately, the existence of good information does not mean consumers will use it in their decision making. At times, the information is ignored or misunderstood, especially by those needing it most (such as the poor); thus, consumer education is needed. Most state departments of education in the United States have consumer education staffs. Such states as Illinois, Oregon, Wisconsin, Florida, Kentucky, and Hawaii require public high school students to take a consumer education course. And hundreds of programs are conducted by all levels of government, as well as by private profit and nonprofit groups. The programs typically cover how to purchase goods and services; key features of credit agreements, contracts, and warranties; and consumer protection laws.

[32]Ken Kasriel, "Hungary Cracks Down on Ad Claims," *Advertising Age* (June 22, 1992), pp. I-1, I-31; and Christopher Condon, "Hungary Regulations Could Polish Industry Image," *Advertising Age* (October 11, 1993), p. I-6.

Consumer Safety There is concern over consumer safety because millions of people worldwide are annually hurt and thousands killed in incidents involving products other than motor vehicles. The yearly cost of product-related injuries is several billion dollars. Critics believe up to one-quarter of these injuries could be averted if companies made safer, better-designed products.

The Consumer Product Safety Commission has several enforcement tools, including **product recall.**

The Consumer Product Safety Commission (CPSC) is the federal U.S. agency with major responsibility for product safety. It has jurisdiction over 15,000 product categories—including TVs, bicycles, lamps, appliances, toys, sporting goods, ladders, furniture, housewares, and lawn mowers. It also regulates structural items in homes such as stairs, retaining walls, and electrical wiring. The major products outside the CPSC's authority are food, drugs, cosmetics, tobacco, motor vehicles, tires, firearms, boats, pesticides, and aircraft. Each of these is regulated by other agencies. For example, the Environmental Protection Agency can recall autos not meeting emission standards; and the Food and Drug Administration oversees food, drugs, cosmetics, medical devices, radiation emissions, and similar items.

The CPSC has extensive powers. It can

1. Require products to be marked with clear warnings and instructions.
2. Issue mandatory standards that may force firms to redesign products.
3. Require manufacturers and resellers to notify it if they find a product has a defect that would create a substantial risk of injury.
4. Require manufacturers to conduct reasonable testing programs to make sure products conform to established safety standards.

When the CPSC finds a product hazard, it can issue an order for a firm to bring the product into conformity with the applicable safety rule or repair the defect, exchange the product for one meeting safety standards, or refund the purchase price. Firms found breaking safety rules can be fined, and executives can be personally fined and jailed for up to a year. **Product recall,** whereby the CPSC asks—orders, if need be—firms to recall and modify (or discontinue) unsafe products, is the primary enforcement tool. The CPSC has initiated numerous recalls, and a single recall may entail millions of units of a product. It has also banned such items as flammable contact adhesives, easily overturned refuse bins, asbestos-treated products, and Tris (a flame retardant used in children's clothing that was linked to cancer).

The U.S. motor vehicle industry, overseen by the National Highway Traffic Safety Administration (NHTSA), has had many vehicles recalled for safety reasons. Since 1980, there have been well over 2,000 different U.S. recalls (often voluntary actions under NHTSA prodding) involving millions of cars, trucks, and other vehicles (some of which have been recalled more than once). Despite recent quality improvements, American auto makers are still somewhat more likely to have cars recalled than Japanese auto makers.

A **class-action suit** *can be filed on behalf of many consumers.*

Consumers also have the right to sue the maker or seller of an injurious product. A legal action on behalf of many affected consumers is known as a **class-action suit**. Each year in the United States, 20,000 consumer law suits are filed in federal courts and 90,000 are filed in state courts; these include both individual and class-action suits.[33] Consumer law suits are rarer outside the United States. Yet, this too is changing:

> Japanese consumers have been docile. But now, consumer consciousness is rising. That's causing government to take a hard look at consumer protection. The Social Democratic Party is even drafting Japan's first product-liability law. Such efforts could alter the cushy atmosphere Japanese firms enjoy at home. For years, they've been shielded from product-liability suits. Japanese legal procedures put the burden of proof on plaintiffs, while limiting access to evidence. In 50 years, consumers have won only 150 product-liability cases. In the United States, American and other firms have lost tens of thousands of such suits."[34]

[33]Paula Mergenhagen, "Product Liability: Who Sues," *American Demographics* (June 1995), pp. 48–54.

[34]Ted Holden and Hiromi Uchida, "Consumers Start Telling It to the Judge," *Business Week* (March 9, 1992), p. 50. See also Paul A. Herbig and Frederick A. Palumbo, "Japanese Consumer Protection," *Journal of Consumer Marketing*, Vol. 11 (Number 1, 1994), pp. 5–14.

A firm can reduce the negative effects of product recalls, as well as the possibility of costly class-action suits, by communicating properly when it learns a product is unsafe. This means voluntarily telling affected consumers, citing specific models that are unsafe, making fair adjustment offers (repair, replacement, or refund), and quickly and conveniently honoring those offers.

When consumers have several alternatives available to them, they are given the right to choose.

Consumer Choice The right to choose means people have several products and brands from which to select. Figure 5-10 illustrates this. As noted earlier, the lack of goods and services (of any brand) is a key consumer concern in less-developed and newly free-market nations—where demand often far outstrips the supply for such items as coffee, bread, jeans, shoes, cosmetics, and fresh meat.

To enhance the already extensive consumer choices there, the federal governments in many industrialized countries have taken various actions:

- Patent rights have time bounds; then, all firms can use the patents.
- Noncompetitive business practices, like price fixing, are banned.
- Government agencies review proposed company mergers; in some cases, they have stopped mergers if they felt industry competition would be lessened.
- Restrictions requiring franchisees to purchase all goods and services from their franchisors have been reduced.
- The media are monitored to ensure that advertising space or time is made available to both small and large firms.

FIGURE 5-10
The Right to Choose
Reprinted by permission.

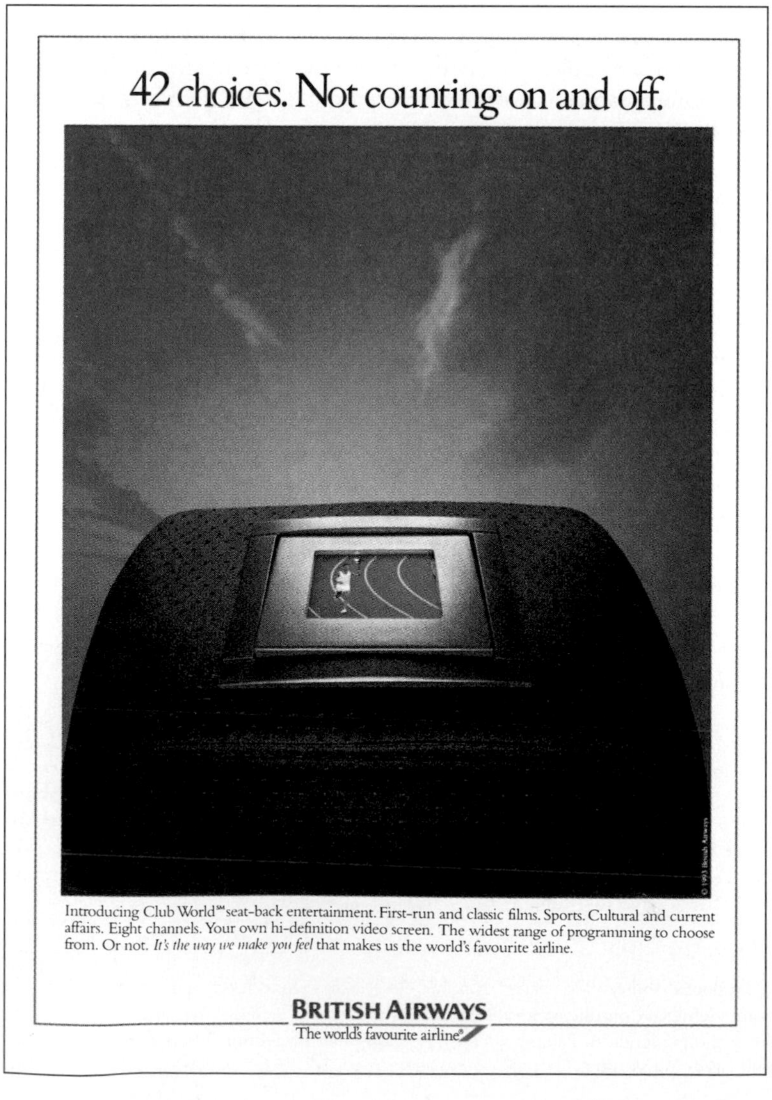

42 choices. Not counting on and off.
Introducing Club World℠ seat-back entertainment. First-run and classic films. Sports. Cultural and current affairs. Eight channels. Your own hi-definition video screen. The widest range of programming to choose from. Or not. *It's the way we make you feel* that makes us the world's favourite airline.
BRITISH AIRWAYS
The world's favourite airline®

- Imports are allowed to compete with domestic-made items.
- Various service industries have been deregulated to foster price competition and encourage new firms to enter the marketplace.

In the United States, consumer choice for some product categories is so extensive that some wonder if there are too many options. According to one prominent social scientist: "We are racing toward 'overchoice'—the point at which the advantages of diversity and individualization are canceled by the complexity of the buyer's decision-making process."[35]

There are various federal, state, and local agencies involved with consumers.

Consumers' Right to Be Heard The right to be heard means people should be able to voice their opinions (sometimes as complaints) to business, government, and other parties. This gives consumers input into the decisions affecting them. To date, no overall U.S. consumer agency exists to represent consumer interests, although several federal agencies regulate various business practices relating to consumers. Their addresses and phone numbers, as well as those of trade associations, are listed in the *Consumer's Resource Handbook* from the U.S. Office of Consumer Affairs. Most states and major cities have their own consumer affairs offices, as do many corporations. Each encourages consumer input.

There are also several consumer groups representing the general public or specific consumer segments. They are quite motivated in their efforts to publicize consumer opinions and complaints, speak at government and industry hearings, and otherwise generate consumer input into the decision processes of government and industry. Because a single consumer rarely has a significant impact, consumer groups frequently become the individual's voice.

The Responses of Business to Consumer Issues

Firms have become much more responsive to consumers, yet questions remain about the effects of consumerism on firms.

Over the last 35 years, in many nations, the business community has greatly increased its acceptance of the legitimacy and importance of consumer rights; many firms now have real commitments to address consumer issues in a positive manner. Nonetheless, a number of companies have raised reasonable questions about consumerism's impact on them. They particularly wonder why there isn't a *business bill of rights* to parallel the consumer's. Here are some of the questions that businesspeople raise:

- Why do different states, municipalities, and nations have different laws regarding business practices? How can a national or international company be expected to comply with each of these laws?
- Don't some government rules cause unnecessary costs and time delays in new-product introductions that outweigh the benefits of these rules?
- Is it the job of business to ensure that consumers obey laws (such as not littering) and use products properly (such as wearing seat belts)?
- Isn't business self-regulation preferred over government regulation?
- Are multimillion dollar jury awards to consumers getting out of hand?

Selected responses to consumer issues by manufacturers, retailers, and trade associations are discussed next.

Manufacturers Numerous manufacturers have long-standing programs to handle consumer issues. In 1961, Maytag introduced Red Carpet Service to improve its appliance repair service. Zenith set up its customer relations department in 1968; Motorola created an Office of Consumer Affairs in 1970; and RCA opened a consumer affairs office at the corporate level in 1972.

General Electric runs the GE Answer Center, which handles consumer phone inquiries 24 hours a day, seven days a week via a toll-free number. It processes millions of calls yearly—questions from potential consumers and do-it-yourselfers, complaints from disgruntled customers, and suggestions regarding company improvements. Via the Answer

[35]Lena Williams, "Free Choice: When Too Much Is Too Much," *New York Times* (February 14, 1990), p. C10.

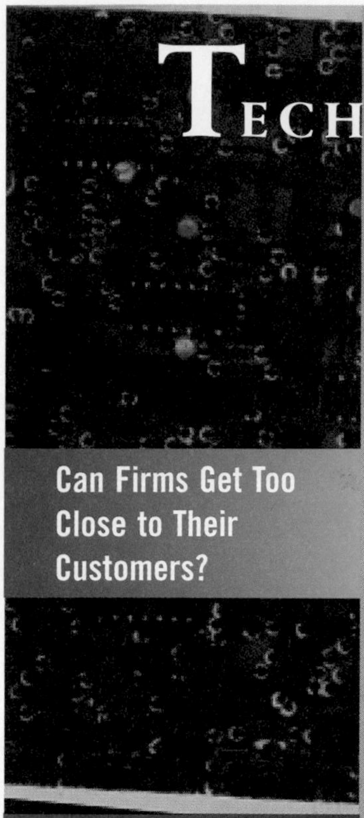

TECHNOLOGY & MARKETING

Can Firms Get Too Close to Their Customers?

It is great that many companies engage in relationship marketing with their customers, and that they stay in regular contact with them. By having good information on customers, companies can tailor marketing efforts to specific customers' needs, provide better follow-up service, and anticipate future customer requests.

Yet, with the rapid advances in business technology, some people now feel especially vulnerable to what they perceive as company abuses in their relationships with customers:

> Imagine you're sorting through your mail at home when you come across a postcard touting an upcoming sale on shirts at the store where you bought a shirt last week. That's funny, you think. You're sure you didn't give the clerk your address. So, how did you end up on the store's mailing list? There's only one explanation: The store must have gotten your address from its credit-card data base because you paid with the store's credit card. Since you're tired of being inundated with junk mail, you angrily toss the postcard in the garbage—after all, you were just at the store last week!

If firms are truly marketing-oriented, they must recognize that different people have different sensitivities regarding information on their behavior and backgrounds being kept in computerized data bases. While one person may prefer that a hotel chain know he or she prefers a nonsmoking room on a high floor, another person may consider that information to be private. Compared to the second person, the first one may value good customer service above privacy or just be less sensitive about who has access to this information. Therefore, companies should train employees who collect customer data to respect a person's request for privacy even if this means not having good information on that person's needs and desires.

As a hotel's marketing manager, present a policy for both acquiring data about customer likes/dislikes and respecting customer privacy.

Source: Based on material in Stephen M. Silverman, "Information Backlash," *Inc. Technology* (June 13, 1995), p. 37.

Center, GE can satisfy current customers and attract potential ones, gather data about consumer demographics, and gain insights about its marketing strategy and possible new products.

In the area of product recalls, many firms are now doing a better job. For instance, LifeScan, a Johnson & Johnson company, makes meters that diabetics use to monitor their sugar levels. When one meter was found to be defective, LifeScan voluntarily recalled its entire product line and notified 600,000 customers within 24 hours. Because of how it handled the recall, LifeScan's market share has increased by seven per cent since that incident.[36]

Despite manufacturers' interest in consumer issues, there are still times when their performance could be better. As a case in point, "Many times, product design is severely deficient in the area of human interface, with insufficient attention paid to how people use—and learn to use—the things in their lives. PCs. Phone systems. Toys requiring assembly. Upscale autos. Even light switches. They all can cause havoc for a person who doesn't read what's in an accompanying 500-page manual, written in 'engineerese.'"[37]

Retailers Various retailers have expressed a positive concern about consumer issues, some for several decades. J.C. Penney first stated its consumer philosophy in 1913, and Macy's formed a Bureau of Standards to test merchandise in 1927. In the 1970s, the Gi-

[36]Tim Triplett, "Product Recall Spurs Company to Improve Customer Satisfaction," *Marketing News* (April 11, 1994), p. 6.

[37]Howard Schlossberg, "Design Disability," *Marketing Management*, Vol. 1 (Spring 1992), p. 6.

ant Food supermarket chain devised its own consumer bill of rights (paralleling the one articulated by President Kennedy):

- Right to safety—no phosphates, certain pesticides removed, toys' age labeled.
- Right to be informed—better labeling, unit pricing, readable dating of perishable items, and nutritional labeling.
- Right to choose—continued sale of cigarettes and food with additives.
- Right to be heard—consumer group meetings, in-house consumer advocate.
- Right to redress—money-back guarantee on all products.
- Right to service—availability of store services and employee attentiveness.

For the last decade, Wal-Mart has had in-store signs to inform consumers about environmentally safe products. It has also run newspaper ads encouraging suppliers to make more environmentally sound products. At 7-Eleven Japan, three times a week, top executives sample foods sold at the chain. The firm's president says, "I won't sell what I wouldn't eat."[38]

With **item price removal,** *prices are displayed only on shelves or signs.*

Retailers and consumer groups have opposing views in one area, involving **item price removal**—whereby prices are marked only on store shelves or aisle signs and not on individual items. Numerous retailers, particularly supermarkets, want to use item price removal because computerized checkouts allow them to computer scan prices through premarked codes on packages. They say this reduces labor costs and that these reductions can be passed on to consumers. Consumer groups believe the practice is deceptive and will make it harder for them to guard against misrings. Item price removal is banned in a number of states and local communities. Giant Food is a leading advocate of item price removal; it passes cost savings along to consumers.

Trade Associations Trade associations represent groups of individual firms. Many have been quite responsive to consumer issues through such actions as coordinating and distributing safety-related research findings, setting up consumer education programs, planning product standards, and handling complaints.

The Major Appliance Consumer Action Panel (MACAP) is an educational and complaint-handling program of the Association of Home Appliance Manufacturers. The Bank Marketing Association has a Financial Advertising Code of Ethics (FACE) for members. The Direct Marketing Association sets industry guidelines and has a consumer action phone line. The National Retail Federation has a Consumer Affairs Committee and offers information to the public. The Alliance Against Fraud in Telemarketing is dedicated to reducing fraudulent practices and consists of consumer groups, trade associations, labor unions, phone companies, federal and state agencies, and telemarketers.

The Better Business Bureau (BBB) is the largest and broadest business run U.S. trade association involved with consumer issues. It publishes educational materials, handles complaints, supervises arbitration panels, makes available a Consumer Affairs Audit, outlines ethical behavior, publicizes unsatisfactory practices and the firms involved, and has nationwide offices. It supports self-regulation as a substitute to government regulation. Nationwide, the BBB handles hundreds of thousands of arbitration cases each year. These cases—many involving autos—are decided by impartial arbitrators. Rulings are usually binding on participating firms but not on consumers.

Trade associations may vigorously oppose potential government rules. For example, the Tobacco Institute (funded by tobacco firms) has lobbied against further restrictions on tobacco sales, promotion, distribution, and use.

The Current Role of Consumerism

During the 1980s, there was much less U.S. federal government activity on consumer-related issues than during the 1960s and 1970s—due to the quality of self-regulation, consumerism's success, increased conservatism by Congress and the American people, and the importance of other issues.

[38]Karen Lowry Miller, "Listening to Shoppers' Voices," *Business Week: Reinventing America* (1992), p. 69.

By 1980, many firms had become more responsive to consumer issues. Thus, there was less pressure for government or consumer groups to intervene. There was also a move to industry deregulation as a way of increasing competition, encouraging innovations, and stimulating lower prices. Consumerism activity was also less needed because of the successes of past actions. On all levels, government protection for consumers had improved dramatically since the early 1960s; and class-action suits won large settlements from firms, making it clear that unsafe practices were financially costly. Consumer groups and independent media publicized negative practices, so firms knew such activities would not go unnoticed. In the 1980s, many members of Congress and sectors of the American public became more conservative about the role of government in regulating business. They felt government had become too big, impeded business practices, and caused unneeded costs; as a result, some government agency functions were limited and budgets cut. Consumerism issues were not as important as other factors, including unemployment, the rate of inflation, industrial productivity, and the negative international balance of trade.

Federal U.S. consumerism efforts have picked up, after a relative lull in the 1980s.

After a decade of a "hands-off" approach, a growing number of government leaders, consumer activists, and business leaders in the United States felt that the balance between business and consumer rights had tipped a little too much in favor of business. Hence, there is now a slightly more aggressive federal government posture toward consumer-related issues than in the 1980s, and states and localities are continuing to be heavily involved.

Here are some indications of the enhanced role of the U.S. government:

- In 1990, the Federal Trade Commission settled its first price-fixing case in eight years, brought its first deceptive-advertising case against an ad agency in five years, and filed its first suit regarding a 900 telephone service. Subsequently, it has been tougher on direct-mail catalog claims, telemarketing practices, misleading ads promoting environmental claims, selling tactics of auto dealers, and other unfair methods of competition.
- Since 1990, the Food and Drug Administration has stepped up efforts to curb misleading food advertising and packaging. Among the items whose ads and packages have been changed as a result of FDA actions are Mazola corn oil and Ragú pasta sauce. The FDA even seized 2,400 cases of a now defunct brand of orange juice, until the maker agreed to remove Fresh Choice from its name (as it was made from concentrate). The FDA has also set forth sweeping new rules for nutrition labels appearing on packaged foods.
- Firms now have to report settlements of product-safety law suits involving death or disabling injuries to the CPSC. This helps identify product hazards that would be hidden by sealed court records.

In many countries outside the United States, government, industry, and consumer groups are stepping up their efforts relating to consumer rights—as past efforts have often been lacking in foreign markets. Some nations are making real progress, while others still have a very long way to go. No other nation has gone through as many evolutionary stages or passed as many laws to protect the consumer rights cited in this chapter as the United States. The worldwide challenge of the late 1990s will be for government, business, and consumer groups to work together so the socioecological view of marketing, ethical behavior, consumer rights, and company rights are in balance.

MARKETING IN A CHANGING WORLD

Tough Choices Ahead

It is now harder than ever to make good societal, ethical, and consumer-oriented decisions. Here are two views as to why this is so:

> Marketing was easier when the economy was expanding and consumer income was growing. For decades after World War II, marketing strategies generally were built around the development of growth markets. Satisfying customers was important, but never as important as it has become in the 1990s, with the competitive pressures of largely static markets. Previously, ethical problems were less apparent, not because people did not care, but because society's expectations were different and there was a simple rule for rating marketing practices: caveat emptor [let the buyer beware], within the rule of law. If it was legal to sell a product that might be harmful or not live up to seller promises, then marketing the product was acceptable because the decision to buy was the consumer's. Today, there is widespread concern about ethics in public and private life extending to many areas—politics, education, and health, as well as business. The current period may be called the "ethics era." For marketers, this has meant that standards of acceptable marketing practice have shifted along a continuum, from a position wherein producer interests are paramount to a position wherein consumer interests are more favored. Society's expectations have changed so that if caveat emptor ever was truly an adequate way to evaluate marketing ethics, this is no longer the case.[39]

> Ethical issues are no longer just about what's right and what's wrong. Increasingly, we must choose between two things that are right, such as doing everything we can to save lives or allowing people to die with dignity. Good moral leadership in the next century will be grounded in centuries-old ethics concepts that may never change. Yet, it must also be flexible, adaptable, and inventive. Already, new dilemmas face us at every turn: How should software be protected from unlicensed copying? Only people living in a computer age would want to know. Should we ban dashboard radar detectors, whose sole purpose is to help people disobey traffic laws? The issue didn't arise until high-speed interstate highways and low-cost transistor technology joined hands in the 1980s. Should New England ship its nuclear waste to Texas? Had you asked anyone 50 years ago, you would have been dismissed as a science-fiction freak: No one had ever thought of the problem. Should public school children get free condoms? Before AIDS, the question would have seemed scandalous. Should you and I clone ourselves? The question has yet to come up—but it will.[40]

SUMMARY

1. *To consider the impact of marketing on society* Marketing actions have the potential for both positive and negative consequences regarding such areas as the quality of life and consumer expectations. Various studies have shown that people's perceptions of marketing are mixed. Firms need to recognize that many dissatisfied consumers do not complain; they simply do not rebuy offending products.

2. *To examine social responsibility and weigh its benefits and costs* Social responsibility involves a concern for the consequences of a person's or firm's acts as they might affect the interests of others. It encompasses the socioecological view of marketing, which looks at all the stages of a product's life and includes both consumers and nonconsumers. Social responsibility can pose dilemmas when popular goods and services have potential adverse effects on consumer or societal well-being.

Consumers and marketing practices have led to some resource shortages. To stem their depletion, cooperative efforts among business, stockholders, government, employees, the general public, consumers, and others are needed. Garbage dumps and landfills, discarded beverage containers, and abandoned autos are marring the landscape. As a result, many areas have laws to rectify the situation. Dangerous pollutants need to be removed and safe ones found to replace them; environmental pollution will be an issue for the foreseeable future. Planned obsolescence is a heavily criticized practice that encourages material wearout, style changes, and functional product changes. Marketers say it responds to consumer demand; critics say it increases resource shortages, is wasteful, and adds to pollution.

Socially responsible actions have such benefits as worker and public health, cleaner air, and a more efficient

[39]N. Craig Smith, "Marketing Strategies for the Ethics Era," *Sloan Management Review*, Vol. 36 (Summer 1995), p. 85.

[40]Rushworth M. Kidder, "Tough Choices: Why It's Getting Harder to Be Ethical," *Futurist* (September–October 1995), pp. 29–30.

use of resources. They also have many costs, such as the unequal distribution of benefits, dollar expenditures, and conservative new-product planning. Benefits and costs need to be weighed. Green marketing will continue gaining popularity.

3. *To look into the role of ethics in marketing* Ethical behavior, based on honest and proper conduct, comes into play when people decide whether given actions are ethical or unethical and when they choose how to act. Egoism, utilitarianism, duty-based, and virtue ethics theories help explain behavior. Marketing ethics can be divided into two categories: process-related and product-related.

Ethics may be examined from four vantage points: a business perspective, a consumer perspective, an international perspective, and teachability. A major difficulty of ethics in business relates to setting boundaries for deciding what is ethical. For high ethical standards to be kept, both consumers and firms must engage in proper behavior. For various reasons, ethical standards in an international setting are especially complex. There has been a lot of debate as to whether ethics can be taught.

4. *To explore consumerism and describe the consumer bill of rights* Consumerism deals with the relations of firms and their consumers. It comprises the acts of government, business, and independent organizations that are designed to protect people from practices that infringe upon their rights as consumers.

U.S. consumerism has seen five eras: early 1900s, 1930s to 1950s, 1960s to 1980, 1980s, and 1990 to the present. The third was the most important and began with President Kennedy's announcement of a consumer bill of rights—to information, to safety, to choice, and to be heard. The interest now is in balancing consumer and business rights—in the United States, as well as in other countries.

The right to be informed includes consumer protection against fraudulent, deceitful, grossly misleading, or incomplete information, advertising, labeling, pricing, packaging, or other practices. Consumer education involves teaching people to spend their money wisely.

The concern over the right to safety arises from the large numbers of people who are injured or killed in product-related accidents. The U.S. Consumer Product Safety Commission has the power to order recalls or modifications for a wide range of products; other agencies oversee such products as autos and pharmaceuticals.

The right to choose means consumers should have several products and brands from which to select. In the U.S., some observers wonder if there is too much choice.

The right to be heard means consumers should be able to voice their opinions (and complaints) to business, government, and other parties. A number of government agencies and consumer groups provide this voice.

5. *To discuss the responses of manufacturers, retailers, and trade associations to consumerism and study the current role of consumerism* Many firms and associations are reacting well to consumer issues. A small number intentionally or unintentionally pursue unfair, misleading, or dangerous acts.

The decade of the 1990s is witnessing more activism than in the 1980s and less than in the 1960s and 1970s. Government, business, and consumers will continue working together to resolve consumer issues.

KEY TERMS

social responsibility (p. 114)
socioecological view of marketing (p. 114)
planned obsolescence (p. 119)
green marketing (p. 122)
ethical behavior (p. 122)
process-related ethical issues (p. 124)
product-related ethical issues (p. 124)
cause-related marketing (p. 126)
consumerism (p. 130)
consumer bill of rights (p. 130)
warranty (p. 131)
product recall (p. 133)
class-action suit (p. 133)
item price removal (p. 137)

Review Questions

1. What are some of the areas in which marketing practices have the potential for both positive and negative consequences for society?

2. Define the term *social responsibility*. What are the implications for marketers?

3. Explain the responsibilities of both business and consumers according to the socioecological view of marketing.

4. Describe the pros and cons of planned obsolescence as a marketing practice.

5. What is ethical behavior? Distinguish among the egoism, utilitarianism, duty-based, and virtue ethics theories.

6. Why is cause-related marketing a controversial practice?

7. Why are ethical standards of conduct particularly complex for international marketers?

8. How does consumerism differ from social responsibility?

9. Explain the consumer bill of rights.

10. Describe the current role of consumerism.

Discussion Questions

1. From a company's perspective, why is hidden consumer dissatisfaction a particular problem? How would you go about making dissatisfaction less hidden?
2. Present a seven-point ethics guide for operating internationally.
3. How would you teach marketing ethics to a class of sophomore business majors? What topics would you discuss? Why?
4. As an executive for a leading toy manufacturer, how would you implement a product recall if you discover that one of your toys could easily be swallowed by children under age 3?
5. Do consumers in the United States have too many goods and services from which to choose? Why or why not?

CASE 1

Herman Miller: Evaluating the Actions of an Environmentally-Conscious Firm[*]

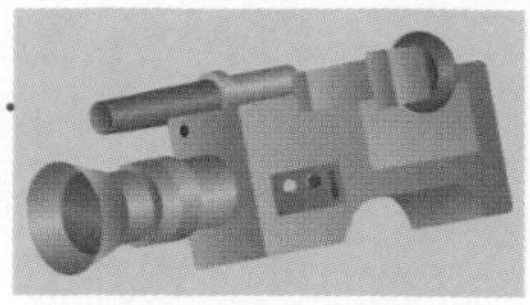

Michigan-based Herman Miller is a leading maker of contemporary-styled furniture and furniture systems for offices and, to a lesser extent, for health-care facilities. Its annual sales exceed $1.1 billion, making it the second-largest U.S. manufacturer of office furniture (after Steelcase). One of its best known products is an office system, consisting of an integrated desk and wall unit, that is used when office space is both limited and costly.

In 1982, long before most firms were concerned with environmental issues, Herman Miller built an $11 million waste-to-energy plant that continues to provide a large portion of its power needs. Instead of burning waste products in landfills, the firm uses its trash to supply all the electricity it needs to heat and air-condition its central factory. Its waste-to-energy plant has reduced the amount of trash the firm discards in landfills by 90 per cent.

Years in advance, the firm set a goal of sending no trash to landfills as of 1995. To reach the goal, it used reduced quantities of packaging and worked with materials that were recyclable. Today, even Herman Miller's scrap fabric is shredded and made into insulation for car-roof linings and dashboards. Not only does this recycling process help the environment, but also it saves the firm $50,000 in annual dumping fees. Overall, according to the vice-president of the Michigan Audubon Society, "Herman Miller has been doing a superb job."

According to the United Nations' Food and Agricultural Organization, 17 million hectares of rain forest are destroyed each year. In March 1990, when Herman Miller's research manager realized that the firm's use of rosewood and Honduran mahogany had resulted in the destruction of tropical rain forests, the company decided not to purchase additional rosewood—a vital ingredient in the company's $2,300 signature-piece chair. As a result, the chair is now made from walnut and cherry woods. According to the firm's chief executive, "We are sharing the growing concern about the tropical rain forests."

The firm's new environmental policy requires that it use only wood from sustained-yield forest sources. This policy was developed in conjunction with the International Hardwood Products Association (IHPA) and the International Timber Trade Organization, a multigovernment agency.

Herman Miller's mission statement highlights its environmental concern: "We are a company that services the built environment with facilities, goods, and services that improve the quality of life and with policies and practices that sustain our environment." Based on its recycling program, Herman Miller was honored with the 1993 Waste Reduction Award from California's Integrated Management Board. It also received the Wildlife Federation Corporate Conservation Council's 1993 Environmental Achievement Award.

Herman Miller's concern with social responsibility extends to employees and customers. As such, it spent $800,000 for two incinerators to burn 98 per cent of the toxic solvents that are emitted from its painting and varnishing operations. These furnaces exceed the standards of the Clean Air Act.

Herman Miller is not content with its environmental actions. The company presently only recycles about 15 per cent of its corrugated cardboard; the balance is burned in its energy plant. It also feels that it needs to burn more of the sawdust that is accumulated as a by-product of producing wooden furniture.

Unlike other companies, Herman Miller does not promote its environmental efforts to its customers. According to its senior vice-president for sales, "green marketing is a ploy that may eventually wear thin with customers."

QUESTIONS

1. Comment on Herman Miller's actions in terms of the socioecological view of marketing.
2. Develop other strategies that Herman Miller can use to increase its social responsibility efforts.
3. Evaluate Herman Miller's refusal to purchase additional rosewood from a product-related ethical issue perspective.
4. Should Herman Miller promote its environmental policies to its customers? Explain your answer.

VIDEO QUESTIONS ON HERMAN MILLER

1. How do its environmental concerns affect Herman Miller's manufacturing and distribution processes?
2. Discuss Herman Miller's application of EPA guidelines.

[*] The data in this case are drawn from Joseph A. Azzarello, "Long-Time Environmental Leadership Pays Off in Many Ways at Herman Miller," *Total Quality Environmental Management* (Winter 1992/1993), pp. 187–191; *Herman Miller, Inc. and Subsidiaries 1994 Annual Report*; and Faye Rice, "Who Scores Best on the Environment," *Fortune* (July 26, 1993), pp. 114–122.

CASE 2

At Starbucks: Is the Customer Always Right?[†]

Starbucks is the country's largest coffee-espresso bar chain with more than 750 stores. The publicly traded firm plans to have 1,500 stores and $1 billion in annual sales by the year 2000. Its sales have increased steadily (in some years by more than 60 per cent chainwide), and profits have been quite strong.

Yet, despite its success, Starbucks recently experienced a situation that could be described as a "public relations nightmare." This is what happened:

A customer, Jeremy Dorosin, became very angry when a Starbucks sales representative would not exchange two espresso machines that he had bought earlier with newer models. Dorosin also felt that Starbucks' employees were rude to him. In response to his frustrations, he placed four ads in the *Wall Street Journal*, with each ad complaining of poor customer service at Starbucks.

After his ads ran, Starbucks sent Jeremy Dorosin an apology letter, offered to exchange his machines for the newer models he initially desired, and even promised him some additional coffee supplies. Dorosin refused this offer, and asked that Starbucks apologize to him in a two-page ad in the *Wall Street Journal*. In addition, he requested that Starbucks build a center for runaway children.

Starbucks steadfastly refused to go beyond its apology letter and its offer of providing new machines and extra supplies. As Starbucks' manager of customer relations, Barbara Reed, said, "We truly believe that we have done everything reasonable to rectify the situation." Starbucks also issued a statement saying, "It is unfortunate that in this particular case we were unable to please Jeremy Dorosin. We regret that our efforts were not sufficient to meet his needs, but there is nothing more we can do."

Starbucks is regarded as having an excellent customer service record:

- It spends about $1,000 to train each new employee during his or her first six months on the job. Although much of the training entails how to make different types of coffee, a customer service philosophy runs throughout the training program. All employees are expected to follow five guiding principles, which include "developing enthusiastically satisfied customers all of the time" and providing a "great work environment."
- It uses mystery shoppers (specially trained employees who are disguised as shoppers) to assess customer service, product quality, and store cleanliness in each store on a monthly basis.
- According to Barbara Reed, "when a situation comes up—we read every letter and respond to every call. We view these comments as opportunities to improve."

In its report on the Dorosin incident, *Sales & Marketing Management* magazine asked two experts (Richard Whiteley, author of *The Customer Driven Company*, and Ron Zemke, author of *The Service Edge*) to comment on Starbucks' offer to Jeremy Dorosin. Whiteley said, "[Dorosin's requests] are outlandish—the fact of the matter is, irate customers are becoming terrorists. The lesson is, you have to nip the problem in the bud, but you don't necessarily give customers everything they think they deserve or want. This seemingly innocent problem has gotten out of hand." To Zemke, "This was a timing problem. You have to start applying bandages early and dramatically, and you have to have a lot of empathy so customers feel they have been heard and dealt with in an expeditious fashion. If you wait and think it through, you are too late. This is not war or famine, this is some customer from hell who is being crazy, and Starbucks has the opportunity to be just as crazy."

QUESTIONS

1. Develop a customer philosophy statement for Starbucks. Refer to the discussion in this chapter on the consumer's bill of rights in your answer.
2. Are Jeremy Dorosin's requests reasonable? Explain your answer.
3. Were Starbucks' rights as a retailer violated by Jeremy Dorosin? Explain your answer.
4. Should Starbucks make another offer to Jeremy Dorosin, such as a better espresso maker than he originally desired or a $200 gift certificate to Starbucks restaurants? Why or why not?

[†]The data in this case are drawn from Allison Lucas, "Trouble Brews for Starbucks," *Sales & Marketing Management* (August 1995), p. 15; and Carol Polsky, "Brewing Ambition," *Newsday* (November 27, 1995), C1–C5.

Chapter 6
Global Aspects of Marketing

Chapter Objectives

1. To define domestic, international, and global marketing
2. To explain why international marketing takes place and study its scope
3. To explore the cultural, economic, political and legal, and technological environments facing international marketers
4. To analyze the stages in the development of an international marketing strategy

Paddling down cow paths in flip-flop sandals or paddling a canoe through piranha-infested creeks, Iraci Macedo da Costa Queiroz lugs from door to door what rain forest dreams are made of: Mesmerize cologne, Forever Fragrance perfume, and Cool Confidence deodorant. With no doorbells to ring at the riverside shanties on stilts, this Avon lady of the Amazon claps her hands and calls out cheerily: "Hi, Honey! I'm here!"

Reprinted by permission.

U.S.-based Avon Products is the world's largest cosmetics firm. In recent years, while its annual U.S. sales have fallen slightly, Avon's foreign sales have risen rapidly (except in Western Europe). As such, foreign sales account for more than 60 per cent of Avon's total revenues. Today, Avon is especially focused on growth opportunities in such emerging markets as Brazil, Argentina, Mexico, China, and Poland. As Avon's chief executive officer says, "we see great promise in these markets, and we feel the growth is sustainable."

U.S. opportunities for Avon have stagnated as a result of more women being in the work force than at home. This trend not only makes it more difficult for Avon to reach customers, but also for Avon to hire qualified salespersons. The firm has tried to attract new U.S. customers with its Avon Select program, which lets customers order cosmetics through a direct-mail catalog or via a toll-free phone number. Unfortunately, sales through this innovative program have been quite low. And Avon's plan to motivate the U.S. sales force to work harder by cutting their commissions and sales incentives also have not worked out well. Instead of motivating the sales force, the plan led to poor morale and lower sales. Under Avon's new president, Christina A. Gold, the old commission structure and bonus system was reinstituted.

Even though Avon has had problems in the United States with its direct selling strategy, this approach has proven ideal for its emerging markets. For example, many countries, such as China and Argentina, lack well-developed infrastructures and distribution systems. And the high potential income is a large attraction for potential sales representatives. In all, Avon is doing business in about 30 developing countries, and the revenues Avon generates in those nations alone exceed its U.S. revenues. Its newest markets are India, South Africa, and Vietnam, all targeted to start operations by 1997.

Avon's largest market in the world, after the United States, is Brazil. Avon's Brazilian sales reached $1 billion in 1995, double the 1993 level. Avon has 480,000 "beauty consultants" in Brazil; this is more than double the size of Brazil's army—and double the number of Amway distributors in the U.S. market. A typical Brazilian sales representative earns between $250 and $700 a month selling Avon products, based on a 30 per cent commission rate. This compares favorably with a national average income of $250 a month in Brazil. "For housewives, there is emancipation," says Eliana Maria Machado de Silva, who supervises 1,000 Avon salespeople in the Amazon region. "They start to have their own financial life. They discover themselves. They gain self-confidence."

Avon knows the Brazilian market is diverse. So, to reach affluent Sao Paulo residents who live in high-security buildings, Avon advertises on cable TV, and it sells to consumers in the Amazon by allowing its salespeople to trade its anti-wrinkle cream for three grams of gold dust.[1]

In this chapter, we will explore the environment facing international marketers and see how to develop an international marketing strategy.

Overview

International business transactions generate trillions of dollars in yearly global sales. And virtually every nation engages in significant international business, whether it be the United States with over $1.5 trillion in yearly exports and imports of goods and services, Namibia (in southern Africa) with $3 billion in exports and imports, or Tonga (in the South Pa-

Due to its impact, international marketing concepts should be understood by all types of firms.

[1]James Brooke, "Who Braves Piranha Waters? Your Avon Lady!" *New York Times* (July 7, 1995), p. A4; and Veronica Byrd and Wendy Zellner, "The Avon Lady of the Amazon," *Business Week* (October 24, 1994), pp. 93–96.

cific) with $100 million in exports and imports. In many areas, the marketplace has a wide variety of foreign firms competing with domestic ones.

Whether a firm is small or large, operates solely in its home nation or in both the home market and abroad, offers goods or services, and is profit- or nonprofit-oriented, it needs to grasp key international marketing concepts and to devise and enact a proper strategy. This means having a broadened marketing perspective. For example, "Most small U.S. businesses never had to look to exports for increased market share. For 45 years, the domestic market—stretching from Maine to Alaska—provided large profits. American firms grew accustomed to being contacted directly by companies overseas for new technology, quality products, and American 'know-how.' Times are changing, however. Small-business owners are starting to review their marketing strategies. They see quality competition from the East, price competition from less-developed countries with cheaper labor, and looming competition from 'Fortress Europe.' U.S. firms of all sizes are now thinking globally."[2]

Domestic marketing *involves the home nation,* **international marketing** *embraces foreign activities, and* **global marketing** *has a worldwide focus.*

By definition, **domestic marketing** encompasses a firm's efforts in its home country. **International marketing** involves marketing goods and services outside a firm's home country, whether in one or several markets. **Global marketing** is an advanced form of international marketing in which a firm addresses global customers, markets, and competition. It is practiced by both multinational and global firms.

A company may act domestically, internationally, or both; efforts vary widely. Here is the range of options that may be pursued:

- A **domestic firm** restricts its efforts to the home market. The firm believes its base market is both large enough and responsive enough to meet its sales and profit goals.
- An **exporting firm** is just embarking on sales expansion beyond its home borders. This company recognizes that the home market is no longer adequate for it fully to meet revenue and profit goals. A firm typically uses exporting when it seeks to sell its traditional products in foreign markets, often via distribution and sales intermediaries. A relatively low percentage of business is outside the domestic market.

A firm may be **domestic, exporting, international, multinational,** *or* **global.**

- An **international firm** goes beyond just exporting existing products. It makes modifications in those items for foreign markets or introduces new products there; the firm knows it must more aggressively cultivate foreign markets. There remains enough strength in the firm's domestic market for that market to remain the dominant one for the company.
- A **multinational firm** is a worldwide player. Although corporate headquarters are in the home nation, the domestic market often accounts for less than 50 percent of sales and profits—and the firm operates in dozens of nations or more. The business scope and search for opportunities are quite broad with regard to geography. Many leading U.S. players (like Boeing, Citicorp, and McDonald's) tend to fall into this category; they market items around the world, but have an American business culture.
- A **global firm** is also a worldwide player. Yet, because its domestic sales are low, it places even more reliance on foreign transactions. It has the greatest geographic business scope. Such firms have been more apt to emerge in smaller nations, where the firms have historically needed foreign markets to survive (in contrast to U.S. firms). The quintessential global firm is Switzerland's Nestlé, which for decades has derived less than 2 per cent of total sales from its home market, makes products in hundreds of plants all over the world, and has employees from 50 nations at headquarters. As illustrated in Figure 6-1, its brands are among the world's most popular. In 1996, Coca-Cola announced that it was converting from a U.S.-based multinational to a global company.[3] See Figure 6-2 on page 148.

[2]Bonnie Heineman Wolfe, "Finding the International Niche: A 'How To' for American Small Business," *Business Horizons*, Vol. 34 (March–April 1991), p. 13.

[3]Joel R. Evans, "What Does Globalization in Business Really Mean?" *Hofstra Horizons* (Spring 1995), pp. 7–9; and Glenn Collins, "Coke Drops 'Domestic' and Goes One World," *New York Times* (January 13, 1996), pp. 35, 37.

Il n'a pas pris
son Nescafé
ce matin.
Ça
commence
bien
le matin.
NESCAFÉ

FIGURE 6-1
Nescafé by Nestlé: A Long-Time Global Firm
Due to the small size of its home market in Switzerland, Nestlé has been a full-fledged global company for several decades.
Reprinted by permission.

As we move into the 21st century, it is clear that more domestic firms will need to become exporters and then international in orientation. And multinational firms will need to become more global, thereby acting boundaryless and not dominated by a home-country-based corporate culture.

This chapter looks at why international marketing occurs, its scope, its environment, and the components of an international marketing strategy.

Why International Marketing Takes Place

There are several reasons why countries and individual firms are engaging in greater international marketing efforts than ever before. These are shown in Figure 6-3 and are discussed next.

Countries trade items in which they have a **comparative advantage**.

According to the concept of **comparative advantage,** each country has distinct strengths and weaknesses based on its natural resources, climate, technology, labor costs, and other factors. Therefore, nations can benefit by exporting the goods and services with which they have relative advantages and importing the ones with which they have relative disadvantages. Comparative advantages may generally be grouped into two categories: (a) those related to the physical environment of a country (such as natural resources and climate) and (b) those related to the socioeconomic development of a country (such as technological advances or low labor costs). Among the best U.S. comparative advantages are its agricultural productivity, the level of technological prowess, and service industry proveniences.

The domestic economy and demographics affect international efforts.

Economic and demographic trends vary by country. A firm in a nation with adverse domestic conditions (like high inflation) and/or a small or stagnant population base can stabilize or increase sales by marketing products in more favorable foreign markets. Thus,

FIGURE 6-2
Coca-Cola: From U.S. Multinational to Global Firm
Due to the enormous size of its home market in the United States, until recently Coca-Cola was a U.S.-based multinational. Then, in 1996, Coca-Cola decided to eliminate the concepts of "domestic" and "international." Its U.S. business was downgraded to be just one of six global units. Why the change? U.S. sales are now only one-fifth of total company revenues.
Reprinted by permission.

the U.S. market is attractive due to rather low inflation and unemployment rates, as well as the relative affluence of the population. Developing and less-developed countries are potentially lucrative markets due to their population growth; over 90 per cent of world population growth is there. For example, Heinz now targets developing and less-developed nations because of their population growth and nutrition needs. Its brands are established in Africa, China, and the Pacific Rim.

Home competition may lead to international efforts.

Competition in a firm's domestic market may become intense and lead to its expanding internationally, as these examples show:

- The U.S. optical-products marketplace is very competitive. So, U.S.-based Bausch & Lomb is stepping up its activities in countries with growth opportunities. Bausch &

FIGURE 6-3
Why International Marketing Occurs

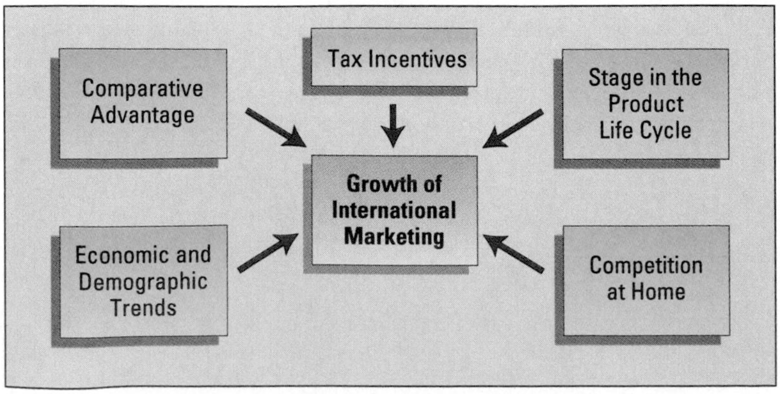

International Marketing in *Action*

Is India the Next Big Marketing Opportunity?

India—with its 900 million people—is the second most-inhabited nation in the world. Yet, for a long time, foreign companies did not view the Indian market as a very attractive one, due largely to the low annual per capita income and the restrictions placed on foreign businesses by the government.

Since the early 1990s, the situation has changed, and foreign firms have invested billions of dollars in India. And 95 per cent of the respondents to a recent survey said they intend to expand their investments:

- India's middle-class market is huge (more than 200 million people).
- Household appliance sales are growing at a double-digit rate. Refrigerator sales are growing at a 15 per cent annual rate and sales of color TVs are growing at an 18 per cent rate.
- India has opened its doors to foreign products by reducing the highest duty rate from 120 to 65 per cent. It also plans to lower duties on imported capital goods.
- Taxes on companies that are incorporated abroad but that earn income in India have been reduced from 65 per cent to 55 per cent.
- To foreign investors, India offers low labor costs and the availability of skilled management and technical personnel. A third resource, research and development opportunities, is tied to the availability of skilled personnel.

Foreign firms do need to be aware of the fragmented nature of the Indian market and of the differences in labor costs, distribution alternatives, and tax rates among Indian regions. Three popular areas for foreign investments are Bombay, Bangalore, and New Delhi. Each one has unique advantages: Bombay is valued for its commercial infrastructure, Bangalore for its software expertise, and New Delhi for the presence of the central government.

As an international marketing consultant, draw up a checklist of factors for Westinghouse's appliance business to consider when investing in India.

Sources: Based on material in Philip Banks and Ganesh Natarajan, "India: The Next Asian Tiger?" *Business Horizons*, Vol. 38 (May–June 1995), pp. 47–50; and Sally D. Goll, "India's Growing Middle Class Buys Stuff Firms' Dreams Are Made Of," *Wall Street Journal* (July 28, 1995), p. B4C.

Lomb's non-U.S. revenues currently represent 45 per cent of the company total, and it markets products in 105 countries.

- In Europe, Germany's Henkel is a leading maker of detergents, cleansers, and personal-care products—as well as industrial chemicals. Yet, it faces European competition from Germany's Hoechst, Dutch-British Unilever, and America's Procter & Gamble. So, it is pumping up efforts in Asia.[4]

International marketing may extend the product life cycle or dispose of discontinued items.

Because products are often in different stages of their life cycles in different nations, exporting may be a way to prolong the cycles. For instance, the U.S. market for tobacco products has been falling, for health and social reasons. To stimulate cigarette sales, Philip Morris and RJR Nabisco (and others) have turned more to foreign sales. The two firms have heightened their efforts in Eastern Europe—where cigarette smoking is popular and

[4]Patrick J. Spain and James R. Talbot (Editors), *Hoover's Handbook of American Business 1996* (Austin, Texas: Reference Press, 1995), pp. 244–245; and Hellmut Schütte, "Henkel's Strategy for Asia Pacific," *Long Range Planning*, Vol. 28 (February 1995), pp. 95–103.

shortages of domestic tobacco products occur. International marketing can also be utilized to dispose of discontinued goods, seconds, and manufacturer remakes (products that have been repaired). These items can be sold abroad without spoiling the domestic market for full-price, first-quality items. However, firms must be careful about selling unsafe products in foreign markets. This can lead to ill will on the part of the governments there.

There may be tax advantages with international marketing. Some countries entice new business from foreign firms by offering tax incentives in the form of low property, import, and income taxes for an initial period. In addition, multinational firms may adjust revenue reports so their largest profits are recorded in nations with the lowest tax rates.

The Scope of International Marketing[5]

The United States is both the world's largest goods and services exporter and importer.

The world's leading export countries are the United States, Germany, Japan, France, and Great Britain. Together, they account for more than $2 trillion annually in goods and services exports. In 1995, U.S. merchandise exports exceeded $550 billion, an amount equaling 7.5 to 8 per cent of the U.S. Gross Domestic Product and 12.5 to 13 per cent of world merchandise exports. Services accounted for another $225 billion in U.S. exports. The leading U.S. exports are capital goods, industrial supplies and materials, food grains, medical equipment, and scientific instruments, and such services as tourism, entertainment, engineering, accounting, insurance, and consulting.

Although 85 per cent of U.S. foreign business revenues are generated by a few hundred multinational firms, 105,000 U.S. firms engage in some level of international marketing. The 50 U.S. firms with the greatest international presence generate over $165 billion in annual foreign revenues, and this figure is deceptively low because it does not include returns on foreign investments and sales by foreign subsidiaries. The leading U.S. firms internationally (in terms of merchandise revenues) are General Motors, Ford, Boeing, Chrysler, General Electric, Motorola, IBM, and Philip Morris.

The United States is also the world's largest importer, followed again by Germany, Japan, France, and Great Britain. In 1995, U.S. merchandise imports were about $740 billion—17 per cent of total world merchandise imports. Service imports were an additional $150 billion. Leading U.S. imports are petroleum, motor vehicles, raw materials, and clothing.

The U.S. has had large merchandise **trade deficits** *and large service* **trade surpluses**.

As a result of the high level of imports in 1995, the United States had a merchandise **trade deficit**—the amount by which the value of imports exceeds the value of exports—of $190 billion. This was by far the greatest merchandise deficit of any country and set a U.S. record. On the other hand, U.S. services continue to be strong, with a service **trade surplus**—the amount by which the value of exports exceeds the value of imports—of $75 billion in 1995. This is by far the greatest service surplus of any nation.

The U.S. merchandise trade deficit is due to a variety of factors:

- The lucrative and attractive nature of the U.S. market. Per-capita consumption is high for most goods and services.
- The slow-growth economies in a number of other countries depressing consumer purchases there.
- Increased competition in foreign markets.
- U.S. dependence on foreign natural resources.
- High U.S. labor costs.
- Trade restrictions in foreign markets.
- U.S. firms virtually exiting such markets as televisions and VCRs.
- Making products in the United States with imported parts and materials.

[5]The data cited in this section are from "U.S. Trade Facts," *Business America* (May 1995), pp. 17–18; "U.S. Trade Deficit Narrows by 13.5% in Export Boom," *New York Times* (February 8, 1996), pp. D1, D16; James Aley, "New Lift for the U.S. Export Boom," *Fortune* (November 13, 1995), pp. 73–78; and Brian Bremner and Edith Hill Updike, "'Made in America' Isn't the Kiss of Death Anymore," *Business Week* (November 13, 1995), p. 62.

- The complacency of some U.S. firms in adapting their marketing strategies to the needs of foreign markets.
- The rather poor image of U.S. products in the eyes of many Americans.
- The emphasis of many U.S. firms on profits over market share. In contrast, Japanese firms try to keep prices stable to maximize market share—even if they must reduce profit margins to do so.

Because U.S. merchandise trade deficits have been so high, American firms are improving their product quality, focusing on market niches, becoming more efficient, building overseas facilities, and engaging in other tactics to improve competitiveness. Some have called for tighter import controls and more access to restricted foreign markets; one outcome of their efforts is the Omnibus Trade and Competitiveness Act that requires the President to press for open foreign markets. The U.S. government has also negotiated with foreign governments to help matters. For example, Japan has agreed to amend some practices to improve its trade balance with the United States. Still, the United States has a trade deficit of $45 billion to $50 billion a year with Japan.

Despite the difficulties it faces, the United States remains a dominant force globally. As one observer noted:

> In blue blazers and white shirts, London schoolchildren may look impeccably British. But these days, many of their shoes are made in America. In Germany, health concerns are forcing the removal of asbestos insulation from countless post-war buildings. The unpleasant work is made easier by equipment manufactured and sold by Critical Industries Inc., of Houston. The success of U.S. businesses in Europe tells of a surprising global turnaround. Americans may still worry that they are on the losing end of international trade. But in Europe, a growing demand for everything from Chrysler minivans to Converse All-Stars has turned a once-yawning U.S. trade deficit [with Europe] into a surplus.[6]

The Environment of International Marketing

Even though the marketing principles described in this book are applicable to international marketing strategies, there are often major environmental differences between domestic and foreign markets—and marketing practices may have to be adapted accordingly. Each market should be studied separately. Only then can a firm decide how much of its domestic marketing strategy can be used in foreign markets and what elements should be modified.

Here's how 3M is expanding globally:

> We like to get in ahead of competitors. We call this our FIDO approach (First In Defeats Others). We start small, with a modest investment, and gradually build a local presence. We make a little, sell a little, and plow profits back into the business. We pick out a few product lines that address the country's most pressing needs—often in the infrastructure. Then, we build up our local capability. Of course, these days when a company goes into a new market, it doesn't have as much time to make a little, sell a little, test it, and see how it all works. Opportunities are shorter than they used to be and competition is more intense. We have to make a bigger commitment than we did in the past.[7]

To gain insights about the global marketplace, useful resources such as these may be consulted:

- National Trade Data Bank (NTDB)—a "one-stop" source for international business data collected by 17 U.S. government agencies. It is updated and released monthly on two CD-ROM disks, with a total of 100,000 documents. The NTDB is also available via the Internet (http://www.stat-usa.gov).

[6]Hilary Stout, "In a Major Turnaround, U.S. Is Posting Surplus in Trade with Europe," *Wall Street Journal* (July 10, 1990), p. A1. See also Dana Milbank, "Made in America Becomes a Boast in Europe," *Wall Street Journal* (January 19, 1994), pp. B1, B6.

[7]Harry Hammerly, "Matching Global Strategies with National Responses," *Journal of Business Strategy*, Vol. 13 (March–April 1992), p. 10.

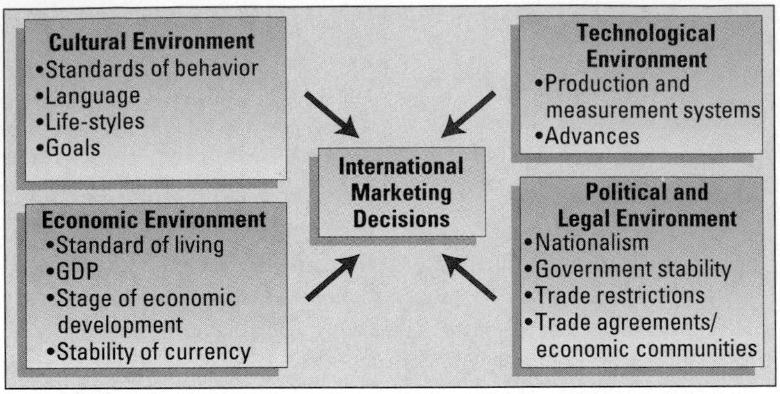

FIGURE 6-4
The Environment Facing International Marketers

- Trade Information Center Fax Retrieval Hotline (1–800-USA-TRADE)—provides general information, listings of state and private organizations, and business contacts. It is accessed through touch-tone phones.
- Export Yellow Pages—a free directory of U.S. manufacturers, banks, service firms, and trading companies looking to do business internationally. It is distributed through local U.S. Department of Commerce offices.[8]

The major cultural, economic, political and legal, and technological environments facing international marketers are discussed next. See Figure 6-4.

The Cultural Environment

Inadequate information about foreign **cultures** *is a common cause of errors.*

International marketers need to be aware of each foreign market's cultural environment. A **culture** consists of a group of people sharing a distinctive heritage. It teaches behavior standards, language, life-styles, and goals; is passed down from one generation to another; and is not easily changed. Almost every country has a different culture; continental differences exist as well. A firm unfamiliar with or insensitive to a foreign culture may try to market goods or services that are unacceptable to that culture. For example, beef and unisex products are rejected by some cultures.

Table 6-1 shows the errors a firm engaged in international marketing could commit due to a lack of awareness about foreign cultures. Sometimes, the firm is at fault because it operates out of a domestic home office and gets little local input. Other times, such as marketing in less-developed countries, information may be limited because a low level of population data exist and mail and phone service are poor. In either case, marketing research—to determine hidden meanings and the ease of pronunciation of brand names and slogans, the rate of product consumption, and reasons for purchases and nonpurchases—would not be fully effective.

Cultural awareness can be improved by employing foreign personnel in key positions, hiring experienced marketing research specialists, locating offices in each country of operations, studying cultural differences, and responding to cultural changes. Table 6-2 shows several cultural opportunities.

This is how Samsung, Korea's largest firm, is improving cultural awareness among its executives:

> Overseas-bound managers attend a month-long boot camp to get lessons on table manners, dancing, and avoiding sexual harassment. In addition, 400 bright junior employees are sent abroad for a year. Their decidedly un-Korean mission: Goof off. "International exposure is important, but you have to develop international tastes. You have to goof off at the mall and watch people." The program costs $80,000 a year per person and takes key people out of their jobs. But, Samsung is convinced cultural immersion will pay off in more astute judgments about what customers want.[9]

[8] "Growing a Global Business," *Wall Street Journal*, 1995 advertising supplement sponsored by Sprint Business.
[9] "Korea's Biggest Firm Teaches Junior Execs Strange Foreign Ways," *Wall Street Journal* (December 30, 1992), p. 1.

Table 6-1

Illustrations of Errors in International Marketing Because of a Lack of Cultural Awareness

In the Czech Republic, Eurotel portable phones did poorly when introduced because they were perceived as walkie-talkies.

Japanese cars had engine trouble in China, where drivers turn off their motors when stopped at red lights. Inasmuch as the air-conditioning in these cars kept going with the motors off, the engines malfunctioned.

At the Moscow Pizza Hut, consumers did not purchase the Moscva Seafood pizza, with sardines and salmon. "Russians have this thing. If it's their own, it must be bad."

Pepsodent failed in Southeast Asia when it promised white teeth to a culture where black or yellow teeth are symbols of prestige.

In Quebec, a canned-fish manufacturer promoted a product by showing a woman dressed in shorts, golfing with her husband, and planning to serve canned fish for dinner. These activities violated cultural norms.

Maxwell House advertised itself as the "great American coffee" in Germany, although Germans have little respect for American coffee.

In Mexico, a U.S. airline meant to advertise that passengers could sit in comfortable leather seats; but the phrase used in its Spanish translation ("sentando en cuero") meant "sit naked."

African men were upset by a commercial for men's deodorant that showed a happy male being chased by women. They thought the deodorant would make them weak and overrun by women.

Source: Compiled by the authors from various publications.

The Economic Environment

A nation's economic environment indicates its present and potential capacities for consuming goods and services. Measures of economic performance include the standard of living, the Gross Domestic Product (GDP), the stage of economic development, and the stability of currency.

Table 6-2

Illustrations of Cultural Opportunities for International Marketers

Globally, the greatest growth in ready-to-eat cereal sales is in Latin America, where there is new interest in convenient foods.

After one year of employment, in most European countries, people receive 20 to 25 days of vacation (compared to 10 days for Canadians and Americans). This means an emphasis on travel, summer homes, and leisure wear.

Japanese consumers are attracted by high-tech vending machines—such as those that play music, talk, dispense free products at random, and use splashy rotating signs.

Worldwide, consumers want the "American look" provided by Levi's jeans.

At Domino's outlets in Australia, the favorite pizzas are those with prawns and pineapple.

In China, the most popular color is red—indicating happiness. Black elicits a positive response because it denotes power and trustworthiness.

French Canadians drink more soda, beer, and wine than their English-speaking counterparts.

Nigerians believe "good beer only comes in green bottles."

British consumers insist on cake mixes that require their adding fresh eggs, as Betty Crocker mixes sold there do.

Source: Compiled by the authors from various publications.

Table 6-3

Ownership and Consumption in Eleven Countries

	PASSENGER CARS (per 100 People)	TV SETS (per 100 People)	RADIOS (per 100 People)	DAILY NEWSPAPER CIRCULATION (per 100 People)	TELEPHONE LINES (per 100 People)	ENERGY CONSUMPTION (Kilograms per Year per Person)
United States	55	81	212	25	56	10,800
Brazil	8	21	44	6	7	800
Canada	46	64	100	23	59	10,900
China	.2	3	19	4	1	800
France	41	50	89	21	52	5,500
Great Britain	35	43	115	40	45	5,400
India	.3	4	8	3	1	340
Italy	48	42	79	11	41	4,000
Japan	31	61	91	59	47	4,750
Nigeria	.9	8	11	2	1	210
Russia	7	37	60	NA	15	6,400

NA = Not available.

Source: United Nations data; and authors' estimates.

The quality of life in a nation is measured by its **standard of living**.

The **standard of living** refers to the average quantity and quality of goods and services that are owned and consumed in a given nation. According to the United Nations and Organization for Economic Cooperation & Development (OECD) data, the United States has the highest standard of living of any industrialized country in the world. By examining a nation's per-capita ownership and consumption across a range of goods and services, a firm can estimate the standard of living there (regarding the average *quantity* of goods and services). Table 6-3 compares data for eleven diverse countries.

The total value of goods and services produced in a nation is its **Gross Domestic Product**.

As noted in Chapter 2, the **Gross Domestic Product (GDP)** is the total value of goods and services produced in a country each year. Total and per-capita GDP are the most frequently used measures of a nation's wealth because they are regularly published and easy to calculate and compare with other nations. Yet, per-capita GDP may be misleading. The figures are means and not income distributions; a few wealthy citizens may boost per-capita GDP, even though the bulk of the population has low income. And due to price and product availability differences, incomes purchase different standards of living in each nation. An income of $30,000 in the United States yields the same standard of living as an income of $13,200 in Brazil, $11,100 in Poland, $6,900 in China, $6,600 in India, and $5,100 in Uganda.[10]

Countries can be classified as **industrialized, developing,** *and* **less developed**.

Marketing opportunities often can be highlighted by looking at a country's stage of economic growth. One way to classify growth is to divide nations into industrialized, developing, and less-developed groups.[11] See Figure 6-5.

Industrialized countries have high literacy, modern technology, and per-capita income of several thousand dollars. They can be placed into two main subgroups: established free-market economies and newly emerging free-market economies. The former include the United States, Canada, Japan, Australia, and countries in Western Europe; they have a large middle class, annual per-capita GDP of $12,000 and up, and plentiful goods and services to satisfy their needs. The latter include Russia and its former republics, as

[10]Peter Fuhrman and Michael Schuman, "Where Are the Indians? The Russians?" *Forbes* (July 17, 1995), pp. 126, 128.

[11]Peter D. Bennett (Editor), *Dictionary of Marketing Terms*, Second Edition (Chicago: American Marketing Association, 1995), various pages.

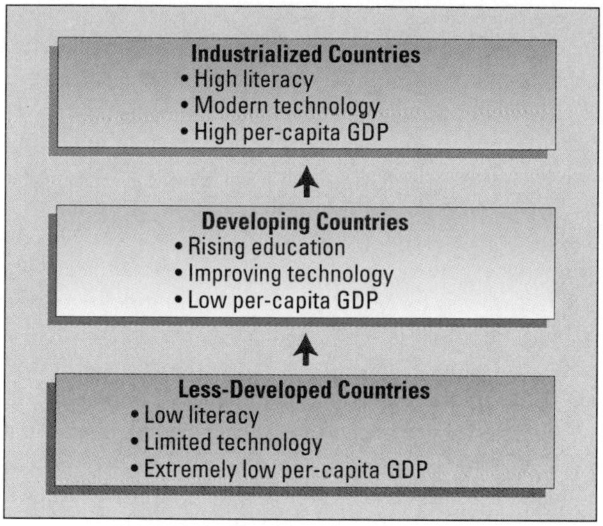

FIGURE 6-5
The Stages of Economic Development

well as other nations in Eastern Europe; although industrialized, they have a smaller middle class, annual per-capita GDP of $5,000 to $8,000, and insufficient goods and services to satisfy all of their needs.

In **developing countries**, education and technology are rising, and per-capita GDP is about $2,000 to $4,000. Included are many Latin American nations. Although developing countries are striving to build their industries, consumers there are limited in what they can purchase (due to the scarcity and relatively high prices of goods and services). These countries account for 20 per cent of world population and almost one-third of its income.

Less-developed countries include a number of nations in Africa and South Asia. Compared to other nations, literacy is lower and technology is more limited. Per-capita GDP is below $1,500 (sometimes less than $500). These nations have two-thirds of world population but under 15 per cent of world income. According to UN data, people in the most affluent one-fifth of the world have 65 times greater per-capita GDP than those in the bottom one-fifth.

The greatest marketing opportunities often occur in industrialized nations due to their higher incomes and standards of living. Yet, industrialized countries have slower rates of population growth, and sales of some product categories may have peaked. In contrast, developing and less-developed nations tend to have more rapidly expanding populations but now purchase few imports. There is long-run potential for international marketers in these nations. For example, Brazilians have only 80 cars per 1,000 population and Indians 3 per 1,000. The 1.2 billion people of China have 2.3 million cars—compared to 1.7 million cars in Denmark, a country with just over five million people.

Currency stability affects foreign sales and profit.

Currency stability should also be considered in international transactions because sales and profits could be affected if a foreign currency fluctuates widely relative to a firm's home currency. For example, during 1995, the value of the Mexican peso against the U.S. dollar fell from 3.26 to 6.65 pesos per dollar—in January 1996, a Mexican consumer had to spend 665 of his or her pesos to buy a $100 U.S. good that cost 326 pesos in January 1995. This decline in the peso's value meant Mexican goods became cheaper for consumers in other nations, while making it more expensive for Mexican consumers to buy foreign products. As a result, foreign firms had some difficulty exporting products to Mexico during this period because their prices became too high.

In recent years, the currencies of both industrialized countries and developing and less-developed nations have fluctuated—some dramatically. As a rule, established free-market industrialized countries' currencies have been more stable than those of other nations.

The Political and Legal Environment

Every nation has a unique political and legal environment. Among the factors for international marketers to study are nationalism, government stability, trade restrictions, and trade agreements and economic communities.

Nationalism *involves a host country's attempts to promote its interests.*

Nationalism refers to a country's efforts to become self-reliant and raise its stature in the eyes of the world community. At times, a high degree of nationalism may lead to tight restrictions on foreign firms to foster the development of domestic industry at their expense. In the past, some nations even seized the assets of multinational firms, revoked their licenses to operate, prevented funds transfers from one currency to another, increased taxes, and/or unilaterally changed contract terms.

Government stability must be studied in terms of two elements: consistency of business policies and orderliness in installing leaders. Do government policies regarding taxes, company expansion, profits, and so on, remain rather unchanged over time? Is there an orderly process for selecting and installing new government leaders? Firms will probably not function well unless both factors are positive. Thus, although Nestlé, PepsiCo, and CPC International have made large investments in developing nations, other food companies have stayed away from some less-developed and developing countries.

A firm can protect itself against the adverse effects of nationalism and political instability. Prior to entering a foreign market, it can measure the potential for domestic instability (riots, government purges), the political climate (stability of political parties, manner of choosing officials), and the economic climate (financial strength, government intervention)—and avoid nations deemed unsuitable. The U.S. government's Overseas Private Investment Corporation (OPIC) insures American investments in more than 70 friendly underdeveloped nations against such perils as asset takeovers and earnings inconvertibility; in addition, private underwriters insure foreign investments. Risks can also be reduced by using foreign partners, borrowing money from foreign governments or banks, and/or utilizing licensing, contract manufacturing, or management contracting (which are covered later in the chapter).

Tariffs, trade quotas, embargoes, *and* **local content laws** *are forms of trade restrictions.*

Another aspect of the international political and legal environment involves trade restrictions. The most common one is a **tariff,** which is a tax placed on imported products by a foreign government. The second major restriction is a **trade quota,** which sets limits on the amounts of products that can be imported into a country. The strictest form of trade quota is an **embargo,** which disallows entry of specified products into a country. The third major restriction involves **local content laws,** which require foreign-based firms to set up local plants and use locally made components. The goal of tariffs, trade quotas, and local content laws is to protect both the economies and domestic employment of the nations involved. Embargoes may also have political ramifications, such as the United States refusing to engage in any trade with Cuba. Here are examples:

- There are U.S. tariffs on imported clothing, ceramic tiles, rubber footwear, brooms, flowers, cement, computer screens, sugar, candy, trucks, and other items. The tariffs raise import prices relative to domestic items.
- Many European nations have pacts with Japan that set voluntary quotas on certain goods exported by Japan to those nations. The agreements limit the sales of VCRs, autos, TVs, quartz watches, and machine tools.
- To stimulate domestic production, in 1984, Brazil placed an embargo on most foreign computer products—thus banning their sales there. The embargo was not lifted until 1990, with some microcomputers still barred until 1992.
- In Italy, food products cannot be called pasta unless they are made from durum wheat, which is the country's major kind of wheat.

Figure 6-6 shows how Toyota is making cars in the United States to maintain a favorable image among American consumers and the general public. Toyota also hopes to avoid local content laws (in place of the voluntary quotas now in existence).

Some barriers among nations have been reduced via trade agreements and economic communities. In 1948, 23 nations, including the United States, signed the General Agreement on Tariffs and Trade (GATT) to foster multilateral trade. By 1994, 115 nations participated in GATT. From its inception, GATT talks helped lower tariffs on manufactured goods. But member nations got bogged down because trade in services, agriculture, textiles, and investment and capital flows was not covered; and GATT let members belong

FIGURE 6-6
A Toyota Car That Is Made in the U.S.A.
Reprinted by permission.

to regional trade associations (economic communities) with fewer trade barriers among the nations involved in those associations than with those not involved.

On January 1, 1995, after eight years of difficult negotiations, GATT was replaced by the **World Trade Organization (WTO)**. About 125 nations have joined the WTO, whose mission is to open up international markets even further and promote a cooperative atmosphere around the globe. These are some of the provisions of the WTO:

The **World Trade Organization** *seeks to eliminate trade barriers.*

- Thousands of tariffs are to be reduced globally by about 40 per cent.
- Intellectual-property protection (such as copyright and patent rights) is to be enacted worldwide. The agreement specifies 20 years protection for patents and up to 50 years for copyrights. This will help book, software, movie, and pharmaceutical companies combat piracy. The United States has to change its rules to comply with this stipulation, since current U.S. laws give protection for 17 years after a patent is granted.
- There are tougher rules regarding price dumping in foreign markets to lessen firms' selling at below-market prices in foreign countries.
- New rules apply to global agricultural and textile products transactions.
- Some nations have agreed to open up their markets for legal and accounting services, as well as computer software. However, the United States did not secure much access to the foreign markets closed to American banks and securities firms, such as those in Japan and other Asian countries.

- Three-person arbitration panels are to rule on disputes between countries.
- Economic communities are still permitted.[12]

The two leading **economic communities** *are the* **European Union** *and the* **North American Free Trade Agreement.**

In contrast to the WTO, which promotes free trade around the world, each **economic community** promotes free trade among its member nations—but not necessarily with nonmember nations. As a result, the best interests of the WTO and economic communities may clash.

The two leading economic communities are the European Union and the North American Free Trade community. The **European Union (EU),** also called the Common Market, consists of Austria, Belgium, Denmark, Finland, France, Germany, Great Britain, Greece, Ireland, Italy, Luxembourg, the Netherlands, Portugal, Spain, and Sweden. Other European nations are expected to join the EU within the next five years. EU rules call for no trade restrictions among members; uniform tariffs with nonmembers; common product standards; and a free flow of people and capital. The aim is for members to have an open marketplace, such as exists among states in the United States. One of the EU's biggest challenges is installing a common currency, which will not occur before the turn of the century. The combined GDP of EU nations is 118 per cent that of the United States; the total population is 1.42 times that of the United States.

In 1988, the United States and Canada reached agreement on a free-trade pact. They then turned to negotiating a free-trade accord with Mexico. On January 1, 1994, the **North American Free Trade Agreement (NAFTA)** was enacted, creating an economic community that links the United States, Canada, and Mexico; over the next several years, tariffs and other trade restrictions among the three countries are to be removed. The NAFTA community and the EU are about the same size in both total GDP and total population (until the EU adds more members). There have been some very preliminary discussions about expanding NAFTA to include such emerging Latin American nations as Brazil and Chile, but, it is quite unlikely that NAFTA will expand in the near future.

Other economic communities include the Andean Pact (with five Latin American members), Association of South East Asian Nations (with six members), Caribbean Common Market (with more than a dozen members), Central American Common Market (with five members), Gulf Cooperation Council (with six Arabic members), Economic Community of West African States (with sixteen members), and Mercosur (with four Latin American members).

As many nations in Eastern Europe and elsewhere have moved to more open economies, they have become quite interested in hiking their participation in world trade. They are deregulating industries, encouraging foreign investment, and seeking trade agreements with free-market nations. In 1990, Eastern Europe's Council for Mutual Economic Assistance announced its own demise—members did not want to be hampered by a "ramshackle trading system." Since then, a number of Eastern European countries have expressed interest in eventually gaining entry into the European Union.[13]

The Technological Environment

International marketing may require adjustments in technology.

Technological factors such as these affect international marketing:

- Technology advances vary around the world. For example, outside the United States, cable TV is more limited. Even in Western Europe, only one-third of households have cable TV (compared to two-thirds in the United States).
- Foreign workers must often be trained to run equipment unfamiliar to them.
- Problems occur if equipment maintenance practices vary by nation or adverse physical conditions exist, such as high humidity, extreme hot or cold weather, or air pollution.

[12]"The Trade Pact's Key Provisions," *Wall Street Journal* (December 2, 1994), p. A8; Paul Lewis, "Trade in Financial Services Is Dealt a Setback by U.S.," *New York Times* (June 30, 1995), pp. D1, D4; and Eduardo Lachica, "U.S. May Be Losing Its Trade-Bully Status," *Wall Street Journal* (October 13, 1995), p. A11.

[13]Tim Carrington, "Anxiety Grows as Comecon's End Nears," *Wall Street Journal* (July 20, 1990), p. B6; Richard W. Stevenson, "East Europe Says Barriers to Trade Hurt Its Economies," *New York Times* (January 25, 1993), pp. A1, D5; and Nathaniel C. Nash, "European Union Offers Timetable for Talks with Applicants," *New York Times* (December 17, 1995), Section 1, p. 17.

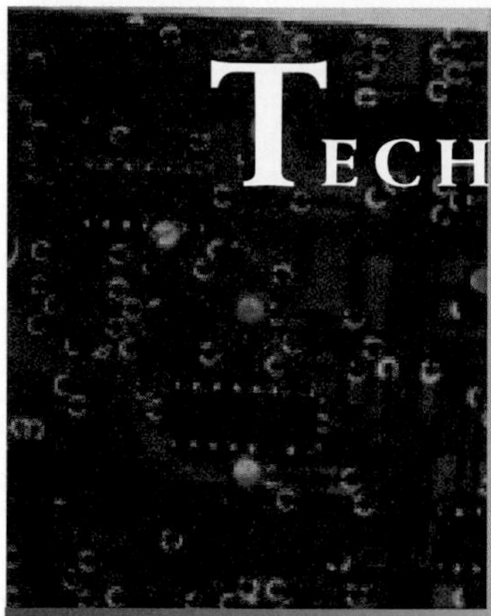

TECHNOLOGY & MARKETING

How Should PCs Be Marketed in Developing Countries?

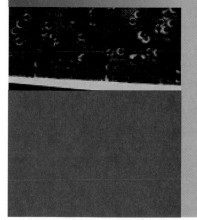

Until recently, both companies and consumers in less-developed nations were unable to purchase PCs and related items due to their high prices. But now, they are able to buy the very affordable PCs and computer networks that are flooding the market. Thus, throughout Latin America, the sales of PCs are hot—with annual growth rates of 25 per cent and more.

Some experts attribute the strong sales to the technological advances of the new PCs (which let businesses use PCs for functions that formerly could only be undertaken by expensive mainframe computers): "Technology is quite reasonably priced for most people, except in the very, very poor nations." Other experts see the high inflation rates in many less-developed countries as an impetus to computer sales. According to that theory, many firms and individuals would rather buy PCs now due to the assumption that they will be much more expensive in the future.

Let's look at PC and workstation sales in Chile: From 1991 to 1995, the annual sales of PCs and workstations in Chile grew from $55 million to $200 million. Still, there were fewer than four PCs for every 100 people as of the end of 1995 (versus more than 30 per 100 people in the United States). Much of Chile's PC sales growth is from small businesses that use computers to track inventories or prepare invoices, from larger firms that use computers to dispatch their salespeople or to track sales of important products, and from electronic banking. In addition, "Chile's export-promotion agency recently connected 160 PCs around the world to a group of Compaq Computer Corp. servers back at its Santiago headquarters, allowing prospective buyers to see exactly what's available, when, and what price."

As the marketing vice-president for a PC manufacturer, what would you do differently in Chile than in the United States?

Source: Based on material in Scott McCartney and Jonathan Friedland, "Computer Sales Sizzles as Developing Nations Try to Shrink PC Gap," *Wall Street Journal* (June 29, 1995), pp. A1, A8.

- Electricity and electrical power needs may vary by nation and require product modifications. For example, U.S. appliances work on 110 volts; European appliances work on 220 volts.
- Although the metric system is the one used in nations with 95 per cent of the world's population, the United States still relies on ounces, pounds, inches, and feet. Thus, auto makers, food processors, beverage bottlers, and many other U.S. firms make items using metric standards—and then list U.S. and metric measures side-by-side on labels and packages. As the United States converts to the metric system (which it has been trying to do since 1866, when Congress passed the first law on the metric system), the American consumer must be re-educated about measurement and learn meters, liters, and other metric standards; this process continues to be a slow one.

On the plus side, various technological advances are easing the growth of international marketing. Such advances involve transactions (automatic teller machines), order processing (computerization), communications (TV satellites, facsimile machines, the Internet), and production (multiplant innovations).

Developing an International Marketing Strategy

The vital parts of an international marketing strategy are explored next: company organization; market entry decisions; the degree of standardization; and product, distribution, promotion, and price planning.

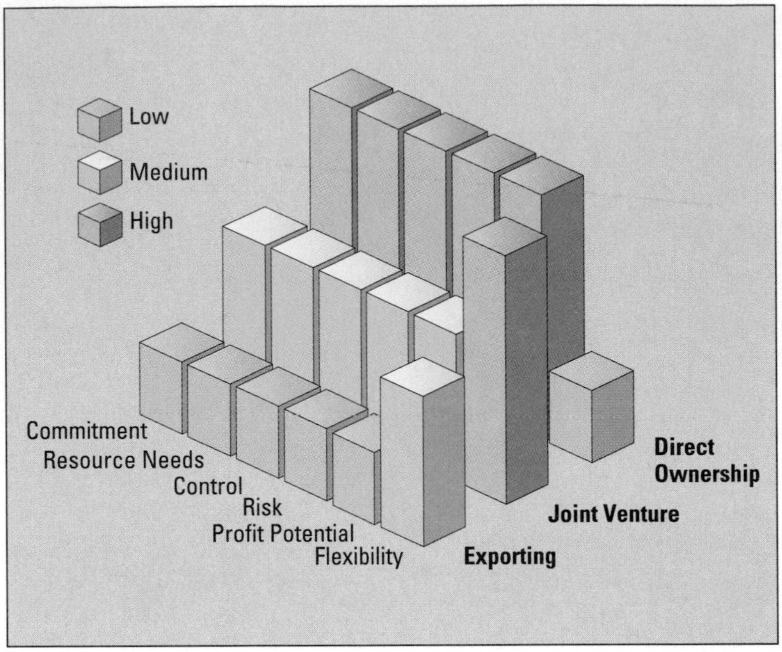

FIGURE 6-7
Alternate Company Organizations for International Marketing

Company Organization

A firm has three organizational formats from which to choose: exporting, joint venture, and direct ownership. They are compared in Figure 6-7.

Exporting *lets a firm reach international markets without foreign production.*

With **exporting**, a firm reaches international markets by selling products made in its home country directly through its own sales force or indirectly via foreign merchants or agents. In direct selling, a firm situates its sales force in a home office or in foreign branch offices. This is best when customers are easy to locate, concentrated, or come to the seller. With indirect selling, a firm hires outside specialists to contact customers. The specialists may be based in the home or foreign country. There are 2,000+ specialized U.S. export management firms marketing products in foreign nations. Indirect selling is best if customers are hard to locate or dispersed, if a potential exporter has limited funds, and/or if local customs are unique.

An exporting structure requires minimal investment in foreign facilities. There is no foreign production by the firm. The exporter may modify packages, labels, or catalogs at its domestic facilities in response to foreign market needs. Exporting embodies the lowest level of commitment to international marketing. Most smaller firms that engage in international marketing rely on exporting. For example, Sharper Finish is a Chicago maker of commercial laundry equipment that works with 300 independent distributors in 30 nations. Sixty per cent of its $3 million in annual sales involves exports.[14]

A **joint venture** *can be based on licensing, contract manufacturing, management contracting, or joint ownership.*

With a **joint venture** (also known as a **strategic alliance**), a firm agrees to combine some aspect of its manufacturing or marketing efforts with those of a foreign company so as to share expertise, costs, and/or connections with important persons. As experts observe: "In this period of advanced technology and global markets, implementing strategies quickly is essential. Forming alliances is often the fastest, most effective method of reaching objectives. However, without the proper partner, a company should not undertake an alliance, even for the right reasons. Partners must be compatible and willing to trust one another."[15]

Here are examples of firms engaged in international joint ventures:

[14]William J. Holstein and Kevin Kelly, "Little Companies, Big Exports," *Business Week* (April 13, 1992), p. 71. See also Stephanie N. Mehta, "Small Companies Look to Cultivate Foreign Business," *Wall Street Journal* (July 7, 1994), p. B1.

[15]Bruce A. Walters, Steve Peters, and Gregory G. Dess, "Strategic Alliances and Joint Ventures: Making Them Work," *Business Horizons*, Vol. 37 (July–August 1994), p. 5.

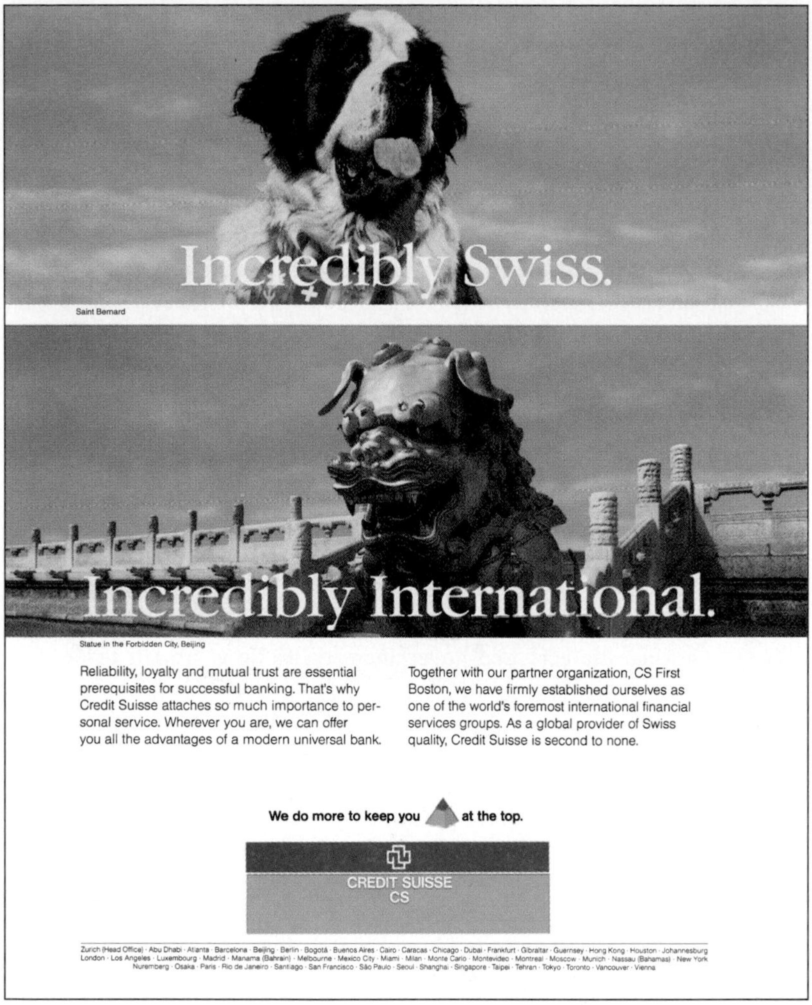

FIGURE 6-8
A Joint Venture That Is "Incredibly International"
Reprinted by permission.

- Credit Suisse (Switzerland) and CS First Boston (United States) are partners in ventures that offer financial services around the world. See Figure 6-8.
- Airbus Industrie, a jet maker, is owned and operated by Aerospatiale (France), Deutsche Airbus (Germany), British Aerospace, and Construcciones Aeronauticas (Spain). It gets financial support from members' governments.
- Charoen Pokphand (Thailand) has a telecommunications venture with Nynex (United States) and a retailing venture with Wal-Mart (United States).
- Monsanto (United States) and PASA (Argentina) are working together to make and market plastics.[16]

A joint venture may lead to reduced costs and favorable trade terms from a foreign government if products are made locally and some degree of foreign ownership is set. Thus, joint ventures between Japanese and U.S. firms are growing because Japanese firms see them as lowering the possibility of U.S. trade restrictions. U.S. firms view the ventures as a means of opening the Japanese market and as a way of observing potential competitors.

A joint venture can involve licensing, contract manufacturing, management contracting, or joint ownership. Licensing gives a foreign firm the rights to a manufacturing process, trademark, patent, and/or trade secret in exchange for a commission, fee, or royalty. Coca-Cola and PepsiCo license products in some nations. Under contract manufacturing, a firm

[16]Patrick J. Spain and James R. Talbot, *Hoover's Handbook of World Business 1995–1996* (Austin, Texas: Reference Press, 1995), various pages; Joyce Barnathan, Pete Engardio, and John Winzenburg, "Asia's New Giants," *Business Week* (November 27, 1995), p. 78; and Geri Smith and John Pearson, "The New World's Newest Trade Bloc," *Business Week* (May 4, 1992), p. 51.

agrees to have a foreign company make its products locally. The firm markets the products itself and provides management expertise. This arrangement is common in book publishing. In management contracting, a firm acts as a consultant to foreign companies. Such hotel chains as Hilton International, Hyatt International, and Sheraton engage in management contracting. With joint ownership, a firm produces and markets products in partnership with a foreign company so as to reduce costs and spread risk. General Electric has a majority interest in Tungsram, a Hungarian light-bulb maker. Sometimes, a foreign government may require joint ownership with local businesses as a condition for entry. In Canada, outsiders must use joint ownership with Canadian firms for new ventures.

Direct ownership *involves total control of foreign operations and facilities by a firm.*

With **direct ownership,** a firm owns production, marketing, and other facilities in one or more foreign nations without any partners. The firm has full control over its international operations in those nations. Thus, Eaton Corporation owns a factory in Belluno, Italy, that makes three million electromagnetic timers a year for use in washing machines. Wholly owned subsidiaries are sometimes established. In the United States, Pillsbury is a subsidiary of Grand Metropolitan of Great Britain and Miles (Alka-Seltzer's maker) is a subsidiary of Bayer of Germany. Similarly, foreign facilities of U.S.-based firms annually yield revenues of hundreds of billions of dollars.

Under direct ownership, a firm has all the benefits and risks of owning a foreign business. There are potential labor savings, and marketing plans are more sensitive to local needs. Profit potential may be high, although costs may also be high. There is a possibility of nationalistic acts, and government restrictions are apt to be stricter. This is the riskiest organization form.

Companies often combine formats. For instance, a firm could use exporting in a country with a history of taking over the assets of foreign businesses and direct ownership in one with tax advantages for construction. McDonald's worldwide efforts combine company-operated stores (20 per cent of outlets), franchisee-operated stores (69 per cent of outlets), and affiliate-operated stores—whereby McDonald's owns 50 per cent or less of assets, with the rest owned by resident nationals (11 per cent of outlets). Company stores are largely in the United States, Canada, France, Great Britain, and Germany; franchisee outlets are mostly in the United States, Canada, France, Germany, and Australia; and affiliate restaurants are common in Latin America, Japan, and other Pacific nations. McDonald's has outlets in 80 countries outside the United States; they generate 50 per cent of systemwide sales.[17]

Market Entry Decisions

A firm needs to determine which and how many foreign markets in which to do business.

There are a number of factors to consider in deciding which and how many foreign markets a firm should enter. Here are several of them:

Which Market(s) to Enter

- Are there cultural similarities between a foreign country and a company's home market? How important is this?
- Are there language similarities between a foreign country and a firm's home market? How important is this?
- Is the standard of living in a foreign country consistent with the goods and services a company would offer there?
- How large is a foreign market for the goods and services a firm would offer there? Is it growing? What is regional potential (e.g., Eastern Europe)?
- Is the technology in a foreign market appropriate for a firm to do business? Is the country's infrastructure appropriate?
- Are there enough skilled workers in a foreign country?
- Are the media in a foreign country adequate for a firm's marketing efforts?
- What is the level of competition in a foreign market?

[17]Spain and Talbot, *Hoover's Handbook of American Business 1996*, pp. 958–959.

- What are the government restrictions a firm would face in a foreign market? The economic communities?
- How stable are the currency and government in a foreign market?
- Is the overall business climate in a foreign country favorable to a firm?

How Many Markets to Enter

- What are the firm's available resources?
- How many foreign markets could a firm's management and marketing personnel properly oversee and service?
- How diverse are multiple foreign markets? What is the geographic proximity?
- What are the marketing economies of scale from being regional or global?
- Are exporting arrangements possible? Are joint ventures?
- What are a firm's goals regarding its mix of domestic and foreign revenues?
- How extensive is competition in a firm's home market?

Standardizing Plans

Under a **global approach**, *a common marketing plan is used for each nation. Under a* **nonstandardized approach**, *each country is given a separate marketing plan. A* **glocal approach** *is a combination strategy.*

A firm engaged in international marketing must determine the degree to which plans should be standardized. Both standardized and nonstandardized plans have benefits and limitations.

With a **standardized (global) marketing approach**, a firm uses a common marketing plan for all nations in which it operates—because the firm assumes that worldwide markets are becoming more homogeneous due to better communications, more open country borders, the move to free-market economies, and other factors. This approach downplays differences among foreign markets. There are marketing and production economies—product design, packaging, advertising, and other costs are spread over a large product base. A uniform image is presented, training foreign personnel is easier, and centralized control is applied. Yet, standardization is insensitive to individual market needs, and input from foreign personnel is limited:

> The increase in global markets and global competition is attributed to many factors. The pressures for growth in slow-growth home markets are driving companies around the world to seek new geographic markets. Converging customer tastes and requirements, the need to gain scale from world market development, shortening product life cycles, and expanding financial markets all have made globalization more necessary and feasible. Government changes, too, are freeing up or encouraging increased global competition.
>
> Yet, the world economy remains mostly local both in market characteristics and in marketing and competitive requirements. Regional conditions and tastes vary to the point where local customization is necessary—often in products and usually in marketing—even within the United States. Many industries can support a business on a local country or regional basis; they need not garner scale from cross-country or cross-region participation. Product development and production technologies, too, are helping provide the flexibility to adjust products for local needs. Finally, as much as government actions are stimulating cross-border competition, they are restricting it as well.[18]

With a **nonstandardized marketing approach,** a firm sees each nation or region as distinct, and requiring its own marketing plan. This strategy is sensitive to local needs and means grooming foreign managers, as decentralized control is undertaken. It works best when distinctive major foreign markets are involved and/or a firm has many product lines. For instance, although Bausch & Lomb has such "global" brands as Ray-Ban sunglasses, its strategy is tailored to individual markets: "In Europe, Ray-Bans tend to be flashier, more avant garde, and costlier than in the United States. In Asia, the company redesigned them to better suit the Asian face—with its flatter bridge and higher cheekbones—and sales took off. Ray-Ban commands an awesome 40 per cent of the world market for premium-priced ($40 to $250) sunglasses."[19]

[18]Marc C. Particelli, "A Global Arena," *Journal of Consumer Marketing*, Vol. 7 (Fall 1990), pp. 43–52.
[19]Rahul Jacob, "Trust the Locals, Win Worldwide," *Fortune* (May 4, 1992), p. 76.

Ethics IN TODAY'S SOCIETY

Why Aren't International Codes of Conduct More Effective?

As a condition for doing business with J.C. Penney, suppliers around the world are required to sign a code of conduct. This code forbids suppliers from violating any local labor law, including the hiring of underage children. The penalty for violating a contract condition is the immediate loss of J.C. Penney's current and future business. According to many industry observers, enforcing such contract clauses is at best very hard and at worse impossible.

As an example, Guatemala is a country with a long history of firms using illegal child labor and paying workers below the minimum wage. Despite codes of conduct, labor law violations are rampant there. Nonetheless, in 1994, 400 Guatemalan firms exported $591 million worth of clothing to the United States.

Guatemalan government labor officials estimate that half of the country's apparel workers are paid below the minimum wage. And one government official says there are 300,000 illegally employed minors in Guatemala. Visits to Guatemalan factories that supply J.C. Penney have turned up children under the age of 14 (the minimum legal age to work), workers who are paid below the country's minimum wage of $2.80 per day, and workers who are forced to toil overtime on an unpaid basis.

According to one market analyst, "Setting standards is 5 per cent of the work; ensuring compliance is 95 per cent." J.C. Penney's difficulty in enforcing standards is compounded by having suppliers in over 50 countries. Many of these suppliers also hire subcontractors to complete their projects. In many cases, J.C. Penney does not even know which factory has produced its products. And some retailers, including Wal-Mart, rely on suppliers to self-police the retailer's code of conduct.

As a clothing buyer for J.C. Penney who does business with Guatemala-based factories, how would you make Penney's international code of conduct more effective?

Source: Based on material in Bob Ortega, "Conduct Codes Garner Goodwill for Retailers, But Violations Go On," *Wall Street Journal* (July 3, 1995), pp. A1, A14.

In recent years, more firms (including Bausch & Lomb) have turned to a **glocal marketing approach**—which stands for *think global and act local*. Under this approach, combining standardized and nonstandardized efforts lets a firm attain production efficiencies, have a consistent image, have some home-office control, and still be sensitive and responsive to local needs. To U.S.-based CPC International (the maker of such brands as Hellmann's Mayonnaise, Knorr soups, Mueller's pasta, Skippy peanut butter, and Mazola corn oil), a glocal approach is "the best of both worlds":

> *We are emphatically global* in our strategy of building a few core businesses worldwide; in the way we share technology, coordinate purchasing, and maximize other CPC worldwide resources; in our application of financial strength to seize opportunities wherever they may be; in our ability to spot worldwide trends before they become locally obvious; in the geographic spread of our businesses that helps us offset economic difficulties in one market with rapid growth in another. At the same time, *we are decisively local* in our detailed understanding of cultures, consumer trends, and competitive environments in 59 countries; in our ability to adapt our products to local eating habits and our marketing programs to local cultural nuances and developing trends; in the entrepreneurial energy that thrives in local CPC teams empowered to act quickly and take risk where we, as the local "home team," have a competitive advantage.[20]

[20]*CPC International 1994 Annual Report.*

FIGURE 6-9
A Modification Strategy for Knorr Products
CPC International markets its Knorr food products around the world. In many cases, it offers specially adapted versions of Knorr sauces, soups, and bouillons—tailored to the tastes of foreign consumers.
Reprinted by permission.

When determining a marketing approach, a firm should evaluate whether differences among countries are sufficiently great to warrant changes in marketing plans, which elements of marketing can be standardized, whether the size of each foreign market would lead to profitable adaptation, and if modifications can be made on a regional rather than a country basis.

Product Planning

Straight extension, product adaptation, backward invention, *and* **forward invention** *are basic methods of international product planning.*

International product planning (including both goods and services) can be based on straight-extension, product-adaptation, backward-invention, and/or forward-invention strategies.

In a **straight-extension** strategy, a firm makes and markets the same products for domestic and foreign sales. The firm is confident successful products can be sold abroad without modifications in the product, its brand name, packaging, or ingredients. This simple approach capitalizes on economies of scale in production. Apple markets the same PCs in the United States and Mexico. Coca-Cola and PepsiCo use straight extension to "cross multitudes of national, regional, and ethnic taste buds trained to a variety of deeply ingrained local preferences of taste, flavor, consistency, effervescence, and aftertaste."[21] Beer makers also use straight extension, and imported beer often has a higher status than domestic beer. Yet, a straight-extension strategy does not take into account differences in customers, laws, customs, technology, and other factors.

With a **product-adaptation** strategy, domestic products are modified to meet foreign language needs, taste preferences, climates, electrical requirements, laws, and/or other factors. It is assumed that new products are not needed and minor changes are sufficient. This is the most often used strategy in international marketing: Knorr Products' food packages are printed in the languages of the nations in which they are sold, as shown in Figure 6-9. Euro Disney in France features Mickey Mouse, Cinderella, and other U.S. Disney characters but also has food concessions and hotels that are adapted to European

[21]Kate Bertrand, "The Pan-American Marketing Motherlode," *Business Marketing* (December 1992), p. 31; and Theodore Levitt, "The Globalization of Markets," *Harvard Business Review*, Vol. 61 (May–June 1983), pp. 92–102.

tastes; KFC has grilled rice balls to go with its fried chicken wings in Japan; PepsiCo's Cheetos cheese-flavored puff snack is cheeseless in China (the two flavors are buttered popcorn and teriyaki); gasoline formulations vary according to a nation's weather conditions; and appliances are modified to accommodate different voltage requirements. This is how Boeing used product adaptation in marketing its 737 jet in the Mideast, Africa, and South America:

> The runways in developing [and less-developed] countries were too short to accommodate the jet, and too soft, made of asphalt instead of concrete. Boeing's engineers redesigned the wings to allow shorter landings and added thrust to the engines for quicker takeoffs. Boeing also redesigned the landing gear and installed low-pressure tires so the plane would stick to the ground when it touched down.[22]

With **backward invention,** a firm appeals to developing and less-developed nations by making products less complex than the ones it sells in its domestic market. This includes manual cash registers and nonelectric sewing machines for consumers in countries without widespread electricity and inexpensive washing machines for consumers in low-income countries. Whirlpool affiliates now build and sell an inexpensive "world washer" in Brazil, Mexico, and India. It is compact, is specially designed (so it does not tangle a sari), handles about one-half the capacity of a regular U.S. washer, and accommodates variations in component availability and local preferences.

In **forward invention,** a company develops new products for its international markets. This plan is riskier and more time-consuming and requires higher capital investments than other strategies. It may also provide the firm with great profit potential and, sometimes, worldwide recognition for innovativeness. Ford's midsized Mondeo car was introduced in Western Europe in 1993. The firm spent $6 billion and used five design studios to develop this front-wheel-drive car, priced at $18,000 (U.S.) in Europe. Ford introduced modified versions (named the Ford Contour and Mercury Mystique)—slightly longer and with more chrome—in the United States in 1994. Today, annual U.S. sales of the two cars total nearly 100,000 units.[23]

Distribution Planning

Channel members and physical distribution methods depend on customs, availability, costs, and other factors.

International distribution planning encompasses the selection and use of resellers and the physical movement of products. A company may sell directly to customers or hire outside distribution specialists—depending on the traditional distribution relationships in a country, the availability of appropriate resellers, differences in distribution practices from those in the home country, government restrictions, costs, and other factors. For example,

- In the Czech Republic, McDonald's employs all local people and must secure 40 separate government permits for each restaurant it opens.
- In Brazil, PepsiCo markets soft drinks through the domestic Brahma beer and soda company because of Brahma's extensive distribution network.
- Amway sells its household products in Japan via hundreds of thousands of local distributors (who are also customers); as in the United States, the distributors earn a commission on their sales.
- International landing rights for U.S. airlines must be negotiated on a government-to-government basis.
- Toys "R" Us has stores in Australia, Belgium, Canada, France, Germany, Great Britain, Hong Kong, Japan, Malaysia, Singapore, Spain, Taiwan, and other countries. Its large full-line outlets compete with "mom-and-pop shops."

[22]Andrew Kupfer, "How to Be a Global Manager," *Fortune* (March 14, 1988), p. 52.

[23]Alex Taylor III, "Ford's $6 Billion Baby," *Fortune* (June 28, 1993), pp. 76–81; Richard W. Stevenson, "Ford Sets Its Sights on a 'World Car,'" *New York Times* (September 27, 1993), pp. D1, D4; and Spain and Talbot, *Hoover's Handbook of American Business 1996*, pp. 622–623.

Hemmet ska vara fullt av liv,
inte avloppet.
KLORIN
När inget annat hjälper.

FIGURE 6-10
Klorin by Colgate-Palmolive: A Nonstandardized Approach to Advertising
This ad appeared in Sweden; the Klorin brand is not marketed in Colgate-Palmolive's U.S. marketplace.
Reprinted by permission.

Physical distribution in international markets often requires special planning: Processing marine insurance, government documents, and other papers may take time. Transportation modes may be unavailable or inefficient. A nation may have inadequate docking facilities, poor highways, or too few motor vehicles. Distribution by ship is slow and subject to delays. Inventory management should take into account the availability of warehousing and the costs of shipping in small quantities. Thus, in Russia, Ben & Jerry's faced difficulties because of the shortage of refrigerated trucks and freezers. So, it brought in Western trucks and freezers that are cold enough to store its ice cream products. Ben & Jerry's learned that "Russia still lacks a developed wholesale-distribution system that will deliver products to stores on time, consistently, and in good condition. To ensure quality, Ben & Jerry's and other companies are themselves creating a soup-to-nuts distribution system. It's expensive, but Ben & Jerry's hopes that by keeping quality high, it can win and keep often-fickle Russian consumers."[24]

Promotion Planning

International promotion planning depends on the overlap of audiences and languages and the availability of media.

Promotion campaigns can be global, nonstandardized, or glocal.[25] Figures 6-10 and 6-11 show examples of nonstandardized and glocal ads.

Firms sometimes use globalized promotion for image purposes: Coca-Cola's "polar bear" TV and print ads have been used around the world, as have various IBM television

[24]Neela Banerjee, "Ben & Jerry's Is Discovering That It's No Joke to Sell Ice Cream to Russians," *Wall Street Journal* (September 19, 1995), p. A18.

[25]See Madu Agrawal, "Review of a 40-Year Debate in International Advertising," *International Marketing Review*, Vol. 12 (Number 1, 1995), pp. 26–48.

FIGURE 6-11
A Glocal Visa Ad
The Visa card is a global symbol that appears in this ad. The copy is adapted to the markets in which various ads appear. The ad depicted here appeared in French-speaking Europe.
Reprinted by permission.

ads that highlight its vast computing strengths. At Revlon, "the intent is to make Revlon more of a global name. All Revlon North America advertising, for all products, whether they are cosmetics, skin care, hair care, or Almay, will be used worldwide."[26]

Companies marketing in various European nations often find that some standardization is desirable due to overlapping readers, listeners, and viewers. For instance, German TV shows are received by a large percentage of Dutch households and *Paris Match* magazine has substantial readership in Belgium, Switzerland, Luxembourg, Germany, Italy, and Holland.

There are also reasons for using nonstandardized promotion. Many countries have distinctions that are not addressed through a single promotion campaign. These differences include customs, language, the meaning of colors and symbols, and literacy rates. Media may be unavailable or inappropriate. In a number of nations, there are few TV sets, ads are restricted, and/or mailing lists are not current. National pride sometimes requires that individual promotions be used. Even within regions that have perceived similarities, such as Western Europe and Latin America, there are differences.

For instance, alcoholic products are banned in some Middle East nations. As a result, Stroh, Heineken, and others market nonalcoholic beers there. Yet, even with nonalcoholic beer, advertising is forbidden. The promotional emphasis is on store displays, spe-

[26]Pat Sloan, "Revlon Eyes Global Image; Picks Y&R," *Advertising Age* (January 11, 1993), pp. 1, 41.

cial promotions, and contests. As Stroh's international general manager said: "The challenge is how do you position a beer-like product not as a beer? One has to be quite sensitive."[27]

Most firms end up utilizing glocal promotion plans:

> Standardized strategies seem most appropriate and effective if a product is utilitarian and the message is informational. Reasons for buying or using the good or service are rational—and less apt to vary in different cultures. Glue, batteries, and gasoline are such products. A standardized approach would also appear appropriate and effective if a brand's identity and desirability are integrally linked to a specific national character. Coca-Cola and McDonald's are marketed worldwide as "quintessential American products"; Chanel is a "quintessential French product."
>
> For most products, it is generally more appropriate and effective to adapt or modify strategies and campaigns to local customs and cultures.
>
> - Often, product usage varies according to the culture. This applies to most foods, and beverages such as coffee and tea.
> - For many products, benefits are more psychological than tangible, requiring an understanding of the psychologies of different cultures. Sweets, snacks, and clothing are products with intangible benefits.
> - When there is an emotional appeal, advertisers must recognize the vast differences in emotional expression that exist in the world. Some societies are demonstrative and open; others are aloof or private.
> - Perhaps the riskiest method of selling is humor. There are differences in humor even within a culture—not to mention differences among cultures. In addition, advertisers must consider a multicultural, adaptable, and flexible strategy or campaign if a brand is in different stages of development or of varying stature across different markets.
> - A commercial for a mature market may not work well in a developing one.
> - A commercial to support a brand's leadership in a market where it is number one may not have the characteristics to succeed in a market where it is number five.
> - A commercial in a market where the product/brand is unique has quite a different task than a commercial where competition is intense.[28]

Price Planning

Major decisions in international price planning involve standardization, levels, currency, and sales terms. **Dumping** *is disliked by host countries.*

The basic considerations in international price planning are whether prices should be standardized, the level at which prices are set, the currency in which prices are quoted, and terms of sale.

Price standardization is hard unless a firm operates within an economic community, such as the EU. Taxes, tariffs, and currency exchange charges are among the costs a firm incurs in international marketing. For example, a 1995 Chrysler Jeep Cherokee made in Toledo, Ohio, had a factory price of $19,100. After an adjustment to reflect the U.S. dollar-Japanese yen exchange rate, the price became $20,433. Shipping to Chiba, Japan, raised the price to $20,633. Customs fees lifted the price to $21,315. The Japanese distributor's profit drove the price to $22,884. "Homologation" (the inspections and modifications needed to meet Japan's standards) and added options sent the price to $25,909. The final sticker price at a Nagoya, Japan, dealer was $31,372.[29]

When setting a price level, a firm would consider such local economic conditions as per-capita GDP. For this reason, many firms try to hold down prices in developing and less-developed countries by marketing simplified product versions or employing less-

[27]Tara Parker-Pope, "Nonalcoholic Beer Hits the Spot in Mideast," *Wall Street Journal* (December 6, 1995), pp. B1, B3.

[28]McCollum Spielman Worldwide, "Global Advertising: Standardized or Multicultural?" *Topline* (Number 37, 1992), pp. 3–4.

[29]Sheryl WuDunn, "An Uphill Journey to Japan," *New York Times* (May 16, 1995), p. D1.

expensive local labor. On the other hand, prices in such industrialized countries as France and Germany can reflect product quality and the added charges of international marketing.

Some firms set lower prices abroad to enhance their international presence and sales or to remove excess supply from their home markets and preserve the prices there. **Dumping** is involved if a firm sells a product in a foreign country at a price much lower than that prevailing in its home market, below the cost of production, or both. In the United States and many other nations, duties may be levied on products "dumped" by foreign firms.

If a firm sets prices on the basis of its own nation's currency, the risk of a foreign currency devaluation is passed along to the buyer and there is better control. But this strategy also has limitations. Consumers may be confused or unable to convert a price into their currency, or a foreign government may insist that prices be quoted in its currency. While Dow Chemical only uses German marks in European transactions to "insulate itself from sharp currency swings," Canondale (a U.S. bicycle maker) does business in 13 European currencies.[30]

Finally, terms of sale need to be set. This involves such judgments as what fees or discounts channel intermediaries get for the tasks they perform, when ownership is transferred, what payment form is required, how much time customers have to pay bills, and what constitutes a proper refund policy.

MARKETING IN A CHANGING WORLD

Do You Want to Work Abroad?

In today's global marketplace, one of the key career decisions that you may have to make involves whether you want to work abroad at some point. For some firms, international assignments are becoming part of a manager's normal work rotation; for others, they are used to groom junior executives for fast-track job advancement. The goal for these firms, in either case, is to develop managers who are "world wise" and have a better and closer understanding of foreign markets.

To prepare for a foreign job assignment, these are some things you should accomplish:

- Learn a foreign language well.
- Study the cultures of foreign countries.
- Travel abroad.
- Study abroad.
- Join and become active in your college's or university's international business organization.

If you are working for a company and asked about undertaking a specific foreign assignment, these are some questions you should ask:

- What specific job is being offered?
- How long will the assignment be?
- What will the compensation be?
- What standard of living will the company support?
- What will be the next job after the return to the home country?[31]

[30]Scott McMurray and Robert L. Simison, "Dow Chemical to Use Only the Mark for All of Its Business Dealings in Europe," *Wall Street Journal* (September 28, 1992), p. A5C; and Robina A. Gangemi, "Invoicing in 13 Currencies," *Sales & Marketing Management* (November 1995), p. 101.

[31]Grace W. Weinstein, "Before Saying Yes to Going Abroad," *Business Week* (December 4, 1995), pp. 130–132. See also Joann S. Lublin, "An Overseas Stint Can Be a Ticket to the Top," *Wall Street Journal* (January 29, 1996), pp. B1, B8.

SUMMARY

1. *To define domestic, international, and global marketing* Domestic marketing encompasses a firm's efforts in its home country. International marketing involves goods and services outside a firm's home country. Global marketing engages a firm in operations in many nations. Companies may be placed into one of five categories: domestic firm, exporting firm, international firm, multinational firm, or global firm. For any type of company (whether domestically or internationally oriented) to succeed in today's competitive marketplace, it must understand key international marketing concepts and act appropriately.

2. *To explain why international marketing takes place and study its scope* International marketing occurs because nations want to exchange goods and services with which they have comparative advantages for those with which they do not. Firms seek to minimize adverse economic conditions and attract growing markets, avoid domestic competition, extend the product life cycle, and get tax breaks.

The United States is the world's largest exporter for both goods and services. About 105,000 U.S. firms engage in some level of international business. The United States is also the world's leading importer, with a huge merchandise trade deficit. In contrast, the United States has a trade surplus for services. There are several reasons for the U.S. merchandise trade deficit, ranging from the American market's allure to the emphasis of U.S. firms on profits over market share. Various actions are under way to reduce this deficit; and the United States is the dominant force worldwide.

3. *To explore the cultural, economic, political and legal, and technological environments facing international marketers* The cultural environment includes the behavior standards, language, lifestyles, and goals of a country's citizens. The economic environment incorporates a nation's standard of living, GDP, stage of economic development, and currency stability. The political and legal environment includes nationalism, government stability, trade rules, and trade agreements and economic communities such as the World Trade Organization, European Union, and the North American Free Trade community. The technological environment creates opportunities and problems, and varies by country.

4. *To analyze the stages in the development of an international marketing strategy* In developing a strategy, a firm may stress exporting, joint ventures, or direct ownership of operations. Each approach has a different commitment, resource needs, control, risk, flexibility, and profit range.

When deciding on which and how many foreign markets to enter, a company should consider several factors. These include cultural and language similarities with the home market, the suitability of the standard of living, consumer demand, its own available resources, and so on.

A firm may adopt a standardized (global), nonstandardized, or glocal marketing approach. Its decision would depend on the differences among the countries served, which marketing elements can be standardized, the size of each market, and the possibility of regional adaptation.

Product planning may extend existing products into foreign markets, modify them, produce simpler items for developing nations, or invent new products for foreign markets. Distribution planning looks at channel relations and sets a network for direct sales or channel intermediaries. Physical distribution features would also be analyzed and adjustments made. Promotion planning would stress global, mixed, or glocal campaigns. Price planning would outline whether prices should be standardized, the price level, the currency in which prices are quoted, and terms of sale.

KEY TERMS

domestic marketing (p. 146)
international marketing (p. 146)
global marketing (p. 146)
domestic firm (p. 146)
exporting firm (p. 146)
international firm (p. 146)
multinational firm (p. 146)
global firm (p. 146)
comparative advantage (p. 147)
trade deficit (p. 150)
trade surplus (p. 150)
culture (p. 152)
standard of living (p. 154)
Gross Domestic Product (GDP) (p. 154)
industrialized countries (p. 154)
developing countries (p. 155)
less-developed countries (p. 155)
nationalism (p. 156)
tariff (p. 156)
trade quota (p. 156)
embargo (p. 156)
local content laws (p. 156)
World Trade Organization (WTO) (p. 157)
economic community (p. 158)
European Union (EU) (p. 158)
North American Free Trade Agreement (NAFTA) (p. 158)
exporting (p. 160)
joint venture (strategic alliance) (p. 160)
direct ownership (p. 162)
standardized (global) marketing approach (p. 163)
nonstandardized marketing approach (p. 163)
glocal marketing approach (p. 164)
straight extension (p. 165)
product adaptation (p. 165)
backward invention (p. 166)
forward invention (p. 166)
dumping (p. 170)

Review Questions

1. Distinguish among domestic, international, and global marketing.
2. Explain the concept of comparative advantage.
3. How can a firm improve its cultural awareness?
4. How can a country's GDP be a misleading indicator of marketing opportunities?
5. Differentiate among industrialized, developing, and less-developed countries.
6. If the value of the Kenyan shilling goes from 42 shillings per U.S. dollar to 50 shillings per U.S. dollar, will U.S. products be more or less expensive in Kenya? Why?
7. Define each of the following:
   a. Local content law.
   b. Tariff.
   c. Embargo.
8. What are the pros and cons of exporting versus joint ventures?
9. Why would a firm use a nonstandardized international marketing strategy? What are the potential disadvantages of this strategy?
10. Distinguish among these product-planning strategies: straight extension, product adaptation, backward invention, and forward invention. When should each be used?

Discussion Questions

1. Cite three basic differences between marketing in the United States and in Mexico.
2. In China, there are 2 cars per 1,000 people, compared with 550 per 1,000 people in the United States. What are the ramifications of this from a marketing perspective?
3. What are the advantages and disadvantages of a country's belonging to an economic community such as the European Union?
4. Develop a 10-question checklist by which a cable television network could determine which and how many foreign markets to enter.
5. Provide a current example of an international ad that you consider to be "glocal." Evaluate the ad.

CASE 1

Can Mercedes Be Less German and More Global?[*]

During 1994, Germany's Mercedes staged a major turnaround, earning a net profit of 1.85 billion marks ($1.35 billion) on sales of 70.7 billion marks ($51.61 billion), a 2.6 per cent profit margin. In contrast, during 1993, it lost 1.2 billion marks ($876 million) on sales of 64.7 billion marks ($47.23 billion). On average, Mercedes' 1994 profit per vehicle was about 2,000 marks ($1,460). By comparison, Germany's Volkswagen earned a profit margin of only 0.2 per cent and had an average profit per car of 48 marks ($35) in 1994.

Despite its return to profitability, Mercedes is concerned about the high value of the German mark relative to other European currencies and the U.S. dollar. According to Helmut Werner, chairman of Mercedes-Benz AG, the high appreciation in the value of the German mark against other European currencies is just as much of a threat to the firm as a falling dollar: "The fundamental problem of German exporters is that we are producing in a country with a hard currency and selling in countries with soft currencies." He concluded that the value of the U.S. dollar needs to move up by about 25 per cent for the firm to make satisfactory profits on cars sold to the U.S. market.

The combination of the mark's strength and recent wage agreements makes German labor 15 to 17 per cent more costly than labor in other European markets. These high costs put Mercedes at a significant disadvantage in such important European markets as Italy and Great Britain. As a result, to guard against the rising costs of German labor and parts, Mercedes plans to make the firm less German and more global. Thus, the firm intends to build more than 10 per cent of all Mercedes outside Germany (in North America, Latin America, and Asia). And between 1995 and 1998, it aims to double the amount of supplies it buys outside Germany. A look at Mercedes' financial statements shows the rising importance of its non-German operations: Foreign subsidiaries now account for 38 per cent of total net profit and non-German sales comprise 62 per cent of overall company sales.

Mercedes also hopes to continue streamlining its manufacturing operations to make itself more efficient. In 1994, it saved about 3.0 billion marks ($2.2 billion) due to lower factory and lower material costs. And the firm wants to obtain additional reductions by having its suppliers perform more work.

German labor unions have not taken kindly to Mercedes' globalization plans. For example, unions have strongly protested the Mercedes' decision to situate a new Swatchmobile minicar plant in France. Although Mercedes originally assumed that placing the plant in France instead of Germany would save the company about 500 marks ($365) per car, these savings have been revised upward by 50 marks (an additional $37). German labor is also sensitive to Mercedes' decision to build its first U.S. plant (in Tuscaloosa, Alabama). In an effort to keep additional Mercedes plants (for the firm's A-1 line) in Germany, German workers recently agreed to a 1 per cent reduction in wages.

Amidst all of these changes in its German-based strategy, Mercedes has been a major advocate of a single currency for Europe. The firm views a single currency as a way to reduce some of the pressure for it to turn to operations outside Germany—and Europe. As Helmut Werner says, "There is a danger that Europe will fall back from an internal market to a large number of individual markets if the currency situation does not become more predictable."

QUESTIONS

1. Evaluate the statement by Helmut Werner, "The fundamental problem of German exporters is that we are producing in a country with a hard currency and selling in countries with soft currencies."
2. What opportunities and threats does Mercedes face by virtue of the European Union (EU)?
3. What are the pros and cons of Mercedes' globalization strategy?
4. Evaluate the pros and cons of Mercedes' using a straight-extension versus a product-adaptation strategy.

[*]The data in this case are drawn from Audrey Choi, "For Mercedes, Going Global Means Being Less German," *Wall Street Journal* (April 27, 1995), p. B4.

CASE 2

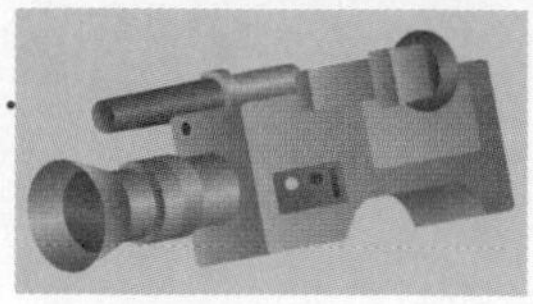

Roadway Express: The Complexities of International Physical Distribution†

International physical distribution is complex because it covers long distances and requires intricate reporting documents. The latter include:

- Bills of lading—forms acknowledging the receipt of goods by carriers that also serve as evidence of title to goods.
- Shippers' export declarations—which state that shippers are authorized to export goods.
- Certificates of origin—that ensure proper tariff collections.

International physical distribution is further complicated by the currency conversions for shipping costs, as well as the need to split the charges for different stages of transportation between buyers and sellers.

Increasingly, both small and large firms have begun using third-party logistics providers, such as Roadway Express, to handle their international shipping and documentation requirements. Roadway Express specializes in long haul, less-than-truckload (LTL) shipments. Unlike other firms that specialize in certain types of shipments over limited distances, Roadway Express is equipped to handle packages of varying weights (including those of 15,000 pounds), and packages shipped over varying distances. It is also able to deliver goods based on different time schedules (such as next day, second day, or within one week). This flexibility enables firms to use Roadway Express as their single carrier.

Roadway Express offers international shipping services to 62 countries on five continents. Customers are served by Roadway's 700 state-of-the-art offices around the world, independently-owned ocean carriers, and a network of agents that provides such services as clearing goods through customs and paying duties. The largest portion of Roadway Express' long-distance foreign transportation involves waterway and motor carrier transportation.

Roadway Express offers customers a choice among shipping alternatives. These include door-to-door, door-to-port, port-to-door, and port-to-port arrangements. For example, a domestic firm selling goods directly to a foreign buyer may desire door-to-door arrangements, whereas a firm selling goods through a major foreign distributor may desire the port-to-port option.

Roadway Express also facilitates customs inspections and declarations. Through use of its PREVIEW pre-arrival clearance system, customs processing can be started prior to the arrival of goods in a foreign destination and thereby reduce customs delays. Roadway Express also offers customers the use of an export documentation system called E-Z. This system automates the filling out of export shipping and documentation forms.

Roadway Express utilizes a single invoice billing system in which all charges are itemized and payable in the payor's currency. The system reduces problems associated with currency exchange rates; and it also lets the proportionate transportation costs be directly charged to the seller and buyer based on the terms of sale.

Roadway Express is considered a technological leader in international distribution. Customers can determine a package's delivery status between 60 countries and 80 ports through use of a single toll-free hot line. High volume customers may use Roadway's MULTISHIP system free of charge. This PC-based system weighs packages, determines rates and routes, and even prints a combination bar code and address label.

Roadway's Global Air unit, which offers overnight service to more than 25,000 locations throughout North America, is one of its fastest-growing divisions. Begun in 1993, Roadway Global Air now has more than 230 air logistics centers. To increase its service reliability, this division centrally manages its pickup and delivery of parcels, air operations, and information systems with its agents and customers.

QUESTIONS

1. What criteria should a firm use in selecting an international physical distribution specialist?
2. How well does Roadway Express meet those criteria? Explain your answer.
3. What special considerations does Roadway Express have in dealing with 62 countries? How should it deal with them?
4. What threats does Roadway Express face in its international marketing efforts? How should it prepare for them?

VIDEO QUESTIONS ON ROADWAY EXPRESS

1. Assess Roadway Express' services in Canada and Mexico.
2. Discuss Roadway Express' services in the European Union.

†The data in this case are drawn from *Roadway Services 1994 Annual Report*; and Cliff Sayreo, "Getting Business," *Distribution* (January 1994), pp. 54–55.

PART 2 CASE

Should International Firms Go Multilingual?

Introduction

Increasingly, firms are serving customers speaking different languages. To compete effectively, many firms find they must provide better service to the growing numbers of linguistic minorities, tourists, and business travelers within domestic markets, as well as expand internationally.

Trade blocs create special new opportunities. For instance, participation in the North American Free Trade Agreement (NAFTA) means American marketers will have more opportunities to serve Spanish-speaking Mexicans and both English- and French-speaking Canadians. Firms in many other countries increasingly face similar challenges, particularly those in the ever-expanding European Union, of which Britain and Ireland are the only two English-speaking members.

Power to Divide

Sir Winston Churchill—whose mother was American—once described the United States and Britain as "two nations divided by a common language." He was referring, of course, to the subtle differences in English usage.

While differences in usage and accent within the same language sometimes lead to misunderstandings or raised eyebrows, they seldom cause serious problems. But in a multilingual context, the choice of which language(s) to use presents all the hazards of entering a minefield without a map—especially for marketers who are responsible for customer service.

Culture has always been expressed through language, and modern concepts of national identity often are centered on people's mother tongues. Deeply held cultural values can find expression in political action to establish official policies of unilingualism. Well-known examples from Western nations range from Canada, where the province of Quebec has moved from official bilingualism to a vigorously enforced policy of French only, to Belgium, where the nation is divided into unilingual French and Dutch regions plus a small German-speaking area, leaving only Brussels and a couple of border towns officially bilingual.

Singapore has made something of a virtue of retaining English as one of its four official languages (the others are Chinese, Malay, and Tamil). This is a major commercial advantage for both business and tourism. Singapore is also well positioned to take advantage of the emerging Chinese market because many citizens are fluent in Mandarin, the official spoken version of Chinese.

Source: Adapted by the authors from Christopher H. Lovelock, "What Language Shall We Put It In?" *Marketing Management* (Winter 1994), pp. 37–48. Reprinted by permission of the American Marketing Association.

Competitive Edge

Today, America is probably as polyglot as at any time in recent history. And as national economies become more multicultural, as people travel more for both business and pleasure, and as markets become more global, doing business only in English may become a competitive disadvantage.

Using another language incorrectly in the eyes and ears of the target customers may also be damaging. And not everyone can even hear speech well. It was not until the screening of the film *Children of a Lesser God* that many people came to realize that sign languages such as Aslan (the American version) are languages in their own right, with specific idioms and grammar.

So, what language should we communicate in? Sometimes, the law tells us what to do, but more often it doesn't. The more relevant questions for marketers are: What language does each potential customer prefer? And what style of that language is most appropriate for the particular context in which communications are taking place with target customers? Language represents an important market segmentation variable—always important in international settings, it's becoming increasingly relevant in domestic markets, too.

Language Segments

The decision to use specific languages in an organization's dealings with customers, suppliers, distributors, and employees should be part of a well-considered strategy. Managers need to recognize that implementation is often situation-specific, being directed at microsegments in locations far from a head office. Failure to oversee and coordinate actions at local levels may result in inconsistencies that present a firm in an unprofessional light.

Recently, the French subsidiary of a major American computer manufacturer teamed up with the Paris office of an American airline to offer in-flight demonstrations of a new notebook PC. First- and business-class passengers flying between France and the United States were handed an announcement in French and English inviting them to test the computers during their trip.

Although English-speaking passengers tend to outnumber French speakers on this airline, four of the five PCs on one flight had French keyboards, whose layout is different from U.S.-English keyboards. The demonstration software allowed users to select either English or French versions of the program, which changed what the keys typed—but not, of course, the symbols or letters embossed on the keys themselves. The English software tutorial was a poor translation of the French, with stilted phrasing and grammatical inaccuracies. The same was true of the accompanying bilingual questionnaire, which asked users for their opinions on the computer and the in-flight test. With this attention to detail, is it any surprise that both sponsoring firms have incurred heavy financial losses on their worldwide operations?

The moral is that marketing plans are too crucial to leave to amateurs who overestimate their language skills. If a firm is already serving customers in many languages, now may be a good time to review existing policies. If it is becoming interested in gaining market share among those whose first language is not English, the time is right to start thinking about how to proceed. A first step is to identify and profile the potential language groups with whom the firm does business or wishes to do business.

International Operations Identifying relevant languages and the number of people who speak them may seem straightforward, but there are traps for the unwary.

The first challenge is that many countries have more than one official language, some of them regional. In India, the national languages are Hindi and English, but 14 regional languages also are recognized officially at the state level. In Spain, Castillian Spanish is the national language, but three other languages have official regional status: Catalan, Galician, and Basque.

Second, the spoken language sometimes differs widely from the written standard, which has important implications for radio and TV ads, promotional tapes and films, and phone-based customer service. In Switzerland, German is the most important of four official languages (the others are French, Italian, and Romansch) and the mother tongue of two-thirds of the people. The written language is virtually the same as the standard—High German—but people at all levels of society actually speak Swiss-German dialects collectively known as Schwytzerdüsch. Many Swiss cannot speak High German; likewise, Germans find it hard to follow Schwytzerdüsch, which has a unique accent and pronunciation—and uses many dialectical words, expressions, and grammatical constructions. Although one instruction manual might be used by German, Austrian, and Swiss-German customers or distributors, inviting the Swiss to call a free help-line based in Cologne or Berlin might be ill-received.

Foreign Tourists and Business Travelers International tourism is a major industry that continues to grow. Business travelers swell the numbers of foreign visitors to domestic markets. In total, 40 million foreign visitors come to the United States yearly, with the largest single nationality being Canadians, of whom one-fifth are French speakers.

The most predominant languages spoken by foreign visitors to the United States (other than Canadians) are Spanish and Japanese (over 4 million each), German (2 million), and French (1 million from Europe). These are followed by Chinese, Dutch, and Korean (about half a million each), as well as a similar number of Portuguese speakers, the great majority of whom come from Brazil.

International tourists and business visitors are of particular interest to marketers in a variety of highly competitive industries, including car rental, hospitality, restaurant, entertainment, and retailing. If you have traveled abroad in an area where you neither speak nor understand the language well, you know how frustrating the absence of multilingual signs and personnel can be for a visitor who wants to obtain information, use a service, or shop.

State and regional tourist boards now track foreign visitors closely and estimate the number of visitors from specific nations. Although some visitors are either native English speakers or speak it well, others have only a limited command of the language or none at all. The friendliness of different service firms may determine if foreign visitors return later or recommend specific companies to other potential travelers back home.

Multilingual Domestic Markets Huge immigration rates in recent decades have enlarged the number of people living in the United States for whom English is either a second language or one that they do not speak at all. Thirty-two million people living in the United States speak a language other than English in their homes.

Census data can help firms estimate the size and geographic location of language-based market segments. If other demographic factors are attractive, then further research may be needed to determine both the English-language skills and the language preferences of the most relevant segments.

Conducting a Language Audit If you're convinced that expanded language capabilities might create a competitive advantage for your firm (or remove a disadvantage), the next step is a "language audit" to evaluate your current communication activities. At a minimum, this should address ten key questions.

(1) Is your current language policy turning off people? Think carefully about how new prospects first learn about your company and its services. Is it via ads, brochures, signs, press stories, or word-of-mouth recommendations? When these are only in English, you (and they) may be missing out. If people find it difficult to do business with your firm, they may not return.

    Surveying customers and prospects informally or through research studies should reveal not only where difficulties occur, but also what languages customers and prospects would prefer to use. Quantifying these results with formal research will indicate the size of each language segment. Specialized firms can help to develop and conduct such surveys in given languages.

(2) In what languages are signs, written information, and electronic information displays currently available? Answering this question requires you to undertake an inventory of information for all goods and services offered by your firm and for all sites it serves directly. If distributors or agents have prepared their own materials to describe your products, include these items, too, in your evaluation.

(3) How good is the quality of each information item in a foreign language? Once items are identified, you're now

in a position to evaluate their quality against two criteria: their visual appearance and their content.

Consistency of appearance—design, printing, paper, or video screen format—may or may not be of great importance to your firm. But ask yourself whether you would wish customers to see handsome materials in English and tacky-looking typewritten photocopies on cheap paper in their own language.

Content evaluation requires help from native speakers of the relevant languages who are also fluent in English. If an item has been translated from English, ask them how close it is to the original. Researchers doing surveys in multiple languages may use reverse translations of questions—such as, English to German and back to English—to verify meanings. Is the translation grammatically accurate? Does it read well or sound stilted and clumsy?

If an item is created specifically for a non-English-speaking audience, review an English translation to ensure that it portrays your firm and its products in a suitable fashion (no outrageous claims, for example).

(4) How easily understood are English materials by non-native speakers? This evaluation may apply to employee materials, as well as items intended for customers. Are the materials written using long words and complex sentences? If so, someone with a limited command of English may find them difficult to understand (even well-educated native English speakers may be turned off by technical jargon and lots of legalese).

(5) If you use symbols in signs or written materials, are they widely recognized and understood? You can conduct surveys and interviews of customers and prospects to answer this question, or seek an expert opinion. If findings are negative, redesign the symbols for greater clarity, choose new ones, or provide a key (in whatever languages are relevant) to explain their meaning.

(6) Has provision been made for visually-impaired or hearing-impaired people? Many organizations provide signs or printed materials in Braille. These items should be easy to read (in any language) and supplemented by audible instructions in specific languages. With hearing-impaired people, make signing interpretations available in person or on video materials, equip handsets or phones with volume control buttons, and offer TTY phone service.

(7) In what languages are incoming phone calls to your firm currently being answered? This question applies to all offices that customers might call, at home and abroad. Solutions include diverting calls to a language specialist and using a third-party phone interpretation service.

(8) Do you know what language skills each employee in your firm has? These findings might surprise you! Some people are immigrants (or children of them), some have lived abroad, and others have studied languages. Be specific in your questioning—ask separately for reading, writing, and speaking. Someone who can read a language well may not be able to speak it, and someone who speaks it fluently may have trouble writing a letter with grammatical accuracy.

Ask about their ability to speak dialects, too (such as Swiss-German, Spanish Creole, or Cantonese-Chinese). You may also learn that some employees have skills in signing (either because they are hearing-impaired or they have lived and worked with deaf people).

Euro Disney makes note of the language capabilities of all employees at its park and resort. If the need arises, management can access the employee by computer (Who do we have on duty who can speak Turkish?) and page him or her immediately by beeper or walkie-talkie. In a medical emergency, this could mean the difference between life and death.

(9) What are competitors' language skills? Within the constraints of what is legal and ethical, learn what you can about each competitor, relative to these same questions. You might learn from their mistakes or emulate what they have done well.

(10) What does the law prescribe for language use? Ask this question for each political jurisdiction in which your firm operates (or wants to operate). Language laws may change in response to political initiatives. The British Parliament recently passed legislation requiring many firms doing business in Wales to provide documentation and billing data in Welsh, as well as English (the law does not apply to England, Scotland, or Northern Ireland).

Package labeling requirements may present a stumbling block to selling existing products in new markets: Wal-Mart has had problems with English-only labeling on products sold in its Mexican stores, and some American exporters balk at the Canadian market because of bilingual labeling laws.

Using the Audit Findings The results of a language audit should reveal.

- The size of different language segments and the extent to which a company is missing opportunities because of deficiencies in specific languages.
- The fit between a firm's current practices and customer preferences.
- Whether there is an advantage or disadvantage relative to competitors and, if so, in what languages and in what specific areas of communication.
- Whether the firm is in compliance with language laws in the areas where it operates and has the capability to enter desired new markets.
- What the internal resources are in terms of existing language skills.

On the basis of the findings, you will be in a position to decide whether changes must be made in your current language strategy (if one exists). Depending on the assessment of threats and opportunities, you might initiate changes in one or more areas—from signs and brochures to personnel.

British Airways (BA) has a language-training unit for cabin crew members to help them become proficient in French, Italian, German, and Spanish. The trainers are crew members who fly for half the year and teach for the other half, so they know and understand job intricacies, the most likely questions, and the most-used vocabulary. Courses last 2.5 months, alternating full-time classroom work with flying duties. Training includes spending a week abroad with a non-English-speaking family and attending a language school.

BA students even learn about national characteristics, interests, customs, traditions, and sensitivities. At the end of the course, participants take a standardized oral test. On the basis of their proficiency, they may be awarded a one-year or three-year flag badge, but they must undergo retesting on a set schedule. BA recruits from numerous countries on its global route network, attracting many employees for whom English is a second language. Collectively, its customer service personnel can speak more than 50 languages.

Some firms train employees to recognize different languages, even if they do not speak them well, so they can direct the customer (or transfer a call) to a colleague or professional interpreter who is able to provide assistance.

QUESTIONS

1. What social responsibility issues are implicitly raised in this case? How would you deal with them?
2. If a company markets its products internationally, how can it encourage more customers to voice their dissatisfaction—rather than hide it?
3. Why would egoism be a poor ethical approach to the international language of business?
4. Should a company print warranty information in the language of every country in which it has customers? Explain your answer.
5. From a marketing perspective, what is the relationship between language and culture?
6. What are the ramifications of the material presented in this case for the tourism board in your state? What do you recommend?
7. What is a language audit? What kinds of firms should conduct such an audit? Why?
8. In entering a non-English-speaking foreign market, would you recommend using unilingual package labels (in only the language of the foreign market) or bilingual package labels (in the language of the foreign market, as well as in English)? Explain your answer.

CONSUMER ANALYSIS

PART 3

UNDERSTANDING AND RESPONDING TO DIVERSITY IN THE MARKETPLACE

In Part 3, we see why consumer analysis is so essential and discuss consumer characteristics, needs, profiles, and decision making—and how firms can devise plans responsive to today's diverse global marketplace.

7

Final Consumer Demographics

This chapter is devoted to final consumer demographics, the objective and quantifiable characteristics that describe the population. We examine population size, gender, age, location, housing, mobility, income, expenditures, occupations, education, marital status, and ethnicity/race—for the United States and a number of other countries around the globe.

8

Final Consumer Life-Styles and Decision Making

Here, we investigate final consumer life-styles and decision making, useful concepts in explaining why and how consumers act as they do. Life-styles encompass various social and psychological factors, many of which we note here. By studying the decision process, we see how consumers move from stimulus to purchase or nonpurchase.

9

Organizational Consumers

In this chapter, we focus on the organizational consumers that purchase goods and services for further production, use in operations, or resale to other consumers. We look at how they differ from final consumers and at their characteristics, buying objectives, buying structure, constraints on purchases, and decision process.

10

Developing a Target Market Strategy

We are now ready to discuss how to plan a target market strategy. Consumer-demand patterns and segmentation bases are examined; and undifferentiated marketing (mass marketing), concentrated marketing, and differentiated marketing (multiple segmentation) are explained and contrasted. The requirements for successful segmentation and the importance of positioning are also considered. We conclude with a discussion of sales forecasting.

Part 3 Video Vignette

MasterCard International

MasterCard International Incorporated (MasterCard) is a rather unique company in that it really has three distinct target markets: the member banks that offer MasterCard® card products, businesses that accept MasterCard cards as a form of customer payment, and the customers that use MasterCard-branded cards when they buy goods and services. There are 150 million MasterCard credit cards in circulation in the United States and 127 million Maestro cards in circulation worldwide. For MasterCard International, each of these target markets must be satisfied; and as the firm's huge success indicates, each is!

To best serve its customers, MasterCard's Acceptance Group is organized on the basis of specialized industry divisions, such as Health Care, Government, and Travel. By doing this, MasterCard can focus on the consumer and merchant needs within the target industries in order to provide superior service.

To best serve its customers, MasterCard's Acceptance Group is organized on the basis of specialized industry divisions, such as Health Care.

In MasterCard's Health Care Marketing division, a key goal is to increase the acceptance of MasterCard cards as payment for health care services and products. Accordingly, the division is targeting the entire health care community (insurers, health care professionals, HMOs, and hospitals; and patients).

Of the various health care market segments for MasterCard, the most saturated is the dental market; 80-plus per cent of dentists accept MasterCard cards. Dentists have high acceptance because comparatively few consumers have dental health coverage. Among physicians, 51 per cent accept MasterCard. In general, larger practices are more prone to accept MasterCard. Smaller, more rural practices and older doctors are less willing.

The most significant emerging health care markets for MasterCard are hospitals, home care, and nursing homes. Traditionally, the government covers the majority of patient care at nursing homes. The balance is paid by the patient or patient's family. According to research by MasterCard, 78 per cent of Americans feel it is appropriate to use credit cards for health care expenses. Of those who have not used a credit card to pay for health care, 10 per cent are unaware that their health care providers accept credit cards.

Recently, MasterCard's Health Care Marketing division ran a special "For a Clean Bill of Health" promotion. The promotion was intended to encourage and reward credit card usage for health care by providing vital health care information, health care financial planning tools, and health care discounts. The goodwill and public relations generated from this promotion were intended to encourage health care providers to accept credit cards. Over eight million inserts were mailed out in monthly credit card statements by several hundred member banks. In addition, advertisements, press releases, and Internet sites were used to communicate with people. When consumers mailed back the form that accompanied the statement insert, they were mailed a free MasterCard Health Care Kit, "For a Clean Bill of Health." This kit contained discount coupons from NordicTrack, Jenny Craig Weight Loss Centres, Smokenders, Pearle Vision, and others. It also had forms for tracking and budgeting annual health care expenses, cooking tips from the American Cancer Society, and useful 800-telephone numbers.

CHAPTER 7

Final Consumer Demographics

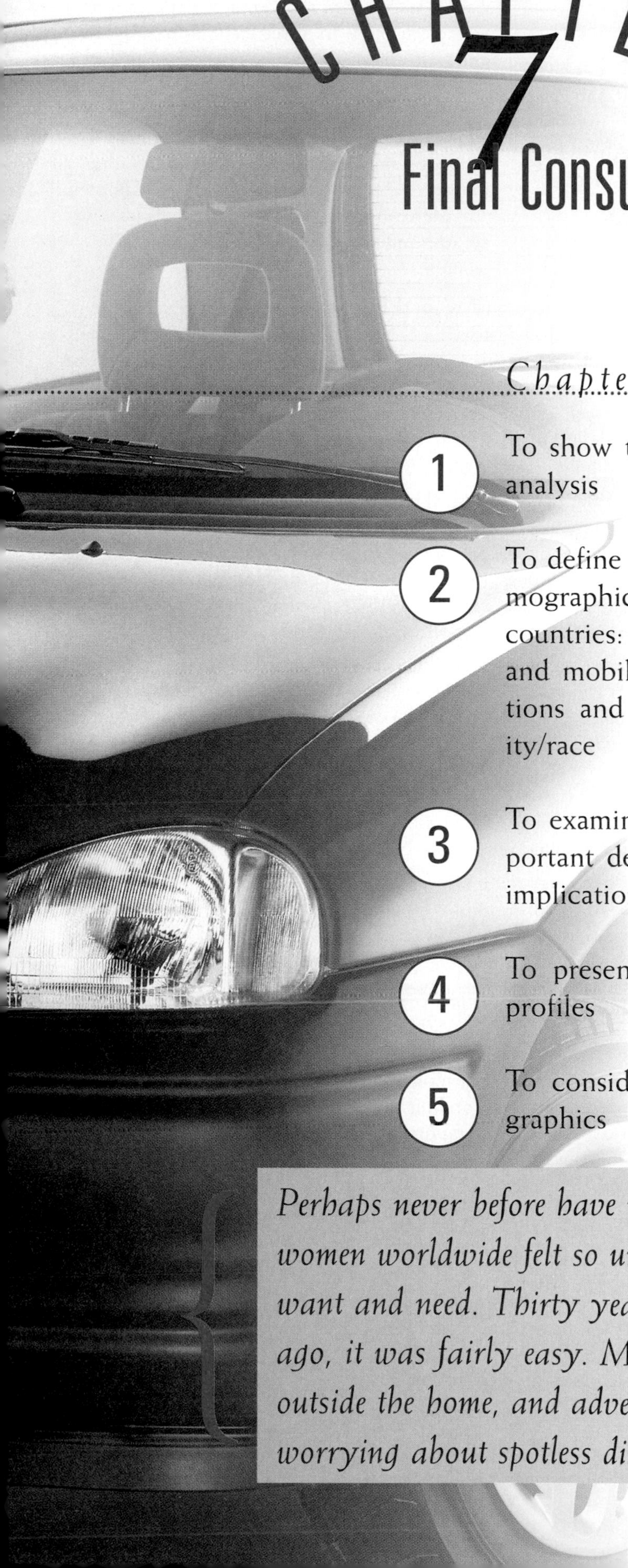

Chapter Objectives

1. To show the importance and scope of consumer analysis

2. To define and enumerate important consumer demographics for the U.S. population and other countries: size, gender, and age; location, housing, and mobility; income and expenditures; occupations and education; marital status; and ethnicity/race

3. To examine trends and projections for these important demographics and study their marketing implications

4. To present examples of consumer demographic profiles

5. To consider the limitations of consumer demographics

Perhaps never before have marketers trying to reach women worldwide felt so unsure about what women want and need. Thirty years ago, even 15 years ago, it was fairly easy. Most women did not work outside the home, and advertising featured them worrying about spotless dishes and clean floors.

Reprinted by permission.

Today, such trends as increased participation by women in the work force, couples having fewer children, and many women's greater focus on career opportunities are having an impact around the globe. For example, research in Australia shows that only 7 per cent of families fit the "traditional" family structure of a working father, a mother at home, and two school-age children.

Here's how marketers throughout the world are responding to the changing demographics of women:

- In Spain, firms are beginning to capitalize on the shortage of time for women. Home food delivery is now a growth industry; it was practically nonexistent a decade ago. One firm alone, TelePizza, has annual sales of $55 million. Campofrío, a leading food marketer, uses the theme "Let Roteta cook" for its Cocina Placer line of microwaveable entrees. Roteta is a well-known Basque chef who has created many of the recipes and endorsed this food line. The concept of the ad campaign is that women can leave food preparation to a highly regarded chef.
- When Opel Spain introduced the Corsa, the firm relied on special presentations to both male and female journalists. It also advertised the product in such women's magazines as the Spanish *Vogue* and *Cosmopolitan* (as well as men's magazines). The ads told the story of a woman going through the day, undertaking different activities, and driving her Corsa. The Corsa model became the fifth best-selling car in Spain—with 46 per cent female buyers, the highest proportion of any Opel model.
- According to the Bureau for Market Research at the University of South Africa, as of the year 2011, women will make up 42.3 per cent of the South African work force, a significant increase from 38.6 per cent in 1991 and 21.1 per cent in 1989. As a result, the sales of convenience foods have increased and will continue to do so. And ads that once depicted women in the home now focus on other roles. More and more firms are also promoting job opportunities for women. One ad, for example, showed a young woman in coveralls and safety glasses welding machinery together. The ad, sponsored by Caltex, a gasoline retailer, described job openings for young people.
- In another South African illustration, Lever Brothers used a unique twist in its TV campaign for Sunlight Micro dishwashing liquid. In the ad, a woman in an evening dress passed the dirty dishes on to a gold-colored male robot, instead of a nearby female domestic. "Sorry, these are a bit greasy, Arthur," she stated, advising him that Sunlight would make his job easier. The ad was developed since images of the housewife "in a tradition role" did not test well, according to Lever Brothers' marketing director.[1]

We have just looked at a few of the demographic changes occurring in Spain and South Africa—and how marketers are responding to them. In this chapter, we will focus on a number of important consumer demographic trends and consider the marketing implications of these trends, looking at the United States and countries throughout the world.

Overview

Consumer analysis is crucial in the diverse global marketplace.

As discussed in Chapters 1 and 2, the consumer is the central focus of marketing. To devise good marketing plans, it is important to study consumer attributes and needs, lifestyles, and purchase processes, and then make proper marketing-mix decisions.

The scope of consumer analysis includes the study of who buys, what they buy, why they buy, how they make decisions to buy, when they buy, where they buy, and how of-

[1]Laurie Freeman, Susan Hack, Deborah Klosky, Geoffrey Lee Martin, Ann Marsh, and Jack Russell, "Changing Demographics: Women," *Advertising Age International* (October 17, 1994), pp. I-14, I-16.

MOUNTAIN GOAT
PUMA
SIR EDMUND HILLARY
ALPINE IBEX
YAK
RANGE ROVER
LAND ROVER
THE BEST 4x4xFAR.
If you'd like a test drive, even if it's only on tarmac, please dial 100 and ask for Freephone Land Rover.

FIGURE 7-1
Creatively Appealing to the Final Consumer of Today
Reprinted by permission.

ten they buy.[2] For example, we might study a college student (who) purchasing textbooks (what) because they are required for various classes (why). The student first looks up the book list at the school store and decides whether to purchase new or used books for each course (how). Then, just before the first week of classes (when), the student goes to the school store to buy the books (where). The student does this three times per year— fall, spring, and summer (how often).

An open-minded, consumer-oriented approach is imperative in today's diverse global marketplace so that a firm can identify and serve its target market, minimize consumer dissatisfaction, and stay ahead of competitors. Why is this so important? As Seagate, a leader in computer data-storage products, noted: "People buy expectations, not just things. Customer satisfaction is dependent not only on our products, but on continuously improving our way of doing business."[3] See Figures 7-1 and 7-2.

Final consumers *buy for personal, family, or household use;* **organizational consumers** *buy for production, operations, or resale.*

In Chapters 7 to 10, the concepts needed to understand consumers in the United States and other nations worldwide, select target markets, and relate marketing strategy to consumer behavior are detailed. Chapters 7 and 8 examine final consumer demographics, life-styles, and decision making. **Final consumers** buy goods and services for personal, family, or household use. Chapter 9 centers on the characteristics and behavior of **organizational consumers**, those buying goods and services for further production, usage in operating the organization; or resale to other consumers. Chapter 10 explains how to devise a target market strategy and use sales forecasts.

[2]Adapted from Leon G. Schiffman and Leslie Lazar Kanuk, *Consumer Behavior*, Fifth Edition (Englewood Cliffs, N.J.: Prentice-Hall, 1994), p. 7.
[3]*Seagate 1992 Annual Report*, p. 9.

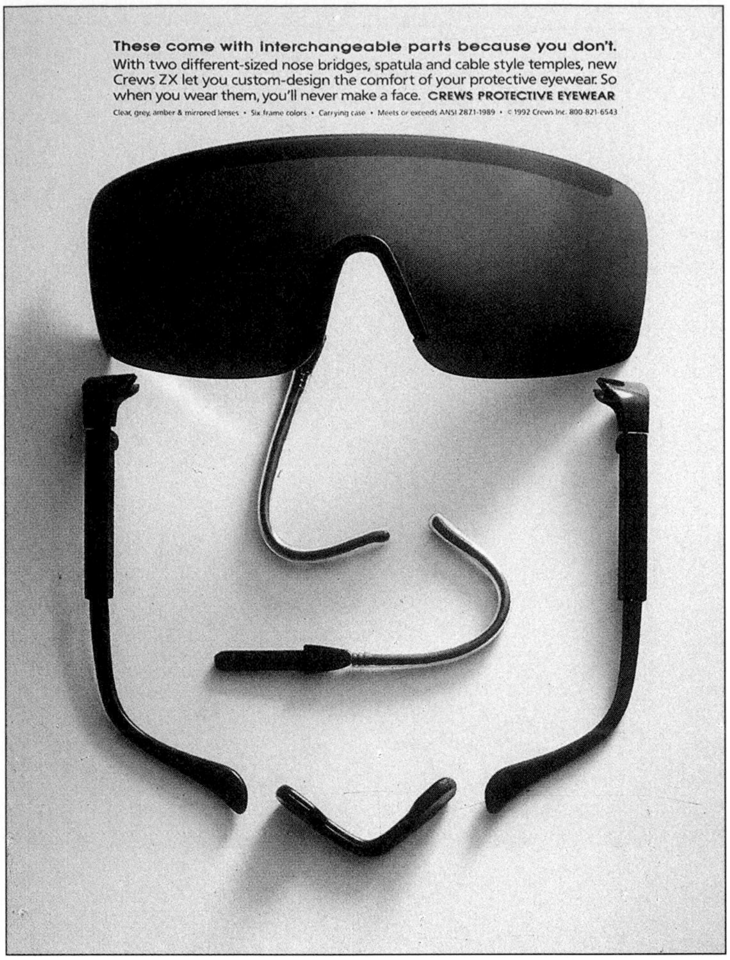

These come with interchangeable parts because you don't.
With two different-sized nose bridges, spatula and cable style temples, new Crews ZX let you custom-design the comfort of your protective eyewear. So when you wear them, you'll never make a face. CREWS PROTECTIVE EYEWEAR
Clear, grey, amber & mirrored lenses • Six frame colors • Carrying case • Meets or exceeds ANSI Z87.1-1989 • © 1992 Crews Inc. 800-821-6543

FIGURE 7-2
Creatively Appealing to the Organizational Consumer of Today
Reprinted by permission.

Demographics Defined and Enumerated[4]

Consumer demographics *are population characteristics that are easy to identify and measure.* **Demographic profiles** *may be formed.*

Consumer demographics are objective and quantifiable population characteristics. They are rather easy to identify, collect, measure, and analyze—and show diversity around the globe. The demographics covered in Chapter 7 are population size, gender, and age; location, housing, and mobility; income and expenditures; occupations and education; marital status; and ethnicity/race.

After separately examining various demographic factors, a firm can form a **consumer demographic profile**—a demographic composite of a consumer group. See Figure 7-3. By establishing consumer profiles, a firm can pinpoint both attractive and declining market opportunities. For example, in highly industrialized nations, the population is growing more slowly, people are older, incomes are higher, more people work in white-collar jobs, and there are smaller households than in less-developed and developing countries. Together, these factors have a great impact on the goods and services that are offered and the marketing strategies for these items.

Several secondary sources offer data on consumer demographics. For U.S. demographics, a key source is the *Census of Population*, a federal government research project providing a wide range of national, state, and local data via printed reports, computer tapes, microfiche, CD-ROM diskettes, and online data bases. Many marketing research firms and state data centers arrange census data by zip code, provide forecasts, and update in-

[4]Unless otherwise indicated, the data presented in this chapter are all from the U.S. Bureau of the Census (various publications); the United Nations (various publications); *International Marketing Data and Statistics 1995* (Great Britain: Euromonitor, 1995); *American Demographics* (various issues); and *World Almanac and Book of Facts 1996* (Mahwah, N.J.: World Almanac Books, 1995).

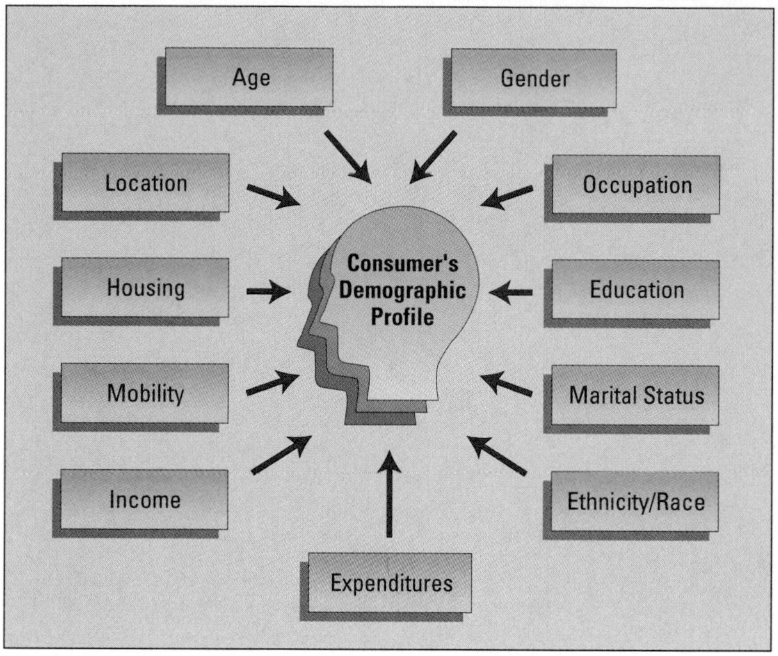

FIGURE 7-3
Factors Determining a Consumer's Demographic Profile

formation. Since complete *Census* data are gathered only once a decade, they must be supplemented by U.S. Bureau of the Census estimates and statistics from chambers of commerce, public utilities, and others.

American Demographics is a monthly magazine dealing mostly with U.S. demographic trends. The *Survey of Buying Power* (published annually by *Sales & Marketing Management*) has current U.S. data by metropolitan area and state, including retail sales by merchandise category, personal disposable income, and five-year estimates. Other U.S. secondary sources are *Editor & Publisher Market Guide, Rand McNally Commercial Atlas & Market Guide, Standard Rate & Data Service*, local newspapers, and regional planning boards.

The United Nations (UN), Euromonitor, and the Organization for Economic Cooperation and Development (OECD) are sources of international demographic data. The UN publishes a *Statistical Yearbook* and a *Demographic Yearbook*. Euromonitor publishes *International Marketing Data and Statistics*. OECD issues demographic and economic reports on an ongoing basis. In highly industrialized nations, demographic data are pretty accurate because actual data are collected on a regular basis. In less-developed and developing nations, demographic data are often based on estimates rather than actual data because such data are apt to be collected on an irregular basis.

Throughout the chapter, information is provided on both U.S. and worldwide demographics. A broad cross-section of country examples is provided to give the reader a good sense of the diversity around the globe.

Population Size, Gender, and Age

Relatively speaking, the U.S. population is expanding slowly. There are also many firstborns, more women than men, and a rising average age.

The world population is expected to grow from 5.7 billion in 1995 to 6.2 billion in 2000, an increase of 1.5 per cent annually. Over the same period, the U.S. population is expected to go from 263 million to 275 million, an annual increase of 1 per cent. Thus, the U.S. population will drop from 4.6 per cent of world population in 1995 to 4.4 per cent in 2000. Figure 7-4 shows world population distribution by region for 1990 and 2000.

Newborns are less than 2 per cent of the population (1.5 per cent in the United States) in industrialized nations—compared with up to 4 per cent or more in nations such as Afghanistan, Syria, and Zaire. For the industrialized countries, a large proportion of the births are firstborns.

Worldwide, males and females comprise roughly equal percentages of the population. Yet, in many industrialized countries, females comprise well over one-half of the popula-

TECHNOLOGY & MARKETING

What's the Deal with Online Census Data?

Need U.S. demographic data in a hurry? Census statistics are now available free of charge to anyone with a computer, a modem, and a public domain graphic interface software package called Mosaic. How popular is this? During its first six months of operation, over one million inquiries—an average of 5,500 per day—were made to the U.S. Bureau of the Census' Internet site. And this number is expected to rise dramatically as more people learn about the service. In the near future, some Census Bureau reports will only be available online as the Bureau attempts to promote electronic access as a way of better serving consumers and to reduce its printing and paper costs.

Marketers interested in analyzing detailed demographic data about a specific state need only to "Enter the Main Data Bank" at the initial menu and select "Statistical Abstract Summaries by States." They are then able to review data on income levels, births and deaths, business failures, and even social insurance programs. Large sets of data can be downloaded by users to their own computers for further analysis.

Another popular program offered at the Census Bureau's Internet site is County Business Patterns. This site features state- and county-based data on employment, payrolls, and establishments. Census Bureau news releases can also be accessed by both subject and date.

The Census Bureau takes great care to protect the confidentiality of its data. By federal law, data provided by individuals or businesses must remain confidential for at least 72 years. Therefore, no data on individuals or businesses is available on the Internet (or through any other access means). The Internet site used by the Census Bureau is also protected by a "firewall" to prevent a user from accessing confidential data.

As a marketing researcher, how would you use online versus published Census Bureau reports?

Source: Based on material in Jackson Morton, "Census of the Internet," *American Demographics* (March 1995), pp. 52–53.

FIGURE 7-4
The World's Population Distribution, 1990 and 2000
Source: U.S. Bureau of the Census.

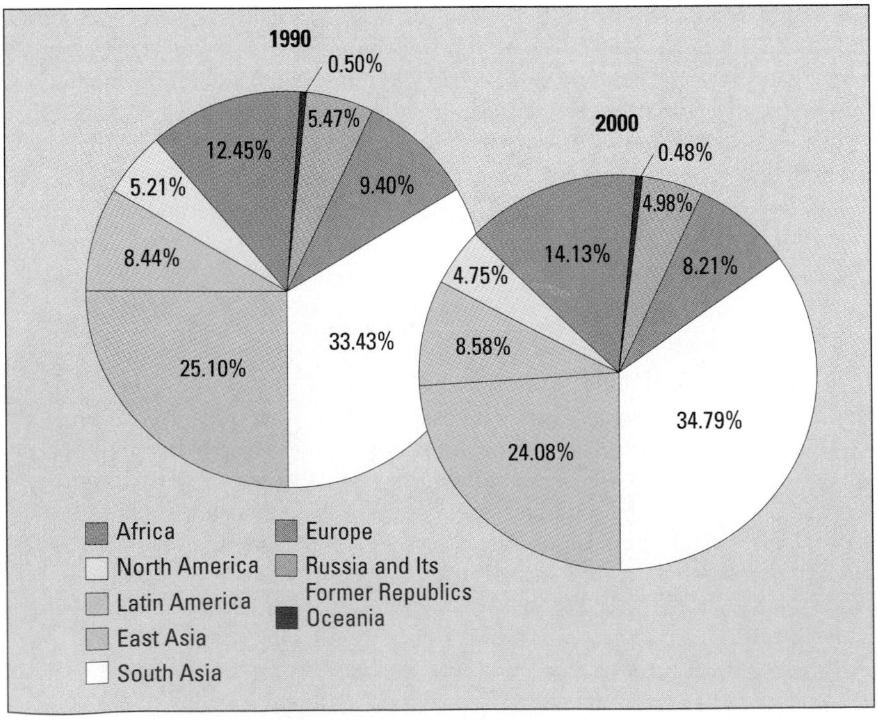

tion—mostly due to differences in life expectancy. For example, the life expectancy for newborn females is 82 years in Canada, 80 in Italy, 80 in the United States, and 74 in Russia; it is 75 years for newborn males in Canada, 76 in Italy, 73 in the United States, and 64 in Russia.

The populations in industrialized nations are older than in less-developed and developing nations. Today, the median age of the population is about 37 years in Japan, 36 in Italy and Great Britain, 34 in the United States, 25 in China, 23 in Brazil, 20 in Mexico, and 16 in Nigeria. In the United States, the average age is predicted to rise to 36 years by the year 2000.

Marketing Implications

Around the world, there are opportunities for marketing all types of goods and services. However, in industrialized countries, the low rate of population growth means that firms there need to focus on specific opportunities, such as firstborns, females, and expanding age groups. There will be heightened battles among firms for market share in industrialized nations.

The number of firstborns is significant because parents have many initial purchases to make, for such items as furniture, clothing, and transportation (stroller, car seat, and so on). On average, parents in industrialized nations spend thousands of dollars (including food, clothing, furniture and bedding, toys, health care, child care, and other items) to raise a first child to just his or her first birthday, far more than on each later child. And today's parents are much more likely to bring their babies with them when they travel. See Figure 7-5.

In the United States, there are over six million more females than males in the total population. This has important implications for marketers of clothing, household services,

There's nothing a Regent concierge can't handle.
Even a lullaby or two.
the Regent
Beverly Wilshire
A Four Seasons • Regent Hotel
AUCKLAND. BANGKOK. BEVERLY HILLS. CHIANG MAI. FIJI. HONG KONG. JAKARTA.
KUALA LUMPUR. LONDON. MELBOURNE. SINGAPORE. SYDNEY. TAIPEI.
CONTACT YOUR TRAVEL COUNSELLOR OR CALL REGENT INTERNATIONAL RESERVATIONS. TOLL FREE: (800) 545-4000.
FOUR SEASONS • REGENT. DEFINING THE ART OF SERVICE AT 40 HOTELS IN 19 COUNTRIES.

FIGURE 7-5
The Pampered Baby
Reprinted by permission.

appliances, cars, and other items where there are differences in needs and buying behavior by gender. Accordingly, more and more companies are gearing their appeals to women. Special interest should be paid to older females, who greatly outnumber their male counterparts.

The shifting age distribution in industrialized countries points up many possibilities. For example, colleges and universities are increasing their recruitment of older, nontraditional students. Sports and recreation companies are becoming more oriented toward the 45+ age group. The over-65 age group represents a growing market for food, medical care, vacation homes, telephone services, travel, entertainment, and restaurants.

On the other hand, the much higher rate of population growth—usually across both genders and all age groups—in less-developed and developing countries means that company opportunities there will be broad-based. There will be openings for companies to substantially increase the overall sales of food, clothing, autos, communications equipment, financial services, and a host of other goods and services—rather than fight over market share or carve up very small market segments. For example, from 1990 to 2000, the total populations in China, Nigeria, and Brazil are expected to rise by 160 million, 42 million, and 28 million people, respectively.

Location, Housing, and Mobility

During this century, there has been a major move of the world population to large urban areas and their surrounding suburbs. As of 1996, over 15 cities had at least 10 million residents each—led by Tokyo/Yokohama and Mexico City. But, as Figure 7-6 shows, the level of urbanization varies greatly by country.

The world is becoming more urban. U.S. urban areas are classed as **Metropolitan Statistical Areas** *and* **Consolidated Metropolitan Statistical Areas**.

Today, 80 per cent of the U.S. population resides in 19 per cent of the land area, often in Metropolitan Statistical Areas (MSAs) or Consolidated Metropolitan Statistical Areas (CMSAs). A **Metropolitan Statistical Area (MSA)** is relatively freestanding and not closely associated with other metropolitan areas. It contains either a city of at least 50,000 population or an urbanized area of 50,000 population (with a total population of 100,000+). Its population can exceed one million. There are 250 MSAs in the United States. A **Consolidated Metropolitan Statistical Area (CMSA)** has two or more overlapping and/or interlocking urban communities, known as Primary Metropolitan Statistical Areas (PMSAs), with a total population of at least one million. CMSAs comprise the 18 largest U.S. metropolitan areas and hold over one-third of the national population. The biggest CMSA is New York-Northern New Jersey-Long Island, New York-New Jersey-Connecticut, with 20 million people and 15 interlocking communities.

In many parts of the world, the majority of people own the homes in which they reside. Here are some examples: Bangladesh, 91 per cent; Paraguay, 81 per cent; New Zealand, 74 per cent; Greece, 73 per cent; Finland, 68 per cent; United States, 65 per cent; and Sri Lanka, 61 per cent.

Globally, many people own homes, and population mobility is high on a worldwide basis.

The worldwide mobility of the population is quite high; annually, millions of people emigrate from one nation to another and hundreds of millions move within their nations. During the last decade, more than eight million people have legally emigrated to the United States. Overall, about 8 per cent of those living in the United States were born in another country. Among U.S. residents, 15 to 20 per cent of all people move annually—64 per cent within the same county, 83 per cent within the same state, and 90 per cent within the same region; only 10 per cent of moves are to a new region or abroad. U.S. population mobility varies by region. From 1990 to 2000, the highest growth will be in the Mountain, Pacific, South Atlantic, and Southwest regions.

Marketing Implications

When a nation's population is urbanized, marketing programs are more cost efficient and it is easier to offer goods and services to large groups of consumers. There are opportunities for mass distribution and advertising. In some regions of the world, suburban shopping has been growing, leading to branch outlets in suburbs and improved transportation and delivery services.

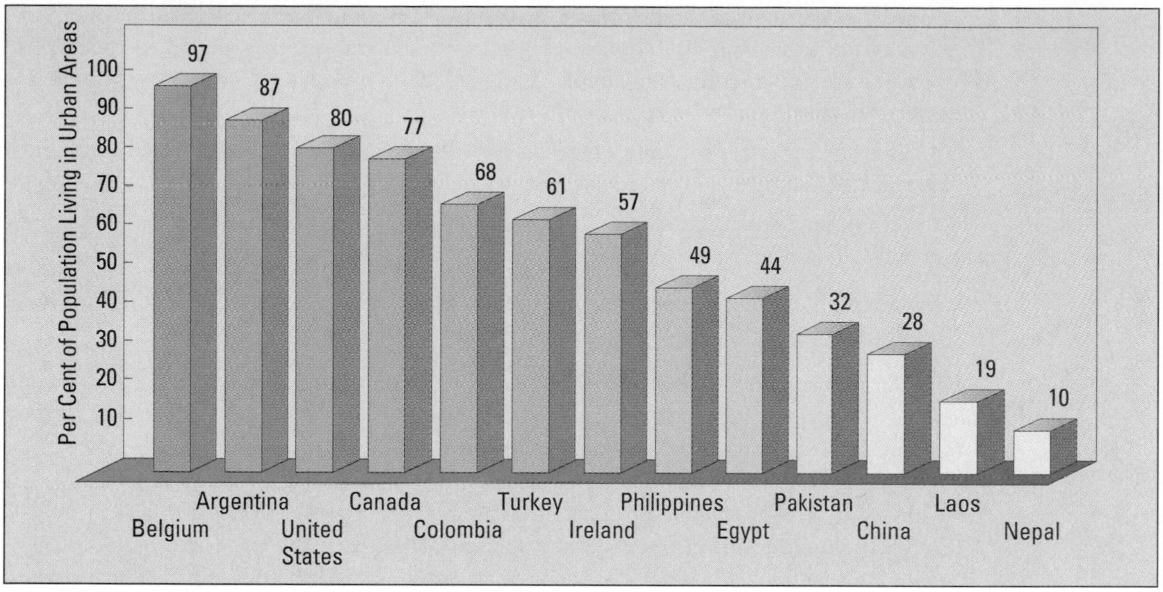

FIGURE 7-6
The Urbanization of Selected Countries
Source: United Nations.

The continuing interest in home ownership offers sales potential for such home-based items as furniture, appliances, carpeting, and insurance. Specially modified products for those occupying small homes and for apartment owners, such as space-efficient washers and dryers, are growing in importance. Because some large-ticket home purchases are greatly affected by the economy, firms need to monitor economic conditions carefully.

Population mobility offers openings for well-advertised global, national, or regional brands; retail chains and franchises; and major credit cards—among others. Their names are well known when consumers relocate and represent an assurance of quality. For example, Crest toothpaste, Heineken beer, British Airways, Honda, McDonald's, and Visa are recognized and successful worldwide, as well as throughout the United States. Macy's department stores do good business in Florida and California because a number of Northeasterners who are loyal Macy's customers have relocated there; yet, Macy's could not build an adequate customer following for its Missouri and Kansas stores and sold them.

Companies often refocus their marketing programs as they anticipate the growth of certain geographic areas and the decline of others. For instance, in the United States, marketing efforts directed at consumers in such states as Arizona, Texas, Florida, and Georgia have risen dramatically. Still, firms should be aware of the rising competition in these states and the possibility of oversaturation. Regions being abandoned by some firms, like the Northeast, should be reviewed by comparing population trends with competition levels.

Income and Expenditures

Country-by-country income data are hard to compare.

Consumer income and expenditure patterns are valuable demographic factors when properly studied. In examining them, these points should be kept in mind:

- Personal income is often stated as GDP per capita—the total value of goods and services produced in a nation divided by population size. This does not report what people really earn, and it inflates per-capita income if a small portion of the population is affluent. A better measure is median income—the income for those at the fiftieth percentile in a nation; it is a true midpoint. Yet, median incomes are rarely reported outside the United States.

- Personal income can be expressed as family, household, and per capita. Because families are larger than households and per-capita income is on an individual basis, these units are not directly comparable. Income can also be stated in pre-tax or after-tax terms, which are not directly comparable.
- Since prices differ by country, a comparison of average incomes that does not take purchasing power into effect will be inaccurate.
- Economic growth is cyclical. At any given time, some countries will be performing well while others are struggling.
- Although the term "poverty" varies greatly by nation, one billion people in the world are characterized by malnutrition, illiteracy, and disease.

During the 1960s and early 1970s, real U.S. income rose considerably. Growth then slowed; and from 1980 to 1982, real income fell. Between 1983 and 1990, real income rose moderately—before falling in 1991. Since then, it has fluctuated slightly each year. Thus, in sum, real U.S. income has gone up rather little over the last 25 years.

In 1995, U.S. median after-tax family income was between $33,000 and $34,000. Although the top one-fifth of families averaged $80,000 (with the top 1 per cent averaging $400,000+ per family), and 14 per cent of all families had incomes of $75,000 and over, the bottom one-fifth averaged just $13,000—and eight million families were at the poverty level. According to recent studies, the top one-fifth of U.S. families have total annual incomes that are nearly 15 times those of the lowest one-fifth. And the OECD reports that the United States has the greatest spread between high-income and low-income families of any industrialized nation in the world.[5]

Worldwide, these are the annual household income distributions:[6]

	PER CENT EARNING $20,000 AND UP	PER CENT EARNING UNDER $5,000
Industrialized countries	65	3
Latin America	27	24
Middle East	18	22
Former Socialist economies	17	21
East Asia/Pacific	4	73
Sub-Saharan Africa	2	75
South Asia	1	75

Changes in the **cost of living** *are measured by a* **consumer price index.**

The slowdown in real U.S. income growth has occurred because income rises have been virtually offset by higher prices. This has led to a higher **cost of living,** the total amount consumers annually pay for goods and services. Over the last 25 years, the greatest price increases have been for medical care, auto insurance, and tobacco products; the smallest have been for phone services, apparel and upkeep, and household furnishings.

Many nations monitor their cost of living via a **consumer price index (CPI),** which measures monthly and yearly price changes (the rate of inflation) for a broad range of consumer goods and services. Since 1983, the overall annual rise in the U.S. CPI has been under 5 per cent (except for 1990, when it rose by 5.5 per cent). In 1995, the CPI rose less than 5 per cent in the United States, France, Great Britain, and Germany. It went up by 10 per cent or more in many developing and less-developed countries.

Global consumption patterns have been shifting. In industrialized nations, the proportion of income that people spend on food, beverages, and tobacco has been declining. The percentage spent on medical care, personal business, and recreation has been ris-

[5]See Joseph Spiers, "Why the Income Gap Won't Go Away," *Fortune* (December 11, 1995), pp. 65–70; Keith Bradsher, "Widest Gap in Incomes? Research Points to U.S.," *New York Times* (October 27, 1995), p. D2; and Don L. Boroughs, "Winter of Discontent," *U.S. News & World Report* (January 22, 1996), pp. 47–54.

[6]Chip Walker, "The Global Middle Class," *American Demographics* (September 1995), p. 44.

International Marketing in *Action*

How Would YOU Do Business in Zambia?

Zambia's economic fortunes have changed dramatically over the past 30 years. At the time of its independence from Great Britain in 1964, the country had the highest standard of living in Black Africa. Unfortunately, Zambia then fell victim to a decline in the price of copper (the country's major export) and years of political control by a dictator.

Now, after holding a multiparty election and enacting economic controls proposed by the International Monetary Fund, Zambia's economic future looks promising. With its Central Africa location, Zambia has common borders with eight other countries; and it is an ideal location as a distribution hub due to the ease of access to 250 million consumers.

Zambia has worked hard to become more attractive to foreign investors. There are no longer restrictions on foreign exchange and investment; new business ventures are exempt from customs duties and sales taxes; firms can take after-tax profits out of the country; and a low income tax rate (a 15 per cent flat tax) is in effect. The nation's annual budget emphasizes such major infrastructure projects as road rehabilitation and rural electrification. The areas luring the most foreign investment are agriculture, mining, and tourism.

Here are some of the key demographic characteristics of Zambia:

- It has a population of 8.1 million people.
- The population density is very low, since Zambia's area is approximately the size of Texas.
- The annual population growth rate is 3.7 per cent.
- The total GDP is $3.5 billion (in U.S. dollars), and per capita income is about $425.
- Its annual inflation rate was reduced from over 200 per cent in 1992 to 35 per cent in 1995.

As an international marketing consultant, what opportunities would you recommend pursuing in Zambia? Why?

Source: Based on material in Christina Lamb, "Zambia: A Model for Africa," *Fortune* (July 24, 1995), Special Advertising Section.

ing. In less-developed and developing nations, the percentage of spending devoted to food remains high. Americans spend 18 per cent of income on food, beverages, and tobacco; and 16 per cent on medical care. In contrast, Argentines spend 40 per cent of income on food, beverages, and tobacco; and 4 per cent on medical care. And Pakistanis spend 47 per cent of income on food, beverages, and tobacco; and 5 per cent on medical care.

Disposable income is a person's, household's, or family's total after-tax income to be used for spending and/or savings. **Discretionary income** is what a person, household, or family has available to spend on luxuries, after necessities are bought. Classifying some product categories as necessities or luxuries depends on a nation's standard of living. In the United States, autos and phones are generally considered necessities; in many less-developed countries, they are typically considered luxuries.

Consumption reflects **disposable income** *and* **discretionary income**.

Marketing Implications

Several marketing implications regarding consumer income can be drawn:

- Companies need to be quite careful in drawing conclusions about the income levels in different countries. Terms must be properly defined and purchasing power, as well as income levels, assessed.
- There is great income diversity among countries. Thus, firms' goods, services, and marketing strategies should be consistent with the income levels in the targeted nations.
- There is tremendous income diversity within countries. This means that even in the same country, some firms can prosper by focusing on lower-income consumers while others succeed by targeting upper-income consumers.
- The cost of living impacts on the discretionary income that people have available to spend. For goods and services perceived as luxuries, consumers need to have discretionary income available.

U.S.-based Whirlpool is a good example of a firm that understands how to react to consumer income levels. It knows that outside the United States and Western Europe, the middle-class consumer is quite different. A consumer has to work 40 to 45 days to afford a washing machine in Poland, 35 days in the Czech Republic, and 30 days in Hungary—versus 5 days in Western Europe. As a result, Whirlpool arranges for more financing in Eastern Europe.[7]

Occupations and Education

The trend to white-collar and service occupations is continuing in industrialized countries.

The labor force in industrialized nations continues to move to white-collar and service occupations. In less-developed and developing nations, many jobs still involve manual work and are more often agriculture-based.

The total employed civilian U.S. labor force is 125 million people—compared with 64 million in Japan, 28 million in Germany, 26 million in Great Britain, 22 million in France, and 20 million in Italy. For the last 30 years, the per cent of U.S. workers in service-related, technical, and clerical white-collar jobs has risen; the per cent as managers, administrators, and sales workers has been constant; and the per cent as nonskilled workers has dropped. Three million U.S. workers have an agriculture-related job.

Women are a large and growing percentage of the worldwide labor force, including 46 per cent in the United States.

Another change in the labor force throughout the world has been the increase in the number and percentage of working women. For example, in 1960, 23 million women comprised 32 per cent of the total U.S. labor force. Today, 58 million women account for 46 per cent of the labor force, and 52 per cent of adult women are working. In Japan and Great Britain, one-half of adult women are in the labor force, while more than 60 per cent of adult women are in the Swedish labor force.

Twelve million married U.S. women, 31 per cent of all married women, were employed in 1960. Now, 33 million married women—59 per cent of all married women—are in the labor force. The per cent of married women with children under age 6 in the U.S. labor force has jumped from 19 per cent in 1960 to 59 per cent currently. Similar increases have also occurred in other nations.

Unemployment rates, which reflect the percentage of adults in the total labor force not working, vary widely by nation. For instance, during 1995, the U.S. unemployment rate was 6 per cent. In contrast, 1995 unemployment rates exceeded 10 per cent in Belgium, Finland, France, Great Britain, and Italy, and Spain's rate was 22 per cent. Even though the U.S. figure was lower, it still meant millions of people without jobs. Some worldwide unemployment has been temporary, due to weak domestic and international economies. Other times, depending on the nation and industry, many job losses have been permanent. Unemployment is often accompanied by cutbacks in discretionary purchases.

[7]Rahul Jacob, "The Big Rise," *Fortune* (May 30, 1994), pp. 74–90.

Global education levels are going up.

Great strides are being made globally to upgrade educational attainment, but the level of education tends to be much higher in industrialized nations than in less-developed and developing ones. One measure of educational attainment is the literacy rate, the percentage of people in a country who can read and write. In industrialized nations such as the United States, this rate exceeds 95 per cent. Here are the rates for some less-developed and developing nations: Bolivia, 78 per cent; Cambodia, 74 per cent; Chad, 30 per cent; China, 78 per cent; Morocco, 50 per cent; and Saudi Arabia, 62 per cent.

Another measure of educational attainment is the level of schooling completed; and compared to other large industrialized nations, the United States is the most educated. A higher percentage of U.S. adults has finished high school and college than those in Canada, France, Germany, Great Britain, Italy, or Japan. As of 1995, 80 per cent of U.S. adults 25 years old and older were high school graduates, and more than 22 per cent were college graduates. Of U.S. adults aged 25 to 34 in 1995, 87 per cent were high school graduates and one-quarter were college graduates. Figure 7-7 compares higher education in the United States with several other nations.

The sharp increase in working women and higher educational attainment have generally contributed to the growing number of people in upper-income brackets; the rather high unemployment rate in some nations and industries, and slow-growth economies, have caused other families to have low incomes.

Marketing Implications

The occupations and education of the population have these marketing implications. A greater number and percentage of the total population are in the labor force than before. This work force needs transportation, clothing, restaurants, and personal services. Stores have opportunities in commercial centers. The market for job-oriented goods and services is growing and the shift in jobs means different needs and aspirations in consumer purchases.

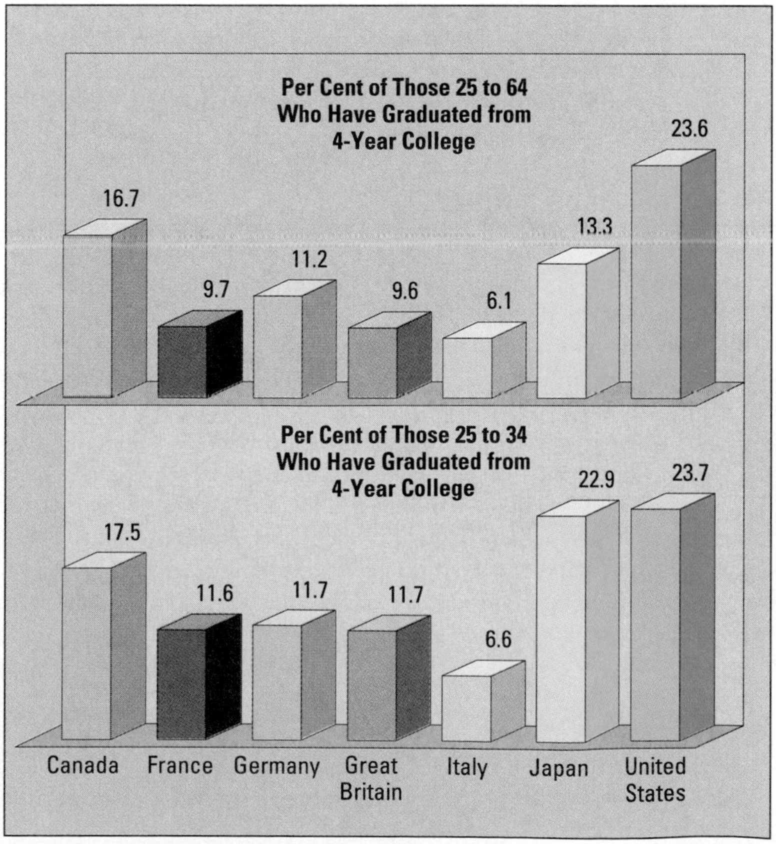

FIGURE 7-7
Educational Attainment by Country

NOTE: These statistics are from 1991, the latest common date available.

Source: Organization for Economic Cooperation and Development data, as reported in *The Condition of Education 1994* (Washington, D.C.: U.S. Department of Education, 1994), p. 70.

Because working women have less time for shopping and operating the home, they tend to be interested in convenience and customer service. They often cannot shop during weekdays, and many require evening and weekend store hours, efficient store layouts, and mail-order and phone purchases. Such time-saving devices as microwave ovens and food processors, prepared foods, pre-wrapped goods, and special services (such as automatic teller machines) appeal to working women. Also, child-related services, such as daytime child care, are particularly important for them. Yet, too few firms help employees in this area, leaving a prime opening for specialized firms to market these services.

As the population's education level rises, firms need to respond in terms of better information, better product quality, better customer service, enhanced safety and environmental controls, greater accuracy in learning and meeting consumer expectations, and improved consumer-complaint departments. At the same time, companies marketing in less-developed and developing countries need to keep the literacy rates of those areas in mind and adapt products, packaging, promotion messages, and operating instructions accordingly.

Marital Status

Marriage and family remain important.

Marriage and family are powerful institutions worldwide, but in some nations, they are now less dominant. Although 2.4 million U.S. couples get married each year, only 60 per cent of U.S. adults are married (down from 76 per cent in 1960); the percentage of married adults in many other nations is much higher. The median U.S. age at first marriage is 27 years for males and 25 years for females—up from 23 and 20 in 1960, as people wait to marry and have children. Thus, the average U.S. family size has gone from 3.7 members in 1960 to 3.2. The male and female ages at first marriage are much lower in less-developed and developing nations, and the average family is bigger there.

*A **family** has related persons residing together. A **household** has one or more persons who may not be related.*

A **family** is a group of two or more persons residing together who are related by blood, marriage, or adoption. A **household** is a person or group of persons occupying a housing unit, whether related or unrelated. In many nations, average household size has been dropping. The U.S. average has gone from 3.3 in 1960 to 2.7 today—due to later marriages, more widows and widowers, a high divorce rate (double that of some industrialized nations), many couples deciding to have fewer children, and the growth of single-person households. Of the nearly 100 million U.S. households, a quarter are one-person units. Family households are 70 per cent of U.S. households—down from 85 per cent in 1960. Figure 7-8 shows household data for several nations.

Marketing Implications

Despite changes over the last 30 or so years, marriage and family are still vital institutions around the world and in the United States. The marketing implications of marital and family status include the following.

There are opportunities for industries associated with weddings (such as caterers and travel agents), family life (such as financial services and full-sized cars), and divorce (such as attorneys). When marriages occur later in individuals' lives, those people have better financial resources and two-income families are more prevalent. This presents opportunities for firms involved with clothing, furniture, entertainment, and recreation.

The growth of single-person households provides opportunities for home and home furnishings industries and those that produce specialized products. These implications also apply to divorced and widowed persons. For example, smaller households have a demand for more petite homes, appropriate-sized furnishings and appliances, and single-serving food packages.

Ethnicity/Race

*Demographically, **ethnicity/race** is one measure of nations' diversity with regard to language, country of origin, or race.*

From a demographics perspective, **ethnicity/race** should be studied to determine the existence of diversity among and within nations in terms of language and country of origin or race.

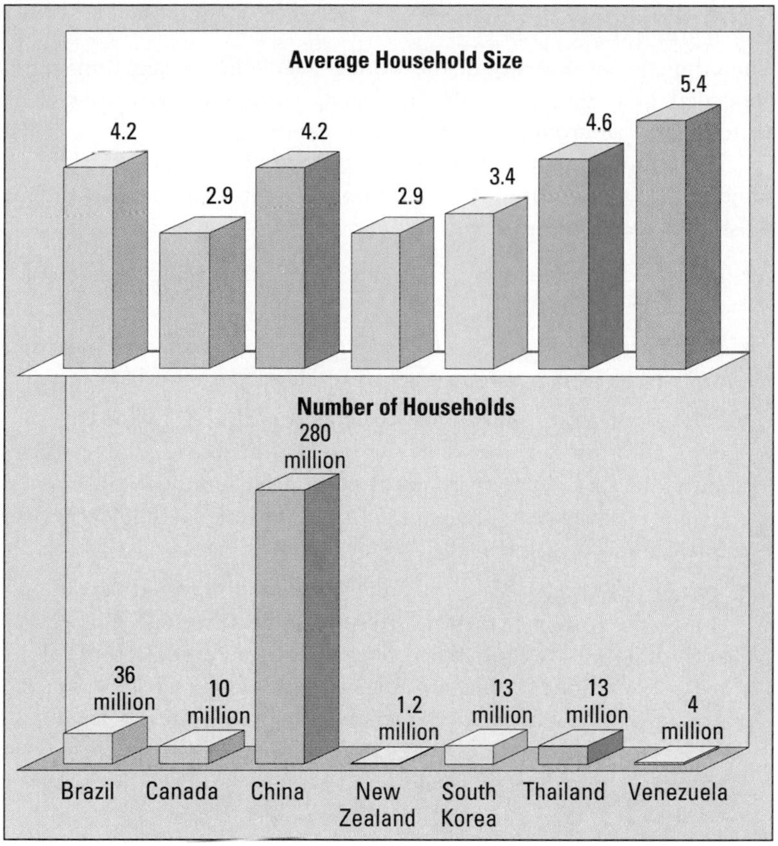

FIGURE 7-8
Household Data by Country

NOTE: These statistics are from 1993, the latest common date available.

Source: International Marketing Data and Statistics 1995 (Great Britain: Euromonitor, 1995), p. 429; and authors' estimates.

Worldwide, there are over 200 different languages spoken by at least one million people each—and 12 of those are spoken by more than 100 million people each (including Mandarin, English, Hindi, and Spanish). Thus, there are vast differences among nations as to the languages commonly spoken. Even within nations, there is often diversity as to the languages spoken. For example, Canada (English and French), Chad (French and Arabic), India (Hindi and English), and Peru (Spanish and Quechua) have two official languages. One of the issues facing the European Community in its unification drive is the multiplicity of languages spoken in the 15 nations.

Most nations consist of people representing different ethnic and racial backgrounds. For instance, among those living in the Philippines are Malays, Chinese, Americans, and Spaniards. Sometimes, the people in various groups continue to speak in the languages of their countries of origin, even though they may have resided in their current nations for one or two generations.

The United States is comprised of people from virtually every ethnic and racial group in the world. The Bureau of the Census uses "black," "white," "Asian," "Pacific Islander," and "American Indian" to delineate U.S. racial groups; "Hispanic" is an ethnic term, denoting people of any race. Although "'African American' is becoming more common as a way to express ethnic pride, 'black' is still used widely, and few are offended by it. Executives should make their own judgments, based on the values of their audience."[8]

The 1995 U.S. population was 73 per cent white, 12.5 per cent black, 10.1 per cent Hispanic, 3.5 per cent Asian and Pacific Islander, and 0.9 per cent American Indian. It is predicted that the 2050 U.S. population will be 52 per cent white, 21 per cent Hispanic, 15.7 per cent black, 10.2 per cent Asian and Pacific Islander, and 1.1 per cent American Indian. These trends will be due to higher birth rates and immigration to the United States by nonwhites.

[8]Eugene Morris, "The Difference in Black and White," *American Demographics* (January 1993), p. 46. See also "People Labels," *U.S. News & World Report* (November 20, 1995), p. 28; and Carolyn Shea, "The New Face of America," *American Demographics* (January 1996), pp. 53–60.

Marketing Implications

The ethnic/racial diversity of the world's population means firms must be careful not to generalize or stereotype—either in dealing with multiple nations or marketing to different ethnic/racial groups within the same nation.

For example, companies marketing goods and services in the United States might miss some prime opportunities if they do not research and adapt to the racial/ethnic characteristics of the marketplace:

- In some of its advertising, Olympus appeals to specific racial/ethnic groups. Figure 7-9 shows one such ad.
- Three-fifths of U.S. Hispanics live in Florida, Texas, and California. More than one-half of U.S. Asians live in California, New York, and Hawaii.
- Direct Language Communications publishes twelve Yellow Pages in Spanish in Northern California. It knows that "Among U.S. Hispanics, 96 per cent speak Spanish fluently; only 41 per cent are fluent in English. Among Northern California Hispanics, 63 per cent say they speak only Spanish at home, while 80 per cent report speaking Spanish more than half the time at home."[9]
- "Several years ago, the Carnation Company discovered that the per-capita consumption of its Instant Breakfast Drink was unusually high among blacks. When mixed with milk, this sweet-flavored powder was intended to serve as a nutritionally complete, low-calorie breakfast. The high usage among blacks was puzzling because blacks generally do not use diet products as heavily as whites. When Carnation investigated, it discovered that blacks were using the product as a supplement. Some customers were even drinking the product and eating a full breakfast simply because they liked the taste."[10]

Uses of Demographic Data

As we noted at the beginning of the chapter, after studying individual demographics, a firm can form consumer demographic profiles to better focus marketing efforts. Here, three examples of demographic profiles are presented.

Profiles of the United States and Mexican populations can be contrasted:

	UNITED STATES	MEXICO
Annual population growth	1%	1.9%
Life expectancy	77 years	74 years
Median age	34 years	20 years
Urban population	80%	71%
Income ratio of top fifth of population to bottom fifth	15	14
Working women as part of total labor force	46	37
Literacy rate	96%	90%
Average household size	2.7	5.6

The typical working woman in Japan is married, in her middle to late 40s, and has children in school. A two-income family can pay for the children's education and meet housing costs. The husband's earnings go to cover housing, household, and other ongoing expenses; the wife's earnings go for children's education, personal needs, social life, and savings. "Japanese women control the household purse strings. Most husbands handed over the pay packet and got an allowance. Today, even with direct deposit, most women

[9] Charles Laughlin, "Speaking in Tongues," *Link* (October 1993), p. 15.
[10] Morris, "The Difference in Black and White," p. 48.

FIGURE 7-9
Marketing to a Diverse Marketplace
Reprinted by permission.

know exactly how much their husbands make, but only a few men know what their wives earn." A full-time working woman spends 7 hours per day on the job, 3.5 hours on household chores and child care, and less than 3 hours on herself.[11]

About 20 million people in the United States engage in woodworking. They spend $15 billion yearly on supplies, materials, and equipment. Eighty four per cent of woodworkers are male, and they average 45 years of age. Four-fifths are married, and the mean household income is $48,000.[12]

Limitations of Demographics

Demographic data may be dated, unavailable, too general, require profile analysis, and not consider reasons for behavior.

In applying demographic data, these limitations should be noted:

- Information may be old. Even in the United States, a full census is done only once per ten years and there are time lags before data are released.
- Data on various demographics may be unavailable in some nations, especially less-developed and developing ones.
- Summary data may be too broad and hide opportunities and risks in small markets or specialized product categories.
- Single demographics may not be useful. A demographic profile may be needed.
- The psychological or social factors influencing people are not considered.

[11]Sandra T. W. Davis, "Japan's Working Women Are a 'New Breed' of Consumer," *Marketing News* (August 17, 1992), p. 12.
[12]"Going with the Grain," *Advertising Age* (September 11, 1995), p. 3.

Ethics IN TODAY'S SOCIETY

Should Public School Districts Accept Advertising?

In the United States alone, children and young adults annually spend more than $100 billion and influence their families to spend an additional $130 billion. Accordingly, marketers are increasingly contacting public school districts to establish ties with them in order to better attract the school-aged market.

Many districts see school bus advertising as a means of increasing their revenues. School bus advertising began in Colorado Springs, Colorado, and was quickly adopted by school districts throughout the United States, including those in Washington, D.C. and New York City.

Each district has its own rules governing school bus ads. Some restrict ads to the placement of logos on the outside of school buses; these ads resemble traveling billboards. Other districts allow advertisers to place brochures and coupons on racks inside school buses. Many districts also control message content by restricting ads to positive messages.

There are also differences in how school bus advertising is implemented. Some districts administer the advertising program themselves. Others, like New York City's Board of Education, plan to develop partnerships with advertising agencies and outdoor media companies. These firms must be willing to absorb all startup costs and to share revenues with the schools.

Supporters of school bus advertising say this is a harmless way of offsetting cuts in federal aid to schools and rising school costs, and that school bus advertising can also involve students in creative projects. In Colorado Springs, for instance, a local Burger King franchisee allowed students to design the logo ads that identified the chain. On the other hand, critics feel bus advertising may be perceived as a product endorsement, that it influences students to purchase unnecessary and sometimes unhealthy items, and that it takes advantage of a captive audience.

As a nonpaid marketing advisor to a local school board, develop a position regarding whether school bus advertising should be accepted by the board.

Sources: Based on material in Kemba Johnson, "NY School Buses Learn to Ad," *Advertising Age* (August 14, 1995), p. 10; and Betsy Wagner, "Our Class Is Brought To You Today By," *U.S. News & World Report* (April 24, 1995), p. 63.

- The decision process that people use in making purchases is not explained.
- Demographics do not delve into the reasons why people make decisions. Why do people with similar demographic profiles buy different products or brands?

For these reasons, Chapter 8 examines the psychological and social factors affecting consumer behavior and the decision process consumers use.

MARKETING IN A CHANGING WORLD

From Boomers to Xers

Two of the key age groups that today's marketers must continually strive to understand and satisfy are *Baby Boomers* and *Generation Xers*. In some cases, the first group includes the parents of the second group.

Baby Boomers are people born between 1946 and 1964, in the aftermath of World War II. By the year 2000, the 77 million U.S. *Baby Boomers* will range in age from 36 to 54, be in their peak earning years, and dominate consumer spending. The older *Baby Boomers* have been heavily influenced by the "Vietnam War, the Civil Rights Movement, and economic expansion." The younger ones have been more affected by "Watergate, the oil embargo, the tough America of the 1970s and 1980s, and a contracting economy." Overall, *Baby Boomers* are "well-educated, high-tech parents who suffer from a lack of leisure time. Despite their financial worries, most can expect a healthy, active, and fun-filled retirement."[13]

Generation Xers—a term coined by marketers and disliked by most in this group (don't YOU dislike this name?)—are people born between 1965 and 1976, a period also known as the "baby bust" in the United States. By the year 2000, *Generation Xers* will range in age from 24 to 35 and will be embarking on major life changes, with regard to getting married, having children, and moving along career ladders. In contrast to *Baby Boomers, Generation Xers* "are more apt to have participated in household chores at an earlier age, so they are more knowledgeable about products at a comparable age. They are more apt to seek a balance of work and leisure activities. They are more diverse and more accepting of diversity, whether it be defined by ethnicity or by sexual preference. And while they are not anti-advertising, they are repulsed by insincerity—and they are experts at spotting it."[14]

SUMMARY

1. *To show the importance and scope of consumer analysis* By analyzing consumers, a firm is better able to determine the most appropriate audience to which to appeal and the combination of marketing factors that will satisfy this audience. This is a critical task given the diversity in today's global marketplace. The scope of consumer analysis includes who, what, why, how, when, where, and how often. This chapter examines consumer demographics. Chapters 8 to 10 focus on the life-style factors affecting the behavior of final consumers, the decision process of final consumers, organizational consumers, the development of a target market, and sales forecasting.

2. *To define and enumerate important consumer demographics for the U.S. population and other countries* Consumer demographics are objective and quantifiable population statistics. They include population size, gender, and age; population location, housing, and mobility; population income and expenditures; population occupations and education; population marital status; and population ethnicity/race.

3. *To examine trends and projections for these important demographics and study their marketing implications* The world population is 5.7 billion people and rising by 1.5 per cent annually. The U.S. population is 263 million people and increasing by one per cent each year. In many nations, a large proportion of births involves firstborns. Worldwide, the number of men and women is roughly equal. However, women generally live longer than men, and the average age of populations in industrialized nations is higher than in less-developed and developing countries.

There has been a significant movement of the world population to large urban areas. The level of urbanization does vary by country, with 80 per cent of the U.S. population living in 19 per cent of the land area. In many countries, the majority of people own the home in which they live, with almost two-thirds of the U.S. population residing in homes they own. Each year, millions of people emigrate from one country to another and hundreds of millions move within their countries. About 800,000 people move to the United States from abroad every year; and about 15 to 20 per cent of the U.S. population moves annually. Major U.S. growth is occurring in the Mountain, Pacific, South Atlantic, and Southwest regions.

[13]Patricia Braus, "The Baby Boom at Mid-Decade," *American Demographics* (April 1995), pp. 40–45.

[14]Karen Ritchie, "Marketing to Generation X," *American Demographics* (April 1995), pp. 34–39; and Susan Mitchell, "Younger Generations Are More Diverse," *Marketing Tools* (January 1996), p. 4.

For several reasons, comparing countries' personal income data can be rather difficult. The 1995 U.S. median after-tax family income was between $33,000 and $34,000—with one-fifth of families having after-tax incomes averaging $80,000 and another one-fifth having after-tax incomes averaging $13,000. Many nations measure their cost of living and rate of inflation via a consumer price index. There are differences in consumption patterns between people in industrialized nations and ones in less-developed and developing countries. When assessing consumption patterns, the distinction between disposable-income spending and discretionary-income expenditures should be kept in mind.

In industrialized nations, the labor force is continuing its movement to white-collar and service occupations; many more jobs in less-developed and developing nations still entail manual work and are agriculture-based. The total employed U.S. civilian labor force is 125 million people. Throughout the world, women comprise a significant portion of the labor force (46 per cent in the United States). Unemployment rates vary widely among nations, based on economic conditions and industry shifts. Globally, educational attainment has gone up—though there are great variations among countries. In the United States, a much larger percentage of people is now graduating high school and attending college than 30 years ago.

Marriage and family are powerful institutions, although less dominant than before for some nations. Three-fifths of U.S. adults are married, with couples waiting until they are older for marriage and having fewer children than in prior decades. A family consists of relatives living together. A household consists of a person or persons occupying a housing unit, related or not. In many nations, both family and household size have declined, due to the growth in single-person households and other factors.

Demographically, ethnicity/race is important as it pertains to the diversity of people among and within nations. Globally, over 200 languages are spoken by at least one million people; and some nations have two or more official languages. Most countries have populations representing different ethnic and racial groups. In the United States, the Bureau of the Census uses the terms "black," "white," "Asian," "Pacific Islander," and "American Indian" to delineate major racial groups and the term "Hispanic" to denote an ethnic group (which includes people of any race).

For each of these demographics, marketing implications are discussed in the chapter.

4. *To present examples of consumer demographic profiles* After looking at demographic factors separately, a firm could develop a consumer demographic profile—a composite description of a consumer group based upon key demographics. Three examples of such profiles are provided.

5. *To consider the limitations of consumer demographics* These limitations of demographics are noted: data may be obsolete; data may be unavailable for some nations; there may be hidden trends or implications; single demographic statistics are often not useful; and demographics do not explain the factors affecting behavior, consumer decision making, and motivation.

KEY TERMS

final consumers (p. 183)
organizational consumers (p. 183)
consumer demographics (p. 184)
consumer demographic profile (p. 184)
Metropolitan Statistical Area (MSA) (p. 188)
Consolidated Metropolitan Statistical Area (CMSA) (p. 188)
cost of living (p. 190)
consumer price index (CPI) (p. 190)
disposable income (p. 191)
discretionary income (p. 191)
family (p. 194)
household (p. 194)
ethnicity/race (p. 194)

Review Questions

1. How does the use of consumer demographics aid marketing decision making?
2. What is the value of a consumer demographic profile?
3. Distinguish between final and organizational consumers.
4. Compare the worldwide and U.S. trends with regard to population growth. Why is this meaningful to marketers?
5. In the United States, how does a Metropolitan Statistical Area differ from a Consolidated Metropolitan Statistical Area?
6. Cite several reasons why it is difficult to contrast personal income data by country.
7. Distinguish between the terms "cost of living" and "consumer price index."
8. In addition to the examples cited in the text, what goods and services should grow as the number of working women and working mothers increases?
9. What is a family? Why are U.S. families getting smaller?
10. Describe the major limitations of demographics.

Discussion Questions

1. Comment on this statement and its marketing ramifications: "Even though the world is getting smaller, there remains tremendous demographic diversity in the marketplace."
2. The biggest CMSA in the United States is New York-Northern New Jersey-Long Island, New York-New Jersey-Connecticut, with 20 million people and 15 PMSAs. What are the pros and cons of marketing products there? Recommend a marketing approach for a local bank.
3. Discuss the country household data in Figure 7-8 and the implications for marketers.
4. Develop a demographic profile of the people residing in your census tract, using the *Census of Population*. What are the marketing overtones of this profile?
5. As the owner-operator of a prospective camera store in Canada, what demographic factors would you study? Describe the demographic profile of your ideal consumer.

CASE 1

America's Changing Demographics: How Should Marketers React?[*]

Let's look at the changes in selected U.S. demographic factors over the 20-year period from 1974 to 1994. While doing so, let's also examine the marketing opportunities and threats that can be anticipated from these trends.

The overall population of the United States rose from 214 million to 260 million people (a 21 per cent increase) over this time period. But not all population age groups had the same growth rate. For example, the population group with people 65 years and older increased by 50 per cent. The substantial increase in the senior citizen population provides major opportunities in terms of retirement housing and medical care. It also means special opportunities for retailers that specialize in the senior market, such as travel agencies that offer grandchild-grandparent travel and special cruise trips.

The inflation-adjusted income of the typical two-parent family increased by only 10 per cent between 1974 and 1994. This increase was very small when compared with the 80 per cent rise recorded from 1954 to 1974. Furthermore, the United States saw a widening gap between low-income households and the incomes of those households that were the best off financially. For example, in 1994, 23 per cent of children aged 18 and under were living in poverty, compared with 15 per cent in 1974. On the other hand, in 1994, after adjusting for inflation, 5.6 million households had incomes over $100,000 (5.8 per cent of all households) compared with 2 million households in 1974 (2.7 per cent of all households). And although many African-American households saw their real income decline from 1974 to 1994, the number of African-American households with incomes over $100,000 increased from 29,000 to 214,000.

The widening gap between wealthy and poor households yields opportunities at both ends of the income spectrum. Wealthy families are a significant market for luxuries such as vacation travel, boating, fine jewelry, and second homes. Nonaffluent families, in contrast, are lured by special buys, discount stores, no-name brands of food products, and do-it-yourself repair projects.

There were also major differences in family structure over the 20-year period. In 1994, there were 1.84 children per family versus 2.14 in 1974; and almost 10 per cent of children in 1994 were living with a parent who had never married at all versus 1.5 per cent in 1974. And in 1994, 16 per cent of all 25- to 34-year-old men lived with their parents versus 10 per cent in 1974.

Clearly, the earlier stereotypes—of a large per cent of the population marrying young and children being raised by two-parent families—are now dated. Among demographic groups, single parents are generally among the most time pressed. This group can be targeted through mail-order catalogs, home delivery, Saturday repair facilities, and pre-wrapped gifts.

Enrollment in two-year colleges increased from 3.4 to 5.8 million from 1974 to 1994. At the same time, enrollment in four-year colleges went from 6.8 to 9.1 million. The increase in college enrollment at both levels means greater demand for college texts, summer internships, air travel (during vacation and summer periods), student housing, and PCs.

Lastly, there was a marked increase in travel during the 20-year time frame. The number of Americans who traveled overseas increased from 7.1 million to 17.1 million. Likewise, visits to the United States by foreigners rose from 3.5 million to 17.3 million.

Increased foreign travel has the effect of opening national borders and making consumer tastes more "borderless." This can be seen in the growing popularity of foreign foods, the brand recognition of popular items throughout the world, and the speed with which foreign fashions are adopted here.

QUESTIONS

1. Describe how a supermarket chain could better attract and service the growing senior citizen market.
2. Discuss the marketing implications of the widening gap between the wealthy and poor segments of the population.
3. Describe how a department store could better appeal to single parents.
4. What are the advantages and disadvantages of applying the demographic data presented in this case?

[*]The data in this case are drawn from David Wessel and Bob Davis, "In the Middle of the Middle: Two Families' Stories," *Wall Street Journal* (March 29, 1995), p. B1.

CASE 2

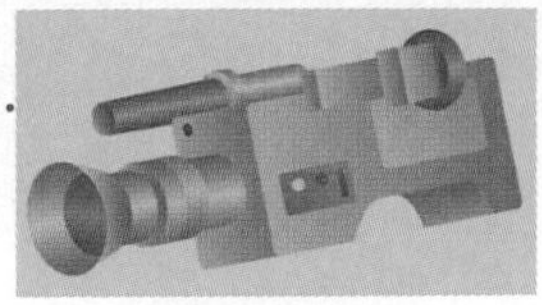

Wellcome: The Influence of Demographic Factors in Taiwan[†]

Many parts of Asia are seen as markets with substantial long-run potential. Some analysts even predict that, over the next decade, more people will become affluent in Asia than anywhere else in the world.

Some forecasters see particularly high growth in Asian grocery marketing, especially for supermarkets. Currently, only 20 per cent of people shop in a supermarket at least once a week in Malaysia, as compared with 35 per cent in Taiwan and 80 per cent in Hong Kong. In contrast, the average U.S. shopper makes 2.2 trips to a supermarket per week and spends a weekly total of $75. As the Gross Domestic Product per capita rises, market analysts forecast that supermarket usage by Asians will significantly increase.

One way to predict the potential number of supermarkets in Asian countries is by extrapolating data from the mature supermarket industry in the United States, using the following formula. Let us apply the formula to Taiwan:

$$\begin{aligned}\text{Potential number of supermarkets in Taiwan} &= \frac{\text{Population of Taiwan}}{\text{Number of people per supermarket in United States}} \times \frac{\text{Per capita income in Taiwan}}{\text{Per capita income in United States}} \\ &= \frac{21{,}500{,}000}{8{,}750} \times \frac{\$10{,}600}{\$24{,}700} \\ &= 2{,}457 \times .429 \\ &= 1{,}054\end{aligned}$$

Thus, based on this formula, there currently is room for 1,054 supermarkets in Taiwan.

One supermarket chain, Dairy Farm (owned by Wellcome, a Hong Kong-based firm with $8 billion in sales), opened its first store in Taiwan in 1987. Dairy Farm's Taiwanese market strategy was to open stores earlier than competitors and to establish economies of scale in advertising, warehousing, and distribution. Dairy Farm now has 80 supermarkets in Taiwan and sees the potential for an additional 250 to 300 markets over the next decade. Although Dairy Farm's Taiwanese stores are small by U.S. standards, they have a large selection of merchandise when compared to the mom-and-pop store competitors in Taiwan.

Among Asian countries, several supermarket executives feel Taiwan will soon represent a more important market than Hong Kong:

- In 1997, Hong Kong is to return to the jurisdiction of China, after being a British Crown Colony.
- There are now 21.5 million people in Taiwan, 25 per cent under the age of 15. The adult population has a literacy rate of 93 per cent.
- Some economic forecasters predict that in the future, Taiwan's GDP per capita will be higher than Australia's. In 1994, Taiwan had a GDP per capita of $10,600, a strong increase over the 1993 level. In comparison, the per capita GDP for Australia was $19,100 in 1994.
- An additional advantage of the Taiwanese market is its high population density. Taiwan has 1,540 people per square mile versus 620 in Great Britain and 72 in the United States.

One obstacle to achieving supermarket success in Taiwan is the long supply chain and the poor infrastructure (roads, warehouses, and communications systems). These items limit expansion opportunities to the larger cities. Another problem relates to the difficulty in getting suppliers to become more efficient. For example, Dairy Farm found that after operating in Taiwan for over seven years, only 10 per cent of its products are delivered to its central warehouse on pallets.

QUESTIONS

1. Comment on the Taiwanese demographic data presented in this case. Besides supermarkets, what other kinds of firms should pursue this market? Why?
2. What kinds of demographic data would be useful in evaluating a particular site in Taiwan as a potential supermarket location?
3. What do you think about the formula used to determine the potential number of supermarkets in Taiwan?
4. Apply the formula to any other country in Asia and compare the results to those shown here for Taiwan.

VIDEO QUESTIONS ON WELLCOME

1. Compare the characteristics of supermarkets in Taiwan with those in the United States.
2. Describe Wellcome's decision making in terms of product width and depth for its Taiwan supermarkets.

[†]The data in this case are drawn from Kevin Coupe, "You Can't Cook a Turkey in a Wok," *Progressive Grocer* (October 1994), pp. 59–60; and "62nd Annual Report of the Grocery Industry," *Progressive Grocer* (April 1995), p. 43.

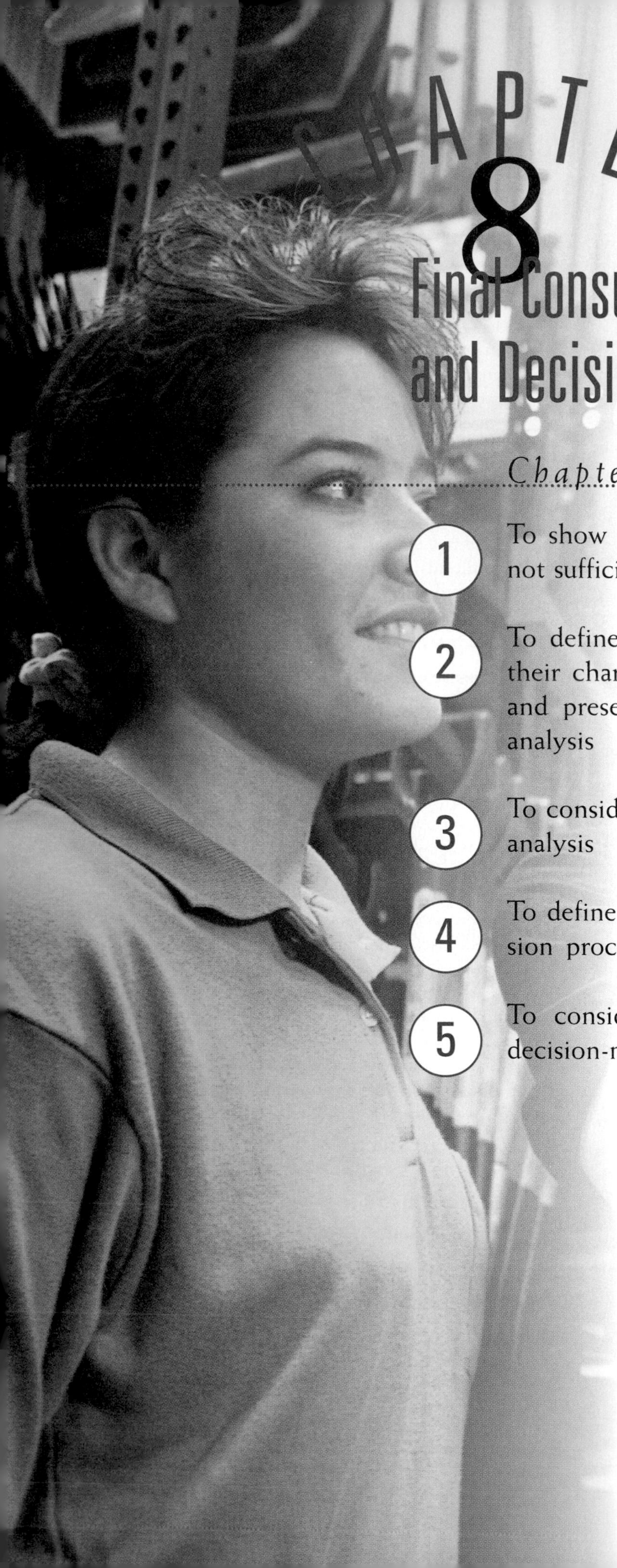

CHAPTER 8

Final Consumer Life-Styles and Decision Making

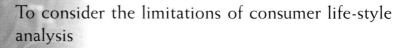

Chapter Objectives

1. To show why consumer demographic analysis is not sufficient in planning marketing programs

2. To define and describe consumer life-styles and their characteristics, examine selected life-styles, and present marketing implications of life-style analysis

3. To consider the limitations of consumer life-style analysis

4. To define and describe the final consumer's decision process and present marketing implications

5. To consider the limitations of final consumer decision-making analysis

> *With an automatic teller machine, you can bank without a banker. With computer software, you can pick a mutual fund without a broker or design a patio deck without an architect. With an online service, you can plan a trip to Paris without a travel agent. You can do these activities when you want— days, nights, or weekends. "In many industries," observes Chris Meyer, a vice-president at Mercer Management Consulting, "you get more choice, more control, and more convenience by doing things yourself."*

In greater numbers, consumers are transporting goods in their own trucks, renovating their homes with their own tools, and managing their own finances with financial software. Although measuring the size of the do-it-yourself market is open to some debate, one study found that if the value of the time spent on such projects was included (based on the cost of a professional), the do-it-yourself market would amount to 40 per cent of the United States' Gross Domestic Product! Another study concluded that the U.S. standard of living is significantly understated because the labor portion of do-it-yourself projects is not included in this measure.

Reprinted by permission.

A glimpse at the do-it-yourself market in the home repair and investment industries also suggests that the size of the overall market is huge. U.S. consumers spend more than $125 billion per year on home-improvement projects, and about 60 per cent of homeowners undertake at least one repair or home renovation project each year. And every year since 1988, discount investment brokers have achieved a larger market share. These brokers rely on computer software so that consumers can evaluate their portfolios and enter purchase orders themselves. Let's look at how Home Depot and Charles Schwab are catering to this large consumer life-style segment.

According to one marketing expert, Home Depot has done more than any company in America to spread the gospel of do-it-yourself to the masses. The chain now operates over 410 warehouse-size stores in 31 states and Canada. Its sales, which hit $15 billion in 1995, have grown at a compound rate of 40 per cent. To help people buy tools for tasks with which they have little experience, Home Depot employs experienced carpenters, plumbers, and electricians as sales associates. Besides helping customers select the appropriate items, these associates teach clinics on such topics as how to plant a tree, install a lighting fixture, or even replace a toilet bowl. They are paid solely on the basis of salary and are encouraged to sell a low-cost replacement part (such as a 15-cent washer) instead of an entire faucet, if the replacement part will suffice.

Charles Schwab, the leading discount broker, currently receives more than 35 per cent of its stock and bond orders via the consumer software that Schwab supplies to its customers. In an effort to satisfy these customers, the firm mails out StreetSmart, a software program that enables customers to look at a stock's past performance, download price quotes, and place buy and sell orders. StreetSmart is used by over 200,000 of Schwab's 3.3 million clients. Recently, Schwab introduced FundMap, software that lets its clients chart the performance of mutual funds by themselves.[1]

By learning more about customers than just their demographics (such as their activities and interests), companies can better pinpoint market needs, reasons for purchases, and changing life-styles and purchase-behavior patterns. In this chapter, we will study the way consumers live and spend time and money—as well as how they make purchase decisions.

Overview

Questions are often unresolved after examining demographics.

Demographic data are often insufficient aids in planning marketing programs for final consumers because these data do not address issues such as these:

- Why do consumers act as they do?
- Why do consumers with similar demographic characteristics act differently?
- To whom do consumers look for advice prior to purchasing?
- Under what situations do families (households) use joint decision making?
- Why does status play a large role in the purchase of some products and a small role in the purchase of others?
- How do different motives affect consumer decisions?
- How does risk affect consumer decisions?
- Why do some consumers act as innovators and buy products before others?
- How important are purchase decisions to consumers?
- What process do consumers use when shopping for various products?
- How long will it take for consumers to reach purchase decisions?
- Why do consumers become brand loyal or regularly switch brands?

To answer these and other questions, marketers, in increasing numbers, are going beyond just demographics in studying final consumers. They are using demographic data in conjunction with and as part of consumer life-style and decision-making analysis. The latter two topics are the focus of this chapter.

Consumer **life-styles** *describe how people live. In making purchases, people use a decision process with several stages.*

A final consumer's **life-style** represents the way in which a person lives and spends time and money. It is based on the social and psychological factors that have been internalized by that person—as well as his or her demographic background.[2] These factors overlap and complement each other; they are not independent or exclusive of one another. The consumer's decision process involves the steps a person uses in buying goods and services: stimulus, problem awareness, information search, evaluation of alternatives, purchase, and post-purchase behavior. Demographics, social factors, and psychological factors all affect the process.

Consumer Life-Styles

The social and psychological characteristics that help form final consumer life-styles are described next.

[1]Ronald Henkoff, "Why Every Red-Blooded Consumer Owns a Truck," *Fortune* (May 29, 1995), pp. 86–100.
[2]Peter D. Bennett (Editor), *Dictionary of Marketing Terms*, Second Edition (Chicago: American Marketing Association, 1995), p. 154.

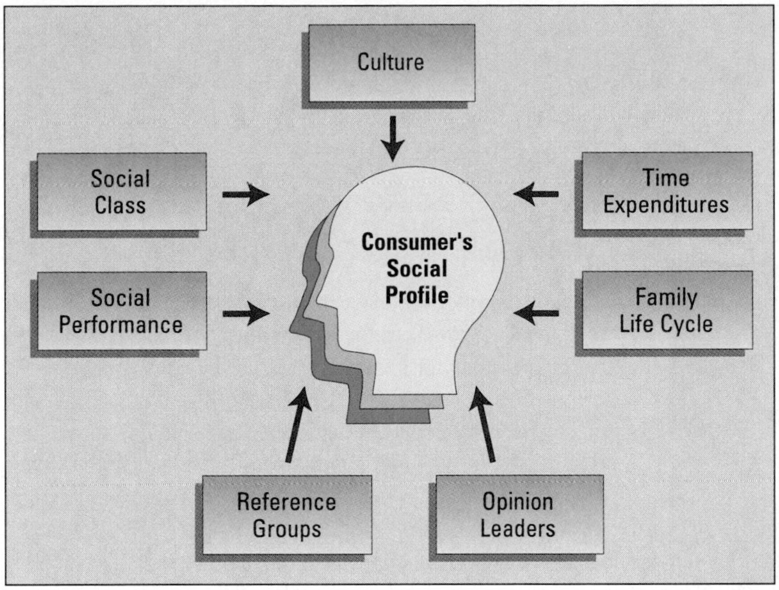

FIGURE 8-1
Factors Determining a Consumer's Social Profile

Social Characteristics of Consumers

The social profile of a final consumer is based on a combination of culture, social class, social performance, reference groups, opinion leaders, family life cycle, and time expenditures (activities). See Figure 8-1.

Each **culture** *transmits socially acceptable behavior and attitudes.*

As discussed in Chapter 6, a **culture** comprises a group of people who share a distinctive heritage, such as Americans or Mexicans. People learn about socially proper behavior and beliefs via their culture. The American culture places importance on achievement and success, activity, efficiency and practicality, progress, material comfort, individualism, freedom, external conformity, humanitarianism, youthfulness, and fitness and health.[3] However, slower economic growth, the rising influence of foreign nations, and a maturing U.S. population may be signaling changes in some of these values.

From a cultural perspective, consumers often have a difficult time when there are dramatic changes in their way of living. This is exemplified by the current situation in eastern Germany:

> People have been propelled into a new consumer society and have had to learn its ways quickly. They remain confused by the huge product choice that has been available to them since the 1990 reunification. Many express the need to relearn consumption and feel inadequate to the task. Not that they get much help; stores may still be poorly laid out, and distribution problems still cause some basics to be out of stock. Sales assistants generally are not equipped to advise consumers, and product literature is absent at the point of sale. Yet, the desire to own western products and luxury items is strong. People are optimistic they will learn to cope with modern consumer society. Yet, they feel that the old way of life, with basic necessities subsidized by the state, had positive points, too.[4]

Social class *separates society into divisions.*

Social class systems reflect a "status hierarchy by which groups and individuals are classified on the basis of esteem and prestige."[5] They exist virtually everywhere and separate society into divisions, informally or formally grouping those with similar values and life-styles. Such systems in industrialized nations have a larger middle class, greater interchange among classes, and less rigidly defined classes than those in less-developed and

[3]Leon G. Schiffman and Leslie Lazar Kanuk, *Consumer Behavior*, Fifth Edition (Englewood Cliffs, N.J.: Prentice-Hall, 1994), pp. 424–437.

[4]Carla Millar and Christine Restall, "The Embryonic Consumer of Eastern Europe," *Marketing Management*, Vol. 1 (Spring 1992), pp. 48–49.

[5]Bennett, *Dictionary of Marketing Terms*, p. 265. See also Chip Walker, "The Global Middle Class," *American Demographics* (September 1995), pp. 40–46; and Aaron Bernstein, "Is America Becoming More of a Class Society?" *Business Week* (February 26 1996), pp. 86–91.

Ethics IN TODAY'S SOCIETY

What Should Be Done with Unethical Consumers?

Although we often dwell on the unethical practices of businesspeople, consumers can also engage in unethical activities. For example, in a retail setting, there are many opportunities for unethical behavior by consumers. These include deliberately misrepresenting where an item was bought in order to get an exchange at a local store, returning merchandise beyond a store's posted return period, misrepresenting a price at another store as a bargaining tactic, buying an item (such as a notebook PC to be used during an out-of-town vacation) with the intention of returning it, offering to pay a retailer in cash to avoid payment of sales taxes, and shoplifting. By one account, there are more than 200 million incidents of U.S. shoplifting each year.

Many consumers try to rationalize their unethical practices as a way of reducing self-blame or to make the activities appear more socially acceptable. Let's look at how people typically seek to rationalize the act of shoplifting:

- Denial of responsibility—"It's not my fault; I had no other choice."
- Denial of injury—"What's the big deal; nobody will miss it?"
- Denial of victim—"It's their fault; if they had been fair with me, I would not have done it."
- Condemning the condemners—"It's a joke they should find fault with me, after the ripoffs they have engineered."
- Appealing to higher loyalties—"To some, what I did may appear wrong, but I did it for my family."

These excuses can also be used to rationalize other unethical practices. For instance, denial of injury can be used to suggest that stores plan for consumer shoplifting in setting their original prices.

As vice-president of operations for a retail chain, how would you try to get shoppers to understand that they too have a responsibility to be ethical?

Source: Based on material in David Strutton, Scott J. Vitell, and Lou E. Pelton, "How Consumers May Justify Inappropriate Behavior in Market Settings: An Application on the Techniques of Neutralization," *Journal of Business Research*, Vol. 30 (July 1994), pp. 253–260.

developing nations. Social classes are based on income, occupation, education, and type of dwelling. Each social class may represent a distinct target market for a firm. Table 8-1 shows the informal U.S. social class structure.

Social performance *describes how people fulfill roles.*

Social performance refers to how a person carries out his or her roles as a worker, family member, citizen, and friend. One person may be an executive, have a happy family life, be active in the community, and have many friends. Another may never go higher than assistant manager, be divorced, not partake in community affairs, and have few friends. Many combinations of social performance are possible—such as vice-president and divorced. The ad in Figure 8-2 (on page 210) is oriented to a person's interest in social performance.

Reference groups *influence thoughts and behavior.*

A **reference group** is one that influences a person's thoughts or actions. For many goods and services, these groups have a large impact on purchases. Face-to-face reference groups, such as family and friends, have the most effect. Yet, other—more general—groups also affect behavior and may be cited in marketing products. Ads showing goods and services being used by college students, successful professionals, and pet owners often ask

Table 8-1

The Informal Social Class Structure in the United States

CLASS	SIZE	CHARACTERISTICS
Upper Americans		
Upper-upper	0.3%	Social elite; inherited wealth; exclusive neighborhoods; summer homes; children attend best schools; money unimportant in purchases; secure in status; spending with good taste
Lower-upper	1.2%	Highest incomes; earned wealth; often business leaders and professionals; college educated; seek best for children; active socially; insecure; conspicuous consumption; money unimportant in purchases
Upper-middle	12.5%	Career-oriented; executives and professionals earning well over $50,000 yearly; status tied to occupations and earnings; most educated, but not from prestige schools; demanding of children; quality products purchased; attractive homes; socially involved; gracious living
Middle Americans		
Middle class	32%	Typical Americans; average-earning white-collar workers and the top group of blue-collar workers; many college educated; respectable; conscientious; try to do the right thing; home ownership sought; do-it-yourselfers; family focus
Working class	38%	Remaining white-collar workers and most blue-collar workers; working class life-styles; some job monotony; job security sought more than advancement; usually high school education; close-knit families; brand loyal and interested in name brands; not status-oriented
Lower Americans		
Upper-lower	9%	Employed, mostly in unskilled or semiskilled jobs; poorly educated; low incomes; rather difficult to move up the social class ladder; protective against lower-lower class; standard of living at or just above poverty; live in affordable housing
Lower-lower	7%	Unemployed or most menial jobs; poorest income, education, and housing; the bottom layer; present-oriented; impulsive as shoppers; overpay; use credit

Sources: This table is derived by the authors from Richard P. Coleman, "The Continuing Significance of Social Class in Marketing," *Journal of Consumer Research*, Vol. 10 (December 1983), pp. 265–280; James F. Engel, Roger D. Blackwell, and Paul W. Miniard, *Consumer Behavior*, Seventh Edition (Hinsdale, Ill.: Dryden, 1993), pp. 117–119; and William L. Wilkie, *Consumer Behavior*, Third Edition (New York: Wiley, 1994), pp. 344–351.

viewers to join the "group" and make similar purchases. By pinpointing reference groups that most sway consumers, firms can better aim their strategies.[6]

Firms want to know which persons in reference groups are **opinion leaders.** These are people to whom other consumers turn for advice and information via face-to-face communication. They tend to be expert about a product category, socially accepted, long-standing members of the community, gregarious, active, and trusted; and they tend to seek approval from others. They normally have an impact over a narrow product range and are perceived as more believable than company-sponsored information.

Opinion leaders *affect others through face-to-face contact.*

The **family life cycle** describes how a family evolves through various stages from bachelorhood to solitary retirement. At each stage, needs, experience, income, family composition, and the use of **joint decision making**—the process whereby two or more people have input into purchases—change. The number of people in different life cycle stages can be obtained from demographic data. Table 8-2 (on page 211) shows the traditional family life cycle and its marketing relevance. The cycle's stages apply to families in all types of nations—both industrialized and less-developed/developing, but, the marketing opportunities in Table 8-2 are most applicable for industrialized countries.

The **family life cycle** *describes life stages, which often use* **joint decision making**. *The* **household life cycle** *includes family and nonfamily units.*

When using life-cycle analysis, the people who do not follow a traditional pattern because they do not marry, do not have children, become divorced, have families with two working spouses (even if there are very small children), and so on, should be noted.

[6]See Basil G. Englis and Michael R. Solomon, "To Be *and* Not to Be: Life-Style Imagery, Reference Groups," *Journal of Advertising*, Vol. 24 (Spring 1995), pp. 13–28.

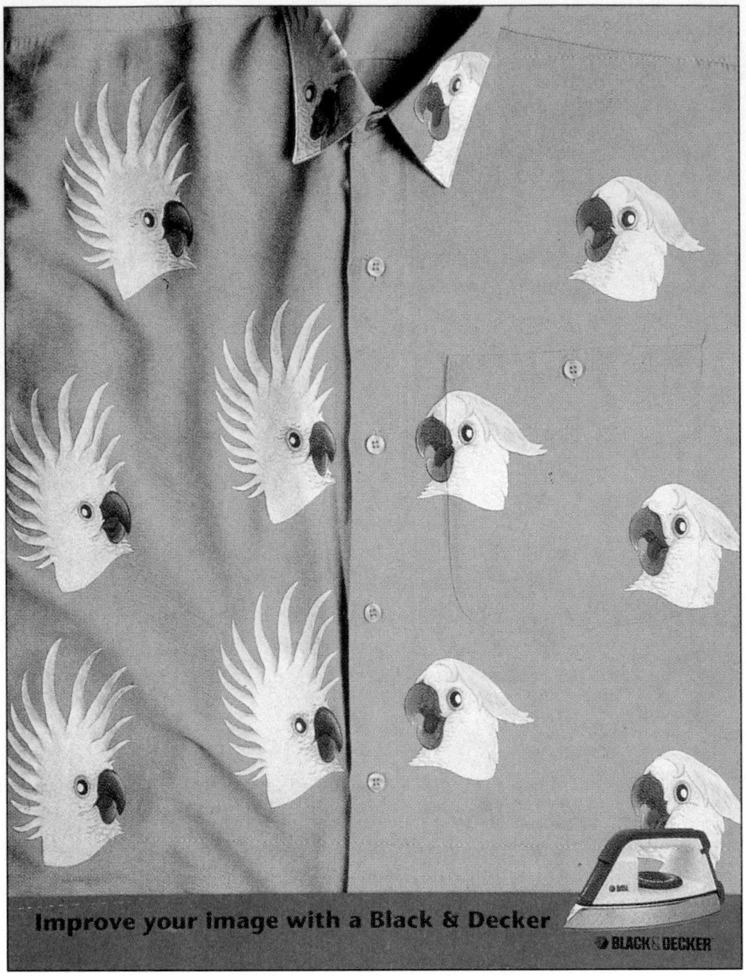

FIGURE 8-2
Appealing to a Consumer's Social Performance
Reprinted by permission.

They are not adequately reflected in Table 8-2, but may represent good marketing opportunities. For that reason, the concept of the **household life cycle**—which incorporates the life stages of both family and nonfamily households—is taking on greater significance.[7] Table 8-3 (page 212) shows the current status of U.S. family and nonfamily households.

Time expenditures *reflect the workweek, family care, and leisure.*

Time expenditures refer to the activities in which a person participates and the time allocated to them. Such activities include work, commuting, personal care, home maintenance, food preparation and consumption, child rearing, social interactions, reading, shopping, self-improvement, recreation, entertainment, vacations, and so on. Although the average U.S. workweek for an individual's primary job has stabilized at 35 to 40 hours weekly, more people are working at two jobs. Americans enjoy TV, phone conversations, pleasure driving, swimming, sightseeing, walking, bicycling, attending spectator events, reading, and playing outdoor games and sports.

Psychological Characteristics of Consumers

The psychological profile of a final consumer involves his or her personality, attitudes (opinions), class consciousness, motivation, perceived risk, innovativeness, and the importance of a purchase. See Figure 8-3 on page 212.

A **personality** *describes a person's composite internal, enduring psychological traits.*

A **personality** is the sum total of an individual's enduring internal psychological traits that make the person unique. Self-confidence, dominance, autonomy, sociability, defensiveness, adaptability, and emotional stability are selected personality traits. Personality has a strong impact on an individual's behavior. For example, a self-confident and sociable person often will not purchase the same goods and services as an inhibited and aloof

[7]Robert E. Wilkes, "Household Life-Cycle Stages, Transitions, and Product Expenditures," *Journal of Consumer Research*, Vol. 22 (June 1995), pp. 27–42.

Table 8-2
The Traditional Family Life Cycle

STAGE IN CYCLE	CHARACTERISTICS	MARKETING OPPORTUNITIES
Bachelor, male or female	Independent; young; early in career; low earnings, low discretionary income	Clothing; auto; stereo; travel; restaurants; entertainment; status appeals
Newly married	Two incomes; relative independence; present- and future-oriented	Apartment furnishings; travel; clothing; durables; appeal to enjoyment and togetherness
Full nest I	Youngest child under 6; one to one-and-a-half incomes; limited independence; future-oriented	Goods and services for the child, home, and family; durability and safety; pharmaceuticals; day care; appeal to economy
Full nest II	Youngest child over 6, but dependent; one-and-a-half to two incomes; at least one spouse set in career; future-oriented	Savings; home; education; family vacations; child-oriented products; some luxuries; appeal to comfort and long-term enjoyment
Full nest III	Youngest child living at home, but independent; highest income level; thoughts of future retirement	Education; expensive durables for children; replacement and improvement of parents' durables; appeal to comfort and luxury
Empty nest I	No children at home; independent; good income; thoughts of self and retirement	Vacation home; travel; clothing; entertainment; luxuries; appeal to self-gratification
Empty nest II	Retirement; less income and expenses; present-oriented	Travel; recreation; new home; health-related items; less interest in luxuries; appeal to comfort at a low price
Sole survivor I	Only one spouse alive; actively employed; present-oriented; good income	Immersion in job and friends; interest in travel, clothing, health, and recreation areas; appeal to productive citizen
Sole survivor II	Only one spouse alive; retired; some feeling of futility; less income	Travel; recreation; pharmaceuticals; security; appeal to economy and social activity

person. It is necessary to remember that a personality is made up of many traits operating in association with one another. See Figure 8-4 on page 213.

Attitudes *can be positive, negative, or neutral.*

Attitudes (opinions) are an individual's positive, neutral, or negative feelings about goods, services, firms, people, issues, and/or institutions. They are shaped by demographics, social factors, and other psychological characteristics. One role of marketing is to generate favorable attitudes; given the intensive competition in many industries, a firm cannot normally succeed without positive consumer attitudes. When studying attitudes, two concepts should often be measured—the attitude itself and the purchase intention toward a firm's brand. For example: (1) Do you like brand A? Would you buy brand A in the future? (2) How does brand A compare with other brands? Would you buy brand A if it were priced higher than other brands?

Class consciousness *is low for inner-directed persons and high for outer-directed ones.*

Class consciousness is the extent to which a person seeks social status. It helps determine his or her interest in social-class mobility, use of reference groups, and the importance of prestige purchases. Inner-directed people want to please themselves and are generally attracted by products that perform well functionally. They are not concerned with social mobility, rely on their own judgment, and do not value prestige items. Outer-directed people want to please the people around them. Upward social mobility, reference group approval, and ownership of prestige items are sought. These people are generally attracted by products providing social visibility, well-known brands, and uniqueness. Functional performance may be less important.

Motivation *is a drive-impelling action; it is caused by* **motives.**

Motivation involves the positive or negative needs, goals, and desires that impel a person to or away from certain actions, objects, or situations.[8] By identifying and appealing to people's **motives**—the reasons for behavior—a firm can produce positive motivation. For example:

[8] Bennett, *Dictionary of Marketing Terms*, pp. 179–180.

Table 8-3

The Current Status of U.S. Family and Nonfamily Households

HOUSEHOLD STATUS	PERCENTAGE OF ALL U.S. HOUSEHOLDS	
Family Households	70	
Married couples, no children under age 18		30
Married couples, with children under age 18		25
Other types of families, no children under age 18		7
Other types of families, with children under age 18[a]		8
Single-Person Households[b]	25	
Age 24 and under		1
Age 25 to 44		8
Age 45 to 64		6
Age 65 and over		10
Other Nonfamily Households	5	
Unmarried couples, no children under age 18		2
Unmarried couples, with children under age 18		1
Other[c]		2
Total	100	100

[a]Includes one-parent families in which married couples are separated but not divorced, one-parent families headed by divorcees, one-parent families headed by widows and widowers, and one-parent families headed by never-married mothers and fathers.

[b]Includes people who have never married, as well as those who are widowed, separated, and divorced.

[c]Includes roommates.

Source: Computed by the authors from U.S. Bureau of the Census, *Current Population Reports*.

FIGURE 8-3
Factors Determining a Consumer's Psychological Profile

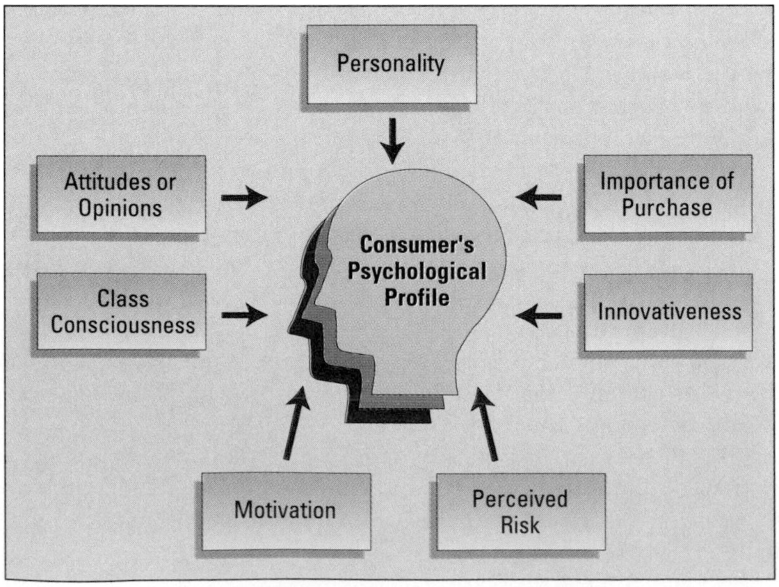

Peel
off
your
inhibitions.
Find your own road.®
The Saab 900 Convertible. Turbocharged or V6 engines available. Fold-down rear seat. Power everything. The four-season,
four-passenger convertible rated #1 by *Car and Driver*,* ahead of BMW and Audi Convertibles. Call 1-800-582-SAAB.
*Car and Driver, 11/94 © 1995 SAAB CARS USA, INC.
SAAB

FIGURE 8-4
Marketing to the Uninhibited
Reprinted by permission.

MOTIVES	**MARKETING ACTIONS THAT MOTIVATE**
Hunger reduction	Television and radio ads for fast-food restaurants
Safety	Smoke detector demonstrations in stores
Sociability	Perfume ads showing social success due to products
Achievement	Use of consumer endorsements in ads specifying how much knowledge can be gained from an encyclopedia
Economy	Newspaper coupons advertising sales
Social responsibility	Package labels that emphasize how easy it is to recycle products

Each person has distinct motives for purchases, and these change by situation and over time. Consumers often combine economic (price, durability) and emotional (social acceptance, self-esteem) motives when making purchases. Figure 8-5 shows some of the motives that Perrier highlights in its ads.

Perceived risk is the level of uncertainty a consumer believes exists as to the outcome of a purchase decision; this belief may or may not be correct. Perceived risk can be divided into six major types:

Perceived risk *is the uncertainty felt by the consumer.*

1. Functional—risk that a product will not perform adequately.
2. Physical—risk that a product will be harmful.
3. Financial—risk that a product will not be worth its cost.
4. Social—risk that a product will cause embarrassment before others.
5. Psychological—risk that one's ego will be bruised.

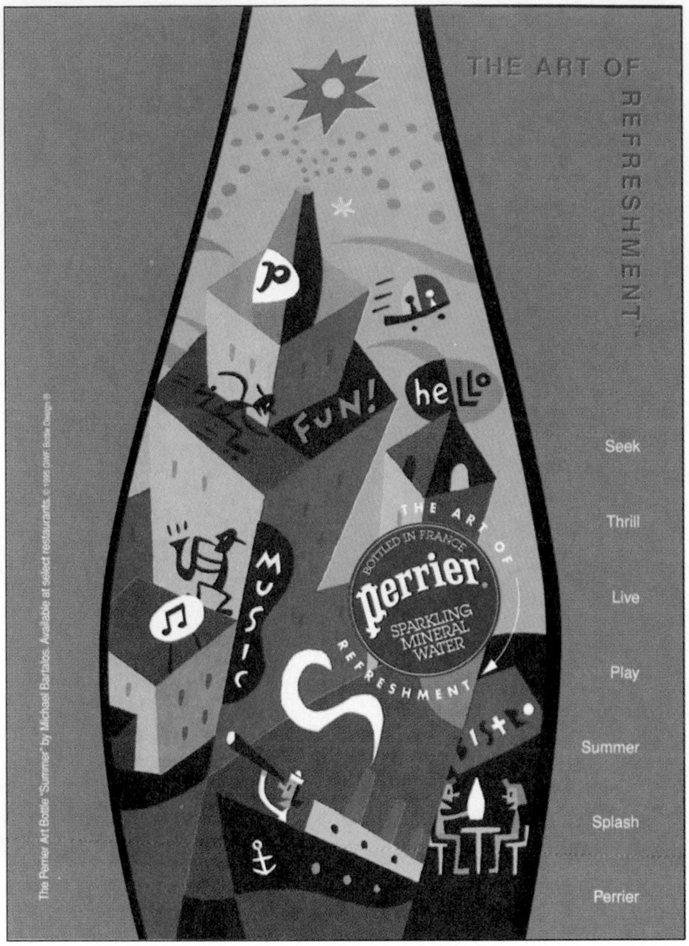

FIGURE 8-5
Reasons to Buy Perrier
Reprinted by permission.

6. Time—risk that the time spent making a purchase will be wasted if the product does not perform as expected.[9]

Because high perceived risk can dampen customer motivation, companies must deal with it even if people have incorrect beliefs. Firms can lower perceived risk by giving more information, having a reputation for superior quality, offering money-back guarantees, avoiding controversial ingredients, and so on.

Innovativeness *is trying a new product others see as risky.*

A person willing to try a new good or service that others perceive as risky exhibits **innovativeness.** An innovator is apt to be young and well educated, and to have above-average income for his or her social class. He or she is also likely to be interested in change, achievement-oriented, open-minded, status-conscious, mobile, and venturesome. Firms need to identify and appeal to innovators when introducing a new good or service.

The **importance of a purchase** *determines the time, effort, and money spent.*

The **importance of a purchase** affects the time and effort a person spends shopping for a product—and the money allotted. An important purchase means careful decision making, high perceived risk, and often a large amount of money. An unimportant purchase means less decision time (an item may be avoided altogether) and low perceived risk, and it is probably inexpensive.

Selected Consumer Life-Styles

Many distinct consumer life-styles are expected to continue, including family values, voluntary simplicity, getting by, "me" generation, blurring of gender roles, poverty of time, and component life-styles.

In some households, **family values** *have a great impact.*

A **family values** life-style emphasizes marriage, children, and home life. It encourages people to focus on children and their education; family autos, vacations, and entertain-

[9]Schiffman and Kanuk, *Consumer Behavior*, pp. 562–564.

ment; and home-oriented products. Yet, as previously noted, the traditional family is becoming less representative of U.S. households. Thus, firms need to be careful in targeting those who say they follow this life-style. They should also keep in mind that a family values life-style remains the leading one in many nations outside the United States. For instance, in Italy, less than one-third of women are in the labor force and the divorce rate is about one-eleventh that of the United States.

Voluntary simplicity is a life-style in which people have an ecological awareness, seek product durability, strive for self-reliance, and buy simple products. People with this life-style are cautious, conservative, and thrifty shoppers. They do not buy expensive cars and clothing, hold on to products for long periods, and rarely eat out or go on pre-packaged vacations. They like going to a park or taking a vacation by car, are more concerned with product toughness than appearance, and believe in conservation. There is an attraction to rational appeals and no-frills retailing.

Voluntary simplicity *is based on ecological awareness and self-reliance.*

Getting by is a frugal life-style pursued by people because of economic circumstances. Those who are getting by seek product durability, self-reliance, and simple products. But, unlike consumers with voluntary simplicity, they do so because they must. In less-developed and developing nations, most people have this life-style; a much smaller proportion do in industrialized countries. Getting by consumers are attracted to well-known brands (to reduce perceived risk), do not try new goods and services, rarely go out, and take few vacations. They look for bargains and tend to patronize local stores. They rarely believe they have any significant discretionary income.

When economic circumstances are tough, people place more emphasis on **getting by.**

A "**me" generation** life-style stresses being good to oneself, self-fulfillment, and self-expression. It involves less pressure to conform, as well as greater diversity; there is also less interest in responsibilities and loyalties. Consumers with this life-style want to take care of themselves. They stress nutrition, exercise, and grooming. They buy expensive cars and apparel, and they visit full-service stores. These people are more concerned with product appearance than durability, and some place below-average value on conservation if it will have a negative effect on their life-style.

The "**me" generation** *stresses self-fulfillment.*

Because many women are working, more men are assuming the once-traditional roles of their wives, and visa versa, thus **blurring gender roles**: "Men are doing more shopping and housework, but only because women are making them change. Knowing how men are changing—and how they aren't—is the key to targeting them. Meanwhile, more women are learning how to buy cars, program VCRs, and use power tools."[10] See Figure 8-6 on the next page.

Blurring gender roles *involves men and women undertaking nontraditional duties.*

The prevalence of working women, the long distances between home and work, and the large number of people working at second jobs contribute to a **poverty-of-time** life-style in many households. For them, the quest for financial security means less free time. This life-style leads people to greater use of time-saving goods and services. Included are convenience foods, quick-oil-change services, microwave ovens, fast-food restaurants, mail-order retailers, one-hour film processing, and professional lawn and household care.

A **poverty of time** *exists when a quest for financial security means less free time.*

Today, more people are turning to a **component life-style**, whereby their attitudes and behavior depend on particular situations rather than an overall life-style philosophy. For example, consumers may take their children with them on vacations (family values), engage in trash recycling programs (voluntary simplicity), look for sales to save money (getting by), take exercise classes ("me" generation), share food shopping chores (blurring gender roles), and eat out on busy nights (poverty of time). As the Roper Organization, a research firm, has noted:

With a **component life-style,** *consumer attitudes and behavior vary by situation.*

> Consumer behavior is becoming more individualistic and less defined by reference to easily identified social groups. Americans are piecing together "component life-styles" for themselves, choosing goods and services that best express their growing sense of uniqueness. A consumer may own a BMW but fill it with self-service gas. Buy take-out fast food for lunch but good wine for dinner. Own expensive photo equipment and low-priced home stereo equipment. Shop for socks at Kmart and suits or dresses at Brooks Brothers.[11]

[10]Diane Crispell, "The Brave New World of Men," *American Demographics* (January 1992), pp. 38, 43.
[11]"31 Major Trends Shaping the Future of American Business," *Public Pulse*, Vol. 2 (Number 1, 1988), p. 1.

FIGURE 8-6
Blurring Gender Roles
Today, more men and women are engaging in nontraditional activities.
Reprinted by permission of SPX Corporation.

Marketing Implications of Life-Style Analysis

Over the years, analysis of the social and psychological characteristics of final consumers has increased dramatically. In this section, we present both general and specific applications of life-style analysis in marketing.

Several organizations are involved with defining and measuring consumer life-styles. They sell this information to client firms, which use it to improve their marketing efforts. These are three of the best-known services:

- *Yankelovich Monitor* tracks over 50 social trends annually, including accommodation to technology, commitment to buy American, need for control, and responsiveness to fantasy. Impermanent consumer profiles are developed, such as "the new establishment," the "discontented," and "traditionalists"—and people are described in terms of their response to the changing environment.
- *VALS (Values and Life-Styles)* is a research program sponsored by SRI International. SRI's VALS 2 classification categorizes consumers into eight basic life-style groups: actualizers, fulfilleds, believers, achievers, strivers, experiencers, makers, and strugglers.
- *PRIZM (Potential Rating Index by Zip Market)* is a program that relies on census data and examines consumer life-styles by zip code. It uses about 60 different neighborhood designations, such as *blue blood* ("old money"), to describe life-styles.

These services have been used by companies marketing financial instruments, cars, health-care products, appliances, women's girdles, liquor, food, and other items.

Studies of consumer life-styles around the world have been conducted. Here are some findings for firms to consider when planning their marketing mixes:

- Although U.S. men go to shopping centers somewhat more often than women, the latter spend nearly 25 per cent more time in a shopping center per visit (and stop at more stores). Two-thirds of women make apparel decisions on their own, compared with 48 per cent of men.
- Russian households prefer and trust ads from western firms over those from local companies. On average, Russians view television nearly three hours per day and enjoy the commercials. Billboards have not been very popular there.

International Marketing in Action

Are Hungarian Life-Styles Ready for ATMs?

Citibank recently opened its first Eastern European retail branch bank in Budapest, Hungary. That branch offers two levels of banking: At the top tier, customers must maintain a $100,000 balance. At the low end, customers must have a $250 minimum balance; this amount is about the average monthly salary in Hungary.

In contrast to competing banks in the region, the Citibank branch is highly automated and offers a flashy decor. Most competing banks still use handwritten ledgers to record deposits and withdrawals. Thus, customers there can spend hours waiting in lines. In contrast, Citibank records all transactions with the swipe of a Citicard. Its customers can also conduct transactions by using automatic teller machines (ATMs) with touch screens or make transactions via telephone. And the Citibank branch's wood veneer paneling is also in sharp contrast to the plain environment at other banks.

In Hungary, Citibank is attempting to make the transition from cash transactions to plastic ones without the introduction of personal checks. The bank has been introducing its Diners Club card to its own banking customers, as well as to others it judges to be creditworthy. It hopes to establish credit bureaus to facilitate this business. So far, Hungarian customers have become comfortable using ATMs for limited transactions.

Citibank faces several challenges in its marketing efforts in Hungary. Unlike Americans, Hungarians are used to paying their bills with cash. In fact, personal checks are virtually unknown in Hungary. As a result, few Hungarian consumers understand how credit works. There are also no credit bureaus to evaluate the creditworthiness of clients. Lastly, much of the data on income that are traditionally used to assess alternate banking sites are unavailable in Eastern Europe.

As a Citibank marketing manager, how would you facilitate Hungary's transition to ATMs?

Source: Based on material in Jane Perlez, "Citibank in Budapest: ATMs and Potted Palms," *New York Times* (June 22, 1995), p. D7.

- European women are less likely than American women to diet and exercise, are more apt to smoke, and have higher self-esteem and optimism for the future.
- In India, the husband in lower-class families usually initiates decisions for appliances and furniture and the wife is more responsible for initiating clothing decisions. For middle-class families, the wife is more influential with all three types of products. For upper-class families, the wife is the initiator for clothing, but there is greater sharing of influence between the husband and wife for appliances and furniture.
- The Japanese are less satisfied with the overall quality of their lives than Americans. They are much less pleased with regard to housing, leisure time, and income.[12]

[12]Dottie Enrico, "Sex Matters," *Newsday* (December 13, 1992), p. 88; Adi Ignatius, "Life-Style Pitch Works in Russia Despite Poverty," *Wall Street Journal* (August 21, 1992), pp. B1, B4; Cyndee Miller, "No Exercise, and They Like to Smoke," *Marketing News* (August 17, 1992), p. 13; Cynthia Webster, "Observation of Marital Roles in Decision Making: A Third-World Perspective" in Robert P. Leone and V. Kumar (Editors), *1992 AMA Educators' Proceedings* (Chicago: American Marketing Association, 1992), p. 517; and Robert Levine, "Why Isn't Japan Happy?" *American Demographics* (June 1992), pp. 58–60.

Table 8-4

Selected Marketing Opportunities of Consumer Life-Styles

LIFE-STYLE CATEGORY	MARKETING OPPORTUNITIES IN APPEALING TO THE LIFE-STYLE
Family values	Family-oriented goods and services Educational devices and toys Traditional family events "Wholesome" entertainment
Voluntary simplicity	Goods and services with quality, durability, and simplicity Environmentally safe products Energy-efficient products Discount-oriented retailing
Getting by	Well-known brands and good buys ("value") Video rentals and other inexpensive entertainment Do-it-yourself projects such as "knock-down" furniture Inexpensive child care
"Me" generation	Individuality in purchases Luxury goods and services Nutritional themes Exercise- and education-related goods and services
Blurring of gender roles	Unisex goods, services, and stores Couples-oriented advertising Child-care services Less male and female stereotyping
Poverty of time	Mail-order and phone sales Service firms with accurate customer appointments Laborsaving devices One-stop shopping
Component life-style	Situational purchases Less social class stereotyping Multiple advertising themes Market niching

Marketing opportunities related to family values, voluntary simplicity, getting by, "me" generation, blurring of gender roles, poverty of time, and component life-style concepts are shown in Table 8-4.

Limitations of Life-Style Analysis

Social and psychological factors can be difficult to measure.

Unlike demographics, many of the social and psychological aspects of final consumer life-styles are difficult to measure, somewhat subjective, usually based on the self-reports of consumers, and sometimes hidden from view (to avoid embarrassment, protect privacy, convey an image, and other reasons). In addition, there are still some ongoing disputes over terminology, misuse of data, and reliability.

The Final Consumer's Decision Process

The **final consumer's decision process** *has many stages, and various factors affect it.*

The **final consumer's decision process** is the way in which people gather and assess information and choose among alternative goods, services, organizations, people, places, and ideas. It consists of the process itself and factors affecting it. The process has six stages: stimulus, problem awareness, information search, evaluation of alternatives, purchase, and

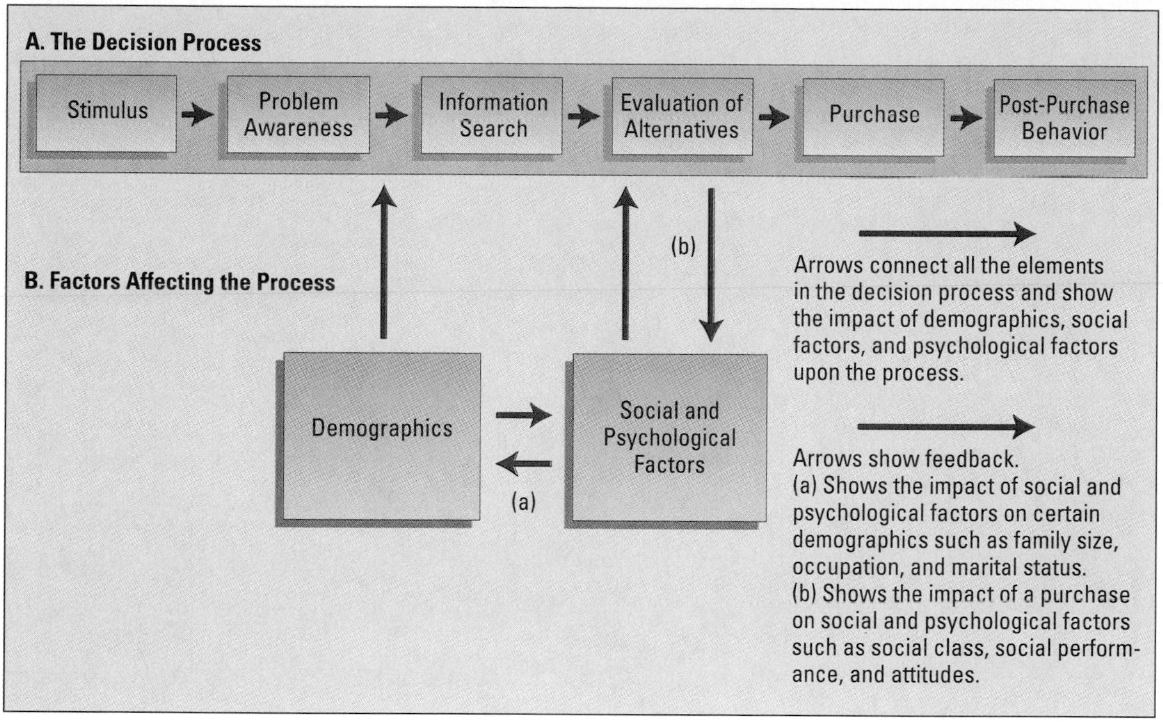

FIGURE 8-7
The Final Consumer's Decision Process

post-purchase behavior. Demographic, social, and psychological factors affect the process. Figure 8-7 shows the total consumer decision-making process.

When a consumer buys a good or service, decides to vote for a political candidate or to donate to a charity, and so on, he or she goes through a decision process. Sometimes, all six stages in the process are used; other times, only a few steps are utilized. For example, the purchase of an expensive stereo requires more decision making than the purchase of a new music video.

At *any* point in the decision process, a person may decide not to buy, vote, or donate—and, thereby, end the process. A good or service may turn out to be unneeded, unsatisfactory, or too expensive.

Stimulus

A **stimulus** *is a cue or drive intended to motivate a consumer.*

A **stimulus** is a cue (social, commercial, or noncommercial) or a drive (physical) meant to motivate a person to act.

A social cue occurs when someone talks with friends, family members, co-workers, and others. It is from an interpersonal source not affiliated with a seller. A commercial cue is a message sponsored by a seller—such as that shown in Figure 8-8—to interest a person in a particular good, service, organization, person, place, or idea. Ads, personal selling, and sales promotions are commercial cues. They are less regarded than social cues because people know they are seller-controlled. A noncommercial cue is a message from an impartial source such as *Consumer Reports* or the government. It has high believability because it is not affiliated with the seller. A physical drive occurs when a person's physical senses are affected. Thirst, hunger, and fear cause physical drives.

A person may be exposed to any or all of these stimuli. If sufficiently stimulated, he or she will go to the next step in the decision process. If not, the person will ignore the cue and delay or terminate the decision process for the given good, service, organization, person, place, or idea.

FIGURE 8-8
A Manufacturer-Sponsored Commercial Stimulus

Reprinted by permission of Wm. Wrigley Jr. Company.

Problem Awareness

Problem awareness *entails recognition of a shortage or an unfulfilled desire.*

At the **problem awareness** stage, a consumer recognizes that the good, service, organization, person, place, or idea under consideration may solve a problem of shortage or unfulfilled desire.

Recognition of shortage occurs when a consumer realizes a repurchase is needed. A suit may wear out. A man or woman may run out of razor blades. An eye examination may be needed. A popular political candidate may be up for re-election. It may be time for a charity's annual fund-raising campaign. In each case, the consumer recognizes a need to repurchase.

Recognition of unfulfilled desire occurs when a consumer becomes aware of a good, service, organization, person, place, or idea that has not been patronized before. Such an item may improve status, appearance, living conditions, or knowledge in a manner not tried before (luxury auto, cosmetic surgery, proposed zoning law, encyclopedia), or it may offer new performance features not previously available (laser surgery, tobacco-free cigarettes). Either way, a consumer is aroused by a desire to try something new.

Many consumers hesitate to act on unfulfilled desires due to greater risks. It is easier to replace a known product. Whether a consumer becomes aware of a problem of shortage or of unfulfilled desire, he or she will act only if the problem is perceived as worth solving.

Information Search

An **information search** *determines alternatives and their characteristics.*

Next, an **Information search** requires listing the alternatives that will solve the problem at hand and determining the characteristics of them.

A list of alternatives does not have to be written. It can be a group of items a consumer thinks about. With internal search, a person has experience in the area being considered and uses a memory search to list the choices to be reviewed. A person with minimal experience will do external search to list alternatives; this can involve commercial sources, noncommercial sources, and/or social sources. Often, once there is a list of choices, items (brands, companies, and so on) not on it do not receive further consideration.

The second phase of information search deals with the attributes of each alternative. This information can also be generated internally or externally, depending on the expertise of the consumer and the level of perceived risk. As risk increases, the information sought increases.

Once an information search is completed, it must be determined whether the shortage or unfulfilled desire can be satisfied by any alternative. If one or more choices are satisfactory, the consumer moves to the next decision. The process is delayed or discontinued when no alternative provides satisfaction.

Evaluation of Alternatives

Evaluating alternatives *consists of weighing features and selecting the most desired product.*

There is now enough information for a consumer to select one alternative from the list of choices. This is easy when one option is clearly the best across all attributes: A product with excellent quality and a low price will be a sure choice over an average-quality, expensive one. The choice is usually not that simple, and a consumer must carefully engage in an **evaluation of alternatives** before making a decision. If two or more alternatives seem attractive, a person needs to determine which criteria to evaluate and their relative importance. Alternatives would then be ranked and a choice made.

Decision criteria are the features a person deems relevant—such as price, style, quality, safety, durability, status, and warranty. A consumer sets standards for the features and forms an attitude on each alternative according to its ability to meet the standards. In addition, each criterion's importance is set because the multiple attributes of a given product are usually of varying weight. For example, a consumer may consider shoe prices to be more important than style and select inexpensive, nondistinctive shoes.

A consumer now ranks alternatives from most to least desirable and selects one. Ranking is sometimes hard because alternatives may have technical differences or be poorly labeled, new, or intangible (such as evaluating two political candidates). On these occasions, options may be ranked on the basis of brand name or price, which is used to indicate overall quality.

In situations where no alternative is satisfactory, a decision to delay or not make a purchase is made.

Purchase

The **purchase act** *includes deciding where to buy, agreeing to terms, and seeing if the item is available.*

After choosing the best alternative, a person is ready for the **purchase act**: an exchange of money, a promise to pay, or support in return for ownership of a specific good, the performance of a specific service, and so on. Three considerations remain: place of purchase, terms, and availability.

Although most items are bought at stores, some are bought at school, work, and home. The place of purchase is picked the same way as a product. Choices are noted, attributes detailed, and a ranking done. The best locale is chosen.

Purchase terms involve the price and method of payment. Generally, a price is the amount (including interest, tax, and other fees) a person pays to gain the ownership or use of a good or service. It may also be a person's vote, time investment, and so on. The payment method is the way a price is paid (cash, short-term credit, or long-term credit).

Availability refers to the timeliness with which a consumer receives a product that he or she buys. It depends on stock on hand (or service capacity) and delivery. Stock on hand (service capacity) relates to a seller's ability to provide a good or service when requested. For items requiring delivery, the period from when an order is placed by a consumer until it is received and the ease with which an item is transported to its place of use are crucial.

A consumer will make a purchase if these elements are acceptable. However, dissatisfaction with any one may cause a consumer to delay or not buy, even though there is no problem with the good or service itself.

Post-Purchase Behavior

Post-purchase behavior *often embodies further buying and/or re-evaluation.* **Cognitive dissonance** *can be reduced by proper consumer after-care.*

Once a purchase is made, a person may engage in **post-purchase behavior,** via further purchases and/or re-evaluation. Many times, one purchase leads to others: A house purchase leads to the acquisition of fire insurance. A PC purchase leads to the acquisition of computer software.

A person may also re-evaluate a purchase after making it: Are expectations matched by performance? Satisfaction usually leads to a repurchase when a good or service wears out, a charity holds a fund-raising campaign, and so on, and leads to positive communication with other people interested in the same item. Dissatisfaction can lead to brand switching and negative communication.

Dissatisfaction is often due to **cognitive dissonance**—doubt that a correct decision has been made. A person may regret a purchase or wish another choice was made. To overcome dissonance, a firm must realize the process does not end with a purchase. Follow-up calls, extended warranties, and ads aimed at purchasers can reassure people.

Factors Affecting the Final Consumer's Decision Process

The decision process is affected by demographic, social, and psychological factors.

Demographic, social, and psychological factors affect the way final consumers make choices and can help a firm understand how people use the decision process. For example, an affluent consumer would move through the process more quickly than a middle-income one due to less financial risk. An insecure consumer would spend more time making a decision than a secure one.

By knowing how these factors influence decisions, a firm can fine-tune its marketing strategies to cater to the target market and its purchase behavior, and answer these questions: Why do two or more people use the decision process in the same way? Why do two or more people use it differently?

Types of Decision Processes

Final consumer decision making can be categorized as **extended, limited,** *or* **routine.**

Each time a person buys a good or service, donates to a charity, and so on, he or she uses the decision process. This may be done subconsciously, with the person not aware of using it. Some situations may let a person move through the process quickly and de-emphasize or skip certain steps; others may require a thorough use of each step. A consumer may use extended, limited, or routine decision making—based on the degree of search, level of experience, frequency of purchase, amount of perceived risk, and time pressure. See Figure 8-9.

Extended consumer decision making occurs when a person fully uses the decision process. Much effort is spent on information search and evaluation of alternatives for expensive, complex items with which a person has little or no experience. Purchases are made infrequently. Perceived risk is high, and the purchase is important. A person has time available to make a choice. Purchase delays often occur. Demographic, social, and

FIGURE 8-9
The Three Types of Final Consumer Decision Processes

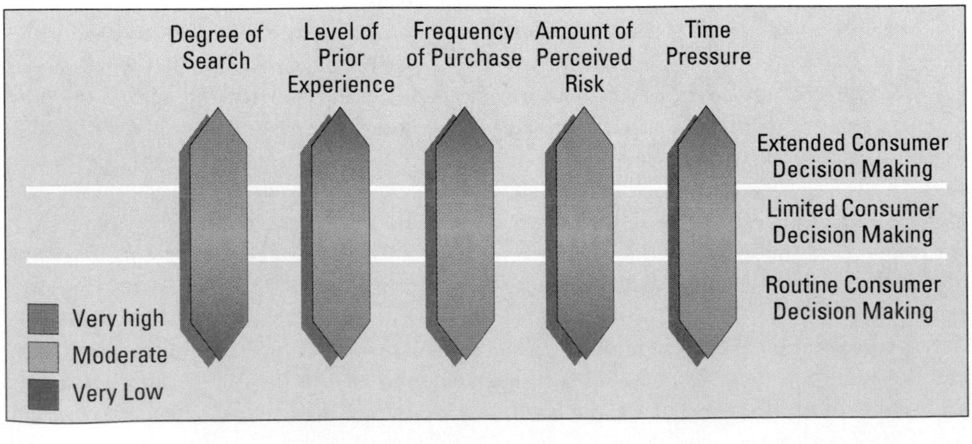

TECHNOLOGY & MARKETING

Will Computers Ever Be Truly "User-Friendly?"

Why is the increased market penetration of PCs accompanied by such high levels of consumer frustration with their computers? Aren't PCs supposed to be "user-friendly?"

Problems often occur because of the complications arising from the wide range of peripherals (such as a modem, CD-ROM player, and mouse) that may be bought to accompany a PC. Many peripherals claim to be fully compatible with a given PC; but they are produced by different firms and often need adjustments in dip switches, memory organization, and interrupt settings that are beyond the capability of most novices. Thus, many consumers have reported spending as much as two days with an "easy-to-install" peripheral such as a CD-ROM player. According to the marketing vice-president for one peripherals manufacturer, "Getting these things to work together is a lot like putting a Chevy engine and a Ford transmission into a Rolls Royce body."

Advanced computer capabilities such as simultaneously displaying graphics and music, jumping from one program to another, and playing audio-based CDs have also made computers more complicated. IBM says it gets 200,000 calls per month on its customer support line.

Microsoft has observed PC users through one-way mirrors in its "usability" labs, and even invested $90,000 in staff time to study how five families used PCs in their homes—to better understand the frustrations of computer novices. To the firm's surprise, its staff found that some people did their budgets with word processing software instead of spreadsheets because the spreadsheets were too intimidating. Microsoft is using the taped sessions to show its programmers the types of problems faced by consumers. It hopes the information will result in more user-friendly products.

As a product manager for Conner Peripherals, a producer of tape drives that back up PC hard drives, describe how you would make your products as user-friendly as possible for the first-time customer.

Source: Based on material in Julie Pitta, "New Hope for Computer Illiterates?" *Forbes* (January 16, 1995), pp. 88–89.

psychological factors have their greatest impact. Extended decision making is often involved in picking a college, a house, a first car, or a location for a wedding.

Limited consumer decision making occurs when a person uses every step in the purchase process but does not spend a great deal of time on some of them. The person has previously bought a given good or service, but makes fresh decisions when it comes under current purchase consideration—due to the relative infrequency of purchase, the introduction of new models, or an interest in variety. Perceived risk is moderate, and a person is willing to spend some time shopping. The thoroughness with which the process is used depends on the amount of prior experience, the importance of the purchase, and the time pressure facing the consumer. Emphasis is on evaluating a list of known choices, although an information search may be done. Factors affecting the decision process have some impact. A second car, clothing, gifts, home furnishings, and an annual vacation typically need limited decision making.

Routine consumer decision making occurs when a person buys out of habit and skips steps in the process. He or she spends little time shopping and often rebuys the same brands (or brands bought before). In this category are items with which a person has much experience. They are bought regularly, have little or no perceived risk, and are relatively low in price. Once a person realizes a good or service is depleted, a repurchase is made. The time pressure to buy is high. Information search, evaluation of alternatives, and post-purchase behavior are normally omitted, as long as a person is satisfied. Factors affecting the process have little impact because problem awareness typically leads to a purchase.

Examples of items routinely purchased are the daily newspaper, a haircut by a regular stylist, and weekly grocery items.

The way the decision process is used varies by country.

There are several differences between consumers in industrialized nations and those in less-developed and developing ones. In general, consumers in less-developed and developing countries

- Are exposed to fewer commercial and noncommercial cues.
- Have access to less information.
- Have fewer goods and services from which to choose.
- Are more apt to buy a second choice if the first one is not available.
- Have fewer places of purchase and may have to wait on long lines.
- Are more apt to find that stores are out of stock.
- Have less purchase experience for many kinds of goods and services.
- Are less educated and have lower incomes.
- Are more apt to rebuy items with which they are only moderately satisfied (due to the lack of choices).

Because many consumers—in both industrialized nations and less-developed nations—want to reduce shopping time, the use of complex decision making, and risk, most purchases are made via routine or limited decision making. Thus, consumers often employ low-involvement purchasing and/or brand loyalty.

Low-involvement purchasing *occurs with unimportant products.*

With **low-involvement purchasing**, a consumer minimizes the time and effort expended in both making decisions about and shopping for those goods and services he or she views as unimportant. Included are "those situations where the consumer simply does not care and is not concerned about brands or choices and makes the decision in the most cognitively miserly manner possible. Most likely, low involvement is situation-based, and the degree of importance and involvement may vary with the individual and with the situation."[13] In these situations, consumers feel little perceived risk, are passive about getting information, act fast, and may assess products after (rather than before) buying.

Firms can adapt to low-involvement purchasing by using repetitive ads to create awareness and familiarity, stressing the practical nature of goods and services, having informed salespeople, setting low prices, using attractive in-store displays, selling in all types of outlets, and offering coupons and free samples. Table 8-5 compares the traditional high-involvement view of consumer behavior with the newer low-involvement view.[14]

Brand loyalty *involves consistent repurchases and preferences of specific brands.*

Once a consumer tries one or more brands of a good or service, **brand loyalty**—the consistent repurchase of and preference toward a particular brand—may take place. With it, a person can reduce time, thought, and risk whenever buying a given good or service. Brand loyalty can occur for simple items such as gasoline (due to low-involvement purchasing) and for complex items like autos (to minimize the risk of switching brands).

Sixty per cent of U.S. adults say they "try to stick with well-known brands." And a lot of people are loyal to one brand of cigarettes, mayonnaise, toothpaste, coffee, hot cereal, ketchup, film, soap, salad dressing, beer, auto, perfume, and gasoline. In Great Britain, France, and Germany, 74 per cent, 54 per cent, and 52 per cent of adults (respectively) say "Once I find a brand, it is very difficult to get me to change brands." In India and China, 35 per cent and 28 per cent of adults (respectively) consider themselves to be "brand loyalists" who buy name brands and remain true to them.[15]

[13]Bennett, *Dictionary of Marketing Terms*, p. 157.

[14]See also Stephen L. Vargo, "Consumer Involvement: An Historical Perspective and Partial Synthesis" in Barbara B. Stern and George M. Zinkham (Editors), *1995 AMA Educators' Proceedings* (Chicago: American Marketing Association, 1995), pp. 139–145.

[15]Adrienne Ward Fawcett, "Life-Style Study: The Latest Results of DDB Needham's 18-Year Survey," *Advertising Age* (April 18, 1994), p. 13; Leo Burnett U.S.A. Research Department, "Consumer Buying Patterns: Beyond Demographics," *Progressive Grocer* (May 1995), pp. 135–138; Nancy Giges, "Europeans Buy Outside Goods, But Like Local Ads," *Advertising Age* (April 27, 1992), pp. I-1, I-26; and Leah Rickard, "Ex-Soviet States Lead World in Ad Cynicism," *Advertising Age* (June 5, 1995), p. 3.

Table 8-5

High-Involvement View of Active Consumers Versus Low-Involvement View of Passive Consumers

TRADITIONAL HIGH-INVOLVEMENT VIEW OF ACTIVE CONSUMERS	NEWER LOW-INVOLVEMENT VIEW OF PASSIVE CONSUMERS
1. Consumers are information processors.	1. Consumers learn information at random.
2. Consumers are information seekers.	2. Consumers are information gatherers.
3. Consumers are an active audience for ads and the effect of ads on them is *weak*.	3. Consumers are a passive audience for ads and the effect of ads on them is *strong*.
4. Consumers evaluate brands before buying.	4. Consumers buy first. If they do evaluate brands, it is done after the purchase.
5. Consumers seek to maximize satisfaction. They compare brands to see which provide the most *benefits* and buy based on detailed comparisons.	5. Consumers seek an acceptable level of satisfaction. They choose the brand least apt to have *problems* and buy based on few factors. Familiarity is key.
6. Life-style characteristics are related to consumer behavior because the product is closely tied to a consumer's identity and belief system.	6. Life-style characteristics are not related to consumer behavior because the product is not closely tied to a consumer's identity and belief system.
7. Reference groups influence behavior because of the product's importance to group norms.	7. Reference groups have little effect on behavior because the product is unlikely to be related to group norms.

Source: Henry Assael, *Consumer Behavior and Marketing Action*, Fourth Edition (Boston: PWS-Kent, 1992), p. 104.

FIGURE 8-10
Osh Kosh: A Reliable Name for More Than 100 Years
Reprinted by permission.

How can companies generate and sustain customer loyalty? As shown in Figure 8-10, Osh Kosh plays up its 100+-year history. And here's the way Bloomingdale's handles this issue:

> Bloomingdale's doesn't want its best cosmetics customers to buy mascara anywhere else again. So, it takes their orders by fax and delivers the makeup to their homes without charge. For other shoppers, Bloomie's sends reminders to husbands to buy birthday or anniversary presents. Still others get on-the-house services like alterations and gift wrapping. The retailer is using an approach traditionally associated with tiny boutiques that know their customers by name. What did these Bloomingdale's customers do to deserve such special treatment? They charged a bundle on their new Bloomingdale's Visa credit cards, and the firm believes they can be milked for even more.[16]

Marketing Implications of the Final Consumer's Decision Process

Over the years, the marketing implications of the final consumer's decision process have been studied in many settings, as these present-day illustrations indicate:

- When acquiring information for a car purchase, people read articles in newspapers and magazines, talk to friends and relatives, and consider their previous experience. On average, U.S. men spend 14 weeks thinking about a new-car purchase; and 32 per cent visit a closed showroom so they can look at models and learn about sticker prices. Once the actual "hunt" starts, men average 14 shopping days to buy a car and visit five dealers. Two-thirds of men say they have a good time when buying a new car.[17]
- Nearly a third of Chinese consumers are "enthusiastic shoppers," who enjoy shopping and like to price bargain. They prepare complete shopping lists before shopping, consult with friends and neighbors prior to making major purchases, and are often innovators and opinion leaders. About 15 per cent of Chinese consumers are "passive shoppers," who consider shopping to be a necessary burden. They are casual shoppers, do not prepare detailed lists before shopping, and do not like price bargaining. They are conservative in their purchase of new products.[18]
- Supermarket shoppers in eastern Germany are much more likely to choose the brands they buy after they enter a store than consumers in the Netherlands, western Germany, Spain, France, Italy, and Great Britain.[19]
- For several reasons, "substantial time often elapses between the time people recognize the need for a product and the time they actually purchase it": People may believe they do not have enough time to devote to the decision. They may feel shopping is an unpleasant experience. They may experience perceived risk. They may need advice from others; and it is not readily available. They may not know how to gather adequate information about products and their attributes. They may expect prices to fall. They may expect improved products to be introduced later.[20]
- Satisfied consumers discuss their experiences with far fewer people than dissatisfied ones. Yet, according to one auto-industry consultant, "It costs you five times as much to get a new customer as to keep an old one."[21]

[16]Laura Bird, "Department Stores Target Top Customers," *Wall Street Journal* (March 8, 1995), p. B1.

[17]"How Men Buy Cars," *Ad Week* (September 18, 1995), p. 21; and "How Guys Buy Cars," *Advertising Age* (September 18, 1995), p. 3.

[18]Zhengyuan Wang, C. P. Rao, and Angela D'Auria, "Measuring Chinese Personal Values and Shopping Behavior: An Empirical Comparison of the Rokeach Value Survey and Perceived Attribute Importance" in Brian T. Engelland and Alan J. Bush (Editors), *Marketing: Advances in Theory and Thought* (Evansville, Ind.: Southern Marketing Association, 1994), pp. 378–381.

[19]"In-Store Promotion Sways Consumers," *Advertising Age* (May 25, 1992), p. I-24.

[20]Eric A. Greenleaf and Donald R. Lehmann, "Reasons for Substantial Delay in Consumer Decision Making," *Journal of Consumer Research*, Vol. 22 (September 1995), pp. 186–199.

[21]Raymond Serafin and Cleveland Horton, "Auto Makers Focus on Service," *Advertising Age* (July 6, 1992), pp. 3, 33.

Limitations of the Final Consumer's Decision Process

The limitations of the final consumer's decision process for marketers lie in the hidden (unexpressed) nature of many elements of the process; the consumer's subconscious performance of the process or a number of its components; the impact of demographic, social, and psychological factors on the process; and the differences in decision making among consumers in different countries.

Much of purchase behavior is hidden or subconscious.

MARKETING IN A CHANGING WORLD

REALLY Understanding Other Cultures[22]

As we discussed before, and again in this chapter, marketers need to do a first-rate job of grasping and appealing to the global marketplace. As such, they must *really* understand other cultures—because of their broad impact on the demographics and life-styles of potential customers, and the way people make consumption decisions. With this in mind, let us explore the distinctions between American and Japanese cultures in greater detail.

According to Koichiro Naganuma, the Japanese chairman of Asatsu/BBDO (an advertising agency):

> In most Western countries, the individual is seen as separate from, and often more important than, the larger community. We Japanese view ourselves as one homogeneous family. Our shared history, traditions, and national cultural identity give us a very strong sense of community. Consequently, the nature of communication within the Japanese culture reflects a commonality of thought, attitude, and circumstance, in what is often an unspoken language understood by us. In contrast to the Japanese, Westerners are direct in face-to-face interaction, conversation, and expression. Western advertising, therefore, tends to fix on a target audience and address it with direct messages which seek to affect the attitude of that audience. Conversely, in the same manner that Japanese find it awkward and even disrespectful to maintain eye contact during conversation, our advertising shuns the directness of the Western method, seeking instead to create a positive, welcoming atmosphere around the product. The Japanese prefer to come to an understanding with little actual conversation. For example, Americans spend 6 1/2 hours in conversation a day, almost double the amount of time we spend conversing with each other.

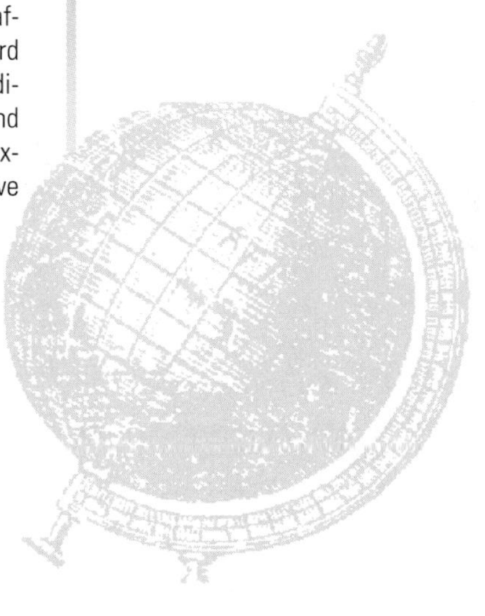

Here are some further comparisons of the American and Japanese cultures:

- American—fight for beliefs. Japanese—harmony is valued.
- American—get the facts straight. Japanese—unspoken agreement.
- American—display emotions. Japanese—hold back emotions.
- American—humor-oriented. Japanese—pun-oriented.
- American—make a long story long. Japanese—make a short story short.
- American—interested in *what* is spoken. Japanese—interested in *who* is speaking.

SUMMARY

1. *To show why consumer demographic analysis is not sufficient in planning marketing programs* Because demographic data do not answer such questions as why consumers act as they do, why demographically similar consumers act differently, how motives and risks affect decisions, and how long it takes people to reach purchase decisions, many firms now analyze the social and psychological aspects of final consumer life-styles, as well as the way in which consumers make decisions—in conjunction with demographics—and then develop descriptive consumer profiles.

2. *To define and describe consumer life-styles and their characteristics, examine selected life-styles, and present marketing implications of life-*

[22]The material in this section is based on Hideo Ishikawa and Koichiro Naganuma, "Exploring Differences in Japan, U.S. Cultures," *Advertising Age* (September 18, 1995), p. I-8.

style analysis A final consumer's life-style is the way in which a person lives and spends time and money. It is a function of the social and psychological factors internalized by that person, along with his or her demographic background. Consumer social profiles are made up of several elements, including culture, social class, social performance, reference groups, opinion leaders, the family life cycle, and time expenditures. Psychological profiles are based on a combination of personality, attitudes (opinions), the level of class consciousness, motivation, perceived risk, innovativeness, and purchase importance.

These seven life-style types are expected to continue, with their popularity often differing by country. A family values life-style emphasizes marriage, children, and home life. With voluntary simplicity, people have an ecological awareness, seek material simplicity, strive for self-reliance, and buy inexpensive product versions. Getting by is a frugal life-style brought on because of economic circumstances. The "me" generation stresses being good to oneself, self-expression, and the acceptance of diversity. With blurring gender roles, more husbands are assuming the once-traditional roles of their wives, and visa versa. A poverty of time occurs for some consumers because the quest for financial security means less free time as the alternatives competing for time expand. In a component life-style, consumer attitudes and behavior depend on particular situations, rather than on an overall life-style philosophy.

Various marketing implications relating to consumer life-styles are discussed.

3. *To consider the limitations of consumer life-style analysis* Many life-style concepts are difficult to measure, somewhat subjective, based on self-reports by consumers, and sometimes hidden from view. There are disputes over terms, misuse of data, and reliability.

4. *To define and describe the final consumer's decision process and present marketing implications* The final consumer's decision process is the procedure by which those consumers collect and analyze information and make choices among alternatives. It consists of the process itself and the factors affecting it (demographic, social, and psychological). It can be delayed or terminated by the consumer at any point.

The process has six steps: stimulus, problem awareness, information search, evaluation of alternatives, purchase, and post-purchase behavior. There are three types of process: extended, limited, and routine. The way people make decisions varies widely between industrialized nations and less-developed and developing nations. Consumers often reduce shopping time, thought, and risk via low-involvement purchasing (for goods and services viewed as unimportant) and brand loyalty (the consistent repurchase of and preference toward a brand).

The marketing implications of the final consumer's decision process have been detailed for years. Several current applications are discussed.

5. *To consider the limitations of final consumer decision-making analysis* The limitations of the decision process for marketers lie in the unexpressed nature of many parts of the process; the subconscious nature of many consumer actions; the impact of demographic, social, and psychological factors; and the intercountry differences in consumer decision making.

KEY TERMS

life-style (p. 206)
culture (p. 207)
social class (p. 207)
social performance (p. 208)
reference group (p. 208)
opinion leaders (p. 209)
family life cycle (p. 209)
joint decision making (p. 209)
household life cycle (p. 210)
time expenditures (p. 210)
personality (p. 210)
attitudes (opinions) (p. 211)
class consciousness (p. 211)
motivation (p. 211)
motives (p. 211)
perceived risk (p. 213)
innovativeness (p. 214)
importance of a purchase (p. 214)
family values (p. 214)
voluntary simplicity (p. 215)
getting by (p. 215)
"me" generation (p. 215)
blurring gender roles (p. 215)
poverty of time (p. 215)
component life-style (p. 215)
final consumer's decision process (p. 218)
stimulus (p. 219)
problem awareness (p. 220)
information search (p. 220)
evaluation of alternatives (p. 221)
purchase act (p. 221)
post-purchase behavior (p. 222)
cognitive dissonance (p. 222)
extended consumer decision making (p. 222)
limited consumer decision making (p. 223)
routine consumer decision making (p. 223)
low-involvement purchasing (p. 224)
brand loyalty (p. 224)

Review Questions

1. Why are demographic data alone frequently insufficient for marketing decisions?
2. How does social class affect an individual's life-style and purchases?
3. Distinguish between the traditional family life cycle and the household life cycle.
4. How does class consciousness differ for inner-directed and outer-directed people? What does this signify for marketers?
5. Distinguish between actual risk and perceived risk. How may a firm reduce each type of perceived risk for a new arthritis pain reliever?
6. Compare the voluntary life-style with the getting by life-style.
7. Differentiate among social, commercial, and noncommercial stimuli. Provide specific examples of each.
8. What causes cognitive dissonance? How may it be reduced?
9. Draw a flowchart showing the steps in routine purchase behavior.
10. Define low-involvement purchasing and explain its use by consumers. Give an example.

Discussion Questions

1. American culture emphasizes achievement and success, activity, efficiency and practicality, progress, material comfort, individualism, freedom, external conformity, humanitarianism, youthfulness, and fitness and health. What are the implications of this for firms marketing the following goods and services?
   a. Motorcycles.
   b. Tanning salons.
   c. Adult education.
   d. Vacation travel.
2. Give examples of current advertisements targeting the
   a. Upper-middle class.
   b. Working class.
   c. Upper-lower class.
3. Distinguish between Tables 8-2 and 8-3. What are the marketing implications of your answer?
4. A large cereal manufacturer has hired you as a marketing consultant. It is particularly interested in learning more about the concept of a component life-style and developing an appropriate strategy.
   a. Explain the relevance of the component life-style concept for the cereal industry.
   b. Suggest various ways in which the cereal manufacturer can appeal to component life-styles.
5. In this chapter, several distinctions are made between consumers in industrialized countries and those in less-developed nations with regard to the final consumer's decision process. How would you deal with these distinctions when marketing to consumers in less-developed and developing countries?

CASE 1

*Will Twentysomethings Buy Levi's Dockers?**

Levi Strauss is in the midst of a major advertising campaign for its Dockers pants. Dockers is currently the best-selling brand of men's pants, with $1 billion in annual wholesale sales. Of Levi Strauss' total advertising budget, about one-quarter is spent on Dockers.

As an addition to its traditional Dockers line of khakis slacks, Levi's recently introduced a new high-fashion khaki line called Dockers Authentics. A cross between khakis and jeans, Dockers Authentics sell for $45 to $48 (versus $35 for Levi's regular khakis). Levi is targeting Dockers Authentics at Generation Xers. Levi realizes that its traditional Dockers brand appeals to an older population group and wants to broaden the brand's appeal beyond baby boomers. Without a successful product aimed at Generation X, the Docker name will become associated with an aging audience.

Levi Strauss is hoping to send the message to men in their 20s that its new khakis are cool. The firm's goal for its advertising campaign is to encourage men to wear khakis in place of jeans and to view Dockers Authentics as a more formal alternative to jeans. And in an attempt not to appear too trendy, Levi's new ads promote Dockers Authentics on the basis of tradition and comfort, not as current fashion.

Levi has used an innovative series of promotions for Dockers Authentics. Early promotions, for example, were based around sponsored rock concerts in six cities. Prior to each concert, Dockers projected a four-minute MTV-style video featuring Dockers Authentics on the side of a nearby building. Each advertisement had the tag line: "Khakis with a blue-jean soul."

Dockers Authentics are being featured in more than 150 department stores (located in large metropolitan markets) via special Authentics departments. The special departments are placed with other mid-priced collections of clothing aimed at young men. Retail analysts expect the Authentics line to compete against Calvin Klein and other brands.

Levi Strauss expects the sales of its Dockers, Dockers Authentics, and Levi's jeans to benefit from the shift to more casual clothing styles on weekends and at work. According to a major marketing research study, almost 90 per cent of all workers say they are "dressing down." Even IBM, once noted for a rigid dress code, has adapted its standards to include more relaxed clothing styles. The study also found that interest in men's suits was down, but interest in casual apparel (like no-iron cotton slacks and sweaters) was up.

Levi Strauss is determined to capitalize on this trend with its casual clothing line. Early research by the company found that although human resources managers favored casual clothing policies, those managers needed Levi's help to convince top management to change their dress codes. So, Levi developed a four-page newsletter filled with reasons why more casual dress codes should be enacted. For example, it noted that letting employees dress casually was a cost-free employee benefit. The newsletter also contained case histories of firms that successfully adopted casual dress codes. In total, Levi Strauss mailed the newsletter to 42,000 human resources managers. Levi Strauss also produced a video on the "fine art of dressing." And in fall 1995, it started hosting casual dress fashion shows at the Dockers shops that the firm owns.

Levi did have one advertising slip-up. In late 1995, it pulled a Dockers' ad from city bus shelters in San Francisco and New York after it was accused of encouraging vandalism. Each ad had a pair of Dockers placed behind a glass plate. Under the pants (seeemingly in anticipation of their theft) was the message: "Apparently, they were very nice pants."

QUESTIONS

1. Which family life-cycle stage is most likely to purchase Dockers? Dockers Authentics? Explain your answers.
2. What forms of perceived risk accompany the purchase of Dockers Authentics by a first-time purchaser? A loyal customer?
3. What consumer life-styles are associated with "dressing down?" Explain your answer.
4. What type of decision process would be used in the purchase of Dockers Authentics? Explain your answer.

*The data in this case are drawn from Alice Z. Cuneo, "Levi's Dons New Men's Wear Appeal," *Advertising Age* (April 24, 1995), p. 12; Cyndee Miller, "A Casual Affair," *Marketing News* (March 13, 1995), pp. 1–2; and Kevin Whitelaw, "Gobbling Up the Gen-X Market," *U.S. News & World Report* (October 9, 1995), p. 68.

CASE 2

Greeting-Card Shopping Behavior in Supermarkets†

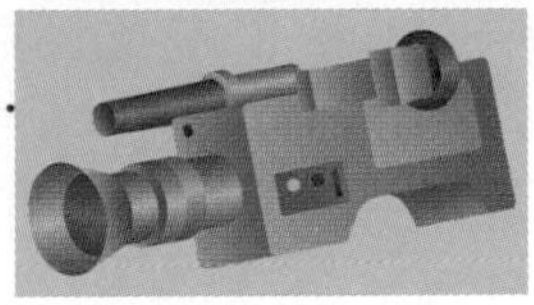

Greeting cards account for 0.7 per cent of sales at the Fred A. Albrecht Grocery Company's 11 conventional supermarkets but more than 10 per cent of the stores' net profits. The high greeting-card profits are due to their 50 per cent gross margin (a $1.50 card yields a $0.75 gross margin). In addition, the operating costs for greeting cards are low because suppliers offer assistance in the form of displays, direct-to-store delivery, and a very favorable return policy on unsold merchandise.

Although some competitors offer substantial discounts on their greeting cards, Albrecht continues to sell them at full price. It competes on the basis of a better presentation, assortment, and promotions. The store's double-digit growth in card sales attests to the chain's superior merchandising ability.

At one of its store units, Albrecht's strength in card sales can be attributed to a full-scale renovation of the card department. This upgrading included taller fixtures (78 versus 66 inches high), the use of 15-tiered fixtures (that display 15 cards at a time versus the old 12-tier fixtures), the use of canopy lighting (no special lighting existed before), and aisle expansion from 3 1/2 feet to 5 feet. According to American Greetings' regional account manager, "The idea is to put our best foot forward by making a major graphic statement with our most popular and high impulse card line."

Even though this prototype design has not been implemented at all of Albrecht's stores, each store now has a special greeting card department located in a conspicuous position near the store entrance. In addition, all of Albrecht's stores rely on cross-merchandising opportunities. These include the sales of paper plates alongside Halloween candies, gift bags in the cosmetics department, birthday candles in the bakery, and higher-priced cards in the floral department. Albrecht even has a Mother's Day promotion, giving 10 minutes of long-distance phone time with the purchase of $10 in greeting cards.

In an effort to learn more about greeting cards, Albrecht read the results of a study conducted by American Greetings, Albrecht's card supplier. This is what Albrecht learned:

- One-half of card purchases were made in card shops 20 years ago; these stores now account for about 30 per cent of sales. Much of this loss in share was to discount stores and supermarkets. In 1993, supermarkets accounted for 18 per cent of purchases, as compared to 12 per cent in 1983.
- 90 per cent of all cards are purchased by women. Women send an average of 17 birthday cards a year versus 10 for men.
- Of all age groups, teenagers (aged 16 to 19) have the highest likelihood of receiving a birthday card.
- One-half of those aged 16 to 19 say they received ten or more cards on their last birthday. About 45 per cent of older Americans (those over the age of 50) also report receiving more than ten cards.
- 50 per cent of cards are now purchased for a seasonal event (such as Valentine's Day, Mother's Day, and Season's Greetings). The balance are purchased on a non-seasonal basis.

†The data in this case are drawn from "Cakes, Cards, and Candles," *American Demographics* (March 1995), pp. 20–22; Susan Chandler, "Can Hallmark Get Well Soon?" *Business Week* (June 19, 1995), pp. 62–63; Kate Fitzgerald, "Hallmark Alters Focus as Life-Styles Change," *Advertising Age* (October 31, 1994), p. 4; and Glenn Snyder, "We Can Outmerchandise Them," *Progressive Grocer* (May 1994), pp. 35–44.

QUESTIONS

1. Discuss how the purchase of a greeting card would differ for a "me" generation person and a voluntary simplicity person.
2. What consumer life-styles and decision making processes can be used to explain the shift in greeting card sales from card shops to supermarkets?
3. Describe the final consumer's decision process for the purchase of a greeting card. Refer to each element in Figure 8-7 in the chapter for your answer.
4. Under what circumstances would buying a greeting card be characterized as a high-involvement purchase?

VIDEO QUESTIONS ON GREETING CARD SHOPPING BEHAVIOR

1. What factors account for the greater importance of supermarkets as a distribution channel for greeting cards?
2. Outline the steps a supermarket operator can take to increase the sales of greeting cards.

CHAPTER 9

Organizational Consumers

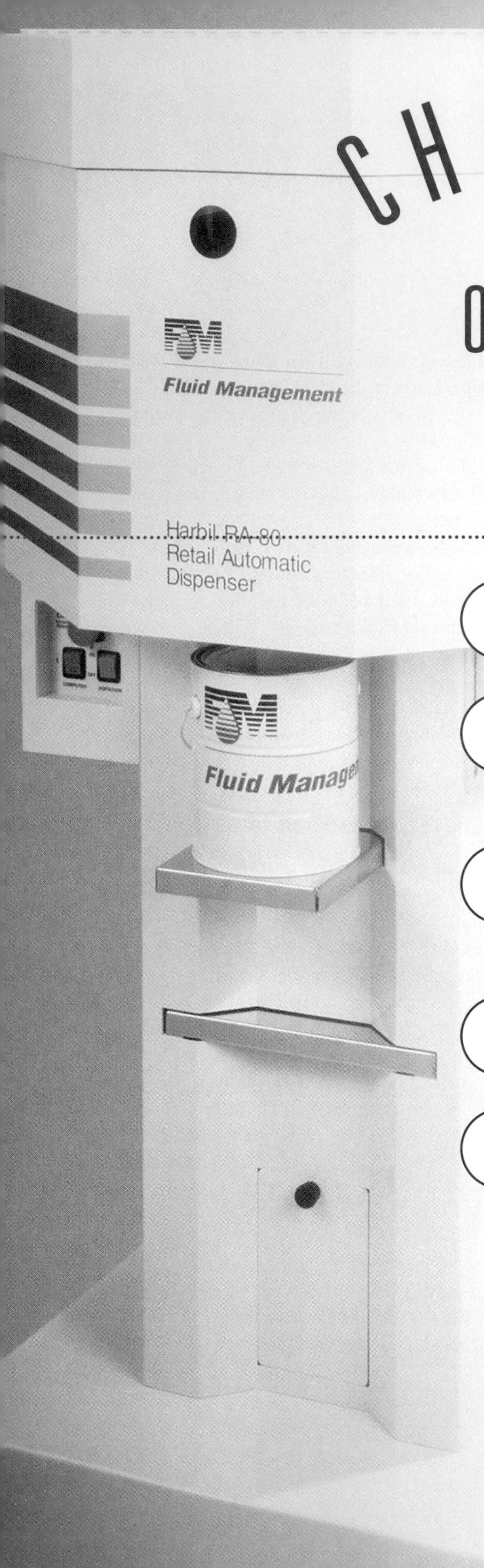

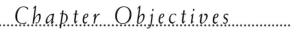

Chapter Objectives

1. To introduce the concept of industrial marketing

2. To differentiate between organizational consumers and final consumers and look at organizational consumers from an international perspective

3. To describe the different types of organizational consumers and their buying objectives, buying structure, and purchase constraints

4. To explain the organizational consumer's decision process

5. To consider the marketing implications of appealing to organizational consumers

In 1989, Fred Brunk, vice-president of sales at Fluid Management, a supplier of paint tinting and mixing equipment, wanted to grow the company's domestic sales. What was missing from his portfolio were the big retailers such as Wal-Mart, which would bring him larger volumes.

Six years later, Brunk got his wish—domestic sales rose dramatically, from $25 million in 1989 to $40 million in 1995, thanks largely to an increase in volume to the mass merchants. But what Brunk did not count on were the tremendous expectations of these companies.

Despite the great opportunities, many small firms find it is more complicated than they expect to sell to large retailers. As Fluid Management's Fred Brunk says, "Even when the details are in place, such as the specific needs of the company and negotiated prices, you have to constantly watch when new stores are opening. There must always be a salesperson ready at a moment's notice to make a trip to the retailer's headquarters." And while Fluid Management may not be able to have its eight-member sales force visit each of Wal-Mart's thousands of stores, the firm's chief executive officer is willing to go to Wal-Mart's Bentonville, Arkansas, headquarters as often as needed.

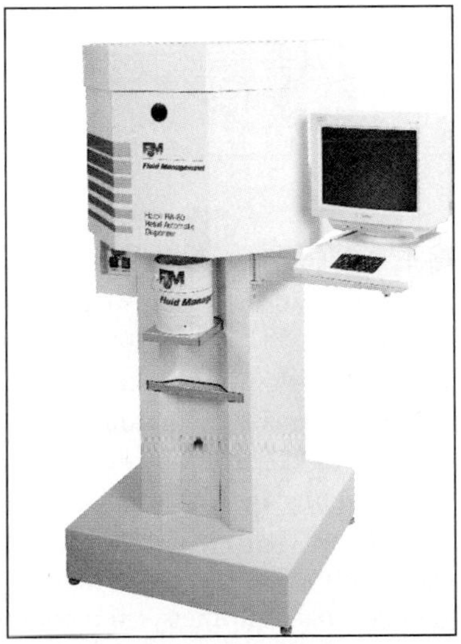

Reprinted by permission.

Here are some other complexities in selling to big accounts like Wal-Mart:

- Wal-Mart does not purchase from wholesalers. Thus, small firms must service the firm on a direct basis. This could be especially tough for a small supplier selling a narrow product line.
- Most small manufacturers do not have the resources to set up offices near Wal-Mart stores.
- Some large retailers require that suppliers take back excess inventories, seek extended payment policies, and even ask that suppliers handle data collection responsibilities. Other demands may include requiring rebates on purchases, adhering to an automatic return policy, and dictating that a supplier give donations to the retailers' favorite charities. A number of small manufacturers say the demands that large retailers place on them are so great that they would lose money selling to those retailers.
- A small supplier's current customers may resent its selling to firms such as Wal-Mart that are viewed as direct competitors.
- The loss of a key account could drive a small supplier into bankruptcy.

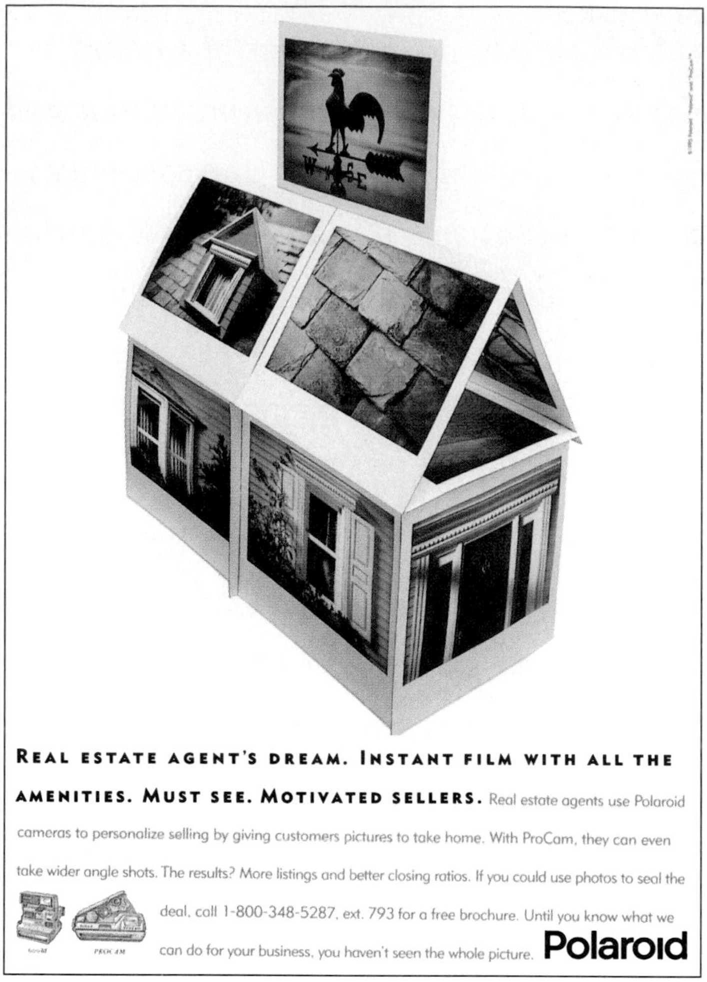

FIGURE 9-1
At Polaroid: A Heightened Emphasis on Industrial Marketing
As Polaroid's core consumer photography business has stagnated, it has turned to imaginative approaches to industrial marketing.
Reprinted by permission.

So, why bother? There are major benefits for a small firm to sell to a large retailer such as Wal-Mart. First, there is the huge sales potential. For example, after Wal-Mart began to upgrade the paint departments in its stores, Fluid Management received more business from Wal-Mart in two months than the firm otherwise received in an entire year. Second, small suppliers can use their contracts with large buyers as a means of getting increased financing or better terms from banks. Third, it may be less costly to sell to large retailers based on their high average sale and the delivery of big orders to a single distribution center instead of to a number of small stores.[1]

In this chapter, we will study much more about the characteristics and behavior of organizational consumers such as Wal-Mart. We will also discuss the different types of organizational customers, their buying objectives, buying structure, and purchase constraints.

Overview

Firms involved with organizational consumers use **industrial marketing.**

As defined in Chapter 8, organizational consumers purchase goods and services for further production, use in operations, or resale to others. In contrast, final consumers buy for personal, family, or household use. Organizational consumers are manufacturers, wholesalers, retailers, and government and other nonprofit institutions. When firms deal with organizational consumers, they engage in **industrial marketing,** as shown in these examples.

Purchasing executives around the world spend trillions of dollars annually for the goods and services their companies require. According to one estimate, "On average, man-

[1]Allison Lucas, "Can You Sell to Wal-Mart?" *Sales & Marketing Management* (August 1995), p. 14.

ufacturers shell out 55 cents of each dollar of revenues on goods and services, from raw materials to overnight mail. By contrast, labor seldom exceeds 6 per cent of sales, overhead 3 per cent."[2]

Although purchasing executives at large corporations often deal with major suppliers, in the United States alone, 100,000 small businesses sell goods and services to these big companies. As one purchasing director noted, "We've discovered that smallness just equates with quality. A tiny company just tends to pay more attention. After all, it's risking everything on a small output. Sloppiness can be ruinous." One-third of the largest U.S. companies use formal programs for seeking out small suppliers. Why then do only 100,000 of the millions of small U.S. firms try to sell to big corporations? They feel there is a "nightmare of paperwork, pre-qualifying inspections, mazes to find the right contact, and the time involved before the contract is signed."[3]

For a long time, Polaroid Corporation earned its reputation (and considerable profits) by making and marketing self-developing cameras for final consumers. But, in recent years, due to the popularity of inexpensive 35-mm cameras and the growth of one-hour photodeveloping labs, Polaroid has reduced its focus on final consumers. Today, Polaroid places greater emphasis on products for organizational consumers, including digital scanners, medical imaging systems, photo ID systems, and security systems.[4] And as Figure 9-1 shows, Polaroid now advertises some of its cameras to such organizational consumers as real-estate brokers.

American Greetings makes cards and other personal-communications products. It is the second-largest firm in the field (behind Hallmark) and markets products in more than 70 nations. Although its products are ultimately sold to final consumers, American Greetings must first get support from organizational consumers—the thousands of retailers (encompassing 97,000 stores) that stock its cards and related items. Accordingly, American Greetings provides research on greeting-cards customers to its retailers, devises and sets up in-store displays, helps computerize transactions, runs special promotions to draw consumers to retail stores, and so on.[5]

Andersen Consulting, a division of Andersen Worldwide, has annual revenues of $3.5 billion and nearly 30,000 consultants in about 50 countries. Its specialties are technical consulting—with which it first became involved in 1954 when helping General Electric install its initial computer—and strategic planning. Its Method/1 approach is a widely used process for teaching clients how to handle any type of computer project in a systematic and cost-efficient manner.[6] See Figure 9-2.

In this chapter, organizational consumers are distinguished from final consumers and an international perspective is provided. The various types of organizational consumers are described. Key factors in organizational consumer behavior are presented. The organizational consumer's decision process is outlined. Marketing implications are offered.

The Characteristics of Organizational Consumers

When undertaking industrial marketing, a firm must recognize that organizational consumers differ from final consumers in several key ways. As shown in Table 9-1, differences are due to the nature of purchases and the nature of the market. A firm must also realize that organizational consumer characteristics vary by nation.

[2]Shawn Tully, "Purchasing's New Muscle," *Fortune* (February 20, 1995), pp. 75–76.

[3]Arthur Bragg, "How to Sell in the Big Time," *Sales & Marketing Management* (February 1990), pp. 42–44; and Michael Selz, "Some Suppliers Rethink Their Reliance on Big Business," *Wall Street Journal* (March 29, 1993), p. B2.

[4]Patrick J. Spain and James R. Talbot (Editors), *Hoover's Handbook of American Business 1996* (Austin, Texas: Reference Press, 1995), pp. 1176–1177.

[5]*American Greetings 1995 Annual Report.*

[6]Lee Berton, "Big Six's Shift to Consulting Services," *Wall Street Journal* (September 21, 1995), pp. B1, B4; and "Andersen Worldwide," *New York Times* (January 23, 1996), p. D7.

Just don't expect it to roar.
In an effort to become swifter and more ferocious, many organizations may be tempted to make superficial changes.
But this approach will rarely improve performance. Especially when information technology is part of the plan.
Which is why Andersen Consulting works with companies to link technology to the heart of their business. Their strategies, operations and human resources.
Because these days, becoming a more aggressive competitor often means transforming the organization. And not just hopping on a technological bandwagon.
ANDERSEN CONSULTING
ARTHUR ANDERSEN & CO., S.C.
Where we go from here.
© 1992 Andersen Consulting. All rights reserved.

FIGURE 9-2
Industrial Marketing for Consulting Services
Reprinted by permission of Andersen Consulting.

Differences from Final Consumers Due to the Nature of Purchases

Organizational and final consumers vary in the way they use goods and services and in the items bought. Organizational consumers purchase capital equipment, raw materials, semifinished goods, and other products for use in further production or operations or for resale to others. Final consumers usually acquire finished items (and are not involved with million-dollar purchases of plant and equipment) for personal, family, or household use. As a result, organizational consumers are more apt to use specifications, multiple-buying decisions, value and vendor analysis, leased equipment, and competitive bidding and negotiation than are final consumers.

Many organizational consumers rely on product specifications in purchase decisions and do not consider alternatives unless they meet minimum standards, such as engineering and architectural guidelines, purity, horsepower, voltage, type of construction, and construction materials. Final consumers more often purchase on the basis of description, style, and color.

Multiple-buying responsibility *may be shared by two or more employees.*

Organizational consumers often use **multiple-buying responsibility**, whereby two or more employees formally participate in complex or expensive purchase decisions. For example, a decision to buy computerized cash registers may involve input from computer personnel, marketing personnel, the operations manager, a systems consultant, and the controller. The firm's president might make the final choice about system characteristics and the supplier. Though final consumers use multiple-buying responsibility (joint decision making), they employ it less frequently and less formally.

Table 9-1

Major Differences Between Organizational and Final Consumers

Differences in Purchases
Organizational consumers
1. buy for further production, use in operations, or resale to others. Final consumers buy only for personal, family, or household use.
2. commonly purchase installations, raw materials, and semifinished materials. Final consumers rarely purchase these goods.
3. often buy on the basis of specifications and technical data. Final consumers frequently buy based on description, fashion, and style.
4. utilize multiple-buying and team-based decisions more often than final consumers.
5. are more apt to apply formal value and vendor analysis.
6. more commonly lease equipment.
7. more frequently employ competitive bidding and negotiation.

Differences in the Market
Organizational consumers
1. derive their demand from that of final consumers.
2. have demand states that are more subject to cyclical fluctuations than final consumer demand.
3. are fewer in number and more geographically concentrated than final consumers.
4. often employ buying specialists.
5. require a shorter distribution channel than do final consumers.
6. may require special relationships with sellers.
7. are more likely than final consumers to be able to make goods and undertake services as alternatives to purchasing them.

Value analysis *reduces costs;* **vendor analysis** *rates suppliers.*

A lot of organizational consumers use value analysis and vendor analysis. In **value analysis**, organizational consumers thoroughly compare the costs and benefits of alternative materials, components, designs, or processes so as to reduce the cost/benefit ratio of purchases.[7] They seek to answer such questions as: What is the purpose of each good or service under purchase consideration? What are the short-run and long-run costs of each alternative? Is a purchase necessary? Are there substitute goods or services that could perform more efficiently? How long will a good or service last before it must be replaced? Can uniform standards be set to ease reordering? In **vendor analysis**, organizational consumers thoroughly assess the strengths and weaknesses of current or new suppliers in terms of quality, customer service, reliability, and price.[8] Satisfaction with current vendors often means customer loyalty. Figures 9-3 and 9-4 illustrate value analysis and vendor analysis.

Organizational consumers of all sizes frequently lease major equipment. Each year, U.S. firms spend over $135 billion in leasing equipment (measured by the original cost of the equipment). Commonly leased equipment includes aircraft, computers, office machinery, and trucks and trailers. The worldwide use of commercial leasing is rising rapidly. Final consumers are less involved with leasing; it is most common in apartment and auto leasing.

In **competitive bidding,** *sellers submit price bids; in* **negotiation,** *the buyer bargains to set prices.*

Organizational consumers often use competitive bidding and negotiation. In **competitive bidding**, two or more sellers submit independent price quotes for specific goods

[7]Peter D. Bennett (Editor), *Dictionary of Marketing Terms*, Second Edition (Chicago: American Marketing Association, 1995), pp. 297–298.
[8]Ibid., p. 299. See also Stephanie Gruner, "The Smart Vendor-Audit Checklist," *Inc.* (April 1995), pp. 93–95.

	Definitely Yes	Probably Yes	Uncertain	Probably No	Definitely No
• Can plastic pipe be substituted to reduce costs?	-----	-----	-----	-----	-----
• Can a standardized 1/3-horsepower motor be used?	-----	-----	-----	-----	-----
• Can an external float-triggered switch be used instead of an internal one?	-----	-----	-----	-----	-----
• Can a noncorrosive base replace the current base which is easily corroded?	-----	-----	-----	-----	-----
• Is a Westinghouse motor more reliable than a GE motor?	-----	-----	-----	-----	-----
• Is a 5-year warranty acceptable?	-----	-----	-----	-----	-----

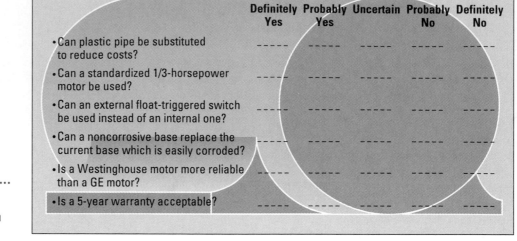

FIGURE 9-3
Value Analysis by a Purchaser of an Electrical Pump

and/or services to a buyer, which chooses the best offer. In **negotiation,** a buyer uses bargaining ability and order size to get sellers' best possible prices. Bidding and negotiation most frequently apply to complex, custom-made goods and services.

Differences from Final Consumers Due to the Nature of the Market

Organizational consumers **derive demand** *from their own customers. With the* **accelerator principle**, *final consumer demand impacts on many organizational consumers.*

Derived demand occurs for organizational consumers because the quantity of the items they purchase is often based on the anticipated level of demand by their subsequent customers for specific goods and services. For example, the demand for the precision rivets used in cruise ships is derived from the demand for new cruise ships, which ultimately is derived from the demand for cruises. Firms know that unless demand is generated at the end-user level, distribution pipelines become clogged and resellers will not buy fresh goods and services. Organizational consumers' price sensitivity depends on end-user demand. If end users are willing to pay higher prices, organizational consumers will not object to increases. However, if end-user demand is low, organizational consumers will reduce purchases, even if prices to them are lowered. Figure 9-5 illustrates derived demand for major household appliances.

Organizational consumers' demand tends to be more volatile than that of final consumers. A small change in the final demand for highly processed goods and services can yield a large change in organizational consumers' demand. This is due to the **accelerator**

	Superior	Average	Inferior
• Speed of normal delivery	------	------	------
• Speed of rush delivery	------	------	------
• Distinctiveness of merchandise	------	------	------
• Availability of styles and colors in all sizes	------	------	------
• Handling of defective merchandise	------	------	------
• Per cent of merchandise defective	------	------	------
• Ability for organizational consumer to make a profit when reselling merchandise	------	------	------
• Purchase terms	------	------	------

FIGURE 9-4
Vendor Analysis of a Sweater Supplier by a Purchaser

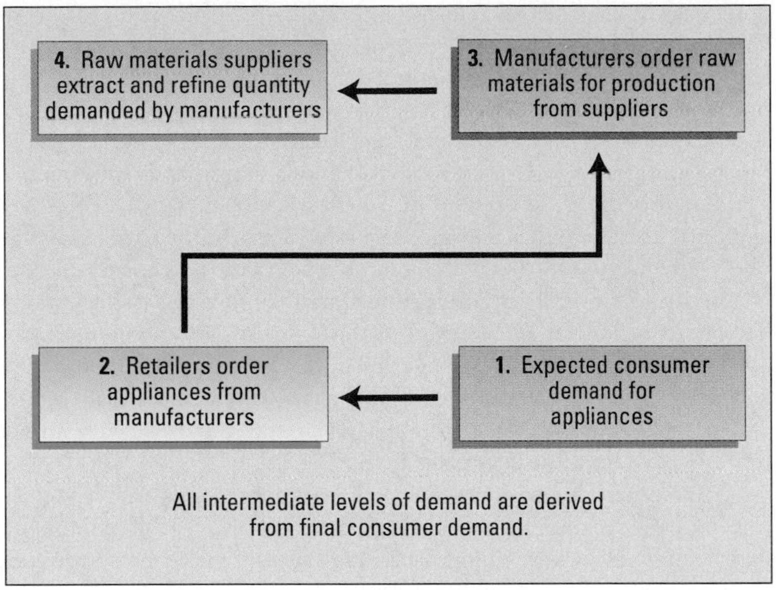

FIGURE 9-5
Derived Demand for Major Appliances

principle, whereby final consumer demand affects many layers of organizational consumers. For example, a drop in auto demand by final consumers reduces dealer demand for cars, auto maker demand for steel, and steel maker demand for iron ore. In addition, capital purchases by organizational consumers are highly influenced by the economy.

Organizational consumers are fewer in number than final consumers. In the United States, there are about 400,000 manufacturing establishments, 500,000 wholesaling establishments (including manufacturer-owned facilities), and 2.5 million retailing establishments, as compared with nearly 100 million final consumer households. In some industries, large organizational consumers dominate, and their size and importance give them bargaining power in dealing with sellers. Over the last several years, Xerox has gone from dealing with 5,000 suppliers to 500, Motorola from 10,000 to 3,000, Ford from 10,000 to 2,300, and Texas Instruments from 22,000 to 14,000. And AlliedSignal has gone from buying valves, pipes, and fittings from more than 400 suppliers to just one. This practice has severely affected those dropped, causing some to go out of business and others to invest considerable amounts to upgrade their facilities and products. Furthermore, the suppliers that are kept are expected to meet the highest levels of quality and customer service—while holding prices down.[9]

Organizational consumers tend to be large and geographically concentrated.

Organizational consumers tend to be geographically concentrated. For instance, eight states (California, New York, Texas, Illinois, Pennsylvania, Ohio, Michigan, and Florida) contain about half of the nation's manufacturing plants. Some industries (such as steel, petroleum, rubber, auto, and tobacco) are even more geographically concentrated.

Because of their size and the types of purchases, many organizational consumers use buying specialists. These people often have technical backgrounds and are trained in supplier analysis and negotiating. Their full-time jobs are to purchase goods and services and analyze purchases. Expertise is high.

Inasmuch as many organizational consumers are large and geographically concentrated, purchase complex and custom-made goods and services, and use buying specialists, distribution channels tend to be shorter than those for final consumers. For example, a laser-printer maker would deal directly with a firm buying 100 printers; a salesperson would call on its purchasing agent. A company marketing printers to final consumers would distribute them via retail stores and expect final consumers to visit those stores.

Systems selling *offers single-source accountability.*

Organizational consumers may require special relationships. They may expect to be consulted while new products are developed; want extra customer services, such as ex-

[9]John R. Emshwiller, "Suppliers Struggle to Improve Quality as Big Firms Slash Their Vendor Rolls," *Wall Street Journal* (August 16, 1991), pp. B1–B2; Kathleen Kerwin and Bill Vlasic, "A Shrinking Supply of Suppliers," *Business Week* (January 8, 1996), p. 83; and Tully, "Purchasing's New Muscle," p. 79.

tended warranties, liberal returns, and free credit; and want close communications with vendors. Systems selling and reciprocity are two specific tactics used in industrial marketing. In **systems selling,** a combination of goods and services is provided to a buyer by one vendor. This gives a buyer one firm with which to negotiate and an assurance of consistency among various parts and components. For example, Hewlett-Packard uses systems selling for its laser printers, personal computers, and servicing.

In **reciprocity,** *suppliers purchase as well as sell.*

Reciprocity is a procedure by which organizational consumers select suppliers that agree to purchase goods and services, as well as sell them. In the United States, the Justice Department and the FTC monitor reciprocity because of its potential lessening of competition. However, in international marketing efforts, sellers may sometimes have to enter into reciprocal agreements (in this case, known as countertrade). For instance, in 1973, because of currency restrictions in the then Soviet Union, PepsiCo began trading soft-drink syrup concentrate for Stolichnaya vodka. Since then, it has exchanged syrup concentrate for more than a million cases of vodka and two Russian-built ships. Its countertrade in today's Russia remains high.[10]

Last, organizational consumers may produce goods and services themselves if they find purchase terms, the way they are treated, or available choices unacceptable. They may sometimes suggest to suppliers that they will make their own goods or perform services so as to improve bargaining positions.

An International Perspective

Foreign organizational consumers must be carefully studied.

As with final consumers, many dissimilarities exist among organizational consumers around the world, and sellers must understand and respond to them. In this section, these topics are discussed: attitudes toward foreign firms as suppliers, the effects of culture on negotiating styles and decision making, the impact of a nation's stage of economic development, the need for an adaptation strategy, and the opportunities available due to new technology.

Firms doing business in foreign markets need to know how organizational consumers in those markets perceive the goods and services of firms from different countries. The attitudes of purchasing agents in foreign nations to U.S. products are often quite positive with regard to high-technology items, professional services, and industrial machinery. Likewise, many U.S. firms believe the product quality and/or prices for some foreign goods and services are better than those of American suppliers. That is why Ortho Biotech, a Johnson & Johnson subsidiary, buys water-purification equipment from Finland and Limited Inc. buys clothing from Hong Kong, Taiwan, and other countries.

Nations' cultures have a large impact on the way their organizational consumers negotiate and reach decisions. Here is an illustration:

> The Chinese believe that one should build the relationship and, if successful, transactions will follow. Westerners build transactions and, if they are successful, a relationship will follow. This difference underlies many negotiating failures.
>
> In China, negotiating responses may be riddled with contradictions. Westerners will see illogical behavior, evasion, deviousness perhaps, where none may be intended. Disentangling these communications supplies much of the challenge that is China. The deadline-driven, transcontinental executive may find it hard to slow down to the pace required to share "a loaf of bread, a jug of wine, and Tao," but marketing in China requires the patient building of relationships. Not that China is slow. The pace can simultaneously be fast and slow. Those involved in negotiations know how long they can drag when the Chinese side is consulting internally or has other reasons for delay, and yet how swiftly they move on other occasions.[11]

The stage of economic development in foreign countries affects the types of goods and services purchased by organizational consumers there. Many less-developed and developing nations do not yet have the infrastructure (electricity, roads, transportation systems, skilled workers) to properly use state-of-the-art machinery and equipment. In addi-

[10]Nathaniel Gilbert, "The Case for Countertrade," *Across the Board* (May 1992), p. 44. See also Peter W. Liesch, "Government-Mandated Countertrade in Australia," *Industrial Marketing Management*, Vol. 23 (October 1994), pp. 299–305.

[11]Tim Ambler, "Reflections in China: Re-Orienting Images of Marketing," *Marketing Management* (Summer 1995), pp. 24, 25–26.

International Marketing in *Action*

Does Country of Origin Affect Industrial Buyers?

In the past, most country-of-origin studies looked at the impact of where a product was made on industrial buyers' quality perceptions. But a more recent study assessed country-of-origin effects by distinguishing between where a good was designed and where it was assembled. That study investigated the perceptions of members of the Canadian Association of Purchasing Managers.

The study suggests that, in general, products designed and assembled in industrialized counties have higher evaluations than those designed and assembled in developing and less-developed nations. Among seven industrialized nations, Japan, Germany, the United States, and Canada rank highest as countries of origin for design and assembly. France, Italy, and Belgium have lower ratings on these two criteria. South Korea, a rapidly industrializing nation, rates almost as highly as France and Italy as a country of assembly and slightly higher than Belgium.

Country of design is a more important cue to purchasing managers than country of assembly for all three product categories evaluated: computer systems, fax machines, and ballpoint pens. It appears that purchasing managers perceive a large difference in design and assembly capabilities based on a country's stage of economic development. And this perceived difference is greater in design than assembly capabilities.

Although brand name has a significant impact in terms of perceived quality and perceived value for both computer systems and fax machines, it has much less impact than both country-of-origin cues. Brand name has no impact on the evaluation of ballpoint pens. In summary, according to this study, brand name plays a limited role as a predictor of quality or purchase value.

As a consultant to a South Korean-based maker of electronic components, how would you incorporate the results of this study into your recommended marketing plan?

Source: Based on material in Sadrudin A. Ahmed, Alain d'Astous, and Mostafa El Adraoui, "Country-of-Origin Effects on Purchasing Managers' Product Perceptions," *Industrial Marketing Management,* Vol. 23 (October 1994), pp. 323–332.

tion, such machinery and equipment may be too expensive for customers in those markets to afford. On the other hand, there is substantial long-term growth potential in those nations due to the scarcity of industrial goods and services there. Firms marketing to less-developed and developing nations need to be patient and flexible in dealing with organizational consumers.

When marketing goods and services to organizational consumers in foreign markets, firms have to consider how much to adapt their strategies to address the unique characteristics and needs of those customers. Because large organizational consumers can account for a significant part of any firm's overall revenues, selling firms are often quite willing to be responsive to customers' desires—by employing personnel who fluently speak the language of the foreign markets, utilizing the most appropriate negotiating styles, and adapting product features and customer service as requested. In general, it is more likely that selling firms will engage in meaningful adaptation of their marketing efforts if a potential customer order is big, the good or service being marketed is complex, and the business cultures and stage of economic development in their domestic and foreign markets are dissimilar.

ORDINARY PHONE LINES CARRY VOICES.
OURS CARRY PEOPLE.
Let GTE Video Conferencing take you to your next out-of-town meeting electronically. By combining live video, text and graphics, you can still be there even if you can't go there. It's amazing what we can do together.™
GTE

FIGURE 9-6
All the World's a Stage—For Business
With such advanced technology as GTE Video Conferencing, the global opportunities for doing business are almost limitless.
Reprinted by permission.

With the new technology now available, there are more opportunities to market to international organizational consumers than ever before. For example, the Internet, E-mail, fax machines, satellite TV, and video conferencing all facilitate buyer-seller communications—and tear down the barriers caused by weak transportation infrastructures, differences in time zones, and the inability of both parties to see each other in regular phone calls. See Figure 9-6.

Types of Organizational Consumers

In devising a marketing plan aimed at organizational consumers, it is necessary to research their attributes: areas of specialization, size and resources, location, and goods and services purchased. As shown in Figure 9-7, organizational consumers can be placed into five broad major categories: manufacturers, wholesalers, retailers, government, and nonprofit.

The **Standard Industrial Classification (SIC)** *provides information on U.S. and foreign organizational consumers.*

The **Standard Industrial Classification (SIC)** may be used to derive information about most organizational consumers. The SIC, compiled by the U.S. Office of Management and Budget, assigns organizations to 11 industrial classifications: agricultural, forestry, and fishing; mining; construction; manufacturing; transportation, communication, electric, gas, and sanitary services; wholesale trade; retail trade; finance, insurance, and real estate; services; public administration; and nonclassifiable establishments. Within these groups, there are over 1,000 more specific industry classifications, such as computer programming services, ice cream makers, and frozen dessert firms.

U.S. data by SIC code are available from various government and commercial publications. The *U.S. Industrial Outlook* (last published in 1994), the *Annual Survey of Manufac-*

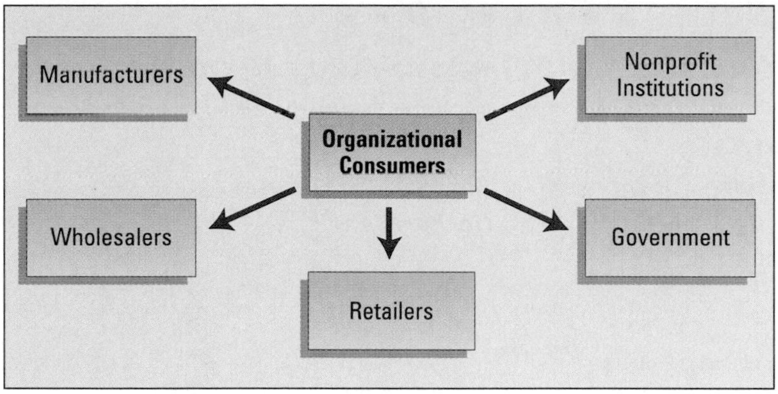

FIGURE 9-7
Types of Organizational Consumers

tures, and the monthly and annual *Current Business Reports* are U.S. Department of Commerce documents with data on hundreds of industries. *Moody's Industry Review* (weekly), *Standard & Poor's Industry Surveys* (weekly), *Predicast's Forecasts* (quarterly), and *Dun's Census of American Business* (annually) also provide data by SIC code and/or geographic area. Data on government institutions are available on a local, state, and federal level from the *Census of Governments*.

Although the SIC code is a U.S. classification system, considerable data on industrial activity and companies in other nations are available in the context of the SIC code. The U.S. Department of Commerce's *Global Trade and Economic Outlook* has information on a number of international industries. Dun & Bradstreet's yearly *Principal International Businesses* directory lists 50,000 firms in 140 different nations. *Predicasts F&S Index Europe* annually cites articles with industry and company data by nation for Western and Eastern Europe, and Russia and the former Soviet republics. *Dun's Latin America's Top* 25,000 annually provides data on companies in 35 countries.

With **end-use analysis**, *a seller studies sales made in different industries.*

End-use analysis is one way in which SIC data can be employed. With it, a seller determines the proportion of sales made to organizational consumers in different industries. Table 9-2 shows end-use analysis for a glue manufacturer (in this example, the seller). First, the firm ascertains the current relative importance of various categories of its customers—9-2(A). It then applies end-use analysis to make an overall sales forecast by estimating the expected growth of each customer category in its geographic area—9-2(B).

Next, several characteristics of manufacturers, wholesalers, retailers, government, and nonprofit organizations as consumers are described.

Manufacturers as Consumers

Manufacturers *make items for resale to others.*

Manufacturers produce products for resale to other consumers. The *Standard Industrial Classification Manual* lists 20 major two-digit industry groups in manufacturing. Each may be divided into three-digit groups and then into four-digit subgroupings. Thus, SIC 23 includes apparel and other textile products; 233, women's and misses' outerwear; and 2331, women's and misses' blouses and shirts. Table 9-3 shows the 20 two-digit groups.

In the United States, one-third of manufacturers have 20 or more workers. The annual costs of their materials are $1.7 trillion. Their expenditures for plant and equipment (from trucks to generator sets) are hundreds of billions of dollars each year. They annually use trillions of BTUs of energy. Annual net sales (including shipments between firms in the same industry category) exceed $3.7 trillion, with the largest 500 industrial firms accounting for 60 per cent of the total.

By knowing where different industries are located, a firm can concentrate efforts and not worry about covering geographically dispersed markets. Because manufacturers' purchasing decisions tend to be made centrally at headquarters or at divisional offices, the seller must identify the location of the proper decision makers.

As consumers, manufacturers buy a variety of goods and services, including land, capital equipment, machinery, raw materials, component parts, trade publications, accounting services, supplies, insurance, advertising, and delivery services. For example, Boeing

Table 9-2

End-Use Analysis for a Regional Glue Manufacturer

(A) SIMPLE END-USE ANALYSIS

SIC Code	*Industry Classification of Customers*	*Current Total Sales (in Per Cent)*[a]
24	Lumber and wood products	25
25	Furniture and fixtures	20
27	Printing and publishing	17
30	Rubber and miscellaneous plastic products	15
31	Leather and leather products	10
39	Miscellaneous manufacturing	13
	Total	100

(B) APPLYING END-USE ANALYSIS TO SALES FORECASTING

SIC Code	*Industry Classification of Customers*	*Per Cent of Current Total Sales*	*Estimated Annual Percentage Growth Rate of Industry*[b]	*Overall Sales Growth Percentage for Glue Manufacturer*[c]
24	Lumber and wood products	25	+1.8	+0.45
25	Furniture and fixtures	20	+3.2	+0.64
27	Printing and publishing	17	+1.9	+0.32
30	Rubber and miscellaneous plastic products	15	+3.0	+0.45
31	Leather and leather products	10	−2.0	−0.20
39	Miscellaneous manufacturing	13	+2.0	+0.26
	Total estimated sales increase			+1.92

[a]Firm examines its sales receipts and categorizes them by SIC group.

[b]Firm estimates growth rate of each category of customer (in its geographic area) on the basis of trade association and government data.

[c]Firm multiplies per cent of current sales in each SIC group by expected growth rate in each industry to derive its own expected sales for the coming year. It expects sales to increase by 1.92 per cent during the next year.

has long- and short-term contracts with suppliers that total $56 billion; and it buys equipment, raw materials, component parts, finished materials, and services from thousands of different subcontractors and other businesses.[12]

Wholesalers as Consumers

Wholesalers *buy or handle merchandise and its resale to nonfinal consumers.*

Wholesalers buy or handle merchandise and its subsequent resale to organizational users, retailers, and other wholesalers. They do not sell significant volume to final users but are involved when services are marketed to organizational consumers. Table 9-4 lists the major industry groups in wholesaling, as well as related transportation industries and business services. Chapter 16 has a broad discussion of wholesaling.

U.S. wholesalers are most prominent in California, New York, Texas, Florida, Illinois, Pennsylvania, Ohio, and New Jersey. Annual wholesaling and related sales (excluding man-

[12]Jeff Cole, "Boeing's Bid to Avoid Swings in Business Falls Short of Hopes," *Wall Street Journal* (February 16, 1993), pp. A1, A12.

Table 9-3
U.S. Manufacturing Industries

SIC CODE	INDUSTRY NAME	SIC CODE	INDUSTRY NAME
20	Food and kindred products	30	Rubber and miscellaneous plastics
21	Tobacco products	31	Leather and leather products
22	Textile mill products	32	Stone, clay, and glass products
23	Apparel and other textile products	33	Primary metal industries
24	Lumber and wood products	34	Fabricated metal products
25	Furniture and fixtures	35	Industrial machinery and equipment
26	Paper and allied products	36	Electronic and electrical equipment
27	Printing and publishing	37	Transportation equipment
28	Chemicals and allied products	38	Instruments and related products
29	Petroleum and coal products	39	Miscellaneous manufacturing

Source: Standard Industrial Classification Manual 1987 (Washington, D.C.: Office of Management and Budget, 1987).

ufacturer wholesaling) exceed $2.2 trillion. Sales are largest for groceries and related products; motor vehicles and related parts and supplies; machinery, equipment, and supplies; professional and commercial equipment and supplies; electrical goods; petroleum products; and farm-product raw materials.

Table 9-4
U.S. Wholesaling and Related Industries

SIC CODE	INDUSTRY NAME	SIC CODE	INDUSTRY NAME
40	Railroad transportation	51	Nondurables
42	Trucking and warehousing		Paper and paper products
44	Water transportation		Drugs, proprietaries, sundries
45	Air transportation		Apparel, piece goods, notions
46	Pipelines, except natural gas		Groceries and related products
47	Transportation service		Farm-product raw materials
50	Durables		Chemicals and allied products
	Motor vehicles, parts, supplies		Petroleum, petroleum products
	Furniture and home furnishings		Beer, wine, liquor
	Lumber and construction materials		Miscellaneous nondurable goods
	Professional, commercial equip.	73	Business services
	Metals and minerals, except petroleum		Advertising
	Electrical goods		Credit reporting, collection
	Hardware, plumbing, heating equipment		Mailing, reproduction, steno
	Machinery, equipment, and supplies		Services to buildings
			Miscellaneous equipment rental
			Personnel supply services
			Computer and related services
			Miscellaneous business services

Source: Standard Industrial Classification Manual 1987 (Washington, D.C.: Office of Management and Budget, 1987).

As consumers, wholesalers buy or handle many goods and services, including warehouse facilities, trucks, finished products, insurance, refrigeration and other equipment, trade publications, accounting services, supplies, and spare parts. A major task in dealing with wholesalers is getting them to carry the selling firm's product line for further resale, thereby placing items into the distribution system. For new sellers or those with new products, gaining cooperation may be difficult. Even well-established manufacturers may have problems with their wholesalers because of the competitive nature of the marketplace, wholesalers' perceptions that they are not being serviced properly, or wholesalers' lack of faith in the manufacturers' products.

Retailers as Consumers

Retailers *sell to the final consumer.*

Retailers buy or handle goods and services for sale (resale) to the final (ultimate) consumer. They usually obtain goods and services from both manufacturers and wholesalers. Table 9-5 lists the major industry groups in retailing, as well as several related service businesses that cater to final consumers. Chapter 17 has a broad discussion of retailing.

Annual U.S. retail sales (both store and nonstore) for firms in SIC codes 52 to 59 exceed $2.5 trillion. Chains operate a quarter of all such stores, accounting for over half of total retail sales. About 500,000 retail stores are operated by franchisees. A large amount of retailing involves auto dealers, food stores, general merchandise stores, eating and drinking places, gas stations, furniture and home furnishings stores, and apparel stores.

As consumers, retailers buy or handle a variety of goods and services, including store locations, facilities, interior design, advertising, resale items, insurance, and trucks. Unlike wholesalers, they are usually concerned about both product resale and the composition of their physical facilities (stores). This is because final consumers usually shop at stores, whereas wholesalers frequently call on customers. Thus, retailers often buy fixtures, displays, and services to decorate and redecorate stores.

Getting retailers to stock new items or continue handling current ones can be difficult because store and catalog space is limited and retailers have their own goals. Many retail chains have evolved into large and powerful customers, not just "shelf stockers."

Table 9-5

U.S. Retailing and Retailed Industries

SIC CODE	INDUSTRY NAME	SIC CODE	INDUSTRY NAME
52	Building materials, garden supplies	70	Hotels and other lodging places
53	General merchandise stores	72	Personal services
54	Food stores	75	Auto repair, services, parking
55	Auto dealers and service stations	76	Miscellaneous repair services
56	Apparel and accessory stores	78	Motion pictures
57	Furniture, home furnishings stores	79	Amusement and recreation, except movies
58	Eating and drinking places		
59	Miscellaneous retail		
60	Depository institutions		
61	Nondepository institutions		
62	Security and commodity brokers		
63	Insurance carriers		
64	Insurance agents and brokers		
65	Real estate		

Source: Standard Industrial Classification Manual 1987 (Washington, D.C.: Office of Management and Budget, 1987).

Table 9-6

U.S. Federal, State, and Local Government (Public Administration)

SIC CODE	INDUSTRY NAME
91	Executive, legislative, and general government, except finance
92	Justice, public order, and safety
93	Public finance, taxation, and monetary policy
94	Administration of human resource programs
95	Administration of environmental quality and housing programs
96	Administration of economic programs
97	National security and international affairs

Source: Standard Industrial Classification Manual 1987 (Washington, D.C.: Office of Management and Budget, 1987).

Some are so powerful that they may even charge *slotting fees* just to carry manufacturers' products in their stores. For instance,

> Nowadays, most supermarket-savvy manufacturers chalk them up as a cost of doing business. But, if fees for shelf-space had been around in the 1980s, products like granola, herbal tea, and yogurt might never have made it into stores and kitchens. These so-called slotting fees (charged by retailers for providing shelf-space) can often exceed $40,000 per retail chain per item, which adds up to millions of dollars for national distribution.[13]

Retailers (and wholesalers) sometimes insist that suppliers make items under the retailers' (wholesalers') names. For private-label manufacturers, the continued orders of these customers are essential. If a large retailer (wholesaler) stops doing business with a private-label manufacturer, then that firm has to establish its own identity with consumers—and it may even go out of business due to the lack of marketplace recognition.

Government as Consumer

Government *purchases and uses a variety of routine and complex products.*

Government consumes goods and services in performing its duties and responsibilities. Federal (1), state (50), and local (87,000) units together account for the greatest volume of purchases of any consumer group in the United States—with all branches spending $1.2 trillion (excluding employee wages) on goods and services each year. The federal government accounts for 40 per cent of that spending. The biggest budget shares (including employee wages) go for operations, capital outlays, military services, postal services, education, highways, public welfare, health care, police, fire protection, sanitation, and natural resources. Data on state and local expenditures by item are annually reported in *Government Finances* and *City Government Finances*. Table 9-6 shows the major SIC codes for government.

Governmental consumers buy a wide range of goods and services, including food, military equipment, office buildings, subway cars, office supplies, clothing, and vehicles. Some purchases involve standard products offered to traditional consumers; others, such as highways, are specially made for a government customer. Although many bigger firms (such as Boeing and Lockheed) derive major percentages of their sales from government contracts, smaller sellers now account for several billion dollars in federal purchases. In fact, 25 per cent of federal agency purchase contracts are with small firms.[14]

[13]Bernice Kanner, "Shelf Control," *New York* (January 22, 1990), p. 22. See also Mary B. W. Tabor, "In Bookstore Chains, Display Space Is for Sale," *New York Times* (January 15, 1996), pp. A1, D8.

[14]Stephanie N. Mehta, "Small Firms Are Getting More Government Contracts," *Wall Street Journal* (April 27, 1995), p. B2.

Some firms are unaccustomed to the bureaucracy, barriers, political sensitivities, and financial constraints of selling to government consumers. To aid them, the federal Government Service Administration's Business Service Centers (BSCs) issue directories, reference data, and technical reports on contracts and contracting procedures, bidding documents, and specifications. Besides BSCs, there are procurement-assistance centers (run by universities or state agencies) spread among more than 40 different states.

Nonprofit Institutions as Consumers

Nonprofit institutions *function in the public interest.*

Nonprofit institutions act in the public interest or to foster a cause and do not seek financial profits. Public hospitals, museums, most universities, political parties, civic organizations, and parks are nonprofit institutions. They buy goods and services in order to run their organizations and also buy items for resale to generate additional revenues to offset costs.

There are many national and international nonprofit institutions, such as the American Cancer Society, the Democratic and Republican parties, the Boy and Girl Scouts, Chambers of Commerce, and the Red Cross. Hospitals, museums, and universities, due to fixed sites, tend to be local nonprofit institutions.

There are no separate SIC codes for nonprofit- versus profit-oriented firms. However, firms in these SIC categories are often nonprofit in nature: 80 (Health services); 82 (Educational services); 83 (Social services); 84 (Museums, art galleries, botanical and zoological gardens); and 86 (Membership organizations).

Key Factors in Organizational Consumer Behavior

Organizational consumer behavior depends on buying objectives, buying structure, and purchase constraints.

Buying Objectives

Organizational buying objectives relate to availability, reliability, consistency, delivery, price, and service.

Organizational consumers have several distinct goals in purchasing goods and services. Generally, these organizational buying objectives are important: availability of items, reliability of sellers, consistency of quality, delivery, price, and customer service. See Figure 9-8.

Availability means a buyer can obtain items when needed. An organizational consumer's production or resales may be inhibited if products are unavailable at the proper times. Seller reliability is based on its fairness in allotting items in high demand, nonadversarial relationships, honesty in reporting bills and shipping orders, and reputation. Consistency of quality refers to buyers' interest in purchasing items of appropriate quality on a regular basis. For example, drill bits should have the same degree of hardness each time they are bought. Delivery goals include minimizing the length of time from placing an order to the receipt of items, minimizing the order size required by the supplier, having

FIGURE 9-8
Goals of Organizational Consumers

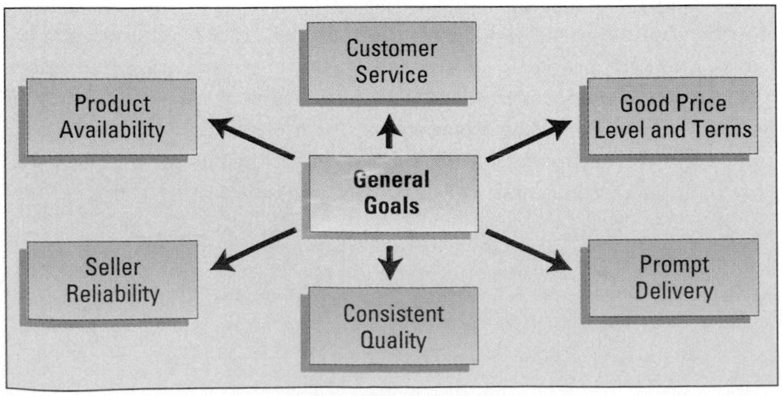

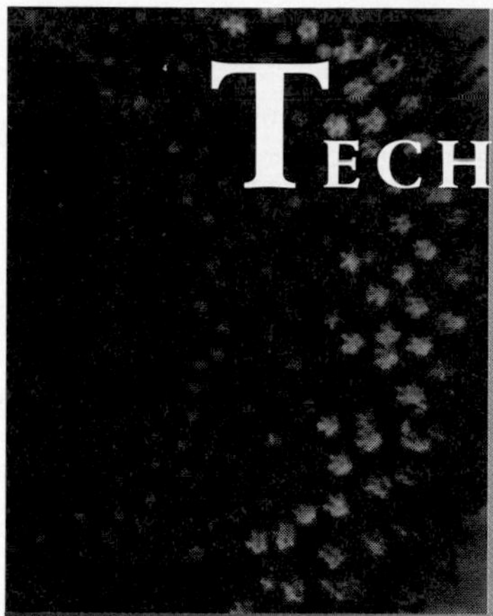

TECHNOLOGY & MARKETING

How Is GE Plastics Marketing Through the Internet?

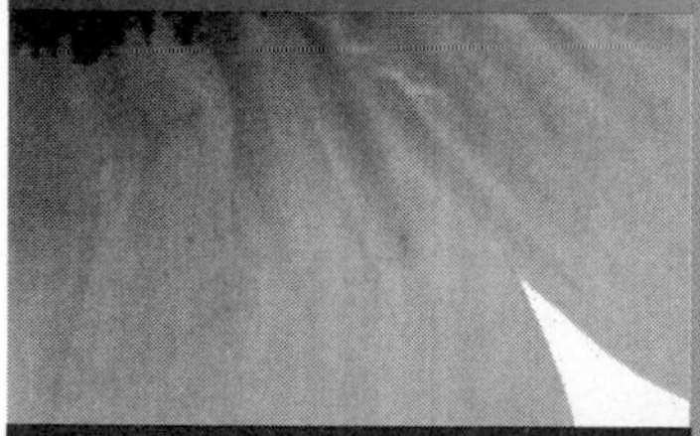

One of the key uses of the Internet involves customer support. Because a firm can use the Internet to communicate with thousands (millions) of current and potential users of a product with a small customer support staff, it is a very cost-effective way of disseminating product information to customers.

GE Plastics is ideally suited to the Internet since almost all of its customers have PCs with modems. Although the firm will not divulge the costs in setting up its Internet site, one analyst estimated them at up to $150,000.

GE Plastics was the first *Fortune 500* firm to use the Internet in a major marketing effort. Its Internet site provides its engineer, designer, and scientist customers with instant access to crucial product and technical information, design guidelines, and graphics. Customers can also communicate and exchange ideas within five newsgroup forums (automotive, building and construction, computers, design, and plastics) that collect information from a variety of sources. This information is updated on a weekly basis.

GE Plastics went online in October 1994. It first had to digitize roughly 1,500 pages of technical literature. An additional challenge it faced was that Internet standards at the time did not allow for a variety of page layouts; it had to find other ways of making documents look good. GE Plastics also hired a software developer to simplify the commands relating to accessing, searching, retrieving, and saving data on the Internet. According to the software developer, "the steps GE took to ease user access to the Internet are highly unusual. Most of the businesses establishing a presence on the Internet leave it up to users to find their own way."

As the customer support manager for GE Plastics, develop specific criteria to evaluate the success of the firm's Internet site.

Source: Based on material in Thayer C. Taylor, "Marketing: The New Generation," *Sales & Marketing Management* (February 1995), pp. 43–44.

the seller responsible for shipments, minimizing costs, and adhering to an agreed-on schedule. Price considerations involve purchase prices and the flexibility of payment terms. Customer service entails the seller's satisfying special requests, having a staff ready to field questions, promptly addressing problems, and having an ongoing dialogue with customers.

Industrial marketers must recognize that price is only one of several considerations for organizational consumers; and it may be lower in importance than availability, quality, service, and other factors:

> Cutting purchasing costs has surprisingly little to do with browbeating suppliers. Purchasers at companies like AT&T and Chrysler aim to reduce the total cost—not just the price—of each part or service they buy. They form enduring partnerships with suppliers that let them chip away at key costs year after year. Purchasing companies are also packing once fragmented purchases of goods and services into companywide contracts for each.[15]

With regard to more specific goals, manufacturers are concerned about quality standards for raw materials, component parts, and equipment. Some like dealing with many suppliers to protect against shortages, foster price and service competition, and be exposed to new products. Others have been reducing the number of suppliers from which they buy, to foster better relationships, cut ordering inefficiencies, and have more clout with each supplier.[16]

[15] Tully, "Purchasing's New Muscle," p. 76.

[16] See Cathy Owens Swift, "Preferences for Single Sourcing and Supplier Selection Criteria," *Journal of Business Research*, Vol. 32 (February 1995), pp. 105–111.

Saleability and exclusivity are keys for wholesalers and retailers.

Wholesalers and retailers consider further saleability (their customers' demand) to be the highest priority. If possible, they seek buying arrangements whereby the number of distribution intermediaries that can carry goods and services in a geographic area is limited. They also seek manufacturers' advertising, transportation, and warehousing support.

Government consumers frequently set exact specifications for some products they buy; as large-volume buyers, they can secure them. Government consumers may sometimes consider the economic conditions in the geographic areas of potential sellers. Contracts may be awarded to the firms with the higher unemployment in their surrounding communities.

Nonprofit consumers stress price, availability, and reliability. They may seek special terms in recognition of their nonprofit status.

Buying Structure

The organization's buying structure depends on its attributes.

The buying structure of an organization refers to the formality and specialization used in the purchase process. It depends on the organization's size, resources, diversity, and format. The structure is apt to be formal (separate department) for a large, corporate, resourceful, diversified, and departmentalized organization. It will be less formal for a small, independently owned, financially limited, focused, and general organization.

Large manufacturers normally have specialized purchasing agents who work with the firms' engineers or production department. Large wholesalers tend to have a single purchasing department or a general manager in charge of operations. Large retailers tend to be quite specialized and have buyers for each narrow product category. Small manufacturers, wholesalers, and retailers often have their buying functions completed by the owner-operator.

Each government unit (federal, state, and local) and division typically has a purchasing department. The General Services Administration (GSA) is the federal office responsible for centralized procurement and coordination of purchases. Each federal unit may buy via the GSA's Bureau of Federal Supply or directly from suppliers; in either case, it must adhere to printed purchasing rules. In a nonprofit organization, there is usually one purchasing department or a member of the operations staff performs buying functions.

Constraints on Purchases

Derived demand is the key constraint on organizational purchases.

For manufacturers, wholesalers, and retailers, derived demand is the major constraint on purchase behavior. Without the demand of consumers, production halts and sales drop as the backward chain of demand comes into play (final consumers → retailers → wholesalers → manufacturers).

Manufacturers also are constrained by the availability of raw materials and their ability to pay for large-ticket items. Wholesalers and retailers are limited by the finances available to make purchases, as well as by the level of risk they are willing to take. In this case, risk refers to the probability that wholesalers or retailers will be able to sell the products they buy in a reasonable time and at a satisfactory profit. Products like fashion clothing have higher risks than such staple items as vitamins and disposable diapers.

Government consumers are constrained by the budgeting process. Approval for categories of purchases must normally be secured well in advance, and deviations must be explained. Budgets must be certified by legislative bodies. For many nonprofit consumers, cash flow (the timing of the money they have coming in versus the money they spend) is the major concern.

The Organizational Consumer's Decision Process

An **organizational consumer's decision process** *is like that of a final consumer.*

Organizational consumers use a decision-making procedure in much the same way as final consumers. Figure 9-9 shows the **organizational consumer's decision process,** with its four components: expectations, buying process, conflict resolution, and situational factors.[17]

[17]The material in this section is drawn from Jagdish N. Sheth, "A Model of Industrial Buyer Behavior," *Journal of Marketing*, Vol. 37 (October 1973), pp. 50–56.

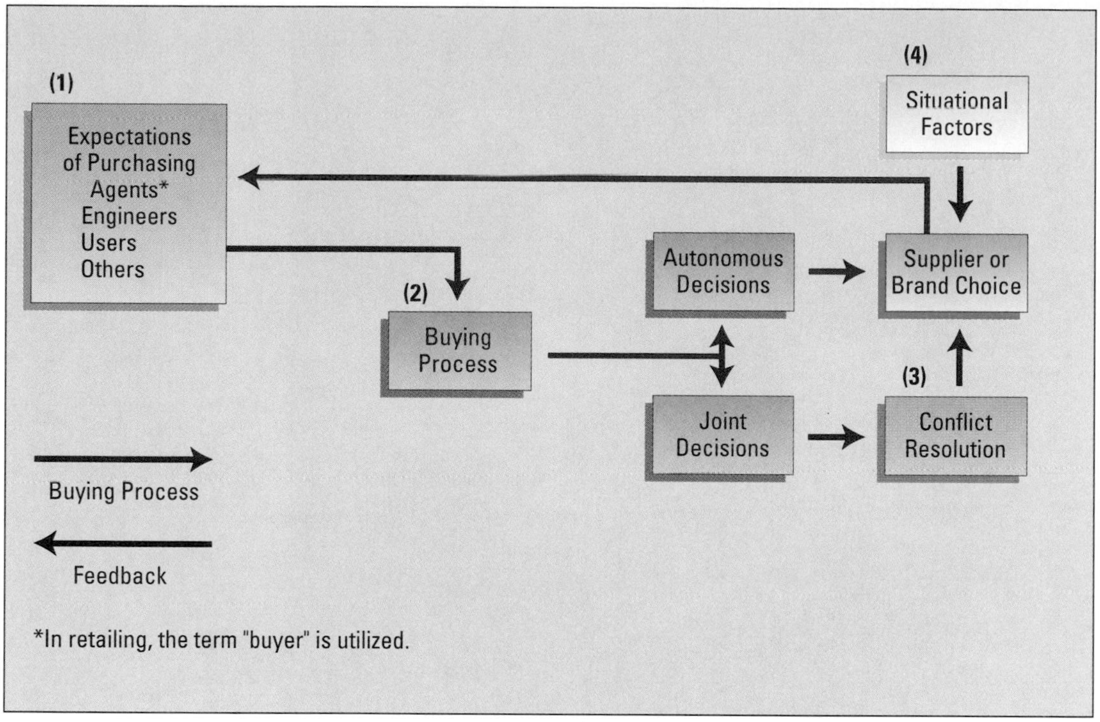

FIGURE 9-9
The Organizational Consumer's Decision Process

Source: Adapted from Jagdish N. Sheth, "A Model of Industrial Buyer Behavior," *Journal of Marketing*, Vol. 37 (October 1973), p. 51. *Reprinted by permission of the American Marketing Association.*

Expectations

Expectations are based on buyers' backgrounds, information, perceptions, and experience.

Purchasing agents, engineers, and users bring a set of organizational consumer expectations to any buying situation: "These expectations refer to the perceived potential of alternative suppliers and brands to satisfy a number of explicit and implicit objectives."[18]

For purchases to be made, buyers must have positive expectations on such supplier attributes as product availability and quality, vendor reliability, delivery time, price, and customer service. Expectations are based on the backgrounds of those participating in the buying process, the information received, perceptions, and satisfaction with past purchases. See Figure 9 10.

Buying Process

During the buying process, a decision as to whether to consider making a purchase is initiated, information gathered, alternative suppliers evaluated, and conflicts among the different representatives of the buyer resolved. The process itself is similar to the final consumer buying process in Figure 8-7.

Autonomous or joint decision making is based on product and company buying factors.

The buying process may involve autonomous (independent) or joint decisions based on product-specific and company-specific factors. *Product-specific buying factors* include perceived risk, purchase frequency, and time pressure. Autonomous decisions occur mostly with low perceived risk, routine products, and high time pressure. Joint ones are more apt to occur with high perceived risk, seldom-bought products, and low time pressure. *Company-specific buying factors* are an organization's basic orientation, size, and level of decision-making centralization. Autonomous decisions most often occur with a high technology or production orientation, small organization, and high centralization. Joint ones are more likely with a low technology or production orientation, large organization, and little centralization in decision making.

[18]Ibid., p. 52.

FIGURE 9-10
Meeting Organizational Consumers' Expectations
Even when marketing such products as corporate jets, consumer expectations must be anticipated. In this case, the long-range flying capacity of Falcon jets is emphasized—which means that nonstop travel over longer distances is now possible.
Reprinted by permission of Dassault Falcon Jet Corporation.

As noted earlier in the chapter, competitive bidding is often used with organizational consumers: potential sellers specify in writing all terms and conditions of a purchase in addition to product attributes; the buyer then selects the best bid. With *open bidding*, proposals can be seen by competing sellers. With *closed bidding*, contract terms are kept secret and sellers are asked to make their best presentation in their first bids. Bidding is used in government purchases to avoid charges of bias or unfair negotiations, and bids for government purchases tend to be closed.

Conflict Resolution

Problem solving, persuasion, bargaining, and politicking lead to **conflict resolution.**

Joint decision making may lead to conflicts due to the diverse backgrounds and perspectives of purchasing agents, engineers, and users. **Conflict resolution** is then needed to make a decision. Four methods of resolution are possible: problem solving, persuasion, bargaining, and politicking.

Problem solving occurs when members of a purchasing team decide to acquire further information before making a decision. This is the best procedure. Persuasion takes place when each member of a team presents his or her reasons why a particular supplier or brand should be selected. In theory, the most logical presentation should be chosen. However, the most dynamic (or powerful) person may persuade others to follow his or her lead.

Under bargaining, team members agree to support each other in different situations, with less attention paid to the merits of a purchase. One member may select the supplier of the current item; in return, another member would choose a vendor the next time. The last, and least desired, method of conflict resolution is politicking. With it, team members try to persuade outside parties and superiors to back their positions, and seek to win at power plays.

Situational Factors

Situational factors *affect organizational consumer decisions.*

A number of **situational factors** can interrupt the decision process and the actual selection of a supplier or brand. These include "temporary economic conditions such as price controls, recession, or foreign trade; internal strikes, walkouts, machine breakdowns, and other production-related events; organizational changes such as merger or acquisition; and ad hoc changes in the marketplace, such as promotional efforts, new-product introduction, price changes, and so on, in the supplier industries."[19]

Purchase and Feedback

After the decision process is completed and situational factors are taken into account, a purchase is made (or the process terminated) and a product is used or experienced. The level of satisfaction with a purchase is then fed back to a purchasing agent or team, and the data are stored for future use.

To maintain customer satisfaction and ensure continued purchases, regular service and follow-up calls by sellers are essential. As one study concluded: "Industrial salespeople today are generally younger, better educated, and more professional in their handling of business activities than in the past. That higher level of education is something that both purchasers and sales professionals benefit from. Both sides appear to be more sensitive to the other's responsibilities. Among purchasers and suppliers interested in developing partnerships, it's not unusual to see sales professionals attending purchasing courses, purchasing agents attending sales courses, and even purchasers and suppliers attending seminars together.[20]

Types of Purchases

Organizational buyers use a **new-task process** *for unique items,* **modified rebuys** *for infrequent purchases, and* **straight rebuys** *for regular purchases.*

A **new-task purchase process** is needed for expensive products an organizational consumer has not bought before. A lot of decision making is undertaken, and perceived risk is high. This is similar to extended decision making for a final consumer. A **modified-rebuy purchase process** is employed for medium-priced products an organizational consumer has bought infrequently before. Moderate decision making is needed. This is similar to limited decision making for a final consumer. A **straight-rebuy purchase process** is used for inexpensive items bought regularly. Reordering, not decision making, is applied because perceived risk is very low. This is like a routine purchase for a final consumer.

Research on the Organizational Consumer's Decision Process

Throughout the world, the organizational consumer's decision process has been heavily researched in recent years. Here are a sampling of the findings:

- There are significant differences in the way that decisions are made by Russian purchasing managers who are 40 years of age or less and those who are older than 40 years of age. The younger managers see entrepreneurs, flexibility, and autonomy rising; their older counterparts do not.[21]
- Nigerian purchasers of capital equipment rely mostly on salesperson visits and manufacturers' catalogs for information; joint decision making is used during all stages of the decision process; and dissatisfaction with existing suppliers is a key reason a detailed decision process is triggered.[22]

[19]Ibid., p. 56.

[20]Derrick C. Schnebelt, "Turning the Tables," *Sales & Marketing Management* (January 1993), p. 23.

[21]John F. Veiga and John N. Yanouzas, "Emerging Cultural Values Among Russian Managers: What Will Tomorrow Bring?" *Business Horizons*, Vol. 38 (July–August 1995), pp. 20–27.

[22]E. D. Bamgboye, "Equipment Buying in Nigeria," *Industrial Marketing Management*, Vol. 21 (August 1992), pp. 181–185.

Ethics IN TODAY'S SOCIETY

Is Environmental Impact an Issue for Purchasing Agents?

How important is social responsibility—a concern for the environmental impact associated with an industrial good or service—to purchasing managers? According to one study, organizations can be placed into four categories:

- Type I (Founder's Ideals)—Social responsibility is an extension of the founder's ideals and values. A social mission for such firms is clearly articulated. This mission often acts as a second "bottom line" by which the firm would be evaluated. For example, "What we're trying to do is to suspend the standard rules in purchasing, which are to get the job done as quickly as possible and as cheaply as possible."
- Type II (Symbolism)—Socially responsible buying is indirectly tied to company success. Firms in this group want to discourage further government regulation. For example, "Now that we buy socially responsible products, people perceive us as green. This is important in getting the company name to where we want it to be."
- Type III (Opportune)—Socially responsible purchasing is seen as a way to lower costs or to increase sales. In one such firm, the purchase of a socially responsible product reduced costs by 70 per cent. Thus, "We do not buy socially irresponsible products, but it isn't as you say for a moral reason. It's for hassle avoidance more than anything else."
- Type IV (Restraint)—There is no deliberate plan as to socially responsible purchasing. And there are negligible "bottom-line" benefits to buying socially responsible products. For example, "If a supplier that we've worked with for 20 years before all the environmental concerns came up didn't share our views, it was hard. I feel much more like an extension of the supplier."

As a product manager for recycled paper, how would you use the preceding typology in marketing to book publishers?

Source: Based on material in Minette E. Drumwight, "Socially Responsible Organizational Buying: Environmental Concern as a Noneconomic Buying Criterion," *Journal of Marketing,* Vol. 58 (July 1994) , pp. 1–9.

- Some Eastern European purchasing agents, due to their lack of experience in a free-market economy, are having a tough time adjusting to situations in which they have more autonomy and a greater voice in decisions.[23]
- High-tech U.S. purchasing agents are apt to stick with existing suppliers if they feel there would be switching costs and compatibility issues with any changes to new vendors. "Out" vendors have the best opportunity to woo these purchasing agents when technological advances are rapid and decisions are important (causing the agents to be more open in vendor analysis).[24]

[23]Johan Roos, Ellen Veie, and Lawrence S. Welch, "A Case Study of Equipment Purchasing in Czechoslovakia," *Industrial Marketing Management*, Vol. 21 (August 1992), pp. 257–263; and Dale A. Lunsford and Bradley C. Fussell, "Marketing Business Services in Central Europe," *Journal of Services Marketing*, Vol. 7 (Number 1, 1993), pp. 13–21.

[24]Jan B. Heide and Allen M. Weiss, "Vendor Consideration and Switching Behavior for Buyers in High-Technology Markets," *Journal of Marketing*, Vol. 59 (July 1995), pp. 30–43.

Marketing Implications

There are many similarities, as well as differences, between organizational and final consumers.

Although organizational and final consumers have substantial differences (as mentioned earlier), they also have similarities. Both can be described demographically; statistical and descriptive data can be gathered and analyzed. Both have different categories of buyers, each with separate needs and requirements. Both can be defined by using social and psychological factors, like operating style, buying structure, purchase use, expectations, perceived risk, and conflict resolution. Both use a decision process, employ joint decision making, and face various kinds of purchase situations.

Industrial marketers must develop plans that reflect the similarities, as well as the differences, between organizational and final consumers. In their roles as sellers, manufacturers and wholesalers may also need two marketing plans—one for intermediate buyers and another for final consumers.

Finally, it must be recognized that purchasing agents or buyers have personal goals, as well as organizational goals. They seek status, approval, promotions, bonuses, and other rewards. And as noted in Figure 9-9, they bring distinct expectations to each buying situation, just as final consumers do.

Industrial marketing strategies should be insightful.

One leading consultant offers these suggestions for industrial marketers:

- *Understand how your customers run their business.*
- *Show how your good or service fits into your customer's business.*
- *Make sure the benefits you sell stay current.*
- *Know how customers buy and fit your selling to their buying process.*
- *When selling, reach everyone on the customer's side involved in the buying decision.*
- *Communicate to each decider the message that will address his or her chief concerns.*
- *Be the person or firm with whom your customers prefer to have a relationship.*
- *Be sure everything you do is consistent with your chosen level of quality, service, price, and performance.*
- *Understand your competitors' strengths and weaknesses.*
- *Strive to dominate your niche.*
- *Train your people in each aspect of your business and that of your customers.*
- *Have a distribution system that meets your needs and those of your customers.*
- *Seek new markets and new applications for your existing products.*
- *Enhance your products with customer service.*
- *Have your goals clearly in mind.*[25]

MARKETING IN A CHANGING WORLD

The Quest for Purchasing Partnerships[26]

In an era when so many purchasing companies are cutting down on the number of suppliers from which they will buy, industrial marketers must be sure they have a strong appreciation of what makes good "purchasing partnerships"—and they must do so from the buyer's point of view.

Purchasing partnerships are "informal or formal agreements between sellers and buyers, in which buyers receive quality products per customer requirements and sellers become primary suppliers. Through such arrangements, partners are able to plan requirements on a mutually beneficial time schedule with mutually satisfactory pricing."

[25]F. Michael Hruby, "17 Tips (Not Just) for Industrial Marketers," *Sales & Marketing Management* (May 1990), pp. 68–76.

[26]The material in this section is based on Eugene H. Fram, "Purchasing Partnerships: The Buyer's View," *Marketing Management* (Summer 1995), pp. 49–55.

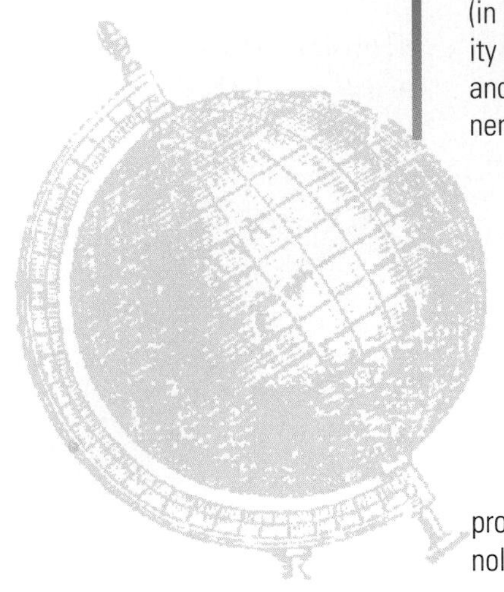

According to a recent study, organizational consumers want to achieve these specific benefits (in the order listed) from purchasing partnerships: better communication, better prices, better quality products, better delivery schedules, development of trust with suppliers, and better forecasting and planning. With regard to communication, organizational consumers expect that purchasing partnerships will result in "more attention" and vendors who "know our business."

Here's what two study participants remarked:

> In business, a relationship is worth a great deal. It is invaluable because the companies can grow together, share information for good planning, and stabilize the pricing environment. We then enter a trust relationship.
>
> Suppliers with ongoing partnerships feel more secure about future business. Consequently, they don't build in contingency costs, and this reduces the cost of our materials. A good working relationship allows for better parts design, standardization, and packaging.

To measure their suppliers' performance, organizational consumers review the quality of the products; on-time delivery; competitive pricing; personnel responsiveness; how well needs, technology, and design are understood; and the ability to resolve problems.

SUMMARY

1. *To introduce the concept of industrial marketing* When firms market goods and services to manufacturers, wholesalers, retailers, and government and other nonprofit institutions, industrial marketing is used.

2. *To differentiate between organizational consumers and final consumers and look at organizational consumers from an international perspective* Organizational consumers buy goods and services for further production, use in operations, or resale to others; they buy installations, raw materials, and semifinished materials. They often buy on the basis of specifications, use joint decision making, apply formal value and vendor analysis, lease equipment, and use bidding and negotiation. Their demand is generally derived from that of their consumers and can be cyclical. They are fewer in number and more geographically concentrated. They may employ buying specialists, expect sellers to visit them, require special relationships, and make goods and undertake services rather than buy them.

There are distinctions among organizational consumers around the globe.

3. *To describe the different types of organizational consumers and their buying objectives, buying structure, and purchase constraints* Organizational consumers may be classified by area of specialization, size and resources, location, and goods and services purchased. The major types of organizational consumers are manufacturers, wholesalers, retailers, government, and nonprofit. The SIC system provides much information on organizational consumers in the United States and the rest of the world.

These consumers have general buying goals, such as product availability, seller reliability, consistent quality, prompt delivery, good prices, and superior customer service. They also have more specific goals, depending on the type of firm involved. An organization's buying structure refers to its level of formality and specialization in the purchase process. Derived demand, availability, further saleability, and resources are the leading purchase constraints.

4. *To explain the organizational consumer's decision process* It includes buyer expectations, the buying process, conflict resolution, and situational factors. Of prime importance is whether an organization uses joint decision making and, if so, how. Some form of bidding may be employed with organizational consumers (most often with government).

If conflicts arise in joint decisions, problem solving, persuasion, bargaining, or politicking is used to arrive at a resolution. Situational factors can intervene between decision making and a purchase. Such factors include strikes, economic conditions, and organizational changes.

New task, modified rebuy, and straight rebuy are the different purchase situations facing organizational consumers.

Research has been done on how organizational consumers in different countries use the decision process.

5. *To consider the marketing implications of appealing to organizational consumers* Organizational consumers and final consumers have many similarities and differences. Industrial marketers must understand them and adapt marketing plans accordingly. Dual marketing campaigns may be necessary for manufacturers and wholesalers that sell to intermediate buyers and have their products resold to final consumers.

Purchasing agents and buyers have personal goals, such as status, promotions, and bonuses; these may have a large impact on decision making.

Industrial marketers can do many things to enhance their chances for success. A number of them are outlined here.

KEY TERMS

industrial marketing (p. 234)
multiple-buying responsibility (p. 236)
value analysis (p. 237)
vendor analysis (p. 237)
competitive bidding (p. 237)
negotiation (p. 238)
derived demand (p. 238)
accelerator principle (pp. 238–239)
systems selling (p. 240)
reciprocity (p. 240)
Standard Industrial Classification (SIC) (p. 242)
end-use analysis (p. 243)
manufacturers (p. 243)
wholesalers (p. 244)
retailers (p. 246)
government (p. 247)
nonprofit institutions (p. 248)
organizational consumer's decision process (p. 250)
conflict resolution (p. 252)
situational factors (p. 253)
new-task purchase process (p. 253)
modified-rebuy purchase process (p. 253)
straight-rebuy purchase process (p. 253)

Review Questions

1. Describe five of the most important differences between organizational and final consumers.
2. Distinguish between vendor analysis and value analysis.
3. What is the relationship between derived demand and the accelerator principle?
4. How is the Standard Industrial Classification a useful marketing tool?
5. What are the most important general organizational consumer-buying objectives?
6. For manufacturers, wholesalers, and retailers, what is the major constraint on their purchase behavior? Why?
7. On what basis are organizational consumer expectations formed?
8. How do product-specific and company-specific buying factors affect the use of autonomous or joint decision making?
9. Which is the worst form of conflict resolution? The best? Explain your answers.
10. Cite several suggestions that industrial marketers should keep in mind when developing and enacting their strategies.

Discussion Questions

1. As a university's purchasing agent, what criteria would you use for competitive bidding in the purchase of new dormitory furniture?
2. As a chemical manufacturer's liaison to China, how would you handle the cultural relationships that would be necessary to win over prospective Chinese business clients?
3. A packaging firm knows its current sales are allocated as follows: 15 per cent to pet food manufacturers (SIC code 2047), 20 per cent to chewing gum manufacturers (SIC code 2067), 30 per cent to soft drink manufacturers (SIC code 2086), 25 per cent to coffee manufacturers (SIC code 2095), and 10 per cent to snack food manufacturers (SIC code 2096). The firm expects next year's industry sales growth in these categories to rise as follows: pet food, 5 per cent; chewing gum, 2 per cent; soft drinks, 3 per cent; coffee, 0 per cent; and snack foods, 5 per cent. According to end-use analysis, by how much should the packaging firm's sales increase next year? Explain your answer.
4. Describe a floral arranger's decision process with regard to what transportation firm to use to ship its products to retailers. Does this process entail a new task, modified rebuy, or straight rebuy? Explain your answer.
5. "It must be understood that organizational purchasing agents or buyers have personal, as well as company goals." Comment on this statement.

CASE 1

Parker Hannifin: The Role of Relationship Marketing[*]

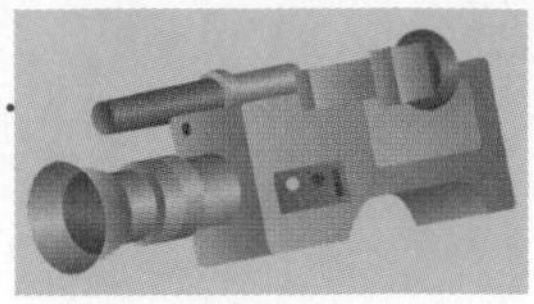

Parker Hannifin (PH) makes a line of motion control products (based on hydraulic, pneumatic, and electromechanical applications) so broad that some analysts refer to it as a "mutual fund of motion control businesses." PH's sales are divided equally between original equipment manufacturers (OEMs) and maintenance, repair, and overhaul (MRO) customers. A large portion of PH's customers are in the tractor, automobile, and jet engine business. In 1994, its sales were $3.2 billion (up 25 per cent from 1993). Net income for 1994 increased to $218 million from $48 million in 1993.

Times were not always so rosy for PH. During the period prior to Duane Collins' becoming chief executive officer (in mid-1993), PH lost much of its business to small competitors. Since PH engineers typically spent little time with clients, many of the firm's smaller competitors were able to attract PH clients by offering them slightly lower prices.

One of the first things that Duane Collins did upon becoming CEO was to invite representatives of each major customer to the firm's headquarters. According to Collins, "We didn't like what we heard. We had increased our productivity by reducing the setup times of our equipment and had increased throughput. But the customer hadn't felt it. If these things aren't being felt by customers, what good are they?"

Collins quickly embraced many of the principles of relationship marketing. These include the importance of customer service, open communication with accounts, and customer retention being viewed to be as important as attracting new customers. Let's look at some of PH's relationship marketing activities.

PH engineers now work closely with customers to design products that are trouble-free. By being aware of PH's engineering sophistication, in many cases, customers delegate product design responsibilities to PH. So, PH engineers can often be found in these customers' plants. This type of close cooperation between PH and its customers highlights the firm's superior technology. And by working closely with a customer, PH engineers are able to better determine the customer's needs and more quickly solve problems.

For example, PH engineers have worked with Oshkosh Truck Corporation (a maker of garbage trucks) to design a new hydraulic system. The system uses PH fittings, tubing, and hose connectors—each of which has a three-year warranty against leakage. PH has the strongest warranty in the business. Similarly, PH's Parflex division and Caterpillar engineers jointly devised thermoplastic hose and fittings to improve the hydraulic system on Caterpillar equipment. As a result of this and other efforts, Caterpillar now ranks Parflex as the number one supplier on the basis of customer service and product quality.

Through other programs, PH uses relationship marketing principles to simplify ordering and customer service. Its Fluid Connections Group now delivers kits of products instead of individual components of merchandise (to facilitate ordering, delivery, and receiving). In addition, this division services key customers via in-plant customer service representatives. PH's motion and control group also reduces ordering chores by letting its customers use a computerized central-ordering system. This system enables a customer to receive a single invoice for multiple orders—reducing its ordering costs. Similar systems are not available from smaller competitors.

PH's concern for long-term customer needs can be seen in the awards given to the firm by customers such as Caterpillar (an earth-moving equipment manufacturer), Tennant (a floor-sweeping equipment manufacturer), Ford, and Toro. PH hopes this recognition will be reflected in its being named as sole supplier to many of these customers.

QUESTIONS

1. Is PH's sale of kits instead of individual components an example of systems selling? Explain your answer.
2. Present a vendor analysis checklist whereby a client could evaluate PH and its competitors.
3. What other relationship marketing principles could PH profitably adopt? Explain your answer.
4. Describe the characteristics of an organizational consumer such as Caterpillar from the perspective of its buying objectives, buying structure, and constraints on purchases.

VIDEO QUESTIONS ON PARKER HANNIFIN

1. Evaluate PH's three-legged strategy for achieving and maintaining growth.

2. Explain how PH can utilize its partnership strategy with its smaller customers.

[*]The data in this case are drawn from *Parker Hannifin Corporation 1995 Annual Report*; and Michael K. Ozanian, "17325 Euclid Avenue," *Financial World* (November 8, 1994), pp. 50–53.

CASE 2

Steel and Aluminum: The Battle for Auto Makers' Business†

There is a huge battle for market share in auto-manufacturing materials between aluminum and steel makers. The car industry is especially important for steel makers since this industry accounts for as much as one-third of total steel sales for some steel makers.

Steel proponents say that the use of steel results in a safer vehicle since steel (as opposed to aluminum) actually becomes stronger in a crash. Steel is also much less costly than aluminum. For example, a steel hood weighing 50 pounds costs $17.50 in material costs, while a comparable hood made of aluminum has a material cost of $35 (even though it weighs only 25 pounds). The steel manufacturers are also quick to cite the long-term experience that car makers have had with steel. Lastly, the labor costs in recycling steel are much lower than with aluminum since scrap steel can be collected with a heavy magnet. The primary benefit to the use of aluminum over steel is in terms of aluminum's weight and ease of forming shapes; aluminum can be extruded while steel must be stamped.

Aluminum has been making significant headway in the auto industry. Since 1980, the proportion of aluminum in an average car has gone from 3.5 per cent to 7 per cent. And in 1995, 15,000 Audi A-8 luxury cars (with aluminum car frames) were sold in Germany. This model was made via a partnership with the Aluminum Corporation of America (Alcoa). Honda also sells some aluminum-based cars.

In the near future, the use of aluminum could skyrocket. Ford and Chrysler have created prototype cars made from aluminum. And Ford executives predict that as of the year 2000 a leading auto maker will begin mass producing an aluminum-based luxury car. In an effort to further increase the inroads made by aluminum, Alcoa recently offered to invest $1 billion in a partnership with any auto maker willing to produce a high-volume aluminum car.

General Motors, Ford, and Chrysler have joined forces to form the Partnership for a New Generation of Vehicles. This group wants to build a fuel-efficient car (which gets up to 80 miles a gallon) that is priced at a comparable level to existing autos. In addition, the group wants to reduce vehicle weight as a means of increasing fuel efficiency. Currently, 55 per cent of the overall weight of the average car is comprised of steel.

The steel industry is not taking aluminum's initiatives lying down. Steel makers are well aware of their loss in market share in the beverage can market over the past 20 years—as aluminum rapidly replaced steel in containers—and this market is currently worth $5 billion per year.

According to a Chrysler purchasing executive, "Steel has changed more in the last five years than in the last 25 years. You can get more strength with lighter kinds of steel." Unlike the aluminum industry, where each company has developed its own production technologies, 31 steel makers from around the world are combining to finance new research. One goal is to make a lighter variation of steel that is still strong enough to be dent resistant.

Both the steel and aluminum industries are concerned about the increasing use of plastics and composites (such as mixtures of carbon fiber) that are being used by car makers. Plastics are currently not strong enough for car bodies and composites are very costly. But, due to engineering advances, it is expected that their use in cars will rise dramatically in the near future.

QUESTIONS

1. Use value analysis to compare aluminum and steel for use in car frames.
2. Describe the importance of derived demand in the sale of steel and aluminum to the auto industry.
3. What other organizational consumers—besides auto makers—should steel firms address? How?
4. What organizational buying objectives should steel makers concentrate on fulfilling? Why?

†The data in this case are drawn from Erle Norton and Gabriella Stern, "Steel and Aluminum Vie Over Every Ounce in a Car's Construction," *Wall Street Journal* (May 9, 1995), pp. A1, A14.

CHAPTER 10

Developing a Target Market Strategy

Chapter Objectives

1. To describe the process of planning a target market strategy
2. To examine alternative demand patterns and segmentation bases for both final and organizational consumers
3. To explain and contrast undifferentiated marketing (mass marketing), concentrated marketing, and differentiated marketing (multiple segmentation)
4. To show the importance of positioning in developing a marketing strategy
5. To discuss sales forecasting and its role in target marketing

"As the world becomes closer due to technological advances in transportation and telecommunications, and with multinational companies expanding worldwide, increasingly there is a great interest in whether individuals in different parts of the world are more alike than different," says Thomas A. W. Miller, senior vice-president of Roper Starch Worldwide.

Roper Starch Worldwide (a marketing research firm) recently conducted a series of studies on global trends. In all, it surveyed nearly 40,000 adults. According to this research, four major shopping styles of consumers are found throughout the world: deal makers, price seekers, brand loyalists, and luxury innovators. And the shopping styles of consumers are heavily influenced by where they live.

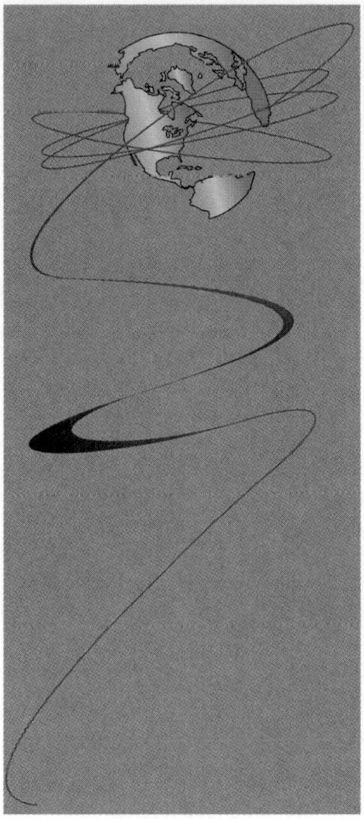

Reprinted by permission.

Let's look at these four consumer segments and their characteristics.

- Deal makers—They enjoy the buying process. This is an educated group, with a median age of 32 years and average affluence and employment. Deal makers make up 29 per cent of all consumers.
- Price seekers—They place major emphasis on the product. This group has the highest per cent of retirees, the lowest education level, and an average level of affluence. Price seekers constitute 27 per cent of all consumers.
- Brand loyalists—They agree that a brand gives good value for the money. This is the least affluent group and is mostly male. Brand loyalists have a median age of 36 and hold average education and employment. They make up 23 per cent of all consumers.
- Luxury innovators—They seek brands that are prestigious and new. This is the most affluent and educated group, with the highest proportion of executives and other professionals. Luxury innovators are mostly male and have a median age of 32. They constitute 21 per cent of all consumers.

The above segment percentages are global figures that vary greatly by country. In the United States, 37 per cent of consumers are deal makers, 36 per cent are price seekers, 17 per cent are luxury innovators, and 11 per cent are brand loyalists. In Mexico, 35 per cent of consumers are deal makers, 23 per cent are price seekers, 20 per cent are luxury innovators, and 19 per cent are brand loyalists. In Saudi Arabia, 40 per cent of consumers are deal makers, 34 per cent are luxury innovators, 15 per cent are brand loyalists, and 9 per cent are price seekers. In the Czech Republic, 27 per cent of consumers are price seekers, 26 per cent are luxury innovators, 24 per cent are brand loyalists, and 23 per cent are deal makers. (Please note that there are rounding errors.) As Thomas Miller notes,

> Price seekers exist more in competitive, developed markets, where shoppers generally cannot haggle or negotiate. Deal makers are more often in developing markets that have less brand competition and a tradition of open air markets, where the process is half the fun. America straddles the two styles because of our more heterogeneous culture and also because shoppers can bargain at many retail outlets and even large category-killer stores."[1]

In this chapter, we will examine each step involved in planning a target market strategy and the related topic of sales forecasting. Life-style segmentation is only one of the ways in which a company may appeal to a target market.

Overview

After gathering data on consumer traits, desires, and decision making; company and industry attributes; and environmental factors; a firm is ready to select the target market(s)

A ***market*** *is all possible consumers for a good or service. Through* ***market segmentation,*** *it can be subdivided.*

[1]Kelly Shermach, "Portrait of the World," *Marketing News* (August 28, 1995), pp. 20–21; and Leah Rickard, "Ex-Soviet States Lead World in Ad Cynicism," *Advertising Age* (June 5, 1995), p. 3.

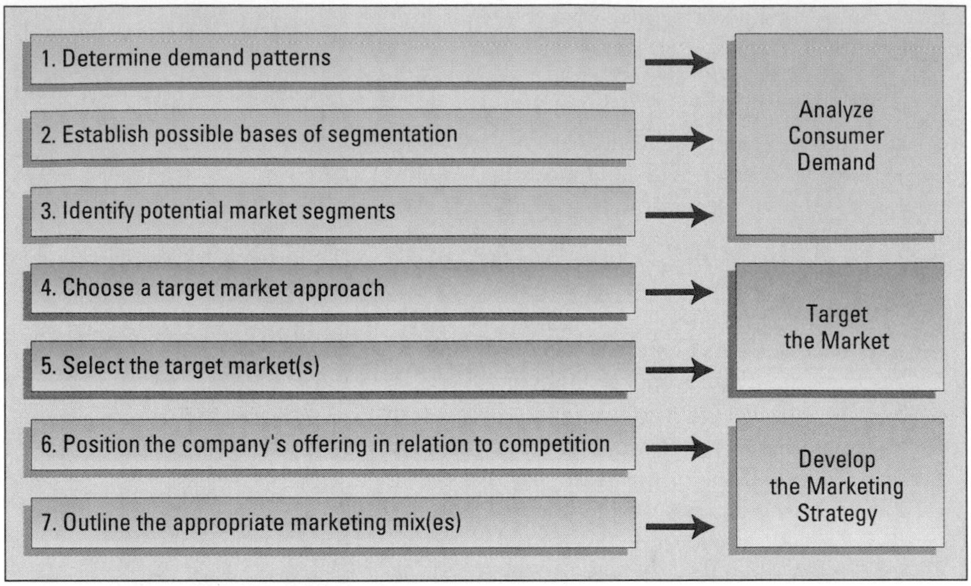

FIGURE 10-1
The Steps in Planning a Target Market Strategy

to which it will appeal and for which it will develop a suitable strategy. The total **market** for a particular good or service consists of all the people and/or organizations who desire (or potentially desire) that good or service, have sufficient resources to make purchases, and are willing and able to buy. Firms often use **market segmentation**—dividing the market into distinct subsets of customers that behave in the same way or have similar needs. Each subset could possibly be a target market.

In a **target market strategy,** *a firm first studies demand.*

Developing a **target market strategy** consists of three general phases: analyzing consumer demand, targeting the market, and developing the marketing strategy. This comprises the seven specific steps shown in Figure 10-1 and described in Chapter 10. First, a firm determines the demand patterns for a given good or service, establishes bases of segmentation, and identifies potential market segments. For example, do prospective consumers have similar or dissimilar needs and desires? What consumer characteristics, desires, and behavior types can be best used to describe market segments?

Targeting approaches are **undifferentiated, concentrated,** *and* **differentiated marketing**.

Second, a firm chooses the target market approach and selects its target market(s). It can use **undifferentiated marketing (mass marketing)**—whereby a company targets the whole market with a single basic marketing strategy intended to have mass appeal; **concentrated marketing**—whereby a company targets one well-defined market segment with one tailored marketing strategy; or **differentiated marketing (multiple segmentation)**—whereby a company targets two or more well-defined market segments with a marketing strategy tailored to each segment.[2]

The marketing strategy is then actually developed, with emphasis on **product differentiation**.

Third, a firm positions its offering relative to competitors and outlines the proper marketing mix(es). Of particular importance here is attaining **product differentiation,** whereby "a product offering is perceived by the consumer to differ from its competition on any physical or nonphysical product characteristic, including price." When differentiation is favorable, it yields a differential advantage. A firm may be able to achieve a key differential advantage by simply emphasizing how its offering satisfies existing consumer desires and needs better than competitors do. However, sometimes demand patterns may have to be modified for consumers to perceive a firm's product differentiation as worthwhile. Thus, Tylenol is promoted as an alternative to aspirin for persons who cannot take aspirin (appealing to existing consumer needs), whereas Dove is marketed as a nonsoap bar cleanser with moisturizing qualities (modifying consumer perceptions of soap's role). If targeted consumers do not believe that moisturizing is a meaningful product attribute, then they will probably not buy Dove—no matter how much better a job of moisturiz-

[2]Peter D. Bennett (Editor), *Dictionary of Marketing Terms*, Second Edition (Chicago: American Marketing Association, 1995), p. 166.

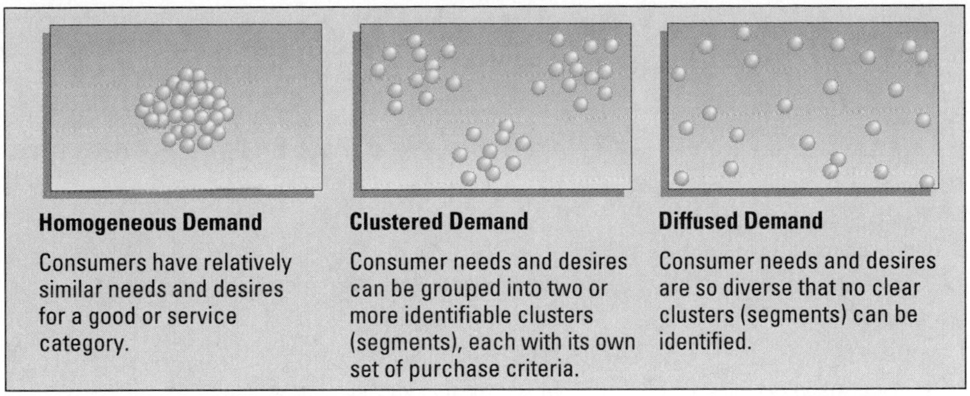

Homogeneous Demand
Consumers have relatively similar needs and desires for a good or service category.
Clustered Demand
Consumer needs and desires can be grouped into two or more identifiable clusters (segments), each with its own set of purchase criteria.
Diffused Demand
Consumer needs and desires are so diverse that no clear clusters (segments) can be identified.

FIGURE 10-2
Alternative Consumer Demand Patterns for A Good or Service Category

ing it does compared to competing soaps. Because Dove's annual U.S. sales are $250 million (and it is the industry leader), moisturizing is clearly a desirable attribute.[3]

In this chapter, the steps in a target market strategy are detailed—as they pertain to both final and organizational consumers. Sales forecasting and its role in developing a target market strategy are also examined.

Analyzing Consumer Demand

The initial phase in planning a target market strategy (analyzing consumer demand) consists of three steps: determining demand patterns, establishing possible bases of segmentation, and identifying potential market segments.

Determining Demand Patterns

Demand patterns *show if consumer desires are similar for a good or service. People may have* **homogeneous, clustered,** *or* **diffused demand**.

A firm must first determine the **demand patterns**—which indicate the uniformity or diversity of consumer needs and desires for particular categories of goods and services—it faces in the marketplace. A firm would face one of the three alternative demand patterns shown in Figure 10-2 and described here for each good or service category it markets.

With **homogeneous demand**, consumers have rather uniform needs and desires for a good or service category. A firm's marketing tasks are straightforward—to identify and satisfy the basic needs of consumers in a superior way. For instance, business customers in the express mail-delivery market are most interested in rapid, reliable delivery and reasonable prices. A firm such as UPS appeals to customers by convincing them it is better than competitors in these areas. As competition picks up, firms may try to modify consumer demand patterns so new-product features become desirable and homogeneous demand turns to clustered demand, with only one or a few firms marketing the new features.

With **clustered demand,** consumer needs and desires for a good or service category can be divided into two or more clusters (segments), each having distinct purchase criteria. A firm's marketing efforts must be geared toward identifying and satisfying the needs and desires of a particular cluster (or clusters) in a superior way. For example, in the auto market, people can be grouped by their interest in price, car size, performance, styling, handling, sportiness, and other factors. Thus, auto makers offer luxury cars, economy cars, full-sized family cars, high-performance vehicles, and sports cars—each appealing to a particular cluster of consumer needs and desires. Clustered demand is the most prevalent demand pattern.

With **diffused demand**, consumer needs and desires for a good or service category are so diverse that clear clusters (segments) cannot be identified. A firm's marketing efforts are complex because product features are harder to communicate and more product versions may be offered. For example, consumers have diverse preferences for lipstick colors; even the same person may desire several colors, to use on different occasions or to switch to avoid boredom. Thus, cosmetics firms offer an array of lipstick colors. It would

[3]Peter R. Dickson and James L. Ginter, "Market Segmentation, Product Differentiation, and Marketing Strategy," *Journal of Marketing*, Vol. 51 (April 1987), pp. 1–10; and "Superbrands '96: Category Charts," *Superbrands 1996: Brandweek's Marketers of the Year* (October 6, 1995), p. 129.

Table 10-1
Possible Bases of Segmentation

BASES	EXAMPLES OF POSSIBLE SEGMENTS
Geographic Demographics	
Population (people or organizations)	
Location	North, South, East, West; domestic, international
Size	Small, medium, large
Density	Urban, suburban, rural
Transportation network	Mass transit, vehicular, pedestrian
Climate	Warm, cold
Type of commerce	Tourist, local worker, resident; SIC codes
Retail establishments	Downtown shopping district, shopping mall
Media	Local, regional, national
Competition	Underdeveloped, saturated
Growth pattern	Stable, negative, positive
Legislation	Stringent, lax
Cost of living/operations	Low, moderate, high
Personal Demographics	
A. Final Consumers	
Age	Child, young adult, adult, older adult
Gender	Male, female
Education	Less than high school, high school, college
Mobility	Same residence for 2 years, moved in last 2 years
Income	Low, middle, high
Occupation	Blue-collar, white-collar, professional
Marital status	Single, married, divorced, widowed
Household size	1, 2, 3, 4, 5, 6, or more
Ethnicity or race	European, American; black, white

be nearly impossible for a firm to succeed with one color or a handful of colors. To make marketing strategies more efficient, firms generally try to modify diffused consumer demand so clusters of at least moderate size appear.

Firms today often try to perform a balancing act with regard to consumer demand patterns. Just as the world marketplace is now getting closer due to more open borders and enhanced communications, there is also more information available on the diversity of the marketplace through customer data bases, point-of-sale scanning in supermarkets, and other emerging data-collection techniques. On the one hand, some firms are looking for demand patterns that let them standardize (perhaps even globalize) their marketing mixes as much as possible—to maximize efficiency, generate a well-known image, and use mass media. On the other hand, some companies are searching for demand patterns that let them pinpoint more specific market segments—to better address the consumer needs in those segments.

Establishing Possible Bases of Segmentation

Next, a company studies possible bases for segmenting the market for each of its products or product lines. See Table 10-1. The firm must decide which of these segmentation bases are most relevant for its particular situation.

Table 10-1 (Cont.)

B. Organizational Consumers	
Industry designation	SIC codes; end-use analysis
Product use	Further production, use in operations, resale to others
Institutional designation	Manufacturer, wholesaler, retailer, government, nonprofit
Company size	Small, medium, large
Industry growth pattern	Slow, moderate, high
Company growth pattern	Slow, moderate, high
Age of company	New, 5 years old, 10 years old or more
Language used	English, French, Japanese
Consumer Life-Styles	
Social class (final consumers)	Lower-lower to upper-upper
Family life cycle (final consumers)	Bachelor to solitary survivor
Buying structure	Informal to formal, autonomous to joint
Usage rate	Light, medium, heavy
Usage experience	None, some, extensive
Brand loyalty	None, some, total
Personality	Introverted-extroverted, persuasible-nonpersuasible
Attitudes	Neutral, positive, negative
Class consciousness	Inner-directed, outer-directed
Motives	Benefit segmentation
Perceived risk	Low, moderate, high
Innovativeness	Innovator, laggard
Opinion leadership	None, some, a lot
Importance of purchase	Little, a great deal

Geographic Demographics **Geographic demographics** are basic identifiable characteristics of towns, cities, states, regions, and countries. A company may use one or a combination of the geographic demographics cited in Table 10-1 to describe its final or organizational consumers.

Geographic demographics *describe towns, cities, states, regions, and countries.*

A segmentation strategy could be geared to geographic differences. For example, it would be useful to know such facts as these about geographic areas: Japanese mail-order shoppers spend twice as much per order as their American counterparts. Per-capita chocolate consumption in Western Europe is two to four times that in the United States, and per-capita consumption of bottled water in Italy is seven times that in the United States. Germans want laundry detergents that are gentle on rivers, and will pay a premium for them; Greeks want small packages to keep down the cost per store visit. Less than 5 per cent of all the life insurance sold in the world is bought by people in Africa and Latin America. Canada and Mexico account for over one-half of steel-mill products exported by U.S. firms. Among U.S. urban areas, annual per-household retail sales are highest in Laredo, Texas, and lowest in New York City; per-household food store sales are 30 per cent higher in Denver than in Chicago; per-household clothing sales are one-third higher

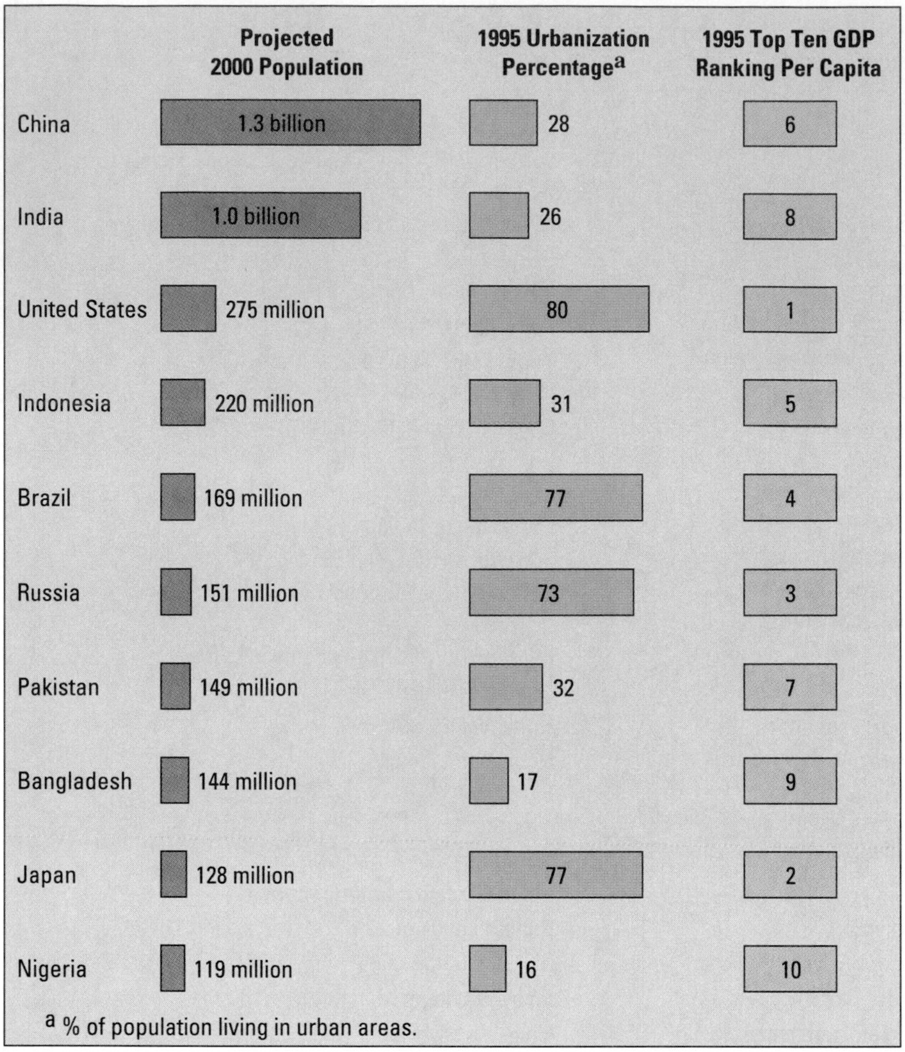

Projected 2000 Population
1995 Urbanization Percentage[a]
1995 Top Ten GDP Ranking Per Capita
China
1.3 billion
28
6
India
1.0 billion
26
8
United States
275 million
80
1
Indonesia
220 million
31
5
Brazil
169 million
77
4
Russia
151 million
73
3
Pakistan
149 million
32
7
Bangladesh
144 million
17
9
Japan
128 million
77
2
Nigeria
119 million
16
10
a % of population living in urban areas.

FIGURE 10-3
Comparing the Ten Most Populated Countries in the World
Source: Compiled by the authors from the U.S. Bureau of the Census International Data Base.

in San Jose, California, than the national average; per-household furniture and appliance sales are about the same in New Orleans and St. Louis; and per-household drugstore sales are 75 per cent higher in Miami than in Atlanta.[4]

Figure 10-3 indicates the population size, urbanization, and per capita GDP ranking of the ten most populated nations of the world. Figure 10-4 shows a demographic map of the United States.

Personal demographics *describe people and organizations. They should be used in studying final and organizational consumers.*

Personal Demographics **Personal demographics** are basic identifiable characteristics of individual final consumers and organizational consumers, and groups of final consumers and organizational consumers. They are often used as a segmentation base because groups of people or organizations with similar demographics may have similar needs and desires that are distinct from those with different backgrounds. Personal demographics may be viewed singly or in combinations.

Final Consumers As noted in Table 10-1, several personal demographics for final consumers may be used in planning a segmentation strategy.

Applications of personal demographic segmentation are plentiful, as these examples indicate: In Latin America, 14 per cent of all urban households are headed by an "emerg-

[4]Sheryl WuDunn, "Japanese Do Buy American: By Mail and a Lot Cheaper," *New York Times* (July 3, 1995), pp. 1, 43; "Who Has the Sweetest Tooth?" *Advertising Age* (July 17, 1995), p. I-3; "Data Watch," *Advertising Age* (February 15, 1993), p. I-22; E. S. Browning, "In Pursuit of the Elusive Euroconsumer," *Wall Street Journal* (April 23, 1992), p. B1; "U.S. Share of Worldwide Insurance Market in Decline," *National Underwriter* (October 5, 1992), pp. 41–43; Marcia Mogelonsky, "America's Hottest Markets," *American Demographics* (January 1996), pp. 20–31; and "1995 Survey of Buying Power," *Sales & Marketing Management* (1995), various pages.

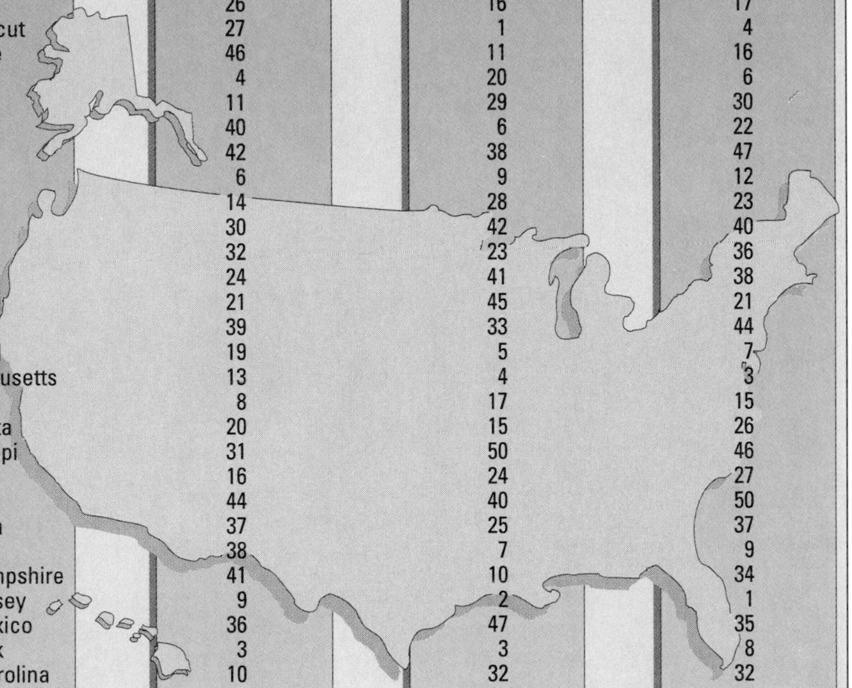

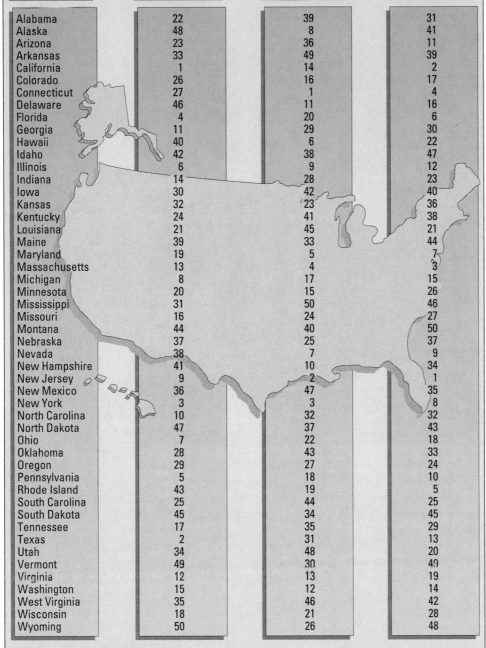

States	1995 Population Ranking	1995 Per Capita Income Ranking	1995 Urbanization Ranking[a]
Alabama	22	39	31
Alaska	48	8	41
Arizona	23	36	11
Arkansas	33	49	39
California	1	14	2
Colorado	26	16	17
Connecticut	27	1	4
Delaware	46	11	16
Florida	4	20	6
Georgia	11	29	30
Hawaii	40	6	22
Idaho	42	38	47
Illinois	6	9	12
Indiana	14	28	23
Iowa	30	42	40
Kansas	32	23	36
Kentucky	24	41	38
Louisiana	21	45	21
Maine	39	33	44
Maryland	19	5	7
Massachusetts	13	4	3
Michigan	8	17	15
Minnesota	20	15	26
Mississippi	31	50	46
Missouri	16	24	27
Montana	44	40	50
Nebraska	37	25	37
Nevada	38	7	9
New Hampshire	41	10	34
New Jersey	9	2	1
New Mexico	36	47	35
New York	3	3	8
North Carolina	10	32	32
North Dakota	47	37	43
Ohio	7	22	18
Oklahoma	28	43	33
Oregon	29	27	24
Pennsylvania	5	18	10
Rhode Island	43	19	5
South Carolina	25	44	25
South Dakota	45	34	45
Tennessee	17	35	29
Texas	2	31	13
Utah	34	48	20
Vermont	49	30	49
Virginia	12	13	19
Washington	15	12	14
West Virginia	35	46	42
Wisconsin	18	21	28
Wyoming	50	26	48

[a] % of population living in urban areas.

FIGURE 10-4
A Demographic Map of the United States

Sources: Compiled by the authors from Bureau of the Census and Bureau of Economic Analysis data.

ing professional elite," people with professional and executive professions. More than one-half of this group is college educated. The "emerging professional elite" represents a strong market for major appliances, credit card services, consumer electronics, and cars.[5] In the United States and other western nations, Clairol and many other companies are now placing greater emphasis on wooing consumers in the early stages of middle age. This group, which is quite large, is particularly interested in slowing the aging process. See Figure 10-5.

Procter & Gamble markets specially designed Luvs Deluxe Diapers for Boys and Luvs Deluxe Diapers for Girls. Whitman Chocolates and Godiva Chocolatier have separate

[5]Jeffery D. Zbar, "Gallup Offers New Take on Latin America," *Advertising Age* (November 13, 1995), p. 21.

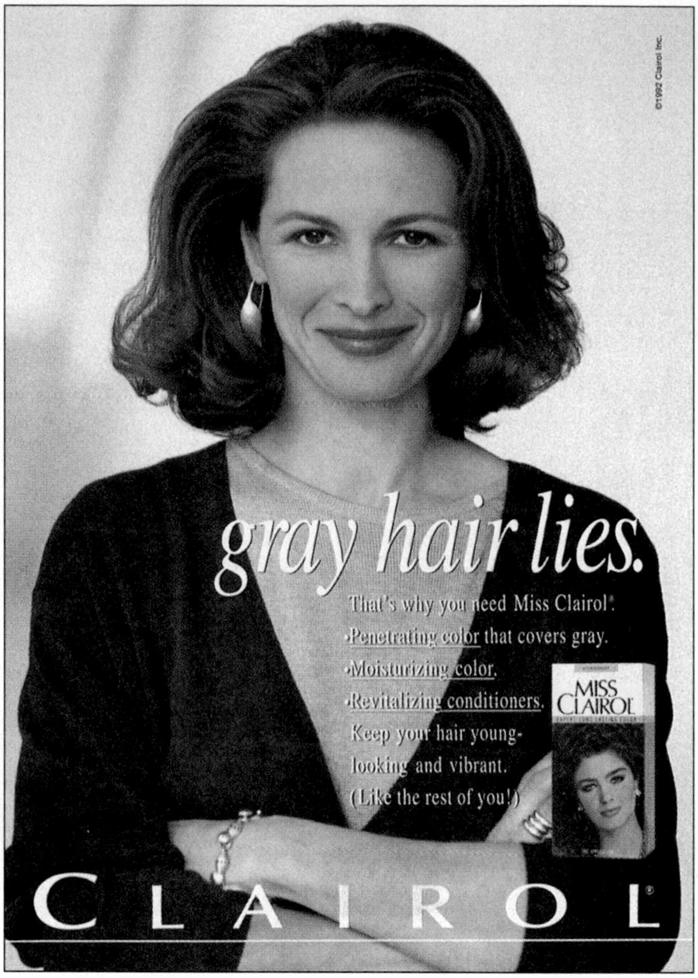

FIGURE 10-5
Wooing Consumers in Early Middle Age
Reprinted by permission.

Valentine's Day promotions aimed at men and women; in the past, all ads were oriented at gift-giving by men. Nike and Reebok are both devoting greater advertising to women's sports shoes and apparel. Why? Women annually spend over $6 billion on athletic shoes—more than men spend.[6]

At Dollar General, a discount "neighborhood" store chain, value-conscious consumers are attracted by low prices; many items are $10 or less. The firm locates mostly in smaller communities, sells many irregulars and factory overruns, and has few employees in each store. In contrast, American Express attracts upper-income consumers with its platinum card. These consumers pay an annual fee of a few hundred dollars and charge tens of thousands of dollars per year; in return, they get special services (such as a worldwide valet service to help them shop, plan trips, and so on) and a high credit line.

Kraft Foods has developed a new line of Valle Lindo cheese products targeted at U.S. Hispanics of Mexican descent. These products melt easily but retain a milky taste. The Spanish advertising asks: "Este queso es de Mexico?" ("Is this cheese from Mexico?") and answers: "No, es de Kraft. ("No, it's from Kraft"). And because the annual spending of African Americans is now $300 billion, specialized goods and services are emerging to satisfy them—including Maybelline's Shades of You cosmetics line, Coca-Cola's 16-ounce sodas, and Inter Image Video's entertainment and educational videos. Overall, it is estimated that marketers spend nearly $1 billion each year to target African Americans.[7]

[6]Maria Mallory, Dan McGraw, Jill Jordan Siedler, and David Fischer, "Women on a Fast Track," *U.S. News & World Report* (November 6, 1995), pp. 60–72; and Joseph Pereira, "Women Jump Ahead of Men in Purchases of Athletic Shoes," *Wall Street Journal* (May 26, 1995), pp. B1, B3.

[7]Yumiko Ono, "Kraft Hopes Hispanic Market Says Cheese," *Wall Street Journal* (December 13, 1995), p. B5; and Adrienne Ward Fawcett, "Marketing to African Americans," *Advertising Age* (July 17, 1995), pp. S-1–S-2.

TECHNOLOGY & MARKETING

How Can You "Net" College Students?

The Internet is a particularly effective medium for providing information and promotions targeting college students. Unlike other populations, a very large proportion of students are computer literate. And currently more than 35 per cent of full-time college students own PCs. At many colleges, such as the University of Wisconsin-Madison, students can access the Internet directly from their dormitory rooms simply by hooking up their PC to a special phone jack. According to a survey by Roper College Track, Internet use among college students doubled between 1994 and 1995 alone.

One important Internet site aimed at the college market is *Link* magazine's *Digital Campus* (http://www.linkmag.com). Introduced in fall 1995, *Digital Campus* already has a circulation of one million plus. *Digital Campus* shows a rendering of a college campus—complete with a library, a bookstore, a student union, and an athletic stadium. Each building in the *Digital Campus* represents an information and service site. For example, students who browse through the bookstore can view flight schedules for Northwest Airlines, apply for an AT&T Universal credit card, order Paco Rabanne men's fragrance, and request free samples of many products.

By clicking on the Specialized Bicycles' icon in the bookstore, students can enter a sweepstakes to win an $800 RockHopper bike, download a screen saver for their computer, and correspond with the manufacturer (via E-mail) about mountain biking. Students can even use a ZIP code-based locator service that lists the nearest authorized Specialized Bicycles' dealer. Specialized Bicycles' marketing director says this about *Digital Campus*, "If you want to play the game, you've got to speak the language."

As the promotion manager for a magazine subscription service, assess the pros and cons of using *Digital Campus* as a vehicle for reaching the college market.

Sources: Based on material in "Hot Wiring the College Crowd," *Promo* (July 1995), pp. 62–63; and Robert McKim, "Constructing Criticism: How to Build a Better Web Site," *Promo* (January 1996), pp. 67–68.

Organizational Consumers Table 10-1 also shows several personal demographics for organizational consumers that may be used in planning a segmentation strategy.

The easiest way to segment organizational consumers is by their industry designation. As an illustration, if a firm studies the information-services industry (SIC codes 7371, 7373, 7374, 7375, 7376, and 7379), it would learn it has 26,000 U.S. businesses, with a total of one million employees, and that global information-services revenues are divided as follows: North America, 48 per cent; Europe, 33 per cent; Asia/Pacific, 17 per cent; Latin America, 1.5 per cent; and Middle East/Africa, 0.5 per cent. The businesses offer electronic information, systems integration, data processing, network services, programming, and consulting and training.[8]

To access potential organizational consumers by institutional type, some sellers rely on trade directories—such as *MacRae's Blue Book* with 60,000 U.S. manufacturers, *Hoover's Masterlist of Major Latin American Companies* with 1,250 businesses, *ABC Europ Production* with 100,000 European manufacturers, and *Scott's Directories* with 50,000 Canadian manufacturers. Mailing lists of organizational consumers may also be bought. The *National Directory of Addresses and Telephone Numbers* includes 140,000 U.S. businesses. And American Business Lists' U.S. lists cite hundreds of thousands of manufacturers and wholesalers, over one million retailers, one million professional service businesses, and 450,000 membership organizations.

Organizational consumers may be divided into small, medium, and large categories. Some companies prosper by marketing goods and services to smaller customers, while others focus on medium and/or large accounts. For example, Panasonic has a line of in-

[8] *U.S. Industrial Outlook 1994* (Washington, D.C.: U.S. Department of Commerce, 1994), pp. 25-1–25-8.

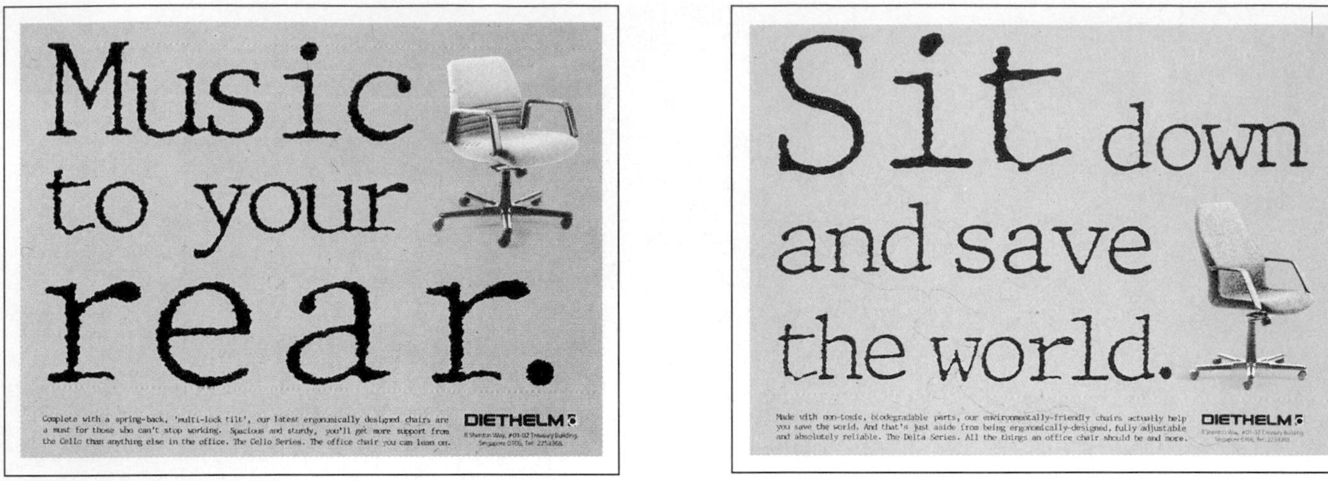

FIGURE 10-6
Applying Benefit Segmentation to Office Furniture
The ad at the left targets people who are interested in comfort, while the one at the right targets people who are attracted to environmentally friendly products.
Reprinted by permission.

expensive fax machines for small customers that cost a few hundred dollars, while Pitney Bowes markets fax machines that cost up to $5,000 and can handle 1,200 pages of text and store 1,000 phone numbers. In the United States, 97.8 per cent of business establishments have under 100 employees, 2 per cent have 100 to 499 employees, and 0.2 per cent have 500 or more employees. Eighty per cent of all U.S. businesses have annual revenues of less than $100,000, 3 per cent have annual revenues between $500,000 and $999,999, and 4 per cent have annual revenues of $1 million or more. The latter account for 89 per cent of all business revenues.[9]

Growth patterns in various industries may give an indication of a firm's future success in marketing to businesses in those industries and provide a good segmentation base. The International Trade Administration of the U.S. Department of Commerce cites electronic information services, health services, pre-recorded music, semiconductors, and surgical and medical instruments as fast-growing industries. Aircraft, paper industries machinery, personal leather goods, farm machinery, and newspapers are slow-growing industries.

Final consumer and organizational consumer segments each can be described on the basis of life-style factors.

Consumer Life-Styles Life-styles are the ways in which people live and spend time and money, and many life-style factors can be applied to both final and organizational consumers. Table 10-1 listed a number of life-style segmentation bases; except where indicated, these factors are relevant when segmenting either final or organizational consumer markets.

Applications of life-style segmentation are abundant, as these examples show: Final consumers may be segmented by social class and stage in the family life cycle. The posh Four Seasons hotel chain appeals to upper-middle-class and upper-class guests with luxurious accommodations, whereas the Hampton Inn chain appeals to middle-class and lower-middle-class consumers with reasonable rates and limited services (such as no restaurant). To attract families with children, various Club Med resorts have day-camp programs.

A **heavy-usage segment** *has a rather large share of sales.*

Final and organizational consumer market segments may be based on their usage rate, the amount of a product they consume. People or organizations can use very little, some, or a great deal. A **heavy-usage segment** (at times known as the **heavy half**) is a consumer group that accounts for a large proportion of a good's or service's sales relative to the size of the market. For instance, women buy 85 per cent of all greeting cards. Heavy yogurt consumers eat nearly double the amount of yogurt as average yogurt consumers. On a per

[9] *Statistical Abstract of the United States 1995* (Washington, D.C.: U.S. Department of Commerce, 1995), various pages; and Karen Maru File, "Is There a Trillion Dollar Family Business Market?" *Industrial Marketing Management*, Vol. 24 (August 1995), pp. 247–255.

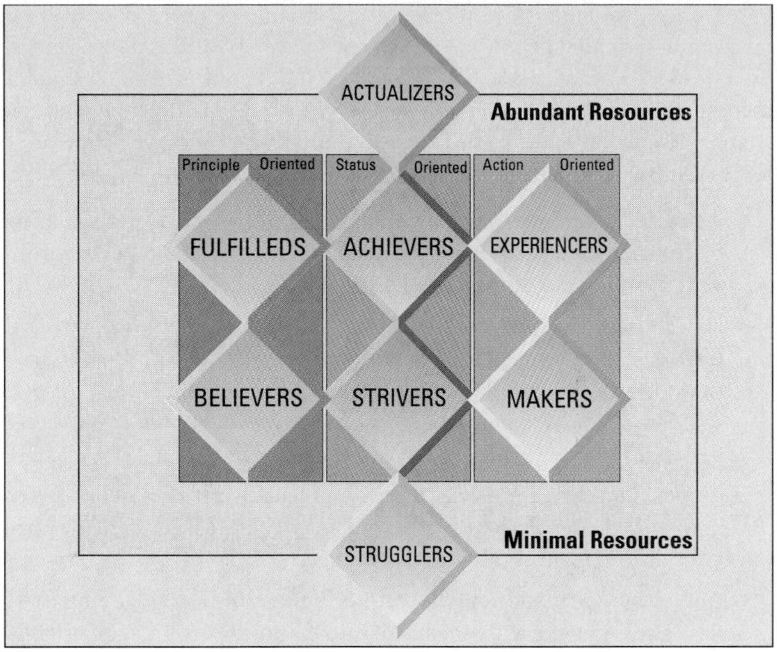

FIGURE 10-7
The VALS 2 Network
Source: Reprinted by permission of SRI International, Menlo Park, California.

capita basis, the Swiss drink 30 times more iced tea than do the French or Portuguese. The roughly 165 tire manufacturing facilities in the United States use about one-half of all general-purpose synthetic rubber. Manufacturers, wholesalers, and retailers account for over 90 per cent of all U.S. equipment leasing, while government and nonprofit organizations make less than 10 per cent of equipment leases.[10] Sometimes, a heavy-usage segment may be attractive because of the volume it consumes; other times, the competition for consumers in that segment may make other opportunities more attractive.

Consumer motives may be used to establish benefit segments. **Benefit segmentation** is a procedure for grouping people into segments on the basis of the different benefits sought from a product. It was first popularized in the late 1960s when Russell Haley divided the toothpaste market into four segments: sensory—people wanting flavor and product appearance; sociable—people wanting bright teeth; worrier—people wanting decay prevention; and independent—people wanting low prices. Since then, benefit segmentation has been applied in many final and organizational consumer settings.[11] Figure 10-6 shows how benefit segmentation may be used to market office furniture.

Benefit segmentation *groups consumers based on their reasons for using products.*

Blending Demographic and Life-Style Factors It is generally advisable to use a mix of demographic and life-style factors to set up possible bases of segmentation. A better analysis then takes place. Two broad classification systems are the **VALS (Values and Life-Styles) program,** which divides final consumers into life-style categories, and the **Social Styles model,** which divides the personnel representing organizational consumers into life-style categories.

VALS *and the* **Social Styles model** *describe market segments in terms of a broad range of factors.*

In the United States, the current VALS 2 typology, shown in Figure 10-7, seeks to explain why and how people make purchase decisions, and places them into segments

[10]Gerri Hirshey, "Happy [ ] Day to You," *New York Times Magazine* (July 2, 1995), p. 27; Henry Assael and David F. Poltrack, "Can Demographic Profiles of Heavy Users Serve as a Surrogate for Purchase Behavior in Selecting TV Programs?" *Journal of Advertising Research*, Vol. 34 (January–February 1994), pp. 11–17; "Brewing Up a Storm," *Advertising Age* (May 15, 1995), p. I-3; *Statistical Abstract of the United States 1995*, various pages; and *U.S. Industrial Outlook 1994*, various pages.

[11]Russell I. Haley, "Benefit Segmentation: A Decision-Oriented Research Tool," *Journal of Marketing*, Vol. 32 (July 1968), pp. 30–35; Russell I. Haley, "Benefit Segments: Backwards and Forwards," *Journal of Advertising Research*, Vol. 24 (February–March 1984), pp. 19–25; James W. Harvey, "Benefit Segmentation for Fund Raisers," *Journal of the Academy of Marketing Science*, Vol. 18 (Winter 1990), pp. 77–86; P. J. O'Connor and Gary L. Sullivan, "Market Segmentation: A Comparison of Benefits/Attributes Desired and Brand Preference," *Psychology & Marketing*, Vol. 12 (October 1995), pp. 613–635; and Chatrathi P. Rao and Zhengyuan Wang, "Evaluating Alternative Segmentation Strategies in Standard Industrial Markets," *European Journal of Marketing*, Vol. 29 (Number 2, 1995), pp. 58–75.

based on self-orientation and resources. Principle-oriented people are guided by their beliefs; status-oriented people are influenced by others; and action-oriented people are guided by a desire for activity, variety, and risk taking. People's resources include their education, income, self-confidence, health, eagerness to buy, intelligence, and energy level; and resources rise from youth to middle age and fall with old age. Here are descriptions of the basic VALS 2 segments (in terms of adult characteristics):

- Actualizers—Highest resources. Successful, sophisticated. Can indulge in any self-orientations. Have a taste for the finer things in life. 8 per cent of population. 95 per cent with at least some college. Median age of 43.
- Fulfilleds—Principle-oriented, abundant resources. Mature, satisfied, comfortable, and reflective. Mostly professional and well educated. As consumers, concerned with functionality, value, and durability. 11 per cent of population. 81 per cent with at least some college. Median age of 48.
- Believers—Principle-oriented, lower resources. Follow routines organized around homes, families, and social or religious organizations. Want American products and known brands. Resources sufficient for needs. 16 per cent of population. 6 per cent with at least some college. Median age of 58.
- Achievers—Status-oriented, second highest resources. Committed to jobs and families, and satisfied with them. Like to be in control. Favor established products that demonstrate their success to peers. 13 per cent of population. 77 per cent with at least some college. Median age of 36.
- Strivers—Status-oriented, lower resources. Values similar to achievers but fewer resources. Unsure of themselves. Concerned about approval from others. Most-desired goods and services generally beyond reach. 13 per cent of population. 23 per cent with at least some college. Median age of 34.
- Experiencers—Action-oriented, acquiring resources. Young, enthusiastic, and rebellious. Seek variety and excitement. Spend much of income on clothing, fast food, music, movies, and videos. 12 per cent of population. 41 per cent with at least some college. Median age of 26.
- Makers—Action-oriented, lower resources. Live in a traditional context of family, work, and physical recreation. Unimpressed by possessions. Like do-it-yourself projects. 13 per cent of population. 24 per cent with at least some college. Median age of 30.
- Strugglers—Lowest resources (too few to include in any self-orientation). Chronically poor, ill-educated, older, and low in skills. Concerned about health, safety, and security. Brand loyal and cautious. 14 per cent of population. 3 per cent with at least some college. Median age of 61.[12]

In conjunction with SRI International (VALS' developer), Market Statistics has devised a high-tech way to use the U.S. VALS 2 model—called GeoVALS. Through GeoVALS, the eight VALS 2 market segments can be broken down by metropolitan area, city, and zip code.[13]

The VALS system is so popular that it is also being applied in Japan and tailored to people there. For example, ryoshiki ("socially intelligent") innovators are career-oriented, middle-aged innovators; ryoshiki adapters are shy and look to ryoshiki innovators; tradition adapters are young and affluent; and low pragmatic are attitudinally negative and oriented to inexpensive products.[14]

According to the Social Styles model, highlighted in Figure 10-8, social styles affect how people react to various stimuli on and off the job. This model looks at two traits—assertiveness and responsiveness—and divides organizational personnel into analyticals, drivers, amiables, and expressives segments. Assertiveness is the degree to which a person

[12]SRI International, Menlo Park, California.

[13]"The Best 100 Sources for Marketing Information," *American Demographics* (January 1995), p. 29.

[14]Lewis C. Winters, "International Psychographics," *Marketing Research*, Vol. 4 (September 1992), pp. 48–49.

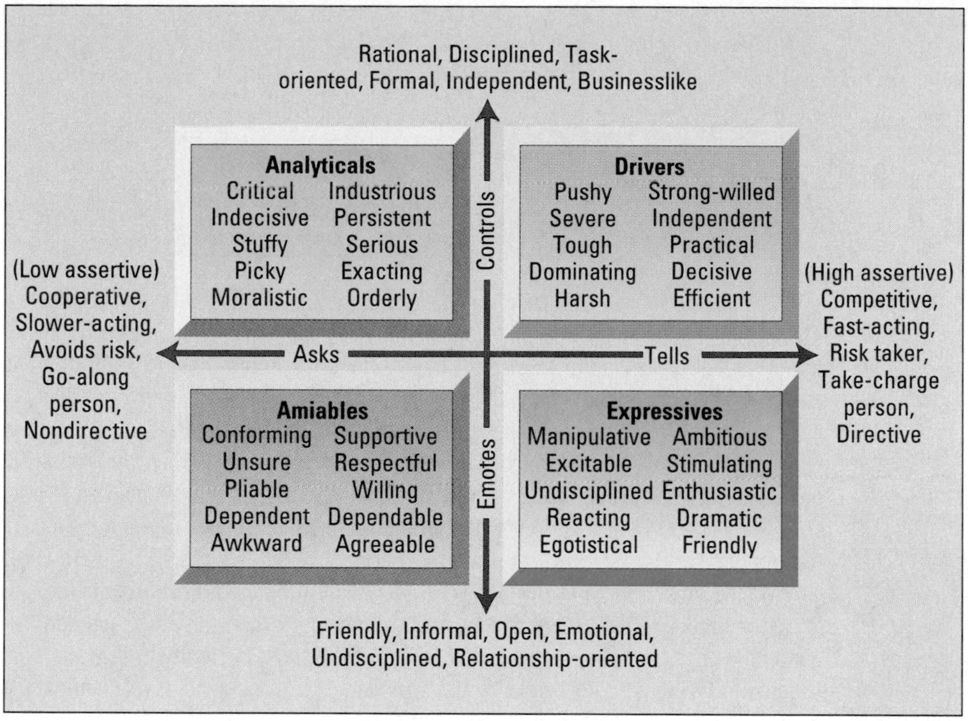

FIGURE 10-8
The Social Styles Model for Organizational Consumers

Sources: Wilson Learning Corporation and Tracom Corporation. *Reprinted by permission of Crain Communications Inc.*, from Tom Eisenhart, "How to Really Excite Your Prospects," *Business Marketing* (July 1988).

states views with assurance, confidence, and force, and the extent to which he or she tries to direct others' actions. Responsiveness is the extent to which a person is affected by appeals, influence, or stimulation and how feelings, emotions, or impressions are shown to others:

- Analyticals—Low in both assertiveness and responsiveness. Like facts and details. Money- and numbers-oriented. Work well alone. Stay under control. Interested in processes. Risk avoiders.
- Expressives—High in both assertiveness and responsiveness. Personality opposites of analyticals. Use hunches to make decisions. Need to be with people. Focus on generalities. Thrive on freedom from outside control. Risk takers, but seek approval for themselves and their firms.
- Drivers—Low in responsiveness and high in assertiveness. Get right to the point. Limited time. "Hard chargers." Self-motivated and impatient. Work well alone. Risk takers. Success-oriented.
- Amiables—Low in assertiveness and high in responsiveness. Team players. Like to build relationships. Friendly and loyal. Need support from others. Careful. Less time-oriented. Can be indecisive. Risk avoiders.[15]

The Social Styles model has been used to classify personnel within industries—including banking, computers and precision instruments, chemicals, pharmaceuticals, telecommunications, aerospace, utilities, and industrial and farm equipment. In all cases, the analyticals segment is the largest.

Identifying Potential Market Segments

Consumer profiles are used in identifying market segments.

After establishing possible bases of segmentation, a firm is ready to construct specific consumer profiles—which identify potential market segments for that firm by aggregating consumers with similar characteristics and needs and separating them from those with different characteristics and needs. Here are some examples.

[15]Tom Eisenhart, "How to Really Excite Your Prospects," *Business Marketing* (July 1988), pp. 44–45 ff.; and Raymond E. Taylor, Lorraine A. Krajewksi, and John R. Darling, "Social Style Application to Enhance Direct Mail Response," *Journal of Direct Marketing*, Vol. 7 (Autumn 1993), pp. 42–53.

International Marketing in Action

How Do Argentines and Venezuelans Spend Their Money?

Roper Reports Americas tracks people's activities in leading Latin American markets, including Argentina and Venezuela. The data it compiles help to highlight target market opportunities in these markets. The data reported below refer to urban adults aged 18 and older.

In a typical month, people in Argentina and Venezuela are more likely than those in the United States to perform job-related duties at home (32 per cent Argentina, 28 per cent Venezuela, and 25 per cent U.S.), make an international phone call (11 per cent Argentina, 14 per cent Venezuela, and 8 per cent U.S.), and take a vacation for 4 or more days (14 per cent Argentina, 10 per cent Venezuela, and 6 per cent U.S.).

On the other hand, in a given month, people in Argentina and Venezuela are less likely than those in the United States to buy clothing for themselves (38 per cent Argentina, 41 per cent Venezuela, and 48 per cent U.S.), use a credit card (21 per cent Argentina, 17 per cent Venezuela, and 44 per cent U.S.), and send or receive a fax at work (7 per cent Argentina, 7 per cent Venezuela, and 15 per cent U.S.).

There are also significant differences between Argentine and Venezuelan consumers. Consumers in Argentina are more apt to buy recorded music (23 per cent in Argentina versus 10 per cent in Venezuela). In contrast, consumers in Argentina are less apt than their Venezuelan counterparts to go away for a weekend (15 per cent in Argentina versus 21 per cent in Venezuela).

As a marketing consultant who works with small U.S. companies that want to market products in Argentina and Venezuela, how would you use these findings?

Source: Based on material in Ignacio Galceran and Jon Berry, "A New World of Consumers," *American Demographics* (March 1995), pp. 26–33.

A supermarket could segment female and male shoppers in terms of their in-store behavior. In general, on each visit, women spend more time shopping, buy more items, are more apt to bring children, and more often use a shopping list than men, and they are equally apt to shop in the evening.

A gas station could divide its potential customers into five life-style market segments (based on extensive research by Mobil): Road Warriors—they drive 25,000 to 50,000 miles per year and buy premium gas with a credit card; True Blues—they are loyal to a brand and sometimes to a particular station; Generation F3—they want fuel and food, and they want it fast; Homebodies—they take a lot of trips around town to transport children and do errands, and use whatever gas station is on the way; and price shoppers—they are not loyal to a brand or a station and rarely buy premium.[16]

A photocopier manufacturer could group the office-copier market into benefit segments, such as: basic copying (satisfied via simple, inexpensive machines that make up to 99 black and white copies of a single page at a time); extensive copying (satisfied via mid-priced machines that make up to 100 or more one- or two-sided copies of multiple pages and then collate them); and desktop publishing (satisfied via expensive, sophisticated machines that make high-quality color copies in big quantities). Both domestic and international prospects for each segment are bright.

[16] Allanna Sullivan, "Mobil Bets Drivers Pick Cappuccino Over Low Prices," *Wall Street Journal* (January 30, 1995), pp. B1, B8.

Targeting the Market

The second phase in planning a target market strategy (targeting the market) consists of choosing the proper approach and selecting the target market(s).

Choosing a Target Market Approach

A firm now decides upon undifferentiated marketing (mass marketing), concentrated marketing, or differentiated marketing (multiple segmentation). These options are shown in Figure 10-9 and Table 10-2, and are discussed next.

Undifferentiated Marketing (Mass Marketing) An undifferentiated marketing (mass marketing) approach aims at a large, broad consumer market via one basic marketing plan. With this approach, a firm believes consumers have very similar desires regarding product attributes or opts to ignore differences among segments. An early practitioner of mass marketing was Henry Ford, who sold one standard car at a reasonable price to many people. The original Model T had no options and came only in black.

With undifferentiated marketing, a firm appeals to a broad range of consumers with one basic marketing plan.

Mass marketing was popular when large-scale production started, but the number of firms using a pure undifferentiated marketing approach has declined a lot in recent years. Among the factors behind the drop are that competition has grown, consumer demand may be stimulated by appealing to specific segments, improved marketing research can better pinpoint different segments' desires, and total production and marketing costs can be reduced by segmentation.

Before engaging in undifferentiated marketing, a firm must weigh several factors. High total resources are needed to mass produce, mass distribute, and mass advertise. Yet, there may be per-unit production and marketing savings because a limited product line is offered and different brand names are not employed. These savings may allow low competitive prices.

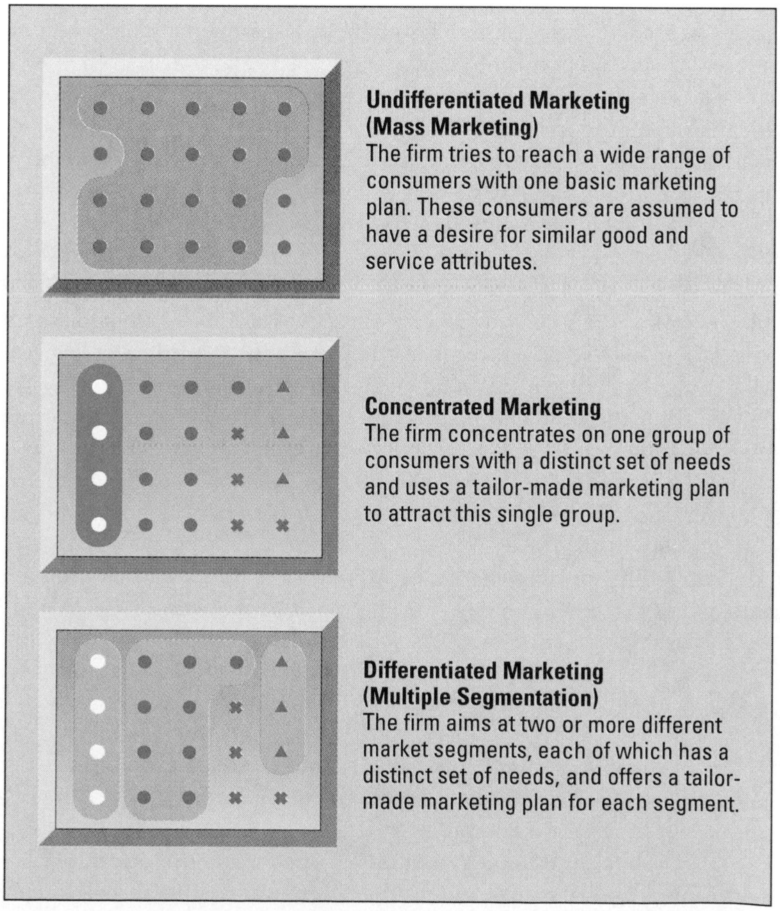
Undifferentiated Marketing (Mass Marketing)
The firm tries to reach a wide range of consumers with one basic marketing plan. These consumers are assumed to have a desire for similar good and service attributes.
Concentrated Marketing
The firm concentrates on one group of consumers with a distinct set of needs and uses a tailor-made marketing plan to attract this single group.
Differentiated Marketing (Multiple Segmentation)
The firm aims at two or more different market segments, each of which has a distinct set of needs, and offers a tailor-made marketing plan for each segment.

FIGURE 10-9
Contrasting Target Market Approaches

Table 10-2
Contrasting Target Market Approaches

STRATEGIC FACTORS	**APPROACHES** *Undifferentiated Marketing*	*Concentrated Marketing*	*Differentiated Marketing*
Target market	Broad range of consumers	One well-defined consumer group	Two or more well-defined consumer groups
Product	Limited number of products under one brand for many types of consumers	One brand tailored to one consumer group	Distinct brand or version for each consumer group
Distribution	All possible outlets	All suitable outlets	All suitable outlets—differs by segment
Promotion	Mass media	All suitable media	All suitable media—differs by segment
Price	One "popular" price range	One price range tailored to the consumer group	Distinct price range for each consumer group
Strategy emphasis	Appeal to a large number of consumers via a uniform, broad-based marketing program	Appeal to one specific consumer group via a highly specialized, but uniform, marketing program	Appeal to two or more distinct market segments via different marketing plans catering to each segment

A major goal of undifferentiated marketing is to maximize sales—that is, a firm tries to sell as many units of an item as possible. Regional, national, and/or international goals are set. Diversification is not undertaken.

For successful pure mass marketing, a large group of consumers must have a desire for the same product attributes (homogeneous demand) so that a firm can use one basic marketing program. Or, demand must be so diffused that it is not worthwhile for a firm to aim marketing plans at specific segments; the firm would try to make demand more homogeneous. Under undifferentiated marketing, different consumer groups are not identified and sought. For example, suppose all consumers buy Morton's salt for its freshness, quality, storability, availability, and fair price. A pure mass marketing strategy is then proper. However, if various consumers want attractive decanters, low-sodium content, larger crystals, and smaller-sized packages (as they now do), Morton would be unable to appeal to all consumers through one basic marketing mix.

With undifferentiated marketing, a firm sells via all possible outlets. Some resellers may be displeased if a brand is sold at nearby locations and insist on carrying additional brands to fill out their product lines. It may be hard to persuade them not to carry competing brands. The shelf space a firm gets is based on its brand's popularity and the promotion support it provides.

An undifferentiated marketing strategy should take both total and long-run profits into account. Firms sometimes may be too involved with revenues and lose sight of profits. For example, for several years, A&P's sales rose as it competed with Safeway for leadership in U.S. supermarket sales. A&P incurred large losses during that period. Only when it began to close some unprofitable stores and stop pursuing sales at any cost did it regain profitability.

A firm and/or its products can ensure a consistent, well-known image with a mass marketing approach. Consumers have only one image when thinking of a firm (or a brand), and it is retained for a number of years.

TV Guide is an example of undifferentiated marketing in action. It is a magazine with television program listings, descriptions, and evaluations, as well as current events and articles on personalities, shows, and the industry. Each week, 14 million copies are sold (down from 18 million a decade ago). It is advertised on TV and in newspapers and stores. It is inexpensive and available at a number of stores and newsstands. Many sales are via subscription. The product itself, the magazine, is the same throughout the United States—except for some differences in program listings (but not in program descriptions, articles, and features) by community. To be more competitive, *TV Guide* now includes cable TV listings and VCR-Plus codes (for easy taping), and it has moved all feature stories to the front of the magazine. *TV Guide* is recognized as the standard in the field. Consumers of varying backgrounds and life-styles buy it for the completeness of listings and the interesting stories.

Concentrated Marketing By means of a concentrated-marketing approach, a firm aims at a narrow, specific consumer segment with one specialized marketing plan catering to the needs of that segment. This is proper to consider if demand is clustered or if diffused demand can be clustered by offering a unique marketing mix.

Via concentrated marketing, a firm appeals to one segment with a tailored marketing plan.

Concentrated marketing has become more popular, especially for smaller firms. With it, a firm does not have to mass produce, mass distribute, or mass advertise. It can succeed with limited resources and abilities by focusing efforts. This method does not usually maximize sales; the goal is efficiency—attracting a large portion of one segment at controlled costs. The firm wants recognition as a specialist and does not diversify.

If concentrated marketing is used, a firm must do better than competitors in tailoring a strategy for its segment. Areas of competitor strength should be avoided and weaknesses exploited. For instance, a new vendor selling standard office stationery would have a harder time distinguishing itself from competitors than a new vendor that provides customers with free recycling services for the office stationery it sells.

When there are two or more attractive market segments from which a firm may choose, it should select the one with the greatest opportunity—while being alert to these two factors: One, the largest segment may not be the best option, due to heavy competition or high consumer satisfaction with competitor offerings. A firm entering this segment may regret it due to the **majority fallacy,** which causes some firms to fail if they go after the largest market segment because competition is intense. See Figure 10-10. Two, a potentially profitable segment may be one ignored by other firms. As an example, Perdue is

To avoid the **majority fallacy,** *a company can enter a smaller, but untapped, segment.*

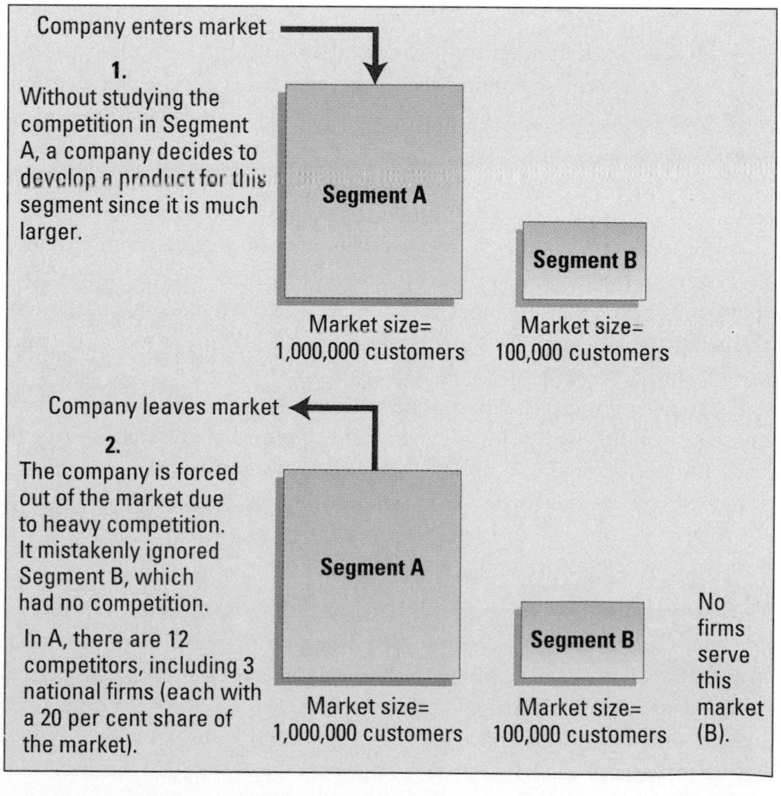
Company enters market
1.
Without studying the competition in Segment A, a company decides to develop a product for this segment since it is much larger.
Segment A
Segment B
Market size= 1,000,000 customers
Market size= 100,000 customers
Company leaves market
2.
The company is forced out of the market due to heavy competition. It mistakenly ignored Segment B, which had no competition.
In A, there are 12 competitors, including 3 national firms (each with a 20 per cent share of the market).
Segment A
Segment B
No firms serve this market (B).
Market size= 1,000,000 customers
Market size= 100,000 customers

FIGURE 10-10
How the Majority Fallacy Occurs

Mita copiers can help any office
get out of the stone age.
Still working with prehistoric office equipment? Get a Mita. Every Mita copier Buyers Lab tested earned their highest rating for uptime. For personal to high-speed copiers, call 1-800-ABC-MITA. The times demand
mita

FIGURE 10-11
Differentiated Marketing in Action: Targeting Organizational Consumers
Mita targets its full line of photocopiers to a wide range of organizational consumers, with different products for each customer type (market segment).

Reprinted by permission of Mita Copystar America, Inc. All rights reserved.

very successful in the poultry business. This is due to its being the first chicken processor to see a market segment desiring superior quality, an identifiable brand name, and a guarantee—and having a willingness to pay premium prices. Previously, chicken was sold as an unbranded commodity.

Concentrated marketing can enable a firm to maximize per-unit profits, but not total profits, because only one segment is sought. It also allows a firm with low resources to vie effectively for specialized markets. There are many local and regional firms that profitably compete in their own markets with national and international companies but that do not have the finances to compete nationally or internationally. However, minor shifts in population or consumer tastes can sharply affect a firm engaging in concentrated marketing.

By carving out a distinct niche via concentrated marketing, a firm may foster a high degree of brand loyalty for a current offering and also be able to develop a product line under a popular name. As long as the firm stays within its perceived area of expertise, the image of one product will rub off on another: Even though it makes several car models, Porsche aims only at the upscale segment of the market—people interested in styling, handling, acceleration, and, of course, status.

In differentiated marketing, two or more marketing plans are tailored to two or more consumer segments.

Differentiated Marketing (Multiple Segmentation) In differentiated marketing (multiple segmentation), a firm appeals to two or more distinct market segments, with a different marketing plan for each. This approach combines the best aspects of undifferentiated marketing and concentrated marketing: A broad range of consumers may be sought and efforts focus on satisfying identifiable consumer segments. Differentiated marketing is appropriate to consider if there are two or more significant demand clusters, or

FIGURE 10-12
Differentiated Marketing in Action: Targeting Final Consumers
These two watch brands are both marketed by SMH, but they are targeted at different market segments.
Reprinted by permission.

if diffused demand can be clustered into two or more segments and satisfied by offering unique marketing mixes to each one.

Some firms appeal to each segment in the market and achieve the same market coverage as with mass marketing. Mita markets photocopiers ranging from the simple and inexpensive to the sophisticated and expensive, thus separately appealing to small and large businesses. Other firms appeal to two or more, but not all, market segments. Thus, Marriott International operates Marriott Hotels and Resorts, Fairfield Inns, Courtyard Hotels, Marriott Suites, and Residence Inns and aims at several—but not all—hospitality segments. And Switzerland's SMH markets Swatch watches for teenagers and young adults, Hamilton watches for adults attracted by classic styles, and upscale Blancpain, Omega, and Tissot brands. See Figures 10-11 and 10-12.

Firms may use both mass marketing and concentrated marketing in their multiple segmentation strategies. They could have one or more major brands aimed at a wide range of consumers (the mass market) and secondary brands for specific segments. Time Warner publishes *Time* and *People* for very broad audiences and *Fortune* and *Sports Illustrated for Kids* for more specialized segments.

Multiple segmentation requires thorough analysis. Company resources and abilities must be able to produce and market two or more different sizes, brands, or product lines. This can be costly, as occurs with high-technology products. However, if a firm sells similar products under its own and retailer brands, added costs are small.

Differentiated marketing lets a firm reach many goals. It can maximize sales: Procter & Gamble is the world leader in laundry products—with such brands as Tide, Bold, Dash,

Cheer, Gain, Oxydol, Era, Ivory Snow, and Ariel. Boeing leads in the global commercial aircraft business—offering planes with different sizes and configurations (including the 737, 747, 757, 767, and 777). Recognition as a specialist can continue if the firm has separate brands for items aimed at separate segments or has a narrow product line: Whirlpool has a clear image under its own label; few people know it also makes products for Sears under the latter's Kenmore brand. Multiple segmentation lets a firm diversify and minimize risks because all emphasis is not placed on one segment: Honda's motorcycles and small engines (for lawn mowers and outboard motors) provide an excellent hedge against a drop in the sales of its cars.

Differentiated marketing does not mean a firm has to enter segments where competitors are strongest and be subjected to the majority fallacy. Its goals, strengths, and weaknesses must be measured against competitors. A firm should target only those segments it can handle. And the majority fallacy can work in reverse. If a firm enters a segment before a competitor, it may prevent the latter from successfully entering that segment in the future.

Although differentiated marketing requires the existence of at least two consumer segments (with distinct desires by each), the more potential segments that exist, the better the opportunity for multiple segmentation. Firms that start with concentrated marketing often turn to multiple segmentation and pursue other segments after they become established in one segment.

Wholesalers and retailers usually find differentiated marketing by their suppliers to be attractive. It lets them reach multiple segments, offers some brand exclusivity, allows orders to be placed with fewer suppliers, and may enable them to carry their own private brands. For the selling firm, several distribution benefits exist. Items can be placed with competing resellers under different brands. Shelf space is given to display various sizes, packages, and/or brands. Price differentials among brands can be maintained. Competitors may be discouraged from entering a distribution channel. Overall, differentiated marketing places the seller in a good bargaining position.

Multiple segmentation can be quite profitable because total profits should rise as a firm increases the number of segments it services. Per-unit profits should also be high if a firm does a good job of enacting a unique marketing plan for each segment. Consumers in each segment would then be willing to pay a premium price for the tailor-made offering.

When a firm serves diverse segments, even though the risks from a decline in any one segment are lessened, extra costs may be incurred by making product variations, selling in more channels, and promoting more brands. The firm must weigh the revenues gained from selling to multiple segments against the costs.

A company must be careful to maintain product distinctiveness for each market segment and guard its overall image. Many consumers still perceive various General Motors' divisions as having "look-alike" cars. And IBM's image has been affected by its past weak performance in the home-PC segment.

Selecting the Target Market(s)

A company now chooses which and how many segments to target.

At this point, a firm has these decisions to make: Which segment(s) offer the best opportunities? How many segments should the firm pursue? In evaluating market segments, a firm should review its goals and strengths, competition, segment size and growth potential, distribution requirements, necessary expenditures, profit potential, company image, ability to create and sustain differential advantages, and other factors.

Based on the target market approach chosen, a firm would then decide whether to pursue one or more segments (or the mass market). For example, due to the high costs of entering the office PC market and the existence of several well-defined demand clusters, it is most likely that a firm new to that industry would start with a concentrated marketing effort. On the other hand, a new sweater maker could easily use differentiated marketing to target boys, girls, men, and women with its products.

These are three examples of target market selection: The Dutch Direktbank caters to the relatively neglected segment of elderly consumers. It focuses on loans to this group in the Netherlands. Pep Boys (the auto repair and parts giant) aims to serve two distinct segments: do-it-yourselfers and professional mechanics. It estimates the total size of the U.S. do-it-yourself segment to be $24 billion per year, while the professional segment is $48 billion per year. Petersen Publishing markets 23 monthly magazines, 9 bimonthly magazines, and 45 annual editions. It targets such different segments as teenage females and teenage and adult male car enthusiasts—with publications for each. Its diverse titles include *Teen, Sassy, Hot Rod, Motor Trend, Sport,* and *Go Cart.* The firm grosses $250 million annually in circulation and ad revenues, although many of its publications have circulations under 150,000. *Teen* and *Sassy* are in the one million circulation range.[17]

Effectiveness requires segments that are distinct, homogeneous, measurable, large enough, and reachable.

Requirements for Successful Segmentation For concentrated marketing or differentiated marketing plans to succeed, the selected market segment(s) have to meet five criteria:

1. There must be *differences* among consumers, or mass marketing would be an appropriate strategy.
2. Within each segment, there must be enough consumer *similarities* to develop an appropriate marketing plan for that segment.
3. A firm must be able to *measure* consumer attributes and needs in order to form groups. This may be hard for some life-style attributes.
4. A segment must be *large enough* to produce sales and cover costs.
5. The members of a segment must be *reachable* in an efficient way. For example, young women can be reached via *Teen* magazine. It is efficient because males and older women do not read the magazine.

The shortcomings of segmentation need to be considered.

Limitations of Segmentation Although segmentation is often a consumer-oriented, efficient, and profitable marketing technique, it should not be abused. Firms could fall into one or more of these traps—which they should try to avoid. Companies may

- Appeal to segments that are too small.
- Misread consumer similarities and differences.
- Become cost inefficient.
- Spin off too many imitations of their original products or brands.
- Become short-run instead of long-run oriented.
- Be unable to use certain media (due to the small size of individual segments).
- Compete in too many segments.
- Confuse people.
- Become locked into a declining segment.
- Be too slow to seek innovative possibilities for new products.

Developing the Marketing Strategy

The third phase in planning a target market strategy (developing the marketing strategy) includes these steps: positioning the company's offering relative to competitors and outlining the appropriate marketing mix(es).

Positioning the Company's Offering in Relation to Competition

A good or service must be carefully positioned against competitors.

Once a firm selects its target market(s), it must identify the attributes and images of each competitor and select a position for its own offering.

[17]Tevfik Dalgic and Maarten Leeuw, "Niche Marketing Revisited: Concept, Applications, and Some European Cases," *European Journal of Marketing*, Vol. 28 (Number 4, 1994), p. 50; Anthony Lin, "Pep Boys Is Undertaking Its Largest Expansion Drive," *Wall Street Journal* (August 10, 1995), p. B4; and Jerry Flint, "The Magazine Factory," *Forbes* (May 22, 1995), pp. 160–162.

Ethics IN TODAY'S SOCIETY

Is There a Market Segment Interested in Eco Tourism?

Maho Bay Camps in St. John is located on privately owned land within the U.S. Virgin Islands National Park. Initially, developer Stanley Selengut planned to build a lavish resort on his property. When environmental opposition mounted, Selengut decided to change his plans to appeal to this market segment, rather than fight against it.

The campground's target market is "eco tourists," consumers interested in getting back to nature and not harming the environment. All aspects of Maho Bay Camps' operation reflect the developer's concern for nature. For example, the tent cottages are placed on simple platforms so as not to disturb the steep hillside. Cables and wires are also attached to the bottoms of walkways instead of being buried underground to reduce soil erosion. Although the campgrounds are far from luxurious (visitors share toilets and have cold-water showers), at $90 a night they are inexpensive by Caribbean standards.

Stanley Selengut's new resort, Harmony, is located next to Maho Bay Camps. Harmony's two-story villas are made almost completely from recycled materials. For example, the villas' rafters and floor beams are made from composite materials derived from wood scraps. Bathroom tiles are made by crushing discarded light bulbs. Even the units' door mats have been produced from old automobile tires. All water is collected rain water and all electricity is provided by solar power; and as part of the daily routine, guests are expected to monitor carefully their water and electricity usage. Harmony's rates are up to $150 a night.

To promote both vacation complexes, Selengut has sent out public relations material to the travel, scientific, and ecological press. So far, Harmony has been solidly booked without a dollar spent on advertising.

As a marketing consultant to Stanley Selengut, outline a target market strategy for both the Maho Bay Camps and Harmony.

Source: Based on material in Suzanne Oliver, "Eco-Profitable," *Forbes* (June 20, 1994), p. 110.

For example, a firm considering entry into the office PC market could describe the key strengths of some of the major competitors as follows:

- IBM—Reliability, service, range of software applications, product variety.
- Apple—Ease of use, graphics, desktop publishing, innovativeness.
- Compaq—Innovativeness, construction, monitor quality, competitive pricing.
- Dell—Low prices, range of accessories carried, direct marketing experience.

In positioning itself against these competitors, the firm would need to present a combination of customer benefits that are not being offered by them and that are desirable by a target market. Customers must be persuaded that there are clear reasons for buying the new firm's computers. It is not a good idea for the firm to go head on against such big, well-known competitors.

As one alternative, the firm could focus on small businesses that have not yet bought a computer and that need a personal touch during both the purchase process and the initial use of the product. It could thus market fully configured PC systems, featuring IBM clones that are installed by the seller (complete with software libraries and customized programs), in-office training of employees, and a single price for a total system. The po-

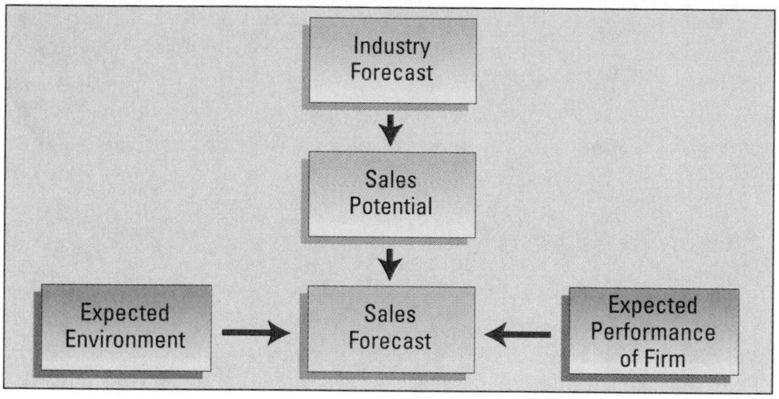

FIGURE 10-13
Developing a Sales Forecast

sitioning emphasis would be "to provide the best ongoing, personalized customer service possible to an underdeveloped market segment, small-business owners."

A fuller discussion of product positioning appears in Chapter 11.

Outlining the Appropriate Marketing Mix(es)

The marketing mix must be attractive to the target market.

The last step in the target-marketing process is for a firm to outline a marketing-mix plan for each customer group it is targeting. Marketing decisions relate to product, distribution, promotion, and price factors.

Here is a logical marketing-mix plan for a firm newly entering the office PC market and concentrating on small-business owners:

- Product—Good-quality, Pentium-based IBM clone with expansion capability; very user-friendly, with a simple keyboard layout; high-resolution color monitor; four speed CD-ROM player and suitable speakers; one gigabyte hard drive; basic software library; customized software; and more.
- Distribution—Direct calls and installations at customers' places of business; follow-up service calls.
- Promotion—Emphasis on personal selling and direct mail; hands-on, on-site training programs; customer referrals.
- Price—Average to above average; customers presented with nonprice reasons for purchase; positioning linked to high value for the price relationship; price of computer, software, and service bundled together.

Sales Forecasting

A ***sales forecast*** *predicts company sales over a specified period.*

As a firm plans a target market strategy, it should forecast its short-run and long-run sales to that market. A **sales forecast** outlines expected company sales for a specific good or service to a specific consumer group over a specific period of time under a specific marketing program. By accurately projecting sales, a firm can better set a marketing budget, allot resources, measure success, analyze sales productivity, monitor the environment and competition, and modify marketing efforts.[18]

A firm should first study industry forecasts; they can strongly affect any company's sales. Next, sales potential outlines the upper limit for the firm, based on marketing and production capacity. A sales forecast then enumerates a firm's realistic sales. The forecast is also based on the expected environment and company performance. Figure 10-13 shows this sales-forecasting process.

[18]See Paul A. Herbig, John Milewicz, and James E. Golden, "The Do's and Don'ts of Sales Forecasting," *Industrial Marketing Management*, Vol. 22 (February 1993), pp. 49–57; Theodore Modis, "Life Cycles: Forecasting the Rise and Fall of Almost Anything," *Futurist* (September–October 1995), pp. 20–25; John B. Mahaffie, "Why Forecasts Fail," *American Demographics* (March 1995), pp. 34–40; and Glen L. Urban, Bruce D. Weinberg, and John R. Hauser, "Premarket Forecasting of Really-New Products," *Journal of Marketing*, Vol. 60 (January 1996), pp. 47–60.

A sales forecast should take into account demographics (such as per capita income), the economy (such as the inflation rate), the competitive environment (such as promotion levels), current and prior sales, and other factors. When devising a forecast, precision is required. A forecast should break sales down by good or service (model 123), consumer group (adult female), time period (July through September), and type of marketing plan (intensive advertising).

Data Sources

A firm can consult several external secondary sources to obtain some of the data needed for a sales forecast. Government agencies provide data on global, national, regional, and local demographic trends; past sales by industry and product; and the economy. Trade associations publish various statistics and often have libraries for member firms. General and specialized media, such as *Business Week* and *Ward's Automotive Reports*, do regular forecasts.

A firm can also obtain data from present and future customers, executives, salespeople, research studies and market tests, and internal records. These data will usually center on company rather than industry predictions.

Methods of Sales Forecasting

Sales forecasting methods range from simple to sophisticated. Among the simple ones are trend analysis, market-share analysis, jury of executive or expert opinion, sales-force surveys, and consumer surveys. Among the more complex ones are the chain-ratio technique, market buildup method, and statistical analyses. At the end of this section, Table 10-3 illustrates each. By combining two or more techniques, a firm can have a better forecast and minimize the weaknesses in any one method.

With simple trend analysis, a firm forecasts sales on the basis of recent or current performance. For example, if sales have risen an average of 10 per cent annually over the last five years, it will forecast next year's sales to be 10 per cent higher than the present year's. Although the technique is easy to use, the problems are that sales fluctuations, changing consumer tastes, changing competition, the economy, and market saturation are not considered. A firm's growth may be affected by these factors.

Market-share analysis is similar to simple trend analysis, except that a company bases its forecast on the assumption that its share of industry sales will remain constant. However, all firms in an industry do not progress at the same rate. Market-share analysis has the same weaknesses as simple trend analysis, but relies more on industry data—and it would let an aggressive or declining firm adjust its forecast and marketing efforts.

A **jury of executive or expert opinion** *has informed people estimate sales.*

A **jury of executive or expert opinion** is used if the management of a firm or other well-informed persons meet, discuss the future, and set sales estimates based on the group's experience and interaction. By itself, this method relies too much on informal analysis. In conjunction with other methods, it is effective because it enables experts to directly interpret and respond to concrete data. Because management lays out goals, sets priorities, and guides a firm's destiny, its input is crucial.

The employees most in touch with consumers and the environment are sales personnel. A sales-force survey allows a firm to obtain input in a structured way. Salespeople are often able to pinpoint trends, strengths and weaknesses in a firm's offering, competitive strategies, customer resistance, and the traits of heavy users. They can break sales forecasts down by product, customer type, and area. However, they can have a limited perspective, offer biased replies, and misinterpret consumer desires.

Many marketers feel the best indicators of future sales are consumer attitudes. By conducting a consumer survey, a firm can obtain information on purchase intentions, future expectations, consumption rates, brand switching, time between purchases, and reasons for purchases. Yet, consumers may not reply to surveys and may act differently from what they say.

With the **chain-ratio method,** *general data are broken down. The* **market buildup method** *adds segment data.*

In the **chain-ratio method,** a firm starts with general market information and then computes a series of more specific information. These combined data yield a sales forecast. For instance, a maker of women's casual shoes could first look at a trade association report to learn the industry sales estimate for shoes, the percentage of sales from women's

Table 10-3
Applying Sales Forecasting Techniques

TECHNIQUE	ILLUSTRATION	SELECTED POTENTIAL SHORTCOMINGS
Simple trend analysis	This year's sales = $2 million; company trend is 5% growth per year; sales forecast = $2,100,000.	Industry decline not considered.
Market share analysis	Current market share = 18%; company seeks stable market share; industry forecast = $10,000,000; company sales forecast = $1,800,000.	New competitors and greater marketing by current ones not considered.
Jury of executive opinion	Three executives see strong growth and three see limited growth; they agree on a 6% rise on this year's sales of $11 million; sales forecast = $11,660,000.	Change in consumer attitudes not uncovered.
Jury of expert opinion	Groups of wholesalers, retailers, and suppliers meet. Each group makes a forecast; top management utilizes each forecast in forming one projection.	Different beliefs by groups about industry growth.
Sales force survey	Sales personnel report a competitor's price drop of 10% will cause company sales to decline 3% from this year's $7 million; sales forecast = $6,790,000.	Sales force unaware a competitor's price cut will be temporary.
Consumer survey	85% of current customers indicate they will repurchase next year and spend an average of $1,000 with the firm; 3% of competitors' customers indicate they will buy from the firm next year and spend an average of $800; sales forecast = $460,000.	Consumer intentions possibly not reflecting real behavior.
Chain-ratio method	Unit sales forecast for introductory marketing text = (number of students) × (% annually enrolled in marketing) × (% buying a new book) × (expected market share) = (10,000,000) × (0.07) × (0.87) × (0.11) = 66,990.	Inaccurate estimate of enrollment in introductory marketing course made.
Market buildup method	Total sales forecast = region 1 forecast + region 2 forecast + region 3 forecast = $2,000,000 + $7,000,000 + $13,000,000 = $22,000,000.	Incorrect assumption that areas will behave similarly in future.
Test marketing	Total sales forecast = (sales in test market A + sales in test market B) × (25) = ($1,000,000 + $1,200,000) × (25) = $55,000,000.	Test areas not representative of all locations.
Detailed statistical analyses	Simulation, complex trend analysis, regression, and correlation.	Lack of understanding by management; all factors not quantifiable.

shoes, and the percentage of women's shoe sales from casual shoes. It would then project its own sales of casual women's shoes to its target market. This method is only as accurate as the data plugged in for each market factor. It is useful since it gets management to think through a forecast and obtain different information.

Opposite to the chain-ratio method is the **market buildup method** by which a firm gathers data from small, separate market segments and aggregates them. For example, the market buildup method lets a company operating in four urban areas develop a forecast by first estimating sales in each area and then adding the areas. With this method, a firm must note that consumer tastes, competition, population growth, and media differ by geographic area. Segments of equal size may present dissimilar sales opportunities; they should not be lumped together without careful study.

Test marketing is a form of market buildup analysis where a firm projects a new product's sales based on short-run, geographically limited tests. With it, a company usually introduces a new product into one or a few markets for a short time and carries out a full marketing campaign there. Overall sales are then forecast from test-market sales. However, test areas may not be representative of all locales, and test-market enthusiasm may not carry into national distribution. Test marketing is discussed further in Chapter 13.

There are a number of detailed statistical methods for sales forecasting. Simulation allows a firm to enter market data into a computer-based model and forecast under varying conditions and marketing plans. With complex trend analysis, the firm includes past sales fluctuations, cyclical factors (such as economic conditions), and other factors when looking at sales trends. Regression and correlation techniques explore mathematical links between future sales and market factors, such as annual family income or derived demand. These methods depend on reliable data and the ability to use them correctly. A deeper discussion is beyond the scope of this text.

Additional Considerations

A forecast for a continuing product should be the most accurate.

The method and accuracy of sales forecasting depend a lot on the newness of a firm's offering. A forecast for a continuing good or service could be based on trend analysis, market-share analysis, executive and expert opinion, and sales-force surveys. Barring major alterations in the economy, industry, competition, or consumer tastes, the forecast should be relatively accurate.

A forecast for an item new to the firm but continuing in the industry could be based on trade data, executive or expert opinion, sales-force and consumer surveys, and test marketing. The first year's forecast should be somewhat accurate, the ensuing years more so. It is hard to project first-year sales precisely since consumer interest and competition may be tough to gauge.

A forecast for a good or service new to both the firm and the industry should rely on sales-force and consumer surveys, test marketing, executive and expert opinion, and simulation. The forecast for the early years may be highly inaccurate since the speed of consumer acceptance cannot be closely determined in advance. Later forecasts will be more accurate. While an initial forecast may be imprecise, it is still needed for setting marketing plans, budgeting, monitoring the environment and competition, and measuring success.

Sales penetration *shows whether a firm has reached its potential.* **Diminishing returns** *may result if it seeks nonconsumers.*

A company must consider **sales penetration**—the degree to which a firm is meeting its sales potential—in forecasting sales. It is expressed as:

Sales penetration = Actual sales/Sales potential

A firm with high sales penetration needs to realize that **diminishing returns** may occur if it seeks to convert remaining nonconsumers because the costs of attracting them may outweigh revenues. Other products or segments may offer better potential. An illustration is shown in Table 10-4.

Table 10-4

Illustrating Sales Penetration and Diminishing Returns

YEAR 1		YEAR 2	
Sales potential =	$1,000,000	Sales potential =	$1,000,000
Actual sales =	$600,000 (60,000 units)	Actual sales =	$700,000 (70,000 units)
Selling price =	$10/unit	Selling price =	$10/unit
Total marketing costs =	$100,000	Total marketing costs =	$150,000
Total production costs (at $8/unit) =	$480,000	Total production costs (at $8/unit) =	$560,000
Sales penetration =	$\frac{\$600{,}000}{\$1{,}000{,}000} = 60\%$	Sales penetration =	$\frac{\$700{,}000}{\$1{,}000{,}000} = 70\%$
Total profit =	$600,000 − ($100,000 + $480,000) = $20,000	Total profit =	$700,000 − ($150,000 + $560,000) = −$10,000

In year 1, sales penetration is 60% and the firm earns a $20,000 profit. In year 2, the firm raises marketing expenditures to increase sales penetration to 70%; as a result, it suffers diminishing returns—the additional $100,000 in actual sales is more than offset by a $130,000 rise in total costs (from $580,000 in year 1 to $710,000 in year 2).

A company must always keep in mind that factors may change and lead to an inaccurate forecast unless it is revised. These include economic conditions, industry conditions, company performance, competition, and consumer tastes.

MARKETING IN A CHANGING WORLD

Targeting the Interactive Marketplace[19]

As companies look ahead to further advances in interactive technology—and the fascinating new marketing opportunities that will accompany such advances, they also need to think about the alternative target market approaches that could be pursued. After all, just like other consumer markets, the interactive marketplace will encompass all sorts of potential segments.

With this in mind, Arbitron's NewMedia Pathfinder Study recently examined the interactive marketplace. Arbitron surveyed thousands of adults and included 612 variables related to demographics, life-styles, current media experiences, and expectations. What did it find? Well, the research firm did come up with some catchy segment names, as well as a lot of implications for marketers. There are fast laners (14 per cent of all respondents), diverse strivers (5 per cent), savvy sophisticates (11 per cent), family-focused (15 per cent), bystanders (16 per cent), sports fanatics (11 per cent), moral Americans (11 per cent), and the settled set (17 per cent).

Let's highlight a few of these segments:

- *Fast laners* are mostly Generation Xers and teens. They are more open to new technology.
- *Savvy sophisticates* are high-income, well-educated baby boomers. They are confident and innovative. More own and use PCs than any other group.
- *Family-focused* consumers are mostly price-oriented women with average income and below-average involvement with PCs and technology.
- *Bystanders* are lowest in confidence and innovativeness. They tend to be baby boomers with an above-average number of children living at home.

As summarized in the *Marketing News*, "Home shopping channels appeal most to fast laners, diverse strivers, family-focused, and bystanders. Infomercials have only average appeal among family-focused and well below-average appeal among bystanders. Savvy sophisticates show the heaviest involvement with on-line and print catalogs. They do not see TV as a purchasing medium." Furthermore, "Internet shoppers are pioneers more in the way they shop than in what they buy."

SUMMARY

1. *To describe the process of planning a target market strategy* After collecting information on consumers and environmental factors, a firm is ready to select the target market(s) to which it will appeal. A potential market contains people with similar needs, adequate resources, and a willingness and ability to buy.

Developing a target market strategy consists of three general phases, comprising seven specific steps: analyzing consumer demand—determining demand patterns (1), establishing bases of segmentation (2), and identifying potential market segments (3); targeting the market—choosing a target market approach (4) and selecting the target market(s) (5); and developing the marketing strategy—positioning the company's offering relative to competitors (6) and outlining the appropriate marketing mix(es) (7). Of particular importance is product differentiation, whereby a product offering is perceived by the consumer to differ from its competition on any physical or nonphysical product characteristic, including price.

2. *To examine alternative demand patterns and segmentation bases for both final and organizational consumers* Demand patterns indicate the uniformity or diversity of consumer needs and desires for particular categories of goods and services. With homogeneous demand, consumers have relatively uniform needs and desires. With clustered demand, consumer needs and desires can be classified into two or more identifiable clusters (segments), with each having distinct purchase requirements. With diffused demand, consumer needs and desires are so diverse that clear clusters (segments) cannot be identified.

[19]The material in this section is based on Kelly Shermach, "Study Identifies Types of Interactive Shoppers," *Marketing News* (September 25, 1995), p. 22.

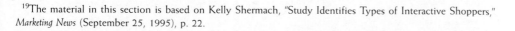

The possible bases for segmenting the market can be placed into three categories: geographic demographics—basic identifiable characteristics of towns, cities, states, regions, and countries; personal demographics—basic identifiable characteristics of individual final consumers and organizational consumers and groups of final consumers and organizational consumers; and life-styles—patterns in which people (final consumers and those representing organizational consumers) live and spend time and money. It is generally advisable to use a combination of demographic and life-style factors to form possible segmentation bases. Although the distinctions between final and organizational consumers should be kept in mind, the three broad segmentation bases could be used in both cases.

After establishing possible segmentation bases, a firm is ready to develop consumer profiles. Such profiles identify potential market segments by aggregating consumers with similar characteristics and needs.

3. *To explain and contrast undifferentiated marketing (mass marketing), concentrated marketing, and differentiated marketing (multiple segmentation)* Undifferentiated marketing aims at a large, broad consumer market via one basic marketing plan. In concentrated marketing, a firm aims at a narrow, specific consumer group via one, specialized marketing plan catering to the needs of that segment. Under differentiated marketing, a firm appeals to two or more distinct market segments, with a different marketing plan for each. When segmenting, a firm must understand the majority fallacy: the largest consumer segment may not offer the best opportunity; it often has the greatest number of competitors.

In selecting its target market(s), a firm should consider its goals and strengths, competition, segment size and growth potential, distribution needs, required expenditures, profit potential, company image, and its ability to develop and sustain a differential advantage.

Successful segmentation requires differences among and similarities within segments, measurable consumer traits and needs, large enough segments, and efficiency in reaching segments. It should not be abused by appealing to overly small groups, using marketing inefficiently, placing too much emphasis on imitations of original company products or brands, confusing consumers, and so on.

4. *To show the importance of positioning in developing a marketing strategy* In positioning its offering against competitors, a firm needs to present a combination of customer benefits that are not being provided by others and that are desirable by a target market. Customers must be persuaded that there are clear reasons for buying the firm's products rather than those of its competitors.

The last step in the target marketing process is for a firm to develop a marketing mix for each customer group to which it wants to appeal.

5. *To discuss sales forecasting and its role in target marketing* Short- and long-run sales should be forecast in developing a target market strategy. This helps a firm compute budgets, allocate resources, measure success, analyze productivity, monitor the environment and competition, and adjust marketing plans. A sales forecast describes the expected company sales of a specific good or service to a specific consumer group over a specific time period under a specific marketing program.

A firm can obtain sales-forecasting data from a variety of internal and external sources. Forecasting methods range from simple trend analysis to detailed statistical analyses. The best results are obtained when methods and forecasts are combined. A sales forecast should consider the newness of a firm's offering, sales penetration, diminishing returns, and the changing nature of many factors.

KEY TERMS

market (p. 262)
market segmentation (p. 262)
target market strategy (p. 262)
undifferentiated marketing (mass marketing) (p. 262)
concentrated marketing (p. 262)
differentiated marketing (multiple segmentation) (p. 262)
product differentiation (p. 262)
demand patterns (p. 263)
homogeneous demand (p. 263)
clustered demand (p. 263)
diffused demand (p. 263)
geographic demographics (p. 265)
personal demographics (p. 266)
heavy-usage segment (heavy half) (p. 270)
benefit segmentation (p. 271)
VALS (Values and Life-Styles) program (p. 271)
Social Styles model (p. 271)
majority fallacy (p. 277)
sales forecast (p. 283)
jury of executive or expert opinion (p. 284)
chain-ratio method (p. 284)
market buildup method (p. 285)
sales penetration (p. 286)
diminishing returns (p. 286)

Review Questions

1. Distinguish between the terms "market" and "market segmentation."
2. What are the three general phases in planning a target market strategy?
3. Explain this comment: "Sometimes a firm can achieve a key differential advantage by simply emphasizing how its offering satisfies existing consumer desires and needs better than its competitors do. Sometimes demand patterns must be modified for consumers to perceive a firm's product differentiation as worthwhile."
4. Differentiate among homogeneous, clustered, and diffused consumer demand. What are the marketing implications?
5. Describe five personal demographics pertaining to organizational consumers.
6. What is the majority fallacy? How may a firm avoid it?
7. Cite the five key requirements for successful segmentation.
8. Why is sales forecasting important when developing a target market strategy?
9. Contrast the jury of executive opinion and the chain-ratio method of sales forecasting.
10. Why are long-run sales forecasts for new products more accurate than short-run forecasts?

Discussion Questions

1. How could an international manufacturer of personal beepers apply geographic-demographic segmentation?
2. Develop a personal-demographic profile of the students in your marketing class. For what goods and services would the class be a good market segment? A poor segment?
3. Describe several potential benefit segments for a firm marketing maintenance services to business clients.
4. Develop a marketing strategy for a utility-vehicle manufacturer that wants to appeal to experiencers (as described in VALS 2). How should the strategy differ if the target market is strivers?
5. A firm has a sales potential of $4,000,000 and attains actual sales of $2,400,000. What does this signify? What should the firm do next?

CASE 1

*Teens as Global Consumers: What Does This Mean for Marketers?**

The worldwide teen (and pre-teen) market is huge. In Europe, Latin America, and the Pacific Rim, there are over 200 million teens—with Mexico, Brazil, and Argentina together having 57 million 10- to 19-year-olds. The United States has 35 million children aged 10 to 19, and each year, U.S. teens spend more than $60 billion of their own money. U.S. teenagers comprise 25 per cent of the market for movie tickets and 27 per cent for all video sales.

A recent study by D'Arcy Masius Benton & Bowles (DMB&B) of more than 6,500 teens in 26 countries concluded that "teens around the world are living very parallel lives." Similarities can be seen in dress (baggy Levi's or Diesel jeans, Doc Martens or Nike shoes, T-shirt, and leather jacket), dining habits (Coca-Cola and Big Macs), and even in the popularity of the same rock group (such as the Red Hot Chili Peppers). See Table 1. A common explanation of the similarity in teen behavior is that the worldwide media (including MTV, the Internet, and satellite television) closely bind teens, the same stores exist in multiple geographic markets, and global events such as the Olympics are appealing around the globe.

The DMB&B study also revealed that teens throughout the world cited the United States as having the greatest influence in fashion and culture. When asked to state which nation had the most impact on their fashion and culture, 54 per cent of American teens, 80 per cent of European teens, 80 per cent of teens from the Far East, and 87 per cent of Latin American teens said the United States. This "Americanization" directly has benefitted U.S. firms.

Still, some experts implore marketers to be aware of the importance of regional or country-based differences. As DMB&B's senior vice-president and director of strategic planning says, "I'm in no way advocating one-size-fits-all communications or advertising. That's just foolish. There will always be local forces that you can't ignore." For example, American advertisers need to realize that although ads aimed for the U.S. market tend to use a lot of superlatives, many Europeans and Asians like more subtle forms of persuasion. Europeans and Asians also do not like comparative ads whereby advertisers compare their offerings to other products or brands.

*The data in this case are drawn from "Teen Interests Appear to be Universal," *Advertising Age* (July 17, 1995), p. A3; Shawn Tully, "Teens: The Most Global Market of All," *Fortune* (May 16, 1994), pp. 90–97; and Cyndee Miller, "Teens Seen as the First Truly Global Consumers," *Marketing News* (March 27, 1995), p. 9.

Table 1

Teenage Wearing Habits In Selected Countries (Per Cent of Teens Who Wear Selected Clothing)

	UNITED STATES	EUROPE	LATIN AMERICA	ASIA	CHINA
Jeans	93	94	86	93	48
T-shirt	93	89	59	96	22
Running shoes	80	79	65	69	36
Blazer	42	43	30	27	43
Denim jacket	39	57	41	23	7

Source: "Teen Interests Appear to be Universal," *Advertising Age* (July 17, 1995), p. A3. Reprinted by permission, The Brain Waves Group.

Other experts say that even though a global teen consumer exists, with the exception of Levi's, America no longer dominates teen culture. They feel the emergence of the European Union has brought European teens closer together. They also see greater influence coming from Europe, Asia, and Latin America.

QUESTIONS

1. How can the product differentiation concept be applied to the teen market?
2. Comment on the "Americanization" versus the "need to reflect cultural differences" theories from the perspective of determining demand patterns.
3. Discuss the "Americanization" versus the "need to reflect cultural differences" theories from the perspective of the establishment of bases for segmentation.
4. Does the teen market represent a heavy-usage segment? Explain your answer.

CASE 2

Gannett: Marketing Newspapers to Women†

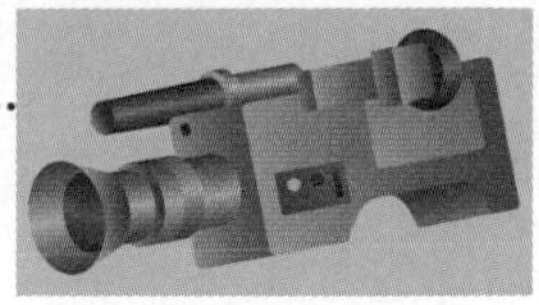

Gannett Co., Inc. is the largest U.S. newspaper group. It owns 82 daily newspapers, including *USA Today*, as well as 50 nondaily publications such as *USA Weekend*. Gannett has an average paid circulation of more than 6.3 million readers per day. In addition to its newspapers and other publications, Gannett owns and operates 10 TV and 10 radio stations in major markets—and North America's largest outdoor advertising group.

Gannett recently started NEWS 2000, a program designed to increase the size and quality of its newspaper audience. As part of this program, Gannett wants to increase its readership among women. Gannett is especially concerned about two disturbing trends: the rising per cent of newspaper readers who do not read the paper every day and low readership levels by women.

This case specifically deals with the strategies a daily newspaper can use to increase its female readership on a regular basis. Much of the material in the case represents the views of key Gannett executives, information from focus groups with women who are regular and irregular newspaper readers, and the views of experts specializing in marketing to females. The strategy of marketing newspapers to female readers can be organized on the basis of content, communication, and time pressures.

Although the first section of a newspaper (called the "A" section by the newspaper industry) is the most widely read section by both men and women, female newspaper readers are slightly less interested in this section than male readers. In total, 95 per cent of men who buy the newspaper read the "A" section, versus 93 per cent of women. Similarly, 55 to 60 per cent of men versus 30 to 34 per cent of women read the sports pages. In contrast, local news is more important to women than to men. Women are also more concerned than men that there is too much coverage of violent crimes, particularly on the first page of each newspaper.

Many women also feel they are portrayed in an overly stereotypical manner by newspapers and their advertisers. According to one expert, women are commonly shown as being "too young, too thin, and too beautiful." Newspapers can increase both their readership and their believability by more accurately portraying females. Many newspaper executives also feel that a newspaper has an obligation to notify the advertisers that inaccurately portray women.

To effectively reach women throughout the week, it is imperative to effectively communicate a newspaper's coverage to women. Some experts feel a newspaper should use its first page to prominently communicate stories of interest to women on a daily basis. For example, issues of importance to women (such as coverage of families, schools, health, and the workplace) should be started on the first page.

Numerous newspaper experts believe women (especially working women with children) face enormous time pressures and that this group cannot read a newspaper on a daily basis. Since many newspapers have weekly sections (on education, entertainment, and shopping) that especially appeal to women, a newspaper could increase sales to women by offering subscriptions that allow them to select specific days of the week. For instance, women could select a Wednesday, Thursday, and Friday subscription based on the special features on shopping, recipes, and entertainment contained in these days.

Like any other large audience, there are different segments of women newspaper readers. Some analysts say the female newspaper audience can be segmented based on their reading the newspaper to relax versus their reading the newspaper to "gear up for the day." Others say segments should be based on a combination of factors such as education, attitude towards women's roles, and the family life cycle stage. Newspapers also need to be careful not to oversegment.

QUESTIONS

1. Is appealing to both male and female newspaper readers an example of undifferentiated marketing or differentiated marketing? Explain your answer.
2. Evaluate the female newspaper market on the basis of the requirements for successful segmentation.
3. What are the pros and cons of selling subscriptions to females based on days that special features appear?
4. Describe how a newspaper could oversegment the female market.

VIDEO QUESTIONS ON GANNETT

1. Evaluate the premise that newspapers are not doing enough to attract women on an everyday basis.
2. How should the first page of a newspaper be laid out to attract a higher proportion of female readers?

†The data in this case are drawn from *Gannett 1994 Annual Report*; and "Marketing Effectively: Issues on Marketing to Women," *Gannett Broadcast* (January 17, 1995).

PART 3 CASE

Digging into the Personalities of Organizational Consumers

Introduction

Final consumer marketers are not the only ones that must worry about how to deal with different kinds of customers. Customer strategies are no less important for industrial marketers. A starting point is studying the types of customers a firm will encounter and then customizing strategies to meet the needs of each. Sound like target marketing? It is, with a small twist.

To study the personality profiles of industrial buyers, a national survey was conducted among managers of firms selling to industrial buyers. The respondents represented a broad spectrum of industries: auto parts, banking, chemical, fast food, consumer credit, food manufacture, forestry, home construction, insurance, plastics, and railroads.

Each manager indicated which of the listed customer types he or she had encountered; an open-ended "other" category was included to cover customers not fitting any type. Through data analysis, nine key prototypical industrial customer personalities emerged, each with different behavioral attributes.

Nine Personality Types

Table 1 shows the typology revealed in the study and notes the descriptive name, the main customer motivation, the marketing strategy that appeals to the customer, a suggested service strategy, and the percentage of all customers that the type represents.

The percentage breakdown an individual firm encounters will vary with the markets it serves. Chiselers, for example, probably make up a larger portion of the customer base for firms selling commodities than for those selling unique, high-end, special-order equipment.

The Chiseler A customer calls to say he/she was shorted on an item. He/she says the only fair solution is a "replacement item plus a trip to Hawaii" for inconvenience.

Chiselers are 15 per cent of the customer base. They are motivated by good deals and low price, but their definition of a good deal is to get something below cost, regardless of how unrealistic that may be. Often, they will try to renegotiate the deal after the fact to squeeze even more out of it.

In general, Chiselers respond to marketing strategies that stress deep discounts, volume, and freebies. Dealing with such customers can be difficult since they often want the same level of service afforded high-margin products.

The Chiseler likes sales presentations filled with dollars and cents deals and cost justifications for any claim made by the salesperson. Because he or she is bottom-line oriented, all marketing promises must go in that direction.

Chiselers have a narrow focus, often being driven by internal pressures to cut costs or get the best deal possible from suppliers. They have a shark-like propensity to go directly for the lowest cost without concern for other aspects of the good or service. Like auctioneers at a community sale trying to take prices up, the Chiseler wants to drive them down. The classic Chiseler initiates competitive bidding between suppliers to drive them to the lowest prices. The victor can win a bidding battle, but lose the profit war.

Here are some quick tips for dealing with Chiselers:

- Never go all the way on price. By beating competitors, you may also beat yourself.
- Cost out all business you quote to a Chiseler. Can you make profits on additional volume if you meet the Chiseler's price?
- If you get an order, next time the Chiseler will expect you to go lower.
- Be prepared to walk away—"Know when to hold 'em, know when to fold 'em."
- Make the relationship two-sided. The Chiseler gets the lowest price on this deal, and you get access to his/her more profitable businesses.
- Give a low price on the product and raise prices on the services that may entail less attention.
- Try to shift the Chiseler from being price-oriented to value-oriented by focusing on the added value of your product.

The Intimidator A fax comes in from a customer that starts, "My lawyer says . . . ." This is the trademark of an Intimidator, a customer who seeks tight control and power.

Representing 5 per cent of customers, Intimidators' definition of a good deal is one in which they dictate terms and the supplier agrees. Control is more important than price. Because they want to dominate the situation, they have done their homework and know what the competition is offering. They're ready to play hard ball and know their legal rights.

Intimidators react well to marketing efforts focusing on detailed product and competitor knowledge, as well as service. Hence, access to engineers and technical expertise must be part of a firm's marketing strategy.

Personnel who deal with Intimidators must be confident and unwilling to back down. These people respect power and an understanding of the rules. Thus, the service strategy must be to let the Intimidator sound off, and then offer an objective and detailed description of the firm's position. It's important to state the position firmly, yet without emotion.

Intimidators look for the firm's weakest person to gain maximum leverage. They are motivated to extract as many

Source: Adapted by the authors from Richard Lancioni and Terence A. Oliva, "Penetrating Purchaser Personalities," *Marketing Management* (Spring 1995), pp. 22–29. Reprinted by permission of the American Marketing Association.

Table 1
Industrial Customer Personality Types

PERSONALITY TYPE	% OF TOTAL	MOTIVATION	MARKETING STRATEGY	SERVICE STRATEGY
Chiseler	15	Low price	Discounts, volume, freebies	Demonstrate value of of the deal
Intimidator	5	Control and power	Detailed specs and procedures	Be firm, follow procedures
Screamer	3	Quick problem resolution	Competitive comparisons	Fast response, empathy
Talker	4	Social interaction	Hand-holding, always available	Refocus on the issue, friendly
Airhead	2	Lazy	No effort, works out of box	Product problem diagnosis
Loyal Customer	62	High degree of comfort	Provide extras	Special first-class treatment
Rude and Irate	3	Poor quality product	Demonstrate product quality	Pre-emptive product fixes ready
Abusive Nitpicker	4	Distrust	Honest, clearly specified terms	Customer-developed solutions
Stereotyper	2	Low ambiguity	Factual competitive comparisons	Have information at fingertips

concessions as possible and can be especially difficult to a new salesperson. They usually play up their position by saying "I am the President" or "This is Doctor Smith."

Here is some advice for dealing with Intimidators:

- Be polite, but do not deviate from company policy or the Intimidator will raise the stakes next time.
- Train employees to recognize and handle Intimidators.
- Refer the Intimidator to a higher authority because he or she is often thwarted by a countervailing power.
- Be patient and never show signs of weakness.

The Screamer Your secretary buzzes to tell you some maniac is at his/her desk screaming and yelling. At first glance, Screamers, who are 3 per cent of the customer base, seem like Intimidators, but they're not.

These people want a quick resolution and use embarrassment and the squeaky-wheel approach as weapons. Some behavior may be driven by their own time constraints and responsibilities; they view any problem as just one more hassle they do not need in their life.

Screamers react best to marketing strategies that promise quick problem resolution, such as a "no-questions-asked money-back guarantee," free product replacements with FedExing parts, and a 24-hour hotline. Service strategies must center on listening, patience, empathy, and above all quick response. Personnel should focus on calming the individual down.

Screamers can be annoying. They will raise their voices over the smallest of issues to force concessions. Unlike Intimidators who work from a power base, Screamers expect that anything will be done to quiet them. It is often senior people who are most susceptible to Screamers.

Here are some suggestions for dealing with Screamers:

- Provide a fast solution. Speed counts because it blunts their leverage.
- Don't react negatively. Have a mechanism for passing them along to your in-house "Screamer expert."
- Have all the facts. This often mollifies a Screamer.

The Talker An intended quick call to a customer becomes an hour-and-a-half talkfest. Talkers, who are 4 per cent of customers, want social interaction. They are motivated by the need to express themselves and their opinions to others. Talkers are usually benign, but use up significant time resources and thereby prevent the firm from adequately serving other customers.

Marketing strategies that push the Talker's button involve personal, "we are always here" approaches. Hand-holding and custom testimonials are very successful with Talkers, who want to belong. Companies that reduce human interaction will lose their business because they do not feel satisfied. Service strategy should be friendly but stress getting to the point.

Talkers are motivated by many factors. First, they often think they know more than a salesperson, and want to demonstrate it. Second, some customers are culturally influenced to talk by virtue of their geographical location. On average, Southern customers engage in more verbal discourse than those in the Northeast. Third, Talkers may be motivated to communicate ideas to others in the industry, and the sales rep provides an ideal conduit. They may start by saying, "This information is confidential," to prolong a conversation. Because the average face-to-face industrial sales call today costs so much, it is critical for companies to develop more cost-effective ways of making a sale.

Here are some tips for making Talkers (or any customers) happy:

- Have an answer for every question raised; preparation is the key.
- Brush up on the Talker's favorite topics—sports, restaurants, wines, etc.—to avoid a lecture and maintain the advantage.
- Be a good listener. Being attuned to what a Talker is saying, regardless of the words, often provides clues to increased sales.
- Don't show signs of frustration, which can cause negative reactions.
- Maintain good eye contact and body language to show interest.

The Airhead You get a letter from a customer who ordered 10,000 type C nuts when he/she needed type B bolts. Why? "The secretary picked the number from the wrong page in the catalog." We call this customer—2 per cent of the base—an Airhead.

Airheads want to exert little effort. They are often lazy, unsure, or tentative. Thus, Airheads find it easier to call than to read the instructions or look things up. Their product problems are often caused by a failure to plug it in or turn it on, or by improper startup procedures.

Marketing strategies to attract Airheads stress the least amount of effort on the customer's part. Programs that preempt customer effort, like calling to see if they need something, are particularly popular. Additionally, it is important to have quick-start instructions, engineering help, troubleshooting guides, and call-back programs to ensure that everything is clear.

Service strategies should facilitate self-learning. In particular, they must help a customer diagnose the problem and offer a fast solution. Airheads are difficult for the firm for which they work and vendors. And they're easy targets for unethical sales reps, often taking a seller's words as gospel.

Such shortcomings offer legitimate firms an opportunity to get and keep Airheads as customers. Yet, you may have to seek them out since they won't have done their homework. Providing Airheads with good products, good service, and a full line of products will build brand loyalty.

Here are some additional suggestions for dealing with Airheads:

- Smother them with service to lock them in and lock out the competition.
- Offer contracts to Airheads to increase their feeling of security.
- Offer warranties or guarantees.
- Provide the Airhead with easy-to-understand instructions.
- Offer one-stop shopping for goods and services.

The Loyal Customer An order has just come in from Susan who has bought from you for the last 12 years. Such customers are critical to success because their loyalty keeps the sales of the firm steady. Loyal Customers are 62 per cent of a company's customer base.

Loyal Customers' needs are being met, but they should not be taken for granted. They like the comfort and lower risk of dealing with a known seller. Strategies should focus on Loyal Customers by selling them new products first, contacting them to diagnose needs, and providing extra service and freebies.

Although this customer group sustains the company, many firms fail to appreciate that fact and take Loyal Customers for granted, focusing marketing efforts instead on "new accounts." A typical example is when discounts or premiums are used as incentives to gain new accounts, but are not offered to established customers, a slight often interpreted by Loyal Customers as a lack of appreciation on the part of the supplier.

Some quick tips for keeping Loyal Customers happy are:

- Make them eligible for all new account bonus programs.
- Seek their advice on re-engineering products, service, or organization.
- Partner with them for inventory planning, new product designs, or old product redesigns.

The Rude and Irate One of your salespeople calls and tells you a customer who is swearing and yelling is demanding to see you. Unlike Screamers, who are motivated to get a fast resolution, Rude and Irate customers are driven by poor quality. These customers feel they have been mistreated or cheated in some way.

The best marketing strategy is to install management procedures that ensure a firm produces high-quality products. And, to lessen problems arising out of possible misunderstandings about what a good or service is supposed to do, salespeople must know your products and those of competitors well.

The best service strategy is to be patient and understanding and to have answers for all possible complaints. This means pre-engineering answers and responses for the most common complaints to ensure a satisfactory resolution.

Rude and Irate customers make up only 3 per cent of the customer base, but can eat up as much as 40 per cent of management's attention. While similar to Intimidators and Screamers, Rude and Irate customers' behavior is spurred by previous interactions with the firm. So, this is payback time for earlier bad experiences—such as problems in receiving shipments on time, incorrect billing, and delays in dealing with returns or defectives.

Having standard service procedures in place is the best solution, but here are some other tips for handling the Rude and Irate customers:

- Learn if their anger is caused by a current issue or rooted in the past.

- Be understanding. Behavior may be due to cultural or regional differences.
- Give factual responses to all questions.
- Respond rapidly to any problem, and you may be able to convert a Rude and Irate customer to a Loyal Customer.

The Abusive Nitpicker Many customers are cautious and may require excruciating detail about a seemingly unimportant issue. Nitpicking is expected in a new relationship, but Abusive Nitpickers carry it to excess.

Driven by distrust, they are ready to swing into action at the slightest provocation to let you know they will check every detail. Hence, any small problem triggers a hostile reaction. To reduce Abusive Nitpickers' distrust, use marketing strategies that focus on guarantees, warranties, and full and detailed disclosure relating to specifications, prices, and return procedures. Factual comparisons with the competition also help allay fears.

Service strategy should stress knowing all the facts about complaints, offering alternative solutions, providing quick responses to remedy problems, and remaining calm and polite throughout the process.

The Abusive Nitpicker–4 per cent of customers–can pose other more serious problems for a firm. The high level of detail demanded about a sale, product, or price can compromise a firm's marketing strategy. For example, he or she may want to know how much profit is being made on a sale. Giving this information to a customer is often inappropriate except in bidding situations where costs must be revealed. And keep in mind that an Abusive Nitpicker may be getting data about the specifics of your product design or marketing strategy to give to a competitor.

When dealing with Abusive Nitpickers, remember the following:

- Tell them only what is important for the sale.
- Determine what information is needed prior to the sales interaction.
- Beware of giving any information to anyone who might be a potential competitor because it could be used against you.

The Stereotyper Some customers categorize suppliers and then formulate a way to deal with them. If these people correctly stereotype and deal with your firm, things can be smooth. Problems only occur when they miscategorize you.

Stereotypers—2 per cent of customers—have a need for certainty. They may have a chip on their shoulder and want to live in a black-and-white world where all is clear. Marketing strategies must use factual comparison charts, well-organized sales presentations, and unambiguous answers to questions.

Because ambiguity reduction is key, service strategy should stress having all key data at one's fingertips. It's crucial to empower employees to resolve problems on the spot and issue status reports on resolution progress.

Other ways to keep Stereotypers happy include:

- Act in a manner consistent with your product or brand image.
- Find out what level of customer service they expect to get to determine if it differs from what they are receiving.
- Avoid making promises you cannot keep.
- Be careful not to box yourself in with the opening deal because it sets the Stereotyper's perceptions for future deals.

QUESTIONS

1. Apply the information in this case to both final and organizational consumers.
2. How would you expect the various industrial customer personality types to utilize vendor and value analysis? Explain your answer.
3. Based on the information in this case, what type of target market strategy would you use in appealing to industrial customers?
4. If an industrial marketer wants to utilize benefit segmentation, what do you recommend?
5. Relate the discussion in this case to the Social Styles model shown in Figure 10-8.
6. As the marketing manager for a small manufacturer of PC-based financial software, how would you handle Chiselers?
7. As the marketing manager for a large umbrella maker, how would you handle the buyer at a large department store chain whom you view as an Airhead?
8. How would you prepare a sales forecast that includes projections for both Loyal Customers and Intimidators?

PRODUCT PLAN

PART 4

To adhere to the marketing concept, a firm needs to devise, enact, and monitor a plan that centers on the four elements of the marketing mix: product, distribution, promotion, and price. We present these elements in Parts 4 to 7, with Part 4 concentrating on product planning.

11 Basic Concepts in Product Planning

Here, we define tangible, augmented, and generic products and distinguish among different types of consumer and industrial products (both goods and services). We look at product mix strategies and product management organizations in detail. We also study product positioning and the product life cycle in depth. The chapter concludes with international dimensions of product planning.

12 Goods Versus Services Planning

Now, we look at the scope of goods and services, and introduce a goods/services continuum. We review goods and services classification systems. Then, we study the special considerations in the marketing of services. We also see that service marketing has lagged behind goods marketing and why this is changing. At this point, our discussion turns to nonprofit marketing and how it is distinct from profit-oriented marketing. We examine how nonprofit organizations can be classified, as well as their role.

13 Conceiving, Developing, and Managing Products

In this chapter, we look at products from their inception to their deletion. We discuss the types of new products, reasons for new-product failures, and the new-product planning process. We explain the growth of products in terms of the adoption and diffusion processes, and note several methods for extending the lives of mature products. We also offer product deletion strategies.

Branding and Packaging

Here, we look at the branding decisions that center on corporate symbols, the branding philosophy, the choice of brand names, and the use of trademarks. We also consider the six basic functions of packaging: containment, usage, communication, market segmentation, channel cooperation, and new-product planning.

Part 4 Video Vignette

Hain Food Group

The Hain Food Group develops, distributes, and markets over 350 food products in more than 30 categories—under six different brand names. The Hain brand features all natural ingredients, with no preservatives or chemical additives. Hain products include rice cakes, soups, nondairy beverages, frozen French toast, snacks, and salad dressings. The Hollywood brand offers vitamin enriched products, such as canola cooking oil and peanut cooking oil. The Estee brand is known for its sugar-free products, ranging from cookies and cereals to chocolate snacks. The Featherweight brand emphasizes low-salt foods, such as crackers and pretzels. The Kineret brand is used for frozen kosher foods, including bread and potato-based products. The Farm Foods brand stands for soy-based foods, such as pizza, frozen desserts, and pocket pitas.

When was the last time you came across a company that sells a healthy baked potato and rice snack (positioned against potato chips) in a Louisiana barbecue flavor?

The Hain Food Group's total annual sales exceed $75 million. What makes it stand out from other food companies? Hain is a leader in natural and specialty foods. The firm offers foods that are healthy *and* delicious *and* high quality *and* innovative. Among its packaging innovations are new cannisters for rice cakes. These cannisters are stackable (good for retailers) and resealable (good for consumers).

If you're skeptical, consider this: When was the last time you came across a company that sells a healthy baked potato and rice snack (positioned against potato chips) in a Louisiana barbecue flavor, a nondairy beverage made of rice and soy, safflower mayonnaise, chocolate animal graham crackers with no saturated fat or cholesterol, a pizza with a wheat crust and reduced calories, or wild blueberry-flavored mini rice cakes? Still skeptical? Maybe these facts will convince you that Hain is the real (pun intended) thing: Total natural food sales in the United States now exceed $8 billion annually, with yearly growth of 20 per cent. And international sales of natural foods are rising just as fast.

Hain's vision, to become the premier specialty food company, drives its product plans and keeps it away from the cluttered part of the market: "This goal will be achieved through a five-pronged strategy designed to build a powerful portfolio of leading niche brands as follows: (1) Solidification and strengthening of core product lines. (2) Innovative product introductions. (3) Strategic alliances with other firms. (4) Acquisition of underdeveloped brand names. (5) Global expansion. The Company will pursue opportunities with good-for-you products in high-growth categories leading to improved corporate profitability. The Company is dedicated to the development and expansion of its Brands. Taste, nutrition, innovation, and quality have always been an integral part of Hain's brand equity. The Company will continue to capitalize on these elements as it expands into new products and categories. It's a Great Time for Hain!"

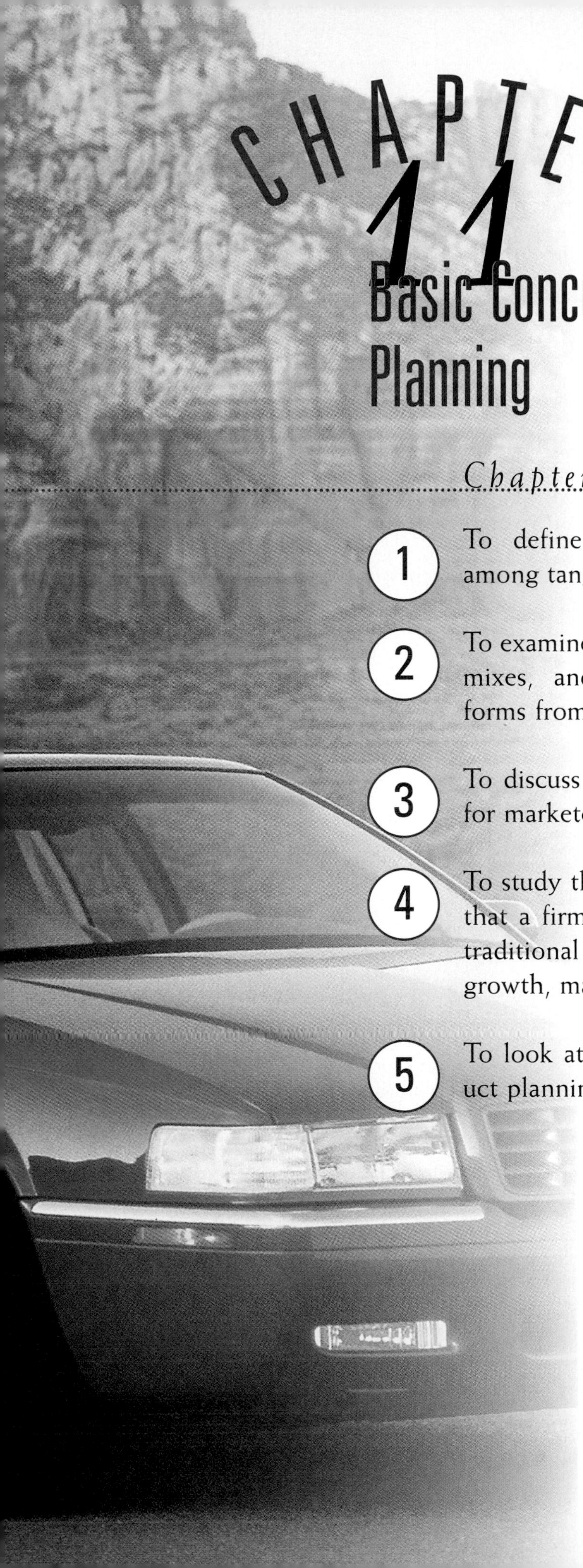

CHAPTER 11

Basic Concepts in Product Planning

Chapter Objectives

1. To define product planning and differentiate among tangible, augmented, and generic products

2. To examine the various types of products, product mixes, and product management organization forms from which a firm may select

3. To discuss product positioning and its usefulness for marketers

4. To study the different types of product life cycles that a firm may encounter and the stages of the traditional product life cycle (introduction, growth, maturity, and decline)

5. To look at the international dimensions of product planning

Upon his appointment as General Motors' (GM's) head of marketing, Ronald L. Zarrella stated that although GM had some of the most recognized car names in the world—from the Buick Roadmaster to the Cadillac Fleetwood—it had failed to keep many of the models up to date enough to be competitive with rivals. "We have too many models and vehicle lines," he said, adding that he counted as many as 77 different car and light-truck varieties in GM's lineup. Zarrella also said a GM survey found that 35 per cent of people shopping for cars didn't even consider a GM model.

Because of GM's weak product positioning strategy, Ronald Zarrella was hired away from Bausch & Lomb and given the job of revamping General Motors' marketing approach. No longer would the company's various divisions be so "muddled" in consumers' minds.

Zarrella announced that the company's vehicle divisions would each become more focused and consistent: "We can't escape the fact that the way our vehicle products have been targeted in the past, many are right on top of one another." To accomplish this, he planned to recruit more marketers to sharpen GM's strategy and to serve as brand managers for the divisions. And to provide inducement for change, each divisional marketing manager will have greater profit-and-loss responsibility.

Here is Zarrella's product positioning vision for GM's vehicle divisions:

- *Chevrolet*—This is GM's high-volume and light-truck division. Chevrolet should offer dependability, reliability, and the widest range of models.
- *Pontiac*—This is GM's sportiest brand. Pontiac should represent youthfulness and spirit and feature "in-your-face styling."
- *Saturn*—It should target import buyers and younger buyers. Saturn needs to stand for "dependability, intelligence, and friendliness." Saturn needs also to retain its "overall shopping, buying, and ownership experience."
- *Oldsmobile*—It should represent the logical trade-up alternative for Saturn owners as they become more affluent and want larger cars. Oldsmobile should compete for market share with Audi, Acura, and entry-level Infiniti and Lexus purchasers.
- *Buick*—It should represent GM's "premium American car." Buick should offer products that are "substantial, distinctive, powerful, mature." Buick needs to target baby boomers in their 50s.

- *Cadillac*—It is GM's luxury car division. Cadillac should represent "sophisticated, highly perfected cars." Cadillac needs to compete against Mercedes, BMW, Jaguar, and Lexus "in all of the markets of the world." Cadillac is especially seen as attracting foreign buyers willing to pay for a large, luxury automobile.
- *GMC*—This is GM's "premium truck brand with differentiated products from Chevrolet." High-end sports-utility vehicles are in the domain of GMC. These vehicles need to be differentiated from Chevrolet's mainstream truck business. For efficiency purposes, Pontiac and GMC vehicles will now be sold only at joint dealerships, and overall marketing management of the two brands will be combined.

Ronald Zarrella also sees Saturn, Chevrolet, and Cadillac as global divisions that should sell more cars and light trucks outside of North America. And he intends to convey brand identities through easy-to-remember ads, like those used by consumer products manufacturers such as Procter & Gamble.[1]

In this chapter, we will look at several basic product-planning decisions a firm must make, including those involving product management organizations and product positioning.

Overview

Product planning *means devising and managing* **products** *that satisfy consumers.*

Product planning is systematic decision making relating to all aspects of the development and management of a firm's products, including branding and packaging. Each **product** consists of a bundle of attributes (features, functions, benefits, and uses) capable of exchange or use, usually a mix of tangible and intangible forms. Thus,

> a product may be an idea, a physical entity (a good), or a service, or any combination of the three. It exists for the purpose of exchange in the satisfaction of individual and organizational objectives.[2]

A well-structured product plan lets a company pinpoint opportunities, develop appropriate marketing programs, coordinate a mix of products, maintain successful products as long as possible, reappraise faltering products, and delete undesirable products.

A firm should define its products in three distinct ways: tangible, augmented, and generic. By considering all three definitions, the company is better able to identify consumer needs, competitive offerings, and distinctive product attributes. This is illustrated in Figure 11-1.

A **tangible product** *has precise specifications, while an* **augmented product** *includes image and service features.*

A **tangible product** is a basic physical entity, service, or idea; it has precise specifications and is offered under a given description or model number. Windows 95 software, a Caterpillar diesel engine, the *Wall Street Journal*, a seven-day Caribbean cruise on the QE2 (Queen Elizabeth 2), and a proposal to cut state income taxes by 3.5 per cent are examples of tangible products. Color, style, size, weight, durability, quality of construction, price, and efficiency in use are some tangible product features.

An **augmented product** includes not only the tangible elements of a product, but also the accompanying cluster of image and service features. For example, one political candidate may receive more votes than another because of charisma (augmented product), despite identical platform issues (tangible product). Rolex watches are popular chiefly due to the image of luxury and status they convey. At Cummins Engine, offering augmented products means "helping our customers be successful, not simply supplying them with quality engines. Increasingly, the value we bring to customers can be described as *smart power*, which is a value-added package of products, information systems, and support services that provides improved performance and business solutions to our customers."[3]

[1]Gabriella Stern, "GM's New Marketing Chief Seeks Clarity Amid Muddle of Overlapping Car Lines," *Wall Street Journal* (May 1, 1995), pp. A3, A5; and Gabriella Stern, "GM May Merge Pontiac, GMC Sales Units," *Wall Street Journal* (January 12, 1996), pp. A3, A12.

[2]Peter D. Bennett (Editor), *Dictionary of Marketing Terms*, Second Edition (Chicago: American Marketing Association, 1995), p. 219.

[3]*Cummins Engine Company 1994 Annual Report.*

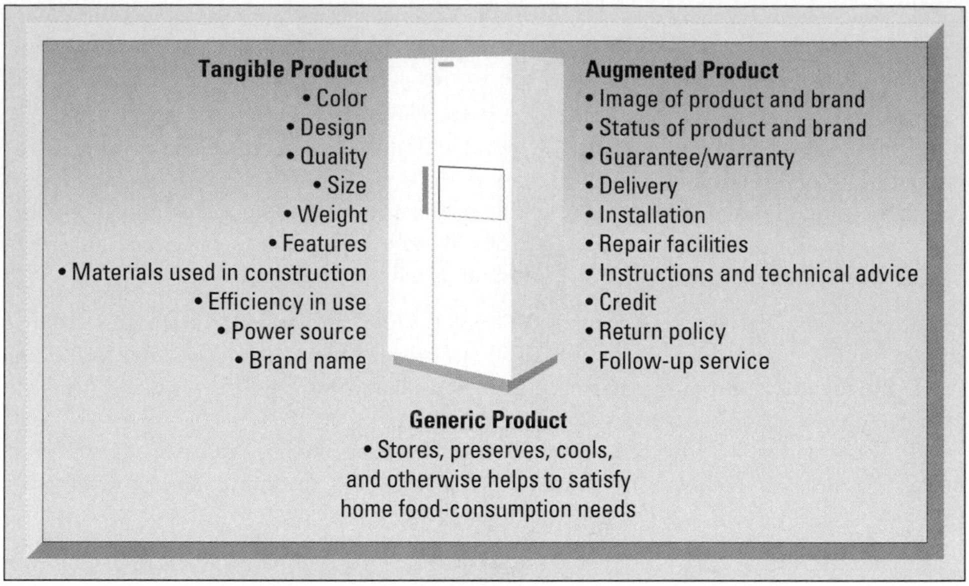

FIGURE 11-1
Illustrating the Three Product Definitions

A **generic product** *centers on consumer benefits.*

A **generic product** focuses on what a product means to the customer, not the seller. It is the broadest definition and is consistent with the marketing concept:

- "In the factory we make cosmetics, and in the drugstore we sell hope." (Charles Revson, founder of Revlon)
- "We know our customers come to us to buy more than bearings and steel. They come to us looking for solutions." (Timken Company)

When applying the generic product concept, these points should be kept in mind. First, because a generic product is a consumer view of what a product represents, a firm should learn what the product means to the consumer before further product planning—as shown in Figure 11-2. Second, inasmuch as people in various nations may perceive the same product (such as a car) in different generic terms (such as basic transportation versus comfortable driving), a firm should consider the impact of this on a possible global strategy.

This chapter provides an overview of product planning. It examines the basic areas in which a firm must make decisions: product type(s), product mix, product management organization, and product positioning. It also covers the product life cycle and its marketing relevance, and presents considerations for international marketers. Chapter 12 covers the planning involved with goods versus services. Chapter 13 presents an in-depth discussion of how to manage products over their lives, from finding new product ideas to deleting faltering products. Chapter 14 concentrates on two specialized aspects of product planning: branding and packaging.

Types of Products

The initial product-planning decision is choosing the type(s) of products to offer. Products can be categorized as goods or services and as consumer or industrial. Categorization is important because it focuses on the differences in the characteristics of products and the resulting marketing implications.

Goods marketing *relates to selling physical products.* **Service marketing** *includes rented-goods services, owned-goods services, and nongoods services.*

Fundamental Distinctions Between Goods and Services

Goods marketing entails the sale of physical products—such as furniture, heavy machinery, food, and stationery. **Service marketing** encompasses the rental of goods, servicing goods owned by consumers, and personal services—such as vehicle rentals, house painting, and accounting.

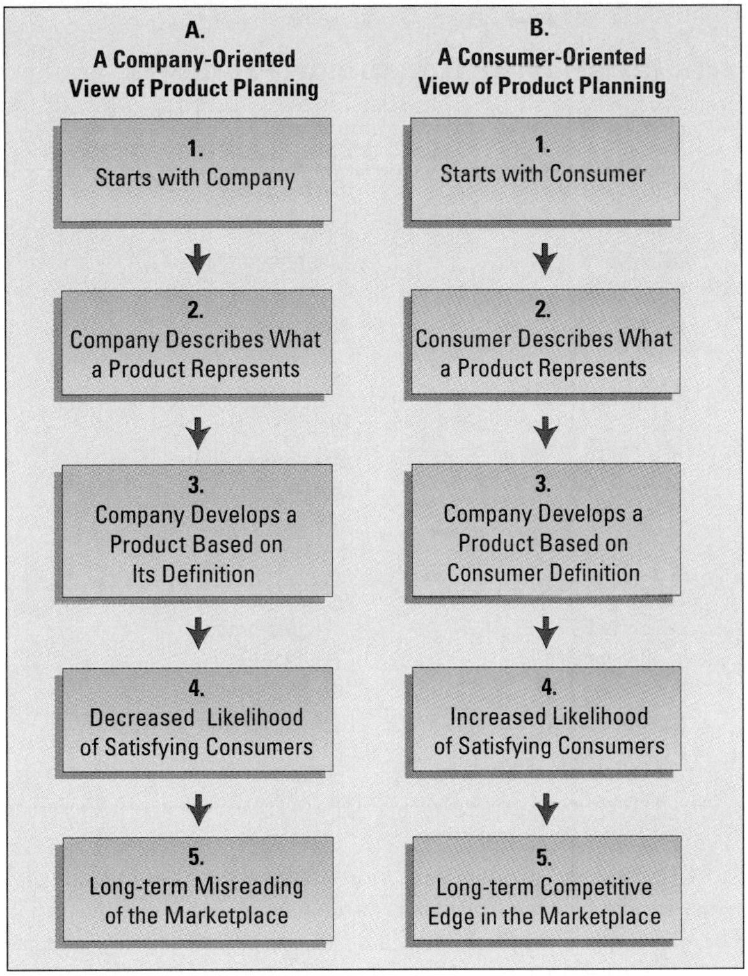

FIGURE 11-2
Applying the Generic Product Concept
In A, the firm is not properly employing the generic product concept and does not understand its customers' needs. In B, the firm is properly using the generic product concept and is successful with its customers.

Source: Adapted by the authors from Leon G. Schiffman and Elaine Sherman, "Value Orientations of New-Age Elderly: The Coming of an Ageless Market," *Journal of Business Research,* Vol. 22 (March 1991), p. 193.

Four attributes generally distinguish services from goods: intangibility, perishability, inseparability from the service provider, and variability in quality. Their impact is greatest for personal services—which are usually more intangible, more perishable, more dependent on the skills of the service provider (inseparability), and have more quality variations than rented- or owned-goods services.

The sales of goods and services are frequently connected. For instance, a tractor manufacturer may provide—for an extra fee—extended warranties, customer training, insurance, and financing. In goods marketing, goods dominate the overall offering and services augment them. In service marketing, services dominate the overall offering and goods augment them.

The distinctions between goods and services planning are more fully discussed in Chapter 12.

Consumer Products

Consumer products *are final consumer goods and services.*

Consumer products are goods and services destined for the final consumer for personal, family, or household use. The use of a good or service designates it as a consumer product. For example, a calculator, dinner at a restaurant, phone service, and an electric pencil sharpener are consumer products only if purchased for personal, family, or household use.

Consumer products may be classed as convenience, shopping, and specialty products—based on shoppers' awareness of alternative products and their characteristics prior to a shopping trip and the degree of search people will undertake. Thus, placing a product into one of these categories depends on shopper behavior. See Table 11-1.

Table 11-1
Characteristics of Consumer Products

CONSUMER CHARACTERISTICS	TYPE OF PRODUCT		
	Convenience	*Shopping*	*Specialty*
Knowledge prior to purchase	High	Low	High
Effort expended to acquire product	Minimal	Moderate to high	As much as needed
Willingness to accept substitutes	High	Moderate	None
Frequency of purchase	High	Moderate or low	Varies
Information search	Low	High	Low
Major desire	Availability without effort	Comparison shopping to determine best choice	Brand loyalty regardless of price and availability
Examples	(a) Staple: cereal (b) Impulse: candy (c) Emergency: tire repair	(a) Attribute-based: name-brand clothes (b) Price-based: budget hotel	Hellmann's mayonnaise

Convenience products *are purchased with minimum effort and are categorized as staples, impulse products, and emergency products.*

Convenience products are those bought with a minimum of effort because a consumer has knowledge of product attributes prior to shopping and/or is pressed for time. The person does not want to search for much information and will accept a substitute (Libby's instead of Green Giant corn) rather than visit more than one store. Marketing tasks center on distribution at all available outlets, convenient store locations and hours, the use of mass advertising and in-store displays, well-designed store layouts, and self-service to minimize purchase time. Resellers often carry many brands.

Convenience products can be subdivided into staples, impulse products, and emergency products. Staples are low-priced and routinely purchased on a regular basis—such as detergent, mass transit, and cereal. Impulse products are items or brands a person does not plan to buy on a specific store trip—such as candy, a magazine, and a lottery ticket. According to a recent study, 70 per cent of brand decisions at supermarkets are made in the stores.[4] Emergency products are bought out of urgent need—such as an umbrella in a rainstorm and aspirin for a headache.

Shopping products *require an information search.*

Shopping products are those for which consumers feel they lack sufficient information about product alternatives and their attributes (or prices), and therefore must acquire further knowledge in order to make a purchase decision. People will exert effort searching for information because shopping products are bought infrequently, have large purchase prices, or require comparisons. The marketing emphasis is on full assortments (such as many colors, sizes, and options), the availability of sales personnel, the communication of competitive advantages, informative ads, well-known brands (or stores), distributor enthusiasm, and customer warranties and follow-up service to reduce perceived risk. Shopping centers and downtown business districts ease shopping behavior by having many adjacent stores.

Shopping products may be attribute- or price-based. With attribute-based shopping products, consumers get information on product features, performance, and other factors. Items with the best combination of attributes are bought. Sony electronics and Calvin Klein clothes are marketed as attribute-based shopping products. With price-based shop-

[4] "POPAI's 1995 Study: 'More Purchase Decisions Made In-Store,'" *Promo* (October 1995), p. 15.

TECHNOLOGY & MARKETING

Will Cars of the Future Be Smarter Than Their Drivers?

Passenger car makers have come up with many new optional features that add convenience, safety, and comfort for drivers and their passengers. Let's look at some of these innovations.

Several car makers have begun to market devices based on satellite-linked navigational systems. GM's system, Guidestar, uses a voice synthesizer that provides directions to lost motorists. Guidestar is currently available on some Oldsmobile models as a $2,000 option. Volvo's Dynaguide Info System is similar to Guidestar, but also includes specific traffic report information. Not to be outdone, Lincoln's Remote Emergency Satellite Cellular Unit (RESCU) will notify the nearest police department, fire department, medical unit, and tow truck in the event of an emergency. The unit dials 911 and then uses satellite information to tell the rescuing unit your car's exact location. RESCU is available as an option on the Lincoln Continental.

Another safety-related option would properly adjust driver and passenger headrests every time the car is started. The option, in final development by Lear Seating, uses ultrasonic sensors that determine the proper positions and adjust each headrest automatically. Improperly positioned headrests provide little protection from whiplash.

Other options are designed to ease the tasks of driving. The Mitsubishi Galant LS and Infinity I30, for example, include a single transmitter that controls a garage door, car doors, and windows. Robert Bosch Corporation, a major parts supplier, has devised an electronic rain sensor that automatically turns the windshield wipers on and closes the sunroof at the first sign of rain or snow. The sensor then continually adjusts the windshield wiper speed based on weather conditions.

As a marketing consultant to Oldsmobile, develop a brief report on how Guidestar and other options can be used as part of a product life cycle strategy.

Sources: Based on material in Kathleen Kerwin, "The Smart Cars Ahead," *Business Week* (May 1, 1995), p. 158 E-6; and Angelo Henderson, "Coming in Tomorrow's Car Seat: Storage, Built-In Safety Belts, and Surround Sound," *Wall Street Journal* (January 22, 1996), pp. B1–B2.

ping products, people feel the choices are relatively similar and shop for the best prices. Budget hotels and low-end electronics are marketed as price-based shopping products.

Consumers are loyal to **specialty products.**

Specialty products are particular brands, stores, and persons to which consumers are loyal. People are fully aware of these products and their attributes prior to making a purchase decision. They will make a significant effort to acquire the brand desired and will pay an above-average price. They will not buy if their choice is unavailable: Substitutes are unacceptable. The marketing emphasis is on maintaining the attributes that make the products so unique to loyal consumers, reminder ads, proper distribution (Hellmann's mayonnaise and *Business Week* require different distribution to loyal customers: supermarkets versus home subscriptions), brand extension to related products (such as Hellmann's tartar sauce), product improvements, ongoing customer contact (such as *Nintendo Power* magazine for owners of Nintendo game consoles), and monitoring reseller performance.

Because many people may view the same products differently, the preceding classification is excellent for segmentation. For example, Tylenol pain reliever may be a convenience product for some people (who will buy another brand if Tylenol is unavailable), a shopping product for others (who read ingredient labels), and a specialty product for still others (who insist on Tylenol). Johnson & Johnson, maker of Tylenol, must understand how Tylenol fits into the various categories and plan its marketing strategy accordingly.

Industrial Products

Industrial products *are organizational consumer goods and services.*

Industrial products are goods and services purchased for use in the production of other goods or services, in the operation of a business, or for resale to other consumers. A cus-

Table 11-2
Characteristics of Industrial Products

	TYPE OF PRODUCT						
CHARACTERISTICS	***Installations***	***Accessory Equipment***	***Raw Materials***	***Component Materials***	***Fabricated Parts***	***Supplies***	***Services***
Degree of consumer decision making	High	Moderate	Low	Low	Low	Very low	Low to high
Per-unit costs	High	Moderate	Low	Low	Low	Very low	Low to moderate
Rapidity of consumption	Very low	Low	High	High	High	High	Low to high
Item becomes part of final product	No	No	Sometimes	Yes	Yes	No	Sometimes
Item undergoes changes in form	No	No	Yes	Yes	No	No	Sometimes
Major consumer desire	Long-term facilities	Modern equipment	Continuous, low-cost, graded materials	Continuous, low-cost, specified materials	Continuous, low-cost, fabricated materials	Continuous, low-cost efficient supplies	Efficient, expert services
Examples	Production plant	Forklift truck	Coal	Steel	Thermostat	Light bulb	Machinery repair, accounting

tomer may be a manufacturer, wholesaler, retailer, or government or other nonprofit organization.

Products may be categorized by the degree of decision making involved in a purchase, costs, consumption rapidity, the role in production, and the change in form. Since industrial-products sellers tend to visit customers, store shopping behavior is often not involved. Installations, accessory equipment, raw materials, component materials, fabricated parts, business supplies, and business services are types of industrial products—as shown in Table 11-2.

Installations *and* **accessory equipment** *are expensive and do not become part of the final product.*

Installations and **accessory equipment** are capital goods. They are used in the production process and do not become part of the final product. Installations are nonportable, involve considerable consumer decision making (usually by upper-level executives), are very expensive, last many years, and do not change form. The key marketing tasks are direct selling from producer to purchaser, lengthy negotiations on features and terms, having complementary services such as maintenance and repair, tailoring products to buyers' desires, and offering technical expertise and team selling (in which various salespeople have different expertise). Examples are buildings, assembly lines, major equipment, large machine tools, and printing presses.

Accessory equipment consists of movable goods that require moderate consumer decision making, are less costly than installations, last many years, and do not become part of the final product or change form. The key marketing tasks are tying sales to those of installations; providing various choices in price, size, and capacity; having a strong distribution channel or sales force; stressing durability and efficiency; and having maintenance and technical support. Examples are drill presses, trucks, vans, and lathes.

Raw materials, component materials, *and* **fabricated parts** *are consumed in production.*

Raw materials, component materials, and **fabricated parts** are used up in production or become part of final products. They are expense rather than capital items. They require limited consumer decision making, are low cost on a per-unit basis, and are rapidly consumed. Raw materials are unprocessed primary materials from extractive and agricultural industries—minerals, coal, and crops, for example. Component materials are semimanufactured goods that undergo further changes in form—steel, textiles, and basic chemicals, for example. Fabricated parts are placed in products without changes in form—electric motors, thermostats, and microprocessors, for example. The major marketing tasks for materials and parts are to ensure consistent quality, continuity in shipments, and prompt delivery; pursue reorders; have competitive prices; seek long-term contracts; use assertive distributors or sales personnel; and meet buyer specifications.

Industrial supplies are convenience goods used in a firm's daily operation. They can be maintenance supplies, such as light bulbs, cleaning materials, and paint; repair supplies, such as rivets, nuts, and bolts; or operating supplies, such as stationery, pens, and business cards. They require little consumer decision making, are very low cost on a per-unit basis, are rapidly consumed, and do not become part of the finished product. Marketing emphasis is on availability, promptness, and ease of ordering.

Industrial supplies *are used daily, and* **industrial services** *are classified as maintenance and repair, and business advisory.*

Industrial services involve maintenance and repair services, and business advisory services. Maintenance and repair services (like janitorial services and machinery repair) usually involve little consumer decision making, are rather inexpensive, and are consumed quickly. They may become part of a final product (for example, keeping for-sale equipment in good working condition) or involve a change in form (for example, janitorial services converting a dirty office into a clean one). The key marketing thrust is on consistent, efficient service at a reasonable price. Business advisory services (like accounting and legal services) may involve a moderate to high level of consumer decision making when these services are first purchased. Ongoing costs tend to be low to moderate, while benefits may be long-lasting. These services do not become part of the final product. The major marketing task is to present an image of expertise and convey the reasons for a client to use the service.

Elements of a Product Mix

After determining the type(s) of products to offer, a firm needs to outline the variety and assortment of those products. A **product item** is a specific model, brand, or size of a product that a company sells, such as a college course on the principles of marketing, a General Motors truck, or Sony 3.5-inch diskettes for PCs. Usually a firm sells a group of closely related product items as part of a **product line.** In each product line, the items have some common characteristics, customers, and/or uses; they may also share technologies, distribution channels, prices, related services, and so on.[5] As an example, Revlon markets lipstick, eye makeup, and other cosmetics. Caterpillar makes several different tractor models. Prentice Hall publishes various college textbooks on aspects of marketing. Many local lawn-service firms offer lawn mowing, landscaping, and tree-trimming services.

A **product item** *is a specific model; a* **product line** *has related items; a* **product mix** *is all a firm's lines.*

The **product mix** consists of all the different product lines a firm offers. For instance, Heinz markets ketchup, tuna fish, low-calorie foods, frozen french fries, soup, pet food, and various other food products in over 200 countries around the globe. Metropolitan Life operates North America's largest life insurer (MetLife), and concentrates on insurance and related services. Tyco Laboratories is a worldwide manufacturing company with three major product lines: fire protection/flow control, electric and electronic components, and packaging materials.

A product mix can be described in terms of its width, depth, and consistency. The *width of a product mix* is based on the number of different product lines a company offers. A wide mix lets a firm diversify products, appeal to different consumer needs, and encourage one-stop shopping. A narrow mix requires lower resource investments and does not call for expertise in different product categories.

A product mix has levels of width, depth, and consistency.

The *depth of a product mix* is based on the number of product items within each product line. A deep mix can satisfy the needs of several consumer segments for the same product, maximize shelf-space, discourage competitors, cover a range of prices, and sustain

[5] Bennett, *Dictionary of Marketing Terms*, p. 222.

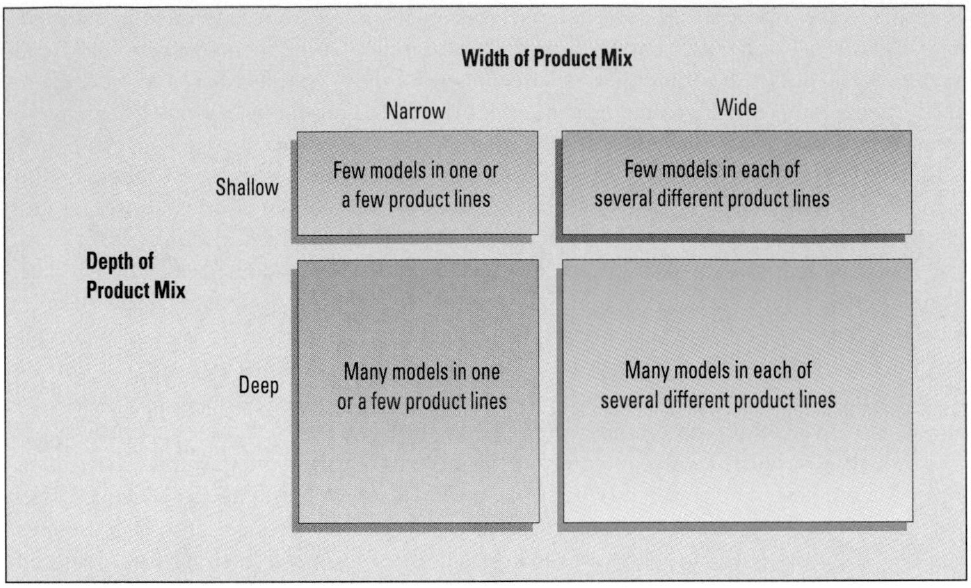

FIGURE 11-3
Product Mix Alternatives

dealer support. A shallow mix imposes lower costs for inventory, product alterations, and order processing; and there are no overlapping product items.

The *consistency of a product mix* is based on the relationship among product lines in terms of their sharing a common end-use, distribution outlets, consumer group(s), and price range. A consistent mix is generally easier to manage than an inconsistent one. It allows a firm to concentrate on marketing and production expertise, create a strong image, and generate solid distribution relations. However, excessive consistency may leave the firm vulnerable to environmental threats, sales fluctuations, or decreased growth potential, since emphasis is on a limited product assortment. Figure 11-3 above shows product mix alternatives in terms of width and depth. On pages 310–311, Figure 11-4 highlights ConAgra's broad product mix, and Figure 11-5 displays Gumout's deep product line.

Product-mix decisions can have both positive and negative effects on companies,[6] as these examples demonstrate:

- Wrigley's strategy is to concentrate on chewing-gum products and not to market even closely related items such as hard candies: "If you are thinking of chewing gum, you are thinking Wrigley's." The firm is so successful that it dominates the sugared gum and sugar-free gum markets. It has a 49 per cent market share of the U.S. gum market; and Extra, Doublemint, Spearmint, and Juicy Fruit are among the world's best-known brands. Wrigley's annual total sales are $1.7 billion, 40 per cent outside the United States.[7]
- Canada's Bombardier Corporation is booming because of its product mix diversification strategy. The firm began in the 1960s as the maker of Ski-Doo snowmobiles. Now, Bombardier manufactures aircraft for commuter airlines and corporate air fleets, railroad and subway cars, and Sea-Doo personal watercraft—as well as Ski-Doo snowmobiles. Its annual revenues have gone from $8 million in 1964 to nearly $5 billion today.[8]
- "Occasionally, Heinz has strayed from its niche leadership strategy—to its regret. One of the company's most notorious marketing failures was its 'Great American Soup' campaign. This ready-to-serve product—a direct assault on Campbell's condensed soups—was the most expensive TV ad ever produced up to that time. Heinz, in fact, spent so much on making the ad, it couldn't afford national media placement. The

[6]See John A. Quelch and David Kenny, "Extend Profits, Not Product Lines," *Harvard Business Review*, Vol. 72 (September–October 1994), pp. 153–160.

[7]"Wm. Wrigley Jr. Co.," *Advertising Age* (September 27, 1995), p. 62.

[8]Patrick J. Spain and James R. Talbot (Editors), *Hoover's Handbook of World Business 1995–1996* (Austin, Texas: Reference Press, 1995), pp. 138–139.

Table 11-3

Comparing Product Management Organizations

	CHARACTERISTICS		
ORGANIZATION	***Staffing***	***Ideal Use***	***Permanency***
Marketing manager system	Key functional areas of marketing report directly to a senior marketer with a lot of authority.	A company makes one product line, has a dominant line, or uses broad category marketing managers.	The system is ongoing.
Product (brand) manager system	There is a layer of middle managers, with each focusing on a single product or a group of related products.	A company makes many distinct products, each requiring expertise.	The system is ongoing.
Product planning committee	Senior executives from various functional areas participate.	The committee should supplement another product organization.	The committee meets irregularly.
New-product manager system	Separate middle managers focus on new products and existing products.	A company makes several existing products, and substantial time, resources, and expertise are needed for new products.	The system is ongoing, but new products are shifted to product managers after introduction.
Venture team	An independent group of company specialists guides all phases of a new product's development.	A company wants to create vastly different products from those currently offered and needs an autonomous structure to aid development.	The team disbands after a new product is introduced, with responsibility going to a product manager.

product never caught on and was dropped from the market. Not that we gave up on soup. A more successful strategy was to withdraw from the branded competition in the U.S. market and build our private-label business. As a result, Heinz is now by far the leading maker of private label soup in the United States."[9]

- Because TRW's product mix had grown to more than 100 categories of high-technology industrial goods and services, some of these products were not performing up to company goals. As a result, TRW decided to sell off businesses generating $500 million in annual sales, including its popular computer repair and servicing division.[10]

Product Management Organizations

A firm may select from among several organizational forms of product management, including: marketing manager, product manager, product planning committee, new-product manager, and venture team.[11] See Table 11-3 above.

Under a **marketing manager system,** an executive is responsible for overseeing a wide range of marketing functions (such as research, target marketing, planning for existing and new products, distribution, promotion, pricing, and customer service) and for coordinat-

One person is directly in charge of a host of marketing tasks, including product planning, with a **marketing manager system.**

[9]Anthony J. F. O'Reilly, "125 Years at the Heinz Table," *Journal of Business Strategy*, Vol. 16 (May–June 1995), p. 11.

[10]Patrick J. Spain and James R. Talbot (Editors), *Hoover's Handbook of American Business 1996* (Austin, Texas: Reference Press, 1995), pp. 1428–1429.

[11]The definitions in this section are drawn from Bennett, *Dictionary of Marketing Terms*, various pages.

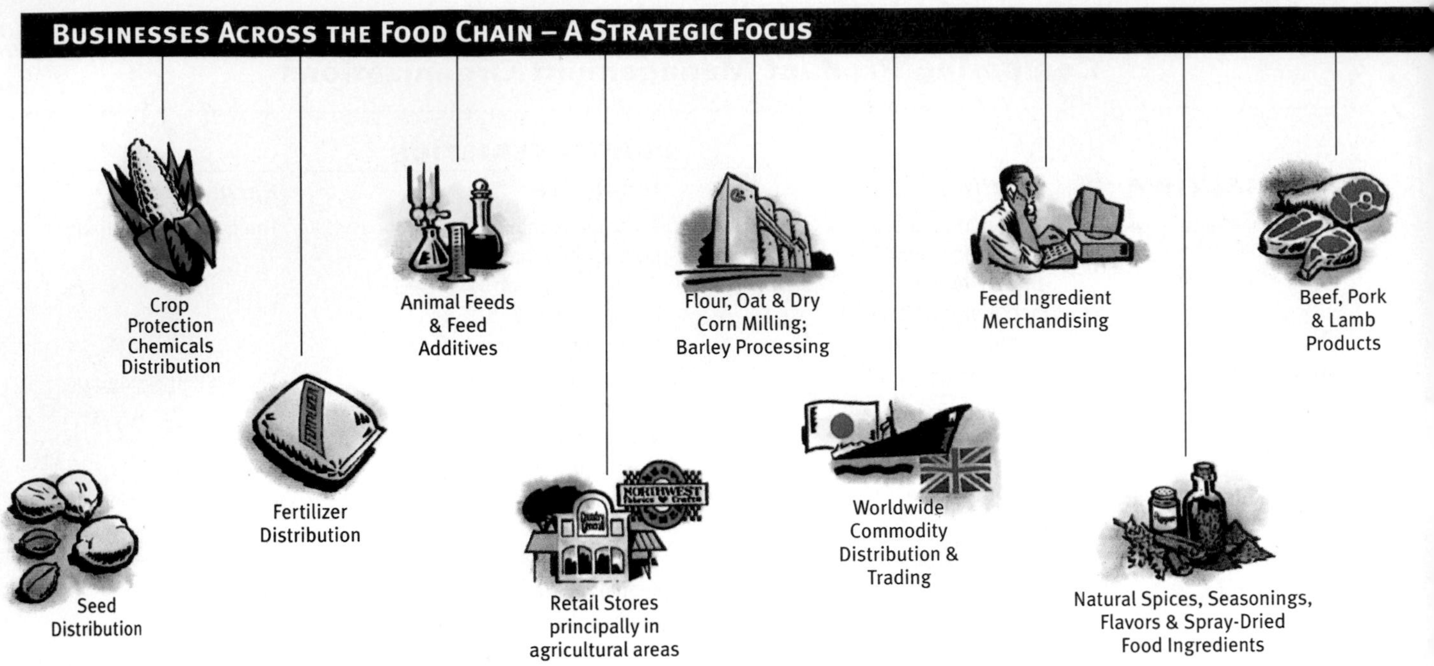

FIGURE 11-4 ConAgra's Broad Product Mix
ConAgra's diversification across the food chain expands opportunities and balances results. About half of ConAgra's earnings are from branded food products, and about half are from foodservice, processing and distribution businesses. *Reprinted by permission.*

ing with other departments that perform marketing-related activities (such as warehousing, order filling, shipping, credit, and purchasing). It works well for firms with a line of similar products or one dominant product line and for smaller firms that want centralized control of marketing tasks. It may be less successful if there are several product lines that require different marketing mixes—unless there are category marketing managers, with each responsible for a broad product line.[12] Pepsi Cola USA, Purex, and Levi Strauss have used some form of marketing manager system.

Middle managers handle new and existing products in a category in the **product (brand) manager system.**

With a **product (brand) manager system,** there is a level of middle managers, each of whom is responsible for planning, coordinating, and monitoring the performance of a single product (brand) or a small group of products (brands). The managers handle both new and existing products and are involved with all the marketing activities related to their product or group of products. The system lets all products or brands get adequate attention. It works well when there are many distinct products or brands, each needing special marketing attention. But, it has two potential shortcomings: lack of authority for the product manager and inadequate attention to new products. Procter & Gamble, RJR Nabisco, and Black & Decker have used product managers.

A **product planning committee** *has top executives involved part-time.*

A **product planning committee** is staffed by high-level executives from various functional areas in a firm, such as marketing, production, engineering, finance, and research and development. It handles product approval, evaluation, and development on a part-time basis. Once a product is introduced, the committee usually turns to other opportunities and completely gives that product over to a product manager. This system lets management have strong input into product decisions, but the committee meets irregularly and must pass projects on to line managers. It functions best as a supplement to other methods and is utilized by many large and small firms.

A **new-product manager system** *has separate middle managers for new and existing products.*

A **new-product manager system** has product managers to supervise existing products and new-product managers to develop new ones. It ensures enough time, resources, enthusiasm, and expertise for new-product planning. Once a product is introduced, it is given to the product manager who oversees the existing products of that line (or brand). The

[12]See "The Dynamics of Category Management," *Promo/Progressive Grocer Special Report* (December 1994).

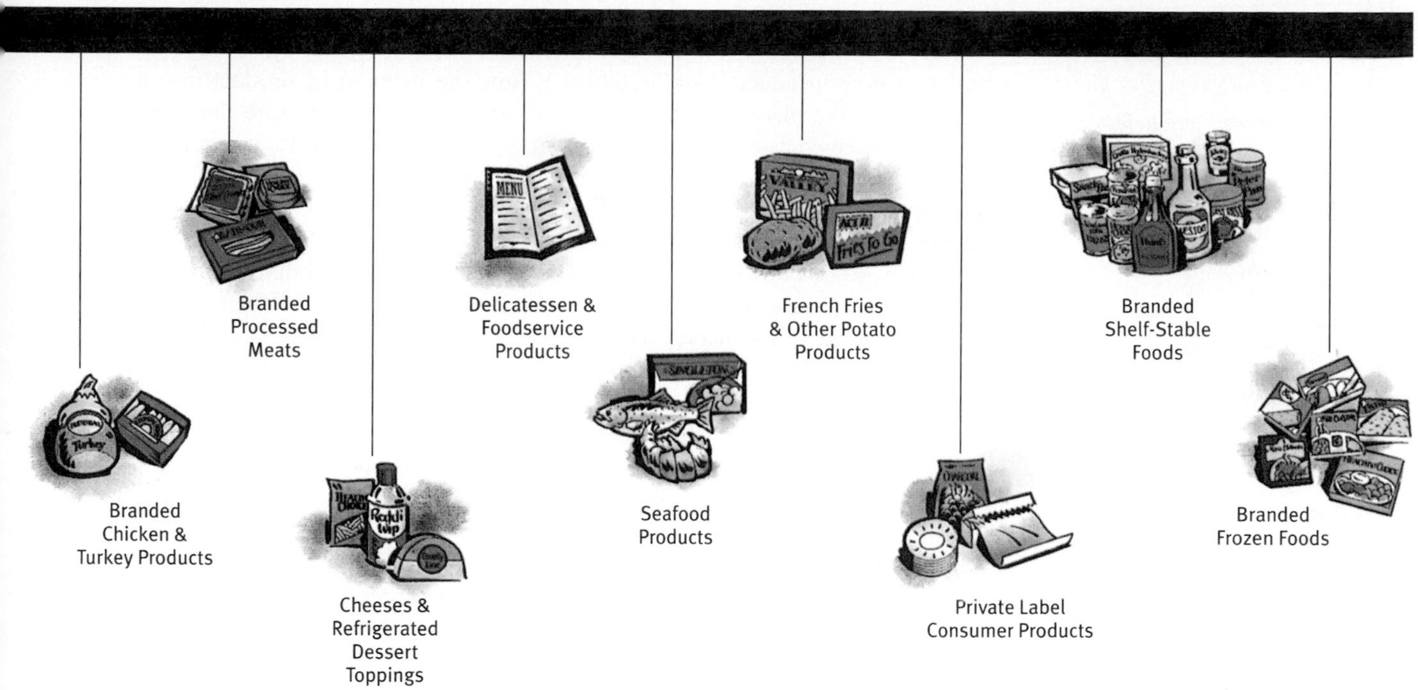

FIGURE 11-4 (cont.)

system can be costly, incur conflicts, and cause discontinuity when an item is introduced. General Foods, General Electric, and Johnson & Johnson have used such managers.

A **venture team** is a small, independent department in a firm that consists of a broad range of specialists—drawn from that firm's marketing, finance, engineering, and other functional departments—who are involved with a specific new product's entire development process. Team members work on a full-time basis and act in a relatively autonomous manner. The team disbands when its new product is introduced, and the product is then managed within the firm's regular management structure. With a venture team, there are proper resources, a flexible environment, expertise, and continuity in new-product planning. It is valuable if a firm wants to be more far-sighted, reach out for truly new ideas, and foster creativity. It is also expensive to establish and operate. Xerox, Polaroid, Monsanto, and 3M have used venture teams.

A **venture team** *is an autonomous new-product department.*

The correct organization depends on the diversity of a firm's offerings, the number of new products introduced, the level of innovativeness, company resources, management expertise, and other factors. A combination organization may be highly desirable; among larger firms, this is particularly common.

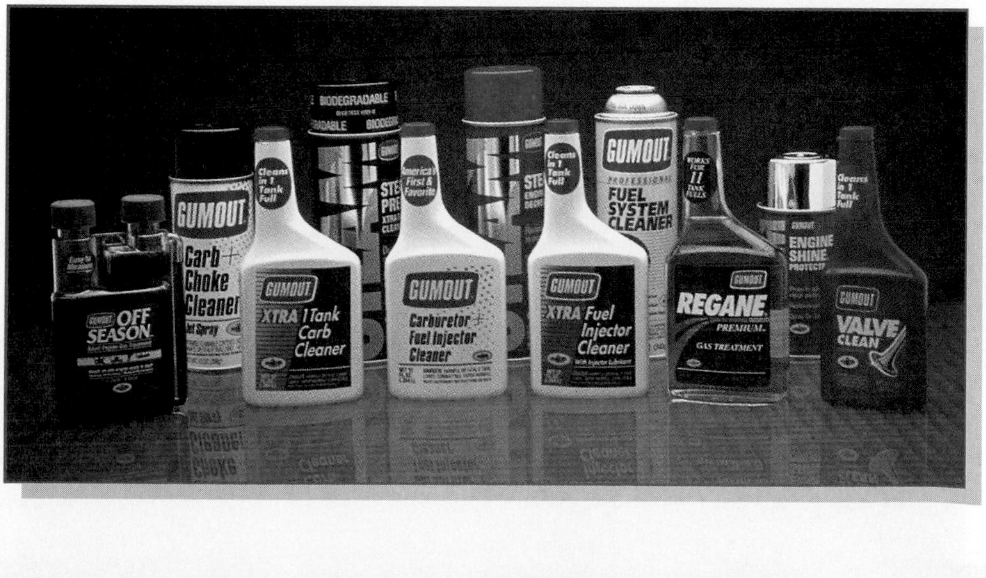

FIGURE 11-5
Gumout's Deep Product Line: Part of Pennzoil's Well-Conceived Product Mix
By offering a full selection of carburetor and fuel injector cleaners, Pennzoil Company is a dominant force in the marketplace—with a strong customer following.
Reprinted by permission.

Product Positioning

Distinctive and desirable product features must be communicated to the marketplace.

Critical to a firm's product-planning efforts is how the items in its product mix are perceived in the marketplace. The firm must work quite hard to make sure that each of its products is perceived as providing some combination of unique features (product differentiation) and that these features are desired by the target market (thereby converting product differentiation to a differential advantage).

When a product is new, a company must clearly communicate its attributes: What is it? What does it do? How is it better than the competition? Who should buy it? The goal is to have consumers perceive product attributes as the firm intends. When a product has an established niche in the market, a company must regularly reinforce its image and communicate the reasons for its success. Once consumer perceptions are formed, they may be hard to alter. And it may also be tough later to change a product's niche in the market (for instance, from low price, low quality to high price, high quality).

Product positioning *maps out consumer perceptions of product attributes.* **Ideal points** *show the most preferred attributes.*

Through **product positioning**, a firm can map each of its products in terms of consumer perceptions and desires, competition, other company products, and environmental changes. Consumer perceptions are the images of products, both a firm's and competitors', in people's minds. Consumer desires refer to the attributes that people would most like products to have—their **ideal points.** If a group of people has a distinctive "ideal" for a product category, that group is a potential market segment. A firm will do well if its products' attributes are perceived by consumers as being close to their ideal.

Both competitive and company product positioning are important.

Competitive product positioning refers to people's perceptions of a firm relative to competitors. The goal is for the firm's products to be perceived as "more ideal" than those of competitors. *Company product positioning* shows a firm how consumers perceive that firm's different brands (items) within the same product line and the relationship of those brands (items) to each other. The goal is for each of the firm's brands to be positioned near an ideal point, yet not too clustered near one another in the consumer's mind—the brands should appeal to different ideal points (market segments).

A firm must monitor the environmental changes that may alter the way its products are perceived. Such changes could include new technology, changing consumer life-styles, new offerings by competitors, and negative publicity.

Product positioning is illustrated in Figure 11-6, which depicts the ice cream marketplace in terms of the consumer desires regarding two key ice-cream attributes: price and richness (level of butterfat content). In this figure, there are six ideal points (target

FIGURE 11-6
The Product Positioning of Ice Cream

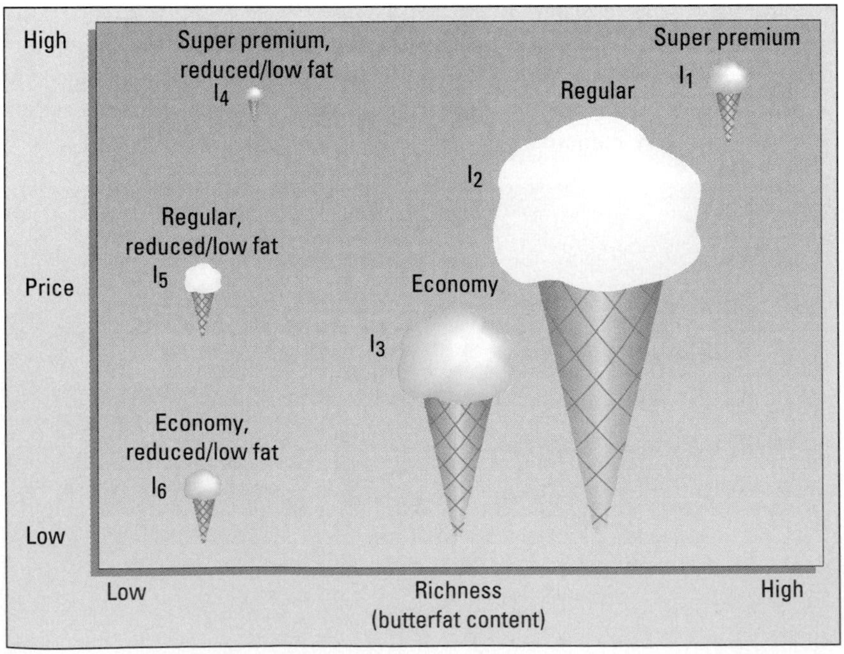

Ethics IN TODAY'S SOCIETY

When Selling a PC, What Does "New" Mean?

As part of a joint 12-state investigation, Florida officials subpoenaed the records of Packard Bell Electronics, a leading manufacturer of home PCs. The investigation began after Compaq Computer—a key competitor—alerted state authorities that Packard Bell had assembled some computers with parts from returned models. In contrast to Packard Bell, Compaq sold all of its returned computers as used equipment in a factory store.

Although Packard Bell's attorneys admitted the firm reused selected parts, they argued that this was a commonly accepted trade practice employed by other PC makers such as Dell and Apple. In addition, Packard Bell's lawyers asserted that it only inserted used parts that were certified to perform as new.

Packard Bell also claimed that although Compaq was aware of Packard Bell's practices since 1992, it only notified state attorney generals in 1995 when Packard Bell had become a formidable foe. Thus, the suit was a competitive tactic by Compaq, not Compaq's response to an ethical issue. One trade report even suggested that Compaq had instituted the suit because it felt Packard Bell's profit margins were too low to withstand the added legal costs.

The distinction between "used" and "new" can sometimes be a hard one to make. Most department stores routinely resell returned goods as new and charge full prices for them. And in contrast to mechanical parts, many PC parts, such as microprocessors, do not deteriorate through normal use. Furthermore, most manufacturers routinely "burn-in" PCs to test their integrity. The burn-in process is considered desirable, not as evidence of a PC's used status.

To address the legal concerns, Packard Bell PCs now contain a statement that they may contain "serviceable" used parts.

As a marketing manager at Packard Bell, how would YOU handle the "new" versus "used" issue?

Sources: Based on material in Larry Armstrong and Gary McWilliams, "A PC War That's Not Exactly P.C.," *Business Week* (July 10, 1995), p. 42; and Jim Carlton, "Florida Subpoenas Data of Packard Bell," *Wall Street Journal* (June 22, 1995), P. B6.

markets)—I1 to I6—each associated with a specific type of ice cream. Here is a brief description of the six categories:

- I1—super premium. The creamiest, richest ice cream (butterfat content of 15 to 18 per cent) with the highest price. Häagen-Dazs, Ben & Jerry's, Frusen Glädje, and Alpen Zauber are in this grouping. This segment represents about 9 per cent of U.S. ice cream sales.
- I2—regular. A creamy, rich ice cream (butterfat content of 10 to 12 per cent) with an average to slightly above-average price. Sealtest, Breyers, Dolly Madison, Dreyer's, and Baskin Robbins are positioned here. This segment is responsible for about 45 per cent of U.S. ice cream sales.
- I3—economy. An average ice cream (butterfat content of 10 per cent) at a below-average price. Private-label brands fit here. This segment embodies about one-quarter of U.S. ice cream sales.

FIGURE 11-7
Wrigley's Spearmint Chewing Gum: Pure Chewing Satisfaction
Reprinted by permission of the Wm. Wrigley Jr. Company.

- I4—super premium, reduced or low fat. A flavorful ice cream with a high price for moderately health-conscious consumers (butterfat content of 5 to 10 per cent). The reduced-fat versions of the leading super premiums go here. This segment represents under 5 per cent of U.S. ice cream sales.
- I5—regular, reduced or low fat. A good-quality ice cream for more health-conscious consumers (butterfat content of less than 8 per cent) at an average price. Weight Watcher's and Light n' Lively are positioned here. This segment accounts for about 8 per cent of U.S. ice cream sales.
- I6—economy, reduced or low fat. An average ice cream for more health-conscious consumers (butterfat content of 4 to 8 per cent) at a below-average price. Private-label brands fit here. This segment accounts for about 8 per cent of U.S. ice cream sales.

An examination of competitive product positioning reveals that there are competing products in each market niche. In some instances, the marketplace is saturated. Nonetheless, the companies in the industry have done a good job in addressing the needs of the various consumer segments and in differentiating the products offered to each segment.

Frusen Glädje, Breyers, Sealtest, and Light n' Lively are all marketed by Unilever. From an analysis of company product positioning, it is clear that Unilever well serves the customers in its markets. However, it must continue to differentiate carefully between Breyers (the "all natural" ice cream) and Sealtest (the "ice-cream parlor" ice cream).

By undertaking product-positioning analysis, a company can learn a great deal and plan its marketing efforts accordingly, as these examples show:

- Wrigley is always on the lookout for positioning opportunities for its chewing gums. Thus, because of the negative attention placed on cigarette smoking, Wrigley recently embarked on a very creative marketing strategy for Wrigley's Spearmint gum—positioning it with the phrase, "When you can't smoke, enjoy pure chewing satisfaction." See Figure 11-7.

FIGURE 11-8
Air Canada: A Customer-Service Positioning Approach
Reprinted by permission.

- Air Canada believes numerous travelers perceive airlines as indifferent and impersonal. To remedy this, it is emphasizing the quality of its service— depicted in ads by the worldwide symbol for outstanding service, the red carpet. See Figure 11-8.
- When marketing its photocopiers and fax machines in the United States, Japan's Konica knows that many potential customers are unfamiliar with the company and its product lines. As a result, the firm has run ads such as the one shown in Figure 11-9—whereby Konica positions its products by aligning itself with another well-known name, in this case, Dutch Boy paint brand (from Sherwin-Williams). Konica must be careful that its positioning message does not get lost in these ads.

The Product Life Cycle

The **product life cycle** *describes each stage in its life.*

Companies often desire a **balanced product portfolio.**

The **product life cycle** is a concept that attempts to describe a product's sales, competitors, profits, customers, and marketing emphasis from its beginning until it is removed from the market.

From a product-planning perspective, there is interest in the product life cycle for several reasons. One, some product lives are shorter than before. Two, new products often require high marketing and other investments. Three, an understanding of the concept lets a firm anticipate changes in consumer tastes, competition, and support from resellers and adjust its marketing plan accordingly. Four, the concept enables a firm to consider the product mix it should offer; many firms seek a **balanced product portfolio,** whereby a combination of new, growing, and mature products is maintained.

The life-cycle concept can be applied to a product class (watches), a product form (quartz watches), and a brand (Seiko quartz watches). Product forms generally follow the traditional life cycle more faithfully than product classes or brands.

FIGURE 11-9
Konica Business Machines U.S.A.: Gaining Positioning Credibility by Affiliating Itself with the Dutch Boy Name
Reprinted by permission.

Product life cycles may be traditional, boom, fad, extended fad, seasonal, revival, or bust.

Product life cycles may vary a lot, both in length of time and shape. See Figure 11-10. A *traditional cycle* has distinct periods of introduction, growth, maturity, and decline. A *boom*, or *classic, cycle* describes a very popular product that sells well for a long time. A *fad cycle* represents a product with quick popularity and a sudden decline. An *extended fad* is like a fad, but residual sales continue at a lower level than earlier sales. A *seasonal*, or *fashion, cycle* results if a product sells well in nonconsecutive periods. With a *revival*, or *nostalgia, cycle*, a seemingly obsolete product achieves new popularity. A *bust cycle* occurs for a product that fails.

Stages of the Traditional Product Life Cycle

The stages and characteristics of the traditional product life cycle are shown in Figure 11-11 and Table 11-4, which both refer to total industry performance during the cycle.

FIGURE 11-10
Selected Product Life-Cycle Patterns

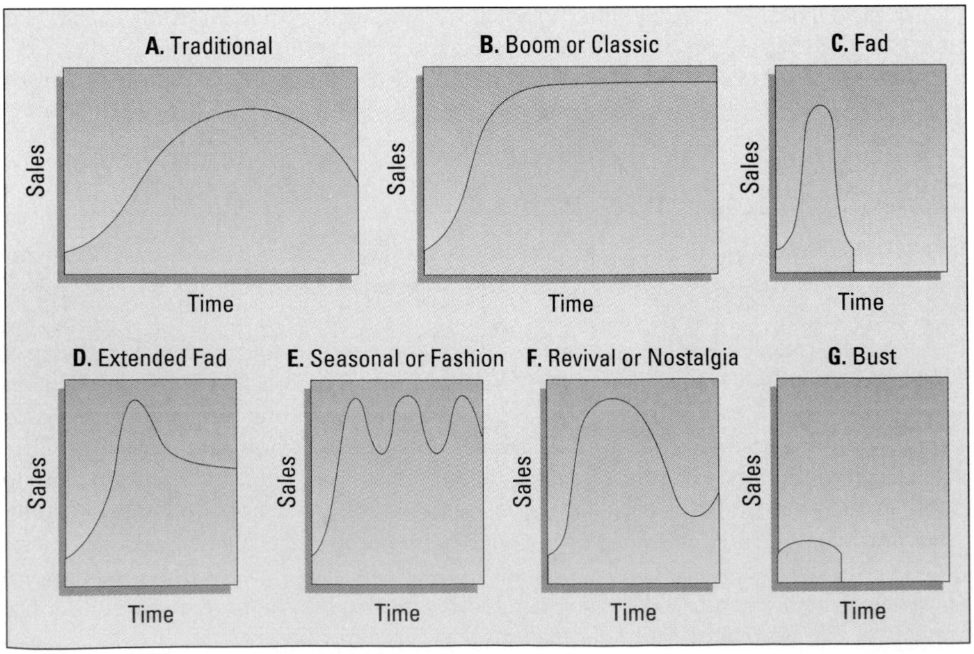

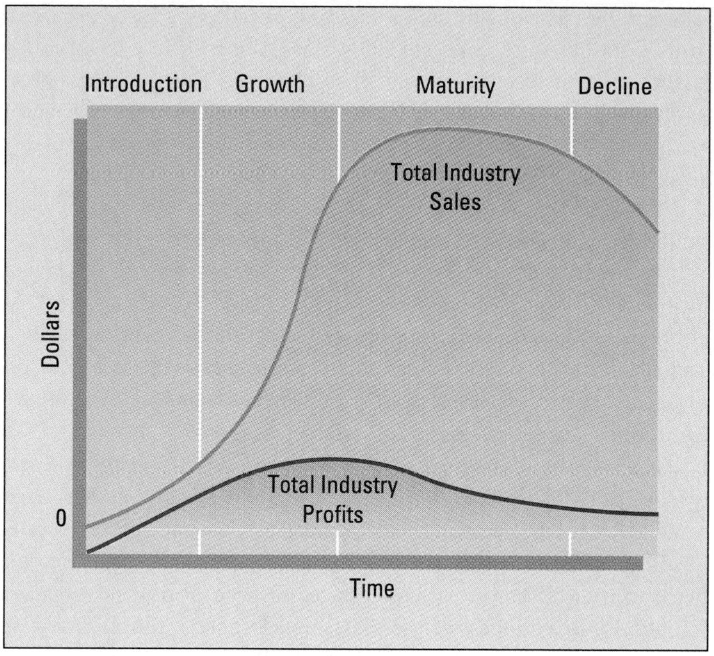

FIGURE 11-11
The Traditional Product Life Cycle

The performance of an individual firm may vary from that of the industry, depending on its specific goals, resources, marketing plans, location, competitive environment, level of success, and stage of entry.

During the **introduction stage of the product life cycle,** a new product is introduced to the marketplace and the goal is to generate customer interest. The rate of sales growth depends on a product's newness, as well as its desirability. Generally, a product modification gains sales faster than a major innovation. Only one or two firms have entered the market, and competition is minimal. There are losses due to high production and marketing costs, and cash flow is poor. Initial customers are innovators who are willing to

In **introduction,** *the goal is to establish a consumer market.*

Table 11-4
The Characteristics of the Traditional Product Life Cycle

	STAGE IN LIFE CYCLE			
CHARACTERISTICS	***Introduction***	***Growth***	***Maturity***	***Decline***
Marketing goal	Attract innovators and opinion leaders to new product	Expand distribution and product line	Maintain differential advantage as long as possible	(a) Cut back, (b) revive, or (c) terminate
Industry sales	Increasing	Rapidly increasing	Stable	Decreasing
Competition	None or small	Some	Substantial	Limited
Industry profits	Negative	Increasing	Decreasing	Decreasing
Customers	Innovators	Resourceful mass market	Mass market	Laggards
Product mix	One or a few basic models	Expanding line	Full product line	Best-sellers
Distribution	Depends on product	Rising number of outlets/ distributors	Greatest number of outlets/ distributors	Decreasing number of outlets/ distributors
Promotion	Informative	Persuasive	Competitive	Informative
Pricing	Depends on product	Greater range of prices	Full line of prices	Selected prices

take risks, can afford to take them, and like the status of buying first. Because one or two firms dominate and costs are high, only one or a few basic product models are sold. For a routine item like a new cereal, distribution is extensive. For a luxury item like a new boat, distribution is limited. Promotion must be informative, and free samples may be desirable. Depending on the product and choice of consumer market, a firm may start with a high status price or low mass-market price.

During **growth,** *firms enlarge the market and offer alternatives.*

Over the **growth stage of the product life cycle,** a new product gains wider consumer acceptance, and the marketing goal is to expand distribution and the range of available product alternatives. Industry sales increase rapidly as a few more firms enter a highly profitable market that has substantial potential. Total and unit profits are high because an affluent (resourceful) mass market buys distinctive products from a limited group of firms and is willing to pay for them. To accommodate the growing market, modified versions of basic models are offered, distribution is expanded, persuasive mass advertising is utilized, and a range of prices is available.

In **maturity,** *companies work hard to sustain a differential advantage.*

During the **maturity stage of the product life cycle,** a product's sales growth levels off and firms try to maintain a differential advantage (such as a lower price, improved features, or extended warranty) for as long as possible. Industry sales stabilize as the market becomes saturated and many firms enter to capitalize on the still sizable demand. Competition is at its highest. Thus, total industry and unit profits drop because discounting is popular. The average-income mass market makes purchases. A full product line is made available at many outlets (or via many distributors) and at many prices. Promotion becomes very competitive.

In **decline,** *firms reduce marketing, revive a product, or end it.*

In the **decline stage of the product life cycle,** a product's sales fall as substitutes enter the market or consumers lose interest. Firms have three options. They can cut back on marketing, thus reducing the number of product items they make, the outlets they sell through, and the promotion used; they can revive a product by repositioning, repackaging, or otherwise remarketing it; or they can drop the product. As industry sales decline, many firms exit the market, since customers are fewer and they have less money to spend. The product mix keys on best-sellers, selected outlets (distributors) and prices, and promotion stressing—informatively—availability and price.

The bulky, electric-powered portable calculator is a good example of a product form that moved through the life cycle. It went from an exclusive, expensive item to a widespread, moderately priced item to a mass-marketed, inexpensive item to an obsolete item. Today, earlier versions of the portable calculator have been replaced by technologically advanced product forms such as credit-card sized, solar-powered calculators.

Evaluating the Product Life-Cycle Concept

The product life cycle provides a good framework for product planning, but, it has not proven very useful in forecasting. In using the product life-cycle concept, these key points should be kept in mind:

1. The stages, the time span, and the shape of the cycle (such as flat, erratic, or sharply inclined) vary by product.
2. Such external factors as the economy, inflation, and consumer life-styles may shorten or lengthen a product's life cycle.
3. A firm may do better or worse than the industry "average" at any stage in the cycle. An industry's being in the growth stage for a product does not mean success for every firm in the market, nor does its being in the decline stage for a product mean lower sales for every firm.
4. A firm may not only be able to manage a product life cycle, it may also be able to extend it or reverse a decline. Effective marketing may lure a new market segment, find a new product use, or foster better reseller support.

A **self-fulfilling prophecy** *may occur when a firm reduces marketing.*

5. Many firms may engage in a **self-fulfilling prophecy,** whereby they predict falling sales and then ensure this by reducing or removing marketing support. See Figure 11-12. With proper marketing, some products might not fail.

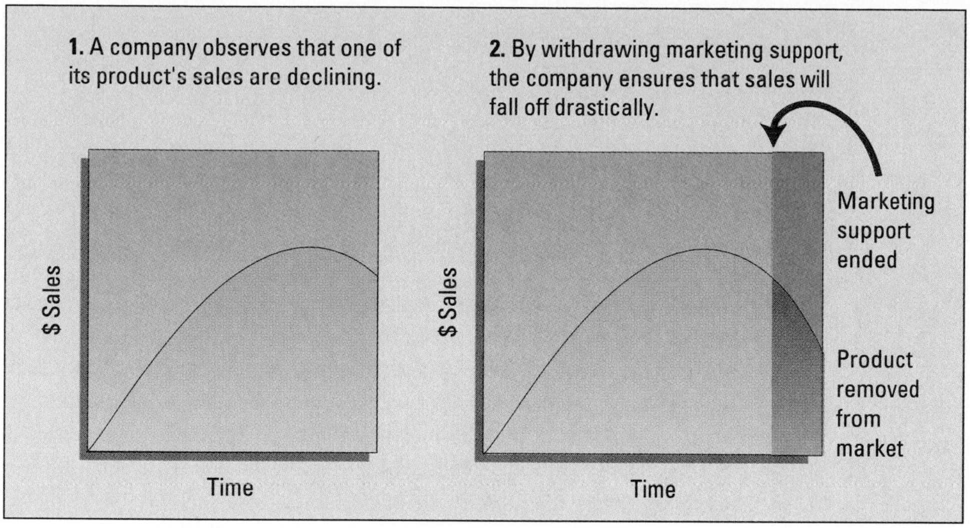
1. A company observes that one of its product's sales are declining.
2. By withdrawing marketing support, the company ensures that sales will fall off drastically.
$ Sales
Time
$ Sales
Time
Marketing support ended
Product removed from market

FIGURE 11-12
A Self-Fulfilling Prophecy

The International Dimensions of Product Planning

When a product plan is being devised, such points as these should be kept in mind with regard to international marketing:

- Although a firm may offer the same products in countries around the globe, these products can have distinct generic meanings in different countries.
- In developing and less-developed countries, product "frills" are often less important than in industrialized countries.
- Due to their intangibility, perishability, inseparability, and variability, the international marketing efforts for services are often more complex than those on behalf of goods.
- The concept of convenience, shopping, and specialty products is less valid in markets where distribution is limited or consumers have few choices.
- Installations and accessory equipment may be hard to ship overseas.
- Marketing all of the items in a wide and/or deep product mix may not be appropriate or economically feasible on an international basis.
- The diversity of international markets may necessitate a decentralized product management organization, with some executives permanently assigned to foreign countries.
- For many products, there are differences in product positioning and consumer ideal points by country or region. Simple positioning messages travel better than more complicated ones.
- Some products are in different stages of their life cycles in developing and less-developed countries than in industrialized countries.
- Expectations regarding goods/services combinations (discussed in the next chapter) may differ by country.
- A product modification or minor innovation in a home market may be a major innovation internationally, necessitating different marketing approaches.
- The characteristics of the market segments—innovators, early adopters, early majority, late majority, and laggards—in the diffusion process (covered in Chapter 13) often differ by country.
- Even though global branding and packaging may be desirable, various nations may have special needs or requirements.

International Marketing in Action

Are the Positioning Factors Used by MBA Students "Universal"?

As consumers, how do MBA students decide on a product's positioning? To answer this question, a marketing research study was conducted to evaluate the importance of brand name, price, physical appearance, and retailer reputation as indicators of product quality for consumer electronics. A questionnaire was completed by 640 beginning MBA students from 38 mostly Western industrialized countries and Japan. The respondents were matched on such factors as age, education, professional goals, and income; and they were separated into four cultural groups: North American countries (the U.S. and Canada), EU member countries, European countries not belonging to the EU, and others.

The researchers found that brand name cues are more important than price or physical appearance—regardless of cultural group. And price and physical appearance are more important than a retailer's reputation in positioning a product's overall quality. The findings support the notion that the value of certain product positioning cues does not vary by culture.

The study's authors suggest that culture or country boundaries are less important in product positioning than these five factors:

- The more consumers rely on a particular quality cue, the more they also want information from other sources.
- Consumers who are willing to accept certain forms of risk also tend to use positioning cues the most.
- Brand-prone consumers are less price sensitive.
- The use of brand and price as signals increases when people have a greater intention to buy a product or when they perceive product benefits as high.
- The use of specific positioning cues decreases as a consumer's education increases and when the consumer is more technologically oriented.

As a Sony Walkman marketing manager, responsible for U.S. and Canadian markets, how would you use these results in catering to educated young adults?

Source: Based on material in Niraj Dawar and Philip Parker, "Marketing Universals: Consumers' Use of Brand Name, Price, Physical Appearance, and Retailer Reputation as Signals of Product Quality," *Journal of Marketing,* Vol. 58 (April 1994), pp. 81–95.

MARKETING IN A CHANGING WORLD

Even Toyota's Not Infallible[13]

Toyota—with its stable of Toyota and Lexus vehicles—has been one of the most respected manufacturers in the world for decades. Toyota is admired for its ability to read the market, its deep product mix, the quality of its vehicles, its ability to position its models in the marketplace (especially the upscale Lexus brand), and its strong customer following. And lest we forget, Toyota's annual sales exceed $100 billion and it is very profitable.

Yet, despite its prowess, this manufacturing dynamo recently had a major stumble in its home Japanese market with the redesigned Corolla. What does this signify? Careful product planning turns into successful product planning only if the consumer says so.

[13]The material in this section is based on Andrew Pollack, "The Risks of Cutting Too Far," *New York Times* (December 21, 1995), pp. D1, D8.

Here's what happened: "For years, Japanese car makers built base models that were luxurious by other makers' standards. And the Toyota Corolla was Japan's best-selling car for 26 years. Thus, when Toyota—worried that sticker prices had grown too steep—did a full remodeling and stripped features from the Corollas it sells in Japan, consumers rebelled. Toyota responded by restoring some of the removed features in a midyear replacement model."

Before the remodeling, a basic Toyota Corolla sold for $10,700 in Japan. Standard features included an AM-FM stereo, self-adjusting air-conditioning, and bumpers painted to match the car's color. The remodeled Corolla sold for $9,750—due to a simplified engine, an AM mono radio, partially vinyl seats, bumpers being left black, and manual-control air-conditioning. Said one dealer, the car "looked cheaper" and "the interior was much poorer."

Once Toyota saw the consumer reaction to the redesign, it had a revamped Corolla at dealer showrooms within five months. The remodeled $10,400 basic Corolla included full-fabric seats, power windows, automatic door locks, and a driver's airbag (which is not legally mandated in Japan). As Toyota learned, "cutting costs too much—or too obviously—can backfire, turning consumers off," even if prices are cut, too.

SUMMARY

1. *To define product planning and differentiate among tangible, augmented, and generic products* Product planning systematically allows a firm to pinpoint opportunities, develop marketing programs, coordinate a product mix, maintain successful products, reappraise faltering ones, and delete undesirable products.

Products should be defined in a combination of ways. A tangible product is a basic physical entity, service, or idea with precise specifications; it is offered under a given description or model number. An augmented product includes not only tangible elements, but also the accompanying cluster of image and service features. A generic product focuses on the benefits a buyer desires; this concept looks at what a product means to the consumer rather than the seller.

2. *To examine the various types of products, product mixes, and product management organization forms from which a firm may select* Goods marketing entails the sale of physical products. Service marketing includes goods rental, servicing goods owned by consumers, and personal services. Goods and services often differ in terms of intangibility, perishability, inseparability from the service provider, and variability in quality.

Consumer products are goods and services for the final consumer. They can be classified as convenience, shopping, and specialty items. These products are differentiated on the basis of consumer awareness of alternatives prior to the shopping trip and the degree of search and time spent shopping. Industrial products are goods and services used in the production of other goods or services, in the operation of a business, or for resale. They include installations, accessory equipment, raw materials, component materials, fabricated parts, business supplies, and business services. They are distinguished on the basis of decision making, costs, consumption, the role in production, and the change in form.

A product item is a specific model, brand, or size of a product sold by a firm. A product line is a group of closely related items sold by a firm. A product mix consists of all the different product lines a firm offers. The width, depth, and consistency of the product mix are important.

A firm may choose from or combine several product management structures, including: marketing manager system, product (brand) manager, product planning committee, new-product manager system, and venture team. Each has particular strengths and best uses.

3. *To discuss product positioning and its usefulness for marketers* A firm must ensure that each of its products is perceived as providing some combination of unique features and that they are desired by the target market. Via product positioning, a firm can map its offerings with regard to consumer perceptions, consumer desires, competition, its own products in the same line, and the changing environment. Competitive positioning, company positioning, and consumers' ideal points are key concepts.

4. *To study the different types of product life cycles that a firm may encounter and the stages of the traditional product life cycle* The product life cycle seeks to describe a product's sales, competitors, profits, customers, and marketing emphasis from its inception until its removal from the market. Many firms desire a balanced product portfolio, with products in various stages of the life cycle. The product life cycle has several derivations, ranging from traditional to fad to bust. The traditional cycle consists of four stages: introduction, growth, maturity, and decline. During each stage, the marketing objective, industry sales, competition, industry profits, customers, and the marketing mix change. While the life cycle is useful in planning, it should not be a forecasting tool.

5. *To look at the international dimensions of product planning* If a firm intends to market products internationally, several points should be kept in mind—such as the distinctive generic meanings of products in different nations and the complexity of marketing services in foreign markets.

KEY TERMS

product planning (p. 301)
product (p. 301)
tangible product (p. 301)
augmented product (p. 301)
generic product (p. 302)
goods marketing (p. 302)
service marketing (p. 302)
consumer products (p. 303)
convenience products (p. 304)
shopping products (p. 304)
specialty products (p. 305)
industrial products (p. 305)
installations (p. 306)
accessory equipment (p. 306)
raw materials (p. 306)
component materials (p. 306)
fabricated parts (p. 306)
industrial supplies (p. 307)
industrial services (p. 307)
product item (p. 307)
product line (p. 307)
product mix (p. 307)
marketing manager system (p. 309)
product (brand) manager system (p. 310)
product planning committee (p. 310)
new-product manager system (p. 310)
venture team (p. 311)
product positioning (p. 312)
ideal points (p. 312)
product life cycle (p. 315)
balanced product portfolio (p. 315)
introduction stage of the product life cycle (p. 317)
growth stage of the product life cycle (p. 318)
maturity stage of the product life cycle (p. 318)
decline stage of the product life cycle (p. 318)
self-fulfilling prophecy (p. 318)

Review Questions

1. Why is it so important to understand the concept of a generic product?

2. Distinguish between a consumer product and an industrial product.

3. How can the same product be a convenience, shopping, *and* specialty product? What does this mean to marketers?

4. What are the similarities and differences between raw materials and component parts?

5. What is a wide/shallow product mix? State the advantages and disadvantages of such a mix.

6. Under what circumstances is a product manager system appropriate? A new-product manager system?

7. What is the role of product positioning for a new product? A continuing product?

8. How do competitive positioning and company positioning differ? Give an example of each.

9. Explain the basic premise of the product life cycle. What is the value of this concept?

10. What is the key marketing objective during the growth stage of the product life cycle? Why?

Discussion Questions

1. For each of the following, describe the tangible, augmented, and generic product:
   - **a.** A review course for the Graduate Management Aptitude Test (GMAT).
   - **b.** A computer mouse.
   - **c.** A Hootie and the Blowfish compact disc.
   - **d.** Highway paving materials.

2. Develop a marketing plan for a firm making installations.

3. Evaluate the product mix for ConAgra, shown in Figure 11-4.

4. What product management organization would you recommend for a large firm that makes, installs, and services home security systems? The firm is thinking about getting involved with auto alarms, fire detectors, and/or television satellite dishes. Explain your answer.

5. How has the positioning of the cellular telephone changed since the product has been on the market? Why?

CASE 1

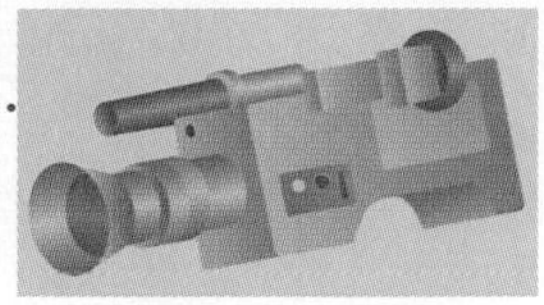

*Raychem: Applying the Generic Product Concept**

Raychem Corporation produces such materials-science products as wiring and cable, heat-shrinkable tubing, circuit protection devices, and splice closures (for joining wire and cable). Its annual sales exceed $1.5 billion.

Raychem believes in continuous product improvement through research and development. The firm's search for new materials and new processes means a continuous stream of new products. For example, new products introduced within the period from 1990 to 1995 accounted for 26 per cent of the firm's 1995 revenues. And many of its new products are more reliable, have a longer life expectancy, and have higher levels of sales growth than earlier ones. Raychem's recent new products include new sealing and protection solutions for automobile manufacturers, and polymer insulators and circuit breakers.

Raychem's sealing and protection solutions for automobiles are designed to reduce the impact of temperature extremes, the impact of water and fluids, corrosion, and vibration on a car's electrical and mechanical systems. Thus, its new LMx process-sealing products are based on a hot-melt adhesive that can seal as many as 100 wires at the same time. These products use two components: a polymer comb that separates each wire and heat-shrinkable tubing that slides over the wires. The new system lets wires be sealed in less than 30 seconds—versus three minutes for conventional heat-shrink products. An additional benefit is that the risk of overheating wires is lessened with the LMx process since the bundle is uniformly heated. Furthermore, based on massive cost cutting and increased volume, Raychem is able to sell the LMx product line at a fraction of the price it received for a similar product that the firm initially developed for the U.S. government for use on tanks. Innovative products such as the LMx process have increased the use of Raychem products by auto manufacturers. Between 1990 and 1995, for instance, the average value of Raychem products in midsize cars grew from $2 per car to $5 per car.

Raychem's polymer insulators and circuit breakers are used by electrical utilities, PC makers, and battery makers. As an example, Raychem's new miniSMD resettable fuse is now bought by makers of hard disk drives for personal computers, PC expansion cards, and cellular phones. The miniSMD fuse is 40 per cent smaller than the next smallest resettable fuse currently on the market. The new fuse is so tiny that it can even be integrated into the disk drive of subnotebook PCs. In comparison to standard SMD fuses, the miniSMD fuse is also 300 per cent faster to trip (resulting in greater protection to printed circuit boards) and 25 per cent lower in cost.

To improve the reliability of its products, Raychem subjects them to a variety of tests. In one test of polymers, Raychem simulates aging by subjecting different formulations to salt water and high humidity. This test enables Raychem to judge which additives have the greatest resistance to ultraviolet light and oxidation. Raychem hopes this product testing will result in higher quality, greater brand loyalty, and less price sensitivity.

Its efforts at continuous product improvement have earned Raychem recognition from customers such as Matsushita Battery, which recently designated Raychem a "Supplier of the Year."

QUESTIONS

1. Describe Raychem's product-planning strategy from the perspective of the generic product concept.
2. How can Raychem be sure that it follows the generic product concept in the future?
3. How wide and deep should Raychem's product mix be? Explain your answer.
4. How could Raychem apply product positioning to its miniSMD resettable fuses? Develop an appropriate positioning map.

VIDEO QUESTIONS ON RAYCHEM

1. What type of industrial products does Raychem produce? Refer to the material just presented in the text case, as well as the information in the video.
2. What are the advantages to a battery manufacturer's using Raychem's Polyswitch polymer circuit breaker over one with traditional materials?

*The data in this case are drawn from Ronald Henkoff, "Getting Beyond Downsizing," *Fortune* (January 10, 1994), pp. 58–64; "Induction Heating Sales Auto Wiring," *Machine Design* (August 22, 1994), p. 36; Seth Lubove, "A Long, Long Last Mile," *Forbes* (October 10, 1994), pp. 66–69; and *Raychem Annual Report 1995.*

CASE 2

Arm & Hammer Baking Soda: A Positioning Powerhouse[†]

Baking soda (sodium bicarbonate) was originally formulated for use in kitchens in the 1830s by Dr. Austin Church, a physician. In the 1840s, Dr. Church's brother-in-law, John Dwight, marketed baking soda as a time-saver for homemakers who made yeast-based breads and biscuits. When the product was combined with vinegar, buttermilk, or molasses, it released carbon dioxide, which created an instant leavening agent. Early in its history, baking soda was also used to neutralize stomach acids. Over time, other household uses were discovered. These include baking soda's use as a refrigerator freshener, garage floor cleaner, toothpaste ingredient to deter the formation of plaque, and fire extinguisher for grease-based fires. Many of these applications were discovered by consumers who communicated them to Dwight & Church, the parent company of Arm & Hammer.

Marketing research studies show that 90 per cent of U.S. households have at least one box of baking soda in their home. Each year, one billion pounds of baking soda are sold in North America alone. And Arm & Hammer has the lion's share of sales for this product category.

Although most people associate baking soda with home-based uses, the product has over 300 significant industrial applications. For example, more baking soda is now used as an ingredient in cattle feed than for any other application. Beef cattle are given baking soda to speed up digestion of their high-energy, low-fiber diet. And dairy cows are fed baking soda to increase their milk production. Baking soda has also been applied as a cleaning agent for the interior of the Statue of Liberty, as an ingredient in kidney dialysis solutions, and to reduce environmental pollution.

At Arm & Hammer, sales of baking soda for environmental applications have grown more than 25 per cent a year for the past five years. According to a spokesperson for Church & Dwight, "The possibilities for sodium bicarbonate to react favorably on the environment are almost infinite." Baking soda is even used to keep such toxic materials as lead and copper out of drinking water, help prevent acid rain, reduce smokestack emissions, and clean building facades. Let's look at these environmental applications.

Until ten years ago, lead pipes were commonly used in water systems. But, unfortunately, when these pipes begin to corrode, lead is distributed into the public's drinking water. Baking soda, when added to the water supply, bonds with the dissolving lead to produce a coating on the inside of lead pipes. This coating prevents further leaching of lead into the drinking water. In the past, phosphates were used by many municipalities to prevent lead contamination. However, unlike baking soda, phosphates had a detrimental effect on the ecosystem.

In recent years, factories and municipal waste plants in more than 60 cities have begun to use baking soda to help prevent acid rain. Using technology developed by Church & Dwight, these factories and plants now shoot baking soda into smokestacks and flues. The baking soda effectively absorbs acid gases before they enter the air. As a result, acid rain emissions have been controlled.

Baking soda is also being utilized to remove grime, paint, and graffiti from buildings. Unlike sandblasting and chemical solvents, baking soda does not damage the surface or release dangerous chemical fumes.

According to the president of the nationwide Earth Day Network, "It [baking soda] is a perfect example of using an environmentally sound product to make money. We'd be in much better shape if we realized what's good for the environment is also good for business."

QUESTIONS

1. Describe Arm & Hammer's product mix based on its width, depth, and consistency.
2. What product management organization is most appropriate for Church & Dwight? Explain your answer.
3. Present a product positioning strategy for Arm & Hammer's baking soda.
4. Evaluate the success of Arm & Hammer's baking soda from the perspective of the product life-cycle concept.

[†]The data in this case are drawn from Suzanne Hamlin, "Baking Soda to the Rescue!" *New York Times* (July 19, 1995), pp. C1, C6.

CHAPTER 12
Goods Versus Services Planning

Chapter Objectives

1. To examine the scope of goods and services, and explain how goods and services may be categorized

2. To discuss the special considerations in the marketing of services

3. To look at the use of marketing by goods versus services firms and provide illustrations of service marketing

4. To distinguish between nonprofit and profit-oriented marketing

5. To describe a classification system for nonprofit marketing, the role of nonprofit marketing in the economy, and applications of nonprofit marketing

It's no secret that service businesses are winning the fast-growing, job adding, tax-paying race. Services, in fact, account for nine of ten of the small-firm dominated businesses that will log the fastest employment growth through 2005, according to an analysis by the Small Business Administration (SBA). Strategic planners, however, need specifics. Which industries, to start with? What will the typical company in that sector be like? And where are they now in the growth curve?

Reprinted by permission of Sunrise Assisted Living.

According to the SBA, the fastest-growing small-business service will be residential care facilities with 150 per cent projected growth through 2005. In comparison, the other service-based industries on the SBA's fastest-growing list are forecast to have employment increases of between 54 and 89 per cent. So, let's examine residential care facilities for the elderly and day care centers for the young—two industries with very high growth rates—and see what factors are behind their anticipated growth.

The forecasted growth in residential care services is attributable to the "graying of the West." In the United States and other highly industrialized Western countries, the number of people over the age of 65 will continue to grow dramatically. Thus, many of the residential care facilities for the elderly serve as a bridge between traditional nursing homes that offer skilled around-the-clock medical care in an institutional environment and independent retirement housing where residents receive no assistance.

One estimate, by Standish Care (a Boston-based assisted-living company), is that assisted-living facilities costs are about 40 per cent those of a traditional nursing home. Residents are also able to have greater freedom of choice. According to David Peete, vice-president of marketing and education at Sunrise Assisted Living in Fairfax, Virginia, "It's not 'Mrs. Jones, it's bath time.' Here, Mrs. Jones picks her own time to bathe and whether or not she needs much assistance." Some facilities, such as National Guest Homes in Houston, even organize cruise trips for residents.

The increase in child care opportunities is due to two trends, a 10 per cent increase in the population under the age of 13 and the increase in working mothers. Day-care center owners also expect growth from their part-time programs that cater to parents who work on a part-time or flex-time arrangement, from corporate-sponsored programs, and from programs offering child supervision before or after school. One firm, American Child Care Centers, based in Tempe, Arizona, has been particularly successful in setting up child care programs that are subsidized by employers. Likewise, Mulberry Child Care Centers, based in Needham, Massachusetts, receives about 25 per cent of its total revenues from corporate sponsored programs.

Despite the growth prospects, some industry experts warn that it is tough to make money in child care. For-profit centers typically compete with nonprofit centers run by religious organizations. Nonprofit centers benefit from lower costs due to tax advantages (they are exempt from property tax and sales taxes), rent subsidies, and volunteer assistance. Many child care centers have high turnover among employees, as well as clients. This imposes large training and marketing costs.[1]

In this chapter, we will study key concepts pertaining to the marketing of services. We will also focus on the differences and similarities between goods and services marketing.

Overview

When devising and enacting product plans, a firm must fully comprehend the distinctions between goods and services—beyond the brief coverage in Chapter 11. Although the planning process is the same for goods and services, their differences need to be reflected by the decisions made in the process.

Chapter 12 covers the scope of goods and services, a goods/services continuum, goods and services classifications, special considerations in service marketing, and the use of marketing by goods and services firms. Also included is information on nonprofit marketing because most nonprofits (such as colleges, health facilities, and libraries) are involved with services.

The Scope of Goods and Services

Goods marketing entails the sale of physical products. **Durable goods** are physical products that are used over an extended period of time, such as furniture and heavy machinery. **Nondurable goods** are physical products made from materials other than metals, hard plastics, and wood; they are rather quickly consumed or worn out; or they become dated, unfashionable, or otherwise unpopular. Examples are food and office supplies.

Goods marketing *involves the sale of* **durable** *and* **nondurable goods.**

Service marketing includes the rental of goods, the alteration or maintenance/repair of goods owned by consumers, and personal services. **Rented-goods services** involve the leasing of goods for a specified period of time—such as auto, hotel room, office building, and tuxedo rentals. **Owned-goods services** involve alterations or maintenance/repairs of goods owned by consumers—such as house painting, clothing alterations, lawn care, equipment maintenance, and machinery repair. **Nongoods services** involve personal service on the part of the seller—such as accounting, legal, consulting, and tutoring services; they do not involve goods.

Service marketing *covers* **rented-goods, owned-goods,** *and* **nongoods services.**

Overall, the value of manufacturers' shipments of U.S.-made nondurable goods slightly exceeds that of durable goods. The leading durable products are transportation equipment, electronic and electrical equipment, machinery, and fabricated metal products. Among U.S. final consumers, nondurables comprise nearly three-quarters of all goods purchases—led by food products. Because nondurables are bought more often and consumed more quickly, sales are more influenced by ads and sales promotions.

In industrialized nations, services account for a substantial share of Gross Domestic Product, generally well over one-half of the GDP. In developing and less-developed nations, services account for a lower share of GDP; goods production (including agricultural items and extracted resources) is more dominant. Yet, even there, the role of services is growing rapidly.

Service marketing is huge in industrialized nations, with the United States being the world leader.

The United States is the world's leading service economy: Services account for $4.5 billion in annual output—60 per cent of the GDP. And as noted in Chapter 6, on an international level, the United States is by far the leading service exporter. Three-fifths of the spending on services in the United States is by final consumers; the rest is by businesses, government, and other nonprofit institutions. Among the leading U.S. service in-

[1]Jenny McCune, "Business 2005: The Face of Tomorrow," *Journal of Business Strategy*, Vol. 16 (May–June 1995), pp. 50–55.

dustries are housing and household operations, medical care, personal services, transportation services, and repair services. More than 75 per cent of the private sector U.S. labor force is in service jobs. Among the other nations with at least 50 per cent of their labor forces in service jobs are Australia, Canada, Great Britain, France, Japan, and Germany.[2]

These reasons have been cited for the worldwide growth of final consumer services: the rising living standard of the population; the complex goods that require specialized installation and repair; the lack of consumers' technical skills; the high purchase prices of items that can be rented rather than bought; and the greater need for health care, child care, and educational services. In the industrial sector, here are some of the services experiencing the greatest growth: computer repair and training, management consulting, engineering, and equipment leasing. There are 650,000 people in the United States working for consulting and other management service firms; these companies generate $18 billion in revenues.[3]

The **hidden service sector** *refers to services offered by goods-oriented firms.*

The scope of services is sometimes underestimated because services may be lumped together with goods in assigning revenues. The **hidden service sector** encompasses the delivery, installation, maintenance, training, repair, and other services provided by firms that emphasize goods sales. For instance, although IBM is a manufacturer, its Integrated Systems Solutions division now generates billions of dollars in revenues. Through outsourcing, IBM "takes back a company's data-processing operations and then sells back computing service or simply runs the operation for a fixed annual fee. Campbell Soup recently signed a $600 million deal for IBM to run its data center, network, and 7,000 desktop computers for ten years."[4]

Categorizing Goods and Services

Goods and services can be categorized in two ways. They can be located on a goods/services continuum; and they can be placed into separate classification systems.

A Goods/Services Continuum

With a **goods/services continuum,** *products are positioned from pure goods to pure services.*

A **goods/services continuum** categorizes products along a scale from pure goods to pure services. With pure goods, the seller offers the consumer only physical goods without any accompanying services. With pure services, the seller offers the consumer only nongoods services without any accompanying physical goods. Between the two extremes, the seller would offer good/service combinations to the consumer.

Figure 12-1 shows a goods/services continuum with four different examples. In each one, a pure good is depicted on the far left and a pure service is depicted on the far right. Moving from left to right, within each example, the combined good/service offerings become more service-oriented. Here is the reasoning behind the continuum examples in Figure 12-1:

- A computer diskette is usually marketed as a pure good—a product free from defects. With most computer software, there is a telephone hotline to answer questions. A PC is typically set up (configured) by the seller, pre-loaded with software, and accompanied by on-site servicing. Computer programming involves labor-intensive service on a physical good. Systems design entails professional consultation regarding a client's information system needs; the seller provides a pure service and does not sell or service goods.
- When a consumer purchases such exercise equipment as a stationary bicycle, he or she obtains ownership of a pure good. If a person rents a stationary bicycle for the

[2]Bureau of Economic Analysis, U.S. Commerce Department; and *Statistical Abstract of the United States 1995* (Washington, D.C.: U.S. Department of Commerce, 1995), various pages. See also Fanglan Du, Paula Mergenhagen, and Marlene Lee, "The Future of Services," *American Demographics* (November 1995), pp. 30–47.

[3]Michael J. Mandel, "White Collar Jobs Are Coming Back in Style," *Business Week* (November 30, 1992), pp. 110–111; and Du, Mergenhagen, and Lee, "The Future of Services," p. 44.

[4]Ira Sager, "The View from IBM," *Business Week* (October 30, 1995), p. 145.

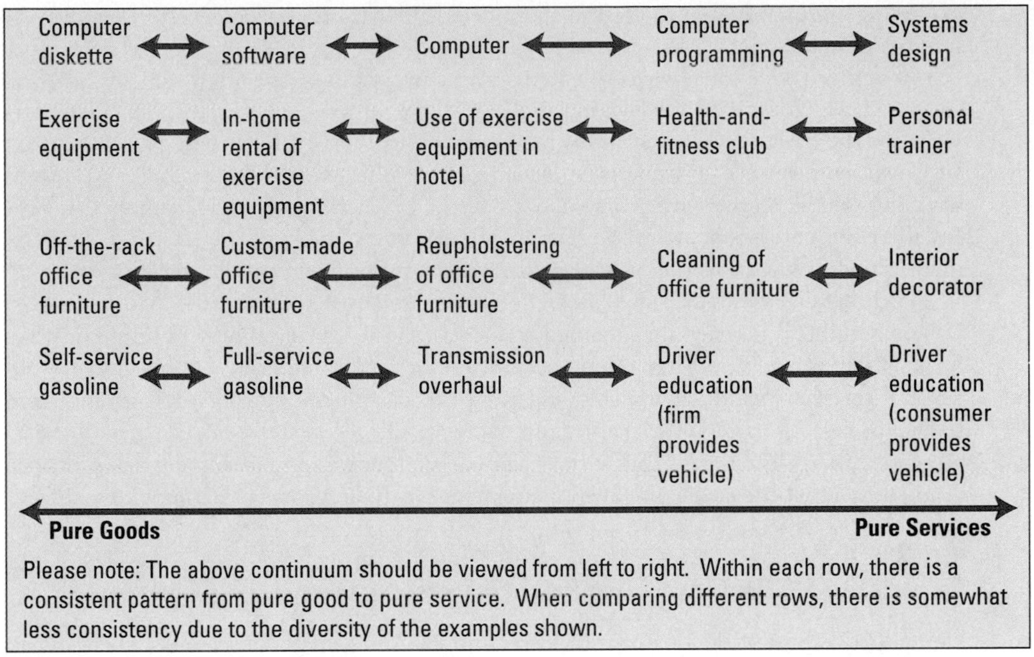

FIGURE 12-1
Illustrating the Goods/Services Continuum

home, that individual obtains the use of a physical product. When a person uses a stationary bicycle at a hotel, he or she obtains the use of a physical product and the related facilities. If a person joins a health-and-fitness club, he or she not only gets to use the physical facilities but also can participate in exercise classes under the direction of various instructors. When a person hires a personal trainer, he or she is acquiring the pure service of an expert teacher in exercise and motivation.

- Off-the-rack office furniture may be marketed as a pure good—with the buyer responsible for delivery and set up. Custom-made office furniture is made on the basis of buyer specifications and buyer/seller consultations; delivery and set-up are included. Furniture reupholstering involves labor-intensive service on a physical good; the seller is marketing a service along with a physical good (the fabric used in the reupholstering). The cleaning of office furniture entails a labor-intensive service on a physical good; the seller is marketing a service (the value of the cleaning solution is minor). An interior decorator offers professional consultation regarding a client's office furniture, wall coverings, flooring materials, layout, and so on; the seller provides a pure service and does not sell or service goods.
- Self-service gas is marketed as a pure good, with no accompanying service. With full-service gas, a station attendant pumps the gas—sometimes washing the windshield and performing other minor tasks. A transmission overhaul is a labor-intensive service on a physical good; the seller markets both a physical product (new parts) and service. In driver education, where the driving school provides the vehicle, the seller teaches a potential driver how to drive in a school car; the major offering is the education provided. In driver ed, where the trainee supplies his or her own vehicle, the driving school markets a pure service; it is not offering the use of a vehicle.

Several things can be learned from a goods/services continuum. First, it applies to both final consumer and organizational consumer products. Second, most products embody goods/services combinations; the selling firm must keep this in mind. Third, each position along the continuum represents a marketing opportunity. Fourth, the bond between a goods provider and its customers becomes closer as the firm moves away from marketing pure goods. Fifth, a firm must decide if it is to be perceived as goods- or services-oriented.[5]

By adding **peripheral services** *to their* **core services,** *firms can create a competitive advantage.*

Whether goods- or services-oriented, a company needs to specify which are core services and which are peripheral—and the level of peripheral services to offer. **Core services** are the basic services that firms must provide to their customers to be competitive. At Casio, core services include prompt delivery, credit, advertising support, and returns handling for the retailers that carry its watches in 150 nations around the globe. At Federal Express, core services involve taking phone orders, picking up packages, tracking them, shipping them overnight, and delivering them the next morning or afternoon.

Peripheral services are supplementary (extra) services that firms provide to customers. Casio's peripheral services are extended credit terms and advice on how to set up displays for its retailers, and a toll-free phone number for consumer inquiries. Federal Express' peripheral services include giving shipping advice to customers, making address labels and special packaging materials available, and tracing packages in transit. Although these services may increase a firm's costs, require added employee and management skills, and be time-consuming, they may also help a company create and sustain a competitive advantage.[6]

Goods and Services Classification Systems

Goods may be classified as to market, durability, value added, goals, regulation, distribution channel, and customer contact.

Figure 12-2 shows a detailed, seven-way classification system for goods. It is useful in demonstrating the diversity of goods marketing.

In selecting a market segment, a goods seller should remember that final and organizational consumers have similarities and differences. The same good may be offered to each segment. The major distinctions between the segments are the reasons for purchases, the amount bought, and the features desired.

Durable goods marketers have a particular challenge. On the one hand, they want to emphasize the defect-free, long-running nature of their products. On the other hand, inasmuch as they need to generate repeat business from current customers, they must continually strive to add unique features and enhance the performance of new models—and then convince people to buy again while the durable goods they own are still functional. For nondurable goods marketers, the key task is to engender brand loyalty, so consumers rebuy the same brands.

High value-added goods are those where manufacturers convert raw materials or components into distinctive products. The more value firms add to the goods they sell, the better the chance for a goods-based differential advantage. Low value-added goods are those where manufacturers do little to enhance the raw materials or components they extract or buy. These firms often must compete on price since their goods may be seen as commodities. Superior customer service can be a major differential advantage and enable marketers of low value-added goods to avoid commodity status.

For the most part, goods-oriented firms are profit-oriented. Sometimes, as noted in Figure 12-2, goods are marketed by nonprofit organizations—usually as a way of generating revenues to support the organizations' activities. Nonprofit marketing is discussed in depth later in this chapter.

Goods may be grouped by the extent of government regulation. Some items, such as those related to the health and safety of people and the environment, are highly regulated. Others, generally those not requiring special health and safety rules, are subject to less regulation.

Distribution channel length refers to the number of intermediaries between goods producers and consumers. Final consumer goods tend to have more intermediaries than organizational consumer ones due to the size and importance of the latter. Furthermore,

[5]See Ralph W. Jackson, Lester A. Neidell, and Dale Lunsford, "An Empirical Investigation of the Differences in Goods and Services as Perceived by Organizational Buyers," *Industrial Marketing Management*, Vol. 24 (March 1995), pp. 99–108.

[6]See James C. Anderson and James A. Narus, "Capturing the Value of Supplementary Services," *Harvard Business Review*, Vol. 73 (January–February 1995), pp. 75–83.

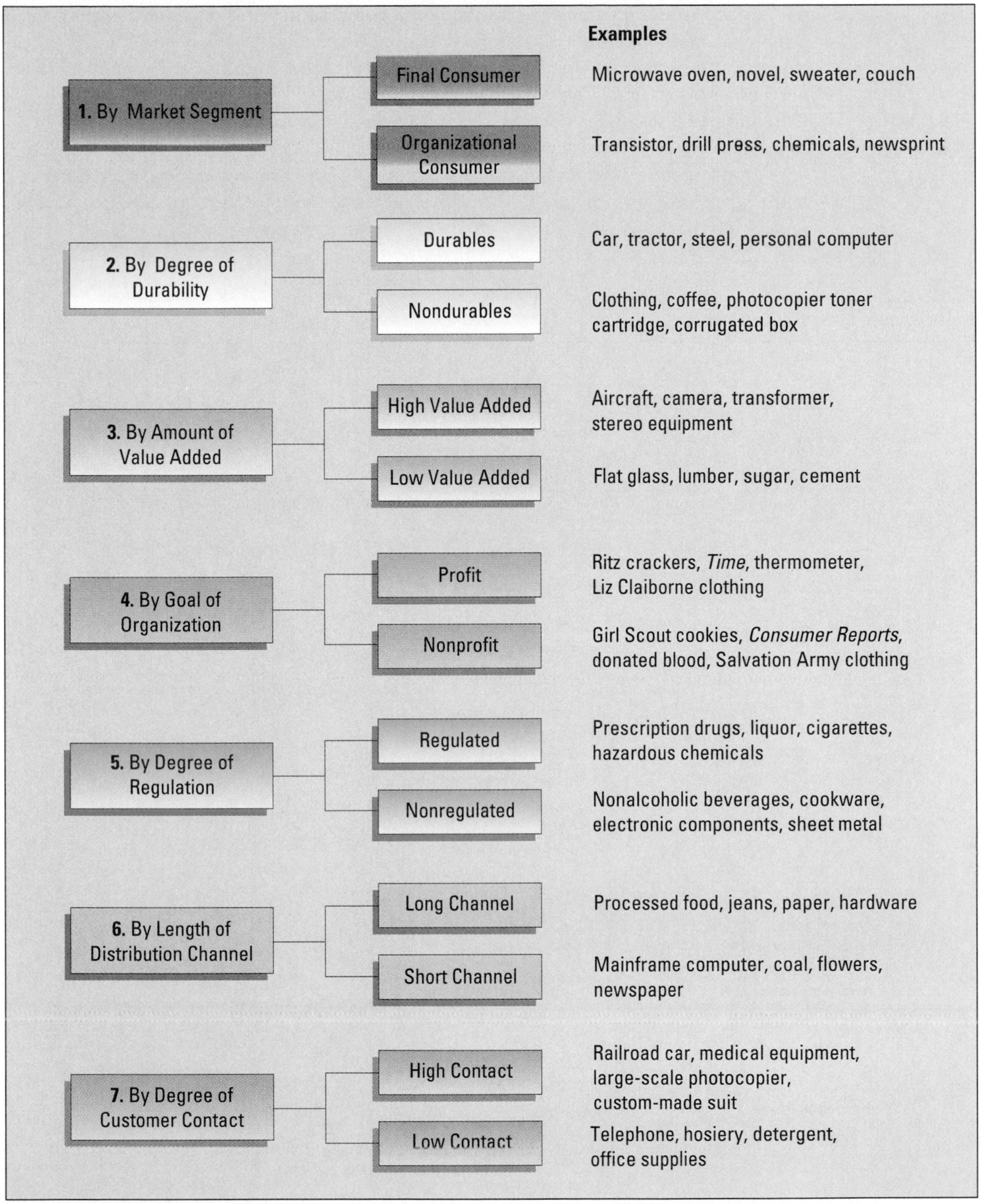

FIGURE 12-2
A Classification System for Goods

goods that are complex, expensive, bulky, and perishable are more apt to have shorter channels.

Goods may be classified by the degree of customer contact between sellers and buyers. Contact is greater for sophisticated equipment, items requiring some training, and custom-made goods. In these instances, proper employee training is needed. Low customer contact is required for goods that consumers are able to buy and use with little assistance from sellers.

A good would normally be classified on a combination of the factors in Figure 12-2. *Time* magazine appeals to final consumers, is nondurable, has a high value added, is profit-oriented, is subject to few regulations, is sold through newsstands (long channel) and home delivery (short channel), and has low customer contact.

Services may be classified as to market, tangibility, skill, goals, regulation, labor intensity, and customer contact.

Figure 12-3 displays a detailed, seven-way classification system for services. It is helpful in showing the diversity of service marketing.

As with goods, final and organizational consumers have similarities and differences, so the same basic service may be offered to each segment. Both groups can counter high

FIGURE 12-3
A Classification System for Services

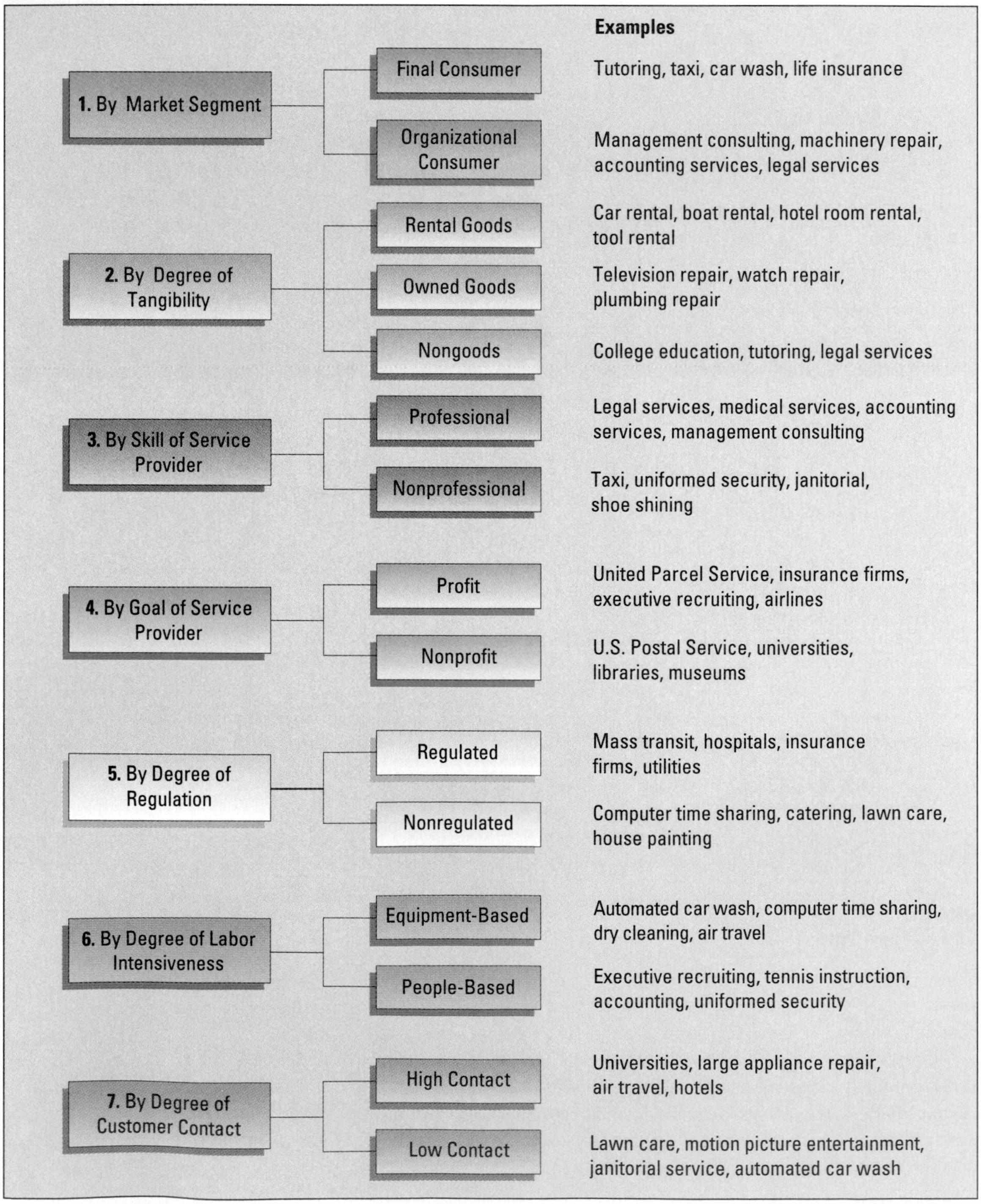

prices or poor service by doing some tasks themselves. The major differences between the segments are the reasons for the service, the quantity of service required, and the complexity of the service performed.

In general, the less tangible a service, the less service marketing resembles goods marketing. For nongoods services, performance can be judged only after the service is completed, and consistency is hard to maintain. Rentals and owned-goods services involve physical goods and may be marketed in a manner somewhat similar to goods.

Services may be provided by persons of greatly varying skills. For services requiring high skill levels, customers are quite selective in picking a provider. That is why professionals often achieve customer loyalty. For services requiring low levels of skill, the range of acceptable substitutes is usually much greater.

Service firms may be profit- or nonprofit-oriented. Nonprofit service marketing may be undertaken by government or private organizations. The major distinctions between profit- and nonprofit-oriented marketing are noted later in this chapter.

Services may be classed by the extent of government regulation. Some firms, such as insurance companies, are highly regulated. Others, such as caterers and house painters, are subject to limited regulation.

The traditional view of services has been that they are performed by one person for another. However, this view is too narrow. Services do differ in labor intensity—such as automated versus teller-oriented bank services. Labor intensity rises if highly skilled personnel are involved and/or services must be provided at the customer's home or business. Some labor-intensive services may be done by do-it-yourself consumers—for example, home repair.

Services may be grouped by their degree of customer contact. If contact is high, training personnel in interpersonal skills is essential, in addition to the technical schooling needed to perform a service properly. Such personnel as appliance repairpeople and car mechanics may be the only contact a person has with a firm. If contact is low, technical skills are most essential.

A service would typically be classified on a combination of the factors in Figure 12-3. A firm tutoring students for college board exams appeals to final consumers, has an intangible service, requires skill by the service provider, is profit-oriented, is not regulated, has many trainers, and has high customer contact. A company may also operate in more than one part of a category (this also applies to goods marketers): A CPA may have both final and organizational consumer clients.

Special Considerations in the Marketing of Services

Services differ from goods in terms of **intangibility, perishability, inseparability,** *and* **variability.**

Services have four attributes that typically distinguish them from goods (as noted in Chapter 11): higher intangibility, greater perishability, inseparability of the service from the service provider, and greater variability in quality. Their effect is greatest for personal services.

The **intangibility of services** means they often cannot be displayed, transported, stored, packaged, or inspected before buying. This occurs for repair services and personal services; only the benefits to be derived from the service experience can be described. The **perishability of services** means many of them cannot be stored for future sale. If a painter who needs eight hours to paint a single house is idle on Monday, he or she will not be able to paint two houses on Tuesday; Monday's idle time is lost. A service supplier must try to manage consumer usage so there is consistent demand over various parts of the week, month, and/or year.

The **inseparability of services** means a service provider and his or her services may be inseparable. When this occurs, the service provider is virtually indispensable, and customer contact is often considered an integral part of the service experience. The quality of machinery repair depends on a mechanic's skill and the quality of legal services depends on a lawyer's ability. **Variability in service quality**—differing service performance from one purchase occasion to another—often occurs even if services are completed by the

TECHNOLOGY & MARKETING

Is Banking Finally Coming Home?

Home banking services can now be conducted on an around-the-clock basis by phone or a modem-equipped personal computer: Consumers use either their phones or PCs to transfer money between accounts, to verify their balances, and even to apply for credit cards. Although many consumers do engage in phone-based banking, banking by computer has not taken off. According to a recent study, only one per cent of consumers bank via their personal computers. Thus, there is much debate over the potential of home banking via PCs.

Some experts say consumers will soon embrace computers for home banking functions. As a manager at one large accounting firm says, "The Nintendo generation will be coming into substantial amounts of money by the time they're ready to do their personal banking, and then you'll see this market explode." In anticipation of the growth of home banking by PC, BankAmerica and NationsBank recently purchased Meca Software, a developer of personal finance software. And twelve other banks have begun to offer updated home banking service via PC through Intuit's Quicken personal finance software.

Other experts wonder about the growth of computer-based home banking services. Even though Citibank reduced the fees for customers who use its home banking products, the bank's management still has doubts as to the long-term growth of PC-based home banking. As Citibank's marketing director says, "People will still want branches to get advice and seek help with financial planning." And the fees that many banks charge to use home banking services (ranging from $8 to $20 per month) are an additional deterrent to customer interest. Furthermore, the electronic payment of bills is now most suitable only for bills that are due periodically (such as utility and mortgage bills).

As the marketing manager for Citibank, what marketing strategies (aside from a price reduction) would you enact to expand the use of computer-based home banking services?

Source: Based on material in Timothy L. O'Brien, "Home Banking: Will It Take Off This Time?" *Wall Street Journal* (June 8, 1995), pp. B1, B4.

same person. This may be due to a service firm's difficulty in problem diagnosis (for repairs), customer inability to verbalize service needs, and the lack of standardization and mass production for many services.

In planning its marketing strategy, a service firm needs to consider how intangible its offering is, how perishable its services are, how inseparable performance is from specific service providers, and the potential variability of service quality. Its goal would be to prepare and enact a marketing strategy that lets consumers perceive its offering in a more tangible manner, makes its services less perishable, encourages consumers to seek it out but enables multiple employees to be viewed as competent, and makes service performance as efficient and consistent as possible.

Service intangibility makes positioning decisions more complex.

Service intangibility can make positioning harder. Unlike goods positioning, which stresses tangible factors and consumer analysis (such as touching and tasting) prior to a purchase, much service positioning must rely on performance promises (such as how well a truck handles after a tune-up), which can only be measured once a purchase is made. But, there are ways to use positioning to help consumers perceive a service more tangibly. A firm can

- Associate an intangible service with tangible objects better understood by the customer. Figure 12-4 shows how United Airlines does this.
- Focus on the relationship between the company and its customers. It can sell the competence, skill, and concern of employees.
- Popularize the company name.

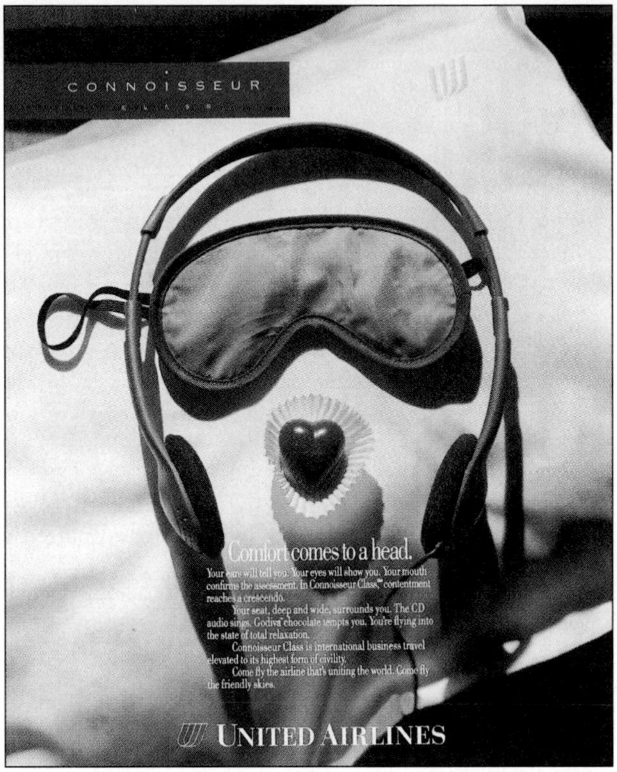

FIGURE 12-4
United Airlines: Associating an Intangible Service with Tangible Objects
Reprinted by permission.

- Offer tangible benefits, such as AccuFunds' promoting specific reasons for people to buy mutual funds from it. See Figure 12-5.

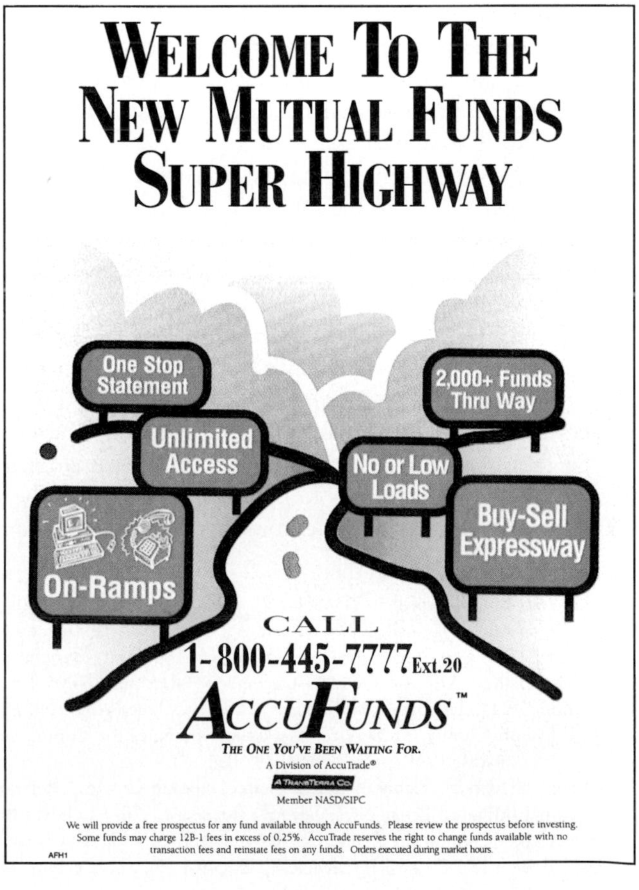

FIGURE 12-5
AccuFunds: Offering Tangible Benefits
Reprinted by permission.

- Establish a unique product position, such as 24-hour, on-site service for the repair of office equipment.[7]

Service intangibility may be magnified if only a small portion of the provided service is visible to the consumer. For example, in-shop repairs are normally not seen by consumers. Although a repairperson may spend two hours on a facsimile machine and insert two parts priced at $35, when the consumer sees a bill for $145, he or she may not appreciate the service time involved. Thus, a firm must explain how much time is needed to render each aspect of service—and the tasks performed—to make that service more tangible to customers.

Services often cannot be stored for later sale, so demand must be carefully matched with supply.

Because of service perishability, a service firm needs to match demand and supply patterns as well as it can. Thus, it might have to alter the timing of consumer demand and/or exert better control over the supply of its service offering. It should try to avoid situations in which excess demand goes unsatisfied and cases in which excess capacity causes an unproductive use of resources. To better match demand with supply, a firm can:

- Market similar services to segments having different demand patterns.
- Market new services with different demand patterns from existing services.
- Market new services that complement existing ones.
- Market service "extras" during nonpeak periods.
- Market new services not affected by existing capacity constraints.
- Train personnel to perform multiple tasks.
- Hire part-time employees during peak periods.
- Educate consumers to use services during nonpeak periods.
- Offer incentives and price reductions in nonpeak periods.[8]

Interpersonal skills are crucial for service businesses.

The existence of a close service provider/consumer relationship makes employee interpersonal skills important. The work force must be trained to interact well with people in such diverse situations as selling and performing services, handling payments, and delivering repaired goods. Generally, more personal involvement, personal contact, and customer input are needed to market services than to market goods. Thus, employee empowerment can be quite beneficial. Those who participate in the marketing of complex services often act as *relationship managers*. As such, the quality of the relationship between a firm's employees and its customers "determines the probability of continued interchange between those parties in the future." Enterprise Rent-a-Car goes so far as to pick up customers who cannot make it to an Enterprise location—and even brings cars to people who are stranded.[9]

In planning a service provider/consumer relationship, this should also be kept in mind: Many customers of personal service firms become loyal to a particular employee rather than the company. If that person leaves the firm, he or she may take some customers with him or her. That is why it is important for a firm to show its customers that multiple employees are equally capable of providing excellent service.

The **industrialization of services** *can lower inefficiency and excessive variability via hard technologies, soft technologies, or hybrid technologies.*

By their nature, many services have the potential for great variability in their quality. It is hard for lawn care firms to mow lawns in exactly the same way each week, for marketing consultants to make sales forecasts for clients that are always accurate, and for each

[7]Gordon H. G. McDougall and Douglas W. Snetsinger, "The Intangibility of Services: Measurement and Competitive Perspectives," *Journal of Services Marketing*, Vol. 4 (Fall 1990), pp. 27–40.

[8]Leonard L. Berry, A. Parasuraman, and Valarie A. Zeithaml, "Synchronizing Demand and Supply in Service Businesses," *Business*, Vol. 34 (October–December 1984), pp. 36–37; James L. Heskett, W. Earl Sasser, Jr., and Christopher W. L. Hart, *Service Breakthroughs* (New York: Free Press, 1990), pp. 135–158; and Donald J. Shemwell, Jr. and J. Joseph Cronin, Jr., "Services Marketing Strategies for Coping with Demand/Supply Imbalances," *Journal of Services Marketing*, Vol. 8 (Number 4, 1994), pp. 14–24.

[9]Lawrence A. Crosby, Kenneth R. Evans, and Deborah Cowles, "Relationship Quality in Services Selling: An Interpersonal Influence Perspective," *Journal of Marketing*, Vol. 54 (July 1990), p. 68; and Gabriella Stern, "If You Don't Feel Like Fetching the Rental Car, It Fetches You," *Wall Street Journal* (June 9, 1995), pp. B1, B13. See also David E. Bowen and Edward E. Lawler III, "Empowering Service Employees," *Sloan Management Review*, Vol. 36 (Summer 1995), pp. 73–84.

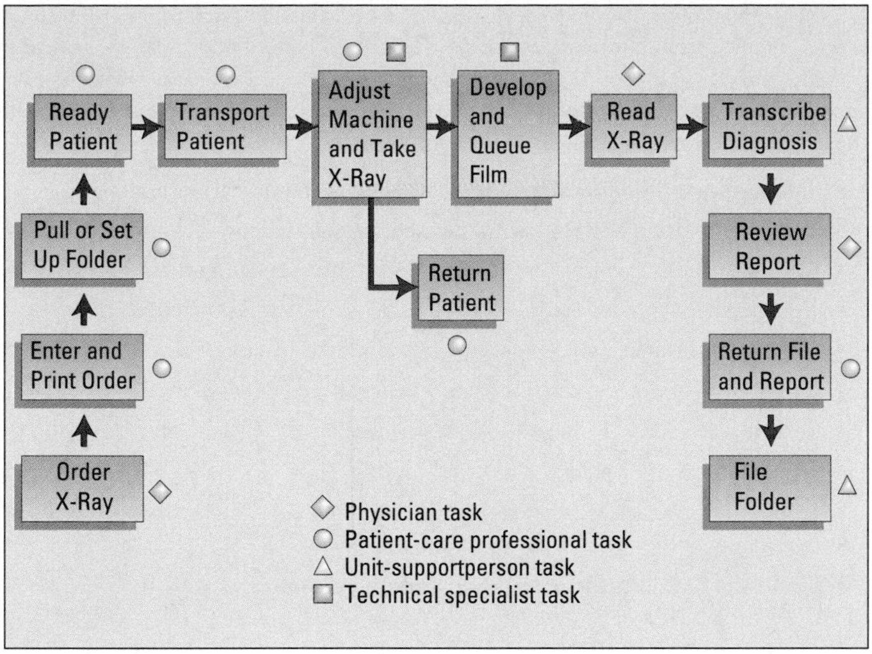

FIGURE 12-6
A Service Blueprint for an X-Ray
This service blueprint depicts the thirteen steps involved in a typical hospital's X-ray process. The steps can be completed in under one hour and they require multiple employees. Without such a blueprint, the X-ray process would probably be less systematic, more time-consuming, and less efficient.

Source: Stephen H. Baum, "Making Your Service Blueprint Pay Off!" *Journal of Services Marketing,* Vol. 4 (Summer 1990), p. 49. *Reprinted by permission.*

airline flight to arrive on time. But what service firms can do is strive to make their performance as efficient and consistent as possible. One solution to the issue of high costs (inefficiency) and low reliability (performance variability) is the **industrialization of services** by using hard, soft, and hybrid technologies.[10] Service reliability can also be improved by setting high-level standards and by tying employee pay and promotions to performance levels.

Hard technologies substitute machinery for people, such as the implementation of an electronic credit authorization system instead of manual credit checks. Hard technologies cannot be as readily applied to services requiring extensive personal skill and contact—such as medical, legal, and hairstyling services. *Soft technologies* substitute pre-planned systems for individual services. For example, travel agents sell pre-packaged vacation tours to standardize transportation, accommodations, food, and sightseeing. *Hybrid technologies* combine both hard and soft technologies. Examples include muffler repair and quick-oil-change shops.

This is how Continental Airlines vastly improved its on-time flight performance by industrializing its service activities:

> Continental launched a complex rescheduling in every hub; for example, it employed an airspace model developed for NASA to test different routings and schedules at its Newark hub. Continental also overhauled airport procedures: It painted more detailed airplane pathways to the gates so crowded planes don't block each other and better positioned luggage carts on the tarmac for exchanging connecting flights' baggage. It studied the most common connections at hubs and grouped those flights' gates and times close together.[11]

To industrialize their services better, many firms use a **service blueprint,** which is a visual portrayal of the service process: "It displays each subprocess (or step) in the service system, linking the various steps in the sequence in which they appear. A service blueprint is essentially a detailed map or flowchart of the service process."[12] Figure 12-6 shows how a service blueprint can be used in administering an X-ray to a patient.

A **service blueprint** *enhances productivity.* **Service gaps** *must be reduced.*

[10]Theodore Levitt, *The Marketing Imagination* (New York: Free Press, 1983), pp. 50–71; and James S. Hensel, "Service Quality Improvement and Control: A Customer-Based Approach," *Journal of Business Research*, Vol. 20 (January 1990), pp. 43–54. See also Myron Magnet, "Good News for the Service Economy," *Fortune* (May 3, 1993), pp. 46–52.

[11]Scott McCartney, "How to Make an Airline Run on Schedule," *Wall Street Journal* (December 22, 1995), pp. B1, B5.

[12]Valarie A. Zeithaml, A. Parasuraman, and Leonard L. Berry, *Delivering Quality Service* (New York: Free Press, 1990), p. 158. See also Susan J. Devlin and H. K. Dong, "Service Quality from the Customers' Perspective," *Marketing Research* (Winter 1994), pp. 5–13.

While planning their marketing strategies, it is also important for firms to understand service quality from the perspective of their customers. They must try to minimize any possible **service gap**—as represented by the difference between customer expectations and actual service performance. Consumer expectations regarding service companies cover these ten areas:

- Tangibles—facilities, equipment, personnel, communication materials.
- Reliability—ability to perform a desired service dependably and accurately.
- Responsiveness—willingness to provide prompt service and assist customers.
- Competence—possession of the necessary skills and knowledge.
- Courtesy—respect, politeness, and friendliness of personnel.
- Credibility—honesty, trustiness, and believability of service performers.
- Security—freedom from risk, doubt, or danger.
- Access—ease of contact.
- Communication—keeping customers informed in a clear manner and listening to comments.
- Understanding the customer—knowing the customer's needs.[13]

The Use of Marketing by Goods and Services Firms

Goods and services firms have differed in their use of marketing, but service firms are now better adapting to their special circumstances than in the past.

A Transition in the Marketing of Services

The low use of marketing for services has been due to small firm size, an emphasis on technical expertise, limited competition, negative attitudes, and other factors.

Service firms have tended to lag behind manufacturers in the use of marketing for several reasons. One, many service firms are so small that marketing specialists cannot be afforded. Two, because manufacturers often have a larger geographic market, they can more efficiently advertise. Three, a lot of service firms are staffed by people with technical expertise in their fields but limited marketing experience. Four, strict licensing provisions sometimes limit competition among service firms and the need for marketing; in most industries, manufacturers have faced intense competition for years. Five, consumers have held some service professionals, such as doctors and lawyers, in such high esteem that marketing has not been needed. Six, in the past, some professional associations banned advertising by members; this was changed by various court rulings that now permit it. Seven, there are still service professionals who dislike marketing, do not understand it, or question the use of marketing practices, such as advertising, in their fields. Finally, many manufacturers have only recently set up services as profit centers.

Service providers' use of marketing practices is expected to continue increasing in the future.

Over the next few years, the use of marketing for services will continue to rise, due to a better understanding of the role of customer service in gaining and retaining consumers; worldwide service opportunities; deregulation in the banking, transportation, and communication industries; competition among service providers; consumer interest in renting/leasing rather than buying; the aggressive marketing of services by firms that once focused on manufacturing (such as IBM); the advent of high-technology services (such as video conferencing); the growth of do-it-yourselfers because of high service costs; and the number of service professionals with formal business training.

Illustrations of Service Marketing

This section examines the use of marketing by hotels, auto repair and servicing firms, and lawyers. The examples represent rented-goods services, owned-goods services, and nongoods services. They differ by the degree of tangibility, the service provider skill, the degree of labor intensiveness, and the level of customer contact. But, in all three instances, the use of marketing practices is expanding.

[13]Zeithaml, Parasuraman, and Berry, *Delivering Quality Service*, pp. 18–22.

"Here's to long commutes, bad meetings, worse weather, and being as far away as possible from all of them."
Feel The Hyatt Touch.
Orlando, Florida
HYATT
REGENCY
GRAND CYPRESS
A HYATT RESORT
For reservations or more information about Hyatt Hotels and Resorts worldwide, call your travel planner or 1-800-233-1234.

FIGURE 12-7
The Hyatt Touch
Reprinted by permission.

Hotels may target one or more market segments: business travelers, through tourists (who stay one night), regular tourists (who stay two or more nights), extended-stay residents (who stay up to several months or even longer), and conventioneers. Each requires different services. The business traveler wants efficient service, a desk in the room, and convenient meeting rooms. A through tourist wants a convenient location, low prices, and quick food service. A regular tourist wants a nice room, recreational facilities, and sightseeing assistance. An extended-stay resident wants an in-room kitchen and other apartmentlike amenities. Conventioneers want large meeting rooms, pre-planned sightseeing, fax machines, computer access, and hospitality suites.

To attract and keep customers, hotels are upgrading, adding new services, opening units in emerging markets around the world, and improving marketing efforts.[14] Elaborate, distinctive lobby areas and immaculate grounds are popular among resort hotels. See Figure 12-7. First-run movies that can be viewed in the room, frequent-stay bonus plans, and special promotions are some of the amenities offered. For example, Sheraton has the largest international frequent-stay program, with a data base of over one million members.

Hotels' marketing efforts now entail more reliance on research, publicity, TV ads, well-conceived slogans, personal attention for consumers, and product positioning. An innovative cooperative project is one by the Hospitality and Tourism Skills Board, an industry trade association. Its "skill standards" project intends to better identify the skills necessary to perform various hospitality jobs (such as front desk clerk and food service

[14]Laura Koss-Feder, "Pricier Hotels Are Piling on the Extras," *Business Week* (October 23, 1995), p. 138; Alan Salomon, "Hotels Rise in Emerging Markets as Business Occupies Vacancies," *Advertising Age* (October 16, 1995), pp. I-20, I-22; and Chad Rubel, "Hotels Help Lodgers Who Help Themselves," *Marketing News* (May 8, 1995), p. 6.

worker) and to set detailed standards for them. For each job, it is focusing on three questions: What work is being done? What are the criteria for outstanding performance? What does an individual employee have to know, be, and do?[15]

Hotels are even trying to resolve consumer complaints more effectively. For instance, business travelers are quite concerned about overbooking, long waiting lines, late check-in times, and unresponsive or discourteous staffs. In response, many of today's hotels arrange for alternative accommodations if they are overbooked, have computerized check-ins, offer express checkout (with bills placed under room doors or mailed to guests' businesses or homes), serve free drinks and provide baggage handling if check-in times are late, and give workers more flexibility. At the Ritz-Carlton, front-desk clerks are empowered to take up to $2,000 dollars off a bill if a guest is displeased: "When a guest complains, we call that an opportunity to make things better."[16]

Repair and servicing firms operate in a variety of product categories—including motor vehicles, computers, TVs and appliances, industrial equipment, watches and jewelry, and a host of others. These firms fix malfunctioning products, replace broken parts, and provide maintenance. Let us highlight the auto repair and servicing industry.

Auto repairs and servicing are carried out via manufacturer-owned or sponsored dealers and independent service centers.[17] New-car dealers actually generate over 85 per cent of their profits from parts and servicing. In total, $125 billion is spent annually on U.S. auto repairs and servicing (including parts and labor), one-third at new-car dealers and two-thirds at independents. For example, General Motors cars can be repaired and serviced via the firm's Mr. Goodwrench program, available at approved GM dealerships; independent repair and maintenance shops; tire, muffler, and battery outlets; mass merchants (such as Sears); and service stations. Independents handle many makes and models. Among the largest independent specialists are Jiffy Lube (oil and lubricating fluids), Midas (mufflers), and Aamco (transmissions).

How has the auto repair and servicing business changed? According to the executive director of the Gasoline and Automotive Services Association, "The old type of gas station with the dirty rags and cigar-smoking mechanic no longer exists. We have evolved due to the technology needed to service, repair, and diagnose modern-day vehicles. It has forced shops to upgrade their tools and equipment. Where it may have cost several thousand dollars in the past, now it can cost several hundred thousand dollars."[18] In addition, there has been an influx of companies such as quick-oil-change firms:

> You can do it on your lunch hour. Usually at the dealerships, you have to check your car in for the day. The average length of time that a car stays on the road is far longer than it used to be. When you start holding cars longer, you try to maintain them better, so you're more likely to change the oil regularly.[19]

In 1977, the U.S. Supreme Court ruled that lawyers could not be prohibited from advertising their services. Since then, legal services advertising has risen significantly and many marketing innovations have been implemented. And today, all U.S. professionals are able to advertise their services.

It is estimated that 20 to 30 per cent of new clients now choose their attorneys on the basis of the latter's marketing efforts; the rest rely on personal referrals.[20] Thus, many attorneys advertise in the Yellow Pages and have printed brochures. Some advertise in newspapers and magazines; and certain ones use TV and radio ads. Various law firms send out newsletters, employ public relations firms, and have sessions where partners and associates practice selling services to clients.

[15]Hospitality and Tourism Skills Board and CHRIE, *Building Skills by Building Standards* (Washington, D.C.: Council on Hotel, Restaurant and Institutional Education, 1995).

[16]James S. Hirsch, "Now Hotel Clerks Provide More Than Keys," *Wall Street Journal* (March 5, 1993), pp. B1, B6.

[17]Bureau of Economic Analysis, U.S. Commerce Department; Julie Edelson Halpert, "Who Will Fix Tomorrow's Cars?" *New York Times* (November 7, 1993), Section 3, p. 4; and authors' estimates.

[18]Du, Mergenhagen, and Lee, "The Future of Services," p. 35.

[19]Ibid.

[20]Jennifer Fulkerson, "When Lawyers Advertise," *American Demographics* (June 1995), pp. 54–55.

FIGURE 12-8
Nonprofit Marketing in Action
Nonprofit marketing is very broad in scope and growing in stature. In this advertisement, the state of Massachusetts is promoting itself as "The Home of America's Greatest Debaters" and seeking to attract tourists to visit there.
Reprinted by permission.

A growing number of firms even hire jury consultants: "Target marketing tools aren't just for business. They are also being used in courtrooms to help attorneys understand what motivates jury decisions. Target marketers use focus groups to understand consumers; jury consultants use mock juries to understand jurors."[21] Overall, lawyers spend 4 per cent of gross revenues on marketing activities—up from 1 per cent a few years ago.

Law clinics and franchised law firms have grown. These firms concentrate on relatively routine legal services. They have large legal staffs, convenient locations (such as in shopping centers), standardized fees and services (such as $100 or so for a simple will), and plain fixtures and furniture. The largest franchised firms have hundreds of attorneys, cover a wide geographic area, advertise heavily, and set fees in advance and in writing.

Legal-services marketing has been met with resistance from a number of attorneys. They criticize price advertising for stressing price at the expense of quality and mass-marketing techniques as eliminating personal counseling. They feel the public's confidence in the profession is falling, information in ads may be inaccurate, and overly high consumer expectations are created. Most lawyers still do not advertise in mass media; they rely totally on referrals.

Nonprofit Marketing

Nonprofit marketing is conducted by organizations and individuals that operate in the public interest or that foster a cause and do not seek financial profits. It may involve organizations (charities, unions, trade associations), people (political candidates), places (resorts, convention centers, industrial sites), and ideas ("stop smoking"), as well as goods and services. See Figure 12-8.

Nonprofit marketing *serves the public interest and does not seek financial profits.*

Although nonprofit organizations conduct exchanges, they do not have to be in the form of dollars for goods and services. Politicians request votes in exchange for promises of better government services. The U.S. Postal Service wants greater use of zip codes in

[21]Joe Schwartz, "Marketing *the* Verdict," *American Demographics* (February 1993), p. 52.

International Marketing in *Action*

How Can Middle East Tourism Be Increased?

Market analysts agree that the most promising areas for the development of Middle East tourism are Egypt, Israel, Jordan, and Lebanon. In one recent year, Egypt's tourist revenues were $1.03 billion, versus $1.67 billion for Israel and $532 million for Jordan. No data were available for Lebanon.

One key to developing and promoting tourism in the region is joint tourist efforts by Egypt, Israel, and Jordan. Tourist officials in each of these countries feel the overall region will be more attractive to tourists who can visit two or three of these countries on a single trip. The Israeli Ministry of Tourism forecasts that Israel's 1993 record of two million tourists could easily double or even triple by 1998.

Some tour officials see Jordan as particularly gaining from this alliance. Jordan has the spectacular ancient city of Petra, world-class beaches, and a modern capital. Until recently, these attractions were not accessible by Israelis. Today, demand is so great that Jordan has been forced to limit the number of visitors to Petra. At the same time, there is also a shortage of hotels and taxis. And while Jordanian land is cheap, hotel development is impeded by the lack of an infrastructure.

Lebanon is another potential bright spot. Before its civil war in 1975, Lebanon had close to 570 hotels, impressive ski resorts, and great beaches. Many of these facilities were destroyed by the civil war. Foreign investors are now renovating and rebuilding the hotels that were wrecked. Lebanon is working with the World Tourism Organization and the United Nations Development Program to develop pamphlets depicting its important archeological treasures.

As a marketing consultant retained by a hotel chain that operates hotels in Israel, Jordan, Egypt, and Lebanon, develop a plan for increasing tourism in the area.

Source: Based on material in Mary A. Kelly, "Tourists Return to Calmer Middle East," *Advertising Age* (April 17, 1995), p. I-12.

exchange for improved service and lower rate hikes. The Red Cross seeks funds to help victims of all kinds of disasters.

Prices charged by nonprofit organizations often have no relation to the cost or value of their services. The Girl Scouts of the USA sells cookies to raise funds; only part of the price goes for the cookies. In contrast, the price of a chest X-ray at an overseas health clinic may be below cost or free.

Due to its unique attributes, marketing by nonprofit organizations rates a thorough discussion—from a product-planning perspective. In the following sections, nonprofit marketing is examined in terms of a comparison with profit-oriented marketing, a classification system, and its extent in the economy. Three detailed examples of nonprofit marketing are also presented.

Nonprofit Versus Profit-Oriented Marketing

Nonprofit marketing has both similarities with and distinctions from profit-oriented marketing.

There are a number of marketing similarities between nonprofit and profit-oriented firms. In today's uncertain and competitive arena, nonprofit organizations must apply appropriate marketing concepts and strategies if they are to generate adequate support—financial and otherwise.

With both nonprofit and profit-oriented organizations, people usually can choose among competing entities; the benefits provided by competitors differ; consumer segments may have distinct reasons for their choices; people are lured by the most desirable prod-

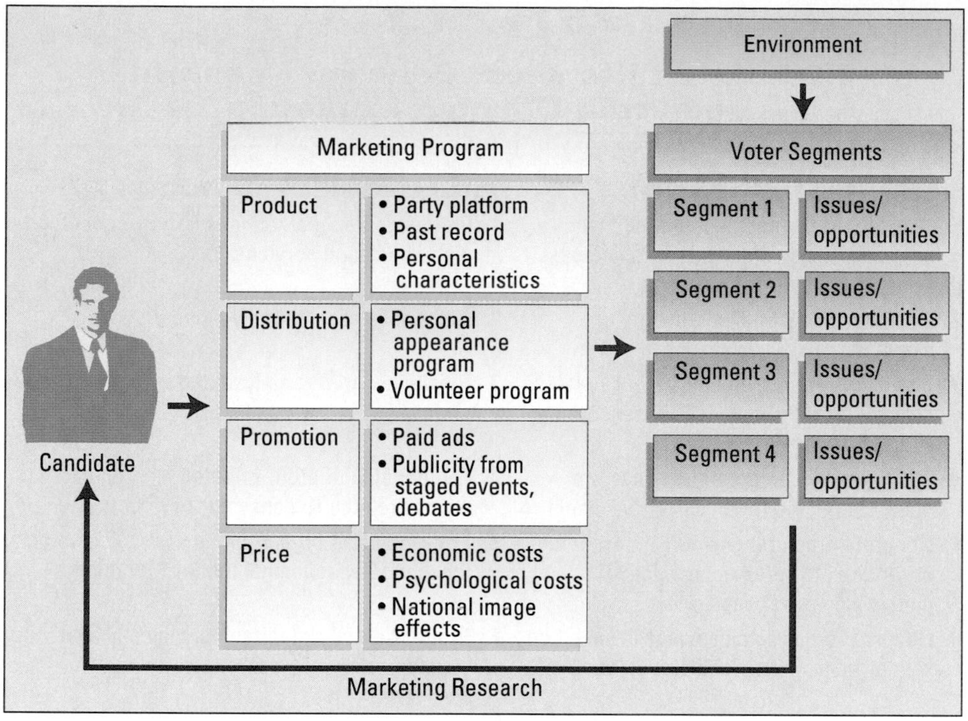

FIGURE 12-9
The Political Marketing Process
Source: Adapted by the authors from Phillip B. Niffenegger, "Strategies for Success from the Political Marketers," *Journal of Consumer Marketing,* Vol. 6 (Winter 1989), p. 46. *Reprinted by permission.*

uct positioning; and they are either satisfied or dissatisfied with performance. Figure 12-9 shows how a political candidate could seek various voter segments via a well-conceived marketing mix and careful product positioning (party platform, past record, and personal traits). This approach is like the one a profit-oriented firm would use.

Doesn't this sound like the approach a profit-oriented firm would take?

> A decade ago, a small Texas company created a long-range planning committee, instituted customer-focused marketing strategies, and forged an innovative set of service-quality initiatives. Since then, it has grown eight-fold, halved development cycle time, and produced five top blockbuster products. Compaq Computer? No, the nonprofit Dallas Symphony. Components of its marketing initiatives include frequent and informative communications with existing subscribers, targeted marketing to specific market segments, and free "samples" of concert performances.[22]

There are also some basic differences in marketing between nonprofit and profit-oriented organizations. They are highlighted in Table 12-1 and described in the following paragraphs.

Nonprofit marketing is broad in scope and frequently involved with **social marketing.**

Nonprofit marketing includes organizations, people, places, and ideas, as well as goods and services. It is much more apt to be involved with social programs and ideas than is profit-oriented marketing. Examples include AIDS prevention, recycling, highway safety, family planning, gun control, and energy conservation. The use of marketing to increase the acceptability of social ideas is referred to as **social marketing.**[23]

The nonprofit exchange process can include nonmonetary and monetary transactions. Nonmonetary transactions can be votes, volunteers' time, blood donations, and so forth. Monetary transactions can be donations, magazine subscriptions, tuition, and so on. Sometimes, nonprofit marketing does not generate revenues in day-to-day exchanges; instead, it may rely on infrequent fund-raising efforts. In addition, a successful marketing campaign may actually lose money if services or goods are provided at less than cost. Thus, operating budgets must be large enough to serve the number of anticipated clients, so none are poorly treated or turned away.

[22]Betsy Wiesendanger, "Profitable Pointers from Nonprofits," *Journal of Business Strategy*, Vol. 15 (July 1994), p. 33.

[23]See Alan R. Andreasen, "Social Marketing: Its Definition and Domain," *Journal of Public Policy & Marketing*, Vol. 13 (Spring 1994), pp. 108–114; and Patricia Braus, "Selling Good Behavior," *American Demographics* (November 1995), pp. 60–64.

Table 12-1

The Basic Differences Between Nonprofit and Profit-Oriented Marketing

NONPROFIT MARKETING	PROFIT-ORIENTED MARKETING
1. Nonprofit marketing is concerned with organizations, people, places, and ideas, as well as goods and services.	1. Profit-oriented marketing is largely concerned with goods and services.
2. Exchanges may be nonmonetary or monetary.	2. Exchanges are generally monetary.
3. Objectives are more complex because success or failure cannot be measured strictly in financial terms.	3. Objectives are typically stated in terms of sales, profits, and recovery of cash.
4. The benefits of nonprofit services are often not related to consumer payments.	4. The benefits of profit-oriented marketing are usually related to consumer payments.
5. Nonprofit organizations may be expected or required to serve economically unfeasible market segments.	5. Profit-oriented organizations seek to serve only those market segments that are profitable.
6. Nonprofit organizations typically have two key target markets: clients and donors.	6. Profit-oriented organizations typically have one key target market: clients.

Goals may be complex because success or failure cannot be measured just in financial terms. A nonprofit organization might have this combination of goals: raise $250,000 from government grants, increase client usage, find a cure for a disease, change public attitudes, and raise $750,000 from private donors. Goals must include the number of clients to be served, the amount of service to be rendered, and the quality of service to be provided.

Consumer benefits may not be related to their payments.

The benefits of nonprofit organizations may not be allotted on the basis of consumer payments. Only a small portion of the population contracts a disease, requires humanitarian services, visits a museum, uses a public library, or goes to a health clinic in a given year; yet the general public pays to find cures, support fellow citizens, or otherwise assist nonprofit organizations. Many times, the people who would benefit most from a nonprofit organization's activities may be the ones least apt to seek or use them. This occurs for libraries, health clinics, remedial programs, and others. With profit-oriented organizations, benefits are usually distributed equitably, based on consumers' direct payments in exchange for goods or services.

Nonprofit organizations may be expected, or required, to serve markets that profit-oriented firms find uneconomical. For example, the U.S. Postal Service must have rural post offices, and Amtrak must offer passenger rail service over some sparsely populated areas. This may give profit-oriented firms an edge; they can concentrate on the most lucrative market segments.

Nonprofit organizations must satisfy **clients** *and* **donors.**

Profit-oriented firms have one major target market—clients (customers)—to whom they offer goods and services and from whom they receive payment; a typical nonprofit organization has two: **clients**—to whom it offers membership, elected officials, locations, ideas, goods, and services—and **donors**—from whom it receives resources (which may be time from volunteers or money from foundations and individuals). There may be little overlap between clients and donors.

Private nonprofit organizations have been granted many legal advantages. These include tax-deductible contributions, exemptions from most sales and real-estate taxes, and reduced postal rates. Profit-oriented firms often feel they are harmed competitively by these legal provisions.[24]

[24]Edward T. Pound, Gary Cohen, and Penny Loeb, "Tax Exempt!" *U.S. News & World Report* (October 2, 1995), pp. 36–51; and John R. Emshwiller, "More Small Firms Complain About Tax-Exempt Rivals," *Wall Street Journal* (August 8, 1995), pp. B1–B2.

Classifying Nonprofit Marketing

The classification of nonprofit marketing may be based on tangibility, structure, goal, and constituency.

Nonprofit organizations may be classified in terms of tangibility, structure, goals, and constituency. This is shown in Figure 12-10. An organization would be classed by a combination of factors. For example, postage stamps for collectors are tangible, distributed by the federal government, intended to reduce the Postal Service's deficit, and aimed at the general public.

As already noted, nonprofit marketing may involve organizations, people, places, ideas, goods, and services. Organizations include foundations, universities, religious insti-

FIGURE 12-10
A Classification System for Nonprofit Marketing

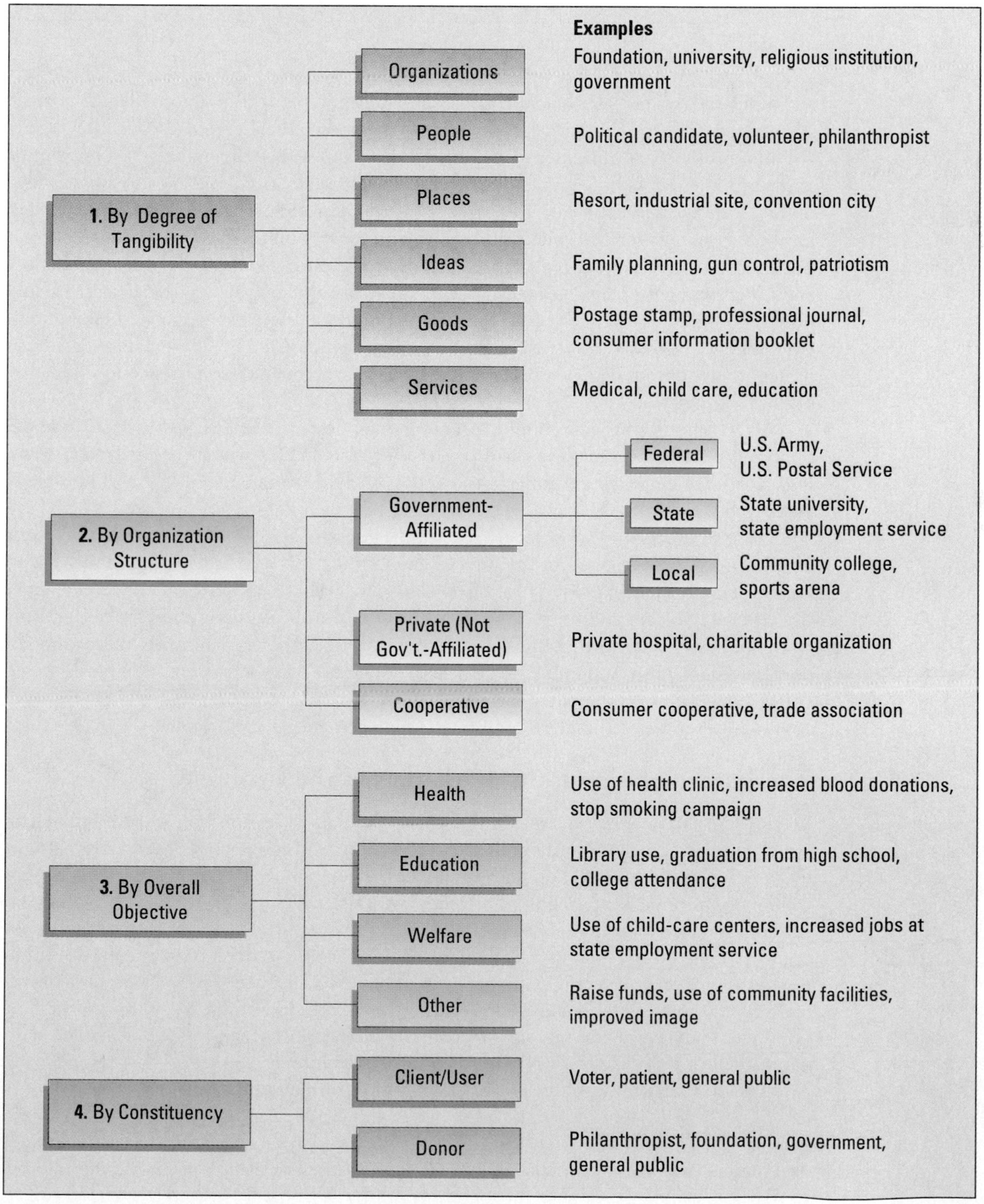

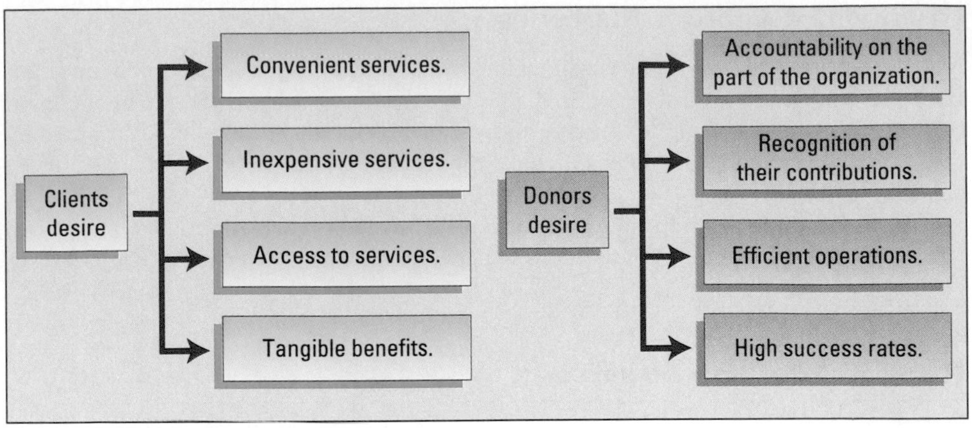

FIGURE 12-11
Clients Versus Donors

tutions, and government; people include politicians and volunteers; places include resorts and industrial centers; ideas include family planning and patriotism; goods include postage stamps and professional journals; and services include medical care and education.

Nonprofit organizations may have a government-affiliated, private, or cooperative structure. The federal government markets military service to recruits, postal services, and other goods and services; state governments market universities and employment services; local governments market colleges, libraries, and sports arenas. Government marketing is also used to increase voter registration, secure bond approval, and gain passage of school and library budgets. Private organizations market hospitals, charities, social services, and other goods and services. They also use marketing to increase membership and donations. Cooperative organizations (such as the Better Business Bureau) aid consumers and/or businesses; their success depends on their securing a large membership base and efficiently performing functions.

Overall nonprofit marketing goals may be divided into health (increase the number of nonsmokers), education (increase usage of the local library), welfare (list more job openings at a state employment office), and other (increase membership in the Boy Scouts) components.

Nonprofit organizations usually require the support of both clients/users and donors. Clients/users are interested in the direct benefits they get by participating in an organization, such as their improved health, education, or welfare. Donors are concerned about the efficiency of operations, success rates, the availability of goods and services, and the recognition of their contributions. For each constituency, an organization must pinpoint its target market. For example, the League of Women Voters might focus on unregistered voters during an enrollment drive and seek funds from corporate foundations. Figure 12-11 shows some of the differing interests between clients and donors.

The Extent of Nonprofit Marketing in the Economy

There are millions of nonprofit organizations in the world, and their use of marketing is increasing.

Worldwide, millions of organizations and people engage in nonprofit marketing. There are 1.1 million U.S. nonprofit organizations (24,000 of which are national or international in scope) with 7.5 to 8 million paid employees. They annually generate revenues of $1.1 trillion and receive $130 billion in private contributions, about 88 per cent from individual donors. On average, Americans allocate 2 to 3 per cent of their incomes to nonprofit organizations. Nearly one-half of the households earning under $10,000 make contributions; those that do average $200 per year. Ninety-six per cent of the households earning $60,000 to $74,999 make contributions; those that do average $1,600 per year. The U.S. mass media provide billions of dollars in advertising space for public-service messages. Half of U.S. adults engage in some form of volunteer work.[25]

This further demonstrates the scope of nonprofit marketing:

[25]Pound, Cohen, and Loeb, "Tax Exempt!" pp. 36–38; *Statistical Abstract of the United States 1995*, various pages; Anna Mulrine, "Who Gives What?" *U.S. News & World Report* (December 4, 1995), p. 87; and Keith Hammonds and Sandra Jones, "Good Help Really Is Hard to Find," *Business Week* (April 4, 1994), pp. 100–101.

- The American Red Cross is just one of a number of nonprofit organizations that operates an Internet site (http://www.crossnet.org). It covers such topics as: "What Do We Do?," "Where We Are," and "How to Help."[26]
- After a survey showed that 92 per cent of the world's population was unaware of its social and humanitarian activities, the United Nations enacted its first major advertising campaign. Ninety advertising agencies in 30 nations donated their time, and they sought $53 million in free media space.[27]
- Many countries use tourism boards to market foreign travel to those nations. The French Ministry of Tourism spends tens of millions of dollars annually on promotion. The British Tourist Authority works with airlines, hotels, and credit-card firms to create and publicize special offers. The Spanish Tourism Institute has used the slogan, "Passion for Life." The German Tourist Board distributes brochures describing lower-priced accommodations.
- In 1996, candidates for the U.S. Congress were expected to spend nearly $1 billion on their election campaigns. Expenditures were for TV and radio ads, campaign staffs, public appearances, travel, campaign buttons and bumper stickers, public relations, direct mail, and fund-raising events.
- The American Cancer Society annually sponsors the Great American Smokeout, which encourages people to stop smoking for one day (in the hope that they will quit for life). It promotes the Smokeout months in advance and receives a lot of free media time and space to do so. Twenty per cent of smokers participate in the Smokeout each year, but it is not known how many stop smoking permanently.[28]

Illustrations of Nonprofit Marketing

This section examines marketing by the U.S. Postal Service, colleges and universities, and the United Way. The activities of these organizations differ due to their degree of tangibility, structure, objectives, and constituencies.

The U.S. Postal Service is an independent federal agency with 825,000 employees and yearly revenues of more then $50 billion. It delivers 175 billion pieces of mail annually (40 per cent of the world's total mail) and runs 40,000 post offices.[29] Competition is intense, and it must deliver all mail, no matter how uneconomical. The Postal Service often runs an annual deficit, and all rate increases must be approved by a Board of Governors.

To protect itself against competitors and stimulate consumer demand, the Postal Service has enacted a strong marketing program—comprising a mix of continuing and new offerings and extensive advertising. With Express Mail, packages and letters are delivered overnight; the items can be dropped at special boxes or picked up for a small fee (to eliminate waiting lines). Priority Mail is an inexpensive service, with two- to three-day delivery anywhere in the United States. ZIP + 4 is an improved zip-code service that offers cost savings for both the Postal Service and its business customers, but it has not been used by customers as much as the Postal Service desires.

The Postal Service has $300 million sales per year via its commemorative stamp program, which it hopes will grow to $1 billion within the next five years. To stimulate sales, it is featuring more celebrities (for example, the Elvis Presley stamp generated $40 million in sales). Many post offices now sell such items as hand-held scales, padded envelopes for packages, air mail markers, and devices to adhere stamps to envelopes. Self-service stamp vending machines are in shopping centers. Some post offices are "postal stores"—with interior space divided into two sections, one for specialized postal services and one for retail sales. The retail part of the stores carries stamps, envelopes, packing material, posters, T-shirts, coffee mugs, pen-and-pencil sets, and earrings. The Postal Service's an-

[26]Timothy M. Ito, "Hands Across the Web," *U.S. News & World Report* (December 4, 1995), p. 82.
[27]Nan O'Neal, "U.N. Taps Ad Group," *Advertising Age* (October 29, 1990), p. 12.
[28]Katherine T. Beddingfield, "Sizing Up the Biggest," *U.S. News & World Report* (December 4, 1995), p. 90.
[29]*World Almanac and Book of Facts 1996* (Mahwah, N.J.: Funk & Wagnalls, 1995), various pages; and Christy Fisher, "Postal Service Looks to Stamp Out Woes," *Advertising Age* (September 12, 1994), p. 4.

Ethics IN TODAY'S SOCIETY

Is the Arthritis Foundation Risking a Consumer Backlash?

Nonprofit organizations are increasingly licensing their names and symbols for use with certain products and then collecting fees based on product sales. According to the Arthritis Foundation's president, "It is the prototype for future relationships between nonprofit organizations and corporate America."

The Arthritis Foundation has an arrangement with Johnson & Johnson's McNeil division, whereby McNeil markets all Arthritis Foundation brand over-the-counter arthritis management medications. Under this arrangement, McNeil gets the right to use the Arthritis Foundation logo and brand name on these products, and the Arthritis Foundation offers a free one-year membership (valued at $20) to consumers who purchase any of these medications.

Each pain reliever box in this arrangement contains information about the Arthritis Foundation, as well as a membership application. As a result of this tie-in, the Arthritis Foundation expects to attract 500,000 new members over a two-year period. McNeil also pledges that it will donate over $1 million for arthritis research each year.

Proponents of this relationship say both groups win. McNeil increases its visibility and sales, and gains increased credibility. At the same time, the Arthritis Foundation expands its membership roster and upgrades its research efforts.

However, licensing arrangements by nonprofit organizations are not without critics. Some question whether any nonprofit organization should endorse products. There is also the question as to which products should be endorsed. For example, should a nonprofit organization endorse a product that is of better value or a product that has a higher royalty rate? Still others feel that donations may suffer if the nonprofit organization derives too much of its funds from licensing arrangements.

As the marketing vice-president for the Arthritis Foundation, present a policy for selecting and controlling licensing arrangements.

Sources: Based on material in Jeff Smyth, "Nonprofits Get Market Savvy," *Advertising Age* (May 29, 1995), pp. 1, 7; and "McNeil Finds Cause to Celebrate," *Promo* (August 1994), p. 23.

nual ad budget is $140 million (up from $90 million in 1992), with large sums going to Express Mail and Priority Mail, direct-mail ads for business accounts, and commemorative stamps.[30]

Colleges and universities realize that the population trends in many industrialized nations (such as smaller households and a relatively low birth rate) have been affecting their enrollment pools, especially with the number of 18- to 24-year-olds falling in some areas. For example, from 1977 to 1991, the number of U.S. high school graduates fell steadily and did not begin to go up again until 1992. Thus, new markets are being targeted and marketing strategies are being used by more educational institutions than ever before.

Many schools are actively seeking nontraditional students: Today, 43 per cent of U.S. college students attend part-time; and nearly one-half of college students are at least 25 years old. In addition, about 20 million people are now in adult higher-education programs at U.S. colleges, universities, and private firms. The adult market needs convenient

[30]Cyndee Miller, "U.S. Postal Service Discovers the Merits of Marketing," *Marketing News* (February 1, 1993), pp. 9, 18; Fisher, "Postal Service Looks to Stamp Out Woes," p. 4; and Mark Lewyn, "Repackaging the Post Office," *Business Week* (January 8, 1996), p. 39.

FIGURE 12-12
The Marketing of Higher Education
Reprinted by permission.

sites and classes not infringing on work hours. At New York University, the School of Continuing Education offers 2,000 courses to 60,000 students per year.[31]

Traditional students are also being sought vigorously. Schools often spend hundreds of dollars—or more—on recruitment efforts for each new student who enrolls. Many buy direct-mailing lists of prospective students from the Educational Testing Service (which administers college-board examinations). And a number of colleges distribute recruiting films or videocassettes, costing tens of thousands of dollars (and up) to produce, to high schools.

The heightened use of marketing is not limited to poor- or average-quality schools. For example, New York's Hofstra University runs a regional full-color ad campaign, using the theme "We Teach Success." See Figure 12-12. Bryn Mawr, Duke, Harvard, and Stanford are among the 750 colleges and universities that let prospective students submit applications on computer diskettes based on CollegeLink software, which enables applicants to enter standardized data just once and then add the customized information for each college. The California Institute of Technology (Cal Tech) has receptions and slide shows for accepted students in two dozen cities and holds "pre-frosh weekends"—complete with a barbecue, a visit to Magic Mountain amusement park, and a tour of the Jet Propulsion Labs (run by Cal Tech for the National Aeronautics Administration). Ohio's Case Western spends over $2,000 per freshman for promotional videos, mailings, and other "courting efforts." Its admissions dean says, "Students have choices they've never had before among good universities."[32]

[31]*Projections of Education Statistics* (Washington, D.C.: U.S. National Center for Education Statistics, 1992); Bickley Townsend, "Lifelong Learning," *American Demographics* (February 1990), pp. 38–39; and Shannon Dortch, "Colleges Come Back," *American Demographics* (May 1995), pp. 4–6.

[32]Marc Spiegler, "Students Apply Themselves," *American Demographics* (January 1996), pp. 16–17; Gary Putka, "With Applications Down, Top Colleges Get Friendlier," *Wall Street Journal* (April 7, 1989), p. B1; Alan Deutschman, "Why Universities Are Shrinking," *Fortune* (September 24, 1990), pp. 105–108; and Steve Stecklow, "Some Colleges Hire Recruiters to Get Bigger Freshman Class," *Wall Street Journal* (September 5, 1995), pp. A1, A8.

This is a crucial time for the United Way of America, which has more than 2,000 chapters and annual fund-raising efforts yielding $3 billion. It supports such groups as Boys Clubs, the Girl Scouts, the Red Cross, centers for children with learning disabilities and other problems, immigration centers, and mental health and drug rehabilitation programs. Yet, although contributions have doubled since 1980, the percentage of total philanthropic giving received by the United Way has dropped—from 3 per cent in 1980 to just over 2 per cent today—and total contributions have leveled off (partly due to the negative publicity about its former chief executive, who misused United Way funds). Most donations come from deductions made from workers' paychecks. In contrast, such organizations as the Salvation Army generate most of their donations from nonworkplace sources. The Salvation Army receives $725 million in yearly contributions from its sources.[33]

For years, the United Way has had an outstanding marketing orientation. It is well known for its long-run association with the National Football League (NFL) and the touching ads that appear during each NFL game. Employees in affiliated chapters are trained in marketing. Periodic conferences are held, such as a yearly marketing and advertising conference. Affiliated chapters present United Way home videos, films, and slide-show programs to potential contributors and volunteers. The United Way even published a book, *Competitive Marketing*, so other charitable groups could learn from it.

The United Way's present situation can be summed up thusly: "Keen competition and urgent need cry out for creativity. For an organization that has thrived on automatic generosity, that is a challenge."[34]

MARKETING IN A CHANGING WORLD

Health Care Services—The Thorniest Issue of All

As the 21st century approaches, by far the toughest issue we must address is how health care services will be marketed. Why is this *the* thorniest issue on the horizon? Consider a few facts: In the United States alone, government, industry, and private individuals now pay more than $1 trillion yearly on medical services and related products (such as prescription drugs and medical equipment)—an amount equal to nearly one-seventh of the GDP. During the last decade, spending on medical care has doubled. The 3,200 U.S. nonprofit hospitals now generate annual revenues of $350 billion. The federal Medicare program serves 37 million people, at a cost of more than $175 billion per year. And finally, according to the U.S. consumer price index, over the past 15 years, the prices of medical services and related products have risen more than in any other category measured.[35]

The marketing of health care services is complicated because there are so many interests and perspectives at stake. Here are just some of them:

- Forty million Americans have no health care insurance and rely on hospital emergency rooms and low-cost private clinics. How should they be served, especially the children involved? And who pays the bill?
- Through their jobs, millions of Americans have medical insurance tied into an HMO (health maintenance organization) that requires them to be served by designated doctors and hospitals. This category is growing rapidly. It caps health care costs because doctors, pharmacies, and hospitals agree to a pre-set fee schedule.
- Millions of other Americans, either through their jobs or their own funding, participate in traditional health insurance—whereby they can choose their own doctors and hospitals. In re-

[33]Keith H. Hammonds and Morton D. Sosland, "Even the United Way Is Struggling to Make Ends Meet," *Business Week* (November 5, 1990), p. 102; Rayna Skolnik, "Rebuilding Trust," *Public Relations Journal*, Vol. 49 (September 1993), pp. 29–32; "United Way Polishes Its Tarnished Image," *Sales & Marketing Management* (September 1995), p. 15; Molly McKaughan, "Is Corporate Philanthropy Drying Up?" *Across the Board* (April 1995), pp. 21–26; and Manny Topol, "Spots That Don't Fade," *Newsday* (January 27, 1996), pp. A42–A43.

[34]Hammonds and Sosland, "Even the United Way Is Struggling to Make Ends Meet," p. 102.

[35]*World Almanac and Book of Facts 1996*, various pages; and *Statistical Abstract of the United States 1995*, various pages.

turn, there are higher deductibles and higher fees. These people do not want their medical choices restricted.

- Many health care providers are upset because they believe their rights to recommend patient procedures, set fees, and earn a living are being abridged by HMOs. Others feel the HMOs give them a steady income stream.

Will the following be the wave of the future in the marketing of medical services?

> Now found in California, Florida, and a handful of other states, medical malls reflect the health care industry's effort to keep patients out of the hospital. The malls have soothing environments dressed up with fountains, food courts, and other amenities found in the retail world. They have lower overhead than traditional hospitals because they don't have emergency rooms, neonatal care units, or other services that require a lot of staff and expensive equipment. Instead, they concentrate on primary care, diagnostic services, and outpatient surgery and therapy. The malls' builders expect doctors and patients to like the convenience of getting tests, meeting doctors, having procedures done, and recuperating in the same place.[36]

SUMMARY

1. *To examine the scope of goods and services, and explain how goods and services may be categorized* Goods marketing encompasses the sales of durable and nondurable physical products; service marketing involves goods rental, goods alteration and maintenance/repair, and personal services. In the United States, the revenues from nondurable goods are slightly higher than those from durable goods—and final consumers spend three times as much on nondurables as on durables. Services account for a very large share of the GDP in industrialized nations, a smaller share in developing and less-developed nations. The United States has the world's largest service economy. Both final consumer and business services have seen significant growth in recent years. The scope of services is sometimes underestimated due to the hidden service sector.

With a goods/services continuum, products can be positioned on a scale from pure goods to goods/services combinations to pure services. Much can be learned by studying this continuum, including its use for final and organizational consumer products, the presence of unique marketing opportunities, and the changing relationship between sellers and buyers as pure goods become goods/services combinations. Both goods- and services-oriented firms need to identify core and peripheral services.

Goods can be classed by market, product durability, value added, company goal, degree of regulation, distribution channel length, and extent of customer contact. Services can be classed by market, level of tangibility, service provider skill, service provider goals, degree of regulation, labor intensiveness, and amount of customer contact. A firm would be categorized on the basis of a combination of these factors.

2. *To discuss the special considerations in the marketing of services* Services are generally less tangible, more perishable, less separable from their provider, and more variable in quality than goods that are sold. The effect of these factors is greatest for personal services. Service firms need to enact strategies that enable consumers to perceive their offerings more tangibly, make their offerings less perishable, encourage consumers to seek them out but enable multiple employees to be viewed as competent, and make performance as efficient and consistent as possible. Such approaches as the industrialization of services, the service blueprint, and gap analysis enable service firms to better devise and implement marketing plans by improving their performance.

3. *To look at the use of marketing by goods versus services firms and provide illustrations of service marketing* Many service firms have lagged behind manufacturers in the use of marketing because of their small size, the larger geographic coverage of goods-oriented companies, their technical emphasis, less competition and the lack of need for marketing, the high esteem of consumers for certain service providers, past bans on advertising, a dislike of marketing by some service professionals, and the reluctance of some manufacturers to view services as profit centers. Yet, for a number of reasons, this has been changing, and the marketing of services is now expanding greatly.

The marketing practices of hotels, repair and servicing firms, and lawyers are highlighted.

4. *To distinguish between nonprofit and profit-oriented marketing* Nonprofit marketing is conducted by organizations and people that operate for the public good or to foster a cause and not for financial profits. It is both similar to and different from profit-oriented marketing. These are some of the differences: Nonprofit marketing is more apt to involve organizations, people, places, and ideas. Nonprofit firms' exchanges do not have to involve money, and goals can be hard to formulate. The benefits of nonprofit firms may be

[36]Robert Tomsho, "At Medical Malls, Shoppers Are Patients," *Wall Street Journal* (December 29, 1995), pp. B1–B2.

distributed unequally, and economically unfeasible market segments may have to be served. Two target markets must be satisfied by nonprofit organizations: clients and donors. 5. *To describe a classification system for nonprofit marketing, the role of nonprofit marketing in the economy, and applications of nonprofit marketing* Nonprofit organizations can be classed on the basis of tangibility, organization structure, objectives, and constituency. A nonprofit organization would be categorized by a combination of these factors.

Worldwide, there are millions of organizations and people engaged in nonprofit marketing. There are 1.1 million nonprofit organizations in the United States, generating $1.1 trillion in annual revenues (including contributions). Their marketing efforts have increased greatly in a very short time. They play a key role in the U.S. economy.

The marketing practices of the U.S. Postal Service, colleges and universities, and the United Way are highlighted.

KEY TERMS

goods marketing (p. 327)
durable goods (p. 327)
nondurable goods (p. 327)
service marketing (p. 327)
rented-goods services (p. 327)
owned-goods services (p. 327)
nongoods services (p. 327)
hidden service sector (p. 328)
goods/services continuum (p. 328)
core services (p. 330)
peripheral services (p. 330)
intangibility of services (p. 333)
perishability of services (p. 333)
inseparability of services (p. 333)
variability in service quality (p. 333)
industrialization of services (p. 337)
service blueprint (p. 337)
service gap (p. 338)
nonprofit marketing (p. 341)
social marketing (p. 343)
clients (p. 344)
donors (p. 344)

Review Questions

1. Differentiate among rented-goods services, owned-goods services, and nongoods services.
2. What is a goods/services continuum? Why should firms be aware of this concept?
3. Distinguish between core and peripheral services. What is the marketing role of each?
4. How can a service be positioned more tangibly?
5. Describe how hard, soft, and hybrid technologies may be used to industrialize services.
6. Why have service firms lagged behind manufacturers in the development and use of marketing strategies?
7. What are some of the similarities and differences involved in the marketing efforts used by nonprofit and profit-oriented organizations?
8. When is an organization engaged in social marketing?
9. Discuss the factors that may be used to classify nonprofit marketing.
10. How do the goals of clients and donors differ?

Discussion Questions

1. Present a goods/services continuum related to entertainment. Discuss the implications of this continuum for a firm interested in developing a marketing plan in the entertainment field.
2. Give several ways that a car rental agency can match demand and supply on days following holidays.
3. Draw and discuss a service blueprint for an insurance broker dealing with small-business clients.
4. Present five objectives that could be used to evaluate the effectiveness of a public television station.
5. Discuss several innovative fund-raising programs for the Pediatric Aids Foundation.

CASE 1

Olsten Corporation: Creating Differential Advantages for a Service Business*

Olsten Corporation is North America's largest provider of home health-care services and one of the world's leading providers of staffing services. The firm operates 1,200 offices in the United States, Canada, Mexico, and Great Britain and has annual revenues of $2.3 billion. The firm is divided into two major divisions: health-care services and staffing services.

Olsten's health-care service unit provides home health care, management services for hospital-based home-health agencies, and institutional staffing in the United States and Canada. This unit is comprised of Olsten Kimberly Quality Care (U.S. and Canada) and ASB Meditest (U.S.). It serves over 400,000 patient accounts through a variety of compensation systems (such as Medicare, Medicaid, and state and county contracts). Forty-seven per cent of Olsten's total revenues are health-care based.

The company's staffing services unit is comprised of Olsten Staffing Services (U.S. and Canada), Office Angels (Great Britain), and Olsten STAFF (Mexico). This unit provides temporary office employees (including clerical, accounting, legal, technical, and production specialities) in the United States, Canada, Great Britain, and Mexico. It serves over 100,000 client accounts in business, industry, and government. Fifty-three per cent of Olsten's total revenues are in staffing services.

Several industrywide developments have affected the market for temporary workers: the ability of clients to "test drive" a temporary employee, clients' desires to reduce the number of temporary suppliers with which they deal, the increased popularity of "vendor-on-premises" contracts, and the growing concern over cost containment by clients. Each of these developments has a positive impact on Olsten.

Many firms like initially hiring an employee on a temporary basis. This allows the firm to see how well a worker performs without having to make a formal job offer, explain why a worker is fired, and so forth. Employees also like to "test drive" an employer or see the differences in job dynamics in different industries. According to a survey by the National Association of Temporary Staffing Services (NATSS), three-quarters of respondents said they became temporary workers as a way of looking for a full-time position. And 40 per cent of those respondents stated that they received permanent job offers.

A lot of firms are reducing the number of temporary firms with which they deal. These firms favor this approach because it increases their bargaining power. A national partnership with a major manufacturer or bank could be worth $100 million per year to Olsten. As partners, agencies also are expected to develop special electronic billing and training for their leading clients. In one such partnership with Columbia/HCA Healthcare, Olsten now manages the home health agencies at 22 Columbia/HCA hospitals.

With "vendor-on-premises" contracts, temporary agencies set up offices at each major client's factory or office. This enhances the customer service provided. For instance, Olsten operates offices at AT&T, Bristol-Myers Squibb, and the computer services unit of General Electric. Olsten hires, trains, and schedules the temporary workers for these clients.

Temporary workers are a means of cost containment for firms. Client firms need only pay for temporary workers in busy seasons or provide coverage for time periods corresponding to regular employees' absences. Health-care employees can even be hired on a temporary basis to correspond with a person's illness.

QUESTIONS

1. Classify Olsten's two divisions based on the dimensions of Figure 12-3.
2. Discuss the difficulties in the marketing of temporary services based on their intangibility, perishability, inseparability, and variability.
3. How can Olsten industrialize its services? Discuss specific concepts that relate to hard, soft, and hybrid technologies.
4. What are the pros and cons of a "vendor-on-premises" contract to Olsten? What are the pros and cons of a "vendor-on-premises" contract to a manufacturer?

VIDEO QUESTIONS ON OLSTEN

1. Outline the specific responsibilities of Olsten's on-site administrator.
2. Explain how Parker Hannifin and the Chicago Mercantile Exchange benefited from Olsten's on-site program.

*The data in this case are drawn from James Aley, "The Temp Biz Boom: Why It's Good," *Fortune* (October 16, 1995), p. 53; Barnaby J. Feder, "Bigger Roles for Suppliers of Temporary Workers," *New York Times* (April 1, 1995), p. 39; *Olsten Corporation 1994 Annual Report*; and "Temp Work on the Rise—For Now," *Newsday* (October 18, 1995), p. A39.

CASE 2

Airlines' Shifting Winds: Less for Consumers†

Even though airline passengers are already dissatisfied with their limited seating space and the lack of food served, several airlines are instituting further cutbacks in both areas.

A common complaint of airline passengers is their cramped quarters. Thus, when Trans World Airlines removed seats on its planes and began to promote itself as "The Most Comfortable Way to Fly," passengers quickly took notice. According to a survey by J.D. Power & Associates, the marketing research firm, TWA was named the top carrier for long domestic flights and second best for shorter flights. Nonetheless, soon thereafter, TWA again began to cram 425 passengers onto flights to popular destinations.

A major airline's load factor (the per cent of seats filled with paying passengers) averages 66 per cent; but more than half of all flights have a load factor of 80 per cent or more. Flights to popular destinations have even higher load factors. This means that removing just four of the 141 seats from a MD-80 jet could cause the loss of $87,603 in annual revenues.

To increase revenues, airlines have resorted to narrower seats and reduced legroom. In many cases, the seat width has been narrowed from 22 inches to 19 inches and the space from the front of one seat to the back of the seat in front of it has shrunk from 34 inches to 31 inches. Yet, as the president of an aircraft interior-design firm says, "You can't overcome the seat problem. It's like wearing a pair of shoes that are too small: You won't walk right."

Food service is another area of consumer dissatisfaction. Since 1992, many airlines have radically reduced their food service. To reduce labor costs, some airlines now hand out brown bags to passengers at the gate instead of serving the meal on the plane. And on flights less than two hours long, airlines may provide either no food whatsoever or limit food to snacks. Thus, a passenger traveling close to four hours (on two consecutive two-hour flights) would not be served a meal. Passenger displeasure is particularly high on flights that begin in the early morning or in the late evening. People on these flights who count on being fed by the airline may not be served a meal. A spokesperson for Northwest Airlines concedes that "It's lunch time less and less often around here, and I don't think we're alone in that."

To compound the situation, there are no "hard and fast rules" as to whether passengers will be fed a meal. At American Airlines, no food is served on flights shorter than two hours—and that food is served during "traditional meal hours, taking into account time zones and competitiveness and so on." The guidelines for other airlines contain phrases such as "with exceptions on a competitive basis," "we serve what we feel is appropriate for the time of day," and "with markets and competition taken into account." As a result, some experienced airline travelers pack snacks into their carry-on luggage or arrive early and eat a meal at the airport, in case they are not fed on board. As one passenger remarked, "I used to be rather bashful eating fast food in front of other people. Now, I'm thinking about picking up six extra sandwiches and selling them on the plane."

Airlines defend their practices as a way of offering lower prices and say they are needed to stay competitive with the newer discount airlines (that often have cost advantages due to lower labor costs and the purchase of used aircraft).

QUESTIONS

1. Describe airline services in terms of the goods/services continuum shown in Figure 12-1. Comment on your answer.
2. Evaluate the airlines' space-saving strategy.
3. How do airlines match supply and demand for their service?
4. What are the pros and cons of communicating an airline's food policy (as to whether nothing, a snack, or a full meal will be served) to passengers on a flight-by-flight basis versus having an overall policy?

†The data in this case are drawn from Lisa Miller, "Airlines and Hotels Say Nuts to Nourishment," *Wall Street Journal* (October 6, 1995), pp. B1, B10; and Michael J. McCarthy, "Airline Squeeze Play: More Seats, Less Legroom," *Wall Street Journal* (April 18, 1994), pp. B1, B8.

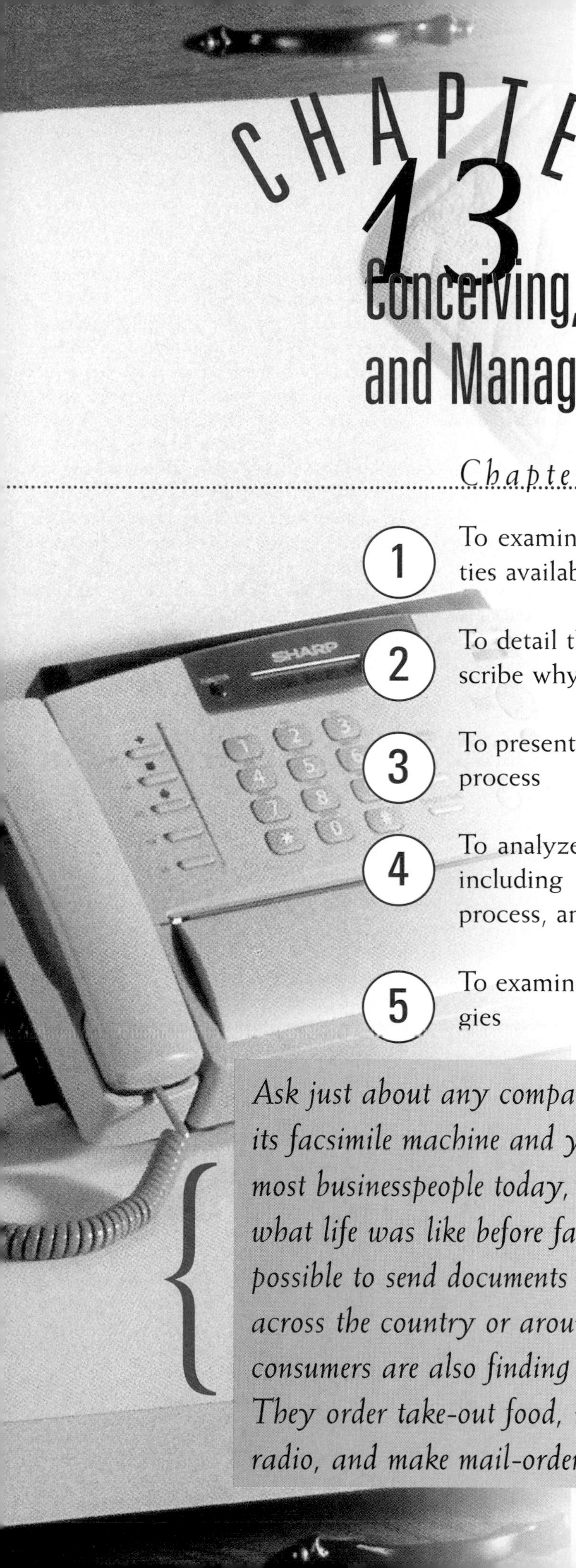

CHAPTER 13

Conceiving, Developing, and Managing Products

Chapter Objectives

1. To examine the types of new-product opportunities available to a firm
2. To detail the importance of new products and describe why new products fail
3. To present the stages in the new-product planning process
4. To analyze the growth and maturity of products, including the adoption process, the diffusion process, and extension strategies
5. To examine product deletion decisions and strategies

Ask just about any company these days to give up its facsimile machine and you're in for a fight. For most businesspeople today, it's difficult to remember what life was like before fax machines made it possible to send documents easily and cheaply across the country or around the world. Final consumers are also finding uses for the fax machine. They order take-out food, request a song on the radio, and make mail-order purchases via fax.

Reprinted by permission of Sharp Electronics Corporation.

According to a recent survey, two-thirds of U.S. adults have either received or sent a fax message at some point (usually at work). Yet, even though PC sales have successfully made the transition from office to home, just 7 per cent of U.S. households now own a freestanding fax machine. In contrast, 40 per cent of U.S. households own PCs.

The survey just cited also indicates that fax machine manufacturers will have to work awfully hard to increase their market penetration in the home market. Seventy-one per cent of U.S. adults feel there is no benefit to being able to send and receive faxes while at home. Of the 28 per cent who believe there are benefits to having a fax machine at home, only 11 per cent (equal to 3 per cent of all U.S. adults) think there is a great benefit. Among the key benefits to home faxes are their quickness, the ability to work at home, not having to leave the house to send a fax, and the speed of a facsimile message versus mail or express carriers.

According to the survey, among people who would purchase fax equipment for home use, one-half of them would prefer a fax machine built into their home computer. (Note: While a built-in computer fax modem can generally be bought for less than $100, it cannot be used to send documents that are not part of a computer file—but a fax modem can receive noncomputerized documents). A fourth would buy a freestanding machine, and 25 per cent do not know what type of machine they would purchase.

Many consumers are also uncertain about the cost of a freestanding fax machine, where they would buy it, and the name of a good brand. On average, consumers expect to pay $640 for a freestanding machine—double today's real "street prices." Price expectations vary with the person's previous experience with fax machines. More experienced shoppers plan to pay less (an average price of $540) than nonusers (an average price of $860). The place to shop for a freestanding fax machine that people mention most is electronics stores (35 per cent of respondents), followed by office supply stores (15 per cent), and then mail-order catalogs (12 per cent). Most people do not know the name of a good brand of fax machine; some even mention names of firms that do not produce freestanding fax machines.[1]

Next, we will study how new products are developed, the factors causing rapid or slow growth for new products, how to manage mature products, and what to do when existing products falter. As our home fax discussion illustrates, it takes a lot of work—and persistence—to stay ahead.

Overview

Product planning involves new and existing products.

In Chapter 13, the conception and development of new products, the management of growing and mature products through their life cycle, and the termination of undesirable products are discussed.

While any product combines tangible and intangible features to satisfy consumer needs, a **new product** involves a modification of an existing product or an innovation the consumer perceives as meaningful. To succeed, a new product must have desirable attributes, be unique, and have its features communicated to consumers. Marketing support is necessary.[2]

New products *may be* **modifications, minor innovations,** *or* **major innovations.**

Modifications are alterations in or extensions of a firm's existing products and include new models, styles, colors, features, and brands. **Minor innovations** are items not previ-

[1]Susan Reda, "Home Faxes Fail to Strike," *Stores* (April 1995), pp. 28–29.

[2]See Roger J. Calantone, C. Anthony Di Benedetto, and Ted Haggbloom, "Principles of New Product Management: Exploring the Beliefs of Product Practitioners," *Journal of Product Innovation Management*, Vol. 12 (June 1995), pp. 235–247.

ously marketed by a firm that have been marketed by others (like the Universal credit card by AT&T). **Major innovations** are items not previously sold by any firm (like the first cellular telephone). If a firm works with major innovations, the costs, risks, and time required for profitability all rise. Overall, most new products are modifications; few are major innovations.

New products may be conceived of and developed by a company itself or purchased from another firm. With the latter, a company may buy a firm, buy a specific product, or sign a licensing agreement (whereby it pays an inventor a royalty fee based on sales). Acquisitions may reduce risks and time demands, but they rely on outsiders for innovations and may require large investments.

Early in a product's life, there is usually strong sales growth, as more people purchase and repurchase. This is an exciting time; and if a product is popular, it can last for quite a while. Next, the market becomes more saturated and competition intensifies. At that point, a firm can maintain high sales by adding features that provide convenience and durability, using new materials in construction, offering a range of models, stressing new packaging, and/or adding customer services. It can also reposition a product, enter untapped geographic markets, demonstrate new uses, offer new brands, set lower prices, use new media, and/or appeal to new segments. Then, for many products, at some point down the road firms must decide whether those items have outlived their usefulness and should be dropped.

The Importance of New Products

A firm's product policy should be future-oriented and recognize that products, no matter how successful, tend to be mortal—they usually cannot sustain a peak level of sales and profits indefinitely: "Innovation can give a company a competitive advantage and profits, but nothing lasts forever. Success brings on imitators, who respond with superior features, lower prices, or some other new way to draw customers. Time ultimately renders nearly all advantages obsolete."[3] So, replacements should be constantly planned and a balanced product portfolio pursued—by both small and large firms.

New products offer differential advantages.

Introducing new products is important for several reasons. Desirable differential advantages can be attained. The Seiko Kinetic Quartz watch is the first quartz watch that does not require a battery or have to be wound. It is advertised as "No more batteries. No more winding. No more hassles." See Figure 13-1. American Home Products' CholesTrac is the first in-home test kit for people to check their cholesterol count without having to visit a doctor. Goodyear's "smart tire" for trucks is embedded with a computer chip allowing drivers to easily see the wear and air pressure of tires; this improves tire life and fuel efficiency. By being first on the market with wrinkle-free pants, Haggar is better competing with the best-selling Dockers brand. New products often enhance a firm's image and position it as an innovator.

New products lead to sales growth or stability.

New products may be needed for continued growth. That is why Quaker Oats has a new line of rice cakes; due to their poor taste, prior Quaker Rice Cakes did not attain company goals—as Quaker admits in Figure 13-2. At Timken, a nearly 100-year-old U.S.-based maker of industrial roller bearings, "Today's bearing is a dramatically different product than it was ten years ago, and we would be very surprised if the 2005 version is anything like we're making today." By thinking like this, Timken still holds a one-third share of the world market for tapered roller bearings.[4] For firms with cyclical or seasonal sales, new products can stabilize revenues and costs. Union Carbide manufactures medical-testing equipment to reduce its dependence on cyclical chemicals. Black & Decker has cut back on lawn mowers and looks for new opportunities in less seasonal products (such as power tools for the home).

New products can take time.

Planning for growth must take into consideration the time it takes for a new product to move from idea stage to commercialization. For instance, in 1983, Canadian Brian

[3]Jeffrey R. Williams, "How Sustainable Is Your Competitive Advantage?" *California Management Review*, Vol. 34 (Spring 1992), p. 29.

[4]Eric S. Hardy, "The Soul of an Old Company," *Forbes* (March 13, 1995), pp. 70–71.

FIGURE 13-1
Creating a Differential Advantage
Reprinted by permission. Courtesy of Seiko Corporation of America.

Maxwell came up with the idea for a food bar for exercise enthusiasts that would let them fuel for long workouts while circumventing the stomach problems that often accompany eating while exercising. He immediately began experimenting with various recipes; it then took three years and 800 experimental recipes to find one that worked: "For three years, people would say the texture wasn't right, the bar was upsetting their stomachs, or there was something wrong with the taste." At that point, Maxwell and his partner, Jennifer Biddulph, invested their life savings to contract for a 50,000-bar production run and start a mail-order business. In 1989, they opened their first plant. And in 1993, Powerfood Inc. became a PriceCostco vendor. Today, the maker of PowerBar has annual revenues of more than $30 million and does business in thirty countries.[5]

New products can increase profits and control.

New products can lead to larger profits and give a company better control over a marketing strategy. For example, the new Lincoln line of cars is quite popular. Thus, the cars have been selling at close to the "sticker" price, with dealers earning gross profits of up to $10,000 on each car sold. Because there are fewer Lincoln dealers relative to lower-priced cars, they do not use much price discounting and have firm command over their marketing efforts.

Risk may be lessened through diversity.

To limit risk, many firms seek to reduce dependence on one product or product line. That is why many movie theaters converted to multiplexes; their revenues are not tied to any one film's performance. Hewlett-Packard makes electronic components and test equipment, medical electronic equipment, and analytical instrumentation—besides its core computing and printing products; and it regularly adds new products. Turtle Wax, the world's

[5]Tod Jones, "The Power of Persistence," *PriceCostco Connection* (June 1995), p. 15.

FIGURE 13-2
Better-Tasting Rice Cakes from Quaker Oats
Reprinted by permission.

leader in car-care products, now makes shoe polish, household cleaners, and fabric protectors.

New products may improve distribution.

Firms may look to improve the efficiency of their established distribution systems by placing new products in them. They can then spread advertising, sales, and distribution costs among several products, gain dealer support, and discourage other companies from entering the market. Manufacturers like AT&T, Unilever, and Revlon can place new products in many outlets quickly. Service firms such as the Royal Bank of Canada also can efficiently add new products (financial services) into their distribution networks.

Technology can be exploited.

Firms often seek technological breakthroughs. For instance, Electronic Realty Associates, a Kansas City-based real-estate broker, has an interactive, visual, worldwide, computerized data base of its listings: "The system allows our brokers to show houses anywhere in the country, in fact, anywhere in the world—from any office."[6] And Japan's Ricoh, one of the world's largest office equipment firms, has a new digital color copier with fast first copies, the highest-quality color copies, and a "Display Editor." See Figure 13-3.

Waste materials can be used.

Sometimes, firms want to find uses for waste materials from existing products—to aid productivity or be responsive to recycling. Just over a decade ago, the chicken industry found that "we have four billion broilers, and the consumer generally doesn't want the necks and backs. What do we do? We grind them into baloney and hot dogs."[7] The sales of these products have skyrocketed since then. For environmental and cost reasons, Johnson Controls makes auto batteries from recycled lead and plastic; Reynolds Metals uses

[6]Nick Ravo, "House-Hunting by Interactive Computer," *New York Times* (November 22, 1992), Section 10, p. 1.
[7]N. R. Kleinfield, "America Goes Chicken Crazy," *New York Times* (December 9, 1984), Section 3, p. 9.

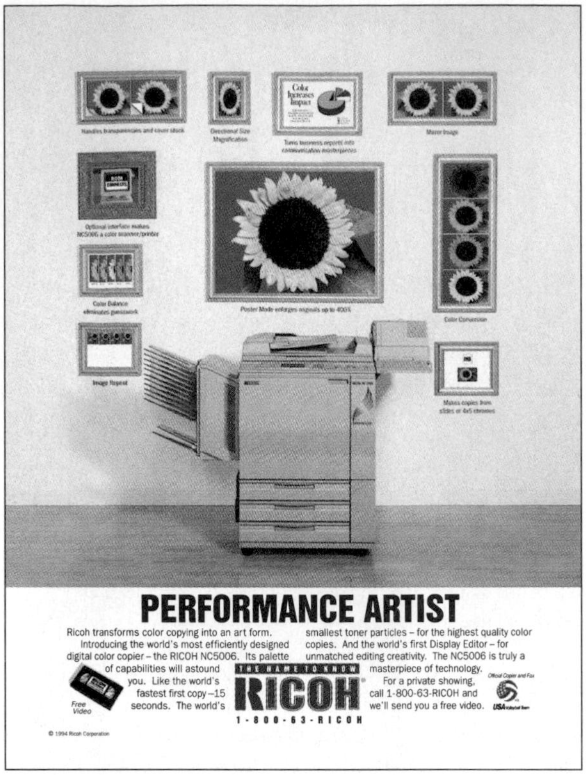

FIGURE 13-3
Capitalizing on New Technology
Reprinted by permission of Ricoh Corporation. Ad agency: Gigante Vaz & Partners Advertising.

recycled paperboard in foil and wax paper packaging; and Scotch-Brite steel wool pads are made from recycled bottles and packaged in recycled paper.

New products respond to consumer needs.

Companies may bring out new products to respond to changing consumer demographics and life-styles. Single-serving pre-packaged foods are aimed at smaller households. Kodak and Fuji have introduced a full line of single-use disposable cameras that appeal to people interested in convenience. Microsoft offers a computer keyboard that is easier on the wrist. Breed Technologies of Florida markets an air bag for installation in used cars that are not equipped with air bags as original equipment. Nabisco's Snackwell foods appeal to consumers interested in good-tasting, low-fat snack foods.

Government mandates are addressed.

New products may have to be developed in response to government mandates. For example, to address growing concerns about battery disposal (and concerns about the carcinogenic properties of nickel cadmium batteries), battery makers (led by Rayovac) have introduced rechargeable batteries that can be recharged up to 25 times or more. Rayovac even hired Michael Jordan as a celebrity endorser of its Renewal batteries. Although sales of rechargeable batteries are still rather low, they are expected to rise rapidly in the next few years.

Good long-run new-product planning requires systematic research and development, matching the requirements of new-product opportunities against company abilities, emphasizing consumer desires, properly spending time and money, and defensive—as well as offensive—planning. A firm must accept that some new products may fail; a progressive firm will take risks:

> Innovation is a risky business, and failure is commonplace. Rewarding success is easy, but rewarding intelligent failure is more important. Don't judge people strictly by results; try to judge them by the quality of their efforts. People should take intelligent business risks without also risking their compensation or their careers.[8]

There also has been some criticism about the negative effects of many U.S. firms' short-run, bottom-line orientation on their level of innovativeness (and willingness to take risks).

[8] "How Can Big Companies Keep the Entrepreneurial Spirit Alive?" *Harvard Business Review*, Vol. 73 (November–December 1995), p. 190.

TECHNOLOGY & MARKETING

Will Virtual Reality Really Boom?

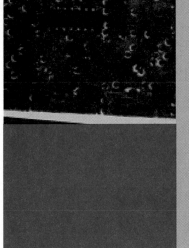

There used to be a common saying among computer programmers: "Virtual reality can be fast, pretty, or cheap—but you can choose only two of the three." Thus, an interactive simulation that was fast and had excellent graphics was also costly. For example, a realistic computer simulation for pilot training used to cost $2 million or more.

In 1990, Silicon Graphics introduced an $80,000 workstation that was able to reproduce realistic backgrounds that simulated motion. This hardware changed forever the "two-of-three" rule.

Using Silicon Graphics equipment, three young programmers (aged 29 to 35) started Paradigm Simulation. Since then, Paradigm software has been used by the U.S. government to test missile designs, the Federal Aviation Administration to evaluate new flight control console designs, and an Italian firm to develop a model of a Renaissance city for an educational project.

Until recently, the landing lights at an airport could be simulated only by writing 3,000 lines of computer code. With Paradigm software, these lights can now be added by simply moving a cursor to an icon labeled "Light Lobes" and clicking a mouse button. Customers can even adjust the size and intensity of the landing lights through another window. Similarly, users can adjust the time of day, weather conditions, add special effects like explosions, and even include computer-controlled objects such as highway traffic.

Paradigm's software prices range from $3,500 to $40,000. Although the software for ship design is especially costly, architectural renderings can be simulated with a $10,000 program. The hardware needed to run Paradigm's most-popular software costs approximately $300,000. Paradigm's total sales exceed $5 million, 40 per cent defense-related.

As a marketing manager for Paradigm, develop a concept test to evaluate a new application of its virtual-reality business software.

Source: Based on material in R. Lee Sullivan, "Virtual Reality Made Easy," *Forbes* (January 2, 1995), pp. 66–67.

Why New Products Fail

Despite better product-planning practices today than ever before, the failure rate for new products is quite high. According to the consulting firm of Booz, Allen & Hamilton, an average of 35 per cent of new industrial and consumer products fail. Others say the rate may be even greater.[9]

With **absolute product failure,** *costs are not regained. With* **relative product failure,** *goals are not met.*

Product failure can be defined in both absolute and relative terms. **Absolute product failure** occurs if a firm is unable to regain its production and marketing costs. It incurs a financial loss. **Relative product failure** occurs if a firm makes a profit on an item but that product does not reach profit goals and/or adversely affects a firm's image. In computing profits and losses, the impact of the new product on the sales of other company items must be measured.

Even firms with good new-product records have had failures along the way. These include "light" pizza (Pizza Hut), *TV-Cable Week* (Time Inc.), Crystal Pepsi (PepsiCo), Bic perfume, McLean Deluxe (McDonald's), "new" Coke (Coca-Cola), Telaction interactive cable-TV shopping service (J.C. Penney), Premier smokeless cigarettes (R.J. Reynolds), and *Junior* (the Universal movie starring Arnold Schwarzenegger, Danny DeVito, and Emma Thompson).

[9]See Cyndee Miller, "Survey: New Product Failure Is Top Management's Fault," *Marketing News* (February 1, 1993), p. 2; Erik Jan Hultink and Henry S. J. Robben, "Measuring New Product Success: The Difference That Time Perspective Makes," *Journal of Product Innovation Management*, Vol. 12 (November 1995), pp. 392–405; James Dao, "From a Collector of Turkeys, A Tour of a Supermarket Zoo," *New York Times* (September 24, 1995), Section C, p. 12; and Ulrike de Brentani, "New Industrial Service Development: Scenarios for Success and Failure," *Journal of Business Research*, Vol. 32 (February 1995), pp. 93–103.

Leading to failure are lack of an advantage, poor planning and timing, and excess enthusiasm.

Numerous factors may cause new-product failure. The key ones are lack of a differential advantage, poor planning, poor timing, and excessive enthusiasm by the sponsor. Illustrations of poor performance due to those factors follow.

When introduced, Federal Express expected its Zap Mail to change the way business customers sent documents. With it, a customer could send a document almost anywhere in the United States in under two hours. The sender called a Federal Express operator, who had a courier pick up a document and take it to a Zap Mail office, which forwarded a copy to a receiving site. The copy was delivered by courier. Yet, within three years, Zap Mail was off the market. Although Federal Express felt Zap Mail would have clear advantages, it failed for three reasons: computer modems let customers communicate instantly and without a delivery firm; many clients did not believe two-hour service (at a high price) was better than overnight service; and as Zap Mail started, inexpensive fax machines began to flood the market.[10]

A small firm, Thermalux, was the only U.S. maker of aerogels, "special substances that look like glass, feel like styrofoam, and are as light as a feather. They are great insulators." Despite the seeming potential, after two years of poor planning, Thermalux had no customers; its aerogels remained "a solution looking for a problem." At first, the firm thought refrigerator makers would be the best market since they were under pressure not to use insulation materials made from certain fluorocarbons and to cut energy use. But, it underestimated competition from other insulation-materials firms. Thermalux also had a tough time setting the prices of its aerogels, and when aerogel insulation was tested in refrigerators, it did not show the benefits expected. Finally, Thermalux could not produce aerogels in sufficient quantity.[11]

Anheuser-Busch's LA beer failure was due to poor timing. LA beer was positioned as having half the alcohol of regular beer and was supported with a strong marketing effort. What happened? Soon after it came out, nonalcohol beers arrived. The market "evolved into an all-or-none situation, where drinkers wanted regular beer or beer with no alcohol." LA beer was dropped in 1990, as Anheuser-Busch turned to O'Doul's—its own premium-priced nonalcohol beer. By 1995, more than 12 million cases of O'Doul's were being sold annually. Yet in Europe, even nonalcohol beer has flopped: "People don't feel the pressure to be seen drinking beer anymore. Now, there's a wider range of adult soft drinks available, and it's socially acceptable to drink a soft drink."[12]

Excessive enthusiasm caused RCA to overinvest in its videodisc player, causing a loss of nearly $600 million before the product was dropped. RCA felt the player's superior picture quality and low price would lead to success with the mass market. It underestimated consumer interest in recording programs (which the videodisc player could not do, but a VCR could). Firms with more focused goals, such as Hitachi, have done well marketing videodisc players to business customers as aids in sales training and point-of-purchase displays. Pioneer has laser videodisc players that "marry the superb sound of audio compact discs with crisp pictures." Philips has interactive players.[13]

New-Product Planning

The **new-product planning process** *moves goods and services from ideas to commercialization.*

The **new-product planning process** involves a series of steps from idea generation to commercialization. See Figure 13-4. During the process, a firm generates ideas, evaluates them, weeds out poor ones, obtains consumer feedback, develops the product, tests it, and brings

[10]Federal Express Corporation reports.

[11]John R. Emschwiller, "Thermalux Seeks Customers for a New Technology," *Wall Street Journal* (February 15, 1991), p. B2.

[12]"Anheuser-Busch Pulls Plug on LA, a Low-Alcohol Beer," *Wall Street Journal* (May 30, 1990), p. B3; Marj Charlier, "Big Beer Makers Go After the Sober Set with Assortment of Nonalcoholic Brews," *Wall Street Journal* (March 30, 1992), pp. B1, B12; and Tara Parker-Pope, "Brewers Dismayed as Drinkers Decide That Suds Are a Dud Without Alcohol," *Wall Street Journal* (July 6, 1995), p. A5C.

[13]Sandra Salmans, "RCA Defends Timing of Videodisc Canceling," *New York Times* (April 6, 1984), pp. D1, D15; Marcia Watson, Jeff Kemph, and Judith Steele, "Marketing Muscle and the Videodisc," *Business Marketing* (June 1985), pp. 130–140; Brian O'Reilly, "Pioneer's Bright Picture," *Fortune* (August 13, 1990), p. 89; and "How to Sell Yourself on a CD-Interactive Player from Philips," *Wall Street Journal* (May 1, 1992), p. A13.

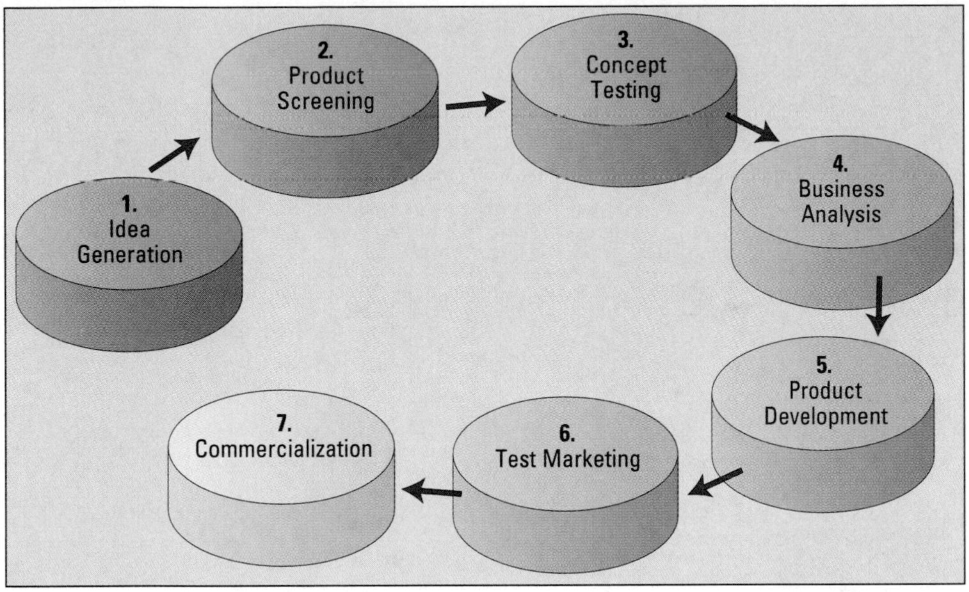

FIGURE 13-4
The New-Product Planning Process

it to market. An idea can be terminated at any time; costs rise as the process goes on. The process could be used by firms of any size or type, and applies to goods and services.

Booz, Allen & Hamilton says it generally takes a firm an average of seven well-defined ideas to yield one commercially successful new product. But, this number can be much higher. A study of new-product managers found that it took nearly 75 ideas to yield one successful new product. In the pharmaceuticals industry, it may take up to 10,000 compounds to come up with one drug that is approved by the Food and Drug Administration.[14]

During the new-product planning process, a firm needs to endeavor to balance such competing goals as these:

- A systematic process should be followed; however, there must be flexibility to adapt to each unique new-product opportunity.
- The process should be thorough, yet not unduly slow down introductions.
- True innovations should be pursued, yet fiscal constraints must be considered.
- An early reading of consumer acceptance should be sought, but the firm must not give away too much information to potential competitors.
- There should be an interest in short-run profitability, but not at the expense of long-run growth.[15]

Figure 13-5 highlights 3M's perspective on new-product planning: The "unique 3M culture, passed on from generation to generation, has resulted in more than 60,000 small miracles that make our lives safer, easier, better."

Idea Generation

Idea generation *is the search for opportunities.*

Idea generation is a continuous, systematic search for new product opportunities. It involves new-idea sources and ways to generate ideas.

Sources of ideas may be employees, channel members, competitors, outside inventors, customers, government, and others. *Market-oriented sources* identify opportunities based on consumer needs and wants; laboratory research is used to satisfy them. Light beer,

[14]Miller, "Survey: New Product Failure Is Top Management's Fault," p. 2; T. Erickson and L. Brenkus, *Healthcare R & D: Tools and Tactics* (Cambridge, Mass.: Arthur D. Little, October 1986), meeting notes; and Laura Jereski, "Block That Innovation!" *Forbes* (January 18, 1993), p. 48.

[15]See Robert G. Cooper and Elmo J. Kleinschmidt, "Benchmarking the Firm's Success Factors in New Product Development," *Journal of Product Innovation Management*, Vol. 12 (November 1995), pp. 374–391; and James M. Higgins, "Innovate or Evaporate," *Futurist* (September–October 1995), pp. 42–48.

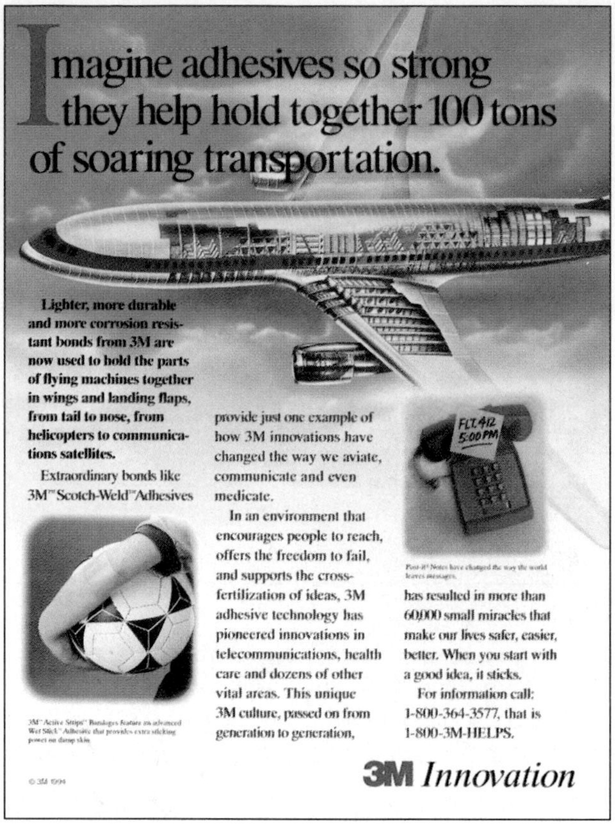

FIGURE 13-5
The 3M Approach to New-Product Planning
Reprinted by permission.

many ice cream flavors, and easy-to-open soda cans have evolved from market-oriented sources. *Laboratory-oriented sources* identify opportunities based on pure research (which seeks to gain knowledge and indirectly leads to specific new-product ideas) or applied research (which uses existing scientific techniques to develop new-product ideas). Penicillin, antifreeze, and synthetic fibers have evolved from laboratory sources.

Methods for generating ideas include brainstorming (small-group sessions to come up with a variety of ideas), analyzing current products, reading trade publications, visiting suppliers and dealers, and doing surveys. An open perspective is key: different people should be consulted; many ideas should be offered; and ideas should not be criticized, no matter how offbeat:

> Think of the *worst* possible idea you can for a new soup. How about a soup with rocks in it? Or a soup made of green slime? Terrible ideas, right? Maybe not. Thinking about a soup with rocks in it could inspire you to invent a new, extra-chunky brand of soup. Thinking about green slime soup could lead you to create a new $100-million line of "Slime Soups" for young boys, who we know like anything and everything that's "gross."[16]

Product Screening

Product screening *weeds out undesirable ideas.*

Once a firm spots potential products, it must screen them. In **product screening,** poor, unsuitable, or otherwise unattractive ideas are weeded out from further consideration. Today, many firms use a new-product screening checklist for preliminary analysis. In it, they list the attributes deemed most important and rate each idea on those attributes. The checklist is standardized and allows ideas to be compared.

Figure 13-6 shows a new-product screening checklist with three major categories: general characteristics, marketing characteristics, and production characteristics (which can be applied to both goods and services). In each category, there are several product attributes to assess. They are scored from 1 (outstanding) to 10 (very poor) for each product idea. In addition, the attributes would be weighted because they vary in their impact

[16]Bryan W. Mattimore, "Eureka! How to Invent a New Product," *Futurist* (March–April 1995), p. 34.

General Characteristics of New Products	**Rating**
Profit potential	------
Existing competition	------
Potential competition	------
Size of market	------
Level of investment	------
Patentability	------
Level of risk	------
Marketing Characteristics of New Products	
Fit with marketing capabilities	------
Effect on existing products (brands)	------
Appeal to current consumer markets	------
Potential length of product life cycle	------
Existence of differential advantage	------
Impact on image	------
Resistance to seasonal factors	------
Production Characteristics of New Products	
Fit with production capabilities	------
Length of time to commercialization	------
Ease of production	------
Availability of labor and material resources	------
Ability to produce at competitive prices	------

FIGURE 13-6
A New-Product Screening Checklist

on new-product success. For every idea, the checklist would yield an overall score. Here is an example of how a firm could develop overall ratings for two product ideas. Remember, in this example, the best rating is 1 (so, 3 is worse than 2):

1. Product idea A gets an average rating of 2.5 on general characteristics, 2.9 on marketing characteristics, and 1.4 on production characteristics. Product idea B gets ratings of 2.8, 1.4, and 1.8, respectively.
2. The firm assigns an importance weight of 4 to general characteristics, 5 to marketing characteristics, and 3 to production characteristics. The best overall rating is 12 $[(1 \times 4) + (1 \times 5) + (1 \times 3)]$. The poorest possible overall average rating is 120 $[(10 \times 4) + (10 \times 5) + (10 \times 3)]$.
3. Idea A gets an overall rating of 28.7 $[(2.5 \times 4) + (2.9 \times 5) + (1.4 \times 3)]$. B gets an overall rating of 23.6 $[(2.8 \times 4) + (1.4 \times 5) + (1.8 \times 3)]$.
4. Idea B's overall rating is better than A's because of its better marketing evaluation (the characteristics judged most important by the firm).

A **patent** *gives exclusive selling rights to an inventor.*

In screening, patentability must often be determined. A **patent** grants an inventor of a useful product or process exclusive selling rights for a fixed period. An invention may be patented if it is a "useful, novel, and nonobvious process, machine, manufacture, or composition of matter" and not patented by anyone else. Separate applications are needed for protection in foreign markets. Many nations have simplified matters via patent cooperation treaties; however, some do not honor such treaties. Today, in the United States and the other members of the new World Trade Organization, patents last for 20 years from the date that applications are filed. Until June 1995, U.S. patents lasted for 17 years from the date they were granted. Each year, about 120,000 patent applications are filed in the United States. About 45 per cent of U.S. patents involve foreign firms; in contrast, 17 per cent of Japanese patents are held by foreigners.[17]

A company should answer these kinds of patent questions in the screening stage: Can the proposed new product be patented by the firm? Are competitive items patented? When

[17]Teresa Riordan, "Patents," *New York Times* (June 12, 1995), p. D2; Neil Gross, "New Patent Office Pending," *Business Week* (October 23, 1995), p. 130; and Masaaki Kotabe, "A Study of Japanese Patent Systems," *Journal of International Business Studies*, Vol. 23 (First Quarter 1992), pp. 147–168.

do competitors' patents expire? Are patents on competing items available under a licensing agreement? Would the firm be free of patent liability (infringement) if it introduces the proposed new product?

Concept Testing

Concept testing *determines customer attitudes before product development.*

Next, a firm needs consumer feedback about the new-product ideas that pass through screening. **Concept testing** presents the consumer with a proposed product and measures attitudes and intentions at an early stage of the new-product planning process.

Concept testing is a quick, inexpensive way to assess consumer enthusiasm. It asks potential consumers to react to a picture, written statement, or oral product description. This lets a firm learn initial attitudes prior to costly, time-consuming product development. Heinz, Kodak, Sony, and Sunbeam are among those using concept testing. Figure 13-7 shows a concept test for a proposed service: a pre-paid telephone card to be used with pay phones. This card is popular in Europe, but it has not yet taken off in the United States (where personal identification numbers must be entered when making pre-paid calls).

Concept testing generally asks consumers these types of questions:

- Is the idea easy to understand?
- Would this product meet a real need?
- Do you see distinct benefits for this product over those on the market?
- Do you find the claims about this product believable?
- Would you buy the product?
- How much would you pay for it?
- Would you replace your current brand with this new product?
- What improvements can you suggest in various attributes of the concept?
- How frequently would you buy the product?
- Who would use the product?[18]

Business Analysis

Business analysis *looks at demand, costs, competition, etc.*

At this point, a firm does business analysis for the new-product concepts that have thus far been deemed attractive. **Business analysis** involves the detailed review, projection, and evaluation of such factors as consumer demand, production costs, marketing costs, break-even points, competition, capital investments, and profitability for each proposed new product. It is much more detailed than product screening.

Here are some of the considerations at this planning stage:

CRITERIA	SELECTED CONSIDERATIONS
Demand projections	Short- and long-run sales potential; speed of sales growth; price/sales relationship; seasonality; rate of repurchases
Production cost projections	Total and per-unit costs; startup vs. continuing costs; estimates of raw materials and other costs; economies of scale; break-even points
Marketing cost projections	Product planning (patent search, product development, testing); promotion; distribution; marketing research; break-even points
Competitive projections	Short-run and long-run market shares of company and competitors; competitors' strengths and weaknesses; potential competitors; likely strategies by competitors in response to firm
Capital investment projections	Need for new equipment and facilities vs. use of existing facilities and resources
Profitability projections	Time to recoup initial costs; short- and long-run total and per-unit profits; reseller needs; control over price; return on investment; risk

[18]Adapted from Philip Kotler, *Marketing Management: Analysis, Planning, Implementation, and Control*, Eighth Edition (Englewood Cliffs, N.J.: Prentice-Hall, 1994), p. 331.

A U.S. long-distance telephone-service company is considering the introduction of a pre-paid card for use with pay phones. Here's how it would work: The caller inserts the card (resembling a credit card) in a special slot at a pay phone and leaves it there during a call; the cost of the call is automatically deducted from the value of the card. The caller does not have to stock up on change and pays a slightly discounted rate. The card is like cash; can be bought in denominations of $10, $25, $50, and $100; and is discarded when used up. This telephone card is already popular in Europe.

Would you please answer some questions to give us a better idea of the pre-paid telephone card's marketability?

1. React to the overall concept of a pre-paid telephone card.

2. In what situations would the pre-paid telephone card be most beneficial to consumers?

3. What else would you like to know about this concept?

4. Do you have any suggestions about the features of the pre-paid telephone card?

5. How likely would you be to purchase a pre-paid telephone card within the next year? Check one answer.
Very likely ____ ____ ____ ____ ____ Very unlikely
Why? ____________________________________

FIGURE 13-7
A Brief Concept Test for a Proposed New Telephone Service

Because the next step is expensive and time-consuming product development, critical use of business analysis is essential to eliminate marginal items.

Product Development

Product development *focuses on devising an actual product and a broad marketing strategy.*

During **product development,** an idea for a new product is converted into a tangible form and a basic marketing strategy is identified. Depending on the product involved, this stage in the planning process encompasses product construction, packaging, branding, product positioning, and consumer attitude and usage testing.

Product construction decisions include the type and quality of materials comprising the product, the method of production, production time, production capacity, the assortment to be offered, and the time needed to move from development to commercialization. Packaging decisions include the materials used, the functions performed, and alternative sizes and colors. Branding decisions include the choice of a name, trademark protection, and the image sought. Product positioning involves selecting a target market and positioning the new good or service against competitors and other company offerings. Consumer testing studies perceptions of and satisfaction with the new product.

If a modification is involved, product-development costs may be relatively low. However, an innovation may be costly (up to several million dollars or even more) and time-consuming (up to four years for a new car). And this is true of services, as well as goods. When Club Med built a resort in Copper Mountain, Colorado, it invested millions of dollars and many years in planning and construction. The Copper Mountain village has a seven-story ski lodge, a theater, a boutique, a ski-rental shop, a sauna, restaurants, various winter sports, instructional classes, a jacuzzi and a sauna, a cocktail lounge, a large fireplace, and more.

Besides being costly and time-consuming, product development can be quite complicated. For example,

> Boeing's traditional method for designing new aircraft is surprisingly primitive. The process has three phases. First, engineers design a plane's shape and components. Then, they hand blueprints to manufacturing experts, who plan the production of components and final assembly. Finally, the manufacturing plan goes to tooling specialists who design specialized production machinery. Since the phases are completed in sequence, they take a long time, and the system forces each group to turn out reams of corrections, consuming millions of hours a year in engineering time.
>
> Once final drawings are ready, carpenters and artisans go to work. They build a full-scale mock-up of the plane incorporating replicas of every part. Converted for the first time from drawings to three-dimensional reality, parts don't necessarily fit. Electricians stringing mock instrument wires through the model, for instance, may discover that a structural beam gets in the way. Result: more expensive changes, as engineers redesign the beam so it has a hole in the center and tool makers reconfigure machines to accommodate the fix. Similar mistakes inevitably plague construction of the first few planes. And since subsequent planes must be tailored to the customer, Boeing goes through a minor version of the same tortuous process with each order.[19]

Test Marketing

Test marketing *occurs in selected areas and observes real performance.*

Test marketing involves placing a fully developed new product (a good or service) in one or more selected areas and observing its actual performance under a proposed marketing plan. The purpose is to evaluate the product and pre-test marketing efforts in a real setting prior to a full-scale introduction. Rather than just study intentions, test marketing lets a firm monitor actual consumer behavior, competitor reactions, and reseller interest. After testing, the firm could decide to go ahead, modify the product and then go ahead, modify the marketing plan and then go ahead, or drop the product. Procter & Gamble, Time Warner, AT&T, Levi Strauss, and McDonald's are among the companies that use test marketing.

Consumer products firms are much more apt to engage in test marketing than industrial products firms:

> In consumer products, test marketing is a science dominated by marketing consultants, database collection firms, and electronic test marketing services. The business is so sophisticated that Information Resources Inc. of Chicago, which runs several electronic test markets, not only measures what every member of its participating households buys but also identifies exactly which television ads propelled them into stores.
>
> By contrast, the test marketing of business-to-business products has only recently become a widespread practice. In the past, a manufacturer created a product, ran it by a few executives, and hoped customers would buy it. Thus, manufacturers often spent huge sums on parts and labor to fix any problems that cropped up after installation. Now, a growing number of man-

[19]Shawn Tully, "Can Boeing Reinvent Itself?" *Fortune* (March 8, 1993), p. 72. See also Alex Taylor III, "Boeing Sleepy in Seattle," *Fortune* (August 7, 1995), pp. 92–98.

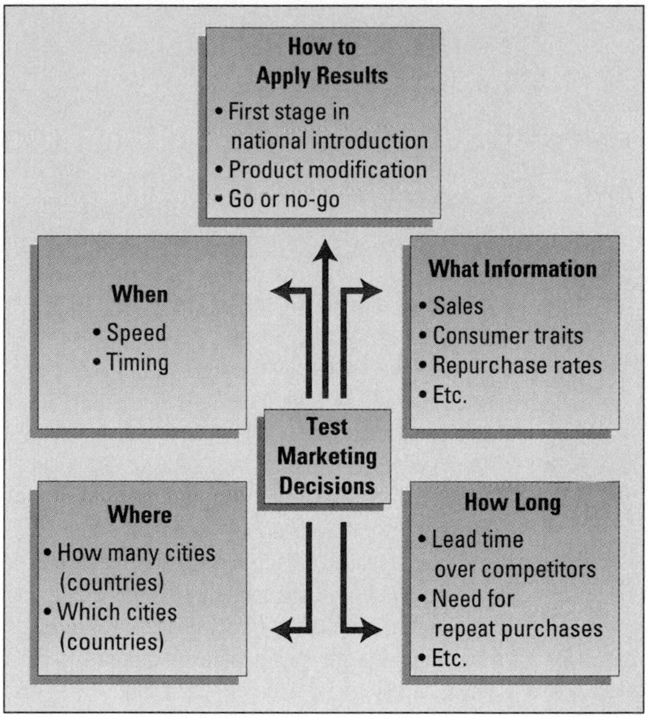

FIGURE 13-8
Test Marketing Decisions

ufacturers in such diverse industries as computers, electronics, industrial chemicals, cleaning equipment, maintenance products, and insurance have begun intensive on-site tests of new products. In most cases, these tests are conducted with anywhere from five to fifty clients and last from two to six months.[20]

The test-marketing process requires several decisions: when to test, where to test, how long to test, what test information to acquire, and how to apply test results. Figure 13-8 shows the criteria to weigh in making the choices.

Although test marketing has been beneficial in many cases, some firms now question its effectiveness and downplay or skip this stage in new-product planning. Dissatisfaction arises from test marketing's costs, the time delays before full introduction, the information being provided to competitors, the inability to predict national (global) results based on limited test-market areas, and the impact of such external factors as the economy and competition on test results. Test marketing can even allow nontesting competitors to catch up with an innovative firm by the time a product is ready for a full rollout.

Commercialization

Commercialization *involves a major marketing commitment.*

When testing goes well, a firm is ready to introduce a new product to its full target market. This involves **commercialization** and corresponds to the introductory stage of the product life cycle. During commercialization, the firm enacts a total marketing plan and works toward production capacity. Among the factors to be considered are the speed of acceptance by consumers and distribution intermediaries, the intensity of distribution (how many outlets), production capabilities, the promotion mix, prices, competition, the time until profitability, and commercialization costs.

Commercialization may require large outlays and a long-term commitment. For example, manufacturers spend an average of more than $5 million for a national rollout in U.S. supermarkets—nearly half on consumer promotion and the rest on product costs, market research costs, and promotions for supermarkets. Yet, commercialization costs can go much higher. When Pepcid, an over-the-counter antacid that promises to relieve and prevent heartburn and acid indigestion, recently entered the national U.S. market to vie

[20]Aimee L. Stern, "Testing Goes Industrial," *Sales & Marketing Management* (March 1991), p. 30. See also Steve Blount, "It's Just a Matter of Time," *Sales & Marketing Management* (March 1992), pp. 32–43.

Ethics IN TODAY'S SOCIETY

Is There a Future for the Electric Car (in This Century)?

GM's new electric car, the EV1, is a "zero emission vehicle" that eliminates the pollutants emitted by gas-powered cars. Until recently, GM worked on the EV1 only because large states such as California had set a mandate that 2 per cent of the cars offered for sale in 1998 have zero emissions. But, in the absence of a commercially viable car, states pulled back from insisting on electric vehicles. So, the question is: After 75 years of research, will we ever see a successful electric car? GM is unsure. That is why the late 1996 launch of the EV1 was planned for just two states—California and Arizona—and in limited quantities.

Unlike electric cars based on traditional gas-powered car designs, the EV1 has been designed from scratch. Thus, it has some innovative features: It is so aerodynamic that it has half the resistance of traditional cars. A dashboard meter constantly recalculates the remaining distance before the car must be recharged (based on the amount of electricity remaining and the rate of electric usage). The fuel cost is low when compared to gas-powered cars. The cost of charging the EV1's batteries averages $1.70; this works out to half the fuel cost per mile of a comparably sized gas-based vehicle.

Despite these innovations, the EV1 has some major handicaps that greatly limit the market potential for the car. As with most electric-powered vehicles, the EV1 has a limited driving range between charges (70 to 90 miles). Although the car can be fully charged in two to three hours with a special 220-volt outlet, with regular household voltage, the recharging time is about 10 hours. The EV1 is also only being offered as a two-seater. Many analysts feel these characteristics would limit buyers to consumers needing a car to drive short distances and households that already have one or two cars. And it is priced at over $30,000.

As a GM marketing manager, offer a plan to commercialize the EV1.

Sources: Based on material in Matthew L. Wald, "Future Shock: Driving an Electric Prototype," *New York Times* (April 2, 1995), Section F, p. 1; and Matthew L. Wald, "Betamax Redux: Big 3 Brawl on Electric Cars," *New York Times* (February 4, 1996), Section 11, p. 1.

with Tums, Mylanta, Tagament, and other antacids, it had a $100 million marketing budget—for TV and print ads, coupons, in-store promotions, and doctor samples.[21]

The commercialization of a new product sometimes must overcome consumer and reseller reluctance because of ineffective prior company offerings. This occurred with Texas Instruments in the business computer market, after it bowed out of the home computer market. Atari, the video-game manufacturer, is another firm for which earlier difficulties have had negative effects on the commercialization of new products.

Growing Products

Once a new product is commercialized, the goal is for consumer acceptance and company sales to rise rapidly. This occurs in some cases; in others, it may take a long while. The growth rate and total sales level of new products rely heavily on two related consumer behavior concepts: the adoption process and the diffusion process. In managing

[21]Pam Weisz, "Marketers of the Year: Pharmaceuticals," *Superbrands 1996: Brandweek's Marketers of the Year* (October 6, 1995), pp. 98–99.

growing products, a firm must understand these concepts and plan its marketing efforts accordingly.

The **adoption process** is the mental and behavioral procedure an individual consumer goes through when learning about and purchasing a new product. It consists of these stages:

*The **adoption process** explains the new-product purchase behavior of individual consumers.*

1. Knowledge—A person (organization) learns of a product's existence and gains some understanding of how it functions.
2. Persuasion—A person (organization) forms a favorable or unfavorable attitude about a product.
3. Decision—A person (organization) engages in actions that lead to a choice to adopt or reject a product.
4. Implementation—A person (organization) uses a product.
5. Confirmation—A person (organization) seeks reinforcement and may reverse a decision if exposed to conflicting messages.[22]

The rate (speed) of adoption depends on consumer traits, the product, and the firm's marketing effort. Adoption is faster if consumers have high discretionary income and are willing to try new offerings; the product has low perceived risk; the product has an advantage over other items on the market; the product is a modification and not an innovation; the product is compatible with current consumer life-styles or ways of operating a business; product attributes can be easily communicated; product importance is low; the product can be tested before a purchase; the product is consumed quickly; the product is easy to use; mass advertising and distribution are used; and the marketing mix adjusts as the person (organization) moves through the adoption process.

The **diffusion process** describes the manner in which different members of the target market often accept and purchase a product. It spans the time from product introduction through market saturation and affects the total sales level of a product as it moves through the life cycle:

*The **diffusion process** describes when different segments are likely to purchase.*

1. Innovators are the first to try a new product. They are venturesome, willing to accept risk, socially aggressive, communicative, and worldly. It must be determined which innovators are opinion leaders—those who influence others. This group is about 2.5 per cent of the market.
2. Early adopters are the next to buy a new product. They enjoy the prestige, leadership, and respect that early purchases bring—and tend to be opinion leaders. They adopt new ideas but use discretion. This group is about 13.5 per cent of the market.
3. The early majority is the initial part of the mass market to buy a product. They have status among peers and are outgoing, communicative, and attentive to information. This group is about 34 per cent of the market.
4. The late majority is the second part of the mass market to buy. They are less cosmopolitan and responsive to change, and include people (firms) with lower economic and social status, those past middle age (or set in their jobs), and skeptics. This group is about 34 per cent of the market.
5. Laggards purchase last, if at all. They are price-conscious, suspicious of change, low in income and status, tradition bound, and conservative. They do not adopt a product until it reaches maturity. Some sellers ignore them because it can be hard to market a product to laggards. Thus, concentrated marketing may do well by focusing on products for laggards. This group is about 16 per cent of the market.[23]

Growth for a major innovation often starts slowly because there is an extended adoption process and the early majority may be hesitant to buy. Sales may then rise quickly. As an illustration, the PC was first marketed in 1977; yet, by the end of 1981, less than 10 per cent of U.S. businesses and under 2 per cent of U.S. households owned one. Con-

[22]Everett M. Rogers, *Diffusion of Innovations*, Third Edition (New York: Free Press, 1982), pp. 164–175.
[23]Ibid., pp. 246–261.

FIGURE 13-9
Turning Any Phone to a WorldPhone
Reprinted by permission of MCI.

sumers were hesitant to make a purchase due to high initial prices, the perceived difficulty of mastering the PC, its early image as a game console, and the limited software. Sales then grew dramatically, going from 1.1 million units in 1981 to over 7.5 million in 1984; inexpensive models entered the market, PCs became more user-friendly, the product lost its game image, and software became widely available.

By 1995, U.S. businesses owned about 40 million PCs and U.S. households nearly 40 million. In contrast, at that time, a total of 40 million PCs were owned by organizational and final consumers in the European Union and fewer than 20 million PCs were owned by organizational and final consumers in Japan. Why has ownership been so low in Japan? It is due to skepticism about the benefits of PCs among Japanese businesspeople, limited office and household space, and rather high prices (compared to the United States).[24]

For minor innovations or product modifications, growth is much faster. As an example, in 1994, MCI introduced WorldPhone service: "All you need to know is the WorldPhone access number for the country you happen to be in. Dial this access number, and you will get an operator who speaks your language, and economical rates from overseas." Due to the popularity of MCI services and the easily understandable premise of WorldPhone, this new service attracted customers in rapid fashion. See Figure 13-9.

These products are among those now in the growth stage of the product life cycle. They represent good opportunities for firms: CD-ROM software, cellular phones and related phone services, anti-lock car brakes, men's hair-coloring products, solar-powered products, generic drugs, plain-paper fax machines, stereo TVs, international financial services, adult education, rechargeable batteries, subnotebook PCs, and business-to-business video conferencing.

[24]*U.S. Industrial Outlook 1994* (Washington, D.C.: U.S. Department of Commerce, 1993), pp. 26-16–26-21; Jim Carlton, "Foreign Markets Give PC Makers a Hearty Hello," *Wall Street Journal* (September 15, 1995), pp. B1, B4; and authors' estimates.

Mature Products

Proper marketing can let mature products maintain high sales.

Products are in the maturity stage of the life cycle when they reach the late majority and laggard markets. Goals turn from growth to maintenance. Because new products are so costly and risky, more firms are placing marketing emphasis on mature products with steady sales and profits, and minimal risk.

In managing mature products, a firm should examine the size, attributes, and needs of the current market; untapped market segments; competition; the potential for product modifications; the likelihood of new company products replacing mature ones; profit margins; the marketing effort required for each sale; reseller attitudes; the promotion mix; the impact of specific products on the overall product line; each product's effect on company image; the number of remaining years for the products; and the management effort needed.

Popular mature brands offer several benefits for companies.

There are many possible benefits if a firm has a popular brand in a mature product category. First, the life cycle may be extended almost indefinitely. Budweiser beer, Coke Classic soda, Goodyear tires, Ivory soap, Lipton tea, Maxwell House coffee, Life Savers mints, Sherwin-Williams paints, and Quaker Oats oatmeal are among the leaders in their product categories; each is well over 75 years old. Second, the brand attracts a loyal customer group and has a stable, profitable position in the market. Third, the likelihood of future low demand is greatly reduced; this is a real risk for new products. Fourth, a firm's overall image is enhanced. This may allow the firm to extend a popular name to other products. Fifth, there is more control over marketing efforts and more precision in sales forecasting. Sixth, mature products can be used as cash cows to support spending on new products. However, some marketing support must be continued if a mature product is to remain popular.

Successful industries and companies market products that stay in maturity for long periods, as the following illustrate:

- The paper clip was invented in 1899 by Norwegian Johan Vaaler. Since then, "several hundred inventors have patented paper clips in every conceivable shape—square, round, oval, triangular, teardrop, and arrowhead." Today, it is more popular than ever due to its ease of use, flexible applications, and large customer following. It seems that, after nearly 100 years, there is still nothing to match a paper clip. Twenty billion are sold yearly.[25]
- Chlorine is a chemical produced by the electrolysis of brine. It is used to process organic chemicals and in the production of pulp, paper, and other industrial goods. In industrialized nations, chlorine is a mature product—with stable sales in the United States and negative sales growth in Canada, Japan, and Europe. But sales are growing in Asia, Latin America, Africa, and the Middle East. Thus, chlorine producers' marketing efforts are now quite aggressive in developing and less-developed nations.[26]
- "Whether clothes are lean or loose, short or long, there's a common thread running through much of today's fashion: Lycra—DuPont's trademark for spandex fiber that started out in the 1950s as a substitute for rubber in girdles." After sales stagnated for a while, the fiber gained attention in the 1980s with the advent of cycling pants and leggings, and technological advances that let Lycra fibers be used in sheer hosiery. Lycra is now "in everything from long, willowy cotton and linen sheaths by Liz Claiborne's Lizsport to crewneck bodysuits from Anne Klein II and tank dresses from designer Donna Karan's DKNY division." In certain parts of Europe, the Lycra name has a consumer recognition rate of 98 per cent, and expansion in Latin America and the Far East are under way.[27]
- For decades, Ralston Purina has dominated the pet food market with its Purina Dog Chow and Purina Cat Chow. Although it regularly adds updated product versions, the company also encourages its customers to seek a consistent diet for their pets by

[25]Amal Kumar Naj, "Hey, Get a Grip! Your Basic Paper Clip Is Like a Mousetrap," *Wall Street Journal* (July 24, 1995), pp. A1, A5.

[26]"Chloralkali Industry Sees Changes," *Chemical Marketing Reporter* (September 21, 1992), pp. 3, 16.

[27]Pat Sloan, "Lycra Stretches Fashion Appeal," *Advertising Age* (November 2, 1992), pp. 3, 36.

Sudden changes in your dog's diet can lead to stomach discomfort.
By suddenly introducing your dog to a new diet, you could be treating him to a stomach ache. The fact is, a consistent diet of one nutritionally complete and balanced food is actually better for dogs. And that's why you can feel good about feeding your dog Purina Dog Chow brand dog food each and every day. With all the taste and nutrition dogs need.
Because, after all, dogs never get sick of good nutrition.
Purina Dog Chow Every Day.

FIGURE 13-10
Promoting Customer Loyalty to a Mature Brand
Reprinted by permission.

regularly buying its mature brands. Figure 13-10 shows how Ralston Purina promotes customer loyalty to Purina Dog Chow.

There are many options available for extending the mature stage of the product life cycle. Table 13-1 shows seven strategies and examples of each.

Table 13-1

Selected Strategies for Extending the Mature Stage of the Product Life Cycle

STRATEGY	EXAMPLES
1. Develop new uses for products	Jell-O used in garden salads WD-40 used in the maintenance of kitchen appliances
2. Develop new product features and refinements	Zoom lenses for 35mm cameras Battery-powered televisions
3. Increase the market	American Express accounts for small businesses International editions of major magazines
4. Find new classes of consumers for present products	Nylon carpeting for institutional markets Johnson & Johnson's baby shampoo used by adults
5. Find new classes of consumers for modified products	Industrial power tools altered for do-it-yourself market Inexpensive copy machines for home offices
6. Increase product usage among current users	Multiple packages for soda and beer Discounts given for increased long-distance phone calls
7. Change marketing strategy	Greeting cards sold in supermarkets Office furniture promoted via mail-order catalogs

International Marketing in Action

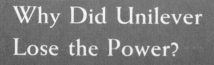

Why Did Unilever Lose the Power?

Dutch-British Unilever is one of the world's global giants, with annual sales of nearly $50 billion—including $11 billion from laundry detergents. Yet, the firm recently suffered a major embarrassment with its new Power detergent, which featured a "patented, stain-annihilating, manganese-based catalyst" known as Accelerator. Just months after it was introduced, Power had to be pulled from the market because it damaged clothes. "It's the greatest marketing setback we've seen," said Sir Michael Perry, Unilever Chairman.

Why did this happen? According to one expert, "The $300 million Power introduction is a cautionary tale highlighting the pressure multinational firms face to come up with winning products that work internationally—and roll them out faster. With only half of P&G's detergent sales, Unilever was desperate to parlay its technology breakthrough into a greater market share."

Specifically, here's what Unilever did:

- It ignored a pre-introduction warning from arch-rival Procter & Gamble that Power could damage clothes.
- It was so enthusiastic that it skipped test marketing and placed Power into full commercialization right after product development.
- It was a victim of its own efficiency. Until recently, it took Unilever up to three years to roll out a new product in 16 European countries. Today, such a rollout is done in a few months, leaving no real chance to catch product errors early in commercialization.
- It decided not to create a strong new brand and "piggybacked" Power onto two of its existing brands, hence Omo Power and Persil Power.
- It underestimated the marketing blitz that P&G would use to call public attention to Power's potentially damaging effect on clothing.

As Unilever's laundry detergent manager, how would you avoid such errors, while still being an aggressive competitor?

Source: Laurel Wentz, "Unilever's Power Failure a Wasteful Use of Haste," *Advertising Age* (March 6, 1995), p. 42.

Not all mature products can be revived or extended. Consumer needs may disappear, as when frozen juice replaced juice squeezers. Life-style changes may lead to less interest in products, such as teller services in banks. Better and more convenient products may be devised, such as CD players to replace record players. The market may be saturated and further marketing efforts may be unable to garner enough sales to justify time and costs, which is why Japan's NEC has a diminished role in consumer electronics.

Product Deletion

Products need to be deleted if they have consistently poor sales, tie up resources, and cannot be revived.

Products should be deleted from a firm's offerings if they offer limited sales and profit potential, reflect poorly on the firm, tie up resources that could be used for other opportunities, involve large amounts of management time, create reseller dissatisfaction due to low inventory turnover, and divert attention from long-term goals.

However, there are many points to weigh before deleting a product: As a product matures, it blends in with existing items and becomes part of the total product line (mix). Customers and distribution intermediaries may be hurt if an item is dropped. A firm may not want competitors to have the only product for customers. Poor sales and profits may be only temporary. The marketing strategy, not the product, may be the cause of poor results. Thus, a systematic procedure should be used to handle faltering products.

As these examples show, low-profit or rapidly declining products are often dropped or de-emphasized:

- After seven years on the market, the Cadillac Allante, a $62,000 General Motors' two-seat luxury roadster, was discontinued due to weak sales. Although the car was profitable, only 2,000 units were sold during its last year. And the Allante was very complicated to build, with undercarriages made in Detroit and bodies and interiors made in Italy.
- Despite annual revenues of $3.3 billion, Sears dropped its 97-year-old mail-order catalog. It was a large money loser—because of high production and mailing costs, as well as the inventory costs involved with a wide and deep product assortment. And Sears was seeing more of its business go to specialized catalog firms and to discounters like Wal-Mart.
- "If business is a jungle, then the rise and fall of the typewriter is one of its more cherishable demonstrations of evolution, of the little creature that could. As Smith Corona filed for bankruptcy protection last week [July 1995], one of the final signals in the triumph of PCs and software over the typewriter [originally patented in 1868] was at hand."[28]

During deletion, customer and distributor needs must be considered.

In discontinuing a product, a firm must take replacement parts, the notification time for customers and resellers, and the honoring of warranties/guarantees into account. For example, a company planning to delete its line of office telephones must resolve these questions: (1) Replacement parts—Who will make them? How long will they be made? (2) Notification time—How soon before the actual deletion will an announcement be made? Will distributors be alerted early enough so they can line up other suppliers? (3) Warranties—How will warranties be honored? After they expire, how will repairs be handled?

MARKETING IN A CHANGING WORLD

Inventors Beware

Gemstar Corporation was started with a $50,000 loan, as founders Henry Yuen and Daniel Kwoh (then co-workers at TRW) developed VCR Plus—a hand-held device that lets TV viewers easily program their VCRs by entering a code number obtained from a television program listing guide. More than three million VCR Plus units (at about $60 each, retail) were sold in the first two years alone. The product is now being marketed in the United States, Canada, Europe, Japan, and Latin America. In addition, some VCR makers bundle VCR Plus with their products (and pay Gemstar to do so).

Sounds simple, right? You invent a product, prepare a marketing plan, and—presto—you're a millionaire. Unfortunately, it's not so simple. In fact, according to experts, for every patented invention that succeeds, about 98 fail. And sometimes, inventors may be disheartened about what others say about their ideas and mistakenly give up—although the ideas may later prove to be blockbusters: "As recently as 1977, Kenneth Olsen, the founder of the Digital Equipment Corporation (DEC), told the World Future Society, 'There is no reason for any individual to have a computer in his or her home.'"[29]

These are some of the hard challenges facing today's inventors:

[28]Francis X. Clines, "An Ode to the Typewriter," *New York Times* (July 10, 1995), p. D5.

[29]Laura Pedersen, "Invented a Gadget? Don't Quit Your Job," *New York Times* (September 10, 1995), Section 3.

- Acquiring marketing and business prowess—Technical proficiency does not mean "business smarts."
- Financing a startup—Banks, venture capitalists, and others may be reluctant to underwrite a new product unless the inventor has a track record or collateral to back up a loan.
- Marketplace clutter—This can be a double whammy. How do you get resellers to carry new products when existing shelf space is tight? How do you get consumers to pay attention, since thousands of new products come out yearly?
- Marketplace skepticism—So many products have been "hyped" that consumers are often unwilling to believe that new items can really do what they say.
- Inaccurate forecasting—This means budget projections about sales, profits, and so forth will tend to be off target (as will inventor earnings).

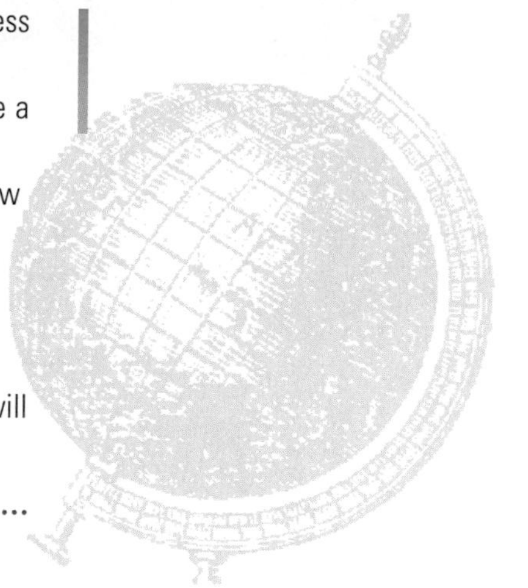

SUMMARY

1. *To examine the types of new-product opportunities available to a firm* Product management entails creating and overseeing products over their lives. New products are modifications or innovations that consumers see as substantive. Modifications are improvements to existing products. Minor innovations have not been previously sold by the firm but have been sold by others. Major innovations have not been previously sold by anyone.

2. *To detail the importance of new products and describe why new products fail* New products are important because they may foster differential advantages, sustain sales growth, require a lot of time for development, generate large profits, enable a firm to diversify, make distribution more efficient, lead to technological breakthroughs, allow waste products to be used, respond to changing consumers, and address government mandates.

When a firm suffers a financial loss, a product is an absolute failure. When it makes a profit but does not attain its goals, a product is a relative failure. Failures occur because of such factors as a lack of a significant differential advantage, poor planning, poor timing, and excessive enthusiasm by the product sponsor.

3. *To present the stages in the new-product planning process* New-product planning involves a comprehensive, seven-step process. During idea generation, new opportunities are sought. In product screening, unattractive ideas are weeded out via a new-product screening checklist. At concept testing, the consumer reacts to a proposed idea. Business analysis requires a detailed evaluation of demand, costs, competition, investments, and profits. Product development converts an idea into a tangible form and outlines a marketing strategy. Test marketing, a much-debated technique, involves placing a product for sale in selected areas and observing performance under actual conditions. Commercialization is the sale of a product to the full target market. A new product can be terminated or modified at any point in the process.

4. *To analyze the growth and maturity of products, including the adoption process, the diffusion process, and extension strategies* Once a new product is commercialized, the firm's goal is for consumer acceptance and company sales to rise as rapidly as possible. However, the growth rate and level for a new product are dependent on the adoption process—which describes how a single consumer learns about and purchases a product—and the diffusion process—which describes how different members of the target market learn about and purchase a product. These processes are faster for certain consumers, products, and marketing strategies.

When products mature, company goals turn from growth to maintenance. Mature products can provide stable sales and profits and loyal consumers. They do not require the risks and costs of new products. There are several factors to consider and alternative strategies from which to choose when planning to sustain mature products. It may not be possible to retain aging products if consumer needs disappear, life-styles change, new products make them obsolete, or the market becomes too saturated.

5. *To examine product deletion decisions and strategies* At some point, a firm may have to determine whether to continue a faltering product. Product deletion may be difficult because of the interrelation of products, the impact on customers and resellers, and other factors. It should be done in a structured manner; and replacement parts, notification time, and warranties should all be considered in a deletion plan.

KEY TERMS

new product (p. 356)
modifications (p. 356)
minor innovations (p. 356)
major innovations (p. 357)
absolute product failure (p. 361)
relative product failure (p. 361)
new-product planning process (p. 362)
idea generation (p. 363)
product screening (p. 364)
patent (p. 365)
concept testing (p. 366)
business analysis (p. 366)
product development (p. 367)
test marketing (p. 368)
commercialization (p. 369)
adoption process (p. 371)
diffusion process (p. 371)

Review Questions

1. Distinguish among a product modification, a minor innovation, and a major innovation. Present an example of each for a hospital.
2. Give four reasons why new products are important to a company.
3. Explain the new-product planning process.
4. How does product screening differ from business analysis?
5. What are the major tasks during product development?
6. What are the pros and cons of test marketing?
7. How can a firm speed a product's growth?
8. Is the maturity stage a good or bad position for a product to occupy? Why?
9. Cite five ways in which a firm could extend the mature stage of the product life cycle. Provide an example of each.
10. Why is a product deletion decision so difficult?

Discussion Questions

1. Comment on the following statement: "We never worry about relative product failures because we make a profit on them. We only worry about absolute product failures."
2. Develop a ten-item new-product screening checklist for a CD-ROM software developer. How would you weight each item?
3. Construct a 50- to 75-word concept statement and six pertinent questions relating to potential consumer interest in new contact lenses that could be left in the eyes for one year without ever having to be removed. Whom would you question in your concept test? Why? What would you expect to learn from this test?
4. Differentiate between the commercialization strategies for a product modification and a major innovation. Relate your answers to the adoption process and the diffusion process.
5. Select a product that has been in existence for 20 or more years and explain why it has been successful for so long.

CASE 1

*Can Swatch Make a Comeback?**

Swatch is owned by SMH, the firm that produces such well-known and highly respected Swiss watches as Blancpain, Omega, and Tissot. In 1983, SMH revolutionized the watch industry by introducing Swatch in the United States. The original Swatch marketing strategy combined the use of advanced technology (drawn from the $16,000 Concord Delirium model), low-cost production (the average Swatch included 51 parts instead of an industry average of 91 and had a plastic case and band), and the marketing of a constant stream of new models (and dropping older models). Unlike other watches, Swatch was not sold in jewelry stores (which the company felt were not progressive enough) or discount stores (which SMH thought would tarnish the product's Swiss image).

Because Swatch was seen as a fashion accessory and not just a timekeeping mechanism, its young customers were encouraged to buy more than one at a time. In addition, limited-edition Swatch watches were sold as collectors' items, and some of them highly escalated in value. For example, a limited-edition model (one of 140) Swatch designed by a pop artist sold at Sotheby's for $45,000—the record for a Swatch sold at auction. Since 1983, over 150 million inexpensive Swatch watches have been sold, at an average retail price of $50.

Swatch's runaway success did not go unnoticed at Timex, a leading U.S. competitor with a traditionally high market share in this price range. Timex, with annual sales of $600 million, introduced its own Guess? line of watches with metal cases and leather bands. Timex correctly reasoned that Swatch's plastic watch cases and bands and bright colors were not as attractive as its new Guess? product line to many people. According to Timex, its Guess? line sold $75 million in watches in 1994—versus Swatch's sales of $20 to $30 million. In addition, market leader Fossil sold $100 million in watches in 1994. According to Timex's chief executive, "The world passed Swatch by as fashion watches moved away from plastic." In addition to poor sales, Swatch lost 1,800 of its 3,000 U.S. distribution outlets between 1994 and 1995.

Swatch is now fighting back with a revitalized marketing strategy. As Swatch's founder and head says, "We were stupid enough to continue letting department stores sell the product as a fashion item alone. We forgot to market Swatch not only as an emotional product but also as a technically advanced product." The overriding question facing Swatch is whether the firm's typical watch product is a fad whose time has passed or whether it can be regenerated with its new marketing strategy.

Swatch recently hired the former head of Swatch in Italy to turn the company around. It has introduced a line of heavier metal watches (priced at $55 to $75)—designed to appeal to older customers. Although its earlier ads were cute and provocative, Swatch's current ads simply portray its watches against a metal backdrop. Swatch's new head of U.S. marketing, in commenting about its older ads, noted, "We were trying to be crazy, a little provocative, and it didn't work [long] in the United States." To drive home its new products and revised target market strategy, Swatch doubled its 1994 advertising budget in 1995 (to around $12 million). And, Swatch invested $40 million to become the official timekeeper for the 1996 Summer Olympic Games in Atlanta. SMH hoped the Olympic Games expenditure would result in the general public perceiving the Swatch name more as a precision timekeeping mechanism than as a fashion item.

QUESTIONS

1. Characterize Swatch's original and current watch models in terms of their being modifications, minor innovations, and major innovations. Explain your answer.
2. Describe the differential advantages of Swatch's current watch models. What results must these watches achieve to be deemed a "success"? Why?
3. What other strategies can Swatch use to prolong the maturity stage of the product life cycle for its watches?
4. Discuss the diffusion process as it pertains to Swatch watches.

*The data in this case are drawn from Joshua Levine, "Swatch Out!" *Forbes* (June 5, 1995), pp. 150–152.

CASE 2

Allegheny Ludlum: Extending the Product Life Cycle for Stainless Steel†

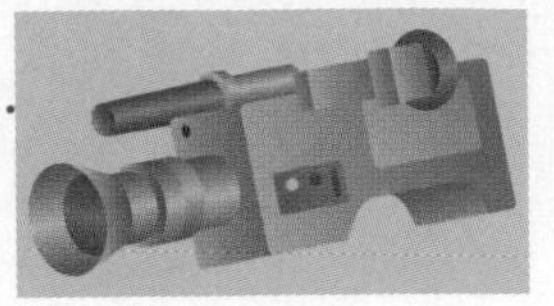

Allegheny Ludlum is North America's largest producer of specialty steel products, with annual sales exceeding $1 billion. Two-thirds of revenues are from consumer durables industries; the rest are from capital goods industries. Stainless steel accounts for 78 per cent of company sales, silicon electrical steel 13 per cent, and other specialty alloys 9 per cent.

In recent years, the annual industry sales-growth rate for stainless steel has been in the double-digit range. Nonetheless, Allegheny Ludlum predicts that long-term annual growth for stainless steel will be in the four to six per cent range. At Allegheny Ludlum, this solid growth will be due to its constant attention to improving production efficiency to control costs and the regular introductions of new applications of this mature product.

A recent *Harvard Business Review* article cited Allegheny Ludlum for embracing lean manufacturing practices. Through these practices, Allegheny Ludlum doubled its capacity at a melt shop without the need for any physical expansion. In its "lean" manufacturing, the firm actively uses team-based decision making. For example, one team concentrates on increasing batch sizes, a second focuses on reducing the time between batches, and a third develops computer programs to increase control over the melting process.

Its production efficiency gives Allegheny Ludlum a big cost advantage over other producers. It also lets the firm price products on a more competitive basis with such substitutes as aluminum, brass, and coated carbon steel.

Stainless steel's continued popularity is also due to its versatility. Firms can vary the alloys used in stainless steel to change its resistance to corrosion, heat, and abrasion. In addition, by varying alloys, the strength, toughness, hardness, and hygienic properties can be modified. Thus, stainless steel is now more widely used in autos, processing applications, and household appliances.

During the last 18 years, the auto industry has increased its use of stainless steel per vehicle from 10 pounds to over 70 pounds. By the end of this decade, some analysts believe the amount will rise to 100 pounds per car. Newer applications of stainless steel involve catalytic convertors—made with Allegheny Ludlum's proprietary ALFA IV alloy. These converters are smaller, lighter, and more effective than conventional converters. The use of stainless steel in fuel tanks, fuel hoses, and other parts is also expected to increase due to the corrosive nature of ethanol and methanol—which are used to reduce automobile emissions.

When stainless steel was first introduced, one of its early applications was for food and dairy processing equipment due to the sanitary nature of this metal. Today, Paul Mueller Company uses thousands of tons of stainless steel sheet to produce processing tanks used in the dairy, beverage, food, and chemical processing industries. Some of the firm's processing silos have capacities as large as 60,000 gallons and are 72 feet high.

Allegheny Ludlum provides a major component for AURA superinsulation, a new product by Owens-Corning. A one-inch panel of this material provides as much insulation as almost twelve inches of standard fiberglass insulation or five inches of refrigeration foam-based insulation. AURA superinsulation is used by Whirlpool in the United States and Europe, and by Lec Refrigeration in Great Britain. AURA enables refrigerator makers to meet demanding energy efficiency standards while having larger interiors (due to the ultra-high efficiency of the insulation).

QUESTIONS

1. How would you explain the long life cycle for stainless steel?
2. Apply the strategies suggested in Table 13-1 to stainless steel.
3. As a purchasing agent, what factors would you consider in deciding whether to buy Allegheny Ludlum's proprietary ALFA IV alloy? Why?
4. What criteria should Allegheny Ludlum use to determine which stainless steel applications it should drop? Explain your answer.

VIDEO QUESTIONS ON ALLEGHENY LUDLUM

1. What properties of stainless steel make it particularly attractive as a basic ingredient in new products?
2. What new products and markets does the video identify that have successfully utilized stainless steel since 1936?

†The data in this case are drawn from *Allegheny Ludlum Corporation 1994 Annual Report*; Robert H. Hayes and Gary P. Pisano, "Beyond World Class: The New Manufacturing Strategy," *Harvard Business Review*, Vol. 72 (January–February 1994), pp. 77–86; and "Stainless Shines," *Forbes* (January 30, 1995), p. 145.

14 Branding and Packaging

Chapter Objectives

1. To define and distinguish among branding terms and to examine thc importance of branding

2. To study the key branding decisions that must be made regarding corporate symbols, the branding philosophy, the choice of brand names, and the use of trademarks

3. To define and distinguish among packaging terms and to examine the importance of packaging

4. To study the basic functions of packaging, key factors in packaging decisions, and criticisms of packaging

Louis Vuitton, the French maker of luxury products, has had to fight against fake goods since the very beginnings of the company. In 1896, Georges Vuitton created the famous "LV" monogram (in honor of his father, Louis Vuitton) precisely to stop counterfeiting of the canvas used to cover his baggage trunks.

Genuine bag at left, fake at right. Reprinted by permission of Louis Vuitton Malletier.

According to the International Anti-Counterfeiting Coalition, each year, companies around the world lose hundreds of billions of dollars on products that are either outright counterfeits or pirated versions of trademarked or copyrighted materials. Counterfeit products involve everything from Louis Vuitton leather bags to Head & Shoulder's shampoo.

Because counterfeiting is a serious problem, the Louis Vuitton Malletier company invests considerable resources to fight against this fraud throughout the five continents. For instance, by taking steps to dismantle illegal manufacturing and distribution networks, the firm tries to remove the sources of operations, which are sometimes very professionally organized. Thus, it initiates seizures of fake goods around the world with the assistance of local police and customs officials, and systematically takes legal action.

In the United States, Louis Vuitton Malletier's anti-counterfeiting fight stretches from New York to Texas and from California to Florida, where the various forms of counterfeiting take place: importers and wholesalers in Los Angeles, New York City, and Atlanta; specialized retail stores in tourist areas; street vendors in New York City; and flea markets in Florida and middle America. Most counterfeit goods are imported from Southeast Asia, mainly South Korea, via Los Angeles.

There is close cooperation between Louis Vuitton Malletier and U.S. officials (Customs and FBI officials, as well as state and local authorities) to conduct raids, seize counterfeit goods, and arrest offending parties. Recent passage of tougher U.S. and state anti-counterfeiting laws (especially in New York, California, and Florida) reflects a growing recognition of this problem and certainly helps the battle against counterfeiting.

At the same time, Louis Vuitton Malletier tries to increase consumers' awareness of counterfeiting. As the firm says, "It goes without saying that the poor quality of the counterfeits has nothing in common with the superb craftsmanship which sets apart the genuine Louis Vuitton products. Thus, the actual and potential clients must be aware that Louis Vuitton products are exclusively sold at the company's stores and leased departments in upscale department stores. A 'Louis Vuitton' product bought in a flea market, in the street, or even at 'home parties' is definitely a fake."

The company even issues consumer tips: "Know a fake when you see one. Some details easily help you to distinguish an authentic Louis Vuitton bag from a counterfeit. A genuine Louis Vuitton always has a leather trim, never plastic; and never bears any patch logo on the outside." See the photos above.

Trademark owners and consumers both always lose in counterfeiting. The rightful trademark owners must incur costs to investigate the source of the counterfeit products, make consumers aware of the counterfeit products, and offer restitution. Consumers also lose in terms of poorer quality products, possible safety risks, and the inconvenience in returning products.[1]

Next, we will study various aspects of both branding and packaging. We will see how firms make such decisions as what corporate symbols to use, what emphasis to place on manufacturer versus private brands, and the basic functions of packaging.

[1] 1996 correspondence from Louis Vuitton Malletier; and Laurel Wentz, "Cachet and Carry," *Advertising Age* (February 12, 1996), pp. I-15–I-16, I-18.

Overview

Brands *identify a firm's products;* **packages** *are product containers that serve many functions.*

When conceiving, developing, and managing its products, a firm needs to make and enact a variety of decisions regarding the brand and package used with each item. A **brand** is a name, term, design, symbol, or any other feature that identifies the goods and services of one seller from those of other sellers. A **package** is a container used to protect, promote, transport, and/or identify a product.[2] It may consist of a product's physical container, an outer label, and/or inserts.

In this chapter, the various types of brand designations, key branding decisions, the basic functions of packaging, key packaging decisions, and selected criticisms of packaging are discussed.

Branding

Branding involves **brand names, brand marks, trade characters,** *and* **trademarks.**

An important part of product planning is *branding*, the procedure a firm follows in researching, developing, and implementing its brand(s). As just noted, a brand is a name, term, design, or symbol (or combination of these) that identifies the products of a seller or group of sellers. By establishing well-known brands, firms are better able to obtain acceptance, distributor cooperation, and above-average prices.

There are four types of brand designation:

1. A **brand name** is a word, letter (number), group of words, or letters (numbers) that can be spoken. Examples are Magnavox, Windows 95, and Lipton Cup-a-Soup.
2. A **brand mark** is a symbol, design, or distinctive coloring or lettering that cannot be spoken. Examples are Lexus' stylized L crest, Ralston Purina's checkerboard, and Prudential's rock.
3. A **trade character** is a brand mark that is personified. Examples are Qantas Airlines' koala bear, McDonald's Ronald McDonald, and the Pillsbury Doughboy.
4. A **trademark** is a brand name, brand mark, or trade character or combination thereof that is given legal protection. When it is used, a registered trademark is followed by ®. Examples are Scotch Brand® tape and MasterCard®.

Brand names, brand marks, and trade characters do not offer legal protection against use by competitors, unless registered as trademarks (which all of the preceding examples have been). Trademarks ensure exclusivity for trademark owners or those securing their permission and provide legal remedies against firms using "confusingly similar" names, designs, or symbols. Trademarks are discussed more fully later in the chapter.

Branding started during the Middle Ages, when craft and merchant guilds required producers to mark goods so output could be restricted and inferior goods traced to each producer. The marks also served as standards for quality when items were sold outside the local markets in which the guilds operated. The earliest and most aggressive promoters of brands in the United States were patent medicine manufacturers. Examples of current U.S. brands that started more than 100 years ago are Borden's Eagle Brand Condensed Milk, Vaseline Petroleum Jelly, and Pillsbury's Best Flour. Morton Salt's little girl with an umbrella is an 85-year-old trade character that has been used with the slogan, "When it rains it pours." Although Morton's little girl has never aged, she has been updated with new hairstyles and dresses several times over the years.

Worldwide, there are now millions of brand names in circulation. Each year, the top hundred U.S. advertisers spend over $45 billion advertising their brands. Permanent media expenditures (such as company logos, stationery, brochures, business forms and cards, and vehicular and building signs) for brands are another large marketing cost. For instance, when Allied-Signal decided to remove its hyphen and become AlliedSignal, it cost $500,000 for new stationery, signs, and so forth.

[2]Peter D. Bennett (Editor), *Dictionary of Marketing Terms*, Second Edition (Chicago: American Marketing Association, 1995), pp. 27, 201.

FIGURE 14-1
The Most Popular and Powerful Brand in the World
Reprinted by permission.

A key goal of firms is to develop brand loyalty, which allows them to maximize sales and maintain a strong brand image. As one expert noted:

> Brands work by facilitating and making more effective the customer's choice process. Every day an individual makes hundreds of consumer decisions. He or she is besieged by countless products and messages competing for attention. To make life bearable and to simplify this decision-making process, the individual looks for shortcuts. The most important of these is to rely on habit—buy brands that have proved satisfactory in the past.[3]

Sometimes, brands do so well that they gain "power" status—they are both well known and highly esteemed. At present, according to a survey of 25,300 people in 16 nations, the world's ten most powerful brands are (in order) Coca-Cola, Kodak, Sony, Mercedes-Benz, Pepsi-Cola, Nestlé, Gillette, Colgate, Adidas, and Volkwagen. The ten brands with the greatest "vitality"—global growth potential—are Coca-Cola, Nike, Adidas, Sony, Ferrari, Reebok, Disney, Porsche, Pepsi-Cola, and Mercedes-Benz.[4] See Figure 14-1.

Brand rankings do differ by region. Thus, in China, six of the top ten brands are from Japan, led by Hitachi; three are from the United States—Coca-Cola, Mickey Mouse, and Marlboro; and one is from China—Tsing Tao (beer).[5] Europeans favor such brands as BMW, Porsche, and Rolls-Royce. Sony is the most powerful brand for Japanese consumers. To Americans, the top brands include Coca-Cola, Campbell, Disney, Pepsi-Cola, Kodak, NBC, Black & Decker, Kellogg, McDonald's, and Hershey.

The use of popular brands can also speed up public acceptance and gain reseller cooperation for new products. For instance, here's a product that gained quick public approval and dealer enthusiasm:

> In mid-1992, Gillette Company unveiled its Sensor for Women razor. Within six months, the stout green-and-white gadgets—designed to give women a better shave in the shower—had a

[3]Peter Doyle, "Building Successful Brands: The Strategic Options," *Journal of Consumer Marketing*, Vol. 7 (Spring 1990), p. 7.

[4]Laurel Wentz, "Upstart Brands Steal Spotlight from Perennials," *Advertising Age* (September 19, 1994), pp. I-13–I-14.

[5]Kevin Goldman, "U.S. Brands Lag Behind Japanese in Name Recognition by Chinese," *Wall Street Journal* (February 16, 1995), p. B8.

> 36 per cent dollar share of the total U.S. women's razor market. Sensor for Women represents Boston-based Gillette's best effort yet to pitch shavers to women. Although Gillette also sells such products as Oral-B toothbrushes and Soft & Dri deodorant, to many consumers its name is synonymous with razors and blades.[6]

Today, annual sales of Sensor for Women exceed $50 million. And it is, by far, the leading product in its category—with foreign revenues growing rapidly.

Gaining and maintaining brand recognition is often a top priority for all kinds of firms. As an example, the major U.S. TV networks (ABC, CBS, Fox, and NBC) "are facing increasing competition and are very conscious of the need to get their brands out there. As more choices are given to consumers, networks have to make sure their viewers understand who they are and what they offer. That can mean anything from a logo subtly popping up in the corner of the viewer's TV screen to a major cross-promotion with some big-name packaged goods marketers."[7]

Brand equity *represents a brand's worth.*

In recent years, a new branding concept—which more concretely recognizes the worth of brands—has emerged. It is known as **brand equity** and measures the "financial impact associated with an increase in a product's value accounted for by its brand name above and beyond the level justified by its quality (as determined by its configuration of brand attributes, product features, or physical characteristics)."[8] As one expert noted,

> In a general sense, brand equity is defined in terms of the marketing effects uniquely attributable to the brand—for example, when certain outcomes result from the marketing of a good or service because of its brand name that would not occur if the same good or service did not have that name. A brand is said to have positive (negative) customer-based brand equity if consumers react more (less) favorably to the product, price, promotion, or distribution of the brand than they do the same marketing-mix element when it is attributed to a fictitiously named or unnamed version of the good or service.[9]

According to *Financial World*, the fifteen most valuable brands in the world—based on sales, profitability, and growth potential—are Coca-Cola, Marlboro, IBM, Motorola, Hewlett-Packard, Microsoft, Kodak, Budweiser, Kellogg, Nescafé, Intel, Gillette, Pepsi-Cola, GE, and Levi's.[10]

Here is an example of how the brand equity concept can be applied. When Cadbury Schweppes acquired the Hires and Crush soda lines from Procter & Gamble, it paid $220 million. Twenty million dollars of that amount was for physical assets and the balance was for "brand value."[11] Brand equity is even higher when licensing royalties can be generated from other firms' use of the brand, such as occurs with trade characters like Walt Disney's Mickey Mouse. Nonetheless, there are no widely approved techniques for assessing overall brand equity.

Branding creates identities, assures quality, and performs other functions. **Brand images** *are the perceptions that consumers have of particular brands.*

These reasons summarize why branding is important:

- Product identification is eased. A customer can order a product by name instead of description.
- Customers are assured that a good or service has a certain level of quality and that they will obtain comparable quality if the same brand is reordered.

[6]Kathleen Deveny, "Sensor Gets Big Edge in Women's Razors," *Wall Street Journal* (December 17, 1992), pp. B1, B10. See also Laurie Freeman, "Sensor Still Helping Gillette Fend Off Razor Challenges," *Advertising Age* (September 28, 1994), p. 21; and Barbara Carton, "Gillette Looks Beyond Whiskers to Big Hair and Stretchy Floss," *Wall Street Journal* (December 14, 1994), pp. B1, B4.

[7]Cyndee Miller, "Stay Tuned for TV Networks as Brands," *Marketing News* (October 9, 1995), pp. 1, 10.

[8]Morris B. Holbrook, "Product Quality, Attributes, and Brand Names as Determinants of Price: The Case of Consumer Electronics," *Marketing Letters*, Vol. 1 (1992), p. 72.

[9]Kevin Lane Keller, "Conceptualizing, Measuring, and Managing Customer-Based Brand Equity," *Journal of Marketing*, Vol. 57 (January 1993), pp. 1, 8. See also David A. Aaker, *Managing Brand Equity* (New York: Free Press, 1991); David C. Bello and Morris B. Holbrook, "Does an Absence of Brand Equity Generalize Across Product Categories?" *Journal of Business Research*, Vol. 34 (October 1995), pp. 125–131; and Betsy Morris, "The Brand's the Thing," *Fortune* (March 4, 1996), pp. 72–86.

[10]"Coke Is Still It," *Advertising Age* (July 17, 1995), p. 8.

[11]Peter H. Farquhar, Julia Y. Han, and Yuji Ijiri, "Brands on the Balance Sheet," *Marketing Management*, Vol. 1 (Winter 1992), pp. 16–22.

International Marketing in *Action*

Will Owens-Corning's Panther Be Pink in Europe?

To boost its brand image in Europe, Owens-Corning Fiberglas Corporation recently acquired the global rights to the Pink Panther through the year 2000. The Pink Panther has been the firm's U.S. trade character since 1980.

Owens-Corning was able to secure these rights after IBM let its exclusive global rights to the character expire in 1994. IBM decided to create and reinforce a single image for its PC line (not tied to a trade character) throughout the world. Owens-Corning's director for global branding programs noted that, "The money IBM spent on the Panther could help us in the notoriety of our character."

According to Owens-Corning's director for global branding programs, "The Panther has been very strong for us; he's catchy, he's different, and he's been a terrific ambassador for us in the United States." To coordinate its overall branding program with the Pink Panther, Owens-Corning even trademarked the color pink for its insulation material.

Although the Pink Panther is well known in Europe due to its use by IBM, Owens-Corning decided to thoroughly research the Pink Panther's image. It also studied the attitudes of European contractors and homeowners regarding the use of the color pink for its insulation. Market analysts estimate that the home improvement market in Europe is $73 billion a year, as compared to the $117 billion U.S. market.

Some marketing experts say it is common for trade characters, such as Snoopy, to be used by multiple firms. There are also promotional economies to using a single trade character in multiple markets with regard to reduced production costs for advertising and the spillover of promotions from one market area to another.

As a marketing consultant to Owens-Corning, evaluate its decision to use the Pink Panther as its trade character on a worldwide basis.

Source: Based on material in Kim Cleland, "Owens Takes Brand Abroad," *Business Marketing* (December 1994), p. 2.

- The firm responsible for the product is known. The producer of unbranded items cannot be as directly identified.
- Price comparisons are reduced when customers perceive distinct brands. This is most likely if special attributes are linked to different brands.
- A firm can advertise (position) its products and associate each brand and its characteristics in the buyer's mind. This aids the consumer in forming a **brand image**, which is the perception a person has of a particular brand. It is "a mirror reflection (though perhaps inaccurate) of the brand personality or product being. It is what people believe about a brand—their thoughts, feelings, expectations."[12]
- Branding helps segment markets by creating tailored images. By using two or more brands, multiple market segments can be attracted. Figure 14-2 highlights Black & Decker's DeWalt brand and the image it presents.
- For socially-visible goods and services, a product's prestige is enhanced via a strong brand name.

[12]Bennett, *Dictionary of Marketing Terms*, p. 28. See also Ernest Dichter, "What's in an Image," *Journal of Product & Brand Management*, Vol. 1 (Spring 1992), pp. 54–60.

FIGURE 14-2
Differentiated Marketing Through the DeWalt Brand
When Black & Decker determined that professional tool users did not have a high enough regard for the Black & Decker tool line (which appealed mostly to the do-it-yourself market), the firm introduced a new tool line under the DeWalt name. DeWalt tools are bright yellow and black, have more features, and are sturdier than Black & Decker tools. They are also very popular with their chosen target market.
Reprinted by permission.

- People feel less risk when buying a brand with which they are familiar and for which they have a favorable attitude. This is why brand loyalty occurs.
- Cooperation from resellers is greater for well-known brands. A strong brand also may let its producer exert more control in the distribution channel.
- A brand may help sell an entire line of products, such as Kellogg cereals.
- A brand may help enter a new product category, like Reese's peanut butter.
- "A product is something made in a factory [or offered by a service firm]; a brand is something bought by a customer. A product can be copied by a competitor; a brand is unique. A product can be quickly outdated; a successful brand is timeless."[13]

There are four branding decisions a firm must undertake. These involve corporate symbols, the branding philosophy, choosing a brand name, and using trademarks. See Figure 14-3.

Corporate Symbols

Corporate symbols *help establish a companywide image.*

Corporate symbols are a firm's name (and/or divisional names), logo(s), and trade character(s). They are significant parts of an overall company image. If a firm begins a business; merges with another company; reduces or expands product lines; seeks new geographic markets; or finds its name to be unwieldy, nondistinctive, or confusing, it needs to evaluate and possibly change its corporate symbols. Here are examples of each situation.

Fifteen years ago, a new PC maker hired a consultant to devise a company name. It wanted a name that "would be memorable and at the same time take command of the idea of portableness; something that would distinguish it from all other IBM PC compatibles." The consultant recommended a name combining two syllables representing "communications" and "small but important." Today, Compaq is one of the 100 largest firms in the United States.[14]

As a result of mergers, Burroughs and Sperry are now Unisys; the Bank of Virginia and Maryland's Union Trust are Signet; Bristol-Myers and Squibb are Bristol-Myers Squibb;

[13]Stephen King, WPP Group, London, as quoted in Aaker, *Managing Brand Equity*, p. 1.

[14]Robert A. Mamis, "Name-Calling," *Inc.* (July 1984), pp. 67–74; and "Fortune 500," *Fortune* (May 15, 1995), pp. F-3–F-4.

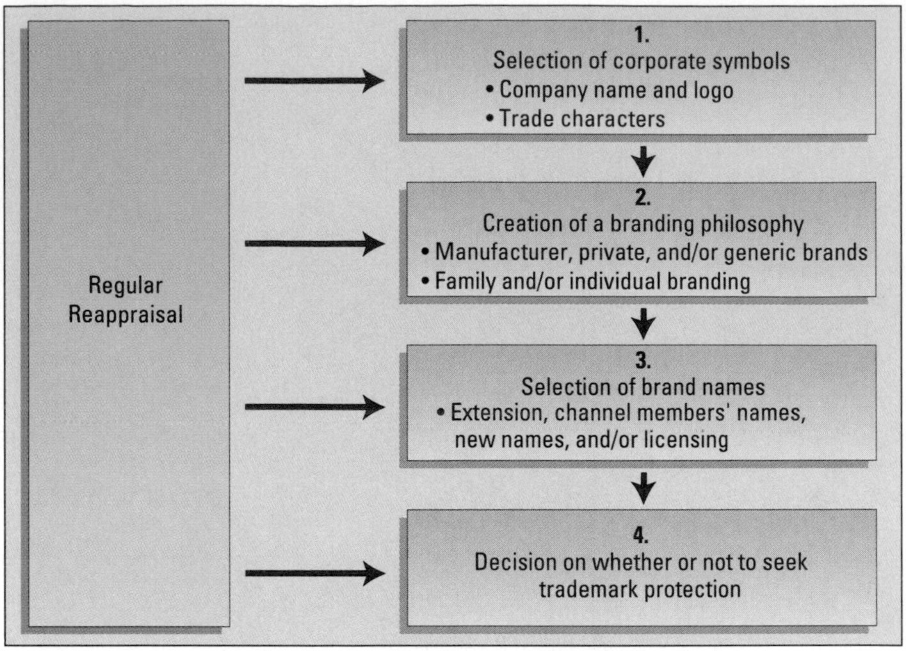

FIGURE 14-3
Branding Decisions

Time Inc. and Warner Communication are Time Warner; and General Cinema and Harcourt Brace & Company are Harcourt General. And after Sony acquired Loews Theatres, it converted the name to Sony Theatres.

Because the nature of its business changed, International Harvester is now Navistar International (after selling its farm equipment business) and General Shoe Corporation is Genesco (a diversified retailer). Boston Chicken recently switched to Boston Market due to its expanded restaurant menu—which includes turkey, ham, meat loaf, and so forth, as well as chicken.

When it expanded into new geographic markets, Allegheny Airlines changed its name to USAir; the old name suggested a small regional airline. The Exxon name was developed because the firm's regional brands, including Esso and Humble, could not be used nationwide, and other brands had unfortunate foreign connotations (for example, Enco means "stalled car" in Japanese).

The National Railroad Passenger Corporation was an unwieldy name; it became Amtrak. Federal Express now promotes the FedEx name, since it is easier to say. United Telecommunications converted its nondistinctive name to Sprint, in recognition of its leading brand. The name of the upscale Holiday Inn Crowne Plaza hotels was changed to Crowne Plaza to avoid confusion about the middle-class Holiday Inn name.

Developing and maintaining appropriate corporate symbols are not easy tasks. For example, when Nissan Motor Corporation changed the name of its U.S. car division from Datsun to Nissan (to have a global brand), sales fell dramatically, despite a major ad campaign. It took years for the Nissan name to reach the level of brand awareness that Datsun had attained. Along the way, Nissan had numerous clashes with dealers not wanting the name change.

Branding Philosophy

While developing a brand strategy, a firm needs to determine its branding philosophy. This philosophy outlines the use of manufacturer, private, and/or generic brands, as well as the use of family and/or individual branding.

Manufacturer brands *are well known and heavily promoted.*

Manufacturer, Private, and Generic Brands[15] **Manufacturer brands** use the names of their makers. They generate the vast majority of U.S. revenues for most prod-

[15]For a good overview of this topic, see John A. Quelch and David Harding, "Brands Versus Private Labels," *Harvard Business Review*, Vol. 74 (January–February 1996), pp. 99–109; Marcia Mogelonsky, "When Stores Become Brands," *American Demographics* (February 1995), pp. 32–38; and "Special Report: Brand Power," *Progressive Grocer* (October 1994), supplement.

uct categories, such as over 85 per cent of food, all autos, 75 per cent of major appliances, and more than 80 per cent of gasoline. They appeal to a wide range of people who desire low risk of poor product performance, good quality, routine purchases, status, and convenience shopping. The brands are often well known and trusted because quality control is strictly maintained. They are identifiable and present distinctive images. Producers may have a number of product alternatives under their brands.

Manufacturers have better channel control over their own brands, which may be sold via many competing intermediaries. Yet, individual resellers can have lower investments if the brands' pre-sold nature makes turnover high—and if manufacturers spend large sums promoting their brands and sponsor cooperative ads with resellers (so costs are shared). Prices are the highest of the three brands, with the bulk going to the manufacturer (which also has the greatest profit). The marketing goal is to attract and retain loyal consumers for these brands, and for their makers to direct the marketing effort for the brands.

Private (dealer) brands *enable channel members to get loyal customers.*

Private (dealer) brands use names designated by their resellers, usually wholesalers or retailers—including service providers. They account for sizable U.S. revenues in many categories, such as 50 per cent of shoes, one-third of tires, 14 per cent of food items, and one-quarter of major appliances. And unit market shares are even higher. For instance, private brands account for 20 per cent of unit food sales in supermarkets. Some firms, such as The Limited and McDonald's, even derive most revenues from their own brands. Private-brand foods are more popular in Europe than in the United States. They generate 28 per cent of revenues in British grocery stores and about 20 to 24 per cent in French and German ones.[16]

Private brands appeal to price-conscious people who buy them if they feel the brands offer good quality at a lower price. They accept some risk as to quality, but reseller loyalty causes the people to see the brands as reliable. Private brands often have similar quality to manufacturer brands, with less emphasis on packaging. At times, they are made to dealer specifications. Assortments are smaller and the brands are unknown to people not shopping with a given reseller. Resellers have more exclusive rights for these brands, and are more responsible for distribution and larger purchases. Inventory turnover may be lower than for manufacturer brands; and promotion and pricing are the reseller's job. Due to lower per-unit packaging and promotion costs, resellers can sell private brands at lower prices and still have better per-unit profits (due to their higher share of the selling price). The marketing goal is to attract people who become loyal to the reseller and for that firm to exert control over marketing. Large resellers advertise their brands widely. Some private brands, such as Sears' Kenmore brand, are as popular as manufacturer brands; and firms like Sherwin-Williams are both manufacturers and retailers.

Generic brands *are low-priced items with little advertising.*

Generic brands emphasize the names of the products themselves and not manufacturer or reseller names. They started in the drug industry as low-cost alternatives to expensive manufacturer brands. Today, generics have expanded into cigarettes, batteries, motor oil, and other products. Forty per cent of U.S. prescriptions are filled with generics; but, due to their low prices, this is only 8 per cent of prescription-drug revenues. Although 85 per cent of U.S. supermarkets stock generics, they account for under 1 per cent of supermarket revenues. Generics appeal to price-conscious, careful shoppers, who perceive them as being a very good value, are sometimes willing to accept lower quality, and often purchase for large families or large organizations.

Generics are seldom advertised and receive poor shelf locations; consumers must search out these brands. Prices are less than other brands by anywhere from 10 to 50 per cent, due to quality, packaging, assortment, distribution, and promotion economies. The major marketing goal is to offer low-priced, lower-quality items to consumers interested in price savings. Table 14-1 compares the three types of brands.

[16]Chad Rubel, "Price, Quality Important for Private Label Goods," *Marketing News* (January 2, 1995), p. 24; E. S. Browning, "Europeans Witness Proliferation of Private Labels," *Wall Street Journal* (October 20, 1992), pp. B1, B5; Laurel Wentz, "Private Labels March in Europe Too," *Advertising Age* (May 9, 1994), p. 53; and Tara Parker-Pope, "U.K. Grocer Aims to Bag U.S. Customers," *Wall Street Journal* (May 16, 1995), p. A14.

Table 14-1
Manufacturer, Private, and Generic Brands

CHARACTERISTIC	MANUFACTURER BRAND	PRIVATE BRAND	GENERIC BRAND
Target market	Risk avoider, quality conscious, brand loyal, status conscious, quick shopper	Price conscious, comparison shopper, quality conscious, moderate risk taker, dealer loyal	Price conscious, careful shopper, willing to accept lower quality, large family or organization
Product	Well known, trusted, best quality control, clearly identifiable, deep product line	Same overall quality as manufacturer, less emphasis on packaging, less assortment, not known to nonshoppers of the dealer	Usually less overall quality than manufacturer, little emphasis on packaging, very limited assortment, not well known
Distribution	Often sold at many competing dealers	Usually only available from a particular dealer in the area	Varies
Promotion	Manufacturer-sponsored ads, cooperative ads	Dealer-sponsored ads	Few ads, secondary shelf space
Price	Highest, usually suggested by manufacturer	Moderate, usually controlled by dealer	Lowest, usually controlled by dealer
Marketing focus	To generate brand loyalty and manufacturer control	To generate dealer loyalty and control	To offer a low-priced, lesser-quality item to those desiring it

A **mixed-brand strategy** *combines brand types.*

Many companies—including service firms—use a **mixed-brand strategy,** thereby selling both manufacturer and private brands (and maybe generic brands). This benefits manufacturers and resellers: There is control over the brand bearing each seller's name. Exclusive rights to a brand can be gained. Multiple segments may be targeted. Brand and dealer loyalty are fostered, shelf locations coordinated, cooperation in the distribution channel improved, and assortments raised. Production is stabilized and excess capacity used. Sales are maximized and profits fairly shared. Planning is better. For example, in Japan, Kodak markets its own brand of film and COOP private-brand film (for the 2,500-store Japanese Consumer Cooperative Union). By doing this, it hopes to make a dent in Fuji's 75 per cent share of the Japanese market. To date, Kodak does not market private-brand film in the United States.[17]

In the **battle of the brands,** *the three brand types compete.*

Manufacturer, private, and generic brands also repeatedly engage in a **battle of the brands,** in which each strives to gain a greater share of the consumer's dollar, control over marketing strategy, consumer loyalty, product distinctiveness, maximum shelf space and locations, and a large share of profits. In recent years, this battle has been intensifying:

> You know the old joke: Just because you're paranoid doesn't mean that they're not out to get you. In a nutshell, that describes how manufacturers of brand-name products react to competition from private labels. On one hand, manufacturers have the right to be concerned: There are more private labels on the market than ever before. Collectively, private labels in the United States command higher unit shares than the strongest national brands in 77 of 250 supermarket product categories. But on the other hand, many manufacturers have overreacted to the threat posed by private labels without fully recognizing two essential points. First, private-label strength generally varies with economic conditions. Second, through their actions, manufacturers of brand-name products can temper the challenge posed by private labels.[18]

[17]Wendy Bounds, "Kodak Pursues a Greater Market Share in Japan with New Private-Label Film," *Wall Street Journal* (March 7, 1995), p. B9.

[18]Quelch and Harding, "Brands Versus Private Labels," pp. 99–100.

Family (blanket) branding *uses a single name for many products.*

Family and Multiple Branding In family (blanket) branding, one name is used for two or more individual products. Many firms selling industrial goods and services (such as Boeing and Airborne Express), as well as those selling consumer services (such as Teléfonos de México), use some form of family branding for all or most of their products. Other companies employ a family brand for each category of products. For example, Sears has Kenmore appliances and Craftsman tools. Family branding can be applied to both manufacturer and private brands, and to both domestic and international (global) brands.

Family branding is best for specialized firms or ones with narrow product lines. Companies capitalize on a uniform, well-known image and promote the same name regularly—keeping promotion costs down. The major disadvantages are that differentiated marketing opportunities may be low (if only one brand is used to target all of a firm's customers), company image may be adversely affected if vastly different products (such as men's and women's cologne) carry one name, and innovativeness may not be projected to consumers.

Brand extension *gains quick acceptance.*

Brand extension, whereby an established name is applied to new products, is an effective use of family branding. Quick customer acceptance may be gained since people are familiar with existing products having the same name, a favorable brand image can be carried over to a new product, and the risk of a failure is less. Figure 14-4 shows how Campbell has applied brand extension to its chicken noodle soup line. Keep in mind that brand extension may have a negative effect if people do not see some link between the original product and a new one. Most new products now use some form of brand extension.

These are seven situations in which brand extension could be effective:

1. Same product in a different form—example, Jell-O Pudding Pops.
2. Distinctive taste/ingredient/component in a new item—example, Arm & Hammer detergent.
3. New companion product—example, Colgate Plus toothbrush.
4. Same customer franchise for a new product (a different product offered to the same target market)—example, Visa traveler's checks aimed at Visa credit-card customers.
5. Expertise conveyed to new product—example, Canon bubble-jet printers.
6. Benefit/attribute/feature conveyed to new product—example, Ivory shampoo (which connotes mildness).
7. Designer image/status conveyed to new product—example, Pierre Cardin sunglasses.[19]

Individual (multiple) branding *uses distinct brands.*

With **individual (multiple) branding,** separate brands are used for different items or product lines sold by a firm. For example, in ConAgra's wide and deep product mix are 21 food brands that each chalk up annual retail sales of $100 million or more. See Figure 14-5.

Through individual branding, a firm can create multiple product positions (separate brand images), attract various market segments, increase sales and marketing control, and offer both premium and low-priced brands. Individual branding also lets manufacturers secure greater shelf space in retail stores. However, each brand requires its own promotion costs and there is no positive brand image rub-off. Economies from mass production may be lessened. New products may not benefit from an established identity. And there may be some cannibalization among company brands. Consumer products firms are more likely than industrial products firms to engage in individual branding.

To gain the benefits of family and individual branding, many firms combine the approaches. A firm could have a flagship brand and other secondary brands: One-third of Heinz's products have the Heinz name; the rest have names like StarKist, 9-Lives, Ore-Ida, and Weight Watchers. Or, a family brand could be used together with individual brands: At Honda, upscale Acura and mainstream Honda are the two auto lines. The Honda line includes the Honda Accord, Honda Civic, and Honda Prelude. It has an overall image and targets a specific market. New models gain from the Honda name, and there

[19]Edward M. Tauber, "Brand Leverage: Strategy for Growth in a Cost-Controlled World," *Journal of Advertising Research*, Vol. 28 (August–September 1988), pp. 26–30.

FIGURE 14-6
Co-Branding: The Seiko Mickey Mouse Alarm Chronograph
Reprinted by permission.

may want to make into global brands, brands often must also reflect the cultural and societal divergencies in the way products are positioned and used in different nations. This illustrates why:

> The Lewis Woolf Griptight company makes infant and toddler products such as pacifiers. These products are sold in Great Britain and the United States. When it talked to parents in Great Britain about the Griptight brand name being used before a new line was launched, the company discovered that it was 'the most un-user-friendly name.' People thought it was a carpet glue, a denture fixative, a kind of tire. The brand name became Kiddiwinks, a British word for children. In the United States, however, recognition of the name Binky was high, with some consumers using it as a generic term for pacifiers—hence, the name Binkykids.[21]

Figure 14-7 shows CPC International's approach to international branding.

The **consumer's brand decision process** *moves from nonrecognition to insistence (or aversion).*

When branding, a firm should plan for the stages in the **consumer's brand decision process,** as displayed in Figure 14-8. For a new brand, a consumer begins with nonrecognition of the name, and the seller must make the person aware of it. He or she then moves to recognition, wherein the brand and its attributes are known, and the seller stresses persuasion. Next, the person develops a preference (or dislike) for a brand and buys it (or opts not to buy); the seller's task is to gain brand loyalty. Last, some people show a brand insistence (or aversion) and become loyal (or never buy); the seller's role is to maintain loyalty. Often times, people form preferences toward several brands but do not buy or insist upon one brand exclusively.

By using brand extension, a new product would begin at the recognition, preference, or insistence stage of the brand decision process because of the carryover effect of the established name. However, consumers who dislike the existing product line would be unlikely to try a new product under the same name, but they might try another company product under a different brand.

[21]Cyndee Miller, "Kiddi Just Fine in the U.K., But Here It's Binky," *Marketing News* (August 28, 1995), p. 8. See also Martin S. Roth, "The Effects of Culture and Socioeconomics on the Performance of Global Brand Image Strategies," *Journal of Marketing Research*, Vol. 32 (May 1995), pp. 163–175.

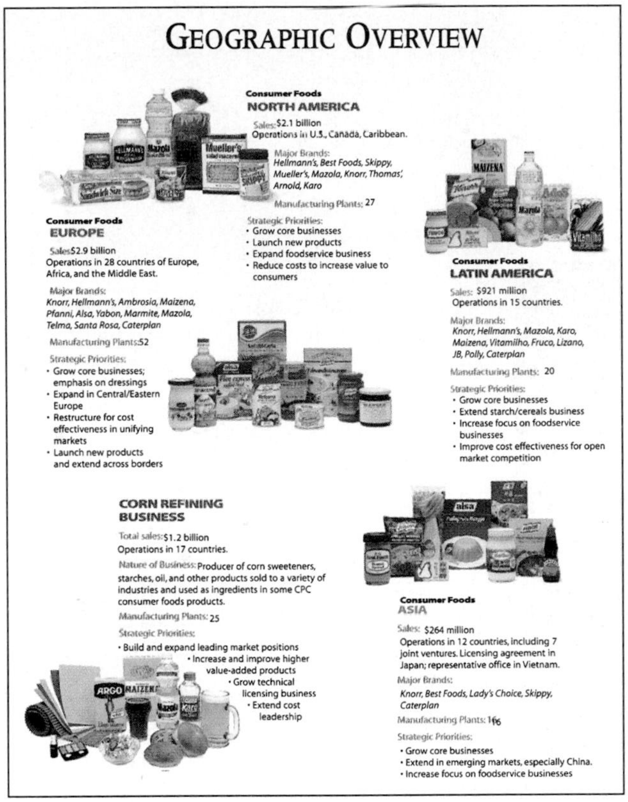

FIGURE 14-7
How CPC International Uses Its Brands Around the World
Reprinted by permission.

The Use of Trademarks

Trademark protection grants exclusive use of a brand or mark for as long as it is marketed.

Finally, a firm must decide whether to seek trademark protection.[22] In the United States, it would do so under either the federal Lanham Act (updated by the Trademark Law Revision Act) or state law. Trademarking gives a firm the exclusive use of a word, name, symbol, combination of letters or numbers, or other devices—such as distinctive packaging—to identify the goods and services of that firm and distinguish them from others for as long as they are marketed. Both trademarks (for goods) and service marks (for services) are covered by trademark law; and there are nearly 150,000 U.S. filings each year.

Trademarks are voluntary and require registration and implementation procedures that can be time-consuming and expensive (challenging a competitor may mean high legal fees and many years in court). A multinational firm must register trademarks in every nation in which it operates; even then, trademark rights may not be enforceable. For a trademark to be legally protected, it must have a distinct meaning that does not describe an entire

[22]See Dorothy Cohen, *Legal Issues in Marketing Decision Making* (Cincinnati: South-Western, 1995), pp. 111–136.

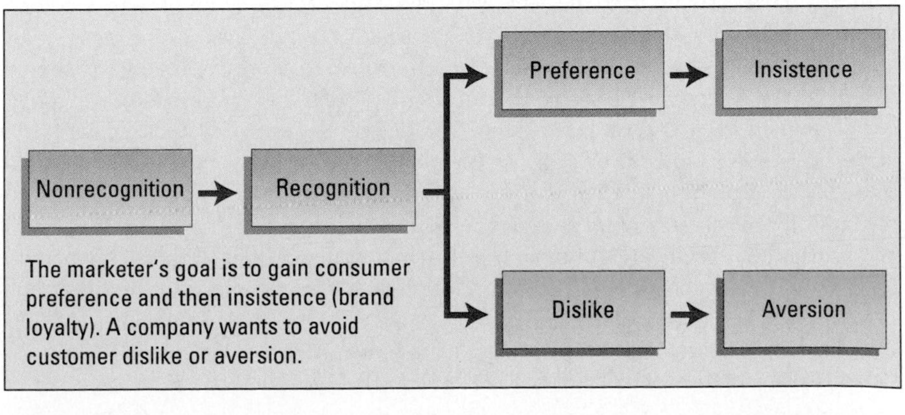

Nonrecognition
Recognition
Preference
Insistence
Dislike
Aversion
The marketer's goal is to gain consumer preference and then insistence (brand loyalty). A company wants to avoid customer dislike or aversion.

FIGURE 14-8
The Consumer's Brand Decision Process

Ethics IN TODAY'S SOCIETY

Is Going from "Light" to "Right" All Right?

According to the new U.S. Nutrition Labeling and Education Act, a food using the term "light" or "lite" must have half the fat content of the original product. To comply with the terms of this law, manufacturers can rename their products using different terms, such as "light taste," "right," "medium," or "smart" or remove more of the fat from these products.

The law does not impose maximum fat requirements on foods described as "light taste," "right," "medium," or "smart." However, it allows the use of the term "reduced fat" only if a "light" product has 25 per cent less fat than the original one.

The labeling law creates an ethical dilemma for a manufacturer when a brand name implies that the product is healthier than it really is. For example, Procter & Gamble (P&G) decided to rename its Pringles Light Chips, which contain one-third less fat than its regular potato chips, as Pringles Right Crisps. Despite the healthy-sounding name, Pringles Right Crisps are still high in fat content. Just 16 chips contain 11 per cent of an adult's daily fat. According to a P&G spokesperson, cutting more fat out was not possible without making the chips taste "very dry." A spokesperson for the American Dietetic Association says that many snack food and ice cream products labeled as "light" foods are still not healthy, despite reduced fat content.

In some cases, manufacturers have chosen not to reduce the fat content due to taste factors. These firms fear that poor tasting products will reduce brand loyalty and that taste may be a more important buying factor than health. So, they are not using any of the legally approved terms noted above.

As a newly appointed product manager for Pringles Right Crisps, prepare a report assessing its branding strategy.

Source: Based on material in Yumiko Ono, "Let There Be 'Right.' Food Marketers Seek Appetizing Alternatives to 'Light'," *Wall Street Journal* (August 4, 1994), pp. B1, B12.

product category, be used in interstate commerce (for federal protection), not be confusingly similar to other trademarks, and not imply attributes a product does not possess. A surname by itself cannot be registered because any person can generally do business under his or her name; it can be registered if used to describe a specific business (for example, McDonald's restaurants). The U.S. Supreme Court recently ruled that the color of a product could receive trademark protection, as long as it had achieved "secondary meaning," whereby the color distinguishes a particular brand and indicates its "source." The Court said: "If a shape, a sound, and a fragrance can act as symbols, can a color not do the same?"[23]

When brands become too popular or descriptive of a product category, they run the risk of becoming public property. A firm then loses its trademark position. Brands fighting to remain exclusive trademarks include L'eggs, Rollerblade, Xerox, Levi's, Plexiglas, Formica, Kleenex, and Teflon. Former trademarks that are now considered generic—and, thus, public property—are cellophane, aspirin, shredded wheat, cola, linoleum, monopoly, and lite beer.

DuPont has used careful research to retain a trademark for Teflon. Company surveys have showed that most people identify Teflon as a brand name. On the other hand, the

[23]Maxine S. Lans, "Supreme Court OKs Color as Trademark," *Marketing News* (May 8, 1995), p. 13; and Andrea Sachs, "High Court's Ruling May Color Ad Plans," *Advertising Age* (April 10, 1995), p. 30.

U.S. Supreme Court ruled that *Monopoly* was a generic term that could be used by any game maker; and a federal court ruled that Miller could not trademark the single word Lite for its lower-calorie beer.

Packaging

Packaging *involves decisions as to a product's physical container, label, and inserts.*

Packaging is the part of product planning where a firm researches, designs, and produces package(s). As noted at the beginning of the chapter, a package consists of a product's physical container, label, and/or inserts.

The physical container may be a cardboard, metal, plastic, or wooden box; a cellophane, waxpaper, or cloth wrapper; a glass, aluminum, or plastic jar or can; a paper bag; styrofoam; some other material; or a combination of these. Products may have more than one container: Cereal is individually packaged in small cardboard boxes, with inner waxpaper wrapping, and shipped in large corrugated boxes; watches are usually covered with cloth linings and shipped in plastic boxes. The label indicates a product's brand name, the company logo, ingredients, promotional messages, inventory codes, and/or instructions for use. Inserts are (1) instructions and safety information placed in drug, toy, and other packages or (2) coupons, prizes, or recipe booklets. They are used as appropriate.

Prior to the advent of the modern supermarket and department store, manufacturers commonly shipped merchandise in such bulk containers as cracker barrels, sugar sacks, and butter tubs. Retail merchants repackaged the contents into smaller, more convenient units to meet customer needs. With the growth of mass merchants and self-service, manufacturers came to realize the value of packaging as a marketing tool. Today, it is a vital part of a firm's product development strategy; a package may even be the product itself (such as the Reynolds Wrap shown in Figure 14-9) or an integral part of the product (such as the aerosol can for shaving cream).

Packaging plays a key role in helping consumers form perceptions about a product (brand). As one packaging expert noted, "Our experience, supported by research, indicates that the consumer does not conceptually strip away the packaging and consider the actual product when making a buying decision. For instance, in the case of food and bev-

FIGURE 14-9
The Package as the Product
Reprinted by permission.

erages, the package communicates a promise of quality, taste, and enjoyment, and the consumer expects the product inside to measure up. If it does not, or if the package fails to deliver on the product's promise, another product failure is the likely result."[24]

About 10 per cent of a typical product's final selling price goes for its packaging. The amount is higher for such products as cosmetics (as much as 40 per cent or more). The complete package redesign of a major product might cost millions of dollars for machinery and production. Packaging decisions must serve both resellers and consumers. Plans are often made in conjunction with production, logistics, and legal personnel. Errors in packaging can be costly.

Package redesign may occur when a firm's current packaging receives a poor response from channel members and customers or becomes too expensive; the firm seeks a new market segment, reformulates a product, or changes or updates its product positioning; or new technology becomes available. For instance,

> When Beverly Seckinger and Lee Buford started their gourmet-cookie company, they always carried cookie tins on sales calls to the Ritz-Carlton, Saks, and Neiman-Marcus. As annual sales reached $2 million, the partners heard complaints about their somewhat stark packages and hired a design firm. They needed a softer look, a color scheme to match stores' other gift items, and a picture of the product on the package to cultivate product identity. They got all that. The new packaging also includes an 800 number through which callers can find local retailers that carry the cookies. Seckinger-Lee spent $250,000—about 12 per cent of sales—on the entire process. Previously, the firm spent only 5 per cent of revenues on sales and marketing yearly. But the new look paid off. At the Fancy Food trade shows in Atlanta and New York City, the firm booked 50 per cent more orders than at the prior year's shows. A buyer from Macy's decided to put the product in the New York store after almost 10 years of courting, citing the new packaging as the reason.[25]

The basic functions of packaging, factors considered when making packaging decisions, and criticisms of packaging are described next.

Basic Packaging Functions

Packaging functions *range from containment and protection to product planning.*

The basic **packaging functions** are containment and protection, usage, communication, segmentation, channel cooperation, and new-product planning:

- Containment and protection—Packaging enables liquid, granular, and other divisible products to be contained in a given quantity and form. It also protects a product while it is shipped, stored, and handled.
- Usage—Packaging lets a product be easily used and re-stored. It may even be reusable after a product is depleted. Packaging must also be safe to all who use it, from the youngest child to the oldest senior. See Figure 14-10.
- Communication—Packaging communicates a brand image, provides ingredients and directions, and displays the product. It is a major promotion tool.
- Segmentation—Packaging can be tailor-made for a specific market group. If a firm offers two or more package shapes, sizes, colors, or designs, it may employ differentiated marketing.
- Channel cooperation—Packaging can address wholesaler and retailer needs with regard to shipping, storing, promotion, and so on.
- New-product planning—New packaging can be a meaningful innovation for a firm and stimulate its sales.

Factors Considered in Packaging Decisions

Several factors must be weighed in making packaging decisions.

What image is sought?

Because package design affects the image a firm seeks for its products, color, shape, and material all influence consumer perceptions. For example, "After 115 years, Lister-

[24]Primo Angeli, "Thinking Out of the Box: A New Approach to Product Development," *Business Horizons*, Vol. 38 (May–June 1995), p. 18.

[25]Sarah Schafer, "When It's Time for a Makeover," *Inc.* (December 1995), p. 118.

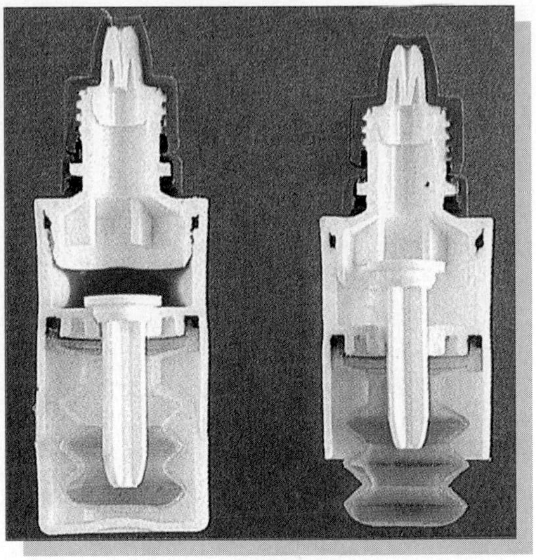

FIGURE 14-10
Using Packaging to Facilitate Product Use
Timpilo, a product for control of glaucoma, is packaged in a unique, award-winning dual-chambered vial. A sight-threatening disease, glaucoma can be controlled with regular applications of two medications, one taken twice a day and the other four times a day. This regimen can be hard for patients to follow; and the medications cannot be combined because the two substances must be stored in different solutions to prevent their deterioration. To solve the problem, Merck's packaging engineers designed a bottle with separate chambers for the two substances *(left)*, which are not mixed together until a patient presses the bottom of the vial, displacing a plug *(right)*.
Reprinted by permission.

ine Antiseptic changed from glass to plastic in its most popular bottle sizes, as well as redesigned the classic barbell-shaped package that signified amber mouthwash—and 'medicine-y' taste to generations of consumers. The product inside is the same. But, we wanted to update and modernize it from the package in your grandmother's medicine cabinet."[26]

Should family packaging be used?

In family packaging, a firm uses a common element on each package in a product line. It parallels family branding. Campbell has virtually identical packages for its traditional soups, distinguished only by flavor or content identification. American Home Products, the maker of Advil and Anacin pain relievers, does not use family packaging with the two brands; they have distinct packages to attract different segments.

Should standard packages be used worldwide?

An international firm must determine if a standardized package can be used worldwide (with only a language change on the label). Standardization boosts global recognition. Thus, Coke and Pepsi have standard packages when possible. Yet, some colors, symbols, and shapes have negative meanings in some nations. For example, white can mean purity or mourning, two vastly different images.

What should costs be?

Package costs must be considered on both a total and per-unit basis. As noted earlier, total costs can run into the millions of dollars, and per-unit costs can go as high as 40 per cent of a product's selling price—depending on the purpose and extent of packaging.

What materials and innovations are right?

A firm has many packaging materials from which to select, such as paperboard, plastic, metal, glass, styrofoam, and cellophane. In the choice, trade-offs are probably needed: Cellophane allows products to be attractively displayed, but it is highly susceptible to tearing; paperboard is relatively inexpensive, but it is hard to open. A firm must also decide how innovative it wants its packaging to be. Figure 14-11 displays some of the innovative packaging from Sonoco.

What features should the package incorporate?

There is a wide range of package features from which to choose, depending on the product. These features include pour spouts, hinged lids, screw-on tops, pop-tops, see-through bags, tuck- or seal-end cartons, carry handles, product testers (for items like batteries), and freshness dating. They may provide a firm with a differential advantage.

What sizes, colors, and shapes are used?

A firm has to select the specific sizes, colors, and shapes of its packages. In picking a package size, shelf life (how long a product stays fresh), convenience, tradition, and competition must be considered. In the food industry, new and larger sizes have captured

[26]Glenn Collins, "New Looks for 2 Staples of the Medicine Cabinet," *New York Times* (July 19, 1994), p. D4.

FIGURE 14-11
Innovative Packaging from Sonoco
Sonoco's consumer packaging operations are known around the world for innovative packaging solutions. These products include composite canisters, plastic tennis ball containers, capseals, plastic and fiber caulk cartridges, carry-out plastic bags for supermarkets and high-volume retail stores, plastic produce roll bags, agricultural film, pressure-sensitive labels, promotional coupons, screen process printing for vending machine graphics, screen printing for fleet graphics, flexible packaging, specialty folding cartons, coasters, and glass covers.
Reprinted by permission.

high sales. The choice of package color depends on the image sought. Mello Yello, a citrus soft drink by Coca-Cola, has a label with bright orange and green lettering on a lemon-yellow background. Package shape also affects a product's image. Hanes created a mystique for L'eggs pantyhose via the egg-shaped package. The number of packages used with any one product depends on competition and the firm's use of differentiated marketing. By selling small, medium, and large sizes, a firm may ensure maximum shelf space, appeal to different consumers, and make it difficult and expensive for a new company to gain channel access.

How should the label and inserts appear?

The placement, content, size, and prominence of the label must be set. Both company and brand names (if appropriate) need to appear on the label. The existence of package inserts and other useful information (some of which may be required by law) should be noted on the label. Sometimes, a redesigned label may be confusing to customers and hurt a product's sales. As one analyst noted, "Marketers are always trying to improve things, and they may end up causing problems for themselves."[27]

Should multiple packaging be used?

Multiple packaging couples two or more product items in one container. It may involve the same product (such as razor blades or soda) or combine different ones (such as a comb and a brush or a first-aid kit). The goal is to increase usage (hoarding may be a problem), get people to buy an assortment of items, or have people try a new item (such as a new toothpaste packaged with an established toothbrush brand). Many multiple packs, like cereal, are versatile—they can be sold as shipped or broken into single units.

Should items be individually wrapped?

Individually wrapping portions of a divisible product may offer a competitive advantage. It may also be costly. Kraft has done well with its individually wrapped cheese slices. Alka-Seltzer sells tablets in individually wrapped tin-foil containers, as well as in a bottle without wrapping.

Should a package have a pre-printed price and use the **Universal Product Code (UPC)***?*

For certain items (such as shirts, magazines, watches, and candy), some resellers may want pre-printed prices. They then have the option of charging those prices or adhering their own labels. Some resellers prefer only a space for the price on the package and insert their own price labels automatically. Because of the growing use of computer technology by resellers in monitoring their inventory levels, more of them are insisting on pre-marked inventory codes on packages. The National Retail Federation endorses the Universal Product Code as the voluntary vendor marking standard in the United States.

[27]Stuart Elliott, "Advertising," *New York Times* (January 28, 1993), p. D20.

TECHNOLOGY & MARKETING

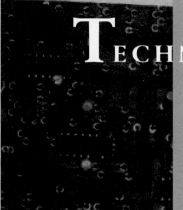

Why Hasn't Milk in a Box Made It in the USA?

Several years ago, Parmalat (Italy's largest milk producer) developed a superheated milk product that is packaged in special aseptic cartons (also known as drink boxes). The major advantage of Parmalat's processed milk is that it can be kept without refrigeration for at least six months. As a result, Parmalat milk accounts for 70 per cent of the total fresh milk consumed by Europeans, and annual sales are almost $2 billion. In contrast, the product accounts for less than 1 per cent of U.S. fresh milk sales.

Parmalat has learned that Americans like to purchase their milk fresh and cold. This means they are suspicious of Parmalat milk. Many consumers think the milk is irradiated or produced from specially treated cows. And Parmalat's higher price (20 per cent more than regular milk) may also reduce consumer demand. Although American consumers may be suspicious of the taste, a test by a noted U.S. food critic found only subtle differences between Parmalat and regular whole milk.

To broaden its appeal in the U.S. market, Parmalat has given out leaflets explaining that it uses heat (not radiation) to preserve the milk, its process does not destroy nutrition, and its milk tastes the same as traditional milk. To underscore the point, some Parmalat packages even contain the wording "Not Irradiated" and "No Preservatives" in large letters.

Parmalat has spent millions of dollars to promote its product to U.S. consumers. Its TV ads highlight the convenience of nonrefrigerated milk and stress the ease of children handling the package. It has distributed discount coupons and free samples. Parmalat even added a two-quart carton to appeal to large American-sized refrigerators and kitchen cabinets. To date, none of these strategies has significantly increased sales.

As a branding and packaging consultant to Parmalat, develop a marketing strategy to increase its market penetration in the U.S. market.

Sources: Based on material in John Tagliabue, "Unchilled Milk: Not Cool Yet," *New York Times* (June 10, 1995), pp. 33–34; and Carolyn Shea, "Parmalat Pours It On," *Promo* (October 1995), pp. 94–99.

With the **Universal Product Code (UPC)**, manufacturers pre-mark items with a series of thick and thin vertical lines. Price and inventory data codes are represented by these lines, which appear on outer package labels—but are not readable by employees and customers. The lines are "read" by computerized optical scanning equipment at the checkout counter. In these instances, the cashier does not have to ring up a transaction manually and inventory data are instantly transmitted to the main computer of the retailer (or the manufacturer). In the UPC system, human-readable prices must still be marked on items, either by the manufacturer or the reseller.[28]

How does the package interrelate with other marketing variables?

Last, a firm must be sure the package design fits in with the rest of its marketing mix. A well-known perfume brand may be extravagantly packaged, distributed in select stores, advertised in upscale magazines, and sold at a high price. In contrast, a firm making perfumes that imitate leading brands has more basic packaging, distributes in discount stores, does not advertise, and uses low prices. The two perfume brands may cost an identical amount to make, but the imitator would spend only a fraction as much on packaging.

Criticisms of Packaging

Packaging is faulted for waste, misleading labels, etc.

The packaging practices of some industries and firms have been heavily criticized and regulated in recent years due to their impact (or potential impact) on the environment and scarce resources, the high expenditures on packaging, questions about the honesty of la-

[28]See Barry Berman and Joel R. Evans, *Retail Management: A Strategic Approach*, Sixth Edition (New York: Prentice Hall, 1995), pp. 232–234.

FIGURE 14-12
Packaging and Social Responsibility: A Team Effort
Reprinted by permission of Knight-Ridder.

bels and the confusion caused by inconsistent designations of package sizes (such as large, family, super), and critics' perceptions of inadequate package safety.

Yet, consumers—as well as business—must bear part of the responsibility for the negative results of packaging. See Figure 14-12. Throwaway bottles (highly preferred by consumers) use almost three times the energy of returnable ones. Shoplifting annually adds to packaging costs because firms must add security tags and otherwise alter packages.

In planning their packaging programs, firms need to weigh the short-term and long-term benefits and costs of providing environmentally safer ("green"), less confusing, and more tamper-resistant packages. Generally, firms are responding quite positively to the criticisms raised here. These issues were examined further in Chapter 5.

MARKETING IN A CHANGING WORLD

The Long-Run Power of Power Brands

Although AT&T is no longer one of the world's 25 most powerful brands, it still packs a strong wallop. Here we are, well past the 1984 breakup of "Ma Bell," and AT&T still dominates the seven "Baby Bells." Before reading the next paragraph, tell us, how many of the Baby Bells can you name? Yet, if you were to do a poll of Americans, more than 90 per cent would know the AT&T name.

The Baby Bells are Ameritech, Bell Atlantic, BellSouth, Nynex, Pacific Telesis, Southwestern Bell, and US West (pending proposed mergers). For the most part, they have done well since being separated from their parent. They dominate their local phone service markets and have branched into cable TV, cellular phone services, and overseas marketing of telecommunications equipment.

One of the primary battles that lies ahead for AT&T and the Baby Bells involves the desire of each to enter the other's telephone service turf. AT&T wants to return to its roots: local telephone service; and the Baby Bells want to be permitted to offer long-distance telephone service. In the current deregulated environment, with the enactment of the Telecommunications Act of 1996, both should get their wish.

Who will win the battle? Consider: After competing with MCI, Sprint, and numerous others for more than a decade for long-distance supremacy, AT&T's U.S. market share is above 55 per cent—MCI's is 18 per cent.[29]

Furthermore, according to a recent survey of 2,000 people throughout the United States, AT&T would clobber *each* of the Baby Bells if people were to choose just one firm for both local and long-distance telephone service:

- Ameritech territory—40 per cent pick AT&T; 27 per cent Ameritech.
- Bell Atlantic territory—49 per cent pick AT&T; 30 per cent Bell Atlantic.
- BellSouth territory—54 per cent pick AT&T; 18 per cent BellSouth.
- Nynex territory—44 per cent pick AT&T; 31 per cent Nynex.
- Pacific Telesis territory—54 per cent pick AT&T; 9 per cent Pacific Telesis.
- Southwestern Bell territory—45 per cent pick AT&T; 21 per cent Southwestern Bell.
- US West territory—49 per cent pick AT&T; 29 per cent US West.[30]

Our conclusion: The Baby Bells should be aware of the old adage that goes, "Be careful what you wish for. You may get it."

SUMMARY

1. *To define and distinguish among branding terms and to examine the importance of branding* Branding is the procedure a firm follows in planning and marketing its brand(s). A brand is a name, term, design, or symbol (or a combination) that identifies a good or service. A brand name is a word, letter (number), or group of words or letters (numbers) that can be spoken. A brand mark is a symbol, design, or distinctive coloring or lettering. A trade character is a personified brand mark. A trademark is a brand name, brand mark, or trade character given legal protection.

There are millions of brand names in circulation worldwide. Ad spending on them is many billions of dollars annually. Through strong brands, brand loyalty can be secured. Popular brands also speed up the acceptance of new products. Gaining and keeping brand recognition is a top priority, as are the development of brand equity and a brand image. Branding benefits all parties: manufacturers, distribution intermediaries, and consumers.

2. *To study the key branding decisions that must be made* Four fundamental decisions are necessary in branding. First, corporate symbols are determined and, if applicable, revised. The company's name (and/or divisional names), logo(s), and trade characters set its overall image. Second, a branding philosophy is set, which includes the proper use of manufacturer, private, and/or generic brands, as well as family and/or individual branding. At this stage, a mixed-brand strategy, the battle of the brands, and brand extension (a popular approach) are also assessed.

Third, a brand name is chosen from one of several sources, including brand extension from existing names, private brands, licensing a name from another firm, and co-branding. With a new brand, the consumer's brand decision process moves from nonrecognition to recognition to preference (dislike) to insistence (aversion). With a continuing name applied to a new product, the brand decision process would begin at recognition, preference (dislike), or insistence (aversion). Fourth, the use of trademarks is evaluated and planned.

3. *To define and distinguish among packaging terms and to examine the importance of packaging* Packaging is the procedure a firm follows in planning and marketing product package(s). A package consists of a physical container, label, and/or inserts. Today, packaging is an integral part of a firm's new-product planning strategy.

Ten per cent of a typical product's final selling price goes for packaging. Package redesign can be quite expensive. Both channel member and final consumer needs must be taken into consideration. Errors can be quite costly.

[29]Kate Fitzgerald, "New Rules Fire Up Ad Joust in Donnybrook Among Telcos," *Advertising Age* (September 27, 1995), pp. 3, 59; and Gautam Naik, "Landmark Telecom Bill Becomes Law," *Wall Street Journal* (February 9, 1996), p. B3.

[30]Kim Cleland, "AT&T Ringing Up 5 Regional Units," *Advertising Age* (December 11, 1995), p. 3.

CASE 2

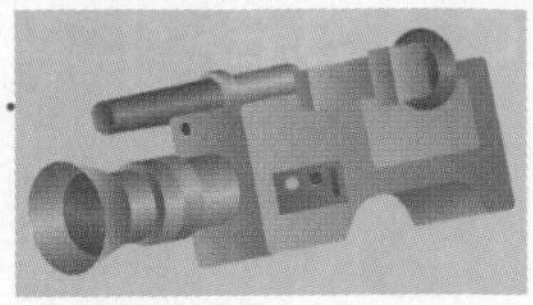

Roadway Package System: Utilizing Package Bar Codes†

Roadway Package System (RPS), a division of Roadway Services, serves customers in the small-package market throughout North America. It has a "commitment to quality and customer satisfaction by providing unsurpassed service, industry leadership in technology and product innovation, motivated employees and contractors, supplier partnerships, and conformance to budget."

RPS delivery routes cover 100 per cent of the United States and 90 per cent of Canada. This means the company serves Puerto Rico, Alaska, and Hawaii via its coordinated ground/air network. Unlike United Parcel Service, which emphasizes the business-to-final consumer segment, most of RPS' service is business-to-business.

RPS is among the most technologically advanced transportation firms, and many of the services it offers to shippers are linked to its state-of-the-art bar-coding system. With bar coding, a symbol—similar to a Universal Product Code (UPC)—is used. While all of a vendor's products of a given size, color, and quality have the same UPC symbol, a unique bar code also identifies each specific package shipped by a firm. The bar code can be placed on a package by a Roadway customer, a Roadway driver, or a Roadway employee at a distribution center. The bar code symbol can be used to identify a package's location as it moves from vendor to shipper to business customer via equipment that scans all packages. There are many different types of bar-coding standards. The ones used by Roadway are the UCC 128 or the UCC EAN bar code system. These codes are already used by many of Roadway's customers.

RPS offers shippers and their customers various services that are based on the bar code technology. Each service enables a client to trace a package throughout Roadway's distribution system and confirm that it is delivered. This assures superior channel communication (in terms of delivery status and detailed billing information), as well as increased channel cooperation (for example, bar coding can be used to assemble a multiple-package shipment so that all packages are received by a customer at the same time). Three of the services offered are RPS Multiship, RPS Star System, and RPS Access.

RPS Multiship is a combination hardware and software system that weighs, rates, routes, and prints bar codes and addresses for RPS clients. Multiship can also be tied into a firm's marketing information system by constantly updating sales, inventory, and distribution data as goods are sold and delivered. Multiship is installed by RPS free-of-charge for its high-volume clients.

The RPS Star System is based on a hand-held microcomputer that is tied into a national cellular network. This system allows customers to receive verbal confirmation of a delivery on the next business day after goods are scheduled to be received by clients. The Star system can be accessed by clients calling a toll-free phone number.

RPS Access lets clients link their computer system with the RPS data base. Using Access enables a customer to more quickly trace packages than with the Star system. In addition, clients can receive proof of delivery through an image-processing system. This service lets Roadway customers obtain a delivery signature for each individual package directly on their computer system.

Through bar code scanning, Roadway can also provide other key information to its customers. For example, with bar coding, Roadway can develop detailed reports of a customer's shipping activity. These reports itemize all packages sent to each individual account by weight, date, and cost.

QUESTIONS

1. Contrast the Universal Product Code as used in supermarkets with bar coding as used by Roadway Package System.
2. Describe how bar coding can perform the basic packaging functions of channel cooperation and market segmentation.
3. Differentiate between the role of packaging for organizational consumers as opposed to final consumers.
4. Evaluate how RPS uses its bar-coding system.

VIDEO QUESTIONS ON ROADWAY PACKAGE SYSTEM

1. Differentiate between Roadway's Tracpack and Roadpack systems.
2. Describe the benefits available to a customer using RPS' return-to-vendor system.

†The data in this case are drawn from *Roadway Services 1994 Annual Report*; and Clyde E. Witt, "Changing the Face and Pace of LTL Shipping," *Material Handling Engineering* (November 1994), pp. 45–47.

PART 4 CASE

Using Packaged-Goods Strategies in Service Marketing

Introduction

An innovative manufacturer can protect its new-product investment through patenting (for example, Gillette's Sensor razor). McDonald's can protect its burger recipe, but can't be sure each burger is served exactly as intended. Because people provide the service, the quality may be inconsistent. Moreover, McDonald's defining competitive advantage of speedy, friendly service cannot be patented or otherwise legally protected.

When Clorox announced its new combination detergent and bleach, P&G counterattacked by speeding up its own introduction of Tide with Bleach. The attacker's advantage of a potentially superior product was quickly trumped. However, service quality is inseparable from the providers and the setting, so it's often more difficult to prevent competitive incursions.

Just as retailers restock shelves from inventory, families buy packaged goods in bulk and draw down their supply over time. This practice is exploited by product managers to reduce the trial of a new brand. The incumbent brand is promoted heavily to fill home storage space and keep people out of the market, away from a new competitor. Because services are perishable, marketers have no household inventory to manipulate. Consumers can buy enough soap to last for months, but they can't "stock up" on phone calls or banking transactions.

Even though many successful defensive moves by goods marketers cannot be applied directly to services, some strategies can be. The key is knowing why a strategy works and then adapting it to service markets.

Defending Against Entry

Market entry consists of pre-entry, introduction, and post-entry. Each step means a greater commitment to compete for customers and profits—and more expenditures. Due to the cycle of investing, monitoring, and decision making, incumbents can exploit the entry process itself to form defensive strategies. Because entrants have different goals at each stage, incumbents' goals change as well. With these changes are opportunities to use strategies to block potential entrants, retaliate in introduction, or adapt to the new competitor.

Stage 1: Pre-Entry/Blocking Before introduction, potential entrants decide which markets offer the best expected return based on their ability to meet market needs and surmount entry barriers. Although incumbents cannot affect potential rivals' abilities, they can block entry by raising the costs of success or reducing expected rewards.

Make performance guarantees. For service marketers, these guarantees are similar to manufacturer patents—which ensure that inventors get revenues for their innovations and serve as an entry barrier. Since competitors can't just copy successful products, they must do some research and development. Such costs lower the prospects for easy entry until patent protection expires.

Performance guarantees have the same effect on potential service entrants. For new services to compete via full-satisfaction guarantees, there must be a comparable service delivery system. Federal Express fended off the U.S. Postal Service's Express Mail because FedEx was built for speed from day one. In contrast, USPS is volume-driven; it couldn't afford the required capital and technology to make its next-morning delivery service competitive.

Performance guarantees must be used to shape the service organization to high quality levels. Car mechanics who say, "If it's not right, we'll make it right," are heading in the right direction but are not quite there. Customers see performance guarantees as preventing problems rather than rectifying them.

Intensify advertising. High ad spending erects a barrier to entry in most packaged-goods markets. Many millions are spent on introductory ads for major new brands of soft drinks, cereal, coffee, you name it.

An ad blitz can create a barrier to entry in some service markets. Yet, the unique experiential quality of services influences how effective ads are. Service quality is subjective; people can't easily judge it without actual experience. Ads compensate by showing the benefits of a given service. We see flights departing on time and listen in on crystal-clear phone conversations.

Because ad claims shape the expectations of potential consumers, promoting service quality can backfire if customers expect too much. Nordstrom cut its public relations efforts heralding its occasionally heroic customer service because some new customers were dissatisfied with sales associates who only provided excellent service.

Control location. Coca-Cola built its empire by being everywhere there are thirsty people. Its strategy is "to make it impossible for the consumer to escape Coca-Cola." By granting exclusive territories to franchised bottlers, Coke could grow rapidly and dominate the soft-drink business.

In the past, a factory's location affected whether it would succeed, since access to cheap power, raw materials, and labor were critical. Although these factors may be less important to today's manufacturers, location continues to play a key role for service businesses such as hotels and child-care centers.

Source: Adapted by the authors from Thomas S. Gruca, "Defending Service Markets," *Marketing Management*, Vol. 3 (No. 1, 1994), pp. 31–38. Reprinted by permission of the American Marketing Association.

For location to pre-empt entry, the incumbent must be positioned with access to good sites. As populations shift and grow, the advantage of current locations might change. The decay of center-city shopping areas, for example, corresponded with population shifts to the suburbs. Potential entrants cannot be prevented from entering if they believe the market will grow over time. The hospitality industry's failure to read capacity signals was as much to blame as the slow-growth economy of the early 1990s for today's glut of U.S. hotel rooms. When forecasts in demand growth are not shared by all, too many service outlets in one place will drive all of the profitability out of the market.

Build switching costs. Product managers sometimes gain customer loyalty by building switching costs—the monetary, psychological, or social expenses that consumers must incur if they change brands—into their products. Years ago, IBM did this by making software that worked only with IBM hardware. Woolite dominates its segment of the laundry soap market by positioning itself as the only choice for hand-washing expensive and delicate clothing. Ads promise you can "Trust Woolite for all your fine washables."

For services, the prospects for creating switching costs depend on the customer's time horizon. If the service is provided over time, the provider can build a relationship with the customer that locks out another competitor. Although the nature of some services is consistent with building long-term relationships, others have no natural follow-through or continuity. For these transaction-type services, shaping switching costs is hard but not impossible. The trick is to turn transactions into relationships. Airline frequent-flier programs and hotels' frequent-guest programs discourage consumers from using other providers and build long-term relationships.

The best defense. A satisfied customer is not an inviting target for new entrants. Striving to keep people happy and tracking company performance are two sides of the same coin. Successful service marketers never stop trying to improve their offerings while always asking, "How are we doing?" There are many methods available to monitor and improve quality—mystery shoppers, consumer advisory panels, 800 hotlines, and so on. Firms just need to make sure the right things are being measured.

The consumer's view of what makes a satisfying service encounter may differ radically from that of the service provider. One patient satisfaction survey used by a hospital includes questions about whether the staff called the patient by the right name and whether anyone followed up after discharge to see if the person was doing OK. Other hospital administrators might not be interested in answers to these questions because they have nothing to do with the clinical abilities of the physicians and nurses. However, such details may spell the difference between a return visit or a switch to another provider.

Stage 2: Introduction/Retaliation With deregulation, new competitors have made major inroads into industries such as communications, trucking, and air travel. The lines between banks, insurance firms, and investment brokers are blurring. And legal, optical, and medical clinics are replacing solo practitioners. Clearly, service markets are now more competitive, and entry often cannot be prevented. Yet, strong action by incumbents can shape entering firms' decisions during introduction.

When a firm enters a new market, it has some expectations for sales, share, and margins in the early stages of introduction. If the new venture does not perform as expected, the firm gets out. It is in this initial period when the competitor is deciding whether or not to commit more resources to a given market that the incumbent has a chance to retaliate.

Reduce trial. When Formula 409 faced the prospect of P&G invading the spray cleaner market in the late 1960s, David slew Goliath with a classic maneuver. Just before the P&G launch, Formula 409 ran a promotion that loaded up customers with a large inventory of the cleaner while tying up available shelf and warehouse space.

Even though services can't be inventoried, they can be pre-paid. Long-term contracts in relationship services can keep customers from investigating a new competitor. Health clubs keep members from switching clubs by reducing renewal fees as the length of contract increases. For transaction services such as video rental, multiple purchases at a special price can keep customers loyal.

It's critical to keep customers from sampling the services of new rivals, for two reasons. First, retaining a current customer is cheaper and much more valuable than converting new customers. Second, once they switch over to another service provider, you have to pay to win them back.

Localize the damage. A widely used product strategy is to launch a "me-too" fighting brand to reduce the impact of a new entrant. Coca-Cola uses its lemon-lime Sprite to keep 7 Up in line and its own "pepper" formulation, Mr. Pibb, to deal with Dr Pepper.

Federal Express used this approach to defend itself against the U.S. Postal Service's Express Mail. The advantage of Express Mail was a lower price for a lesser service—next afternoon delivery. FedEx matched the performance guarantee with a new service called Standard Overnight, while its existing service became Priority Overnight. By localizing the competition between the firms to the next day afternoon service, FedEx kept its higher margins on Priority Overnight and weakened the impact of Express Mail.

Develop a reputation for standing your ground. Some packaged-goods firms are so tough that their reputation deters new entrants. In *The Marketing Revolution*, Kevin Clancy and Robert Shulman related a story of one food processor's response to the introduction of a new food product. Instead of an anticipated 80 per cent increase in advertising and promotional expenditures by the incumbent, the entrant faced a 630 per cent surge—almost eight times larger than anticipated!

The entrant knows the incumbent can't sustain greatly increased marketing spending or deep price cuts forever and that such aggressive actions have to be scaled back eventually. Yet, the extreme response indicates an incumbent's commitment.

Hit 'em with everything you've got (sometimes). The continuing battle in the retail coffee market shows how not to retaliate against a new entrant. The vigorous response greeting Folgers as it entered the stronghold of Maxwell House has raged undiminished for 20 years. The parents of these two proud brands, P&G and General Foods, appear locked in a death grip—squeezing until all the profits are gone. In 1990, *Fortune* asked, "Can Anyone Win the Coffee War?" Since both firms have other resources to draw on, the fight for supremacy in this market may continue indefinitely.

When Citibank faced the prospect of competing with AT&T's Universal Card, it mounted a strong but measured counterattack. Citibank canceled its AT&T long-distance service, added price protection, and tried to block further entry of nonbanking entities. These aggressive actions emphasized the extent of Citibank's displeasure with AT&T, but did not prevent the phone giant from becoming the third-largest U.S. card issuer. They also did not discourage GM, GE, and Prudential Life from moving ahead with their own plastic plans.

Was Citibank's retaliation a failure? Maybe not. No matter how solid the pre-entry marketing research, some uncertainty always remains about how well a service will be received by the public. The services battlefield is littered with the corpses of popular new communications services—until you asked someone to pay for them. Incumbents can at least keep nagging doubts alive.

New services often require deep pockets, and firms like AT&T have them. Although AT&T now has more cardholders than expected, the Universal Card did not turn a profit until two years after introduction. Committed to expanding beyond communications services, AT&T had the resources to wait for results.

Stage 3: Post-Entry/Adaptation During introduction, the incumbent seeks to derail the attacking firm's commitment to entry. In post-entry, adaptation takes the entrant's foothold in the market as a given. The transition from counterattack to adaptation marks a change to a longer-term adjustment for an incumbent.

Meet 'em to beat 'em. Packaged-goods firms know that although the best ideas may come from small competitors, dominant players often are the ones to profit. Minnetonka introduced the first pump toothpaste and Royal Crown had the first successful caffeine-free cola. Incumbents in these markets met the challenges posed by adding features to their core brands (Crest, Colgate) or launching flanker products (Pepsi Free, caffeine-free Coke).

Service marketers can sometimes try to match the strengths brought to the market by a new competitor. When Marshall Field faced the entry of Nordstrom into its home turf, the incumbent began preparing years ahead of Nordstrom's opening. It increased the size of the women's department—the area accounting for 60 per cent of Nordstrom's sales—and extended the shoe selection. It also upgraded sales associate training.

Grow the whole pie. Wrigley dominated the chewing gum market for decades with Juicy Fruit, Double Mint, and Spearmint. Yet, it was so slow to react to the sugar-free gum trend that inroads by Warner-Lambert (Trident) and Nabisco (CareFree) were made. While it took its time devising the ultimately successful Extra sugar-free gum, Wrigley also created Freedent, a brand that expanded the total gum category by bringing back some former product users. Freedent was created for denture wearers who would otherwise be unable to chew gum. Since its introduction, no comparable U.S. gum has been successfully introduced and—with the aging of the population—Freedent has positioned Wrigley as a strong player for the future.

Fast-food franchisers are going to the customer rather than trying to get the customer to come to them. In its home state of Illinois, McDonald's can be found at an interstate rest stop in Dekalb and on the campus of Moraine Valley Community College. Some franchisors even have outlets in mass merchandisers; Little Caesar's pizza is at Kmart.

Concentrate on niches. As a last resort, the incumbent may have to give up the fight and concentrate on profitable niches. Faced with price competition from superstores such as Barnes & Noble, small booksellers have begun focusing on specialty subjects like women writers or foreign novelists.

When cellular phones began their assault on the pager business, Nynex gave up, selling its operations to a competitor. Others are digging deeper to find uses for the technology among the 97 per cent of the population who have never used a pager.

Masters of Defense

Here are some additional tips:

- Attack yourself first. Don't be afraid to make your own service obsolete by replacing it with a better performer. Packaged-goods giants are a constantly moving target to potential rivals because they do not wait until one of their brands is under attack to bring out a new and better version. Tide detergent has been upgraded and improved no less than 30 times in its life.
- Think about imitation barriers rather than entry barriers. AT&T blindsided financial institutions that issue credit cards because they only worried about each other. However, the core competencies needed to compete in the credit-card market are transaction processing and marketing, not financial management acumen. Once AT&T paved the way, the entries of GM and GE were inevitable. To avoid a similar surprise, ask, "Who else might have the competencies to compete for my customers?"
- React to new competitors by building value for consumers. Under attack from cheaper private-label brands, P&G cut prices while maintaining high quality. This

value-enhancement strategy is paying off for P&G. Assess all defensive moves by how much value they give to customers.

QUESTIONS

1. How can both goods and service marketers use the generic product concept?
2. What product life-cycle concepts could be learned from this case?
3. Relate the goods/services continuum to pre-entry planning by an existing service marketer. A new service marketer.
4. Because services are more intangible and inseparable from providers, what features should a child-care center promote to prospective customers?
5. As the manager of a new optical center, how would you market yourself versus Pearle or another large chain?
6. What do you think about this retaliatory strategy: "develop a reputation for standing your ground"? For what kinds of firms is it *not* suited?
7. Can new services be test marketed? Why or why not?
8. Comment on each of these defenses:
   a. Attack yourself first.
   b. Think about imitation barriers rather than entry barriers.
   c. React to new competitors by building value for customers.

DISTRIBUTION PLANNING

PART 5

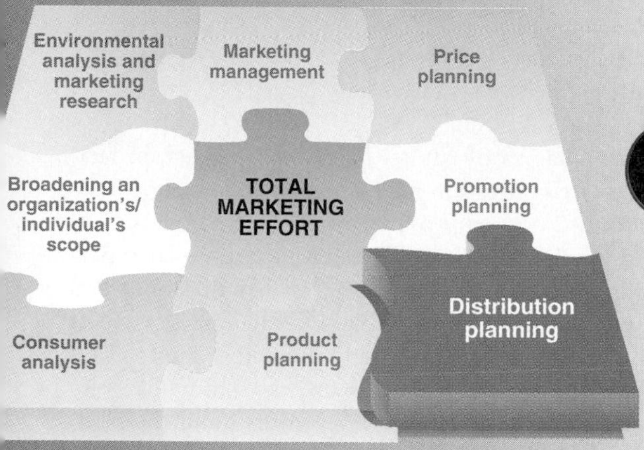

Part 5 deals with the second major element of the marketing mix, distribution.

15 Considerations in Distribution Planning and Physical Distribution

Here, we broadly study distribution planning, which involves the physical movement and transfer of ownership of a product from producer to consumer. We explore the functions of distribution, types of channels, supplier/distribution intermediary contracts, channel cooperation and conflict, the industrial channel, and international distribution. We also look at physical distribution, in particular at transportation and inventory management issues.

16 Wholesaling

In this chapter, we examine wholesaling, which entails buying and/or handling goods and services and their subsequent resale to organizational users, retailers, and/or other wholesalers. We show the impact of wholesaling on the economy, its functions, and its relationships with suppliers and customers. We describe the major types of company-owned and independent wholesalers and note recent trends in wholesaling.

17 Retailing

Here, we concentrate on retailing, which consists of those business activities involved with the sale of goods and services to the final consumer. We show the impact of retailing on the economy, its functions in distribution, and its relationship with suppliers. We categorize retailers by ownership, store strategy mix, and nonstore operations. We also describe several retail planning considerations and note recent trends in retailing.

Part 5 Video Vignette
Hain Food Group

As part of its expansion plans, the Hain Food Group is looking to increase its distribution network in the United States and internationally. Until a few years ago, natural foods (as a category) were most likely to be found in small health food stores; traditional supermarkets devoted little space to this category. Many supermarket operators perceived natural foods as a fad desired by a small market segment. But, my, how times have changed!

Industrywide, there has been a proliferation of natural food supermarkets. In fact, 60 per cent of all natural food store sales are realized in medium-to-large and supermarket-size stores, although they represent only 24 per cent of natural food store outlets. And there is a heightened emphasis on natural foods in traditional supermarkets because of the growing customer desire for healthy foods and the new FDA labeling requirements for packaged foods. The new labels make it much easier for shoppers to understand ingredient tables.

"The natural foods category is one of the fastest-growing food categories, and we are the company that will lead it."

Interestingly, U.S. shoppers in the South are much more likely to shop at a health food store than those in the Northeast and the Midwest. There are more than 12,000 specialty/health food stores in the United States, and it is estimated that these stores alone account for several billion dollars in yearly sales.

Today, Hain brands are marketed through traditional supermarkets, natural food stores (including natural food supermarkets), specialty grocery stores, mass merchandisers, convenience stores, drugstores, and elsewhere. A large percentage of its sales are from supermarkets, including Albertson's, A&P, Bruno's, Kroger, Publix, Vons, and Waldbaum's. Hain is also in such natural food stores as Fresh Fields, Whole Foods, Wild by Nature Market, and Wild Oats Market. And the firm is adding vending machines and warehouse clubs to its distribution mix.

Hain stores and ships its products out of six public warehouses around the United States, where items are received from the firm's co-packers. Some retailers pick up the products themselves directly from the warehouses.

Hain uses food brokers (who work on a commission) and merchant wholesalers (who buy products from Hain and then service their own retail customers). These wholesalers are also known as food distributors. Fleming and SuperValu are among the wholesalers that buy from Hain. In addition to outside parties, Hain has its own in-house sales force that works with key accounts, and its Hollywood brand is sold directly to chain stores only.

What's in store for Hain next? It is looking to move into Canada, Mexico, Great Britain, and France. As Irwin Simon, Hain's chief executive says, "We will continue to seek niche growth markets and deliver excellence in products that meet consumer demand. The natural foods industry is one of the fastest-growing food categories, and we are the company that will lead it."

CHAPTER 15

Considerations in Distribution Planning and Physical Distribution

Chapter Objectives

1. To define distribution planning and to examine its importance, distribution functions, the factors used in selecting a distribution channel, and the different types of distribution channels

2. To describe the nature of supplier/distribution intermediary contracts, and cooperation and conflict in a channel of distribution

3. To examine the special aspects relating to a distribution channel for industrial products and to international distribution

4. To define physical distribution and to demonstrate its importance

5. To discuss transportation alternatives and inventory management issues

Letting others take the lead may be outré at Paris salons, but it's a winning style at VF. By sticking mostly to timeless apparel staples, finely honing its "second-to-the-market" approach, and bringing high technology to the nitty-gritty details of distribution, VF—based in Wyomissing, Pennsylvania—has avoided the financial gyrations that beset many clothing makers. Says VF CEO Lawrence R. Pugh: "Clearly, there is less risk."

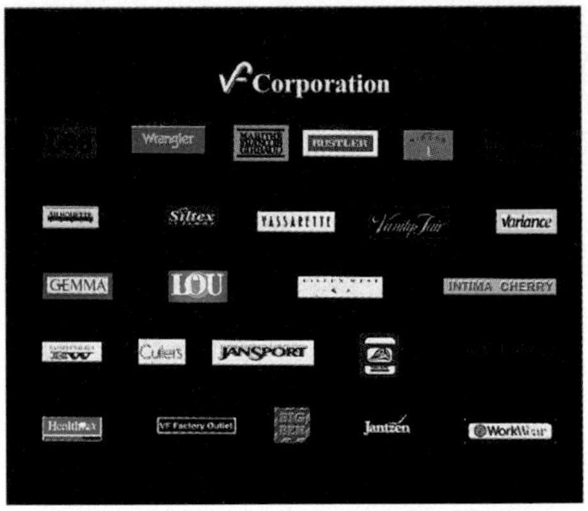

For the last several years, VF has increased both its income and sales at an annual compound rate of 20 per cent. Few companies can boast such a record. And it has generated these impressive gains while selling such low-fashion products as Lee and Wrangler jeans and Vanity Fair women's undergarments. Chief executive Pugh credits VF's computerized quick response (QR) inventory system with making the firm the market share leader in the U.S. jeans market.

Although a follower in clothing designs, VF is an acknowledged innovator in devising and implementing QR inventory systems that let retailers improve their inventory productivity. VF's system tracks customer preferences by analyzing purchases and allows the firm to consistently deliver replacement merchandise in an accurate and timely manner. VF's QR inventory system reduces retailers' inventory investments, as well as their inventory risks (because fewer poor-selling products are overstocked and then sold at a discount). The system also makes sure that VF retailers replenish those sizes and styles that are good sellers. Although it may take Levi Strauss up to one month to restock Levi's jeans, VF jeans generally arrive within three days of an order.

Because VF sells its products to tens of thousands of retailers, setting up and maintaining a quick response system is an arduous task. VF now has more than 350 retailers that are fully using its program, and it manages inventory levels at more than 40,000 store locations. About 40 per cent of the company's output is currently based on automatic replenishment. For example, every night, Wal-Mart sends its computerized Wrangler sales data directly to VF, which then reorders the jeans automatically. If VF has exact replacements in stock, the goods are shipped right to the Wal-Mart store the next day. If the goods are not in stock, newly made ones are shipped within a week. Thus, Wal-Mart's merchandise manager for men's and boys' goods says the system "has enabled us to get merchandise into the stores in a more timely manner, closer to buying decisions by the customer."

VF vows to continue refining its quick response system and keep its lead in logistics support systems. With its experimental Trendsetter system, VF can track the sales of groups of products—such as jeans and shirts of various styles and colors—and ascertain their sales patterns. These patterns can then be used to forecast ideal inventory levels for individual retailers. VF has also developed a new program, called VF Ready, for small retailers. The program, using scanners to record sales at the end of the day, even accommodates retailers that do not have point-of-sale systems.[1]

In this chapter, we will learn more about the decisions made in distribution planning and the activities involved in physical distribution, including quick response inventory systems.

Overview

Distribution planning is systematic decision making regarding the physical movement of goods and services from producer to consumer, as well as the related transfer of ownership (or rental) of them. It encompasses such diverse functions as transportation, inventory management, and customer transactions.

Distribution planning *involves movement and ownership in a* **channel of distribution**. *It consists of* **channel members**.

Functions are carried out via a **channel of distribution**, which is comprised of all the organizations or people involved in the distribution process. Those organizations or people are known as **channel members** and may include manufacturers, service providers, wholesalers, retailers, marketing specialists, and/or consumers. When the term **distribution intermediaries** is used, it refers to wholesalers, retailers, and marketing specialists (such as transportation firms) that act as facilitators (links) between manufacturers/service providers and consumers.

Distribution intermediaries *often have a channel role.*

This chapter presents an in-depth look at distribution planning and looks at the role of physical distribution. Chapter 16 covers wholesaling's role in the distribution process. Chapter 17 discusses retailing.

Distribution Planning

A channel of distribution can be simple or complex. It can be based on a handshake agreement between a small manufacturer and a local reseller or require detailed written contracts among numerous manufacturers, wholesalers, and retailers. Some firms seek widespread distribution and need independent wholesalers and/or retailers to carry their merchandise and improve cash flow. Others want direct customer contact and do not use independent resellers. Industrial channels usually have more direct contact between manufacturers/service providers and customers than final consumer channels. International channels also have special needs.

Distribution arrangements vary widely.

The importance of distribution planning, the range of tasks performed in the distribution process, the criteria to consider in picking a distribution channel, supplier/distribution intermediary contracts, channel cooperation and conflict, the industrial channel of distribution, and international distribution are discussed next.

The Importance of Distribution Planning

Distribution decisions have a great impact on a company's marketing efforts. Because intermediaries can perform a host of functions, a firm's marketing plan will differ if it sells direct rather than via intermediaries, and a decision to sell in stores rather than through the mail or the World Wide Web requires a different marketing orientation and tasks.

The choice of a distribution channel is one of the most critical decisions a firm will make. Close ties with intermediaries and/or customers may take time to develop; if there are existing bonds among channel members, it may be hard for a new firm to enter. Once channel alliances are achieved, suitable new products can be put into distribution more easily. Channel members need to act in a coordinated way. Strong resellers enhance manufacturers' marketing abilities. Consumers like to buy products the same way over time.

Today, more companies recognize the value of having good relationships throughout the distribution channel. As a result, many firms now engage in relationship marketing, whereby they seek to develop and maintain continuous long-term ties with suppliers, distribution intermediaries, and customers. By doing so, these firms ensure a more consistent

Through relationship marketing, companies strive for ongoing ties with suppliers, intermediaries, and customers.

[1]Gary Robins, "Pushing the Limits of VMI," *Stores* (March 1995), pp. 42–44; and Joseph Weber, "Just Get It to the Stores on Time," *Business Week* (March 6, 1995), pp. 66–67.

FIGURE 15-1
Relationship Marketing and ConAgra
To enhance its relationship marketing efforts, ConAgra is dramatically increasing its in-store sales force to serve retail customers more effectively. This is part of an overall program to provide greater ordering and display support, as well as to encourage more frequent communication.
Reprinted by permission.

flow of goods and services from suppliers, encourage intermediaries to act more as partners than adversaries, and increase the likelihood of having loyal customers. They improve employee morale by empowering them to respond positively to reasonable requests—in the employees' judgment—from suppliers, intermediaries, and/or customers. They get earlier and better data on prospective new products and the best strategies for continuing ones. They also lower operating and marketing costs, thus improving efficiency. As one expert noted, with relationship marketing, it is "traumatic to leave someone who you believe is responsive to your personal needs. We don't change doctors, lawyers, or accountants at the drop of a hat. Firms want to build the same relationships with suppliers, distribution intermediaries, and customers so they won't leave every time they get a better offer."[2] See Figures 15-1 and 15-2.

These are several recommendations as to how effective relationship marketing in a distribution channel may be achieved:

- Relationship marketing should be conducted as a continuous and systematic process that incorporates both buyer and seller needs.
- Relationship marketing needs top management support; and its principles should permeate a firm's corporate culture.
- At a minimum, relationship marketing means understanding consumer expectations, building service partnerships, empowering employees, and total quality management (from buyer and seller perspectives).
- Suppliers, intermediaries, and customers should be surveyed—by category—to determine the aspects of relationship marketing to be emphasized for them.
- Although increased profitability is a desirable result from relationship marketing, other important measures of success are customer satisfaction, customer loyalty, and product quality.
- Both positive and negative feedback (going far beyond just passively receiving customer complaints) can provide meaningful information.
- Sellers need to communicate to their customers that relationship marketing involves responsibilities, as well as benefits, for both parties.

[2]Aimee L. Stern, "Courting Consumer Loyalty with the Feel-Good Bond," *New York Times* (January 17, 1993), Section 3, p. 10. For further information on relationship marketing, see Barry Berman, *Marketing Channels* (New York: Wiley, 1996), pp. 201–239; "Special Issue on Relationship Marketing," *Journal of the Academy of Marketing Science*, Vol. 23 (Fall 1995); Robert M. Morgan and Shelby D. Hunt, "The Commitment-Trust Theory of Relationship Marketing," *Journal of Marketing*, Vol. 58 (July 1994), pp. 20–38; Robert D. Buzzell and Gwen Ortmeyer, "Channel Partnerships Streamline Distribution," *Sloan Management Review*, Vol. 36 (Spring 1995), pp. 85–96; and Gregory T. Gundlach, Ravi S. Achrol, and John T. Mentzer, "The Structure of Commitment in Exchange," *Journal of Marketing*, Vol. 59 (January 1995), pp. 78–92.

FIGURE 15-2
What Relationship Marketing Means to Litton Industries
Litton is a global design, engineering, integration, installation, and service firm for integrated manufacturing systems. Many components in the systems are outsourced to suppliers to keep costs down, assure better quality, and allow more control over Litton assets. Data management expertise enables Litton to offer total solutions to customers' material handling, material flow, and information needs.
Reprinted by permission of Litton Industries, Inc.

- Mutually agreeable (by buyers and sellers) contingency plans should be devised in case anything goes awry.[3]

Costs, as well as profits, are affected by the selection of a particular type of distribution channel. A firm doing all functions must pay for them itself; in return, it reaps all profits. A firm using intermediaries reduces per-unit distribution costs; it also reduces per-unit profits because those resellers receive their share. With intermediaries, a firm's total profits would rise if there are far higher sales than the firm could attain itself.

Distribution formats are long-standing in some industries. For example, in the beverage and food industry, manufacturers often sell through wholesalers that then deal with retailers. Auto makers sell through franchised dealers. Mail-order firms line up suppliers, print catalogs, and sell to consumers. So, firms must frequently conform to the channel patterns in their industries.

A firm's market coverage is often influenced by the location and number, market penetration, image, product selection, services, and marketing plans of the wholesalers, retailers, and/or marketing specialists with which it deals. In weighing options, a firm should note that the more intermediaries it uses, the less customer contact it has and the lower its control over marketing.

These examples show the scope of distribution planning:

- Sherwin-Williams distributes its paints via more than 2,000 company-owned stores, as well as through independent paint stores, mass merchandisers, and wholesale distributors. It also has a direct sales force for certain industrial markets, and employs distributors in nearly 40 nations.[4]
- Shoppers Advantage is a member-based shopping service that operates exclusively through the World Wide Web (http://www.cuc.com). It has a data base of 250,000

[3]Joel R. Evans and Richard L. Laskin, "The Relationship Marketing Process: A Conceptualization and Application," *Industrial Marketing Management*, Vol. 23 (December 1994), p. 451.
[4]*Sherwin-Williams Co. 1995 Annual Report.*

Ethics IN TODAY'S SOCIETY

Can New Firms Use an "Honor System" to Gain Distribution?

McAfee Associates markets two computer software packages: VirusScan, which protects a PC from viruses, and Netshield, which monitors security in local area networks. The firm's annual sales revenues exceed $30 million.

Unlike many other similar firms, both of McAfee's products are shareware. Thus, these programs can be downloaded from electronic bulletin boards by anyone with a modem and a personal computer. In theory, consumers are given a 60-day trial period. Those who wish to continue using the products are expected to pay a $100 fee for access to technical support and for future upgrades. However, in practice, most consumers do not pay the fee, realizing that it is quite difficult for any shareware provider to enforce payment.

About 100,000 potential customers download McAfee's software packages each month. Of this group, about 20 per cent eventually remit the $100 fee. In some cases, McAfee's technical supportpeople have fielded questions from nonpaying users. Why? The firm is careful not to offend nonpayers, hoping they will pay for the programs they use. McAfee also realizes that many of these "freeloaders" are responsible for publicizing its software within their firms.

Unlike hobbyists, almost all corporate users are quick to pay for the shareware they use. As a result, the majority of McAfee's actual sales are from corporate users. Ford Motor Company, for instance, has a license for 52,000 users and Mobil Corporation has one for over 36,000 computers.

Shareware is typically marketed by small software firms that cannot afford to get distribution through traditional channels. These companies typically concentrate on the hobbyist market. In many cases, shareware authors also do not have the resources to properly test and refine their products.

As a channels manager for McAfee, evaluate the pros and cons of the firm's continued use of shareware. What would you do next? Why?

Source: Based on material in Julie Pitta, "Honor System," *Forbes* (October 24, 1994), pp. 258–260.

brand-name products that are offered at a discount. Shoppers Advantage "acts as an online broker, displaying wares and taking orders and payment. Orders are passed on to distributors, manufacturers, and vendors, which ship products to, or book reservations for, customers."[5]

- Century 21 is the world's largest residential real-estate broker. It relies on 6,000 franchisee-operated offices in eleven countries.[6]
- Singer and its affiliates operate 1,300 stores throughout the globe. Of these, nearly 600 are in Asia, more than 250 are in Latin America, and about 30 are in Africa and the Middle East. Independent dealers and mass merchants represent another 59,000 Singer distribution points. In developing nations, a total of 13,000 door-to-door salespeople are used in conjunction with retail stores.[7]

[5]Peter H. Lewis, "Online Middleman Opens for Business," *Wall Street Journal* (October 2, 1995), p. D5.
[6]Suzanne Woolley, "I Want My Century 21!" *Business Week* (January 15, 1996), pp. 72–73.
[7]*Singer Company 1995 Annual Report.*

Channel Functions and the Role of Distribution Intermediaries

Intermediaries can perform **channel functions** *and reduce costs, provide expertise, open markets, and lower risks.*

For most goods and services, the **channel functions** shown in Figure 15-3 and described here must be undertaken. They must be completed somewhere in the distribution channel and responsibility for them assigned.

Distribution intermediaries can play a vital role in marketing research. Due to their closeness to the market, they generally have good insights into the characteristics and needs of customers.

In buying products, intermediaries sometimes pay as items are received; other times, they accept items on consignment and do not pay until after sales are made. Purchase terms for intermediaries may range from net cash (payment due at once) to net 60 days (payment not due for 60 days) or longer. If intermediaries do not pay until after resale, manufacturers risk poor cash flow, high product returns, obsolescence and spoilage, multiple transactions with the intermediaries, and potentially low sales to customers.

Manufacturers and service firms like H&R Block often take care of national (international) ads when assigning promotion roles. Wholesalers may help coordinate regional promotions among retailers and may motivate and train retail salespeople. Most retailers undertake local ads, personal selling, and special events.

Customer services include delivery, credit, in-office and in-home purchases, training programs, warranties, and return privileges. Again, these services can be provided by one channel member or a combination of them.

Distribution intermediaries can contribute to product planning in several ways. They often provide advice on new and existing products. Test marketing requires their cooperation. And intermediaries can be helpful in positioning products against competitors and suggesting which products to drop.

Wholesalers and retailers often have strong input into pricing decisions. They state their required markups and then price-mark products or specify how they should be marked. Court rulings limit manufacturers' ability to control final prices. Intermediaries thus have great flexibility in setting them.

Distribution incorporates three major factors: transportation, inventory management, and customer contact. Goods must be shipped from a manufacturer to consumers; intermediaries often provide this service. Because production capabilities and customer demand frequently differ, inventory levels must be properly managed (and items may require storage in a warehouse before being sold). Consumer transactions may require a store or other seller location, long hours of operation, and store fixtures (such as dressing rooms).

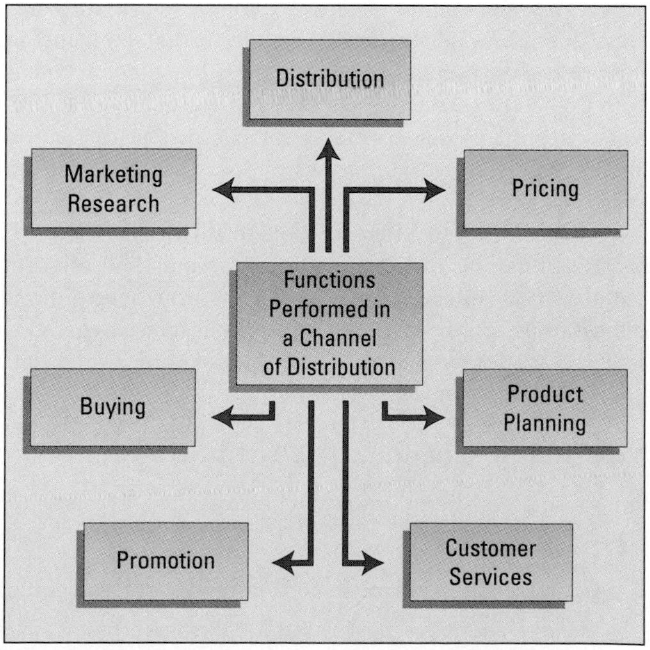

FIGURE 15-3
Channel Functions

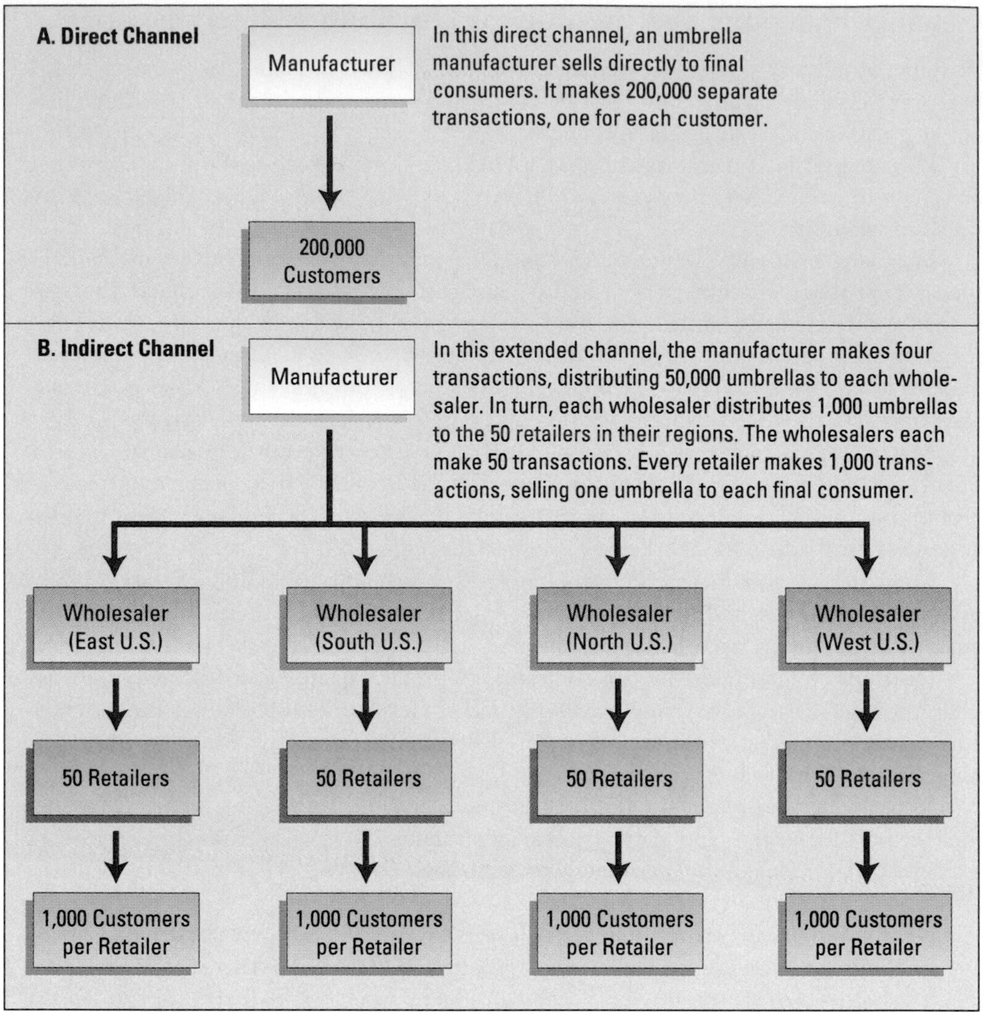

FIGURE 15-4
Transactions in a Direct Versus an Indirect Channel

Manufacturers typically like to make a limited variety of items in large quantities and have as few transactions as possible to sell their entire output. On the other hand, consumers tend to want a variety of brands, colors, sizes, and qualities from which to select—and opt to buy a small amount at a time. Manufacturers might also prefer to sell products from the factory, have 9-to-5 hours and spartan fixtures, and use a limited sales force. Yet, organizational consumers may want salespeople to come to their offices and final consumers may want to shop at nearby locations and visit attractive, well-staffed stores on weekends and evenings.

The **sorting process** *coordinates manufacturer and consumer goals.*

To resolve these differences, intermediaries can be used in the **sorting process**, which consists of four distribution functions: accumulation, allocation, sorting, and assorting. Accumulation is collecting small shipments from several firms so shipping costs are lower. Allocation is apportioning items to various consumer markets. Sorting is separating products into grades, colors, and so forth. Assorting is offering a broad range of products so the consumer has many choices.

Selecting a Channel of Distribution

In choosing a distribution channel, several key factors must be considered:

Channel choice depends on consumers, the company, the product, competition, existing channels, and legalities.

- *The consumer.*

  Characteristics—number, concentration, average purchase size.

  Needs—shopping locations and hours, assortment, sales help, credit.

  Segments—size, purchase behavior.

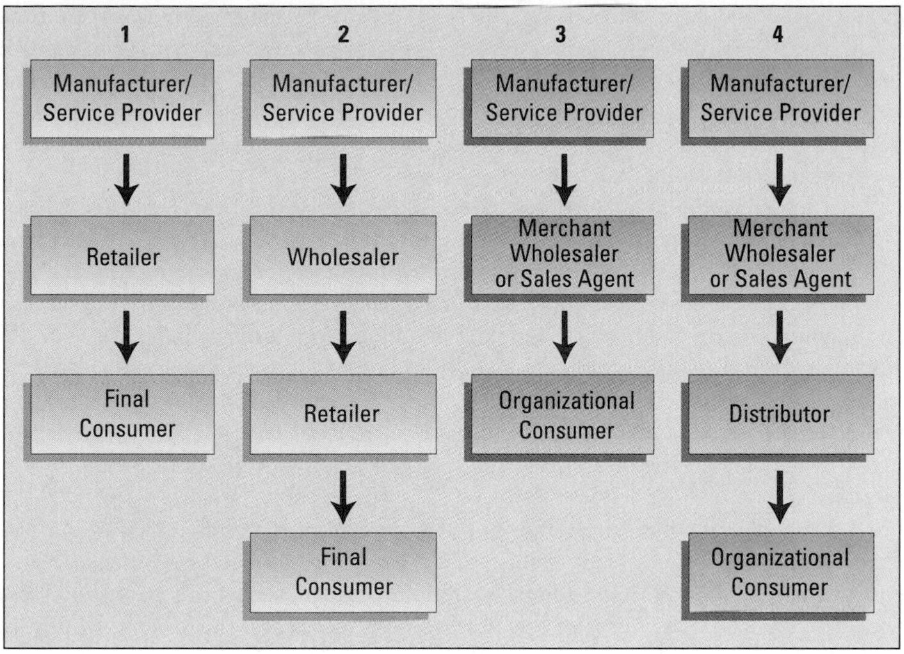

FIGURE 15-5
Typical Indirect Channels of Distribution

- *The company.*

  Goals—control, sales, profit, timing.

  Resources—level, flexibility, service needs.

  Expertise—functions, specialization, efficiency.

  Experience—distribution methods, channel relationships.
- *The product.*

  Value—price per unit.

  Complexity—technical nature.

  Perishability—shelf life, frequency of shipments.

  Bulk—weight per unit, divisibility.
- *The competition.*

  Characteristics—number, concentration, assortment, customers.

  Tactics—distribution methods, channel relationships.
- *Distribution channels.*

  Alternatives—direct, indirect.

  Characteristics—number of intermediaries, functions performed, tradition.

  Availability—exclusive arrangements, territorial restrictions.
- *Legalities*—current laws, pending laws.

While assessing the preceding factors, a firm would make decisions about the type of channel used, contractual arrangements or administered channels, channel length and width, channel intensity, and the use of dual channels.

In a **direct channel,** *one firm performs all tasks. An* **indirect channel** *has multiple firms.*

There are two basic types of channels: direct and indirect. A **direct channel of distribution** involves the movement of goods and services from producer to consumers without the use of independent intermediaries. An **indirect channel of distribution** involves the movement of goods and services from producer to independent intermediaries to consumers. Figure 15-4 shows the transactions necessary for the sale of 200,000 men's umbrellas under direct and indirect channels. Figure 15-5 shows the most common indirect channels for final consumer and organizational consumer products.

If a manufacturer or service provider sells to consumers via company-owned outlets (for example, Exxon-owned gas stations), this is a direct channel. In an indirect channel, a manufacturer may employ several layers of independent wholesalers (for example, regional, state, and local) and sell via different kinds of retailers (such as discount, department, and specialty stores). A direct channel is most used by firms that want control over their entire marketing programs, desire close customer contact, and have limited markets. An indirect channel is most used by firms that want to enlarge their markets, raise sales volume, give up distribution functions and costs, and are willing to surrender some channel control and customer contact.

Because an indirect channel has independent members, a way is needed to plan and assign marketing responsibilities. With a *contractual channel arrangement*, all the terms regarding distribution tasks, prices, and other factors are stated in writing for each member. A manufacturer and a retailer could sign an agreement citing promotion support, delivery and payment dates, and product handling, marking, and displays. In an *administered channel arrangement*, the dominant firm in the distribution process plans the marketing program and itemizes and coordinates each member's duties. Depending on their relative strength, a manufacturer/service provider, wholesaler, or retailer could be a channel leader. Accordingly, a manufacturer with a strong brand could set its image, price range, and selling method.

Channel length *describes the levels of independents.* **Channel width** *refers to the independents at one level.*

Channel length refers to the levels of independent members along a distribution channel. In Figure 15-4, *A* is a short channel and *B* is a long channel. Sometimes, a firm shortens its channel by acquiring a company at another stage, such as a manufacturer merging with a wholesaler. This may let the firm be more self-sufficient, ensure supply, control

Table 15-1
Intensity of Channel Coverage

ATTRIBUTES	EXCLUSIVE DISTRIBUTION	SELECTIVE DISTRIBUTION	INTENSIVE DISTRIBUTION
Objectives	Prestige image, channel control and loyalty, price stability and high profit margins	Moderate market coverage, solid image, some channel control and loyalty, good sales and profits	Widespread market coverage, channel acceptance, volume sales and profits
Resellers	Few in number, well-established, reputable firms (outlets)	Moderate in number, well-established, better firms (outlets)	Many in number, all types of firms (outlets)
Customers	Final consumers: fewer in number, trend setters, willing to travel to store, brand loyal Organizational consumers: focus on major accounts, service expected from manufacturer	Final consumers: moderate in number, brand conscious, somewhat willing to travel to store Organizational consumers: focus on many types of accounts, service expected from manufacturer or intermediary	Final consumers: many in number, convenience-oriented Organizational consumers: focus on all types of accounts, service expected from intermediary
Marketing emphasis	Final consumers: personal selling, pleasant shopping conditions, good service Organizational consumers: availability, regular communications, superior service	Final consumers: promotional mix, pleasant shopping conditions, good service Organizational consumers: availability, regular communications, superior service	Final consumers: mass advertising, nearby location, items in stock Organizational consumers: availability, regular communications, superior service
Major weakness	Limited sales potential	May be difficult to carve out a niche	Limited channel control
Examples	Autos, designer clothes, capital equipment, complex services	Furniture, clothing, mechanics' tools, industrialized services	Household products, groceries, office supplies, routine services

channel members, lower distribution costs, and coordinate timing throughout the channel. Critics of the practice believe it limits competition, fosters inefficiency, and does not result in lower consumer prices.

Channel width refers to the number of independent members at any stage of distribution. In a narrow channel, a manufacturer or service provider sells via few wholesalers or retailers; in a wide channel, it sells via many. If a firm wants to enhance its position at its stage of the channel, it may buy other companies like itself, such as one janitorial-services firm buying another. This lets a firm increase its size and share of the market, improve bargaining power with other channel members, enlarge its market, and utilize mass promotion and distribution techniques more efficiently.

Exclusive, selective, *and* **intensive distribution** *depend on goals, sellers, customers, and marketing.*

In selecting a distribution channel, a firm would decide on the intensity of its coverage. Under **exclusive distribution**, a firm severely limits the number of resellers utilized in a geographic area, perhaps having only one or two within a specific shopping location. It seeks a prestige image, channel control, and high profit margins and accepts lower total sales than in another type of distribution. With **selective distribution**, a firm employs a moderate number of resellers. It tries to combine some channel control and a solid image with good sales volume and profits. A firm uses a large number of resellers in **intensive distribution**. Its goals are to have wide market coverage, channel acceptance, and high total sales and profits. Per-unit profits are low. It is a strategy aimed at the greatest number of consumers. See Table 15-1.

A **dual channel** *lets a company reach different segments or diversify.*

Some additional factors are noteworthy in selecting a channel. First, a firm may use a **dual channel of distribution**, whereby it appeals to different market segments or diversifies business by selling through two or more separate channels. A company could use selective distribution for a prestige brand of watches and intensive distribution for a discount brand, or use both direct and indirect channels (such as an insurance firm selling group health insurance directly to large businesses and individual life insurance indirectly to final consumers via independent agents). See Figure 15-6. Second, a firm may go from exclusive to selective to intensive distribution as a product passes through its life cycle. Yet, it would be hard to go from intensive to selective to exclusive distribution. For example, designer jeans rapidly moved from prestige stores to better stores to all types of outlets. This process would not have worked in reverse. Third, a firm may distribute products in a new way and achieve great success. The sale of women's hosiery was revolutionized when L'eggs products were placed in supermarkets.

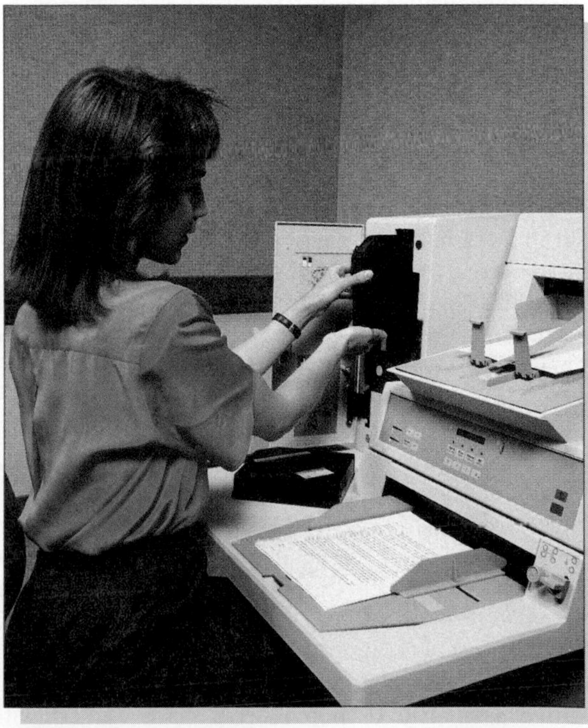

FIGURE 15-6
How Kodak Uses Dual Channels of Distribution
Kodak uses a three-tiered distribution approach for microfilm, supplies, and imaging systems and software: (1) Kodak has its own sales representatives who concentrate on complex document-imaging systems. (2) Well-trained brokers market such Kodak equipment as reader-printers and other stand-alone components; they must be certified to sell and service each product line carried. (3) Other intermediaries handle film sales, film processing, and delivery to all business clients in their territories.
Reprinted by permission.

Supplier/Distribution Intermediary Contracts

Supplier/distribution intermediary contracts cover prices, sale conditions, territories, commitments, timing, and termination.

Supplier/distribution intermediary contracts focus on price policies, conditions of sale, territorial rights, the services/responsibility mix, and contract length and conditions of termination. The highlights of a basic contract follow.

Price policies largely deal with the discounts given to intermediaries for their functions, quantity purchases, and cash payments, and with commission rates. Functional discounts are deductions from list prices given to intermediaries for performing storage, shipping, and other jobs. Quantity discounts are deductions for volume purchases. Cash discounts are deductions for early payment. Some intermediaries are paid commissions for their tasks.

Conditions of sale cover price and quality guarantees, payment and shipping terms, reimbursement for unsaleable items, and return allowances. A guarantee against a price decline protects one intermediary from paying a high price for an item that is then offered to others at a lower price; if prices are reduced, the original buyer receives a rebate so its product costs are like those of competitors. Otherwise, it could not meet the prices that competitors charge customers. Suppliers sometimes employ full-line forcing, whereby intermediaries are required to carry an entire line of products. This is legal if they are not prevented from also buying items from other suppliers.

Territorial rights outline the geographic areas (such as greater Paris) in which resellers may operate and/or the target markets (such as small business accounts) they may contact. In some cases, they have exclusive territories, as with McDonald's franchisees; in others, many firms are granted territorial rights for the same areas, as with retailers selling Sharp calculators.

The services/responsibility mix describes the role of each channel member. It outlines such factors as who delivers products, stores inventory, trains salespeople, writes ad copy, and sets up displays; and it sets performance standards. If included, a hold-harmless clause specifies that manufacturers or service providers—and not resellers—are accountable for law suits arising from poor product design or negligence in production.

Contract length and conditions of termination protect an intermediary against a manufacturer or service provider prematurely bypassing it after a territory has been built up. The manufacturer or service provider is shielded by limiting contract duration and stating the factors leading to termination.

Not all relationships among channel members are so formal. Some firms rely on handshake agreements. However, without a contract, the danger exists that there will be misunderstandings regarding goals, compensation, tasks to be performed, and the length of the agreement. The one constraint of a written contract may be its inflexibility under changing market conditions.

Channel Cooperation and Conflict

Channel member goals need to be balanced.

All firms in a distribution channel have similar general goals: profitability, access to goods and services, efficient distribution, and customer loyalty. Yet, the way these and other goals are achieved often leads to differing views, even if the parties engage in relationship marketing. For example: How are profits allocated along a channel? How can manufacturers sell products via many competing resellers and expect the resellers not to carry other brands? Which party coordinates channel decisions? To whom are consumers loyal—manufacturers/service providers, wholesalers, or retailers?

There are natural differences among the firms in a distribution channel by virtue of their channel positions, the tasks performed, and the desire of each firm to raise its profits and control its strategy. A successful channel will maximize cooperation and minimize conflict. Table 15-2 cites causes of channel conflict. Table 15-3 (on page 426) shows how channel cooperation can reduce these conflicts.

In the past, manufacturers dominated channels because they had the best market coverage and recognition; resellers were small and localized. Now—with the growth of large national (and international) wholesalers and retailers, the volume accounted for by them, and the popularity of private brands—the balance of power has shifted more to resellers. As one expert said, "In highly competitive markets, with so many manufacturers compet-

Table 15-2

Potential Causes of Channel Conflict

FACTOR	MANUFACTURER'S/ SERVICE PROVIDER'S GOAL	DISTRIBUTION INTERMEDIARY'S GOAL
Pricing	To establish final price consistent with product image	To establish final price consistent with the intermediary's image
Purchase terms	To ensure prompt, accurate payments and minimize discounts	To defer payments as long as possible and secure discounts
Shelf space	To obtain plentiful shelf space with good visibility so as to maximize brand sales	To allocate shelf space among multiple brands so as to maximize total product sales
Exclusivity	To hold down the number of competing brands each intermediary stocks while selling via many intermediaries	To hold down the number of competing intermediaries carrying the same brands while selling different brands itself
Delivery	To receive adequate notice before deliveries are required	To obtain quick service
Advertising support	To secure ad support from intermediaries	To secure ad support from manufacturers/service providers
Profitability	To have adequate profit margins	To have adequate profit margins
Continuity	To receive orders on a regular basis	To receive shipments on a regular basis
Order size	To maximize order size	To have order size conform with consumer demand to minimize inventory investment
Assortment	To offer a limited variety	To secure a full variety
Risk	To have intermediaries assume risks	To have manufacturers/service providers assume risks
Branding	To sell products under the manufacturer's/service provider's name	To sell products under private brands, as well as manufacturers'/service providers' brands
Channel access	To distribute products wherever desired by the manufacturer/service provider	To carry only those items desired by intermediaries
Importance of account	To not allow any one intermediary to dominate	To not allow any one manufacturer/service provider to dominate
Consumer loyalty	To have consumers loyal to the manufacturer/service provider	To have consumers loyal to the intermediary
Channel control	To make key channel decisions	To make key channel decisions

ing for the same customers, distributors and dealers can afford to be choosy about which firms' products they will push. Getting them to push your products is what motivation in marketing channels is all about. With so many U.S. manufacturers interested in marketing products overseas, and needing foreign dealers and distributors to do so, the motivation of channel partners needs to be addressed from an international perspective, as well as a domestic one."[8]

If conflicts are not resolved cooperatively, confrontations may occur. A manufacturer or service provider may then ship late, refuse to deal with certain resellers, limit financing, withdraw promotional support, or use other tactics. Similarly, a reseller may make late payments, give poor shelf space, refuse to carry items, return many products, and apply other tactics. A channel cannot function well in a confrontational framework. These are two examples of channel conflict:

- Until a few years ago, Goodyear-brand tires were only sold via 3,000 independent Goodyear dealers. Since then, Goodyear has allowed Sears, Wal-Mart, Montgomery Ward, and others to carry the firm's namesake tires. Although this strategy has boosted

[8]Bert Rosenbloom, "Motivating Your International Channel Partners," *Business Horizons*, Vol. 33 (March–April 1990), p. 53.

Table 15-3
Methods of Channel Cooperation

FACTOR	MANUFACTURER'S/SERVICE PROVIDER'S ACTIONS	DISTRIBUTION INTERMEDIARY'S ACTIONS
New-product introduction	Thorough testing, adequate promotional support	Good shelf location and space, enthusiasm for product, assistance in test marketing
Delivery	Prompt filling of orders, adherence to scheduled dates	Proper time allowed for delivery, shipments immediately checked for accuracy
Marketing research	Data provided to resellers	Data provided to manufacturers/service providers
Pricing	Prices to intermediaries let them gain reasonable profits, intermediary flexibility encouraged	Infrequent sales from regular prices, maintaining proper image
Promotion	Training reseller's salespeople, sales force incentives, developing appropriate ad campaign, cooperative ad programs	Attractive store displays, knowledgeable salespeople, participation in cooperative programs
Financing	Liberal financial terms	Adherence to financial terms
Product quality	Product guarantees	Proper installation and servicing of products for customers
Channel control	Shared and specified decision making	Shared and specified decision making

Goodyear's overall revenues, many dealers have been very upset. One said, "It's not the same old Goodyear. I don't think their ultimate goal is to have a win-win situation."[9]

- Elizabeth Arden had to postpone the introduction of its new Liz Taylor's Black Pearls fragrance after three department store operators—Federated, Dillard, and May—refused to carry the line. Why did they do this? Arden wanted to contribute only 3 per cent of sales to the retailers' sales staffs (down from the traditional 5 per cent). And it also wanted to stop sharing the costs of advertising, catalogs, and window displays. By delaying the product, Arden lost $15 million in development and marketing costs. After several months of negotiations, Arden restored the traditional sales commissions and introduced Black Pearls.[10]

In a **pushing strategy**, *there is cooperation. With* **pulling**, *a firm generates demand before channel support.*

A thriving existing manufacturer or service provider can often secure reseller support and enthusiasm when introducing new products and continuing popular ones. This occurs because resellers know the manufacturer's or service provider's past track record, the promotion support that will be provided, and the manufacturer's or service provider's reliability in future deliveries. Thus, a **pushing strategy** is used, whereby the various firms in a distribution channel cooperate in marketing a product. With this approach, a manufacturer or service provider uses relationship marketing.

As a rule, it is harder for a new manufacturer or service provider to break into an existing channel. Resellers are unfamiliar with the firm, not able to gauge its sales potential, and wonder about its support and future deliveries. So, a new firm would need a **pulling strategy**, whereby it first stimulates consumer demand and then gains dealer support. This means heavy promotion expenses, fully paid by the manufacturer or service provider; it must often offer guarantees of minimum sales or profits to resellers—and make up shortfalls. Figure 15-7 contrasts pushing and pulling strategies.

[9] "Goodyear to Sell Tires at 350 Montgomery Ward & Co. Outlets," *Wall Street Journal* (June 14, 1995), p. A6; and Zachary Schiller, "And Fix That Flat Before You Go, Stanley," *Business Week* (January 16, 1995), p. 35.

[10] Teri Agins, "Arden Cancels Fall Launch of Liz Taylor's Fragrance," *Wall Street Journal* (August 30, 1995), p. B1; and Teri Agins, "Liz's Perfume Gets Star Role in Prime Time," *Wall Street Journal* (February 15, 1996), pp. B1, B6.

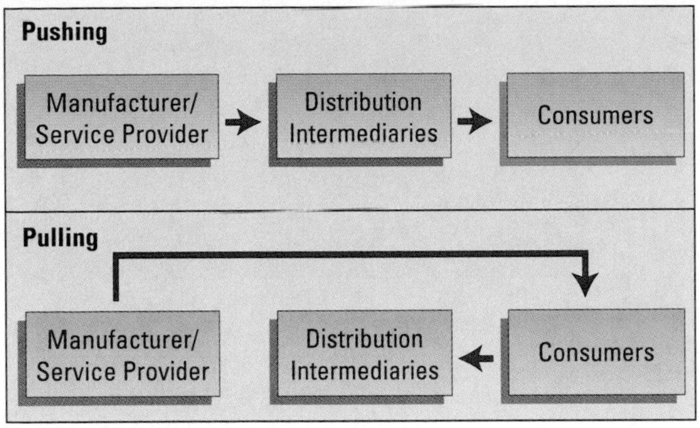

FIGURE 15-7
Pushing Versus Pulling Strategies

In today's competitive environment, with so many new domestic and foreign products being introduced each year, even market-leading firms must sometimes use pulling strategies. They have to convince resellers that consumer demand exists for their products, before the resellers agree to tie up shelf space.

The Industrial Channel of Distribution

An industrial channel has unique characteristics.

The distribution channel for industrial products differs from that for consumer products in the following key ways:

1. Retailers are typically not utilized.
2. Direct channels are more readily employed.
3. Transactions are fewer and orders are larger.
4. Specification selling is more prevalent.
5. Intermediaries are more knowledgeable.
6. Team selling (two or more salespeople) may be necessary.
7. Distinct intermediaries specialize in industrial products.[11]
8. Leasing, rather than selling, is more likely.
9. Customer information needs are more technical.
10. Activities like shipping and warehousing may be shared.

International Distribution Planning

International distribution requires particular planning.

When devising an international distribution plan, a number of factors should be kept in mind. Here are several of them.

Channel length often depends on a nation's stage of economic development and consumer behavior patterns. Less-developed and developing nations tend to use shorter, more direct channels than industrialized ones. They have many small firms marketing goods and services to nearby consumers, and the more limited transportation and communications networks foster local shopping. At the same time, cultural norms in nations—both developing and industrialized—affect the expected interactions between sellers and consumers. For instance, in Japan, people treasure personal attention when making purchases, especially of expensive products. Unlike American shoppers, Japanese consumers are not used to making purchases by telephone.

Distribution practices and formats vary by nation, as these examples show:

- Great Britain has the largest retail chains in Europe. The other nations have more independent retailers; but, with the opening of European borders, the growth of chains will accelerate in the future.

[11]See Kris Frieswick, "Surviving the Mass Merchant Diagnosis," *Industrial Distribution* (September 1995), pp. 28–35.

International Marketing in Action

How Do Mexican Distributors Rate U.S. Manufacturers?

To answer this question, a survey was mailed to Mexican distributors in four industries: industrial machinery, parts and components, chemicals and allied products, and office equipment. A total of one hundred distributors responded. By using distributor *importance* ratings for several attributes, as well as ratings of manufacturer *performance* on these same attributes, the study researchers developed performance "gap" measures.

Respondents were first asked to evaluate the importance of 11 types of support that manufacturers typically provide to distributors. Two of the 11 items related to distributors' terms: adequacy of profit margins and territorial exclusivity. The others related to the manufacturer support provided (such as financial assistance, sales force training, and advertising assistance). According to study results, "quick responses to requests for information" and "adequate profit margins" were the most important factors.

To assess how well U.S. manufacturers performed, the distributors then assessed the manufacturers on each of the 11 factors, and gap measures were generated by subtracting the performance ratings from the importance ratings. Where importance ratings were higher than performance ratings, manufacturers were deemed "underperforming." The opposite results would be categorized as "overperforming." For items rated as important, manufacturers should have high performance ratings. Very high ratings on items viewed as less important indicate that resources could be allocated to other support activities.

In the study, all performance ratings were lower than their importance ratings. This indicates underperformance by manufacturers. Items of high importance with large performance gaps included: "quick responses to requests for information," "training for your salespeople," "materials to assist your salespeople," "advertising to your customers," and "exclusive territories."

As a sales manager for a firm selling products via Mexican distributors, integrate these findings into your overall distributors' sales strategy.

Source: Based on material in Lance Leuthesser, Douglas W. LaBahn, and Katrin R. Harich, "Assessing Cross-National Business Relationships," *Industrial Marketing Management*, Vol. 24 (January 1995), pp. 61–68.

- Some Mexican supermarkets shut their electricity overnight to hold down costs. Thus, items such as dairy products have a much shorter shelf life and must be more frequently delivered than in the United States.
- Large Japanese firms often set up *keiretsus*. A vertical keiretsu is an integrated network of suppliers, manufacturers, and resellers. A horizontal keiretsu typically consists of a money-center bank, an insurance company, a trust banking company, a trading company, and several major manufacturers. U.S. firms have some channels that resemble vertical keiretsus, but they do not have networks that emulate horizontal keiretsus.[12]
- Although it has more than three times as many people as the United States, India has roughly the same number of retail establishments, and just one-quarter of them are

[12]Roy L. Simerly, "Should U.S. Companies Establish Keiretsus?" *Journal of Business Strategy*, Vol. 13 (November–December 1992), pp. 58–61.

in metropolitan areas. "Pan-bidi" are the popular neighborhood grocery and general stores that offer very low prices.[13]

If a firm enters a foreign market for the first time, it must resolve various questions, including: Should products be made domestically and shipped to the foreign market or made in the foreign market? If products are made domestically, what form of transportation is best? What kind of distribution intermediaries should be used? Which specific intermediaries should be used? The U.S. Department of Commerce runs district offices nationwide to assist small firms seeking advice on international distribution. It has computerized market data on more than 150 nations and contacts in a number of them. For a modest fee, an Agent/Distributor Service (ADS) can locate potential foreign distributors that will to carry a firm's line in a given market.

Legal requirements regarding distribution differ by country—and some have strict laws as to hours, methods of operation, and sites. In France, there are severe limits on Sunday retail hours. In Germany, there are strict limits on store size and Sunday hours. And many nations have complex procedures for foreign firms to distribute products there. Thus, firms interested in standardized (global) distribution may be stymied in their efforts.

What is likely to cause a company to be more or less satisfied with its international distribution channel? According to one study: The better a firm's domestic channel performs relative to its international channel, the lower its satisfaction with the international channel. The more experience a firm has in foreign markets, the greater its satisfaction with its existing international channel. A firm is more satisfied with an existing international channel if it believes it has the ability to change channels. A firm has less satisfaction with its existing international channel if environmental uncertainty is high. A firm is less satisfied with its existing international channel if it is difficult to monitor the behavior of channel members.[14]

Physical Distribution

Physical distribution (also known as **logistics**) encompasses the broad range of activities concerned with efficiently delivering raw materials, parts, semifinished items, and finished products to designated places, at designated times, and in proper condition. It may be undertaken by any member of a channel, from producer to consumer.

Physical distribution (logistics) *involves the location, timing, and condition of deliveries. An* **order cycle** *covers many activities.*

Physical distribution involves such functions as customer service, shipping, warehousing, inventory control, private trucking-fleet operations, packaging, receiving, materials handling, and plant, warehouse, and store location planning. The physical distribution activities involved in a typical **order cycle**—the period of time that spans a customer's placing an order and its receipt—are illustrated in Figure 15-8.

The Importance of Physical Distribution

Physical distribution is important for a number of reasons: its costs, the value of customer service, and its relationship with other functional areas.

Costs Physical distribution costs amount to 10 to 12 per cent of the U.S. GDP, with transportation (freight) accounting for over one-half of that total. To contain costs, firms have been working hard to improve efficiency. Today, physical distribution tasks are completed faster, more accurately, and with fewer people than 20 years ago. Due to greater computerization and improved transportation, firms have reduced their inventory levels by tens of billions of dollars, thus saving on warehousing and interest expenses.

Cost control is a major goal.

Distribution costs vary widely by industry and company type. At individual firms, total physical distribution costs depend on such factors as the nature of the business, the geographic area covered, the tasks done by other channel members, and the weight/value

[13]Janet Zhang, "Asia: Opportunities Large and Small," *Chain Store Age Executive* (January 1995), Section 3, p. 7.
[14]Saul Klein and Victor J. Roth, "Satisfaction with International Marketing Channels," *Journal of the Academy of Marketing Science*, Vol. 21 (Winter 1993), pp. 39–44.

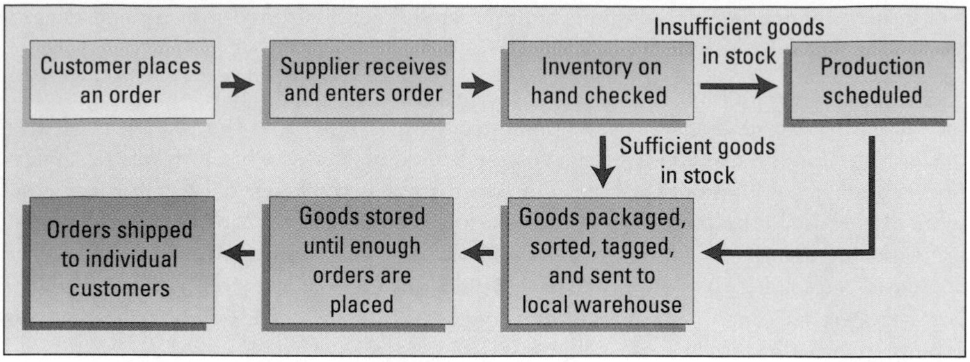

FIGURE 15-8
Selected Physical Distribution Activities Involved in a Typical Order Cycle

ratio of the items involved. For example, while many retailers spend 2 to 3 per cent of their revenues on transportation from vendors and receiving, marking, storing, and distributing goods; petroleum refiners spend almost one-quarter of their sales just on inbound and outbound transportation. And whenever the U.S. Postal Service raises rates, shipping costs are dramatically affected for all kinds of firms.

Firms must identify the symptoms of poor distribution systems and strive to be more efficient. Up to one-fifth of the perishable items carried by U.S. grocers, like fish and dairy items, are lost to spoilage due to breakdowns in shipping or too much time on store shelves. To reduce losses, many grocers now insist on smaller, more frequent deliveries and have upgraded their storage facilities. Table 15-4 shows several cost ramifications of poor distribution.

Customer Service A major concern in planning a firm's physical distribution program is the level of customer service it should provide. Decisions involve delivery frequency, speed, and consistency; emergency shipments; whether to accept small orders; warehousing; coordinating assortments; whether to provide order progress reports; and other factors. Weak performance may lose customers.

Accordingly, distribution standards—clear and measurable goals as to service levels in physical distribution—must be devised. Examples are filling 90 per cent of orders from

Table 15-4
Selected Symptoms of a Poor Physical Distribution System

SYMPTOM	COST RAMIFICATIONS
1. Slow-turning and/or too-high inventory	Excessive capital is tied up in inventory. The firm has high insurance costs, interest expenses, and high risks of pilferage and product obsolescence. Merchandise may be stale.
2. Inefficient customer service	Costs are high relative to the value of shipments; warehouses are poorly situated; inventory levels are not tied to customer demand.
3. A large number of interwarehouse shipments	Merchandise transfers raise physical distribution costs because items must be handled and verified at each warehouse.
4. Frequent use of emergency shipments	Extra charges add significantly to physical distribution costs.
5. Peripheral hauls and/or limited backhauling	The firm uses its own trucking facilities; but many hauls are too spread out and trucks may only be full one way.
6. A large number of small orders	Small orders often are unprofitable. Many distribution costs are fixed.

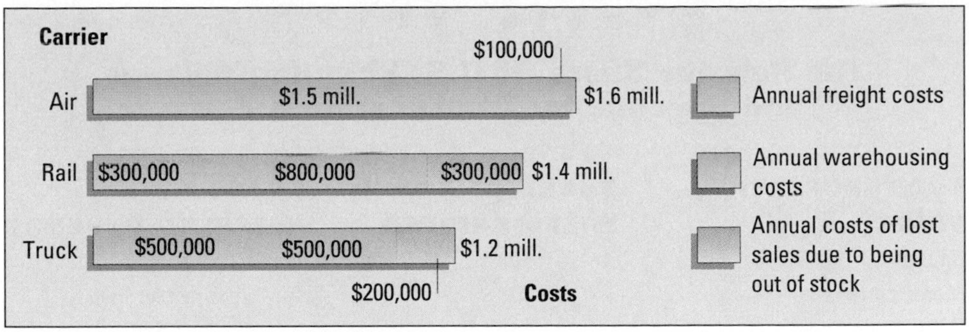

FIGURE 15-9
An Illustration of the Total-Cost Approach in Distribution

existing inventory, responding to customer requests for order information within two hours, filling orders with 99 per cent accuracy, and limiting goods damaged in transit to two per cent or less.

The **total-cost approach** *considers both costs and opportunities.*

One way to set the proper customer service level is the **total-cost approach**, whereby the distribution service level with the lowest total costs—including freight (shipping), warehousing, and lost business—is the best service level. An ideal system seeks a balance between low expenditures on distribution and high opportunities for sales. Seldom will that be at the lowest level of distribution spending; lost sales will be too great. Figure 15-9 illustrates the total-cost approach.

By offering superior customer service, a firm may establish a significant competitive advantage. The opposite is also true: "Customers increasingly demand on-time delivery from their suppliers. If they don't get it, they go elsewhere. The standard delivery window in supermarkets used to be four hours. Now, top suppliers deliver within an hour of their promised times, sometimes within fifteen minutes. The trend toward more reliable delivery times reaches across all industries."[15]

Physical distribution must be coordinated with other areas.

Physical Distribution and Other Functional Areas There is an interaction between physical distribution and every aspect of marketing, as well as other functional areas in the firm, as the following indicate.

Product variations in color, size, features, quality, and style impose a burden on a firm's distribution facilities. Greater variety means lower volume per item, which increases unit shipping and warehousing costs. Stocking a broader range of replacement parts also becomes necessary.

Physical distribution is related to an overall channel strategy. A firm seeking extensive distribution needs dispersed warehouses. One involved with perishables needs to be sure that most of a product's selling life is not spent in transit.

Because promotion campaigns are often planned well in advance, it is essential that distribution to resellers be done at the proper times to ensure ample stocks of goods. Resellers may get consumer complaints for not having sufficient quantities of the items they advertise, although the manufacturer is really at fault. Some new products fail due to poor initial distribution.

Physical distribution also plays a key part in pricing. A firm with fast, reliable delivery and an ample supply of replacement parts—that ships small orders and provides emergency shipments—may be able to charge higher prices than one providing less service.

A distribution strategy has a link with production and finance functions. High freight costs inspire firms to put plants closer to markets. Low average inventories in stock allow firms to reduce finance charges. Warehouse receipts may be used as collateral for loans.

Overall, there are many decisions to be made and coordinated in planning a physical distribution strategy: the transportation form(s) used, inventory levels and warehouse form(s), and the number and sites of plants, warehouses, and shopping facilities. A strategy can be simple: A firm can have one plant, focus on one geographic market, and ship to resellers or customers without the use of decentralized warehouses. On the other hand,

[15]Anil Kumar and Graham Sharman, "We Love Your Product, But Where Is It?" *Sloan Management Review*, Vol. 33 (Winter 1992), p. 92. See also Ronald Henkoff, "Delivering the Goods," *Fortune* (November 28, 1994), pp. 64–78.

Table 15-5

The Relative Share of U.S. Shipping Mileage and Revenue by Transportation Form

TRANSPORTATION FORM	SHARE OF TON MILES SHIPPED	SHARE OF SHIPPING REVENUE
Railroads	38%	9%
Motor carriers	28	79
Waterways	15	6
Pipelines	18	2
Airways	less than 0.5	4

Sources: Adapted by the authors from Frank A. Smith, *Transportation in America*, 11th Edition (Lansdowne, Virginia: Transportation Foundation, 1993); and *Statistical Abstract of the United States 1995* (Washington, D.C.: U.S. Department of Commerce, 1995).

a strategy can include multiple plants, assembly and/or warehouse locations in each market, thousands of customer locations, and several transportation forms.

The rest of this chapter looks at two central aspects of a physical distribution strategy: transportation and inventory management.

Transportation

Transportation is rated on speed, availability, dependability, capability, frequency, losses, and cost.

There are five basic transportation forms: railroads, motor carriers, waterways, pipelines, and airways. Table 15-5 shows the share of U.S. mileage and revenue by each. Table 15-6 ranks them on seven operating characteristics.

The deregulation of U.S. transportation industries has greatly expanded the competition in and among these industries. Deregulation generally allows transportation firms greater flexibility in entering markets, expanding their businesses, the products carried, price setting, and the functions performed. It also means greater choices for those shipping goods.

Each transportation form and three transport services are studied next.

Railroads *ship mostly heavy items over long distances.*

Railroads **Railroads** usually carry heavy, bulky items that are low in value (relative to weight) over long distances. They ship items too heavy for trucks. Despite their dominant position in ton miles shipped, railroads have had various problems. Fixed costs are high due to investments in facilities. Shippers face railroad car shortages in high-demand months for agricultural goods. Some tracks and railroad cars are in serious need of repair. Trucks are faster, more flexible, and packed more easily. In response to these problems, railroads are relying on new shipping techniques, operating flexibility due to deregulation, and mergers to improve efficiency.

Motor carriers *handle small shipments for short distances.*

Motor Carriers **Motor carriers** predominantly transport small shipments over short distances. They handle about 80 per cent of U.S. shipments weighing less than 500 or 1,000 pounds. Seventy per cent of all motor carriers are used for local deliveries and two-thirds of total truck miles are local. For these reasons, motor carriers account for a large share of shipping revenue. Motor carriers are more flexible than rail because they can pick up packages at a factory or warehouse and deliver them to the customer's door. They are often used to supplement rail, air, and other forms that cannot deliver direct to customers. In addition, trucks are faster than rail for short distances. Like railroads, the trucking industry has been deregulated since 1980.

Waterways *specialize in low-value, high-bulk items.*

Waterways In the United States, **waterways** involve the movement of goods on barges via inland rivers and on tankers and general-merchandise freighters through the Great Lakes, intercoastal shipping, and the St. Lawrence Seaway. They are used primarily for transporting low-value, high-bulk freight (such as coal, iron ore, gravel, grain, and ce-

Table 15-6

The Relative Operating Characteristics of Five Transportation Forms

OPERATING CHARACTERISTICS	RANKING BY TRANSPORTATION FORM[a]				
	Railroads	*Motor Carriers*	*Waterways*	*Pipelines*	*Airways*
Delivery speed	3	2	5	4	1
Number of locations served	2	1	4	5	3
On-time dependability[b]	3	2	4	1	5
Range of products carried	1	2	3	5	4
Frequency of shipments	4	2	5	1	3
Losses and damages	5	4	2	1	3
Cost per ton mile	3	4	1	2	5

[a] 1 = highest ranking.

[b] Relative variation from anticipated delivery time.

Sources: Adapted by the authors from Donald J. Bowersox and David J. Closs, *Logistical Management: The Integrated Supply Chain Process* (New York: McGraw-Hill, 1996); Ronald H. Ballou, *Business Logistics Management: Planning and Control*, Third Edition (Englewood Cliffs, N.J.: Prentice Hall, 1992); and James C. Johnson and Donald F. Wood, *Contemporary Logistics*, Fourth Edition (New York: Macmillan, 1990).

ment). Waterways are slow and may be closed by ice in winter, but rates are quite low. Various improvements in vessel design have occurred over the last several years. For example, many "supervessels" now operate on the Great Lakes and other waterways. They can each carry up to 60,000 gross tons or more of iron-bearing rock (or similar heavy materials) in one trip. Their conveyor systems are twice as efficient as the ones on older boats. Navigation is computer controlled.

Pipelines Within **pipelines**, there is continuous movement and there are no interruptions, inventories (except those held by a carrier), and intermediate storage sites. Handling and labor costs are minimized. Although pipelines are very reliable, only certain commodities can be moved through them. In the past, emphasis was on gas and petroleum-based products. Pipelines have now been modified to accept coal and wood chips, which are sent as semiliquids. Still, the lack of flexibility limits their potential. Some pipelines are enormous. The Trans-Alaska Highway pipeline is 48 inches in diameter and 800 miles long. It carries 25 per cent of all the U.S. crude oil produced. It can discharge up to two million barrels daily. Oil is loaded from the pipeline to supervessels and then sent by water to the lower 48 states.

Pipelines *center on liquids, gases, and semiliquids.*

Airways **Airways** are the fastest and most expensive transportation form. High-value, perishable, and emergency goods dominate air shipments. Although air transit is costly, it may lower other costs, such as the need for outlying or even regional warehouses. The costs of packing, unpacking, and preparing goods for shipping are lower than for other transportation forms. Airfreight has been deregulated since the late 1970s. So, many firms have stepped up their cargo operations. Some now use wide-bodied jets for large containers. Modern communications and sorting equipment have also been added to airfreight operations. Firms specializing in air shipments have done well by stressing speedy, guaranteed service at acceptable prices.

Airways *handle valuable, perishable, and emergency items.*

Transportation Services Transportation service companies are marketing specialists that chiefly handle the shipments of small and moderate-sized packages. Some pick up at the sender's office and deliver direct to the addressee. Others require packages to be brought to a service company outlet. The major kinds of transportation service firms are government parcel post, private parcel, and express.

These transportation service companies ship packages: government parcel post, private parcel, and express.

Government parcel post operates out of post offices and has rates based on postal zones, of which there are eight in the United States. Parcel post can be insured or sent

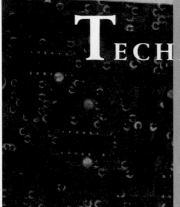

TECHNOLOGY & MARKETING

How Are Carriers Weblike in Tracking Shipments?

According to experts, the role of the Internet has gone from being a library of data (phase one) to a provider of important customer services (phase two). In its third phase, the Internet will enable customers to better handle financial transactions. Evidence of the transition from phase one to phase two is the use of the Internet's World Wide Web by business customers to track packages shipped by Federal Express and United Parcel Service (UPS).

Since November 1994, all Federal Express customers have been able to log on to the FedEx home page on the World Wide Web and enter their bill-tracking numbers into online package-tracking forms. Within minutes, the Internet server connects with Federal Express' main computer and returns reports to customers on the locations of their packages. As packages move through the FedEx distribution system, the data passed on to clients are constantly updated by Federal Express personnel.

Although Federal Express had to design special software and contract with an Internet provider, the overall costs of implementing its system have been very low. In addition, the FedEx site—which receives 4,500+ inquiries per day—saves money for the firm by reducing the need for customer service personnel. All customers have access to this Internet-based service, but larger ones can also access the firm's private network. According to a Federal Express spokesperson, 60 per cent of all package tracking is now done through automated procedures.

Likewise, UPS has begun to offer package tracking on the Internet. As with Federal Express, UPS' site was not started to save money for the firm, but is less costly than other package tracking methods.

As a customer service supervisor for Federal Express, outline the pros and cons of using the World Wide Web to automate package tracking.

Source: Based on material in Laurie Flynn, "Companies Use Web Hoping to Save Millions," *New York Times* (July 17, 1995), p. D5.

COD (collect on delivery). Regular service is completed in a few days. Special handling is available to expedite shipments. Express mail is available for next-day service from a post office to an addressee.

Private parcel services specialize in small-package delivery, usually less than 50-pound shipments. Most shipments go from businesses to their customers. Regular service usually takes two to three days. More expensive next-day service is also available from many carriers. The largest private firm is United Parcel Service (UPS), a multibillion-dollar, international company. See Figure 15-10.

Specialized express companies, such as Federal Express and Emery Air Freight, typically provide guaranteed nationwide delivery of small packages for the morning after pickup. The average express delivery is under 10 pounds.

Containerization *and* **freight forwarding** *simplify intermodal shipping.*

Coordinating Transportation Because a single shipment may involve a combination of transportation forms—a practice known as *intermodal shipping*, coordination is needed. A firm can enhance its ability to coordinate shipments via containerization and freight forwarding.

With **containerization**, goods are placed in sturdy containers that can be loaded on trains, trucks, ships, or planes. The marked containers are sealed until delivered, thereby reducing damage and pilferage. Their progress and destination are monitored. The containers are mobile warehouses that can be moved from manufacturing plants to receiving docks, where they remain until the contents are needed.

In **freight forwarding**, specialized firms (freight forwarders) collect small shipments (usually less than 500 pounds each) from several companies. They pick up merchandise at each shipper's place of business and arrange for delivery at buyers' doors. Freight for-

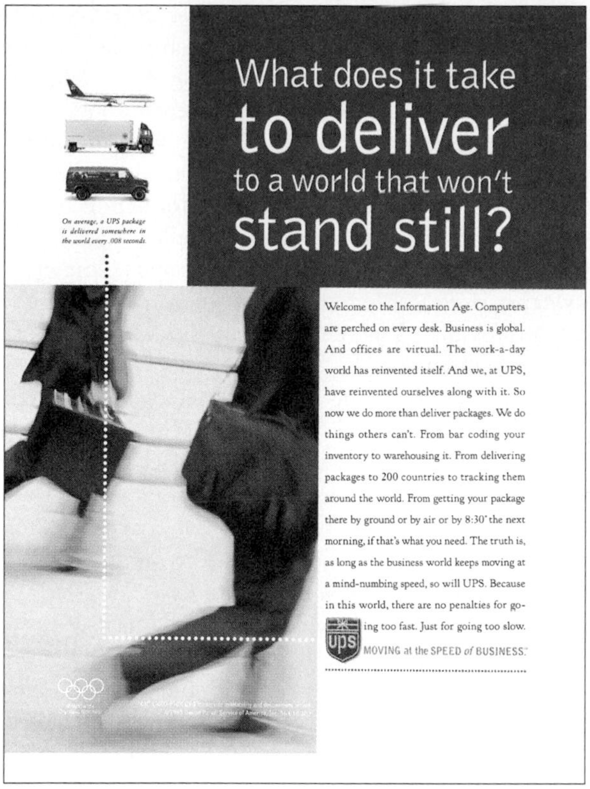

FIGURE 15-10
1–800-PICK-UPS
Reprinted by permission.

warders prosper because less than carload (lcl) shipping rates are sharply higher than carload (cl) rates. They also provide traffic management services, such as selecting the best transportation form at the most reasonable rate.

Carriers are classified as **common, contract, exempt,** *or* **private.**

The Legal Status of Transportation Firms Transportation firms are categorized as common, contract, exempt, and/or private carriers. **Common carriers** must transport the goods of any company (or individual) interested in their services; they cannot refuse any shipments unless their rules are broken (such as packing requirements). Common carriers provide service on a fixed and publicized schedule between designated points. A fee schedule is published. All railroads and petroleum pipelines and some air, motor vehicle, and water transporters are common carriers.

Contract carriers provide transportation services to one or more shippers, based on individual agreements. Contract carriers do not have to maintain set routes or schedules and may negotiate rates. Many motor vehicle, inland waterway, and airfreight transporters are contract carriers. Firms can operate as both common and contract carriers, depending on their services.

Exempt carriers are excused from legal regulations and must only comply with safety rules. They are specified by law. Some commodities moved by water and most agricultural goods are exempt from many legal restrictions.

Private carriers are firms with their own transportation facilities. They are subject to safety rules. In the United States, there are over 100,000 private carriers.

Inventory Management

Inventory management *deals with the flow and allocation of products.*

The intent of **inventory management** is to provide a continuous flow of goods and to match the quantity of goods kept in inventory as closely as possible with customer demand. When production or consumption is seasonal or erratic, this can be particularly difficult.

Inventory management has broad implications: A manufacturer or service firm cannot afford to run out of a crucial part that could put a halt to its business. Yet, inventory on hand should not be too large because the costs of storing raw materials, parts, and/or finished products can be substantial. If models change yearly, as with autos, large inven-

Just-in-time (JIT) *and* **quick response (QR) inventory systems** *closely monitor inventory levels.*

tories can adversely affect new-product sales or rentals. Excessive stock may also lead to stale goods, cause a firm to mark down prices, and tie up funds.

To improve their inventory management, a lot of companies are now applying either or both of two complementary concepts: a just-in-time inventory system and electronic data interchange. With a **just-in-time (JIT) inventory system**, a purchasing firm reduces the amount of inventory it keeps on hand by ordering more often and in lower quantity. This requires better planning and information on the part of the purchaser, geographically closer sellers, improved buyer-seller relationships, and better production and distribution facilities. To retailers, a JIT system is known as a **quick response (QR) inventory system**—a cooperative effort between retailers and suppliers to reduce retail inventory while providing a merchandise supply that more closely addresses the actual buying patterns of consumers.[16]

JIT and QR systems are being used by auto makers, Hewlett-Packard, Canon, DuPont, Ryder, Whirlpool, The Limited, Levi Strauss, Wal-Mart, J.C. Penney, Motorola, Premier Industrial, General Electric, Deere, Black & Decker, Boeing, and many other large and small firms. For example, when a Camry lands at Toyota's Kentucky paint shop, a seat order—color, fabric, and type (bench or bucket)—is sent by computer to a nearby Johnson Controls factory. Four hours later, the seat can be installed in the Camry. Johnson Controls also provides similar service for GM, Chrysler, Ford, and Nissan.[17] Figure 15-11 highlights the JIT systems used by DuPont and Rider.

With **electronic data interchange (EDI)**, *computers are used to exchange information between suppliers and their customers.*

Through **electronic data interchange (EDI)**, suppliers and their manufacturers/service providers, wholesalers, and/or retailers exchange data via computer linkups. This lets firms maximize revenues, reduce markdowns, and lower inventory-carrying costs by speeding the flow of data and products. For EDI to work well, each firm in a distribution channel must use the Universal Product Code (UPC) and electronically exchange data. Although all major food makers use the UPC, many makers of general merchandise do not. However, the number of general merchandise manufacturers using the UPC on their products has been rising, and more will begin using the UPC in the near future.

Four specific aspects of inventory management are examined next: stock turnover, when to reorder, how much to reorder, and warehousing.

Stock turnover *shows the ratio between sales and average inventory.*

Stock Turnover **Stock turnover**—the number of times during a stated period (usually one year) that average inventory on hand is sold—shows the relationship between a firm's sales and the inventory level it maintains. It is calculated in units or dollars (in selling price or at cost):

$$\text{Annual rate of stock turnover} = \frac{\text{Number of units sold during year}}{\text{Average inventory on hand (in units)}}$$

or

$$= \frac{\text{Net yearly sales}}{\text{Average inventory on hand (valued in sales dollars)}}$$

or

$$= \frac{\text{Cost of goods sold}}{\text{Average inventory on hand (valued at cost)}}$$

For example, in retailing, average annual stock turnover ranges from less than 3 in jewelry stores to more than 30 in gasoline service stations.

[16]See Jitendra Chhikara and Elliott N. Weiss, "JIT Savings—Myth or Reality?" *Business Horizons*, Vol. 38 (May–June 1995), pp. 73–78; Susan R. Helper and Mari Sako, "Supplier Relations in Japan and the United States: Are They Converging?" *Sloan Management Review*, Vol. 36 (Spring 1995), pp. 77–84; Lisa Phillips and Cornelia Dröge, "Quick Response: A Theoretical Framework" in David W. Stewart and Naufel J. Vilcassim (Editors), *1995 AMA Winter Educators' Proceedings* (Chicago: American Marketing Association, 1995), pp. 295–302; Paul F. Christ and Jack Gault, "The Benefits, Costs, and Strategic Implications of Quick Response Systems" in Barbara B. Stern and George M. Zinkham (Editors), *1995 AMA Educators' Proceedings* (Chicago: American Marketing Association, 1995), pp. 485–491; and Jonathan Friedland, "VW Puts Suppliers on Production Lines," *Wall Street Journal* (February 15, 1996), p. A11.

[17]Marcia Berss, "Watizzit?" *Forbes* (August 28, 1995), p. 100.

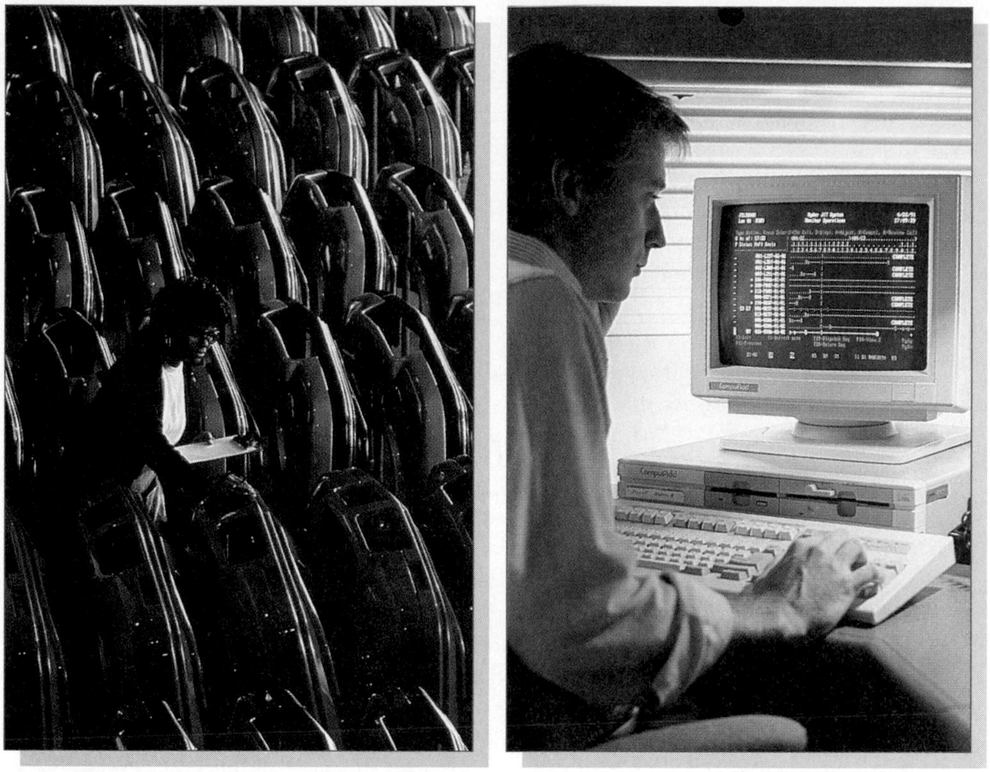

FIGURE 15-11
JIT in Action
At its Kansas City facility (left), DuPont paints, assembles, and delivers auto body parts to a nearby General Motors assembly plant on a just-in-time basis. Through its JIT system (right), Ryder tracks deliveries for the business customers that utilize its full-service truck leases.
Reprinted by permission of DuPont Company and Ryder System.

A high stock turnover rate has many advantages: inventory investments are productive, items are fresh, losses from style changes are reduced, and inventory costs (such as insurance, breakage, warehousing, and credit) are lower. Turnover can be improved by reducing assortments, dropping slow-selling items, keeping only small amounts of some items, and buying from suppliers that deliver on time. On the other hand, too high a turnover rate may have adverse effects: small purchases may cause a loss of volume discounts, low product assortment may reduce sales volume if consumers do not have enough choice or related items are not carried, discounts may be needed to lift sales volume, and chances of running out of stock go up when average inventory size is low. Figure 15-12 shows how people can act should a firm run out of stock.

Knowing when to reorder merchandise helps protect against stockouts while minimizing inventory investments.

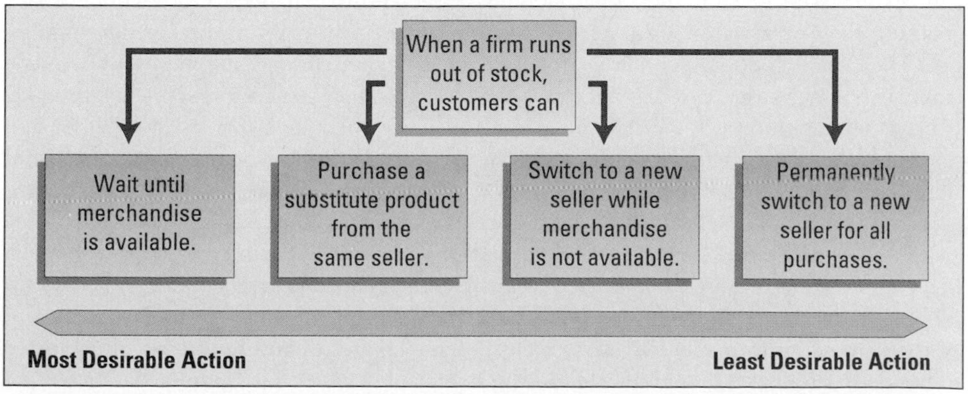

FIGURE 15-12
What Happens When a Firm Has Stock Shortages

The **reorder point** *is based on lead time, usage, and safety stock.*

When to Reorder Inventory By having a clear **reorder point** for each of its products (or raw materials or parts), a firm sets the inventory levels at which to place new orders. A reorder point depends on order lead time, the usage rate, and safety stock. Order lead time is the period from the date an order is placed until the date items are ready to sell or use (received, checked, and altered, if needed). Usage rate is the average unit sales (for a reseller) or the rate at which a product is used in production (for a manufacturer). Safety stock is extra inventory kept to guard against being out of stock due to unexpectedly high demand or production and delivery delays.

The reorder point formula is

$$\text{Reorder point} = (\text{Order lead time} \times \text{Usage rate}) + (\text{Safety stock})$$

For instance, a wholesaler that needs four days for its purchase orders to be placed and received, sells ten items per day, and wants to have ten extra items on hand in case of a supplier's delivery delay of one day, has a reorder point of 50 [(4 × 10) + (10)]. Without safety stock, the firm would lose ten sales if it orders when inventory is forty items and the items are received in five days.

How Much to Reorder A firm must decide its order size—the right amount of products, parts, and so on, to buy at one time. Order size depends on volume discounts, the firm's resources, the stock turnover rate, the costs of processing each order, and the costs of holding goods in inventory. If a firm places large orders, quantity discounts are usually available, a large part of its finances are tied up in inventory, its stock turnover rate is relatively low, per-order processing costs are low, and inventory costs are generally high. The firm is also less apt to run out of goods. The opposite is true for small orders.

Economic order quantity (EOQ) *balances ordering and inventory costs.*

Many companies seek to balance their order-processing costs (filling out forms, computer time, and product handling) and their inventory-holding costs (warehouse expenses, interest charges, insurance, deterioration, and theft). Processing costs per unit fall as orders get bigger, but inventory costs rise. The **economic order quantity (EOQ)** is the order volume corresponding to the lowest sum of order-processing and inventory-holding costs.

Table 15-7 demonstrates three ways to compute EOQ. In this illustration, a firm has an annual demand of 3,000 units for a product; the cost of each unit is $1; order-processing costs are $3 per order; and inventory-holding costs equal 20 per cent of each item's cost. As shown in the table, the economic order quantity is 300 units. Thus, the firm should place orders of 300 units and have 10 orders per year.

Warehousing *involves storing and dispatching goods.*

Warehousing **Warehousing** involves the physical facilities used to store, identify, and sort goods in expectation of their sale and transfer within a distribution channel. Warehouses can be used to store goods, prepare goods for shipment, coordinate shipments, send orders, and aid in product recalls.

Private warehouses are owned and operated by firms that store and distribute their own products. They are most likely to be used by those with stable inventory levels and long-run plans to serve the same geographic areas.

Public warehouses provide storage and related distribution services to any interested firm or individual on a rental basis. They are used by small firms that do not have the resources or desire to have their own facilities, larger firms that need more storage space (because their own warehouses are full), or any size of firm entering new geographic areas. They offer shipping economies for users by allowing carload shipments to be made from such warehouses in local markets; then short-distance, smaller shipments are made from warehouses to customers. Firms can also reduce their investments in facilities and maximize flexibility by using public warehouses. If products must be recalled, these warehouses can be used as collection points, where items are separated, disposed of, and/or salvaged. There are thousands of public warehouses in the United States.

Public warehouses can accommodate both bonded warehousing and field warehousing. In bonded warehousing, imported or taxable goods are stored and can be released for sale only after applicable taxes are paid. This enables firms to postpone tax payments until they are ready to make deliveries to customers. Cigarettes and liquor are often stored in bonded warehouses. In field warehousing, a receipt is issued by a public warehouse for

Table 15-7
Computing an Economic Order Quantity

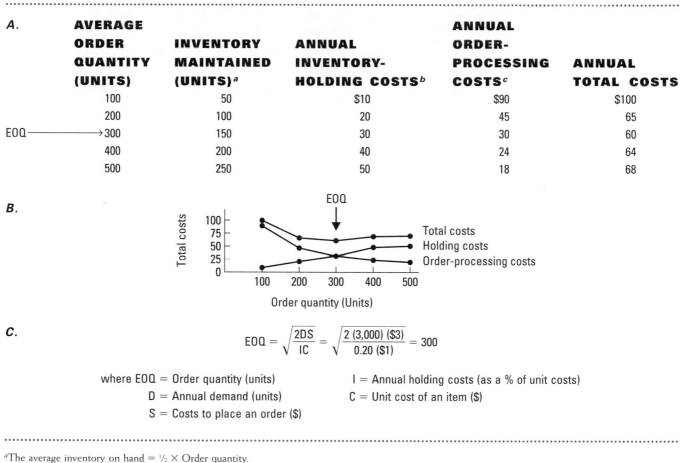

A.

	AVERAGE ORDER QUANTITY (UNITS)	INVENTORY MAINTAINED (UNITS)[a]	ANNUAL INVENTORY-HOLDING COSTS[b]	ANNUAL ORDER-PROCESSING COSTS[c]	ANNUAL TOTAL COSTS
	100	50	$10	$90	$100
	200	100	20	45	65
EOQ ⟶	300	150	30	30	60
	400	200	40	24	64
	500	250	50	18	68

B.

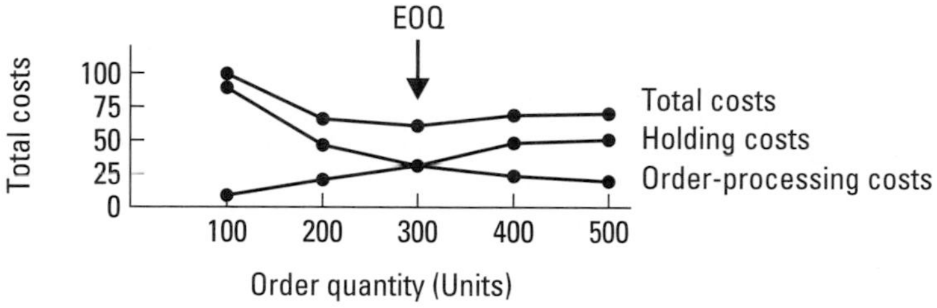

C.

$$EOQ = \sqrt{\frac{2DS}{IC}} = \sqrt{\frac{2\,(3{,}000)\,(\$3)}{0.20\,(\$1)}} = 300$$

where EOQ = Order quantity (units)
D = Annual demand (units)
S = Costs to place an order ($)
I = Annual holding costs (as a % of unit costs)
C = Unit cost of an item ($)

[a]The average inventory on hand = ½ × Order quantity.

[b]Inventory-holding costs = Annual holding costs as a per cent of unit cost × Unit cost × Average inventory.

[c]Order-processing costs = Number of annual orders × Costs to place an order. Number of orders = Annual demand/Order quantity.

goods stored in a private warehouse or in transit to consumers. The goods are put in a special area, and the field warehouser is responsible for them. A firm may use field warehousing because a warehouse receipt serves as collateral for a loan.

MARKETING IN A CHANGING WORLD

Being Aware of the Problem of Export Diversion[18]

As companies expand globally, they face a greater chance of dealing with unscrupulous foreign distributors. Why? There are two major reasons: One, it is difficult to do the proper background checks on such distributors—and less is known about them than about domestic distributors. Two, it is hard to monitor distributor performance in distant markets.

A particularly troublesome distribution practice for U.S. manufacturers is known as "export diversion." This hypothetical example shows how it works:

1. A U.S. manufacturer sells 100,000 widgets to Europe-based ABC Distributors for $10 each (half the U.S. wholesale price) so as to gain access to Kazakhstan.

[18]The material in this section is based on Amy Borrus, "Exports That Aren't Going Anywhere," *Business Week* (December 4, 1995), pp. 121, 124.

2. The manufacturer ships the widgets to Rotterdam, while ABC secretly pre-sells them to U.S. supermarket chains and wholesalers for $15 apiece. In Rotterdam, the widgets are repackaged and sent back to the United States duty-free as "American goods returned."
3. ABC earns $500,000—the difference between the manufacturer's export price and the price paid by the U.S. supermarkets and wholesalers.
4. The returned widgets are sold in the United States, and the manufacturer cannot understand why some of its supermarket customers are no longer buying from it.

Johnson & Johnson, a very sophisticated U.S.-based manufacturer, recently learned that export diversion is not just "hypothetical":

> It seemed like the perfect opportunity to break into an important emerging market. At least that's what LifeScan Inc., a Johnson & Johnson subsidiary, thought when it agreed to sell $400,000 worth of glucose test strips at half the U.S. wholesale price. The buyer, Swiss-based Anglo-American Foundation, promised to distribute LifeScan's devices to needy diabetics in the former Soviet Union. But the deal was costly—particularly when LifeScan discovered that its strips never even left U.S. shores. Instead, they allegedly were diverted by Anglo-American to a New Jersey warehouse and then resold to local wholesalers for a tidy profit.

Because of export diversion, international companies now have one more illegal and unethical business practice to worry about—and to police.

SUMMARY

1. *To define distribution planning and to examine its importance, distribution functions, the factors used in selecting a distribution channel, and the different types of distribution channels* Distribution planning is systematic decision making as to the physical movement of goods and services from producer to consumer, as well as the related transfer of ownership (or rental). A channel of distribution consists of the organizations or people—known as channel members or distribution intermediaries—involved in the distribution process.

Distribution decisions often affect a firm's marketing plans. For many firms, the choice of a distribution channel is one of the most important decisions they make. More companies now realize the value of relationship marketing and work for long-term relations with suppliers, intermediaries, and customers. Both costs and profits are affected by the channel chosen. Firms may have to conform to existing channel patterns; and their markets' size and nature are also influenced by the channel employed.

No matter who does them, channel functions include research, buying, promotion, customer services, product planning, pricing, and distribution. Intermediaries can play a key role by doing various tasks and resolving differences in manufacturer and consumer goals via the sorting process.

In selecting a method of distribution, these factors must be considered: the consumer, the company, the product, the competition, the distribution channels themselves, and legal requirements.

A direct channel requires that one party do all distribution tasks; in an indirect channel, tasks are done by multiple parties. In comparing methods, a firm must weigh its costs and abilities against control and total sales. An indirect channel may use a contractual or an administered agreement. A long channel has many levels of independent firms; a wide one has many firms at any stage. A channel may be exclusive, selective, or intensive, based on company goals, resellers, customers, and marketing. A dual channel lets a company operate via two or more distribution methods.

2. *To describe the nature of supplier/distribution intermediary contracts, and cooperation and conflict in a channel of distribution* In contracts between suppliers and distribution intermediaries, price policies, sale conditions, territorial rights, the services/responsibility mix, and contract length and termination conditions are specified.

Cooperation and conflict may both occur in a distribution channel. Conflicts must be settled fairly because confrontation can cause hostility and negative acts by all parties. Frequently, a pushing strategy—based on channel cooperation—can be employed by established firms. But a pulling strategy—based on proving that consumer demand exists prior to gaining intermediary support or acceptance—must be used by many new companies.

3. *To examine the special aspects relating to a distribution channel for industrial products and to international distribution* An industrial channel normally does not use retailers; it is more direct, entails fewer transactions and larger orders, requires specification selling and knowing resellers, uses team selling and special intermediaries, includes more leasing, provides more technical data, and embraces shared activities.

Channel length depends on a nation's stage of economic development and consumer behavior. Distribution practices and structures differ by nation. International decisions must be made as to shipping and intermediaries. Each country has distinct legal provisions pertaining to distribution.

4. *To define physical distribution and to demonstrate its importance* Physical distribution (logistics) involves efficiently delivering products to designated places, at designated times, and in proper condition. It may be undertaken by any member of a channel, from producer to consumer.

There are various reasons for studying physical distribution: its costs, the value of customer service, and its relationship with other functional areas in a firm. With the total-cost approach, the service level with the lowest total cost (including freight, warehousing, and lost business) is the best one. In a physical distribution strategy, decisions are made as to transportation, inventory levels, warehousing, and facility locations.

5. *To discuss transportation alternatives and inventory management issues* Railroads typically carry bulky goods for long distances. Motor carriers dominate small shipments over short distances. Waterways primarily ship low-value freight. Pipelines provide ongoing movement of liquid, gaseous, and semiliquid products. Airways offer fast, expensive movement of perishables and high-value items. Transportation service firms are specialists that mostly handle small and medium-sized packages. Coordination can be improved via containerization and freight forwarding. There are common, contract, exempt, and private carriers.

Inventory management is needed to provide a continuous flow of goods and to match the stock kept in inventory as closely as possible with demand. In a just-in-time (JIT) or quick response (QR) system, the purchasing firm reduces the stock it keeps on hand by ordering more often and in lower quantity. With electronic data interchange (EDI), channel members exchange information via computer linkages.

The interplay between a firm's sales and the inventory level it keeps is expressed by stock turnover. A reorder point shows the inventory level when goods must be reordered. The economic order quantity (EOQ) is the optimal amount of goods to order based on order-processing and inventory-holding costs. Warehousing decisions include selecting a private or public warehouse and examining the availability of public warehouse services.

KEY TERMS

distribution planning (p. 415)
channel of distribution (p. 415)
channel members (p. 415)
distribution intermediaries (p. 415)
channel functions (p. 419)
sorting process (p. 420)
direct channel of distribution (p. 421)
indirect channel of distribution (p. 421)
channel length (p. 422)
channel width (p. 423)
exclusive distribution (p. 423)
selective distribution (p. 423)
intensive distribution (p. 423)
dual channel of distribution (p. 423)
pushing strategy (p. 426)
pulling strategy (p. 426)
physical distribution (logistics) (p. 429)
order cycle (p. 429)
total-cost approach (p. 431)
railroads (p. 432)
motor carriers (p. 432)
waterways (p. 432)
pipelines (p. 433)
airways (p. 433)
containerization (p. 434)
freight forwarding (p. 434)
common carriers (p. 435)
contract carriers (p. 435)
exempt carriers (p. 435)
private carriers (p. 435)
inventory management (p. 435)
just-in-time (JIT) inventory system (p. 436)
quick response (QR) inventory system (p. 436)
electronic data interchange (EDI) (p. 436)
stock turnover (p. 436)
reorder point (p. 438)
economic order quantity (EOQ) (p. 438)
warehousing (p. 438)

Review Questions

1. What is relationship marketing?
2. Explain the sorting process. Provide an example in your answer.
3. Which factors influence the selection of a distribution channel?
4. Under what circumstances should a company engage in direct distribution? Indirect distribution?
5. What is meant by a short, narrow channel of distribution?
6. Explain how a product could move from exclusive to selective to intensive distribution.
7. Compare motor carrier and waterway deliveries on the basis of the total-cost approach.
8. The average stock turnover rate in jewelry stores is less than 3. What does this mean? How could a jewelry store raise its turnover rate?
9. Two wholesalers sell identical merchandise. Yet, one plans a safety stock equal to 20 per cent of expected sales, while the other plans no safety stock. Comment on this difference.
10. Why would a firm use both private and public warehouses?

Discussion Questions

1. What distribution decisions would a new firm that rents vans to small, seasonal businesses have to make?
2. Devise distribution channels for the sale of a daily newspaper, pianos, and cellular phones. Explain your choices.
3. Present a checklist that a firm could use in making international distribution decisions on a country-by-country basis.
4. Develop a list of distribution standards for a firm delivering fresh fruit to supermarkets.
5. Are there any disadvantages to a JIT or QR system? Explain your answer.

CASE 1

*Pendleton Mills: An 85-Year-Old Distribution Strategy**

Pendleton Woolen Mills makes bright plaid-design woolen shirts for men and skirts, sweaters, blouses, and jackets for women in similar patterns. The majority of the items in its product line have above-average prices. For example, its men's outdoor shirts (the firm's most popular item—accounting for 40 per cent of total sales) cost $68, while skirts and coordinate outfits for women sell for $350 or so.

Pendleton, with 13 mills located from Washougal, Washington, to Dorr, New Hampshire, is family-owned. Although the firm zealously guards its financial data, market analysts estimate that its annual sales are $150 million. And the analysts assume that Pendleton's sales have been stagnant in recent years.

Pendleton's clothing sells best with the 50+ age group; many of these customers started wearing Pendleton clothes when they were in their teens and twenties. In recent years, Pendleton has also begun to seek out a younger target market by offering more updated items. For example, the firm now has a zippered, hooded shirt to appeal to younger males, and it has added rugged-looking slacks and jackets as part of a new women's clothing line.

What is quickly apparent to most observers is that Pendleton has little in common with most apparel firms. It is vertically integrated, produces the overwhelming majority of its apparel in the United States, refuses to sell to retailers that seek unfair terms, and will not sell surplus stock to closeout retailers. Let's look at Pendleton's distribution strategy.

Unlike other clothing firms, Pendleton is vertically integrated. Pendleton employees buy wool from farmers; sort, grade, and clean fibers; spin fibers into yarn; weave the yarn into fabric; and then sew the garments. Finally, about 15 per cent of the firm's production is ultimately sold in Pendleton's own stores. In contrast, competitors usually just purchase processed fabrics from wholesalers, sew the garments (or arrange to have the garments sewn by contractors), and sell the finished apparel through independent retailers.

Although Pendleton could easily reduce overall expenses by relying on inexpensive foreign labor, it insists on having the majority of production done in the United States. In comparison to the overall apparel industry—which does 70 per cent of manufacturing overseas, Pendleton prides itself on doing 95 per cent of its manufacturing in the United States. The firm is concerned about keeping jobs in America and about its relationship with employees. Of its 2,000 employees, 160 have worked for the company 25 years or longer. Pendleton shifted 5 per cent of production to China and Mexico only after the North American Free Trade Agreement (NAFTA) passed.

Pendleton also plays by its own rules when dealing with department stores. For example, it has steadfastly refused to share advertising costs (through cooperative advertising programs), reimburse stores for markdowns, and take back unsold items to gain and keep department stores' business. According to a retail consultant, "They're [Pendleton] the Snow White of the business. They insist on doing things according to their own principles." While some department stores (such as Macy's and Bloomingdale's) no longer carry the Pendleton line, others (such as Lord & Taylor, Dillard, and Nordstrom) stock it due to the loyal customer base. In addition, many small, local specialty clothing stores continue to carry the products. Some of these stores are so successful that sales average $1,000 a square foot (versus the average $250–$300 per square foot in annual sales for clothing-based retailers).

Pendleton is careful not to sell its excess merchandise to outlet stores or mass merchandisers (such as Wal-Mart). It is leery of generating ill will with its traditional retailer customers.

QUESTIONS

1. Evaluate the pros and cons of Pendleton's direct channel strategy.
2. What degree of intensity of channel coverage is most appropriate for Pendleton? Explain your answer.
3. How does Pendleton effectively utilize dual channels of distribution?
4. Discuss the demands of departments stores from the perspective of channel cooperation and conflict.

*The data in this case are drawn from Phyllis Berman, "From Sheep to Shirt," *Forbes* (May 22, 1995), pp. 162–164.

CASE 2

CSX: An Intermodal Shipping Strategy†

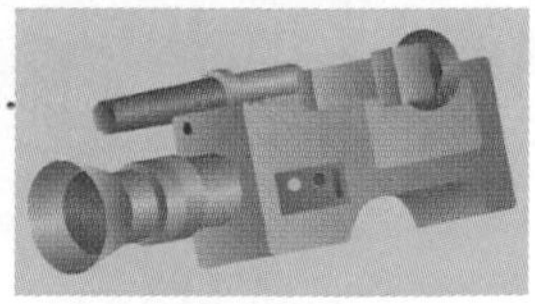

CSX Corporation is a diversified international transportation company that offers a variety of container shipping, intermodal shipping (ship to truck to train), waterway barging, and distribution services. The firm has annual revenues of $10 billion and an operating income of $1.2 billion.

CSX Corporation operates CSX, America's largest railroad in terms of revenues. CSX has an 18,779-mile rail system that links 20 states in the eastern, midwestern, and southern United States and Ontario, Canada. The firm also operates American Commercial Lines (a leading inland barge line), Sea-Land Service (the largest U.S. flag container shipping company), and CSX Intermodal Inc. (CSXI)—which is the nation's only full-service coast-to-coast intermodal transportation company.

All of CSX Corporation's units are involved with containerization and intermodal shipping. Among the types of intermodal transportation offered are fishyback (waterways and motor carriers), piggyback (rail and motor carriers), COFC (container on flat cars), rail-water, airtruck, and trainship. For example, Sea-Land owns 93 container ships (and about 188,000 containers) that serve 120 ports in 80 nations and territories. It features the world's largest container fleet: with standard-sized 20-foot and 40-foot containers, as well as 45-foot containers, refrigerated containers, and specialized containers (that house garments on hangers) and open-top containers for oversized loads.

A major advantage of intermodal transportation is that it enables the most efficient transportation mode to be used for each part of an overall transportation system. For instance, through piggyback, a firm could combine the advantages of the low-cost operations of a railroad with the flexibility (in terms of the number of pickup and delivery locations served) of a motor carrier. In addition, containerization also reduces pilferage, allows loading and unloading to be automated, and reduces handling and storage costs at terminals. As a result of these benefits, demand for piggybacking services is increasing. An Association of American Railroads study found that a record seven million trailers and their containers now "hitch a ride" on U.S. railroads. And 90 per cent of intermodal piggyback services are from five firms: CSX, Conrail, Union Pacific, Santa Fe, and Norfolk Southern.

One major drawback in using piggyback-based intermodal transportation is that there are wide swings between peak and minimum demand for containers and their trailers. Because a new container costs an average of $10,400 and the trailer costs an additional $8,000, most shipping firms cannot afford to have enough containers and trailers to accommodate peak demand—since this would result in idle equipment during periods of slow demand.

One way to facilitate the use of containers is to boost the container turnover rate. A recent study found the percentage of a container's turnaround time accounted for by activity: in-transit (29 per cent), delivery (23 per cent), awaiting dispatch (18 per cent), destination awaiting delivery (13 per cent), pickup (11 per cent), loading (4 per cent), and out of service (2 per cent). To reduce nonproductive container time, some firms are providing an incentive to truckers that turn in containers prior to the posted deadline. In addition, all carriers charge truckers a penalty if they turn in containers late.

CSX Intermodal has increased its supply of containers by privatizing (owning) its trailer fleet. Privatizing ensures that the newest and best parts of CSX's fleet will be available to its own customers.

QUESTIONS

1. Discuss the pros and cons of an intermodal transportation system.
2. Explain how container usage facilitates inventory management.
3. How can freight forwarders utilize intermodal transportation through containerization.
4. Describe other measures that can be used by CSX Corporation to increase the turnover rate of containers.

VIDEO QUESTIONS ON CSX

1. Describe the systems Sea-Land uses to track shipments.
2. Discuss CSX's advances in containerization.

†The data in this case are drawn from "Balancing Supply and Demand," *Distribution* (January 1995), p. 18; "Capacity Dampens Intermodal Growth," *Distribution* (February 1994), p. 14; *CSX Corporation 1994 Annual Report and Form 10-K*; and Gregory D. L. Morris, "CSX Practices the Art of Tracking," *Chemical Week* (May 4, 1994), p. 34.

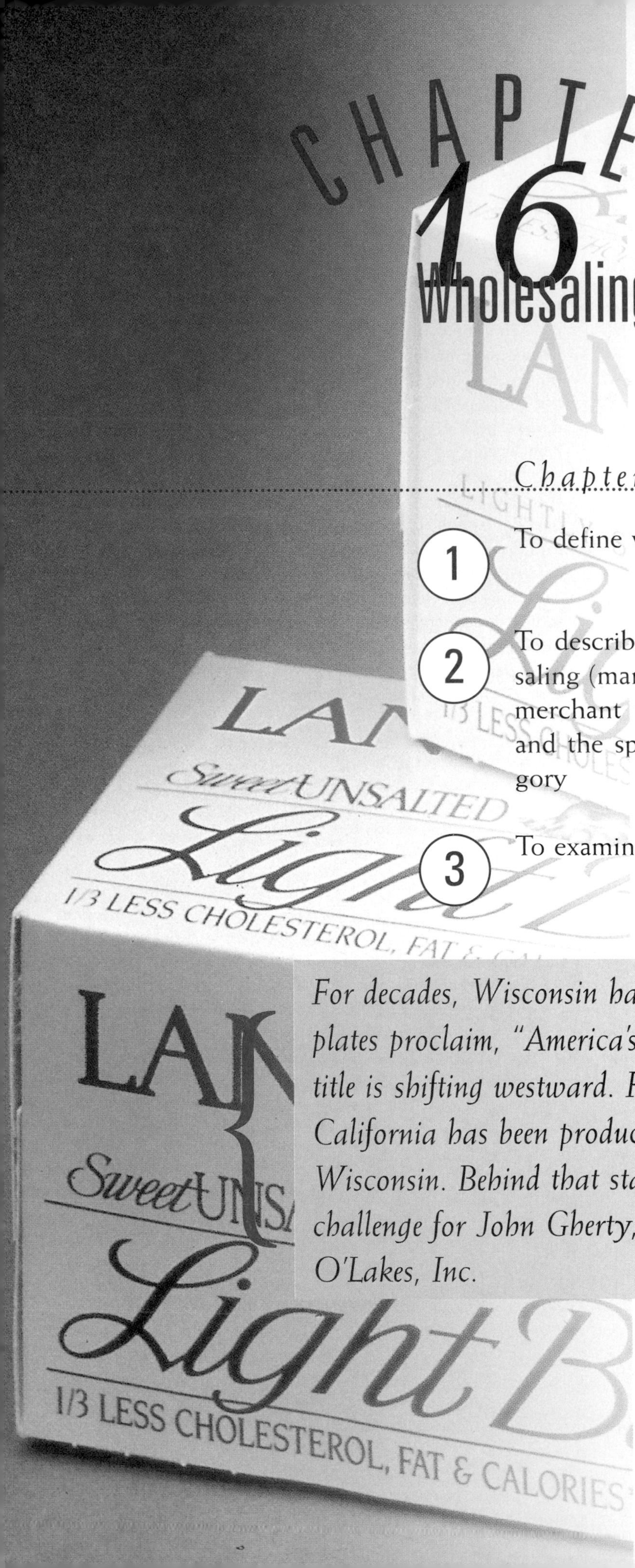

CHAPTER 16
Wholesaling

Chapter Objectives

1. To define wholesaling and show its importance

2. To describe the three broad categories of wholesaling (manufacturer/service provider wholesaling, merchant wholesaling, and agents and brokers) and the specific types of firms within each category

3. To examine recent trends in wholesaling

For decades, Wisconsin has been, as its license plates proclaim, "America's Dairyland." Now, the title is shifting westward. For the last few years, California has been producing more milk than Wisconsin. Behind that statistic lies a tough challenge for John Gherty, chief executive of Land O'Lakes, Inc.

Reprinted by permission.

Land O'Lakes is a wholesale cooperative owned by about 8,000 dairy and livestock farmers and 1,000 local cooperatives that are based in the Midwest and the Pacific Northwest. By virtue of its size, Land O'Lakes can reduce its members' costs by pooling purchases—as well as arrange for the storage, transportation, and selling of their output. Land O'Lakes also sells its members' products under the well-regarded Land O'Lakes brand name. Like most wholesale cooperatives, Land O'Lakes disburses its annual profits to members in the form of a special dividend.

Many Land O'Lakes members own and operate small farms. The firm's average farm member earns about $20,000 per year—too low a figure to finance the purchase of larger livestock herds and more modern equipment. As a result, despite their hard work, a number of Land O'Lakes members are inefficient when compared to larger agricultural operations. For example, Minnesota dairy farms average 48 milk cows; the average farm in California has 280. In addition, California dairy farms typically milk six to twelve cows at a time using automatic equipment. In contrast, Land O'Lakes members' cows are generally milked two to four at a time with older equipment.

Land O'Lakes' John Gherty has tried to convince members to become more efficient by increasing the size of their livestock herds and by making investments in new barns and machinery. However, many members have either been resistant to the notion of enlarging or been unable to obtain the necessary financing. As one observer noted, "A farmer in his or her fifties isn't going to invest $500,000 to expand a few years before retirement. And younger producers have a tough time getting the financing to expand."

Recently, when Land O'Lakes paid its member farmer/owners $12.90 per hundred pounds of milk (which is used in the cooperative's butter, cheese, and sour cream products), cooperatives on the West Coast purchased milk at $12.00 per hundred pounds from their members. This put Land O'Lakes at a major cost disadvantage for its dairy business. Thus, Land O'Lakes' profits have suffered accordingly. In some years, its net profits before tax have been as low as four-tenths of one per cent of sales.

To adapt to its situation, Land O'Lakes has increased its production and distribution of such nondairy-based farm products as fertilizers, seeds, and animal feed. Although these products account for one-half of total sales, they contribute over 90 per cent of the cooperative's pre-tax income. Some industry observers regard this change in marketing strategy as positive for the cooperative and its members. Yet, they fear that this may not stop the decline of the dairy industry in the Midwest relative to California.[1]

In this chapter, we will further study wholesalers' relationships with their suppliers and customers. We will also examine the different types of firms that perform wholesaling activities and the strategies they use to compete in the marketplace, including wholesale cooperatives such as Land O'Lakes.

Overview

Wholesaling encompasses the buying and/or handling of goods and services and their subsequent resale to organizational users, retailers, and/or other wholesalers—but not the sale of significant volume to final consumers. Wholesaling undertakes many vital functions in a channel of distribution, particularly those in the sorting process.

Wholesaling *is the buying/handling of products and their resale to organizational buyers.*

Manufacturers and service providers sometimes are their own wholesalers; other times, independent firms are employed. Independents may or may not take title to or possession of products, depending on the type of wholesaling. Some independents have limited tasks; others do a wide range of functions.

[1]William M. Stern, "Land O'Low Returns," *Forbes* (August 15, 1994), p. 90.

Industrial, commercial, and government institutions are wholesalers' leading customers, followed closely by retailers. Sales from one wholesaler to another also represent a significant proportion of wholesaling activity. The following show the diversity of transactions considered as wholesaling:

- Sales of goods and services to manufacturers, service providers, oil firms, fisheries, railroads, public utilities, and government departments.
- Sales of office or laboratory equipment, supplies, and services to such professionals as doctors and dentists.
- Sales of building materials and services to contractors, except when they buy on behalf of homeowners.
- All purchases of farm products for sale to other than individual consumers, regardless of whether purchases are made from farmers or intermediaries.
- All sales by supply houses, as long as purchases are not by final consumers.
- Sales to grocery stores, restaurants, hotels, clothing stores, shoe repair firms, video rental stores, and all other retailers.
- Manufacturer/service provider sales to wholesalers, and wholesaler sales to other wholesalers.[2]

In this chapter, the importance of wholesaling, the different types of wholesaling, and recent trends in wholesaling are all discussed in depth.

The Importance of Wholesaling

Wholesaling is an important aspect of distribution because of its impact on the economy, its functions in the distribution channel, and its relationships with suppliers and customers.

Wholesaling's Impact on the Economy

Wholesale sales are high; and wholesalers greatly affect final prices.

In the United States, there are about 500,000 wholesale establishments with total annual sales exceeding $3.3 trillion (including manufacturers with wholesale facilities); yet, although wholesale revenues are higher than those in retailing, there are five times as many retail establishments as wholesale. According to the National Association of Wholesaler-Distributors, U.S. wholesalers will generate 18 per cent of their total revenues from foreign markets by the year 2000, nearly double the current share.[3]

Revenues are high because wholesaling involves any purchases made by organizational consumers. Some products also move through multiple levels of wholesalers (e.g., regional, then local); an item can be sold twice or more at the wholesale level. There are more retailers because they serve individual, geographically dispersed final consumers; wholesalers handle fewer, larger, more concentrated customers.

From a cost perspective, wholesalers have a great impact on prices. Table 16-1 shows the per cent of wholesale selling prices that go to selected wholesalers to cover their operating expenses and pre-tax profits. For example, 31 per cent of the price that a general merchandise wholesaler charges its retailers covers that wholesaler's operating and other expenses (29 per cent) and pre-tax profit (2 per cent). Operating costs include inventory charges, sales force salaries, advertising, and rent.

Wholesaler costs and profits depend on inventory turnover, the dollar value of products, the functions performed, efficiency, and competition.

[2] Adapted by the authors from C. Glenn Walters and Blaise J. Bergiel, *Marketing Channels*, Second Edition (Hinsdale, Ill.: Scott, Foresman, 1982), p. 108.

[3] Barry Berman, *Marketing Channels* (New York: Wiley, 1996), pp. 147–148; and "The Emerging Role of International Distribution," *Industrial Distribution* (September 1995), Supplement, p. S5.

Table 16-1

Selected Performance Data for U.S. Wholesalers (All Sizes) by Product Category[1]

PRODUCT CATEGORY OF WHOLESALER	GROSS PROFIT (AS PER CENT OF SALES)[a]	OPERATING EXPENSES (AS PER CENT OF SALES)	ALL OTHER EXPENSES (AS PER CENT OF SALES)	PROFIT BEFORE TAXES (AS PER CENT OF SALES)
Building materials	25.3	22.5	0.4	2.3
Chemicals and allied products	28.8	25.7	0.3	2.8
Coffee, tea, and spices	29.0	25.4	1.1	2.5
Drugs, drug proprietaries, and druggists' supplies	29.3	25.0	0.5	3.8
Electronic parts and equipment	29.7	26.5	0.5	2.6
Fish and seafoods	15.2	12.9	0.4	1.8
Flowers, nursery stock, and florists' supplies	33.7	30.3	0.9	2.4
General groceries	18.2	16.4	0.4	1.5
General merchandise	31.3	28.4	0.7	2.2
Hardware and paints	29.9	26.8	0.6	2.4
Jewelry	28.2	24.6	0.9	2.7
Motor vehicle supplies and new parts	30.9	27.3	0.7	2.9
Wine, liquor, and beer	23.7	20.9	0.4	2.4

[1]In interpreting these data, RMA cautions that the Studies be regarded only as a general guideline and not as an absolute industry norm. This is due to limited samples within categories, the categorization of firms by their primary Standard Industrial Classification (SIC) number only, and different methods of operations by firms within the same industry. For these reasons, RMA recommends that the figures be used only as general guidelines in addition to other methods of financial analysis.

[a]Total costs of wholesaling, which include expenses and profit. There are some rounding errors.

Source: Adapted from *RMA Annual Statement Studies 1995* (Philadelphia: Robert Morris Associates, 1995). © 1995, Robert Morris Associates; reprinted by permission.

The Functions of Wholesalers

Wholesalers do tasks ranging from distribution to risk taking.

With regard to functions performed, wholesalers can

- Enable manufacturers and service providers to distribute locally without making customer contacts.
- Provide a trained sales force.
- Provide marketing and research assistance for manufacturers, service providers, and retail or institutional consumers.
- Gather assortments for customers and let them make fewer transactions.
- Purchase large quantities, thus reducing total physical distribution costs.
- Provide warehousing and delivery facilities.
- Offer financing for manufacturers and service providers (by paying for products when they are shipped, not when they are sold) and retail or institutional consumers (by granting credit).
- Handle financial records.

Ethics IN TODAY'S SOCIETY

What Responsibility Do Big Customers Have to Their Suppliers?

According to a Dun & Bradstreet (D&B) survey, in recent years, companies with 500 or more employees have begun to pay their small suppliers' bills more slowly. And a study by the National Association of Credit Management found that almost two-thirds of its members cited slow-paying customers as a moderate to severe problem.

A D&B spokesperson says that some large firms are paying their bills 60 days late, and that many smaller suppliers accept the late payments "out of desperation to get business." In many cases, however, the small suppliers are unaware that continued late payments by major accounts can significantly reduce the small firms' cash flow, as well as the capital they require to expand. For example, one firm, Earthly Elements, a small manufacturer of dried floral gifts and accessories, ultimately closed down due to the cash crunch from a late-paying customer. By the time the customer paid (close to three months past due), it was too late.

In response to large customers not only paying late, but also deducting a discount for early payment, Caruthers Raisin Packing Company was forced to stop offering its time-based discounts to anyone (even those paying within the stipulated time). Other small firms are being even more aggressive. Truck Brokers Inc., a transportation brokerage company, demands cash payments from customers with a reputation or track record of late payment. Says the owner of the firm, "If there's any question about payment, we're saying, make it cash."

To better cope with slow-paying accounts, Dun & Bradstreet recommends that small firms reduce their reliance on large accounts, develop cash reserves, and arrange to stretch out their own accounts payable.

As the sales manager for a small manufacturer, develop a policy for dealing with a major account that repeatedly pays late.

Sources: Based on material in Michael Selz, "Big Customers' Late Bills Choke Small Suppliers." *Wall Street Journal* (July 22, 1994), p. B1; and Christina Duff, "Big Stores' Outlandish Demands Alienate Small Suppliers," *Wall Street Journal* (October 27, 1995), pp. B1, B5.

- Process returns and make adjustments for defective merchandise.
- Take risks by being responsible for theft, deterioration, and obsolescence of inventory.[4]

Wholesalers that take title to and possession of products usually perform several or all of these tasks. Agents and brokers that facilitate sales, but do not take title or possession, tend to concentrate on more limited duties.

The use of independent wholesalers varies by industry. Most consumer products, food items, replacement parts, and office supplies are sold via independent wholesalers. In other industries, including heavy equipment, mainframe computers, gasoline, and temporary employment, manufacturers and service providers may bypass independent resellers.

Without independent wholesalers, organizational consumers would have to develop supplier contacts, deal with a number of suppliers and coordinate shipments, do more distribution functions, stock greater quantities, and place more emphasis on an internal purchasing agent or department. Many small retailers and other firms might be avoided as customers because they might not be profitably reached by a manufacturer or service provider, and they might not be able to buy necessary items elsewhere.

[4]Adapted by the authors from Walters and Bergiel, *Marketing Channels*, p. 109; and Louis W. Stern, Adel L. El-Ansary, and James R. Brown, *Management in Marketing Channels* (Englewood Cliffs, N.J.: Prentice Hall, 1989), pp. 98–99.

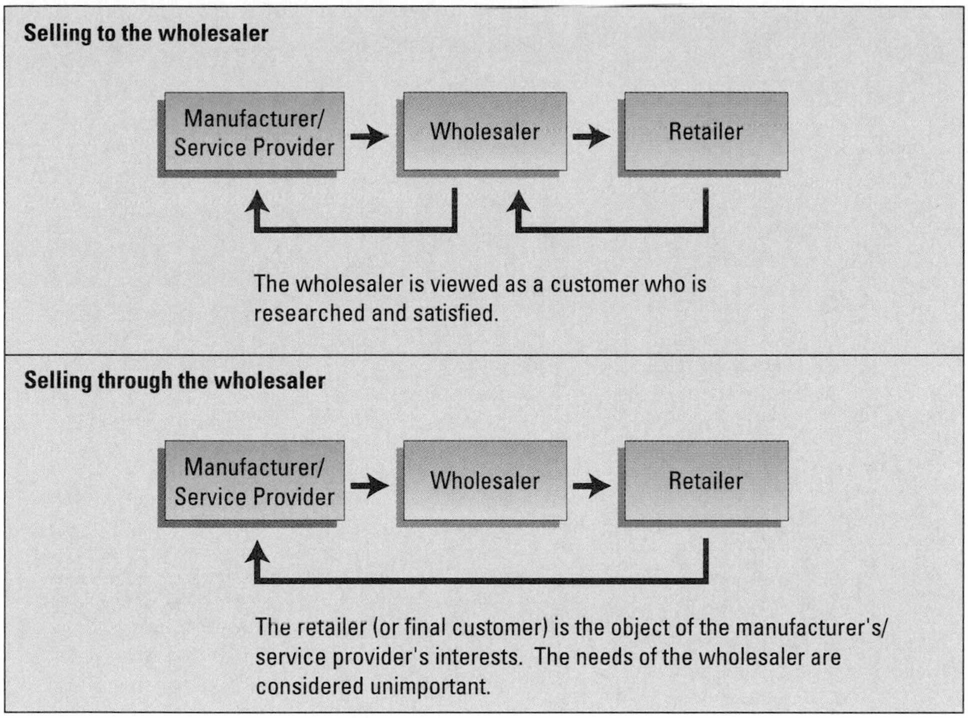

FIGURE 16-1
Selling To Vs. Selling Through the Wholesaler

An illustration of wholesaling's value is the U.S. auto parts industry, in which there used to be thousands of firms making a wide range of products and marketing them via a multitude of sales organizations. At that time, customers (mostly specialty stores and service stations) faced constant interruptions by salespeople, and manufacturers' sales costs were high. A better system exists today with the organized use of a moderate number of independent distributors.

Wholesalers' Relationships with Suppliers and Customers

Wholesalers have obligations to both suppliers and customers.

Independent wholesalers are often very much "in the middle," not fully knowing whether their allegiance should be to manufacturers/service providers or their own customers. These comments show the dilemma many wholesalers face: "The challenge is to find ways individually, and as an industry, to show our customers and manufacturers exactly where and how we do and can add value. Our roles and performance are in a state of flux. The new theory is to cut out the wholesaler to reduce costs."[5]

Many wholesalers feel they get scant support from manufacturers/service providers. They desire training, technical assistance, product literature, and advertising. They dislike it when vendors alter territory assignments, shrink territory size, add new distributors to cover an existing geographic area, or decide to change to a direct channel and perform wholesale tasks themselves. Wholesalers want manufacturers/service providers to sell to them and not through them. Selling to the wholesaler means a distributor is viewed as a customer to be researched and satisfied. Selling through the wholesaler means retailers or final consumers are objects of manufacturers'/service providers' interest and wholesaler needs are less important. See Figure 16-1.

To remedy the situation, this is how many wholesalers are reacting:

> Wholesalers have traditionally viewed themselves as extensions of either their suppliers or customers. Wholesalers that saw themselves as extensions of suppliers adopted the mindset of their suppliers, structured operations to best assist suppliers, and viewed customers as "outside" this relationship. And wholesalers that saw their role as extensions of their customers adopted that mindset and business structure and viewed the supplier as "outside." In short, wholesalers have typically viewed themselves as "distributors."

[5] R. Craig MacClaren, "Squeezed Brokers Position for Value-Added Services," *Promo* (February 1995), p. 36; and Stephen Bennett, "Working the Middle Ground," *Progressive Grocer* (August 1995), p. 147.

Factors	Manufacturer/Service Provider Wholesaling	Merchant Wholesaling	Agents and Brokers
Control/ Functions	• The manufacturer/ service provider controls wholesaling and performs all functions.	• The wholesaler controls wholesaling and performs many or all functions.	• The manufacturer/ service provider and wholesaler each have some control and perform some functions.
Ownership	• The manufacturer/ service provider owns products until they are bought by retailers or other organizational consumers.	• The wholesaler buys products from the manufacturer/ service provider and resells them.	• The manufacturer/ service provider owns the products and pays the wholesaler a fee/commission.
Cash Flow	• The manufacturer/ service provider does not receive payment until the retailer or other customer buys products.	• The manufacturer/ service provider is paid when the wholesaler purchases products.	• The manufacturer/ service provider does not receive payment until products are sold.
Best Use(s)	• The manufacturer/ service provider deals with a small group of large and geographically concentrated customers; rapid expansion is not a goal.	•The manufacturer/service provider has a large product line that is sold through many small and geographically dispersed customers; expansion is a goal.	• The manufacturer/ service provider is small, has little marketing expertise, and is relatively unknown to potential customers; expansion is a goal.

FIGURE 16-2
The Broad Categories of Wholesaling

Today, more wholesalers feel they are in the "marketing support business." They view themselves as marketing *with* their suppliers and customers, not just being distributors. They recognize their primary role is to help both suppliers and customers devise better marketing programs. The marketing support-oriented wholesaler is willing to perform any task, activity, or function for either suppliers or customers that will result in more effective and efficient marketing for the entire channel.[6]

Types of Wholesaling

The three broad categories of wholesaling are outlined in Figure 16-2: manufacturer/service provider wholesaling, merchant wholesaling, and agents and brokers. Table 16-2 contains detailed descriptions of every type of independent wholesaler and shows their functions and special features.

Manufacturer/Service Provider Wholesaling

In **manufacturer/service provider wholesaling,** *a firm acts via its own sales or branch offices.*

In **manufacturer/service provider wholesaling,** a producer does all wholesaling functions itself. This occurs if a firm feels it is best able to reach retailers or other organizational customers by being responsible for wholesaling tasks itself. The format accounts for 32 per cent of U.S. wholesale revenues and 7 per cent of establishments. Manufacturer/service provider wholesalers include General Motors, IBM, Frito-Lay, Hanes, Pitney Bowes, Prudential, Citicorp, and public utilities.

[6]Robert F. Lusch, Deborah Zizzo, and James M. Kenderdine, "Strategic Renewal in Distribution," *Marketing Management*, Vol. 2 (Number 2, 1993), p. 25.

Table 16-2
Characteristics of Independent Wholesalers

	MAJOR FUNCTIONS						
WHOLESALER TYPE	*Provides Credit*	*Stores and Delivers*	*Takes Title*	*Provides Merchandising and Promotion Assistance*	*Provides Personal Sales Force*	*Performs Research and Planning*	**SPECIAL FEATURES**
I. Merchant wholesaler							
A. Full service							
1. General merchandise	Yes	Yes	Yes	Yes	Yes	Yes	Carries nearly all items a customer normally needs
2. Specialty merchandise	Yes	Yes	Yes	Yes	Yes	Yes	Specializes in a narrow product range, extensive assortment
3. Rack jobber	Yes	Yes	Yes	Yes	Yes	Yes	Furnishes racks and shelves, consignment sales
4. Franchise	Yes	Yes	Yes	Yes	Yes	Yes	Use of common business format, extensive management services
5. Cooperative							
a. Producer-owned	Yes	Yes	Yes	Yes	Yes	Yes	Farmer controlled, profits divided among members
b. Retailer-owned	Yes	Yes	Yes	Yes	Yes	Yes	Wholesaler owned by several retailers
B. Limited service							
1. Cash and carry	No	Stores, no delivery	Yes	No	No	No	No outside sales force, wholesale store for business needs
2. Drop shipper	Yes	Delivers, no storage	Yes	No	Yes	Sometimes	Ships items without physically handling them
3. Truck/wagon	Rarely	Yes	Yes	Yes	Yes	Sometimes	Sales and delivery on same call
4. Mail order	Sometimes	Yes	Yes	No	No	Sometimes	Catalogs used as sole promotion tool
II. Agents and brokers							
A. Agents							
1. Manufacturers' (service providers')	No	Sometimes	No	Yes	Yes	Sometimes	Sells selected items for several firms
2. Selling	Sometimes	Yes	No	Yes	Yes	Yes	Markets all the items of a firm
3. Commission (factor) merchants	Sometimes	Yes	No	No	Yes	Yes	Handles items on a consignment basis
B. Brokers							
1. Food	No	Sometimes	No	Yes	Yes	Yes	Brings together buyers and sellers
2. Stock	Sometimes	Sometimes	No	Yes	Yes	Yes	Brings together buyers and sellers

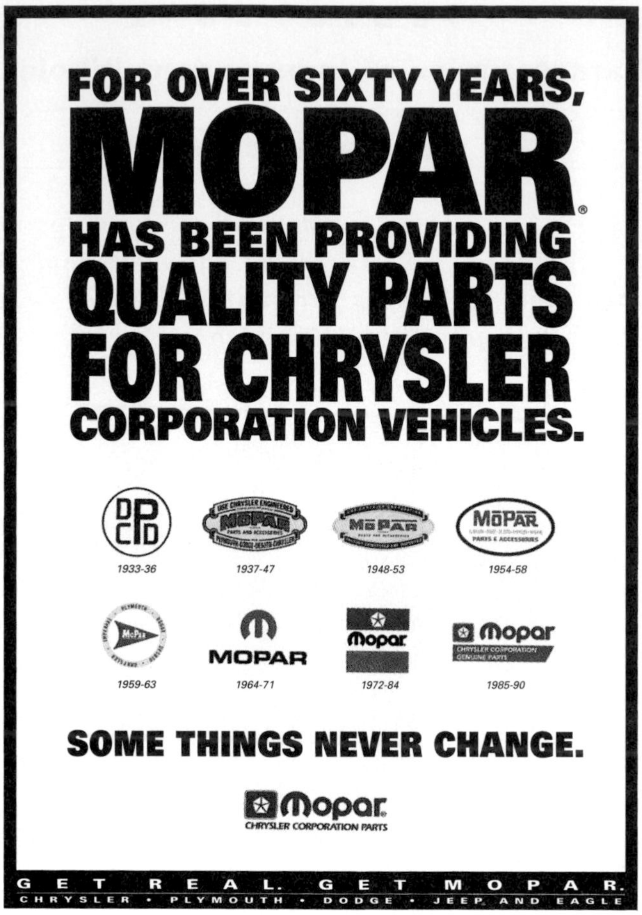

FIGURE 16-3
Manufacturer Wholesaling by Chrysler
Reprinted by permission.

Wholesale activities by a manufacturer or service provider may be carried out via sales offices and/or branch offices. A sales office is located at a firm's production facilities or a site close to the market. No inventory is carried there. In contrast, a branch office has facilities for warehousing products, as well as for selling them.

Manufacturer/service provider wholesaling is most likely if independent intermediaries are unavailable, existing intermediaries are unacceptable to the manufacturer or service provider, the manufacturer or service provider wants control over marketing, customers are relatively few in number and each is a key account, customers desire personal service from the producer, customers are near to the firm or clustered, a computerized order system links a firm with customers, and/or laws (particularly in foreign markets) limit arrangements with independent resellers.

For instance, because Boeing makes multimillion dollar aircraft and individual customer orders can be in the billions of dollars, manufacturer wholesaling is a must. When Boeing recently sold $3 billion in jets to General Electric, the complex negotiations took over a year.[7] And at Chrysler, manufacturer wholesaling means closer relationships with its auto dealers. Chrysler distributes its Mopar brand replacement parts directly to the retailers and works with them to market the parts. See Figure 16-3.

Merchant Wholesaling

Merchant wholesalers *buy products and are* **full** *or* **limited service**.

Merchant wholesalers buy, take title, and take possession of products for further resale. This is the largest U.S. wholesale category in sales—57 per cent of the total—and establishments—84 per cent of the total.

As an example, Sysco is a merchant wholesaler that buys and handles 150,000 products from 3,000 producers of food and related products from around the world. It resells

[7]Jeff Cole and Susan Carey, "Boeing Co. to Get GE Job Valued at Over $3 Billion," *Wall Street Journal* (January 8, 1996), pp. A3–A4.

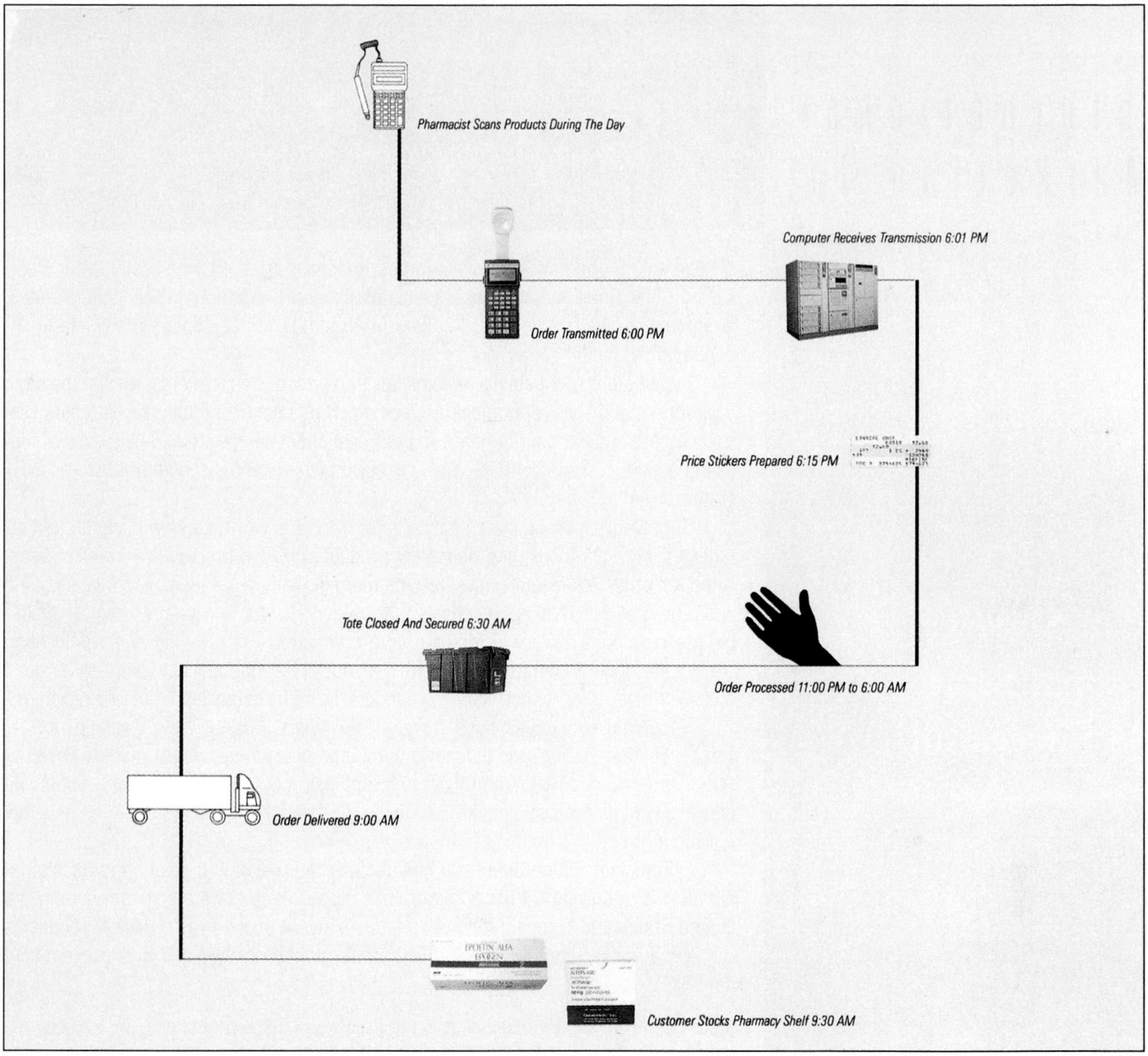

FIGURE 16-4
Bergen Brunswig Corporation: A Full-Service Merchant Wholesaler
Bergen Brunswig is a pharmaceutical wholesaler. It provides a wide range of services for customers, including automated order processing. The firm's computer network is linked to drugstores and hospitals. In general, a customer prepares an order during the day for transmission in the late afternoon. The order is filled at night and delivered early the next morning.
Reprinted by permission.

these products and offers many customer services to its 250,000 clients—restaurants, hotels, schools, hospitals, fast-food chains, and other organizations in the United States and Canada.[8]

Full-service merchant wholesalers perform a full range of distribution tasks. They provide credit, store and deliver products, offer merchandising and promotion assistance, have a personal sales force, offer research and planning support, pass along information to suppliers and customers, and give installation and repair services. They are prevalent for grocery products, pharmaceuticals, hardware, plumbing equipment, tobacco, alcoholic beverages, and television program syndication. See Figure 16-4.

[8]Patrick J. Spain and James R. Talbot (Editors), *Hoover's Handbook of American Business 1996* (Austin, Texas: Reference Press, 1995), pp. 1368–1369.

International Marketing in *Action*

Will Supervalu's Global Strategy Be Successful?

Supervalu is the nation's second-largest independent food wholesaler, after Fleming Companies, Inc. Its annual revenues exceed $17 billion. In the United States, Supervalu serves nearly 4,700 retailers in 48 states. Its customers are primarily independently owned supermarkets.

Supervalu is a full-service wholesaler that provides customers with site location, accounting, and store operations assistance. These services help its customers better compete against their regional and national chain competitors. Besides its wholesaling activities, Supervalu operates 300 supermarkets and discount food stores in 31 states.

Supervalu's mission statement calls for it to be a world-class wholesaler and retailer of food, nonfoods, and pharmacy products through grocery-driven businesses. Although other wholesalers have become more globally oriented in recent years, none has a greater international emphasis than Supervalu. As its vice-president of strategic planning says, "We will take our core competency in retailing and wholesaling and locate opportunities throughout the world, in nations not as advanced as ours. This will give us an opportunity to replicate in other countries what we did here."

Supervalu executives have traveled to Japan, Russia, New Zealand, Korea, Turkey, Eastern Europe, and Indonesia pursuing opportunities. Most grocery stores in those nations are small, with 90 per cent being 1,000 square feet or less. Supervalu plans to compete in some markets by using limited assortment stores it will develop. In others, it will use joint ventures or acquisitions.

One market where Supervalu has declined an ownership position is Russia. Instead, it is supplying a Russian store with 90 per cent of its merchandise from the United States and Europe. Much of the store's inventory involves private-label goods.

As a market analyst, assess Supervalu's global strategy and make recommendations.

Sources: Patrick J. Spain and James R. Talbot (Editors), *Hoover's Handbook of American Business 1996* (Austin, Texas: Reference Press, 1995), pp. 1366–1367; and Steve Weinstein, "Spanning the Globe," *Progressive Grocer* (October 1992), pp. 65–70.

Limited-service merchant wholesalers do not perform all the functions of full-service merchant wholesalers. For instance, they may not provide credit, merchandising assistance, or marketing research data. They are popular for construction materials, coal, lumber, perishables, equipment rentals, and specialty foods.

On average, full-service merchant wholesalers require more compensation than limited-service ones because they perform greater functions.

Full-Service Merchant Wholesalers Full-service merchant wholesalers can be divided into general merchandise, specialty merchandise, rack jobber, franchise, and cooperative types.

General-merchandise wholesalers *sell a range of items.*

General-merchandise (full-line) wholesalers carry a wide product assortment—nearly all the items needed by their customers. Thus, some general-merchandise hardware, drug, and clothing wholesalers stock many products, but not much depth in any one line. They seek to sell their retailers or other organizational customers all or most of their products and develop strong loyalty and exclusivity with them.

Specialty-merchandise (limited-line) wholesalers concentrate on a rather narrow product range and have an extensive selection in that range. They offer many sizes, colors, and models—and provide functions similar to other full-service merchant wholesalers. They are popular for health foods, seafood, retail store displays, frozen foods, and video rentals.

Specialty-merchandise wholesalers *sell a narrow line.*

Rack jobbers furnish the racks or shelves on which products are displayed. They own the products on the racks, selling them on a consignment basis—so their clients pay after goods are resold. Unsold items are taken back. Jobbers set up displays, refill shelves, price-mark goods, maintain inventory records, and compute the amount due from their customers. Heavily advertised, branded merchandise that is sold on a self-service basis is most often handled. Included are magazines, health and beauty aids, cosmetics, drugs, hand tools, toys, housewares, and stationery.

Rack jobbers *set up displays and are paid after sales.*

In **franchise wholesaling**, independent retailers affiliate with an existing wholesaler to use a standardized storefront design, business format, name, and purchase system. Many times, suppliers produce goods and services according to specifications set by the franchise wholesaler. This form of wholesaling is utilized for hardware, auto parts, and groceries. Franchise wholesalers include Independent Grocers Alliance (IGA), Ben Franklin Stores, Western Auto, and Walgreen. At IGA, affiliated retailers are supplied with such services as site selection, store engineering, interior design, and merchandising assistance. See Figure 16-5.

With **franchise wholesaling**, *retailers join with a wholesaler.*

Wholesale cooperatives are owned by member firms to economize functions and provide broad support. Producer-owned cooperatives are popular in farming. They market, transport, and process farm products—as well as make and distribute farm supplies. These cooperatives often sell to stores under their own names, such as Blue Diamond, Farmland,

Producers or retailers can set up **wholesale cooperatives**.

FIGURE 16-5
IGA: A Franchise Wholesaler
IGA assists its affiliated food retailers with such services as in-store displays and store layout planning.
Reprinted by permission of IGA, Inc., Chicago.

Land O'Lakes, Ocean Spray, Sunkist, and Welch's. With retailer-owned cooperatives, independent retailers form associations that purchase, lease, or build wholesale facilities. The cooperatives take title to merchandise, handle cooperative advertising, and negotiate with suppliers. They are used by hardware and grocery stores.

Limited-Service Merchant Wholesalers Limited-service merchant wholesalers can be divided into cash-and-carry, drop shipper, truck/wagon, and mail-order types.

In **cash-and-carry wholesaling,** *the customer drives to a wholesaler.*

In **cash-and-carry wholesaling,** small businesspeople drive to wholesalers, order products, and take them back to a store or business. These wholesalers offer no credit or delivery, no merchandising and promotion help, no outside sales force, and no research or planning assistance. They are good for fill-in items, have low prices, and allow immediate product use. They are common for construction materials, electrical supplies, office supplies, auto supplies, hardware products, and groceries.

Drop shippers (desk jobbers) *buy goods, but do not take possession.*

Drop shippers (desk jobbers) buy goods from manufacturers or suppliers and arrange for their shipment to retailers or industrial users. They have legal ownership, but do not take physical possession of products and have no storage facilities. They purchase items, leave them at manufacturers' plants, contact customers by phone, set up and coordinate carload shipments from manufacturers directly to customers, and are responsible for items that cannot be sold. Trade credit, a personal sales force, and some research and planning are provided; merchandising and promotion support are not. Drop shippers are often used for coal, coke, and building materials. These goods have high freight costs, in relation to their value, because of their weight. Thus, direct shipments from suppliers to customers are needed.

Truck/wagon wholesalers *offer products on a sales route.*

Truck/wagon wholesalers generally have a regular sales route, offer items from a truck or wagon, and deliver goods while they are sold. They do provide merchandising and promotion support; however, they are considered limited service because they usually do not extend credit and offer little research and planning help. Operating costs are high due to the services performed and low average sales. These wholesalers often deal with goods requiring special handling or with perishables—such as bakery products, tobacco, meat, candy, potato chips, and dairy products.

Mail-order wholesalers *sell through catalogs.*

Mail-order wholesalers use catalogs, instead of a personal sales force, to promote products and communicate with customers. They may provide credit but do not generally give merchandising and promotion support. They store and deliver goods, and offer some research and planning assistance. These wholesalers are found with jewelry, cosmetics, auto parts, specialty food product lines, business supplies, and small office equipment.

Agents and Brokers

Agents *and* **brokers** *do not take title to products.*

Agents and **brokers** perform various wholesale tasks, but do not take title to products. Unlike merchant wholesalers, who make profits on the sales of products they own, they work for commissions or fees as payment for their services. They account for 11 per cent of wholesale sales and 9 per cent of wholesale establishments. The main difference between agents and brokers is that agents are more apt to be used on a permanent basis.[9]

Agents and brokers let a manufacturer or service provider expand sales volume despite limited resources. Their selling costs are a pre-determined per cent of sales; and they have trained salespeople. There are manufacturers'/ service providers' agents, selling agents, and commission (factor) merchants.

Manufacturers'/service providers' agents *work for many firms and carry noncompeting items.*

Manufacturers'/service providers' agents work for several manufacturers/service providers and carry noncompetitive, complementary products in exclusive territories. By selling noncompetitive items, the agents eliminate conflict-of-interest situations. By selling complementary products, they stock a fairly complete line of products for their market areas. They do not offer credit but may store and deliver products and give limited

[9]See Reva Berman Brown and Richard Herring, "The Role of the Manufacturer's Distributor," *Industrial Marketing Management*, Vol. 24 (August 1995), pp. 285–295.

research and planning aid. Merchandising and promotional support are provided. These agents may supplement the sales efforts of their clients, help introduce new products, enter dispersed markets, and handle items with low average sales. They may carry only some of a firm's products; a manufacturer/service provider may hire many agents. Larger firms may hire a separate one for every product line. Agents have little say on marketing and pricing. They earn commissions of 5 to 10 per cent of sales, and are popular for auto products, iron, steel, footwear, textiles, and commercial real-estate and insurance. See Figure 16-6.

Selling agents are responsible for marketing the entire output of a manufacturer/service provider under a contractual agreement. They become the marketing departments for their clients and can negotiate price and other conditions of sale, such as credit and delivery. They perform all wholesale tasks except taking title. While a firm may use several manufacturers'/service providers' agents, it may employ only one sales agent. These agents are more apt to work for small firms than large ones. They are common for textile manufacturing, canned foods, metals, home furnishings, apparel, lumber, and metal products.

Selling agents *market all the products of a manufacturer or service provider.*

FIGURE 16-6
Citizens Business Insurance: A Service Providers' Agent
Reprinted by permission.

Anything
Can appen.
H
Citizens has all the insurance coverage.
Group life and health. Worker's comp
and financial planning. Plus lots more.
So drop by or give us a call. Because the
best time to protect your business from a
disaster is before one happens.
Citizens
Business Insurance
111 S.E. Third Street · Post Office Box 99 · Evansville, Indiana 47701 · 812-428-2830

Because they perform more tasks, they often get higher commissions than manufacturers'/service providers' representatives.

Commission (factor) merchants *assemble goods from local markets.*

Commission (factor) merchants receive goods on consignment, accumulate them from local markets, and arrange for their sale in a central location. They may offer credit; they do store and deliver goods, provide a sales force, and offer research and planning help. They normally do not assist in merchandising and promotion, but they can negotiate prices with buyers, provided the prices are not below sellers' stated minimums. They may act in an auction setting; commissions vary. These wholesalers are used for agricultural and seafood products, furniture, and art.

Brokers are common for food and financial services. They are well informed about market conditions, terms of sale, sources of credit, price setting, potential buyers and sellers, and the art of negotiating. They do not take title and usually are not allowed to complete a transaction without approval.

Food brokers *and* **commercial stock brokers** *unite buyers and sellers to conclude sales.*

Food brokers introduce buyers and sellers of food and related general-merchandise items to one another and bring them together to complete a sale. They operate in specific locales and work for a limited number of food producers. Their sales forces call on chain-store buyers, store managers, and purchasing agents. Food brokers work closely with ad agencies. They generally represent the seller, who pays the commission; they do not actually provide credit but may store and deliver. Commissions are 3 to 5 per cent of sales.

Commercial stock brokers are licensed sales representatives who advise business clients, take orders, and then acquire stocks and/or bonds for the clients. They may aid the firms selling the stocks or bonds, represent either buyers or sellers (with both buyers and sellers paying commissions), and offer some credit. Although operating in particular areas, they typically sell the stocks and bonds of firms from throughout the United States—even around the world. They deal a lot over the phone and may help publicize new stock or bond offerings. The average commission for commercial stock brokers is 1 to 10 per cent of sales, depending on volume and stock prices.

Recent Trends in Wholesaling

During the last 15 years, wholesaling has changed dramatically, with independent wholesalers striving to protect their place in the channel. Among the key trends are those related to the evolving wholesaler mix, productivity, customer service, international opportunities, and target markets.

Firms are becoming larger and more productive.

Since the early 1980s, the proportion of total sales volume contributed by manufacturer wholesaling, merchant wholesaling, and agents and brokers has stayed rather steady. However, manufacturer wholesalers now operate far fewer establishments (due to the consolidation of facilities) and merchant wholesalers operate many more (to provide better customer service). Overall, 280,000 companies currently engage in some form of U.S. wholesaling, down from 364,000 companies a decade ago. Thus, today, the average annual sales for the 36,000 U.S. manufacturer wholesaling establishments are $30 million—compared with $4.5 million for the 415,000 merchant wholesaling establishments and $8 million for the 45,000 agent/broker establishments. The 50 largest manufacturer wholesalers account for 50 per cent of sales in that category; the 50 biggest merchant wholesalers account for 16 per cent of sales in that category; and the 50 biggest agents/brokers account for 18 per cent of category sales. The National Association of Wholesaler-Distributors forecasts that the trend toward bigger firms will continue well into the future.[10]

Since wholesalers' profit margins are small (such as 1.5 per cent of sales for food wholesalers and less than 3 per cent of sales for general merchandise wholesalers), they are constantly seeking gains in productivity. For example, at McKesson Corporation (the largest U.S. pharmaceutical wholesaler),

[10] *U.S. Industrial Outlook 1994* (Washington, D.C.: U.S. Department of Commerce, 1994), pp. 38-1–38-4; Berman, *Marketing Channels*, pp. 148–155; and Ryan Mathews, "Industry Consolidation: Is a New Day Dawning?" *Progressive Grocer* (June 1995), pp. 38–44.

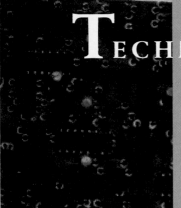

TECHNOLOGY & MARKETING

Can Food Brokers Build Channel Relationships Via Micromarketing?

Micromarketing is an approach which recognizes that different marketing strategies may be necessary on a store-by-store basis to maximize a reseller's sales and profitability. Micromarketing opportunities are facilitated when retailers and suppliers are able to share vital information. This process increases trust between both parties. According to Ed Fargo, a vice-president of Eisenhart & Associates, a food brokerage firm, "When we can show a food retailer what's selling, who's buying, where those buyers live and what they like, we have won that food retailer's attention."

As a service to customers, Eisenhart & Associates compiles and evaluates research data on product sales, consumer demographics, life-styles, and local advertising expenditures. Eisenhart's analysis relies on its computer-generated profiles of the typical users and heavy users of each account's product line. Thus, it can estimate a chain's market share in selected merchandise categories as compared with local supermarkets, mass merchandisers, and drug stores. Although a chain can develop similar analysis, Fargo realizes that "not all retailers can afford the time and effort to analyze hundreds of categories in this manner."

On the basis of this analysis, Eisenhart & Associates determines which stores in a chain would most benefit from special displays and in-store demonstrations, and which ones should be sold together via joint promotions. In many cases, Eisenhart is able to show that a product's contribution to sales and profits is greater than its proportionate use of shelf space.

Eisenhart & Associates then seeks to increase product positions on shelves (such as from ankle to eye level) or to add new items to a product line. For example, in one case, Fargo was able to convince a supermarket to add seven new items to a line of light yogurt.

As a food broker, what other opportunities exist for the building of channel relationships via micromarketing?

Source: Based on material in "Building Bridges," *Promo/Progressive Grocer Special Report* (October 1994), p. 9.

Accuracy and efficiency in filling customers' orders are significantly enhanced with the deployment of the new Acumax Plus warehouse management system. "Acumax Plus is the most advanced materials tracking tool available in the distribution industry," McKesson Drug President Jim Smith says. Because of Acumax and other advances, McKesson's drug division added more than $800 million in revenue, while selling and distribution expenses rose only $1 million.[11]

Wholesalers are emphasizing customer service and looking to international markets.

Wholesalers have learned that customer service is extremely important in securing a competitive advantage, developing client loyalty, and attaining acceptable profit margins. Here is what three are doing:

- W.W. Grainger—an Illinois-based wholesaler of maintenance, repair, and operating supplies—offers a "value package" that includes electronic ordering and payment, cost-reduction consulting services, and so forth. As a Grainger vice-president says, "On sales calls these days, we seldom talk about why the motor we sell is better than someone else's motor; we talk about value-added services."[12]

[11] *McKesson Corp. 1995 Annual Report.*

[12] Thomas A. Stewart, "The Information Wars: What You Don't Know Will Hurt You," *Fortune* (June 12, 1995), pp. 120–121.

- Pacific Periodicals Services of Tacoma, Washington, is a magazine wholesaler that uses a "pre-delivery interbody system." By delivering magazines several days early, its retail customers can use less expensive night personnel to process the orders.[13]
- Fleming, the largest U.S. food wholesaler, uses FOODS (Fleming's online operational distribution system) computer-based technology to provide many services to its customers. For instance, FOODS can manage item data, arrange store shipments, update retail scanning files, generate purchase orders, manage work force productivity, automate accounts payable and accounts receivable, and support electronic data interchanges with vendors.[14]

More U.S. wholesalers are turning to foreign markets for growth. As an example, Ocean Spray (the giant U.S. food cooperative) plans on reaching $500 million in annual sales to 25 foreign countries around the globe by the year 2000. In general terms, according to one expert, "The Pacific Rim especially represents a huge potential for wholesalers in terms of sheer size, growing earning power, disposable incomes, and the amount of investment going on. In Latin America, Chile and Brazil are attractive, as well. However, learning how to do business in these regions will take a lot of time and cost a lot of money. But, it's the age-old mercantile equation: high growth and high profit always equals high risk."[15]

Target market strategies are more complex.

In large numbers, wholesalers are diversifying the markets they serve or the products they carry: Farm and garden machinery wholesalers now sell to florists, hardware dealers, and garden supply stores. Plumbing wholesalers have added industrial accounts, contractors, and builders. Grocery wholesalers deal with hotels, airlines, hospitals, schools, and restaurants. Some food wholesalers have moved into apparel retailing and opened auto-parts stores.

Yet, some wholesalers are taking the opposite approach and seeking to appeal to one customer niche or need. Thus, Wallace Company focuses on pipe, valves, and fittings for the oil and chemical industries. In 1990, it became the first wholesaler to win the Malcolm Baldridge National Quality Award for small businesses. It has "a passion for total quality management."[16] Ten years ago, 75 per cent of Wallace's deliveries to customers arrived on time; today 98 per cent arrive on time.

MARKETING IN A CHANGING WORLD

How Manufacturers'/Service Providers' Agents Are Staying the Course[17]

For some time now, many manufacturers'/service providers' agents (MSPAs) have been on the endangered species list. Why? One, some large retail chains such as Wal-Mart insist on interacting face-to-face with manufacturers/service providers and will not even schedule appointments with MSPAs. Two, because of the competition for their shelf space, loads of retailers have stopped buying from small manufacturers/service providers—the same firms that the MSPAs represent. Three, the technological advances (particularly, electronic data interchange) that make today's distribution so efficient are also reducing the MSPAs' role—or at least, greatly modifying it.

The initial MSPAs appeared in the mid-1880s. Since it was inconvenient and expensive to send salespeople and samples to distant locales, MSPAs were hired locally by railroad manufacturers to market equipment to railroad builders. In some regards, MSPAs have not changed much: They still

[13]Christina Veiders, "Magazine Distributors Widening Role," *Supermarket News* (May 15, 1995), p. 54.

[14]Michael Garry, "Linchpin of the New Fleming," *Progressive Grocer* (January 1995), p. 58.

[15]Joseph Pereira, "Unknown Fruit Takes on Unfamiliar Markets," *Wall Street Journal* (November 9, 1995), pp. B1, B10; and "The Emerging Role of International Distribution," p. S8.

[16]Joseph Weber, "The Practice of Making Perfect," *Business Week* (January 14, 1991), p. 66.

[17]The material in this section is based on Melissa Campbell, "Agents of Change," *Sales & Marketing Management* (February 1995), pp. 71–75.

offer localized customer attention. Since a set commission is specified in advance, sales costs are predictable. Health benefits, training, and turnover are also eliminated.

Nonetheless, MSPAs are adapting to their current situation. And the most far-sighted ones are performing very well. Here's some of what they are doing:

- They are becoming more "technologically savvy," learning and applying everything from EDI to computerized inventory controls. This benefits the small firms that they represent (which do not have these capabilities themselves) and lets them gain entry to big retailers such as Target Stores.
- They are helping to develop new products, based on the feedback from their own customers.
- They are hiring their own support staffs, providing marketing services, and turning into product specialists—an even narrower niche than being industry specialists.
- They are offering such marketing services as telemarketing and direct mail programs for the firms they represent.

In sum, as one MSPA expert says, "The focus of the MSPA has been modified. MSPAs no longer peddle products in the traditional sense. They work closely with the manufacturers they serve, identify the needs of their customers, and then provide the product and service solutions to meet those needs."

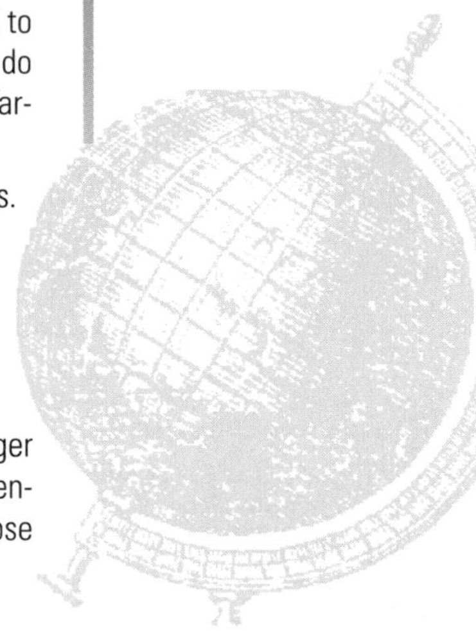

SUMMARY

1. *To define wholesaling and show its importance* Wholesaling involves the buying and/or handling of goods and services and their resale to organizational users, retailers, and/or other wholesalers but not the sale of significant volume to final consumers. In the United States, about 500,000 wholesale establishments distribute over $3.3 trillion in goods and services annually.

Wholesale functions encompass distribution, personal selling, marketing and research assistance, gathering assortments, cost reductions, warehousing, financing, returns, and risk taking. These functions may be assumed by manufacturers/service providers or shared with independent wholesalers. The latter are sometimes in a precarious position because they are located between manufacturers/service providers and customers and must determine their responsibilities to each.

2. *To describe the three broad categories of wholesaling (manufacturer/service provider wholesaling, merchant wholesaling, and agents and brokers) and the specific types of firms within each category* In manufacturer/service provider wholesaling, a producer undertakes all wholesaling functions itself. This form of wholesaling can be conducted through sales or branch offices. The sales office carries no inventory.

Merchant wholesalers buy, take title, and possess products for further resale. Full service merchant wholesalers gather assortments of products, provide trade credit, store and deliver products, offer merchandising and promotion assistance, provide a personal sales force, offer research and planning support, and complete other functions as well. Full-service merchant wholesalers fall into general merchandise, specialty merchandise, rack jobber, franchise, and cooperative types. Limited-service merchant wholesalers take title to products but do not provide all wholesale functions. Limited-service merchant wholesalers are divided into cash-and-carry, drop shipper, truck/wagon, and mail-order types.

Agents and brokers provide various wholesale tasks, such as negotiating purchases and expediting sales, but they do not take title. They are paid commissions or fees. Agents are used on a more permanent basis than brokers. Types of agents are manufacturers'/service providers' agents, selling agents, and commission (factor) merchants. Food brokers and commercial stock brokers are two key players in wholesale brokerage.

3. *To examine recent trends in wholesaling* The nature of wholesaling has changed over the last several years. Trends involve the evolving wholesaler mix, productivity, customer service, international openings, and target markets.

KEY TERMS

wholesaling (p. 445)
manufacturer/service provider wholesaling (p. 450)
merchant wholesalers (p. 452)
full-service merchant wholesalers (p. 453)
limited-service merchant wholesalers (p. 454)
general-merchandise (full-line) wholesalers (p. 454)
specialty-merchandise (limited-line) wholesalers (p. 455)
rack jobbers (p. 455)
franchise wholesaling (p. 455)
wholesale cooperatives (p. 455)
cash-and-carry wholesaling (p. 456)
drop shippers (desk jobbers) (p. 456)
truck/wagon wholesalers (p. 456)
mail-order wholesalers (p. 456)
agents (p. 456)
brokers (p. 456)
manufacturers'/service providers' agents (p. 456)
selling agents (p. 457)
commission (factor) merchants (p. 458)
food brokers (p. 458)
commercial stock brokers (p. 458)

Review Questions

1. Why does wholesale sales volume exceed retail sales volume?
2. Differentiate between selling to a wholesaler and selling through a wholesaler.
3. Under what circumstances should a manufacturer or service provider undertake wholesaling?
4. Distinguish between a manufacturer's/service provider's branch office and a manufacturer's/service provider's sales office.
5. Which wholesaling functions are performed by merchant wholesalers? Which are performed by agents and brokers?
6. Distinguish between limited-service merchant wholesalers and full-service merchant wholesalers.
7. What are the unique features of cash-and-carry and truck/wagon merchant wholesalers?
8. Why are drop shippers frequently used for coal, coke, and building materials?
9. How do manufacturers'/service providers' agents and selling agents differ?
10. What is the role of the commercial stock broker?

Discussion Questions

1. "Wholesalers are very much in the middle, often not fully knowing whether their first allegiance should be to the manufacturer/service provider or the customer." Comment on this statement. Can they rectify this situation? Why or why not?
2. The marketing vice-president of American Express has asked you to outline a support program to improve relations with the retailers that accept its cards. Prepare this outline.
3. As a member of a producer-owned wholesale cooperative, what factors would you study to determine whether your firm is being well served?
4. Develop a short checklist that Sony Music Entertainment could use in determining whether to use merchant wholesalers or agents/brokers in different countries around the world.
5. Discuss how and why a perfume manufacturer would use a combination of manufacturer/service provider wholesaling, merchant wholesaling, and agents/brokers.

CASE 1

*The Home-Market Dominance of Japanese Wholesalers**

The Japanese distribution system has often been knocked as restricting the entry of foreign goods into Japanese channels. Due to their great channel power, the critical role of Japanese wholesalers is often cited by experts.

Japanese wholesalers ("tonya") have three traits that are different from typical Western wholesalers. One, besides the marketing functions generally offered by Western wholesalers, tonya provide financing, insurance, and management consulting services for manufacturers. Two, Japanese wholesaling is more multitiered than in the West. Therefore, a typical Japanese distribution channel has two or more levels of wholesalers between manufacturers and retailers. Three, tonya supply Japan with critical imports. Today, Japanese wholesalers have taken on a significant new role through "supervised exports" in which the production processes of foreign companies are controlled. Collectively, these factors give wholesalers a large degree of channel power.

Tonya have been criticized as having so much power that foreign goods are placed at a disadvantage in Japan. One professor, who researched the history of tonya, says their power is due to historical, political, and economic forces—and not based on culture. Therefore, the tonya's modern role is better understood by examining the history of the Japanese distribution system.

In the 1100s, a rigid four-tier caste system evolved in Japan. The system placed the samurai (whose status was inherited) at the top, followed by farmers, artisans, and then merchants. The samurai were not permitted to engage in any form of business. Thus, even though Japanese wholesalers had low prestige, as members of the merchant class, they rapidly gained power and wealth through political protection and patronage. Part of their power was also due to their high wealth in comparison to the state government.

The power of wholesalers was consolidated in the 1600s, due to three factors: the functions performed by tonya for the state, the development of trade associations that represented tonya, and the financial dependence of the samurai class on wealthy wholesalers. At that time, wholesalers in Western Japan were responsible for storing, transporting, and marketing the rice tax for the state. Samurai were still restricted from business activities. Trade associations enhanced the power of wholesalers by offering insurance and extending credit to members, by lobbying activities, and by granting control of trade routes. The samurai class also needed the services of wholesalers, since the latter maintained the price of rice against the price levels of other commodities (as a means of protecting the samurai's income stream).

During the 1870s, the Japanese defense, manufacturing, and finance sectors were modernized. Yet, its distribution system hardly changed. As a result, many small manufacturers stayed dependent on powerful wholesalers for capital, materials, and marketing. Today, the Japanese distribution system still has resemblances to a feudal era.

The power of the tonya has continued into modern times, even with the increased presence of foreign businesses. For example, retail distribution in Japan is still characterized by single-product-line stores. These small independent retailers have little channel power relative to their wholesalers. And foreign firms must use a number of strategies to penetrate a Japanese distribution system that is dominated by strong wholesalers. Thus, Schick bypassed the traditional Japanese distribution channel by using a major cutlery wholesaler to market its razor blades. Johnson & Johnson engaged in piggybacking—whereby it piggybacked onto the distribution system of a manufacturer selling noncompeting goods to the same market—to sell its health-care supplies. And Maxwell House used a partnership arrangement to gain access to the strong distribution network controlled by a major food company.

QUESTIONS

1. Describe the notion of a wholesaler's being "in the middle" with reference to the role of Japanese wholesalers.
2. What types of wholesalers are described in this case? Refer to Table 16-2.
3. Explain the significance of this statement: "The power of wholesalers in Japan is based on historical, political, and economic forces, not culture."
4. Evaluate each of the different types of channel strategies used by U.S. firms to penetrate the Japanese distribution system.

*The data in this case are drawn from Barry Berman, *Marketing Channels* (New York: John Wiley & Sons, 1996), p. 614; and Susan Kitchell, "Tonya, the Japanese Wholesalers: Why Their Dominant Position?" *Journal of Macromarketing*, Vol. 15 (Spring 1995), pp. 21–31.

CASE 2

Nash Finch: A Food Wholesaler's Marketing Strategy†

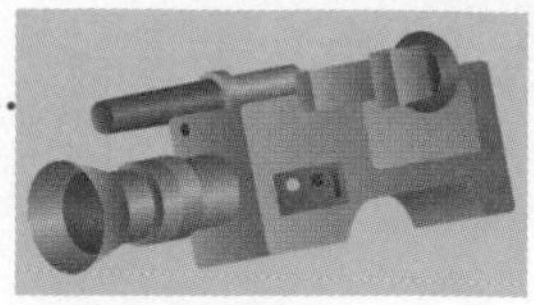

Nash Finch is the fourth-largest U.S. food wholesaler, with annual sales of $3 billion. While the firm operates its own food stores (under names such as Econofoods, Sun Mart, Family Thrifty Center, Food Folks, and Easter's), wholesale operations account for two-thirds of revenues. Unlike Supervalu or Fleming (other major food wholesalers), most of Nash Finch's business is in rural areas. Its net income as a per cent of sales has averaged 0.5 per cent or less of sales, below the median of the eight leading firms in the industry.

Via its distribution centers, it supplies food and general merchandise to 700 affiliated supermarkets—and 5,000 independent supermarkets, military bases, convenience stores, and other customers in 31 states. Affiliated food stores get such support services as site-location planning, store planning, advertising assistance, and trouble-shooting help from Nash Finch.

Nash Finch is using two strategies to grow: With market penetration, it seeks to increase market share in existing markets by sponsoring special events in existing stores and by adding additional stores in markets where the firm is currently strong, such as the Midwest. With market development, it is growing by acquiring food wholesalers in territories where it has had weak distribution. For example, in 1989, the firm acquired Timberlake Grocery Company, Georgia's second-largest food wholesaler. Timberlake supplies a full line of food and other products to supermarkets and convenience stores in Georgia and northern Florida. In 1990, it bought Tidewater Wholesale Grocery, which distributes grocery products to military commissaries in Washington, D.C., and seven Middle Atlantic states. Nash Finch has also been entering new territories, such as Tennessee and Alabama.

Nash Finch is interested in becoming even more efficient, to better enable its customers to be cost effective. Thus, it is actively involved in enacting efficient consumer response (ECR), a systems approach that seeks to reduce inefficiencies in the food distribution chain. ECR works to get manufacturers, wholesalers, and retailers to cooperate more closely with each other to reduce duplication in work and inventories. Among the elements of ECR that have been adopted by Nash Finch are electronic data interchange, continuous inventory replenishment, computer-assisted ordering, and scanning. It has also begun to regionally centralize its buying operations to reduce purchasing and handling costs, as well as to enhance its negotiating ability. As contrasted with a pure centralized program, Nash Finch's regional buying program will enable it to better meet special local preferences.

Nash Finch has long provided affiliated food stores with successful promotions. Its top promotion has been an annual Summer Circus Sale, which started about 30 years ago as a way to increase business for the slow period during the first two weeks of August. These two weeks are now the busiest two weeks of the year, with the exception of the Christmas holiday. To better capitalize on the Summer Circus Sale and other special promotions, Nash Finch prepares colorful point-of-sales materials, sponsors contests, and distributes sales flyers. Affiliated stores can choose the most suitable promotions for their markets. For example, the Spring Jubilee Sale is the best promotion in small towns. Stores are also able to modify particular promotions to meet their own needs.

QUESTIONS

1. What are the pros and cons of Nash Finch's operating its own retail stores? Take the perspective of an independently owned supermarket that is supplied by Nash Finch.
2. What are the pros and cons of Nash Finch's use of regional purchasing versus a pure centralized purchasing program?
3. Describe the advantages of efficient consumer response (ECR) to Nash Finch.
4. Evaluate Nash Finch's overall wholesale strategy.

VIDEO QUESTIONS ON NASH FINCH

1. Describe the merchandising and sales promotion services that Nash Finch offers to its retailer customers.
2. Describe the full range of store counseling and supervision services that Nash Finch offers to its retailer customers.

†The data in this case are drawn from *Nash Finch Company 1994 Annual Report*; Kerry Dolan, "Food Distributors," *Forbes* (January 1, 1996), pp. 136–138; Steve Weinstein, "Central Buying: The Best Buy . . . And Sell," *Progressive Grocer* (August 1994), pp. 40–44; and Steve Weinstein, "On the Cutting Edge," *Progressive Grocer* (August 1995), pp. 34–36.

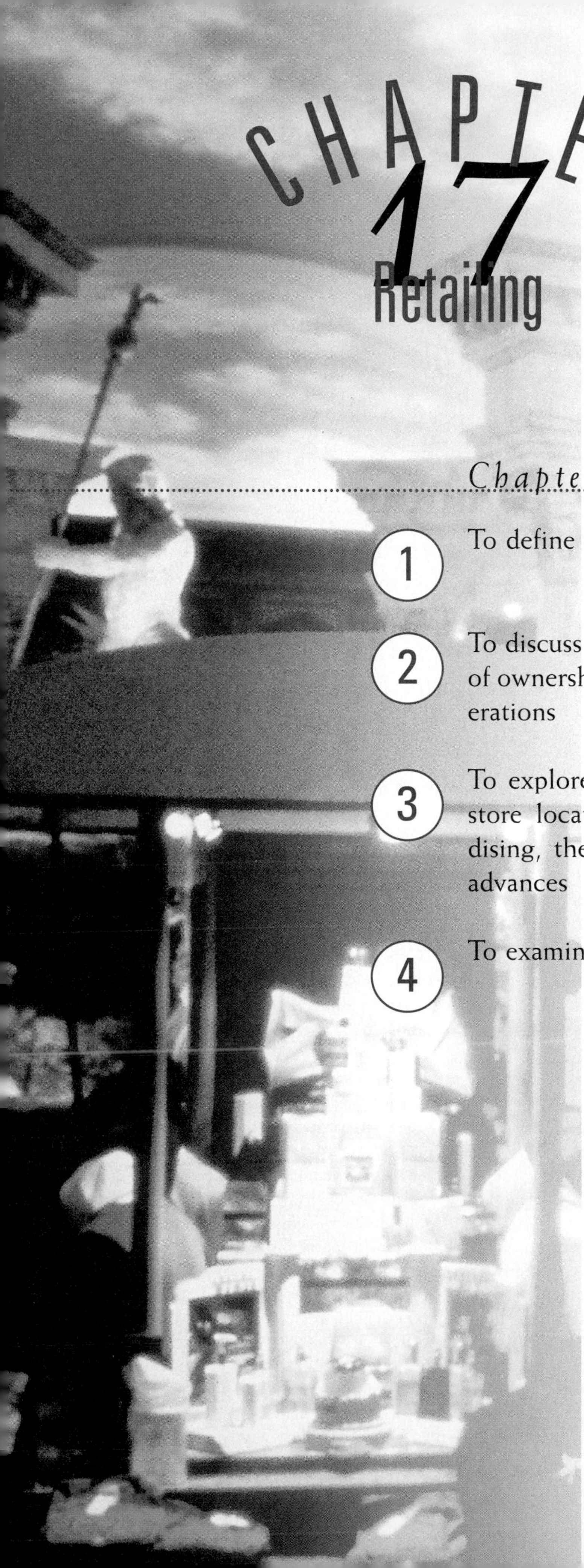

CHAPTER 17
Retailing

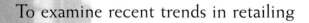

Chapter Objectives

1. To define retailing and show its importance

2. To discuss the different types of retailers, in terms of ownership, store strategy mix, and nonstore operations

3. To explore five major aspects of retail planning: store location, atmosphere, scrambled merchandising, the wheel of retailing, and technological advances

4. To examine recent trends in retailing

The experts say that over the next few years as many as 300 of the roughly 1,800 regional and super-regional malls in the United States—those with over 400,000 square feet of space—will be either shut down or converted to the warehouse-style retailing that do-it-yourselfers favor. Says Carl Steidtmann, director of research at Management Horizons, a retail consulting division of Price Waterhouse: "Regional malls clearly have a life cycle, and a lot of them are in their last throes."

Those that survive will have to reinvent themselves somehow. They will have to become primary destinations once again, catering to a consumer generation no longer willing to drift through loads of boutiques while slowly annihilating the family budget.

The Forum Shops at Caesars. Reprinted by permission.

One way to reinvent the shopping center is to offer shoppers on-premises entertainment. Many centers have added such tenants as movie theaters, video arcades, and fancy restaurants to enhance the shopping experience. Even some factory outlet malls now offer festivals, concerts, and book signings as a means of attracting greater consumer traffic. As one real-estate executive says, "The idea is to give people multiple reasons to come to your center."

Industry experts have been carefully studying the success of two projects of the Simon Property Group, a leading mall developer based in Indianapolis: the Forum Shops at Caesars in Las Vegas and the Mall of America, located in Minneapolis. Let's take a glimpse at these two popular shopping centers that integrate entertainment and shopping experiences.

The Forum Shops is housed in a wing of Caesars Palace, directly next to the hotel's casino. The atmosphere in the mall has been thoughtfully planned. It approximates a Roman street with such features as a polished flagstone floor and a painted-sky ceiling. The ceiling color changes hourly to mark the time of day. And each hour, the statues that line the Festival Fountain come alive and put on a show, complete with music, sound effects, audio animatronics, lasers, and special scenic projections on the dome, that combine together with a computer-controlled waterscape effect. While marketing analysts can debate whether they like the glitz factor, there is little question about the success of this shopping center. The Forum Shops (which includes Gucci, Louis Vuitton, and Gianni Versace) are averaging annual sales of $1,000 per square foot, making it one of the most productive retail malls in the United States.

The Mall of America includes four department stores, over 400 specialty shops, an amusement park (with a roller coaster), a 14-screen movie complex, 45 restaurants, and even a wedding chapel—all under one roof. In addition to having a wide variety of stores, many retailers in the Mall of America use interactive merchandising to provide consumer entertainment. For instance, Oshman's (a sporting-goods retailer) operates a basketball court and a rollerskating track so that customers can test a planned purchase before leaving the store. Some skeptics were initially critical of the mall's huge overall size. But, as with the Forum Shops, few can now dispute its success. These are some of Mall of America's numbers: it attracts 35 million visitors per year; it has a 94 per cent occupancy rate; and annual sales are $425 per square foot for specialty retailers in the mall (versus $200 to $400 for the average shopping center).[1]

In this chapter, we will examine various aspects of retailing—including trends affecting shopping centers—and consider their ramifications.

Overview

Retailing, *the last channel stage, entails selling to final consumers.*

Retailing encompasses those business activities involved with the sale of goods and services to the final consumer for personal, family, or household use. It is the final stage in a channel of distribution. Manufacturers, importers, and wholesalers act as retailers when they sell products directly to the final consumer.

The average retail sale per shopping trip is small, about $40 for U.S. department stores and $50 for specialty stores. Convenience stores, such as 7-Eleven, have average sales of just a few dollars (not including gasoline). U.S. chain supermarkets average nearly $20 per customer transaction.[2] Accordingly, retailers try to increase their sales volume by using one-stop shopping appeals, broadening merchandise and service assortments, increasing customer shopping frequency, and encouraging more family members to go shopping. Inventory controls, automated merchandise handling, and electronic cash registers enable retailers to reduce their transaction costs.

Despite the low average size of customer transactions, about one-half of sales for such retailers as department stores involve some form of customer credit. This means these retailers must pay a percentage of each transaction to a bank or other credit-card service company or absorb the costs of their own credit programs—in return for increased sales.[3] For example, Sears and J.C. Penney each have tens of millions of holders of their own credit cards; these people buy billions of dollars in goods and services every year.

Whereas salespeople regularly visit organizational consumers to initiate and conclude transactions, most final consumers patronize stores. This makes the location of the store, product assortment, store hours, store fixtures, sales personnel, delivery, customer service, and other factors critical tools in drawing customers to the store. See Figure 17-1.

Final consumers make many unplanned purchases. In contrast, those that buy for resale or use in production (or operating a business) are more systematic in their purchasing. Therefore, retailers need to place impulse items in high-traffic locations, organize store layout, train sales personnel in suggestion selling, place related items next to each other, and sponsor special events to stimulate consumers.

In this chapter, the importance of retailing, the various types of retailers, considerations in retail planning, and recent trends in retailing are all discussed in detail.

[1]Kenneth Labich, "What It Will Take to Keep People Hanging Out at the Mall," *Fortune* (May 29, 1995), pp. 102–106; and Mitchell Pacelle, "Malls Add Fun and Games to Attract Shoppers," *Wall Street Journal* (January 23, 1996), pp. B1, B9.

[2]"Retailing: Basic Analysis," *Standard & Poor's Industry Surveys* (June 15, 1995), p. R82.

[3]"Survey of Retail Payment Systems," *Chain Store Age* (January 1996), Section Two.

FIGURE 17-1
Customer Service at Radio Shack
To provide excellent customer service, Radio Shack has thousands of convenient locations, 20,000 well-trained employees, and "simple" answers to "complicated" questions—all backed by a 70-year company tradition.
Reprinted by permission.

The Importance of Retailing

Retailing is a significant aspect of distribution because of its impact on the economy, its functions in the distribution channel, and its relationships with suppliers.

Retailing's Impact on the Economy

Retailing embodies high annual sales, employment, and costs.

Retail sales and employment account for substantial amounts of sales and employment. Annual U.S. retail store sales volume exceeds $2.5 trillion; this does not include most vending machine, direct selling, and direct marketing revenues or many retail services. The world's top 100 retailers (38 of which reside in the United States) generate $1.3 trillion in total annual revenues and include firms from 14 different nations. The largest retailer on the planet, by far, is U.S.-based Wal-Mart—with annual sales approaching $100 billion (over 95 per cent in the United States), nearly 3,000 stores, and multiple store formats (such as Wal-Mart and Sam's Clubs).[4]

According to the Bureau of Labor Statistics, almost one-sixth of the labor force is employed in 2.4 million retail establishments in the United States. Wal-Mart's work force alone is more than 500,000. Industrywide and around the globe, a wide range of retailing career opportunities is available, including store management, merchandising, and owning one's own retail business.[5]

From a cost perspective, retailing is a significant field. For example, on average, 38 to 40 cents of every dollar a consumer spends in a U.S. department or specialty store goes

[4] "State of the Industry," *Chain Store Age* (August 1995), Section Two; "The Shopping Spree That Wasn't," *Wall Street Journal* (January 5, 1996), p. B1; Coopers & Lybrands, "Global Powers of Retailing," *Chain Store Age* (December 1995), Section Two; Zina Moukheiber, "The Great Wal-Mart Massacre, Part II," *Forbes* (January 22, 1996), p. 44; and Louise Lee and Kevin Hellicker, "Humbled Wal-Mart Plans More Stores," *Wall Street Journal* (February 23, 1996), pp. B1, B4.

[5] A discussion of careers in retailing can be found in Barry Berman and Joel R. Evans, *Retail Management: A Strategic Approach*, Sixth Edition (New York: Prentice Hall, 1995), pp. A1–A13.

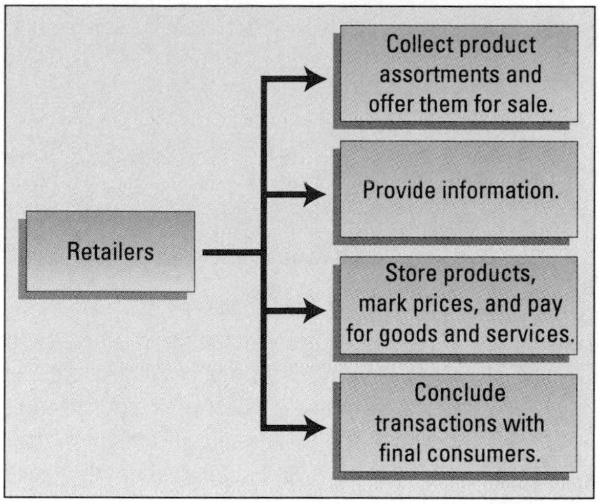

FIGURE 17-2
Key Retailing Functions

to it as compensation for the functions it performs. The corresponding figure is 22 cents for a supermarket. This compensation—known as gross margin—is for rent, taxes, fuel, advertising, management, personnel, and other retail costs, as well as profits. One of the reasons for Wal-Mart's success is that its operating costs are so low (16 per cent of sales) compared to other firms. For instance, Kmart's operating costs are 22 per cent of sales and Federated Department Stores' are 33 per cent.[6]

Although comprehensive retail data are not available on a global basis, these statistics indicate the magnitude of retailing around the world: Annual retail store sales are about $300 billion in China, $200 billion in Canada, $35 billion in South Africa, $25 billion in New Zealand, $15 billion in Mexico, and $2.5 billion in Nigeria. British retailers sell $35 billion of women's apparel each year, while German retailers sell $40 billion. China has almost 12 million retail stores; Brazil and Japan each have over 1.5 million; South Korea and Spain each have 500,000.[7]

Retailing Functions in Distribution

Retailers undertake four key functions.

As highlighted in Figure 17-2, retailers generally perform four distinct functions. They

- Engage in the sorting process by assembling an assortment of goods and services from a variety of suppliers and offering them for sale. The width and depth of assortment depend on the individual retailer's strategy.
- Provide information to consumers via ads, displays and signs, and sales personnel. And marketing research support (feedback) is given to other channel members.
- Store products, mark prices, place items on the selling floor, and otherwise handle products. Retailers usually pay for items before selling them to final consumers.
- Facilitate and complete transactions by having appropriate locations and hours, credit policies, and other services (like delivery).

The Relationship of Retailers and Suppliers

Retailers deal with two broad supplier categories: those selling goods or services for use by the retailers and those selling goods or services that are resold by the retailers. Examples of goods and services purchased by retailers for their use are store fixtures, computer equipment, management consulting, and insurance. Resale purchases depend on the lines sold by the retailer.

[6]*Stores*, various issues; "Progressive Grocer Annual Report," *Progressive Grocer* (April 1996); and Mary Kuntz, et al., "Reinventing the Store," *Business Week* (November 27, 1995), p. 92.
[7]Data estimated by the authors, based on several sources.

Ethics IN TODAY'S SOCIETY

How Should Retailers Deal with Vendor Kickback Efforts?

As a housewares buyer for J.C. Penney, Jimmy Locklear earned $56,000 per year. However, according to some estimates, he supplemented this salary by as much as $1.5 million through bribes and kickbacks over a four-year period. In exchange for these payments, Locklear offered suppliers large profitable orders or access to confidential data (such as a competing firm's bid).

Locklear's case is unusual in that Penney sought both criminal and civil prosecution (to recover damages). Many times, retailers are more interested in gaining restitution in exchange for an offer not to prosecute. Unlike other dishonest buyers who typically perform poorly, Locklear was considered a first-rate buyer. Under his direction, Penney's annual sales of housewares rose from $25 to $45 million dollars over four years. And Locklear was named a buyer of the year for three consecutive years.

Some critics believe Penney should have been aware of Jimmy Locklear's lavish life-style relative to his salary. Furthermore, three years before Locklear was prosecuted, a cutlery supplier told a Penney personnel director that Locklear was taking kickbacks. Penney says that when it investigated these and other past complaints it found no evidence of wrongdoing. Then, in July 1992, Locklear admitted taking a $200,000 payment from a manufacturer's representative after Penney received an anonymous letter.

The Locklear incident also highlights differences in conflict-of-interest policies among retailers. For instance, Wal-Mart does not allow a buyer to accept even a cup of coffee from a vendor. In contrast, J.C. Penney's policy is that as long as buyers feel there is an opportunity to reciprocate, they may accept dinners, theater tickets, or golf dates. And Penney does not plan to tighten its ethics code based on this incident.

As a J.C. Penney personnel manager, evaluate the firm's strategy in dealing with Jimmy Locklear.

Source: Based on material in Andrea Gerlin, "How a Penney Buyer Made Up to $1.5 Million On Vendors' Kickbacks," *Wall Street Journal* (February 7, 1995), pp. A1, A16.

Suppliers must have knowledge of their retailers' goals, strategies, and methods of business operation to sell and service accounts effectively. Retailers and their suppliers may have divergent viewpoints, which must be reconciled. Here are two examples:

> Current and former Reebok insiders say the toughest fight with Nike is being waged at Woolworth Corporation's Foot Locker unit—and Reebok is losing. With little fanfare, the shoe retailer has grown into a behemoth: Its 2,800 outlets chalk up about 23 per cent of U.S. sneaker sales. When a retailer achieves such dominance in a product category, it expects to get preferred terms from manufacturers, early looks at new models, and speedy shipments. Nike has played the game. Reebok has not. Thus, in 1995, Foot Locker's Nike sales were $750 million, while Reebok's were only $172 million.[8]

> A few years ago, Steve DiFillippo, owner of a swank Italian restaurant in Boston, was one of American Express's most vocal critics, going so far as to cut up an American Express card before newspaper photographers. In response to DiFillippo and others, American Express did what it said it wouldn't do: It lowered transaction fees paid by merchants to bring them closer to

[8]Joseph Pereira, "In Reebok-Nike War, Big Woolworth Chain Is a Major Battlefield," *Wall Street Journal* (September 22, 1995), p. A1.

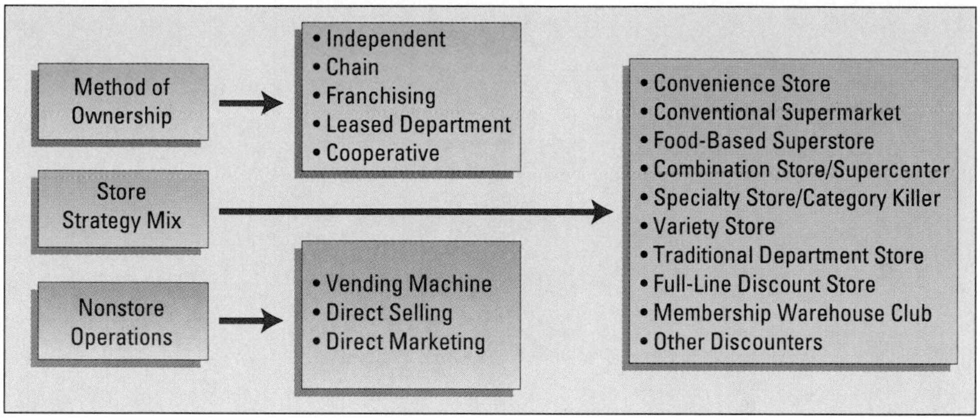

FIGURE 17-3
Categorizing Retailers

those of bank-card rivals. Equally important, it shifted its marketing emphasis to keeping existing merchants happy, rather than focusing too much on adding new ones. DiFillippo now says, "They're great. They've been transformed."[9]

Types of Retailers[10]

Retailers can be categorized by ownership, store strategy mix, and nonstore operations. See Figure 17-3. The categories overlap; that is, a firm can be correctly placed in more than one grouping. For example, 7-Eleven is a chain, a franchise, and a convenience store. The study of retailers by group provides data on their traits and orientation, and the impact of environmental factors.

By Ownership

An **independent retailer** *has one store, while a* **retail chain** *has multiple outlets.*

An **independent retailer** operates only one outlet and offers personal service, a convenient location, and close customer contact. Nearly 80 per cent of U.S. retail establishments (including those staffed solely by the owners and their families)—and an even higher percentage in some foreign nations—are operated by independents, including many dry cleaners, beauty salons, furniture stores, gas stations, and neighborhood stores. This large number is due to the ease of entry because various kinds of retailing require low investments and little technical knowledge. Therefore, competition is plentiful. Numerous retailers do not succeed because of the ease of entry, poor management skills, and inadequate resources. According to the U.S. Small Business Administration, about one-third of new retailers do not last one full year and two-thirds do not make it past the first three years.

A **retail chain** involves common ownership of multiple outlets. It usually has central purchasing and decision making. Although independents have simple organizations, chains tend to rely on specialization, standardization, and elaborate control systems. Chains can serve a large, dispersed target market and have a well-known company name. They operate 20 per cent of U.S. retail outlets, but account for well over one-half of all retail store sales. About 550 chains have over 100 units; yet they generate 35 per cent of U.S. store sales. Chains are common for department stores, supermarkets, and fast-food outlets, among others. Examples of chains are Wal-Mart, Kroger, and Dillard.

Retail franchising *uses an established name and operates under certain rules.*

Retail franchising is a contractual arrangement between a franchisor (a manufacturer, wholesaler, or service sponsor) and a retail franchisee, which allows the latter to run a certain form of business under an established name and according to specific rules. It is a form of chain retailing that lets a small businessperson benefit from the experience, buy-

[9]Peter Pae, "American Express Rings Up Praise from Merchants," *Wall Street Journal* (October 21, 1992), p. B4.
[10]Unless otherwise indicated, the statistics in these subsections are the authors' current projections, based on data from *1992 Census of Retail Trade* (Washington, D.C.: U.S. Bureau of the Census); *Stores*; *Progressive Grocer*; *Discount Store News*; *Inc.*; *Vending Times Census of the Industry* (1995); *Direct Marketing*; and Berman and Evans, *Retail Management: A Strategic Approach*.

FIGURE 17-4
Pizza Hut: A Leader in Franchising
PepsiCo serves as the franchisor for Pizza Hut, KFC, and Taco Bell—the big guns in their respective market niches. Of the 12,000 Pizza Hut restaurants around the world, over 4,000 are franchised; the rest are owned and operated by PepsiCo.
Reprinted by permission.

ing abilities, and name of a large multiunit retailer. Many times, the franchisee gets management training and engages in cooperative buying and advertising. The franchisor benefits by obtaining franchise fees and royalties, faster payments, strict operating controls, consistency among outlets, and motivated owner-operators. Franchises annually account for more than $750 billion in U.S. retail sales via 500,000 outlets. One-third of U.S. franchisors have stores in foreign markets, a number growing rapidly. Franchising is popular for auto and truck dealers, gas stations, fast-food outlets, hotels and motels, service firms, and convenience-foods stores. Examples of retail franchises are Chevrolet dealers, Pizza Hut, and H&R Block. See Figure 17-4.

A **leased department** *is one rented to an outside party.*

A **leased department** is a section of a retail store rented to an outside party. The lessee operates a department—under the store's rules—and pays a percentage of sales as rent. Lessors gain from the reduced risk and inventory investment, expertise of lessees, lucrative lease terms, increased store traffic, and appeal to one-stop shopping. Lessees gain from the location in established stores, lessor name awareness, overall store traffic, one-stop customers attracted to stores, and whatever services (such as ads) lessors provide. Leased departments are popular for beauty salons, jewelry, photo studios, shoes and shoe repairs, and cosmetics. In U.S. department stores, such departments generate $12 billion to $15 billion in annual sales. Meldisco leases departments in 2,600 stores (mostly Kmarts) for its shoe lines.

With a **retail cooperative**, *stores organize to share costs.*

With a **retail cooperative**, independent retailers share purchases, storage and shipping facilities, advertising, planning, and other tasks. Individual stores remain independent—but agree on broad, common policies. Cooperatives are growing due to chains' domination of independents. They are popular for liquor stores, hardware stores, and gro-

Table 17-1

Key Characteristics of Retail Ownership Forms

	CHARACTERISTICS		
OWNERSHIP FORM	***Distinguishing Features***	***Major Advantages***	***Major Disadvantages***
Independent	Operates one outlet, easy entry	Personal service, convenient location, customer contact	Much competition, poor management skills, limited resources
Retail chain	Common ownership of multiple units	Central purchasing, strong management, specialization of tasks, larger market	Inflexibility, high investment costs, less entrepreneurial
Retail franchising	Contractual arrangement between central management (franchisor) and independent businesspersons (franchisees) to operate a specified form of business	To franchisor: investments from franchisees, faster growth, entrepreneurial spirit of franchisees To franchisee: established name, training, experience of franchisor, cooperative ads	To franchisor: some loss of control, franchisees not employees, harder to maintain uniformity To franchisee: strict rules, limited decision making ability, payments to franchisors
Leased department	Space in a store leased to an outside operator	To lessor: expertise of lessee, little risk, diversification To lessee: lower investment in store fixtures, customer traffic, store image	To lessor: some loss of control, poor performance reflects on store To lessee: strict rules, limited decision-making ability, payments to store
Retail cooperative	Purchases, advertising, planning, and other functions shared by independent retailers	Independence maintained, efficiency improved, enhances competitiveness with chains	Different goals of participants, hard to control members, some autonomy lost

cery stores. Associated Food Stores and Certified Grocers are cooperatives. *Retail cooperative* and *retailer-owned wholesale cooperative* are synonymous terms.

Table 17-1 compares the retail ownership forms.

By Store Strategy Mix

A **retail store strategy mix** *combines the hours and products, etc., offered.*

Firms can be classed by the store strategy mix they undertake. A typical **retail store strategy mix** consists of an integrated combination of hours, location, assortment, service, ad-

FIGURE 17-5
Harris Teeter: A Popular Conventional Supermarket Chain
There are 140 Harris Teeter supermarkets in several states in the Southeast. It offers a wide variety of staples, as well as perishable goods and specialty items, at competitive prices. Most outlets feature a full-service deli, bakery, and fresh seafood and meat counters. The chain has a reputation for top-quality goods and services.
Reprinted by permission of the Ruddick Corporation.

vertising, prices, and other factors retailers employ. Store strategy mixes vary widely, as the following indicate.

A **convenience store** *stresses fill-in items.*

A **convenience store** is usually a well-situated, food-oriented store with long hours and a limited number of items. In the United States, these stores have annual sales of $80 billion, including gasoline, and account for 7 to 8 per cent of total grocery sales. The average store has yearly sales that are a fraction of those of a conventional supermarket. Consumers use a convenience store for fill-in merchandise, often at off-hours. Gasoline, milk, groceries, newspapers, soda, cigarettes, beer, and fast food are popular items. 7-Eleven, Circle K, and Arco operate convenience stores.

A **conventional supermarket** *is a large, self-service food store.*

A **conventional supermarket** is a departmentalized food store with minimum annual sales of $2 million; it emphasizes a wide range of food and related products—general merchandise sales are limited. It originated in the 1930s, when food retailers realized a large-scale operation would let them combine volume sales, self-service, low prices, impulse buying, and one-stop grocery shopping. The car and refrigerator aided the supermarket's success by lowering travel costs and adding to perishables' life spans. These stores today account for 45 per cent of total U.S. supermarket sales (which exceed $300 billion) and nearly two-thirds of supermarket outlets. Kroger, American, and Safeway are among the large chains operating conventional supermarkets. Figure 17-5 features Harris Teeter—a strong regional chain.

A **food-based superstore** *stocks food and other products for one-stop shoppers.*

A **food-based superstore** is a diversified supermarket that sells a broad range of food and nonfood items. The latter account for 20 to 25 per cent of sales. A food-based superstore typically has greeting cards, floral products, VCR tapes, garden supplies, some apparel, wine, film developing, and small household appliances—besides a full line of

FIGURE 17-6
The Body Shop: A Focused Specialty Store Chain
Around the world, Great Britain-based The Body Shop offers a deep selection of goods and services—all related to its natural cosmetics and personal-care products. Shown here is Anita Roddick, the founder and managing director.
Reprinted by permission.

supermarket items. Although a conventional U.S. supermarket has 15,000 to 20,000 square feet of space and average annual sales of $7.5 million, a food-based superstore has 25,000 to 50,000 square feet and $16 million in average sales. About 6,000 superstores account for nearly 30 per cent of all U.S. supermarket sales. Several factors have caused many conventional supermarkets to switch to superstores: consumer interest in one-stop shopping, the leveling of food sales due to population stability and competition from fast-food stores and restaurants, and higher margins on general merchandise (double those of food items). For large food chains, the superstore is now the preferred supermarket format.

A **combination store** *offers a large assortment of general merchandise, as well as food. One type is a* **supercenter**.

A **combination store** unites food/grocery and general merchandise sales in one facility, with general merchandise providing 25 to 40 per cent or more of sales. It goes further than a food-based superstore in appealing to one-stop shoppers and occupies 30,000 to 100,000 square feet or more. It lets a retailer operate efficiently, expand the number of people drawn to a store, raise impulse purchases and the size of the average transaction, sell both high-turnover/low-profit food items and lower-turnover/high-profit general merchandise, and offer fair prices. A **supercenter** is a combination store that integrates an economy supermarket with a discount department store, with at least 40 per cent of sales from nonfood items. It is 75,000 to 150,000 square feet in size and carries 50,000 or more items. Among the firms with combination stores are Wal-Mart, Jewel, Albertson's, and France's Carrefour.

A **specialty store** *emphasizes one kind of product, with a* **category killer** *store being a large version.*

A **specialty store** concentrates on one product line, such as stereo equipment or hair-care services. Consumers like these stores since they are not faced with racks of unrelated products, do not have to search through several departments, are apt to find informed salespeople, can select from tailored assortments, and may avoid crowding. Specialty stores are quite successful with apparel, appliances, toys, electronics, furniture, personal care products, and personal services. The total annual sales of the 20 largest U.S. specialty stores are $75 billion annually. Specialty stores include The Limited, LensCrafters, and The Body Shop. See Figure 17-6.

A rather new type of specialty store—the category killer—is now gaining strength. The **category killer** is an especially large specialty store. It features an enormous selection in its product category and relatively low prices, and consumers are drawn from wide geographic areas. Toys "R" Us, The Limited, The Gap, Sam Goody, and Barnes & Noble are among the many specialty store chains that are opening new category killer stores to complement their existing stores. Blockbuster, Sports Authority, Home Depot, and Staples are among the chains fully based on the category-killer store concept.

A **variety store** *sells an assortment of lower-priced items.*

A **variety store** sells a wide assortment of inexpensive and popularly priced merchandise. It features stationery, gift items, women's accessories, toiletries, light hardware, toys, housewares, and confectionery items. U.S. sales are $6 billion per year. With the growth of other retail store strategy mixes, U.S. variety stores have lost a lot of ground in recent years. F.W. Woolworth has dominated U.S. variety store sales, but it is now emphasizing its specialty-store divisions (such as Kinney and Foot Locker).

A department store employs at least 50 people and usually sells a general line of apparel for the family, household linens and textile products, and some mix of furniture, home furnishings, appliances, and consumer electronics. It is organized into separate departments for purposes of buying, promotion, service, and control. There are two types of department store: the traditional department store and the full-line discount store.

A **traditional department store** *is a fashion leader with many customer services.*

A **traditional department store** has a great assortment of goods and services, provides many customer services, is a fashion leader, and often serves as an anchor store in a shopping district or shopping center. Prices are average to above average. It has high name recognition and uses all forms of media in ads. In recent years, traditional department stores have set up more boutiques, theme displays, and designer departments to compete with other firms. They face intense competition from specialty stores and discounters. Annual U.S. sales, including mail order, are nearly $100 billion. Traditional department stores include May, Dayton Hudson, Macy's, and Bloomingdale's.

A **full-line discount store** *has self-service and popular brands.*

A **full-line discount store** is a department store with lower prices, a broad product assortment, a lower-rent location, more emphasis on self-service, brand-name merchandise, wide aisles, shopping carts, and more goods displayed on the sales floor. U.S. full-line discounters annually sell over $125 billion in goods and services. They are among the largest retailers of apparel, housewares, electronics, health and beauty aids, auto supplies, toys, sporting goods, photographic products, and jewelry. Wal-Mart, Kmart, and Target account for three-quarters of U.S. full-line discount store sales.

A **membership warehouse club** *offers deep discounts to its member customers.*

With a **membership warehouse club**, final consumers and businesses pay small yearly dues for the right to shop in a huge, austere warehouse. Products are often displayed in their original boxes, large sizes are stocked, and some product lines vary by time period (since clubs purchase overruns and one-of-a-kind items that cannot always be replaced). Consumers buy items at deep discounts. For a decade, this retailing format, whose annual sales skyrocketed from $2.5 billion in 1985 to $20 billion (excluding sales to business customers) in 1995, was the fastest-growing form of retailing in the United States. Lately, growth has slowed due to marketplace saturation and overexpansion. The leading clubs are Sam's Club and PriceCostco.

In recent years, other forms of low-price retailing have also grown. Among them are warehouse-style food stores, off-price specialty chains, discount drugstore chains, and factory outlet stores. These retailers all hold their prices down by maximizing inventory turnover, using plain store fixtures, locating at inexpensive sites, running few ads, and offering less customer service. They appeal to price-sensitive consumers. These retailers include Marshalls (an off-price chain) and Kids Port USA (a factory outlet chain).

Table 17-2 shows the differences between discount store and traditional department store strategies.

By Nonstore Operations

Nonstore retailing *is nontraditional.*

With **nonstore retailing**, a firm uses a strategy mix that is not store-based to reach consumers and complete transactions. It does not involve conventional store facilities.

Vending machines *allow 24-hour, self-service sales.*

A **vending machine** uses coin- or card-operated machinery to dispense goods (such as beverages) or services (such as life insurance policies at airports). It eliminates the need for salespeople, allows 24-hour sales, and can be placed outside rather than inside a store. Its sales are concentrated on a few products—beverages, food items, and cigarettes yield 95 per cent of the U.S. total. Machines may need intensive servicing due to breakdowns, stock-outs, and vandalism. Improved technology lets vending machines make change for bills, "talk" to consumers, use video screens to show products, brew coffee, and so on. Yearly U.S. sales are $27 billion.

Direct selling *encompasses personal contacts with consumers in nonstore settings.*

Direct selling involves personal contact with consumers in their homes (and other nonstore locations) and phone solicitations initiated by the retailer. Cosmetics, vacuum cleaners, encyclopedias, household services (like carpet cleaning), dairy products, and newspapers are sometimes marketed via direct selling. In a cold canvass, a salesperson calls people or knocks on doors to find customers. With referrals, past buyers recommend friends to the salesperson. In the party method, one consumer acts as host and invites people to a sales demonstration in his or her home (or other nonstore site). To some con-

Table 17-2

Typical Retail Strategy Mixes—A Discount Store Versus a Traditional Department Store

DISCOUNT STORE STRATEGY	DEPARTMENT STORE STRATEGY
1. Less expensive rental location—lower level of pedestrian traffic. (Note: Some discount stores are using more expensive locations.)	**1.** More expensive rental location in shopping center or district—higher level of pedestrian traffic.
2. Simpler fixtures, linoleum floor, central dressing room, fewer interior and window displays.	**2.** More elaborate fixtures, carpeted floor, individual dressing rooms, many interior and exterior displays.
3. Promotional emphasis on price. Some discounters do not advertise brand names, but say "famous brands."	**3.** Promotional emphasis on full service, quality brands, and store image.
4. Fewer alterations, limited phone orders, delivery, and gift wrapping; less availability of credit.	**4.** Many alterations included in prices, phone orders accepted, and home delivery at little or no fee; credit widely available.
5. More reliance on self-service, plain displays with piles of merchandise; most merchandise visible.	**5.** Extensive sales assistance, attractive merchandise displays, a lot of storage in back room.
6. Emphasis on branded products; selection may not be complete (not all models and colors). Some discounters feature "seconds," remove labels from goods if asked by manufacturers, and stock low-price, nonbranded items.	**6.** Emphasis on a full selection of branded and privately branded first-quality products; does not stock closeouts, discontinued lines, or seconds.
7. Year-round use of low prices.	**7.** Sales limited to end-of-season clearance and special events.

sumers, direct selling has a poor image. In addition, sales force turnover is high and many people are not home during the day. To increase business, salespeople for firms such as Avon now target working women via office presentations during breaks and lunch hours. Direct selling has yearly U.S. revenues of $15 billion. Avon, Mary Kay, Tupperware, and Amway are leading direct selling organizations.

In **direct marketing**, *a seller first communicates with consumers via nonpersonal media.*

Direct marketing occurs when a consumer is first exposed to a good or service by a nonpersonal medium (such as direct mail, TV, radio, magazine, newspaper, or PC) and then orders by mail, phone, or PC. More than one-half of U.S. households make such purchases each year—mostly due to convenience. The popularity of both manufacturer brands and the private brands of many direct marketing firms (and consumer confidence in them), the large number of working women, and the belief that direct marketing is a good way to shop are all fueling its growth:

> When you shop, you're not hemmed in by time or space. A night owl can buy a scarf at 3 A.M.; a city dweller can purchase cheese made in the Vermont countryside. Shoppers can peruse several malls' worth of items and buy from an armchair, without driving, bumping elbows with other shoppers, or waiting in line.[11]

For retailers, direct marketing offers low operating costs, coverage of a wide geographic area, and new market segments. Direct marketing is used by specialized firms, as well as store retailers that apply it to supplement their regular business. Among the most popular direct-marketing items are books, tapes and CDs, clothing, magazines, insurance,

[11]"Mail-Order Shopping: Which Catalogs Are Best?" *Consumer Reports* (October 1994), p. 621.

FIGURE 17-7
The Many Faces of Spiegel Catalogs
Reprinted by permission of Spiegel, Inc. All rights reserved.

home accessories, and sports equipment. Yearly U.S. retail sales are more than $135 billion, up from $70 billion a decade ago. Spiegel, L.L. Bean, J.C. Penney, Dell Computer, and QVC are direct marketers. See Figure 17-7.

Globally, the United States, Europe, and Japan account for 95 per cent of the world's mail order business. The United States alone is responsible for 47 per cent of the total.[12]

Considerations in Retail Planning

There are many factors for retailers to weigh in devising marketing plans—and manufacturers, service providers, and wholesalers to keep in mind. Five key factors are store location, atmosphere, scrambled merchandising, the wheel of retailing, and technological advances.

Store Location

Store location is meaningful because it helps determine the customer mix and competition faced. Once selected, it is also inflexible. The basic forms of store location are the isolated store, the unplanned business district, and the planned shopping center.

An **isolated store** *is a freestanding outlet on a highway or side street.*

An **isolated store** is a freestanding retail outlet located on a highway or street. There are no adjacent stores with which the firm competes, but there are also no stores to help draw shoppers. Customers may hesitate to travel to an isolated store unless it has a good product assortment and an established image. This site may be used by discount stores due to low rent and supplier desires for them to be far enough away from stores selling goods and services at full prices. Some Kmart and 7-Eleven stores are isolated.

In an **unplanned business district**, *stores locate together with no prior planning.*

An **unplanned business district** exists where multiple stores are located close to one another without prior planning as to the number and composition of stores. The four unplanned sites are central business district, secondary business district, neighborhood business district, and string.

A central business district (CBD) is the hub of retailing in a city and is sometimes called "downtown." It has the most commercial, employment, cultural, entertainment, and shopping facilities in a city—with at least one major department store and a broad group-

[12]For an in-depth look at the global opportunities available to direct marketers, see Richard Miller, *Multinational Direct Marketing: The Methods and the Markets* (New York: McGraw-Hill, 1995).

ing of specialty and convenience stores. CBDs have had some problems with crowding, a lack of parking, older buildings, limited pedestrian traffic when offices close, nonstandardized store hours, crime, and other elements. Yet, in many urban areas, CBD sales remain strong. Among the tactics being used to strengthen CBDs are modernizing storefronts and equipment, improving transportation, closing streets to vehicular traffic, developing strong merchant associations, planting trees to make areas more attractive, and integrating the commercial and residential environment.

A secondary business district (SBD) is a shopping area bounded by the intersection of two major streets. Cities tend to have several SBDs, each with at least one branch department store, a variety store, and/or some larger specialty stores, as well as several smaller shops. Compared to a CBD, an SBD has less assortment and a smaller trading area (the geographic area from which customers are drawn), and sells more convenience-oriented items.

A neighborhood business district (NBD) satisfies the convenience-shopping and service needs of a neighborhood. It has a number of small stores, with the major retailer being a supermarket, a large drugstore, or a variety store. An NBD is located on the major street in a residential area.

A string is ordinarily composed of a group of stores with similar or compatible product lines that situate along a street or highway. Because this location is unplanned, various store combinations are possible. Car dealers, antique stores, and clothing stores are retailers often locating in strings.

A **planned shopping center** has centrally owned or managed facilities; it is planned and operated as an entity, ringed by parking, and based on balanced tenancy. With balanced tenancy, the number and composition of stores are related to overall shopper needs—stores complement each other in the variety and quality of their offerings. To ensure balance, a center may limit the products a store carries. Planned centers account for 40 per cent of total U.S. retail-store sales (including autos and gas); unplanned business districts and isolated stores account for the rest. The three types of planned center are regional, community, and neighborhood.

A **planned shopping center** *is centrally planned and has balanced tenancy.*

A regional shopping center sells mostly shopping goods to a geographically dispersed market. It has at least one or two department stores and up to a hundred or more smaller stores. People will drive as much as a half hour to reach such a center. As with CBDs, many regional centers (especially those built a while ago) need renovation. Enhancements include bringing in "hot" new retailers, enclosing more malls, erecting new store directories, redesigning storefronts, adding trees and plants, and replacing concrete in parking lots.

A community shopping center has a branch department store, a variety store, and/or a large specialty store as its major retailer, with several smaller stores. It sells both convenience- and shopping-oriented items. A neighborhood shopping center sells mostly convenience-oriented goods and services. It has a supermarket and/or drugstore, and a few smaller stores.

Atmosphere

Atmosphere is the sum total of the physical attributes of a retail store or group of stores that are used to develop an image and draw customers. It affects the target market attracted, the customer's shopping mood and time spent in the store, impulse purchases, and store positioning; and is related to the strategy chosen. As was shown in Table 17-2, a discount store would have simple fixtures, linoleum floors, and crowded displays. A full-service store would have elaborate fixtures, carpeted floors, and attractive displays.

Atmosphere *consists of a store's exterior, general interior, layout, and displays.*

There are four basic components of a store's atmosphere:

- Exterior—elements such as the storefront, the marquee, entrances, display windows, store visibility, store design, the surrounding area, and traffic congestion.
- General interior—elements such as flooring, colors, scents, lighting, fixtures, wall textures, temperature, aisle width, vertical transportation, personnel, cash register placement, and overall cleanliness.

FIGURE 17-8
The Appealing Atmosphere of the Hulen Mall
The Hulen Mall in Fort Worth, Texas, is the dominant regional center in its market.
Reprinted by permission of The Rouse Company.

- Store layout—elements such as the floor space allotted for customers, selling, and storage; product groupings; and department locations.
- Interior (point-of-sale) displays—elements such as merchandise cases and racks, mobiles, in-store ads, posters, and mannequins.

See Figure 17-8.

Canada's West Edmonton Mall—the world's largest planned shopping center— uses an innovative atmosphere to draw millions of people annually, some from as much as 750 miles or more away. It has 11 department stores, over 800 other shops, a mile-long concourse, and 58 entrances. Its size equals 115 football fields. The mall contains an amusement park, an ice-skating rink, a miniature golf course, and other attractions. It has parking for 20,000 vehicles. Total construction costs exceeded $700 million.[13]

Scrambled Merchandising

In **scrambled merchandising**, *a retailer adds items to obtain one-stop shopping, higher margins, and impulse purchases.*

Scrambled merchandising occurs if a retailer adds goods and services that are unrelated to each other and the firm's original business. Examples are supermarkets adding videocassette rentals, department stores offering theater ticket services, restaurants carrying newspapers, and car washes stocking postcards.

There are several reasons for the popularity of scrambled merchandising: Retailers seek to convert their stores to one-stop shopping centers. Scrambled merchandise is often fast selling, generates store traffic, and yields high profit margins. Impulse purchasing is increased. Different target markets can be attracted. And the effects of seasonality and competition may be lessened.

On the other hand, scrambled merchandising can spread quickly and cause competition among unrelated firms. For instance, when supermarkets branch into nonfood personal-care items, drugstore sales fall. This forces the drugstores to scramble into stationery and other product lines, which has a subsequent impact on specialty store sales. The situation is illustrated in Figure 17-9.

[13]Triple Five Corporation Ltd. correspondence.

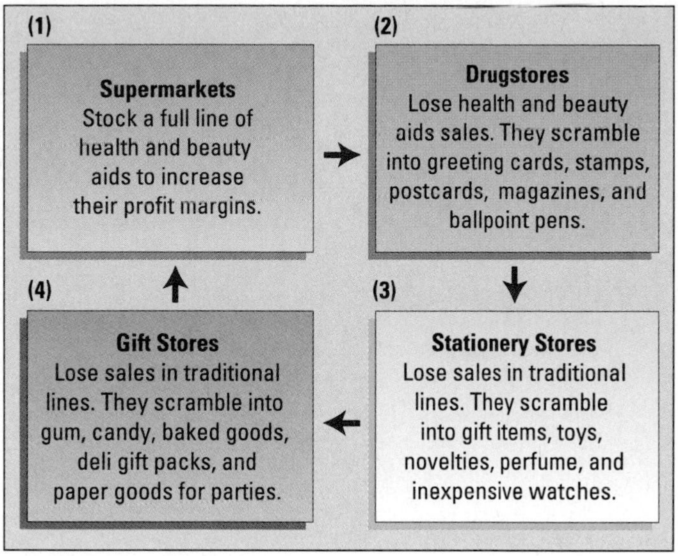

FIGURE 17-9
The Self-Perpetuating Nature of Scrambled Merchandising

There are limits to how far a firm should go with scrambled merchandising, especially if adding unrelated items would reduce buying, selling, and service effectiveness. Furthermore, stock turnover might be low for certain product lines should a retailer enter too many diverse product categories. Finally, due to scrambled merchandising, a firm's image may become fuzzy to consumers.

The Wheel of Retailing

The **wheel of retailing** *shows how strategies change, leaving opportunities for new firms.*

The **wheel of retailing** describes how low-end (discount) strategies can evolve into high-end (full service, high price) strategies and thus provide opportunities for new firms to enter as discounters. According to the wheel, retail innovators often first appear as low-price operators with low profit-margin requirements and low costs. As time passes, the innovators look to increase their sales and customer base. They upgrade product offerings, facilities, and services and turn into more traditional retailers. They may expand the sales force, move to better sites, and usher in delivery, credit, and alterations. The improvements lead to higher costs, which in turn cause higher prices. This creates openings for a new generation of retailers to emerge by appealing to the price-conscious shoppers who are left behind as existing firms move along the wheel. Figure 17-10 shows the wheel in action.

There are some limitations in applying the wheel-of-retailing theory too literally, these two in particular: many retailers do not follow the pattern suggested, and trying to move

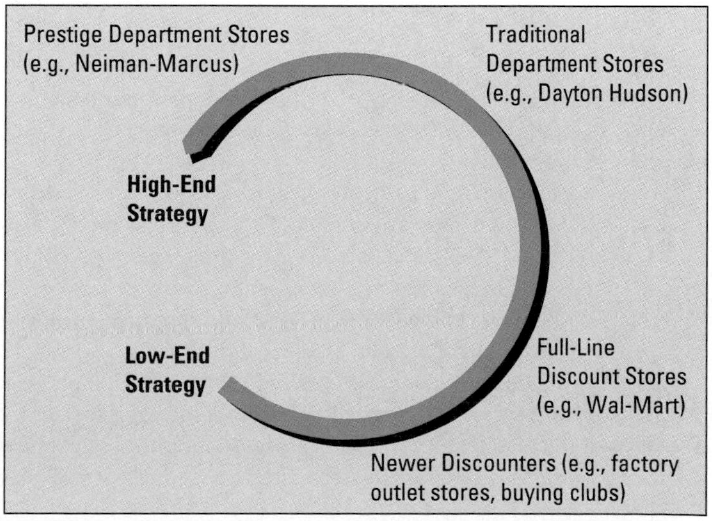

FIGURE 17-10
The Wheel of Retailing in Action

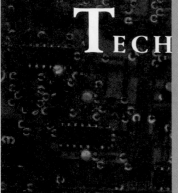

TECHNOLOGY & MARKETING

Self-Scanning: Will Consumers Pass the Honesty Test?

Several supermarket chains are now testing a scanning system that lets consumers scan their groceries as they shop and then ring up and total their purchases. In most of the tests, shoppers receive a hand-held scanner as they enter the supermarket. They then scan items as they are picked and deposited into their shopping carts. Items that are returned to the shelves (because a shopper changed his or her mind) can be easily deducted from the bill.

At the end of the shopping trip, the scanner system prints out a shopper's total bill. In some stores, a customer can pay the bill on his or her credit card by swiping the card through the scanner. Many stores are also providing a take-home container that fits compactly into the shopping cart. This container eliminates the need to unpack and then repack the shopping cart.

According to market analysts, the real test of self-scanning is with consumers' honesty, not with the equipment. Although tests of this system in the Netherlands showed that retail shoplifting actually dropped because of self-scanning, many experts feel that the Dutch experience may not be replicated in the United States. Other potential problems relate to using self-scanning with fruits and vegetables (consumers must know the proper variety and then weigh the foods selected), dealing with items that do not properly scan, and the embarrassment to shoppers who, during a random check by a store employee, discover they inadvertently forgot to scan an item or two.

Supermarkets hope that self-scanning will attract shoppers interested in reducing the time spent on checkout lines. Other advantages include shoppers being able to calculate their total bill during the shopping process (to stay within budget) and their better access to price information.

As the manager of an independent supermarket, would you recommend self-scanning? Why or why not?

Sources: Based on material in Tara Parker-Pope, "New Devices Add Up Bill, Measure Shoppers' Honesty," *Wall Street Journal* (June 6, 1995), pp. B1, B6; and Emily Nelson, "Finast Tests Scanners to Shorten Time Needed for Customers to Check Out," *Wall Street Journal* (October 25, 1995), p. B5.

along the wheel may cause a firm to lose its loyal customers. The best use of the wheel is in understanding that there can be distinct low-end, medium, and high-end strategies pursued by retailers.

Technological Advances

Technological advances range from computerized-checkout systems to enhanced operating efficiency.

Over the last several years, a number of technological advances related to retailing have emerged. The most dramatic involve the computerized-checkout system, video-shopping services, data warehousing, computer-aided site selection, electronic banking, and enhanced operating efficiency.

In a computerized-checkout (electronic point-of-sale) system, a cashier manually rings up a sale or passes an item over or past an optical scanner; a computerized register instantly records and displays a sale. The customer gets a receipt, and inventory data are stored in the computer's memory bank. Such a system reduces checkout time, employee training, misrings, and the need for price marking on all products. It also generates a current listing of the merchandise in stock without taking a physical inventory, improves inventory control, reduces spoilage, and aids ordering. See Figure 17-11.

Video-shopping services let retailers efficiently, conveniently, and promptly present information, receive orders, and process transactions. These services can be divided into two basic categories: merchandise catalogs, and in-store and in-home ordering systems.

FIGURE 17-11
A Computerized-Checkout System in Action
Through its state-of-the-art, electronic point-of-sale system, Mercantile Stores is able to speed up transaction times for customers, collect data so that it can engage in quick response inventory planning, and automatically restock best-selling items as selling seasons progress. Mercantile has over 100 department stores operating under about a dozen different store names.
Reprinted by permission of Mercantile Stores.

Video catalogs (shown on special monitors or via disc players/VCRs using conventional TV sets) allow consumers to view pre-recorded product and sales presentations in store and nonstore settings without the seller having to set up costly displays. With such catalogs (sometimes called kiosks), supermarkets can market appliances, airports can market watches, department stores can market gourmet foods, and mail-order firms can have offerings come to life.

With an in-store video-ordering system, a consumer orders products by entering data into a self-prompting computer, which processes the order. After placing the order, the consumer usually goes to a checkout area where the item can be picked up and an invoice received. The consumer then pays a cashier. Such a system is used by Service Merchandise. For an in-home system, goods and services are listed or displayed and then consumers order directly via special toll-free 800 phone numbers or via their PCs. To date, most in-home ordering has been from consumer phone responses to TV shows offered by such firms as the Home Shopping Network and QVC.

Through "data warehousing," more retailers are embracing data-base marketing. For example,

> Each week, information from the Lands' End order processing and customer mailing systems is added to the catalog company's data warehouse. Detailed information is kept on some 20 million customers, enabling Lands' End decision makers to find and analyze data by customer, product, and transaction. The transaction information available through the data warehouse includes not only purchases, but also requests for catalogs, shipping dates, and orders for merchandise that was not in stock.[14]

The availability of inexpensive computerized site-selection software is so prevalent that retailers of any size and type can now use it. For as little as $500, a retailer can buy

[14]Gary Robins, "Data Warehousing: Retailers on the Cutting Edge," *Stores* (September 1995), pp. 19, 24.

International Marketing in Action

What's Next for Retailing in China?

Retail experts predict that China's retail sales will more than double between 1995 and the year 2000. In 1993, the latest year for which data are available, the sales of China's state-owned department store chain, Shanghai No. 1, rose by 44 per cent and after-tax profit rose by 78 per cent over 1992.

State retailers are working hard to deal with China's increasingly sophisticated consumers. Thus, to better compete against domestic and international competitors, China's state-owned retailers are teaming up with foreign partners. Generally, China's retailers are trading their land-rights usage (as a state enterprise they have rent-free status) and their ability to cut through China's bureaucracy in return for their foreign partners' superior management skills and financial resources.

One significant joint venture is Nextage Shanghai (short for next stage), a partnership of Shanghai No. 1 Department Store Company and Japan's Yaohan Group. Nextage Shanghai is a $200-million complex that features department and specialty stores, an ice-skating rink, an automobile dealership, fast-food outlets, and sports and entertainment facilities. One marketing characteristic of Nextage Shanghai is its focus on higher-fashion clothing. To appeal to fashion-oriented firms such as Esprit, Donna Karan, Ralph Lauren, and Yves Saint Laurent, Nextage Shanghai will provide manufacturers with greater control over merchandise presentation by offering them consignment sales opportunities. Nextage Shanghai hopes to attract these designers, many of whom had shunned state-owned department stores in previous years.

High growth prospects and the easing of government investment restrictions have also accelerated the growth of foreign retailer competition. Among the retailers that have recently announced plans to enter China or have already entered are: Wal-Mart Stores, Walt Disney, Esprit, Jusco (Japan), and Au Printemps (France).

As a marketing consultant to a U.S. retailer, assess Nextage's strategy.

Source: Based on material in Sally D. Goll, "China's Big State-Owned Retail Stores Form New Ventures with Foreign Firms," *Wall Street Journal* (March 13, 1995), p. A11C.

tate employees among tasks to lessen boredom, reward good performance with bonuses, and encourage the best employees to pursue full-time career paths in retailing.

Foreign opportunities are plentiful.

For firms with proper resources and management prowess, there are numerous retailing opportunities in foreign markets. These are several examples:

- Toys "R" Us does well in Europe and Japan because of the wide merchandise selection in its stores, especially compared to local retailers.[21]
- "Direct marketing is in its infancy in Russia. In the decade ahead, and based on what has been accomplished in a short time, we expect to witness a commercial environment intertwined with direct marketing applications. That process is certain to become more important and a more integrated function in the new Russian economy. This is especially true in view of the large distances and great span of the country, requiring the vital communication function that direct marketing can provide."[22]

[21]Carla Rapoport and Justin Martin, "Retailers Go Global," *Fortune* (February 20, 1995), pp. 104, 106.
[22]Mark D. Mariska, "Direct Marketing in Russia," *Direct Marketing* (January 1995), p. 41.

- Because of the lack of discounters in South Korea, the Seoul Price Club has attracted 100,000 members. In contrast, the typical U.S. Price Club has 45,000 members.[23]
- McDonald's is building hundreds of restaurants in Central Europe, an underserved area for fast-food outlets. It is also expanding rapidly in Latin America and Asia.[24]
- Annual worldwide direct selling revenues are estimated to be $50 billion (including the United States). This form of retailing is now significantly more popular outside the United States than within the United States, due to consumer demographics and other factors.[25]
- France's Carrefour is the leading retailer in Argentina, with $1.5 billion in annual revenues.[26]

MARKETING IN A CHANGING WORLD

Competing in the Age of Wal-Mart

For thousands of retailers competing in the age of Wal-Mart, the lyrics of an old rock song seem unfortunately on target: "Another one bites the dust." Why? These days, it seems the 35-year-old Wal-Mart is virtually unstoppable with its low prices and large assortments. Wal-Mart stores and Sam's Clubs blanket the United States; and the firm is rapidly expanding in Canada, Mexico, Hong Kong, and elsewhere. In its wake, vulnerable (unprepared) retailers keep falling by the wayside.

Nonetheless, as we have noted throughout *Marketing*, when companies follow sound marketing principles, they greatly increase their chances of success. And this is just as true of retailers in the age of Wal-Mart as in any other situation.

Each year, *Chain Store Age* and Ernst & Young recognize a number of owner-managed and middle-market retail businesses as "Entrepreneurs of the Year"—based on such factors as financial growth, firm history, current stage of development, future prospects, business experience, major accomplishments, and community involvement. Let us look at a few of the recent award recipients to see how they are competing:

- Tires Plus Groupe is an upscale tire retailer with 70 stores in the Upper Midwest. Tires Plus stores have tile floors and waiting rooms with TVs, newspapers, magazines, and free coffee to foster a friendly atmosphere.
- Gourmet to Go is a St. Louis retailer with two take-out gourmet food shops. It prepares moderately priced, healthy meals that can be ordered in advance and picked up on the way home. People can also enter a shop, pick an entrée, choose a side dish and dessert, and have a hot meal packed for later eating.
- Dots is an off-price women's apparel chain with nearly 250 stores in the Midwest and on the East Coast. All items sell for $10 or less. For an off-price chain, it has a strong customer service orientation, exemplified by its "unconditional" return policy.
- Cele Peterson's Fashions operates one women's apparel store in Tucson, Arizona. It carries fashionable, upscale apparel. What makes the firm unique is its community involvement—ranging from the Tucson Children's Museum to the Steel Memorial's Children's Research Center. The company's founder even helped start the Tucson Opera Company and Arizona Theater Company.[27]

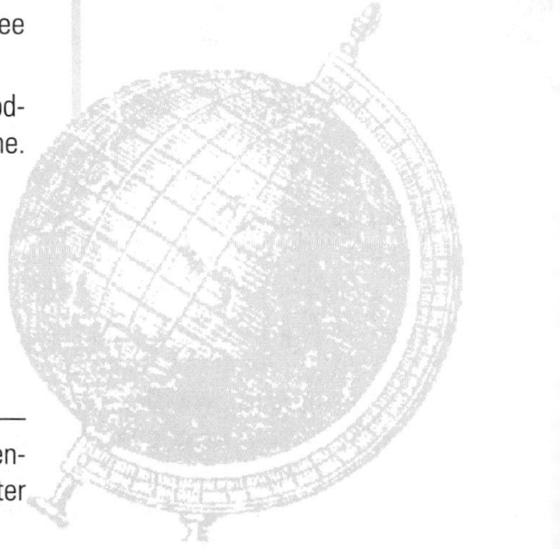

[23]Gale Eisenstodt, "Park Gui-Sook's Reading List," *Forbes* (September 11, 1995), pp. 72–76.

[24]Jeanne Whalen, "McDonald's Cooks Worldwide Growth," *Advertising Age* (July 17, 1995), p. I-4; and Richard Gibson, "McDonald's Accelerates Store Openings in U.S. and Abroad, Pressuring Rivals," *Wall Street Journal* (January 18, 1996), p. A3.

[25]Direct Selling Education Foundation.

[26]Jonathan Friedland, "Big Discounters Duel Over Hot Market," *Wall Street Journal* (August 23, 1995), p. A8.

[27]"Retail Entrepreneurs of the Year," *Chain Store Age* (December 1995), pp. 47–102.

SUMMARY

1. *To define retailing and show its importance* Retailing encompasses those business activities involved with the sale of goods and services to the final consumer for personal, family, or household use. It is the final stage in a distribution channel. Average retail sales are small, yet the use of credit is widespread. Final consumers generally visit a retail store to make a purchase, and they also make many unplanned purchases.

Retailing has an impact on the economy because of its total sales and the number of people employed. Retailers provide a variety of functions, including gathering a product assortment, providing information, handling merchandise, and completing transactions. Retailers deal with suppliers that sell products the retailers use in operating their businesses, as well as suppliers selling items the retailers will resell.

2. *To discuss the different types of retailers, in terms of ownership, store strategy mix, and nonstore operations* Retailers may be categorized in several ways. The basic ownership formats are independent—a retailer operating only one outlet; chain—a retailer operating two or more outlets; franchise—a contractual arrangement between a franchisor and a franchisee to conduct a certain business; leased department—a department in a store that is leased to an outside party; and retail cooperative—an enterprise shared by retail owners. The ease of entry into retailing fosters competition and results in many new firms failing.

Different strategy mixes are used by convenience stores—well-situated, food-oriented retailers; conventional supermarkets—departmentalized food stores with minimum annual sales of $2 million; food-based superstores—diversified supermarkets that sell a broad range of food and nonfood items; combination stores (including supercenters)—outlets that go further than food-based superstores in carrying both food and general merchandise; specialty stores (including category killers)—outlets that concentrate on one merchandise or service line; variety stores—outlets selling a wide assortment of inexpensive and popularly priced merchandise; traditional department stores—outlets that have a great assortment, provide customer services, are fashion leaders, often dominate surrounding stores, and have average to above-average prices; full-line discount stores—department stores with a low-price, moderate-service orientation; membership warehouse clubs—stores that offer very low prices in austere settings; and other discounters—including limited-line stores and off-price chains.

Nonstore retailing occurs when a firm uses a strategy mix that is not store-based. Vending machines use coin- or card-operated machinery to dispense goods and services. Direct selling involves both personal contact with consumers in their homes (or other places) and phone solicitations initiated by retailers. Direct marketing occurs when consumers are exposed to goods and services through nonpersonal media and then order via mail and phone. It is now a large part of retailing.

3. *To explore five major aspects of retail planning: store location, atmosphere, scrambled merchandising, the wheel of retailing, and technological advances* A firm may select from among three forms of store location: an isolated store—a freestanding outlet located on a highway or street; an unplanned business district—in which two or more stores locate close to one another without prior planning as to the number and composition of stores; and a planned shopping center—which is centrally managed, as well as planned and operated as an entity. Only planned shopping centers utilize balanced tenancy, thus relating the store mix to consumer needs.

Atmosphere is the sum total of a store's physical characteristics that help develop an image and attract customers. It depends on the store's exterior, general interior, layout, and interior displays.

Scrambled merchandising occurs when a retailer adds products unrelated to its original business. The goals of scrambled merchandising are to encourage customer one-stop shopping, increase sales of high-profit items and impulse purchases, attract different target markets, and balance sales throughout the year.

The wheel of retailing explains low-end and high-end retail strategies and how they emerge. As low-cost, low-price innovators move along the wheel, they leave opportunities for newer, more cost-conscious firms to enter the market.

A number of technological advances have emerged over the past several years. These include computerized checkouts, video-shopping services, data warehousing, computerized site selection, electronic banking, and techniques to improve operating efficiency.

4. *To examine recent trends in retailing* The nature of retailing has changed dramatically in recent years. Among the key trends retailers are adapting to are those relating to consumer demographics and life-styles, competitive forces, operating costs, the labor force, and international opportunities.

KEY TERMS

retailing (p. 467)
independent retailer (p. 471)
retail chain (p. 471)
retail franchising (p. 471)
leased department (p. 472)
retail cooperative (p. 472)
retail store strategy mix (p. 473)
convenience store (p. 474)
conventional supermarket (p. 474)
food-based superstore (p. 474)
combination store (p. 475)
supercenter (p. 475)
specialty store (p. 475)
category killer (p. 475)
variety store (p. 475)
traditional department store (p. 476)
full-line discount store (p. 476)
membership warehouse club (p. 476)
nonstore retailing (p. 476)
vending machine (p. 476)
direct selling (p. 476)
direct marketing (p. 477)
isolated store (p. 478)
unplanned business district (p. 478)
planned shopping center (p. 479)
atmosphere (p. 479)
scrambled merchandising (p. 480)
wheel of retailing (p. 481)
debit transactions (p. 484)

Review Questions

1. Describe the four basic functions performed by retailers.
2. What are the disadvantages of an independent retailer in competing with retail chains?
3. What are the benefits of retail franchising to the franchisee? To the franchisor?
4. Why would a store want to have leased shoe departments rather than operate these departments itself?
5. Compare the strategies of full-line discount stores and membership warehouse clubs.
6. Distinguish between direct marketing and direct selling. Which has greater sales? Why?
7. What are the pros and cons of scrambled merchandising?
8. Explain the wheel of retailing from the perspective of the battle between traditional department stores and full-line discount stores for market share.
9. Differentiate between credit cards and debit cards. What is the benefit of debit cards to retailers?
10. Why are attracting and retaining a quality labor force so difficult for many U.S. retailers?

Discussion Questions

1. The typical retailer earns a profit of 3 per cent or less on its sales revenues. How can this amount be so low if 38 to 40 cents of every customer dollar spent in department stores and specialty stores go to the retailers?
2. As a prospective franchisee for a Dunkin' Donuts outlet, what criteria would you use in deciding whether Dunkin' Donuts is right for you? What criteria do you think Dunkin' Donuts should use in assessing potential franchisees? Explain the differences in your answers to these two questions.
3. Develop a discount-store strategy for an art gallery. How would the strategy differ from that for an upscale art gallery?
4. Select a planned shopping center near your college or university and evaluate it.
5. How can a nonstore retailer create a good shopping atmosphere for its customers?

CASE 1

*At Woodworkers Warehouse Stores: No One's Afraid of Home Depot**

At one time, Stanley Black (a high school dropout from a poor family) had two small businesses. One sold metal fasteners; the other sold tools used by furniture makers, repairpersons, and upholsters. In 1982, Black realized that much of the demand for his products came from shops selling to woodworking hobbyists. So, he rented mailing lists of such hobbyists and produced a mail-order catalog called *Trend-lines*.

In 1986, Stanley Black opened his first Woodworkers Warehouse store. During 1994, Trend-lines raised $22 million by selling 35 per cent of the company's stock. Black and his wife own 65 per cent of the company. Their stock ownership in Trend-lines is valued at about $55 million.

Today, Massachusetts-based Trend-lines Inc. has 75 woodworking stores, a *Trend-lines* catalog that goes to 1.5 million customers, and Golf-Day (a golf-supply retail chain and mail-order catalog division). In fiscal 1995, Trend-lines had sales of $128 million and after-tax profits of $5 million. For fiscal 1996, sales were expected to reach $185 million; and profits of $7.5 million were forecast.

Many of Trend-lines' 5,000-square-foot Woodworkers Warehouse stores are located within a few blocks of Home Depot (whose stores are ten times or more larger) and other major home improvement stores. Some are literally next door to a Home Depot. But in comparison to Home Depot (which carries a much wider product assortment), Woodworkers Warehouse's has a more extensive selection within its chosen product lines—woodworking tools and supplies. For example, Home Depot stores typically carry 30 or so power drills; Woodworker Warehouse stores carry about 70. And many of the specialty items carried by Woodworkers Warehouse, such as a dovetail jig, are not even available at Home Depot. As a result, many Home Depot salespeople refer customers to Woodworkers Warehouse for specialty items. According to a top executive at Black & Decker, "Woodworkers Warehouse typical customers are like avid fishermen, hunters, and golfers. They want the best and newest products in their hobby. It's a toy store for these people."

There is plenty of untapped growth among woodworking hobbyists. The magazine *American Woodworker* estimates that there are now 17 million woodworking hobbyists. To capitalize on this demand, Black wants to open another 40 stores per year. And Trend-lines' new 286,000-square-foot warehouse has the capacity to supply 375 stores, five times the current level.

Trend-lines acquired Golf-Day in 1989 for $100,000. Golf-Day complements the firm's woodworking business because sales of golf supplies (such as clubs and golf-cart seat covers) are busiest in the spring and summer—when woodworking sales are slowest. The division's opposite seasonal sales pattern from woodworking supplies and tools (whose sales are busiest in the fall and winter) increases the efficiency of Trend-lines' warehouse operations and sales staff. Golf-Day's ten stores and 700,000 customer mailing list account for over 20 per cent of Trend-lines' companywide revenues.

Although Stanley Black is very aggressive in pursuing sales, he is also known for his desire to reduce operating and other costs. For example, Black initially rejected purchasing Golf-Day for $600,000. A year later he was able to purchase the firm and its then 200,000-person mailing list for $100,000. In outfitting Trend-lines' new offices, Black selected used partitions, purchased at 15 per cent of the cost of comparable new fixtures. He even buys surplus and misprinted cartons to save money. Thus, some merchandise is delivered to customers in cartons with a frozen food manufacturer's name imprinted.

QUESTIONS

1. Contrast Woodworkers Warehouse's overall retail strategy with Home Depot's.
2. How can an independent retailer effectively compete against Woodworkers Warehouse?
3. What type of store location is most suitable for Woodworkers Warehouse stores? Explain your answer.
4. Explain the strategic fit of the Golf-Day acquisition to Trend-lines.

*The data in this case are drawn from Matthew Schifrin, "What Do Woodworkers Do in the Summer?" *Forbes* (May 22, 1995), pp. 116–117.

CASE 2

Incredible Universe: A Power Retailing Strategy[†]

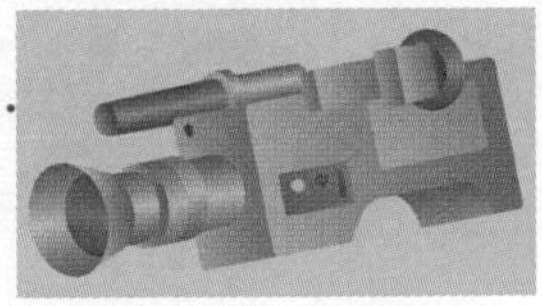

Tandy Corporation is comprised of three major retail units: Radio Shack, Computer City, and Incredible Universe. Its annual overall sales are $6 billion, and it operates nearly 7,000 stores (well over 90 per cent of which are under the Radio Shack format). Tandy's fastest-growing divisions are Computer City and Incredible Universe, both of which have seen their revenues explode. While Tandy does not break out profitability by division, company reports indicate that both Incredible Universe and Computer City operate on lower profit margins (but also have lower selling, general, and administrative expenses) than Radio Shack. This case focuses on Incredible Universe.

Incredible Universe stores carry consumer electronics, computers, and appliances. When they opened in 1992, the first two Incredible Universe stores had total sales of $34 million. By 1994, the nine Incredible Universe stores accounted for sales of $382 million. And in 1995, the 17 Incredible Universe stores amassed sales of $725 million. It is no wonder that Tandy planned to open more stores in 1996 and expects to have as many as 30 Incredible Universe stores by the year 2000, with mature locations bringing in $80 million to $100 million in yearly revenues.

To distinguish its stores from competitors' large stores, Tandy classifies Incredible Universe stores as "gigastores." The average size of an Incredible Universe location is 184,000 square feet, equal to three football fields. In comparison, Circuit City's average store size is 30,000 square feet and Best Buy's is 50,000 square feet. Incredible Universe's size enables it to offer an unmatched selection of merchandise in its product categories (85,000 items versus 5,000 to 7,000 at competitors).

Store atmosphere is an essential part of Incredible Universe's overall strategy. TVs, for example, are displayed in large demonstration rooms with a wide-screen format. Car stereos can be heard when a shopper (called a "guest") sits behind the wheel of a vintage model auto. And unlike other stores where customers are told to keep their hands off merchandise, customers at Incredible Universe are encouraged to "please, play with the merchandise!"

In keeping with the emphasis on store atmosphere, all Incredible Universe sales personnel and their managers are trained by Disney. The Incredible Universe also uses Disney's terms of "producers" and "directors" for managers, "cast members" for sales staff, "scenes" for departments, and "guests" for customers. And as a consumer leaves the store, he or she can read an overhead sign that says, "We Hope You Enjoyed the Show." In contrast to competitors that use high-pressure sales techniques, all Incredible Universe salespeople are noncommissioned.

Each store's size and merchandise mix is so big that an estimated 700,000 customers visit each location annually. And the typical Incredible Universe store attracts 10,000 customers daily on weekends. The drawing power of each store is so great that 10 per cent of its customers travel more than 100 miles to visit.

Incredible Universe appeals both to bargain hunters and to consumers who want top-of-the-line models—due to its full merchandise selection and superior demonstration capabilities. As a result, Tandy feels Incredible Universe can sell higher-end products better than competitors due to its superior demonstration capabilities, and these products usually have better profit margins than lower-end ones. A low-price guarantee is offered to assure customers of Incredible Universe's competitive pricing.

Because of the high investment in Incredible Universe stores and the huge inventory carried, the chain has yet to turn a profit. In 1995, losses were $26 million.

QUESTIONS

1. What types of store locations are best for an Incredible Universe?
2. What opportunities for scrambled merchandising exist for Incredible Universe?
3. How can a traditional appliance store compete against a newly opened Incredible Universe located in its trading area?
4. Evaluate the overall retail strategy of Incredible Universe.

VIDEO QUESTIONS ON INCREDIBLE UNIVERSE

1. Evaluate the pros and cons of Incredible Universe's vast selection strategy.
2. Incredible Universe calls its stores "electronics trade shows." Comment on this description.

[†]The data in this case are drawn from Bruce Fox, "Not Just the Design is Incredible," *Chain Store Age Executive* (January 1994), pp. 89–95; Mary Kuntz, et al., "Reinventing the Store," *Business Week* (November 27, 1995), p. 86; and Stephanie Anderson Forest, "Incredible Universe: Lost in Space," *Business Week* (March 4, 1996), p. 70.

PART 5 CASE

Relationship Marketing and Distribution Networks

Introduction

Like nations, corporations must court allies to promote their own survival and prosperity. Thus, a major consequence of the global economy is the proliferation of alliances, partnerships, and other cooperative agreements between corporations. They give rise to "strategic network competition" and also give new meaning to the concept "relationship marketing."

New Era of Competition

In this era of strategic network competition, managers must understand the processes involved in establishing, nurturing, developing, and maintaining successful relationships with all the firm's exchange partners—be they suppliers, competitors, nonprofit organizations, government agencies, or even the firm's own divisions and employees.

Traditional Competition Figure 1 illustrates the traditional view of competition, using the auto industry as an example. Competition is horizontal and firm-to-firm at each level: Auto makers compete with other auto makers, materials' suppliers compete with other materials' suppliers, ad agencies compete with other ad agencies, and so on.

The advantages of traditional competition in such an industry structure are numerous, both for individual firms and society as a whole:

- All firms specialize in those activities they do best—core competencies.
- All firms are optimally positioned to take advantage of economies of scale because market forces punish firms that are either too large or too small.
- The discipline of marketplace price ensures efficiency because all firms negotiate at "arms length."
- The capital investment of each firm is kept to the absolute minimum.
- All firms can (and must) adapt quickly to environmental changes, such as technological advances. Thus, if a new firm devises a radically new battery that would make obsolete all the capital equipment of current battery producers, auto makers could adopt the new battery without thinking about the investment losses of current battery suppliers.

Hierarchical Competition Although traditional firm-to-firm competition has many advantages, it also has inherent disadvantages; so some companies engage in a kind of integration that results in competition between "hierarchies." In its early days, Ford was really "just" an assembler of autos—connecting parts made by others. Over the years, however, Ford adopted the structure in Figure 2, integrating backward to such an extent that at one time it even made its own steel!

In contrast with firm-to-firm competition, highly integrated firms have:

- Lower transaction costs, realized by not having to buy and sell goods/services from independent suppliers.
- Less likelihood of being the victim of opportunistic behavior, such as suppliers not fulfilling their contractual responsibilities.
- More autonomy through increased control over the resources necessary for survival and growth.
- Better coordination of activities.
- Greater opportunity to plan for the future.

By 1980, Ford was one of the most highly integrated companies in the world (as were Chrysler and GM). The benefits of integration, thought many, exceeded the disadvantages: less competency fit, potential diseconomies of scale, lack of price discipline on components produced "in-house," high investment expense, and a lack of flexibility and adaptability.

Strategic Network Competition During the 1980s, theorizing began about a form of competition that could potentially combine the best parts of traditional and hierarchical competition without incurring the disadvantages of either. This resulted in strategic network competition, as illustrated in Figure 3.

Formally speaking, a network is a group of independently owned and managed firms that agree to be partners and not adversaries. Because each partner's individual success is tied to the success of the overall network, the firms pursue common goals. They engage in cooperative behavior and coordinated activities in such areas as marketing, production, finance, purchasing, and R&D. Although each firm is independently owned, the extent of cooperation and coordination among the firms is so great that company boundaries become "fuzzy," as illustrated by the broken lines surrounding each firm in Figure 3.

Network competition best describes the current auto industry. Ford no longer just vies with Nissan and Volkswagen. Ford *and all its partners* compete with Nissan *and its partners* and VW *and its partners*. Although (arguably) not as far along as the auto industry, competition in computers, communications, and consumer electronics increasingly is leaning to a network orientation. Firms are turning from discrete, arms-

Source: Adapted by the authors from Shelby D. Hunt and Robert M. Morgan, "Relationship Marketing in the Era of Network Competition," *Marketing Management*, Vol. 3 (No. 1, 1995), pp. 19–27. Reprinted by permission of the American Marketing Association.

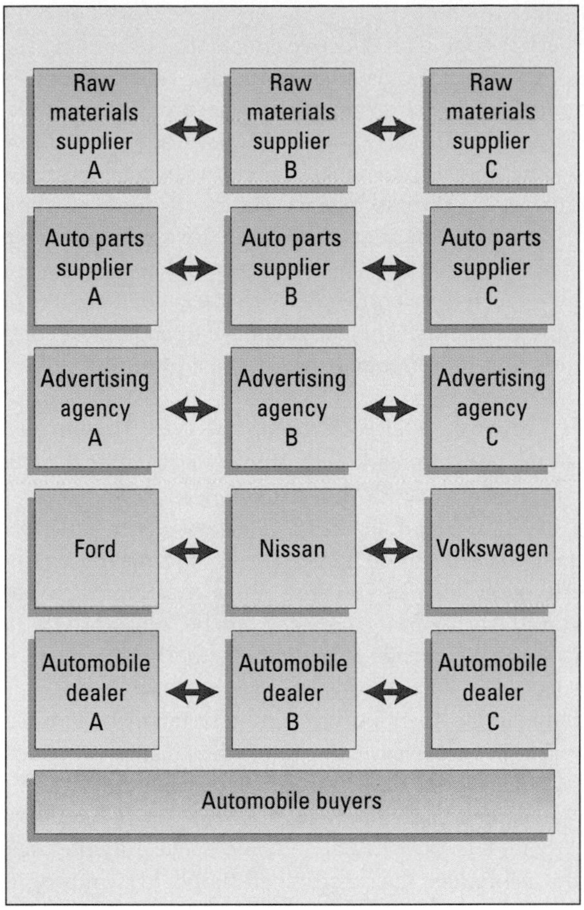

FIGURE 1
Traditional View of Competition

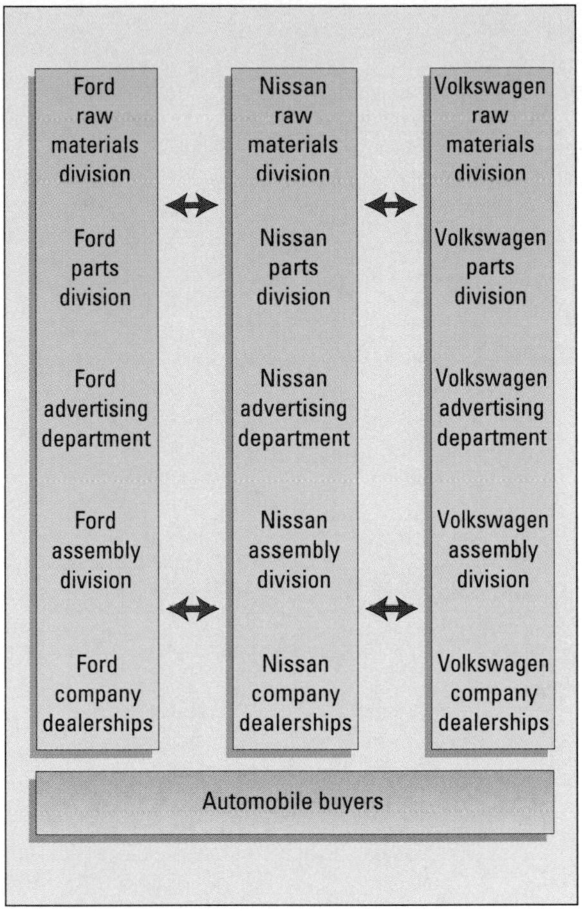

FIGURE 2
Hierarchical View of Competition

length exchanges with many suppliers to long-term, "relational" exchanges with few partners.

Relational exchanges in network competition occur between firms and their (1) goods suppliers, as in just-in-time procurement; (2) services providers, as in integrated marketing efforts among sales promotion, ads, and marketing research agencies; (3) competitors, as in strategic alliances; (4) nonprofit organizations, as in ties with universities, the Olympics, and green marketing groups; (5) government entities, as in joint R&D; (6) ultimate customers, as in data-base marketing; (7) intermediate customers, as in franchising and distribution channels; (8) functional departments, as in cross-functional project teams; (9) employees, as in internal marketing and total quality management; and (10) business units, as in cooperation across corporate divisions, subsidiaries, or other strategic groupings.

IBM alone has more than 500 strategic alliances, and other examples of relationship marketing abound. All of these firms are cooperating to compete successfully:

- Procter & Gamble has assigned permanent employees to live and work at Wal-Mart's headquarters to coordinate sales of P&G products.
- Corning now defines itself as a "network of organizations."
- Levi Strauss, using electronic data interchange (EDI), monitors daily product sales at major retailers to better coordinate purchasing, manufacturing, and inventory.
- Motorola allies itself with 11 partners in Iridium, a consortium for developing a global wireless communication system.
- Revlon works with the National Breast Cancer coalition to develop relationships with women by supporting cancer research and early breast-cancer detection.
- AT&T develops relationships with small businesses through its Customer Access Program.

Relationship Marketing No matter how many partnerships make up an overall network, the success of each partner depends on the network's success. It is crucial for each firm to manage relationships with its partners. "Relationship marketing" refers to the marketing activities directed at forming, developing, and keeping successful relational exchanges in all partnerships.

Some partnerships are much more successful than others. Though estimates vary, about one-third of all strategic al-

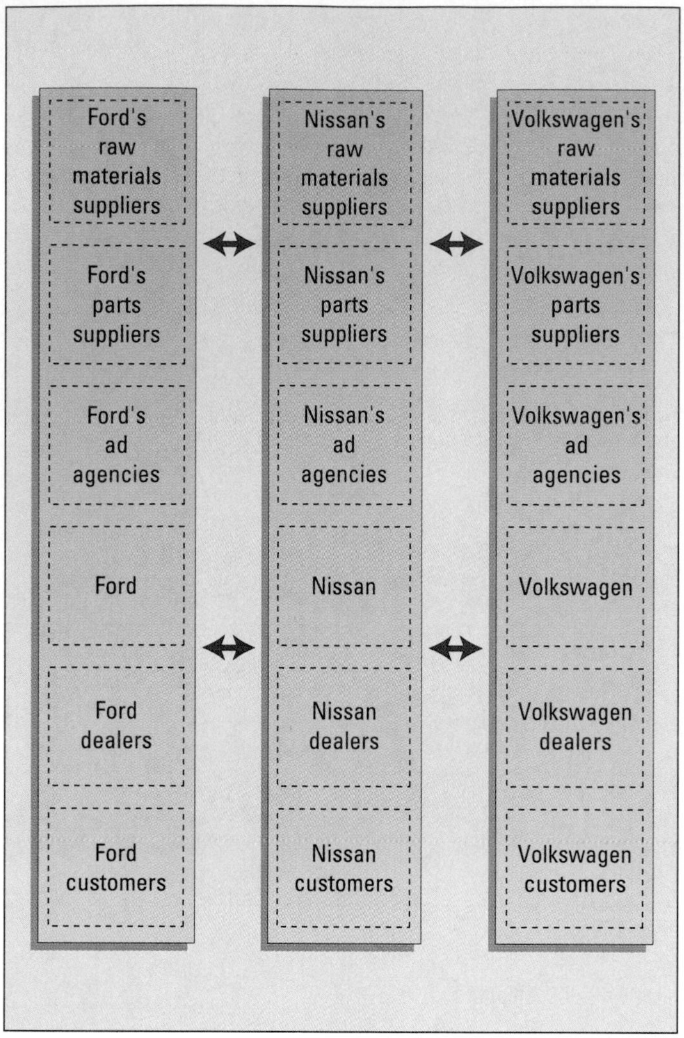

FIGURE 3
Network View of Competition

liances appear to be outright failures, and many others are only moderately successful, as judged by the participants. A study of 895 strategic alliances across 23 industries found that participants rated them to be successful only 45.3 per cent of the time.

As a case in point, consider the auto industry. Although the Ford/Mazda strategic alliance is widely regarded to be an extraordinary success, industry observers generally view the General Motors/Daewoo, Chrysler/Mitsubishi, and Fiat/Nissan alliances as either outright failures or significantly less successful. Because all the alliances were cross-cultural and all the partners brought complementary resources to the table, neither of these factors can explain the disparity between the marketing success of Ford/Mazda and the disappointing results of the other auto partnerships.

Ford/Mazda's success results from the partners managing the relationship to maximize the likelihood of effective cooperation. The paradox of relationship marketing is that being an effective competitor in the era of network competition also means being an effective cooperator. Examining the details of the Ford/Mazda alliance reveals it has been managed—purposefully or accidentally—to promote commitment and trust: Both parties must perceive each cooperative project to be mutually beneficial; senior managements must be sure there is an overall balance of benefits for both companies. Top management sets the "tone" for the relationship by letting it be known in no uncertain terms that middle managers are expected to cooperate with their counterparts to achieve these benefits. The partners have open lines of communication and hold frequent face-to-face meetings.

Perfect Unions Our research on the commitment-trust theory of relationship marketing prompts us to offer the following maxims for relationship marketing success:

Choose Partners Carefully Partnerships mean major investments of time, money, personnel, and maybe equipment. Although such investments signal relationship commitment to the other party, they also can be "sunk costs" with little salvage value outside a specific relationship. Since ending unsuccessful relationships can be costly, it makes one partner vulnerable to opportunistic behavior by the other.

For example, a partner can exploit the alliance for short-term advantage by not abiding by (formal and informal) terms of the agreement. Not long ago, GM tore up hundreds of supplier contracts and demanded immediate, double-digit price cuts. Moreover, GM distributed suppliers' own proprietary blueprints to rivals to satisfy its quest for lower prices.

With network competition, firms should maintain traditional relationships with those that have opportunistic tendencies and form partnerships with trustworthy firms. Thus, Inverness Castings Group in Grand Rapids, Michigan, is a major partner of Chrysler Corporation. Chrysler recently purchased a new part from Inverness that cost 30 per cent more than the part it replaced. Why? Because Inverness' research showed that the new part would save on assembly time and result in a higher quality final product.

In all relationships, disagreements are inevitable. The real issue is, do the partners see these disagreements as an effective way of bringing problems into the open or do they get angry and begin looking for other partners? Our research suggests that parties who trust each other will handle disagreements or conflicts in a positive manner, working to identify ways to solve the underlying problems leading to a disagreement. Because communication is an important part of this process, a key concern in choosing a partner should be its willingness to share timely, meaningful information.

Shared values signal a potentially trustworthy partner. Firms should seek out partners that hold similar beliefs about what business behaviors are appropriate or inappropriate, right or wrong, proper or improper, and acceptable or unacceptable. In cross-cultural partnerships, one factor that can make an alliance difficult is a potential lack of shared values, even though global corporations are becoming more cosmopolitan. One should approach cross-cultural partnerships very, very carefully.

Structure Partnerships Carefully The key structural issue in relationship marketing stems from its raison d'etre: exchanging resources to provide mutual benefits and reach mutual goals.

Consider Ford's relationship with Excel Industries, a maker of car windows. Ford discovered that windows produced by Excel reduced inventory requirements and assembly costs. Ford was so impressed that it not only "deintegrated" by selling its own Fulton, Kentucky, window company to Excel, but also guaranteed Excel 70 per cent of its window business. Thus emboldened, Excel plowed $4 million more into better manufacturing systems. As a result, Excel's sales and profits have flourished, and it now equips new Ford models a year faster. Structuring partnerships for mutual benefits, therefore, leads to better products, lower costs, and relationship marketing success.

Allow Time for Relationship Growth Because commitment and trust develop slowly, start with small projects with a new partner and expand the scope of the relationship gradually. As the relationship grows, a complex set of norms will evolve for making the relationship work. These norms cover such aspects of the relationship as how each party will exchange information of value to the other and how each party must act to safeguard a relationship in the face of unexpected circumstances. Norms, then, substitute for formal contract clauses.

When Harley-Davidson cut 200 members from its supplier roster and entered long-term relations with its other 120 suppliers, Harley's legal department suggested a 40-page book to codify every detail of the relationship. Harley's president disregarded that advice and signed brief documents with each supplier outlining goals and a way to resolve disputes. Harley-Davidson now relies on informal norms, not clauses in formal contracts.

Maintain Open Lines of Communication Network organizations should have multiple points of contact because communications—formal and informal—let partners align their expectations of what the partnership can produce. Informal socializing builds personal relationships that contribute significantly to developing trust.

Consider the Blimpie sandwich chain. As rival Subway began to corner the submarine sandwich market, Blimpie ignored its franchisees to focus on new Mexican food concepts. When the franchisees complained, the chain's co-founder sought to rebuild trust by opening communications. He met the franchisees personally and discussed their problems, formed a franchisee advisory council to get continuing input on key issues, launched a newsletter to communicate with franchisees, set up an 800-number franchising tips hotline, and gave franchisees more control over their ads via regional advertising cooperatives. And, recognizing that all partners in a network must share, Blimpie let some franchisees in distress divert their 6 per cent royalty fees to advertising.

Maintain a Corporate Culture That Is Trustworthy In the global village, there is no place for opportunists to hide. Having a reputation for corporate integrity is critical. Character counts, and opportunism brings short-term gains at the expense of long-term success.

Consider the billing fraud at Sears' auto service centers. The California Department of Consumer Affairs accused Sears of overcharging repair customers 90 per cent of the time at 33 Sears centers, with overcharges averaging $223. Sears' response was to drop commissions and product sales goals for auto center employees nationwide. Maybe Sears can regain consumers' trust and maybe not. But wouldn't it have been better for Sears to monitor the behavior of its own employees to ensure that such policies as commissions and sales goals were not encouraging unethical, if not illegal, behavior?

Research on corporate culture and relationship building implies that if a firm uses honesty, fairness, responsibility, and competence in its relations with its own employees, this in turn helps ensure that employees perform their jobs in a way that portrays the firm as a trustworthy partner for others.

QUESTIONS

1. Distinguish among the views of competition shown in Figures 1, 2, and 3.
2. Which view of competition most resembles a direct channel of distribution? Explain your answer.
3. What do you recommend to raise the odds of strategic networks working out?
4. Apply the concept of dual distribution to this case. In what situations would it be most effective? Least effective? Why?
5. What are the ramifications of strategic network competition for merchant wholesalers?
6. Based on the material in this case, what role should selling agents play for small manufacturers? Explain your answer.
7. Does this case accurately reflect the changing power relationships of manufacturers and chain retailers? Why or why not?
8. Can manufacturers and retailers really be partners, given their differing roles and perspectives?

PROMOTION PLANNING

PART 6

Part 6 covers the third major element of the marketing mix, promotion.

18 The Context of Promotion Planning

Here, we broadly discuss promotion planning, which involves all communication used to inform, persuade, and/or remind people about an organization's or individual's goods, services, image, ideas, community involvement, or impact on society. We describe the basic types of promotion and the stages in a channel of communication. Next, we present the steps in developing an overall promotion plan. We conclude the chapter with international promotion considerations, and the legal environment and criticisms of promotion.

19 Advertising and Public Relations

In this chapter, we examine two of the four types of promotion: advertising and public relations. We define advertising as paid, nonpersonal communication by an identified sponsor, and public relations as any form of image-directed communication by an identified sponsor or the independent media. We detail the scope of advertising and public relations and their attributes, and we describe the role of publicity. We discuss the development of advertising and public relations plans in depth.

20 Personal Selling and Sales Promotion

Here, we focus on the two other key elements of a promotion mix: personal selling and sales promotion. We define personal selling as oral communication with one or more prospective buyers by paid representatives for the purpose of making sales, and we define sales promotion as the paid marketing communication activities (other than advertising, publicity, or personal selling) that stimulate consumer purchases and dealer effectiveness. We describe the scope, characteristics, and stages in planning for both personal selling and sales promotion.

Part 6 Video Vignette

FD&B Inc.

FD&B Inc. has a four-part credo that guides operations:

1. "To make a difference, today's marketers need the capabilities of an advertising agency that has the experience, talent, and desire to deliver targeted creative solutions to marketing problems—quickly and efficiently.
2. "To make a difference, the agency must create and execute effective advertising, as well as strategically integrated promotion, public relations, and direct marketing.
3. "To make a difference, the agency must understand the multiplicity of media available, discern their efficiency, synergistically plan for the media, and maintain the know-how to negotiate and purchase media time or space economically.
4. "And to make a difference, the agency must base all efforts on a deeply defined strategy. At FD&B, this process is called STRATEGICS (Synergistic Thinking Rigorously Applied To Efficiently Generate Integrated Creative Solutions)." The FD&B STRATEGICS matrix disciplines the agency and the client in pursuit of a marketing and advertising program that will be unquestionably appropriate, have the highest probability of success, and above all, be cost effective."

Through its public relations efforts, FD&B clients' products are mentioned in articles or stories (in addition to paid advertising).

FD&B's activities span all sorts of media. Thus, it prepares creative copy and places ads in newspapers and magazines and on TV. The agency's MasterCard International campaign "For a Clean Bill of Health" appeared in Sunday newspapers with 20 million circulation (representing the top 20 U.S. markets). Its ads for Watson Pharmaceuticals run in such trade publications as *Drug Store News* and *U.S. Pharmacist*.

FD&B is especially active in promotions, including in-store displays, coupon offers, and sweepstakes. For Eight O'Clock Bean Coffee, the agency devised in-store displays to motivate consumers to "Taste the difference of **really** fresh-ground coffee! Fresh-ground not pre-ground." These displays were accompanied by a series of TV ads using the same slogan. When possible, FD&B helps its clients participate in cooperative promotions. One such effort is Watson's share in Pharmacy PoweRx-Pak, which combines inserts from several health-oriented companies and is sent to pharmacies.

Through its public relations efforts, FD&B clients' products are mentioned in articles or stories (in addition to paid advertising). It has secured coverage from such sources as the *New York Times* and the *Evening News with Dan Rather*. FD&B also works with clients, such as the Hain Food Group, to prepare and distribute image-related videos that are targeted to potential resellers and investors.

FD&B recognizes the growing role of direct marketing—which occurs when a consumer is first exposed to a product by a nonpersonal medium (such as direct mail, magazine, or PC) and then orders by mail, phone, or PC—and is acting accordingly.

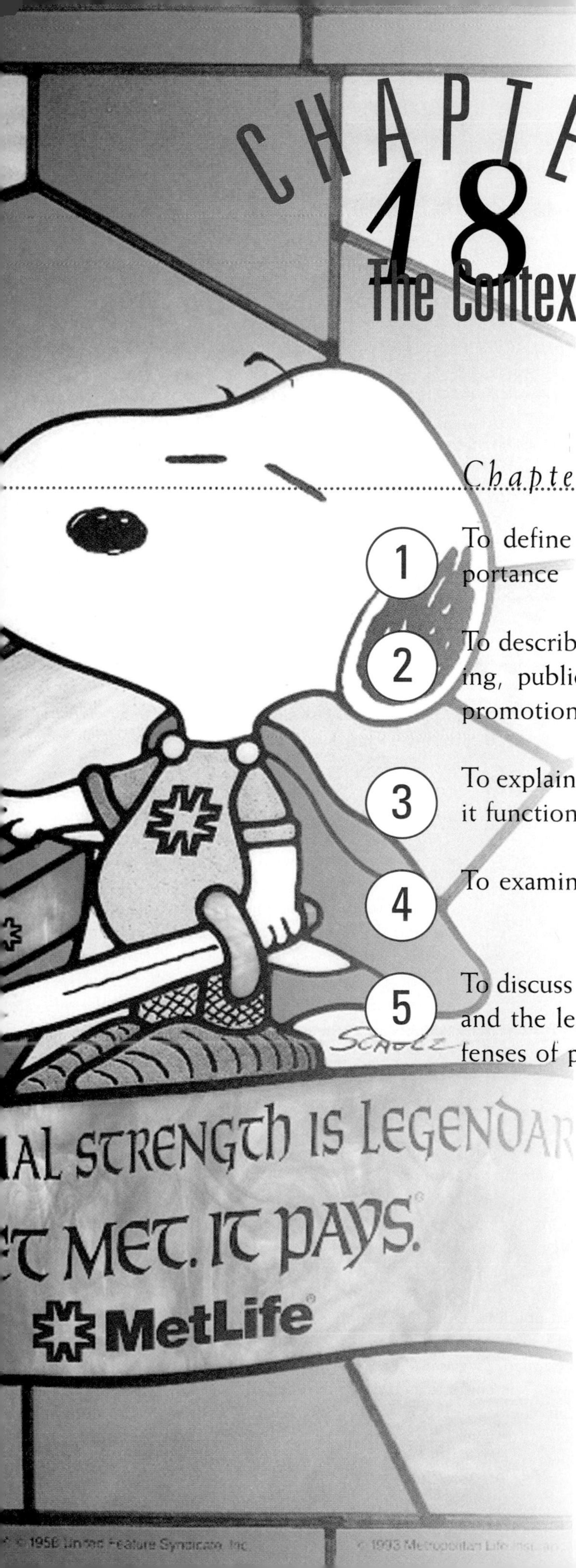

AL STRENGTH IS LEGENDAR
T MET. IT PAYS.
MetLife

CHAPTER 18
The Context of Promotion Planning

Chapter Objectives

1. To define promotion planning and show its importance

2. To describe the general characteristics of advertising, public relations, personal selling, and sales promotion

3. To explain the channel of communication and how it functions

4. To examine the components of a promotion plan

5. To discuss international promotion considerations, and the legal environment and criticisms and defenses of promotion

> *You have to have something that sets you apart from the competition—whether it be a particular product, quality, or service. And, burnt by the foibles of human celebrity spokespeople, more and more companies are turning their corporate images (and fortunes) over to animated characters. After all, you have almost no chance of being embarrassed by Fred Flintstone, the Pink Panther, or Snoopy. These characters can help you maintain visibility and to stay favorably in the public eye.*

Reprinted by permission.

In particular, says John Lister (chief executive officer of Lister Butler, a corporate and brand identity consultant), animated characters can bring warmth and feeling to an otherwise boring category of products: "The goal of using a cartoon is to complement the product, not eclipse it, take top billing, or conflict with the intended message." Let's look at how Owens-Corning and Metropolitan Life use animated characters—the Pink Panther and the *Peanuts* group of figures—in their advertising programs.

For a decade and a half, Owens-Corning has utilized the Pink Panther in ads for its insulation products. The character is especially effective in reassuring people that insulating their attics is a task they can easily accomplish. This is an important message since marketing research studies have found that many consumers view this project as too difficult for the typical do-it-yourselfer.

The Pink Panther is a natural communicator because of its affable nature and color. And Owens-Corning is the only firm that markets a pink-colored insulation. The Pink Panther-based campaign is instrumental in allowing Owens-Corning to maintain an eight-to-one brand preference over its closest U.S. competitor. According to John Lister, Owens-Corning's success is due to the "masterful job of integrating the character into the product's identity."

In the mid-1980s, Metropolitan Life Insurance chose to hire *Peanuts* characters to help generate more warmth and feeling toward the company and its products. As a Metropolitan Life account executive noted, "We wanted to convey a warm and friendly personality, which we think we have. The characters convey a kind of trust and goodwill."

The MetLife *Peanuts* campaign continues to this day, with the characters used in everything from print media to TV ads. The firm believes the feelings that the *Peanuts* characters engender, "particularly of security," are a part of the insurance firm's positioning in the marketplace.

As with live actors, a company using animated characters as endorsers needs to safeguard its interests. A major concern is that a popular character could be used in so many product categories that its image becomes blurry. To avert this potential problem, MetLife has "an exclusive in the financial services market." According to a senior vice-president at Young & Rubicam, the advertising agency that handles the MetLife account, "We have an equity in the characters, and we can't afford to have that equity diluted."[1]

In this chapter, we will study many dimensions of promotion planning, including the usefulness of celebrities (human or animated) as sources in the channel of communication. Our discussion will also cover how the channel of communication works and the roles of the source, encoding, the message, the media, decoding, the audience, and feedback.

Overview

Promotion is any communication used to inform, persuade, and/or remind people about an organization's or individual's goods, services, image, ideas, community involvement, or impact on society. **Promotion planning** is systematic decision making relating to all aspects of an organization's or individual's communications efforts.

Promotion planning *focuses on a total* **promotion** *effort—informing, persuading, and reminding.*

Communication occurs through brand names, packaging, company marquees and displays, personal selling, customer service, trade shows, sweepstakes, and messages in mass media (such as newspapers, television, radio, direct mail, billboards, magazines, and transit). It can be company sponsored or controlled by independent media. Messages may emphasize information, persuasion, fear, sociability, product performance, humor, and/or comparisons with competitors.

In this chapter, the context of promotion planning is provided. Included are discussions on promotion's importance, the basic promotion types, the channel of communication, promotion planning, international considerations, the legal environment, and general criticisms and defenses of promotion. Chapter 19 covers advertising and public relations. Chapter 20 deals with personal selling and sales promotion.

The Importance of Promotion

Promotion is a key element of the marketing mix. For new products, people must be informed about items and their features before they can develop favorable attitudes toward them. For products with some consumer awareness, the focus is on persuasion: converting knowledge to liking. For very popular products, the focus is on reminding: reinforcing existing consumer beliefs.

The people and/or organizations at whom a firm's promotional efforts are aimed may fall into various categories: consumers, stockholders, consumer advocacy groups, government, channel members, employees, competitors, and the general public. Communication often goes on between a firm and each of these audiences, not just with consumers. In addition, communication with each may be different because each has distinct goals, knowledge, and needs.

Within an audience category (like consumers), a firm needs to identify and appeal to opinion leaders—those who influence others' decisions. It also should understand **word-of-mouth communication**, the process by which people express opinions and product-related experiences to one another. Unless there is sustained, positive word-of-mouth communication, it is hard to succeed.[2]

Word-of-mouth communication *occurs as people state opinions to others.*

A company's promotion plan usually stresses individual goods and services, with the intent of moving people from awareness to purchase. Yet, the firm may also convey its overall image (industry innovator), views on ideas (nuclear energy), community service (funding a new hospital), or impact on society (the size of its work force). Table 18-1 shows many valuable promotion functions.

[1]Christine Unruh, "Snap, Crackle, Pop," *Journal of Business Strategy*, Vol. 16 (March–April 1995), pp. 39–43.

[2]See Paula Fitzgerald Bone, "Word-of-Mouth Effects on Short-Term and Long-Term Product Judgments," *Journal of Business Research*, Vol. 32 (March 1995), pp. 213–223; and Chip Walker, "Word of Mouth," *American Demographics* (July 1995), pp. 38–44.

Table 18-1
The Value of Promotion

Promotion

- Establishes an image for a company and its goods and services.
- Communicates features of goods and services.
- Creates awareness for new goods and services.
- Keeps existing goods and services popular.
- Can reposition the images or uses of faltering goods and services.
- Generates enthusiasm from channel members.
- Notes where goods and services can be purchased.
- Can persuade consumers to trade up from one product to a more expensive one.
- Alerts consumers to sales.
- Justifies (rationalizes) the prices of goods and services.
- Answers consumer questions.
- Closes transactions.
- Provides service for consumers after transactions are completed.
- Reinforces loyal consumers.
- Places the firm and its goods and services in a favorable light, relative to competitors.

A good promotion plan complements the product, distribution, and price aspects of the marketing mix, and it is properly designed. For example, Allen Edmonds—a maker of quality shoes—distributes its products via finer stores and sets premium prices. It advertises in such magazines as *GQ* and *Fortune* and expects retailers to provide first-rate personal selling. Ads are in color and refer to product features, not prices. See Figure 18-1.

Well-conceived promotion plans are feasible even if companies have limited resources. For instance:

> Until 1989, Straight Arrow Products, a 25-year-old Pennsylvania company, couldn't afford to do much marketing. Sales at the time were only $500,000 annually. Fast-forward five years: Sales reached $50 million and current owner W. Roger Dunavant was running a $3.5 million ad campaign. What happened? During 1989, without a bundle to spend on advertising, Dunavant (then the firm's director of sales and marketing) began to hit the road to sell the company's wares. The goods: grooming products that horse owners use on their animals—and themselves. The strategy: play up the novelty for all it was worth. Dunavant attended horse shows and handed out samples of Mane 'n Tail shampoo and conditioner and a cream called Hoofmaker (for equestrians' hands, not feet). He encouraged horse owners to use Mane 'n Tail on both themselves and their horses. One person he met at a show turned out to be a radio announcer who invited him for an interview. Once the show aired, other journalists from print and radio began calling. Dunavant bought Straight Arrow in 1993. He handled his own bookings until that year, when he hired a public relations firm. In 1994 alone, he gave 140 radio interviews. The result: skyrocketing sales and *Wall Street Journal* coverage.[3]

Promotion's importance is also evident from the expenditures and jobs in this area. The world's 50 largest advertising agencies have overall annual billings of $20 billion. The International Advertising Association's thousands of members are from 90 nations. In the United States alone, each year, retailers spend $9 billion, auto makers $9 billion, and industrial-materials firms $140 million on media ads; 15 million people work in sales; 320 billion coupons are given out; and there are 4,000 trade shows.[4]

[3]Jeffrey A. Tannenbaum, "Priceless Promotions," *Wall Street Journal* (May 22, 1995), p. R20.

[4]"Agency Report," *Advertising Age* (April 10, 1995); Stuart Elliott, "The Industry Is Set to Start a Global Self-Promotion," *New York Times* (September 28, 1992), p. D7; "Total Measured U.S. Ad Spending by Category & Media," *Advertising Age* (September 27, 1995), p. 62; U.S. Department of Labor, Bureau of Labor Statistics; "The 1995 Annual Report on the Promotion Industry," *Promo Magazine's SourceBook '96*, p. 15; and Srinath Gopalakrishna, Gary L. Lilien, Jerome D. Williams, and Ian K. Sequeira, "Do Trade Shows Pay Off?" *Journal of Marketing*, Vol. 59 (July 1995), p. 75.

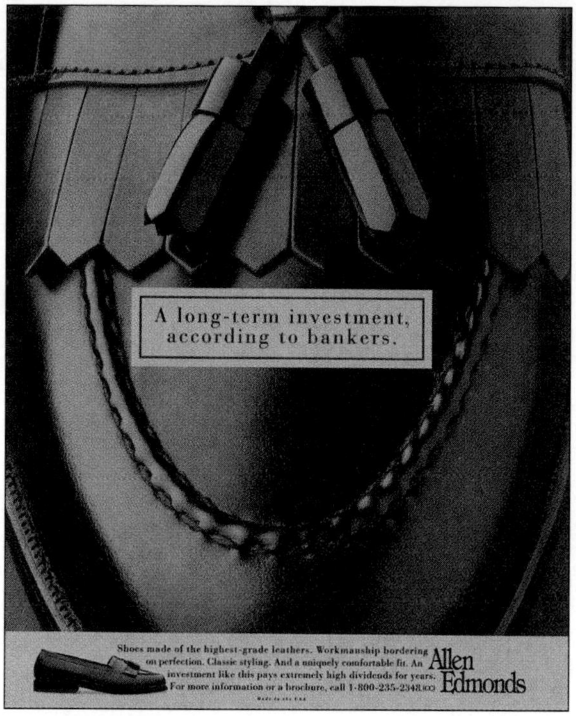

FIGURE 18-1
The Consistent, High-Quality Promotional Emphasis of Allen Edmonds
Reprinted by permission.

Types of Promotion

In their communications programs, organizations use one or more of four basic types of promotion:

Advertising, public relations (publicity), personal selling, *and* **sales promotion** *are the four key promotion types.*

- **Advertising** is paid, nonpersonal communication regarding goods, services, organizations, people, places, and ideas that is transmitted through various media by business firms, government and other nonprofit organizations, and individuals who are identified in the advertising message as the sponsor. The message is generally controlled by the sponsor.
- **Public relations** includes any communication to foster a favorable image for goods, services, organizations, people, places, and ideas among their publics—such as consumers, investors, government, channel members, employees, and the general public. It may be nonpersonal or personal, paid or nonpaid, and sponsor controlled or not controlled. **Publicity** is the form of public relations that entails nonpersonal communication passed on via various media but not paid for by an identified sponsor. Wording and placement of publicity messages are generally media controlled.
- **Personal selling** involves oral communication with one or more prospective buyers by paid representatives for the purpose of making sales.
- **Sales promotion** involves paid marketing communication activities (other than advertising, publicity, or personal selling) that are intended to stimulate consumer purchases and dealer effectiveness. Included are trade shows, premiums, incentives, giveaways, demonstrations, and various other efforts not in the ordinary promotion routine.[5]

The general characteristics of each type of promotion are shown in Table 18-2. As discussed later in the chapter, many firms in some way combine them into an integrated promotional blend. This lets them reach their entire target market, present both persuasive and believable messages, have personal contact with customers, sponsor special events, and balance the promotional budget.

[5]Adapted by the authors from Peter D. Bennett (Editor), *Dictionary of Marketing Terms*, Second Edition (Chicago: American Marketing Association, 1995), pp. 6, 206, 231, 232, and 253.

Table 18-2

Characteristics of Promotional Types

FACTOR	ADVERTISING	PUBLICITY FORM OF PUBLIC RELATIONS[a]	PERSONAL SELLING	SALES PROMOTION
Audience	Mass	Mass	Small (one-to-one)	Varies
Message	Uniform	Uniform	Specific	Varies
Cost	Low per viewer or reader	None for media space and time; can be some costs for media releases and publicity materials	High per customer	Moderate per customer
Sponsor	Company	No formal sponsor in that media are not paid	Company	Company
Flexibility	Low	Low	High	Moderate
Control over content and placement	High	None (controlled by media)	High	High
Credibility	Moderate	High	Moderate	Moderate
Major goal	To appeal to a mass audience at a reasonable cost, and to create awareness and favorable attitudes	To reach a mass audience with an independently reported message	To deal with individual consumers, to resolve questions, to close sales	To stimulate short-run sales, to increase impulse purchases
Example	Television ad for a Sony CD player for use in cars	Magazine article describing the unique features of a Sony CD player for cars	Retail sales personnel explaining how a Sony CD player for cars works	A Sony CD player for cars exhibited at trade shows

[a]*Please note:* When public relations embodies advertising (an image-related message), personal selling (a salesperson describing his or her firm's public service efforts to college students), and/or sales promotion (distributing special discount coupons to low-income consumers), it takes on the characteristics of those promotional types. However, the goal would be more image-related than sales-related.

The Channel of Communication

A message is sent to an audience via a **channel of communication**.

To develop a proper promotion mix and interact effectively with a target audience, the **channel of communication (communication process)** shown in Figure 18-2 must be understood. Through such a channel, a source develops a message, transmits it to an audience via some medium, and gets feedback from the audience. The components of a communication channel are discussed next.

FIGURE 18-2
A Channel of Communication

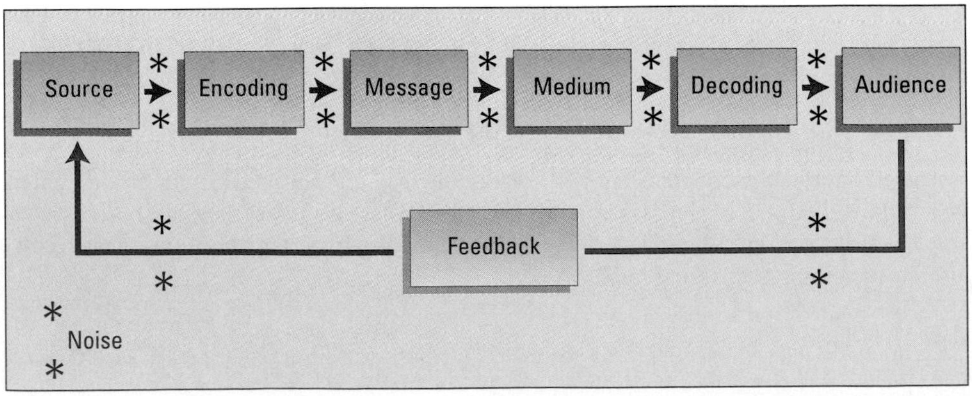

Ethics IN TODAY'S SOCIETY

Is It Getting Harder to Tell the TV Programs from the Ads?

A product placement occurs when a branded product is shown during a TV show or movie, often being used by an actor—such as when James Bond (Pierce Brosnan) drove a new BMW Z3 roadster in the movie *GoldenEye*.

In the United States, the Federal Communications Commission requires full disclosure of all product placement fees that are paid directly by companies to TV show producers. However, companies can bypass this provision by paying product-placement firms instead. To protect themselves from legal action, all TV networks require producers to sign a statement indicating that they have not received a product-placement fee.

Marketers favoring the use of product placements feel this is a relatively inexpensive way of gaining recognition for a new product or reinforcement for an existing one. A $20,000 product placement, for example, can reach more people for a longer time period than a $250,000, 30-second commercial. Networks also benefit from product placements by getting free props.

Those that question the use of product placements cite both implementation and societal concerns. On an implementation level, product placements can be hit or miss. Product visibility can be poor due to a camera's panning too quickly and/or a brand name being out of focus. Like publicity, a firm cannot overly rely on product placement. There are also concerns when too many brands are placed on the same show.

On a societal level, product placements can blur the distinction between advertising and program content. According to the executive director of the Center for Science in the Public Interest, "You can zap a commercial. But you can't zap something that's on a program."

As an advertising consultant, give a strategy for using product placements on *Seinfeld*, the popular TV comedy. In the past, Snapple iced tea, Rold Gold pretzels, diet Coke, and Columbo frozen yogurt were featured on the show.

Sources: Based on material in Fara Warner, "Why It's Getting Harder to Tell the Shows From the Ads," *Wall Street Journal* (June 15, 1995), pp. B1, B11; and Daniel Shannon, "Nobody Does It Better," *Promo* (January 1996), p. 10.

The Source

A **source** *presents a message.*

The **source** of communication is usually a company, an independent institution, or an opinion leader seeking to present a message to an audience. A firm communicates through a(n) spokesperson, celebrity, actor playing a role, representative consumer, and/or salesperson.

A company spokesperson is typically a long-time employee who represents the company in communications. The spokesperson has an aura of sincerity, commitment, and expertise. Sometimes the spokesperson is a top executive, like Wendy's Dave Thomas. Other times, front-line workers are used, such as a Nynex repairwoman or a Sheraton hotel chef. In general, this source has been quite effective.

A celebrity is used when the goal is to gain the audience's attention and improve product awareness. Problems can arise if the celebrity is perceived as insincere or unknowledgeable. Popular celebrities include Michael Jordan for Nike, Candice Bergen for Sprint, Kathie Lee Gifford for Carnival Cruises, and Snoopy and other *Peanuts* characters for Metropolitan Life Insurance.

Many ads have actors playing roles rather than celebrity spokespeople. In these commercials, the emphasis is on presenting a message about a good, service, or idea—rather than on the consumer recognizing a celebrity. The hope is that the consumer will learn more about product attributes.

A representative consumer is one who likes a product and recommends it in an ad. The person is shown with his or her name and hometown. The intent is to present a real consumer in an actual situation. A hidden camera or blind taste test is often used with this source. Today, viewers are more skeptical about how "representative" the endorser is.

Finally, a firm may use a salesperson to communicate with consumers. Many salespeople are knowledgeable, assertive, and persuasive. However, consumers may doubt their objectivity and tactics. Auto salespeople rate particularly low in consumer surveys.

An independent institution is not controlled by the firms on which it reports. It presents information in a professional, nonpaid (by the firms) manner. Consumers Union and the local newspaper restaurant critic are examples of independent sources. They have great credibility for their readers because they discuss both good and bad points, but some segments of the population may not be exposed to these sources. The information presented may differ from that contained in a firm's commercials or sales-force presentations.

An opinion leader is a person who has face-to-face contact with and influences other potential consumers. Because he or she deals on a personal level, an opinion leader often has strong persuasive impact and believability, and he or she can offer social acceptance for followers. Thus, firms often address initial messages to opinion leaders, who then provide word-of-mouth communication to others. Many marketers believe opinion leaders not only influence, but also are influenced by, others (opinion receivers); even opinion leaders need approval for their choices.

In assessing a source, these questions are critical: Is he/she believable? Is he/she convincing? Does he/she present an image consistent with the firm? Do consumers value the message of the source? Is he/she seen as knowledgeable? Does the source complement the product he/she communicates about, or does the source overwhelm it? Do significant parts of the market dislike the source?

Encoding

*In **encoding**, a source translates a thought into a message.*

Encoding is the process whereby a thought or idea is translated into a message by the source. At this stage, preliminary decisions are made as to message content, such as the use of symbolism and wording. It is vital that the thought or idea be translated exactly as the source intends. For example, a firm wanting to stress its product's prestige would include the concepts of status, exclusive ownership, and special features in a message. It would not emphasize a price lower than competitors, availability in discount stores, or the millions of people who have already purchased.

The Message

*A **message** combines words and symbols.*

A **message** is a combination of words and symbols transmitted to an audience. Its thrust depends on whether a firm's goal is to inform, persuade, or remind its audience. Almost all messages include some information on the company name, the product name, the desired image, differential advantages, and product attributes. A firm would also give information about availability and price at some point during the consumer's decision process.

Most communication involves one-sided messages, in which only the benefits of a good, service, or idea are cited. Fewer firms use two-sided messages, in which both benefits and limitations are noted. Firms are not anxious to point out their shortcomings, although consumer perceptions of honesty may be improved via two-sided messages. For example, a few years ago, "Continental Airlines admitted a variety of problems with past service (delays, canceled flights, and lost luggage), but assured passengers that those problems had been eliminated through an intensified commitment to quality." Continental ran this ad campaign to regain customer confidence, which had deteriorated.[6]

[6]Ayn E. Crowley and Wayne D. Hoyer, "An Integrative Framework for Understanding Two-Sided Persuasion," *Journal of Consumer Research*, Vol. 20 (March 1994), p. 561.

FIGURE 18-3
A Humorous U.S. Ad: There's a New Grandma in Town
Reprinted by permission.

Many messages use symbolism and try to relate safety, social acceptance, or sexual appeal to a purchase. In symbolic messages, a firm stresses psychological benefits rather than tangible product performance. Clothing ads may offer acceptance by peers; toothpaste may brighten teeth and make a person more sexually attractive. One type of symbolism, the use of fear appeals, has had mixed results. Although people respond to moderate fear appeals, strong messages may not be as well received:

> Fear appeals can be useful. Ads alerting people to potential natural resource depletion, the danger of forest fires, drunk driving ramifications, the potential health hazards of permissive sexual behavior, and the like, are examples. The public good and advertisers' self-interest are compatible. In addition, these ads have an educational value which may prove useful over an extended period. Yet, marketers must undertake the ads in such a way that a great deal of anxiety or discomfort by recipients is avoided.[7]

Humor is sometimes used to gain audience attention and retain it. Two popular examples are the Bud Light "I love you, man" commercials and basketball player Larry Johnson as "Grandma" in Converse shoe ads. However, a firm needs to be careful to get across the intended message when using humor—which should not make fun of the company, its goods, or its services; and humor should not dominate a message so the brand name or product's attributes go unnoticed. Figure 18-3 shows a U.S.-based Larry Johnson ad.

[7]Michael S. LaTour and Shaker A. Zahra, "Fear Appeals as Advertising Strategy: Should They Be Used?" *Journal of Consumer Marketing*, Vol. 6 (Spring 1989), p. 67. See also Tony L. Henthorne, Michael S. LaTour, and Rajan Nataraajan, "Fear Appeals in Print Advertising: An Analysis of Arousal and Ad Response," *Journal of Advertising*, Vol. 22 (June 1993), pp. 59–69; and James B. Hunt, John F. Tanner, Jr., and David P. Eppright, "Forty Years of Fear Appeal Research: Support for the Ordered Protection Motivation Model" in David W. Stewart and Naufel J. Vilcassim (Editors), *1995 AMA Winter Educators' Proceedings* (Chicago: American Marketing Association, 1995), pp. 147–153.

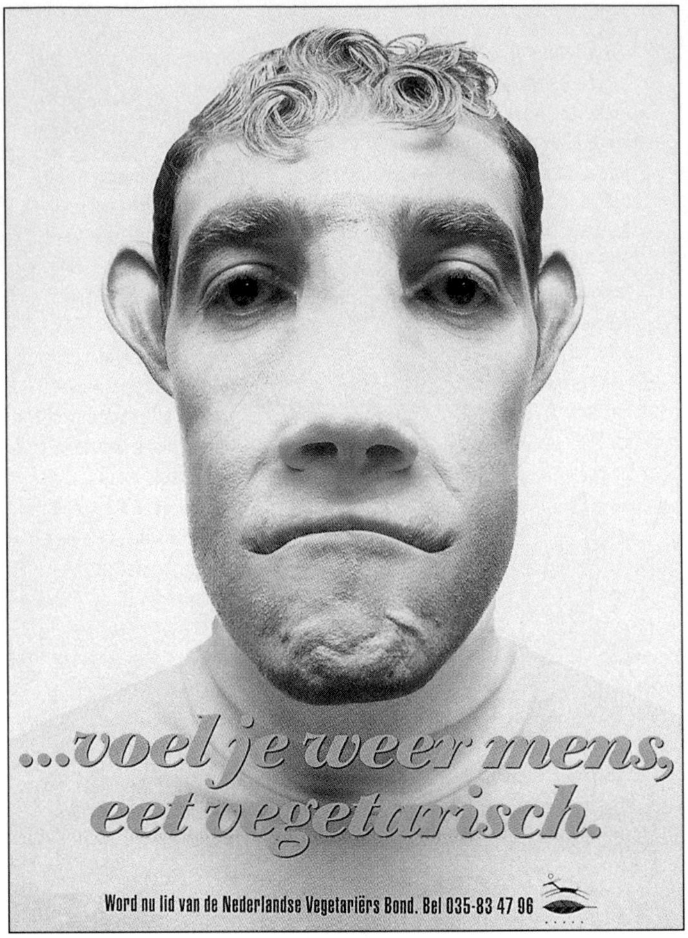

FIGURE 18-4
A Humorous Dutch Ad: Feel Human Again, Eat Vegetarian
Reprinted by permission.

Figure 18-4 has a Netherlands Vegetarian Council ad. Because humor has cultural underpinnings, these U.S. and Dutch ads would probably not work well in the other's country.

Comparative messages *position a firm versus competitors.*

Comparative messages implicitly or explicitly contrast a firm's offerings with those of competitors. Implicit comparisons use an indirect brand X or leading brand approach ("Our industrial glues are more effective than other leading brands"). Explicit comparisons use a direct approach (such as this Nissan print ad, "We can see by your face that you've priced the new Camry" from Toyota). Comparative messages, in one form or another, are used in various TV and radio commercials, print ads, and other media. In addition, salespeople often compare their products' attributes with those of competitors. When using comparative messages, a firm has to be quite careful not to turn off consumers, place too much emphasis on a competitor's brand, or lose sight of its own differential advantages that should be promoted. See Figure 18-5.

A message must be presented in a desirable, exclusive, and believable way. The good, service, or idea must be perceived as something worth buying or accepting. It also must be seen as unique to the seller—that is, it cannot be gotten elsewhere. Finally, the message must make believable claims.

Massed *or* **distributed promotion** *and the* **wearout rate** *must be carefully planned.*

Message timing must also be carefully planned. First, during what times of the year should a firm advertise, seek publicity, add salespeople, or run sales promotions? In **massed promotion**, communication efforts are concentrated in peak periods, like holidays. In **distributed promotion**, communication efforts are spread throughout the year. Figure 18-6 compares massed and distributed promotion.

Second, the **wearout rate**—the time it takes for a message to lose its effectiveness—must be determined. Some messages wear out quickly; others last for years. The wearout rate depends on the frequency of communications, message quality, the number of different messages used by a firm, and other factors. Ford has done such a good job with its "Quality is Job 1" message that it is still strong after many years.

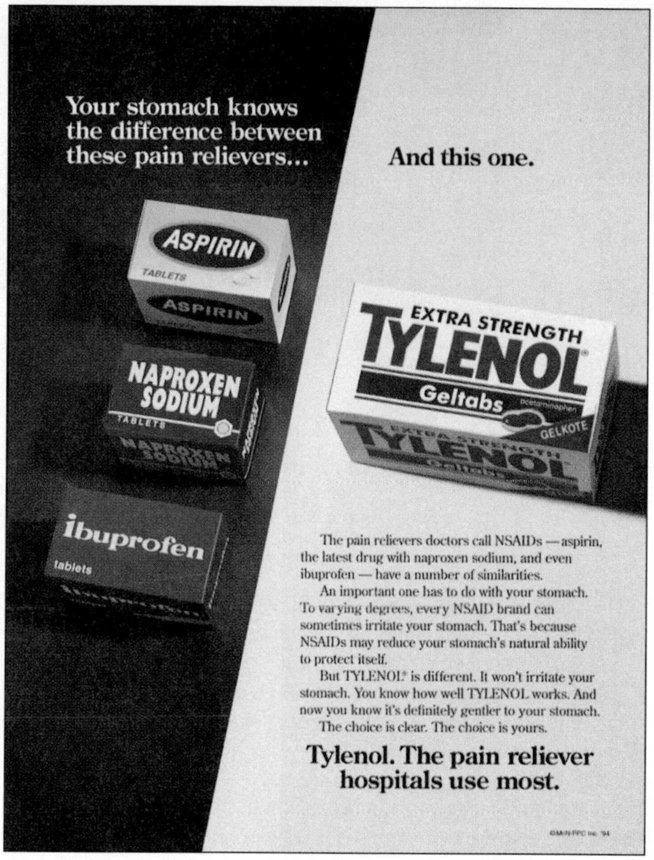

FIGURE 18-5
Comparative Advertising, the Tylenol Way
Reprinted by permission.

The Medium

The **medium** is the personal or nonpersonal means used to send a message. Personal media are company salespeople and other representatives, as well as opinion leaders. Nonpersonal (mass) media include newspapers, television, radio, direct mail, billboards, magazines, and transit.

A **medium** *is a personal or nonpersonal channel for a message.*

Personal media offer one-to-one audience contact. They are flexible, can adapt messages to individual needs, and can answer questions. They appeal to a small audience and are best with a concentrated market. Nonpersonal media have a large audience and low per-customer costs. They are not as flexible and dynamic as one-to-one contacts. They work best with a dispersed target market.

In deciding between personal and nonpersonal media, a firm should consider both total and per-unit costs, product complexity, audience attributes, and communication goals. The two kinds of media go well together since nonpersonal media generate consumer interest and personal media help close sales.

Decoding

Decoding is the process by which a message sent by a source is interpreted by an audience. The interpretation is based on the audience's background and on message clarity and complexity. For example, a housewife and a working woman might have different interpretations of a message on the value of child-care centers. Usually, as symbolism and complexity increase, clarity decreases. "*National Geographic*: Connect. Convince." is not as understandable a message as "Yellow Pages. It Pays. We'll Prove It." As noted earlier, it is essential that a message be decoded in the manner intended by the source (encoding = decoding). Is the business-to-business ad depicted in Figure 18-7 (on page 511) too provocative, or merely attention grabbing? Is the serious message buried in the imagery, or quite clear to the targeted audience?

In **decoding**, *the audience translates the message sent by the source.*

Subliminal advertising is a highly controversial kind of promotion because it does not enable the audience to consciously decode a message. With it, visual or verbal mes-

Subliminal advertising *aims at a consumer's subconscious.*

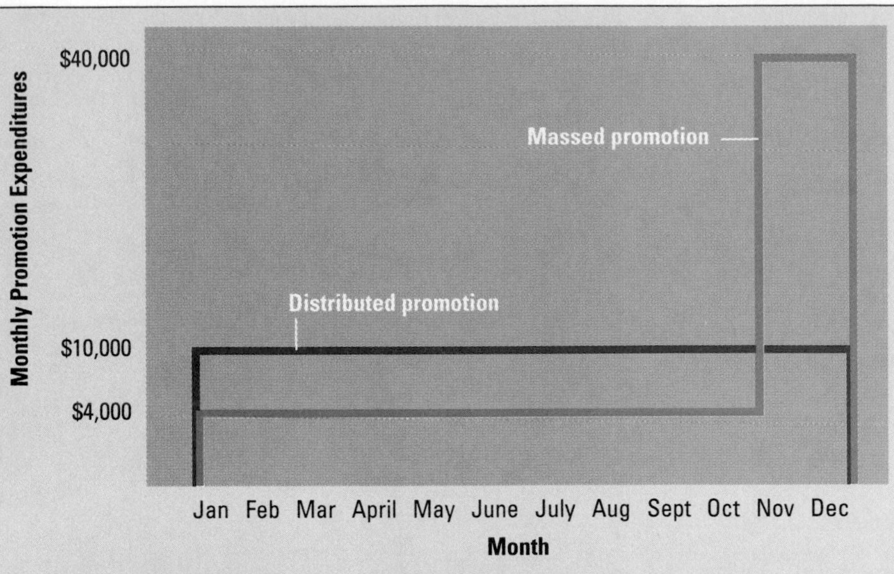

With a total promotion budget of $120,000, a hosiery manufacturer employs distributed promotion and spends $10,000 each month throughout the year. With the same budget, a toy manufacturer uses massed promotion and spends $80,000 from November 1 through December 31 (the remaining $40,000 is spent over the other 10 months). In both cases, monthly promotion expenditures are linked to monthly sales.

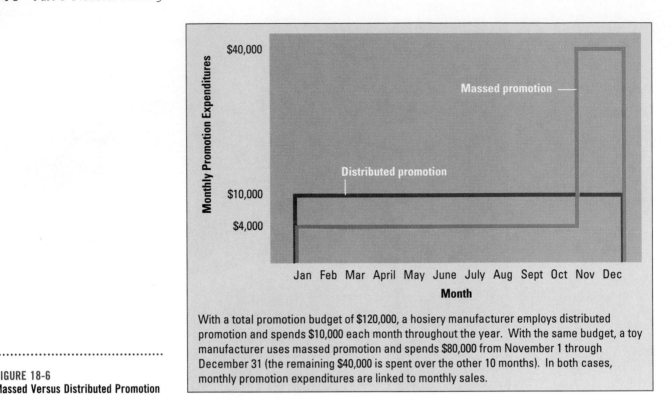

FIGURE 18-6
Massed Versus Distributed Promotion

sages are presented so quickly that people do not see, hear, or remember them. Yet, the assumption is that they will buy goods and services because of subconscious impulses stimulated by these messages. The overwhelming evidence shows that subliminal ads cannot get people to buy things they do not want. In addition, subliminal ads are often misinterpreted; clear, well-labeled ads are much more effective. In the United States, state laws and self-regulation by business associations (such as the National Association of Broadcasters) have all but eliminated subliminal ads.[8]

The Audience

The **audience** *is usually the target market, but the target can also be others.*

An **audience** is the object of a source's message. In most marketing situations, it is the target market. However, a source may also want to communicate an idea, build an image, or give information to stockholders, independent media, the public, government officials, and others.

The way a communication channel is used by a firm depends on the size and dispersion of the audience, demographic and life-style audience traits, and the availability of appropriate media. Thus, because the communication process should be keyed to the audience, AIDS prevention groups have had a tough time getting their message across to teens and young adults:

> Past AIDS-related public service announcements have defined the problem as one of HIV/AIDS awareness, the assumption being that once young people are aware of AIDS, they will be motivated to practice APBs (AIDS preventive behaviors). However, this definition is outdated. It is now evident that AIDS awareness has been accomplished among teens and young adults. They are already aware that sexual intercourse and IV drug use represent the major modes of AIDS transmission. The challenge facing communicators is how to convert AIDS awareness into APBs. Although there is some need to keep generic AIDS messages before the public, rudimentary information/awareness-based appeals are of little use to a market that knows the elementary facts or when there is little evidence that basic knowledge leads to adoption of APBs.[9]

[8]See Carl L. Witte, Madhavan Parthasarathy, and James W. Gentry, "Subliminal Perception Versus Subliminal Persuasion: A Re-Examination of the Basic Issues" in Barbara B. Stern and George M. Zinkham (Editors), *1995 AMA Educators' Proceedings* (Chicago: American Marketing Association, 1995), pp. 133–138.

[9]Kristina D. Frankenberger and Ajay S. Sukhdial, "Segmenting Teens for AIDS Preventive Behaviors with Implications for Marketing Communications," *Journal of Public Policy & Marketing*, Vol. 13 (Spring 1994), p. 134.

TAKE TWO AND CALL US IN THE MORNING. Healthcare professionals take Polaroid photos with healthy results. Our GridFilm is used to measure and enhance written descriptions of wounds. Our MicroCam instantly records microscopic specimens. We've even created an imaging system that's revolutionizing radiology departments. If your business needs to document information stat, call 1-800-348-5287, ext.793 for a free brochure. Until you know what we can do for your business, you haven't seen the whole picture.
Polaroid

FIGURE 18-7
Is This Business-to-Business Ad Easily Decoded?
Reprinted by permission.

To make matters still tougher for marketers, a recent global consumer survey found that people are rather down on promotion messages:

- 72 per cent believe marketers exaggerate health benefits.
- 70 per cent do not believe marketers respect consumers' intelligence.
- 70 per cent believe marketers brainwash children.
- 62 per cent do not believe marketers give accurate information.
- 55 per cent do not believe marketers sponsor worthwhile events.
- 40 per cent do not believe ads are creative and entertaining.[10]

Feedback

Feedback is the response an audience has to a message. It may be a purchase, an attitude change, or a nonpurchase. A firm must understand that each of these responses is possible and devise a way for monitoring them.

Feedback *consists of purchase, attitude, or nonpurchase responses to a message.*

The most desirable kind of feedback occurs if a consumer buys a good or service (or accepts an idea) after communication with or from the firm. This means a message is effective enough to stimulate a transaction.

A second type of feedback takes place if a firm finds its promotion efforts elicit a favorable audience attitude toward it or its offerings. For new goods or services, positive attitudes must usually be formed before purchases (awareness → favorable attitude → purchase). With existing products, people may have bought another brand just before receiving a message or be temporarily out of funds; generating their favorable attitudes may lead to future purchases.

The least desirable feedback is if the audience neither makes a purchase nor develops a favorable attitude. This may happen for one of several reasons: There is no recall

[10]Roper Starch, "The World's View of Marketers," *Advertising Age* (January 15, 1996), p. I-10.

International Marketing in Action

What Kind of Communication Strategy Should Be Used in Tanzania?

Tanzania, located in the southern tier of Africa, has a population of 30 million people. After years of socialism, high import restrictions, and very low per capita income, conditions in Tanzania have recently improved. Thus, several large firms have recently been drawn to Tanzania (such as PepsiCo, Coca-Cola, and Sterling Health)—based on the country's good resource base, stable political government, and fast-growing economy.

According to the executive chairman of ScanAd, Tanzania's largest advertising agency, when the company opened in 1990, "The Tanzanian population was literally starved of basic consumer needs. In the rural areas, people didn't know how to use toothpaste and they ate their bread dry."

Despite the recent growth, marketers in Tanzania still face various challenges. Tanzania's annual per-capita GDP is around $600. Total yearly advertising expenditures are currently under $3 million (versus $32 million in Kenya with a population of 26 million and $30 million in Zimbabwe with a population of 14 million).

Promotional media are also very limited. For example, Radio Tanzania is the only real national medium because the country's two television stations only reach the 2 million inhabitants of Dar es Salaam. And though Tanzania's national literacy rate is about 45 per cent, its national newspaper's sales are hampered by its basic printing techniques and by road conditions so poor that newspapers can take four days to arrive. Even the most popular English-language daily newspaper, *The Daily News*, sells only 22,000 copies per day.

ScanAd does business in Tanzania with such large international clients as SwissAir, Toyota, and Sterling Health—while other agencies are content to plan advertising campaigns from nearby Nairobi, Kenya.

As the advertising manager for SwissAir (the international airline), develop a communication strategy to be used for the Tanzanian market.

Source: Based on material in Karen Yates, "Advertising's Heart of Darkness," *Advertising Age* (May 15, 1995), pp. I-10–I-15.

of the message. There is contentment with another brand. The message is not believed. No differential advantage is perceived.

Noise

Noise *may interfere with the communication process at any stage.*

Noise is interference at any point along a channel of communication. Because of it, messages are sometimes encoded or decoded incorrectly or weak audience responses are made. Examples of noise are

- A phone call interrupting a company's marketing manager while he or she is developing a promotional theme.
- A salesperson misidentifying a product and giving incorrect information.
- An impatient customer interrupting a sales presentation.
- A conversation between two consumers during a TV commercial.
- A direct-mail ad being opened by the wrong person.
- A consumer seeing a sale on a competitor's item while waiting at an office-supply store's checkout counter.

Promotion Planning

After a firm gains an understanding of the communication process, it is ready to develop an overall promotion plan. Such a plan consists of three parts: objectives, budgeting, and the promotion mix.

Objectives

Promotion objectives can be divided into two main categories: stimulating demand and enhancing company image.

In setting demand goals, the **hierarchy-of-effects model** should be used. It outlines the sequential short-term, intermediate, and long-term promotion goals for a firm to pursue—and works in conjunction with the consumer's decision process that was discussed in Chapter 8:

The **hierarchy-of-effects model** *outlines demand goals.*

1. Provide information—Obtain consumer product recognition, then gain consumer knowledge of product attributes.
2. Develop positive attitudes and feelings—Obtain favorable attitudes, then gain preference for the company's brand(s) over those of competitors.
3. Stimulate purchases and retain desires—Obtain strong consumer preference, gain purchase of good or service, encourage continued purchases (brand loyalty).

By applying the hierarchy-of-effects model, a company can move from informing to persuading and then to reminding consumers about its offerings. At the early stages of the model, when a good or service is little known, **primary demand** should be sought. This is consumer demand for a product category. At later stages, with preference the goal, **selective demand** should be sought. This is consumer demand for a particular brand. Sometimes organizations may try to sustain or revitalize interest in mature products and revert to a primary demand orientation. Thus, the Florida Tomato Committee sponsors ads to generate primary demand for tomatoes. See Figure 18-8.

Primary demand *is for a product category;* **selective demand** *is for a brand.*

FIGURE 18-8
Generating Primary Demand
Reprinted by permission of the Florida Tomato Committee.

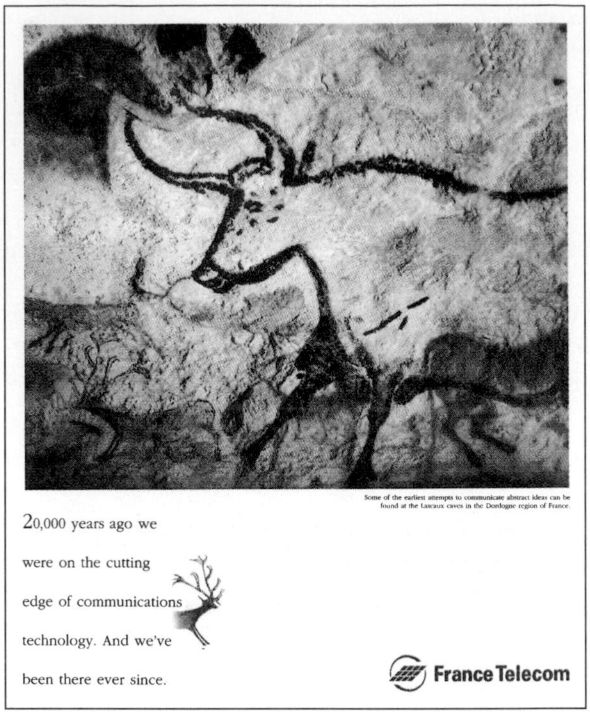

Some of the earliest attempts to communicate abstract ideas can be found at the Lascaux caves in the Dordogne region of France.
20,000 years ago we were on the cutting edge of communications technology. And we've been there ever since.
France Telecom

FIGURE 18-9
Institutional Advertising by France Telecom
Reprinted by permission.

Institutional advertising *is involved with image goals.*

If promotion goals are image-oriented, a firm engages in public relations efforts—via suitable advertising, publicity, personal selling, and/or sales promotion (as noted in Table 18-2). **Institutional advertising** is used when the advertising goal is to enhance company image—and not to sell goods or services. This is illustrated in Figure 18-9. Estimates are that more than one-half of the leading advertisers in the United States run such ads.

Budgeting

Budgeting methods are **all you can afford, incremental, competitive parity, percentage of sales,** *and* **objective and task.**

There are five basic ways to set a total promotion budget: all you can afford, incremental, competitive parity, percentage of sales, and objective and task. The choice depends on the requirements of the individual firm. Budgets can range from 1 to 5 per cent of sales for industrial-products firms to up to 20 to 30 per cent of sales for consumer-products firms.[11]

In the **all-you-can-afford method**, a firm first allots funds for other elements of marketing; any remaining marketing funds then go to the promotion budget. It is the weakest technique and is used most often by small, production-oriented firms. It gives little importance to promotion, spending is not linked to goals, and there is a risk of having no promotion budget if finances are low.

With the **incremental method**, a company bases its new promotion budget on the previous one. A percentage is added to or subtracted from this year's budget to determine next year's. The technique is also used by small firms. It has these advantages: a reference point, a budget based on a firm's feelings about past performance and future trends, and easy calculations. Important disadvantages do exist: budget size is rarely tied to goals, "gut feelings" are overemphasized, and it is hard to evaluate success or failure.

In the **competitive parity method**, a firm's promotion budget is raised or lowered according to competitors' actions. It is useful to both large and small firms. The benefits are that it is keyed to a reference point, market-oriented, and conservative. The shortcomings are that it is a follower and not a leadership approach, it is difficult to get competitors' promotion data, and there is an assumption of a similarity between the firm and its competitors (as to years in business, goods or services, image, prices, and so on). However, firms usually have basic differences from competitors.

[11]See Cyndee Miller, "Marketing Industry Report: Who's Spending What on Biz-to-Biz Marketing," *Marketing News* (January 1, 1996), pp. 1, 7.

With the **percentage-of-sales method**, a firm ties its promotion budget to sales revenue. In the first year, a promotion-to-sales ratio is set. During succeeding years, the ratio of promotion to sales dollars is constant. The benefits are the use of sales as a base, the adaptability, and the link of revenues and promotion. However, there is no relation to promotion goals; promotion is a sales follower, not a sales leader; and promotion cuts occur in poor sales periods (when increases could help). The technique yields too large a budget in high sales periods and too small a budget in low sales periods.

Under the **objective-and-task method**, a firm sets promotion goals, determines the activities needed to satisfy them, and then establishes the proper budget. It is the best method. The advantages are that goals are clearly stated, spending is related to goal-oriented tasks, adaptability is offered, and it is rather easy to evaluate performance. The major weakness is the complexity of setting goals and specific tasks, especially for small firms. Most large companies use some form of objective-and-task technique.

During promotional budgeting, a firm should keep the concept of marginal return in mind. The **marginal return** is the amount of sales each increment of promotion spending will generate. When a product is new, the marginal return is high because the market is expanding. When a product is established, the marginal return is lower because each additional increment of promotion has less of an impact on sales (due to a saturated target market).

The **marginal return** *is the sales generated by incremental promotional spending.*

The Promotion Mix

After establishing a total promotion budget, a company must determine its **promotion mix**. This is the firm's overall and specific communication program, including its involvement with advertising, public relations (publicity), personal selling, and/or sales promotion. Seldom does a company use just one type of promotion—such as a mail-order firm relying on ads, a hospital on publicity, or a flea market vendor on selling. Typically, a promotion mix is used.

A **promotion mix** *somehow combines advertising, public relations, personal selling, and/or sales promotion. When done well,* **integrated marketing communications (IMC)** *results.*

When a well-coordinated promotion mix is involved, a firm is undertaking **integrated marketing communications (IMC)**. As defined by the American Association of Advertising Agencies, IMC "recognizes the value of a comprehensive plan that evaluates the strategic roles of a variety of communication disciplines—advertising, public relations, personal selling, and sales promotion—and combines them to provide clarity, consistency, and maximum communication impact."[12] For example, Frito-Lay has a sales force that visits every store stocking its products, advertises in papers and magazines and on TV, and distributes cents-off coupons. Hitachi has a large technical sales force, advertises in business and trade publications, and sends representatives to trade shows.

Each type of promotion has a distinct function and complements the other types. Ads appeal to big audiences and create awareness; without them, selling is more difficult, time consuming, and costly. The publicity aspect of public relations provides credible information to a wide audience, but content and timing cannot be controlled. Selling has one-to-one contact, flexibility, and the ability to close sales; without it, the interest caused by ads might be wasted. Sales promotion spurs short-run sales and supplements ads and selling.

The selection of a promotion mix depends on company attributes, the product life cycle, media access, and channel members. A small firm is limited in the kinds of ads it can afford or use efficiently; it may have to stress personal selling and a few sales promotions. A large firm covering a sizable geographic area could combine many ads, personal selling, and frequent sales promotions. As products move through the life cycle, promotion emphasis goes from information to persuasion to reinforcement; different media and messages are needed at each stage. Some media may not be accessible (no cigarette ads on TV) or require lengthy lead time (Yellow Pages). Channel members may demand special promotions, sales support, and/or cooperative advertising allowances.

[12]Adapted by the authors from Janet Smith, "Integrated Marketing," *Marketing Tools* (November–December 1995), p. 64.

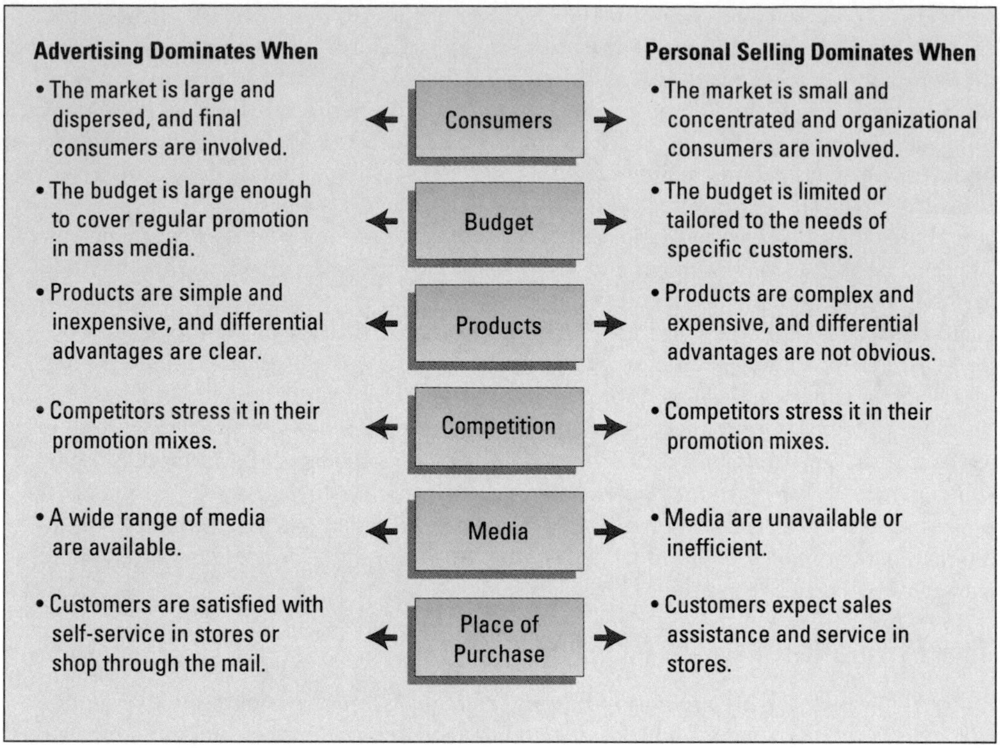

Advertising Dominates When
• The market is large and dispersed, and final consumers are involved.
• The budget is large enough to cover regular promotion in mass media.
• Products are simple and inexpensive, and differential advantages are clear.
• Competitors stress it in their promotion mixes.
• A wide range of media are available.
• Customers are satisfied with self-service in stores or shop through the mail.
Consumers
Budget
Products
Competition
Media
Place of Purchase
Personal Selling Dominates When
• The market is small and concentrated and organizational consumers are involved.
• The budget is limited or tailored to the needs of specific customers.
• Products are complex and expensive, and differential advantages are not obvious.
• Competitors stress it in their promotion mixes.
• Media are unavailable or inefficient.
• Customers expect sales assistance and service in stores.

FIGURE 18-10
Contrasting Promotion Mixes

It is the job of a firm's marketing director (or vice-president) to set up a promotion budget and a promotion mix, as well as to allocate resources to each aspect of promotion. In large firms, there may be separate managers for advertising, public relations, personal selling, and sales promotion. They report to, and have their efforts coordinated by, the marketing director.

Figure 18-10 contrasts promotion mixes in which advertising and personal selling would dominate.

International Promotion Considerations

International promotion decisions should not be made until each market is carefully studied.

While preparing a promotion strategy for foreign nations, the channel of communication, promotion goals, budgeting, and the promotion mix should be carefully reviewed as they pertain to each market.

With regard to the channel of communication, a firm should recognize that

- Source recognition and credibility vary by nation or region. As celebrities, Elizabeth Taylor, Sean Connery, Sylvester Stallone, and Sophia Loren have high recognition rates in both the United States and Japan. Jodie Foster and Julia Roberts are not well known in Japan, despite their U.S. popularity.
- Encoding messages can be quite challenging, particularly if the messages must be translated into another language.
- Because the effects of message symbolism depend on the nation or region, care must be taken if fear, humorous, and/or sexual messages are used. Themes have to correspond to local customs. Thus, French print ads are more apt to have emotional, humorous, and sexual themes than U.S. ones.
- In some locales, few residents have TVs, a limited number of newspapers and magazines are printed, and programs (channels) limit or do not accept ads.

- As with encoding, ensuring that messages are decoded properly can be demanding: "To promote its Wash & Go shampoo, Procter & Gamble blanketed Polish TV and mailed samples. Poles found the dubbed ad culturally out of touch: It showed a woman popping out of a swimming pool and into a shower. 'We don't have swimming pools, and most of us don't have showers. We have baths,' sniffed Eugeniusz Smilowski, president of a Warsaw research group."[13]
- Making assumptions about audience traits in foreign markets without adequate research may lead to wrong assumptions: "An *average* U.S. farmer uses a $100,000 combine while an *average* Chinese farmer uses an ox-pulled hand plow. However, niche marketing, along with the media ability to reach just those customers who have a need for specific products, lets a John Deere economically reach the 30,000 U.S. farmers and the 2,000 Chinese cooperatives who can afford and who need a $100,000 combine."[14]
- Global techniques for measuring promotion effectiveness are emerging.

In terms of promotion goals, budgeting, and the promotion mix, these points should be considered:

- For nations where a firm and its brands are unknown, there must be a series of promotion goals—as people are taken through the hierarchy-of-effects model. For nations in which a product category is new, primary demand must be created before selective demand is gained. To show goodwill, image ads may be even more important in foreign than in domestic markets.
- The promotion budgets in foreign countries must be keyed to the size of the markets and the activities required to succeed there. The objective-and-task method is highly recommended in setting international promotion budgets.
- Due to cultural, socioeconomic, infrastructure, and other differences, promotion mixes must be consistent with the countries served. In Western Europe, Germans listen to the most radio; the Dutch and British watch the most TV. And when Procter & Gamble mailed free samples (a form of sales promotion) of Wash & Go shampoo to people's homes in Poland, thieves broke into mailboxes to get the samples—which they resold. As a Procter & Gamble manager said, "The tools we were using were new to that area."[15]

The Legal Environment of Promotion

Federal, state, and local governmental bodies—in the United States and other nations around the globe—have laws and rules regarding promotion practices. These regulations range from banning billboards in some locales to requiring celebrity endorsers to use products if they say they do. The U.S. agencies most involved with promotion are the Federal Trade Commission and the Federal Communications Commission. Table 18-3 shows selected U.S. regulations.

There are five major enforcement tools to protect consumers and competing firms from undesirable promotion practices: full disclosure, substantiation, cease-and-desist orders, corrective advertising, and fines.

Full disclosure, substantiation, cease-and-desist orders, corrective advertising, *and* **fines** *are major governmental limits on promotion activities.*

Full disclosure requires that all data necessary for a consumer to make a safe and informed decision be provided in a promotion message. That is why Alka-Seltzer must mention that its regular version contains aspirin, and diet products must note how many calories they contain. In this way, consumers can assess the overall benefits and risks of a purchase.

[13]Gail E. Schares, "Colgate-Palmolive Is Really Cleaning Up in Poland," *Business Week* (March 15, 1993), p. 56.

[14]Tom Duncan, "Standardized Global Marketing Communication Campaigns Are Possible, They're Just Hard to Do" in Robert P. Leone and V. Kumar (Editors), *1992 AMA Educators' Proceedings* (Chicago: American Marketing Association, 1992), p. 355.

[15]"Data Watch," *Advertising Age* (October 26, 1992), p. I-10; and E. S. Browning, "Eastern Europe Poses Obstacles for Ads," *Wall Street Journal* (July 30, 1992), p. B6.

Table 18-3
Selected U.S. Regulations Affecting Promotion

FACTOR	LEGAL ENVIRONMENT
Access to media	Cigarettes and liquor have restricted access. Legal, medical, and other professions have been given the right to advertise.
Deception	It is illegal to use messages that would mislead reasonable consumers and potentially harm them.
Bait-and-switch	It is illegal to lure a customer with an ad for a low-priced item and then, once the customer talks to a salesperson, to use a strong sales pitch intended to switch the shopper to a more expensive item.
Door-to-door selling	Many locales restrict door-to-door sales practices. A cooling-off period allows a person to cancel an in-home sale up to three days after an agreement is reached.
Promotional allowances	Such allowances must be available to channel members in a fair and equitable manner.
Comparative advertisements	Claims must be substantiated. The Federal Trade Commission favors naming competitors in ads (not citing a competitor as brand X).
Testimonials or endorsements	A celebrity or expert endorser must actually use a product if he or she makes such a claim.

Substantiation requires a firm to be able to prove all the claims it makes in promotion messages. This means thorough testing and evidence of performance are needed before making claims. If a tire maker says a brand will last for 70,000 miles, it must be capable of verifying this with test results.

Under a **cease-and-desist order**, a firm must discontinue a promotion practice that is deemed deceptive and modify a message accordingly. The firm is often not forced to admit guilt or pay fines, as long as it obeys the order. For example, under FTC pressure, Pioneer Enterprises agreed no longer to use misleading direct-mail offers of such prizes as diamond watches and Hawaiian vacations to sell its products. In letters they received, consumers had been led to believe they had "won" stated prizes, but when they made calls to Pioneer to claim the prizes, they were told they had to buy vitamins or other items before being eligible to win.

Corrective advertising requires a firm to run new ads to correct the false impressions left by previous ones. Several years ago, Listerine was told to spend $10.2 million on ads to correct prior messages claiming it was a cold remedy. Listerine decided to run the ads (with the phrase "Listerine will not help prevent colds or sore throats or lessen their severity") after learning it would not otherwise be permitted to continue any advertising.

The last major remedy is fines, which are dollar penalties for deceptive promotion. A company may have to pay a sum to the government, as with Pfizer's Plax mouth rinse, or be forced to provide consumer refunds, as with mail-order firms not meeting delivery dates. Pfizer had to pay ten states a total of $70,000 for misrepresenting the effectiveness of Plax in treating and preventing tooth and gum disease.

A decade ago, the FTC made two key changes in the way U.S. promotion is regulated. Thus, it is easier for firms to substantiate claims made in ads and sales presentations since less evidence is needed, and the current definition of deceptive advertising includes only promotional claims that would mislead a "reasonable" consumer and result in "injury" (physical, financial, or other).

Besides government rules, the media have their own voluntary standards for promotion practices. The National Association of Broadcasters monitors ads on TV and radio.

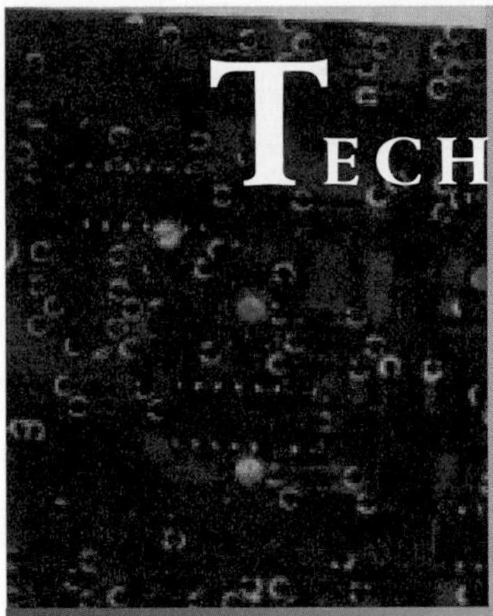

TECHNOLOGY & MARKETING

How Do You Avoid the Legal Pitfalls of Promoting in Cyberspace?

According to experts in the field, there are many legal risks associated with using the Internet for promotions. They advise marketers to keep this seven-point checklist in mind when planning and evaluating Internet-based promotions:

1. All Internet domain names and E-mail addresses are trademarks that must be cleared to ensure they are not owned by others and then legally protected.
2. A firm operating a bulletin board may be liable for the information showing up there. In a case involving slanderous information, Prodigy was held responsible for the same standards as traditional publishers.
3. The Screen Actors Guild claims jurisdiction over the employment of actors used in the production of online and CD-ROM programs. This affects videos initially made for television that are now used in the Internet.
4. As with other media, an individual's name, photograph, or likeness cannot be used in connection with any promotion without his or her written permission.
5. Because the Internet is worldwide in terms of distribution, its use is subject to the laws in countries where the messages are reproduced.
6. The rights of company photographers and free-lance photographers may be affected by use of their materials on the Internet.
7. Marketers should reserve the right to cancel any Internet-based promotion in the event it is infected with a virus or otherwise cannot properly run.

As the advertising manager for Aiwa, you are responsible for devising an Internet-based promotion for a new line of surround-sound stereo receivers. How can you best assure that your promotion meets the legal guidelines listed above?

Source: Based on material in Douglas J. Wood and Linda A. Goldstein, "Seven Legal Pitfalls of Promoting in Cyberspace," *Promo* (July 1995), p. 21.

General industry groups, such as the Better Business Bureau, the American Association of Advertising Agencies, and the International Advertising Association, also participate in the self-regulation of promotion.

Criticisms and Defenses of Promotion

Promotion controversies center on materialism, honesty, prices, symbolism, and consumer expectations.

For many years, various industry trade groups have campaigned to improve the overall image of promotion, as illustrated in Figure 18-11. According to the general director of the International Advertising Association, "There's been enough talk about the bad—the clutter, the obtrusiveness, the stuffed mailboxes. It's time that people know about the good."[16]

Nonetheless, promotion is the most heavily criticized area of marketing. Here are a number of criticisms and the defenses of marketers to them:

DETRACTORS FEEL THAT PROMOTION	MARKETING PROFESSIONALS ANSWER THAT PROMOTION
Creates an obsession with material possessions.	Responds to consumer desires for material possessions. In affluent societies, these items are plentiful and paid for with discretionary earnings.

[16]Cyndee Miller, "The Marketing of Advertising," *Marketing News* (December 7, 1992), p. 2.

FIGURE 18-11
A Strong Defense of Promotion by the American Association of Advertising Agencies
Reprinted by permission.

Is basically dishonest.	Is basically honest. The great majority of companies abide by all laws and set strict self-regulations. A few dishonest firms give a bad name to all.
Raises the prices of goods and services.	Holds down prices. By increasing consumer demand, promotion enables firms to use mass production and mass distribution and reduce per-unit costs. Employment is higher when demand is stimulated.
Overemphasizes symbolism and status.	Differentiates goods and services through symbolic and status appeals. Consumers desire distinctiveness and product benefits.
Causes excessively high expectations.	Keeps expectations high; it thereby sustains consumer motivation and worker productivity in order to satisfy expectations.

MARKETING IN A CHANGING WORLD

What's Ahead for Integrated Marketing Communications?

According to Don E. Schultz, Stanley Tannenbaum, and Robert F. Lauterborn (in their best-selling *Integrated Marketing Communications: Pulling It All Together and Making It Work*), IMC has four fundamental goals:

- To ensure that all communications with consumers are coordinated.
- To make the consumer—not the product—the focal point of communication.

- To foster one-on-one communication with consumers.
- To engender two-way communication between a firm and its consumers.[17]

These sound like admirable objectives, so what's the problem? In a word: implementation. Says one expert, "Integrated marketing communications is the buzz in today's business world. Unfortunately, it usually ends there—a buzz lacking a bite." In fact, one survey of business marketers found that only one-quarter of the respondents had developed an annual IMC plan.[18]

Let us see why implementation is so rough and how it may be worked out:

> At a recent Marketing Sciences Institute conference on marketing communications, one firm after another recounted various attempts to overcome vertical silos [departmental turfs] and to create cross-organizational marketing integration. IBM told of multiple experiments, moving from centralized communications to a decentralized team approach, and then to a marketing services "account manager" approach. Currently, the company is attempting to dismantle its vertical marketing functions completely in favor of cross-functional teams that reside in and work for sponsoring companies.
>
> Organizational resistance is a common impediment because marketing departments—whether arranged by product or by function—are accustomed to autonomy and see IMC as a threat to their resources and decision-making power. Some firms try to tackle this problem by creating marketing service functions that gradually build on some small successes. As the company demonstrates the value of cooperation to marketing or product managers, resistance gradually gives way to rising demand for further integration.[19]

SUMMARY

1. *To define promotion planning and show its importance* Promotion involves any communication that informs, persuades, and/or reminds people about an organization's or individual's goods, services, ideas, community involvement, or impact on society. Promotion planning is systematic and relates to all aspects of communication.

Promotion efforts are needed for both new products and existing ones. The audience for promotion may be consumers, stockholders, consumer advocacy groups, government, channel members, employees, competitors, and the public. With word-of-mouth communication, people express opinions and product-related experiences to one another. A firm may communicate its image, views on ideas, community involvement, or impact on society—as well as persuade people to buy. Good promotion enhances the other elements of the marketing mix. Promotion is a major activity around the world.

2. *To describe the general characteristics of advertising, public relations, personal selling, and sales promotion* Advertising is paid, nonpersonal communication transmitted through various media by organizations and individuals who are in some way identified as the sponsor. Public relations includes any communication (paid or nonpaid, nonpersonal or personal, sponsored by a firm or reported by an independent medium) designed to foster a favorable image. Publicity is the nonpaid, nonpersonal, nonsponsored form of public relations. Personal selling involves oral communication with one or more prospective buyers by paid representatives for the purpose of making sales. Sales promotion involves paid marketing activities to stimulate consumer purchases and dealers.

3. *To explain the channel of communication and how it functions* A source sends a message to its audience via a channel of communication. A channel consists of a source, encoding, the message, the medium, decoding, the audience, feedback, and noise.

A source is a company, an independent institution, or an opinion leader that seeks to present a message to an audience. Encoding is the process by which a thought or an idea is translated into a message by the source. A message is a combination of words and symbols transmitted to the audience. A medium is a personal or nonpersonal channel used to convey a message. Decoding is the process by which a message sent by a source is translated by the audience. The audience is the object of a source's message. Feedback is the response the audience makes to a message: purchase, attitude change, or nonpurchase. Noise is interference at any stage.

4. *To examine the components of a promotion plan* Promotion goals may be demand- or image-oriented. Demand goals should correspond to the hierarchy-of-effects model, moving a consumer from awareness to purchase. Primary demand is total

[17]Don E. Schultz, Stanley Tannenbaum, and Robert F. Lauterborn, *Integrated Marketing Communications: Pulling It All Together and Making It Work* (Lincolnwood, Ill.: NTC Business Books, 1993).

[18]Kim Cleland, "Few Wed Marketing, Communications," *Advertising Age* (February 27, 1995), p. 10.

[19]Smith, "Integrated Marketing," p. 65.

consumer demand for a product category; selective demand refers to consumer interest in a particular brand. Institutional advertising is used to enhance company image.

Five ways to set a promotion budget are all you can afford (the weakest method), incremental, competitive parity, percentage of sales, and objective and task (the best method). Marginal return should be considered when budgeting.

A promotion mix is the overall and specific communication program of a firm, including its use of advertising, public relations (publicity), personal selling, and/or sales promotion. The mix can be well rounded through integrated marketing communications. Many factors need to be considered in developing a promotion mix.

5. *To discuss international promotion considerations, and the legal environment and criticisms and defenses of promotion* When devising an international promotion plan, the channel of communication, promotion goals, budgeting, and promotion mix should be studied for and applied to each market.

There are many laws and rules affecting promotion. The major ways to guard against undesirable promotion are full disclosure, substantiation, cease-and-desist orders, corrective advertising, and fines.

Critics are strong in their complaints about promotion practices and their effects. Marketers are equally firm in their defenses.

KEY TERMS

promotion (p. 501)
promotion planning (p. 501)
word-of-mouth communication (p. 501)
advertising (p. 503)
public relations (p. 503)
publicity (p. 503)
personal selling (p. 503)
sales promotion (p. 503)
channel of communication (communication process) (p. 504)
source (p. 505)
encoding (p. 506)
message (p. 506)
comparative messages (p. 508)
massed promotion (p. 508)
distributed promotion (p. 508)
wearout rate (p. 508)
medium (p. 509)
decoding (p. 509)
subliminal advertising (p. 509)
audience (p. 510)
feedback (p. 511)
noise (p. 512)
hierarchy-of-effects model (p. 513)
primary demand (p. 513)
selective demand (p. 513)
institutional advertising (p. 514)
all-you-can-afford method (p. 514)
incremental method (p. 514)
competitive parity method (p. 514)
percentage-of-sales method (p. 515)
objective-and-task method (p. 515)
marginal return (p. 515)
promotion mix (p. 515)
integrated marketing communications (IMC) (p. 515)
full disclosure (p. 517)
substantiation (p. 518)
cease-and-desist order (p. 518)
corrective advertising (p. 518)

Review Questions

1. Why is promotion planning important?
2. Distinguish among advertising, public relations, personal selling, and sales promotion.
3. What is the role of an opinion leader in a channel of communication?
4. What is a two-sided message? Why do few companies use such messages?
5. What should be the relationship between encoding and decoding messages? Why?
6. A consumer listens to a sales presentation but does not make a purchase. Has the presentation failed? Explain your answer.
7. Explain the hierarchy-of-effects model. How is it related to demand objectives?
8. Describe each of the methods of promotional budgeting.
9. When should personal selling dominate the promotion mix?
10. State the basic criticisms and defenses of promotion.

Discussion Questions

1. What are the advantages and disadvantages of changing messages (themes) infrequently?
2. Present a promotion campaign to increase APBs (AIDS preventive behaviors) among teens.
3. As the marketing manager for a small U.S.-based Portuguese book publisher that is entering the Brazilian market for the first time, devise a promotion budget relying on the objective-and-task method.
4. Develop a promotion mix for
- **a.** A global restaurant chain.
- **b.** A small janitorial service.
- **c.** A four-person dental practice.
- **d.** A medium-sized sporting-goods manufacturer.

5. Comment on this statement: "Full disclosure confuses consumers by giving them too much information. It also raises costs."

CASE 1

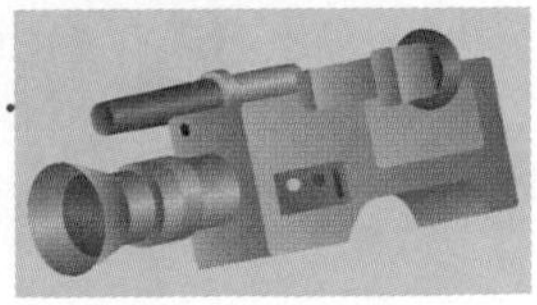

*The Advertising Council: Developing a Communication Strategy**

Since 1942, the nonprofit Advertising Council has developed and placed public service messages. Among its better known campaigns are "The Mind Is a Terrible Thing to Waste" (United Negro College Fund—from Young & Rubicam), "The Toughest Job You'll Ever Love" (Peace Corps—from Red Bates & Co.), and "Drinking and Driving Can Kill a Friendship" (U.S. National Highway Traffic Safety Administration—from Foote, Cone & Belding/Leber Katz Partners).

One of the council's earliest efforts was aimed at preventing forest fires. Its long-running campaign featuring Smokey the Bear was created by Foote, Cone & Belding, Los Angeles. Smokey the Bear was first used in print media and then in television. It is one of the most enduring and recognizable symbols in the history of advertising.

Among the most acclaimed ads was a 30-second spot done by Marsteller (now part of Young & Rubicam), entitled "Indian in Canoe." Run as part of the "Keep America Beautiful" campaign, the ad opened with an Indian being increasingly distraught and ultimately being driven to tears due to the environmental pollution he saw around his canoe.

A newer Ad Council campaign on anti-discrimination is sponsored by the Leadership Conference Education Fund, a nonprofit coalition of about 180 civil rights groups. The coalition is providing guidance for the ads and covering the production costs. The television ads show that too often children avoid others who are different from them in terms of race, creed, culture, or physical abilities. These public service announcements urge children to rise above their initial fears and carry the message "Don't Be Afraid, Be a Friend." The ads have run in children's consumer magazines, and on English- and Hispanic-language TV programs.

As a policy, the Advertising Council only accepts campaign proposals from government or nonprofit associations. For a campaign to be considered, it must be noncontroversial (as an example, the Ad Council will not accept a proposal for a gun control ad) and aimed at a national problem. Political advertising also is not accepted. All commercials devised by the Ad Council are directed at promoting an activity (such as healthy eating), not joining an organization (like the American Heart Association). Its campaigns stress what an individual should do, in addition to publicizing a social problem. Campaigns are created by advertising agency volunteers and then coordinated by volunteers from corporate advertising, communications, or public affairs departments. If a campaign is accepted, the Ad Council works to recruit sponsoring organizations to fund the costs of producing the commercials. The Ad Council then helps get media to contribute advertising time (for broadcast media) and space (for print media). The Ad Council views the media's willingness to run a particular ad as the first test of that ad's effectiveness.

According to a spokesperson for the Ad Council, the annual donated air time for TV is worth about $250 million. Thus, if the Ad Council was an advertising agency, it would rank among the top 20 agencies in the United States. Although the Ad Council is the largest public service advertising source, there are many other groups on local and regional levels that perform similar services. An example of another nonprofit advertising organization is the Partnership for a Drug-Free America.

QUESTIONS

1. Evaluate the policies of the Advertising Council.
2. Apply the stages in the channel of communication to the Advertising Council's anti-discrimination campaign.
3. Relate the stages in promotion planning—objectives, budgeting, and the promotion mix—to the anti-discrimination campaign undertaken by the Advertising Council.
4. Describe how the Advertising Council can evaluate the effectiveness of the anti-discrimination campaign.

VIDEO QUESTIONS ON THE ADVERTISING COUNCIL

1. Evaluate the Advertising Council's eight techniques of effective television advertising.
2. Why does a nonprofit group need both 30- and 60-second commercials?

*The data in this case are drawn from "Fifth Estater: Ruth Ann Wooden," *Broadcasting* (November 2, 1992), p. 79; and Robert G. Goldsborough, "Put Service Before Profits," *Advertising Age* (Spring 1995), p. 51.

CASE 2

Can a Firm Succeed by Poking Fun at Itself?[†]

An increasing number of firms have begun to mock their past behavior in their advertising. Examples of self-deprecating ads include those for Thom McAn shoes and 7-Eleven stores. For example, a recent ad for Thom McAn said, "Please excuse some of our shoe styles in the past. Through a fluke computer error, the office-supply store repeatedly sent us the wrong desk calendar and we still thought it was 1976." Another ad even stated, "Please excuse some of our shoe styles in the past. For years, our new and updated shoes were rerouted by a disgruntled worker and abandoned under a bridge near Chicago."

7-Eleven's ads have poked fun at the stores' past high prices, cramped interiors, and food that wasn't always fresh. In one ad, comedian Louie Anderson remarked, "They're so small that there's barely room for me and a Big Gulp." Another ad featuring Brett Butler (of the TV series *Grace Under Fire*) expressed surprise at the gourmet coffee and frozen yogurt at a 7-Eleven. She also said, "Are women running 7-Eleven now?" and "Pork rinds and Perrier. Is this heaven or what?"

After tough times, both Thom McAn and 7-Eleven poked fun at their past strategies as a way of promoting their new images. For example, in 1981, Thom McAn had sales of $440 million through 1,200 outlets, but 1995 sales had sunk to $275 million from 400 stores. And 7-Eleven had difficulty convincing consumers that its grocery products were delivered daily, versus every four to five days. The chain also had a blue-collar male image that was not attractive to females and higher-income professionals. As 7-Eleven's director of advertising and sales promotion noted, "We needed to communicate the magnitude of our changes."

Marketing analysts have mixed views on the effectiveness of advertising that makes fun of a firm's past. Advocates of this technique feel this approach is perceived as honest. They also say this strategy is most effective when a company's/brand's image has hit rock-bottom, and when the current reality is better than the public's perceptions. According to the head of Thom McAn's advertising agency, "There's nothing new in just saying, 'Come see us, we have changed.' A lot of people do that, and there's no reason to believe them. So you have to use a bit of self-deprecation to get people to take you seriously."

Those who question this technique, however, have a different viewpoint. One marketing expert suggests that, "It's foolish to talk about the past and remind people of things that may have not made a difference. Consumers want to know what's in your stores now." Another cautions advertisers about using this technique: "You had better be certain that your product or service fulfills the promise of the apologizing advertising."

Most marketing observers do agree that poking fun at oneself will work only when a firm has made meaningful changes in its overall marketing strategy. Therefore, in addition to changing its advertising, Thom McAn introduced more contemporary shoe styles, a spiffy new logo, more modern store colors, and a private label that offers fashionable shoes targeted at younger, more fashion-conscious shoppers.

An example of an ineffective self-deprecating ad was Oldsmobile's, "This is not your father's Oldsmobile" campaign, which aired in the late 1980s. Although the campaign lured a young target market to Oldsmobile dealerships, few browsers actually bought a car resembling their "father's Oldsmobile."

QUESTIONS

1. How does a self-deprecating ad differ from a two-sided message?
2. What are the similarities between a self-deprecating ad and a two-sided message?
3. What are the pros and cons of the use of humor in advertising?
4. Explain how Thom McAn can develop a budget for its advertising using the objective-and-task technique.

[†]The data in this case are drawn from Joshua Levine, "Please Excuse Our Shoe Styles of the Past," *Forbes* (January 2, 1995), p. 64; and Fara Warner, "'We Goofed, Forgive Us,' New Ads Plead," *Wall Street Journal* (May 25, 1995), pp. B1, B8.

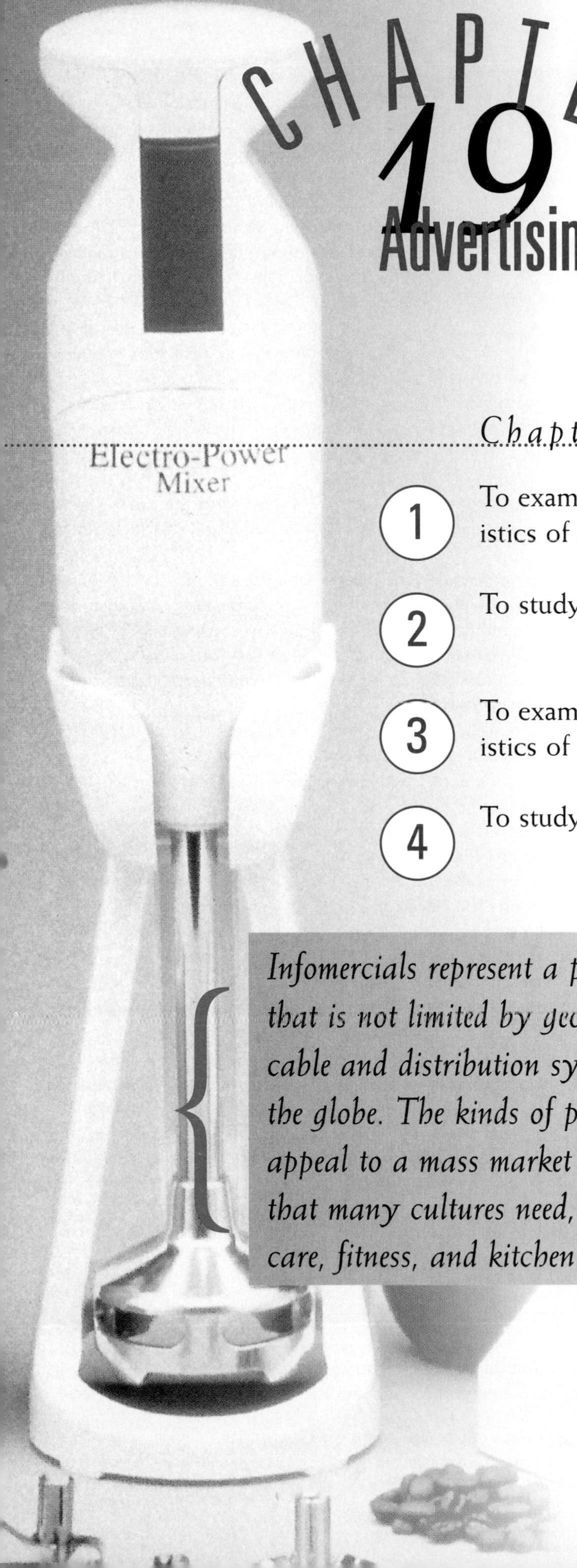

CHAPTER 19
Advertising and Public Relations

Chapter Objectives

1. To examine the scope, importance, and characteristics of advertising
2. To study the elements in an advertising plan
3. To examine the scope, importance, and characteristics of public relations
4. To study the elements in a public relations plan

Infomercials represent a powerful marketing vehicle that is not limited by geographic borders. New cable and distribution systems are exploding around the globe. The kinds of products that sell on TV appeal to a mass market and fall into categories that many cultures need, like cosmetics, personal care, fitness, and kitchen items.

Reprinted by permission of Home Shopping Network.

An infomercial is a full-length TV advertising program (typically 30 minutes) that airs on cable television—or on broadcast media at a fringe time. While watching infomercials, consumers call in orders, and items are then delivered directly to their homes or offices. An infomercial is especially useful for products requiring demonstrations to show their benefits.

Infomercials are successfully promoting a variety of goods and services—including food preparation devices (such as juice preparation machines and pasta makers), cosmetics, exercise equipment, instructional videos on computer software, and car waxes. Through its infomercials, Home Shopping Network Direct (HSN Direct) sold 60,000 of its Electro-Power Mixers internationally in just six months. This mixer is an exclusive product of HSN Direct.

There are several factors behind a good infomercial. They relate to the use of testimonials, program length, product pricing, two-step offers, and production considerations. Let's now review each.

A key to the success of any infomercial is the proper use of testimonials. A testimonial is particularly important with two types of infomercials—those that sell a product replacing an "earlier generation" item and the "I made a ton of money and so can you" types of programs. Testimonials do not have to come from a celebrity; they can come from satisfied customers. Some celebrity testimonials can be very effective; however, celebrities can also double an infomercial's production cost.

Even though the usual infomercial is 30 minutes long, most viewers watch only part of a show. Therefore, infomercial sponsors often divide their programs into self-sustaining parts (such as three 10-minute segments) and give people a chance to order merchandise during each portion of the program.

According to one industry expert, the price of a product appearing on an infomercial should exceed $40 to $50, due to the high production costs and media expenditures. If an appropriate item is priced at a lower amount, sponsors may sell the product as a package of three for $49.95 or as part of a "Buy two for $49.95, get one free" promotion.

Some products require a two-step offer, in which a sponsor first generates a list of prospects from an infomercial and then makes separate calls to try to close sales. Two-step offers are appropriate to screen prospects by getting additional information about the prospects' needs, product use, or company size. A negative element of the two-step approach is that the sponsor needs to sell the potential consumer twice, on both the initial inquiry and close.

Producers must include several production considerations in planning and implementing infomercials: The offer should be listed as available for a limited time only to increase sales responses. A toll-free number should be clearly listed. Humor can be used in establishing rapport with the customer, but infomercial experts warn against using humor when promoting a product. And lastly, the qualifications of an "expert host" should be mentioned in the infomercial to enhance credibility.[1]

In this chapter, we will study both the advertising and public relations aspects of promotion.

Overview

Advertising and public relations are two of the major forms of promotion.

This chapter covers two promotion forms: advertising and public relations. As defined in Chapter 18, advertising is paid, nonpersonal communication regarding goods, services,

[1]Kim Cleland, "Infomercial Audience Crosses Over Cultures," *Advertising Age* (January 15, 1996), p. I-8; Hershell Gordon Lewis, "Information on Infomercials," *Direct Marketing* (March 1995), pp. 30–32; and Zachary Schiller and Ron Grover, "And Now, A Show from Your Sponsor," *Business Week* (May 22, 1995), pp. 100–104.

Table 19-1

Advertising Expenditures by Medium: United States Versus Western Europe

***IN THE UNITED STATES*[a]**

Media	*Per Cent of Total Expenditures*
Newspapers	22.9
Television	22.8
Direct mail	19.7
Radio	7.0
Yellow Pages	6.6
Magazines	5.3
Business publications	2.2
Outdoor	0.8
Farm publications	0.2
Miscellaneous	12.5
Total	100.0

***IN WESTERN EUROPE*[a]**

Media	*Per Cent of Total Expenditures*
Newspapers	32.0
Television	25.0
Magazines	17.4
Direct mail	16.2
Outdoor	4.7
Radio	3.5
Cinema	0.7
Miscellaneous	0.5
Total	100.0

[a]The media designations in the two areas differ because the sources for the U.S. data are different from the sources for the European data.

Sources: Estimated by the authors from data reported in various issues of *Advertising Age*.

organizations, people, places, and ideas; it may be used by businesses, government and other nonprofit organizations, and individuals. Its distinguishing features are that a sponsor pays for its message, a set format is sent to an entire audience through mass media, the sponsor's name is clearly presented, and the sponsor controls the message.

In contrast, public relations involves communication that fosters a favorable image for goods, services, organizations, people, places, and ideas among their various publics. Its unique features are that it is more image- than sales-oriented; it embodies image-oriented advertising, personal selling, and sales promotion; and it often seeks favorable publicity for a firm. As an aspect of public relations, publicity entails nonpersonal communication that is transmitted via mass media but not paid for by an identified sponsor. The media usually control the wording and placement of publicity messages.

The distinctions between advertising and publicity are in part revealed by this statement: "Advertising is paid for, publicity is prayed for."

The scope and importance, characteristics, and planning considerations are examined in Chapter 19 for both advertising and public relations.

The Scope and Importance of Advertising

In 1996 alone, it is estimated that $375 billion was spent on advertising around the world—nearly $175 billion in the United States and just over $200 billion outside the United States (half in Western Europe).[2] Table 19-1 shows expenditures by medium for the United States and Western Europe. In both areas, newspapers and TV are the preferred media, but newspapers are more popular for Western European advertisers, partly due to greater U.S. media choice. Direct mail is also a key and growing medium in each area. The largest media difference is with magazines, which are more popular in Western Europe.

[2]Stuart Elliott, "Advertising," *New York Times* (December 5, 1995), p. D10; and Sally Goll Beatty, "Agencies See Record Ad Spending in '96, Slowing Growth Thereafter," *Wall Street Journal* (December 5, 1995), p. B12.

Table 19-2
Advertising in Selected U.S. Industries, 1995

INDUSTRY	ADVERTISING AS PER CENT OF SALES	INDUSTRY	ADVERTISING AS PER CENT OF SALES
Games and toys	13.3	Hospitals	4.1
Hand tools	9.7	Books	3.6
Soaps and detergents	9.7	Financial services	3.0
Perfume	8.2	Paper mills	1.9
Beverages	8.2	Security brokers	1.2
Mail-order catalogs	7.7	Grocery stores	1.1
Educational services	7.4	Lumber	1.0
Food products	6.5	Computer & office equipment	0.9
Adhesives and sealants	5.4	Electronic components	0.9

Source: Derived from Schonfeld & Associates, "1995 Advertising to Sales Ratios for the 200 Largest Ad Spending Industries," *Advertising Age* (August 14, 1995), p. 26.

Three-quarters of U.S. firms spend less than 4 per cent of sales on advertising. Ads are most important for standardized products aimed at large markets.

Advertising as a per cent of sales varies by industry and firm, and company advertising as a per cent of sales is very low. See Tables 19-2 and 19-3. During 1995, expenditures were less than 2.0 per cent of sales in 40 per cent of U.S. industries; 2.0 to 3.9 per cent of sales in 35 per cent of U.S. industries; and at least 4.0 per cent of sales in 25 per cent of U.S. industries.[3] Among the leading advertisers, such as Procter & Gamble, the percentages often far exceed industry averages.

An advertising emphasis is most likely if products are standardized, have easily communicated features, appeal to a large market, have low prices, are marketed via independent resellers, and/or are new. Leading brands often get large ad budgets to hold their positions. For example, at Charles Schwab, the discount stock broker, ads stress two themes: low prices and quality service. It has an in-house ad agency and runs ads on traditional and cable TV. Through advertising, it has raised investor awareness and introduced new products.

As a senior executive at the J. Walter Thompson advertising agency once noted, "Advertising works on television and it works in print. What's more, it especially pays to advertise during recessions. All too often, by focusing on the bottom line, firms sacrifice the long-term, brand-building gains advertising makes possible. In our view, this is a serious mistake."[4]

The following observations can be made as to the impact of advertising: Due to low-involvement purchases, consumer behavior may be easier to change than attitudes. One ad can have a strong effect on brand awareness. By advertising, it is easier to raise people's opinions for a little-known product than a well-known one. Ad effectiveness often rises over long-term campaigns.

The Characteristics of Advertising

Advertising attracts an audience, has low per-customer costs, offers varied media, is surrounded by information, and aids selling.

On the positive side, advertising reaches a large, geographically dispersed market; and, for print media, circulation is supplemented by the passing of a copy from one reader to

[3]Computed by the authors from Schonfeld & Associates, "1995 Advertising to Sales Ratios for the 200 Largest Ad Spending Industries," *Advertising Age* (August 14, 1995), p. 26.

[4]Peter Kim, "Does Advertising Work: A Review of the Evidence," *Journal of Consumer Marketing*, Vol. 9 (Fall 1992), p. 5.

Table 19-3

The Leading Advertisers in the World (1994 Data)

IN THE UNITED STATES			***OUTSIDE THE UNITED STATES***		
Company	***Advertising Expenditures***	***Advertising as Per Cent of U.S. Sales***	***Company***	***Advertising Expenditures***	***Advertising as Per Cent of Non-U.S. Sales***
Procter & Gamble	$2,698,800,000	16.6	Unilever	$2,208,800,000	6.1
Philip Morris	$2,413,300,000	5.9	Procter & Gamble	$2,199,500,000	12.8
General Motors	$1,929,400,000	1.6	Nestlé	$1,216,800,000	3.6
Ford	$1,186,000,000	1.3	Philip Morris	$ 778,300,000	3.2
Sears	$1,134,100,000	NA	Peugeot-Citroën	$ 773,300,000	3.0
AT&T	$1,102,700,000	1.6	Toyota	$ 697,400,000	NA
PepsiCo	$1,097,800,000	5.4	Volkswagen	$ 696,900,000	1.5
Chrysler	$ 971,600,000	2.1	General Motors	$ 650,500,000	2.0
Walt Disney	$ 934,800,000	12.1	Nissan	$ 611,000,000	NA
Johnson & Johnson	$ 933,700,000	12.0	Mars	$ 604,200,000	NA

NA = Not available.

Sources: Derived from "100 Leading National Advertisers," *Advertising Age* (September 27, 1995); and "Top 50 Non-U.S. Spenders," *Advertising Age* (November 20, 1995), p. I-20. *Reprinted by permission of* Advertising Age. *Copyright 1995 by Crain Communications Inc. All rights reserved.*

another. The costs per viewer or listener are low. For example, a single TV ad may cost $360,000 to air and reach 30 million people—a cost of $0.012 per person (for media time). A broad range of media is available: from national (international) television to local newspapers. Thus, a firm's goals and resources may be matched with the most appropriate medium.

A sponsor has control over message content, graphics, timing, and size or length, as well as the audience targeted. A uniform message is sent to the whole audience. With print media, people can study and restudy messages. Editorial content (a news story or segment of a broadcast show) often borders an ad. This can raise readership or viewing/listening, enhance an image, and create the proper mood for an ad. A firm may even seek specialized media or sections of media (like a newspaper's sports section for a men's clothing ad).

Ads ease the way for personal selling by creating audience awareness and liking for brands. They also enable self-service wholesalers and retailers to operate, and they sustain an industry—mail order. With a pulling strategy, advertising enables a firm to show its resellers that consumer demand exists.

Advertising is inflexible and can be wasteful, costly, and limit information and feedback.

On the negative side, because messages are standardized, they are rather inflexible and not responsive to consumer questions. This makes it hard to satisfy the needs of a diverse audience. And since many media appeal to broad audiences, a large portion of viewers or readers may be wasted for a sponsor. For instance, a single-unit health spa or a local roofing-materials firm might find that only one-fifth of a newspaper's readers live in its shopping area.

Advertising sometimes requires high total expenditures, although costs per viewer or reader are low. This may keep smaller firms from using some media. In the example earlier in this section, it was said that a TV ad might cost only $0.012 per viewer. Yet, media time alone for that ad would be $360,000—for one ad, placed once. Also, because high costs lead to brief messages, most ads do not provide much information. TV commercials are very short, averaging 30 seconds or less; few are as long as one minute. Further, because ads are impersonal, feedback is harder to get and it may not be immediately available.

International Marketing in *Action*

Which Soft Drink Is the Real Thing in Brazil?

With $6 billion in annual sales, Brazil has the world's fourth-largest soft-drink consumption after the United States, Mexico, and Germany. About 45 million of the country's residents are aged 10 to 24, the prime soda-drinking age group. Brazil's average per capita consumption is about 24 liters.

In a effort to gain additional market share in the Brazilian market, PepsiCo has invested more than $500 million in advertising and distribution facilities since 1994. Because of this initiative, Pepsi has increased its overall market share of the Brazilian soda market from 5 per cent to 6 per cent. During the same period, Coca-Cola's overall soda market share has dropped by 1.5 per cent—to 38 per cent. In the cola segment, Pepsi has a 7 per cent share; Coca-Cola's is nearly 88 per cent.

Pepsi has devised 20 different TV commercials targeted specifically at the Brazilian market. One of these commercials shows Coca-Cola executives worrying about Pepsi's revised look, reformulated taste, and new distribution prowess. In response, Coca-Cola is increasing its advertising budget and running a new campaign—with a photocopy salesperson, who, while demonstrating the world's most advanced copy machine, says that no one can copy Coca-Cola.

Royal Crown Cola (RC) is entering the Brazilian market via an alliance with a local distributor. Using the firm's "Shake things up" international advertising slogan, RC invested $750,000 in a promotional campaign aimed at three Brazilian test market areas. After a national rollout, RC hopes to go from 0 per cent to 3 per cent market share in the cola segment by the end of 1997.

As the advertising manager for RC, what would you do to compete with Coke and Pepsi in Brazil?

Source: Based on material in Claudia Penteado, "Pepsi Challenges Coke in Brazil," *Advertising Age* (January 16, 1995), p. 12.

Mass media are used by many people who do not view or listen to ads. They watch TV, read print media, and so on, but ignore ads and discard direct mail. Of concern to television advertisers is "zapping," whereby a viewer uses a remote-control device to switch programs when an ad comes on.

Developing an Advertising Plan

The development of an advertising plan consists of the nine steps shown in Figure 19-1. These steps are now highlighted.

Setting Objectives

An organization's advertising goals can be divided into demand and image types, with image-oriented ads being part of its public relations effort. Table 19-4 cites several goals. Usually, a number of them are pursued in an advertising plan.

As an example, the American Institute of Certified Public Accountants recently ran a $3 million image-oriented ad campaign with very clear goals: to expand the public's un-

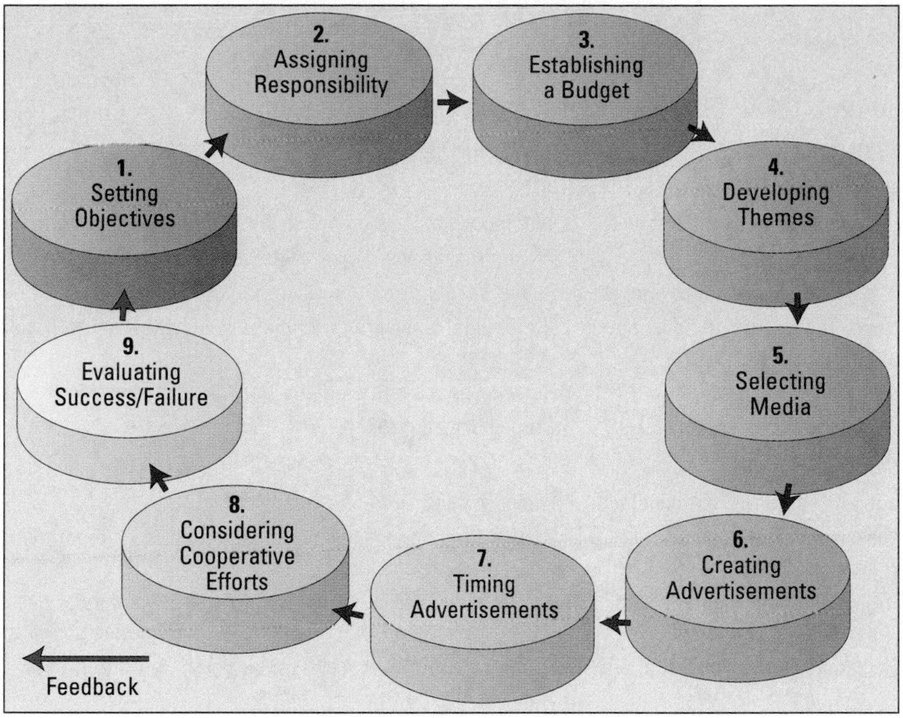

FIGURE 19-1
Developing an Advertising Plan

derstanding of what CPAs do and to show how they add value. Thus, the campaign emphasized that "CPAs can see things beyond the numbers the rest of us can't. The CPA. Never Underestimate the Value."[5]

[5]Lee Berton, "Accountants Group to Spend $3 Million on Ad Campaign," *Wall Street Journal* (September 27, 1995), p. B2.

Table 19-4
Illustrations of Specific Advertising Objectives

TYPE OF OBJECTIVE	ILLUSTRATIONS
Demand-Oriented	
Information	To create target market awareness for a new brand To acquaint consumers with new business or store hours To reduce the time salespeople take to answer basic questions
Persuasion	To gain brand preference To increase store traffic To achieve brand loyalty
Reminding (retention)	To stabilize sales To maintain brand loyalty To sustain brand recognition and image
Image-Oriented	
Industry	To develop and maintain a favorable industry image To generate primary demand
Company	To develop and maintain a favorable company image To generate selective demand

Table 19-5
Advertising Themes

THEME	EXAMPLE
Good or Service Related	
Dominant features described	Whirlpool washers emphasize dependability and durability.
Competitive advantages cited	Aiwa stresses the superior quality of its portable stereos.
Price used as dominant feature	Suave beauty products advertise low prices.
News or information domination	New-model laser printers point out enhancements in color and fonts.
Size of market detailed	Hertz emphasizes its leading position in car rentals.
Primary demand sought	Grapes are advertised.
Consumer Related	
Good or service uses explained	Pillsbury ads have cake recipes.
Cost benefits of good or service shown	Owens-Corning states how consumers reduce heating bills with Fiberglas insulation.
Emphasis on how good or service helps consumer	The Regent Beverly Wilshire hotel mentions that its customer service is so good that it gives clients complete peace of mind.
Threatening situation	The American Heart Association points out the risks of smoking.
Incentives given to encourage purchases	An ad mentions $1 off the purchase as an introductory offer for a new brand of coffee.
Institutional Related	
Favorable image sought	Mobil explains how it is searching for new energy sources.
Growth, profits, and potential described to attract investors	Companies regularly take out full-page ads in business sections of major newspapers.

Assigning Responsibility

In assigning advertising responsibility, a firm can rely on its internal personnel involved with marketing functions, use an in-house advertising department, or hire an outside advertising agency. Although many firms use internal personnel or in-house departments, most firms involved with advertising on a regular or sizable basis employ outside agencies (some in addition to their own personnel or departments). Diversified firms may hire a different agency for each product line. A firm's decision to use an outside agency depends on its own expertise and resources and on the role of advertising for the firm.

An **advertising agency** *may work with a firm to develop its ad plan, conduct research, or provide other services.*

An **advertising agency** is an organization that provides a variety of advertising-related services to client firms. It often works with clients in devising their advertising plans—including themes, media choice, copywriting, and other tasks. A large agency may also offer market research, product planning, consumer research, public relations, and other services.

Establishing a Budget

After figuring its overall advertising spending by the all-you-can-afford, incremental, competitive parity, percentage-of-sales, or objective-and-task method, a firm sets a detailed ad budget—to specify the funds for each type of advertising (such as product and institutional messages) and each medium (such as newspapers and radio). Because demand-oriented ads generate revenues, firms should be cautious about reducing these budgets. A better campaign, not a lower budget, may be the answer if performance does not reach goals.

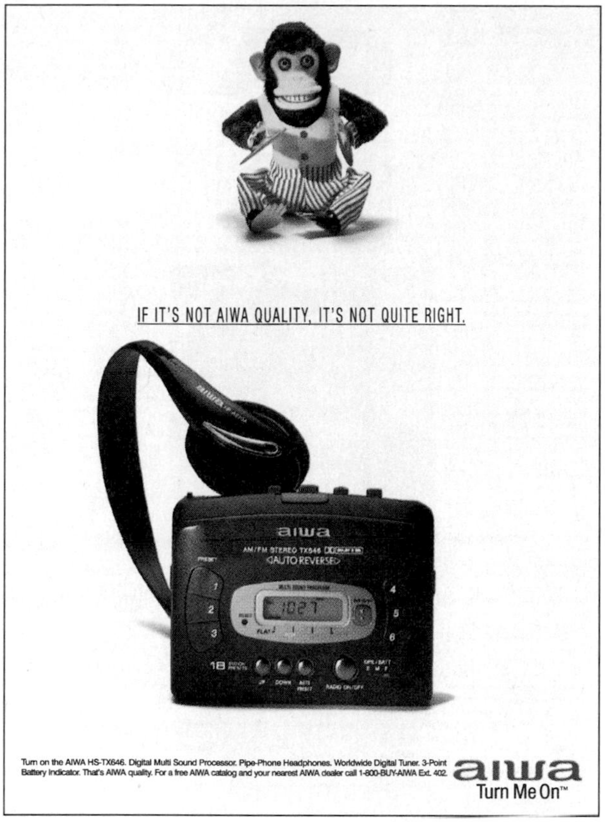
IF IT'S NOT AIWA QUALITY, IT'S NOT QUITE RIGHT.
aiwa
AUTO REVERSE
Turn on the AIWA HS-TX646. Digital Multi Sound Processor. Pipe-Phone Headphones. Worldwide Digital Tuner. 3-Point Battery Indicator. That's AIWA quality. For a free AIWA catalog and your nearest AIWA dealer call 1-800-BUY-AIWA Ext. 402.
aiwa
Turn Me On™

FIGURE 19-2
Aiwa: Citing Competitive Advantages
Reprinted by permission.

These points should be addressed: What do various alternatives cost for time or space (a 30-second TV spot versus a full-page magazine ad)? How many placements are needed for an ad to be effective (if it takes four telecasts of a single ad to make an impact, a budget must allow four placements)? How have media prices risen recently? How should a firm react during an industry sales slump? What channel members are assigned which promotion tasks? Do channel members require contributions toward advertising? What does it cost to produce an ad? How should a budget be allocated for domestic versus international ads?

According to a recent survey of international advertising executives, 28 per cent of firms allow personnel in each pan-geographic region to determine their own needs and then petition headquarters for a budget, 28 per cent allow each individual market to have its own advertising strategy and budget, and 20 per cent control budgeting decisions from their world headquarters. Airlines are most likely to use the pan-geographic approach. Consumer products and high-tech companies are most apt to have individual market budgeting.[6]

Developing Themes

Basic **advertising themes** *are product, consumer, and/or institutional appeals.*

A firm next develops **advertising themes**, the overall appeals for its campaign. A good or service appeal centers on the item and its attributes. A consumer appeal describes a product in terms of consumer benefits rather than its features. An institutional appeal deals with a firm's image. Table 19-5 presents a full range of advertising themes from which a firm may select. Figures 19-2, 19-3, and 19-4 show thematic ads from Aiwa, Owens-Corning, and the Regent Beverly Wilshire.

[6]Jan Jaben, "Ad Decision Makers Favor Regional Angle," *Advertising Age* (May 15, 1995), pp. I-3, I-16.

FIGURE 19-3
Owens-Corning: Emphasizing Cost Benefits
Reprinted by permission.

Leaving you at peace with yourself. *It's all part of Regent's truly attentive service.*
the Regent
AUCKLAND. BANGKOK. BEVERLY HILLS. CHIANG MAI. FIJI. HONG KONG. JAKARTA. KUALA LUMPUR. LONDON. MELBOURNE. SINGAPORE. SYDNEY. TAIPEI.
CONTACT YOUR TRAVEL COUNSELLOR OR CALL REGENT INTERNATIONAL RESERVATIONS. TOLL FREE: (800) 545 4000.
FOUR SEASONS • REGENT. DEFINING THE ART OF SERVICE AT 40 HOTELS IN 19 COUNTRIES.

FIGURE 19-4
The Regent Beverly Wilshire: Promoting How Its Service Helps the Consumer
Reprinted by permission.

Selecting Media

There are many media available, as noted in Table 19-6 on pages 536–537. In selecting them, costs, reach, waste, narrowcasting, frequency, message permanence, persuasive impact, clutter, lead time, and media innovations should be reviewed.

Advertising media costs are outlays for media time or space. They are related to ad length or size, as well as media attributes. First, the total costs to place an ad in a given medium should be computed—for example, $30,000 for a full-page color ad in a magazine. Second, per-reader or viewer costs should be derived (stated on a per-thousand basis). If a $30,000 ad goes in a magazine with a 500,000 circulation, the cost per thousand is $60.

Advertising media costs *include total and per person costs.*

Reach refers to the number of viewers, readers, or listeners in a medium's audience. For TV and radio, it is the total number of people who watch or listen to an ad. For print media, it has two aspects: circulation and passalong rate. Circulation is the number of copies sold or distributed to people. The passalong rate is the number of times each copy is read by another reader. For instance, each copy of *Newsweek* is read by several people. The magazine passalong rate is much higher than that for daily papers.

Reach *includes circulation and passalongs.*

Waste is the part of a medium's audience not in a firm's target market. Because media appeal to mass audiences, it can be a big factor. This can be shown by continuing the magazine example noted in media costs. If the magazine is a special-interest one for amateur photographers, a film producer would know that 450,000 readers might have an interest in a new fast-speed film; 50,000 would have no interest. The latter represents the wasted audience for its ad. So, the real cost is $66.67 ($30,000/450,000 × 1,000 = $66.67) per-thousand circulation. The firm also knows a general-interest magazine runs ads for film. That magazine sells one million copies and a full-page ad costs $40,000—$40 per thousand. Yet, the firm expects only 200,000 people to have an interest in photography. Thus, the real cost is $200 ($40,000/200,000 × 1,000 = $200) per-thousand circulation. See Figure 19-5 below.

Waste *is the audience segment not in the target market.*

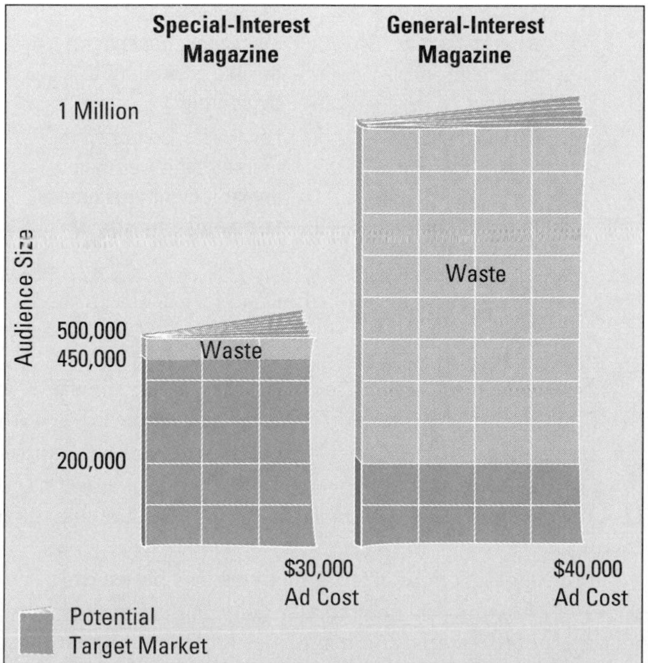

Even though the general-interest magazine attracts a much larger overall audience than the special-interest magazine (at little additional cost), a large portion of its audience is wasted – many people are not part of the potential target market.

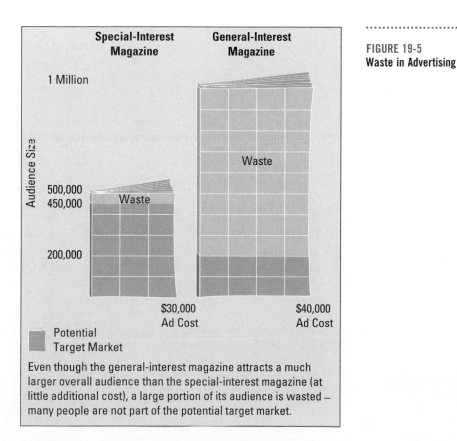

FIGURE 19-5
Waste in Advertising

Table 19-6
Advertising Media

MEDIUM	MARKET COVERAGE	BEST USES	SELECTED ADVANTAGES	SELECTED DISADVANTAGES
Daily newspaper	Entire metropolitan area; local editions used sometimes	Medium and large firms	Short lead time, concentrated market, flexible, high frequency, passalongs, surrounded by content	General audience, heavy ad competition, limited color, limited creativity
Weekly newspaper	One community	Local firms	Same as daily	Heavy ad competition, very limited color, limited creativity, small market
Commercial television	Regional, national, or international	Regional manufacturers and large retailers; national, large manufacturers and largest retailers	Reach, low cost per viewer persuasive impact, creative options, flexible, high frequency, surrounded by programs	High minimum total costs, general audience, lead time for popular shows, short messages, limited availability
Cable television	Local, regional, national, or international	Local, regional, and national manufacturers and retailers	More precise audience and more creative than commercial television	Not all consumers hooked up; ads not yet fully accepted on programs
Direct mail	Advertiser selects market	New products, book clubs, financial services, catalog sales	Precise audience, flexible, personal approach, less clutter from other messages	High throwaway rate, receipt by wrong person, low credibility
Magazines	Local, national, or international (with regional issues)	Local service retailers and mail-order firms; major manufacturers and retailers	Color, creative options, affluent audience, permanence of messages, passalongs, flexible, surrounded by content	Long lead time, poor frequency (if monthly), ad clutter, geographically dispersed audience
Radio	Entire metropolitan area	Local or regional firms	Low costs, selective market, high frequency, immediacy of messages, surrounded by content	No visual impact, commercial clutter, channel switching, consumer distractions

In **narrowcasting**, *advertisers seek to reduce waste.*

Narrowcasting, which presents advertising messages to rather limited and well-defined audiences, is a way to reduce the audience waste with mass media. It may be done via direct mail, local cable TV, specialty magazines, and other targeted media. In narrowcasting, a firm gets less waste in return for a smaller reach. Now that the majority of U.S. homes get cable TV programs, this medium has great potential for local narrowcasting.

Frequency *is highest for daily media.*

Frequency is how often a medium can be used. It is greatest for newspapers, radio, and TV. Different ads may appear daily and a strategy may be easily changed. Phone directories, outdoor ads, and magazines have the poorest frequency. A Yellow Pages ad may be placed only once per year.

Message permanence *refers to exposures per ad.*

Message permanence refers to the number of exposures one ad generates (repetition) and how long it remains available to the audience. Outdoor ads, transit ads, and phone directories yield many exposures per message; and many magazines are retained by consumers for long periods. On the other hand, radio and TV ads last only 5 to 60 seconds and are over.

Table 19-6 (Cont.)

MEDIUM	MARKET COVERAGE	BEST USES	SELECTED ADVANTAGES	SELECTED DISADVANTAGES
Business publications	National, regional, or international	Corporate advertising, industrial firms	Selective market, high readability, surrounded by content, message permanence, passalongs	Restricted product applications, may not be read by proper decision maker, not final-consumer oriented
Outdoor	Entire metropolitan area or one location	Brand-name products, nearby retailers, reminder ads	Large size, color, creative options, repetition, less clutter, message permanence	Legal restrictions, consumer distractions, general audience, inflexible, limited content, lead time
Transit	Urban community with a transit system	Firms located along transit route	Concentrated market, message permanence, repetition, action-oriented messages, color, creative options	Clutter of ads, consumer distractions, geographically limited audience
Telephone directories	Entire metropolitan area (with local supplements)	All types of retailers, professionals, service companies	Low costs, permanence of messages, repetition, coverage of market, specialized listings, action-oriented messages	Clutter of ads, limited creativity, very long lead time, low appeal to passive consumers
Internet	Local, national, or international	All types and sizes of firms	Low costs, huge potential audience, vast geographic coverage, amount of information conveyed, interactivity	Clutter of ads, viewed as a novelty by some, goals unclear (advertising vs. entertainment and education), no set rate structure
Flyers	Single neighborhood	Local firms	Low costs, market coverage, little waste, flexible	High throwaway rate, poor image

Persuasive impact is the ability of a medium to stimulate consumers. Television often has the highest persuasive impact because it is able to combine audio, video, color, and animation. Magazines also have high persuasive impact. Many newspapers are improving their technology to feature color ads and increase their persuasive impact.

Persuasive impact *is highest for TV.*

Clutter involves the number of ads found in a single program, issue, and so forth, of a medium. It is low when few ads are presented, such as Hallmark placing only scattered commercials on the TV specials for which it is the exclusive sponsor. It is high when there are many ads, such as the large amount of supermarket ads in a newspaper's Wednesday issue. Overall, magazines have the highest clutter. And TV is criticized for allowing too much clutter, particularly for assigning more time per hour to commercials and for letting firms show very brief messages (e.g., 15 seconds or shorter). About one-third of all television ads are 15-second spots.[7]

Clutter *occurs when there are many ads.*

[7]Robert J. Kent, "Competitive Clutter in Network Television Advertising: Current Levels and Advertiser Responses," *Journal of Advertising Research*, Vol. 35 (January–February 1995), pp. 49–57.

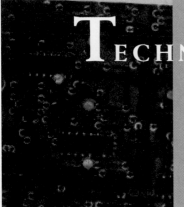

TECHNOLOGY & MARKETING

A New Service for Hotel Guests: Interactive Yellow Pages?

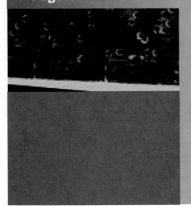

US West Marketing Resources has invested millions of dollars to develop an electronic hotel Yellow Pages service. This service provides hotel guests with a dining guide (including restaurant menus), shopping sources, a directory of local attractions (with onscreen tours), a nightlife directory, and a listing of available hotel services.

Soon, the system will let a guest automatically phone for reservations, print maps, and list directions. In addition, in-room shopping services (including delivery to a guest's hotel room or home) are planned. Currently, 15 to 20 per cent of the guests in hotels equipped with US West's system use it. The average use time is 14 minutes.

US West's new system is quite different from traditional video advertising that has been available for years. The system enables hotel guests to focus on a specific area of interest. It also has the potential to send an unlimited number of ads, versus a 30-minute ad "loop." Lastly, advertisers can monitor usage. According to the advertising coordinator for a San Francisco specialty store, "We know exactly how many people are watching us for how long."

In San Francisco, advertisers pay US West about $9,000 per year to run a 60-second video ad. This is half the cost of a full-page ad in a hotel magazine. Rates for national advertisers are comparable to cable television costs for a comparable audience.

Setting up the system in hotels is costly for US West. The system requires that one or more computer servers (costing $8,500 per server) be connected to a hotel's interactive TV system (one delivering such services as pay-per-view and video checkout). US West also has to pay a commission to SpectraVision or On Command Video for signing up hotels. To encourage hotels to sign up, they can carry the system and advertise on it at no cost.

As the business manager of a four-star restaurant located in downtown San Francisco, what are the pros and cons of advertising on US West's system?

Source: Based on material in Neil Weinberg, "Push 6 for Seafood," *Forbes* (December 5, 1994), p. 270.

Lead time *is needed for placing an ad.*

Lead time is the period required by a medium for placing an ad. It is shortest for newspapers and longest for magazines and phone directories. Popular TV shows may also require a lengthy lead time since the number of ads they can carry is limited. Because a firm must place ads well in advance, a long lead time risks improper themes in a changing environment.

There have been many media innovations in recent years. These include the online computer services such as America Online and other fast-emerging services that let people "surf the Web"; regional editions and special one-sponsor issues ("advertorials") to revitalize magazines; specialized Yellow Pages; televised ads in supermarkets, movie theaters, and aircraft; more radio stations handling ads in stereo; better quality in outdoor signs; full-length televised advertising programs ("infomercials"); and direct-mail ads with CD-ROM diskettes.

Creating Advertisements

Ad creation involves content, scheduling, media placement, and variations.

In creating ads, there are four fundamental decisions:

1. Determine message content and devise ads. Each ad needs a headline or opening to create consumer interest and copy that presents the message. Content decisions also involve the use of color and illustrations, ad size or length, the source, the use of symbolism, and the adaptations needed for foreign markets. The role of these factors depends on a firm's goals and resources. Figure 19-6 shows a full-page color ad for the $325 Parker Duofold pen. The ad does a superior job of product positioning.

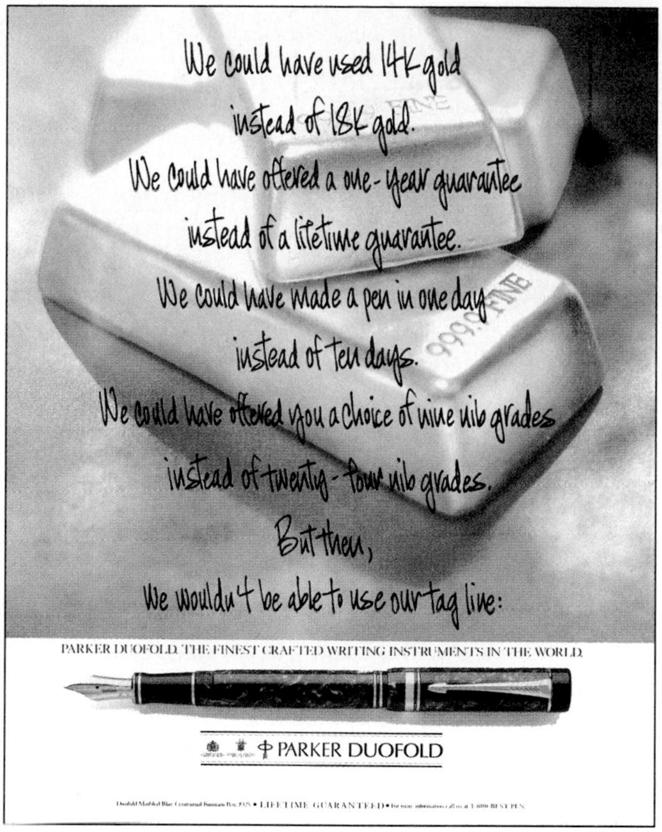

We could have used 14K gold
instead of 18K gold.
We could have offered a one-year guarantee
instead of a lifetime guarantee.
We could have made a pen in one day
instead of ten days.
We could have offered you a choice of nine nib grades
instead of twenty-four nib grades.
But then,
we wouldn't be able to use our tag line:
PARKER DUOFOLD. THE FINEST CRAFTED WRITING INSTRUMENTS IN THE WORLD.
PARKER DUOFOLD
LIFETIME GUARANTEED

FIGURE 19-6
Message Content
Reprinted by permission.

2. Outline a promotion schedule. This should allow for all copy and artwork and be based on the lead time needed for the chosen media.
3. Specify each ad's location in a broadcast program or print medium. As costs have risen, more firms have become concerned about ad placement.
4. Choose how many variations of a basic message to use. This depends on the frequency of presentations and the ad quality. As Figure 19-7 illustrates, due to the consistently high quality of its ads, Sony has been able to run its "There's Nothing Like a Real Trinitron" message for years.

Timing Advertisements

Timing refers to how often an ad is shown and when to advertise during the year.

There are two major decisions about the timing of advertisements: how often a given ad is shown and when to advertise during the year. First, a firm must balance audience awareness and knowledge versus irritation if it places an ad a number of times in a short period. Thus, McDonald's runs its ads repeatedly, but changes them often. Second, a firm must choose whether to advertise throughout the year or in concentrated periods. Distributed ads maintain brand recognition and increase sales in nonpeak periods. They are used by most manufacturers and general-merchandise retailers. Massed ads are concentrated in peak periods to generate short-run consumer enthusiasm; they ignore sales in nonpeak periods. Specialty manufacturers and retailers use this method.

Other timing considerations include when to advertise new products, when to stop advertising existing products, how to coordinate advertising and other promotional tools, when to change basic themes, and how to space messages during the hierarchy-of-effects process.

Considering Cooperative Efforts

In **cooperative advertising**, *costs are shared by multiple parties.*

To stimulate advertising by channel members and/or to hold down its own ad budget, a firm should consider cooperative efforts. With **cooperative advertising**, two or more firms

FIGURE 19-7
Sony's Use of a Long-Time Advertising Message
Reprinted by permission.

share some advertising costs. In a vertical cooperative-advertising agreement, firms at different stages in a distribution channel (such as a manufacturer and a wholesaler) share costs. In a horizontal cooperative-advertising agreement, two or more independent firms at the same stage in a distribution channel share costs (such as retailers in a mall).

Good cooperative agreements state the share of costs paid by each party, the functions and responsibilities of each party, the advertisements to be covered, and the basis for termination. They also benefit each participant.

Each year, about $15 billion in vertical-cooperative advertising support is made available by manufacturers in the United States. Yet, distribution intermediaries actually use only about two-thirds of this amount. The nonuse by so many resellers is due to their perceptions of manufacturer inflexibility involving messages and media, the costs of cooperative advertising to the resellers, restrictive provisions (such as high minimum purchases to be eligible), and the emphasis on the manufacturer's name in ads. To remedy this, more manufacturers are now flexible as to the messages and media they will support, pay a larger share of advertising costs, have eased restrictive provisions, and feature reseller names more prominently in ads.

Evaluating Success or Failure

Advertising's success or failure depends on how well it helps an organization to achieve promotion goals. Creating customer awareness and increasing sales are distinct goals; success or failure in reaching them must be measured differently. In addition, advertising can be quite difficult to isolate as the single factor leading to a certain image or sales level.

Here are various examples dealing with the evaluation of advertising's success or failure:

- The typical U.S. consumer is bombarded with 300 advertising messages each day—about 110,000 per year. According to one major research study, two-thirds of people believe a nationally advertised brand creates the perception that it is of better quality than brands that are not heavily advertised, and in choosing among two unfamiliar brands, two-thirds of people will select the one that is advertised most.[8]

- A survey of consumers in 22 nations found that advertising is favorably regarded, although opinions differ by country: "Individuals in former Communist nations are among the most enthusiastic supporters of advertising, apparently reflecting their current desire to embrace consumer-oriented Western capitalism. Egypt was the only market where respondents were consistently anti-advertising."[9]
- Young adults (those 18 to 34) account for one-third of all Yellow Pages use. They are more apt than older adults to rely on information in display ads and less likely to have a specific company name in mind when consulting the Yellow Pages.[10]
- A study for the Association of National Advertisers indicates that advertising is a reliable way to boost sales but is less consistent in raising market share and profits.[11]
- *Business Marketing* annually honors the best business-to-business ads. It uses criteria like these in picking winners: visual magnetism, the target audience, the message, readability, and the firm's character.

The Scope and Importance of Public Relations

Public relations efforts can have a major impact.

Each firm would like to foster the best possible relations with its publics and to receive favorable publicity about its offerings or the firm itself, such as "State Farm Insurance is considered one of the five best insurance firms by this magazine." Sometimes, as with restaurant or theater reviews, publicity can greatly increase sales or virtually put a firm out of business.

In the United States, over 5,400 firms and 500 trade associations have their own public relations departments, and there are more than 1,800 public relations agencies. Worldwide, the International Public Relations Association has 1,000 members from 60 nations, yet the role of public relations varies greatly by nation: "In many foreign areas, the term *public relations* really means *press relations*. Working with the press abroad is not easy; there may be a language barrier, and many times, government controls the media."[12]

The competition to gain media attention for publicity is intense. After all, in the United States, there are rather few national television networks and only 85 magazines and newspapers with circulations of one million or more. Nonetheless, there are many opportunities for publicity—with 4,900 AM radio stations, 5,100 FM radio stations, 1,500 conventional television stations, 12,000 newspapers, and 11,000 periodicals around the United States. In addition, there are 11,000 cable television systems.[13]

Some firms have poor policies to deal with their publics and the media, and to develop a sustained public relations effort. Table 19-7 shows several public relations-related situations and how a firm could deal with them. Since unfavorable publicity can occur, a firm must be ready to deal with it in the best way possible. Negative publicity can happen to any firm; a successful one will have a plan to handle it. A firm may get the media on its side by being candid and acting promptly; media may be used to help explain complex issues; and by cooperating with reporters, preconceived notions may be dispelled.

Public relations encompasses image-directed ads, selling, and sales promotion—as well as publicity.

The interrelationship of public relations and other promotion forms must be understood. If advertising, personal selling, and sales promotion are image-oriented, public relations is involved. If they are demand-oriented, it is not. Figure 19-8 shows the interface

[8]Michael J. McCarthy, "Mind Probe," *Wall Street Journal* (March 22, 1991), p. B3; and "Advertising Makes the Difference," *Advertising Age* (January 15, 1996), p. 30.

[9]Laurel Wentz, "Major Global Study Finds Consumers Support Ads," *Advertising Age* (October 11, 1993), pp. I-1, I-21.

[10]Jeffrey Casey, "How Do We Get Into This Person's Head?" *Link* (October–November 1995), pp. 37–45.

[11]Gary Levin, "Ads Show Power to Help Sales," *Advertising Age* (December 13, 1993), p. 28.

[12]Fraser P. Seitel, *The Practice of Public Relations*, Sixth Edition (New York: Prentice Hall, 1995), various pages.

[13]*Statistical Abstract of the United States 1995* (Washington, D.C.: U.S. Department of Commerce, 1995), various pages.

Table 19-7

Public Relations-Related Situations and How a Firm Could Respond to Them

SITUATION	POOR RESPONSE	GOOD RESPONSE
Fire breaks out in a company plant	Requests for information by media are ignored.	Company spokesperson explains the fire's causes and the precautions to avoid it and answers questions.
New product introduced	Advertising is used without publicity.	Pre-introduction news releases, product samples, and testimonials are used.
News story about product defects	Media requests for information are ignored, blanket denials are issued, and there is hostility to reporters.	Company spokesperson says tests are being done, describes the procedure for handling defects, and takes questions.
Competitor introduces new product	A demand-oriented advertising campaign is stepped up.	Extensive news releases, statistics, and spokespeople are made available to media to present firm's competitive features.
High profits reported	Profits are justified and positive effects on the economy are cited.	Profits are explained, comparative data are provided, and profit uses are noted: research and community development.
Overall view of public relations	There is an infrequent need for public relations; crisis fighting is used when bad reports are circulated.	There is an ongoing need for public relations, strong planning, and plans to counter bad reports.

between public relations and other promotion tools. Figures 19-9 and 19-10 show two effective institutional ads.

For organizations of all sizes and types,

> Public relations is a necessary part of the marketing mix. This is as true for the two-person SOHO (small office/home office) operation as it is for the multinational corporation. Lack of a big budget for PR is no excuse: Public relations has been called the last free thing in America, and that's very nearly true. It's possible to run a whole PR campaign with a pen, a fax ma-

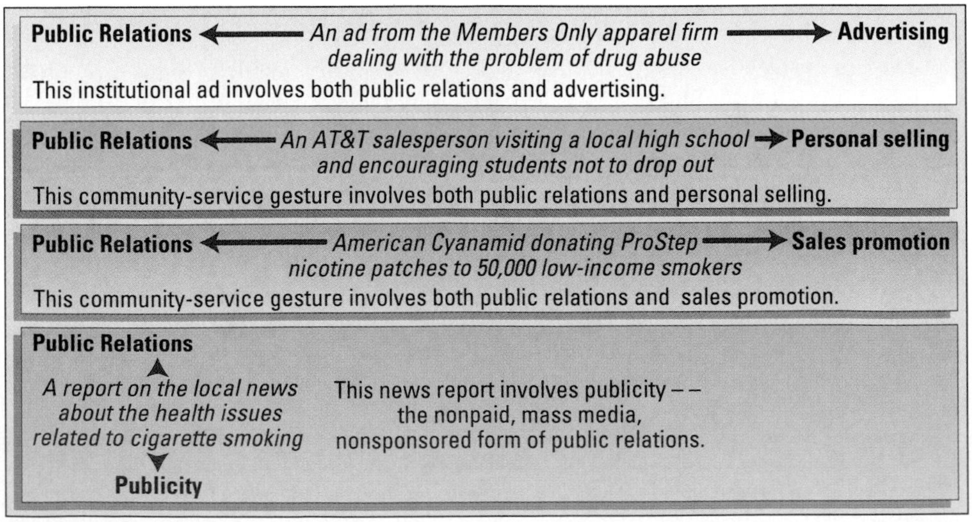

Public Relations
An ad from the Members Only apparel firm dealing with the problem of drug abuse
Advertising
This institutional ad involves both public relations and advertising.
Public Relations
An AT&T salesperson visiting a local high school and encouraging students not to drop out
Personal selling
This community-service gesture involves both public relations and personal selling.
Public Relations
American Cyanamid donating ProStep nicotine patches to 50,000 low-income smokers
Sales promotion
This community-service gesture involves both public relations and sales promotion.
Public Relations
A report on the local news about the health issues related to cigarette smoking
Publicity
This news report involves publicity -- the nonpaid, mass media, nonsponsored form of public relations.

FIGURE 19-8
The Relationship Between Public Relations and the Other Elements of the Promotion Mix

FIGURE 19-9
A Socially Responsible Public Relations Campaign
Reprinted by permission.

chine, and a little brainpower. A lot of PR has to do with timing. The real name of the game in public relations is contacts—the editors, reporters, and other media people you need to get your story out.[14]

The Characteristics of Public Relations

Public relations engenders good feelings; publicity has no time costs, a large audience, high credibility, and attentiveness.

Public relations offers several benefits. Since it is image-oriented, good feelings toward a firm by its external publics can be fostered. In addition, employee morale (pride) is enhanced if the firm is community and civic minded.

When publicity is involved, there are no costs for message time or space. A prime-time television ad may cost $300,000 to $750,000 or more per minute of media time; a five-minute report on a network newscast does not cost anything for media time. Yet, there are costs for news releases, a public relations department, and so on. As with advertising, publicity reaches a mass audience. In a short time, new products or company policies are well known.

Message believability is higher with publicity because stories appear in independent media. A newspaper's movie review is more credible than an ad in the same paper—the reader links independence with objectivity. Similarly, people may pay more attention to news than to ads. *Women's Wear Daily* has both fashion reports and ads; people read the stories, but flip through ads. There are a dozen or more ads in a half-hour TV show and hundreds of them in a typical magazine; feature stories are fewer in number and stand out more.

Public relations may be downplayed by some firms; publicity cannot be controlled or timed accurately by a company.

Public relations also has limitations, compared to other promotion forms. Some firms question the value of image-oriented communications and are disinterested in activities not directly tied to sales and profits. They may give the poor responses that were indicated in Table 19-7.

[14]Gene Koprowski, "Extra: Smart Companies Use Public Relations Tactics to Get Good Ink," *Marketing Tools* (October 1995), p. 48.

FIGURE 19-10
A Community-Oriented Public Relations Campaign
Reprinted by permission.

With publicity, a firm has less control over messages and their timing, placement, and coverage by the media. It may issue detailed press releases and find only parts cited in the media, and media may be more critical than a firm would like. Media tend to find disasters, scandals, and product recalls more newsworthy than press releases. This shows how intense bad publicity can be:

> When Rich Koch, a computer salesperson from Florida bought a new $13,000 Dodge Neon, it quickly developed glitches. The driver's door latch sometimes refused to release, the plastic liners inside both fenders rattled, and sealant oozed from around the rear window. So Koch posted an electronic memo on Prodigy detailing his car's woes for the online service's 1.2 million subscribers. "I'd never buy another," he wrote in disgust. Unfortunately for Chrysler, Koch wasn't the only one taking aim at its quality problems. In its annual survey of auto quality, J.D. Power & Associates ranked Chrysler cars below industry averages. And *Consumer Reports* warned readers to be wary of the Dodge Intrepid, Jeep Cherokee pickup, and Dodge Ram pickup—all of which had above-average chances of landing in the repair shop.[15]

A firm may want publicity during certain periods, such as when a new product is introduced or a new store opened, but the media may not provide coverage until much later. Similarly, the media determine a story's placement; it may follow a crime or sports report. Finally, the media choose whether to cover a story at all and the amount of coverage for it. A firm-sponsored jobs program might go unreported or get three-sentence coverage in a local paper.

Publicity may be hard to plan in advance because newsworthy events occur quickly and unexpectedly. Thus, short-run and long-run public relations plans should differ in ap-

[15]David Woodruff, "An Embarrassment of Glitches Galvanizes Chrysler," *Business Week* (April 17, 1995), p. 76.

proach. Publicity must complement advertising and not be a substitute. The assets of each (credibility and low costs for publicity, control and coverage for ads) are needed for a good communications program.

To optimize their public relations efforts, at many companies:

- Public relations personnel have regular access to senior executives.
- The publicity value of annual reports is recognized.
- Public relations messages are professionally prepared (with the same care as used in writing ad copy) and continuously given to media.
- Internal personnel and media personnel interaction is fostered.
- Public-service events are planned to obtain maximum media coverage.
- Part of the promotion budget goes to publicity-generating tasks.
- There is a better understanding of the kinds of stories the media are apt to cover and how to present stories to the media.

Developing a Public Relations Plan

Developing a public relations plan is much like devising an advertising plan. It involves the steps shown in Figure 19-11 and described next.

Setting Objectives

Public relations goals are image-oriented (firm and/or industry). The choice guides the entire public relations plan.

These are some goals that could be set:

- To gain placement for news releases and company spokespersons with a variety of media.
- To have the media report on the accomplishments of the company.
- To have the company's position presented when controversy arises.
- To coordinate publicity with advertising.
- To gain more media coverage than competitors.
- To sustain favorable publicity as long as possible.
- To reach out to community groups.
- To have publics view the firm and its industry favorably.

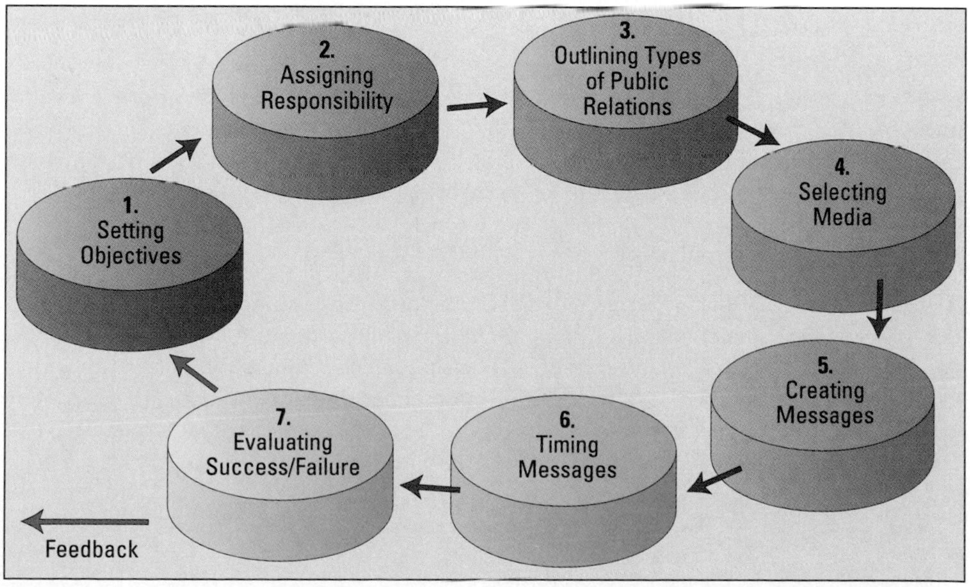

FIGURE 19-11
Developing a Public Relations Plan

Ethics IN TODAY'S SOCIETY

What Would Firms Do If They Had to Prove EVERY Promotion Claim?

Currently, advertising "puffery" does not have any legal status because the Federal Trade Commission considers most puffery statements, such as "this carpet will wear like iron" or "this car is the ultimate driving machine," to be so vague that they will not be taken literally by consumers. According to a law firm specializing in advertising-related issues, with puffery cases, the seller often has prevailed as courts have ruled it unreasonable to conclude that people relied on puffery as the basis for purchasing a product.

However, some consumer advocates have suggested that the U.S. Uniform Commercial Code be amended so that puffery in advertising would be considered an "express warranty" or a statement that consumers could depend on in buying a product. The possible revisions would affect legal interpretation in 49 states (all but Louisiana), the District of Columbia, and Puerto Rico.

If the puffery revisions are enacted, consumers who feel a product does not fulfill the statements made about it could sue the offending firm. The revisions would also force an advertiser to either substantiate its claim or prove that no reasonable person would rely on the puffery as a basis for buying a product.

Many advertisers have been taking a "wait and see" approach to the proposed legal changes. For example, BMW of North America's legal department reviewed the proposed changes, but did not offer a comment to law makers. According to a BMW spokesperson, "While we don't agree with the commissioners, if it's enacted, we will find a way to abide by it." The chairperson of the committee drafting the revisions also does not believe that revisions would lead to a large number of class-action legal suits.

As a public relations consultant for BMW, what would you recommend with regard to the firm's "the ultimate driving machine" tag line if the proposed legal changes about puffery go into effect?

Sources: Based on material in Fara Warner, "'Puffing' Marketers Would Bear Burden of Proof If Code Is Revised," *Wall Street Journal* (May 17, 1995), p. B3; and Chuck Ross, "Marketers Fend Off Shift in Rules for Ad Puffery," *Advertising Age* (February 19, 1996), p. 41.

While setting goals, this truism should be kept in mind: "PR involves both *performance* and *recognition*. It is possible to boast excellent performance without being properly recognized, but it is not possible to earn recognition that is not based on solid performance. Woe to the firm that tries to get the R (recognition) without the P (performance)."[16]

Assigning Responsibility

A firm can use an in-house department, hire an outside ad agency, or hire a specialist.

A firm has three options in assigning public relations responsibility: it may use its existing marketing personnel, an in-house public relations department, or an in-house publicity department; it may have an outside advertising agency handle public relations; or it may hire a specialized public relations firm. Internal personnel or an in-house department ensure more control and secrecy. An outside firm often has better contacts and expertise. Each approach is popular, and they may be combined.[17]

[16]Nat B. Read, "Sears PR Debacle Shows How Not to Handle a Crisis," *Wall Street Journal* (January 11, 1993), p. A16.

[17]See Gene Koprowski, "Hiring an Agency," *Marketing Tools* (October 1995), pp. 48–49.

Procter & Gamble has an in-house publicity department and several outside public relations agencies. In contrast, some smaller firms rely on the services of specialists, which may charge retainer fees of $25,000 to $50,000 per year. Computer software, such as PRpower, can also let smaller firms easily set up media mailing lists.

Outlining the Types of Public Relations to Be Used

In this step, a firm first chooses the mix of institutional advertising, image-oriented personal selling, image-oriented sales promotion, and publicity to incorporate into an overall promotion plan. Next, public relations efforts must be coordinated with the demand-oriented promotion activities of the firm.

Finally, the general **publicity types** must be understood and envisioned. Each can play a role in an integrated public relations program:

Publicity types *include news, features, releases, background material, and emergency information.*

- *News publicity* deals with international, national, regional, or local events. Planned releases can be prepared and regularly given out by a firm.
- *Business feature articles* are detailed stories about a company or its offerings that are given to business media.
- *Service feature articles* are lighter stories focusing on personal care, household items, and similar topics that are sent to newspapers, cable TV stations, and magazines.
- *Finance releases* are stories aimed at the business sections of newspapers, TV news shows, and magazines.
- *Product releases* deal with new products and product improvements; they aim at all media forms.
- *Pictorial releases* are illustrations or pictures sent to the media.
- *Video news releases* are videotaped segments supplied to the media.
- *Background editorial material* is extra information given to media writers and editors; it enhances standard releases and provides filler for stories (like the biography of the chief executive of a company).
- *Emergency publicity* consists of special spontaneous news releases keyed to unexpected events.[18]

Selecting the Media for Public Relations Efforts to Appear

For institutional ads, personal selling, and sales promotion, traditional nonpersonal and/or personal media would be used. For publicity, a firm would typically focus on newspapers, television, magazines, radio, and business publications. Due to the infrequent nature of many magazines and some business publications, publicity-seeking efforts may be aimed at daily or weekly media.

Public relations executives rank newspapers and business publications the highest. The *Wall Street Journal, New York Times*, and *USA Today* are preferred newspapers. *Business Week, Fortune*, and *Forbes* are preferred business publications. *Time, Newsweek*, and *U.S. News & World Report* are preferred general news magazines.

Creating Messages

The creation of public relations messages entails the same factors as other promotion forms—content, variations, and a production schedule. Messages can be conveyed in one or a combination of forms, such as news conferences, media releases, phone calls or personal contacts, media kits (a combination of materials on a story), special events (Macy's Thanksgiving Parade), or videos.

Because it is essential that the media find a firm's publicity messages to be useful, these points need to be kept in mind:

[18] H. Frazier Moore, *Public Relations: Principles, Cases, and Problems*, Eighth Edition (Homewood, Ill.: Richard D. Irwin, 1981), pp. 163–167.

1. Messages should be newsworthy.
2. Reporter deadlines should be respected.
3. Appropriate company representatives should be accessible to reporters.
4. "Mind-fogging" jargon should be avoided.
5. The phrase "no comment" should not be used.
6. Attribution rules (making the source and the content of a story "on" or "off" the record) should be set in advance.
7. A reporter should not be asked to kill a story.
8. Releases should be both easy to read, view, or hear and to use.
9. There should be no hesitancy to volunteer a "bad" story (it will probably get out anyway).
10. Attention should be paid to the needs of each type of medium.[19]

Timing Messages

Public relations efforts should precede new-product introductions and generate excitement for them. For emergencies, media releases and spokespeople should be immediately available. For ongoing public relations, messages should be properly spaced through the year. As already noted, a firm may find it hard to anticipate media coverage for both unexpected and planned publicity because the media control timing.

Evaluating Success or Failure

There are several straightforward ways to rate a public relations campaign's success or failure. With institutional ads, image-oriented personal selling, and image-oriented sales promotion, a firm can conduct simple surveys to see how well these communications are received and their impact on its image. With publicity, a firm can count the stories about it, analyze coverage length and placement, review desired with actual timing of stories, evaluate audience reactions, and/or compute the cost of comparable advertising.

Here are some measures of public relations' success:

- California's National Advancement Corporation, a computer-repair training service with $2 million in annual sales, spent $20,000 to produce a video news release (VNR). The VNR showed an undercover "sting" operation whereby six computer repair firms "scammed" a customer. The VNR was so effective that network TV affiliates in six of the largest twenty markets ran it.[20]
- Wal-Mart now tracks the *quality*, as well as the quantity of media coverage. It classifies items as news stories, letters to the editor, editorials, or opinion articles—for each market area.[21]
- According to various surveys, many chief executive officers feel effective public relations contributes to profits.[22]

[19]Christel K. Beard and H. J. Dalton, Jr., "The Power of Positive Press," *Sales & Marketing Management* (January 1991), pp. 37–43. See also Daniel P. Dern, "News That's Fit to Print," *Marketing Tools* (October 1995), pp. 52–53.

[20]Robina A. Gangemi, "Your Company: On TV," *Inc.* (July 1995), p. 91.

[21]Don E. Shinkle, "PR Measurement Is the Answer," *Public Relations Quarterly*, Vol. 39 (Fall 1994), pp. 16–17.

[22]Bristol Voss, "Measuring the Effectiveness of Advertising and PR," *Sales & Marketing Management* (October 1992), p. 123; Catherine B. Campbell, "Does Public Relations Affect the Bottom Line?" *Public Relations Journal*, Vol. 49 (October 1993), pp. 14–17; and Koprowski, "Extra: Smart Companies Use Public Relations Tactics to Get Good Ink," pp. 46–53.

MARKETING IN A CHANGING WORLD

Dos and Don'ts for Using the Web[23]

Since October 1994, HotWired (http://www.hotwired.com) has operated a Web site—complete with advertising—on the Internet. These are some of the lessons it has learned and wants to pass along:

- *The most important decision.* A company must be clear about why it wants to be on the Web. Is the goal brand building, publicity, selling products, giving information, customer service, or order tracking?
- *The only valid measure is response.* An actual customer has much more value than an anonymous impression.
- *Bandwidth is still limited.* Because so many people are joining the Web, the average access speed is slowing. Thus, a company should keep its image, video, and text files small—and not waste customers' time.
- *Bigger is not always better.* A 1,000-page Web site may not be better than a one-page site. The best Web sites are quick, personalized, and user-friendly.
- *Static sites are toxic.* The easiest way to lose traffic is to set up a site and not change its look often enough.
- *It's more than advertising.* "Marketing on the Web is about providing information and entertainment, and about fostering community. Many companies have also discovered that Web-based customer service functions are improving customer relations and saving money."
- *If it's not part of your media mix, you lose.* To succeed, a company must commit itself to the Web as an integral part of its media mix.
- *Don't ignore demographics or life-styles.* "All sites are not equal any more than all magazines or TV shows are equal."
- *No "Under Construction" signs.* "Vaporware is not appreciated. Don't open your site until it's ready."
- *No shovelware.* "TV isn't just radio with pictures, and the Net isn't just a brochure with buttons. It's a whole new medium, with a whole new dynamic."

SUMMARY

1. *To examine the scope, importance, and characteristics of advertising* Advertising is paid, nonpersonal communication sent through various media by identified sponsors. U.S. ad spending is $175 billion annually and non-U.S. spending exceeds $200 billion per year via such media as newspapers, TV, direct mail, Yellow Pages, radio, magazines, business publications, outdoor, and farm publications. In many industries, advertising is under 2.0 per cent of sales.

It is most apt with standardized products and when features are easy to communicate, the market is large, prices are low, resellers are used in distribution, and/or products are new. In general, behavior is easier to change than attitudes; one ad can have an impact; ads do well with little-known products; and effectiveness rises during extended campaigns.

Among advertising's advantages are its appeal to a geographically dispersed audience, low per-customer costs, the availability of a broad variety of media, the firm's control over all aspects of a message, the surrounding editorial content, and how it complements personal selling. Disadvantages include message inflexibility, some viewers or readers not in the target audience, high media costs, limited information provided, difficulty in getting audience feedback, and low audience involvement.

2. *To study the elements in an advertising plan* An advertising plan has nine steps: setting goals—demand and image types; assigning duties—internal and/or external; setting a budget; developing themes—good/service, consumer, and institutional; selecting media—based on costs, reach, waste, narrowcasting, frequency, message permanence, persuasive impact, clutter, lead time, and media innovations; creating ads—including content, placement, and variations; timing ads; considering cooperative efforts—both vertical and horizontal; and evaluating success or failure.

[23]The material in this section is based on HotWired, "How *Not* to Advertise on the Web," *Advertising Age* (December 4, 1995), p. 17.

3. *To examine the scope, importance, and characteristics of public relations* Public relations includes any communication that fosters a favorable image among a firm's various publics. It is more image- than sales-oriented; embodies image-oriented ads, personal selling, and sales promotion; and seeks favorable publicity—the nonpersonal communication sent via various media but not paid for by identified sponsors. There are thousands of companies with their own public relations departments and many specialized public relations firms. Companies try to get positive publicity and to avoid negative publicity. Competition is intense for placing publicity releases. Some firms have ineffective policies to deal with independent media or develop a sustained publicity campaign.

Among its advantages are the image orientation, the positive effects on employee morale, and—for publicity—the lack of costs for message time, the high credibility, and audience attentiveness. The disadvantages of public relations—compared with other promotion forms—include the lack of interest by some firms in image-oriented communications and the lesser control of publicity placements by the firm, the media interest in negative events, and the difficulty of planning publicity in advance.

4. *To study the elements in a public relations plan* A public relations plan has seven steps: setting goals—company and/or industry; assigning duties—internally and/or externally; outlining types of public relations—the mix of image-oriented promotion forms and the categories of publicity (news publicity, business and service feature articles, finance releases, product and pictorial releases, video news releases, background editorial releases, and emergency publicity); choosing media; creating messages; timing messages; and weighing success or failure.

KEY TERMS

advertising agency (p. 532)
advertising themes (p. 533)
advertising media costs (p. 535)
reach (p. 535)
waste (p. 535)
narrowcasting (p. 536)
frequency (p. 536)
message permanence (p. 536)
persuasive impact (p. 537)
clutter (p. 537)
lead time (p. 538)
cooperative advertising (p. 539)
publicity types (p. 547)

Review Questions

1. Explain the statement "Advertising is paid for, publicity is prayed for."
2. Under what circumstances is advertising most likely to be used?
3. List five objectives of advertising and give an example of how each may be accomplished.
4. A small firm has an overall annual budget of $50,000 for advertising. What specific decisions must it make in allocating the budget?
5. Differentiate among these advertising concepts: reach, narrowcasting, waste, clutter, and frequency.
6. What are the pros and cons of cooperative advertising?
7. Describe the role of public relations in many foreign countries.
8. What is a video news release?
9. According to public relations executives, which are the two most preferred media for receiving publicity?
10. State three ways for a firm to evaluate the success or failure of its public relations efforts.

Discussion Questions

1. Devise an advertising plan for generating primary demand for American-made TVs.
2. A hotel chain knows a full-page ad in a general-interest magazine would cost $85,000; the magazine's total audience is 2.5 million—800,000 of whom are part of the chain's target market. A full-page ad in a travel magazine would cost $25,000; its total audience is 375,000—300,000 of whom are part of the chain's target market. Which magazine should be selected? Why?
3. Present and evaluate current examples of companies using institutional advertising, image-oriented personal selling, image-oriented sales promotion, and publicity.
4. Why do you think so many firms handle public relations-related situations poorly?
5. How would you obtain publicity for a small company that has developed a "talking" computer—one that gives instructions on how to set up the computer, how to use various software, and how to diagnose and correct computer errors.

CASE 1

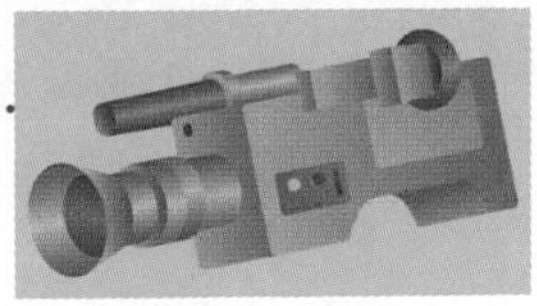

Acuvue: Developing an Advertising Campaign for Disposable Contact Lenses[*]

Vistakon, a division of Johnson & Johnson Vision products, is the largest U.S. contact lens company, with a 25 per cent market share. It produces and markets lenses under the Acuvue brand name. Major competitors are Bausch & Lomb and Ciba Vision; both firms market similar disposable contact lenses.

In 1988, Acuvue was introduced by Vistakon as the nation's first disposable lenses. The lenses were approved to be worn continuously for one week at a time by the Food and Drug Administration; after the week, the lenses were to be discarded. The major attraction of Acuvue lenses was that they required less cleaning and care than traditional soft lenses, which generally last for about a year. Yet, while a regular pair of soft contact lenses cost about $350 to buy (including costs of doctor's visits), a pair of Acuvue contacts cost about $500 a year (also including doctor's visits). Within three years of Acuvue's introduction, worldwide sales exceeded $225 million.

Lintas New York, Vistakon's advertising agency, conducted market research studies to determine consumer opinions about Acuvue's benefits. Focus group participants repeatedly told the agency that Acuvue's primary benefit over traditional contact lenses was that Acuvue required only minimal daily cleaning. A secondary benefit was that Acuvue lens wearers did not have to purchase or apply disinfecting solutions. The agency also determined that, of the 1.1 million known contact lens users, college-educated adults aged 18–34, with incomes of $30,000 or more, were Acuvue's most appropriate target market.

Acuvue's initial ads required elaborate preparation to accurately show the lenses, as well as to set the tone for a major new medical product. The person speaking the voice-over was carefully chosen, as was the background music. Initial ads used the theme, "The best solution is no solution." In addition, Acuvue's ad campaign offered current contact lens wearers free trial lenses—without any further obligation. Johnson & Johnson felt it needed this type of campaign due to the product's expense and the high risk felt by many people.

Despite strong Acuvue sales growth, Vistakon does not feel the market is saturated. Unlike the market for traditional contact lenses, which has been flat for a decade, disposable and frequent-replacement-lens sales have been growing. Among adults under age 35, one-quarter wear prescription eyeglasses and 15 per cent wear contacts. Among those 35 to 54 years old, bifocals (14 per cent usage) are more common than contacts (12 per cent); and among those 55 and older, only 3 per cent wear contact lenses. Some analysts feel younger people may continue to wear contacts when they get older or switch to contacts from bifocals when their need for vision correction goes beyond reading.

Vistakon is aware of substantial foreign growth opportunities. Fifteen per cent of the U.S. population requiring corrective lenses wears contacts; in foreign markets, under 5 per cent of corrective lens users choose contacts. Vistakon is well-positioned for foreign growth. Johnson & Johnson's affiliate companies in over 50 countries are able to distribute Acuvue. And Acuvue has been marketed in such nations as Japan (the second-largest contact lens market in the world, after Denmark) and in Latin America, another major market.

Vistakon has also introduced Surevue, which is similar to Acuvue, but designed to be discarded after two weeks. Although Surevue costs more per lens, it costs less in the long run due to its durability.

QUESTIONS

1. Outline specific demand- and image-oriented advertising objectives for Acuvue that were appropriate at the time of its market introduction.
2. Describe how the demographic data in this case could be used to select advertising media.
3. Develop a cooperative advertising strategy for Acuvue.
4. How would you advertise Surevue without adversely affecting Acuvue?

VIDEO QUESTIONS ON ACUVUE

1. Discuss the use of focus groups in developing the theme for Acuvue's advertising.
2. Describe the types of decisions that had to be made in the process of creating Acuvue's first advertisement.

[*]The data in this case are drawn from Diane Crispell, "Contact Lenses or Glasses?" *American Demographics* (June 1995), pp. 38–39; "How Manufacturing Can Make Low-Tech Products High-Tech," *Harvard Business Review*, Vol. 73 (September–October 1995), p. 98; Jennifer Reingold, "Above the Neck," *Financial World* (January 18, 1994), pp. 30–32; and Joseph Weber, "How J&J's Foresight Made Contact Lenses Pay," *Business Week* (May 4, 1992), p. 132.

CASE 2

Intuit and Intel: Two Different Reactions to Negative Publicity[†]

When a California sculptor found a serious error in MacIn-Tax, the version of TurboTax software for Apple Macintosh users, he complained to Intuit (the software's developer). After the firm brushed off the complaint, the sculptor took his story to the *San Francisco Chronicle*.

Right after a newspaper story appeared, Scott D. Cook, Intuit's chairman, admitted the firm's tax software had a number of errors that could produce inaccurate calculations. And Intuit offered to replace the diskettes of all 1.7 million MacIn-Tax customers, even though the calculation errors affected less than 1 per cent of them. Those consumers desiring to quickly correct their software were given the opportunity to download the corrected version from commercial online services. Along with the replacement software, Cook sent an apology letter to registered users. In addition, Intuit complied with consumer requests for refunds.

According to experts, errors in tax packages are inevitable due to the short time a firm has to adapt its software to the latest changes in the tax code. In total, only 75,000 of Intuit's 1.4 million registered users requested the new diskette, and about 3,000 consumers downloaded the corrected program from online services.

Intuit's handling of its problem was in sharp contrast to Intel's reaction to the flawed Pentium chip, which generated division errors in complex mathematical calculations. Although the flaw was discovered in November 1994, only after weeks of pressure from final and intermediate customers (including IBM and Gateway 2000), did Intel offer to replace the flawed chips. At first, Intel asked customers to prove they were affected by the flaw. The firm also took the position that errors would occur in only one of 9 billion calculations. Furthermore, Intel knowingly sent defective chips to customers prior to correcting the problem, instead of immediately stopping production.

Because of its unpopular approach, Intel was berated in an almost endless stream of negative TV, newspaper, and Internet reports. Then, on December 12, 1994, IBM announced it was temporarily stopping the sale of Pentium-based computers (based on IBM's estimate that errors could occur as frequently as once every 24 days for heavy users). IBM also pledged to replace defective Pentium chips free of charge. Soon thereafter, other manufacturers of PCs agreed to "no questions asked" free replacements.

Eventually, Intel capitulated. As Andrew Grove, Intel's chief executive officer said then, "We got caught between our mindset, which is a fact-based, analysis-based engineer's mindset, and the customers' mindset, which is not so much emotional but accustomed to making their own choice. I think the kernel of the issue we missed was that we presumed to tell somebody what they should or shouldn't worry about, or should or shouldn't do."

Although Intel will not disclose actual numbers, analysts estimate the total Pentium chip return rate was less than 10 per cent, compared with initial estimates of about 25 per cent. Market analysts estimated that half of corporate users and 10 per cent of final consumers would ask for replacement chips. However, the actual replacement rate was 25 per cent for corporate users and between 1 and 3 per cent for final consumers.

Some marketing experts say the high initial customer outcry, followed by such a low return rate, was a sign that people were more concerned with Intel's attitude than with the actual defect.

QUESTIONS

1. Develop appropriate public relations objectives for both Intuit and Intel in handling their product recalls.
2. Why do you think that Intuit acted so much more quickly than Intel to recall its defective product?
3. Do you think the barrage of media criticism that Intel faced was "fair"? Explain your answer.
4. How can Intel ensure that a similar situation (in terms of negative publicity) does not happen again?

[†]The data in this case are drawn from Jim Carlton and Stephen Kreider Yoder, "Humble Pie: Intel to Replace Its Pentium Chips," *Wall Street Journal* (December 21, 1994), pp. B1, B6; Dean Foust, "Good Instincts and Intuit," *Business Week* (March 27, 1995), p. 46; and G. Christian Hill, "Despite Furor, Most Keep Their Pentium Chips," *Wall Street Journal* (April 13, 1995), pp. B1–B2.

CHAPTER 20

Personal Selling and Sales Promotion

Chapter Objectives

1. To examine the scope, importance, and characteristics of personal selling
2. To study the elements in a personal selling plan
3. To examine the scope, importance, and characteristics of sales promotion
4. To study the elements in a sales promotion plan

Timothy C. Gercke, who lectures on behalf of the National Automobile Dealers Association, is an avatar of an industrywide effort to turn salespeople into "sales professionals" and buff the business' greasy image. The auto companies have inaugurated numerous training programs because they believe that as quality gaps narrow, the salesperson is the key to keeping customers loyal in a market jammed with competitors selling what Gercke, with typical sweep, refers to as "this thing called a car."

NADA CERTIFIED

SOCIETY OF AUTOMOTIVE SALES PROFESSIONALS

Reprinted by permission.

The training program sponsored by the National Automobile Dealers Association consists of an eight-hour class and twelve hours of home study. After passing a multiple-choice exam, working for six months at a dealership, and completing product training for the vehicles they sell, salespeople become certified as members of the Society of Automobile Sales Professionals.

The program suggests some dos and don'ts for car salespeople:

- Do tell the truth.
- Do greet customers with a handshake, eye contact, and a genuine smile, not exaggerated.
- Do carefully check your appearance in a full-length mirror before leaving for work.
- Do promise to find the answer to a customer's question if you do not know it. You should never fake an answer.
- Do answer questions posed by a customer's children.
- Don't swear, or use expressions such as "you know" or "yeah."
- Don't treat men and women differently.
- Don't refer to women as "babe," "honey," or "sweetheart."
- Don't use high-pressure tactics.
- Don't display cartoons that could be considered as offensive.

Although the ideals of the National Automobile Dealers Association are laudatory, it recognizes the difficulties in accomplishing its goals. Among the major problems are the continued use of commissions and the difficult environment facing many salespeople.

With few exceptions, auto dealers pay their salespeople on the basis of the gross profit of each transaction, with most salespeople receiving between 20 and 25 per cent of the dealer's gross profit. Thus, salespeople have an incentive to overcharge an unknowing customer, offer a customer lower value for his or her trade-in, and even disregard a dealer's advertised price when speaking with an unsuspecting customer.

On the other hand, not all of the gamesmanship comes from the salespeople. Auto salespeople are also confronted with customers who overestimate the condition of their trade-in (some trade-ins that customers say have never been in an accident have more dimples than a golf ball) and lie about the best deal they've been offered elsewhere. And after completing reams of paperwork, a salesperson could also find that a customer's credit rating is much poorer than stated by that person. One salesperson completing the training program told of having 17 credit rejections in a row. These experiences can make a salesperson quite cynical.

So far, the association has signed up only 350 of its 19,400 members to attend the program. The fee for the program is $1,295 per dealership and an additional $295 per attendee.[1]

Next, we will study the personal selling and sales promotion aspects of promotion and see how these tools (including sales training) can be used effectively.

Overview

Personal selling is one-on-one with buyers. Sales promotion includes paid supplemental efforts.

This chapter looks at the two other major promotion forms: personal selling and sales promotion. As defined in Chapter 18, personal selling involves oral communication with one or more prospective buyers by paid representatives for the purpose of making sales. It re-

[1]James Bennet, "A Charm School for Car Salesmen," *New York Times* (March 29, 1995), pp. D1, D8.

lies on personal contact, unlike advertising and the publicity aspect of public relations. Its goals are similar to other promotion forms: informing, persuading, and/or reminding.

Sales promotion involves paid marketing communication activities (other than advertising, publicity, or personal selling) that stimulate consumers and dealers. Among the kinds of promotion classed as sales promotion are coupons, trade shows, contests and sweepstakes, and point-of-purchase displays.

The scope and importance, characteristics, and planning considerations for both personal selling and sales promotion are examined in Chapter 20.

The Scope and Importance of Personal Selling

In the United States, 15 million people work in the sales positions defined by the Department of Labor; millions more in other nations are also employed in sales jobs. Professional salespeople generate new customer accounts, ascertain needs, interact with consumers, emphasize knowledge and persuasion, and offer substantial service. They include stockbrokers, insurance agents, manufacturer sales representatives, and real-estate brokers. Top ones can earn over $100,000 per year. Clerical salespeople answer simple queries, retrieve stock from inventory, recommend the best brand in a product category, and complete transactions by receiving payments and packing products. They include retail, wholesale, and manufacturer sales clerks.

From a marketing perspective, personal selling really goes far beyond the people in identified sales positions because every contact between a company representative and a customer entails some personal interaction. Lawyers, plumbers, hairdressers, and cashiers are not defined as salespeople. Yet, each undertakes a lot of customer contact. PPG and Tupperware are two of the many firms that know the value of customer contact. See Figures 20-1 and 20-2.

Selling is stressed when orders are large, consumers are concentrated, items are expensive, and service is required.

In various situations, a strong personal-selling emphasis may be needed. Large-volume customers require special attention. Geographically concentrated consumers may be more efficiently served by a sales force than via ads in mass media. Custom-made, expensive, and complex goods or services require in-depth consumer information, demonstrations, and follow-up calls. Tangential sales services—like gift wrapping and delivery—may be requested. If ads are not informative enough, questions can be resolved only by personal selling. New products may need personal selling to gain reseller acceptance. Foreign-market entry may be best handled by personal contacts with prospective resellers and/or consumers. Finally, many organizational customers expect a lot of personal contact. Generally, a decision to stress personal selling depends on such factors as costs, audience size and needs, and a desire for flexibility.

Selling costs are often greater than advertising costs. Auto parts firms, office and equipment firms, and appliance makers all spend far more on selling than on ads. Fuller

FIGURE 20-1
The Value of Customer Contact with Organizational Consumers
PPG places a high value on salesperson interactions with the firm's business accounts. Shown is a PPG account representative (right) in discussion with a "team advisor" from Cross Pointe Paper (a PPG customer). PPG's SansInk chemical de-inking system makes it possible for Cross Pointe Paper to remove the laser print from paper and recycle it into fresh sheets.
Reprinted by permission.

FIGURE 20-2
How Tupperware Uses Personal Selling to Reach Final Consumers
Through parties and demonstrations, in and outside the home, Tupperware salespeople encourage consumers to learn about products, converse among themselves, and make purchases.
Reprinted by permission of Tupperware Home Parties.

Brush sales commissions range up to 50 per cent of sales. The average cost of a single business-to-business field sales call is several hundred dollars; and it may take several visits to make a sale.[2]

High selling costs have led to a concern for efficiency. In **telemarketing**, *phone calls initiate sales or set up sales appointments.*

A number of strategies have been devised to keep selling costs down and improve the efficiency of the sales force, as these examples show:

- Many firms are more effectively routing salespeople to minimize travel time and expenses. Some firms are bypassing smaller customers in their personal selling efforts and specifying minimum order sizes for personalized service. This means opportunities for sellers willing to serve small accounts.
- With **telemarketing**, telephone communications are used to sell or solicit business or to set up an appointment for a salesperson to sell or solicit business. By using it, salespeople can talk to several consumers per hour, centralize operations and lower expenses, screen prospects, process orders and arrange shipments, provide customer service, assist the field sales staff, speed communications, and increase repeat business. A lot of companies rely on telephone personnel to contact customers; outside sales personnel (who actually call on customers) are then more involved with customer service and technical assistance. A broad range of both small and large firms use some form of telemarketing.
- Computerization is improving sales efficiency by providing salespeople with detailed—and speedy—data, making ordering easier, coordinating orders by various salespeople, and identifying the best prospects and their desires (such as preferred brands)—based on prior purchases. About 3.5 million U.S. salespeople now have notebook PCs: "Anything that allows reps to squeeze a couple more hours out of their day has great benefits."[3] Figure 20-3 illustrates the value of computerization in sales.
- Many firms now view computerized customer data bases as among their most valuable sales resources. These data bases enable the firms to focus their efforts better,

[2]Allison Lucas, "Portrait of a Salesperson," *Sales & Marketing Management* (June 1995), p. 13; and Richard T. Hise and Edward L. Reid, "Improving the Performance of the Industrial Sales Force in the 1990s," *Industrial Marketing Management*, Vol. 23 (October 1994), pp. 273–279.

[3]Tom Dellecave, Jr., "Getting the Bugs Out," *Sales & Marketing Management* (December 1995), Part 2, p. 27.

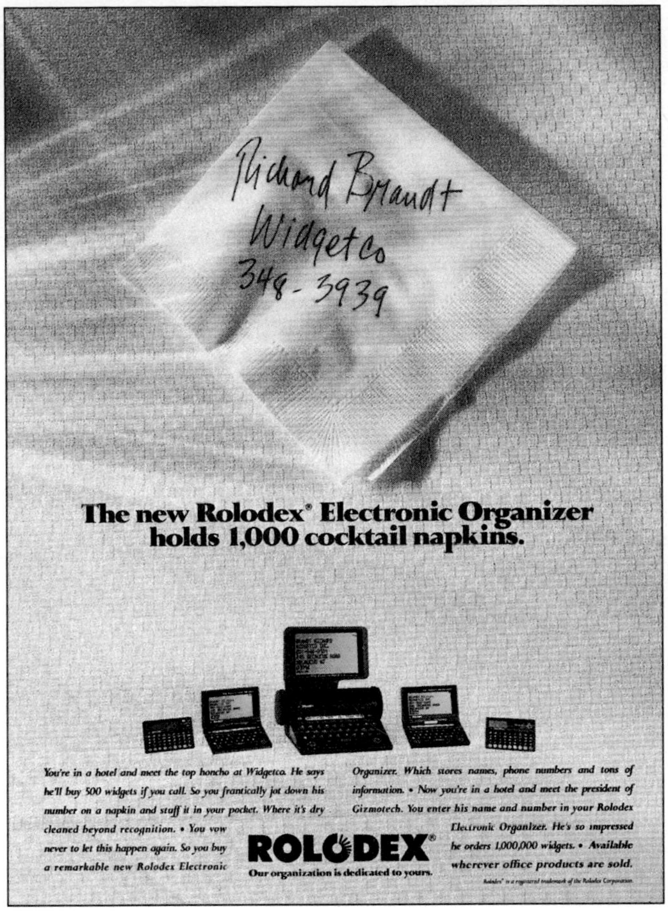

FIGURE 20-3
Why Should Salespeople Carry Portable Computers?
Reprinted by permission.

make sure their key accounts are regularly serviced, and use direct mailings to complement telephone calls and salesperson visits.

The Characteristics of Personal Selling

Selling uses a **buyer-seller dyad** *and is flexible and efficient, closes sales, and provides feedback.*

On the positive side, personal selling provides individual attention for each consumer and passes on a lot of information. There is a dynamic interplay between buyer and seller. This lets a firm use a **buyer-seller dyad**, the two-way flow of communication between both parties. See Figure 20-4. That is not possible with advertising. Thus, personal selling can be flexible and adapted to specific consumer needs. For example, a real-estate broker can use one sales presentation with a first-time buyer and another with a person who has already bought a home. A salesperson can also apply as much persuasion as needed and balance it against the need for information. Furthermore, through the buyer-seller dyad, a "relationship selling" approach is possible, whereby customer friendships may be developed.[4]

Personal selling targets a more defined and concentrated audience, which means less waste than with advertising. In addition, people who enter a store or who are contacted by a salesperson are more apt to buy a product than those watching an ad on TV. Because ads stimulate interest, those who make it to the personal selling stage are often key members of the target market. When unsolicited, direct selling has the most waste in personal selling.

Selling clinches sales and is usually conducted during the purchase stage of the consumer's decision process, taking place after information search and exposure to ads. It holds

[4]See John J. Withey and Eric Panitz, "Face-to-Face Selling: Making It More Effective," *Industrial Marketing Management*, Vol. 24 (August 1995), pp. 239–246.

International Marketing in *Action*

Door-to-Door *Car* Sales (the Japanese Way)?

According to the Japan Automobile Dealers Association, as many as half of all cars in Japan are bought via direct selling. Toyota alone has over 100,000 door-to-door salespeople. This is equivalent to 50 per cent of the sales force for all brands of cars in the United States. Toyota's sales force in Japan is so strong that many Japanese car buyers never have to go into a dealership.

Eiko Shiraishi is a typical Toyota salesperson. He represents Toyota in a south-west Tokyo territory, comprised of 3,000 households. He has already sold cars to 370 of these prospects. And he has many repeat customers. Shiraishi sells about seven cars a month and earns a salary of $70,000 per year. Almost all of his income is from a salary; very little is due to sales commissions.

Shiraishi times his visits so that he stops by his customers' homes just before their cars reach three years of age. He also calls on customers every two years thereafter. Why? At these times, car owners must replace several costly parts as part of the Japanese government's inspection system.

He is careful not to call on housewives early in the morning (when children are being sent off to school) or in late afternoon (when dinner is being prepared). As with most door-to-door car salespeople, Eiko Shiraishi personally delivers his customers' new vehicles right to their homes. He even drives trade-in vehicles back to the dealership.

Shiraishi's job does not end with the sale of a car. Afterwards, he always calls to see how well the car is running, writes handwritten greeting cards, and sends out special invitations for low-cost oil changes and other services.

As a sales manager for Ford, evaluate the pros and cons of using direct selling. Could it be used in the United States? Why or why not?

Source: Based on material in Valarie Reitman, "In Japan's Car Market, Big Three Face Rivals Who Go Door-to-Door," *Wall Street Journal* (September 28, 1994), pp. A1, A13.

repeat customers and those already convinced by advertising—and resolves any concerns of undecided consumers by answering questions about price, warranty, and other factors. It settles service issues, like delivery and installation. Feedback is immediate and clear-cut: Consumers may be asked their feelings about product features or they may complain, and salespeople may unearth a marketing program's strengths and weaknesses.

Selling has a limited audience, high costs per customer, and a poor image.

On the negative side, selling is ineffective for generating awareness because salespeople can handle only a limited number of consumers. A retail furniture salesperson may be able to talk to fewer than 20 people per day if the average length of a customer con-

FIGURE 20-4
The Buyer-Seller Dyad

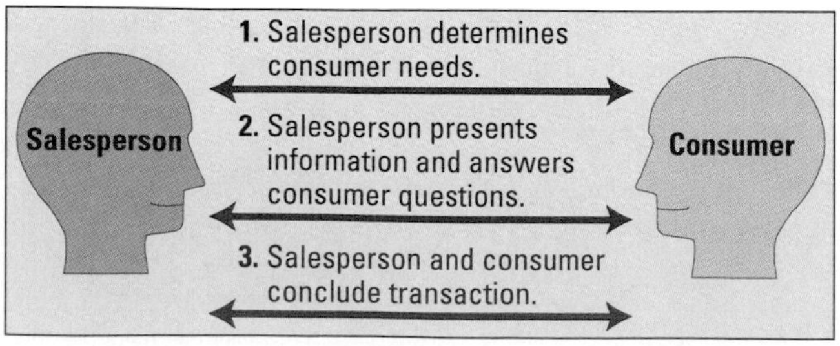

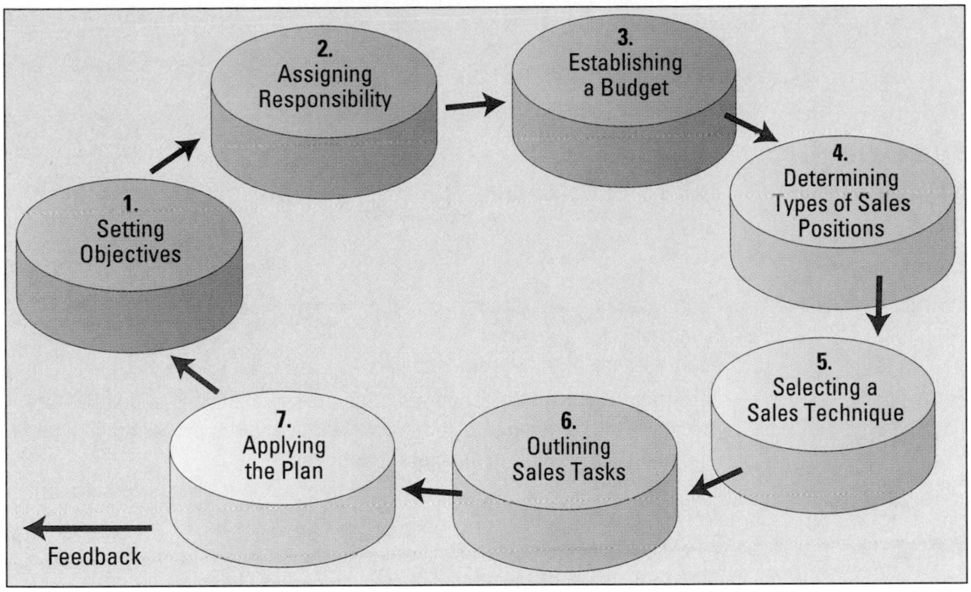

FIGURE 20-5
Developing a Personal Selling Plan

tact is 15 minutes to a half hour. Sales personnel who call on customers can handle even fewer accounts, due to travel. In addition, many consumers drawn by advertising may want self-service. This is discouraged by some aggressive salespeople.

Personal selling costs per customer can be very high due to the one-on-one nature of selling. An in-store furniture salesperson who talks to 20 customers daily might cost a firm $7 per presentation ($140/day compensation divided by 20), an amount much higher than an ad's cost per-customer contact. For outside salespeople, hotel stays, meals, and transportation can amount to $250 or more daily per salesperson, and compensation must be added to these costs.

Finally, personal selling, especially among final consumers, has a poor image. It is criticized for a lack of honesty and pressure tactics:

> The public's consistent interpretation of the term *salesperson* has provided fodder for many dramatic works, anecdotes, and jokes that reflect the widely held negative stereotype of salespeople. As a result, people may avoid them deliberately. The consumer practice of visiting car dealerships after business hours personifies a common reaction to salespeople. This practice may be due to beliefs that consumers can evaluate alternative cars better in the absence of the "dreaded" salesperson. Sometimes, salespeople may even inhibit, rather than facilitate, mutually satisfying exchanges.[5]

The situation can be improved by better sales-force training and the use of consumer-oriented rather than seller-oriented practices.

Developing a Personal Selling Plan

A personal selling plan can be divided into the seven steps shown in Figure 20-5 and highlighted here.

Setting Objectives

Selling goals can be demand- and/or image-oriented. When image-oriented, they involve public relations. Although many firms have some interest in information, reminder, and image goals, the major goal usually is persuasion: converting consumer interest into a sale. Examples appear in Table 20-1.

[5]Barry J. Babin, James S. Boles, and William R. Darden, "Salesperson Stereotypes, Consumer Emotions, and Their Impact on Information Processing," *Journal of the Academy of Marketing Science*, Vol. 23 (Spring 1995), p. 94.

Table 20-1
Specific Personal Selling Objectives

TYPE OF OBJECTIVE	ILLUSTRATIONS
Demand-Oriented	
Information	To fully explain all attributes of goods and services To answer any questions To probe for any further questions
Persuasion	To distinguish attributes of goods or services from those of competitors To maximize the number of purchases relative to the presentations made To convert undecided consumers into buyers To sell complementary items—e.g., a telephoto lens with a camera To placate dissatisfied customers
Reminding	To ensure delivery, installation, etc. To follow-up after a good or service has been purchased To follow-up when a repurchase is near To reassure previous customers as they make a new purchase
Image-Oriented	
Industry and company	To have a good appearance for all personnel having customer contact To follow acceptable (ethical) sales practices To be respected by customers, employees, and other publics

Assigning Responsibility

A manager must oversee selling functions.

The personal selling function may be assigned to a marketing or sales manager who oversees all areas of selling, from planning to sales force management. A small or specialized firm is likely to have its marketing manager oversee selling or use one general sales manager. A large or diversified firm may have multiple sales managers—assigned by product line, customer type, and/or region.

These are the basic responsibilities of a sales manager:

- To understand the firm's goals, strategies, market position, and basic marketing plan and to convey them to the sales force.
- To determine and outline a sales philosophy, sales force characteristics, selling tasks, a sales organization, and methods of customer contact.
- To prepare and update sales forecasts.
- To allocate selling resources based on sales forecasts and customer needs.
- To select, train, assign, compensate, and supervise sales personnel.
- To synchronize selling tasks with advertising, product planning, distribution, marketing research, production, and other activities.
- To assess sales performance by salesperson, product, product line, customer, customer group, and geographic area.
- To continuously monitor competitors' actions.
- To make sure the sales force acts in an ethical manner.
- To convey the image sought by the company.

Table 20-2

A Sales-Expense Budget for a Small Manufacturer Specializing in Business Machinery, 1997

ITEM	ESTIMATED ANNUAL COSTS (REVENUES)
Sales Forecast	$1,950,000
Overhead (1 sales manager, 1 office)	$100,000
Sales force compensation (2 salespeople)	90,000
Sales expenses	40,000
Sales meetings	5,000
Selling aids	15,000
Sales management costs	10,000
Total personal-selling budget	$260,000
Personal selling costs as a percentage of sales forecast	13.3

Establishing a Budget

A **sales-expense budget** allots selling costs among salespeople, products, customers, and geographic areas for a given period. It is usually tied to a sales forecast and relates tasks to goals. It should be somewhat flexible in case sales are not reached or are exceeded.

A **sales-expense budget** *assigns spending for a specific time.*

These items should be covered in a budget: sales forecast, overhead (manager's compensation, office costs), sales force compensation, sales expenses (travel, lodging, meals, entertainment), sales meetings, selling aids (including computer equipment), and sales management (employee selection and training) costs. Table 20-2 shows a budget for a small maker of business machinery.

The budget will be larger if customers are dispersed and a lot of travel is required. Complex products need costly, time-consuming sales presentations and result in fewer calls per salesperson. An expanding sales force needs expenditures for recruiting and training.

Determining the Type(s) of Sales Positions

Salespeople can be broadly classed as order takers, order getters, or support personnel. Some firms employ one type of salesperson, others a combination.

An **order taker** processes routine orders and reorders. This person is involved more with clerical than creative selling, typically for pre-sold goods or services. He or she arranges displays, restocks items, answers simple questions, writes up orders, and completes transactions. He or she may work in a warehouse (manufacturer clerk) or store (retail clerk) or call on customers (a field salesperson). An order taker has these advantages: compensation is rather low, little training is required, both selling and nonselling tasks are performed, and a sales force can be expanded or contracted quickly. Yet, an order taker is an improper choice for goods and services that need creative selling or extensive information for customers. Personnel turnover is high. Enthusiasm may be limited due to the low salary and routine tasks.

An **order taker** *handles routine orders and sells items that are pre-sold.*

An **order getter** generates customer leads, provides information, persuades customers, and closes sales. He or she is the creative salesperson used for high-priced, complex, and/or new products. There is less emphasis on clerical work. The person may be inside (jewelry store salesperson) or outside (Xerox salesperson).[6] He or she is expert and enthusiastic,

An **order getter** *obtains leads, provides information, persuades customers, and closes sales.*

[6]See Kris Frieswick, "Inside Sales Takes Center Stage," *Industrial Distribution* (October 1995), pp. 24–27.

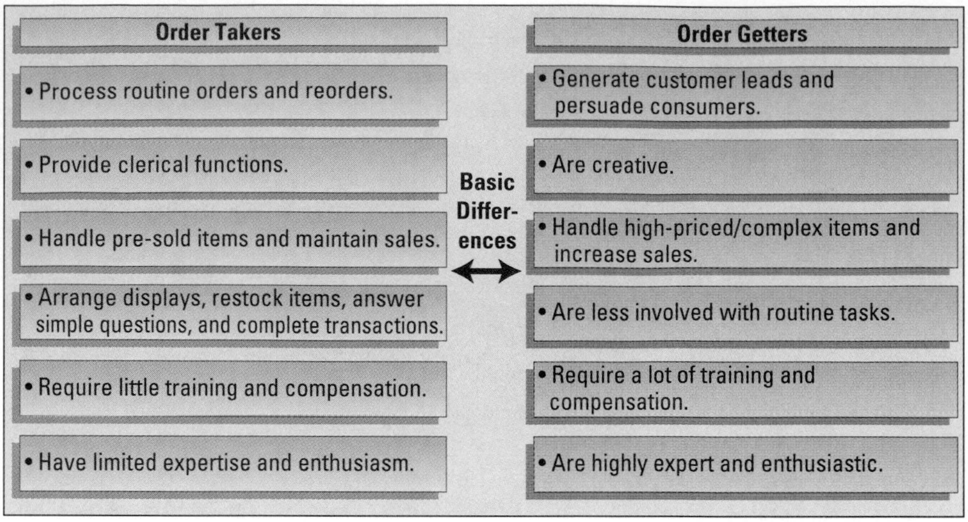

Order Takers
• Process routine orders and reorders.
• Provide clerical functions.
• Handle pre-sold items and maintain sales.
• Arrange displays, restock items, answer simple questions, and complete transactions.
• Require little training and compensation.
• Have limited expertise and enthusiasm.
Basic Differ- ences
Order Getters
• Generate customer leads and persuade consumers.
• Are creative.
• Handle high-priced/complex items and increase sales.
• Are less involved with routine tasks.
• Require a lot of training and compensation.
• Are highly expert and enthusiastic.

FIGURE 20-6
Contrasting Order Takers and Order Getters

expands sales, and can convince undecided customers to buy or decided customers to add peripheral items—such as carpeting and appliances along with a newly built house. Yet, for many people, the order getter has a high-pressure image. He or she may also need expensive training. Such nonsales tasks as writing reports may be avoided because they take away from a seller's time with customers and are seldom rewarded. Compensation can be very high for salespersons who are effective order getters. Figure 20-6 contrasts order takers and order getters.

Missionary salespersons, sales engineers, *and* **service salespersons** *are support personnel.*

Support personnel supplement a sales force. A **missionary salesperson** gives out information on new goods or services. He or she does not close sales but describes items' attributes, answers questions, and leaves written matter. This paves the way for later sales and is commonly used with prescription drugs. A **sales engineer** accompanies an order getter if a very technical or complex item is involved. He or she discusses specifications and long-range uses, while the order getter makes customer contacts and closes sales. A **service salesperson** ordinarily deals with customers after sales. Delivery, installation, and other follow-up tasks are done.

Selecting a Sales Technique

The **canned sales presentation** *is memorized and nonadaptive.*

The two basic techniques for selling are the canned sales presentation and the need-satisfaction approach. The **canned sales presentation** is a memorized, repetitive presentation given to all customers interested in a given item. It does not adapt to customer needs or traits but presumes a general presentation will appeal to everyone. Although criticized for its inflexibility and a nonmarketing orientation, it does have some value:

> Inexperienced salespeople who are lacking in selling instinct and confidence will benefit from the professionalism, anticipation of questions and objections, and other fail-safe mechanisms often inherent in a company-prepared memorized, audiovisual, or flip-chart presentation. Consequently, this method should be considered when qualified new salespeople are scarce and when brevity of training is essential.[7]

The **need-satisfaction approach** *adapts to individual consumers.*

The **need-satisfaction approach** is a high-level selling method based on the principle that each customer has different attributes and wants, and therefore the sales presentation should be adapted to the individual consumer. With this technique, a salesperson first asks such questions of the consumer as: What type of product are you looking for? Have you ever purchased this product before? What price range are you considering? Then the sales presentation is more responsive to the particular person, and a new shop-

[7]Marvin A. Jolson, "The Underestimated Potential of the Canned Sales Presentation," *Journal of Marketing*, Vol. 39 (January 1975), p. 78.

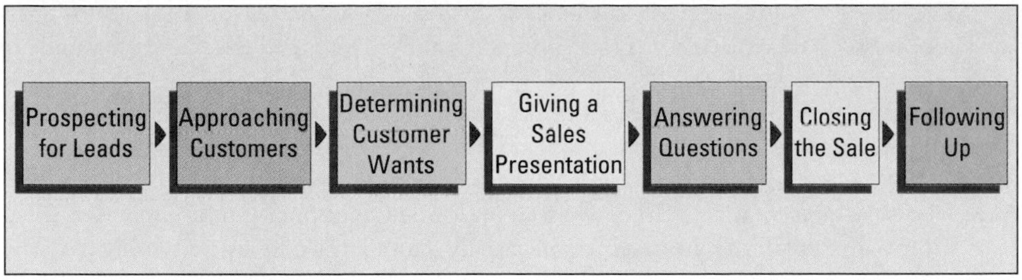

FIGURE 20-7
The Selling Process

per is treated quite differently from an experienced one. The need-satisfaction approach is more popular and customer-oriented; however, it requires better training and skilled sales personnel. This approach includes

- Using the buyer-seller dyad to generate two-way respect.
- Listening well.
- Making presentations based on a good grasp of the facts.
- Spending time on pre-sales research ("homework").
- Being punctual for appointments (and willing to leave when the allotted time is over).
- Allowing the customer to talk.
- Offering "solutions," not goods and services.
- Showing competence.
- Acknowledging if a question cannot be answered, but getting back to the customer immediately with the correct answer.
- Not wasting a prospect's time.
- Providing superior service after the sale.[8]

The canned sales presentation works best with inexpensive, routine items that are heavily advertised and relatively pre-sold. The need-satisfaction approach works best with more expensive, more complex items that have moderate advertising and require substantial additional information for consumers.

Outlining Sales Tasks

The **selling process** *consists of seven steps.*

The tasks to be performed by the personal sales force need to be outlined. The **selling process** consists of prospecting for leads, approaching customers, determining consumer wants, giving a sales presentation, answering questions, closing the sale, and following up. See Figure 20-7.

Prospecting *creates customer leads.*

Outside selling requires a procedure, known as **prospecting**, to generate a list of customer leads. Blind prospecting uses phone directories and other general listings of potential customers; with it, a small percentage of those contacted will be interested in a firm's offering. Lead prospecting depends on past customers and others for referrals; thus, a greater percentage of people will be interested because of the referral from someone they know. Inside selling does not involve prospecting because customers have already been drawn to a store or office through ads or prior purchase experience.

The pre-approach and greeting are the two parts of **approaching customers**.

Approaching customers is a two-stage procedure: pre-approach and greeting. During pre-approach, a salesperson tries to get information about the customer from the firm's data base, census materials, and/or other secondary data—as well as from referrals. The salesperson is then better equipped to interact with that customer. Inside retail salespeople may be unable to use a pre-approach; they often know nothing about a consumer until he or she enters the store. During the greeting, a salesperson begins a conversation. The intention is to put the customer at ease and build rapport.

[8]Adapted by the authors from James E. Lukaszewski and Paul Ridgeway, "To Put Your Best Foot Forward, Start by Taking These 21 Simple Steps," *Sales & Marketing Management* (June 1990), pp. 84–86. See also Fiona Gibb, "The New Sales Basics," *Sales & Marketing Management* (April 1995), p. 81.

The next step is to ascertain customer wants by asking the person a variety of questions regarding past experience, price, product features, intended uses, and the kinds of information still needed.

The **sales presentation** *converts an uncertain consumer.*

The **sales presentation** includes a verbal description of a product, its benefits, options and models, price, associated services like delivery and warranty, and a demonstration (if needed). A canned sales presentation or need-satisfaction method may be used. The purpose of a sales presentation is to convert an undecided consumer into a purchaser.

After a presentation, the salesperson usually must answer questions from the consumer. Questions are of two kinds: the first request more information; the second raise objections that must be settled before a sale is made.

The **closing** *clinches a sale.*

Once any questions have been answered, a salesperson is ready for **closing the sale**. This means getting a person to agree to a purchase. The salesperson must be sure no major questions remain before trying to close a sale. In addition, a salesperson must not argue with a consumer.

For a large purchase, the salesperson should follow-up after the sale to make sure the customer is pleased. That achieves three goals: the customer is better satisfied, referrals are stimulated, and repurchases are more likely. "Relationship selling is not about getting an order; it is about convincing customers that you will be there after an order, no matter what. Relationships are based on doing what is right, not doing what you can get way with."[9]

Besides the tasks in the selling process, a firm must clearly enumerate the nonselling tasks it wants sales personnel to perform. Among the nonselling tasks that may be assigned are setting up displays, writing up information sheets, marking prices on products, checking competitors' strategies, doing test marketing analysis and consumer surveys, and training new employees.

Applying the Plan

Sales management *tasks range from employee selection to supervision.*

Sales management—planning, implementing, and controlling the personal sales function—should be used in applying a personal selling plan. It covers employee selection, training, territory allocation, compensation, and supervision.

In selecting sales personnel, a combination of personal attributes should be assessed: mental (intelligence, ability to plan), physical (appearance, speaking ability), experiential (education, sales/business background), environmental (group memberships, social influences), personality (ambition, enthusiasm, tact, resourcefulness, stability), and willingness to be trained and to follow instructions.[10] Contrary to earlier beliefs, it is now pretty much accepted that good salespeople are not necessarily born; they are carefully selected and trained: "How would you describe the ideal salesperson? Extroverted, aggressive? Quick to develop a rapport? A good sense of humor, a competitive spirit, charisma? This has been a popular stereotype, to be sure, and no doubt there are some excellent sales professionals out there who actually do possess these qualities. On the other hand, it's also a popular misconception. The truth is, these factors aren't always the most important ones to consider when selecting and training top salespeople."[11]

The traits of potential salespeople must be compatible with the customers with whom they will interact and the requirements of the good or service being sold. The buyer-seller dyad operates better when there are some similarities in salesperson and customer characteristics. And certain product categories require much different education, technical training, and sales activities than others (such as jewelry versus computer sales).

Once these factors are studied, the firm would develop a formal selection procedure that specifies the personal attributes sought, sources of employees (such as colleges and employment agencies), and methods for selection (such as interviews and testing). It would be based on the firm's overall selling plan.

[9]Michael Collins, "Breaking into the Big Leagues," *Marketing Tools* (January–February 1996), p. 28.

[10]Adapted by the authors from William J. Stanton, Richard H. Buskirk, and Rosann L. Spiro, *Management of a Sales Force*, Ninth Edition (Homewood, Ill.: Richard D. Irwin, 1995).

[11]Thomas Rollins, "How to Tell Competent Salespeople from the Other Kind," *Sales & Marketing Management* (September 1990), p. 116.

Salesperson training may take one or a combination of forms. A formal program uses a trainer, a classroom setting, lectures, and printed materials. It may also include role playing (in which trainees act out parts) and case analysis. Field trips take trainees out on actual calls so they can observe skilled salespeople in action. On-the-job training places trainees in their own selling situations under the close supervision of the trainer or a senior salesperson. Training often covers a range of topics; it should teach selling skills and include information on the firm and its offerings, the industry, and employee duties. At Caterpillar (the industrial and farm equipment manufacturer), "We train our sales force to understand why our customers buy our products, what their needs are, the importance of follow-up, the need to let a customer vent his/her anger, and how to help a customer resolve problems without passing the responsibility on to someone else in the company."[12] Besides initial training, continuous training or retraining of sales personnel may teach new techniques, explain new products, or improve performance.

A **sales territory** *contains the area, customers, and/or products assigned to a salesperson.*

Territory size and salesperson allocation are decided next. A **sales territory** consists of the geographic area, customers, and/or product lines assigned to a salesperson. If territories are assigned by customer type or product category, two or more salespeople may cover the same geographic area. Territory size depends on customer locations, order size, travel time and expenses, the time per sales call, the yearly visits for each account, and the amount of hours per year each salesperson has for selling tasks. The mix of established versus new customer accounts must also be considered. Allocating salespeople to specific territories depends on their ability, the buyer-seller dyad, the mix of selling and nonselling functions (such as one salesperson training new employees), and seniority. Proper territory size and allocation provide adequate coverage of customers, minimize territory overlap, recognize geographic boundaries, minimize travel expenses, encourage solicitation of new accounts, provide enough sales potential for good salespeople to be well rewarded, and are fair to the whole sales force.

Sales compensation may be **straight salary, straight commission**, *or a* **combination** *of the two.*

Salespeople can be compensated by straight salary, straight commission, or a combination of salary and commission or bonus. With a **straight salary plan**, a salesperson is paid a flat amount per time period. Earnings are not tied to sales. The advantages are that both selling and nonselling tasks can be specified and controlled, salespeople have security, and expenses are known in advance. The disadvantages are the low incentive to increase sales, expenses not being tied to productivity, and the continuing costs even if there are low sales. Order takers are usually paid straight salaries.

With a **straight commission plan**, a salesperson's earnings are directly related to sales, profits, customer satisfaction, or some other type of performance. The commission rate is often keyed to a quota, which is a productivity standard. The advantages of this plan are the use of motivated salespeople, no fixed sales compensation costs, and expenses being tied to productivity. The disadvantages are the firm's lack of control over nonselling tasks, the instability of a firm's expenses, and salesperson risks due to variable pay. Insurance, real estate, and direct-selling order getters often earn straight commissions. A real-estate salesperson might receive a 3 per cent commission of $4,500 for selling a $150,000 house.

To gain the advantages of both salary- and commission-oriented methods, many firms use elements of each in a **combination compensation plan**. Such plans balance company control, flexibility, and employee incentives; and some award bonuses for superior individual or company performance. All types of order getters work on a combination basis. According to various studies, about two-thirds of U.S. firms compensate sales personnel via some form of combination plan, one-fifth use a straight-salary plan, and the rest use straight commissions. Smaller firms are more apt to use a straight-salary plan and less apt to use a combination plan.

Supervision involves motivation, performance measures, nonselling tasks, and modifying behavior.

Supervision encompasses four aspects of sales management: One, sales personnel must be motivated. Their motivation depends on such factors as the clarity of the job (what tasks must be performed), the salesperson's desire to achieve, the variety of tasks performed, the incentives for undertaking each task, the style of the sales manager, flexibility, and recognition. Two, performance must be measured. To do this, achievements must

[12]Geoffrey Brewer, "Caterpillar Inc.: Industrial & Farm Equipment," *Sales & Marketing Management* (September 1993), p. 61.

Ethics IN TODAY'S SOCIETY

Do Life Insurance Agents "Churn" So Much to Earn So Much?

Prudential and other agents have recently been scrutinized for "churning" insurance policies. Under this practice, agents recommend that customers use the built-in cash value from old policies to purchase new ones. Churning is often practiced by agents as a way of increasing their commission income from loyal accounts. Because a new policy often generates a sales commission equal to half of the first year's premium, churning is highly profitable to agents.

Unfortunately, people are often not fully briefed about the consequences of switching policies. In one instance, an unsuspecting consumer was advised by an agent to borrow against the cash value in an existing policy so that the customer could purchase more insurance coverage. However, in such instances, the cash value of the old policy could run out, while the interest on the loan increases. The customer would then be forced to pay off the debt.

Churning is also generally not profitable for the insurance company. It often takes at least six years of payments for a new policy to be profitable due to the company's cost of sales commissions, administrative costs, and medical testing fees.

Despite these problems, it is hard to reduce churning activity. In many sales offices, monitoring this activity falls under the jurisdiction of junior managers. Because these managers are evaluated on the basis of the sales revenues of their agents, churning increases their income. In addition, many insurance agents represent multiple firms. An independent agent can easily churn a policyholder from one insurance provider to another. Finally, many insurance firms do not want to come down too hard on productive independent agents since they can easily switch their loyalty from one insurance company to another.

As a Prudential marketing executive, how would you discourage independent agents from churning?

Source: Based on material in Leslie Scism, "Some Agents Churn Life-Insurance Policies, Hurt Their Customers," *Wall Street Journal* (January 3, 1995), pp. 1, 4.

be gauged against such goals as sales and calls per day. The analysis should take into account territory size, travel time, and experience. Salesperson failure is often related to poor listening skills, the failure to concentrate on priorities, a lack of effort, the inability to determine customer needs, a lack of planning for presentations, overpromising on product performance, and inadequate knowledge. Three, the sales manager must ensure that all nonselling tasks are completed, even if sales personnel are not rewarded for them. Four, if a salesperson's performance does not meet expectations, then some action may be needed to modify behavior.[13]

There are more women in sales than ever before, and international markets require special decisions.

In sales management, these key factors should also be taken into account: the evolving role of women in selling and the special nature of selling in foreign markets.

With regard to women in personal selling, "perhaps the most radical change in the U.S. industrial sales force over the last two decades has been the accelerated recruitment

[13]Thomas N. Ingram, Charles H. Schwepker, Jr., and Don Hutson, "Why Salespeople Fail," *Industrial Marketing Management*, Vol. 21 (August 1992), pp. 225–230; and "Pipe Down," *Sales & Marketing Management* (January 1994), p. 22. See also Goutam N. Challagalla and Tasadduq A. Shervani, "Dimensions and Types of Supervisory Control: Effects on Salesperson Performance and Satisfaction," *Journal of Marketing*, Vol. 60 (January 1996), pp. 89–105.

FIGURE 20-8
Personal Selling in an International Setting
In many Arab countries, negotiations—particularly bargaining—are viewed as an enjoyable activity or even as a social event. Foreign salespeople need to respect the religious traditions of their Arab customers and recognize that Arab personnel may not be available at all times. In addition, they are known to refrain from saying "no" and to engage in contract renegotiations if the need arises. Arabs end negotiations by orally committing themselves, rather than doing so in writing.
Reprinted by permission of Texaco.

of women into traditionally male-dominated sales positions."[14] According to the U.S. Bureau of Labor Statistics, 25 years ago, women made up 5 to 6 per cent of the industrial sales force. Today, they represent 26 per cent, and as two researchers have noted:

> Sales managers do not have to provide special considerations or training programs for female salespersons to facilitate their socialization into the industrial sales force. Consequently, sales managers should not be concerned with incurring additional training expenses for females, nor do they need to behave more solicitously in their management practices toward women than toward men. To do otherwise will probably result in the demotivation of male salespersons, and will probably handicap females by intimating they are deficient in some way and require additional assistance. Instead, sales managers should include women equally in all sales training, motivation, and socialization activities, just as these opportunities are extended to men.[15]

When firms go international, "they are faced with the task of establishing and managing sales forces in foreign markets. Once in place, they must then decide how much home-office influence to exert on subsidiary sales policies. When faced with the diversity of the international marketplace, top marketing management is often uncertain about how much it should influence its overseas sales forces. Management benefits from knowing which sales decisions are suited to home-office input and, just as important, which are not."[16] In particular, the attributes of salespeople; salesperson training, compensation, and supervision; the dynamics of the buyer-seller dyad; and the selling process may need to be tailored to different foreign markets. See Figure 20-8.

The Scope and Importance of Sales Promotion

Sales promotion efforts are now quite extensive.

Due to intense competition in their industries, numerous firms are aggressively seeking every marketing edge possible. Thus, sales promotion activities worldwide are at their highest level. According to *Promo*, in the United States alone, spending exceeds $200 billion a year.[17]

[14]Patrick L. Schul and Brent M. Wren, "The Emerging Role of Women in Industrial Selling: A Decade of Change," *Journal of Marketing*, Vol. 56 (July 1992), p. 38.

[15]Judy A. Siguaw and Earl D. Honeycutt, Jr., "An Examination of Gender Differences in Selling Behaviors and Job Attitudes," *Industrial Marketing Management*, Vol. 24 (January 1995), p. 51. See also Nancy Arnott, "It's a Woman's World," *Sales & Marketing Management* (March 1995), pp. 54–59.

[16]John S. Hill, Richard R. Still, and Ünal O. Boya, "Managing the Multinational Sales Force," *International Marketing Review*, Vol. 8 (Number 1, 1991), pp. 19–31. See also Earl D. Honeycutt and John B. Ford, "Guidelines for Managing an International Sales Force," *Industrial Marketing Management*, Vol. 24 (March 1995), pp. 135–144.

[17]Please note: There is an overlap in the expenditures reported for advertising and sales promotion because some sales promotion activities (such as direct mail and promotion-oriented ads) may also be viewed as advertising.

The extent of sales promotion activities can be shown via the following:

- About 320 billion coupons are distributed annually in the United States. In a typical year, most American households use coupons, half on a regular basis. Yet, people redeem only 2 per cent of distributed coupons.[18]
- Business-to-business firms spend about 13 per cent of their marketing budgets on trade shows and exhibits. Fifty per cent of industrial trade show attendees report signing a purchase order as a result of a trade show visit.[19]
- According to International Events Group, firms spend $4.5 billion annually to sponsor special events—two-thirds on sports-related events. Bausch & Lomb, Kodak, John Hancock Life Insurance, and Visa USA are among the companies that have already signed up as sponsors for the 1998 Winter Olympics and 2000 Summer Olympics.[20]
- Vons, the California-based supermarket chain, has 4 million members in its VonsClub frequent-shopper program. Customers are rewarded with special discounts, and Vons is able to build its customer data base.[21]
- $17 billion is spent on point-of-purchase displays in U.S. stores each year.[22] These displays stimulate impulse purchases and provide information. Besides traditional cardboard, metal, and plastic displays, more stores are now using digital electronic signs and video displays. Figure 20-9 shows the sales-oriented displays in a Saturday Matinee store.
- In rural India (with its 650-million population), fewer than 15 per cent of the people use toothpaste. So, Colgate-Palmolive hires "video vans" to regularly visit local villages. The vans show a 27-minute infomercial on the value of toothpaste; free samples are then given out and tooth brushing demonstrations are provided.[23]

Several factors account for the strength of sales promotion as a marketing tool. As noted at the beginning of this section, firms are looking for any competitive edge they can get, and this often involves some kind of sales promotion. The various forms of sales promotions are more acceptable to firms and consumers than in the past. Quick returns are possible, and numerous firms want to improve short-run profits. Today, more consumers look for promotions before buying, and resellers put pressure on manufacturers for promotions. In economic downturns, even more shoppers look for value-oriented sales promotions. Due to rising costs, advertising and personal selling have become more expensive relative to sales promotion. Technology advances make aspects of sales promotion, like coupon redemption, easier to administer.

The Characteristics of Sales Promotion

Sales promotion lures customers, maintains loyalty, creates excitement, is often keyed to patronage, and appeals to channel members.

Sales promotion has many advantages. It helps attract customer traffic and keep brand or company loyalty: New-product samples and trial offers draw customers. A manufacturer can retain brand loyalty by giving gifts to regular customers and coupons for its brands. A reseller can retain loyal customers by having incentives for frequent shoppers and using store coupons.

Rapid results can be gained. Some sales promotions provide consumer value and are retained by them (such as calendars, matchbooks, T-shirts, pens, and posters with the firm's

[18]"The 1995 Annual Report on the Promotion Industry," *Promo* (July 1995), p. 38.

[19]Cyndee Miller, "Marketing Industry Report: Who's Spending What on Biz-to-Biz Marketing," *Marketing News* (January 1, 1996), p. 1; and John F. Tanner, Jr. and Lawrence B. Chonko, "Trade Show Objectives," *Industrial Marketing Management*, Vol. 24 (August 1995), pp. 257–264.

[20]"The 1995 Annual Report on the Promotion Industry," p. 40; and Jeff Jensen, "IOC Re-Signing Sponsors for '98, 2000 Games," *Advertising Age* (January 15, 1996), p. 3.

[21]Leah Haran, "With 4M+ Cards, VonsClub Helps Target Shoppers," *Advertising Age* (October 16, 1995), pp. 24–26.

[22]Leah Haran, "Point of Purchase," *Advertising Age* (October 23, 1995), p. 33.

[23]Miriam Jordan, "In Rural India, Video Vans Sell Toothpaste and Shampoo," *Wall Street Journal* (January 10, 1996), pp. B1, B5.

FIGURE 20-9
Saturday Matinee's Sales-Oriented Displays
Saturday Matinee's in-store displays greatly enhance the consumer's shopping experience. Special Kids' Matinee display areas appeal to children ages 4 to 12.

Reprinted by permission of Trans World Entertainment Corporation.

name); they provide a reminder function. Impulse purchases can be stimulated via in-store displays. For example, an attractive supermarket display for batteries can dramatically raise sales. In addition, a good display may lead a shopper to a bigger purchase than originally intended.

Excitement is created via certain short-run promotions involving gifts, contests, or sweepstakes; and high-value items or high payoffs encourage consumers to participate. Contests offer the further benefit of customer involvement (through the completion of some skill-oriented activity). Many promotions are keyed to customer patronage—with the awarding of coupons, frequent-shopper gifts, and referral gifts directly related to purchases. In these cases, promotions can be a fixed percentage of sales and their costs not incurred until transactions are completed. And resellers may be stimulated if sales-promotion support is provided in the form of displays, manufacturer coupons, manufacturer rebates, and trade allowances.

Sales promotion may hurt image, cause consumers to wait for special offers, and shift the focus from the product.

Sales promotion also has limitations. A firm's image may be lessened if it always runs promotions. People may view discounts as representing a decline in product quality and believe a firm could not sell its offerings without them. Profit margins are often lower for a firm if sales promotion is used. When coupons, rebates, or other special deals are employed frequently, people may not buy when products are offered at regular prices; they will stock up each time there is a promotion. Some consumers may even interpret a regular price as an increase for items that are heavily promoted.

Some promotions shift the marketing focus away from the product itself to secondary factors. People may be lured by calendars and sweepstakes instead of product quality and features. In the short run, this generates consumer enthusiasm. In the long run, it may adversely affect a brand's image and sales because a product-related advantage has not been communicated. Sales promotion can enhance—not replace—advertising, personal selling, and public relations.

Developing a Sales Promotion Plan

A sales promotion plan consists of the steps shown in Figure 20-10 and explained next.

Setting Objectives

Sales promotion goals are usually demand-oriented. They may be related to channel members and to consumers.

Objectives associated with channel-member sales promotions include gaining distribution, receiving adequate shelf space, increasing dealer enthusiasm, raising sales, and getting cooperation in sales promotion expenditures. Objectives pertaining to consumer sales promotions include boosting brand awareness, increasing product trials, hiking average purchases, encouraging repurchases, obtaining impulse sales, emphasizing novelty, and supplementing other promotional tools.

Assigning Responsibility

Sales promotion duties are often shared by advertising and sales managers, with each directing the promotions in his or her area. Thus, an advertising manager would work on coupons, customer contests, calendars, and other mass promotions. A sales manager would work on trade shows, cooperative promotions, special events, demonstrations, and other efforts involving individualized attention directed at channel members or consumers.

Some companies have their own specialized sales-promotion departments or hire outside promotion firms, like Donnelly Marketing. Outside sales-promotion firms tend to operate in narrow areas—such as coupons, contests, or gifts—and generally can develop a sales promotion campaign at less expense than the user company could. These firms offer expertise, swift service, flexibility, and, when requested, distribution.

Outlining the Overall Plan

Next, a sales promotion plan should be outlined and include a budget, an orientation, conditions, media, duration and timing, and cooperative efforts. In setting a sales promotion budget, it is important to include all costs. For example, the average face value of a grocery coupon is over 65 cents; supermarkets receive a handling fee for each coupon they redeem; and there are costs for printing, mailing, and advertising coupons.

Sales promotion orientation *may be toward channel members and/or final consumers.*

Sales promotion orientation refers to its focus—channel members or consumers—and its theme. Promotions for channel members should raise their product knowledge, provide sales support, offer rewards for selling a promoted product, and seek better co-

FIGURE 20-10
Developing a Sales Promotion Plan

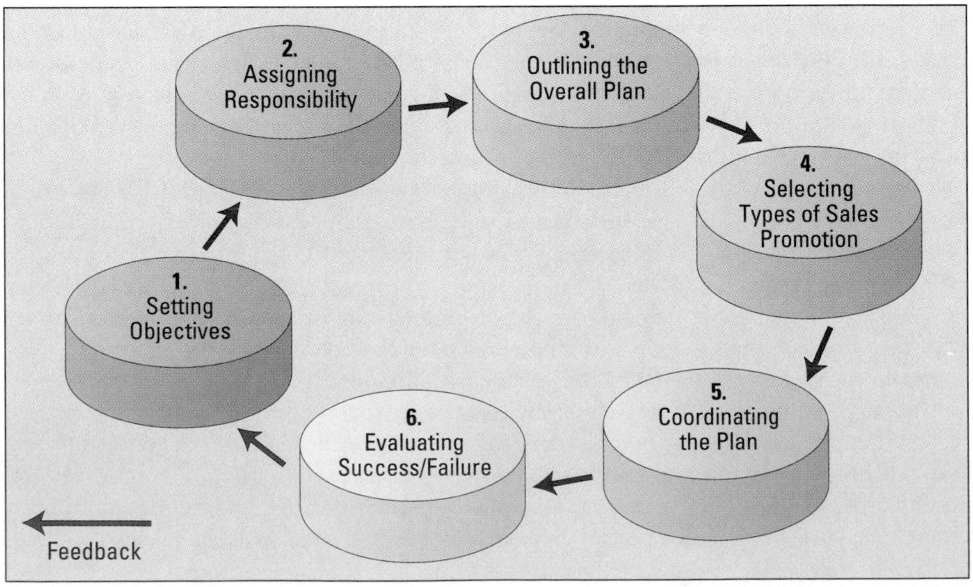

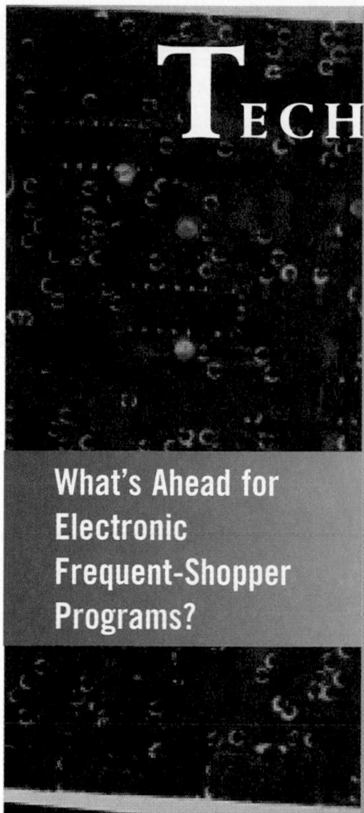

TECHNOLOGY & MARKETING

What's Ahead for Electronic Frequent-Shopper Programs?

According to Brian P. Woolf, president of the Retail Strategy Center, a retailer should "treat all customers equally, but reward them differently." He bases this advice on the fact that a firm's best customers can spend 50 times the amount of its worst customers.

One way to enact a differential reward strategy is to use an electronic frequent-shopper program. Such programs rely on the use of shopper information that has been captured by retailers at the point-of-sale.

There are various types of frequent-shopper programs. Some are price-based, with frequent shoppers getting price reductions on their total bill or special offers not available to the general public. In another type of program, retailers contribute money to charities based on frequent-shopper purchases. Other programs offer different point values keyed to the products purchased. Some state-of-the-art programs even automatically accumulate shopper transactions. Until recently, retailers had to design and implement frequent-shopper programs on their own.

According to Brian Woolf, in over 90 per cent of the instances where retailers have introduced frequent-shopper programs, they have achieved a 6 per cent increase in same store sales. However, to achieve these results, a frequent-shopper program must be at the center of the retailer's overall marketing strategy.

Recently, Safeway Stores' Eastern Division announced a simple program available to marketers of packaged goods. These marketers can now participate in special targeted promotions aimed at Safeway's 1.2-million-member Savings Club data base. This data base contains purchase histories of consumers all the way down to the individual item level.

As marketing manager for Heinz ketchup, how would you tie into Safeway's Savings Club data base?

Source: Based on material in R. Craig MacClaren, "The Future Is in the Cards," *Promo* (July 1995), p. 56.

operation and efficiency. Promotions for consumers should induce impulse and larger-volume sales, sustain brand-name recognition, and gain participation. A promotion theme refers to its underlying channel member or consumer message—such as a special sale, store opening, new-product introduction, holiday celebration, or customer recruitment. See Figure 20-11.

Sales promotion conditions are requirements channel members or consumers must meet to be eligible for a specific sales promotion. These may include minimum purchases, performance provisions, and/or minimum age. A channel member may have to stock a certain amount of merchandise to receive a free display case from a manufacturer. A consumer may have to send in proofs of purchase to get a refund or gift. In some cases, strict time limits are set as to the closing dates for participation in a sales promotion.

Sales promotion conditions *are eligibility requirements.*

The media are the vehicles through which sales promotions reach channel members or consumers. They include direct mail, newspapers, magazines, television, the personal sales force, trade shows, and group meetings.

A promotion's duration may be short or long, depending on its goals. Coupons usually have quick closing dates because they are used to increase store traffic. Frequent-shopper points often can be redeemed for at least one year; their goal is to maintain loyalty. As noted earlier, if promotions are lengthy or offered frequently, consumers may come to expect them as part of a purchase. Some promotions are seasonal, and for these timing is crucial. They must be tied to such events as fall school openings, or model or style changes.

Finally, the use of shared promotions should be decided. With cooperative efforts, each party pays some costs and gets benefits. These promotions can be sponsored by industry trade associations, manufacturers and/or service firms, wholesalers, and retailers.

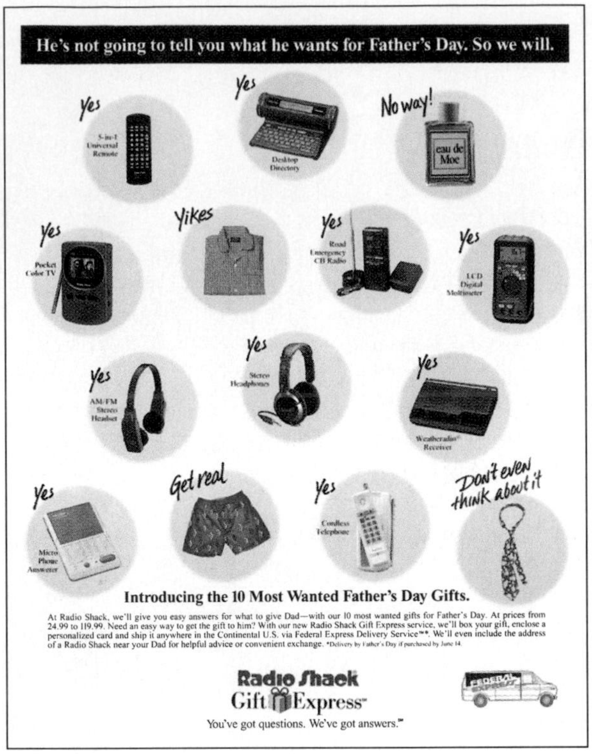

FIGURE 20-11
Happy Father's Day
Reprinted by permission.

For example, "McDonald's realizes the strength of the Walt Disney Co. and its strength with animated films, and Disney made a conscious decision to work with us, to our mutual advantage. So, in March 1996, McDonald's headlined a two-tier promotion that included an instant-win trivia game for adults and a kid-targeted Happy Meals promotion. The entire effort surrounded Walt Disney Home Video's top-selling Masterpiece Collection of 13 videos, including *The Lion King* and *Pocahontas*."[24]

Selecting the Types of Sales Promotion

There is a wide range of sales promotion tools available. The attributes of several promotion tools oriented to channel members are shown in Table 20-3. The attributes of several consumer-oriented sales-promotion tools are noted in Table 20-4. Examples for each tool are also provided in these tables.

The selection of sales promotions should be based on such factors as company image, company goals, costs, participation requirements, and the enthusiasm of channel members or customers.

Coordinating the Plan

Advertising and sales promotion should be integrated.

It is essential that sales promotion activities be well coordinated with other elements of the promotion mix. In particular:

- Advertising and sales promotion plans should be integrated.
- The sales force should be notified of all promotions well in advance and trained to implement them.
- For special events, such as the appearance of a major celebrity, publicity should be generated.
- Sales promotions should be consistent with channel members' activities.

[24]Kate Fitzgerald, "McDonald's Scores Big Promo Role with Disney," *Advertising Age* (January 8, 1996), p. 8.

Table 20-3

Selected Types of Sales Promotion Directed at Channel Members

TYPE	CHARACTERISTICS	ILLUSTRATION
Trade shows or meetings	One or a group of manufacturers invites channel members to attend sessions where products are displayed and explained.	The annual National Home Center Show attracts more than one thousand exhibitors and tens of thousands of attendees.
Training	The manufacturer provides training for personnel of channel members.	Compaq trains retail salespeople in how to operate and use its computers.
Trade allowances or special offers	Channel members are given discounts or rebates for performing specified functions or purchasing during certain time periods.	A local distributor receives a discount for running its own promotion for GE light bulbs.
Point-of-purchase displays	The manufacturer or wholesaler gives channel members fully equipped displays for its products and sets them up.	Coca-Cola provides refrigerators with its name on them to retailers carrying minimum quantities of Coca-Cola products.
Push money	Channel members' salespeople are given bonuses for pushing the brand of a certain manufacturer. Channel members may not like this if their salespeople shift loyalty to the manufacturer.	A salesperson in an office-equipment store is paid an extra $50 for every desk of a particular brand that is sold.
Sales contests	Prizes or bonuses are distributed if certain performance levels are met.	A wholesaler receives $2,500 for selling 1,000 microchips in a month.
Free merchandise	Discounts or allowances are provided in the form of merchandise.	A retailer gets one case of ballpoint pens free for every 10 cases purchased.
Demonstration models	Free items are given to channel members for demonstration purposes.	A hospital-bed manufacturer offers demonstrator models to its distributors.
Gifts	Channel members are given gifts for carrying items or performing functions.	During one three-month period, a book publisher gives computerized cash registers to bookstores that agree to purchase a specified quantity of its books.
Cooperative promotions	Two or more channel members share the costs of a promotion.	A manufacturer and retailer each pay part of the costs for T-shirts with the manufacturer's and retailer's names embossed.

Evaluating Success or Failure

The success or failure of some sales promotions is simple to measure.

The success or failure of many types of sales promotions is straightforward to measure since the promotions are so closely linked to performance or sales. By analyzing before-and-after data, the impact of these promotions is clear. Trade show effectiveness can be gauged by counting the number of leads generated from a show, examining the sales from those leads and the cost per lead, getting customer feedback about a show from the sales force, and determining the amount of literature given out at a show. Companies can verify changes in sales as a result of dealer-training programs. Firms using coupons can review sales and compare redemption rates with industry averages. Surveys of channel members and consumers can indicate satisfaction with promotions, suggestions for improvements, and the effect of promotions on image.

Some sales promotions—such as event sponsorships and T-shirt giveaways—are more difficult to evaluate. Objectives are less definitive.

Here are three examples relating to the effectiveness of sales promotion:

- About two-thirds of supermarket shoppers say that end-aisle displays and circular coupons "frequently" catch their attention.[25]

[25] "Impact in the Aisles: The Marketer's Last Best Chance," *Promo* (January 1996), p. 26.

Table 20-4

Selected Types of Sales Promotion Directed at Consumers

TYPE	CHARACTERISTICS	ILLUSTRATION
Coupons	Manufacturers or channel members advertise special discounts for customers who redeem coupons.	P&G mails consumers a 50-cents-off coupon for Sure deodorant, which can be redeemed at any supermarket.
Refunds or rebates	Consumers submit proof-of-purchases (usually to the manufacturer) and receive an extra discount.	First Alert provides rebates to consumers submitting proofs of purchase for its fire alarms.
Samples	Free merchandise or services are given to consumers, generally for new items.	America Online offers a free one-month trial of services.
Contests or sweepstakes	Consumers compete for prizes by answering questions (contests) or filling out forms for random drawings of prizes (sweepstakes).	Publishers Clearing House sponsors annual sweepstakes and awards cash and other prizes.
Bonus packs or multipacks	Consumers receive discounts for purchasing in quantity.	An office-supply store runs a "buy one, get one free" sale on desk lamps.
Shows or exhibits	Many firms co-sponsor exhibitions for consumers.	The Auto Show is annually scheduled for the public in New York.
Point-of-purchase displays	In-store displays remind customers and generate impulse purchases.	*TV Guide* sales in supermarkets are high because displays are placed at checkout counters.
Special events	Firms sponsor the Olympics, fashion shows, and other activities.	Visa USA is a worldwide sponsor of the Olympics.
Product placements	Branded goods and services are depicted in movies and TV shows.	Nike sneakers appear in the movie *Forrest Gump.*
Gifts	Consumers get gifts for making a purchase or opening a new account.	Savings banks offer a range of gifts for consumers opening new accounts or expanding existing ones.
Frequent-shopper gifts	Consumers get gifts or special discounts, based on cumulative purchases. Points are amassed and exchanged for gifts or money.	Airline travelers can accumulate mileage and receive free trips or gifts when enough miles have been earned.
Referral gifts	Existing customers are given gifts for referring their friends to the company.	Tupperware awards gifts to the woman hosting a Tupperware party in her home.
Demonstrations	Goods or services are shown in action.	Different models of Apple computers are demonstrated in a complimentary lesson.

- BMW received 6,000 pre-orders for its Z3 roadster after it was seen in the James Bond thriller *GoldenEye*. The car wasn't commercially available until several months after the movie opened.[26]
- In many countries outside the United States, coupons hold little attraction. As one Egyptian consumer says, "When I lived in the States, we used coupons all the time, but here I never believed the shop would actually apply the discount. If more people offered coupons and were trustworthy, I would use them." And according to a Canadian shopper, "Why should you buy peanut butter with 50 cents off, when you can get no-name peanut butter more cheaply?"[27]

[26]Blair R. Fischer, "Making Your Product the Star Attraction," *Promo* (January 1996), p. 88.
[27]Jan Jaben, "Shoppers Tell Marketers to Save Breath on Offers," *Advertising Age* (January 15, 1996), p. I-2.

MARKETING IN A CHANGING WORLD

Sales Training the 3M Way[28]

3M is taking a very novel approach to sales training for its veteran salespeople, and others can learn from its experiences. As one observer noted, "While innovation was long a part of the research, product development, and manufacturing processes at 3M, it wasn't as conspicuous in sales. 3M sales training, although always high-quality, was not focused as well as it might have been on customer needs. That's changed. Three years ago, innovation struck sales training: the firm started asking customers to tell it where salespeople needed to improve skills or get additional training."

The new sales-training approach is a big departure from prior 3M practice, when the company relied on broad customer satisfaction surveys rather than specific measures of salesperson performance. 3M now surveys customers to determine how its sales representatives are performing in terms of specific skills. In a typical year, 1,000 or so business customers are surveyed.

The new program is called A.C.T.—assessment and analysis, curriculum content, and training transfer. It provides "customer-focused, just-in-time, on-demand sales training." This is how A.C.T. works:

- A written questionnaire assesses selling skills in six areas: knowledge of products and services, strategic skills critical to best using the time spent with the customer, interpersonal selling, sales negotiation, internal influence and teamwork, and customer-focused quality.
- Each participating salesperson personally gives the questionnaire to a select group of about six customers. The customers then rate the importance of each of the skill areas, and how well the salesperson is performing them.
- Completed questionnaires go to an outside tabulation firm. (Sales managers only receive composite scores for their salespeople, but not the results of individual salespeople.) Results are computed and the gaps in salesperson performance are derived.
- Each salesperson works with his or her sales manager to set up a training curriculum to correct key weaknesses, and to undergo appropriate training.
- The last step is transfer, whereby each salesperson applies what he or she has learned to actual customer situations.

SUMMARY

1. *To examine the scope, importance, and characteristics of personal selling* Personal selling involves oral communication with one or more prospective buyers by paid representatives for the purpose of making sales. About 15 million people work in U.S. selling jobs; millions more work in sales jobs outside the United States. Yet, these numbers understate the value of personal selling because every contact between a company employee and a customer involves some degree of selling.

Selling is emphasized with high-volume clients, geographically concentrated customers, expensive and/or complex products, customers wanting sales services, and entries into foreign markets. Selling also resolves questions and addresses other issues. Selling costs are higher than advertising costs at many firms. An average business-to-business sales call costs several hundred dollars. Thus, efficiency is important.

Selling fosters a buyer-seller dyad (a two-way communication flow), offers flexibility and adaptability, adds to relationships with customers, results in less audience waste, clinches sales, and provides immediate feedback. Yet, personal selling can handle only a limited number of customers, is rather ineffective for creating consumer awareness, has high costs per customer, and has a poor image for some consumers.

2. *To study the elements in a personal selling plan* A selling plan has seven steps: setting goals—demand- and/or image-related; assigning oversight—to one manager or to several

[28]The material in this section is based on William Keenan, Jr., "Getting Customers into the A.C.T.," *Sales & Marketing Management* (February 1995), pp. 58–63.

managers; setting a budget; choosing the type(s) of sales positions—order takers, order getters, and/or support salespeople; selecting a sales technique—the canned sales presentation or the need-satisfaction approach; outlining tasks—including each of the relevant steps in the selling process and nonselling tasks; and applying the plan—which centers on sales management.

3. *To examine the scope, importance, and characteristics of sales promotion* Sales promotion encompasses paid marketing communication activities (other than advertising, publicity, or personal selling) that stimulate consumer purchases and dealer effectiveness. In the United States, sales promotion expenditures are more than $200 billion annually.

The rapid growth of sales promotion is due to firms aggressively looking for a competitive edge, the greater acceptance of sales promotion tools by both firms and consumers, quick returns, the pressure by consumers and channel members for promotions, the popularity during economic downturns, the high costs of other promotional forms, and technological advances.

A sales promotion helps attract customer traffic and loyalty, provides value and may be retained by people, increases impulse purchases, creates excitement, is keyed to patronage, and improves reseller cooperation. Yet, it may hurt a firm's image, encourage consumers to wait for promotions before making purchases, and shift the focus away from product attributes. Sales promotion cannot replace other forms of promotion.

4. *To study the elements in a sales promotion plan* A promotion plan has six steps: setting goals—ordinarily demand-oriented; assigning responsibility—to advertising and sales managers, company departments, and/or outside specialists; outlining the overall plan—including orientation, conditions, and other factors; selecting the types of sales promotion; coordinating the plan with the other elements of the promotion mix; and evaluating success or failure.

KEY TERMS

telemarketing (p. 556)
buyer-seller dyad (p. 557)
sales-expense budget (p. 561)
order taker (p. 561)
order getter (p. 561)
missionary salesperson (p. 562)
sales engineer (p. 562)
service salesperson (p. 562)
canned sales presentation (p. 562)
need-satisfaction approach (p. 562)
selling process (p. 563)
prospecting (p. 563)
approaching customers (p. 563)
sales presentation (p. 564)
closing the sale (p. 564)
sales management (p. 564)
sales territory (p. 565)
straight salary plan (p. 565)
straight commission plan (p. 565)
combination compensation plan (p. 565)
sales promotion orientation (p. 570)
sales promotion conditions (p. 571)

Review Questions

1. The Department of Labor lists 15 million people in sales positions in the United States. Why does this figure understate the importance of personal selling?
2. Under what circumstances should personal selling be emphasized? Why?
3. Draw and explain the buyer-seller dyad.
4. Distinguish among order-taker, order-getter, and support sales personnel.
5. When is a canned sales presentation appropriate? When is it inappropriate?
6. Outline the steps in the selling process.
7. Why is sales promotion growing as a marketing tool?
8. What are the limitations associated with sales promotion?
9. Differentiate between sales promotion orientation and conditions.
10. Why is the success or failure of many types of sales promotion relatively easy to measure?

Discussion Questions

1. Comment on this statement: "Although its role may differ, telemarketing may be successfully used during the selling process for any type of good or service."
2. How would you handle these objections raised at the end of a sales presentation?
  a. "I saw the price of the same item at a competing store for 10 per cent less than what you are asking."
  b. "Your warranty period is much too short."
  c. "None of the alternatives you showed me is satisfactory."
3. Present a checklist for a medium-sized apparel manufacturer to use in setting up a sales force in a foreign market.
4. List several sales promotion techniques that would be appropriate for a university. List several that would be appropriate for a minor league baseball team. Explain the differences in your two lists.
5. How could a sales promotion be *too* successful?

CASE 1

Rhodes Furniture: A Personal Selling Strategy[*]

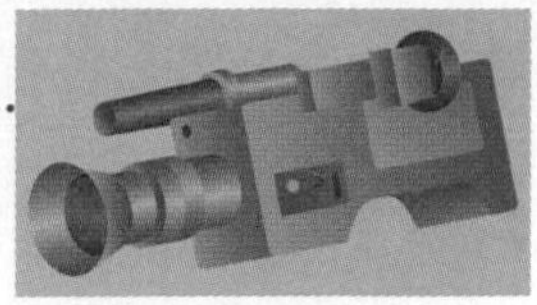

Rhodes Furniture is a regional U.S. retail chain featuring medium-priced home furniture and furnishings. Its stores are concentrated in major urban market areas, so that Rhodes can attain efficiencies in both its advertising and delivery. In the past, all of its stores were in high-growth states such as Alabama, Florida, Georgia, Mississippi, North Carolina, and South Carolina. Now it is expanding into other areas, such as the Midwest. Rhodes' total net sales are nearly $350 million, with net income after tax of $12 million.

Many furniture retailers center their marketing strategies around extensive selections, immediate delivery, and/or the lowest possible prices. However, personal selling and customer service are the long-term cornerstones of Rhodes' marketing strategy. For example, the firm has developed and implemented a highly respected and continuous sales training program (complete with video instructional materials).

The emphasis on personal selling provides these benefits to Rhodes:

- It increases the size of the typical sales transaction because salespeople encourage customers to buy accessories, such as lamps with sofas.
- Customers are often persuaded to purchase higher-quality merchandise. Typically, more expensive products have higher profits.
- The proportion of customers who purchase extended warranties with their furniture is increased.
- Customer satisfaction is enhanced when sales personnel are knowledgeable, helpful in coordinating furniture (such as the various pieces in a bedroom set), and polite.

Two aspects of the personal sales process for which Rhodes has developed extensive training materials are the approach/greeting and the follow-up/complaint handling. For example,

- Approach/greeting—"Introduce yourself. Be knowledgeable about all products on the sales floor, especially currently promoted products. Gain customer confidence and trust. Complement people on their taste in furniture and in clothing. Keep a comfortable distance from the customer. Get the customer's name and use it as often as you can during the sale. Make sure to smile. The expression on your face is very important." Rhodes' sales training materials encourage the salesperson to get the customer talking right away and to ask what the salesperson can show the customer. However, they also suggest that the salesperson should not pressure a customer who says he or she is "just looking." It also cautions salespeople against pre-judging a customer on the basis of his or her appearance or attitude.
- Follow-up/handling complaints—"It is virtually impossible for a customer to be abusive to a 'smiling voice.' Sound happy and enthusiastic, and soon your customer will too. Never argue with a customer. A customer can't maintain anger with someone who agrees with him or her. Use the customer's name often during the conversation. Be a good listener. Assure the customer that we will take care of the problem. Rebuild our reputation by reminding the customer that we usually don't make this kind of error."

QUESTIONS

1. What is the ideal role for personal selling at Rhodes? What should be the roles for the other elements of its promotion mix? Why?
2. Why do you think that Rhodes places so much importance on the approach/greeting and the follow-up/complaint phases in the personal selling process?
3. Develop three effective strategies for closing a sale at Rhodes for an expensive bedroom set to a newly married couple.
4. What are the pros and cons of Rhodes using a straight-commission compensation plan for its salespeople?

VIDEO QUESTIONS ON RHODES FURNITURE

1. Evaluate the dos and don'ts presented in this video.
2. What is the ideal use of the approach/greeting for Rhodes Furniture? Integrate your answer with the other stages in the personal selling process.

[*]The data in this case are drawn from "Rhodes Plans to Open 23 Stores by February 1997, Including Some New Markets," *Furniture Today* (August 15, 1994), p. S25; "Rhodes Reports Sales of $325.3 Million in Fiscal Year Ended February 28, 1994, Up 13.5 Per Cent Versus $286.5 Million in Previous Year," *Furniture Today* (April 18, 1994), p. 203.

CASE 2

In Sales Promotion: Does a Free Lunch Work?†

According to Donnelley Marketing's *Survey of Promotional Practices*, marketers cite these as their top reasons for product sampling: introduce a new product, launch line extensions, build a customer franchise, defend against brand competition, add consumer value, gain retail distribution, and defend against private label competition.

Among the well-known firms that have developed major sampling promotions are Taco Bell, Dunkin' Donuts, and Keebler. Each of these firms has recently used product sampling to increase trial rates and to convert nonusers to product users. Let's now examine each of their strategies.

In 1995, Taco Bell, a division of PepsiCo, decided to offer free samples of its new Border Lights low-fat foods for an entire day. The company's goal was to quickly generate trial and use of this line of foods. According to Taco Bell's chairman and chief executive officer, "We knew that once consumers took their first bite, they would love the taste." Taco Bell expected sales of its Border Lights products to reach $800 million by the end of 1995.

Dunkin' Donuts used sampling to increase the trial of its coffee. During summer 1995, it used four custom vans (which traveled to beaches, festivals, and other high-traffic locations) to give out free samples of its new flavored Hazelnut and Vanilla Nut coffees. Unlike Taco Bell, which handled its own sampling distribution, Dunkin' Donuts hired a sampling firm to plan and implement its sampling effort. Dunkin' Donuts also decided to go to its customers (rather than to provide the coffee samples in its stores) to increase the trial rate.

As Dunkin' Donuts' marketing development manager said, "Today, people live in the here and now. Even getting a coupon for a free product is considered a lot of work because they have to go to the store to get it. Sampling is intrusive and is a way to create awareness of our brands and get them into the consumers' mouths immediately."

After reformulating its Pizzarias snack product, Keebler realized that product sampling was the fastest and most efficient way to make its teenage customer market aware of the chips' superior taste. Working with a promotion agency, Keebler distributed a million free Pizzarias samples at over 200 arcades, tieing its sampling activity to *Brutal Paws of Fury* (GameTek's new video game). In addition to the free sample, teenagers received tear pads inviting them to a special offer upon purchasing a regular size bag of Pizzarias. The offer included a free demo of *Brutal Paws*, as well as a chance to win various prizes. Keebler's integrated marketing program even included retail displays, shelf talkers, and local radio tie-ins.

To date, Keebler has been "extremely pleased" with the results of this marketing effort. However, according to Keebler's brand manager, if the firm were to again use product sampling for Pizzarias, he would use more in-store sampling. This would facilitate the consumer's purchase of a desired product.

One way to assess the effectiveness of product sampling is to compute the break-even conversion rate. The conversion rate represents how many consumers buy a product after trying a free sample.

Mathematically, this is equal to a product's distribution costs (including the cost of manufacturing the samples) divided by the annual profit per user. Thus, if these costs equal $1 per unit and 750,000 samples are distributed, the firm's investment would equal $750,000. The annual profit per user can be calculated by multiplying the average annual use of the product by its profit margin. If the average annual use is 12 and the profit per unit is $1, the annual profit per user is $12. Thus, the break-even conversion rate is 62,500 (the $750,000 investment divided by the $12 profit per user).

QUESTIONS

1. Under what conditions should a firm employ an outside agency to handle its sampling effort?
2. Evaluate Dunkin' Donuts' strategy to sample its flavored coffees from vans rather than from its stores.
3. Discuss the pros and cons of product sampling versus coupons.
4. If a product's distribution costs are $3, one million samples are distributed, the annual usage rate is 6, and the product has a profitability of $1 per unit, what is the break-even conversion rate? Is this good or bad? Why?

†The data in this case are drawn from Kerry J. Smith, "Free Lunch," *Promo* (September 1995), pp. 93–96, 105.

PART 6 CASE

The Changing Role of Salespeople

Introduction

Intense global competition, slow growth in many markets, and demanding customers are forcing many companies to change their sales strategies and structures. Reinventing the sales organization is becoming a critical item on the agenda as firms restructure to lower costs and leverage their capabilities to build customer satisfaction. Examples of the changes under way include devising a customer orientation throughout an organization, building strong internal and external relations, creating multifunctional teams to manage key processes, and reshaping the organization's traditional pyramid structure.

There is perhaps no better illustration of these changes than American Express Financial Advisors (AEFA), which sells financial products such as mutual funds and insurance. AEFA's financial performance has been good, but management's long-term vision about the financial services market is guiding major changes in the company's sales strategy.

AEFA's 8,000 planners are building long-term client relationships. The planners get special training to help them shift into relationship building, and software to increase productivity and reduce response time. Commission pay has been scrapped in favor of bonuses that reward planners and managers for scoring well on customer satisfaction. Sales teams now manage processes like client satisfaction and account relations. AEFA's performance targets include 95 per cent client retention, 80 per cent planner retention after four years, and annual sales growth of 18 per cent.

AEFA's experience previews changes under way in many firms. The reforming process requires redesigning the traditional sales organization, leveraging information technology to lower costs and provide quick response, designing the sales strategy to meet different customer needs, and building long-term relationships with customers and business partners. The sales force is still a key contributor in organizations like AEFA, but salespeople are being asked to assume new responsibilities, and the methods for keeping score are changing.

Building Relationships

Building customer relationships is the core sales strategy of Marriott International Inc.'s business travel sales organization. The travel manager is the target for the 2,500-person sales organization. The key features of the major account sales strategy are to:

Source: Adapted by the authors from David W. Cravens, "The Changing Role of the Sales Force," *Marketing Management* (Fall 1995), pp. 49–57. Reprinted by permission of the American Marketing Association.

- Choose customers wisely.
- Understand what drives customer value and satisfaction.
- Lead with learning by following a step-by-step sales process.
- Invest in the customer's goal-setting process, rather than Marriott's.
- Develop a relationship strategy with a sense of purpose, trust, open access, shared leadership, and continuous learning.

Marriott knows regular customers are valuable assets who demand continuous attention by high-performance teams. Rapidly changing markets and customer diversity add to the importance of strong ties with key customers.

Setting Priorities Relationship marketing means getting and keeping customers via cooperation, trust, commitment, and sharing information. Besides Marriott, the firms with these strategies include American Express, AT&T, Electronic Data Systems, Motorola, and Owens-Corning.

A recent study by Learning International found that 96 per cent of the sales executives surveyed consider "building long-term relationships with customers" to be the most important activity affecting sales productivity. Only 39 per cent saw incentive programs as a key driver of sales productivity.

Sales reps and managers are front-line customer contacts, and relationship marketing is altering their traditional roles. The most sweeping change is that the entire firm is responsible for customer satisfaction. The era of "lone wolf" salespeople is giving way to building customer relationships involving all business functions. Importantly, a commitment to relationship marketing increases a sales organization's opportunity for internal support in its sales strategy. Greater involvement of other business functions in the customer relationship also changes selling from individuals to teams.

Assessing Customer Value Relationship building is a good strategy when there are large differences in the value of customers. High-value customers might want close collaboration from suppliers in product design, inventory planning, and order processing. Some customers might want collaboration. And buyer/seller collaboration is essential in total quality management. The goal is to focus buyer and seller efforts on relationships where both can benefit from close collaboration.

Implementing the Relationship Strategy Relationship building places new demands on all those involved in the process. The issues to be considered include:

- Deciding what criteria to use in partner selection.
- Recognizing that both partners must be willing to collaborate.

- Devising and enacting operating guidelines for the relationship strategy.

Relationship building requires careful planning and implementation. It is a long-term proposition built on foundations of trust and commitment. Deciding the value and feasibility of relationship building is the starting point.

Fostering Change

Complacency can have dire consequences, as illustrated by the experience of Encyclopedia Britannica Corp. First published 225 years ago in Edinburgh, Scotland, peak sales for Encyclopedia Britannica were $650 million in 1990, with profits of $40 million. During the early 1990s, CD-ROM technology gained acceptance in the encyclopedia market, but Britannica's management did not respond to the threat and continued to deploy a direct sales force of 2,300.

By 1994, Britannica's sales force was cut by half. Competitors had entered the market with CD-ROM encyclopedias, priced from $99 to $395, and targeted an estimated 7 million U.S. households. The typical $1,500 Encyclopedia Britannica pays a sales commission of $300, but it's tough to sell against a low-priced, high-tech version. The company now is in severe financial trouble.

Removing Barriers to Change During the 1990s, managers have aggressively reduced the size and altered the structures of their sales organizations. Flexible, adaptable structures are essential for competing today. One unique aspect of the new organizations is that they are complex networks of independent companies and units linked to share competencies and buffer risk and uncertainty. The changes are altering how sales organizations are designed and used to implement strategies.

IBM's search for the perfect organizational design highlights the changes taking place in sales organizations. There is perhaps no other company that has restructured so many times in recent years (17 revampings by one count).

The firm announced another reorganization in 1994, one with major changes in IBM's country chiefs. The actions would eliminate one or more management layers and simplify the hierarchical network of sales branches, trading area managers, and regional sales managers. The aim is to convert account managers from order takers into teams of business consultants.

How Organizations Are Changing Organizations are becoming flatter and focused on the management of core processes, like customer service. Multifunctional teams are responsible for client relations and new-product planning. Sales managers and salespeople need to develop new skills such as multifunctional collaboration and teamwork, and they will assume different responsibilities. The selling process is shifting from a short-term focus to problem solving aimed at customer satisfaction.

Specific customers and market segments are increasingly the basis for designing the sales organization and deploying salespeople. This means sales managers will be responsible for multiple sales strategies.

Consider how pharmaceutical sales organizations are being redesigned to target different market segments. Merck and its strategic partner, Swedish Astra AB, formed Astra/Merck to sell drugs. The new sales organization has a much smaller sales force than the typical pharmaceutical firm. By reducing the levels between salespeople and the CEO to only three and using information technology, Astra/Merck has lower costs and closer ties with customers.

Laptop computers help salespeople access data relevant to each customer's needs. Thus, a doctor gets research data on treatment costs. Other market segments targeted by Astra/Merck are health care organizations concerned about economic factors, traditional MDs seeking the right drugs for the treatment of different diseases, and medical thought leaders interested in new therapies.

Firms are examining the logic of specialized sales forces—responsible for certain products. Sales forces are being merged to reduce duplication in customer coverage and enhance customer coordination. These changes create different responsibilities for salespeople and could result in layoffs because multiple sales calls from specialized sales forces are eliminated.

The changes at Kraft Foods are illustrative. This new Philip Morris food division combines Kraft, General Foods, Oscar Mayer Foods, and Maxwell House products. The 3,500 people from the specialized sales forces are now one unit, organized in 300 marketing support teams—each assigned to a chain of stores. The salesperson is now responsible for a wide range of grocery products.

Making It Happen These organizational design issues need to be considered by sales managers:

- The typical pyramid organization of the 1970s and 1980s—with a chief sales executive, regional managers directing district managers, and eight or ten salespeople per district—is being redesigned to improve customer satisfaction and reduce costs.
- Red flags signaling the need to rethink the sales structure include high expense-to-sales ratios, loss of customers, large sales variations across territories, merging sales forces, and salesperson turnover. Benchmarking successful sales organizations can provide useful comparisons.
- A firm's process management calls for more participation by other business functions in the sales process, and for new ways to organize salespeople.
- Multiple sales channels for customers mean changing the sales structure and the method of customer coverage to leverage each channel's advantages.

Revamping traditional sales structures promises to be an exciting, though demanding, experience for sales managers and salespeople. Finding a viable sales organization design promises much trial and evaluation. Sales structures are apt to change more often in the future, creating new challenges for managers and salespeople, making agility and flexibility key requirements.

Gaining Commitment

The popularity of teams comprising people from different business functions has escalated. The intent is to get people from the different areas to work together rather than each person and department performing tasks and then passing them on to the next function. Deciding how to form and use sales teams in customer relationships, and how sales managers and salespeople are to participate in other team relationships, are important sales management issues.

The Value of Teams Teams can produce impressive results. Publishing Image, a small newsletter publisher, uses self-managed work teams to improve effectiveness. The firm has doubled its 1993 sales and increased its profit margin from 3 per cent to 20 per cent. The CEO of the 26-employee firm credits the success to the firm's four teams, each responsible for a customer group.

Each team has an account executive (salesperson), editorial specialists, and production workers. Every team member has unique skills but also performs other members' functions when needed. An account executive might do research for writers, proofread copy, and assist in layout. The experience gives each member a view of the entire operation. The team becomes involved in the sales process when client contact is initiated. Publishing Image's teams have raised efficiency, curtailed employee turnover, and improved customer satisfaction.

Removing Functional Barriers Though the team concept is compelling, making it work is another thing. A functionally organized company presents major obstacles. The restructuring of Corporate America successfully removed some functional barriers, but also required major changes in corporate culture, priorities, attitudes, work processes, and incentives.

Decisions must be made concerning the selection of team members, reporting relationships (and authority), job responsibilities, performance assessment, and incentive compensation. The company cannot respond to these issues without establishing a culture conducive to team relationships and providing training for leaders and members. For example, leaders of IBM's client teams spend three weeks at the Harvard Business School learning about business operations, consulting, and the client's industry. During the rest of the year, they work on case studies and write a thesis on the customer. Harvard professors grade assignments and students who pass are certified. The program is not mandatory.

IBM sales teams have the flexibility to recommend the products that best meet customer requirements—including competitors' products. The objective is helping the customer solve problems rather than selling IBM's products.

Leveraging Team Experience People who have completed major account management programs have valuable experience and skills in team building. Working with both customer buying center participants and people from various internal functions, they have been in the middle of turf battles and learned how to develop a consensus.

Sales managers face several challenges in organizations wanting to build multifunctional relationships. These are some of them:

- Is there a shared vision in the organization about the value of teams?
- Should there be client teams and, if so, what are the responsibilities?
- What is a salesperson's role on internal teams and customer-linked teams?
- What guidelines are needed for team member selection and team operations?

Many firms are committed to employing teams as a way of organizing work activities. If used in situations where their capabilities are needed and properly implemented, teams can produce impressive results. They work best in a corporate culture where strong functional hurdles are not present.

Coaching Vs. Commanding

Discussions with sales executives in many firms indicate that managers are coaching salespeople, directing their activities, and monitoring what they do. Although the tight control management style is losing favor, responses show that sales managers believe some monitoring and directing is still essential.

Shifting Styles A survey of managers points to several shifts: (1) collaboration rather than control, (2) coaching instead of criticizing, (3) employee empowerment rather than domination, (4) sharing information instead of withholding it, and (5) adapting to individual salespeople rather than treating everyone the same.

Some managers sense the changing business environment and adjust their management processes accordingly. But not all managers recognize these demands and not all corporate cultures accommodate change. Shifting from commanding to coaching is a challenge for both managers and salespeople. And some managers might be unwilling or unable to make the transition.

Firms planning to change practices should first review their recruiting, selection, and training of managers and salespeople. It's easier to create a coaching culture in a new firm than to alter an existing command-and-control organization. Coaching calls for a specific type of leadership style.

Keeping Score

Sales volume has been the way of keeping score. The salesperson or sales manager who meets and exceeds objectives (quotas) is considered to be doing well. Yet, scorekeeping in the sales organization also is undergoing change. Managers continue to track sales, but now add other measures such as customer satisfaction, profit contribution, share of customer (share of product category sales), and customer retention to evaluate salespeople and managers.

The Rules Are Changing The changes in performance evaluation are driven by three factors. First, total quality management and customer relationship building encourage a long-term orientation. Sales results are important, but so are building relationships. Second, primary emphasis on sales volume might lead to overselling customers and excessive inventory problems, causing customer dissatisfaction. Third, in organizations where pay is closely tied to sales, it's tough to encourage salespeople to develop new accounts, provide customer service, and emphasize all the products that are important to the company.

Activity or Outcome? Performance evaluation options range from primary emphasis on what the salesperson does (e.g., building effective relationships with customers) to emphasis on outcomes (e.g., sales). Either system is effective when matched to the right selling situation. Emphasis on activities works best when the sales strategy is to build long-term collaborative relationships with customers. Companies such as American Airlines, Caterpillar, IBM, and Procter & Gamble use a blend of activity and outcome control. Direct-selling organizations like Avon, Mary Kay, and Tupperware base compensation primarily on commissions.

A key issue is deciding the amount of salary compared to incentive pay. Managers who want to foster relationship strategies and form multifunctional teams will undoubtedly have to modify how they compensate salespeople.

Leveraging Technology

Sales force automation is changing both the effectiveness of selling and how it is done. PCs, telecommunications, and software give sales managers and salespeople a powerful array of capabilities. Information technology is now indispensable in many companies. For example, Godiva Chocolates' salespeople use portable PCs to process orders, plan their time, forecast sales, and communicate with internal personnel and customers. While in the department store candy buyer's office, the salesperson calculates the order cost, sends the order, and obtains a delivery date. He/she uses the customer's phone and his/her computer to communicate with the order processing center.

The investment in applying these technologies is high, but well-designed and implemented systems give valuable capabilities to the sales force. The equipment, software, and training costs for automating the sales force range from $2,500 to $5,000 or more per person. One firm, which spent $2.5 million to equip its 300-person sales staff with computers and software, considers the investment worthwhile because of increased sales and reduced costs.

Salespeople can analyze sales history much better and much faster than in the past. On the road or in the customer's office, information is at their fingertips to answer questions and solve problems. Visual displays show products, applications, and performance information. Motorola salespeople, for example, are able to design phone pagers in the customer's office by combining various design modules from a PC.

QUESTIONS

1. What do you recommend to enable salespeople to be viewed as more credible sources in a channel of communication?
2. What should be the role of consumer products salespeople in a promotion mix? The role of industrial products salespeople? Why?
3. How does marginal return apply to personal selling?
4. How could a personal sales force be used in a firm's public relations efforts? Explain your answer.
5. Recommend five specific things that a firm could do to foster a greater customer orientation among its salespeople.
6. Why won't a "lone wolf" type of salesperson be good for most companies? What would you do to convert a lone wolf to one of the pack?
7. Comment on this statement: "Multiple sales channels for customers mean changing the sales structure and the method of customer coverage to leverage each channel's advantages."
8. To a sales manager, what is the difference between coaching and commanding? Which is the preferred method today? Why?

PRICE PLANNING

PART 7

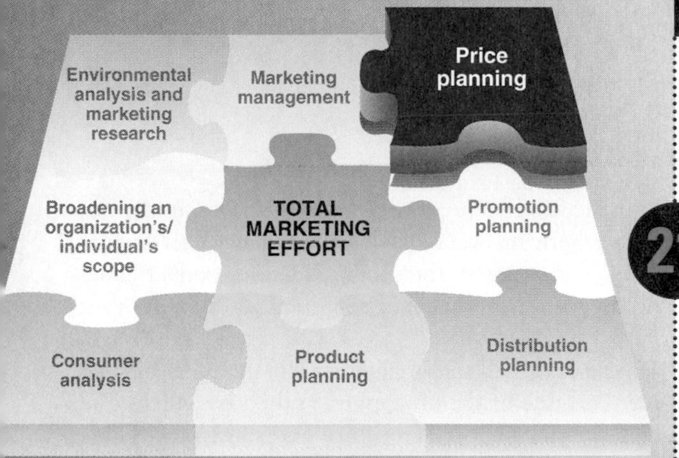

Part 7 covers the fourth and final element of the marketing mix, pricing.

21 Considerations in Price Planning

In this chapter, we study the role of price, its importance in transactions, and its interrelationship with other marketing variables. We contrast price-based and nonprice-based approaches. We also look at each of the factors affecting price decisions in depth: consumers, costs, government, channel members, and competition.

22 Developing and Applying a Pricing Strategy

Here, we explain how to construct and enact a pricing strategy. First, we distinguish among sales, profit, and status quo objectives. Next, we discuss the role of a broad price policy. Then, we introduce three approaches to pricing (cost-, demand-, and competition-based) and show how they may be applied. We also explain why cost-, demand-, and competition-based pricing methods should be integrated. We examine a number of pricing tactics, such as customary and odd pricing. We conclude the chapter by noting methods for adjusting prices.

Part 7 Video Vignette

Watson Pharmaceuticals

According to Watson Pharmaceuticals, the pricing strategy for generic (off-patent) drugs depends on whether a particular drug is the first, second, or third generic to be produced after a branded drug goes off-patent. Why? There is a long-term advantage to being the first generic on the market.

Consumers—in this case, pharmacists and physicians—are reluctant to switch among generic manufacturers once they start using a particular generic drug. Also, the first generic product on the market initially has the entire generic market to itself. Subsequent generics generally receive progressively lower shares. For example, the second generic product could capture a 30 to 40 per cent share, and the third generic could capture a 10 to 15 per cent share.

While generic drugs result in lower prices to final consumers, they also provide higher markups for wholesalers and pharmacies.

In general, generic drugs sell for 40 per cent less than the branded version of a product. This rule of thumb applies to the first and second FDA-approved generics in a category. The third and subsequent FDA-approved generics often sell at 60 to 70 per cent less. Yet, despite the increased presence of generics, the branded versions of drugs are rarely reduced in price after they go off-patent. The branded-version manufacturers count on the fact that 15 to 20 per cent of users never switch to a generic after their products lose patent protection. These users are extremely brand loyal.

While generic drugs result in lower prices to final consumers, they also provide higher markups for wholesalers and pharmacies. Thus, patients (or insurers) have an incentive to buy generics, and wholesalers and pharmacies have an incentive to sell them. The reduced prices for generics are largely due to their lower research and development expenditures.

Pharmaceutical products are distributed in a number of ways. Of the major channels of distribution, mail-order pharmacies account for 10 to 12 per cent of total pharmaceutical sales; chain pharmacies account for 50 per cent of sales; and 30 per cent of sales are to independent pharmacies and hospitals. HMOs exert their influence in all channels. In some cases, they require members to use mail-order pharmacies; in others, members can purchase generics through neighborhood-based independent or chain pharmacies.

Pharmacies play a key role in the generic drug sector. They control which generic is purchased by the consumer (unless the physician states "dispense as written," which means no generic substitution). Pharmacies do not want to stock multiple brands of generic drugs. They traditionally stock only one. Pharmacies can also be gatekeepers by telling physicians that they are out of a branded drug, but have a generic in stock.

CHAPTER 21
Considerations in Price Planning

Chapter Objectives

1. To define the terms price and price planning
2. To demonstrate the importance of price and study its relationship with other marketing variables
3. To differentiate between price-based and non-price-based approaches
4. To examine the factors affecting pricing decisions

"We have been slowly pricing ourselves out of the competition with our biggest competitors, which are the old airplanes in the fleets," says Ronald Woodward, president of commercial-jetliner manufacturing for Boeing. The pressure on air fares is taking root and appears "irreversible," he adds. "Deregulation is hitting the manufacturers now."

Reprinted by permission.

What does this mean? According to some experts, aircraft pricing finally is reflecting the deregulation of airline fares, airlines' preoccupation with reducing costs, and many airlines' delay in purchasing new aircraft. And it is a good thing, since the list price of smaller jetliners reached $50 million in 1995—with the list price of the largest jumbo jets hitting $175 million each!

Today, there is much greater flexibility in the pricing of commercial aircraft as manufacturers are more willing to offer substantial discounts from a plane's list price. Even Boeing, the world's leading commercial aircraft manufacturer and the United States' largest exporter, has embarked on a new pricing strategy. Gordon Bethune, the chief executive of Continental Airlines and a former senior executive at Boeing, says that Boeing has changed from its "fair price" notion to offering planes at prices airlines will pay.

Central to Boeing's current pricing strategy is its massive cost-reduction program. It consists of reduced staffing requirements, reduced cycle times (the time from the beginning of work on a plane to a plane's delivery), and standardized parts.

During one recent two-year period, Boeing laid off thousands of production and managerial personnel. It has lowered its cycle time by 45 per cent and plans another 20 per cent reduction. The firm has also begun standardizing parts on all of its planes. Previously, each part was individually engineered. Boeing estimates the parts standardization program will save it between $2 and $5 billion when the program is fully implemented.

Boeing's pricing program has increased interest among airlines for newer planes that are more fuel efficient, have better seat configurations, and fully meet new noise abatement standards at major airports. Airlines that might not have considered buying or leasing new planes are expressing greater enthusiasm. Furthermore, the pace of negotiations with such firms as International Lease Corp., the largest lessor of new aircraft, has increased. The firm plans to buy 40 to 50 new 737 jets from Boeing.

An example of Boeing's new aggressiveness can be seen in its winning an order for 41 planes from Scandinavian Airlines System (SAS). By some accounts, Boeing and its engine supplier, General Electric, agreed to sell the 100 passenger 737–600 jets for about $20 million each. That would be a 38 per cent discount from list price. The sale was particularly disheartening to McDonnell Douglas because SAS had been McDonnell Douglas' most loyal customer. Boeing's Robert Woodward remarked that his firm won the sale because "the value of our product was better."[1]

Boeing is so committed to its value pricing plan that it intends to give up some of the escalator clauses it has placed in long-term aircraft contracts (to protect itself against the effects of inflation).

In this chapter, we will learn more about the importance of price and its relationship with other marketing variables. We will also examine factors affecting pricing decisions: consumers, costs, government, channel members, and competition.

Overview

Through **price planning**, *each* **price** *places a value on a good or service.*

A **price** represents the value of a good or service for both the seller and the buyer. **Price planning** is systematic decision making by an organization regarding all aspects of pricing.

The value of a good or service can involve both tangible and intangible factors. An example of a tangible factor is the cost saving a soda distributor obtains from buying a new bottling machine; an example of an intangible factor is a consumer's pride in the ownership of a Porsche rather than another brand of car.

[1]Jeff Cole, "Boeing Is Offering Cuts in Prices of New Jets, Rattling the Industry," *Wall Street Journal* (April 24, 1995), pp. A1, A6; and Lawrence M. Fisher, "Boeing Beats Rival for $12.7 Billion Order," *New York Times* (November 15, 1995), pp. D1, D7.

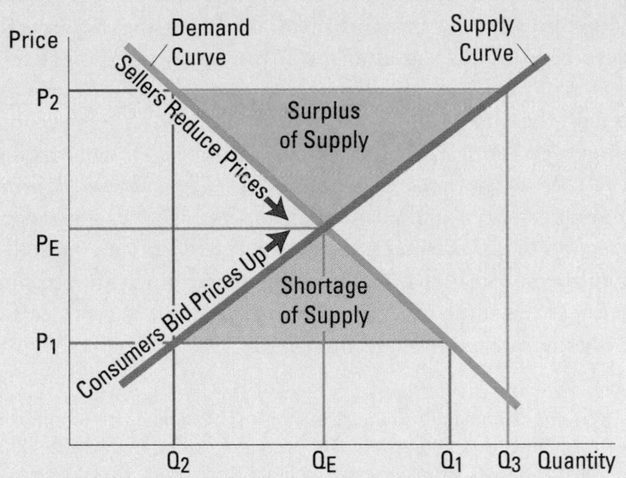

At equilibrium (P_E Q_E), the quantity demanded equals the supply.
At price P_1, consumers demand Q_1 of an item. However, at this price, suppliers will make available only Q_2. There is a shortage of supply of Q_1 - Q_2. The price is bid up as consumers seek to buy greater quantities than offered at P_1.
At price P_2, suppliers will make available Q_3 of an item. However, at this price, consumers demand only Q_2. There is a surplus of supply of Q_3 - Q_2. The price is reduced by sellers in order to attract greater demand by consumers.

FIGURE 21-1
The Role of Price in Balancing Supply and Demand

For an exchange to take place, both the buyer and seller must feel that the price of a good or service provides an equitable ("fair") value. To the buyer, the payment of a price reduces the purchasing power available for other items. To the seller, the receipt of a price is a source of revenue and a key determinant of sales and profit levels.

Many words are substitutes for the term *price*, including admission fee, membership fee, rate, tuition, service charge, donation, rent, salary, interest, retainer, and assessment. No matter what it is called, a price refers to all the terms of purchase: monetary and nonmonetary charges, discounts, handling and shipping fees, credit charges and other forms of interest, and late-payment penalties.

A nonmonetary exchange would be a department store awarding a gift to a person who gets a friend to shop at that store or an airline offering tickets as payment for advertising space and time. Monetary and nonmonetary exchanges may be combined. This is common with autos, where the buyer gives the seller money plus a trade-in. That combination leads to a lower monetary price.

From a broader perspective, price is the mechanism for allocating goods and services among potential buyers and for ensuring competition among sellers in an open marketplace. If demand exceeds supply, prices are usually bid up by consumers. If supply exceeds demand, prices are usually reduced by sellers. See Figure 21-1.

In this chapter, the importance of price and its relationship to other marketing variables, price-based and nonprice-based approaches, and the factors affecting price decisions are studied. Chapter 22 deals with devising and enacting a price strategy, and applying techniques for setting prices.

The Importance of Price and Its Relationship to Other Marketing Variables

The stature of price decisions has risen because more firms recognize their far-reaching impact.

The importance of price decisions has risen considerably over the last 30 years. First, because price in a monetary or nonmonetary form is a component of the exchange process, it appears in every marketing transaction. More firms now realize the impact of price on image, sales, and profits. Second, deregulation in several industries has led to more price competition among firms in them. Third, in the 1970s and early 1980s, U.S. costs and prices rose rapidly—leading both firms and consumers to be price-conscious. In some other nations, costs and prices continue to escalate very quickly. Fourth, in the 1970s through the mid-1980s, a strong U.S. dollar with respect to other currencies gave foreign competitors a price advantage in U.S. markets. Today, the dollar is weaker relative to such currencies as the Japanese yen, and a larger number of firms monitor international currency fluctuations and adapt their marketing strategies accordingly. Fifth, the rapid pace of technological advances has caused intense price competition for such products as PCs, CD players, and VCRs. Sixth, service-based firms are placing more emphasis on how they set prices. Seventh, in slow economic times, it is hard for firms to raise prices.

Many marketers share this view:

> Pricing is managers' biggest marketing headache. It's where they feel the most pressure to perform and the least certain that they are doing a good job. The pressure is intensified because, for the most part, managers believe they don't have control over price: It is dictated by the market. Moreover, pricing is often seen as a difficult area in which to set goals and measure results. Ask managers to define the firm's manufacturing function, and they will cite a concrete goal, such as output and cost. Ask for a measure of productivity, and they will refer to cycle times. But pricing is hard to pin down. High unit sales and increased market share sound promising, but they may in fact mean a price is too low. And foregone profits do not appear on any scorecard.[2]

Inasmuch as a price places a value on the overall marketing mix offered to consumers (such as product features, product image, store location, and customer service), pricing decisions must be made in conjunction with product, distribution, and promotion plans. For instance, Parfums de Coeur makes imitations of expensive perfumes from Chanel, Estée Lauder, and Giorgio and sells them for one-third to one-fifth the price of those perfumes. It uses similar ingredients but saves on packaging, advertising, and personal selling costs. It distributes via such mass merchandisers as Kmart.

These are some basic ways in which pricing is related to other marketing and company variables:

- Prices ordinarily vary over the life of a product category, from high prices to gain status-conscious innovators to lower prices to lure the mass market.
- Customer service is affected since low prices are often associated with less customer service.
- From a distribution perspective, the prices charged to resellers must adequately compensate them for their functions, yet be low enough to be competitive with other brands at the wholesale or retail level.
- There may be conflict in a distribution channel if a manufacturer tries to control or suggest final prices.
- Product lines with different features—and different prices—can attract different market segments.
- A sales force may need some flexibility in negotiating prices and terms, particularly with large business accounts.
- The roles of marketing and finance personnel must be coordinated. Marketers often begin with the prices that people are willing to pay and work backward to ascertain acceptable company costs. Finance people typically start with costs and add desired profits to set prices.
- As costs change, decisions must be made as to whether to pass these changes on to consumers, absorb them, or modify product features.

[2]Robert J. Dolan, "How Do You Know When the Price Is Right?" *Harvard Business Review*, Vol. 73 (September–October 1995), p. 174.

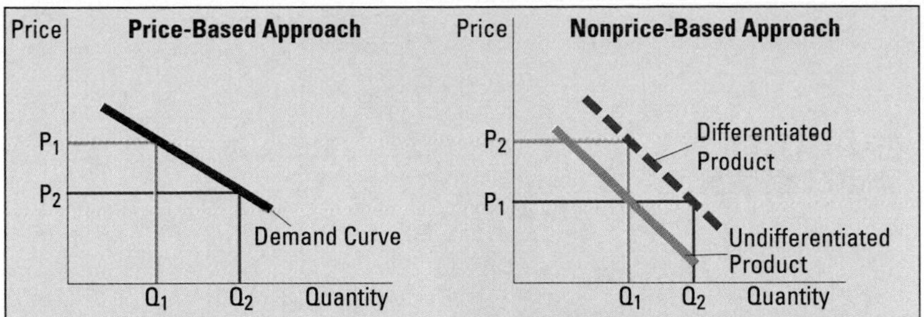

A company operating at P_1 Q_1 may increase sales by lowering its price to P_2. This increases demand to Q_2.

A firm relying on a price-based approach must lower its prices to increase sales.

Through a nonprice-based approach, the firm shifts the consumer demand curve to the right by successfully differentiating its products from competitors. This enables the firm to:
(a) increase demand from Q_1 to Q_2 at price P_1, or
(b) raise the price from P_1 to P_2 while maintaining a demand of Q_1.

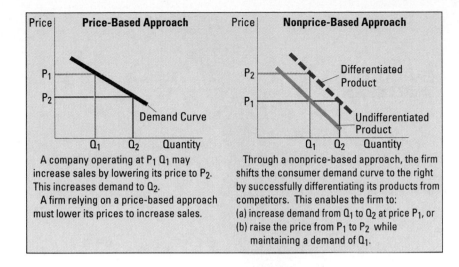

FIGURE 21-2
Price-Based and Nonprice-Based Approaches

Pricing internationally can be quite complicated.

If firms market products in foreign markets, "One of the most significant and perplexing of decisions has to do with pricing. Determining what prices to charge and when to change those prices are almost always tough decisions, but they become even more complicated when a company begins offering products to customers in several international markets." The greater complexity is typically due to the divergent company goals in different markets, the varying attributes of each market, and other factors. Furthermore, the ability to set prices in foreign markets may be affected by variations in government rules, competition, currency exchange rates, anti-dumping laws, operating costs, the rate of inflation, the standard of living, and so on.[3]

Price-Based and Nonprice-Based Approaches

A **price-based approach** *occurs when sellers stress low prices; a* **nonprice-based approach** *emphasizes factors other than price.*

With a **price-based approach**, sellers influence consumer demand primarily through changes in price levels. With a **nonprice-based approach**, sellers downplay price as a factor in consumer demand by creating a distinctive good or service via promotion, packaging, delivery, customer service, availability, and other marketing factors. The more unique a product offering is perceived by consumers, the greater a firm's freedom to set prices above competitors'. See Figure 21-2.

In a price-based approach, sellers move along a demand curve by raising or lowering prices. This is a flexible marketing technique because prices can be adjusted quickly and easily to reflect demand, cost, or competitive factors. Yet, of all the controllable marketing variables, price is the easiest for a competitor to copy. This may result in "me-too" strategies or even in price wars. Furthermore, the government may monitor anti-competitive aspects of price-based strategies.

In a nonprice-based approach, sellers shift consumer demand curves by stressing the distinctive attributes of their products. This lets firms increase unit sales at a given price or sell their original supply at a higher price. The risk with a nonprice strategy is that consumers may not perceive a seller's product as better than a competitor's. People would then buy the lower-priced item believed to be similar to the higher-priced one.

These are examples of price- and nonprice-oriented strategies:

- Since their introduction in 1983, more than 150 million low-price Swatch watches have been sold. These watches are fashionable, yet have fewer working parts than more costly models. The newest Swatch line is called Irony—featuring metal bands (instead of plastic ones). The Irony line retails for $55 to $75. See Figure 21-3.
- "Call it the Great Grape Squeeze. The price of first-class Bordeaux rose a head-spinning 30 per cent last year, and topflight California wines kept pace. But don't reach

[3]James K. Weekly, "Pricing in Foreign Markets: Pitfalls and Opportunities," *Industrial Marketing Management*, Vol. 21 (May 1992), pp. 173–179.

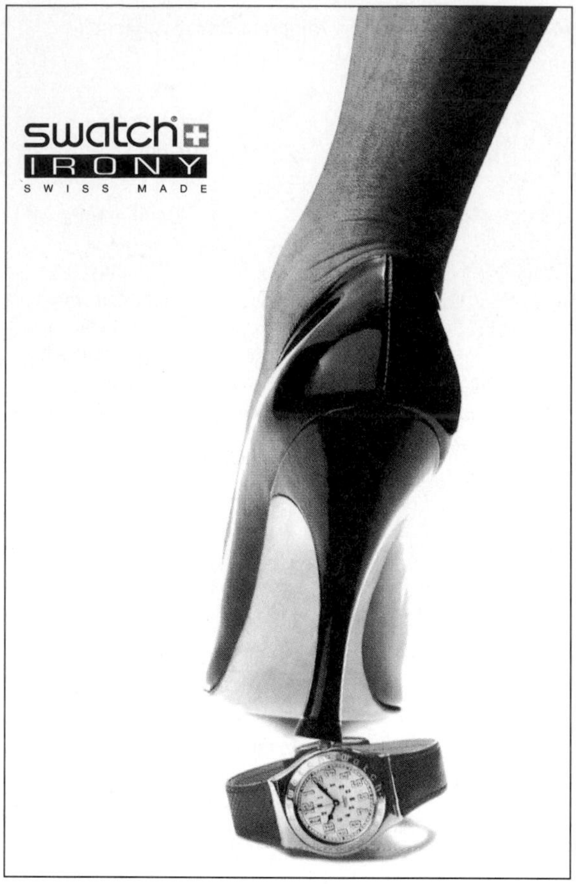

FIGURE 21-3
Swatch's Price-Oriented Strategy
Swatch watches sell for $50 to $75. The new Irony series retails for $55 to $75.
Reprinted by permission.

for Chateau Screw Cap just yet: There are solutions for the wannabe wine maven. Those with a nose for a bargain, as well as a bouquet, can slash their wine bills by shopping around. The mail-order Wine Club in California, for one, has a wide selection and charges just 12 per cent above wholesale, compared with 33 per cent or more for many stores. But a $37 shipping charge outside California can easily swallow the savings for out-of-towners."[4]

- Lenox makes fine china and crystal, which are elegant and expensive. Ads rarely mention price, but focus on product quality and design. "Lenox—Because art is not an extravagance" is one of its slogans. See Figure 21-4.
- Gucci is the Italian designer/manufacturer of upscale fashion accessories. ("Everyone in Hollywood has to have Gucci's velvet hip-huggers—and the suede loafers with the classic horse's bit on top of a lug sole are selling as fast as Gucci can deliver them.") Its shoes are priced from $160 to $1,050, handbags go for $335 to $8,995, and women's apparel prices are $110 to $9,000. The company recently scrapped some of its cheaper items, such as canvas and plastic handbags.[5]

Factors Affecting Pricing Decisions

Before a firm develops a pricing strategy (which is described in Chapter 22), it should analyze the outside factors affecting decisions. Like distribution planning, pricing depends heavily on elements external to the firm. This contrasts with product and promotion decisions, which are more controlled by a firm (except for publicity). Sometimes, outside

[4]Richard S. Teitelbaum, "When Bargain Meets Bouquet," *Fortune* (February 5, 1996), p. 137.
[5]John Tagliabue, "Gucci Gains Ground with Revival of Style," *New York Times* (December 14, 1995), pp. D1, D6.

Shown: Chateau China, Clarity Crystal
LENOX
Because art is never an extravagance.

FIGURE 21-4
Lenox's Nonprice-Oriented Strategy
Reprinted by permission. Not to be reproduced without authorization of Lenox China and Crystal.

elements greatly influence the ability to set prices; in other cases, they have little impact. Figure 21-5 outlines the major factors, which are discussed next.

Consumers

According to the **law of demand**, *more is bought at low prices;* **price elasticity** *explains reactions to changes.*

Company personnel involved with pricing decisions must understand the relationship between price and consumer purchases and perceptions. This relationship is explained by two economic principles—the law of demand and the price elasticity of demand—and by market segmentation.

The **law of demand** states that consumers usually purchase more units at a low price than at a high price. The **price elasticity of demand** indicates the sensitivity of buyers to price changes in terms of the quantities they will purchase.[6]

Price elasticity represents the percentage change in the quantity demanded relative to a specific percentage change in the price charged. This formula shows the percentage change in demand for each 1 per cent change in price:

$$\text{Price elasticity} = \frac{\dfrac{\text{Quantity 1} - \text{Quantity 2}}{\text{Quantity 1} + \text{Quantity 2}}}{\dfrac{\text{Price 1} - \text{Price 2}}{\text{Price 1} + \text{Price 2}}}$$

[6]See N. Carroll Mohn, "Price Research for Decision Making," *Marketing Research* (Winter 1995), pp. 11–19; Stephen J. Hoch, Byung-Do Kim, Alan L. Montgomery, and Peter E. Rossi, "Determinants of Store-Level Price Elasticity," *Journal of Marketing Research*, Vol. 32 (February 1995), pp. 17–29; and Francis J. Mulhern and Robert P. Leone, "Measuring Market Response to Price Changes: A Classification Approach," *Journal of Business Research*, Vol. 33 (July 1995), pp. 197–205.

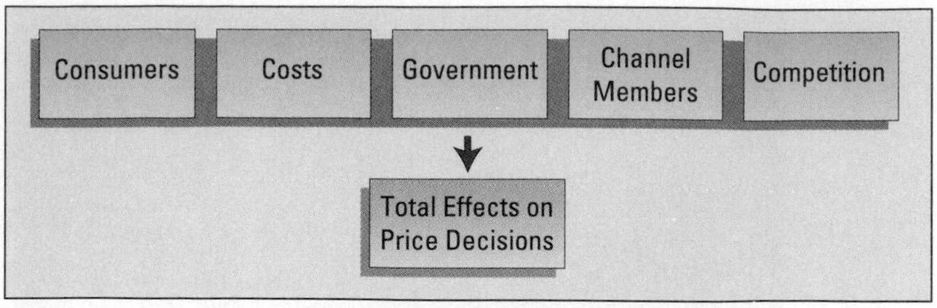

FIGURE 21-5
Factors Affecting Price Decisions

Because the quantity demanded usually falls as price rises, elasticity is a negative number. However, for purposes of simplicity, elasticity calculations are usually expressed as positive numbers.

Demand may be **elastic, inelastic,** *or* **unitary.** *It depends on the availability of substitutes and the urgency of need.*

Elastic demand occurs if relatively small changes in price result in large changes in quantity demanded. Numerically, price elasticity is greater than 1. With elastic demand, total revenue goes up when prices are decreased and goes down when prices rise. **Inelastic demand** takes place if price changes have little impact on the quantity demanded. Price elasticity is less than 1. With inelastic demand, total revenue goes up when prices are raised and goes down when prices decline. **Unitary demand** exists if price changes are exactly offset by changes in the quantity demanded, so total sales revenue remains constant. Price elasticity is 1.

Demand elasticity is based mostly on two criteria: availability of substitutes and urgency of need. If people *believe* there are many similar goods or services from which to choose or have no urgency to buy, demand is elastic and greatly influenced by price changes: Price increases lead to purchases of substitutes or delayed purchases, and decreases expand sales as people are drawn from competitors or move up the date of their purchases. For some people, the airfare for a vacation is highly elastic. If prices go up, they may travel to a nearer location by car or postpone a trip.

If consumers believe a firm's offering is unique or there is an urgency to buy, demand is inelastic and little influenced by price changes: Neither price increases nor declines will have much impact on demand. In most locales, when heating oil prices go up or down, demand remains relatively constant because there is often no feasible substitute—and homes and offices must be properly heated. Brand loyalty also generates inelastic demand; consumers then feel their brands are distinctive and do not accept substitutes. Finally, emergency conditions increase demand inelasticity. A truck driver with a flat tire would pay more for a replacement than a driver with time to shop around. Figure 21-6 illustrates elastic and inelastic demand.

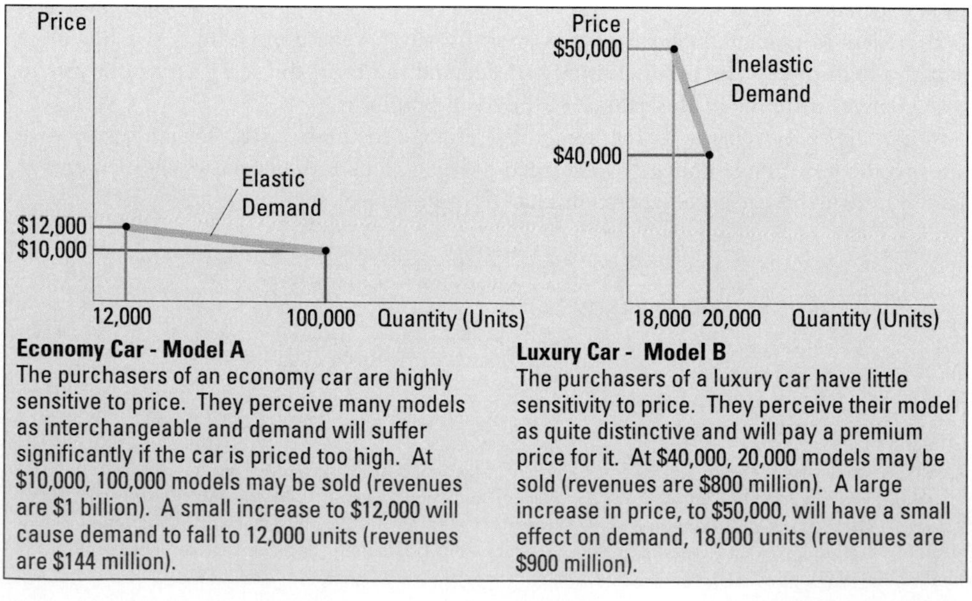
Price
Elastic Demand
$12,000
$10,000
12,000
100,000
Quantity (Units)
Economy Car - Model A
The purchasers of an economy car are highly sensitive to price. They perceive many models as interchangeable and demand will suffer significantly if the car is priced too high. At $10,000, 100,000 models may be sold (revenues are $1 billion). A small increase to $12,000 will cause demand to fall to 12,000 units (revenues are $144 million).
Price
$50,000
Inelastic Demand
$40,000
18,000
20,000
Quantity (Units)
Luxury Car - Model B
The purchasers of a luxury car have little sensitivity to price. They perceive their model as quite distinctive and will pay a premium price for it. At $40,000, 20,000 models may be sold (revenues are $800 million). A large increase in price, to $50,000, will have a small effect on demand, 18,000 units (revenues are $900 million).

FIGURE 21-6
Demand Elasticity for Two Models of Automobiles

It should be noted that demand elasticity usually varies over a wide range of prices for the same good or service. At very high prices, even revenues for essential goods and services may fall (mass-transit ridership would drop a lot if fares rise from $1.50 to $3; driving would become a more reasonable substitute). At very low prices, demand cannot be stimulated further; market saturation is reached and consumers may begin to perceive quality as inferior.

Table 21-1 shows the price-elasticity calculations for an office-equipment repair business. There is a clear relationship between price and demand. At the lowest price, $60, daily demand is greatest: 10 service calls. At the highest price, $120, demand is least: 5 service calls. Demand is inelastic between $60 and $84; total service-call revenues (price × quantity) rise as price increases. Demand is unitary between $84 and $96; total service-call revenues remain the same ($672). Demand is elastic between $96 and $120; total service-call revenues decline as the price rises within this range.

Although a fee of either $84 or $96 yields the highest total service-call revenues, $672, other criteria must be evaluated before selecting a price. The repair firm in Table 21-1 should consider costs per service call; the number of servicepeople required at different levels of demand; the overall revenues generated by each service call, including

Table 21-1

Price Elasticity for Service Calls by an Office-Equipment Repair Business

PRICE OF SERVICE CALL	SERVICE CALLS DEMANDED PER DAY	REVENUES FROM SERVICE CALLS	PRICE ELASTICITY OF DEMAND[a]	TYPE OF DEMAND
$ 60.00	10	$600.00		
			$E = \frac{(10-9)}{(10+9)} \Big/ \frac{(\$60-\$72)}{(\$60+\$72)} = 0.58$	Inelastic
$ 72.00	9	$648.00		
			$E = \frac{(9-8)}{(9+8)} \Big/ \frac{(\$72-\$84)}{(\$72+\$84)} = 0.76$	Inelastic
$ 84.00	8	$672.00		
			$E = \frac{(8-7)}{(8+7)} \Big/ \frac{(\$84-\$96)}{(\$84+\$96)} = 1.00$	Unitary
$ 96.00	7	$672.00		
			$E = \frac{(7-6)}{(7+6)} \Big/ \frac{(\$96-\$108)}{(\$96+\$108)} = 1.31$	Elastic
$108.00	6	$648.00		
			$E = \frac{(6-5)}{(6+5)} \Big/ \frac{(\$108-\$120)}{(\$108+\$120)} = 1.73$	Elastic
$120.00	5	$600.00		

[a]Expressed as positive numbers.

parts and additional labor charges; travel time; the percentage of satisfied customers at different prices, as expressed by repeat business; and the potential for new-customer referrals.

Consumers can be segmented in terms of their price orientation.

Price sensitivity varies by market segment because all people are not equally price-conscious. Consumers can be divided into such segments as these:

- Price shoppers—They are interested in the "best deal" for a product.
- Brand-loyal customers—They believe their current brands are better than others and will pay "fair" prices for those products.
- Status seekers—They buy prestigious brands and product categories and will pay whatever prices are set; higher prices signify greater status.
- Service/features shoppers—They place a great value on customer service and/or product features and will pay for them.
- Convenience shoppers—They value ease of shopping, nearby locations, long hours by sellers, and other approaches that make shopping simple; they will pay above-average prices.

A firm must determine which segment or segments are represented by its target market and plan accordingly.

A consumer's perception of a price level is the **subjective price**.

The consumer's (market segment's) perception of the price of a good or service as being high, fair, or low—its **subjective price**—may be more important than its actual price. For example, a consumer may feel a low price represents a good buy or inferior quality—or a high price represents status or poor value, depending on his/her perception.

Such factors as these affect a consumer's (market segment's) subjective price: Purchase experience with a particular good or service—"How much have I paid in the past?" Purchase experience with other, rather similar goods or services—"What's a fair price for an item in the same or adjacent product category that I bought before?" Self-image—"How much should a person like me pay for something like this?" Social situation—"How much do the people around me expect me to pay for something like this?" Context of the purchase—"What should this cost in these circumstances?"[7]

Kaufman Broad, a leading home developer, strives very hard to offer prices perceived as fair by its target market. Its homes have energy-saving features, water-saving fixtures, and low-maintenance roofs. Because the firm identifies growing communities and buys land before prices become inflated, it controls land costs. It also works with clients to gain attractive mortgage financing. A Kaufman Broad residential unit is "not just a house, it's a home."[8]

Costs

The costs of raw materials, supplies, labor, transportation, and other items are commonly beyond a firm's control. Yet, they have a great impact on prices. In the United States, from the early 1970s into the 1980s, many costs rose rapidly and pushed prices to high levels before leveling off. For example,

- The minimum wage rose from $1.60 per hour in 1970 to $3.35 per hour in 1981. This affected fast-food retailers and other firms relying on semiskilled and unskilled labor. The minimum wage remained the same until 1990, when it rose to $3.80. The amount went to $4.25 in 1991, and stayed there until $5.15 was proposed in 1996.
- Mortgage interest rates more than doubled between 1977 and 1981, severely dampening the housing market, before starting to decline in 1983. Since 1993, they have been at 25-year lows.

[7] G. Ray Funkhouser, "Using Consumer Expectations as an Input to Pricing Decisions," *Journal of Product & Brand Management*, Vol. 1 (Spring 1992), p. 48. See also Richard W. Olshavsky, Andrew B. Aylesworth, and DeAnna S. Kempf, "The Price-Choice Relationship: A Contingent Processing Approach," *Industrial Marketing Management*, Vol. 33 (July 1995), pp. 207–218; and John R. Johnson, "How Valuable Is Value Added?" *Industrial Distribution* (May 1995), pp. 35–38.

[8] Kaufman Broad correspondence.

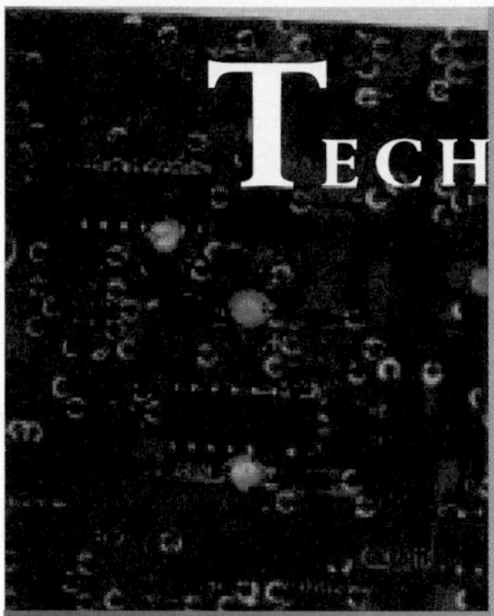

TECHNOLOGY & MARKETING

New Technology *and* Lower Prices?

Three years ago, when Computer Associates introduced its *Simply Money* accounting software, the firm decided to offer the package free of charge to consumers. Computer Associates correctly assumed the favorable publicity that a no-cost offer would generate was worth much more than the cost of producing the diskettes. Furthermore, Computer Associates felt the zero-price strategy would increase its data base of customers, creating a ready-made market for upgrades and other programs.

According to marketing experts, the massive cost reductions attributable to new technologies now call for redefining value. These experts say that companies need to establish long-term relationships with customers—even if it means giving the first generation of a product away for free.

Companies are reacting to the combination of declining costs and better product quality by using radically different marketing strategies. For example, due to their market dominance, Intel and Microsoft have kept above-average prices compared to smaller competitors. And while clone makers like Packard Bell compete mostly on price, firms such as Compaq and Dell look to differentiate their products by offering superior customer service, distinctive product features, and more competitive prices.

In many instances, technological growth has been so great that it has played havoc with pricing. For example, the sound quality of inexpensive CD players is so good that some consumers use them instead of costly audio systems. And a five-dollar quartz watch is as accurate as a model costing 100 times its price.

An executive with the Japan Institute of Office Automation says these advances create real pricing dilemmas. He asks, "How do you assign prices or value in a world where quality is perfect and nothing breaks?"

As a Computer Associates marketing executive, under what conditions would you recommend another product giveaway? When would you avoid giveaways? Why?

Source: Based on material in Neil Gross, Peter Coy, and Otis Port, "The Technology Paradox," *Business Week* (March 6, 1995), pp. 76–84.

- The cost of prime-time TV ads have gone up dramatically. A 30-second ad on the 1972 Super Bowl cost $100,000. In 1996, the cost was $1.3 million.
- Fuel costs went up almost 500 per cent, before falling considerably in 1985 and 1986. This placed pressure on airlines, the trucking industry, and the auto industry. Since then, with scattered fluctuations, fuel costs have increased only a little—and sometimes even declined. In 1995, the prices for unleaded gasoline were lower than in 1980. But they rose considerably in 1996.
- Silver and gold prices were very volatile. Silver went from $6 per ounce to more than $50 per ounce, before dropping down. This caused problems for the photography industry, which uses silver as an ingredient in film. In 1996, silver was selling for $5 to $7 per ounce. Gold went from $45 per ounce to $1,000 per ounce, before settling at $300 to $500 per ounce. This affected dentists and jewelers.

Over the past 15 years, overall U.S. cost increases have been rather low. Although the 1980 inflation rate was 13.5 per cent, the 1996 rate was under 5 per cent. This means better cost control and more stable prices for most firms. Yet, unexpected events can still strike specific industries. As an example, a few years ago, the price of rhodium, a precious metal used to make catalytic converters for cars, rapidly rose from $1,750 to $7,000 per ounce due to problems at a refinery. Rhodium's cost per car went from $15 to $60.[9]

[9] "Scarce Metal Hits $7,000 an Ounce," *New York Times* (July 4, 1990), pp. 43, 48.

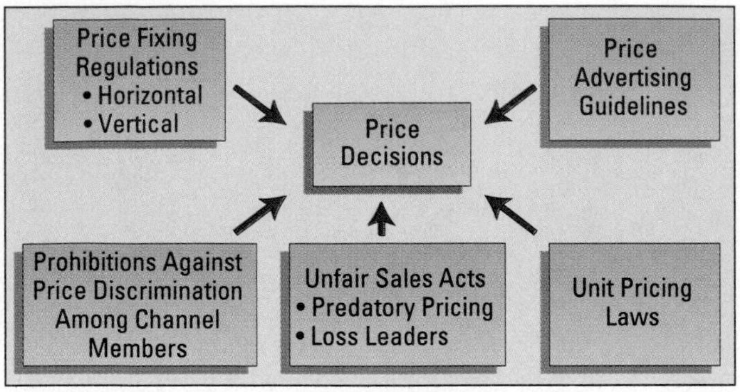

FIGURE 21-7
Selected U.S. Government Actions Affecting Price Decisions

When costs rise, companies pass along increases, alter products, or delete some items.

During periods of rapidly rising costs, firms can react in one or more ways: They can leave products unchanged and pass along all of their cost increases to consumers, leave products unchanged and pass along part of their increases and absorb part of them, modify products to hold down costs and maintain prices (by reducing size, using lesser-quality materials, or offering fewer options), modify products to gain consumer support for higher prices (by increasing size, using better-quality materials, offering more options, or upgrading customer service), and/or abandon unprofitable products. For instance, in response to a 50 to 60 per cent increase in the cost of pulp paper, Scott decided to reduce the number of sheets in the smallest roll of Scott Clean paper towels from 96 to 60—and *lower* the price by 10 per cent.[10]

Despite a firm's or an industry's best intentions, it may sometimes take years to get runaway costs (and prices) under control. A good illustration is the U.S. auto industry, where costs and prices have risen substantially since 1970. The average new car had a retail price of under $3,500 then; the average price is now about $20,000. Among the costs that auto executives have had to deal with are billions of dollars in retooling from large to small cars; high fixed costs for plant, equipment, and unionized labor; hundreds of millions of dollars for anti-pollution and safety devices; and investments of up to $1 billion or more to develop each major new model. Therefore, pricing decisions have to be made far in advance, and flexibility is limited.

Cost decreases have mostly positive benefits for marketing strategies.

If costs decline, firms can drop selling prices or raise profit margins, as these examples show: The use of microchips has reduced PC costs by requiring less wiring and assembly time in production, improving durability, and enlarging information-processing capability. PC prices have gone down steadily, thus expanding the market. On the other hand, low sugar prices let candy makers increase package size (and profits) without raising prices.

Sometimes, low costs can actually have a negative long-run impact:

> Since the oil price collapse of 1986, years of relatively cheap energy prices have brought the march toward greater efficiency to a virtual halt. And that has stymied the efforts to temper the indirect social and economic costs associated with energy use: increased dependence on foreign oil, which retards progress in cutting the trade deficit, and pollution and environmental damage—including the uncertain but potentially catastrophic effects of global warming.[11]

Government

U.S. government (federal and/or state) actions related to pricing can be divided into the five major areas shown in Figure 21-7 and discussed next.

Horizontal price fixing *is illegal and results from agreements among companies at the same stage in a channel.*

Price Fixing There are restrictions pertaining to horizontal and vertical price fixing. **Horizontal price fixing** results from agreements among manufacturers, among wholesalers, or among retailers to set prices at a given stage in a channel of distribution. Such agree-

[10]Chad Rubel, "Marketers Try to Ease Sting of Price Increases," *Marketing News* (October 9, 1995), pp. 5–6.
[11]"Why Lower Energy Prices Can Be a Mixed Blessing," *Business Week* (February 8, 1993), p. 16.

ments are illegal according to the federal Sherman Antitrust Act and the Federal Trade Commission Act, regardless of how "reasonable" prices are.

When violations are found, federal penalties may be severe: A company can be fined up to $10 million, and individuals can be fined up to $350,000 each and imprisoned for up to three years. The Justice Department investigates 140 price-fixing cases annually.[12]

In the 1990s, nine major airlines agreed to pay $14 million in cash and $396 million in discount fare coupons to resolve a price-fixing lawsuit. Two firms agreed to pay $11.5 million in federal fines and $19.5 million in state fines for engaging in a bid-rigging scheme in Florida; they had agreed to rotate low bids on contracts with schools and military installations for milk, juice, and ice cream. A participant in a price-fixing scheme involving the interstate sale of real estate (whereby pre-arranged bids were made at public auctions) was sentenced to four months in jail and fined $65,000. Several soda-distributor executives got jail time and paid fines of up to $100,000 each for partaking in price-fixing deals with competitors.[13]

To avoid price-fixing charges, a firm must be careful not to

- Coordinate discounts, credit terms, or conditions of sale with competitors.
- Talk about price levels, markups, and costs at trade association meetings.
- Plan with competitors to issue new price lists on the same date.
- Plan with competitors to rotate low bids on contracts.
- Agree with competitors to limit production to keep high prices.
- Exchange information with competitors, even informally.

Under **vertical price fixing**, *manufacturers or wholesalers try to control resale prices. This practice is now limited.*

Vertical price fixing occurs when manufacturers or wholesalers seek to control the final selling prices of their goods or services. Until 1976, the Miller-Tydings Act allowed these firms to set and strictly enforce resale prices if they so desired. This practice was known as fair trade. It protected small resellers and maintained brand images by forcing all resellers within fair-trade states to charge the same price for affected products. Fair trade was criticized by consumer groups and many resellers and manufacturers as being noncompetitive, keeping prices too high, and rewarding reseller inefficiency. Thus, the Consumer Goods Pricing Act terminated all interstate use of fair trade or resale price maintenance as of March 1976.

Today, resellers cannot be forced to adhere to manufacturer or wholesaler list prices. Most times, they are free to set their own prices. As a result, in 1995, Reebok entered into a consent decree with the FTC, whereby it agreed "not to try to set or control the prices at which retailers sell or advertise their prices—and not to threaten retailers with suspension or termination if they don't go along with suggested prices." In addition, Reebok agreed to pay state fines of $9.5 million.[14]

Manufacturers or wholesalers may control final prices only by one of these methods:

- Manufacturer or wholesaler ownership of sales facilities.
- Consignment selling. The manufacturer or wholesaler owns items until they are sold and assumes costs normally associated with the reseller, such as advertising and selling.
- Careful screening of the channel members that sell goods or services. A supplier can bypass or drop distributors if they are not living up to the supplier's performance standards, as long as there is no collusion between the supplier and other distributors. (A firm must be careful not to threaten channel members that do not adhere to suggested prices.)

[12]Allison Lucas, "Price Fixing Plays a More Visible Hand," *Sales & Marketing Management* (December 1995), p. 11.

[13]Joe Davidson, "Big Airlines Settle U.S. Suit on Price Fixing," *Wall Street Journal* (March 18, 1994), p. A2; Karen Blumenthal, "Southland Corp., Borden Inc. Admit Guilt in Milk Case," *Wall Street Journal* (March 2, 1990), p. D13; Paul M. Barrett, "Justice Department Acts Aggressively on Cases of Bid-Rigging, Price-Fixing," *Wall Street Journal* (December 17, 1990), p. B6A; and Andrew Galvin, "The Price of Fixing Prices," *Journal of Pricing Management*, Vol. 1 (Summer 1990), pp. 46–51.

[14]Viveca Novak and Joseph Pereira, "Reebok and FTC Settle Price-Fixing Charges," *Wall Street Journal* (May 5, 1995), pp. B1, B10.

- Suggesting realistic selling prices.
- Pre-printing prices on products.
- Establishing customary prices (such as 50 cents for a newspaper) that are accepted by consumers.

The **Robinson-Patman Act** *prohibits price discrimination when selling to channel members.*

Price Discrimination The **Robinson-Patman Act** prohibits manufacturers and wholesalers from price discrimination in dealing with different channel-member purchasers of products with "like quality" if the effect of such discrimination is to injure competition. Covered by the act are prices, discounts, rebates, premiums, coupons, guarantees, delivery, warehousing, and credit rates. Terms and conditions of sale must be made available to all competing channel-member customers on a proportionately equal basis.

The Robinson-Patman Act was enacted in 1936 to protect small retailers from unfair price competition by large chains. It was feared that small firms would be driven out of business due to the superior bargaining power (and the resultant lower selling prices) of chains. This act requires that the price differences charged to competing resellers be limited to the supplier's cost savings in dealing with the different resellers. It remains an important legal restraint on pricing, as evidenced by the multimillion dollar 1996 law suits brought by Rite Aid, Albertson, Kroger, and other pharmacy owners against 15 leading pharmaceutical manufacturers. The pharmacy owners accused the manufacturers of giving unfair discounts to bulk buyers such as HMOs (health maintenance organizations).[15]

There are some exceptions to the Robinson-Patman Act. Price discrimination within a channel is allowed if each buyer purchases products with substantial physical differences, if noncompeting buyers are involved, if prices do not injure competition, if price differences are justified by costs, if market conditions change (such as production costs rising), or if the seller reduces prices in response to another supplier.

Discounts are permissible if a seller demonstrates that they are available to all competing resellers on a proportionate basis, sufficiently graduated so both small and large buyers can qualify, or cost-justified. For instance, a seller must prove that discounts for cumulative purchases (total volume during the year) or multistore purchases by chains are based on cost savings.

Although the Robinson-Patman Act is oriented toward sellers, it provides specific liabilities for purchasing firms under Section 2(F): "It shall be unlawful for any person engaged in commerce, in the course of such commerce, knowingly to induce or receive a discrimination in price which is prohibited in this section." Accordingly, resellers should try to get the lowest prices charged to any competitor in their class, but not bargain so hard that their discounts cannot be explained by one of the acceptable exceptions to the act.

Unfair-sales acts *protect small firms from* **predatory pricing** *by large companies and restrict the use of* **loss leaders**.

Minimum Prices A number of states have enacted **unfair-sales acts (minimum price laws)** to prevent firms from selling products for less than their cost plus a fixed percentage that includes overhead and profit. About one-half of the states have unfair-sales acts covering all kinds of products and retail situations; approximately two-thirds have laws involving specific products, such as bread, dairy items, and liquor. Unfair-sales acts are intended to protect small firms from predatory pricing by larger competitors and to limit the use of loss leaders by retailers.

With **predatory pricing**, large firms cut prices on products to below their cost in selected geographic areas so as to eliminate small, local competitors. At the federal level, predatory pricing is banned by the Sherman and Clayton Acts. Manufacturers, wholesalers, and retailers are all subject to these acts.[16]

Loss leaders, items priced below cost to attract customers to a seller—usually in a store setting—are also restricted by some state unfair-sales acts. Sellers use loss leaders, typically well-known and heavily advertised brands, to increase their overall sales. They

[15]Laurie P. Cohen, "Pharmacists Assail Drug Accord as a Bitter Pill," *Wall Street Journal* (February 12, 1996), pp. A3–A4.

[16]See Gregory T. Gundlach, "Price Predation: Legal Limits and Antitrust Considerations," *Journal of Public Policy & Marketing*, Vol. 14 (Fall 1995), pp. 278–289.

Ethics IN TODAY'S SOCIETY

Can Pricing Be More Consumer-Friendly?

Some marketing critics compare the buying of products such as liquid detergent to tricky high school math problems. For example, which is cheaper, a 50-ounce bottle of regular liquid detergent at $4.99 or a 32-ounce bottle of concentrated liquid detergent at $3.49?

If the concentrated detergent washes the same amount of clothes as the regular version, it is cheaper. Unfortunately, many consumers still mistakenly buy the regular detergent, incorrectly believing that a larger-sized bottle washes more clothes. This matter is significant since concentrated liquid detergent now accounts for 60 per cent of the total liquid and powder detergent market. The president of the American Association of Family and Consumer Sciences calls this "a packaging and labeling discrepancy."

In the states with unit-pricing laws, only the price per ounce has been shown on supermarket shelves—despite the fact that the 50-ounce bottle and the 32-ounce bottle each clean 16 laundry loads. Thus, although the 50-ounce bottle's unit price is 10 cents per ounce versus 11 cents per ounce for the concentrated version, by the washload, the larger bottle costs 31 cents as compared with 22 cents for the concentrated version. This means that in addition to encouraging consumers to purchase a more costly product, the larger size package is also worse for the environment.

According to a coordinator for the federal Office of Weights and Measures, resolving this problem is not easy because it requires that the members of the Soap and Detergent Association define exactly what constitutes a "washload."

Despite the absence of standards, Safeway and Giant Foods have begun to compute unit prices on the basis of washloads. However, Kroger, Winn-Dixie, and A&P continue to compute unit prices based on ounces.

As a vice-president of consumer affairs for a major supermarket chain, develop a strategy for the unit pricing of detergents.

Source: Based on material in "Consumer-Friendly Labels Sought for Laundry Soap," *Marketing News* (January 30, 1995), p. 9.

assume customers drawn by loss leaders will also buy nonsale items. Because consumers benefit, loss-leader laws are rarely enforced.

With **unit pricing**, *consumers can compare prices for different-sized packages.*

Unit Pricing The lack of uniformity in package sizes has led to unit-pricing legislation in many states. **Unit pricing** lets consumers compare price per quantity for competing brands and for various sizes of the same brand.

Food stores are most affected by unit-pricing laws; they often must show price per unit of measure, as well as total price. For example, through unit pricing, a shopper could learn that a 12-ounce can of soda selling for 35 cents is priced at 2.9 cents per ounce, whereas a 67.6-ounce (2-liter) bottle of the same brand selling for $1.79 is priced at 2.6 cents per ounce. The larger size is cheaper than the smaller one.

Retailers' unit-pricing costs include computing per-unit prices, printing shelf labels, and maintaining computer records. The costs are affected by the number of stores in a chain, the sales per store, the number of items under unit pricing, and the frequency of price changes.

When unit-pricing laws were first enacted in the early 1970s, research found that people generally did not use the data and that low-income consumers (for whom the laws were most intended) were least apt to look at unit prices. So, critics felt the laws were costly without providing benefits. More recent research has shown that unit pricing is effective and suggests that consumer learning and the subsequent behavioral changes take time. However, upscale suburban residents are still more prone to use the data than others.

FTC guidelines establish standards for price ads.

Price Advertising Price advertising guidelines have been developed by the FTC and various trade associations, such as the Better Business Bureau. The FTC's guidelines specify standards of permissible conduct in several categories:

- A firm may not claim or imply that a price has been reduced from a former level unless the original price was offered to the public on a regular basis during a reasonable, recent period of time.
- A firm may not claim its price is lower than that of competitors or the manufacturer's list price without verifying, via price comparisons involving large quantities of merchandise, that an item's price at other companies in the same trading area is in fact higher.
- A suggested list price or a pre-marked price cannot be advertised as a reference point for a sale or a comparison with other products unless the advertised product has really been sold at that price.
- Bargain offers (such as "free," "buy one, get one free," and "half-price sale") are considered deceptive if their terms are not disclosed at the beginning of a sales presentation or in an ad, the stated regular price of an item is inflated to create an impression of savings, or the quality or quantity of a product is lessened without informing the consumer. A firm may not continuously advertise the same product as being on sale.
- **Bait-and-switch advertising** is an illegal practice whereby customers are lured to a seller that advertises items at very low prices and then told the items are out of stock or of poor quality. Salespeople try to switch shoppers to more expensive substitutes, and there is no intent to sell advertised items. Signs of bait-and-switch are refusals to demonstrate sale items, the belittling of sale items, inadequate quantities of sale items on hand, refusals to take orders, demonstrations of defective items, and the use of compensation plans encouraging salespeople to use the tactic.

Under **bait-and-switch advertising**, *sellers illegally draw customers by deceptive pricing.*

Channel Members

Generally, each channel member seeks to play a significant role in setting prices so as to generate sales volume, obtain adequate profit margins, have a suitable image, ensure repeat purchases, and meet specific goals.

A manufacturer can gain greater control over prices by using an exclusive distribution system or avoiding price-oriented resellers; pre-marking prices on products; owning sales outlets; offering products on consignment; providing adequate margins to resellers; and, most importantly, by having strong brands to which people are brand loyal and for which they will pay premium prices.

A wholesaler or retailer can gain better control over prices by stressing its importance as a customer to the supplier, linking resale support to the profit margins allowed by the supplier, refusing to carry unprofitable items, stocking competing items, having strong private brands so people are loyal to the seller and not the supplier, and purchasing outside traditional channels.

To increase private brand sales, some channel members **sell against the brand.**

Wholesalers and retailers may engage in **selling against the brand**, whereby they stock well-known brands, place high prices on them, and then sell other brands for lower prices. This is done to increase sales of their private brands. The practice is disliked by manufacturers because the sales of their brands decline.

Gray market goods *bypass authorized channels.*

Sometimes, wholesalers and retailers go outside traditional distribution channels and buy **gray market goods**—foreign-made products imported into countries such as the United States by distributors (suppliers) that are not authorized by the products' manufacturers. Personal stereos, VCRs, car stereos, watches, and cameras are just some of the

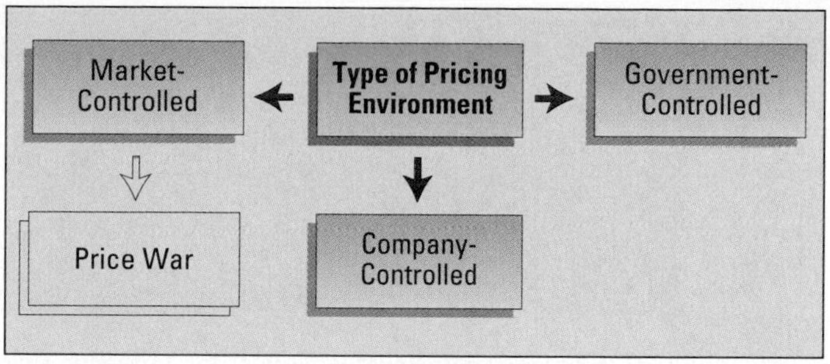

FIGURE 21-8
The Competitive Environments of Pricing

items handled in this way. If wholesalers and retailers buy gray market goods, their purchase prices are less than they would be otherwise and they have greater control over their own selling prices. The result is often discounted prices for consumers, which may be upsetting to manufacturers and authorized dealers.[17]

To maximize channel-member cooperation regarding price decisions, these factors should be considered: channel-member profit margins, price guarantees, special deals, and the impact of price increases. Wholesalers and retailers require appropriate profit margins to cover their costs (such as shipping, storage, credit, and advertising) and earn reasonable profits. Thus, the prices that are charged to them must take these profit margins into account. An attempt to reduce traditional margins for channel members may lose their cooperation and perhaps find them unwilling to carry a product. Pricing through a distribution channel is discussed further in Chapter 22.

Price guarantees *reassure channel members.*

Channel members may seek price guarantees to maintain inventory values and profit. **Price guarantees** assure resellers that the prices they pay are the lowest available. Any discount given to competitors will also be given to the original purchasers. Guarantees are most frequently requested for new firms or new products that want to gain entry into an established channel.

Special deals—consisting of limited-time discounts and/or free products—are often used to stimulate purchases by resellers. The deals may require channel members to share their savings with final consumers to increase the latter's demand. For example, soda bottlers normally give retailers large price discounts on new products to encourage them to make purchases and then offer low introductory prices to consumers.

The effects of price increases on channel members' behavior must also be assessed. When firms raise prices to resellers, these increases tend to be passed along to consumers. This practice is more difficult for items with customary prices, such as candy, where small cost rises may be absorbed by the resellers. In any event, cooperation depends on an equitable distribution of costs and profit within the channel.

Competition

A firm may face a **market-controlled, company-controlled,** *or* **government-controlled price environment.**

Another factor contributing to the degree of control a firm has over prices is the competitive environment within which it operates. See Figure 21-8.

A **market-controlled price environment** is characterized by a high level of competition, similar goods and services, and little control over prices by individual firms. Those trying to charge much more than the going price would attract few customers because demand for any single firm is weak enough that customers would switch to competitors. There would similarly be little gained by selling for less because competitors would match price cuts.

A **company-controlled price environment** is characterized by moderate competition, well-differentiated goods and services, and strong control over prices by individual firms. Companies can succeed with above-average prices because people view their offerings as unique. Differentiation may be based on brand image, features, associated services, assortment, or other elements. Discounters also can carve out a niche in this environment by attracting consumers interested in low prices.

[17] See Gert Assmus and Carsten Wiese, "How to Address the Gray Market Threat Using Price Coordination," *Sloan Management Review*, Vol. 36 (Spring 1995), pp. 31–41.

International Marketing in Action

Will the Euro Ever Come to Pass?

For several years, most leaders of the European Union have agreed that a uniform currency should be established to further unify Europe. This would also eliminate currency losses among EU members, make it unnecessary for travelers to exchange currencies in each European country, and reduce the cross-border shopping that is caused when products have different prices due to the value of countries' currencies.

Plans now call for the new common currency to be called "Euro" and for it to be fully adopted by the year 2002. These are some of the major events scheduled for the Euro:

- Early 1998—Decision on which nations qualify for the monetary union. A European Central Bank is created.
- January 1, 1999—Permanent exchange rates set for qualifying nations. The European Central Bank takes over monetary policy. Government debt is issued in Euros.
- Early 2002—Circulation of Euro notes begins. Stores price goods and services in Euros.
- June 2002—Old national currencies no longer legal tender. Only Euros used in member countries.

Despite these plans, several experts question whether the Euro will ever be the currency of Europe. Here are three reasons why. One, at present, very few EU members meet eligibility requirements in terms of the inflation rate, total government debt as a percentage of Gross Domestic Product, and the annual budget deficit as a percentage of Gross Domestic Product. Two, the governments of some EU members, especially the British government, look at a unified currency as an infringement on national sovereignty. Three, it will not be easy to re-educate the citizens in member countries.

As a consultant to the EU, develop a strategy for resolving these hurdles.

Source: Based on material in Nathaniel C. Nash, "Europeans Agree on New Currency," *New York Times* (December 16, 1995), pp. 1, 40.

A **government-controlled price environment** is characterized by prices being set or strongly influenced by some level of government. Examples are public utilities, mass transit, insurance, and state universities. In each case, government bodies determine or affect prices after obtaining input from the relevant companies, institutions, and/or trade associations, as well as other interested parties (such as consumer groups).

Companies may have to adapt to a changing competitive environment in their industries. Firms in the transportation, telecommunications, and financial industries have seen their price environment shift from government- to market-controlled—although some strong firms in these industries have managed to develop a company-controlled price environment.

Price wars *occur when competitors constantly lower prices.*

Because price strategies are rather easy and quick to copy, competitors' reactions are predictable if the firm initiating a price change does well. Thus, marketers must view price from both short- and long-run perspectives. Excessive price competition may lead to lengthy and costly **price wars**, in which various firms continually try to undercut each other's prices to draw customers. These wars often result in low profits or even losses for the participants and in some companies being forced out of business.

In recent years, there have been price wars among some car-rental firms, airlines, blank videocassette tape manufacturers, PC makers, semiconductor manufacturers, supermarkets, insurance companies, and others. Although price wars have been more common in the United States (due to fierce competition in some industries), they are now spreading overseas—particularly to Europe and, to a lesser extent, to Japan.

MARKETING IN A CHANGING WORLD

Will "Pre-Owning" Catch On?[18]

As the prices of such products as in-line skates ($170 for a pair of Rollerblade Lightning), guitars ($550 to $650 for a Fender Stratomaster), and cribs ($250 to $325 for a Simmons model) keep creeping up, some consumers are turning to "pre-owned" versions of these items.

Here's how:

> Retailing, meet recycling. Regional and national chains of thrift boutiques are doing a brisk business in used but perfectly usable stuff, from golf clubs to baby cribs, at 20 per cent to 60 per cent below the prices charged by discounters on new items. (Hagglers can sometimes do even better.) In 1995, Grow Biz International, a Minneapolis-based franchisor, had 814 outlets around the country, including Play It Again Sports, Once Upon a Child, Music-Go-Round, and Disc Go Round—with another 400 more stores planned for 1996. Children's Orchard, based in Ann Arbor, Michigan, has 50 stores in 12 states.
>
> Much of the merchandise comes from local individuals who sell it outright or on consignment or trade it in for other products. (Most shops pay sellers 25 to 35 per cent of the price of the item when new or about 60 per cent of the take for a consignment item, or exchange the item for a store credit worth about 40 per cent of its original price.)

Despite the seeming popularity of shopping for pre-owned items—after all, we have been buying used cars for decades—questions still remain: Is this a fad that will fade away in a short time? If someone's old Rollerblade skates are priced at $122 when new ones (fresh out of the box) sell for $170, will very many people really want the pre-owned ones? For what types of products will pre-owned merchandise sell best? Will status seekers be drawn to pre-owned goods because they still have prestige names (which the consumers might not otherwise be able to afford)? Should traditional retailers think about stocking both new and pre-owned items? What kinds of warranties and return policies should be made available?

SUMMARY

1. *To define the terms price and price planning* A price represents the value of a product for both the seller and the buyer. Price planning is systematic decision making relating to all aspects of pricing by a firm; it involves both tangible and intangible factors, purchase terms, and the nonmonetary exchange of goods and services. Exchange does not take place unless the buyer and seller agree that a price represents an equitable value. Price also balances supply and demand.

2. *To demonstrate the importance of price and study its relationship with other marketing variables* During the last three decades, price decisions have become more important to business executives. This is due to price (monetary or nonmonetary) being part of every type of exchange, deregulation, cost increases, currency rates, technological advances, the greater emphasis by service companies, and periodic economic slowdowns.

Price decisions must be made in conjunction with other marketing-mix elements. And pricing is often related to the product life cycle, customer service levels, and other specific marketing and company variables. In addition, setting prices for international markets can be complex and influenced by country factors.

3. *To differentiate between price-based and nonprice-based approaches* Under a price-based approach, sellers influence demand primarily via changes in price levels; they move consumers along a demand curve by raising or lowering prices. With a nonprice-based approach, sellers downplay price and emphasize such other marketing attributes as image, pack-

[18]The material in this section is based on Kerry Hannon, Sally Deneen, Melanie Mavrides, and Jill Jordan Sieder, "Think of It as 'Pre-Owned,'" *U.S. News & World Report* (June 5, 1995), pp. 61–64.

aging, and features; they shift the demand curves of consumers by stressing product distinctiveness.

4. *To examine the factors affecting pricing decisions* Several factors affect pricing decisions: consumers, costs, government, channel members, and competition. The law of demand states that consumers usually buy more units at a low price than at a high price. The price elasticity of demand explains the sensitivity of buyers to price changes in terms of the amounts they buy. Demand may be elastic, inelastic, or unitary; and it is impacted by the availability of substitutes and urgency of need. Consumers can be divided into segments based on their level of price sensitivity. Subjective price may be more important than actual price.

The costs of raw materials, supplies, labor, ads, transportation, and other items affect prices. Large increases often lead firms to raise prices, modify products, or abandon some offerings. Cost declines benefit marketing strategies by improving firms' ability to plan prices.

Government restrictions affect a broad variety of pricing areas. Price fixing, both horizontal and vertical, is subject to severe limitations. The Robinson-Patman Act bans most price discrimination to resellers that is not justified by costs. A number of states have unfair-sales acts (minimum price laws) to protect small firms against predatory pricing. Unit-pricing laws require specified retailers to post prices in terms of quantity. The FTC has a series of guidelines for price advertising.

Often, each channel member seeks a role in pricing. Manufacturers exert control via exclusive distribution, preticketing, opening their own outlets, offering goods on consignment, providing adequate margins, and having strong brands. Resellers exert control by making large purchases, linking sales support to margins, refusing to carry items, stocking competing brands, developing private brands, and purchasing outside traditional channels. Reseller profit margins, price guarantees, special deals, and the ramifications of price increases all need to be considered.

A market-controlled price environment has a high level of competition, similar products, and little control over prices by individual firms. A company-controlled price environment has a moderate level of competition, well-differentiated products, and strong control over prices by individual firms. In a government-controlled price environment, the government sets or influences prices. Some competitive actions may result in price wars, in which firms try to undercut each other's prices.

KEY TERMS

price (p. 586)
price planning (p. 586)
price-based approach (p. 589)
nonprice-based approach (p. 589)
law of demand (p. 591)
price elasticity of demand (p. 591)
elastic demand (p. 592)
inelastic demand (p. 592)
unitary demand (p. 592)
subjective price (p. 594)
horizontal price fixing (p. 596)
vertical price fixing (p. 597)
Robinson-Patman Act (p. 598)
unfair-sales acts (minimum price laws) (p. 598)
predatory pricing (p. 598)
loss leaders (p. 598)
unit pricing (p. 599)
bait-and-switch advertising (p. 600)
selling against the brand (p. 600)
gray market goods (p. 600)
price guarantees (p. 601)
market-controlled price environment (p. 601)
company-controlled price environment (p. 601)
government-controlled price environment (p. 602)
price wars (p. 602)

Review Questions

1. Cite at least three reasons why price decisions are so important today.
2. Explain the role of price in balancing supply and demand. Refer to Figure 21-1.
3. What is the risk with using a nonprice-oriented strategy?
4. Distinguish between elastic and inelastic demand. Why is it necessary for a firm to understand these differences?
5. At a price of $40, a firm could sell 900 units. At a price of $25, it could sell 1,200 units. Calculate the elasticity of demand and state what price the firm should charge—and why.
6. If costs rise rapidly, how could a company react?
7. Is horizontal price fixing always illegal? Explain your answer.
8. Does the buyer have any potential liability under the Robinson-Patman Act? Why or why not?
9. In what way are loss leaders different from bait-and-switch advertising?
10. How can a firm turn a market-controlled price environment into a company-controlled one?

Discussion Questions

1. How could a firm estimate price elasticity for a new industrial product? A mature industrial product?
2. When would you pass along a cost decrease to consumers? When would you not pass the decrease along?
3. You are the marketing vice-president of a telemarketing firm that sells chimney cleaning services at prices ranging from $200 to $600 (depending on the size and condition of the chimney). What would you do to persuade consumers that you offer fair prices?
4. Present five examples of price advertising for a hardware store that would violate FTC guidelines.
5. Describe several advantages and disadvantages of a government-controlled price environment.

CASE 1

*Here Come $20 Eyeglasses**

Optometrist Robert Morrison and his son Jim own Morrison International, a firm specializing in the manufacture and sale of inexpensive prescription eyeglasses. The firm's main product, Instant Eyeglasses, is especially easy to assemble and retails for about $20 a pair. Morrison's most expensive product— bifocal sunglasses with an anti-scratch coating—sells for $39.95.

To keep its costs low, Morrison International has reinvented the way eyeglasses are made. Although traditional eyeglasses are custom ground to accommodate the different sizes and shapes of various frames, Morrison's eyeglasses utilize pre-molded lenses. These lenses can be snapped into frames and adjusted to fit any size face. They can also be rotated to one of 180 positions in the frame. Each position accommodates a different prescription. Thus, Morrison can fill 27,000 prescriptions from an inventory of 152 lenses.

From a cost perspective, Instant Eyeglasses are not only inexpensive to produce, but they are also efficient to store (due to the high inventory turnover of lenses and their frames). This enables Instant Eyeglasses to be sold at rock-bottom prices.

Morrison has two target markets: consumers who want a spare pair of inexpensive glasses (and would not pay the average retail price of $135), and charities that provide glasses for the needy in the U.S. and international markets. Eyeglasses sold to the spare-pair market are sold through mail order and through kiosks. Morrison markets the glasses to the spare-frame market as a profit-making venture, but sells to the poor on a nonprofit basis.

Morrison is reaching the U.S. poor through a $500,000 laboratory on wheels. The equipment and supplies for this lab have been paid through a grant from the Hershey Foods Corporation. In one recent 18-month period, the lab traveled throughout the United States and provided eye examinations and eyeglasses to 18,000 people—free of charge.

The company also rents mobile clinics to charities in Atlanta and Tampa. These clinics can evaluate a person's vision and then make a pair of Instant Eyeglasses in minutes. In a typical arrangement, Morrison provides the eyeglasses at cost (between $10 and $12) to the charities, which then sells the glasses at cost to the poor. Morrison is negotiating similar arrangements in foreign markets.

According to Dean Butler, the founder of LensCrafters, the world's largest optical retailer, "Doggone, he is onto something." Butler, who sold LensCrafters in 1988, is on the board of Optical Care Ltd., which has the right to distribute Instant Eyeglasses in the former Soviet Union, Eastern Europe, India, and Pakistan. As Optical Care's chairman says, "The need is enormous." For instance, 40 per cent of the Russian adults who need glasses do not have them. In nations where there are few eye doctors, Optical Care plans to put equipment in stores to test people's vision. Optical Care estimates that it will sell $55 million worth of Instant Eyeglasses per year in the former Eastern Bloc markets over the next five years.

Instant Eyeglasses is not Robert Morrison's first invention. In 1963, he worked with Czech scientists to develop the first soft contact lens. And briefly in the 1960s, Morrison's lab manufactured every soft lens that was sold in the United States. He later sold out his share in the business to his partners in exchange for royalty income. According to the chairman of the opthalmology department at Penn State University, "He dramatically refined contact lenses from an experimental concept into a successful product."

QUESTIONS

1. Apply the concept of price and nonprice competition to Instant Eyeglasses.
2. Describe the impact of price elasticity of demand for Instant Eyeglasses' spare eyeglasses market.
3. How does a consumer's subjective price affect Instant Eyeglasses' market strategy?
4. If Morrison's costs go up by 15 per cent, should it pass along the full increase? Why or why not?

*The data in this case are drawn from Amy Borrus, "Eyeglasses for the Masses," *Business Week* (November 20, 1995), pp. 104–105.

CASE 2

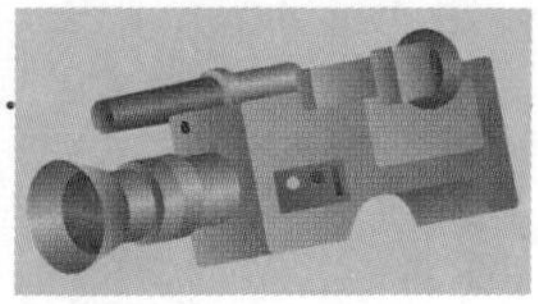

Charles Schwab Corporation: An Analysis of a Pricing Strategy[†]

Charles Schwab Corporation was among the first brokerage firms to develop a low-cost distribution channel to attract the clients who did not require all of the services performed by traditional full-service brokers. Because Schwab does not have market analysts, it can operate at a much lower cost structure than full-service brokers. For example, a small-volume trade priced at $75 with a full-service broker may be as little as $39 through Schwab.

In 1980, discount brokers handled a small fraction of all retail stock trades. Today, their overall market share has risen to 14 per cent; and some industry analysts project the market share to be 20 per cent as of the year 2000. Schwab has a 44 per cent market share among discount brokers.

A key to Schwab's success is its extensive use of technology to facilitate customer access. During 1989, Schwab introduced automated touchpad trading and in 1993, its *StreetSmart for Windows* software package became available. *StreetSmart* lets customers enter trades via computer modem. In 1994, Schwab brought out *Custom Broker*—a combination phone, fax, and paging service for active traders.

One of Schwab's most significant innovations is OneSource, a series of no-load mutual funds overseen by dozens of money managers. Through OneSource, Schwab became one of the top U.S. mutual fund distributors. By just its second year, OneSource generated 6.4 per cent of all mutual fund sales conducted by brokers (amounting to over 500,000 accounts and $16 billion in assets).

Above its daily break-even level of 22,400 trades, Schwab has a profit margin of 90 per cent. And it is averaging 40,000 or so trades a day. More than one-half of Schwab's revenues comes from its retail brokerage business. Although its profit margin on mutual fund sales is smaller, its revenue stream is more stable. As a result, in 1994, when most brokers reported that their profits dropped by 30 per cent, Schwab continued its profit growth.

Schwab's prices for implementing trades are low versus full-service brokers, but it is not the least expensive discount broker. An analysis of commissions and fees among 19 discount brokers by *Smart Money* found that its fees were the highest for the three sample trades conducted (100 shares of a $20 listed stock, 500 shares of a $20 listed stock, and 100 shares of a $50 over-the-counter stock). Schwab's total price quote for these trades was $220, while the lowest-priced firm (E*Trade) charged $69.85. To better appeal to high-trade customers who make an average of 48 or more commission trades a year and have at least $50,000 in assets with the company, Schwab offers discounts of 10 to 20 per cent.

Unlike Schwab, E*Trade relies on computer online fees: Its customers are given 12 fee minutes of computer time to complete a trade. Higher charges are incurred if a trade takes longer. Some E*Trade customers have complained that it takes longer than 12 minutes to complete a trade and download statements.

According to *Smart Money*, Schwab shines in its offering of a large selection of top-performing no-load (no sales commission) mutual funds to its customers. Of the 345 funds offered by Schwab, 90 have performed in the top 25 per cent of their sector groupings. According to *Smart Money*, "Nobody else even comes close."

QUESTIONS

1. Evaluate Schwab's overall pricing strategy for its brokerage services.
2. What type of customer should Schwab seek? Why?
3. Discuss the role of costs in Schwab's overall pricing strategy.
4. Describe the competitive environment within which Schwab operates.

VIDEO QUESTIONS ON SCHWAB

1. Compare Schwab's target market to that of other discount brokers.
2. How does Schwab attempt to differentiate itself from other discount brokerage firms?

[†]The data in this case are drawn from Peggy Edersheim Kalb, "The Best and Worst Discount Brokers," *Smart Money* (July 1995), pp. 92–101; Adrian J. Slywotzky, "Taking the Low Road," *Sales & Marketing Management* (January 1996), pp. 53, 55, 60; and Sandra Ward, "Sincere Flattery," *Barron's* (May 15, 1995), pp. 18–19.

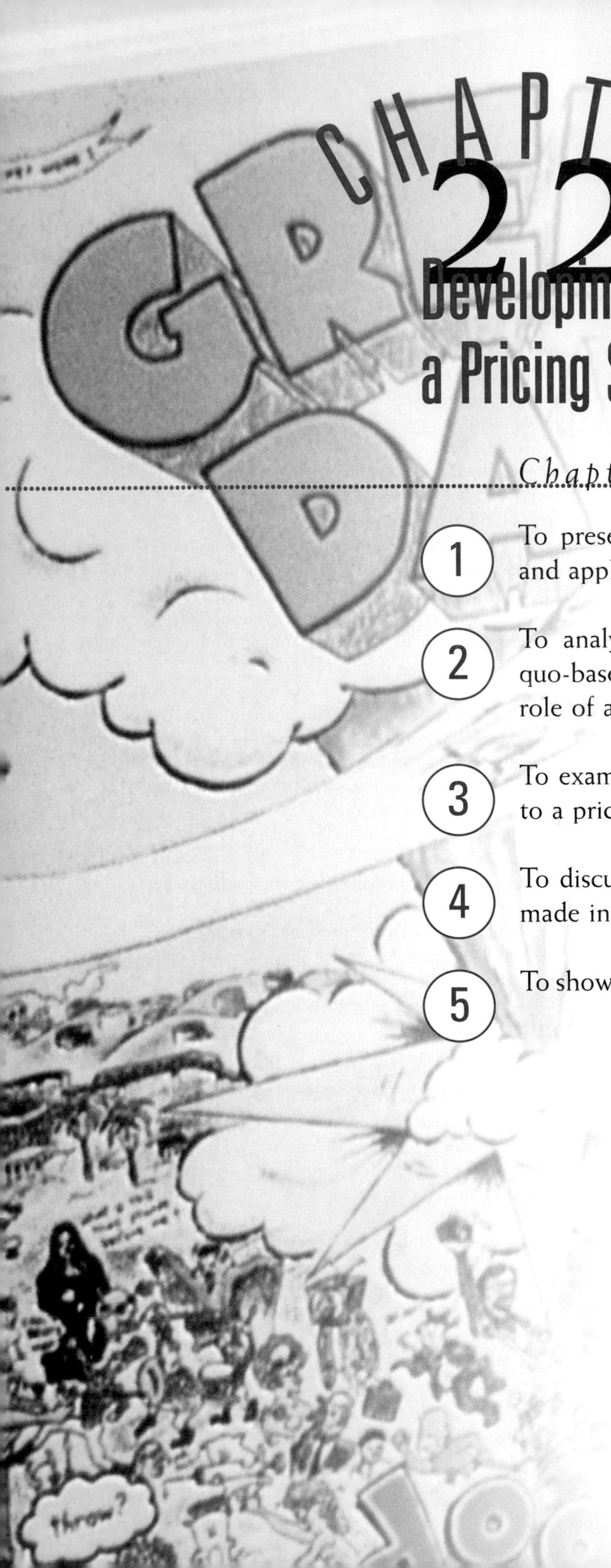

CHAPTER 22 Developing and Applying a Pricing Strategy

Chapter Objectives

1. To present an overall framework for developing and applying a pricing strategy

2. To analyze sales-based, profit-based, and status quo-based pricing objectives, and to describe the role of a broad price policy

3. To examine and apply the alternative approaches to a pricing strategy

4. To discuss several specific decisions that must be made in implementing a pricing strategy

5. To show the major ways that prices can be adjusted

Recent growth in the music business has been set off by an explosion of new recording talent, the coming of age of Walkman-toting Generation Xers, and ever more ways to deliver tunes. "Music is a more important part of more people's lives than ever before," explains David Geffen, billionaire record impresario and co-founder of DreamWorks SKG. "Young people listen to more music than [baby boomers] did. They buy more music than we did. And we're still buying it, too."

Reprinted by permission.

The total sales of pre-recorded music in the United States (and around the world) have increased dramatically in recent years. Globally, annual pre-recorded music sales are approaching $40 billion. In the United States alone, annual pre-recorded music revenues exceed $13 billion—with $9 billion from the CD format. From 1985 to 1995, total U.S. pre-recorded music sales rose by 300 per cent and CD sales went up 2,200 per cent.

The largest firm in the recording business is Warner Bros., with a 22+ per cent market share. Warner has many established recording artists, as well as such newer stars as Hootie & the Blowfish and Green Day.

Although close to 80 per cent of new releases fail, successful recordings are *very* profitable. A CD is relatively inexpensive to produce, usually costing less than $500,000. And besides the profits from CD sales, there are proceeds from catalog and music publishing sales.

It once took a group several years—and many road tours—to obtain a following. But now, through MTV rock videos and the Internet, a group can receive incredible recognition and sales from its first recorded effort. The debut albums *Dookie* and *Cracked Rear View*, from Green Day and Hootie & the Blowfish, respectively, each sold more than six million copies. *Cracked Rear View* remained on the music charts for well over a year.

The high sales and profit potential have generated increased attention for the CD business. Both the News Corporation and Viacom have been looking at opportunities in the recording industry. Existing recording companies such as MCA and Warner Bros. are also launching new labels—at a cost of $50 to $100 million per label (the same amount needed to bankroll a major action movie).

Let's look at the economics of producing and marketing a typical CD: A CD usually sells for $15.98 to $16.98 at retail. Since the standard wholesale cost for a major release is $10.00, the retailer's markup (at retail selling price) is as high as 40 per cent [($16.98 − $10.00)/$16.98]. The $10.00 wholesale price represents the sales revenue to a recording company per CD.

From its $10.00, the recording company must pay for overhead and profits, artist royalties and copyright fees, marketing expenses, and CD manufacturing costs. Of these items,

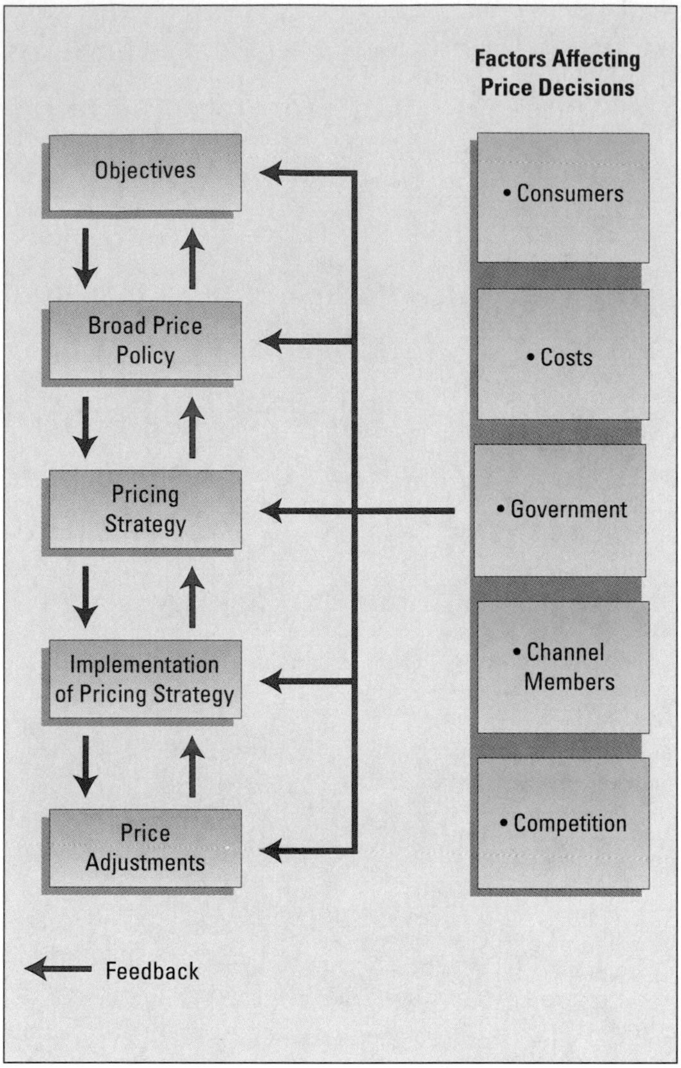

FIGURE 22-1
A Framework for Developing and Applying a Pricing Strategy

overhead (comprising record company administration expenses, recording costs, returns, and profits) is the largest category, amounting to $4.25 to $5.25 per CD. The next largest expense, artist royalties and copyright fees, is $2.00 to $3.00 per CD. Marketing expenses for advertising, public relations, and physical distribution activities total $1.45. Lastly, manufacturing costs are $1.30; this consists of CD production ($0.75), the jewel box container ($0.30), and the printed booklet ($0.25) that accompany the CD.[1]

In this chapter, we will look at the overall process of developing and applying a pricing strategy—including the setting of pricing objectives, the use of various pricing approaches, how a pricing strategy is implemented, and how prices can be adjusted.

Overview

As Figure 22-1 shows, a pricing strategy has five steps: objectives, broad policy, strategy, implementation, and adjustments. All of them are affected by the outside factors noted in Chapter 21. Like any planning activity, a pricing strategy begins with a clear statement of goals and ends with an adaptive or corrective mechanism. Pricing decisions are integrated with the firm's overall marketing program during the broad price-policy step.

[1]Thom Geier, Betsy Streisand, and Kevin Whitelaw, "Recording Sound Sales," *U.S. News & World Report* (September 25, 1995), pp. 67–72.

The development of a pricing strategy is not a one-time occurrence. It needs to be reviewed when a new product is introduced, an existing product is revised, the competitive environment changes, a product moves through its life cycle, a competitor initiates a price change, costs rise or fall, the firm's prices come under government scrutiny, and/or other events take place.

These are some indications a pricing strategy may be performing poorly:

- Prices are changed too frequently.
- Pricing policy is difficult to explain to consumers.
- Channel members complain that profit margins are inadequate.
- Price decisions are made without adequate marketing-research information.
- Too many different price options are available.
- Too much sales personnel time is spent in bargaining.
- Prices are inconsistent with the target market.
- A high percentage of goods is marked down or discounted late in the selling season to clear out surplus inventory.
- Too high a proportion of customers is price-sensitive and attracted by competitors' discounts. Demand is elastic.
- The firm has problems conforming with pricing legislation.

This chapter describes in detail the pricing framework outlined in Figure 22-1.

Pricing Objectives

A pricing strategy should be consistent with and reflect overall company goals. It is possible for different firms in the same industry to have dissimilar objectives and, therefore, distinct pricing strategies.

There are three general pricing objectives from which a firm may select: sales-based, profit-based, and status quo-based. See Figure 22-2. With sales-based goals, a firm is interested in sales growth and/or maximizing market share. With profit-based goals, it is interested in maximizing profit, earning a satisfactory profit, optimizing the return on investment, and/or securing an early recovery of cash. With status quo-based goals, it seeks to avoid unfavorable government actions, minimize the effects of competitor actions, maintain good channel relations, discourage the entry of competitors, reduce demands from suppliers, and/or stabilize prices.

A company may pursue more than one pricing goal at the same time, such as increasing sales by 5 to 10 per cent each year, achieving a 15 per cent return on capital investments, and keeping prices near those of competitors. It may also set distinct short- and long-run goals. In the short run, it may seek high profit margins on new products; in the long run, these profit margins would drop to discourage potential competitors.

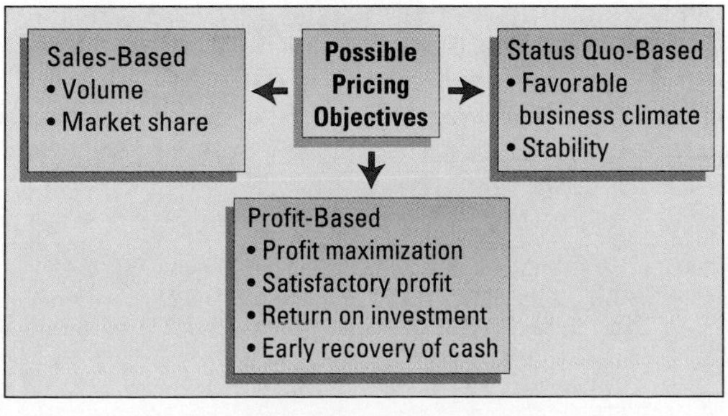

FIGURE 22-2
Pricing Objectives

Sales-Based Objectives

Sales-based objectives *seek high volume or market share.*

A firm with **sales-based pricing objectives** is oriented toward high sales volume and/or expanding its share of sales relative to competitors. The company focuses on sales-based goals for either (or all) of three reasons: It sees market saturation or sales growth as a major step leading to market control and sustained profits. It wants to maximize unit sales and will trade low per-unit profits for larger total profits. It assumes greater sales will enable it to have lower per-unit costs.

Penetration pricing *aims at the mass market.*

To gain high sales volume, **penetration pricing** is often employed—whereby low prices are used to capture the mass market for a good or service. It is a proper approach if customers are highly sensitive to price, low prices discourage actual and potential competitors, there are economies of scale (per-unit production and distribution costs fall as sales rise), and a large consumer market exists. Penetration pricing also recognizes that a high price may leave a product vulnerable to competition.

Penetration pricing is used by such companies as Compaq, Malt-O-Meal, and Kellwood. Compaq now markets a $1,500 "entry level" PC whose price includes a monitor, a 100-megahertz Pentium chip, a one-gigabyte hard drive, eight megabytes of memory, and a fast modem. As one observer says, "The closer you get to $1,000, the bigger the market will be." Malt-O-Meal makes no-frills cereals and sells them in bags rather than boxes. Its prices are half those of better-known brands. Cape Cod-Cricket Lane is a division of Kellwood Corp. that makes "knockoff" apparel for such retailers as J.C. Penney and Target. It produces items like rayon jackets and skirts—priced at $24.99 and $19.99, respectively (at retail).[2]

Penetration pricing may even tap markets not originally anticipated. For example, few people forecast that cordless phones would reach the sales volume attained during their peak. The market expanded rapidly after prices fell below $100. It grew again as new models were introduced for $60 and less.

Profit-Based Objectives

Profit-based objectives *range from maximization to recovery of cash. Goals can be per unit or total.*

A company with **profit-based pricing objectives** orients its strategy toward some type of profit goals. With profit-maximization goals, high dollar profits are sought. With satisfactory-profit goals, stability over time is desired; rather than maximize profits in a given year (which could result in declines in nonpeak years), steady profits for a number of years are sought. With return-on-investment goals, profits are related to investment costs; these goals are often pursued by regulated utilities as a way of justifying rate increases. With early-recovery-of-cash goals, high initial profits are sought because firms are short of funds or uncertain about their future.

Profit may be expressed in per-unit or total terms. Per-unit profit equals the revenue a seller receives for one unit sold minus its costs. A product like custom-made furniture has a high unit profit. Total profit equals the revenue a seller receives for all items sold minus total costs. It is computed by multiplying per-unit profit times the number of units sold. A product like mass-marketed furniture has a low unit profit; success is based on the number of units sold (turnover). Products with high per-unit profits may have lower total profits than ones with low per-unit profits if the discount prices of the latter generate a much greater level of consumer demand. However, this depends on the elasticity of demand.

Skimming pricing *is aimed at the segment interested in quality or status.*

Skimming pricing uses high prices to attract the market segment more concerned with product quality, uniqueness, or status than price. It is proper if competition can be minimized (via patent protection, brand loyalty, raw material control, or high capital requirements), funds are needed for early cash recovery or further expansion, consumers are

[2]Jim Carlton, "Compaq and Acer Are Slashing Prices on Entry-Level PCs to Expand Market," *Wall Street Journal* (November 17, 1995), pp. A3, A8; Richard Gibson, "Quaker Oats Co. Will Begin Marketing Value-Priced Cereals Under Its Brand," *Wall Street Journal* (January 23, 1995), pp. 88, 90; and Teri Agins, "Why Cheap Clothes Are Getting More Respect," *Wall Street Journal* (October 16, 1995), pp. B1, B3.

insensitive to price or willing to pay a high initial price, and unit costs remain equal or rise as sales increase (economies of scale are absent).

Skimming prices are used by such firms as Genentech, Canondale, and British Airways. Genentech is the maker of Activase, a patented brand of TPA (tissue plasminogen activator), a product that quickly clears the blood clots associated with heart attacks and effectively treats certain kinds of strokes. It sells Activase for about $1,500 per dose. Canondale's Super V bikes retail for $3,500 each. They have rear shock absorbers to boost comfort, rear frames that pivot vertically to keep the back wheels in constant contact with bumpy roads, light aluminum frames to maximize pedaling efficiency, and front suspensions that ease steering and ensure smoother rides. British Airways recently overhauled its first-class cabins to provide passengers with fully reclining seats, greater privacy, and more room. It is targeting those willing to pay $6,600 for a round-trip ticket between London and New York.[3]

Firms sometimes first employ skimming pricing and then penetration pricing, or they market both a premium brand and a value brand. There are many advantages to this approach: One, high prices are charged when competition is limited. Two, high prices help cover development and introductory advertising costs. Three, the first group of customers to buy a new product is usually less price-sensitive than later groups. Four, high initial prices portray a high-quality image. Five, raising initial prices may be resisted by consumers; lowering them is viewed more favorably. Six, after the initial market segment is saturated, penetration pricing can be used to appeal to the mass market and expand total sales volume. Seven, multiple segments can be reached.

Status Quo-Based Objectives

Status quo-based objectives *seek good business conditions and stability.*

Status quo-based pricing objectives are sought by a firm interested in continuing a favorable business climate for its operations or in stability. The pricing strategy is used to minimize the impact of such outside parties as government, competitors, and channel members—and to avoid sales declines.

One should not infer that status quo goals require no effort. A firm must instruct salespeople not to offer different terms to competing channel members or else the government may accuse it of a Robinson-Patman Act violation. It may have to match competitors' price cuts to keep customers—while striving to avoid price wars. It may have to accept lower profit margins in the face of rising costs to hold channel cooperation. It may have to charge penetration prices to discourage competitors from also marketing certain product lines.

Broad Price Policy

A **broad price policy** *links prices with the target market, image, and other marketing elements.*

A **broad price policy** sets the overall direction (and tone) for a firm's pricing efforts and makes sure pricing decisions are coordinated with the firm's choices as to a target market, an image, and other marketing-mix factors. It incorporates short- and long-term pricing goals, as well as the role of pricing. Pricing can play a passive role—with customer purchases based on superior service, convenience, and quality—or it can play an active role—with purchases based on discount prices. Thus, a high-income segment buying status brands at upscale stores would expect premium prices. A moderate-income segment buying private brands at flea markets would expect low prices.

A firm outlines a broad price policy by placing individual decisions into an integrated format. It then decides on the interrelationship of prices for items within a product line, how often special discounts are used, how prices compare to competition, the frequency of price changes, and the method for setting new-product prices. As such, "Marketing

[3]Ralph T. King, Jr., "TPA Scores Big in Treatment of Stroke," *Wall Street Journal* (December 14, 1995), p. 8; Ron Stodghill II, "Joe Montgomery's Wild Ride," *Business Week* (April 19, 1993), pp. 50, 52; and Charles Goldsmith, "Jet Ahoy! First-Class Fliers Go 'Yachting,'" *Wall Street Journal* (December 4, 1995), pp. B1, B10.

International Marketing in Action

Can Reebok's Global Hopscotching Pay Off in Lower Costs?

Ten years ago, most of Reebok's shoes and sneakers were produced in South Korea and Taiwan. However, as labor costs in these nations rose, Reebok sought new production facilities. Now, China and Indonesia account for 60 per cent of Reebok's annual worldwide production. That is almost 170 million pairs of sneakers and shoes. Only 9 per cent of Reebok footwear is still produced in South Korea.

Reebok is not alone in changing production sites on the basis of costs. According to the Athletic Footwear Association, a pair of sneakers costs about $20 to manufacture in East Asia and sells for $70 in the United States. Nonetheless, after deducting operating expenses, a sneaker manufacturer is left with an average profit of just over $6 per pair. Thus, most manufacturers play a game of global hopscotching in their vendor sourcing.

Different parts of the same shoe are even produced in different countries. For Reebok's Kamikaze II sneaker, a basketball high top, cushioning materials are made in Southern California and then shipped along with molded shoes to Reebok plants in South Korea and China for final assembly. Different types of sneakers are also made in different countries. Generally, a new production facility first produces a simple version of a running shoe or an aerobic shoe. After workers learn to perfect their skills, more costly lines of shoes are then manufactured there.

All of its Asian factories are evaluated through the six-point Reebok Supplier Certification Program, which ranks suppliers on the basis of such attributes as the number of defective sneakers returned by retailers and on-time delivery. In addition, suppliers must comply with the firm's human-rights production standards.

As a consultant to Reebok, discuss the pros and cons of its global hopscotching approach.

Source: Based on material in David Fischer, "Global Hopscotch," *U.S. News & World Report* (June 5, 1995), pp. 43–45.

strategies attempt to define where the firm wants to be in the marketplace, and how it plans to get there. They provide the larger framework within which pricing and other programs are developed. Correspondingly, there should be a clear link between strategies and individual programs."[4]

Pricing Strategy

A pricing strategy may be cost-, demand-, and/or competition-based. When the three approaches are integrated, combination pricing is involved. See Figure 22-3. Next, each technique is explained and illustrations provided.

Cost-Based Pricing

Under **cost-based pricing,** *expenses are computed, profit is projected, and a* **price floor** *set.*

In **cost-based pricing,** a firm sets prices by computing merchandise, service, and overhead costs and then adding an amount to cover its profit goal. Table 22-1 defines the key concepts in cost-based pricing and how they may be applied to big-screen television sets.

[4]Michael H. Morris and Roger J. Calantone, "Four Components of Effective Pricing," *Industrial Marketing Management*, Vol. 19 (November 1990), p. 327.

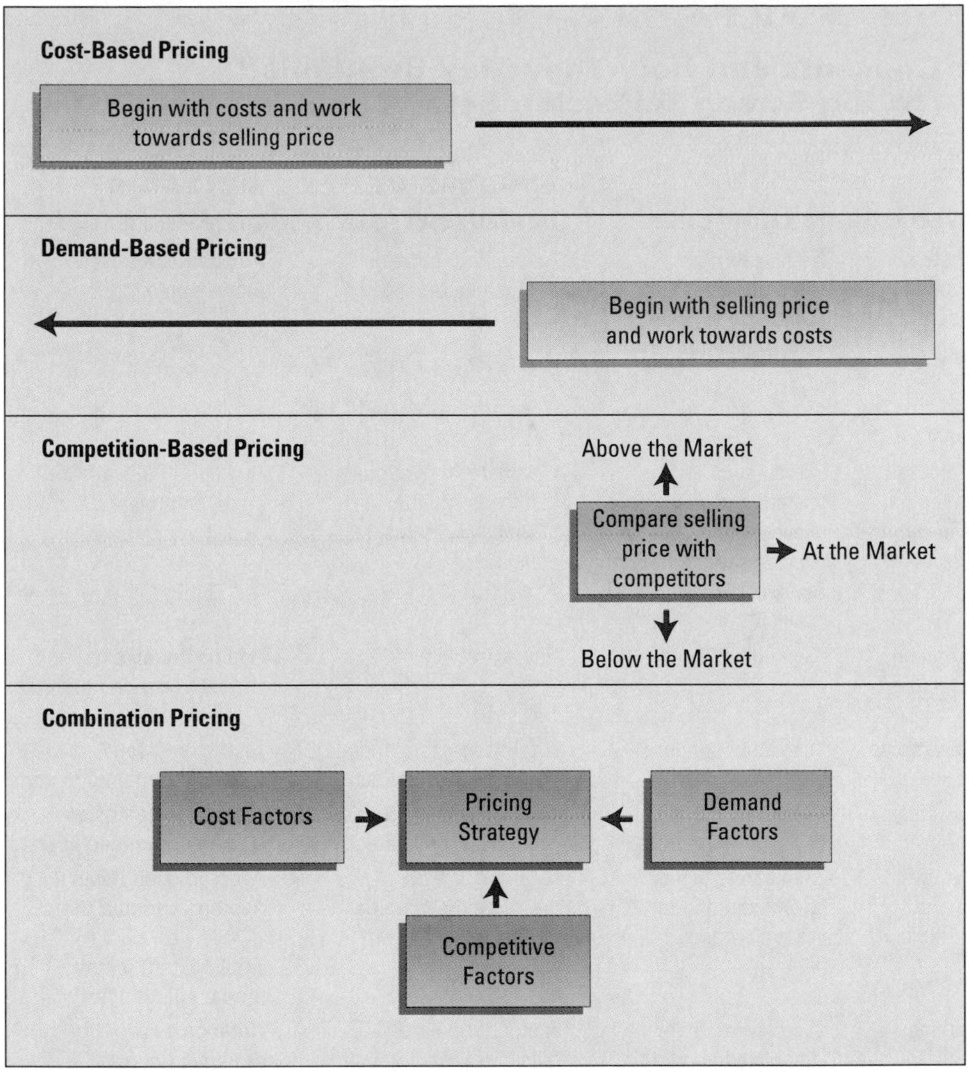

FIGURE 22-3
The Alternative Ways of Developing a Pricing Strategy

Cost-based prices are rather easy to derive because there is no need to estimate elasticity of demand or competitive reactions to price changes. There is also greater certainty about costs than demand or competitor responses to prices. Finally, cost-based pricing seeks reasonable profits since it is geared to covering all types of costs. It is often used by firms whose goals are stated in terms of profit or return on investment. A **price floor** is the lowest acceptable price a firm can charge and attain its profit goal.

When used by itself, cost-based pricing does have some significant limitations. It does not consider market conditions, the full effects of excess plant capacity, competitive prices, the product's phase in its life cycle, market share goals, consumers' ability to pay, and other factors.

Sometimes, it is hard to figure how such overhead costs as rent, lighting, personnel, and other general expenses should be allocated to each product. These costs are often assigned on the basis of product sales or the personnel time associated with each item. For instance, if product A accounts for 10 per cent of sales, it might be allotted 10 per cent of overhead costs. If product B receives 20 per cent of personnel time, it might be allotted 20 per cent of overhead costs. Yet, problems may arise since different methods for assigning costs may yield different results: How would costs be allocated if product A yields 10 per cent of sales and requires 20 per cent of personnel time?

In the following subsections, five cost-based pricing techniques are covered: cost-plus, markup, target, price-floor, and traditional break-even analysis. Figure 22-4 gives a synopsis of each technique. And at the end of these subsections, Table 22-2 contains numerical examples of them.

Table 22-1

Key Cost Concepts and How They May Be Applied to Big-Screen Television Sets

COST CONCEPT	DEFINITION	EXAMPLES[a]	SOURCES OF INFORMATION	METHOD OF COMPUTATION
Total fixed costs	Ongoing costs not related to volume. They are usually constant over a given range of output for a specified time.	Rent, salaries, electricity, real-estate taxes, plant, and equipment.	Accounting data, bills, cost estimates.	Addition of all fixed cost components.
Total variable costs	Costs that change with increases or decreases in output (volume).	Parts (such as tuners and speakers), hourly employees who assemble sets, and sales commissions.	Cost data from suppliers, estimates of labor productivity, sales estimates.	Addition of all variable cost components.
Total costs	Sum of total fixed and total variable costs.	See above.	See above.	Addition of all fixed and variable cost components.
Average fixed costs	Average fixed costs per unit.	See above under total fixed costs.	Total fixed costs and production estimates.	Total fixed costs/ Quantity produced in units.
Average variable costs	Average variable costs per unit.	See above under total variable costs.	Total variable costs and production estimates.	Total variable costs/ Quantity produced in units.
Average total costs	Sum of average fixed costs and average variable costs.	See above under total fixed and total variable costs.	Total costs and production estimates.	Average fixed costs + Average variable costs or Total costs/Quantity produced in units.
Marginal costs	Costs of making an additional unit.	See above under total fixed and total variable costs.	Accounting data, bills, cost estimates of labor and materials.	(Total costs of producing current quantity + one unit) − (Total costs of producing current quantity).

[a]Such marketing costs as advertising and distribution are often broken down into both fixed and variable components.

Cost-plus pricing *is the easiest form of pricing, based on units produced, total costs, and profit.*

Cost-Plus Pricing For **cost-plus pricing,** prices are set by adding a pre-determined profit to costs. It is the simplest form of cost-based pricing.

Generally, the steps for computing cost-plus prices are to estimate the number of units to be produced, calculate fixed and variable costs, and add a desired profit to costs. The formula for cost-plus pricing is

$$\text{Price} = \frac{\text{Total fixed costs} + \text{Total variable costs} + \text{Projected profit}}{\text{Units produced}}$$

This method is easy to compute; yet, it has shortcomings. Profit is not expressed in relation to sales but in relation to costs, and price is not tied to consumer demand. Adjustments for rising costs are poorly conceived, and there are no plans for using excess capacity. There is little incentive to improve efficiency to hold down costs, and marginal costs are rarely analyzed.

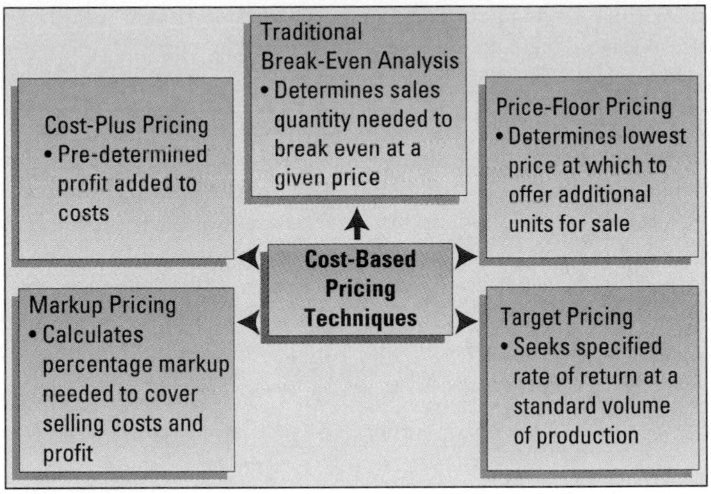

FIGURE 22-4
Cost-Based Pricing Techniques

Cost-plus pricing is most effective when price fluctuations have little influence on sales and when a firm is able to control prices. For example, the prices of custom-made furniture, ships, heavy machinery, and extracted minerals typically depend on the costs incurred in producing these items; thus, companies set prices by computing costs and adding a reasonable profit. Cost-plus pricing often allows firms to get consumer orders, produce items, and then derive prices after total costs are known. This protects sellers.

Markup Pricing In **markup pricing**, a firm sets prices by computing the per-unit costs of producing (buying) goods and/or services and then determining the markup percentages needed to cover selling costs and profit. It is most commonly used by wholesalers and retailers, although it is employed by all types of organizations. The formula for markup pricing is[5]

Markup pricing *considers per-unit product costs and the markups required to cover selling costs and profits. Markups should be expressed in terms of price rather than cost.*

$$\text{Price} = \frac{\text{Product cost}}{(100 - \text{Markup per cent})/100}$$

There are several reasons why markups are commonly stated in terms of selling price instead of cost. One, since expenses, markdowns, and profits are computed as percentages of sales, when markups are also cited as percentages of sales, they aid in profit planning. Two, firms quote their selling prices and trade discounts to channel members as percentage reductions from final list prices. Three, competitive price data are more readily available than cost data. Four, profitability appears smaller if based on price rather than on cost. This may be useful to avoid criticism over high earnings.

Markup size depends on traditional profit margins, company selling and operating expenses, suggested list prices, inventory turnover, competition, the extent to which products must be serviced, and the effort needed to complete transactions. Due to differences in selling costs among products, some firms use a **variable markup policy**, whereby separate categories of goods and services receive different percentage markups. Variable markups recognize that some items require greater personal selling, customer service, alterations, and end-of-season markdowns than others. For example, expensive cosmetics need more personal selling and customer service than paperback books, suits need greater custom alterations than shirts, and fashion items are marked down more than basic clothing late in the selling season.

A **variable markup policy** *responds to differences in selling costs among products.*

Markup pricing, while having many of cost-plus pricing's limitations, is popular. It is fairly simple, especially for firms with uniform markups for several items. Channel members get fair profits. Price competition is less if firms have similar markups. Resellers can

[5]Markup can be calculated by transposing the formula above into

$$\text{Markup percentage} = \frac{\text{Price} - \text{Product cost}}{\text{Price}} \times 100$$

show their actual prices compared to suggested prices. Adjustments can be made as costs rise. Variable markups are responsive to selling cost differences among products or channel members.

Target pricing *enables a rate of return on investment to be earned for a standard volume of production.*

Target Pricing In **target pricing**, prices are set to provide a particular rate of return on investment for a standard volume of production—the level of production a firm anticipates achieving. For example, in the paper industry, the standard volume of production is usually set at around 90 to 92 per cent of plant capacity.[6] For target pricing to operate properly, a company must sell its entire standard volume at specified prices.

Target pricing is used by capital-intensive firms (like auto makers) and public utilities (like water companies). The prices charged by utilities are based on fair rates of return on invested assets and must be approved by regulatory commissions. Mathematically, a target price is computed as

$$\text{Price} = \frac{\text{Investment costs} \times \text{Target return on investment (\%)}}{\text{Standard volume}} + \text{Average total costs (at standard volume)}$$

Target pricing has five major shortcomings. First, it is not useful for firms with low capital investments; it understates selling price. Second, because prices are not keyed to demand, the entire standard volume may not be sold at the target price. Third, production problems may hamper output and standard volume may not be attained. Fourth, price cuts to handle overstocked inventory are not planned under this approach. Fifth, if the standard volume is reduced due to expected poor sales performance, the price would be raised under a target-pricing calculation.

Price-floor pricing *may be used if there is excess capacity.*

Price-Floor Pricing A firm's usual goal is to set prices to cover the sum of average fixed costs, average variable costs, and profit per unit. But when a firm has excess (unused) capacity, it may use **price-floor pricing** to determine the lowest price at which it is worthwhile to increase the amount of goods or services it makes available for sale.

The general principle in price-floor pricing is that the sale of additional units can be used to increase profits or help pay for fixed costs (which exist whether or not these items are made), as long as marginal revenues are greater than marginal costs. Although a firm cannot survive in the long run unless its average total costs are covered by prices, it may improve performance through price-floor pricing. The formula is

$$\text{Price-floor price} = \text{Marginal revenue per unit} > \text{Marginal cost per unit}$$

Traditional break-even analysis *computes the sales needed to break even at a specific price.*

Traditional Break-Even Analysis Like target pricing, traditional break-even analysis looks at the relationship among costs, revenues, and profits. While target pricing yields the price that results in a specified return on investment, **traditional break-even analysis** finds the sales quantity in units or dollars that is needed for total revenues (price × units sold) to equal total costs (fixed and variable) at a given price. If sales exceed the break-even quantity, a firm earns a profit. If sales are less than the break-even quantity, it loses money. Traditional break-even analysis does not consider return on investment, but can be extended to take profit planning into account. It is used by all kinds of sellers.

The break-even point can be computed in terms of units or sales dollars:

$$\text{Break-even point (units)} = \frac{\text{Total fixed costs}}{\text{Price} - \text{Variable costs (per unit)}}$$

$$\text{Break-even point (sales dollars)} = \frac{\text{Total fixed costs}}{1 - \dfrac{\text{Variable costs (per unit)}}{\text{Price}}}$$

These formulas are derived from the equation: Price × Quantity = Total fixed costs + (Variable costs per unit × Quantity).

[6]*U.S. Industrial Outlook 1994* (Washington, D.C.: U.S. Department of Commerce, 1994), pp. 10-1–10-2.

Break-even analysis can be adjusted to take into account the profit sought by a firm:

$$\text{Break-even point (units)} = \frac{\text{Total fixed costs} + \text{Projected profit}}{\text{Price} - \text{Variable costs (per unit)}}$$

$$\text{Break-even point (sales dollars)} = \frac{\text{Total fixed costs} + \text{Projected profit}}{1 - \dfrac{\text{Variable costs (per unit)}}{\text{Price}}}$$

Table 22-2
Examples of Cost-Based Pricing Techniques

Cost-Plus Pricing—A custom-sofa maker has total fixed costs of $50,000, variable costs of $500 per sofa, desires $10,000 in profits, and plans to produce 100 couches. What is the selling price per couch?

$$\text{Price} = \frac{\text{Total fixed costs} + \text{Total variable costs} + \text{Projected profit}}{\text{Units produced}}$$

$$= \frac{\$50{,}000 + \$500(100) + \$10{,}000}{100} = \underline{\underline{\$1{,}100}}$$

Markup Pricing—A retailer pays $30 for touch-tone phones and wants a markup on selling price of 40 per cent (30 per cent for selling costs and 10 per cent for profit). What is the final selling price?

$$\text{Price} = \frac{\text{Merchandise costs}}{(100 - \text{Markup per cent})/100} = \frac{\$30}{(100 - 40)/100} = \underline{\underline{\$50}}$$

Target Pricing—A specialty auto maker has spent $160,000,000 for a new plant. It has a 25 per cent target return on investment. Standard production volume for the year is 5,000 units. Average total costs, excluding the new plant, are $14,000 for each car (at a production level of 5,000 cars). What is the selling price to the firm's retail dealers?

$$\text{Price} = \frac{\text{Investment costs} \times \text{Target return on investment (\%)}}{\text{Standard volume}}$$

$$+ \text{ Average total costs (at standard volume)}$$

$$= \frac{\$160{,}000{,}000 \times .25}{5{,}000} + \$14{,}000 = \underline{\underline{\$22{,}000}}$$

Price-Floor Pricing—A big-screen TV manufacturer's plant capacity is 1,000 units. Its total fixed costs are $500,000 and variable costs are $375 per unit. At full production, average fixed costs are $500 per unit. The firm sets a price of $1,100 to retailers and gets orders for 800 TVs at that price. It must operate at 80 per cent of capacity, unless it re-evaluates its pricing strategy. With price-floor pricing, it can sell the 200 additional sets to retailers. How?

The firm could let resellers buy one TV at $425 for every four they buy at $1,100. Then, it earns a profit of $90,000 [revenues of ($1,100 × 800) + ($425 × 200) less costs of ($875 × 1,000)]. If it just makes and sells 800 TVs at full price, it earns $80,000 [revenues of ($1,100 × 800) less variable costs of ($375 × 800) and fixed costs of $500,000]. The higher profits are due to marginal revenue > marginal cost.

Traditional Break-Even Analysis—A small candy maker has total fixed costs of $150,000 and variable costs per unit of $0.25. It sells to retailers for $0.40 per bar. What is the break-even point in units? In sales dollars?

$$\text{Break-even point (units)} = \frac{\text{Total fixed costs}}{\text{Price} - \text{Variable costs (per unit)}} = \frac{\$150{,}000}{\$0.40 - \$0.25} = \underline{\underline{1{,}000{,}000}}$$

$$\text{Break-even point (sales dollars)} = \frac{\text{Total fixed costs}}{1 - \dfrac{\text{Variable costs (per unit)}}{\text{Price}}} = \frac{\$150{,}000}{1 - \dfrac{\$0.25}{\$0.40}} = \underline{\underline{\$250{,}000}}$$

There are limitations to traditional break-even analysis. First, as with all forms of cost-based pricing, demand is not considered. The presumption is that wide variations in quantity can be sold at the same price; this is highly unlikely. Second, it is assumed that all costs can be divided into fixed and variable categories. Yet some, like advertising, are difficult to define; advertising can be fixed or a per cent of sales. Third, it is assumed that variable costs per unit are constant over a range of quantities. However, purchase discounts or overtime wages may alter these costs. Fourth, it is assumed that fixed costs remain constant; but increases in production may lead to higher costs for new equipment, new full-time employees, and other items.

By including demand considerations, each of the cost-based techniques can be improved. Demand-based pricing techniques are discussed next.

Demand-Based Pricing

Under **demand-based pricing,** *consumers are researched and a* **price ceiling** *set.*

With **demand-based pricing,** a firm sets prices after studying consumer desires and ascertaining the range of prices acceptable to the target market. This approach is used by companies that believe price is a key factor in consumer decision making. These companies identify a **price ceiling,** which is the maximum amount consumers will pay for a given good or service. If the ceiling is exceeded, consumers will not make purchases. Its level depends on the elasticity of demand (availability of substitutes and urgency of need) and consumers' subjective price regarding the particular good or service.

Demand-based techniques require consumer research as to the quantities that will be purchased at various prices, sensitivity to price changes, the existence of market segments, and consumers' ability to pay. Demand estimates tend to be less precise than cost estimates. Also, firms that do inadequate cost analysis and rely on demand data may end up losing money if they make unrealistically low cost assumptions.

Under demand-based pricing, very competitive situations may lead to small markups and lower prices because consumers will purchase substitutes. In these cases, costs must be held down or prices will be too high—as might occur via cost-based pricing. For noncompetitive situations, firms can set large markups and high prices since demand is rather inelastic. There is less emphasis on costs when setting prices in these situations. With cost-based pricing, firms are more apt to set overly low prices in noncompetitive markets.

Four demand-based pricing techniques are reviewed next: demand-minus, chain-markup, modified break-even, and price discrimination. Figure 22-5 gives a synopsis of each technique. And at the end of these subsections, Table 22-3 (on page 623) contains numerical examples of them.

In **demand-minus pricing,** *selling price, then markup, and finally maximum product costs are computed.*

Demand-Minus Pricing Through **demand-minus (demand-backward) pricing,** a firm finds the proper selling price and works backward to compute costs. This approach stipulates that price decisions revolve around consumer demand rather than company operations. It is used by firms selling directly to consumers.

Demand-minus pricing has three steps: Selling price is determined via consumer surveys or other research. The required markup percentage is set based on selling expenses

FIGURE 22-5
Demand-Based Pricing Techniques

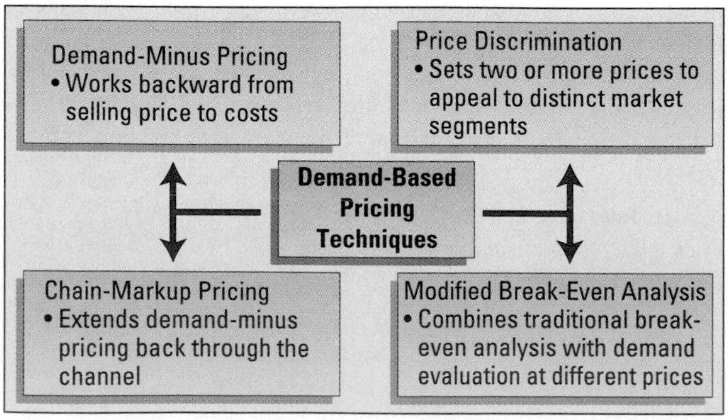

and desired profits. The maximum acceptable per-unit cost for making or buying a product is computed. This formula is used:

$$\text{Maximum product cost} = \text{Price} \times [(100 - \text{Markup per cent})/100]$$

It shows that product cost is derived after selling price and markup are set.

The difficulty in demand-minus pricing is that marketing research may be time-consuming or complex, particularly if many items are involved. Also, new-product pricing research may be particularly inaccurate.

Chain-Markup Pricing **Chain-markup pricing** extends demand-minus calculations all the way from resellers back to suppliers (manufacturers). With it, final selling price is determined, markups for each channel member are examined, and the maximum acceptable costs to each member are computed.

Chain-markup pricing *traces demand-minus calculations from channel members to suppliers.*

In a traditional consumer-goods channel, the markup chain is composed of

1. $\text{Maximum selling price to retailer} = \text{Final selling price} \times [(100 - \text{Retailer's markup})/100]$
2. $\text{Maximum selling price to wholesaler} = \text{Selling price to retailer} \times [(100 - \text{Wholesaler's markup})/100]$
3. $\text{Maximum product cost to manufacturer} = \text{Selling price to wholesaler} \times [(100 - \text{Manufacturer's markup})/100]$

By using chain-markup pricing, price decisions can be related to consumer demand and each reseller is able to see the effects of price changes on the total distribution channel. The interdependence of firms becomes more clear; they cannot set prices independently of one another.

Modified Break-Even Analysis **Modified break-even analysis** combines traditional break-even analysis with an evaluation of demand at various levels of price. Traditional analysis focuses on the sales needed to break even at a given price. It does not indicate the likely level of demand at that price, examine how consumers respond to different levels of price, consider that the break-even point can vary greatly depending on the price the firm happens to select, or calculate the price that maximizes profits.

Melding traditional break-even analysis with demand evaluation at various prices is **modified break-even analysis**.

Modified analysis reveals the price-quantity mix that maximizes profits. It shows that profits do not inevitably rise as the quantity sold increases because lower prices may be needed to expand demand. It also verifies that a firm should examine various price levels and select the one with the greatest profits. Finally, it relates demand to price, rather than assuming that the same volume could be sold at any price.

Price Discrimination With a **price discrimination** approach, a firm sets two or more distinct prices for a product so as to appeal to different final consumer or organizational consumer segments. Higher prices are offered to inelastic segments and lower prices to elastic ones. Price discrimination can be customer-based, product-based, time-based, or place-based.

Setting distinct prices to reach different market segments is **price discrimination**.

In customer-based price discrimination, prices differ by customer category for the same good or service. Price differentials may relate to a consumer's ability to pay (doctors, lawyers, and accountants partially set prices in this manner), negotiating ability (the price of an office building is usually set by bargaining), or buying power (discounts are given for volume purchases).

Through product-based price discrimination, a firm markets a number of features, styles, qualities, brands, or sizes of a product and sets a different price for each product version. Price differentials are greater than cost differentials for the various versions. For example, a dishwasher may be priced at $400 in white and $450 in brown, although the brown color costs the manufacturer only $10 more. There is inelastic demand by customers desiring the special color, and product versions are priced accordingly.

Under time-based price discrimination, a firm varies prices by day versus evening (movie theater tickets), time of day (telephone and utility rates), or season (hotel rates). Consumers who insist on prime-time use pay higher prices than those who are willing to make their purchases during nonpeak times.

Ethics IN TODAY'S SOCIETY

How Much Do People Really Pay for Pay Phones?

Since the deregulation of telephone services, the only U.S. long-distance rates still subject to federal oversight are AT&T's. Why? In deregulating phone services, the Federal Communications Commission (FCC) assumed that new "operator service providers" (OSPs) would offer lower prices due to intense competition and that they would increase the number of pay phones. And even the restrictions on AT&T have been eased.

One of the FCC's goals has clearly been met: The number of pay phones has increased by 325 per cent since deregulation. One in six pay phones is now either independently owned or served by an OSP.

However, in too many instances, the FCC's other major goal has not been achieved: unscrupulous OSPs charge very high prices. In 1994 alone, the FCC received close to 2,500 complaints about the high charges at public phones—nearly twice the number of complaints received in 1993. In some cases, calls for which AT&T would have charged $1.25 or less were billed at up to $5.95 (due to high surcharges or handling fees).

OSPs say these fees are required because they must shell out commissions to whomever controls the space where the phone is installed (such as a hotel, hospital, or shopping mall operator). For example, Oncor Communications spends about $55 million in yearly commissions (29 cents of every dollar collected from its calls). In addition, the firm compensates distributors with $15 for every phone they sign up. Oncor has even acknowledged raising its rates due to the large proportion of customers who circumvent Oncor by using an AT&T or MCI access code. Many hotel, hospital, and shopping mall owners note that they are unaware of the actual fees paid by phone users at their locations.

As an FCC consultant, develop a strategy to resolve unfairness in pay phone pricing.

Sources: Based on material in Penny Loeb, Warren Cohen, Gary Cohen, and Katia Hetter, "Watch that Pay Phone," *U.S. News & World Report* (June 26, 1995), pp. 60–62; and Daniel Pearl, "Why Pay-Phone Calls Can Get So Expensive and Spark Complaints," *Wall Street Journal* (May 30, 1995), pp. A1, A6.

For place-based price discrimination, prices differ by seat location (sports and entertainment events), floor location (office buildings, hotels), or geographic location (resort cities). The demand for locations near the stage, elevators, or warm climates drives the prices of these locations up. General admission tickets, basement offices, and moderate-temperature resorts are priced lower to attract consumers to otherwise less desirable purchases.

Yield management pricing *lets firms optimize price discrimination efforts.*

When a firm engages in price discrimination, it should use **yield management pricing**—whereby it determines the mix of price-quantity combinations that generates the highest level of revenues for a given period. A company wants to make sure that it gives itself every opportunity to sell as many goods and services at full price as possible, while also seeking to sell as many units as it can. It does not want to sell so many low-price items that it jeopardizes full-price sales. Thus, a 1,000-seat theater offering first-run plays must determine how many tickets to sell as orchestra (at $50 each) and how many to sell as general admission (at $25 each). If it tries to sell too many orchestra tickets, there may

Table 22-3
Examples of Demand-Based Pricing Techniques

Demand-Minus Pricing—A mail-order CD-ROM encyclopedia publisher has done consumer research and found people are willing to spend $60.00 for its brand. Its selling expenses and profits are expected to be 35 per cent of the selling price. What is the maximum it can spend to develop and produce each encyclopedia CD-ROM?

$$\text{Maximum merchandise costs} = \text{Price} \times [(100 - \text{Markup per cent})/100]$$
$$= \$60.00 \times [(100 - 35)/100] = \underline{\underline{\$39.00}}$$

Chain-Markup Pricing—A ladies' shoe maker knows women will pay $50.00 for a pair of its shoes. It sells via wholesalers and retailers. Each requires a markup of 30 per cent; the manufacturer wants a 25 per cent markup. (a) What is the maximum price that retailers and wholesalers will spend for a pair of shoes? (b) What is the maximum the manufacturer can spend to make each pair of shoes?

(a) $$\text{Maximum selling price to retailer} = \text{Final selling price} \times [(100 - \text{Retailer's markup})/100]$$
$$= \$50.00 \times [(100 - 30)/100] = \underline{\underline{\$35.00}}$$

$$\text{Maximum selling price to wholesaler} = \text{Selling price to retailer} \times [(100 - \text{Wholesaler's markup})/100]$$
$$= \$35.00 \times [(100 - 30)/100] = \underline{\underline{\$24.50}}$$

(b) $$\text{Maximum merchandise costs to manufacturer} = \text{Selling price to wholesaler} \times [(100 - \text{Manufacturer's markup})/100]$$
$$= \$24.50 \times [(100 - 25)/100] = \underline{\underline{\$18.38}}$$

Modified Break-Even Analysis—An aspirin maker has total fixed costs of $2,000,000 and variable costs of $1.50 per bottle. Research shows the following demand schedule. At what price should the company sell its aspirin?

Selling Price	*Quantity Demanded*	*Total Revenue*	*Total Cost*	*Total Profit (Loss)*	
$3.00	2,000,000	$ 6,000,000	$5,000,000	$1,000,000	Maximum
2.50	3,200,000	8,000,000	6,800,000	1,200,000 ←	profit at
2.00	5,000,000	10,000,000	9,500,000	500,000	price of $2.50

Price Discrimination—A sports team knows people will pay different prices for tickets, based on location. It offers 10,000 tickets at $30 each, 25,000 at $20 each, and 20,000 at $12 each. What are profits if total costs per game are $750,000?

$$\text{Profit} = (\text{Revenues from Segment A} + \text{Segment B} + \text{Segment C}) - \text{Total costs}$$
$$= (\$300,000 + \$500,000 + \$240,000) - \$750,000 = \underline{\underline{\$290,000}}$$

be empty seats during a performance. If it looks to sell too many general admission tickets, the theater may be full—but total revenues may be unsatisfactory.[7]

Before using price discrimination, a firm should consider these questions: Are there distinct market segments? Do people communicate with each other about product features and prices? Can product versions be differentiated? Will some consumers choose low-priced models when they might otherwise buy high-priced models if those are the only ones available? How do the marginal costs of adding product alternatives compare with marginal revenues? Will channel members stock all models? How difficult is it to explain product differences to consumers? Under what conditions is price discrimination legal (a firm would not want to violate the Robinson-Patman Act)?

[7]See Edwin McDowell, "His Goal: No Room at the Inns," *New York Times* (November 23, 1995), pp. D1, D8.

Competition-Based Pricing

Competition-based pricing *is setting prices relative to other firms.*

In **competition-based pricing**, a firm uses competitors' prices rather than demand or cost considerations as its primary pricing guideposts. The company may not respond to changes in demand or costs unless they also have an effect on competitors' prices. It can set prices below the market, at the market, or above the market, depending on its customers, image, marketing mix, consumer loyalty, and other factors. This approach is applied by firms contending with others selling similar items (or those perceived as similar).

Competition-based pricing is popular. It is simple, with no reliance on demand curves, price elasticity, or costs per unit. The ongoing market price level is assumed to be fair for both consumers and companies. Pricing at the market level does not disrupt competition and, therefore, does not lead to retaliations. However, it may lead to complacency, and different firms may not have the same demand and cost structures.

Two aspects of competition-based pricing are discussed in the following subsections: price leadership and competitive bidding.

Price leadership *occurs when one or a few firms initiate price changes in an industry; they are effective when others follow.*

Price Leadership **Price leadership** exists in situations where one firm (or a few firms) is usually the first to announce price changes and others in the industry follow. The price leader's role is to set prices that reflect market conditions, without disrupting the marketplace—it must not turn off consumers with price increases perceived as too large or precipitate a price war with competitors by excessive price cuts.

Price leaders are generally firms that have significant market shares, well-established positions, respect from competitors, and the desire to initiate price changes. As an illustration, a frequent price leader in the newsprint industry has been Canada's Abitibi-Price. It is the world's largest newsprint maker, has the largest production capacity, and has the dominant market share. Because over one-half of its revenues are in newsprint, the firm has a strong commitment to maintain stable prices.

Over the last several years, the role of price leaders has been greatly reduced in many industries, including steel, chemical, glass container, and newsprint, as many smaller firms have sought to act more independently. Even Abitibi-Price has been affected by this trend. At various times, it has announced higher newsprint prices, but had to backtrack—after competitors decided not to go along.

Announcements of price changes by industry leaders must be communicated through the media. It is illegal for firms in the same industry or in competing ones to confer with one another regarding the setting of prices.

Competitive Bidding Through competitive bidding (discussed in Chapter 9), two or more firms independently submit prices to a customer for a specific good, project, and/or service. Sealed bids may be requested by some government or organizational consumers; each seller then has one chance to make its best offer.

Various mathematical models have been applied to competitive bidding. All use the expected profit concept, which states that as the bid price increases the profit to a firm increases, but the probability of its winning a contract decreases. Although a firm's potential profit (loss) at a given bid amount can usually be estimated accurately, the probability of getting a contract (underbidding all other qualified competitors) can be hard to determine.

Combination Pricing

It is essential that companies integrate cost, demand, and competitive pricing techniques via **combination pricing**.

Although cost-, demand-, and competition-based pricing methods have been discussed separately, aspects of the three approaches should be integrated into a **combination pricing** approach. This is done often in practice. A cost-based approach sets a price floor and outlines the various costs incurred in doing business. It establishes profit margins, target prices, and/or break-even quantities. A demand-based approach finds out the prices consumers will pay and the ceiling prices for each channel member. It develops the price-quantity mix that maximizes profits and allows a firm to reach different market segments (if it so desires). A competition-based approach examines the proper price level for the firm in relation to competitors.

Unless the approaches are integrated, critical issues may be overlooked. Table 22-4 shows a list of questions a firm should consider in setting prices.

Implementing a Pricing Strategy

Implementing a pricing strategy involves a wide variety of separate but related specific decisions, besides the broader concepts just discussed. The decisions involve whether and how to use customary versus variable pricing, a one-price policy versus flexible pricing, odd pricing, the price-quality association, leader pricing, multiple-unit pricing, price lining, price bundling, geographic pricing, and purchase terms.

Customary Versus Variable Pricing

With **customary pricing**, *one price is maintained over an extended period. Under* **variable pricing**, *prices reflect costs or differences in demand.*

Customary pricing occurs when a firm sets prices and seeks to maintain them for an extended time. Prices are not changed during this period. Customary pricing is used for items like candy, gum, magazines, restaurant food, and mass transit. Rather than modify prices to reflect cost increases, firms may reduce package size, change ingredients, or have a more restrictive transfer policy among bus lines. The assumption is that consumers prefer one of these alternatives to a price hike.

Variable pricing allows a firm to intentionally alter prices in response to cost fluctuations or differences in consumer demand. When costs change, prices are lowered or raised accordingly; the fluctuations are not absorbed and product quality is not modified to maintain customary prices. Through price discrimination, a firm can offer distinct prices to appeal to different market segments. In this way, the prices charged to diverse consumers

Table 22-4

Selected Issues to Consider When Combining Pricing Techniques

Cost-Based

What profit margin does a price level permit?

Do markups allow for differences in product investments, installation and servicing, and selling effort and merchandising skills?

Are there accurate and timely cost data by good, service, project, process, and/or store?

Are cost changes monitored and prices adjusted accordingly?

Are there specific profit or return-on-investment goals?

What is the price-floor price for each good, service, project, process, and/or store?

What are the break-even points for each good, service, project, process, and/or store?

Demand-Based

What type of demand does each good, service, project, process, and/or store face?

Have price elasticities been estimated for various price levels?

Are demand-minus, chain-markup, and modified break-even analyses utilized?

Has price discrimination been considered?

How loyal are customers?

Competition-Based

How do prices compare with those of competitors?

Is price leadership used in the industry? By whom?

How do competitors react to price changes?

How are competitive bids determined?

Is the long-run expected profit concept used in competitive bidding?

are not based on costs, but on consumer sensitivity to price. Many firms use some form of variable pricing.

It is possible to combine customary and variable pricing. For example, a magazine may be $3 per single copy and $24 per year's subscription ($2 an issue)—two customary prices are charged, and the consumer selects the offer he or she finds most attractive.

A One-Price Policy Versus Flexible Pricing

All buying the same product pay the same price under a **one-price policy**. *Different customers may pay different prices with* **flexible pricing**.

A **one-price policy** lets a firm charge the same price to all customers seeking to purchase a good or service under similar conditions. Prices may differ according to the quantity bought, time of purchase, and services obtained (such as delivery and installation), but all consumers are given the opportunity to pay the same price for the same combinations of goods and services. This builds consumer confidence, is easy to administer, eliminates bargaining, and permits self-service and catalog sales. Today, throughout the United States, one-price policies are the rule for most retailers. In industrial marketing, a firm with a one-price policy would not allow sales personnel to deviate from a published price list.

With **flexible pricing,** a firms sets prices based on the consumer's ability to negotiate or on the buying power of a large customer. For instance, people who are knowledgeable or are good bargainers would pay lower prices than those who are not knowledgeable or are weaker bargainers. Jewelry stores, car dealers, flea markets, real-estate brokers, antique shops, and many types of industrial marketers frequently use flexible pricing. In some cases, salesperson commissions are keyed to the profitability of orders; this encourages salespeople to solicit higher prices. Flexible prices to resellers are subject to the Robinson-Patman restrictions explained in Chapter 21. Flexible pricing is much more prevalent outside the United States, where this practice (sometimes known as "haggling") may be culturally ingrained.

One result of flexible pricing is the practice whereby consumers gather information from full-service sellers, shop around for the best available price, and then challenge discount sellers to "beat the lowest price." This practice is detrimental to full-service firms and allows discounters to hold down selling costs (and encourage further bargaining).

Odd Pricing

Odd prices *are those set below even-dollar values.*

Odd pricing is used when selling prices are set at levels below even dollar values, such as 49 cents, $4.95, and $199. It has proven popular for several reasons: People like getting change. Because the cashier must make change, employers ensure that transactions are properly recorded and money is placed in the cash register. Consumers gain the impression that a firm thinks carefully about its prices and sets them as low as possible. They may also believe that odd prices represent price reductions; a price of $8.95 may be viewed as a discount from $10.

Odd prices one or two cents below the next even price (29 cents, $2.98) are common up to $4 or $5. Beyond that point and up to $50 or so, five-cent reductions from the highest even price ($19.95, $49.95) are more usual. For expensive items, odd endings are in dollars ($499, $5,995).

Odd prices may help consumers stay within their price limits and still buy the best items available. A shopper willing to spend "less than $20" for a tie will be attracted to a $19.95 tie and might be as likely to purchase it as a $17 tie because it is within the defined price range. Yet, the imposition of sales tax in 45 states has the effect of raising odd prices into higher dollar levels and may reduce the impact of odd pricing as a selling tool.

The Price-Quality Association

The **price-quality association** *deals with perceptions.* **Prestige pricing** *indicates that consumers may not buy when a price is too low.*

According to the **price-quality association,** consumers may believe high prices represent high quality and low prices represent low quality. This association tends to be most valid when quality is difficult to judge on bases other than price, buyers perceive large differences in quality among brands, buyers have little experience or confidence in assessing quality (as with a new product), high prices are used to exclude the mass market, brand names are unknown, or brand names require certain price levels to sustain their images.

If brand names are well known and/or people are confident of their ability to compare different brands in terms of nonprice factors, the price-quality association may be less valid. Then, many consumers may be more interested in the perceived value they receive for their money—and not necessarily believe a higher price represents better quality. It is essential that prices properly reflect both the quality and the image a firm seeks for its offerings.

With **prestige pricing,** a theory drawn from the price-quality association, it is assumed that consumers will not buy goods or services at prices they consider to be too low. Most people set their own price floors and will not purchase at prices below those floors—because they feel quality and status would be inferior at extremely low prices. Most people also set ceilings with regard to the prices they consider acceptable for particular goods or services. Above those ceilings, items would be seen as too expensive. For each good or service, a firm should set its prices in the target market's acceptable range between the floor and ceiling. See Figure 22-6.

Leader Pricing

Leader pricing *is used to attract customers to low prices.*

With **leader pricing,** a firm advertises and sells key items in its product assortment at less than their usual profit margins. For a wholesaler or retailer, the goal is to increase customer traffic. For a manufacturer, the goal is to gain greater consumer interest in its overall product line. In both cases, it is hoped that consumers will buy regularly priced merchandise in addition to the specially priced items that attract them.

Leader pricing is most used with well-known, high-turnover, frequently bought products. For example, in some drugstores, one of the best-selling items in terms of dollar sales is Kodak film. To stimulate customer traffic into these stores, film may be priced very low; in some cases, it is sold at close to cost. Film is a good item for leader pricing because consumers are able to detect low prices and they are attracted into a store by a discount on the item, which regularly sells for several dollars.

There are two kinds of leader pricing: loss leaders and prices higher than cost but lower than regular prices. As stated in Chapter 21, the use of loss leaders is regulated or illegal in a number of states.

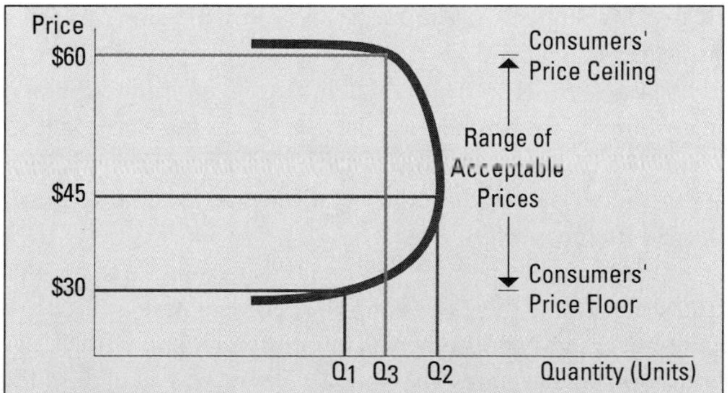

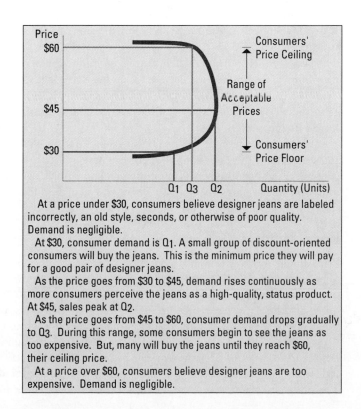

At a price under $30, consumers believe designer jeans are labeled incorrectly, an old style, seconds, or otherwise of poor quality. Demand is negligible.

At $30, consumer demand is Q_1. A small group of discount-oriented consumers will buy the jeans. This is the minimum price they will pay for a good pair of designer jeans.

As the price goes from $30 to $45, demand rises continuously as more consumers perceive the jeans as a high-quality, status product. At $45, sales peak at Q_2.

As the price goes from $45 to $60, consumer demand drops gradually to Q_3. During this range, some consumers begin to see the jeans as too expensive. But, many will buy the jeans until they reach $60, their ceiling price.

At a price over $60, consumers believe designer jeans are too expensive. Demand is negligible.

FIGURE 22-6
Demand for Designer Jeans Under Prestige Pricing

FIGURE 22-7
Price Lining and Target Stores
By offering products at several different price points, Target addresses the needs of all of its customers.
Reprinted by permission.

Multiple-Unit Pricing

With **multiple-unit pricing,** *quantity discounts are intended to result in higher sales volume.*

Multiple-unit pricing is a practice whereby a firm offers discounts to consumers to encourage them to buy in quantity, so as to increase overall sales volume. By offering items at two for 89 cents or six for $139, a firm attempts to sell more units than would be sold at 50 cents or $25 each.

There are four major benefits from multiple-unit pricing: Customers may increase their immediate purchases if they feel they get a bargain. They may boost long-term consumption if they make larger purchases, as occurs with soda. Competitors' customers may be attracted by the discounts. A firm may be able to clear out slow-moving and end-of-season merchandise.

Multiple-unit pricing will not be successful if consumers merely shift their purchases and do not hike their consumption. For example, multiple-unit pricing for Heinz ketchup may not result in consumers using more ketchup with their meals. Thus, it would not raise total dollar sales; consumers would simply buy ketchup less frequently because it can be stored.

Price Lining

Price lining *sets a range of selling prices and price points within that range.*

Price lining involves selling products at a range of prices, with each representing a distinct level of quality (or features). Instead of setting one price for a single version of a good or service, a firm sells two or more versions (with different levels of quality or features) at different prices. Price lining involves two decisions: prescribing the price range (floor and ceiling) and setting specific price points in that range.

A price range may be low, intermediate, or high. For example, inexpensive radios may be priced from $8 to $20, moderately priced radios from $22 to $50, and expensive radios from $55 to $120. After the range is chosen, a limited number of price points is set. The price points must be distinct and not too close together. Inexpensive radios could be priced at \$8, \$12, and \$20. They would not be priced at \$8, \$9, \$10, \$11, \$12, \$13, \$14, \$15, \$16, \$17, \$18, \$19, and \$20. This would confuse consumers and be inefficient for the firm. Figure 22-7 illustrates how Target uses price lining for vacuum cleaners.

When price lining, a firm must consider these factors: Price points must be spaced far enough apart so customers perceive differences among product versions—otherwise, consumers might view the price floor as the price they should pay and believe there is no difference among models. Price points should be spaced farther apart at higher prices because consumer demand becomes more inelastic. Relationships among price points must be kept when costs rise, so clear differences are retained. If radio costs rise 25 per cent, prices should be set at \$10, \$15, and \$25 (up from \$8, \$12, and \$20).

Price lining offers benefits for both sellers and consumers. Sellers can offer a product assortment, attract market segments, trade up shoppers within a price range, control inventory by price point, reduce competition by having versions over a price range, and increase overall sales volume. Consumers are given an assortment from which to choose, confusion is lessened, comparisons may be made, and quality options are available within a given price range.

Price lining can also have constraints: Consumers may feel price gaps are too large—a \$25 handbag may be too low, while the next price point of \$100 may be too high. Rising costs may squeeze individual prices and make it hard for a firm to keep the proper relationships in its line. Markdowns or special sales may disrupt the balance in a price line, unless all items in the line are proportionately reduced in price.

Price Bundling

A firm can use **bundled** *or* **unbundled pricing**.

Some form of price bundling can be used in a strategy. With **bundled pricing**, a firm sells a basic product, options, and customer service for one total price. An industrial-equipment manufacturer may have a single price for a drill press, its delivery, its installation, and a service contract. Individual items, such as the drill press, would not be sold separately.

With **unbundled pricing**, a firm breaks down prices by individual components and allows the consumer to decide what to purchase. A discount appliance store may have separate prices for a refrigerator, its delivery, its installation, and a service contract.

Many companies choose to offer consumers both pricing options and allow a slight discount for bundled pricing. See Figure 22-8.

FIGURE 22-8
Price Bundling for a Bookcase

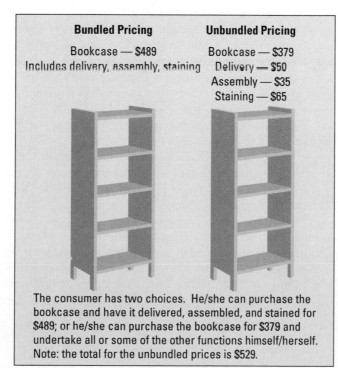

Bundled Pricing	**Unbundled Pricing**
Bookcase — \$489	Bookcase — \$379
Includes delivery, assembly, staining	Delivery — \$50
	Assembly — \$35
	Staining — \$65

The consumer has two choices. He/she can purchase the bookcase and have it delivered, assembled, and stained for \$489; or he/she can purchase the bookcase for \$379 and undertake all or some of the other functions himself/herself. Note: the total for the unbundled prices is \$529.

Geographic Pricing

Geographic pricing *alternatives are FOB mill (factory), uniform delivered, zone, and base-point pricing.*

Geographic pricing outlines responsibility for transportation charges. Many times, it is not negotiated but depends on the traditional practices in the industry in which the firm operates, and all companies in the industry normally conform to the same geographic pricing format. Geographic pricing often involves industrial marketing situations.

These are the most common methods of geographic pricing:

- *FOB mill (factory) pricing*—The buyer picks a transportation form and pays all freight charges, the seller pays the costs of loading the goods (hence, "free on board"), and the delivered price to the buyer depends on freight charges.
- *Uniform delivered pricing*—All buyers pay the same delivered price for the same quantity of goods, regardless of their location; the seller pays for shipping.
- *Zone pricing*—It provides for a uniform delivered price to all buyers within a geographic zone; through a multiple-zone system, delivered prices vary by zone.
- *Base-point pricing*—Firms in an industry establish basing points from which the costs of shipping are computed; the delivered price to a buyer reflects the cost of transporting goods from the basing point nearest to the buyer, regardless of the actual site of supply.

Purchase Terms

Purchase terms *outline pricing provisions.*

Purchase terms are the provisions of price agreements. They include discounts, the timing of payments, and credit arrangements.

Discounts are the reductions from final selling prices that are available to resellers and consumers for performing certain functions, paying cash, buying large amounts, buying in off-seasons, or enhancing promotions. As an example, a wholesaler may buy goods at 40 per cent off the manufacturer's suggested final list selling price. This 40 per cent covers the wholesaler's expenses, profit, and discount to the retailer. The retailer could buy goods for 25 per cent off list (the wholesaler keeping 15 per cent for its costs and profit). In giving discounts, firms must make them proportionately available to all competing channel members, to avoid violating the Robinson-Patman Act.

Payment timing must be specified in a purchase agreement. Final consumers may pay immediately or after delivery. In credit transactions, payments are not made until bills are received; they may be made over time. Organizational consumers are also quite interested in the timing of payments and negotiate for the best terms. For example, terms of net 30 mean products do not have to be paid for until 30 days after receipt. They must then be paid for in full. Terms of 2/10, net 30 mean a buyer receives a 2 per cent discount if the full bill is paid within 10 days after merchandise receipt. The buyer must pay the face value of a bill within 30 days after the receipt of products. Various time terms are available.

When marketing internationally, sellers must sometimes be prepared to wait an extended period to receive payments. At one time, it took U.S. firms an average of 337 days to get paid by Iranian businesses, 129 days to get paid by Kenyan businesses, 123 days to get paid by Argentine businesses, and 119 days to get paid by Brazilian clients.[8]

Open *and* **revolving credit accounts** *are possible.*

A firm that allows credit purchases may use open accounts or revolving accounts. With an **open credit account,** the buyer receives a monthly bill for the goods and services bought during the preceding month. The account must be paid in full each month. With a **revolving credit account,** the buyer agrees to make minimum monthly payments during an extended period of time and pays interest on outstanding balances. Today, various types of firms (from Xerox to many colleges) offer some form of credit plan. Auto makers provide their own cut-rate financing programs to stimulate sales and leasing.

[8]"Your Check Is in the Mail," *Wall Street Journal* (December 8, 1992), p. 2.

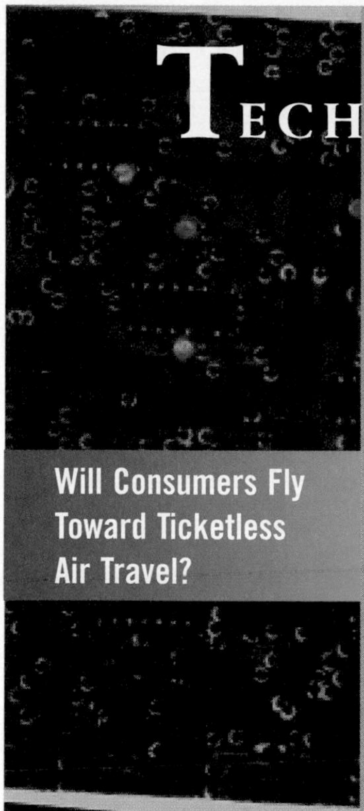

TECHNOLOGY & MARKETING

Will Consumers Fly Toward Ticketless Air Travel?

Many airlines are now seriously considering the substitution of electronic ticketing for traditional paper-based tickets. With electronic ticketing, passengers no longer have to worry about losing or misplacing their tickets. And airlines can save millions of dollars by eliminating accounting positions.

ValuJet Airlines, the leader in ticketless air travel, has used this form of ticketing since this discount carrier began in 1993. In its system, passengers book seats either directly through the airline or by way of travel agents. Instead of getting plane tickets, ValuJet passengers receive personal confirmation numbers when they book flights. At flight time, they are issued boarding passes at the gate after they give their names and confirmation numbers to an attendant. The firm provides receipts upon request.

As ValuJet's director of communications says, "We were clearly the trend setter. Our goal was to simplify the travel process. From an accounting perspective, once the flight has taken off, that revenue is automatically posted as flown revenues. We have no accounting department that requires 200 to 300 people."

In 1995, Southwest Airlines began offering ticketless reservations. During the first year, about 30 per cent of its passengers used that option, and the airline estimated it would trim $25 million in costs.

Although ticketless reservation systems have been used by hotels and car rental firms for years, airlines have been slow to change. Furthermore, ticketless travel "terrifies travel agents because consumers will think that they don't need them anymore." United Airlines, for example, is bypassing travel agents through its CompuServe site.

As a marketing executive for American Airlines, would you recommend the use of a ticketless reservation system? Explain your answer.

Sources: Based on material in Bridget O'Brian, "Ticketless Plane Trips, New Technology Force Travel Agencies to Change Course," *Wall Street Journal* (September 13, 1994), pp. B1, B5; and Michael Wilke, "Nix to Tix at Some Airlines," *Advertising Age* (August 14, 1995), pp. 1, 10.

Price Adjustments

List prices, escalator clauses, surcharges, additional markups, markdowns, *and* **rebates** *are key pricing tools.*

After a price strategy is enacted, it often requires continuous fine-tuning to reflect changes in costs, competitive conditions, and demand. Prices can be adjusted via alterations in list prices, escalator clauses and surcharges, added markups, markdowns, and rebates.

List prices are the regularly quoted prices provided to customers. They may be preprinted on price tags, in catalogs, and in dealer purchase orders. Modifications in list prices are necessary if there are sustained changes in labor costs, raw material costs, and market segments, and as a product moves through its life cycle. When these events are long-term in nature, they enable customary prices to be revised, new catalogs to be printed, and adjustments to be completed in an orderly fashion.

Costs or economic conditions may sometimes be so volatile that revised list prices cannot be printed or distributed efficiently. Escalator clauses or surcharges can then be used. Both allow prices to be adjusted quickly. With **escalator clauses,** a firm is contractually allowed to raise the prices of items to reflect higher costs in those items' essential ingredients without changing printed list prices. It may even be able to set prices at the time of delivery. **Surcharges** are across-the-board published price increases that supplement list prices. These may be used with catalogs because of their simplicity; an insert is distributed with the catalog.

When list prices are not involved, **additional markups** can be used to raise regular selling prices if demand is unexpectedly high or costs are rising. There is a risk to this.

For example, supermarkets get bad publicity for relabeling low-cost existing items at higher prices so they match those of newer merchandise purchased at higher costs.

Markdowns are reductions from items' original selling prices. All types of sellers use them to meet the lower prices of competitors, counteract overstocking of merchandise, clear out shopworn merchandise, deplete assortments of odds and ends, and increase customer traffic.

Although manufacturers regularly give discounts to resellers, they may periodically offer cash **rebates** to customers to stimulate the purchase of an item or a group of items. Rebates are flexible, do not alter basic prices, involve direct communication between consumers and manufacturers (since rebates are usually sent to consumers by manufacturers), and do not affect resellers' profits (as regular price reductions do). Price cuts by individual resellers may not generate the same kind of consumer enthusiasm. Rebate popularity can be traced to their usage by the auto industry to help cut down on inventory surpluses. Rebates have also been offered by Fedders, Gillette, Polaroid, Minolta, and a number of others. The major disadvantage is that so many firms have used rebates that their impact may be lessened.

Whenever adjustments are needed, channel members should cooperatively agree on their individual roles. Price hikes or cuts should not be unilateral.

MARKETING IN A CHANGING WORLD

Dealing with Slow-Paying Customers[9]

One of the problems facing many firms today is that more customers seem to be paying late (or sometimes not paying at all). When customers buy goods and services through their revolving credit accounts, there is usually a simple remedy: interest charges accrue. And since some revolving credit costs more than 20 per cent in annual interest rates, late payments can be quite profitable—as long as customers do not default.

A company may encounter real trouble when a customer requests a service and then decides to pay late or not at all. What do you do then? You cannot repossess the service. Rural Metro, a Scottsdale, Arizona-based ambulance service, is asking itself that very question.

Rural Metro operates a fleet of 650 ambulances in 80 communities covering ten states. This is what it has encountered:

> Ambulance service is a tough product to make money on. True, demand is—as economists say—price inelastic: Anyone who needs the service is unlikely to haggle over its price. On the other hand, costs in the business are high and fixed: An ambulance costs $70,000 to buy and around $450,000 a year to operate. And revenues are variable: Once a customer has used the service, there's not much a provider can do to make the person pay the bill. Ambulance companies' average bill for emergency transports runs from $250 to $550 a patient, but the companies collect only 60 to 70 per cent of their bills.

As a result, Rural Metro is forced to use "account collectors" to call customers with past-due bills, send frequent computerized bills and rebills, and engage in other aggressive tactics—through no fault of its own.

[9] The material in this section is based on Nina Munk, "Making the Customer Pay," *Forbes* (February 13, 1995), pp. 74–75.

SUMMARY

1. *To present an overall framework for developing and applying a pricing strategy* A pricing strategy has five stages: objectives, broad policy, strategy, implementation, and adjustments. The stages are affected by outside factors and must be integrated with a firm's marketing mix.

2. *To analyze sales-based, profit-based, and status quo-based pricing objectives, and to describe the role of a broad price policy* Sales goals center on volume and/or market share. In penetration pricing, a company sets low prices to capture a mass market. Profit goals focus on profit maximization, satisfactory profits, optimum return on investment, and/or early cash recovery. In skimming pricing, a firm seeks to capture the segment less concerned with price than quality or status. Status quo goals are geared toward minimizing the impact of outside parties and ensuring stability. Two or more pricing objectives may be combined.

A broad price policy sets the overall direction for a firm's pricing efforts. Through it, a firm decides if it is price- or nonprice-oriented.

3. *To examine and apply the alternative approaches to a pricing strategy* A price strategy may be cost-based, demand-based, competition-based, or a combination of these.

With cost-based pricing, a firm computes merchandise, service, and overhead costs and then adds an amount to cover profit. Cost-plus pricing adds costs and a desired profit to set prices. In markup pricing, a firm sets prices by calculating the per-unit costs of producing (buying) goods and/or services and then determining the markup percentages needed to cover selling costs and profit; a variable markup policy allows different markups for distinct products. In target pricing, prices are set to provide a specified rate of return on investment for a standard volume of production. When a firm has excess capacity, it may use price-floor pricing, in which prices are set at a level above variable costs rather than total costs. Traditional break-even analysis determines the sales quantity at which total costs equal total revenues for a chosen price.

With demand-based pricing, a firm sets prices after doing consumer research and learning the range of acceptable prices to the target market. In demand-minus pricing, a firm determines the proper selling price and works backward to compute costs. Chain-markup pricing extends demand-minus calculations all the way from resellers back to suppliers (manufacturers). Modified break-even analysis combines traditional break-even analysis with an evaluation of demand at various levels of price. Price discrimination is a technique whereby a firm sets two or more distinct prices for a product so as to appeal to different market segments.

In competition-based pricing, a firm uses competitors' prices as its main guideposts. Prices may be below, at, or above the market. A firm would determine whether it has the ability and the interest to be a price leader or a price follower. Under competitive bidding, two or more firms independently submit prices in response to precise customer requests.

These three pricing approaches should be integrated via combination pricing, so that a firm includes all necessary factors in its pricing strategy. Otherwise, critical decisions are likely to be overlooked.

4. *To discuss several specific decisions that must be made in implementing a pricing strategy* Enacting a price strategy involves a variety of interlocking specific decisions. Customary pricing is employed when a firm sets prices for an extended period. With variable pricing, a firm alters prices to coincide with cost or consumer demand fluctuations.

In a one-price policy, all consumers purchasing under similar conditions pay the same price. Flexible pricing allows a firm to vary prices based on a shopper's ability to negotiate or the buying power of a large customer.

Odd-pricing is used if selling prices are set below even-dollar values. According to the price-quality association, consumers may believe there is a correlation between price and quality. With prestige pricing, it is assumed that consumers do not buy products at prices that are considered too low. They set price floors, as well as price ceilings.

Under leader pricing, key items are sold at less than their usual profit margins to increase consumer traffic. Multiple-unit pricing is a practice in which a company offers discounts to consumers for buying in quantity.

Price lining involves the sale of goods and services at a range of prices, with each embodying a distinct level of quality (or features). In bundled pricing, a firm offers a basic product, options, and customer service for one total price; through unbundled pricing, it breaks down prices by individual components and lets consumers decide what to buy.

Geographic pricing outlines the responsibility for transportation. Purchase terms are the provisions of price agreements, including discounts, timing of payments, and credit.

5. *To show the major ways that prices can be adjusted* Once a pricing strategy is implemented, it usually needs regular fine-tuning to reflect cost, competition, and demand changes. Prices can be adjusted by changing list prices, including escalator clauses and surcharges in contracts, marking prices up or down, and offering direct rebates.

KEY TERMS

sales-based pricing objectives (p. 612)
penetration pricing (p. 612)
profit-based pricing objectives (p. 612)
skimming pricing (p. 612)
status quo-based pricing objectives (p. 613)
broad price policy (p. 613)
cost-based pricing (p. 614)
price floor (p. 615)
cost-plus pricing (p. 616)
markup pricing (p. 617)
variable markup policy (p. 617)
target pricing (p. 618)
price-floor pricing (p. 618)
traditional break-even analysis (p. 618)
demand-based pricing (p. 620)
price ceiling (p. 620)
demand-minus (demand-backward) pricing (p. 620)
chain-markup pricing (p. 621)
modified break-even analysis (p. 621)
price discrimination (p. 621)
yield management pricing (p. 622)
competition-based pricing (p. 624)
price leadership (p. 624)
combination pricing (p. 624)
customary pricing (p. 625)
variable pricing (p. 625)
one-price policy (p. 626)
flexible pricing (p. 626)
odd pricing (p. 626)
price-quality association (p. 626)
prestige pricing (p. 627)
leader pricing (p. 627)
multiple-unit pricing (p. 628)
price lining (p. 628)
bundled pricing (p. 629)
unbundled pricing (p. 629)
geographic pricing (p. 630)
purchase terms (p. 630)
open credit account (p. 630)
revolving credit account (p. 630)
list prices (p. 631)
escalator clauses (p. 631)
surcharges (p. 631)
additional markups (p. 631)
markdowns (p. 632)
rebates (p. 632)

Review Questions

1. Explain this statement: "It should not be inferred that status quo objectives require no effort on the part of the firm."

2. When should a firm pursue penetration pricing? Skimming pricing?

3. Why are markups usually computed on the basis of selling price?

4. A firm requires a 14 per cent return on a $700,000 investment in order to produce a new electric garage-door opener. If the standard volume is 50,000 units, fixed costs are $500,000, and variable costs are $48 per unit, what is the target price?

5. A company making office desks has total fixed costs of $2 million per year and variable costs of $450 per desk. It sells the desks to retailers for $750 apiece. Compute the traditional break-even point in both units and dollars.

6. Discuss chain-markup pricing from the perspective of a retailer.

7. What is yield management pricing? Why is it important for sellers to understand this concept?

8. Contrast customary pricing and variable pricing. How may the two techniques be combined?

9. Under what circumstances is the price-quality association most valid? Least valid?

10. How does price lining benefit manufacturers? Retailers? Consumers?

Discussion Questions

1. A movie theater has weekly fixed costs (land, building, and equipment) of $3,500. Variable weekly costs (movie rental, electricity, ushers, etc.) are $1,800. From a price-floor pricing perspective, how much revenue must a movie generate during a slow week for it to be worthwhile to open the theater? Explain your answer.

2. A retailer determines that customers are willing to spend $27.95 on a new John Grisham (author of *The Client* and other best-sellers in the legal arena) novel. The publisher charges the retailer $22.50 for each copy. The retailer wants a 30 per cent markup. Comment on this situation.

3. a. A wholesaler of small industrial tools has fixed costs of $350,000, variable costs of $20 per tool, and faces this demand schedule from its hardware-store customers:

Price	Quantity Demanded
$24	100,000
$27	85,000
$30	65,000
$33	40,000

At what price is profit maximized?

b. If the company noted in Question 3a decides to sell 40,000 small tools at $33 and 45,000 of these tools at $27, what will its profit be? What are the risks of this approach?

4. Develop a price-lining strategy for each of these firms:
a. A restaurant.
b. A CPA firm specializing in large-business accounts.
c. A video-rental firm.

5. A wholesaler of plumbing supplies recently added a new line of kitchen sinks and priced them at $109 each (to plumbers). The manufacturer has just announced a 10 per cent price increase on the sinks—due to higher materials and labor costs. Yet, for this wholesaler, the initial response of plumbers to the sinks has been sluggish. Also, some competing wholesalers are selling the sinks for $99—$30 under the manufacturer's new suggested list price. What should the wholesaler do next?

CASE 1

*The Science and Art of Pricing**

According to a seminar at the University of Chicago, pricing decisions must reflect an upper boundary (the price an informed consumer is willing to pay for a product) and a lower boundary (determined by a product's variable costs). The upper boundary should be based on comparisons of a firm's products with competitors, an analysis of the best available alternative products and their relative benefits, and an assignment of value to each benefit. Let's first look at the upper boundary pricing decisions by Datastorm (a Columbia, Missouri-based, software company) and Sears. We will then look at lower boundary decision making using an airline example.

Datastorm faced a tough decision in the initial pricing of its Procomm Plus software, a product that links computers to networks and bulletin board systems through a modem. When the product was introduced in 1991, competitive products were priced at premium prices. And despite high prices, the sales of these products were growing at a rapid pace.

In comparison with competitors, Datastorm set its prices to attract a cost-conscious market segment that did not own communications software. At its inception, Procomm Plus sold for $179 retail, a price far below competitors. Datastorm then kept Procomm Plus at this price for over four years. Market analysts credit the company's pricing strategy as a major factor contributing to its current 85 per cent market share among IBM compatible users.

What Datastorm did, whether or not the firm knew it, was to follow the three Cs of pricing: customer, company, and competition. Datastorm set its new product's price based on its perception of what price would be fair to its customers. Part of this analysis was also keyed to the competition.

Sears' pricing strategy for an ultrasonic appliance (that cleaned dentures and tools) illustrates what can happen when a firm misjudges its customer's upper boundary. Even though the product and its suggested price were reviewed by a sample of 400 targeted customers, the cleaner was unsuccessful when actually commercialized. Sears' customers had hoped for a much lower price (closer to $20) than the $39.95 price that Sears thought was appropriate for the product. As a former manager of marketing research at Sears said, "I'm sure they looked at it and compared it to a mixer or a coffee maker."

According to one marketing analyst, Sears should have tested the $39.95 price before it produced the product. Sears did this when it subsequently introduced a new trash compactor. It tested the compactor price in three different markets. The pricing data from the research project was then incorporated into the final product's price.

One University of Chicago marketing professor suggests that a common problem in determining the lower pricing boundary is that often firms lump variable and fixed costs together: "In an airline, if you have a seat, and you take the average cost of the plane, the crew, and the pilot, it might turn out that your average cost per seat is $10. But if the plane is sitting on the runway, ready to take off, the variable cost might be as low as $1." Thus, obtaining a price over $1 (to cover the variable cost of the snack served on a short-term flight) would contribute to the firm's overhead costs and profits. "Firms that inflate variable costs tend not to reduce their prices much. They don't realize the true incremental revenue they gain from a discount."

After a firm sets upper and lower price boundaries, it then must look at particular aspects of price, such as fairness. Some research suggests that although consumers may view price increases based on higher costs of doing business as fair, they do not look kindly at price differences based on customer characteristics.

QUESTIONS

1. Evaluate Datastorm's pricing strategy.
2. Explain the significance of this statement: "Firms that inflate their variable costs tend not to reduce their prices much. They don't realize the true incremental revenue they can gain from a discount."
3. What is the major drawback of a firm's long-term use of price-floor pricing?
4. If demand determines the price ceiling and cost determines the price floor, what is the role of competition?

*The data in this case are drawn from Gene Koprowski, "The Price Is Right," *Marketing Tools* (September 1995), pp. 56–61.

CASE 2

The Pricing of Beef at Supermarkets†

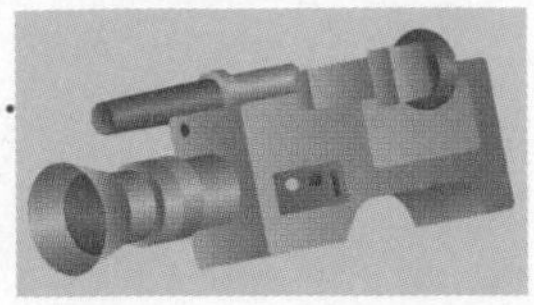

According to *Progressive Grocer*, meat and seafood together account for 16 per cent of sales in an average supermarket. (The industry does not break out data for beef.) This case discusses two major developments affecting the sales and profitability of beef in supermarkets: the use of vitamin E supplements for cattle and the sales of ready-to-cook meat.

Vitamin E, when given to cattle in the final days of their feeding, has been shown to be effective in retarding the oxidation of beef. At the same time, Vitamin E does not affect beef's tenderness, juiciness, or flavor. With oxidation, beef loses its desirable "cherry red" color and becomes brown, and brown-colored beef generally has to be marked down in order to be sold.

A recent study, sponsored by the National Cattleman's Association, compared markdowns for two samples of beef: one from cattle fed with vitamin E and the other from cattle fed in a traditional manner. Both samples were graded Choice and Select, vacuum packaged, and aged for a 12-day period. Table 1 outlines the price reductions by cut for both samples during the first four days of sale in a chain supermarket.

As shown in the table, Vitamin E beef required much lower markdowns than traditional beef. Customers also reported that the Vitamin E beef retained its "bright cherry red" color longer than traditional beef. Based on its study, the National Cattleman's Association concluded that the use of Vitamin E could save the retail industry about $1 billion per year in markdowns.

Supermarkets are also considering expanded sales of ready-to-cook meats as a way to raise profits. And in devising a marketing strategy for ready-to-cook meats, supermarket managers need to evaluate sourcing (whether items should be purchased from a supplier, prepared on the premises, or prepared at a central kitchen for a chain operation), as well as the variety of meats offered for sale. For example, too few items could lead to low sales while too much choice could result in consumer confusion and waste due to poor sales of some items. Market analysts familiar with ready-to-cook items also note that there are high labor costs associated with this department.

One chain that has done well with ready-to-cook meats is Giant Foods. Giant monitors what products sell best by examining the chain's scanning data. Among its best-selling items are marinated London broil, beef for stir fry, chicken cutlet with lemon and herb seasoning, and marinated beef kabobs. To ensure uniformity, one person from each store's meat department is responsible for its prepared meats. That employee decides how much to produce each day, taking into account the product's high perishability. For example, sales of some meats expand significantly during weekends.

Although ready-to-cook meat prices are very high on a cost-per-pound basis, most consumers look at prices on a per-serving basis. Thus, a well-run ready-to-cook department can be extremely profitable. One supplier of ready-to-cook foods estimates that its products sell for $3.99 to $5.99 per pound and that most retailers use 20 to 30 per cent markups with its products. Most of its packages range in weight from 1.0 to 1.3 pounds.

Table 1

Necessary Price Reductions by Cut for Vitamin E-Treated and Traditional Beef

	PRICE REDUCTION NEEDED DURING FIRST FOUR DAYS	
Cut	***Vitamin E–Treated Beef***	***Traditional Beef***
Top Loin	0.0%	7.1%
Tenderloin	0.0	12.5
Cross Rib Steak	3.5	39.1

QUESTIONS

1. What other factors should be examined before a supermarket decides whether to purchase Vitamin E-treated beef?
2. Present additional strategies to reduce markdowns on beef.
3. Describe the costs associated with producing ready-to-cook meat on the premises versus costs for marketing outsourced meat.
4. How can a supermarket utilize price discrimination in its meat department?

VIDEO QUESTIONS ON VITAMIN E: THE INDUSTRY'S HELPER

1. Evaluate the data in this video.
2. How much extra could cattle growers charge for Vitamin E treated beef based on the data in the video?

†The data in this case are drawn from Stephen Bennett, "Ready for Ready-to-Cook," *Progressive Grocer* (September 1995), pp. 133–136; and "Annual Report of the Grocery Industry," *Progressive Grocer* (April 1995), pp. 26, 37. Video published and coprighted by Retail Insights, a division of Progressive Grocer Associates, L.L.C.

PART 7 CASE

Yield Management Pricing: Improving Capacity-Allocation Guesswork

Introduction

Yield management (YM) is an integrated demand-management, capacity-planning process that focuses on two aspects of service quality: order-change responsiveness and delivery reliability. Unlike service design, advertised image, or positioning, these two traits of service quality are process-based and difficult for competitors to imitate. Thus, a corporate strategy expressed using yield management can provide a source of sustainable price premiums.

For the individual service firm, segmenting markets and setting pricing differentials are complicated by the perishability of service capacity, the inability to change prices easily and quickly in response to unexpected demand shifts, and the need to make capacity choices before demand is known.

A hospital or an airline must acquire and schedule capacity before demand for elective surgeries or an 11 A.M. flight. Careful scheduling and creative adjustment of a marketing mix can affect the order flow of these businesses, but they can never remove entirely the impact of random demand. And service flows are nonstorable—no revenue can be realized tomorrow from empty airline seats or unused surgical rooms.

Unsold seats and unused operating tables—not to mention the revenue lost from denying service to high-margin, repeat-purchase customers when capacity is sold out—are serious problems critical to the success of many service firms. American Airlines recently calculated the added revenues it has gained from attending to these problems (mostly by employing yield management) to be about $470 million per year.

Segmentation Strategy

In principle, YM can be applied any time sellers of perishable goods or services can segment markets for which capacity must be committed prior to observing demand. YM involves setting differential prices for alternative market segments, product lines, or accounts and then exercising selective order refusals by reallocating fixed capacity between groups as the time of delivery approaches. An airline might deny reservations to price-sensitive, advance-sale customers if above-average numbers of nonprice-sensitive customer reservations are forecast.

Though most linked with such transportation industries as airlines, railroads, and cruise ships—YM is now utilized by hotels, auto rental firms, printing and publishing firms, hospital outpatient services, and broadcast advertising. Future generations of applications can be expected to involve services such as accounting partnerships, entertainment facilities such as Broadway theaters and movies, and flexible manufacturing systems.

Yield Management in Use

A simplified airline-industry example shows how fares are set and seating capacity is allocated for two classes of airline passengers: business and leisure. We make these assumptions:

- The airline has a single 170-seat plane flying between Atlanta and Chicago.
- It has two passenger classes, business and leisure.
- Expected demand (the initial "demand function") for each class is based on past experience and is reasonably stable.
- Past experience tells how reservations come in over time for both passenger classes, so actual reservations can be mapped against expected ones for this flight during the months and weeks prior to departure.
- Fares for the two classes are based on their expected demand functions and expected marginal operating costs, are set months ahead of the flight date, and will not change.

To minimize complexity, we have held fares constant—but in actuality, they will often be adjusted to reflect the changes in market conditions.

Setting Initial Fares and Seat Allocations Let's first look at how fares for the two passenger classes are established and how the 170-seat capacity is allocated to business and leisure fliers. See Table 1. The first three columns show numbers of seats, fares, and marginal revenues for business class travelers.

For example, at a fare of $1,000, only one seat on the entire plane would be sold, and it would go to a business class passenger. If the fare per seat falls to $935, two seats go to business class passengers. At a fare of $870, three seats are taken, and so on.

Marginal revenue (*expected* marginal revenue because the airline must base its fare-setting procedure on historical data) is the increase in total revenue realized from selling one more seat in business class. For example, when a single seat is sold at $1,000, total revenue is also $1,000. When two seats are sold at a fare of $935, however, total revenue jumps to $1,870, and marginal revenue, which is the difference in total revenue realized from selling one more seat, is $1,870 minus

Source: Adapted by the authors from Frederick deB. Harris and Peter Peacock, "Hold My Place, Please," *Marketing Management* (Fall 1995), pp. 34–44. Reprinted by permission of the American Marketing Association.

Table 1
Allocating Airline Capacity[a]

BUSINESS CLASS			LEISURE CLASS			COMBINED CLASSES	
Seats	Fare	Marginal Revenue	Seats	Fare	Marginal Revenue	Total Seats	Marginal Cost
1	$1,000	$1,000				1	$ 87
2	935	870				2	87
3	870	740				3	87
4	803	600				4	87
5	738	480				5	87
10	564	390				10	87
			1	$342	$342		87
			2	331	320		95
			3	319	295		95
			4	311	287		95
20	422	280	5	305	280	25	95
			10	280	255		95
			20	260	240		95
30	358	230	30	250	230	60	100
			40	240	210		100
			50	230	192		100
40	313	180	60	222	180	100	112
			70	214	166		112
50	281	150	80	206	150	130	112
			90	199	141		120
60	256	133	100	192	133	160	125
63	**250**	**130**	**107**	**188**	**130**	**170**	**130**
			110	186	128		140
70	237	122	120	181	122	190	155
			130	176	112		170
80	221	110	140	173	110	220	190

[a]There are rounding errors in this table.

$1,000, or $870. Similarly, the marginal revenue associated with the third seat sold is $2,610 minus $1,870, or $740.

Table 1 shows corresponding information for leisure class passengers. The first leisure class seat is sold at $342, the second at $331, and so on. The last two columns depict total seats sold and marginal cost, which is the incremental cost of serving one additional passenger in either class.

In this simple two-booking-class example, marginal revenue equals rising marginal cost at $130 per seat. (Marginal cost increases by steps with additions of flight attendants needed to serve additional passengers and the additional fuel consumed because of worsening aerodynamics at high load factors.) At marginal cost of $130, optimal fares are obtained by equating individual marginal revenues of both segments and the marginal cost of the last seat expected to be sold (the 170th seat in this example). Business and leisure traveler marginal revenues are $130 at 63 and 107 seats, respectively, and fares of $250 and $188 are optimal at these seat allocation levels.

Next, consider that, in addition to tracing the demand curve for business and leisure passenger classes, historical data provide guidance about the pattern of reservation arrivals over time. Simply put, leisure passenger reservations tend to begin coming in well before business class reservations and according to rather stable patterns given day of the week, seasonality, and other factors such as local economic conditions.

Similarly, stable arrival patterns are usually observable in business class reservations in the absence of large changes in external factors. If the pattern of reservations in either passenger class deviates significantly from the expected pattern over time, the deviation can be interpreted to mean that the underlying demand situation for that class has changed.

Reallocating Seats As reservations are made, they are tracked closely, and large variances from the seat demand forecast are reported. Assume the forecasted "booking curves" are net bookings—new reservations less cancellations—and the curves exhibit the early- and late-arriving patterns of demand usually observed with leisure and business markets. If everything goes according to expectation, actual reservations should track nicely.

In actual yield management decision support systems, "threshold curves" are based on the estimated reservation arrival patterns for a particular flight. They are used to determine whether actual bookings have deviated so far from forecast as to warrant reallocation of capacity. Suppose actual business travel bookings appear to be significantly above the ticket sales forecast 10 days before takeoff. This violation of the threshold sales level raises the question of whether to deny reservations in the leisure class where the fare charged is much lower for the business class segment.

Marginal capacity reallocations are warranted if the expected incremental revenue minus marginal cost—that is, the additional expected contribution to fixed cost—exceeds the incremental cost of added capacity. In capacity reallocation, the incremental cost of added capacity for business travelers is just an opportunity cost—namely, the contribution foregone by not selling another seat in leisure class. At the margin, the airline should reallocate capacity when the expected contribution margin from allocating another seat to a business traveler ($250 − $130) exceeds the lost expected contribution margin from denying the same seat to a leisure traveler ($188 − $130).

Now, suppose an exception report has been received and it appears that the arrival distribution of business travelers on our flight will have a larger average number than assumed initially. Again using the fares of $250 and $188, assume the change in business demand means the new optimal capacity allocation to business class will be 65 seats. (The exact number to be allocated will be generated by an airline decision support system.)

This finding implies that, at present, a reservation maximum of 105 seats should apply to the leisure class bookings and that the extra two seats should be reallocated to business class. Continued monitoring of bookings relative to the forecast thresholds could result in a return of these seats to leisure class or to an additional reallocation of seats to business travelers.

Although the preceding example is set in an airline context, the principles can be applied to many other service industries with constrained capacity.

YM Framework

A fully integrated YM system should include demand estimation, aggregate capacity choice, capacity allocation and scheduling, differential pricing, sales forecasting, dynamic capacity reallocation, and tactical price adjustment. See Figure 1. YM systems should also encompass formal performance evaluation and feedback systems to assess the contribution of each component of the total YM system.

Demand Estimation Effective YM begins with Stage 1: estimating demand for the service. Using forecasting techniques, expert opinion, experiments, and other methodologies, managers make a first cut at determining the levels of demand that exist at prices high enough to cover variable costs for each market segment. Customer segments are identified, the potential impact of competitive rivalry is assessed, and demand projections are made for those submarkets within which the firm considers operating. Demand estimation would usually be conducted yearly as an input to the annual planning process.

Market segments are identifiable groups of customers, each with different price and service-quality elasticities of demand, such as the business and leisure class customers in our airline example.

Market Segmentation With information from the demand-estimation process, managers move to Stage 2:

FIGURE 1
Yield Management Framework

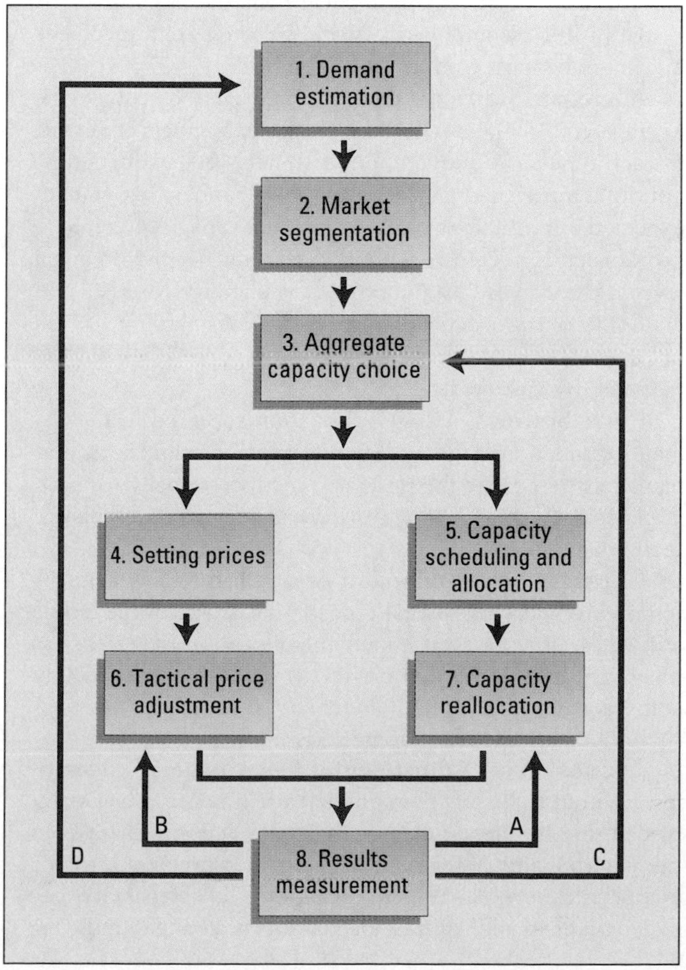

defining the market segments identified in Stage 1—that is, specifying their numerical size and behavioral characteristics. Stable market segments are a key strategic element in positioning and service image, so YM must also establish "fencing" mechanisms to prevent movement across segments.

In the airline case, common ways to achieve this purpose are (1) requiring a discount ticket holder to stay at the destination city over a weekend, (2) making tickets nonrefundable in the event of cancellation, and (3) reserving space and ticketing in the name of the actual traveler.

Marriott has succeeded in segmenting business and leisure travel, even in vacation destinations like Florida. Many $99, no-deposit room nights have been sold to $79 guests with fixed travel plans who will pay in advance or agree to large nonrefundable deposits. This means the revenue opportunity loss from protecting too much capacity for last-minute space requests—the marginal value of unoccupied space—has declined. As a result, late reservations are available at $125 rather than $145. Without the segmentation provided by these fencing restrictions, business travelers, with their volatile travel schedules and change orders, would pay the higher rate. Yield management in this case lowered rates to both leisure and business travelers, raised occupancy, and increased total revenue.

Core Components Stages 3 through 7 in the framework are the major strategic and tactical components of the YM system. All five components should be integrated to achieve maximum benefits from the YM approach.

Aggregate Capacity Choice Managers determine the aggregate level of capacity—for example, numbers of aircraft of each type and configuration—estimating demand, contribution margins, and capacity cost in a manner that equates expected contributions from incremental capacity to unit capacity cost. Expected contribution margins depend on given levels of service quality and product availability. Realized revenue, in contrast, depends on the provider's ability to "sell up" in the event of service denials and random stockouts anticipated by customers.

Price Setting Using information captured in the demand estimation stage and market segmentation decisions, managers determine the price to announce initially for each market segment and allot capacity using marginal analysis techniques.

Capacity Scheduling and Allocation This stage often involves making several types of decisions. In the airline and auto rental cases, it entails the allocation of seat or car inventory across customer classes, as well as fleet scheduling across locations. In the hotel industry, it means room inventory allocation across customer classes.

Tactical Price Adjustment Initial "optimal" prices often turn out to be less than optimal when orders are actually placed due to unanticipated competitor actions, changes in the determinants of segment demand, measurement error, or misspecification of demand equations. Discrepancies between planned and realized load factors or changes in the estimated price and service quality elasticities of demand call for resetting price, as well as reallocating capacity when advance sales data deviate from forecast.

Capacity Reallocation Managers might also have to modify the initial optimal capacity allocations to market segments in response to changes in the market or imperfections in the statistical models of customer response. For example, if reservations for business class airline seats (or full-rate hotel rooms) come in more rapidly than anticipated, reservations for leisure class seats (or economy-rate hotel rooms) should be denied earlier in the booking process.

Results Measurement This last stage of the YM framework recognizes explicitly that market response to tactical repricing and capacity reallocation should be measured systematically and fed back to the other elements of the complete process.

Figure 1 shows two short-run feedback loops—labeled A and B—from the results measurement element to the elements that dynamically reallocate capacity and reset prices. Two other feedback loops are shown: C, a link between results measurement and capacity planning that should be an integral part of the YM approach, and D, the feedback loop that links results back to the demand estimation stage.

Adopting the System

YM presents services marketing challenges and raises the question of how applications should be identified. Are the same marketing and managerial economics techniques employed by airlines appropriate as YM moves across the service sector to hotels, rental cars, hospitals, and professional services? Several industry and firm attributes permit some companies to adopt the YM approach more easily than others in the same industry or than firms in other industries. Success indicators fall into three separate categories:

- Motivating factors—When fixed capacity, perishable inventory, demand uncertainty, and fixed costs are all high, there is a strong motivation for most firms in an industry to adopt YM.
- External enabling factors—Motivating characteristics tend to make a firm willing to use YM; enabling characteristics allow it to use YM. External enabling characteristics include the presence of segmentable markets, the ease of preventing arbitrage, and the quality of advance reservation systems.
- Internal enabling factors—These are historical sales data bases, forecast accuracy, and management informations systems (MIS) sophistication—items that management can manipulate directly to support the application of YM.

QUESTIONS

1. Using the data in Table 1, compute the elasticity of demand for business class passengers if the fare drops from $738 to $564. Comment on your answer.

2. Using the data in Table 1, compute the elasticity of demand for leisure class passengers if the fare drops from $250 to $240. Comment on your answer.
3. Relate the concept of subjective price to yield management pricing.
4. Would yield management pricing work in a market-controlled pricing environment? Why or why not?
5. How are price-floor pricing and yield management pricing interrelated?
6. Should airlines base fares on whether passengers book directly through them versus travel agents (who get paid commissions)? Explain your answer.
7. Discuss whether or not you feel yield management pricing is ethical.
8. Using the data in Table 1, determine the most profitable fare to charge business class passengers and the most profitable fare to charge leisure class passengers. How many total seats will be filled? *NOTE:* Assume there is only ONE business class fare and ONE leisure class fare.

MARKETING MANAGEMENT

PART 8

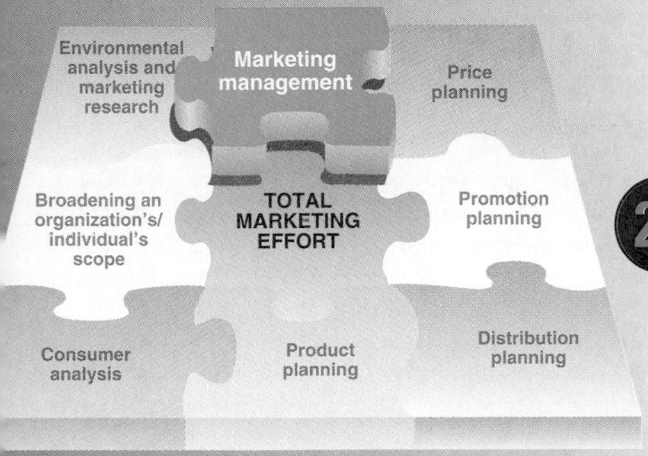

In Part 8, we tie together the concepts introduced in Chapters 1 through 22 and discuss planning for the future.

23 Pulling It All Together: Integrating and Analyzing the Marketing Plan

We first note the value of developing and analyzing integrated marketing plans. Next, we examine the elements in a well-integrated marketing plan: clear organizational mission, long-term competitive advantages, precisely defined target market, compatible subplans, coordination among SBUs, coordination of the marketing mix, and stability over time. Then, we study five types of marketing plan analysis: benchmarking, customer satisfaction research, marketing cost analysis, sales analysis, and the marketing audit. These are important tools for evaluating the success or failure of marketing plans. We conclude with a look at why and how firms should anticipate and plan for the future.

Part 8 Video Vignette
MasterCard International

What drives MasterCard as it prepares for the future? In a recent annual report, subtitled *Staying Ahead in a World of Change*, the company reported that "Our commitment to member [bank] *profitability* remains our primary role. To assist members in their efforts to navigate through the evolving and sometimes unexpected directions of the global payments business, we must anticipate changes in *consumer behavior*. We can then address them by applying emerging *technologies* and leveraging the special characteristics of the global MasterCard family of *brands*. Broadened *competition* will also demand more focused allocation of our resources. Strategic *partnerships* will play a key role in attaining the level of *innovation* needed to provide members and their customers with the ever-increasing levels of *value* that they require. By successfully balancing local needs with global economies of scale, MasterCard will enable members to *stay ahead in a world of change*."

> *"By successfully balancing local needs with global economies of scale, MasterCard will enable members to* stay ahead in a world of change."

MasterCard periodically studies card user satisfaction, especially as it relates to customer service scores, and regularly reviews card acceptance by retailers. To stimulate card usage, card-issuing banks provide superior value to consumers by offering airline miles, increased insurance coverage, and a contribution on affinity card transactions (often tied in to nonprofit organizations).

In planning their marketing strategies, MasterCard's divisions first receive overall annual budgets from top management. The divisions can then form and implement their own programs within these budgets subject to management approval. Sometimes, annual budgets are based on the prior year's performance and expenditures (incremental budgeting). Other times, the previous year's budget is less important because of changing goals or major market developments.

Scenario planning is employed by MasterCard International to identify and be prepared for future events. For instance, MasterCard Health Care Marketing is now analyzing several potential scenarios in order to devise and enact appropriate long-run marketing strategies. According to one possible scenario, the health care market would split into two segments: (1) an increasingly open market that drives down health care costs (because of a greater number of consumers shopping for health care coverage) and (2) the growth of totally managed HMO (health maintenance organization) plans. The first segment would raise their credit card usage as people pay for the services provided. The second segment would involve no exchange of funds for covered services (and no need for credit card use). Yet, according to another scenario, some experts feel that deductibles and annual medical exams may not be covered in basic HMO plans in the future (as they are now), resulting in segment 2 patients also turning to credit card payments.

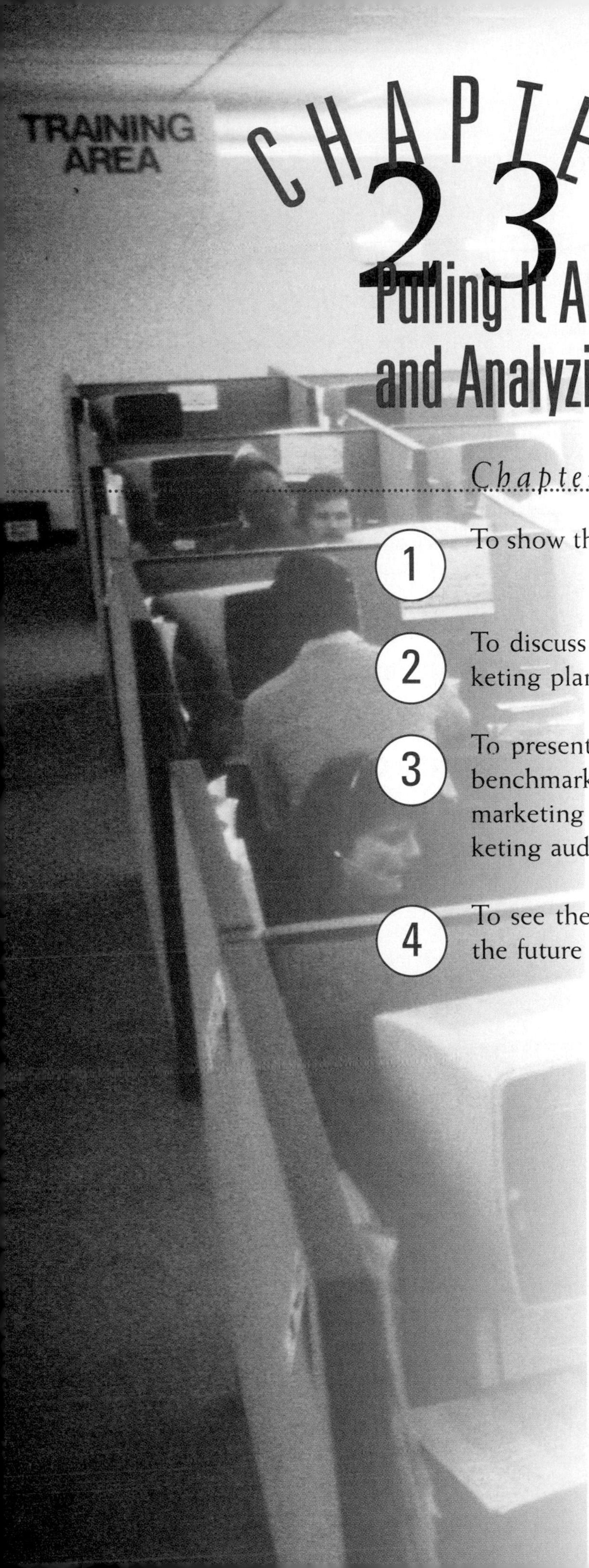

Chapter 23

Pulling It All Together: Integrating and Analyzing the Marketing Plan

Chapter Objectives

1. To show the value of an integrated marketing plan

2. To discuss the elements of a well-integrated marketing plan

3. To present five types of marketing plan analysis: benchmarking, customer satisfaction research, marketing cost analysis, sales analysis, and the marketing audit

4. To see the merit of anticipating and planning for the future

Today's corporate planners, ravaged by the modern scourges of globalization, downsizing, and technological change, look for solutions and security at Motorola, Microsoft, and Springfield ReManufacturing (the guru of open book management). Some 2,000 devotees stream through AT&T Universal Card's super-efficient telephone customer service center in Jacksonville, Florida, every year, at $375 a pop. More than 5,000 supplicants have sojourned at Federal Express' expansive overnight package facility in Memphis for a $250 midnight hub tour and all-day seminar. USAA, the San Antonio-based insurer, has drawn more than 2,100 seekers to its monthly program from such far-flung locales as Australia, Italy, Japan, South Korea, and South Africa.

Reprinted by permission. Courtesy of Lands' End, Inc.

Firms such as Motorola, AT&T, and Federal Express are now viewed as "management meccas." And business visitors are drawn to these meccas to gain benchmarking insights, so they can better set performance standards for their own organizations. Benchmarking is becoming a more widely recognized component of a firm's integrated marketing program.

Each mecca company has been publicly recognized for its excellence in a specific aspect of business—by winning a Baldridge Award for quality, by being lauded in the media, and/or by constantly increasing sales and profits:

- Motorola offers an eight-hour seminar on its famed "six sigma" quality program, which aims for only one defect per 1,000,000-unit production run. The seminar also includes material on how to reduce the time from when a new product idea is approved to when the product is commercialized, as well as Motorola's total customer satisfaction philosophy.
- AT&T's Universal Card walks executives through its customer service center, which handles 1.5 million calls per month. A standout portion of its session features the high-technology system that lets AT&T employees retrieve a customer's bill and payment record even before the phone is picked up.

- Federal Express' session features a full tour of its package-handling facility, a discussion of its customer service policies, and its measurement of service quality.

Visits to management meccas are spreading since more management consulting firms are including them as part of their client training. In contrast to other techniques, such visits enable managers to see how concepts are really enacted, instead of evaluating different theories. "You get a real sense for the culture of the company, for what the people are like, and what the place looks like," says Jay Michaud, a vice-president with CSC Consulting. It also allows executives to talk with others who have had similar experiences.

By visiting such management meccas as General Electric, Lands' End, and Fidelity Investments, GTE found a better way to handle customer service—based on the technology these three firms were utilizing. As a result of its new methods, GTE can now complete a customer order in less than two hours, versus the three to four days it took using the previous technology. And the student has become the professor—as hundreds of managers from other firms visit GTE each year to learn about its high-tech customer service methods.[1]

In this chapter, we will study how a firm can integrate and analyze its marketing plan—and see the value of developing and implementing a clear, forward-looking, cohesive, and adaptable strategy.

Overview

Chapters 1 and 2 introduced basic marketing concepts and described the marketing environment. Chapters 3 and 4 presented the strategic planning process as it applies to marketing and the role of marketing information systems and marketing research. Chapters 5 and 6 broadened our scope to include the societal, ethical, and consumer implications of marketing and international marketing efforts. Chapters 7 to 22 centered on specific aspects of marketing: describing and selecting target markets, and the marketing mix (product, distribution, promotion, and price planning).

This chapter ties things together, and describes how a marketing plan can be integrated and evaluated. It builds on the discussion of strategic planning in Chapter 3—particularly, the total quality approach (whereby a firm strives to fully satisfy customers in an effective and efficient manner). With an integrated marketing effort, individual marketing components are synchronized and everyone is "on the same page." And when an organization wants to appraise performance, capitalize on strengths, minimize weaknesses, and plan for the future, marketing analysis (including benchmarking and customer satisfaction) is necessary.

This is the challenge, as one expert sees it:

> Do you know where your marketing plan is? In a world where competitors observe and rapidly imitate each other's advancements in product development, pricing, packaging, and distribution, internal and external communication is more important than ever as a way of differentiating your business from those of competitors. At its most basic level, a marketing plan defines a business niche, summarizes objectives, and presents strategies for getting from point A to point B. But roadmaps need constant updating to reflect the addition of new routes. Likewise, in a decade in which technology, international relations, and the competitive landscape are constantly changing, the concept of a static marketing plan has to be reassessed.
>
> Two of today's hottest buzzwords are "interactive" and "integrated." A successful marketing plan has to be both. "Interactive" means your marketing plan should be a conversation between your business and your customers. It's your chance to tell customers about your business and to listen and act on their responses. "Integrated" means the message in your marketing is consistently reinforced by every department within your company. Marketing is as much a function of the finance and manufacturing areas as it is the advertising and public relations areas.[2]

[1]John A. Byrne, "Management Meccas," *Business Week* (September 18, 1995), pp. 122–132.

[2]Shelly Reese, "The Very Model of a Modern Marketing Plan," *Marketing Tools* (January/February 1996), pp. 56–59.

Wal-Mart's ten basic rules apply to a wide range of firms.

Thus, every organization can learn from the focused management rules of Wal-Mart, the world's leading retailer. These principles were developed by the late Sam Walton, the firm's founder, and are in his words:

1. "Commit to your business. Believe in it more than anybody else."
2. "Share your profits with all your associates [workers] and treat them as partners. In turn, they will treat you as a partner."
3. "Motivate your partners [workers]. Constantly, day by day, think of new and more interesting ways to motivate and challenge. Set high goals, encourage competition, and keep score."
4. "Communicate everything you possibly can to your partners [workers]. The more they know, the more they'll understand. The more they understand, the more they'll care. Once they care, there's no stopping them."
5. "Appreciate everything your associates do for the business. Nothing else can quite substitute for a few well-chosen, well-timed, sincere words of praise. They're absolutely free and worth a fortune."
6. "Celebrate your successes. Find humor in your failures. Don't take yourself so seriously. Loosen up and everybody around you will loosen up."
7. "Listen to everyone in your company. The folks on the front lines—the ones who actually talk to the customer—are the only ones who really know what's going on out there. You'd better find out what they know. This is really what total quality is all about."
8. "Exceed your customers' expectations. If you do, they'll come back over and over. Make good on all your mistakes, and don't make excuses—apologize. The two most important words I ever wrote were on the first Wal-Mart sign: SATISFACTION GUARANTEED."
9. "Control your expenses better than your competition. This is where you can always find the competitive advantage. You can make a lot of different mistakes and still recover if you run an efficient operation. Or you can be brilliant and still go out of business if you're inefficient."
10. "Swim upstream. Ignore the conventional wisdom. If everybody else is doing it one way, there's a good chance you can find your niche by going in exactly the opposite direction."[3]

Integrating the Marketing Plan

From a total quality perspective, the many parts of a marketing plan should be unified, consistent, and coordinated.

When a marketing plan is properly integrated, all of its various parts are unified, consistent, and coordinated; and a total quality approach can be followed. Although this appears to be a simple task, it is important to recall that a firm may have long-run, moderate-length, and short-run plans; the different strategic business units in an organization may require separate marketing plans; and each aspect of the marketing mix requires planning. For example:

- An overall plan would be poorly integrated if short-run profits are earned at the expense of moderate- or long-term profits. This could occur if marketing research or new-product planning expenditures are reduced to raise profits temporarily. A firm could also encounter difficulties if plans are changed too frequently, leading to a blurred image for consumers and a lack of focus for executives.
- Resources need to be allocated among SBUs, so funds are given to those with high potential. The target markets, product images, price levels, and so on, of each SBU must be distinctive—yet not in conflict with one another. Physical distribution efforts and channel member arrangements need to be timed so the system and its role

[3]Sam Walton and John Huey, *Made in America* (New York: Doubleday, 1992).

in a total quality program are not strained by two or more SBUs making costly demands simultaneously.

- Even though a promotion plan primarily deals with one strategic element, it must also be integrated with product, distribution, and pricing plans. It must reflect the proper image for a firm's products, encourage channel cooperation, and demonstrate that products are worth the prices set.

A well-integrated marketing plan incorporates the elements shown in Figure 23-1. These elements are explained next.

Clear Organizational Mission

The organizational mission should be clear and directive.

A clear organizational mission outlines a firm's commitment to a type of business and a place in the market. It directs the company's total quality efforts. The organizational mission is involved whenever a firm seeks new customer groups or abandons existing ones, adds or deletes product lines, acquires other firms or sells part of its own business, performs different marketing functions, and/or shifts technological focus (as noted in Chapter 3). Both top management and marketing personnel must be committed to an organizational mission for it to be achieved; and the mission must be communicated to customers, company employees, suppliers, and distribution intermediaries. For example, as illustrated in Figure 23-2, PHH has a directive—yet flexible—organizational mission with a total quality approach:

> PHH is in the service business. We don't make cars. We don't own real-estate companies. We aren't a traditional bank. We specialize in business processes that are not an organization's primary focus, but are essential to top performance.
>
> *Vehicle Management Services*—Companies which operate fleets of vehicles turn to PHH for expert assistance in selecting, purchasing, managing, and remarketing their cars, vans, and trucks. Our consultative, information, and administrative services, as well as our extensive national networks of suppliers, help keep a client's drivers safely and productively on the road, while efficiently managing expenses through process improvements and valuable information. And PHH's fuel and service cards mean added driver convenience and client cost-savings through the world's largest fuel, vehicle repair, and maintenance network.
>
> *Relocation and Real-Estate Services*—Mobility for organizations and their employees is a critical factor in business success. PHH companies are dedicated to helping clients manage the complex process of relocating employees where they can be most effective. With comprehensive high-quality services and extensive real estate-related supplier networks, PHH facilitates the process of home selling, home finding, moving, and settling into the new area for the relocating family. PHH also provides property management and marketing services to financial institutions, and location planning and strategic management consulting to businesses and municipalities.
>
> *Mortgage Banking Services*—Finding the right home financing is a complicated business. PHH works with corporations, credit unions, real-estate brokers, and affinity groups to provide a full

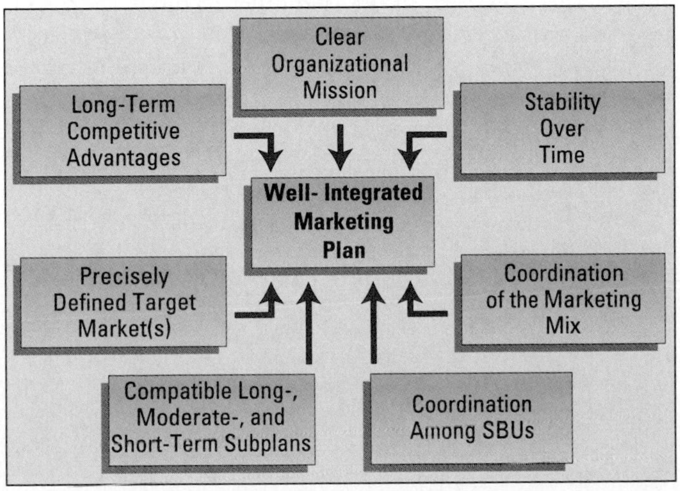

FIGURE 23-1
Elements Leading to a Well-Integrated Marketing Plan

FIGURE 23-2
PHH's Directive Organizational Mission
Within its three core business areas, PHH is constantly looking for creative ways to serve its existing clients and to attract new ones: "Most of all, PHH stands for value, innovation, and commitment to quality service."
Reprinted by permission. Images concept and design: Allemann Almquist & Jones, Philadelphia, PA. Photography: David Fields, Philadelphia, PA.

range of residential first mortgages and casualty insurance-related products. Via customer-focused services, centralized management, and extensive telecommunications and computer capabilities, PHH has grown into one of the top 20 mortgage originators in the United States.[4]

Many experts believe a firm should reappraise its organizational mission if that company has values which do not fit a changing environment, its industry undergoes rapid changes, its performance is average or worse, it is changing size (from small to large or large to small), or opportunities unrelated to its original mission arise.

Long-Term Competitive Advantages

Competitive advantages should center on company, product, and marketing attributes with long-range distinctiveness.

Long-term competitive advantages are company, product, and marketing attributes whose distinctiveness and appeal to consumers can be maintained over an extended period of time. A firm must capitalize on the attributes that are most important to consumers and prepare competitive advantages accordingly. For competitive advantages to be sustainable, consumers must perceive a consistent positive difference in key attributes between the company's offerings and those of competitors; that difference must be linked to a capability gap that competitors will have difficulty in closing (due to patents, superior marketing skills, customer loyalty, and other factors); and the company's offerings must appeal to some enduring consumer need. While concentrating on its competitive advantages, a company should not lose sight of the importance of customer service and its role in a total quality program.

As Michael Treacy and Fred Wiersema say in their best-selling *The Discipline of Market Leaders*:

> Today's market leaders understand the battle they're in. They know they have to redefine value by raising customer expectations in the one component of value they choose to highlight. Casio, for instance, establishes new affordability levels for familiar products such as calculators; Hertz makes car rental nearly as convenient as taking a cab; Lands' End shows individuals that they're not just a number; and Home Depot proves that old-fashioned, knowledgeable advice hasn't gone the way of trading stamps.
>
> But wait a minute. These companies don't shine in every way. A successful company like Wal-Mart doesn't peddle haute couture; Lands' End doesn't sell clothing for the lowest possi-

[4]*PHH Corporation: Your Connection to Quality Business Services* (n.d.).

> ble cost; and Starbucks, the Seattle coffee chain, doesn't slide a cup of java under your nose any faster or more conveniently than anyone else. Yet, all of these companies are thriving because they shine in a way their customers care most about. They have honed at least one component of value to a level of excellence that puts all competitors to shame. Our research shows that no company can succeed today by trying to be all things to all people. It must instead find the unique value that it alone can deliver to a chosen market.[5]

Because smaller firms often cannot compete on the basis of low prices, they tend to concentrate on other competitive advantages, such as:

- Targeting underserved market niches, including international ones.
- Having unique offerings via specialization. Firms can be innovative, process customized orders, or otherwise adapt products for particular customers.
- Stressing product quality and reliability. "The more crucial the performance of a product to customer needs, the lower will be the concern with pricing."
- Engaging in extra efforts to gain customer loyalty. These include making the purchase process easy, giving superior service, and promising the long-term availability of goods and services. As one small-firm manager said, "We know our products are reliable and do not require visits. But when our clients see us physically inspecting machines, sometimes merely dusting them, they have a sense of security and comfort." This is a total quality approach.
- Emphasizing relationship marketing, whereby personal relationships with their suppliers are viewed as important by customers.[6]

When implementing a marketing strategy, a firm should note that its competitive advantages may not apply in all situations. For instance, an advantage can lose its value when transferred to another nation. This can occur because an advantage is not relevant in a different context or because it can easily be countered by local competitors: "Products that are superior in the home market may not offer customer-perceived value in the target country because the price is too high or the degree of sophistication is excessive. The value of well-known brand names and trademarks can be reduced by piracy and imitation. Technological advantages can be neutralized by the weakness of intellectual property law and laxity in enforcing the law. Whether an advantage retains its value depends on the fit between conditions in the target country and the nature of the advantage."[7]

Precisely Defined Target Market(s)

The target market(s) should be identified precisely.

By precisely defining its target market(s), a firm identifies the specific consumers to be addressed in its marketing plans. This guides the firm's current marketing efforts and future direction. For example, as noted in Figure 23-3, Carr Business Machines is a distributor that concentrates on a limited geographic area and knows customers by name, not by zip code: "Because we've been dedicated to the Brooklyn, Queens, Nassau, and Suffolk market [four New York counties] for the last fifty-five years, we're perfectly suited to meet the needs of local businesses of all sizes. In fact, our reputation depends on it." And when a firm engages in differentiated marketing (multiple segmentation), it is essential that each segment be described fully.

A firm's target market approach may have to be fine-tuned due to changing demographics and life-styles—or falling sales. Today, a lot of consumers are more demanding:

> The balance of power between producers and buyers has shifted to the latter. Most industries today are no longer constrained by supply. In fact, an overabundance of suppliers is crowding

[5]Michael Treacy and Fred Wiersema, *The Discipline of Market Leaders* (Reading, Mass.: Addison-Wesley, 1995).
[6]Peter Wright, "Competitive Strategies for Small Business," *Collegiate Forum* (Spring 1983), pp. 3–4; Steven P. Galante, "More Firms Quiz Customers for Clues about Competition," *Wall Street Journal* (March 3, 1986), p. 21; "Hot Growth Companies," *Business Week* (May 27, 1991), pp. 78–84; and Donna Fenn, "Leader of the Pack," *Inc.* (February 1996), pp. 31–38.
[7]Yao-Su Hu, "The International Transferability of the Firm's Advantages," *California Management Review*, Vol. 37 (Summer 1995), p. 83.

International Marketing in Action

Does Korea's Samsung Represent the Conglomerate of the Future?

Under chairman Lee Kun, Samsung is expanding from its traditional businesses—electronics, chemicals, finance, and heavy machinery—into autos, aerospace, transportation, and entertainment. It has also begun to negotiate strategic alliances with such firms as Boeing, Walt Disney, and Nissan. According to its chairman, Samsung Group plans to more than quadruple its 1994 sales level to reach $200 billion in annual sales as of 2001.

More than one-half of its expansion projects are being financed through Samsung Electronics, the firm's semiconductor manufacturing division. If the worldwide demand for memory chips continues, Samsung can become a major conglomerate, on the level of a General Electric. If not, Samsung could be remembered as a firm that gambled with large stakes but lost.

In the past, Samsung's success confounded some critics. For instance, it became the world's top producer of semiconductors in just ten years. However, Samsung now plans on being a major player in some of the world's most competitive and capital-intensive industries. Among its planned projects are:

- A $4.5 billion investment over a three-year period to develop a new line of cars with Nissan.
- A $3 billion investment for three more semiconductor plants (one in North America and one each in Europe and Southeast Asia).
- A $150 million investment as a partner in a Sino-Korean venture to build a jetliner.

Besides being successful in these ventures, some analysts believe Samsung needs to move away from its present discount image. In some markets, Samsung products sell for as much as 30 per cent less than other brands; this reduces the firm's overall profitability.

As a marketing consultant to Samsung, evaluate its strategic plan.

Sources: Based on material in Steve Glain, "Korea's Samsung Plans Very Rapid Expansion into Autos, Other Lines," *Wall Street Journal* (March 2, 1995), pp. A1, A5; and Laxmi Nakami, Kevin Kelly, and Larry Armstrong, "Look Out World—Samsung is Coming," *Business Week* (July 10, 1995), pp. 52–53.

> every part of the market. Customers, who are becoming more astute in their buying practices every day, have tremendous choice in deciding who will get their business. The 1990s have become the "value decade"; buyers carefully examine total offerings to find out which one yields the best overall value compared to alternatives. The challenge is to give customers all of what they want, and none of what they don't want: the best quality *and* the best prices, served quickly *and* with a smile![8]

In this context, a total quality approach is especially crucial in attracting and retaining consumers.

Compatible Long-, Moderate-, and Short-Term Subplans

Long-, moderate-, and short-term subplans must be compatible.

The long-, moderate-, and short-term marketing subplans of a firm need to be compatible with one another. Long-term plans are the most general and set a broad framework

[8]William A. Band, "Customer-Accelerated Change," *Marketing Management* (Winter 1995), pp. 47–48.

FIGURE 23-3
Target Marketing and a Local Distributor
Carr Business Machines markets Mita copiers to business accounts. In its marketing strategy, Carr recognizes the value of a total quality approach and engenders strong relationships with clients, who are not just a "zip code."
Reprinted by permission.

for moderate-term plans. Short-term plans are the most specific, but they need to be derived from both moderate- and long-term plans. At Motorola, this means "placing far-sighted bets on a wide array of technologies while expanding in fast-growing, developing markets. We think we're making balanced investments for the future."[9]

Unfortunately, adequate plans and subplans are not always set—or are not communicated to employees. According to one study of employees at small and midsized U.S. firms, 77 per cent say their firms have a clear organizational mission; 55 per cent feel top management actions support the organizational mission; 57 per cent believe all departments, branches, and divisions have specific and measurable goals; 38 per cent feel all employees understand what is expected of them; and 22 per cent say all employees are held accountable for daily performance.[10] For a total quality program to work, these percentages must be considerably higher.

One important current trend among many companies is the shrinking time frame of marketing plans:

> Because customer priorities are constantly changing, a marketing plan should change with them. For years, conventional wisdom was "prepare a five-year marketing plan and review it every year." But change happens a lot faster than it did 20 or even 10 years ago. For that reason, Bob Dawson of The Business Group, a consulting group in Fremont, California, recommends that firms prepare three-year plans and review them every quarter. Frequent reviews enable companies to identify potential problems and opportunities before the competition does. "Preventative maintenance for a company is as important as putting oil in a car," Dawson says. "You don't wait a whole year to do it. You can't change history, but you can anticipate what's going to happen."[11]

[9]Peter Coy and Ron Stodghill II, "Is Motorola a Bit Too Patient?" *Business Week* (February 5, 1996), pp. 150–151.
[10]Oechsli Institute, "Reality Check," *Inc.* (March 1993), p. 34.
[11]Reese, "The Very Model of a Modern Marketing Plan," pp. 60–61.

Coordination Among SBUs

SBUs should be coordinated.

Coordination among an organization's SBUs is enhanced when the functions, strategies, and resources allocated to each are described in long-term, moderate-term, and short-term plans. For instance, at GE (General Electric), there are now 12 SBUs (in technology, services, and manufacturing)—down from 350 several years ago: "Only businesses that were number one or number two in their markets could win in the increasingly global arena. Those that were not leaders were fixed, closed, or sold." Today, GE's goal is to "attain competitive advantages that let it rank first or second in every market it serves." And its planning and resource allocation are structured accordingly.

Virtually all of GE's SBUs are market leaders, including aircraft engines, circuit breakers, electric motors, engineering plastics, industrial and power systems, nonbank financial services, major appliances, lighting, locomotives, and medical diagnostic imaging. Problematic SBUs are singled out for special attention by top management, which coordinates plans and assigns resources. Thus, when GE decided to hold onto its broadcasting SBU (even though the NBC TV network had fallen to a weak third in audience ratings as of 1993), a renewed commitment was pledged. By 1996, NBC was again number one with such popular shows as *ER*, *Seinfeld*, and *Friends*.[12]

The coordination of SBUs by large multinational firms can be particularly complex. For example, ABB (Asea Brown Boveri) has 175 global managers at its Swiss headquarters. They oversee 200,000 employees and over 1,000 companies that operate in 140 countries around the globe: "ABB isn't Japanese, nor is it Swiss or Swedish. It is a global firm without a national identity, though its mailing address is in Zurich. The company's top 13 managers hold frequent meetings in different countries. Since they share no common first language, they speak only English, a foreign tongue to all but one."[13]

Coordination of the Marketing Mix

The marketing mix within each SBU has to be coordinated.

The components of the marketing mix (product, distribution, promotion, and price) need to be coordinated and consistent with a firm's organizational mission. As an example, Intuit Inc. is a computer software maker, founded in 1984. It specializes in user-friendly, personal-finance programs for PCs. From 1984 to 1986, sales were very low—due to a lack of startup capital: "Without money, there were no distribution channels and no customers. What computer store would carry an unknown software product, unsupported by advertising?" The firm then invested $125,000 in advertising and sales took off. By 1996, Intuit products were carried by virtually every type of computer software store and it had 1.7 million loyal customers.[14] Its current marketing mix is outstanding and adheres to a total quality philosophy:

- Product—Intuit's Quicken software is the leading personal-finance program on the market. It helps consumers balance their checkbooks, set up budgets, and monitor investments. Quicken has been upgraded and improved a number of times. New programs, such as QuickBooks bookkeeping software, are heavily tested before they are introduced.
- Distribution—Intuit products are sold by all types of retailers across the United States and a number of other countries, including Target, Wal-Mart, major computer chains, bookstores, and mail-order firms.

[12]Stephen W. Quickel, "CEO of the Year: Welch on Welch," *Financial World* (April 3, 1990), p. 62; Al Ries, "The Discipline of the Narrow Focus," *Journal of Business Strategy*, Vol. 13 (November–December 1992), p. 5; Noel M. Tichy and Stratford P. Sherman, *Control Your Own Destiny or Someone Else Will* (New York: Doubleday, 1993); and Patrick J. Spain and James R. Talbot (Editors), *Hoover's Handbook of American Business 1996* (Austin, Texas: Reference Press, 1995), pp. 652–653.

[13]Carla Rapoport, "A Tough Swede Invades the U.S.," *Fortune* (June 29, 1992), p. 76; Rich Karlgaard, "Percy Barnevik," *Forbes ASAP* (January 2, 1995), pp. 65–68; and Patrick J. Spain and James R. Talbot (Editors), *Hoover's Handbook of World Business 1995–1996* (Austin, Texas: Reference Press, 1995), pp. 94–95.

[14]John Case, "Customer Service: The Last Word," *Inc.* (April 1991), pp. 88–93; and Intuit advertisement, *ComputerLife* (January 1996).

- Promotion—Although ad expenditures are modest, Intuit runs ads in such magazines as *PC* and *ComputerLife*, and it seeks out publicity. The firm is also quite clever. In one recent ad campaign, it used this approach: "Stop Cheating—yourself out of legitimate, money-saving tax deductions. That's why you need TurboTax, America's #1-selling tax software! Complete Satisfaction—We guarantee you'll be satisfied with TurboTax or your money back." The firm does spend about 10 per cent of revenues on customer service personnel, including technical-support people who handle 800-number telephone calls.
- Price—Quicken, Quicken for Windows, TurboTax, and MacIn-Tax have "street prices" (the discounted prices offered by resellers) of $35 to $45. Included in purchases are a detailed owner's manual, the right to upgrades at a modest price, and telephone support service. Most competing programs are much more expensive than Quicken.

Stability Over Time

The stability of the basic plan should be maintained over time.

A marketing plan must have a certain degree of stability over time for it to be implemented and evaluated properly. This does not mean a plan should be inflexible and therefore unable to adjust to a dynamic environment. Rather, it means a broad marketing plan, consistent with a firm's organizational mission and total quality approach, should guide long-term efforts and be fine-tuned regularly; the basic plan should remain in effect for a number of years. Short-run marketing plans can be much more flexible, as long as they conform to long-term goals and the organizational mission. Thus, low prices might be part of a long-term marketing plan. However, in any particular year, prices might have to be raised in response to environmental forces.

An example of a firm striving to maintain a stable—but flexible—approach is Illinois Tool Works (ITW). It began in 1912 as a maker of machine tools. Today, it is a "multinational manufacturer of highly engineered fasteners, components, assemblies, and systems. ITW businesses are small and focused so they can work more effectively in a decentralized structure to add value to customers' products." After 85 years, ITW's mission is true to its heritage.

ITW has major facilities in 35 countries. Its operating units are divided into two business segments: engineered components, and industrial systems and consumables. Due to the firm's global presence, the ITW designation is now used more often than the full name. Every year since 1987, ITW has been ranked first or second in its industry (metal products) in *Fortune's* annual listing of the most admired corporations in the United States. Figure 23-4 shows one of the company's thousands of products.

In keeping with its strong total-quality orientation, ITW adheres to these principles:

> Managing with a long-term view is key to our success. We do this by emphasizing the basic elements of the business that ultimately result in the creation of inventive new goods and services for our customers. While markets and circumstances change, the continuity found by staying in touch with these fundamental tenets assures our future.
>
> These basics include building partnerships with our customers and focusing on their product quality, growing our core businesses, adapting technologies to new products and systems, improving the manufacturing process, and doing these as an environmentally responsible corporation.
>
> We serve diverse markets throughout the industrial world. To maintain the close contact necessary to respond quickly with value-added solutions to customers' problems, we are organized into more than 150 operating units, aligned into several core businesses. Each of the units is subject to the dynamics of changing composition and direction in the company's markets. Remaining flexible and responsive to these market factors are the true determinants of our future.[15]

[15] *ITW 1994 Annual Report*; Ronald Henkoff, "The Ultimate Nuts & Bolts Co.," *Fortune* (July 16, 1990), pp. 70–73; Reese; and Spain and Talbot, *Hoover's Handbook of American Business 1996*, pp. 766–767.

FIGURE 23-4
ITW's Nexus: $50 Million a Year from Buckles
Nexus buckles are used on products ranging from life jackets to back packs to pet collars.
Reprinted by permission of Illinois Tool Works.

Analyzing the Marketing Plan

Marketing plan analysis *compares actual and targeted achievements.*

Marketing plan analysis involves comparing actual performance with planned or expected performance for a specified period of time. If actual performance is unsatisfactory, corrective action may be needed. Also, plans must sometimes be revised because of the impact of uncontrollable variables.

Five techniques used to analyze marketing plans are discussed in the following sections: benchmarking, customer satisfaction research, marketing cost analysis, sales analysis, and the marketing audit. Though our discussion of these tools is limited to their utility in evaluating marketing plans, they may also be employed when developing and modifying these plans.

Benchmarking

In **benchmarking**, *specific points of comparison are set so performance can be measured.*

For a firm to properly assess the effectiveness of its marketing plans, it must set performance standards. That is, it must specify what exactly is meant by "success." One way to do this is to utilize **benchmarking**, whereby a firm sets its own marketing performance standards based on the competence of the best companies in its industry, innovative companies in other industries anywhere around the world, the prowess of direct competitors, and/or prior actions by the firm itself. Xerox, a leader in this area, uses benchmarking to measure its goods, services, and practices "against the toughest competitors or those recognized as industry leaders."[16] Among the growing number of firms—besides Xerox—

[16]Beth Enslow, "The Benchmarking Bonanza," *Across the Board* (April 1992), p. 17. See also Thomas C. Powell, "Total Quality Management as Competitive Advantage: A Review and Empirical Study," *Strategic Management Journal*, Vol. 16 (January 1995), pp. 15–37; and Roland T. Rust, Anthony J. Zahorik, and Timothy L. Keiningham, "Return on Quality (ROQ): Making Service Quality Financially Accountable," *Journal of Marketing*, Vol. 59 (April 1995), pp. 58–70.

FIGURE 23-5
MetLife: Benchmarking Based on the Clients Served
Reprinted by permission.

now using benchmarking are AT&T, DuPont, Ford, IBM, Kodak, Marriott, Metropolitan Life, and Motorola. As Figure 23-5 illustrates, Metropolitan Life's benchmark is "The Top 100 Companies in the U.S."

Benchmarking may be divided into two main categories:

> *Strategic benchmarks* for business performance are measures which set overall direction, and show managers how others have succeeded in similar circumstances. *Process benchmarks*, in contrast, usually indicate standards which should be achievable in day-to-day operations, given the willingness to learn.[17]

According to one worldwide study of over 580 companies in four industries (computer, auto, health care, and banking), a greater percentage of U.S. firms regularly engage in benchmarking than their Japanese and German counterparts. Nonetheless, there are some "universal truths" about total quality that can aid any firm. Those that do best: communicate the corporate strategic plan to employees, customers, suppliers, and channel members; upgrade and simplify development and production processes; set up formal practices to certify suppliers; and scrutinize and reduce cycle time (how long it takes a firm to get from designing to delivering a good or service).[18]

There are three steps in the benchmarking ladder: novice, journeyman, and master.

The sponsors of the just-mentioned study, Ernst & Young and the American Quality Foundation, recommend that a benchmarking program be approached in three stages.

[17]Tony Clayton and Bob Luchs, "Strategic Benchmarking at ICI Fibres," *Long Range Planning*, Vol. 27 (June 1994), p. 56.

[18]Jeremy Main, "How to Steal the Best Ideas Around," *Fortune* (October 1992), pp. 102–106; Cyndee Miller, "TQM's Value Criticized in New Report," *Marketing News* (November 9, 1992), pp. 1, 16; and Gilbert Fuchsberg, "'Total Quality' Is Termed Only a Partial Success," *Wall Street Journal* (October 1, 1992), pp. B1, B7.

Firms can hurt themselves by setting unrealistic goals if they compare themselves to those at a later stage:

- *Novice*—A firm in this category should strive to emulate direct competitors, not world-class companies. It should rely on customers for new-product ideas and choose suppliers mostly on price and reliability criteria. There should be a focus on cost-reduction potential, with a "don't develop it, buy it" thrust. Workers should be rewarded for teamwork and quality. The firm should identify processes that add value, simplify those processes, and move faster in responding to the marketplace.
- *Journeyman*—A firm in this category should encourage workers to find ways to do their jobs better and to simplify operations. It should strive to emulate market leaders and selected world-class companies. Consumer input, formal marketing research, and internal ideas should be used in generating new products. The firm should select suppliers having good quality, and then look at their prices. Compensation for both workers and managers should be linked to teamwork and quality. The firm should refine practices to improve the value added per employee, the time to market, and customer satisfaction.
- *Master*—A firm in this category relies on self-managed, multiskilled teams that emphasize horizontal processes (like product development and logistics). It measures its product development, distribution, and customer service against the world's best. Consumer input, benchmarking, and internal research and development should be used in generating new products. The firm should select suppliers that are technologically advanced and offer superior quality. Strategic partnerships are employed to diversify production. Compensation for senior executives should be linked to teamwork and quality. The firm should continue to refine its practices to improve the value added per employee, the time to market, and customer satisfaction.[19]

Two especially useful benchmarks are the Malcolm Baldridge National Quality Award criteria and *Fortune's* Corporate Reputations survey criteria. A firm does not have to actually participate in either of these competitions to benefit from the benchmarks. Any organization can internally assess itself and compare its results with others.

The Baldridge Award rates companies in these seven areas: leadership; information and analysis (such as competitive comparisons and benchmarks); strategic quality planning; human resource development and management; management of process quality; quality and operational results; and customer focus and satisfaction. Of the maximum 1,000 points a company can score, 300 are for customer focus and satisfaction. *Fortune's* Corporate Reputations survey rates companies in these eight areas: quality of management; quality of goods or services; innovativeness; long-term investment value; financial soundness; the ability to attract, develop, and keep talented people; responsibility to the community and the environment; and wise use of corporate resources. Companies are rated within their own industry.

Customer Satisfaction Research

Research is needed to gauge **customer satisfaction**. *ACSI is a broad project that is doing so.*

As defined in Chapter 1, **customer satisfaction** is the degree to which there is a match between a customer's expectations of a good or service and the actual performance of that good or service, including customer service. Today, more than ever, companies realize they must measure the level of customer satisfaction through regular research:

> How little we know about these indispensable strangers, our customers. Are they happy? Restless? Was it good for them, too? Will they come back tomorrow? The answers to these questions profoundly affect any business. Indeed, one could say they *define* a business. They also

[19]Otis Port, John Carey, Kevin Kelly, and Stephanie Anderson Forest, "Quality: Small and Midsize Companies Seize the Challenge—Not a Moment Too Soon," *Business Week* (November 30, 1992), pp. 66–72.

> define the meaning of economic activity, for in the largest sense an economy cannot be described by adding up how many passenger-miles of air travel it logs or how much wood its woodchucks chuck per hour. All these count (and we count them). But in the final analysis, what matters is how well an economy satisfies its customers' needs and wants.[20]

The largest ongoing research project on customer satisfaction is the annual American Customer Satisfaction Index (ACSI), a joint effort by the University of Michigan and the American Society for Quality Control. To compute ACSI, 30,000 consumers are surveyed about 3,900 goods and services. The surveys cover "perceptions of service, quality, value, how well the good or service lived up to expectations, how it compared to an ideal, and how willing people were to pay more for it." With a maximum score of 100, these were the highest-rated firms in 1995: Dole (90), Mars (89), Clorox (88), CPC International (88), Hershey (88), American Tobacco (87), Heinz (87), Maytag (87), PepsiCo (87), Procter & Gamble (87), Borden (86), Colgate-Palmolive (86), Honda (86), Mercedes-Benz (86), Nestlé (86), Pillsbury (86), Cadbury Schweppes (85), Coca-Cola (85), Dial (85), and Federal Express (85). The average score for all companies was 73.7.[21]

Any firm can measure its own customer satisfaction. Here is an eight-step process as to how it can do so:

1. "Institute a process to tap management, employees, outside consultants, and industry sources for input on the dimensions critical to customer satisfaction. Environmental scanning of trade publications and competitors and a regular program of internal focus groups can accomplish this."
2. "Use this feedback to develop an ongoing program of customer focus groups and personal interviews to identify critical customer satisfaction dimensions."
3. "Work with a professional staff to develop telephone and/or mail survey instruments to reliably and validly incorporate identified dimensions."
4. "Regardless of whether the people developing the survey are internal or external, make sure they understand the theoretical basis of the instruments and are familiar with standard procedures for developing and testing reliable, valid items. Keep in mind that customer satisfaction survey results that simply describe what was found provide no guidance for developing an action plan to improve satisfaction."
5. "Regularly do surveys and re-evaluate their reliability and validity."
6. "From these data, develop a customer satisfaction metric that not only relates the level of satisfaction of your customers, but also analyzes the importance of the various dimensions of that satisfaction."
7. "Use the dimensional information to develop an action plan for improving each dimension and communicating these improvements to customers. Remember: Delivery of customer satisfaction is not a reality if the customer does not notice it."
8. "Tie the performance evaluation and compensation of each employee involved in the action plan to its accomplishment. This will ensure that the customers' goals match employees' goals. Remember: What gets measured gets rewarded, and what gets rewarded gets done."[22]

[20]Thomas A. Stewart, "After All You've Done for Your Customers, Why Are They Still Not Happy?" *Fortune* (December 11, 1995), p. 179.

[21]Jaclyn Fierman, "Americans Can't Get No Satisfaction," *Fortune* (December 11, 1995), pp. 186–194.

[22]John T. Mentzer, Carol C. Bienstock, and Kenneth B. Kahn, "Benchmarking Satisfaction," *Marketing Management* (Summer 1995), pp. 41–46. See also Dominique V. Turpin, "Japanese Approaches to Customer Satisfaction: Some Best Practices," *Long Range Planning*, Vol. 28 (June 1995), pp. 84–90; Abbie Griffin, Greg Gleason, Rick Preiss, and Dave Shevenaugh, "Best Practice for Customer Satisfaction in Manufacturing Firms," *Sloan Management Review*, Vol. 36 (Winter 1995), pp. 87–98; and William Keenan, Jr., "Customer Service," *Sales & Marketing Management* (January 1996), pp. 63–66.

Ethics IN TODAY'S SOCIETY

How Far Should Customer Satisfaction Guarantees Go?

A money-back guarantee can be an especially strong competitive advantage in attracting skeptical customers. It can also function as an early warning system about potential problems and serve as a motivator to employees. For example, after studying its returns, mail-order retailer L.L. Bean found that "the wrong size" was the most frequent reason for returns. As a result, it revised the size information in all of its catalogs. And besides providing information to correct its operations, the president of Hampton Inns believes the hotel's service guarantee motivates its maids to be sure rooms are especially clean.

An example of an effective satisfaction guarantee is Xerox's "Total Satisfaction Guarantee." It covers the firm's equipment for three years from the date of purchase. Says a Xerox spokesperson, "We're putting the customer in charge. The customer is the sole arbiter and decision maker." Crest toothpaste also offers consumers their money back if they are not satisfied with the results of their dental examinations after six months of use.

Yet, not all companies openly embrace guarantees as a means of building customer loyalty. Some fear that too many customers will ask for a refund on the basis of a trivial complaint. And some companies that promote guarantees extensively in their advertising make it difficult to collect: "A guarantee program can either be the centerpiece of a service company's entire operation or simply a promotional tool. Many businesses continue to make shallow promises with slogans because they are not prepared to guarantee what their customers want, or because the process for getting the company to make good on its offer is overly complicated."

As a marketing manager for a leading hotel chain, develop a money-back guarantee policy that is designed both to reimburse dissatisfied guests and to reduce the lost revenues due to trivial complaints.

Source: Based on material in Jonathan Barsky, "Guarantee; Warranty; Loyalty," *Marketing Tools* (September 1995), pp. 72–75.

Marketing Cost Analysis

Cost efficiency is measured in **marketing cost analysis**.

Marketing cost analysis is used to evaluate the cost efficiency of various marketing factors, such as different total quality configurations, product lines, order sizes, distribution methods, sales territories, channel members, salespersons, advertising media, and customer types. Although a firm may be very profitable, it is highly unlikely that all of its products, distribution methods, and so on, are equally cost efficient (or profitable).

With marketing cost analysis, a firm can determine which factors (classifications) are the most efficient and which are the least efficient, and make appropriate adjustments. It can also generate information that may be needed to substantiate price compliance with the Robinson-Patman Act.

For this type of analysis to work properly, a firm needs to obtain and to use continuous and accurate cost data. Table 23-1 presents several examples of marketing cost analysis.

Marketing cost analysis consists of three steps: studying natural account expenses, reclassifying natural accounts into functional ones, and allocating functional accounts by marketing classification.

Table 23-1

Examples of Marketing Cost Analysis

MARKETING FACTOR	STRATEGY/TACTICS STUDIED	PROBLEM/OPPORTUNITY DISCOVERED	ACTION APPLIED
Customer type	What are the relative costs of selling X-rays to dentists, doctors, and hospitals?	Per-unit costs of hospital sales are lowest (as are prices); per-unit costs of dentist and doctor sales are highest (as are prices).	Current efforts are maintained. Each customer is serviced.
Product	Should a manufacturer accept a retailer's proposal that the firm make 700,000 private-label sneakers?	Substantial excess capacity exists; the private label would require no additional fixed costs.	A contract is signed. Different features for private and manufacturer labels are planned.
Distribution	Should a men's suit maker sell directly to consumers, as well as through normal channels?	Startup and personal selling costs would be high. Additional sales would be minimal.	Direct sales are not undertaken.
Order size	What is the minimum order size a hardware manufacturer should accept?	Orders below $30 do not have positive profit margins; they are too costly to process.	Small orders are discouraged through surcharges and minimum order size.
Advertising media	Which is more effective, TV or magazine advertising?	TV ads cost $0.05 for every potential customer reached; magazine ads cost $0.07.	TV ads are increased.
Personal selling	What are the costs of making a sale?	15 per cent of sales covers compensation and selling expenses, 2 per cent above the industry average.	Sales personnel are encouraged to phone customers before visiting them, to confirm appointments.

Studying Natural Account Expenses The first step is to determine the level of expenses for all **natural accounts,** which report costs by the names of the expenses and not by their purposes. Such expense categories include salaries, rent, advertising, supplies, insurance, and interest. These are the names most often entered in accounting records. Table 23-2 shows a natural-account expense classification.

Natural accounts *are reported as salaries, rent, insurance, and other expenses.*

Table 23-2

A Natural-Account Expense Classification

Net sales (after returns and discounts)	$1,000,000	
Less: Costs of goods sold	450,000	
Gross profit		$550,000
Less: Operating expenses (natural account expenses)		
Salaries and fringe benefits	220,000	
Rent	40,000	
Advertising	30,000	
Supplies	6,100	
Insurance	2,500	
Interest expense	1,400	
Total operating expenses		300,000
Net profit before taxes		$250,000

Table 23-3

Reclassifying Natural Accounts into Functional Accounts

		FUNCTIONAL ACCOUNTS						
NATURAL ACCOUNTS	**TOTAL**	*Marketing Adminis-tration*	*Personal Selling*	*Adver-tising*	*Transpor-tation*	*Ware-housing*	*Marketing Research*	*General Adminis-tration*
Salaries and fringe benefits	$220,000	$30,000	$50,000	$15,000	$10,000	$20,000	$30,000	$65,000
Rent	40,000	3,000	7,000	3,000	2,000	10,000	5,000	10,000
Advertising	30,000			30,000				
Supplies	6,100	500	1,000	500			1,100	3,000
Insurance	2,500		1,000			1,200		300
Interest expense	1,400							1,400
Total	$300,000	$33,500	$59,000	$48,500	$12,000	$31,200	$36,100	$79,700

Functional accounts *denote the purpose or activity of expenditures.*

Reclassifying Natural Accounts into Functional Accounts Natural accounts are then reclassified into **functional accounts,** which indicate the purposes or activities for which expenditures have been made. Included as functional expenses are marketing administration, personal selling, advertising, transportation, warehousing, marketing research, and general administration. Table 23-3 reclassifies the natural accounts of Table 23-2 into functional accounts.

Once functional accounts are established, cost analysis becomes clearer. For instance, if salaries and fringe benefits increase by $25,000 over the prior year, natural account analysis cannot allocate the rise to a functional area. Functional account analysis can pinpoint the areas of marketing having higher personnel costs.

Functional costs are assigned with each marketing classification becoming a profit center.

Allocating Functional Accounts by Marketing Classification The third step assigns functional costs by product, distribution method, customer, or other marketing classification. This reports each classification as a profit center. Table 23-4 shows how costs can be allocated among different products, using the data in Tables 23-2 and 23-3. From Table 23-4, it is clear that product A has the highest sales and highest total profit. However, product C has the greatest profit as a per cent of sales.

In assigning functional costs, these points should be kept in mind. One, assigning some costs—such as marketing administration—to different products, customers, or other classifications is usually somewhat arbitrary. Two, the elimination of a poorly performing classification would lead to overhead costs—such as general administration—being allotted among the remaining product or customer categories. This may actually result in lower overall total profit. Thus, a firm should distinguish between those separable expenses that are directly associated with a given classification category and can be eliminated if a category is dropped and those common expenses that are shared by various categories and cannot be eliminated if one is dropped.[23]

A firm must differentiate between order-generating and order-processing costs (described in Chapter 3) before making any strategic changes suggested by marketing cost analysis:

> After a decade of frantic cost-cutting, the downside of downsizing is beginning to take its toll: Decimated sales staffs turn in lousy numbers. "Survivor syndrome" takes hold, and overburdened staffers just go through the motions of working. New-product ideas languish. Risk-

[23]See Joseph A. Ness and Thomas G. Cucuzza, "Tapping the Full Potential of ABC," *Harvard Business Review,* Vol. 73 (July–August 1995), pp. 130–138.

Table 23-4
Allocating Functional Expenses by Product

	TOTAL		PRODUCT A		PRODUCT B		PRODUCT C	
Net sales	$1,000,000		$500,000		$300,000		$200,000	
Less: Cost of goods sold	450,000		250,000		120,000		80,000	
Gross profit		$550,000		$250,000		$180,000		$120,000
Less: Operating expenses (functional account expenses)								
Marketing administration	33,500		16,000		10,000		7,500	
Personal selling	59,000		30,000		17,100		11,900	
Advertising	48,500		20,000		18,000		10,500	
Transportation	12,000		5,000		5,000		2,000	
Warehousing	31,200		20,000		7,000		4,200	
Marketing research	36,100		18,000		11,000		7,100	
General administration	79,700		40,000		23,000		16,700	
Total operating expenses		300,000		149,000		91,100		59,900
Net profit before taxes		$250,000		$101,000		$88,900		$60,100
Profit as per cent of sales		25.0		20.2		29.6		30.1

> taking dwindles because the culture of cost-cutting emphasizes the certainties of cutting costs over the uncertainties—and expense—of trying something new."[24]

In making cost cuts, a company must be especially sure to judge the effects of those cuts on the total quality of its goods and services.

Sales Analysis

Sales analysis *looks at sales data to assess the effectiveness of a marketing strategy.*

Sales analysis is the detailed study of sales data for the purpose of appraising the appropriateness and effectiveness of a marketing strategy. Without adequate sales analysis, a poor response to the total quality offered by a firm may not be seen early enough, the value of certain market segments and territories may be overlooked, sales effort may be poorly matched with market potential, trends may be missed, or support for sales personnel may not be forthcoming. Sales analysis enables plans to be set in terms of revenues by product, product line, salesperson, region, customer type, time period, price line, method of sale, and so on. It also compares actual sales against planned sales. More firms engage in sales analysis than in marketing cost analysis.

The main source of sales analysis data is the sales invoice, which may be written, typed, or computer generated. An invoice may contain such information as the customer's name and address, the quantity ordered, the price paid, purchase terms, all the different items bought at the same time, the order date, shipping arrangements, and the salesperson. Summary data are generated by adding invoices. The use of computerized marking, cash register, and inventory systems speeds data recording and improves their accuracy.

Control units *are an essential aspect of sales analysis.*

In conducting sales analysis, proper control units must be selected. **Control units** are the sales categories for which data are gathered, such as boys', men's, girls', and women's clothing. Although a marketing executive can broaden a control system by adding several

[24]Bernard Wysocki, Jr., "Some Companies Cut Costs Too Far, Suffer 'Corporate Anorexia,'" *Wall Street Journal* (July 5, 1995), p. A1. See also Robin Cooper and W. Bruce Crew, "Control Tomorrow's Costs Through Today's Designs," *Harvard Business Review*, Vol. 74 (January–February 1996), pp. 88–97.

80-20 Principle

	Annual Sales		Marketing Expenditures	
	$	%	$	%
Product A	1,000,000	50.0	200,000	44.4
Product B	750,000	37.5	150,000	33.3
Product C	250,000	12.5	100,000	22.2
Total	$2,000,000	100.0	$450,000	100.0*

*Rounding error.

Although a company gets only 12.5 per cent of total sales from Product C, it spends 22.2 per cent of its marketing budget on that product.

Sales Exception Reporting

SALES REPORT

	Expected Sales	Actual Sales
Product 1	$50,000	$100,000
Product 2	$50,000	$50,000
Product 3	$75,000	$75,000
Product 4	$75,000	$50,000

A review of the sales report indicates that Product 1 has done much better than expected, while Product 4 has done much worse.

Iceberg Principle

Only the tip of the iceberg is seen with superficial analysis (aggregate data).

FIGURE 23-6
Sales Analysis Concepts

sales categories together, wide categories cannot be broken down into components. Thus, a narrow sales category is preferable to one that is too wide. It is also helpful to select control units consistent with other company, trade association, and government data. A stable classification system is necessary to compare data from different time periods.

A key concept in undertaking sales analysis is that summary data, such as overall sales or market share, are usually insufficient to diagnose a firm's areas of strength and weakness. More intensive investigation is needed. Two sales analysis techniques that offer in-depth probing are the 80–20 principle and sales exception reporting.

The **80–20 principle** *notes that a large share of sales (profits) often comes from few customers, products, or territories. Analysis errors may be due to the* **iceberg principle**.

According to the **80–20 principle,** in many organizations, a large proportion of total sales (profit) is likely to come from a small proportion of customers, products, or territories. Thus, to function as efficiently as possible, firms need to determine sales and profit by customer, product, or territory. Marketing efforts can then be allocated accordingly. Firms err if they do not isolate and categorize data. Through faulty reasoning, they would place equal effort into each sale instead of concentrating on key accounts. These errors are due to a related concept, the **iceberg principle,** which states that superficial data are insufficient to make sound evaluations.

This is how one firm is using the 80–20 principle in its sales analysis:

> Many people have sampled Health Valley's fat-free soups, fruit bars, and cereals. Health Valley can't survey all its supermarket customers, but has learned how to spot its strongest allies. The company identifies them in two ways: One, those who save up 20 bar-code labels for a $5 rebate. Two, those who order Health Valley's books—the $14.95 *Cooking Without Fat* or the $12.95 *Baking Without Fat*. Since 1992, Health Valley has carried both the bar-code and book offers, along with a toll-free number on the packages of 150 of its products. More than 600,000 consumers have responded, boosting membership in Health Valley's Preferred Customer club.[25]

Sales exception reporting *centers on unmet goals or special opportunities.*

Analysis can be further enhanced by **sales exception reporting,** which highlights situations where sales goals are not met or sales opportunities are present. A slow-selling item report cites products whose sales are below forecasts. It could suggest such corrective actions as price reductions, promotions, and sales incentives to increase unit sales. A fast-selling item report cites items whose sales exceed forecasts. It points out openings, as well as items that need more inventory on hand to prevent stockouts. Finally, sales ex-

[25]Susan Greco, "Identify Your Best Customers," *Inc.* (August 1995), p. 97.

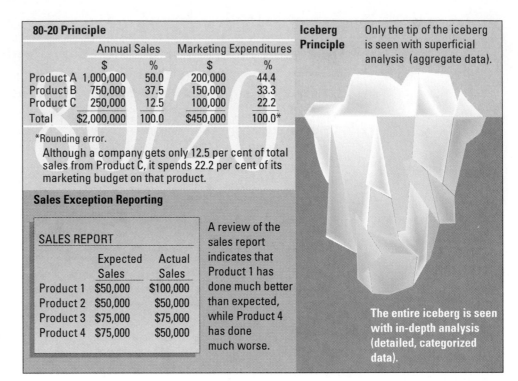

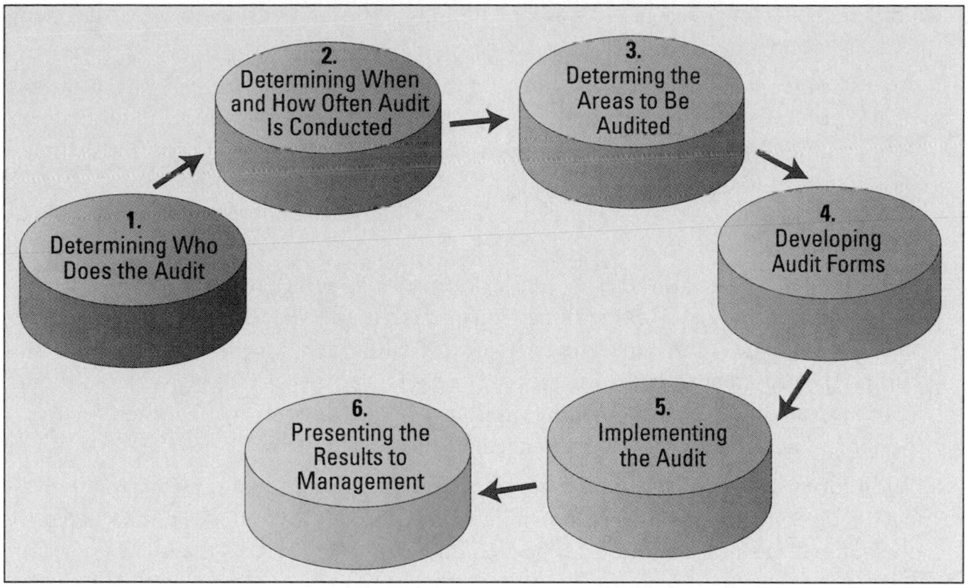

FIGURE 23-7
The Marketing Audit Process

ception reporting enables a firm to evaluate the validity of forecasts and make the proper modifications in them. Figure 23-6 presents examples of the 80–20 principle, the iceberg principle, and sales exception reporting.

Organizations also may use sales analysis to identify and monitor consumer buying patterns by answering such questions as these:

- Who purchases? Organizational vs. final consumer, geographic region, end use, purchase history, customer size, customer demographics
- What is purchased? Product line, price category, brand, country of origin, package size, options purchased
- Where are purchases made? Place of customer contact, purchase location, warehouse location
- How are items purchased? Form of payment, billing terms, delivery form, packaging technique
- When are purchases heaviest and lightest? Season, day of week, time of day
- How much is purchased? Unit sales volume, dollar sales volume, profit margin
- What types of promotion get the best sales results? Advertising, personal selling, sales promotion
- What prices are paid? List prices vs. discounted prices

The Marketing Audit

A **marketing audit** is a systematic, critical, impartial review and appraisal of the basic goals and policies of the marketing function, and of the organization, methods, procedures, and personnel employed to implement the policies and achieve the goals.[26] The purpose of a marketing audit is to determine (1) how well a firm's marketing efforts are being conducted and (2) how they can be improved. Audits should be conducted on a regular basis.

A **marketing audit** *examines a firm in a systematic, critical, and unbiased manner.*

The marketing audit process involves the six steps shown in Figure 23-7:

1. A marketing audit may be conducted by company specialists, by company division or department managers, or by outside specialists. Expertise, access to information,

[26]Christopher H. Lovelock and Charles A. Weinberg, *Public & Nonprofit Marketing*, Second Edition (Redwood City, Calif.: Scientific Press, 1989), pp. 47–48. See also Peter Spillard, Matthew Moriarty, and John Woodthorpe, "The Role Matrix: A Diagnostic of Marketing Health," *European Journal of Marketing*, Vol. 28 (Number 7, 1994), pp. 55–76; and Robert S. Kaplan and David P. Norton, "Using the Balanced Scorecard as a Strategic Management System," *Harvard Business Review*, Vol. 74 (January–February 1996), pp. 75–85.

costs, and potential biases are some of the factors to be considered when choosing audit personnel.

2. An audit may be undertaken at the end of a calendar year, at the end of a firm's annual reporting year, or when conducting a physical inventory. An audit should be performed at least annually, although some firms prefer more frequent analysis. It should be completed during the same time period each year to allow comparisons. In some cases, unannounced audits are useful to keep employees alert and to ensure spontaneous answers.

*A **horizontal audit** studies overall marketing performance; a **vertical audit** analyzes one aspect of marketing.*

3. A **horizontal audit** (also known as a marketing-mix audit) studies the overall marketing performance of a firm with particular emphasis on the interrelationship of variables and their relative importance. A **vertical audit** (also known as a functional audit) is an in-depth analysis of one aspect of a firm's marketing strategy, such as product planning. The two audits should be used in conjunction with one another because a horizontal audit often reveals areas needing further study.
4. Audit forms list the topics to be examined and the exact information required to evaluate each topic. Forms usually resemble questionnaires, and they are completed by the auditor. Examples of audit forms are contained in Figures 23-8 and 23-9.
5. When implementing an audit, decisions need to be made with regard to its duration, whether employees are to be aware of the audit, whether the audit is performed while a firm is open or closed for business, and how the final report is to be prepared.
6. The last step in an audit is to present findings and recommendations to management. However, the auditing process is complete only after suitable responses are taken by management. It is the responsibility of management, not the auditor, to determine these responses.

Despite the merits, many firms still do not use formal marketing audits. Three factors mostly account for this. First, success or failure is difficult to establish in marketing. A firm may have poor performance despite the best planning if environmental factors intervene. On the other hand, good results may be based on a firm's being at the right place at the right time. Second, if marketing audits are completed by company personnel, they may not be comprehensive enough to be considered audits. Third, the pressures of other activities often mean that only a small part of a firm's marketing strategy is audited or that audits are done on a nonregular basis.

Anticipating and Planning for the Future

The next decade promises to be a complex one for marketers everywhere, as they try to anticipate trends and plan long-run strategies. On the positive side, this period should see increasing consumer affluence in many countries, improvements in technological capabilities, expanding worldwide markets, greater deregulation of industry, and other opportunities. On the negative side, the period will probably witness greater competition among firms based in different countries, relatively slow to moderate growth in U.S. and European markets, some resource instability, and an uncertain worldwide economy among the potential problems.

Planning efforts for the future must consider external factors and company abilities.

Long-range plans must take into account both the external variables facing a firm and its capacity for change. Specifically, what variables will affect the firm? What trends are forecast for them? Is the firm able to respond to these trends (for example, does it have the necessary resources and lead time)? A firm that does not anticipate and respond to future trends has a good possibility of falling into Levitt's marketing myopia trap and losing ground to more farsighted competitors:

> Most managers manage for yesterday's conditions because yesterday is where they got their experiences and had their successes. But, management is about tomorrow, not yesterday. Tomorrow concerns what should be done, not what has been done. "Should" is determined by the external environment—what competitors (old, new, and potential) can and might do, the

Does Your Department, Division, or Firm . . .	Answer Yes or No to Each Question
Planning, Organization, and Control	
1. Have specific objectives?	--------
2. Devise objectives to meet changing conditions?	--------
3. Study customer needs, attitudes, and behavior?	--------
4. Organize marketing efforts in a systematic way?	--------
5. Have a market planning process?	--------
6. Engage in comprehensive sales forecasting?	--------
7. Integrate buyer behavior research in market planning?	--------
8. Have strategy and tactics within the marketing plan?	--------
9. Have clearly stated contingency plans?	--------
10. Monitor environmental changes?	--------
11. Incorporate social responsibility as a criterion for decision making?	--------
12. Control activities via marketing cost analysis, sales analysis, and the marketing audit?	--------
Marketing Research	
13. Utilize marketing research for planning, as well as problem solving?	--------
14. Have a marketing information system?	--------
15. Give enough support to marketing research?	--------
16. Have adequate communication between marketing research and line executives?	--------
Products	
17. Utilize a systematic product-planning process?	--------
18. Plan product policy relative to the product life-cycle concept?	--------
19. Have a procedure for developing new products?	--------
20. Periodically review all products?	--------
21. Monitor competitive developments in product planning?	--------
22. Revise mature products?	--------
23. Phase out weak products?	--------
Distribution	
24. Motivate channel members?	--------
25. Have sufficient market coverage?	--------
26. Periodically evaluate channel members?	--------
27. Evaluate alternative shipping arrangements?	--------
28. Study warehouse and facility locations?	--------
29. Compute economic order quantities?	--------
30. Modify channel decisions as conditions warrant?	--------
Promotion	
31. Have an overall promotion plan?	--------
32. Balance promotion components within the plan?	--------
33. Measure the effectiveness of advertising?	--------
34. Seek out favorable publicity?	--------
35. Have a procedure for recruiting and retaining sales personnel?	--------
36. Analyze the sales-force organization periodically?	--------
37. Moderate the use of sales promotions?	--------
Prices	
38. Have a pricing strategy that is in compliance with government regulations?	--------
39. Have a pricing strategy that satisfies channel members?	--------
40. Estimate demand and cost factors before setting prices?	--------
41. Plan for competitive developments?	--------
42. Set prices that are consistent with image?	--------
43. Seek to maximize total profits?	--------

FIGURE 23-8
A Horizontal Marketing Audit Form

Total Quality
Health Check-up Questionnaire

After filling out questionnaire, return to : ______________________

The purpose of this questionnaire is to provide a means for companies to conduct a study of their employees, to determine the degree of involvement and commitment to the principles and practices of Total Quality Management.

The questionnaire is based on the criteria embodied in the Baldridge Quality Award categories (Being employed by many companies as an integrated management system and to conform to requirements in attaining the award).

INDIVIDUAL INSTRUCTIONS

Identify your position title and company department in the spaces below, then respond to each of the following ten statements, indicating your personal opinion as to the degree of compliance with the criteria in company operations. When completed, return to the individual identified at the top of the sheet for tabulation and reporting of results.

Your Position: ______________________ Department: ______________________

QUALITY HEALTH CRITERIA (Circle numbers at right to indicate agreement)	HOW ARE WE DOING? Not true					Very true
1. External customer expectations define the quality of our goods and services.	0	1	2	3	4	5
2. Cross-functional and inter-departmental cooperation are encouraged and supported.	0	1	2	3	4	5
3. There is active leadership for quality improvement at all levels of management.	0	1	2	3	4	5
4. Employees have the authority to act on goods and service quality problems.	0	1	2	3	4	5
5. A team approach is used to solve quality problems and to meet customer expectations.	0	1	2	3	4	5
6. Measures of internal and external customer expectations are well understood.	0	1	2	3	4	5
7. Employees are brought into decisions that affect the quality of their work.	0	1	2	3	4	5
8. There is major emphasis on the prevention and solving of quality problems.	0	1	2	3	4	5
9. Individuals and teams are given recognition for contributions to quality improvement.	0	1	2	3	4	5
10. Systems are in place to assess and respond to changing customer expectations and needs.	0	1	2	3	4	5

FIGURE 23-9
A Total-Quality Vertical-Audit Form

Source: Dick Berry, "How Healthy Is Your Company?" *Marketing News* (February 15, 1993), p. 2. *Reprinted by permission of the American Marketing Association.*

choices this will give customers and those who advise or direct customers, the rules constantly being made by governments and other players, demographic changes, advances in generalized knowledge and technology, changing ecology and public sentiments, and the like.

The most precious thing a manager brings to a job is the wisdom conferred by experience—precisely so that he or she can operate decisively and effectively with limited information, with dispatch and confidence. But when change accelerates, when it comes unexpectedly from constantly unexpected directions, when new technologies and social and environmental conditions occur so disjunctively, the wisdom conferred by experience needs help. That is one reason professional staffs and consultants proliferate. It is also why, in this unaccustomed age of rapid acceleration, this hazardous new age of fast history, managers must take time to carefully think for themselves.[27]

[27]Theodore Levitt, "The Thinking Manager," *Across the Board* (June 1992), pp. 11, 13.

TECHNOLOGY & MARKETING

Can You Predict Where Communications Technology Is Heading?

According to many technology experts, new applications for the "boring" telephone are going to explode in the near future. Here are some predictions:

- Appliances will soon be equipped with phones that are programmed to automatically dial a service center when an internal sensor detects a malfunction.
- Air conditioners will have phones that let people turn them on or off from remote locations.
- Cars will have phones that automatically dial the police or an ambulance in the event an air bag is deployed.

One of the major reasons for the expected increase in phone applications is AT&T's being able to reduce the size of a phone to a computer chip that is the size of a finger nail. This unit can be mass produced at a cost of a few dollars. Accordingly, the small size and low cost will allow phones to be easily installed in household appliances, auto dashboards, and other places.

In the long term, Compaq envisions marketing a central personal computer for the home into which consumers could plug all of their major appliances. And the computer would be connected to a phone line. According to Compaq's vice-president of corporate development, "You might be able to call home and tell 'home' to turn on the oven or to change the code of the security system."

Some analysts caution that consumers may reject innovations that phone designers feel are the most promising. A vice-president at Sony Electronics says that avant garde prototypes become actual products "about as often as concept cars do—not never, but never often."

As vice-president of long-range planning for Whirlpool, plan a major appliance strategy based on the information just provided.

Source: Based on material in Bart Ziegler, "Anytime, Anywhere," *Wall Street Journal* (March 20, 1995), p. R18.

> Average American middle managers think they've beaten the Japanese. They think they've won. They think they're smarter. But they don't understand the nature of the competition. The Japanese have a proven ability to cope with crisis. Japanese companies are, of necessity, becoming world-class experts at managing through tough times. Today, their customers won't spend enough, their currency won't fall enough, and their government won't—or can't—do enough. So Japanese managers are going back to the drawing board, sometimes literally. They are redesigning products, redeploying workers, reconfiguring distribution systems, and generally retooling some of their most storied management practices—from just-in-time production to consensus decision-making, from flexible manufacturing to continuous improvement.[28]

See Figure 23-10.

3M—the giant U.S. firm—illustrates what a firm should do to prepare for the uncertain future: It recently decided to divest itself of businesses with annual sales of $3 billion (including computer diskettes, videotape, and audiotape). 3M believed its long-term prospects in those businesses were not strong. The firm is expanding its efforts in "microreplication" technologies that can "refract light or transport it, strip adhesive from plastic film or serve as a fastener, reduce water drag on boat hulls or polish golf clubs." 3M is more aggressive in obtaining ideas from business customers, and it is extremely interested in gaining insights into the unarticulated needs of those customers. As 3M's chief executive says, "We're going to do two principal things: be very innovative and satisfy our customers in all respects."[29]

[28]Ronald Henkoff, "New Management Secrets from Japan: Really," *Fortune* (November 27, 1995), p. 136.
[29]Thomas A. Stewart, "3M Fights Back," *Fortune* (February 5, 1996), pp. 94–99.

FIGURE 23-10
Facing the Future: Based on Reality
Reprinted by permission.

To prepare for the future, companies can do the following:

- *Company vision planning*—This articulates the firm's future mission.
- *Scenario planning*—This identifies the range of events that may occur in the future.
- *Contingency planning*—This prepares alternative strategies, each keyed to a specific scenario (such as a slow-growth economy).
- *Competitive positioning*—This outlines where a firm will be positioned in the future versus competitors.
- *Competitive benchmarking*—This keeps the firm focused on how well it is doing versus its competitors.
- *Ongoing marketing research*—This entails consumer and other relevant research.[30]

As we look ahead, it is clear that the role of marketing will take on greater importance at many companies. Here is why:

> Marketing is responsible for more than the sale, and its responsibilities differ depending on the level of organization and strategy. It is the management function responsible for making sure that every aspect of the business is focused on delivering superior value [total quality] to customers in the competitive marketplace. The business is increasingly likely to be a network of strategic partnerships among designers, technology providers, manufacturers, distributors, and information specialists. The business will be defined by its customers, not its products or factories or offices. This is a critical point: in network organizations, it is the ongoing relationship with a set of customers that represents the most important business asset. Marketing as a distinct management function will be responsible for being expert on the customer and keeping the rest of the network organization informed about the customer. At the corporate and business unit levels, marketing may merge with strategic planning or, more generally, the strategy development function, with shared responsibility for information, environmental scanning, and coordination of the network activities.[31]

[30]Adapted by the authors from Bernard Taylor, "The New Strategic Leadership: Driving Change, Getting Results," *Long Range Planning*, Vol. 28 (October 1995), pp. 71–81.

[31]Frederick E. Webster, Jr., "The Changing Role of Marketing in the Corporation," *Journal of Marketing*, Vol. 56 (October 1992), p. 14.

MARKETING IN A CHANGING WORLD

Stemming the Tide of Customer Defections[32]

As discussed in this chapter, measuring customer satisfaction is a key task for marketing-oriented firms. Yet, too many companies assume that satisfied customers will automatically be loyal customers. What these companies fail to recognize is that other firms may offer better choices and lure "defectors." For example, even if you are satisfied with American Airlines, might you fly with Southwest Airlines due to its lower prices? Even if you are pleased with a Jeep Cherokee, might you still switch to the more luxurious Range Rover the next time you buy? Of course, the answer to both questions is yes. Customer defections are always possible, and companies must learn to deal with them.

These are among the mistaken impressions that some firms have:

> First, it is sufficient merely to satisfy a customer; as long as a customer responds with at least a satisfied rating, the company-customer relationship is strong. In other words, a level of satisfaction below complete or total satisfaction is acceptable. After all, this is the real world, where goods and services are rarely perfect and people are hard to please. Second, the investment required to change customers from satisfied to completely satisfied will not provide an attractive financial return and probably is not a wise use of resources. There may even be instances—most notably, when competing in a cut-throat commodity market—where it doesn't pay to try to satisfy any customers. Third, each division with a relatively high average rating should focus on the customers in the lowest-satisfaction categories. Striving to understand the causes of their dissatisfaction and concentrating efforts on addressing them is the best use of resources.

To stem the tide of customer defections, instead of relying on the preceding flawed assumptions, firms must see that

- With rare exceptions, complete customer satisfaction is the key to gaining customer loyalty *and* superior long-term financial results.
- Even in relatively noncompetitive markets, providing customers with outstanding value may be the most reliable way to secure sustained customer satisfaction and loyalty.
- Very poor goods and services are not the sole cause—and may not even be the main one—of high customer dissatisfaction. A company may be attracting the wrong customers or have an inadequate process for turning around the right customers after they have bad experiences.
- Different satisfaction levels require different kinds of actions.
- Customer satisfaction surveys alone are insufficient marketing feedback.

SUMMARY

1. *To show the value of an integrated marketing plan* Integrated planning builds upon a firm's strategic planning efforts and its use of a total quality approach. In this way, everyone is "on the same page." An integrated marketing plan is one in which all of its various parts are unified, consistent, and coordinated.

2. *To discuss the elements of a well-integrated marketing plan* There are several major elements in an integrated marketing plan. A clear organizational mission outlines a firm's commitment to a type of business and a place in the market. Long-term competitive advantages are company, product, and marketing attributes—whose distinctiveness and appeal to consumers can be maintained over an extended period of time. A precisely defined target market enables a firm to identify the specific consumers it addresses in a marketing plan.

The long-, moderate-, and short-term marketing subplans of a firm need to be compatible with one another. Coordination among SBUs is enhanced when the functions, strategies, and resources of each are described and monitored by top management. The components of the marketing mix need to be coordinated within each SBU. The plan must have a certain degree of stability over time.

3. *To present five types of marketing plan analysis: benchmarking, customer satisfaction research, marketing cost analysis, sales analysis, and*

[32]The material in this section is based on Thomas O. Jones and W. Earl Sasser, Jr., "Why Satisfied Customers Defect," *Harvard Business Review*, Vol. 73 (November–December 1995), pp. 88–99.

the marketing audit Marketing plan analysis compares a firm's actual performance with its planned or expected performance for a specified period of time. If actual performance is unsatisfactory, corrective action may be needed. Plans may have to be revised because of the impact of uncontrollable variables.

Through benchmarking, a company can set its own marketing performance standards by studying the best firms in its industry, innovative firms in any industry, direct competitors, and/or the company itself. There are strategic benchmarks and process benchmarks. In general, firms progress through three stages as they engage in benchmarking: novice, journeyman, and master. The Malcolm Baldridge National Quality Award and *Fortune's* Corporate Reputations survey are good benchmarking tools.

In customer satisfaction research, a firm determines the degree to which customer expectations regarding a good or service are actually satisfied. The largest research project in this area is the American Customer Satisfaction Index (ACSI), which rates thousands of goods and services. In 1995, the average ACSI score for all companies was 73.7 (out of 100).

Marketing cost analysis evaluates the cost efficiency of various marketing factors, such as different total quality configurations, product lines, order sizes, distribution methods, sales territories, channel members, salespersons, advertising media, and customer types. Continuous and accurate cost data are needed. Marketing cost analysis involves studying natural account expenses, reclassifying natural accounts into functional accounts, and allocating accounts by marketing classification.

Sales analysis is the detailed study of sales data for the purpose of appraising the appropriateness and effectiveness of a marketing strategy. Sales analysis enables plans to be set in terms of revenues by product, product line, salesperson, region, customer type, time period, price line, or method of sale. It also monitors actual sales against planned sales. More firms use sales analysis than marketing cost analysis. The main source of sales data is the sales invoice; control units must be specified. Sales analysis should take the 80–20 principle, the iceberg principle, and sales exception reporting into account.

The marketing audit is a systematic, critical, impartial review and appraisal of a firm's marketing objectives, strategy, implementation, and organization. It contains six steps: determining who does the audit, establishing when and how often the audit is conducted, deciding what the audit covers, developing audit forms, implementing the audit, and presenting the results. A horizontal audit studies the overall marketing performance of a firm. A vertical audit is an in-depth analysis of one aspect of marketing strategy.

4. *To see the merit of anticipating and planning for the future* Long-range plans must take into account both the external variables facing a firm and its capacity for change. A firm that does not anticipate and respond to future trends has a good chance of falling into Levitt's marketing myopia trap—which should be avoided.

KEY TERMS

marketing plan analysis (p. 656)
benchmarking (p. 656)
customer satisfaction (p. 658)
marketing cost analysis (p. 660)
natural accounts (p. 661)
functional accounts (p. 662)
sales analysis (p. 663)
control units (p. 663)
80–20 principle (p. 664)
iceberg principle (p. 664)
sales exception reporting (p. 664)
marketing audit (p. 665)
horizontal audit (p. 666)
vertical audit (p. 666)

Review Questions

1. State five of Wal-Mart's ten focused management rules.
2. Explain Figure 23-1, which deals with a well-integrated marketing plan.
3. Why might competitive advantages not travel well internationally?
4. What is benchmarking? How should a *novice* firm use it differently from a *master* firm?
5. Explain the American Customer Satisfaction Index (ACSI).
6. Why is functional account cost analysis more useful than natural account analysis?
7. Distinguish between marketing cost analysis and sales analysis.
8. When conducting sales analysis, why is it necessary that control units not be too wide?
9. Differentiate between a vertical and a horizontal marketing audit.
10. What are some of the positive and negative trends firms are likely to face over the coming decade?

Discussion Questions

1. Do you think your college or university is applying an integrated marketing approach? Why or why not? What marketing recommendations would you make for your school?

2. Develop a customer satisfaction survey for your local bank. Discuss the kinds of information you are seeking.

3. What data could a manufacturer obtain from a monthly analysis of its sales to wholesalers? How could this information improve marketing plans?

4. Develop a vertical marketing audit form for Sony to appraise its relationship with the retailers that carry its products.

5. As the marketing vice-president for a small book publisher, how would you prepare for the future? What key trends do you foresee over the next decade? How would you address them?

CASE 1

*Full Speed Ahead?**

Some experts suggest that speed in all phases of marketing strategy—from receiving orders to delivering products to answering customer questions—may be replacing total quality management as the latest competitive advantage. Michael Porter, Harvard Business School's strategy guru, says "It's gone from a game of resources to a game of rate-of-progress." The chairman of a software firm concurs, "It's not the big companies that eat the small; its the fast that eat the slow."

Firms in a variety of industries are seeking to boost the speed of their marketing operations. IBM can now build and ship a customized PC within 24 hours of taking an order. Gillette has reduced its new-product development process from three to two years, while Toyota's development process has been cut from 27 months to 19 months. And Westinghouse Electric is aiming to reduce the time it takes to issue an invoice.

There are various approaches to speeding up marketing processes. One technique is to enumerate all of the steps in the process, determine which steps add value to the customer, and then eliminate most of the others. In an application of this approach, a firm found that just filling an order for its business forms took 90 separate steps. The company reengineered the ordering process so sales taxes are automatically calculated (based on the zip code of the customer) and credit checks are no longer required (unless a new order exceeds the previous order by a certain amount). Because of these activities, the company was able to cut the steps required to fill an order to 20. In addition, the firm can now quote an order in one week versus three weeks under the old process.

A second approach to speeding up processes is to use interfunctional teams to design products as units, rather than to work in separate units. With this technique, Chrysler has been able to reduce the number of engineers it needs to develop a new car model (such as the LH design for the Dodge Intrepid, Chrysler Concorde, and Eagle Vision) from 1,400 to 741. Chrysler estimates that its next new cars will be planned by 540 engineers.

Today, Chrysler even chooses outside suppliers before starting work on the design of new cars; and many of its suppliers lease space near Chrysler's design center to facilitate cooperation. Under the old system, Textron, a big supplier to Chrysler, took five days to estimate the costs of alternative dashboard designs. According to the president of the Textron unit, "Now, we can develop a price within 5 per cent inside of a day. We're trying to get it down to half a day."

A third approach involves using computers to speed up processes. For example, PC software can enable a salesperson to determine parts availability and receive price quotes while sitting in a customer's office. Previously, the salesperson had to write down information by hand, travel back to his or her office, and then look up price and item availability information.

Despite all of the excitement associated with speed, managers need to be aware of the potential limitations of speeding up processes: Managers may feel they are under constant pressure to work faster. A slow just-in-time delivery of crucial inventory may cause the temporary shutdown of a plant. Still worse, the emphasis on speed may result in products being commercialized before they are fully tested.

QUESTIONS

1. Discuss the overall advantages and disadvantages to the use of speed in marketing strategy.
2. How can a firm employ benchmarking to assess and revise its speed of operations?
3. Do smaller firms have an advantage in speed over larger ones? Explain your answer.
4. Is speed an aid or inhibitor to integrating a marketing strategy? Why?

*The data in this case are drawn from William M. Bulkeley, "The Latest Big Thing at Many Companies Is Speed, Speed, Speed," *Wall Street Journal* (December 23, 1994), pp. A1, A4; and Valerie Reitman and Robert L. Simpson, "Japanese Car Makers Speed Up Car Making," *Wall Street Journal* (December 29, 1995), pp. B1–B2.

CASE 2

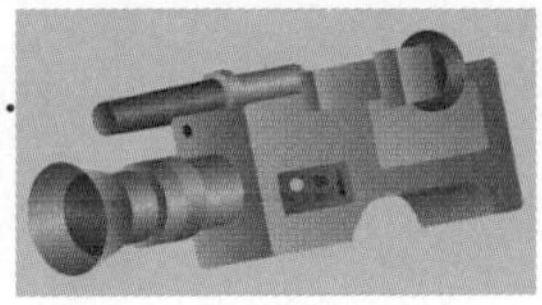

General Electric: An Integrated Marketing Strategy†

The last several years have been good ones for General Electric (GE). Earnings from ongoing operations are rising steadily, with many of its SBUs showing double-digit sales growth. Even the Aircraft Engines SBU, which has had some earnings declines, still produces a yearly profit of half a billion dollars (mostly due to concessions from suppliers and large reductions in the number of vendors used). General Electric attributes much of its success to an integrated strategy consisting of four key dimensions: boundarylessness, speed, stretch, and simplification. Let's now look at each of these.

Boundarylessness consists of finding a better way or a better idea from a colleague, another GE business, another firm that will share its ideas with GE, or a supplier. GE reinforces boundarylessness behavior by recognizing the person who implements an idea as much as its originator.

In one instance of boundarylessness, GE learned that American Standard, one of its big accounts, had successfully installed a "Demand Flow Technology" system that doubled or even tripled inventory turnover rates—working toward a goal of zero working capital. So, GE now uses this technique in its Power Systems, Plastics, and Medical Systems businesses. And the working capital turnover in these businesses has increased by double-digit levels.

Another application of boundarylessness is based on observing Caterpillar, a firm that reduced its service costs and new-product development time by standardizing parts. Using this system, GE has been able to cut new-product introduction times in half in its Appliances and Power Systems businesses.

At GE, speed is viewed as a major competitive advantage. Among the key benefits of shorter production cycles are better asset turnover and increased cash flow. These new-product development examples illustrate the success of GE in the area of speed. The CNBC cable channel was able to develop *America's Talking*, a TV program with 14 hours a day of original programming, from product concept to commercialized product—in less than six months. And in locomotive manufacturing, GE developed a new AC locomotive within 18 months. As of 1995, virtually its entire line of locomotives changed to AC technology (versus the DC technology that characterized its line as recently as 1993).

GE's third major strategy dimension is stretch, the notion that "nothing is impossible," and that tough goals are seen as motivators. While businesses leaders at GE set targets at the beginning of the year (for income, cash flow, and market share), at the end of the year, performance is measured on results as compared to the prior year (and the current environment), not the stretch targets. GE believes that stretch replaces the notion of being "as good as you have to be" with being "as good as you can be." For example, in 1991, GE set two stretch goals: a 10 times inventory turnover and a 15 per cent operating profit margin. At the time, inventory turnover was 5 times and the firm's operating profit was 11 per cent. In 1995, its inventory turnover was 9 times and its operating profit was a record 13.6 per cent. What is important at GE is not whether a target is hit, but whether the firm looks to new targets.

Last, GE wants to simplify all it does and makes. This means fewer parts, simpler product designs, and higher quality. The firm now measures the quality of a design in terms of its simplicity, not its complexity. Simplicity also means communication within GE and with customers must be more straightforward.

QUESTIONS

1. Evaluate General Electric's overall strategy.
2. What overall short- and long-range goals would you recommend for General Electric?
3. Describe how General Electric could use marketing cost analysis in its operations.
4. What factors should General Electric study in a horizontal marketing audit? Explain your answer.

VIDEO QUESTIONS ON GENERAL ELECTRIC

1. Describe two recent GE innovations.
2. Evaluate GE's organization mission.

†The data in this case are drawn from *General Electric 1994 Annual Report*; and Tim Smart and Zachary Schiller, "Just Imagine If Times Were Good," *Business Week* (April 17, 1995), pp. 78–80.

PART 8 CASE

Marketing Under Fire: The Heat Is On

Introduction

That customers today have a variety of high-quality goods and services available at reasonable prices is due, in part, to marketing's ascendancy in the modern firm. Yet, in many firms, marketing seems to have a rather high resource share, inviting intense scrutiny from corporate cost-cutters.

In the past, marketing productivity was viewed in terms of efficiency. Early attempts at improvement focused mostly on minimizing costs. This was driven by the recognition that it was hard to measure the output of marketing adequately. But it was also driven by an implicit belief that marketing did not create value in any tangible sense and, hence, was an activity on which the minimum necessary amount of resources should be expended.

Today, we have ample evidence that well-spent marketing resources can be tremendously productive. For example, the return on $1 of advertising for AT&T's early "Reach out and touch someone" campaign was estimated to be over $4, most of it profit.

Measuring Productivity

There is so much to be gained from improvements in marketing productivity that even imperfect measurements can be of great value. However, we must measure the right things; otherwise, our attempts at improvement will, by definition, be misdirected.

Typically, productivity has been measured as the quantity of output for a given amount of input. Yet, such measures are unsatisfactory in that they fail to adjust for changes in the desirability of the output. If the output of a steel mill is measured in "tons of steel," the fact that the quality and value-added of such steel may increase substantially over time is disregarded.

The Intangibles Factor This problem is especially acute for marketing measurement since marketing deals with so many intangibles. To address it, we suggest that marketing productivity be defined as the amount of desirable output per unit of input; thus, output should be measured in terms of quality, as well as quantity.

Salesperson productivity, for example, is more than the number of calls made or the number of transactions that result. It includes the effectiveness of sales calls (their long-run impact on the relationship with customers), the profitability of resulting transactions, and the impact of today's business mix on the future. Likewise, a productive ad could be defined as one that maximizes the quality-adjusted amount of positive exposure for a given budget.

The desired output of marketing can be stated in simple terms: acquiring and retaining customers profitably. Thus, a good measure of marketing productivity must include the economics of both customer acquisition and retention.

Acquiring Customers This measure consists of the revenues attributable to marketing actions that bring in new customers, divided by the costs of those actions, adjusted by a customer satisfaction index (CSI). This formula reflects the idea that highly satisfying exchanges, rather than "hard sell" techniques or deceptive ads, form the basis of new customer acquisitions. Overpromising and then underdelivering on heightened expectations usually leads to dissatisfaction.

Retaining Customers Since retaining a customer requires more than sustaining high satisfaction, we suggest adjusting the measure of revenues/costs for existing customers by what we call a customer loyalty index (CLI). Even ostensibly satisfied customers can be induced to switch to a rival unless they have been strongly bonded to a firm's offering. The CLI addresses customer "churn," which is a significant problem in a number of industries today.

Effective Efficiency Using this method, a firm's overall marketing productivity would be a weighted combination of the productivity of customer acquisition and customer retention. The weights should reflect the relative importance of acquisition and retention according to the firm's goals. Thus, a startup firm in a growing market would place more emphasis on acquisition, while an established firm in a slow-growing market might be more concerned with keeping its best customers.

Marketing productivity includes both efficiency (doing things right) and effectiveness (doing the right things). Ideally, the marketing function should generate satisfied customers at low cost. Too often, however, companies either create satisfied customers at unacceptably high cost, or alienate customers (as well as employees) in their search for marketing efficiencies.

To make the necessary improvements, we first must adopt a broader view of productivity. Marketing must pursue the ideal of "effective efficiency" in all programs and processes; neither objective is adequate by itself.

Achieving Balance

Marketing's productivity problem is partly due to poor marketing; firms often fail to apply marketing concepts in a balanced way. Too many stress gaining market share over growing a market—a distinction that leads to an escalating spiral of misapplied marketing dollars and heavy retaliation.

Source: Adapted by the authors from Jagdish N. Sheth and Rajendra S. Sisodia, "Feeling the Heat," *Marketing Management* (Fall 1995), pp. 9–22. Reprinted by permission of the American Marketing Association.

Likewise, many companies demonstrate a poor understanding of how marketing mix elements interrelate. For example, if a company misses the fact that its "weak link" is inadequate market coverage, it might lower prices or end up squandering excessive resources on advertising.

A good business strategy makes marketing easier and productivity more achievable. Yet, even productive and enlightened marketing cannot compensate for a flawed strategy in the long run. Marketing can thus be an uphill battle or downhill glide, depending on how sound a business strategy is.

For example, Southwest Airlines has spent less on marketing over the years than rivals, but it has outperformed them on every measure. Southwest knew it didn't have to spend heavily on a message that is intrinsically attractive to a large and growing part of the market. The airline also has been highly consistent in its marketing efforts over the years and advertises on local, rather than national, TV to avoid reaching markets where it has no presence. Where it does serve, Southwest's market share now tops 60 per cent.

We have identified a number of ways to improve marketing productivity and classified them into two broad categories: collaborating and improving marketing efficiency.

Collaborating

Several collaborative marketing approaches help improve productivity. In particular, partnering, relationship marketing, and marketing alliances allow for greater resource efficiency, as well as improved customer satisfaction.

Partnering "Partnering" between members of a value chain, such as retailers and manufacturers, is a major departure from their traditionally antagonistic relationship. Both become part of a single process—distributing products to customers—which technology can greatly streamline and simplify. For example, Black & Decker describes its new distribution philosophy as "Sell one, ship one, build one." Inventory is pulled through the system rather than pushed down, leading to lower average levels of inventory, coupled with higher levels of availability for customers.

Relationship Marketing Related to partnering, but one step short, is relationship marketing—long-term, mutually beneficial arrangements in which buyers and sellers focus on value by creating more satisfying exchanges. At the same time, both buyers and sellers can reduce costs; buyers do it by reducing their search and transaction costs while sellers can lower advertising and selling costs. Implied in the concept of relationship marketing is the idea of customer selectivity. It is neither feasible nor worthwhile to establish such relationships with all customers. By channeling resources into customers who can be served profitably, companies can increase marketing productivity.

Marketing Alliances By combining forces with another company interested in reaching a similar target market with a distinctive or complementary offering, firms can almost double the productivity of some marketing resources. Marketing alliances are most readily formed for advertising, selling, or distribution purposes, but could also extend into product development or other arrangements.

Improving Marketing Efficiency

There are two major ways by which marketing can be made more efficient. The first is by better defining where marketing tasks should be done, up a value chain (outsourcing to suppliers) and down a value chain (having customers take over some tasks). Another possibility is to move marketing tasks into other parts of the firm, which can reach the same results more efficiently or effectively (or both). Thus, certain tasks performed by customer service could be designed into the product, thus reducing the need for customer service.

The second dimension of marketing efficiency relates to the problem of poor resource allocation among the elements of the marketing mix. Productivity can sometimes be improved simply by pulling back in some areas and deploying all or some part of those resources elsewhere. For example, Procter & Gamble has improved its marketing performance by drastically cutting its spending on sales promotions in favor of advertising and R&D.

Competitive pressures have led marketing to add more variations of the marketing mix. If these variations are unrelated to actual differences in customer preferences, they can add complexity and cost without adding value. Thus, the long-distance telephone service industry has proliferated pricing schemes to such a degree that customers are confused and often resentful.

For firms serving a wide range of product markets, marketing activities can become highly scattered and very costly if undertaken in an uncoordinated, excessively decentralized manner. Yet, such firms also have the opportunity to be very productive in their marketing—if they reduce redundancies, increase economies of scale in marketing, engage in cross-marketing, and so on.

Companies can spend marketing dollars at several different levels: brand, divisional, corporate, and even the industry level. Productivity improvements can sometimes be realized simply by shifting resources from one level to the next. Similarly, reassigning marketing dollars between advertising, sales promotion, public relations, and the nurturing/managing of word-of-mouth communications among customers can have a significant impact on marketing productivity. PR and word-of-mouth have gotten too little attention from most companies, but the latter type of communication will likely take on greater import with the higher use of online networks for marketing purposes.

Make Vs. Buy Every marketing activity should be evaluated in terms of a "make vs. buy" decision. Outsourcing should be used when there is a high degree of specialization in performing a marketing activity. Over time, more marketing tasks are becoming specialized, making them good candidates for outsourcing.

By one estimate, PepsiCo outsources 80 per cent of its marketing efforts. R.J. Reynolds outsources many things, including package design. P&G outsources 90 per cent of its custom research projects. With noncore marketing tasks being outsourced and core activities being spread among other functional areas, it is evident that the marketing department is squeezed from two sides.

Some activities, such as advertising, have traditionally been outsourced, and others, such as marketing research, are heading in the same direction. The marketing activities that are candidates for outsourcing include sales, sales management, sales promotion, logistics, marketing information systems, customer service, and so on.

Outsourcing can contribute tremendously to marketing productivity if it takes a secondary or "back-burner" activity and hands it over to a specialist for whom it is a "front-burner" activity. The specialist enjoys economies of scale and scope in doing the activity and provides leading-edge capabilities through investments in emerging technologies. Direct marketer Laura Ashley, for example, successfully outsourced its inbound and outbound logistics functions to Federal Express. The result was a 10 per cent reduction in costs, along with a dramatic improvement in product availability and the launch of a new worldwide, 48-hour direct delivery service.

Bringing Customers Into the Value Chain One of marketing's ironies is that customers are often more satisfied when they perform some tasks that marketers normally would perform. Firms can simultaneously lower costs and increase customer satisfaction by identifying such areas. The leading telecommunications firms have done this by providing billing information to business customers on floppy disk, CD-ROM, or computer tape. Rather than the telecommunications company providing detailed reports, customers use software (also provided by the telecommunications company) to analyze data themselves. And numerous activities—from ATM banking to pumping gas—now are routinely and preferentially done by customers.

The win-win aspect of such changes is critical. Lacking a "win" for the customer, productivity-enhancing measures are viewed as self-serving and lead to customer defections. In some instances, the "win" is not immediately clear, and may require extensive customer education or a continued provision of traditional service for some segments. The "high-tech" aspects of such service changes must be balanced by adequate attention to "high-touch" issues.

In the early 1980s, Citibank attempted to speed the use of ATMs in New York by requiring customers with total account balances below a set amount to use only ATMs for a specified list of transactions. The policy led to protests by customers, adverse publicity, and account closings. Customers like multiple options and usually will not stand for ultimatums.

This checklist can help determine if customers should be asked to perform tasks ordinarily performed by marketing or customer service:

- Does the change save the customer time?
- How much additional effort does it entail?
- Does it protect the customer's privacy?
- Can the customer automate the process to any extent? Can we provide tools to accomplish this?
- Can the customer customize it to a greater degree?
- Does the change keep or raise the accuracy with which a task is performed?
- Is personal help available immediately if the customer needs it?

Reducing Product Proliferation Flexible manufacturing systems and various software-driven manufacturing processes now enable many firms to increase the assortment of products they can make without substantially raising unit costs. This capability frequently contributes to declining marketing productivity because the ability to produce products efficiently does not mean that they can be marketed efficiently.

Many firms have expanded their range product offerings beyond what the market needs. This has fragmented, as well as increased, the need for ads and salespeople. It has also raised the difficulty of forecasting sales, leading to more unsold inventory. As a result, marketing costs for the product line increase substantially, lowering or eliminating profits.

Rethinking Advertising By making information sources such as newspapers, magazines, TV, and radio virtually free to most end users, advertising has had a large role in creating huge and profitable markets for these media. Yet, advertising is so rife with productivity problems that its role is under increasingly harsh scrutiny.

Today, the advertising industry is being transformed through the evolution of information technology. And Ed Artzt, former chairman of Procter & Gamble (the largest U.S. advertiser) has called for the advertising profession to reinvent itself, suggesting that "business as usual" will not work. The key problem is the poor targetability of ads and their highly intrusive nature.

Unfortunately, much advertising still is developed for broadcast to mass markets, many of which long ago fragmented into smaller markets. To succeed in the future, advertising will have to move from a broadcast mode to more narrowcasting and eventually "monocasting" or "pointcasting" to segments of one. Meanwhile, managers can improve ad productivity by managing expectations, budgeting more carefully, adjusting compensation, and recycling campaigns.

Focusing Promotions Sales promotion has gotten out of hand, especially in the packaged-goods industry. While ads can be viewed as an investment, sales promotion is a short-term fix, typically intended to buttress the top line or market share.

Firms such as P&G like to gain trial via advertising, which is considered the highest value way of gaining trial because customers are buying the product "for the right reasons." In other words, they have been convinced a product is superior. Also, P&G believes people who use coupons are very apt to switch again. The implication is that the lifetime value of customers gained via advertising is higher than customers gained from couponing. Unfortunately, there is no reliable way to track ad-driven trial, though that too will change when interactive advertising becomes more widespread.

Dynamic Pricing Many firms still use cost-plus pricing. They tend to sacrifice significant profit opportunities in the long run, as well as hide operating and marketing inefficiencies. By moving to market-driven pricing—and price-based costing—they force costs down; no artificial umbrella exists to shield high costs.

Southwest Airlines has a very low-cost structure that allows it to turn a profit on a $50 ticket. Clearly, it cannot afford to spend $25 of marketing effort on getting a customer! The use of price-based costing leads to a price that "hits the sweet spot" in the market, making marketing's task much easier.

Unbundling and Rebundling Services Many firms are trapped in an escalating spiral of increasing service costs. If service is bundled with a core product, it can rapidly lift marketing costs and erode profits. It also leads to a subsidization of heavy users by light ones, which causes marketing inefficiency and leaves openings for competitors to steal profitable low-service customers by offering them lower prices.

The answer is not to reduce or eliminate service but to package it in different ways. Firms can provide a base level of service to all customers and then offer different levels of service to different customer groups for a fee. Alternatively, they can choose to continue offering the service free to their most frequent and profitable customers.

QUESTIONS

1. Relate the discussion in this case to the buzzwords "interactive" and "integrated" that were noted in Chapter 23.
2. Present five case-related recommendations for a firm that wants to have total quality in its marketing plan.
3. Comment on this statement from a marketing perspective: "Typically, productivity has been measured as the quantity of output for a given amount of input."
4. How could a firm benchmark the performance of its sales force? Include measures of both tangible and intangible factors in your answer.
5. Comment on this statement from the perspective of customer satisfaction research: "Marketing must pursue the ideal of *effective efficiency* in all programs and processes; neither objective is adequate by itself."
6. Distinguish among partnering, relationship marketing, and marketing alliances. What is the value of each?
7. Under what circumstances should a firm outsource marketing tasks to suppliers? To customers? Explain your answer.
8. How would you determine whether a firm offers too many product versions to consumers? What would you do then? Why?

Appendix A

Careers in Marketing

Career opportunities in marketing are quite extensive and diversified. Many marketing positions give a considerable amount of responsibility to people early in their careers. For example, within six months to one year of being hired, assistant retail buyers are usually given budget authority for purchases involving hundreds of thousands of dollars. Beginning salespeople typically start to call on accounts within several weeks of being hired. Marketing research personnel actually develop preliminary questionnaires, determine sampling procedures, and interpret study results within a short time after their initial employment. A marketing career is excellent preparation for a path to top management positions in all types of organizations.

Many marketing positions are highly visible. These include salespeople, sales managers, retail buyers, brand managers, industrial traffic managers, credit managers, and advertising and public relations personnel. For instance, a bank manager of deposits development at Canadian Imperial Bank, one of North America's largest banks, develops localized marketing strategies within bank branches. Such a manager trains branch personnel in identifying market opportunities, using bank data bases, seeking prospects, telemarketing, and writing marketing letters. In general, the visibility of marketing positions allows effective persons to be recognized, promoted, and well compensated.

Marketing offers career opportunities for people with varying educational backgrounds. An associate's or a bachelor's degree is generally required for most management training positions in retailing, inventory management, sales, public relations, and advertising. A master of business administration degree is increasingly necessary for marketing research, marketing consulting, brand management, middle and senior management, and industrial sales positions. Marketing consultants, marketing research directors, and marketing professors frequently have earned Ph.D. degrees in marketing or related subjects.

A marketing background can also train a person to operate his or her own business. Among the entrepreneurial opportunities available are careers as retail store owners, manufacturers' agents, wholesalers, insurance and real-estate brokers, marketing consultants, marketing researchers, and freelance advertising illustrators or copywriters.

Table 1 contains a detailed listing of job titles in marketing. Table 2 shows the types of firms that employ people in marketing positions.

Table 1

Selected Job Titles in Marketing

Job Title	*Description*
Account executive	Liaison between an ad agency and its clients. This person is employed by the agency to study clients' promotion goals and create promotion programs (including messages, layout, media, and timing).
Advertising copywriter	Creator of headlines and content for ads.
Advertising layout person	Producer of illustrations or one who uses other artists' materials to form ads.
Advertising manager	Director of a firm's ad program. He or she determines media, copy, budget size, ad frequency, and the choice of an ad agency.
Advertising production manager	Person who arranges to have an ad filmed (for TV), recorded (for radio), or printed (for newspaper, magazine, etc.).
Advertising research director	Person who researches markets, evaluates alternative ads, assesses media, and tests reactions.
Agent (broker)	Wholesaler who works for a commission or fee.
Catalog manager	Person who determines target market, products, copy, displays, and pricing for sales catalogs.
Commercial artist	Creator of ads for TV, print media, and product packaging. This artist selects photos and drawings, and determines the layout and type of print used in newspaper and magazine ads. Sample scenes of TV commercials are sketched for clients.
Consumer affairs specialist (customer relations specialist)	Firm's contact with consumers. The person handles consumer complaints and attempts to have the firm's policies reflect customer needs. Community programs, such as lectures on product safety, are devised.
Credit manager	Supervisor of the firm's credit process, including eligibility for credit, terms, late payments, consumer complaints, and control.
Customer service representative	Person responsible for order status inquiries, expediting deliveries, field sales support, and returns and claims processing.
Direct-to-home (or office) salesperson	Person who sells goods and services to consumers by personal contact at the consumer's home or office.
Display worker	Person who designs and sets up retail store displays.

(cont. on next page)

Table 1 (Cont.)

Job Title	*Description*
Exporter	Individual who arranges for foreign sales and distribution, mostly for domestic firms having a small presence internationally.
Fashion designer	Designer of such apparel as beachwear, hats, dresses, scarves, and shoes.
Franchisee	Person who leases or buys a business with many outlets and a popular name. A franchisee often has one outlet and engages in cooperative planning and ads. The franchisor sets operating rules for all.
Franchisor	Person who develops a company name and reputation and then leases or sells parts of a firm to independent businesspeople. The franchisor oversees the firm, sets policy, and often trains franchisees.
Freight forwarder	Wholesaler who consolidates small shipments from many companies.
Industrial designer	Person who enhances the appearance and function of machine-made products.
Industrial traffic manager	Arranger of transportation to and from firms and customers for raw materials, fabricated parts, finished goods, and equipment.
International marketer	Person who works abroad or in the international department of a domestic firm and is involved with some aspect of marketing. Positions are available in all areas of marketing.
Inventory manager	Person who controls the level and allocation of merchandise throughout the year. This manager evaluates and balances inventory amounts against the costs of holding merchandise.
Life insurance agent (broker)	Person who advises clients on the policy types available relative to their needs. Policies offer insurance and/or retirement income.
Manufacturers' representative (agent)	Salesperson representing several, often small, manufacturers that cannot afford a sales force. The person often sells to wholesalers and retailers.
Marketing manager (vice-president)	Executive who plans, directs, and controls all of a firm's marketing functions. He or she oversees marketing decisions and personnel.
Marketing research project supervisor	Person who develops the research methodology, evaluates the accuracy of different sample sizes, and analyzes data.
Media analyst	Person who evaluates the characteristics and costs of available media. He or she examines audience size and traits, legal restrictions, types of messages used, and other factors. The effectiveness of company messages is also measured.
Media director (space or time buyer)	Person who determines the day, time (for radio and TV), media, location, and size of ads. The goal is to reach the largest desirable audience efficiently. This person negotiates contracts for ad space or air time.
Missionary salesperson	Support salesperson who provides information about new and existing products.
Order-fulfillment manager	Supervisor responsible for shipping merchandise. He or she verifies orders, checks availability of goods, oversees packing, and requests delivery.
Packaging specialist	Person responsible for package design, durability, safety, appeal, size, and cost. This specialist must be familiar with all key laws.
Political consultant	Person who advises political candidates on media relations, opinion polling, fund raising, and overall campaign strategy.
Pricing economist	Specialist who studies sources of supply, consumer demand, government restrictions, competition, and costs, and then offers short-run and long-run pricing recommendations.
Product manager (brand manager)	Person who supervises the marketing of a product or brand category. In some firms, there are product (brand) managers for existing items and new-product (brand) managers for new items. For a one-brand or one-product firm, this manager is really the marketing manager.
Property and casualty insurance agent (broker)	Person who evaluates client risks from such perils as fire, burglary, and accidents; assesses coverage needs; and sells policies to indemnify losses.
Public relations director	Person who manages firm's efforts to keep the public aware of its societal accomplishments and to minimize negative reactions to its policies and activities. He or she constantly measures public attitudes and seeks to keep a favorable public opinion of a firm.
Purchasing agent	Buyer for a manufacturer, wholesaler, or retailer. He or she purchases the items necessary for operating the firm and usually buys in bulk, seeks reliable suppliers, and sets precise specifications.
Real-estate agent (broker)	Liaison who brings together a buyer and a seller, lessor and lessee, or landlord and tenant. This salesperson receives a commission.

Table 1 (Cont.)

Job Title	*Description*
Retail buyer	Person responsible for purchasing items for resale. The buyer normally concentrates on a product area and develops a plan for proper styles, assortments, sizes, and quantities.
Retail department manager	Supervisor of one retail department, often at a branch store. This is often the first job a college graduate gets after initial training.
Retail merchandise manager	Supervisor of several buyers. He or she sets the retailer's direction in terms of styles, product lines, image, pricing, and other factors and allocates budgets among buyers.
Retail salesperson	Salesperson for a firm that sells to final consumers.
Retail store manager	Supervisor of day-to-day operations of a store. All in-store personnel report to this manager.
Sales engineer	Support salesperson involved with technical goods or services.
Sales manager	Sales force supervisor who is responsible for recruitment, selection, training, motivation, evaluation, compensation, and control.
Salesperson	Company representative who interacts with consumers. He or she may require limited or extensive skills, deal with final or organizational customers, work from an office or go out in the field, and be a career salesperson or progress in management.
Sales promotion director	Person involved with supplementary promotional activities, such as frequent-shopper programs, coupons, contests, and free samples.
Securities salesperson (commodities broker)	Salesperson involved with buying and selling stocks, bonds, government securities, mutual funds, and other financial transactions.
Traffic manager	Supervisor of the purchase and use of alternative transportation methods. This manager routes shipments and monitors performance.
Warehouser	Person responsible for storage and movement of goods within a firm's warehouse facilities. He or she keeps inventory records and makes sure older items are shipped before newer ones (rotating stock).
Wholesale salesperson	Salesperson representing a wholesaler to retailers and other firms.

Table 2

Selected Employers of Marketing Personnel

Advertising agencies	Manufacturers
Agents and brokers	Marketing research firms
Common carriers	Marketing specialists
Computer service bureaus	Media
Consulting firms	Multinational firms
Credit bureaus	Nonprofit institutions
Delivery firms	Product-testing laboratories
Direct marketing businesses	Public relations firms
Educational institutions	Raw material extractors
Entertainment firms	Real-estate firms
Exporting companies	Retailers
Financial institutions	Self-employed
Franchisees	Service firms
Franchisors	Shopping centers
Fund-raising organizations	Sports teams
Government	Transportation firms
Health-care firms	Warehousers
Industrial firms	Wholesalers
International firms	

Jobs in marketing are growing at a much more rapid rate than those in other occupational categories—and this is expected to continue. For example, today there are about 26 million people who work in U.S. retailing and wholesaling activities, representing over one-fifth of all civilian employees 16 years old and over. And according to U.S. Department of Labor projections, employment in marketing, advertising, sales, and public relations occupations will increase much faster than average between now and the year 2000.

The strong demand for marketing personnel is based on several factors. More service firms, nonprofit institutions, political candidates, and others are applying marketing principles. The deregulation of several industries (such as banking, communication, and transportation) has encouraged companies in these industries to increase their marketing efforts. Although production can be mechanized and automated, many marketing activities require personal contact. The rise in foreign competition, the attraction of many international markets, and the maturity of several market segments in the United States are causing more U.S. firms to expand and upgrade their marketing programs.

Such new technologies as electronic checkouts, marketing-based computer software, and single-source data collection techniques are creating marketing opportunities for firms. The changes in U.S. and foreign societies (such as blurring gender roles, recreational activities, and the rise in single-person households) need to be monitored through marketing research and marketing information systems, and adaptations made via careful marketing planning.

Figure 1 shows four potential marketing career paths. They are general and intended to give you a perspective about "moving up the ladder." Individual firms have their own variations of these career paths. Specialized career opportunities also exist in each area shown (such as sales training, support sales, and final consumer versus organizational consumer sales in the sales area); these are not revealed in Figure 1.

Starting salaries for marketing personnel range from $13,000 to $25,000 for those with an associate's degree, $18,000 to $32,000 for those with a bachelor's degree, and $30,000 to $50,000 and more for those with a master of business administration degree. On average, in 1996, those with a bachelor's degree who majored in marketing had beginning salaries of $25,000, and those with an MBA and a nontechnical bachelor's degree had beginning salaries of $37,000. MBAs with a technical bachelor's degree averaged over $40,000. In addition to salary, some marketing positions (especially in sales) provide a company car, bonus, and/or expense account that are not common to other professions.

Worldwide, and especially in the United States, marketing executives often are chosen as the chief executive officers (CEOs) of major industrial and nonindustrial corporations. They each typically earn at least several hundred thousand dollars per year plus bonuses.

Table 3 shows salary ranges for a number of marketing positions. This table focuses on entry level, middle management, and top management positions. Table 4 shows sources that may be contacted for more specific information.

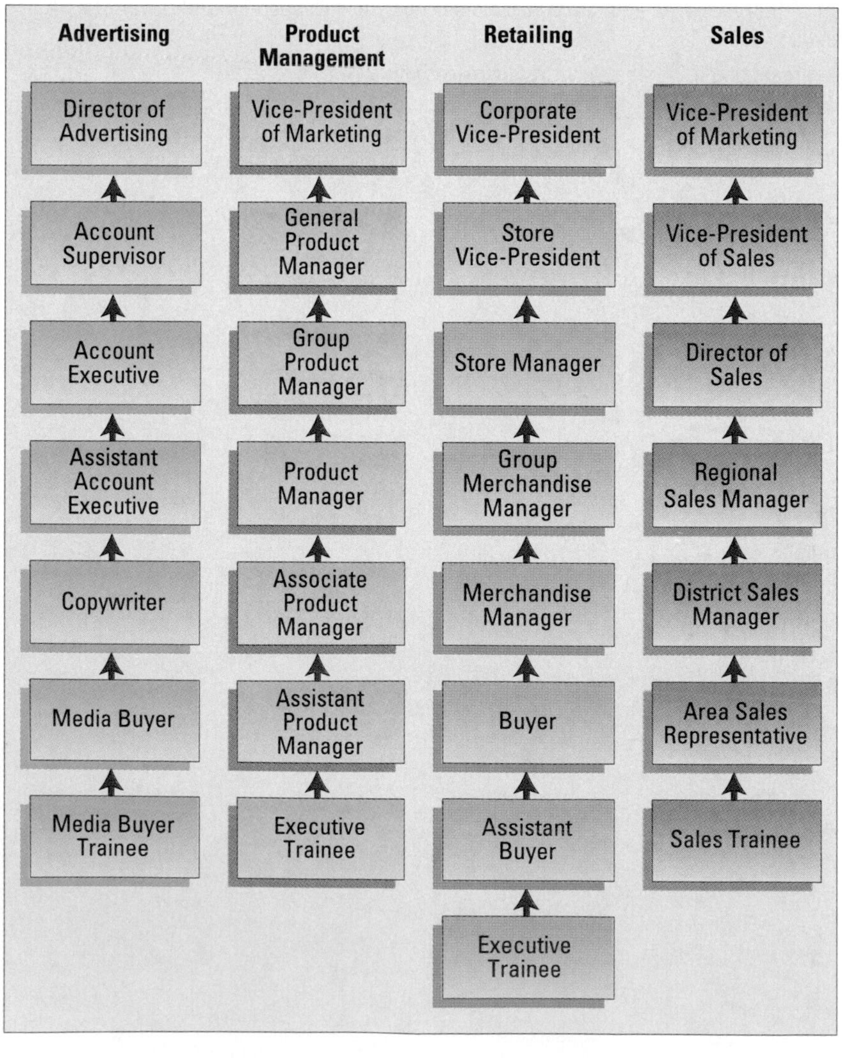

FIGURE 1
Selected Marketing Career Paths

Table 3

Annual Compensation for Personnel in Selected Marketing Positions (Including Bonus)

Advertising Positions	***Compensation***
Assistant media planner	$ 14,000–$ 30,000+
Chief copywriter	$ 40,000–$ 70,000+
Creative director	$ 60,000–$100,000+
Marketing Research Positions	***Compensation***
Junior analyst	$ 17,000–$ 25,000+
Senior analyst/project director	$ 40,000–$ 60,000+
Research director	$ 70,000–$100,000+
Product Management Positions	***Compensation***
Senior marketing analyst	$ 20,000–$ 40,000+
Product manager	$ 40,000–$ 85,000+
Group product manager	$ 50,000–$100,000+
Public Relations Positions	***Compensation***
Account executive	$ 20,000–$ 45,000+
Account supervisor	$ 30,000–$ 60,000+
Retailing Positions	***Compensation***
Assistant buyer	$ 20,000–$ 30,000+
Buyer	$ 30,000–$ 80,000+
General merchandise manager	$ 60,000–$200,000+
Sales Positions	***Compensation***
Sales trainee	$ 20,000–$ 30,000+
Real-estate agent (broker)	$ 20,000–$100,000+
Regional sales manager	$ 50,000–$100,000+
Miscellaneous Marketing Positions	***Compensation***
Customer service representative	$ 20,000–$ 35,000+
Customer service supervisor	$ 30,000–$ 50,000+
Distribution general manager	$ 30,000–$ 90,000+
Sales promotion director	$ 40,000–$ 80,000+
International general sales executive	$ 45,000–$ 75,000+
Top Marketing Positions	***Compensation***
President—distributor	$ 40,000–$200,000+
Senior public relations executive	$ 50,000–$ 80,000+
Senior sales executive	$ 50,000–$100,000+
Branch office manager—advertising agency	$ 50,000–$200,000+
Executive vice-president—advertising agency	$ 75,000–$175,000+
Vice-president of sales	$ 90,000–$260,000+
Vice-president of marketing	$ 95,000–$500,000+
President—advertising agency	$100,000–$400,000+

Sources: Compiled by the authors from various publications.

Table 4

Selected Sources of Additional Marketing Career Information

Career Opportunity	*Sources*
Advertising	American Advertising Federation Education Services Department 1400 K Street NW Washington, DC 20005
	American Association of Advertising Agencies 666 Third Avenue New York, NY 10017
Buying (retail)	National Retail Federation 701 Pennsylvania Avenue NW Washington, DC 20004
Consumer advocate	Consumer Federation of America 1424 16th Street NW Washington, DC 20036
Direct marketing	The Direct Marketing Education Foundation 1120 Avenue of the Americas New York, NY 10036
Direct selling	Direct Selling Association 1776 K Street NW Washington, DC 20006
Industrial design	Industrial Designers Society of America 1142 Walker Road Great Falls, VA 22006
Insurance sales	Independent Insurance Agents of America 127 South Peyton Street Alexandria, VA 22314
	Insurance Information Institute 1101 17th Street NW Washington, DC 20036
Life insurance sales	American Council of Life Insurance 1001 Pennsylvania Avenue NW Washington, DC 20004
Manufacturers' representation	Sales & Marketing Executives International 458 Statler Office Towers Cleveland, OH 44115
Marketing	American Marketing Association 250 S. Wacker Drive Chicago, IL 60606
Marketing research	Marketing Research Association 2189 Silas Deane Highway Rocky Hill, CT 06067
Physical distribution	Council of Logistics Management 2803 Butterfield Road Oak Brook, IL 60521
Public relations	Public Relations Society of America 33 Irving Place New York, NY 10003
Purchasing agents	National Association of Purchasing Management 2055 East Centennial Circle PO Box 22160 Tempe, AZ 85282
	National Contract Management Association 1912 Woodford Road Vienna, VA 22182

Table 4 (Cont.)

Career Opportunity	*Sources*
Real-estate sales	National Association of Realtors 777 14 Street NW Washington, DC 20005
Retailing	International Mass Retailing Association 1901 Pennsylvania Avenue NW Washington, DC 20006
	National Retail Federation 701 Pennsylvania Avenue NW Washington, DC 20004
Sales promotion	Council of Sales Promotion Agencies 750 Summer Street Stamford, CT 06901
Securities sales	Securities Industry Association 120 Broadway New York, NY 10071
Selling	Sales & Marketing Executives International 458 Statler Office Towers Cleveland, OH 44115
Supermarket industry	Food Marketing Institute 800 Connecticut Avenue NW Washington, DC 20006
	National Retail Grocers Association 1825 Samuel Morse Drive Reston, VA 22090
Travel agents	American Society of Travel Agents 1401 New York Avenue NW Washington, DC 20005
Wholesaling	Manufacturers' Agents National Association 23016 Mill Creek Road Laguna Hills, CA 92654
	National Food Brokers Association 1010 Massachusetts Avenue NW Washington, DC 20001

Appendix B

Marketing Mathematics

To design, implement, and review marketing programs properly, it is necessary to understand basic business mathematics from a marketing perspective. Accordingly, this appendix describes and illustrates the types of business mathematics with which marketers should be most familiar: the profit-and-loss statement, marketing performance ratios, pricing, and determining an optimal marketing mix.

The crucial role of marketing mathematics can be seen via the following:

- By utilizing marketing mathematics well, a firm can evaluate monthly, quarterly, and annual reports; and study performance on a product, market, SBU, division, or overall company basis.
- Marketing plans for all types of channel members (manufacturers, wholesalers, and retailers) and all time periods (short term through long term) should be based on marketing mathematics.
- Both small and large, goods and services, and profit and nonprofit organizations need to rely on marketing mathematics in making decisions.
- Marketing mathematics provide a systematic basis for establishing standards of performance, reviewing that performance, and focusing attention on opportunities and problem areas.
- By understanding marketing mathematics, better pricing and marketing mix decisions can be made.
- By grasping marketing mathematics, decision making with regard to entering or withdrawing from a market, budgeting expenditures, and the deployment of marketing personnel can be aided.

The Profit-and-Loss Statement

The **profit-and-loss (income) statement** presents a summary of the revenues and costs for an organization over a specific period of time. Such a statement is generally developed on a monthly, quarterly, and yearly basis. The profit-and-loss statement enables a firm to examine overall and specific revenues and costs over similar time periods (for example, January 1, 1996 to December 31, 1996 versus January 1, 1995 to December 31, 1995) and to analyze its profitability. Monthly and quarterly statements enable a firm to monitor progress toward goals and revise performance estimates.

The profit-and-loss statement consists of these major components:

- **Gross sales**—The total revenues generated by a firm's goods and services.
- **Net sales**—The revenues received by a firm after subtracting returns and discounts (such as trade, quantity, cash, and special promotional allowances).
- **Cost of goods sold**—The cost of merchandise sold by a manufacturer, wholesaler, or retailer.
- **Gross margin (profit)**—The difference between net sales and the cost of goods sold; consists of operating expenses plus net profit.
- **Operating expenses**—The cost of running a business, including marketing.
- **Net profit before taxes**—The profit earned after all costs have been deducted.

When examining a profit-and-loss statement, it is important to recognize a key difference between manufacturers and wholesalers or retailers. For manufacturers, the cost of goods sold involves the cost of producing products (raw materials, labor, and overhead). For wholesalers or retailers, the cost of goods sold involves the cost of merchandise purchased for resale (purchase price plus freight charges).

Table 1 shows an annual profit-and-loss statement (in dollars) for a manufacturer, the General Toy Company. From this table, these observations can be made:

- Total company sales for 1996 were $1,000,000. However, the firm gave refunds worth $20,000 for returned merchandise and allowances. Discounts of $50,000 were also provided. This left the firm with actual (net) sales of $930,000.
- As a manufacturer, General Toy computed its cost of goods sold by adding the cost value of the beginning inventory on hand (items left in stock from the previous period) and the merchandise manufactured during the time period (costs included raw materials, labor, and overhead), and then subtracting the cost value of the inventory remaining at the end of the period. For General Toy, this was $450,000 ($100,000 + $400,000 − $50,000).
- The gross margin was $480,000, calculated by subtracting the cost of goods sold from net sales. This sum was used for operating expenses, with the remainder accounting for net profit.
- Operating expenses involve all costs not considered in the cost of goods sold. Operating expenses for General Toy included sales force compensation, advertising, delivery, administration, rent, office supplies, and miscellaneous costs, a total of $370,000. Of this amount, $225,000 was directly allocated for marketing costs (sales force, advertising, delivery).
- General Toy's net profit before taxes was $110,000, computed by deducting operating expenses from gross margin. This amount would be used to cover federal and state taxes, as well as company profits.

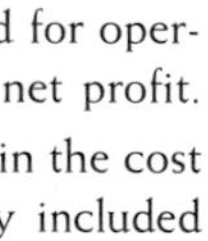

Performance Ratios

Performance ratios are used to measure the actual performance of a firm against company goals or industry standards. Comparative data can be obtained from trade associations, Dun & Bradstreet, Robert Morris Associates, and other sources. Among the most valuable performance ratios for marketing analysis are the following:

$$(1)\quad \begin{array}{l}\text{Sales efficiency ratio}\\ \text{(percentage)}\end{array} = \frac{\text{Net sales}}{\text{Gross sales}}$$

The **sales efficiency ratio (percentage)** compares net sales against gross sales. The highest level of efficiency is 1.00; in that

Table 1

General Toy Company, Profit-and-Loss Statement for the Year January 1, 1996 through December 31, 1996 (in Dollars)

Gross sales			$1,000,000
Less: Returns and allowances		$ 20,000	
Discounts		50,000	
Total sales deductions			70,000
Net sales			$ 930,000
Less cost of goods sold:			
Beginning inventory (at cost)		$100,000	
New merchandise (at cost)[a]		400,000	
Merchandise available for sale		$500,000	
Ending inventory (at cost)		50,000	
Total cost of goods sold			450,000
Gross margin			$ 480,000
Less operating expenses:			
Marketing expenses			
Sales force compensation	$125,000		
Advertising	75,000		
Delivery	25,000		
Total marketing expenses		$225,000	
General expenses			
Administration	$ 75,000		
Rent	30,000		
Office supplies	20,000		
Miscellaneous	20,000		
Total general expenses		145,000	
Total operating expenses			370,000
Net profit before taxes			$ 110,000

[a]For a manufacturer, new-merchandise costs refer to the raw materials, labor, and overhead costs incurred in the production of items for resale. For a wholesaler or retailer, new-merchandise costs refer to the purchase costs of items (including freight) bought for resale.

case, there would be no returns, allowances, or discounts. General Toy had a sales efficiency ratio of 93 per cent ($930,000/$1,000,000) in 1996. This is a very good ratio; anything greater would mean General Toy was too conservative in making sales.

$$(2)\quad \frac{\text{Cost-of-goods-sold ratio}}{\text{(percentage)}} = \frac{\text{Cost of goods sold}}{\text{Net sales}}$$

The **cost-of-goods-sold ratio (percentage)** indicates the portion of net sales used to manufacture or purchase the goods sold. When the ratio is high, a firm has little revenue left to use for operating expenses and net profit. This could mean costs are too high or selling price is too low. In 1996, General Toy had a cost-of-goods-sold ratio of 48.4 per cent ($450,000/$930,000), a satisfactory figure.

$$(3)\quad \frac{\text{Gross margin ratio}}{\text{(percentage)}} = \frac{\text{Gross margin}}{\text{Net sales}}$$

The **gross margin ratio (percentage)** shows the proportion of net sales allocated to operating expenses and net profit. If the ratio is high, a firm has substantial revenue left for these items. During 1996, General Toy had a gross margin ratio of 51.6 per cent ($480,000/$930,000), a satisfactory figure.

$$(4)\quad \frac{\text{Operating expense ratio}}{\text{(percentage)}} = \frac{\text{Operating expenses}}{\text{Net sales}}$$

The **operating expense ratio (percentage)** expresses these expenses in terms of net sales. When the ratio is high, a firm is spending a large amount on marketing and other operating costs. General Toy had an operating expense ratio of 39.8 per cent in 1996 ($370,000/$930,000), meaning that almost 40 cents of every sales dollar went for operations, a moderate amount.

$$(5)\quad \frac{\text{Net profit ratio}}{\text{(percentage)}} = \frac{\text{Net profit before taxes}}{\text{Net sales}}$$

The **net profit ratio (percentage)** indicates the portion of each sales dollar going for profits (after deducting all costs). The net profit ratio varies a lot by industry. For example, in the supermarket industry, net profits are just 1 to 2 per cent of net sales; in the industrial chemical industry, net profits are about 5 per cent of net sales. The 1996 net profit for General Toy was 11.8 per cent of net sales ($110,000/$930,000), well above the industry average.

$$(6)\ \text{Stock turnover ratio} = \frac{\text{Net sales (in units)}}{\text{Average inventory (in units)}}$$

or

$$\frac{\text{Net sales (in sales dollars)}}{\text{Average inventory (in sales dollars)}}$$

or

$$\frac{\text{Cost of goods sold}}{\text{Average inventory (at cost)}}$$

The **stock turnover ratio** shows the number of times during a specified period, usually one year, that average inventory on hand is sold. It can be calculated in units or dollars (in selling price or at cost). In the case of General Toy, the 1996 stock turnover ratio can be calculated on a cost basis. The cost of goods sold during 1996 was $450,000. Average inventory at cost = (Beginning inventory at cost + Ending inventory at cost)/2 = ($100,000 + $50,000)/2 = $75,000. The stock turnover ratio was ($450,000/75,000) = 6. This compared favorably with the industry average. This meant General Toy sold its goods more quickly than competitors.

$$(7)\ \text{Return on investment} = \frac{\text{Net sales}}{\text{Investment}} \times \frac{\text{Net profit before taxes}}{\text{Net sales}}$$

$$= \frac{\text{Net profit before taxes}}{\text{Investment}}$$

The **return on investment (ROI)** compares profitability with the investment necessary to manufacture or distribute merchandise. For a manufacturer, this investment includes land, plant, equipment, and inventory costs. For a wholesaler or retailer, it involves inventory, the costs of land, the outlet and its fixtures, and equipment. To learn General Toy's return on investment, total investment costs are culled from its **balance sheet**, which lists the assets and liabilities of a firm at a particular time.

There are two components to the return on investment measure—investment turnover ratio and net profit ratio (percentage):

$$\text{Investment turnover ratio} = \frac{\text{Net sales}}{\text{Investment}}$$

$$\text{Net profit ratio (percentage)} = \frac{\text{Net profit before taxes}}{\text{Net sales}}$$

The investment turnover ratio computes the sales per dollar of investment. The General Toy management calculated that an overall investment of $550,000 was needed to yield 1996 net sales of $930,000. Thus, its investment turnover ratio was 1.7 times ($930,000/$550,000). Because General Toy's net profit ratio was 11.8 per cent ($110,000/$930,000), the firm's return on investment equaled 20.1 per cent (1.7 × .118). This figure was above the industry norm.

Table 2 shows a percentage profit-and-loss statement for the General Toy Company, using the same period as in Table 1. All figures in the table are computed on the basis of net sales equaling 100 per cent. This table allows a firm to observe quickly such performance measures as the cost-of-goods-sold percentage, operating expense percentage, and net profit percentage.

Pricing

The material here complements Chapters 21 and 22. Five specific aspects of pricing are examined: price elasticity, fixed versus variable costs, markups, markdowns, and profit planning using markups and markdowns.

Price Elasticity

As defined in Chapter 21, **price elasticity** refers to the buyer sensitivity to price changes in terms of the quantities they will purchase. Elasticity is based on the availability of substitutes and the urgency of need. It is expressed as the percentage change in quantity demanded divided by the percentage change in price:

$$\text{Price elasticity} = \frac{\dfrac{\text{Quantity 1} - \text{Quantity 2}}{\text{Quantity 1} + \text{Quantity 2}}}{\dfrac{\text{Price 1} - \text{Price 2}}{\text{Price 1} + \text{Price 2}}}$$

For purposes of simplicity, price elasticity is often expressed as a positive number (as it will be in this section).

Table 3 shows a demand schedule for women's blouses at several different prices. When selling price is reduced by a small percentage, from $40 to $35, the percentage change in quantity demanded rises materially, from 120 to 150 units. Maxine's Blouses then gains a strong competitive advantage. Demand is highly elastic (price sensitive). As price is reduced, total revenues go up:

$$\text{Price elasticity} = \frac{\dfrac{120 - 150}{120 + 150}}{\dfrac{\$40 - \$35}{\$40 + \$35}} = 1.7\ \text{(expressed as a positive number)}$$

At a price of $25, the market becomes more saturated—the percentage change in price, from $25 to $20, is directly offset by the percentage change in quantity demanded, from 240 to 300 units:

$$\text{Price elasticity} = \frac{\dfrac{240 - 300}{240 + 300}}{\dfrac{\$25 - \$20}{\$25 + \$20}} = 1.0\ \text{(expressed as a positive number)}$$

Total revenues remain the same at a price of $25 or $20. This is unitary demand, whereby total revenues stay constant as price changes.

At a price of $20, the market becomes extremely saturated, and further price reductions have little impact on demand. A large percentage change in price, from $20 to $15, results in a small per-

Table 2

General Toy Company, Profit-and-Loss Statement for the Year January 1, 1996 through December 31, 1996 (in Per Cent, with Net Sales = 100.0)

Net sales		100.0
Less cost of goods sold		48.4
Gross margin		51.6
Less operating expenses:		
Marketing expenses	24.2	
General expenses	15.6	
Total operating expenses		39.8
Net profit before taxes		11.8

Table 3

Maxine's Blouses, A Demand Schedule

Selling Price	*Quantity Demanded*	*Elasticity*[a]	*Total Revenue*[b]	
$40	120		$4,800	
		1.7		
35	150		5,250	
		1.5		
30	190		5,700	
		1.3		
25	240		6,000	← Maximum
		1.0		total
20	300		6,000	← revenue
		0.5		
15	350		5,250	
		0.3		
10	390		3,900	

[a]Expressed as positive numbers.

[b]Total revenue = Selling price × Quantity demanded.

centage change in quantity demanded, from 300 to 350 units. Maxine's is able to sell relatively few additional blouses. Demand is inelastic (insensitive to price changes):

$$\text{Price elasticity} = \frac{\dfrac{300 - 350}{300 + 350}}{\dfrac{\$20 - \$15}{\$20 + \$15}} = 0.5 \text{ (expressed as a positive number)}$$

Notice that total revenue falls as demand changes from elastic to inelastic; at this point, price cuts are not effective.

Total revenue is maximized at the price levels where price and demand changes directly offset each other (in this example, $25 and $20). How does a firm choose between those prices? It depends on the marketing philosophy. At a price of $25, profit will probably be higher because the firm needs to produce and sell fewer products, thus reducing costs. At a price of $20, more units are sold; this may increase the customer base for other products the firm offers and thereby raise overall company sales and profits.

Figure 1 graphically depicts demand elasticity for Maxine's Blouses. This figure indicates that a demand curve is not necessarily straight and that a single demand schedule has elastic, unitary, and inelastic ranges.

It is important to remember that price elasticity refers to percentage changes, not to absolute changes. For example, a demand shift from 120 to 150 units involves a greater percentage change than a demand shift from 300 to 350 units. In addition, each product or brand faces a distinct demand schedule. Milk and magazines have dissimilar schedules, despite similar price ranges, because of the different availability of substitutes and urgency of need.

Fixed Versus Variable Costs

In making pricing decisions, it is essential to distinguish between fixed and variable costs. **Fixed costs** are ongoing costs that are unrelated to production or sales volume; they are generally constant over a given range of output for a specific time period. In the short run, fixed costs cannot usually be changed. Examples of fixed costs are rent, full-time employee salaries, physical plant, equipment, real-estate taxes, and insurance.

Variable costs are directly related to production or sales volume. As volume increases, total variable costs increase; as volume declines, total variable costs decline. Per-unit variable costs often remain constant over a given range of volume (e.g., total sales commissions go up as sales rise, while sales commissions as a per cent of sales remain constant). Examples of variable costs are raw materials, sales commissions, parts, salaries of hourly employees, and product advertising.

FIGURE 1
Maxine's Blouses, Demand Elasticity

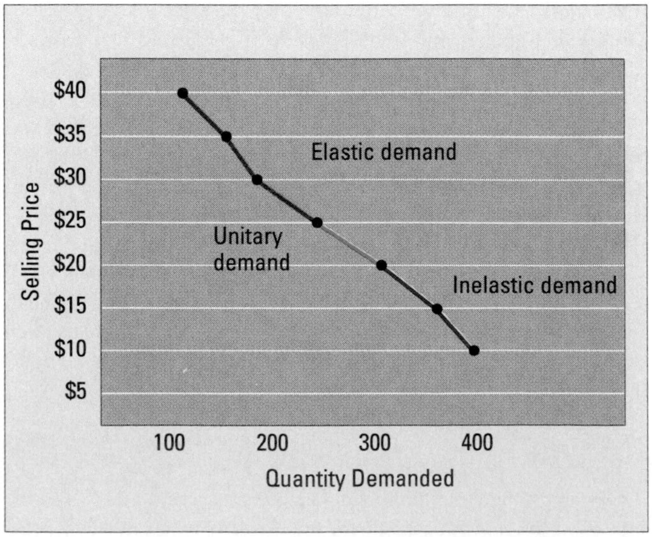

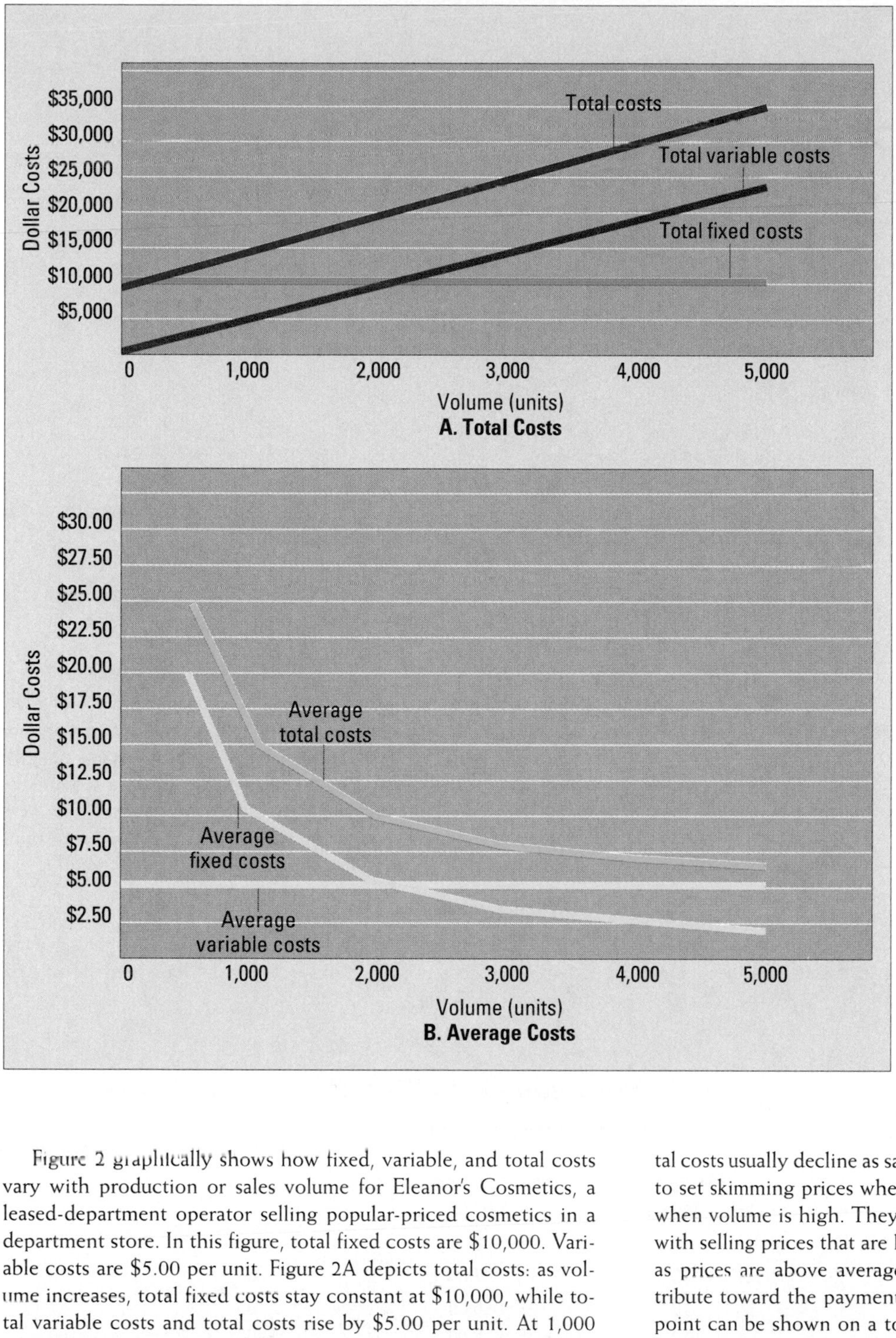

FIGURE 2
Fixed and Variable Costs for Eleanor's Cosmetics

Figure 2 graphically shows how fixed, variable, and total costs vary with production or sales volume for Eleanor's Cosmetics, a leased-department operator selling popular-priced cosmetics in a department store. In this figure, total fixed costs are $10,000. Variable costs are $5.00 per unit. Figure 2A depicts total costs: as volume increases, total fixed costs stay constant at $10,000, while total variable costs and total costs rise by $5.00 per unit. At 1,000 units, total fixed costs are $10,000, total variable costs are $5,000, and total costs are $15,000. At 5,000 units, total fixed costs are $10,000, total variable costs are $25,000, and total costs are $35,000.

Figure 2B depicts average costs: as volume increases, average fixed costs and average total costs decline (because fixed costs are spread over more units), while average variable costs remain the same. At 1,000 units, average fixed costs are $10.00, average variable costs are $5.00, and average total costs are $15.00. At 5,000 units, average fixed costs are $2.00 ($10,000/5,000 units), average variable costs are $5.00, and average total costs are $7.00.

By knowing the relationship between fixed and variable costs, firms are better able to set prices. They recognize that average total costs usually decline as sales volume expands, which allows them to set skimming prices when volume is low and penetration prices when volume is high. They also realize that losses can be reduced with selling prices that are lower than average total costs—as long as prices are above average variable costs, transactions will contribute toward the payment of fixed costs. Finally, the break-even point can be shown on a total-cost curve graph. See Figure 3.

With a selling price of $10.00 per unit, Eleanor's Cosmetics loses money unless 2,000 units can be sold. At that amount, the firm breaks even. For all sales volumes above 2,000 units, the company earns a profit of $5.00 per unit, an amount equal to the difference between selling price and average variable costs (fixed costs are assumed to be "paid off" when sales reach 2,000 units). A sales volume of 5,000 units returns a profit of $15,000 (total revenues of $50,000 − total costs of $35,000).

Markups

A **markup** is the difference between merchandise cost and selling price for each channel member. Markup is usually expressed as a percentage:

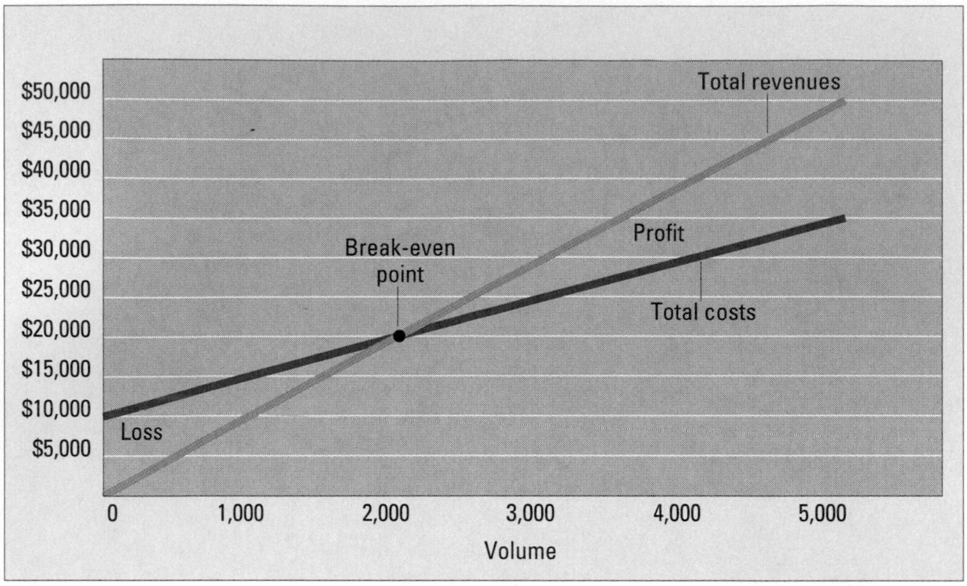

FIGURE 3
Break-Even Analysis for Eleanor's Cosmetics

$$\text{Markup percentage (on selling price)} = \frac{\text{Selling price} - \text{Merchandise cost}}{\text{Selling price}}$$

$$\text{Markup percentage (at cost)} = \frac{\text{Selling price} - \text{Merchandise cost}}{\text{Merchandise cost}}$$

Table 4 shows markup percentages on selling price and at cost for an item selling for $10.00 under varying costs. Because firms often consider a markup percentage as the equivalent of the gross margin percentage discussed earlier in this appendix, they use the markup percentage on selling price in their planning. As with gross margins, firms use their markups to cover operating expenses and net profit.

It is necessary for channel members to understand the discounts provided to them by vendors (suppliers). Besides the markups they receive for providing regular marketing functions, they may also obtain quantity, cash, seasonal, and/or promotional discounts. Transportation costs are added to the final purchase price; they are not discounted.

Table 5 shows the computation of a purchase price by a TV retailer, based on a functional markup of 40 per cent and individual discounts of 10 (quantity), 2 (cash), 5 (seasonal), and 5 (promotional) per cent. The discounts do not total 62 per cent off final selling price. They total 52.2 per cent because the discounts are computed upon successive balances. For example, the 10 per cent quantity discount is computed on $165, which is the purchase price after deducting the functional markup allowed by the vendor.

Markdowns

One of the key price adjustments made by most firms is a **markdown**, which is a reduction in the original selling price of an item

Table 4
Markups on Selling Price and at Cost

Selling Price	*Merchandise Cost*	*Markup (% on Selling Price)*	*Markup (% at Cost)*
$10.00	$9.00	10	11
10.00	8.00	20	25
10.00	7.00	30	43
10.00	6.00	40	67
10.00	5.00	50	100
10.00	4.00	60	150
10.00	3.00	70	233
10.00	2.00	80	400
10.00	1.00	90	900

Formulas to convert markup percentages:

$$\text{Markup percentage (on selling price)} = \frac{\text{Markup percentage (at cost)}}{100\% + \text{Markup percentage (at cost)}}$$

$$\text{Markup percentage (at cost)} = \frac{\text{Markup percentage (on selling price)}}{100\% - \text{Markup percentage (on selling price)}}$$

Table 5

A TV Retailer's Final Purchase Price, After Deducting All Discounts—Model 123

Discounts Offered by Manufacturer (in %)			
Functional	40		
Quantity	10		
Cash	2		
Seasonal	5		
Promotional	5		
Suggested Final Selling Price		$275.00	
Shipping Charges		$ 15.30	
Computation of Purchase Price Paid by Retailer			
List price			$275.00
Less functional markup ($275.00 × 0.40)			110.00
Balance			$165.00
Less quantity discount ($165.00 × 0.10)			16.50
Balance			$148.50
Less cash discount ($148.50 × 0.02)			2.97
Balance			$145.53
Less seasonal discount ($145.53 × 0.05)			7.28
Balance			$138.25
Less promotional discount ($138.25 × 0.05)			6.91
Balance after all discounts			$131.34
Plus shipping charges			15.30
Price to channel member			$146.64
Total of Discounts			$143.66
Total Discount % ($143.66/$275)			52.2

so as to sell it. Markdowns are caused by slow sales, model changes, and other factors.

Markdown percentages can be computed in either of two ways:

$$\text{Markdown percentage (off-original price)} = \frac{\text{Original selling price} - \text{Reduced selling price}}{\text{Original selling price}}$$

$$\text{Markdown percentage (off-sale price)} = \frac{\text{Original selling price} - \text{Reduced selling price}}{\text{Reduced selling price}}$$

For example, the off-original markdown percentage for an item that initially sold for $20 and has been marked down to $15 is ($20 − $15)/$20 = 25. The off-sale markdown percentage is ($20 − $15)/$15 = 33. While the off-original percentage is more accurate for price planning, the off-sale percentage shows a larger price reduction to consumers and may generate increased interest.

Profit Planning Using Markups and Markdowns

Although lower markups (higher markdowns) generally result in higher unit sales, and higher markups (lower markdowns) generally result in lower unit sales, it is essential that a firm determine the effect of a change in selling price on its profitability. The impact of a price adjustment on total gross profit (also known as gross margin) can be determined through the use of this formula:

$$\text{Unit sales required to earn the same total gross profit with a price adjustment} = \frac{\text{Original markup (\%)}}{\text{Original markup (\%)} +/- \text{Price change (\%)}} \times \text{Expected unit sales at original price}$$

For example, if a wholesaler pays $7 to buy one unit of an item and decides to reduce that item's selling price by 10 per cent—from an original price of $10 to $9—its markup on selling price drops from 30 per cent ($3/$10) to 22.2 per cent ($2/$9). Because the wholesaler originally planned to sell 1,000 units at $10, it must now sell 1,500 units at $9 to keep the same gross profitability (30/20 × 1,000). Conversely, if it decides to raise its price by 10 per cent—to $11—its new markup on selling price is 36.4 per cent ($4/$11), and it must sell only 750 units to keep the original gross profit level (30/40 × 1,000).

Determining an Optimal Marketing Mix

When devising, enacting, and assessing a marketing plan, it is necessary to consider the alternative marketing mixes available to a firm and find the most effective one. Because many marketing costs (such as packaging, distribution, advertising, and personal selling) can be both order generating and variable, marketing executives need to estimate and compare revenues for various combinations at various levels of costs. Table 6 shows how a firm could set prices and allocate its $3 million annual marketing budget among product, distribution, advertising, and personal selling—in a manner that maximizes profit. In this situation, the firm would choose a mass marketing mix that results in a low price, a lower-quality product, extensive distribution, and an emphasis on advertising.

The concepts of opportunity costs and sales response curves provide valuable information in determining an optimal marketing mix. **Opportunity costs** measure the foregone revenues (profit) from not using the optimal marketing mix. For example, it may be possible for a firm to sell an additional 10,000 units in a selective marketing strategy by raising advertising expenditures by $100,000 and reducing distribution expenditures by $100,000. A firm that is unaware of this option would have opportunity costs—in terms of profit—of $110,000:

$$\begin{aligned}\text{Opportunity costs} &= (\text{Foregone unit sales} \times \text{Selling price}) - (\text{Added costs})\\ &= (10{,}000 \times \$29.00) - (10{,}000 \times \$18.00)\\ &= \$110{,}000\end{aligned}$$

At its optimal marketing strategy, a firm's opportunity costs equal zero.

Sales response curves show the expected relationships between sales revenue and functional marketing efforts. These curves are estimated on the basis of executives' judgment, surveys, industry data, and/or experiments (whereby marketing mix factors are systematically varied in a controlled way).

Figure 4 shows sales response curves for a firm examining four aspects of its marketing effort: depth of product line, number of outlets carrying products, advertising expenditures, and price level. For each of these factors, the expected impact of a strategy change on sales is shown; it is clear that different actions will result in different sales responses.

When using sales response curves, these points should be kept in mind:

- Sales responsiveness may vary by product and by market segment. For example, marketing expenditures have a much greater

Table 6

Determining an Optimal Marketing Mix for a Company with a $3 Million Annual Marketing Budget

Alternative Marketing Mix	*Selling Price*	*Unit Sales*	*Sales Revenue*	*Total Product Costs*[a]	*Advertising Costs*	*Personal Selling Costs*	*Distribution Costs*	*Total Costs*	*Profit*
Mass marketing	$11.00	2,507,000	$27,577,000	$22,563,000	$1,400,000	$ 300,000	$1,300,000	$25,563,000	$2,014,000
Selective marketing	29.00	432,000	12,528,000	7,776,000	900,000	1,200,000	900,000	10,766,000	1,762,000
Exclusive marketing	43.00	302,000	12,986,000	9,966,000	600,000	1,850,000	550,000	12,966,000	20,000

[a] Mass marketing = $9.00 per unit for labor, materials, and other production costs; selective marketing = $18.00 per unit for labor, materials, and other production costs; and exclusive marketing = $33.00 per unit for labor, materials, and other production costs.

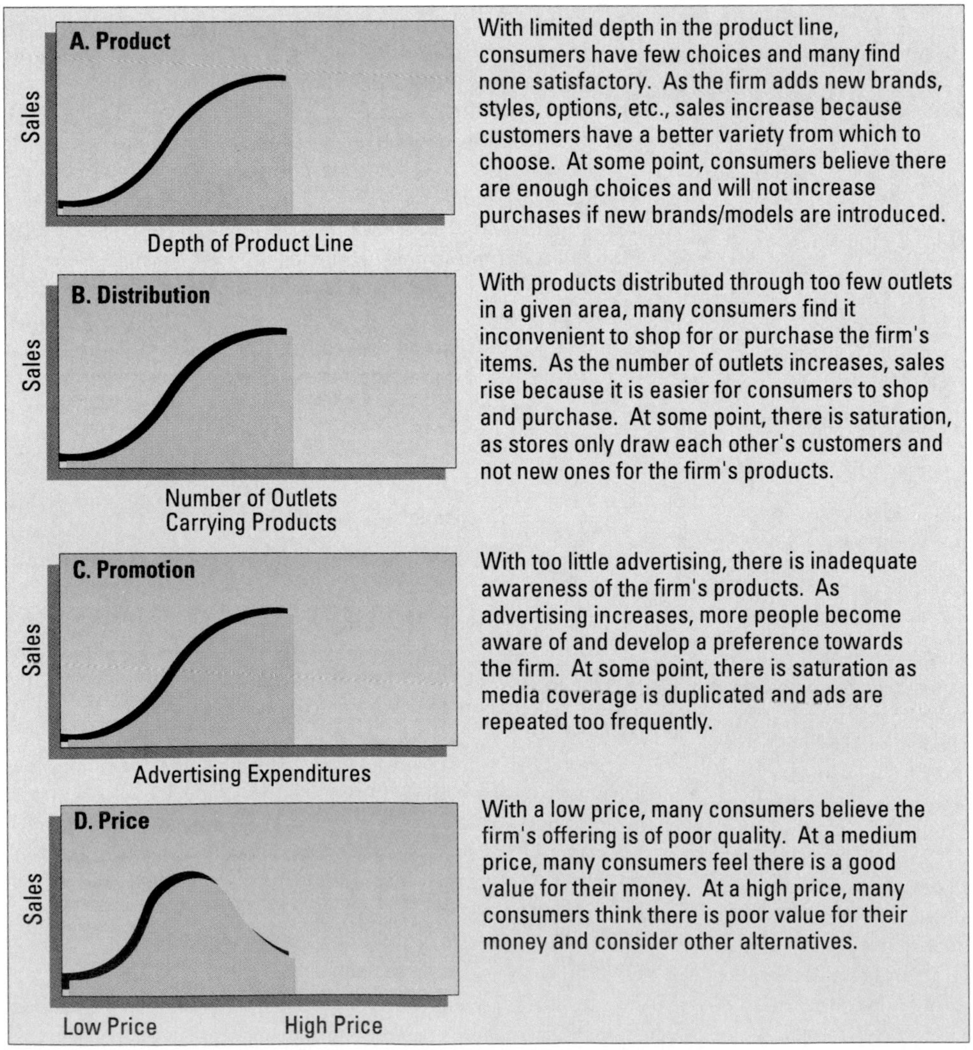

A. Product
Sales
Depth of Product Line
With limited depth in the product line, consumers have few choices and many find none satisfactory. As the firm adds new brands, styles, options, etc., sales increase because customers have a better variety from which to choose. At some point, consumers believe there are enough choices and will not increase purchases if new brands/models are introduced.
B. Distribution
Sales
Number of Outlets Carrying Products
With products distributed through too few outlets in a given area, many consumers find it inconvenient to shop for or purchase the firm's items. As the number of outlets increases, sales rise because it is easier for consumers to shop and purchase. At some point, there is saturation, as stores only draw each other's customers and not new ones for the firm's products.
C. Promotion
Sales
Advertising Expenditures
With too little advertising, there is inadequate awareness of the firm's products. As advertising increases, more people become aware of and develop a preference towards the firm. At some point, there is saturation as media coverage is duplicated and ads are repeated too frequently.
D. Price
Sales
Low Price
High Price
With a low price, many consumers believe the firm's offering is of poor quality. At a medium price, many consumers feel there is a good value for their money. At a high price, many consumers think there is poor value for their money and consider other alternatives.

FIGURE 4
Selected Sales Response Curves for Marketing Mix Functions

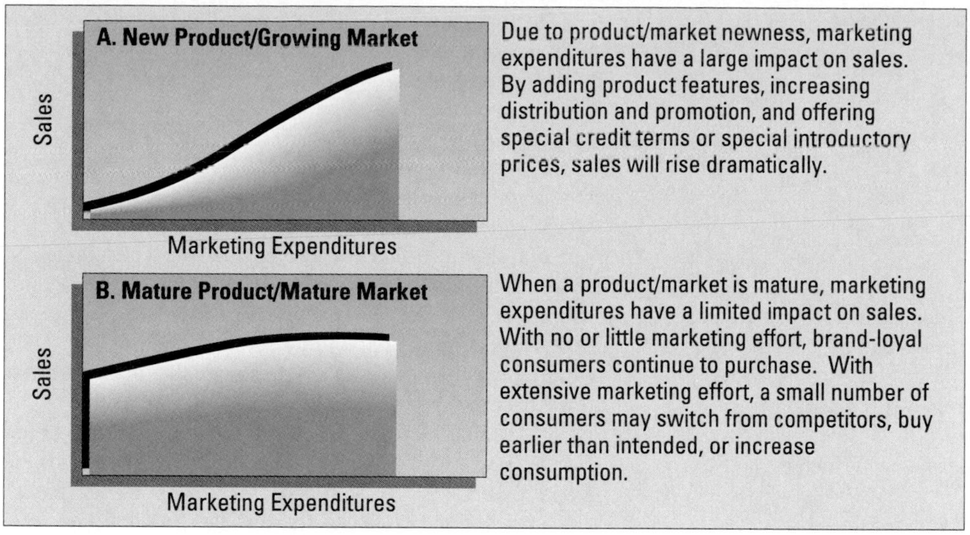
A. New Product/Growing Market
Sales
Marketing Expenditures
Due to product/market newness, marketing expenditures have a large impact on sales. By adding product features, increasing distribution and promotion, and offering special credit terms or special introductory prices, sales will rise dramatically.
B. Mature Product/Mature Market
Sales
Marketing Expenditures
When a product/market is mature, marketing expenditures have a limited impact on sales. With no or little marketing effort, brand-loyal consumers continue to purchase. With extensive marketing effort, a small number of consumers may switch from competitors, buy earlier than intended, or increase consumption.

FIGURE 5
Sales Response Curves and Product/Market Maturity

influence on new products/growing markets than on mature products/mature markets. See Figure 5.

- The range of efficient marketing efforts must be determined. At low levels, marketing activities may be insufficient to generate consumer interest. At high levels, these activities may be redundant and appeal to a saturated market. The range of marketing efforts having the greatest impact on sales is the appropriate one. See Figure 6.
- Sales response curves are related to the combination of marketing mix factors employed by a firm. To determine its overall sales response curve, a company would combine all the individual curves shown in Figure 4 (or use all the data in Table 6).
- Sales response curves examine revenue fluctuations. Before making marketing decisions, profit response curves should also be studied.
- Sales response curves should be projected under different conditions, such as good economy/poor economy or heavy competition/light competition.

FIGURE 6
Optimal Marketing Expenditures

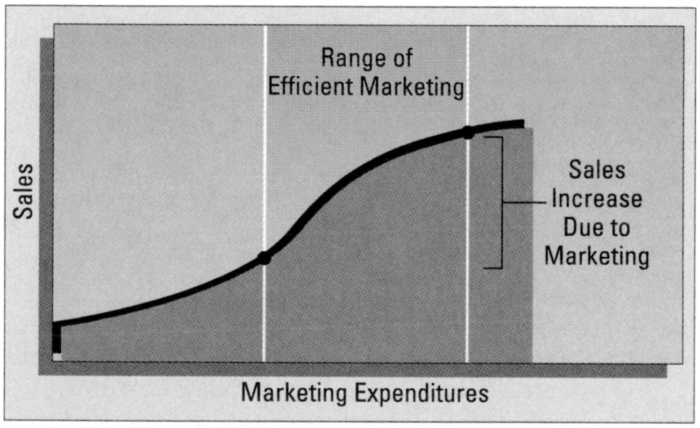
Range of Efficient Marketing
Sales
Sales Increase Due to Marketing
Marketing Expenditures

QUESTIONS

1. What information can a firm obtain from a profit-and-loss statement (in dollars)?
2. Develop a profit-and-loss statement for The Flying Carpet Company, a retail store, based on the following:

Beginning inventory (at cost)	$ 750,000
New merchandise (at cost)	800,000
Ending inventory (at cost)	500,000
Gross sales	2,000,000
Returns and allowances	200,000
Marketing expenses	400,000
General expenses	350,000

3. Using the profit-and-loss statement from Question 2, calculate:
   - **a.** Return on investment. (Assume that investment equals $500,000 plus average inventory.)
   - **b.** Stock turnover ratio.
   - **c.** Net profit ratio (percentage).
   - **d.** Operating expense ratio (percentage).
   - **e.** Gross margin ratio (percentage).
   - **f.** Cost-of-goods-sold ratio (percentage).
   - **g.** Sales efficiency ratio (percentage).
4. How would The Flying Carpet Company determine whether its performance ratios are satisfactory?
5. **a.** What is the impact on return on investment if a firm increases its investment turnover from three times to four times?
   b. List five ways for a firm to increase its investment turnover.
6. A wholesaler estimates that it can sell 10,000 CD changers at $100 each or 6,500 at $115 each. The CD changers cost the wholesaler $70 each.
   - **a.** Calculate the price elasticity between the $100 and $115 price levels.
   - **b.** What factors should determine the price to be set?
7. A full-service car wash has conducted research on its customers' sensitivity to price. These are the results:

Price	Number of Car Washes Demanded in Market Area per Year
$5.25	90,000
5.75	70,000
6.25	60,000
6.75	30,000
7.25	15,000
7.75	10,000

a. Calculate price elasticity for all price levels.
b. At what price is total revenue maximized?
c. What price should be set? Why?
d. What other information, not given in this question, is important in setting price?
e. Which expenses for a car wash are fixed? Which expenses are variable?

8. The car wash in Question 7 can accommodate up to 40,000 cars per year with fixed costs of $80,000. Above 40,000 cars, fixed costs rise to $100,000. Variable costs are $2.50 per car wash.
a. Compute average fixed costs, average variable costs, and average total costs for the car wash at each price.
b. At what price is profit maximized?
c. Why might the car wash set a price that does not maximize profit?

9. A tire manufacturer has fixed costs of $1,000,000 and variable costs of $52.00 per tire.
a. Calculate total costs for volumes of 10,000, 25,000, and 50,000 tires.
b. Calculate average total, fixed, and variable costs for the same volumes.
c. At a volume of 25,000 tires, would the firm make a profit or loss with a wholesale selling price of $68.00? What is the total profit or loss?

10. A supermarket retailer sells medium-sized shaving cream containers for $1.49; they are purchased for $0.97. Large-sized containers sell for $2.09; they are purchased for $1.55.
a. For each size container, determine the markup percentage on selling price and at cost.
b. Why would the retailer use a different markup percentage for medium containers from that for large containers?
c. If a shaving cream manufacturer offers the supermarket a 25 per cent markup on selling price for medium-sized containers, as well as a cash discount of 2 per cent and a quantity discount of 5 per cent, what is the purchase price to the supermarket? What is the overall discount? There are no transportation costs.

11. A wholesaler requires a 50 per cent markup on selling price for profit projections to be met. The merchandise costs $43.00.
a. What must the selling price be for the wholesaler to meet its markup goal?
b. What would be the minimum selling price if the wholesaler has a markup goal of 40 per cent on selling price?

12. Convert the following markups from selling price to cost:
a. 40 per cent markup on selling price.
b. 50 per cent markup on selling price.
c. 60 per cent markup on selling price.

13. Convert the following markups from cost to selling price:
a. 100 per cent markup at cost.
b. 125 per cent markup at cost.
c. 150 per cent markup at cost.

14. An auto parts distributor is offered the following discounts: functional markup, 40 per cent; quantity discount, 5 per cent; cash discount, 2 per cent; and seasonal discount, 3 per cent. If the suggested final selling price of the total order is $1,000 and shipping charges are $50.00, compute the total order cost to the firm.

15. A glove manufacturer originally sold suede gloves for $49 per pair. An end-of-season sale has reduced the price of these gloves to $35.
a. Compute the off-original and off-sale markdown percentages.
b. Why is there a difference in these calculations?

16. **a.** A firm expects to sell 1,000 advanced PC systems yearly at a price of $1,800 per system (including color monitor, four-speed CD-ROM drive, hard drive, keyboard, and graphics board). At the $1,800 price, the company's markup is 15 per cent. How many units would the firm need to sell to earn the same gross profit at a selling price of $2,000 as it would at a selling price of $1,800?
b. How many units must the firm sell to earn the same gross profit at a selling price of $1,600 as it would at a selling price of $1,800?

17. A manufacturer estimates the following relationship between marketing expenses and sales:

Marketing Expenses	*Unit Sales*
$100,000	200,000
200,000	250,000
300,000	290,000
400,000	325,000
500,000	350,000

If a product has a gross profit of $4 per unit and general operating expenses are constant at $100,000, at what marketing expenditure level is profit maximized?

18. Calculate the opportunity costs associated with each marketing expenditure level in Question 17.

19. **a.** Why do most sales response curves have "S" shapes?
b. Under what conditions would sales response curves have different shapes?
c. Draw sales response curves based on the information in Table 6.

Appendix C

Computer-Based Marketing Exercises

This appendix and an accompanying computer diskette allow you to engage in marketing decision making under simulated conditions and to apply many of the concepts studied during your introduction to or survey of marketing course. To use *Computer-Based Marketing Exercises*, you need to purchase a blank 3-1/2 inch formatted computer diskette and make a personal copy of the master exercise disk, which is available to your instructor.

The exercises described in this appendix are designed to reinforce text material; to allow you to manipulate controllable marketing factors and to see their impact on costs, sales, and profits; to have you understand better the influence of uncontrollable factors; and to have you gain experience in using a computer to assess marketing opportunities and to solve marketing problems. All 18 exercises are designed either to be handed in for class assignments or for your own use. The exercises are balanced in terms of subject and level.

These are among the features of *Computer-Based Marketing Exercises*:

- The exercises are linked to key concepts covered throughout *Marketing*, Seventh Edition. Text page references are provided for each exercise both on the computer diskette and in this appendix.
- Although exercises closely parallel the text, they allow great flexibility in data input. You are encouraged to manipulate data and compare the results attained under different assumptions. This provides "hands-on" experience.
- The format of the exercises is very user-friendly. All directions are contained on screens that introduce each exercise, and the exercises are self-prompting. No knowledge of computer programming or computers is needed.
- There is a broad variety of applications.
- All exercises are as realistic as possible.
- The graphics quality is high. Although some exercises use spreadsheet-type analyses, spreadsheet software (such as Lotus or Excel) is not required.
- The software operates on either IBM personal computers or compatibles and with either a color or monochrome monitor. The exercise diskette is available in a 3-1/2 inch format and requires Windows 3.1 or higher.
- After setting up your personal copy of the exercise diskette, your name will appear at the top of each screen and on any pages you print from the screen.

How to Use the Computer-Based Exercise Diskette

Computer Requirements

This version of *Computer-Based Marketing Exercises* requires that users have the following minimum hardware requirements:

- A personal computer that has a 386, 486, or Pentium microprocessor.
- An operating system that runs Windows 3.1 or higher.
- At least 4 MB of RAM (performance increases with 8 MB of memory).
- A hard drive with sufficient space for this program (about 800 KB).
- At least one 3-1/2 inch floppy drive.
- A graphics card that is compatible with Windows 3.1 or later.
- A high-resolution monitor (VGA or SVGA).
- A printer that is supported by Windows.

Although this program can be operated through either traditional keys or a mouse (trackball), a mouse (trackball) is preferable.

Program Installation and Operation

This section explains how to install and operate your copy of the *Computer-Based Marketing Exercises* diskette and how to permanently place your name, class, and section on your diskette (so that assignments may be submitted with your name printed on them). Separate directions are provided for a computer with a hard drive and a network. Since the program contains compressed files, it must be copied onto a hard drive or used on a network.

Using a Computer with a Hard Drive To run *Computer-Based Marketing Exercises* from a computer with a hard drive, your instructor or college computer center must make a copy of the master diskette for you or have you make your own copy of the master diskette (using the proper disk copy command). The instructions below assume you have your own student copy of *Computer-Based Marketing Exercises*, Windows 3.1 or higher is pre-loaded on your hard drive, and "A" or "B" is a 3-1/2 inch drive.

Switch on your computer and then initialize the Windows environment. Insert your *Computer-Based Marketing Exercises* disk into the 3-1/2 inch floppy drive (either A or B). From the Program Manager window, pull down FILE and then choose RUN. In the COMMAND LINE field, type "A:Setup" (without the quotes). (If your 3-1/2 inch drive is designated as B:, type "B:Setup".) Press [ENTER] or click OK with your mouse. (If you get a message to close any running applications before continuing, use the [ALT] + [TAB] keys to switch to other applications and then close them.)

On the CBME Exercise setup screen, click on the underscored C (or hold down the [Alt] key and then press the [C] key if you do not have a mouse or trackball) to transfer the exercise files to your hard disk. The program automatically creates the directory "C:\EXERCISE" for this program. If a directory currently exists with this designation, you will be asked to designate a new drive and path. Use the [Backspace] key to remove the "C:\EXERCISE" drive and/or path. Then, type a new drive and/or path. Click on the underscored C (or hold down the [ALT] key and then press the [C] key) to accept the new drive and/or path that you designated.

A dialog box then appears telling you that your installation is complete. Now click on the OK box (or hold down the [Enter] key). You can remove your disk from the floppy drive. Please store this disk in a location that is not subject to heat or a magnetic field.

You can now run *Computer-Based Marketing Exercises* from your hard drive. If you are still in the Windows environment, open the EXERCISE application by double clicking on the CBME exercises group icon and then double click on the exercises icon. If you do not have a mouse or trackball, you can open this program by pulling down FILE, choosing RUN and typing "C:\EXERCISE\EXERCISE.EXE". If you have designated a different drive or path, use that designation. If you have exited your computer and then return at another time, switch on the computer and initialize the Windows environment. Then, simply adhere to the instructions just cited.

The first time you run *Computer-Based Marketing Exercises*, you will be asked to insert your name, class, and section. Once you enter this information, it will appear on every computer screen and printout—and become a permanent part of your "exercise" program. It will not have to be repeated. The program will do the rest and guide you to the main menu.

Using a Network Some colleges and universities have PC networks for student use. Because there are many differences in the way these networks are set up and operated, please consult with your professor or someone in the computer lab with regard to using *Computer-Based Marketing Exercises*.

How to Use the Main Menu

When running *Computer-Based Marketing Exercises*, all exercises can be accessed from the MAIN MENU. Use the mouse to select an exercise and then double-click at the desired exercise. You can also choose an exercise by repeatedly hitting the tab key until the desired exercise is highlighted; then press the ENTER key. Selecting EXIT (or holding down the [ALT] key and then pressing the [E] key) will enable you to quit the program.

The menu is arranged in the order the topics appear in the text and shows page references so you may review concepts before or while doing an exercise. See Table 1.

How to Operate Each Exercise

At the bottom of each exercise screen, there are a number of commands. They include the EXIT button [E] to quit the program, the MENU button [M] to return to the main menu, the NEXT button [N] to proceed to the following screen, the BACK button [B] to return to the prior screen, the PRINT SCREEN button [P], the ANALYSIS button [A], and the TABLE button [T]. All commands can be executed by either double-clicking your mouse (or trackball) or by holding down the [ALT] key and then hitting the respective letter key. All decisions can be entered by clicking your mouse (or trackball) or by using the [TAB] key and appropriate cursor key.

How to Print from the Exercise Diskette

While using the exercise diskette, you may print any screen for your own reference or for the submission of a class assignment. Simply turn on the printer (either dot-matrix, letter-quality, or laser) that is connected to the computer you are using. Then, dou-

Table 1

Computer-Based Marketing Exercises Main Menu

ble-click on the PRINT SCREEN button [P] located at the bottom of each exercise screen (or hold down the [ALT] key and then press the [P] key). The screen appearing on your computer monitor will automatically be printed—including your name, class, and section.

The Exercises

In the following sections, each exercise is discussed. For every exercise, we present objectives, a list of the relevant key terms and concepts from the text, an explanation of the exercise, and questions/assignments to be answered or completed.

Exercise 1: Marketing Orientation

Objectives

1. To demonstrate selling versus marketing philosophies
2. To see the importance of customer service
3. To illustrate the components of a marketing orientation
4. To show how changes in attitudes affect a marketing orientation

Key Terms and Concepts

production era	*customer service*
sales era	*empowering employees*
marketing department era	*customer satisfaction*
marketing company era	*relationship marketing*
marketing concept	

Explanation of Exercise

As the owner of a local florist, a table allows you to enter your degree of agreement to ten questions (on a five-point scale ranging from strongly agree to strongly disagree). These questions relate to such areas as the importance of various markets, planning for seasonality, forecasting sales and profits, assessing customer needs, understanding the strategies of competitors, and selling flowers with a limited shelf life.

A summary table then rates your overall marketing orientation. For each of the ten questions, the most appropriate answer receives a +2 score, while the least appropriate response generates a score of −2. The total score can vary from +20 to −20, with +20 being the maximum marketing orientation and −20 being the lowest.

By responding differently to the various statements, you can determine an optimal philosophy in terms of the firm's total marketing orientation score.

The exercise is keyed to pages 11–17 in the text.

Questions/Assignments

1. Print out and evaluate your responses to the ten-question marketing orientation checklist.
2. Explain how the checklist is used to compute a firm's overall marketing orientation. Use your response to question/assignment 1 in answering this question.
3. Develop five additional questions that can be used to rate a retailer's overall marketing orientation.
4. What are the difficulties in measuring the overall marketing orientation of a firm through the use of this checklist?

Exercise 2: Boston Consulting Group Matrix

Objectives

1. To apply the Boston Consulting Group matrix to a firm's marketing planning activities
2. To see how a product category's relative market share and industry growth rate affect its placement as a star, cash cow, question mark, or dog
3. To consider the appropriate balance of stars, cash cows, question marks, and dogs for a firm

Key Terms and Concepts

strategic business unit (SBU)	*cash cow*
Boston Consulting Group matrix	*question mark*
star	*dog*

Explanation of Exercise

As a marketing executive for Packard Athletic Shoe Company, a table allows you to enter revised values for the relative market shares and industry growth rates for any or all of Packard's product categories (SBUs). The products are then displayed in a Boston Consulting Group matrix.

In this exercise, the dividing lines between high and low relative market shares, as well as high and low industry growth rates, are the average market share and the average industry growth rate for all of Packard's product categories. The averages change when you vary relative market shares and industry growth rates for individual product categories.

When examining the Boston Consulting Group matrix, study the balance of products in each grouping. For example, are there enough cash cows to support question marks? Also consider the balance of products for future periods. For example, where will future stars come from?

The exercise is keyed to pages 63–65 in the text.

Questions/Assignments

1. Print and evaluate a Boston Consulting Group matrix with these current percentage values for Packard Athletic Shoe Company: All-purpose sneakers—70 (share) and 4 (growth); Tennis sneakers—100 (share) and 6 (growth); Soccer shoes—20 (share) and 10 (growth); Bowling shoes—15 (share) and 3 (growth); Running shoes—250 (share) and 15 (growth); Low-impact aerobic shoes—75 (share) and 5 (growth); Walking shoes—125 (share) and 5 (growth); and Basketball sneakers—50 (share) and 15 (growth).
2. Print and evaluate a Boston Consulting Group matrix with these 2005 projections for Packard Athletic Shoe Company: All-purpose sneakers—150 (share) and 2 (growth); Tennis sneakers—70 (share) and 7 (growth); Soccer shoes—150 (share) and 10 (growth); Bowling shoes—50 (share) and 10 (growth); Running shoes—125 (share) and 7 (growth); Low-impact aerobic shoes—20 (share) and 5 (growth); Walking shoes—35 (share) and 10 (growth); and Basketball sneakers—50 (share) and 15 (growth).
3. Compare the current and projected matrixes. Will Packard Athletic Shoe Company be in a stronger, weaker, or equal position in 2005 than it is now? Explain your answer.
4. What should an ideal projected Boston Consulting Group matrix for Packard Athletic Shoe Company look like? Print the matrix and explain your answer.

5. What additional data do you need to better advise Packard Athletic Shoe Company in its strategic planning efforts?

Exercise 3: Questionnaire Analysis

Objectives

1. To implement a survey dealing with consumer attitudes, usage, and purchase behavior
2. To explore the differences between market segments via a survey
3. To see how data analysis is undertaken
4. To present recommendations based upon survey results

Key Terms and Concepts

marketing research	*research design*
marketing research process	*survey*
primary data	*data analysis*

Explanation of Exercise

In this exercise, you are a market researcher who is requested to collect data for a consumer survey on boom boxes (portable self-contained stereos with multiple speakers). The exercise screens explain how blank copies of the survey may be printed, as well as how the survey may be administered at the computer.

After interviewing respondents, you input their answers into the computer, and a summary of the responses is provided automatically—separated into boom box buyer and nonbuyer segments. The questionnaire consists of several questions and varies slightly for the two segments. For the analysis to be meaningful, you should interview at least 20 respondents; the program will accept as many as 50 respondents.

The exercise is keyed to pages 90–100 in the text.

Questions/Assignments

1. Prepare ten blank questionnaires each for boom box buyers and nonbuyers. Then interview ten boom box buyers and ten nonbuyers. Record their answers on the blank questionnaires (one per respondent) and enter these answers on your exercise program. Print a boom box questionnaire analysis screen summarizing the responses.
2. Analyze the data generated from question/assignment 1. Write a two-page report recapping the findings of your study. Make sure your analysis covers each question (including features, record option pricing, and color and brand preference).
3. Develop specific recommendations for the marketing of boom boxes.
4. Develop specific recommendations for the pricing of the record option, based upon your analysis in question/assignment 2.
5. Evaluate the questionnaire used in this exercise.
   a. Is the wording clear? Why?
   b. What additional questions should be asked?
   c. How else could the attitudes/behavior of recent boom box buyers versus nonbuyers be studied?

Exercise 4: Ethics in Action

Objectives

1. To study ethical behavior in detail
2. To distinguish between process-related and product-related ethical issues
3. To examine ethics from business, consumer, and international perspectives
4. To evaluate marketing strategies on the basis of ethical criteria
5. To see the range of business responses to consumer issues

Key Terms and Concepts

ethical behavior	*product-related ethical issues*
process-related ethical issues	*product recall*

Explanation of Exercise

As a marketing executive for an industrial-goods manufacturer, a table allows you to enter your degree of agreement to ten questions (on a five-point scale ranging from strongly agree to strongly disagree). These questions present a variety of ethical situations relating to salespersons, marketing managers, buyers, retailers, and importers.

A summary table indicates your firm's overall ethical orientation. For each of the ten questions, the most ethical answer receives a +2 score, with the least appropriate response generating a score of −2. The total score can vary from +20 to −20, with +20 being the maximum possible ethical score and −20 being the lowest possible score.

By responding differently to the various statements, you can affect the ethical nature of the industrial-goods manufacturer.

The exercise is keyed to pages 122–130 in the text.

Questions/Assignments

1. Print out and evaluate your responses to the ten-question ethics checklist.
2. Explain how the checklist is used to compute an overall ethics score. Use your response to question/assignment 1 to answer this question.
3. Develop five additional questions that can be used to measure the ethical behavior of a marketer.
4. How could you improve the overall ethical orientation of the industrial-goods manufacturer?
5. Do small firms have a greater difficulty being ethical than large firms? Explain your answer.

Exercise 5: Standardizing Marketing Plans

Objectives

1. To see the dynamics of international marketing
2. To study several components of an international marketing strategy: brand name, product design, manufacturing adaptation, advertising, and pricing
3. To consider the conditions under which a standardized (global), a nonstandardized, or a glocal marketing approach to international marketing is preferred
4. To demonstrate how specific changes in an international marketing strategy affect the overall level of standardization

Key Terms and Concepts

international marketing	*nonstandardized marketing approach*
global marketing	*glocal marketing approach*
standardized (global) marketing approach	

Explanation of Exercise

By answering a series of questions, you—as an international marketing consultant—are able to make decisions regarding the level of standardization for five factors: a product's brand name, its design, its manufacturing process, its advertising, and its pricing. You can vary each factor from pure standardized (global) to glocal to nonstandardized.

Each time you change a factor's level of standardization, the graph on the bottom of the exercise screen automatically moves to reflect the overall degree of standardization for your marketing strategy. All of the five factors are weighted equally. The graphic scale has fifteen gradation points.

This exercise is keyed to pages 163–170 in the text.

Questions/Assignments

1. A small U.S. detergent manufacturer that never exported its products to Mexico is now seeking entry into the Mexican market. The firm hopes that free trade due to the North American Free Trade Agreement (NAFTA) will stimulate demand for its products. Preliminary market research by the firm suggests that many upper-middle-class Mexicans employ domestic help to purchase detergents and wash clothes. These workers generally speak little or no English. The low current value of the Mexican peso relative to the U.S. dollar places many U.S. products out of the price range of low-income Mexican consumers. What do you recommend as the detergent manufacturer's level of standardization for each of the factors covered in this exercise? Print out and comment on your decisions.
2. You have been asked to develop a marketing strategy for a U.S.-based car maker that wants to begin selling four-wheel drive vehicles in Japan.
   a. What important questions regarding consumers, competition, distribution channels, and the legal and economic environment should you resolve prior to recommending a marketing strategy for the firm?
   b. Select an appropriate level of standardization for each of the factors covered in this exercise. Print out and comment on your decisions.
3. a. Under what conditions should a firm adopt a pure standardized marketing strategy? Why?
   b. Under what conditions should a firm adopt a pure nonstandardized marketing strategy? Why?
4. a. What problems would confront a PC maker with a pure standardized approach in all markets? Explain your answer.
   b. What problems would confront a PC maker with a pure nonstandardized approach in all markets? Explain your answer.

Exercise 6: Vendor Analysis

Objectives

1. To show the value of vendor analysis
2. To apply vendor analysis in an organizational consumer purchase situation
3. To show how changes in attribute weights can affect a company's overall vendor rating

Key Terms and Concepts

organizational consumer	*organizational consumer's decision process*
vendor analysis	

Explanation of Exercise

As the purchasing director for a firm, you are to assign weights to eight important vendor attributes: delivery speed, delivery reliability, product quality, quality of final customer support, quality of intermediate customer support, purchase terms, pricing, and availability of styles and colors in all sizes.

A table allows you to enter revised weights for each vendor attribute. The sum of your weights is then converted to 100 per cent automatically by the computer program. In addition, after you enter new weights, the program computes total rating scores for ten potential vendors, as well as the average total score for all vendors. Each vendor is also rated from unsatisfactory to excellent on the basis of its total score.

Mathematically, each vendor's total score equals your assigned weight (in per cent) for each attribute times the pre-assigned evaluation for each attribute (these evaluations cannot be changed by you), summed for all attributes. Attributes with higher assigned weights have the greatest impact on vendor analysis. One of the computer screens enables you to see the pre-assigned evaluations for all ten vendors.

The exercise is keyed to pages 236–240 in the text.

Questions/Assignments

1. Develop vendor analysis weights for the eight attributes for a photography specialty retailer seeking to evaluate multiple vendors. Assume that the retailer appeals to a sophisticated clientele, has high seasonality, and is concerned about product quality (particularly the handling of defective merchandise during the warranty period). Prepare a report evaluating all the vendors, keyed to the vendor data base and your attribute weights.
2. Develop vendor analysis weights for an auto maker that purchases steering wheels (which include airbags and wiring for horns) as complete units. A defective steering wheel can cause consumer dissatisfaction, a major product recall, and dealer service difficulties. Unreliable delivery schedules can cause a major production tie-up. Prepare a report evaluating all the vendors, keyed to the vendor data base and your attribute weights.
3. How do your weights for the vendors in questions/assignments 1 and 2 in this exercise differ? Explain your answer.
4. Develop specific recommendations showing how a poorly rated vendor can improve its evaluation.
5. Evaluate the vendor analysis technique used in this exercise.
   a. Are attributes appropriate? Why or why not? What specific attributes should be added?
   b. Are attributes equally appropriate for manufacturers, wholesalers, and retailers as customers?
   c. Comment on the information shown in the data-base screen.

Exercise 7: Segmentation Analysis

Objectives

1. To better understand the alternatives for developing a target market strategy: undifferentiated marketing (mass marketing), concentrated marketing, and differentiated marketing (multiple segmentation)
2. To show how the choice of a target market approach and alternative marketing budget levels affect a firm's sales and profitability
3. To relate such concepts as product differentiation, demand patterns, the majority fallacy, sales penetration, and diminishing returns to marketing budget allocations

Key Terms and Concepts

market
market segmentation
target market strategy
undifferentiated marketing (mass marketing)
concentrated marketing
differentiated marketing (multiple segmentation)
product differentiation
demand patterns
majority fallacy
sales penetration
diminishing returns

Explanation of Exercise

A table allows you, the vice-president of marketing for a medium-sized local company, to allocate a $3-million annual marketing budget between final and organizational market segments. By varying the budget, unit sales, sales revenues, manufacturing costs, total costs, and profit are affected. Different levels of marketing expenditures are required to be successful in each market segment.

The final consumer segment is large and very competitive. Consumers have many brands from which to choose. Although the organizational segment is much smaller, it has less competition. Selling prices and manufacturing costs also differ between the segments.

The exercise is keyed to pages 275–281 in the text.

Questions/Assignments

1. At what marketing budget level would you be most profitable in the final consumer segment? Print your optimal budget level for this market and explain your answer.
2. At what marketing budget level would you be most profitable in the organizational segment? Print your optimal budget level for this market and explain your answer.
3. Describe the basic differences between the final and organizational segments in terms of the relationship among sales, profits, and marketing expenditures. What does this mean to marketers?
4. At what marketing budget allocation levels would your firm's total profits be maximized? Print your optimal budget allocation and explain your answer. *NOTE:* You may use a differentiated marketing approach.
5. Explain how these concepts relate to the exercise:
   a. Product differentiation.
   b. Demand patterns.
   c. Majority fallacy.
   d. Sales penetration.
   e. Diminishing returns.

Exercise 8: Product Positioning

Objectives

1. To demonstrate the use of a product-positioning map as a tool for studying and evaluating consumer product perceptions
2. To show how a product position can be changed through price and nonprice factors
3. To illustrate how competitive and company product positioning are affected by modifications in marketing strategy
4. To consider which competitive product positioning strategies maximize the market share for a company's brand

Key Terms and Concepts

product positioning
ideal points

Explanation of Exercise

A product positioning map lets you—acting as an outside consultant—evaluate Hewlett Packard's (HP's) personal computer positioning relative to other major brands (Apple, IBM, Packard Bell, Compaq, and Dell). By rating HP's updated image on the basis of a series of statements, a revised product-positioning map for HP and five other brands is generated and displayed. In addition, the computer program calculates revised market shares for HP and the other brands, leading to an adjusted market-share table.

By responding differently to the various product-positioning statements, you can determine the optimal product-positioning strategy for HP, in terms of HP's market share and the market share for the other brands.

The exercise is keyed to pages 312–315 in the text.

Questions/Assignments

1. What series of responses to the statements on the exercise screens would result in HP being positioned in the prestige brands segment? Why? Print your input screens and the related product-positioning map.
2. What series of responses to the statements on the exercise screens would result in HP being positioned in the high-value brands segment? Why? Print your input screens and the related product-positioning map.
3. Which product position for HP results in its achieving a maximum market share? Why? Print your input screens and the related positioning map.
4. Which product position for HP results in its achieving a minimum market share? Why? Print your input screens and the related positioning map.
5. **a.** Evaluate the series of statements used in this exercise.
   b. Make specific recommendations to improve these statements.

Exercise 9: Services Strategy

Objectives

1. To distinguish between core and peripheral services
2. To explore the characteristics of services
3. To illustrate the development of a service marketing strategy

Key Terms and Concepts

service marketing
core services
peripheral services
intangibility of services
perishability of services
inseparability of services
variability in service quality

Explanation of Exercise

By making a number of marketing decisions, you—as a manager of a hotel chain—are able to develop an overall services strategy. You are seeking to increase your hotel's occupancy rate and profits by looking into free breakfasts, exercise facilities, and the use of a print shop. Each of these strategies can be offered at four different levels; cost data are provided for each level. By varying the level of each strategy, total revenues, costs, operating profit, and the hotel's occupancy rate are affected. You can revise your overall strategy by re-entering a new strategy.

This exercise is keyed to pages 327–338 in the text.

Questions/Assignments

1. Which overall strategy maximizes the hotel's sales revenues?
2. Which overall strategy maximizes the hotel's overall profit?
3. Explain the differences in these strategies.
4. The hotel chain is seeking to attract convention customers. Explain your choice of a services strategy for this segment.

5. The hotel chain plans to use a differentiated marketing strategy to attract both businesspersons and tourists. Explain your choice of services strategy for each segment.

Exercise 10: Product Screening Checklist

Objectives

1. To demonstrate the use of a new-product screening checklist as a product evaluation tool
2. To show how the importance of various product characteristics can be denoted
3. To illustrate how different assumptions regarding the importance of product characteristics and the ratings of individual attributes affect a product's overall rating
4. To consider what minimum overall evaluation score would be necessary for a product to successfully pass the product-screening stage of new-product planning

Key Terms and Concepts

modifications
minor modifications
major modifications
new-product planning process
product screening

Explanation of Exercise

A new-product screening checklist lets you—acting as an outside consultant who specializes in new-product concepts—weight the importance of various general, marketing, and production characteristics; and then rate a new product idea in terms of each of these characteristics. The computer program then computes separate indexes for general, marketing, and production factors—as well as an overall evaluation index.

Mathematically, every specific index equals the average of all of its attributes' weights times their ratings. Thus, the general characteristics index equals

$$\frac{\text{The sum of (Each attribute's weight} \times \text{That attribute's rating)}}{\text{The total weights assigned to general characteristics}}$$

The exercise is keyed to pages 362–370 in the text.

Questions/Assignments

1. As a new-product planning analyst at a major computer manufacturer, you have been asked to explore the feasibility of producing an inexpensive desktop computer designed especially for Internet users. Like traditional computers, this model comes complete with a keyboard, modem, floppy disk, and a color monitor. However, unlike traditional desktop units, it is priced at $500 retail—since it contains a slow microprocessor and no hard drive. In comparison, the least expensive computer currently produced by the firm is priced at $2,000 at retail. Preliminary market research reports indicate a large market potential for consumers who would like to "surf the net" but who do not wish to spend $2,000 or more for a computer. Print both the individual weights and ratings that you assign to the product, as well as the overall analysis screen.
2. **a.** Explain your choice of weights and ratings for each of the criteria in the new-product screening checklist for question/assignment 1.
   b. How should the computer manufacturer use concept testing with this product?
   c. Would you recommend that the manufacturer skip test marketing? Why or why not?
3. As a product manager for radios at General Electric (GE), you have been carefully following the new products produced by competitors. The most innovative clock radio of the 1990s is Bose's Wave Radio. Despite its small size, this radio provides sound that is comparable in clarity and richness to many full-sized stereos. Bose has accomplished this via a patented speaker design. In addition to its fine sound, the Bose Wave has features generally not found on a clock radio. These include a remote control device, a consumer's ability to fall asleep listening to one station and to wake up listening to another (also at different volumes), and twin alarms to accommodate different work schedules. GE currently makes clock radios priced from $15 to $75 at retail and is considering producing a $150 unit that incorporates some Wave Radio features. Print both the individual weights and ratings that you assign to GE's proposed new product, and the overall analysis screen.
4. **a.** Explain your choice of weights and ratings for each of the criteria in the new-product screening checklist in question/assignment 3.
   b. Should GE proceed further with this product? Why or why not?
   c. Comment on the risks inherent in marketing the new clock radio. Compare these to the risks in marketing a new personal computer.

Exercise 11: Economic Order Quantity

Objectives

1. To consider the overall ramifications of order size for a firm when it makes purchases
2. To examine the individual components of economic order quantity (EOQ): annual demand, wholesale unit costs, order-processing costs, and inventory-holding costs
3. To calculate economic order quantities
4. To see the impact of different assumptions on economic order quantity

Key Terms and Concepts

just-in-time (JIT) inventory system
quick response (QR) inventory system
stock turnover
economic order quantity (EOQ)

Explanation of Exercise

As the purchasing manager for a firm, you can determine its economic order quantity under various assumptions by answering questions about expected annual demand for a product, its unit cost at wholesale, order-processing costs, and inventory-holding costs (as a percentage of a unit's wholesale cost). The computer program uses the EOQ formula, and a screen graphically displays the results.

Mathematically,

$$\text{EOQ} = \sqrt{\frac{2 \times \text{Annual demand} \times \text{Order-processing costs}}{\text{Inventory-holding costs \%} \times \text{Unit cost}}}$$

The exercise is keyed to pages 435–439 in the text.

Questions/Assignments

1. **a.** How can order-processing and inventory-holding costs be estimated by a company?
   b. Explain how a just-in-time (JIT) inventory system can reduce a firm's order-processing costs.

c. Explain how a just-in-time (JIT) inventory system can reduce a firm's inventory-holding costs.

2. A mail-order office-supply retailer wishes to apply the EOQ concept to its purchases of key items to minimize the sum of its order-processing and inventory-holding costs. For example, it annually buys 2,000 units of an automatic electric stapler. The cost at wholesale is $8.00. Each order the retailer places with its supplier costs the retailer $10.00. Inventory-holding costs are 20 per cent of unit cost. Print and comment on the economic order quantity for the retailer.
3. Determine how each of the following (one at a time) impacts on the EOQ of the mail-order firm noted in question/assignment 2. Discuss these changes and print the relevant screens.
   a. Reduce annual demand from 2,000 to 1,500 units.
   b. Increase the cost at wholesale from $8.00 to $10.00.
   c. Reduce order-processing costs from $10.00 to $7.00.
   d. Raise inventory-holding costs from 20 per cent to 25 per cent.
4. Describe three situations in which the economic order quantity model would be inappropriate for the mail-order retailer.

Exercise 12: Wholesaler Cost Analysis

Objectives

1. To study the functions of wholesalers
2. To consider the characteristics of manufacturer wholesaling
3. To review the characteristics of merchant wholesaling
4. To determine under what circumstances manufacturer wholesaling or merchant wholesaling should be used

Key Terms and Concepts

wholesaling
manufacturer/service provider wholesaling
merchant wholesalers

Explanation of Exercise

As a consultant for a manufacturer, you have been retained to review that firm's selection of manufacturer wholesaling versus merchant wholesaling. The total costs of each wholesaling alternative differ on the basis of sales.

The costs for manufacturer wholesaling and merchant wholesaling are provided. These are based upon estimates of salesperson productivity, salesperson salaries, warehouse administrative costs, functional discounts, and channel manager costs for each wholesaler alternative. In computing these costs, note that some are fixed, while others are based upon sales volume. In addition, some cost elements are unique to the type of wholesaler used. For example, there are no channel manager costs under manufacturer wholesaling and no sales manager costs under merchant wholesaling.

After you enter your sales-volume forecast, the computer program automatically generates a screen showing total planned distribution costs under each alternative.

The exercise is keyed to pages 445–456 in the text.

Questions/Assignments

1. Calculate total distribution costs under manufacturer wholesaling and merchant wholesaling for projected sales volumes of $1 million and $3 million. Print and assess the results.
2. Calculate total distribution costs under manufacturer wholesaling and merchant wholesaling for projected sales volumes of $5 million and $10 million. Print and assess the results.
3. Under what conditions should a manufacturer use manufacturer wholesaling even though merchant wholesaling would be less costly?
4. Under what conditions should a manufacturer use merchant wholesaling when manufacturer wholesaling would be less costly?

Exercise 13: Advertising Budget

Objectives

1. To practice setting an advertising budget—using such concepts as reach, waste, and cost per thousand
2. To examine the characteristics of alternative magazines as advertising media
3. To see how the allocation of an advertising budget among various magazines affects promotion effectiveness
4. To study the match between magazine readership and the target market

Key Terms and Concepts

advertising media costs
reach
waste
cost per thousand
effective cost per thousand
narrowcasting
frequency
clutter
lead time

Explanation of Exercise

As the advertising director for Sunshine Cruise Lines, a leading cruise ship operator, one of your responsibilities is to allocate the firm's ad budget among various magazines via a computerized-spreadsheet table.

You make decisions with regard to the number of insertions (full-page 4-color ads) that Sunshine should make in these magazines during the year and the per cent of each magazine's audience that would be wasted for Sunshine. You are provided with the names of the magazines, their cost per full-page ad (equal to one insertion), and their reach. These data are from *Standard Rate & Data Service*. Based on your decisions, the computer program calculates the budget allocated to each magazine, its cost per thousand, and the effective cost per thousand. For instance, the effective cost per thousand for a specific magazine equals

$$\frac{\text{Advertising budget for a magazine}}{\text{Reach for that magazine} \times (100 - \text{Per cent waste})} \times 1{,}000$$

The program also derives company totals, using weighted averages. As an example, the total waste for Sunshine's magazine advertising equals

(% of magazine ad budget allocated to magazine A × % waste for magazine A)
+ (% of magazine ad budget allocated to magazine B × % waste for magazine B)
+ (other magazines, based on individual budgets and waste)

When choosing among the magazines, note that the number of placements is limited by each magazine's frequency. The computer program limits your placements to match each magazine's frequency. It is also important that your decisions be based upon the target market for Sunshine. Important target markets for the firm are newlyweds, retired couples, and singles.

The exercise is keyed to pages 532–538 in the text.

Questions/Assignments

1. a. Evaluate each of the magazines shown on the computer screen for this exercise in terms of cost per 1-page ad and

reach. These are the full titles of the magazines: *Cruise Travel, Ladies Home Journal, Modern Bride, Modern Maturity, People, Travel & Leisure, Travel Holiday,* and *TV Guide.*

b. Estimate waste as a percentage of reach for each magazine and explain your answer.

c. Allot a $2 million advertising budget roughly equally among all the magazines. Print and comment upon the results.

2. Sunshine's marketing vice-president has given you these guidelines in making your actual magazine budget expenditure decisions: You should spend as close to your entire $2 million magazine advertising budget as possible. You should use no fewer than five magazines. You should allocate no more than 40 per cent of the budget to any one magazine. The effective cost per thousand should be minimized.

a. Develop an advertising budget that meets these guidelines.

b. Print and explain your budget allocations.

c. What is the role of reach in your decision making?

3. Sunshine's marketing vice-president has decided to modify two of the guidelines stated in question/assignment 2. First, you may use as few magazines as you deem proper (you may even use just one magazine). Second, there are no restrictions on the maximum per cent of the $2 million budget that may be spent on any single magazine.

a. Develop an advertising budget that meets these guidelines.

b. Print and explain your budget allocations.

c. What are the pros and cons of concentrating your budget on fewer magazines?

4. Explain how each of these factors would affect your magazine advertising budget decisions:

a. Passalong rates (as a part of reach).

b. Narrowcasting.

c. Frequency.

d. Clutter.

e. Message permanence.

f. Lead time.

Exercise 14: Salesperson Deployment

Objectives

1. To practice setting a sales-expense budget
2. To see how the mix of accounts in a territory affects the required number of salespeople
3. To show how the level of customer service affects the required number of salespeople
4. To study how the use of telemarketing and catalog sales reduces the required number of salespeople

Key Terms and Concepts

sales-expense budget	*sales management*
order taker	*sales territory*
order getter	

Explanation of Exercise

As a regional sales manager, one of your more important responsibilities is to determine the required number of salespeople in your territory. Your firm has four types of industrial accounts ("A", "B", "C", and "D"). "A" accounts are key customers; "B" accounts have high potential but only moderate sales; "C" accounts are smaller firms with lower sales potential; and "D" are the smallest accounts. First, you make decisions on the number of accounts in each group: "A," "B," "C," and "D." Next, you can set the required call frequency for each account type. Finally, you need to determine the desired level of customer service: limited, regular, or intensive.

After you enter your decisions, the computer program generates a screen showing the required number of sales calls per year, the number of calls per salesperson per year, and the required number of salespersons. The required number of salespersons equals

$$\frac{\text{Required number of sales calls per year}}{\text{Number of calls per salesperson per year}}$$

The exercise is keyed to pages 561–567 in the text.

Questions/Assignments

1. Calculate the required number of salespeople when the firm has 50 "A" accounts, 150 "B" accounts, 1,000 "C" accounts, and 2,000 "D" accounts. The required call frequencies per year for "A," "B," "C," and "D" accounts are 50, 25, 10, and 3 respectively. Assume that the firm desires intensive service. Print and assess the results.
2. Calculate the required number of salespeople when the firm has 50 "A" accounts, 150 "B" accounts, 1,000 "C" accounts, and 2,000 "D" accounts. The required call frequency per year for "A," "B," "C," and "D" accounts are 50, 25, 10, and 3 respectively. Assume that the firm desires limited service. Print and compare the results to your answer in question/assignment 1.
3. Under what conditions would you recommend that a firm use limited service? Intensive service?
4. Describe the specific assumptions of the salesperson deployment model used in this exercise.

Exercise 15: Price Elasticity

Objectives

1. To illustrate the law of demand
2. To distinguish among elastic, inelastic, and unitary demand
3. To see how a firm can estimate demand at different price levels
4. To further explore the interrelationship among price, demand, total revenue, and price elasticity

Key Terms and Concepts

law of demand	*inelastic demand*
price elasticity of demand	*unitary demand*
elastic demand	*subjective price*

Explanation of Exercise

As the owner-operator of an auto-repair firm specializing in tune-ups, you are concerned about what price to charge for a basic tune-up. First, you answer a series of questions about the price range to be considered and the expected average amount of consumer demand (which may be expressed in fractions) at various prices. The computer program then calculates elasticity of demand for the various price intervals and graphically displays it.

Your answers affect the type of demand the firm would face at different prices. Demand may be elastic, inelastic, or unitary—based on the price elasticity formula discussed in the text.

The exercise is keyed to pages 591–594 in the text.

Questions/Assignments

1. You are considering the implementation of one of two price strategies: The low-end strategy involves traditional spark plugs and a one-year or 20,000-mile warranty (whichever comes first). In contrast, the high-end strategy involves

platinum-tipped spark plugs and a two-year or 30,000-mile warranty. You have done some preliminary demand analysis and estimate the following demand schedule:

Price	***Average Low-End Demand (Tune-Ups Per Day)***	***Average High-End Demand (Tune-Ups Per Day)***
$ 50	12	15
$ 60	10	12
$ 70	7	10
$ 80	3	7
$ 90	0	5
$100	0	0

Determine the price elasticities at the various prices for the two strategies. Print the computer-generated tables and assess them. Hint: Enter the numbers in two groups (one for low-end demand and another for high-end demand).

2. **a.** Could your firm utilize both a low-end and a high-end marketing strategy? Explain your answer.
   b. Based on the information provided for question/assignment 1, could you determine the most profitable price level for the firm? If yes, what is it? If no, why not?
   c. How could you improve your ability to estimate the demand at various price levels?
3. **a.** Present average customer demand levels so that price elasticity at every interval between $50 and $80 (at $10 intervals) is elastic. Print and discuss your answer.
   b. Present average customer demand levels so that price elasticity at every interval between $70 and $100 (at $10 intervals) is inelastic. Print and discuss your answer.
   c. Is it realistic that demand would always be elastic or always be inelastic over a broad price range? Explain your answer.
4. **a.** Under what conditions would the price elasticity of demand equal 0? Why?
   b. Under what conditions would the price elasticity of demand equal 1? Why?
   c. Print a demand curve screen showing both 0 and 1 price elasticities.

Exercise 16: Key Cost Concepts

Objectives

1. To study fixed and variable cost concepts in detail
2. To distinguish between total and average fixed costs and total and average variable costs
3. To show the effects of changes in fixed and variable costs on a variety of cost components
4. To see how fixed, variable, and total costs are related to the level of production

Key Terms and Concepts

total fixed costs
total variable costs
total costs
average fixed costs
average variable costs
average total costs
marginal costs

Explanation of Exercise

As a pricing consultant for Ultimate Audiovision, you answer questions about the fixed and variable costs of making the home-entertainment system at various production levels. Ultimate Audiovision contains a state-of-the-art 46-inch rear projection TV, a VCR, an AM/FM tuner, two tape decks, a CD player, a turntable, an amplifier, an equalizer, and two 200-watt speakers. The system has an oak-wood look and may be operated via an infrared remote control or manually.

First, you set the total fixed costs at two different production levels. Next, you set the average (per-unit) variable costs at four different production levels. NOTE: You should reduce per-unit variable costs as the production volume increases. After you enter your decisions, the computer program automatically generates a screen showing production levels; total fixed, variable, and overall costs; average fixed, variable, and overall costs; and the change in per-unit costs as volume increases.

The exercise is keyed to pages 614–616 in the text.

Questions/Assignments

1. You have been asked to prepare an analysis of home-entertainment system production costs for the purpose of gathering background data to be used in the development and implementation of Ultimate Audiovision's pricing strategy. You estimate that fixed costs would be $180,000 if 100 to 499 units are produced and $225,000 if production involves 500 or more units. You further estimate that average (per-unit) variable costs would be $3,000 if 100 to 299 units are produced, $2,700 if 300 to 599 units are produced, $2,400 if 600 to 899 units are produced, and $2,200 if 900 or more units are produced. Print and analyze a key cost calculations screen based on these data.
2. Use the same variable costs as in question/assignment 1, but assume that fixed costs are $195,000 for all production levels. Print the key cost calculations screen based on these data and compare it to the one you generated for question/assignment 1.
3. Using all the data from question/assignment 1, what would be the price-floor price at each production level (100 units, 200 units, 300 units, etc.)? Would you be willing to sell your full production of 1,000 units at the price-floor price? Explain your answers.
4. How could you use the information from this exercise to undertake traditional break-even analysis? Modified break-even analysis? What additional data would be needed to complete these analyses?

Exercise 17: Performance Ratios

Objectives

1. To evaluate company efficiency and effectiveness by using performance ratios
2. To apply several company performance ratios: sales efficiency, cost-of-goods-sold, gross margin, operating expense, net profit, stock turnover, and return on investment
3. To show the relationship between profit-and-loss statement values and company performance ratios
4. To build on the data in Appendix B relating to General Toy Company

Key Terms and Concepts

profit-and-loss (income) statement
performance ratios
sales efficiency ratio (percentage)
cost-of-goods-sold ratio (percentage)
gross margin ratio (percentage)
operating expense ratio (percentage)
net profit ratio (percentage)
stock turnover ratio
return on investment (ROI)

Explanation of Exercise

As a General Toy Company executive vice-president, you are quite interested in using performance ratios to measure your company's relative success or failure across several criteria. The pre-set data in this exercise (those programmed into the exercise diskette) are drawn from Appendix B in the text.

By entering new data onto a profit-and-loss screen, you can see the impact of changes in General Toy's sales efficiency, cost of goods sold, gross margin, operating expenses, net profit, stock turnover, and return on investment on the company's related performance ratios. For example, what would happen to ROI if General Toy's assets rise by 5 per cent?

After you input the new data, the computer calculates revised performance ratios and shows a screen summarizing all the ratios. The screen also stipulates whether each ratio is excellent, good, or poor—based on criteria that you may access via the exercise diskette.

The exercise is keyed to pages A-9–A-11 in Appendix B ("Marketing Mathematics").

Questions/Assignments

1. **a.** Evaluate General Toy's performance on the basis of the pre-set data appearing on the exercise screens. Print the relevant screens.
   b. What recommendations would you make to General Toy?
2. Enter these data on the profit-and-loss screen: assets—$1,120,000; gross sales—$1,000,000; returns—$200,000; ending inventory—$100,000; and operating expenses—$400,000. The other data categories should retain the pre-set values. Print the relevant screens and comment on General Toy's performance. Compare your answers with those in question/assignment 1.
3. Enter these revised data on the profit-and-loss screen: assets—$800,000; gross sales—$1,050,000; returns—$50,000; beginning inventory—$150,000; and operating expenses—$300,000. The other data categories should retain the pre-set values. Print the relevant screens and comment on General Toy's performance. Compare the answers with those in questions/assignments 1 and 2.
4. Enter these revised data on the profit-and-loss screen: gross sales—$1,050,000; returns—$50,000; beginning inventory—$50,000; purchases (new merchandise)—$300,000; and ending inventory—$50,000. The other data categories should retain the pre-set values. Print the relevant screens and comment on General Toy's performance. Compare your answers with those in questions/assignments 1, 2, and 3.

Exercise 18: Optimal Marketing Mix

Objectives

1. To apply and compare mass marketing, selective marketing, and exclusive marketing strategies
2. To determine the impact of specific marketing-mix factors on mass, selective, and exclusive marketing strategies
3. To see how the optimal marketing mixes for mass, selective, and exclusive marketing strategies may be calculated
4. To demonstrate the value of sales response curves

Key Terms and Concepts

alternative marketing mixes	*opportunity costs*
optimal marketing mix	*sales response curves*

Explanation of Exercise

A table allows you—the marketing director for a small industrial manufacturer—to make decisions regarding your firm's $3 million annual marketing budget. You have the ability to make decisions regarding the expenditures for advertising, personal selling, and distribution and to set the price for your product for each of three strategy alternatives: mass marketing, selective marketing, and exclusive marketing. Thus, you are involved with two distinct areas of decision making: (1) For each strategy alternative (mass marketing, selective marketing, and exclusive marketing), what is the best marketing mix? (2) Which strategy alternative should your firm pursue?

In setting prices, you must use penetration pricing (a range of $10 to $15) with mass marketing, moderate pricing ($20 to $34) with selective marketing, and skimming pricing (a range of $35 to $99) with exclusive marketing. When allocating the $3 million marketing budget, you assign values to advertising and personal selling; the computer subtracts these figures from $3 million and displays the amount you want to spend on distribution. The costs of making the product depend on which strategy alternative is involved. For example, an exclusive-marketing strategy requires a much higher cost to make the product than a mass-marketing strategy.

Once you enter decisions, the computer program automatically calculates and displays unit sales, revenues, total product costs, total costs, and profit. The results will differ substantially for the three alternative strategies.

The exercise is keyed to pages A-15–A-17 in Appendix B ("Marketing Mathematics").

Questions/Assignments

1. For each strategy alternative (mass marketing, selective marketing, and exclusive marketing), what is the best marketing mix? Print the relevant table and explain it.
2. Which strategy alternative should your firm pursue? Why?
3. If you could reduce your product costs by 10 per cent, which strategy alternative would you choose? Why? *NOTE:* This question/assignment requires you to make some computations with a calculator and should be answered after you respond to questions/assignments 1 and 2.
4. **a.** Develop separate sales response curves for price, advertising, personal selling, and distribution under a mass-marketing strategy.
   b. Develop separate sales response curves for price, advertising, personal selling, and distribution under an exclusive-marketing strategy.
   c. Compare the curves in a and b.

   NOTE: In deriving each sales response curve, vary only the factor for which you are devising that response curve (for example, price). Otherwise, you will not be able to trace the response to the single factor you are studying.

Appendix D

Glossary

A

Absolute Product Failure Occurs if a firm is unable to regain its production and marketing costs. The firm incurs a financial loss.

Accelerator Principle States that final consumer demand affects many layers of organizational consumers.

Accessory Equipment Portable industrial capital goods used in the production process that require moderate consumer decision making, are less costly than installations, last many years, and do not become part of the final product or change form.

Adaptation A firm's responses to the surrounding environment, while continuing to capitalize on differential advantages, including looking for new opportunities and responding to threats.

Additional Markups Can be used to raise regular selling prices if demand is unexpectedly high or costs are rising.

Adoption Process The mental and behavioral procedure an individual consumer goes through when learning about and purchasing a new product. It consists of five stages: knowledge, persuasion, decision, implementation, and confirmation.

Advertising Paid, nonpersonal communication regarding goods, services, organizations, people, places, and ideas that is transmitted through various media by business firms, government and other nonprofit organizations, and individuals who are identified in the advertising message as sponsors.

Advertising Agency An organization that provides a variety of advertising-related services to client firms. It often works with clients in devising their advertising plans—including themes, media choice, copywriting, and other tasks.

Advertising Media Costs Outlays for media time or space. They are related to ad length or size, as well as media attributes.

Advertising Themes The overall appeals for a campaign. Themes can be good or service, consumer, or institutional.

Agents Wholesalers that do not take title to products. They work for commissions or fees as payment for their services and are comprised of manufacturers'/service providers' agents, selling agents, and commission (factor) merchants.

Airways The fastest, most expensive transportation form. They are used for high-value, perishable, and emergency goods.

All-You-Can Afford Method A promotional budget method in which a firm first allots funds for every element of marketing except promotion; any remaining marketing funds then go to the promotion budget.

Approaching Customers The stage in the selling process that consists of the pre-approach and greeting.

Atmosphere The sum total of the physical attributes of a retail store or group of stores that are used to develop an image and draw customers.

Attitudes (Opinions) An individual's positive, neutral, or negative feelings about goods, services, firms, people, issues, and/or institutions.

Audience The object of a source's message in a channel of communication.

Augmented Product Includes not only the tangible elements of a product, but also the accompanying cluster of image and service features.

B

Backward Invention An international product-planning strategy in which a firm appeals to developing and less-developed nations by making products less complex than the ones it sells in its domestic market.

Bait-and-Switch Advertising An illegal practice whereby customers are lured to a seller that advertises items at very low prices and are then told the items are out of stock or of poor quality. There is no intent to sell advertised items.

Balanced Product Portfolio A strategy by which a firm maintains a combination of new, growing, and mature products.

Barter Era People's earliest use of the exchange process. With barter, people trade one resource for another.

Battle of the Brands Manufacturer, private, and generic brands each striving to gain a greater share of the consumer's dollar, control over marketing strategy, consumer loyalty, product distinctiveness, maximum shelf space and locations, and a large share of profits.

Benchmarking A procedure utilized by a firm for setting its own marketing performance standards based on the competence of the best companies in its industry, innovative companies in other industries anywhere around the world, the prowess of direct competitors, and/or prior actions by the firm itself.

Benefit Segmentation A procedure for grouping consumers into segments on the basis of the different benefits sought from a product.

Blanket Branding *See* Family Branding.

Blurring Gender Roles A consumer life-style in which more men are assuming the once-traditional roles of their wives, and vice versa.

Boston Consulting Group Matrix Lets a firm classify each strategic business unit (SBU) in terms of market share relative to major competitors and annual industry growth. The matrix identifies four types of SBUs—star, cash cow, question mark, and dog—and offers strategies for them.

Brand A name, term, design, symbol, or any other feature that identifies the goods and services of one seller from those of other sellers.

Brand Equity A branding concept that recognizes the worth of brands. It measures the financial impact associated with an increase in a product's value accounted for by its brand name above and beyond the level justified by its quality.

Brand Extension A strategy by which an established brand name is applied to new products.

Brand Image The perception a person has of a particular brand.

Brand Loyalty The consistent repurchase of and preference toward a particular brand. With it, people can reduce time, thought, and risk.

Brand Manager System *See* Product Manager System.

Brand Mark A symbol, design, or distinctive coloring or lettering that cannot be spoken.

Brand Name A word, letter (number), group of words, or letters (numbers) that can be spoken.

Broad Price Policy Sets the overall direction (and tone) for a firm's pricing efforts and makes sure pricing decisions are coordinated with the firm's choices as to a target market, an image, and other marketing-mix factors. It incorporates short- and long-term pricing goals, as well as the role of pricing.

Brokers Temporary wholesalers, paid by a commission or fee, who introduce buyers and sellers and help complete transactions.

Bundled Pricing An offering of a basic product, options, and customer service for one total price.

Business Analysis The stage in the new-product planning process which involves the detailed review, projection, and evaluation of such factors as consumer demand, production costs, marketing costs, break-even points, competition, capital investments, and profitability for each new proposed product.

Buyer-Seller Dyad A two-way flow of communication between buyer and seller.

C

Canned Sales Presentation A memorized, repetitive presentation given to all customers interested in a given item. It does not adapt to customer needs or traits but presumes a general presentation will appeal to everyone.

Cash-and-Carry Wholesaling A limited-service merchant wholesaler format in which people from small businesses drive to wholesalers, order products, and take them back to a store or business. No credit, delivery, merchandise, and promotional assistance are provided.

Cash Cow A category in the Boston Consulting Group matrix that describes a leading strategic business unit (high market share) in a mature or declining industry (low growth). A cash cow produces more cash (profit) than is needed to keep its market share.

Category Killer An especially large specialty store that features an enormous selection in its product category and relatively low prices.

Cause-Related Marketing A somewhat controversial practice in which profit-oriented firms contribute specific amounts to given nonprofit organizations for each consumer purchase of certain goods and services during a special promotion.

Cease-and-Desist Order A consumer-protection legal concept which requires a firm to discontinue a promotion practice that is deemed deceptive and modify a message accordingly.

Chain-Markup Pricing A form of demand-based pricing in which final selling price is determined, markups for each channel member are examined, and the maximum acceptable costs to each member are computed. It extends demand-minus calculations all the way from resellers back to suppliers (manufacturers).

Chain-Ratio Method A method of sales forecasting in which a firm starts with general market information and then computes a series of more specific information. These combined data yield a sales forecast.

Channel Functions The functions completed by some member of a channel: marketing research, buying, promotion, customer services, product planning, pricing, and distribution.

Channel Length Refers to the levels of independent members along a distribution channel.

Channel Members Those organizations or people participating in the distribution process. They may be manufacturers, service providers, wholesalers, retailers, and/or consumers.

Channel of Communication (Communication Process) The mechanism through which a source develops a message, transmits it to an audience via some medium, and gets feedback from the audience.

Channel of Distribution Composed of all the organizations or people involved in the distribution process.

Channel Width Refers to the number of independent members at any stage of distribution.

Class-Action Suit A legal action on behalf of many affected consumers.

Class Consciousness The extent to which a person seeks social status.

Clients The constituency for which a nonprofit organization offers membership, elected officials, locations, ideas, goods, and services.

Closing the Sale The stage in the selling process that means getting a person to agree to a purchase. The salesperson must be sure no major questions remain before trying to close a sale.

Clustered Demand A demand pattern in which consumer needs and desires for a good or service category can be classified into two or more clusters (segments), each having distinct purchase criteria.

Clutter Involves the number of ads found in a single program, issue, and so forth of a medium.

CMSA *See* Consolidated Metropolitan Statistical Area.

Co-Branding A strategy in which two or more brand names are used with the same product to gain from the brand images of each.

Cognitive Dissonance Doubt that a correct purchase decision has been made. To overcome dissonance, a firm must realize that the decision process does not end with a purchase.

Combination Compensation Plan A sales compensation plan that uses elements of both salary and commission methods. Such plans balance company control, flexibility, and employee incentives.

Combination Pricing A pricing approach whereby aspects of cost-, demand-, and competition-based pricing methods are integrated.

Combination Store Unites food/grocery and general merchandise sales in one facility, with general merchandise providing 25 to 40 per cent or more of sales.

Commercial Data Bases Contain information on population traits, the business environment, economic forecasts, industry and companies' performance, and other items.

Commercialization The final stage in the new-product planning process in which the firm introduces the product to its full target market. This corresponds to the introductory stage of the product life cycle.

Commercial Stock Brokers Licensed sales representatives who advise business clients, take orders, and then acquire stocks and/or bonds for the clients. They may aid the firms selling the stocks or bonds, represent either buyers or sellers, and offer some credit.

Commission (Factor) Merchants Agents that receive goods on consignment, accumulate them from local markets, and arrange for their sale in a central location.

Common Carriers Companies that must transport the goods of any company (or individual) interested in their services; they cannot refuse any shipments unless their rules are broken. They provide service on a fixed and publicized schedule between designated points. A fee schedule is published.

Communication Process *See* Channel of Communication.

Company-Controlled Price Environment Characterized by moderate competition, well-differentiated goods and services, and strong control over prices by individual firms.

Comparative Advantage A concept in international marketing which states that each country has distinct strengths and weaknesses based on its natural resources, climate, technology, labor costs, and other factors. Nations can benefit by exporting the goods and services with which they have relative advantages and importing the ones with which they have relative disadvantages.

Comparative Messages Implicitly or explicitly contrast a firm's offerings with those of competitors.

Competition-Based Pricing A pricing strategy approach whereby a firm uses competitors' prices rather than demand or cost considerations as its primary pricing guideposts. A firm can set prices below the market, at the market, or above the market.

Competitive Bidding A situation in which two or more sellers submit independent price quotes for specific goods and/or services to a buyer, which chooses the best offer.

Competitive Parity Method A method by which a firm's promotion budget is raised or lowered according to competitors' actions.

Component Life-Style A living pattern whereby the attitudes and behavior of people depend on particular situations rather than an overall life-style philosophy.

Component Materials Semimanufactured industrial goods that undergo further changes in form. They are expense rather than capital items.

Concentrated Marketing Exists when a company targets one well-defined market segment with one tailored marketing strategy.

Concept Testing The stage in the new-product planning process that presents the consumer with a proposed product and measures attitudes and intentions at an early stage of the process.

Conclusive Research The structured collection and analysis of data pertaining to a specific issue or problem.

Conflict Resolution A procedure in organizational buying for resolving disagreements in joint decision making. The methods of resolution are problem solving, persuasion, bargaining, and politicking.

Consolidated Metropolitan Statistical Area (CMSA) Has two or more overlapping and/or interlocking urban communities, known as Primary Metropolitan Statistical Areas, with a total population of at least one million.

Consumer Bill of Rights A statement by President Kennedy saying that all consumers have four basic rights: to information, to safety, to choice in product selection, and to be heard.

Consumer Demand Refers to the attributes and needs of final consumers, industrial consumers, wholesalers and retailers, government institutions, international markets, and nonprofit institutions.

Consumer Demographic Profile A demographic composite description of a consumer group.

Consumer Demographics Objective and quantifiable population characteristics. They are rather easy to identify, collect, measure, and analyze—and show diversity around the globe.

Consumerism Encompasses the wide range of activities of government, business, and independent organizations that are designed to protect people from practices that infringe upon their rights as consumers.

Consumer Price Index (CPI) A monitoring tool of the cost of living for many nations. It measures monthly and yearly price changes (the rate of inflation) for a broad range of consumer goods and services.

Consumer Products Goods and services destined for the final consumer for personal, family, or household use.

Consumer's Brand Decision Process Consists of nonrecognition, recognition, preference (or dislike), and insistence (or aversion) stages that consumers pass through.

Containerization A coordinated transportation practice in which goods are placed in sturdy containers that can be loaded on trains, trucks, ships, or planes. The containers are mobile warehouses.

Continuous Monitoring Used to regularly study a firm's external and internal environment.

Contract Carriers Provide transportation services to shippers, based on individual agreements. Contract carriers do not have to maintain set routes or schedules and may negotiate rates.

Controllable Factors Decision elements internally directed by an organization and its marketers. Some of these factors are directed by top management; others are directed by marketers.

Control Units The sales categories for which data are gathered, such as boys', men's, girls', and women's clothing.

Convenience Products Items bought with a minimum of effort because a consumer has knowledge of product attributes prior to shopping and/or is pressed for time. Types are staples, impulse products, and emergency products.

Convenience Store A retail store that is usually well situated and food-oriented, with long hours and a limited number of items. Consumers use a convenience store for fill-in merchandise, often at off-hours.

Conventional Supermarket A departmentalized food store with minimum annual sales of $2 million that emphasizes a wide range of food and related products.

Cooperative Advertising Allows two or more firms to share some advertising costs. It can be vertical or horizontal.

Core Services The basic services that firms must provide to their customers to be competitive.

Corporate Culture The shared values, norms, and practices communicated to and followed by those working for a firm.

Corporate Symbols A firm's name (and/or divisional names), logo(s), and trade characters. They are significant parts of an overall company image.

Corrective Advertising A consumer-protection legal concept which requires a firm to run new ads to correct the false impressions left by previous ones.

Cost-Based Pricing A pricing strategy approach whereby a firm sets prices by computing merchandise, service, and overhead costs and then adding an amount to cover its profit goal.

Cost of Living The total amount consumers annually pay for goods and services.

Cost-Plus Pricing A form of cost-based pricing in which prices are set by adding a pre-determined profit to costs. It is the simplest form of cost-based pricing:

$$\text{Price} = \frac{\text{Total fixed costs} + \text{Total variable costs} + \text{Projected profit}}{\text{Units produced}}$$

CPI *See* Consumer Price Index.

Culture Consists of a group of people sharing a distinctive heritage.

Customary Pricing Occurs when a firm sets prices and seeks to maintain them for an extended time.

Customer Satisfaction The degree to which there is a match between a customer's expectations of a good or service and the actual performance of that good or service, including customer service.

Customer Service Involves the identifiable, but rather intangible, activities undertaken by a seller in conjunction with the basic goods and/or services it offers.

D

Data Analysis The coding, tabulation, and analysis of marketing research data.

Data-Base Marketing An automated system to identify people—both customers and prospects—by name and to use quantifiable information about them to define the best possible purchasers and prospects for a given offer at a given point in time.

Data Storage Involves retaining all types of relevant company records (such as sales, costs, personnel performance, etc.), as well as the information collected through marketing research and continuous monitoring.

Dealer Brands *See* Private Brands.

Debit Transactions An arrangement in which, when a purchase is made, the amount is immediately charged against a buyer's account; there is no delayed billing without an interest charge.

Decline Stage of the Product Life Cycle The period during which industry sales decline and many firms exit the market since customers are fewer and they have less money to spend.

Decoding The process in a channel of communication by which a message sent by a source is interpreted by an audience.

Demand-Backward Pricing *See* Demand-Minus Pricing.

Demand-Based Pricing A pricing strategy approach whereby a firm sets prices after studying consumer desires and ascertaining the range of prices acceptable to the target market.

Demand-Minus (Demand-Backward) Pricing A form of demand-based pricing whereby a firm finds the proper selling price and works backward to compute costs. The formula used in demand-minus pricing is

$$\text{Maximum product cost} = \text{Price} \times [(100 - \text{Markup per cent})/100]$$

Demand Patterns Indicate the uniformity or diversity of consumer needs and desires for particular categories of goods and services.

Derived Demand Occurs for organizational consumers because the quantity of the items they purchase is often based on the anticipated level of demand by their subsequent customers for specific goods and services.

Desk Jobbers *See* Drop Shippers

Developing Countries Have a rising education level and technology, but a per capita Gross Domestic Product of about $2,000 to $4,000.

Differential Advantages The unique features in a firm's marketing program that cause consumers to patronize that firm and not its competitors.

Differentiated Marketing (Multiple Segmentation) Exists when a company targets two or more well-defined market segments with a marketing strategy tailored to each segment.

Diffused Demand A demand pattern in which consumer needs and desires for a good or service category are so diverse that clear clusters (segments) cannot be identified.

Diffusion Process Describes the manner in which different members of the target market often accept and purchase a product. It spans the time from product introduction through market saturation.

Diminishing Returns May occur in a firm with high sales penetration if the firm seeks to convert remaining nonconsumers because the costs of attracting them may outweigh revenues.

Direct Channel of Distribution Involves the movement of goods and services from producer to consumers without the use of independent intermediaries.

Direct Marketing Occurs when a consumer is first exposed to a good or service by a nonpersonal medium (such as direct mail, TV, radio, magazine, newspaper, or PC) and then orders by mail, phone, or PC.

Direct Ownership A form of international marketing company organization in which a firm owns production, marketing, and other facilities in one or more foreign nations without any partners. The firm has full control over its international operations in those nations.

Direct Selling A nonstore retail operation which involves both personal contact with consumers in their homes (and other nonstore locations) and phone solicitations initiated by the retailer.

Discretionary Income What a person, household, or family has available to spend on luxuries, after necessities are purchased.

Disposable Income A person's, household's, or family's total after-tax income to be used for spending and/or savings.

Distributed Promotion Communication efforts spread throughout the year.

Distribution Intermediaries Refers to wholesalers, retailers, and marketing specialists (such as transportation firms) that act as facilitators (links) between manufacturers/service providers and consumers.

Distribution Planning Systematic decision making regarding the physical movement of goods and services from producer to consumer, as well as the related transfer of ownership (or rental) of them. It encompasses such diverse functions as transportation, inventory management, and customer transactions.

Diversification A product/market opportunity matrix strategy in which a firm becomes involved with new products aimed at new markets.

Dog A category in the Boston Consulting Group matrix that describes a strategic business unit with limited sales (low market share) in a mature or declining industry (low growth). A dog usually has cost disadvantages and few growth opportunities.

Domestic Firm Restricts its efforts to the home market.

Domestic Marketing Encompasses a firm's efforts in its home country.

Donors The constituency from which a nonprofit organization receives resources.

Drop Shippers (Desk Jobbers) Limited-service merchant wholesalers that buy goods from manufacturers or suppliers and arrange for their shipment to retailers or industrial users. They have legal ownership, but do not take physical possession of products and have no storage facilities.

Dual Channel of Distribution A strategy whereby a firm appeals to different market segments or diversifies business by selling through two or more separate channels.

Dumping Selling a product in a foreign country at a price much lower than that prevailing in the exporter's home market, below the cost of production, or both.

Durable Goods Physical products that are used over an extended period of time.

E

Economic Community Promotes free trade among its member nations—but not necessarily with nonmember nations.

Economic Order Quantity (EOQ) The order volume corresponding to the lowest sum of order-processing and inventory-holding costs.

EDI *See* Electronic Data Interchange.

80–20 Principle States that in many organizations, a large proportion of total sales (profit) is likely to come from a small proportion of customers, products, or territories.

Elastic Demand Occurs if relatively small changes in price result in large changes in quantity demanded.

Electronic Data Interchange (EDI) Allows suppliers and their manufacturers/service providers, wholesalers, and/or retailers to exchange data via computer linkups.

Embargo A form of trade restriction which disallows entry of specified products into a country.

Empowering Employees When companies give their workers broad leeway to satisfy customer requests. Employees are encouraged and rewarded for showing initiative and imagination.

Encoding The process in a channel of communication whereby a thought or idea is translated into a message by the source.

End-Use Analysis The process by which a seller determines the proportion of its sales made to organizational consumers in different industries.

EOQ *See* Economic Order Quantity.

Escalator Clauses A form of price adjustment in which a firm is contractually allowed to raise the prices of items to reflect higher costs in those items' essential ingredients without changing printed list prices.

Ethical Behavior Based on honest and proper conduct.

Ethnicity/Race Should be studied from a demographics perspective to determine the existence of diversity among and within nations in terms of language and country of origin or race.

EU *See* European Union.

European Union (EU) Also known as the Common Market. The EU rules call for no trade restrictions among members, uniform tariffs with nonmembers, common product standards, and a free flow of people and capital.

Evaluation of Alternatives The stage in the final consumer's decision process in which criteria for a decision are set and alternatives ranked.

Exchange The process by which consumers and publics give money, a promise to pay, or support for the offering of a firm, institution, person, place, or idea.

Exclusive Distribution A policy in which a firm severely limits the number of resellers utilized in a geographic area, perhaps having only one or two within a specific shopping district.

Exempt Carriers Transporters that are excused from legal regulations and must only comply with safety rules. Exempt carriers are specified by law.

Experiment A type of research in which one or more factors are manipulated under controlled conditions. Experiments are able to show cause and effect.

Exploratory Research Used when a researcher is uncertain about the precise topic to be investigated, or wants to informally study an issue. It is also called "qualitative research."

Exporting A form of international marketing company organization in which a firm reaches international markets by selling products made in its home country directly through its own sales force or indirectly via foreign merchants or agents. An exporting structure requires minimal investment in foreign facilities.

Exporting Firm One that is just embarking on sales expansion beyond its home borders.

Extended Consumer Decision Making Occurs when a person fully uses the decision process. Much effort is spent on information search and evaluation of alternatives for expensive, complex items with which a person has little or no experience.

F

Fabricated Parts Industrial goods placed in products without further changes in form. They are expense rather than capital items.

Factor Merchants *See* Commission Merchants.

Family A group of two or more persons residing together who are related by blood, marriage, or adoption.

Family (Blanket) Branding A strategy in which one name is used for two or more individual products. It can be applied to both manufacturer and private brands, and to both domestic and international (global) brands.

Family Life Cycle Describes how a family evolves through various stages from bachelorhood to solitary retirement. At each stage, needs, experience, income, family composition, and the use of joint decision making change.

Family Values A consumer life-style that emphasizes marriage, children, and home life.

Feedback (Channel of Communication) The response an audience has to a message.

Feedback (Uncontrollable Environment) Information about the uncontrollable environment, the organization's performance, and how well the marketing plan is received.

Final Consumers Buy goods and services for personal, family, or household use.

Final Consumer's Decision Process The way in which people gather and assess information and choose among alternative goods, services, organizations, people, places, and ideas. It has six stages: stimulus, problem awareness, information search, evaluation of alternatives, purchase, and post-purchase behavior. Demographic, social, and psychological factors affect this process.

Flexible Pricing Allows a firm to set prices based on the consumer's ability to negotiate or on the buying power of a large customer.

Food-Based Superstore A diversified supermarket that sells a broad range of food and nonfood items.

Food Brokers Introduce buyers and sellers of food and related general-merchandise items to one another and bring them together to complete a sale.

Forward Invention An international product-planning strategy in which a company develops new products for its international markets.

Franchise Wholesaling A full-service merchant wholesaler format whereby independent retailers affiliate with an existing wholesaler to use a standardized storefront design, business format, name, and purchase system.

Freight Forwarding A transportation service in which specialized firms (freight forwarders) collect small shipments (usually less than 500 pounds each) from several companies. They pick up merchandise at each shipper's place of business and arrange for delivery at buyers' doors.

Frequency How often a medium can be used.

Full Disclosure A consumer-protection legal concept which requires that all data necessary for a consumer to make a safe and informed decision be provided in a promotion message.

Full-Line Discount Store A department store with lower prices, a broad product assortment, a lower-rent location, more emphasis on self-service, brand-name merchandise, wide aisles, shopping carts, and more goods displayed on the selling floor.

Full-Line Wholesalers *See* General-Merchandise Wholesalers.

Full-Service Merchant Wholesalers Perform a full range of distribution tasks. They provide trade credit, store and deliver products, offer merchandising and promotion assistance, have a personal sales force, offer research and planning support, pass along information to suppliers and customers, and give installation and repair services.

Functional Accounts Occur when natural account expenses are reclassified by function to indicate the purposes or activities for which expenditures have been made. Included as functional expenses are marketing administration, personal selling, advertising, transportation, warehousing, marketing research, and general administration.

G

GDP *See* Gross Domestic Product.

General Electric Business Screen Categorizes strategic business units and products in terms of industry attractiveness and company business strengths.

General-Merchandise (Full-Line) Wholesalers Full-service merchant wholesalers that carry a wide product assortment—nearly all the items needed by their customers.

Generic Brands Emphasize the names of the products themselves and not manufacturer or reseller names.

Generic Product The broadest definition of a product, centering on customer need fulfillment. It focuses on what a product means to the customer, not the seller.

Geographic Demographics Basic identifiable characteristics of towns, cities, states, regions, and countries.

Geographic Pricing Outlines responsibility for transportation charges. The most common methods of geographic pricing are FOB (free on board) mill pricing, uniform delivered pricing, zone pricing, and base-point pricing.

Getting By A frugal consumer life-style pursued by people because of economic circumstances.

Global Firm One in which, because domestic sales are low, there is great reliance on foreign transactions.

Global Marketing An advanced form of international marketing in which a firm addresses global customers, markets, and competition.

Global Marketing Approach *See* Standardized Marketing Approach.

Glocal Marketing Approach An international marketing strategy in which combining standardized and nonstandardized efforts lets a firm attain production efficiencies, have a consistent image, have some home-office control, and still be sensitive and responsive to local needs.

Goods Marketing Entails the sale of physical products.

Goods/Services Continuum Categorizes products along a scale from pure goods to pure services.

Government Consumes goods and services in performing its duties and responsibilities. There are 1 federal, 50 state, and 87,000 local governmental units.

Government-Controlled Price Environment Characterized by prices being set or strongly influenced by some level of government.

Gray Market Goods Foreign-made products imported into countries such as the United States by distributors (suppliers) that are not authorized by the products' manufacturers.

Green Marketing A form of socioecological marketing whereby the goods and services sold, and the marketing practices involved in their sale, take into account environmental ramifications for society as a whole.

Gross Domestic Product (GDP) The total annual value of goods and services produced in a country less net foreign investment.

Growth Stage of the Product Life Cycle The period during which industry sales increase rapidly as a few more firms enter a highly profitable market that has substantial potential.

H

Heavy Half *See* Heavy-Usage Segment.

Heavy-Usage Segment (Heavy Half) A consumer group that accounts for a large proportion of a good's or service's sales relative to the size of the market.

Hidden Service Sector Encompasses the delivery, installation, maintenance, training, repair, and other services provided by firms that emphasize goods sales.

Hierarchy-of-Effects Model Outlines the sequential short-term, intermediate, and long-term promotion goals for a firm to pursue—and works in conjunction with the consumer's decision process.

Homogeneous Demand A demand pattern in which consumers have rather uniform needs and desires for a good or service category.

Horizontal Audit Studies the overall marketing performance of a firm with particular emphasis on the interrelationship of variables and their relative importance. It is also known as a marketing-mix audit.

Horizontal Price Fixing Results from agreements among manufacturers, among wholesalers, or among retailers to set prices at a given stage in a channel of distribution. Such agreements are illegal according to the federal Sherman Antitrust Act and the Federal Trade Commission Act, regardless of how "reasonable" prices are.

Household A person or group of persons occupying a housing unit, whether related or unrelated.

Household Life Cycle Incorporates the life stages of both family and nonfamily households.

I

Iceberg Principle States that superficial data are insufficient to make sound marketing evaluations.

Idea Generation The stage in the new-product planning process which involves the continuous, systematic search for product opportunities. It involves new-idea sources and ways to generate ideas.

Ideal Points The combinations of attributes that people would most like products to have.

IMC *See* Integrated Marketing Communications.

Importance of a Purchase Related to the degree of decision making, level of perceived risk, and amount of money to be spent/invested. The level of importance of a purchase affects the time and effort a person spends shopping for a product—and the money allotted.

Incremental Method A promotional budget method in which a company bases its new budget on the previous one. A percentage is added to or subtracted from this year's budget to determine next year's.

Independent Media Communication vehicles not controlled by a firm; yet they influence government, consumer, and publics' perceptions of that firm's products and overall image.

Independent Retailer Operates only one outlet and offers personal service, a convenient location, and close customer contact.

Indirect Channel of Distribution Involves the movement of goods and services from producer to independent intermediaries to consumers.

Individual (Multiple) Branding Separate brands used for different items or product lines sold by a firm.

Industrialization of Services Improves service efficiency and variability by using hard, soft, and hybrid technologies.

Industrialized Countries Have high literacy, modern technology, and per-capita income of several thousand dollars.

Industrial Marketing Occurs when firms deal with organizational consumers.

Industrial Products Goods and services purchased for use in the production of other goods or services, in the operation of a business, or for resale to other consumers.

Industrial Services Involve maintenance and repair services, and business advisory services.

Industrial Supplies Convenience goods used in a firm's daily operation.

Inelastic Demand Takes place if price changes have little impact on the quantity demanded.

Information Search The stage in the final consumer's decision process that requires listing the alternatives that will solve the problem at hand and determining the characteristics of them. Information search may be either internal or external.

Innovativeness The willingness to try a new good or service that others perceive as risky.

Inseparability of Services Means a service provider and his or her services may be inseparable. Customer contact is often considered an integral part of the service experience.

Installations Nonportable industrial capital goods used in the production process that involve considerable consumer decision making, are very expensive, last many years, and do not change form.

Institutional Advertising Used when the advertising goal is to enhance company image—and not to sell goods or services.

Intangibility of Services Means that services often cannot be displayed, transported, stored, packaged, or inspected before buying.

Integrated Marketing Communications (IMC) Recognizes the value of a comprehensive plan that evaluates the strategic roles of a variety of communication disciplines—advertising, public relations, personal selling, and sales promotion—and combines them to provide clarity, consistency, and maximum communication impact.

Intensive Distribution A policy in which a firm uses a large number of resellers in order to have wide market coverage, channel acceptance, and high total sales and profits.

International Firm Goes beyond just exporting existing products by making modifications in those items for foreign markets or introducing new products there.

International Marketing Involves marketing goods and services outside a firm's home country, whether in one or several markets.

Introduction Stage of the Product Life Cycle The period during which only one or two firms have entered the market and competition is limited. Initial customers are innovators.

Inventory Management Involved with providing a continuous flow of goods and matching the quantity of goods kept in inventory as closely as possible with customer demand.

Isolated Store A freestanding retail outlet located on a highway or street.

Issue (Problem) Definition A statement of the topic to be looked into via marketing research. It directs the research process to collect and analyze appropriate data for the purpose of decision making.

Item Price Removal A practice whereby prices are marked only on store shelves or aisle signs and not on individual items.

J

JIT Inventory System *See* Just-in-Time Inventory System.

Joint Decision Making The process whereby two or more people have input into purchases.

Joint Venture (Strategic Alliance) A form of international marketing company organization in which a firm agrees to combine some aspect of its manufacturing or marketing efforts with those of a foreign company so as to share expertise, costs, and/or connections with important persons.

Jury of Executive or Expert Opinion A method of sales forecasting by which the management of a firm or other well-informed persons meet, discuss the future, and set sales estimates based on the group's experience and interaction.

Just-in-Time (JIT) Inventory System A procedure by which a purchasing firm reduces the amount of inventory it keeps on hand by ordering more often and in lower quantity.

L

Law of Demand States that consumers usually purchase more units at a low price than at a high price.

Leader Pricing A firm's advertising and selling key items in its product assortment at less than their usual profit margins. For a wholesaler or retailer, the goal is to increase customer traffic. For a manufacturer, the goal is to gain greater consumer interest in its overall product line.

Lead Time The period required by a medium for placing an ad.

Leased Department A section of a retail store rented to an outside party. The lessee operates a department—under the store's rules—and pays a percentage of sales as rent.

Less-Developed Countries Have low literacy, limited technology, and per capita Gross Domestic Product below $1,500 (sometimes less than $500).

Licensing Agreement A situation in which a company pays a fee to use a name or logo whose trademark rights are held by another firm.

Life-Style Represents the way in which a person lives and spends time and money. It is based on the social and psychological factors that have been internalized by that person—as well as his or her demographic background.

Limited Consumer Decision Making Occurs when a person uses every step in the purchase process but does not spend a great deal of time on some of them. The person has previously bought a given good or service, but makes fresh decisions when it comes under current purchase consideration.

Limited-Line Wholesalers *See* Specialty-Merchandise Wholesalers.

Limited-Service Merchant Wholesalers Buy and take title to products, but do not perform all the functions of full-service merchant wholesalers. They may not provide credit, merchandising assistance, or marketing research data.

Line of Business Refers to the general goods/service category, functions, geographic coverage, type of ownership, and specific business of a firm.

List Prices The regularly quoted prices provided to customers. They may be pre-printed on price tags, in catalogs, and in dealer purchase orders.

Local Content Laws Require foreign-based firms to set up local plants and use locally made components. The goal of these laws is to protect both the economies and domestic employment of the nations involved.

Logistics *See* Physical Distribution.

Loss Leaders Items priced below cost to attract customers to a seller—usually in a store setting.

Low-Involvement Purchasing Occurs when a consumer minimizes the time and effort expended in both making decisions about and shopping for those goods and services he or she views as unimportant.

M

Macroenvironment Encompasses the broad demographic, societal, economic, political, technological, and other factors that an organization faces.

Mail-Order Wholesalers Limited-service merchant wholesalers that use catalogs, instead of a personal sales force, to promote products and communicate with customers.

Major Innovations Items not previously sold by any firm.

Majority Fallacy Concept stating that companies sometimes fail when they go after the largest market segment because competition is intense. A potentially profitable segment may be one ignored by other firms.

Manufacturer Brands Use the names of their makers and generate the vast majority of U.S. revenues for most product categories. The marketing goal for manufacturer brands is to attract and retain loyal consumers, and for their makers to direct the marketing effort for the brands.

Manufacturers Produce products for resale to other consumers.

Manufacturer/Service Provider Wholesaling Occurs when a producer does all wholesaling functions itself. It may be carried out via sales offices and/or branch offices.

Manufacturers'/Service Providers' Agents Agents who work for several manufacturers/service providers and carry noncompetitive, complementary products in exclusive territories. A manufacturer/service provider may use many agents.

Marginal Return The amount of sales each increment of promotion spending will generate.

Markdowns Reductions from items' original selling prices to meet the lower prices of competitors, counteract overstocking of merchandise, clear out shopworn merchandise, deplete assortments of odds and ends, and increase customer traffic.

Market Consists of all the people and/or organizations who desire (or potentially desire) a good or service, have sufficient resources to make purchases, and are willing and able to buy.

Market Buildup Method A method of sales forecasting in which a firm gathers data from small, separate market segments and aggregates them.

Market-Controlled Price Environment Characterized by a high level of competition, similar goods and services, and little control over prices by individual firms.

Market Development A product/market opportunity matrix strategy in which a firm seeks greater sales of present products from new markets or new product uses.

Marketing The anticipation, management, and satisfaction of demand through the exchange process.

Marketing Audit A systematic, critical, impartial review and appraisal of the basic goals and policies of the marketing function, and of the organization, methods, procedures, and personnel employed to implement the policies and achieve the goals.

Marketing Company Era Recognition of the central role of marketing. The marketing department becomes the equal of others in the company. Company efforts are well integrated and regularly reviewed.

Marketing Concept A consumer-oriented, market-driven, value-based, integrated, goal-oriented philosophy for a firm, institution, or person.

Marketing Cost Analysis Used to evaluate the cost efficiency of various marketing factors, such as different total quality configurations, product lines, order sizes, distribution methods, sales territories, channel members, salespersons, advertising media, and customer types.

Marketing Department Era Stage during which the marketing department shares in company decisions but remains in a subordinate position to the production, engineering, and sales departments.

Marketing Environment Consists of controllable factors, uncontrollable factors, the organization's level of success or failure in reaching its objectives, feedback, and adaptation.

Marketing Functions Include environmental analysis and marketing research, broadening an organization's/individual's marketing scope, consumer analysis, product planning, distribution planning, promotion planning, price planning, and marketing management.

Marketing Information System (MIS) A set of procedures and methods designed to generate, analyze, disseminate, and store anticipated marketing decision information on a regular, continuous basis.

Marketing Intelligence Network The part of a marketing information system that consists of marketing research, continuous monitoring, and data storage.

Marketing Manager System A product management organizational format under which a company executive is responsible for overseeing a wide range of marketing functions and for coordinating with other departments that perform marketing-related activities.

Marketing Mix The specific combination of marketing elements used to achieve objectives and satisfy the target market. It encompasses decisions regarding four major variables: product, distribution, promotion, and price.

Marketing Myopia A shortsighted, narrow-minded view of marketing and its environment.

Marketing Organization The structural arrangement that directs marketing functions. It outlines authority, responsibility, and tasks to be done.

Marketing Performers The organizations or individuals that undertake one or more marketing functions. They include manufacturers and service providers, wholesalers, retailers, marketing specialists, and organizational and final consumers.

Marketing Plan Analysis Involves comparing actual performance with planned or expected performance for a specified period of time.

Marketing Research Involves systematically gathering, recording, and analyzing information about specific issues related to the marketing of goods, services, organizations, people, places, and ideas.

Marketing Research Process Consists of a series of activities: defining the issue or problem to be studied; examining secondary data; generating primary data, if necessary; analyzing information; making recommendations; and implementing findings.

Marketing Strategy Outlines the way in which the marketing mix is used to attract and satisfy the target market(s) and achieve an organization's goals.

Market Penetration A product/market opportunity matrix strategy in which a firm seeks to expand the sales of its present products in its present markets through more intensive distribution, aggressive promotion, and competitive pricing.

Market Segmentation Involves subdividing a market into clear subsets of customers that act in the same way or that have comparable needs.

Markup Pricing A form of cost-based pricing in which a firm sets prices by computing the per-unit costs of producing (buying) goods and/or services and then determining the markup percentages needed to cover selling costs and profit. The formula for markup pricing is

$$\text{Price} = \frac{\text{Product cost}}{(100 - \text{Markup per cent})/100}$$

Massed Promotion Communication efforts that are concentrated in peak periods, like holidays.

Mass Marketing *See* Undifferentiated Marketing.

Maturity Stage of the Product Life Cycle The period during which industry sales stabilize as the market becomes saturated and many firms enter to capitalize on the still sizable demand. Companies seek to maintain a differential advantage.

Medium The personal or nonpersonal means in a channel of communication used to send a message.

"Me" Generation A consumer life-style that stresses being good to oneself, self-fulfillment, and self-expression.

Membership Warehouse Club A retailing format in which final consumers and businesses pay small yearly dues for the right to shop in a huge, austere warehouse. Consumers buy items at deep discounts.

Merchant Wholesalers Buy, take title, and take possession of products for further resale. Merchant wholesalers may be full or limited service.

Message A combination of words and symbols transmitted to an audience through a channel of communication.

Message Permanence Refers to the number of exposures one ad generates (repetition) and how long it remains available to the audience.

Metropolitan Statistical Area (MSA) A relatively freestanding area not closely associated with other metropolitan areas, which contains either a city of at least 50,000 population or an urbanized area of 50,000 population (with a total population of 100,000 or more).

Microenvironment Encompasses the forces close to an organization that have a direct impact on its ability to serve customers, including distribution intermediaries, competitors, consumer markets, and the capabilities of the organization itself.

Minimum Price Laws *See* Unfair-Sales Acts.

Minor Innovations Items not previously marketed by a firm that have been marketed by others.

MIS *See* Marketing Information System.

Missionary Salesperson A type of sales support person who gives out information on new goods or services. He or she does not close sales, but describes items' attributes, answers questions, and leaves written matter.

Mixed-Brand Strategy Occurs when a combination of manufacturer and private brands (and maybe generic brands) are sold by manufacturers, wholesalers, and retailers.

Modifications Alterations in or extensions of a firm's existing products. They include new models, styles, colors, features, and brands.

Modified Break-Even Analysis A form of demand-based pricing that combines traditional break-even analysis with an evaluation of demand at various levels of price. It reveals the price-quantity mix that maximizes profits.

Modified Rebuy Purchase Process A moderate amount of decision making undertaken in the purchase of medium-priced products that an organizational consumer has bought infrequently before.

Monitoring Results Involves comparing the actual performance of a firm, business unit, or product against planned performance for a specified period.

Monopolistic Competition A situation in which there are several firms in an industry, each trying to offer a unique marketing mix—based on price or nonprice factors.

Monopoly A situation in which just one firm sells a given good or service and has a lot of control over its marketing plan.

Motivation Involves the positive or negative needs, goals, and desires that impel a person to or away from certain actions, objects, or conditions.

Motives The reasons for behavior.

Motor Carriers Transporters of small shipments over short distances.

MSA *See* Metropolitan Statistical Area.

Multinational Firm One in which corporate headquarters are in the home nation, but the domestic market often accounts for less than 50 per cent of sales and profits. The firm operates in dozens of nations or more.

Multiple Branding *See* Individual Branding.

Multiple-Buying Responsibility Two or more employees formally participating in complex or expensive purchase decisions.

Multiple Segmentation *See* Differentiated Marketing.

Multiple-Unit Pricing A practice whereby a firm offers discounts to consumers to encourage them to buy in quantity, so as to increase overall sales volume.

N

NAFTA *See* North American Free Trade Agreement.

Narrowcasting Presenting advertising messages to rather limited and well-defined audiences. It is a way to reduce the audience waste with mass media.

Nationalism Refers to a country's efforts to become self-reliant and raise its stature in the eyes of the world community. At times, a high degree of nationalism may lead to tight restrictions on foreign firms in order to foster the development of domestic industry at their expense.

Natural Accounts Costs that are reported by the names of the expenses and not by their purposes. Such expense categories include salaries, rent, advertising, supplies, insurance, and interest.

Need-Satisfaction Approach A high-level selling method based on the principle that each customer has different attributes and wants, and therefore the sales presentation should be adapted to the individual consumer.

Negotiation A situation in which a buyer uses bargaining ability and order size to get sellers' best possible prices.

New Product Involves a modification of an existing product or an innovation the consumer perceives as meaningful.

New-Product Manager System A product management organizational format which has product managers to supervise existing products and new-product managers to develop new ones. Once a product is introduced, it is given to the product manager.

New-Product Planning Process Involves a series of steps from idea generation to commercialization. The firm generates ideas, evaluates them, weeds out poor ones, obtains consumer feedback, develops the product, tests it, and brings it to market.

New-Task Purchase Process A large amount of decision making undertaken in the purchase of an expensive product an organizational consumer has not bought before.

Noise Interference at any point along a channel of communication.

Nondurable Goods Physical products that are made from materials other than metals, hard plastics, and wood; are rather quickly consumed or worn out; or become dated, unfashionable, or otherwise unpopular.

Nongoods Services Involve personal service on the part of the seller. They do not involve goods.

Nonprice-Based Approach A pricing strategy in which sellers downplay price as a factor in consumer demand by creating a distinctive good or service via promotion, packaging, delivery, customer service, availability, and other marketing factors.

Nonprofit Institutions Act in the public interest or to foster a cause and do not seek financial profits.

Nonprofit Marketing Conducted by organizations and individuals that operate in the public interest or that foster a cause and do not seek financial profits. It may involve organizations, people, places, and ideas, as well as goods and services.

Nonstandardized Marketing Approach An international marketing strategy in which a firm sees each nation or region as distinct and requiring its own marketing plan.

Nonstore Retailing Occurs when a firm uses a strategy mix that is not store-based to reach consumers and complete transactions.

North American Free Trade Agreement (NAFTA) An agreement that created an economic community linking the United States, Canada, and Mexico. It will remove tariffs and trade restrictions among the three countries over the next several years.

O

Objective-and-Task Method A promotional budget method in which a firm sets promotion goals, determines the activities needed to satisfy them, and then establishes the proper budget.

Observation A research method whereby present behavior or the results of past behavior are observed and noted. People are not questioned, and cooperation is unnecessary.

Odd Pricing Used when selling prices are set at levels below even dollar values, such as 49 cents, $4.95, and $199.

Oligopoly A situation in which a few firms—usually large ones—account for most industry sales and would like to engage in nonprice competition.

One-Price Policy Lets a firm charge the same price to all customers seeking to purchase a good or service under similar conditions.

Open Credit Account A credit arrangement in which the buyer receives a monthly bill for the goods and services bought during the preceding month. The account must be paid in full each month.

Opinion Leaders People to whom other consumers turn for advice and information via face-to-face communication. They normally have an impact over a narrow product range.

Opinions *See* Attitudes.

Order Cycle The period of time that spans a customer's placing an order and its receipt.

Order Getter A type of salesperson who generates customer leads, provides information, persuades customers, and closes sales.

Order Taker A type of salesperson who processes routine orders and reorders. The order taker typically handles goods and services that are pre-sold.

Organizational Consumers Buy goods and services for further production, usage in operating the organization, or resale to other consumers.

Organizational Consumer's Decision Process Consists of expectations, the buying process, conflict resolution, and situational factors.

Organizational Mission Refers to a long-term commitment to a type of business and a place in the market. It can be expressed in terms of the customer group(s) served, the goods and services offered, the functions performed, and/or the technologies utilized.

Owned-Goods Services Involve alterations or maintenance/repairs of goods owned by consumers.

P

Package A container used to protect, promote, transport, and/or identify a product.

Packaging The part of product planning where a firm researches, designs, and produces package(s).

Packaging Functions Consist of containment and protection, usage, communication, segmentation, channel cooperation, and new-product planning.

Patent Grants an inventor of a useful product or process exclusive selling rights for a fixed period.

Penetration Pricing Uses low prices to capture the mass market for a good or service.

Perceived Risk The level of uncertainty a consumer believes exists as to the outcome of a purchase decision; this belief may or may not be correct. Perceived risk can be divided into six major types: functional, physical, financial, social, psychological, and time.

Percentage-of-Sales Method A promotional budget method in which a firm ties its promotion budget to sales revenue.

Peripheral Services Supplementary (extra) services that firms provide to customers.

Perishability of Services Means that many services cannot be stored for future sale. A service supplier must try to manage consumer usage so there is consistent demand over various parts of the week, month, and/or year.

Personal Demographics Basic identifiable characteristics of individual final consumers and organizational consumers and groups of final consumers and organizational consumers.

Personality The sum total of an individual's enduring internal psychological traits that make the person unique.

Personal Selling Involves oral communication with one or more prospective buyers by paid representatives for the purpose of making sales.

Persuasive Impact The ability of a medium to stimulate consumers.

Physical Distribution (Logistics) Encompasses the broad range of activities concerned with efficiently delivering raw materials, parts, semifinished items, and finished products to designated places, at designated times, and in proper condition.

Pipelines A transportation form that involves continuous movement, with no interruptions, inventories, or intermediate storage sites.

Planned Obsolescence A marketing practice that capitalizes on short-run material wearout, style changes, and functional product changes.

Planned Shopping Center A retail location that consists of centrally owned or managed facilities. It is planned and operated as an entity, ringed by parking, and based on balanced tenancy. The three types of planned center are regional, community, and neighborhood.

Porter Generic Strategy Model Identifies two key marketing planning concepts and the options available for each: competitive scope (broad or narrow target) and competitive advantage (lower cost or differentiation).

Post-Purchase Behavior The stage in the final consumer's decision process when further purchases and/or re-evaluation of the purchase are undertaken.

Poverty of Time A consumer life-style where the quest for financial security means less free time.

Predatory Pricing An illegal practice in which large firms cut prices on products to below their cost in selected geographic areas so as to eliminate small, local competitors.

Prestige Pricing Assumes that consumers will not buy goods or services at prices they consider to be too low.

Price Represents the value of a good or service for both the seller and the buyer.

Price-Based Approach A pricing strategy in which sellers influence consumer demand primarily through changes in price levels.

Price Ceiling The maximum amount customers will pay for a given good or service.

Price Discrimination A form of demand-based pricing in which a firm sets two or more distinct prices for a product so as to appeal to different final consumer or organizational consumer segments. Price discrimination can be customer-, product-, time-, or place-based.

Price Elasticity of Demand Indicates the sensitivity of buyers to price changes in terms of the quantities they will purchase. It is computed by dividing the percentage change in quantity demanded by the percentage change in price charged.

Price Floor The lowest acceptable price a firm can charge and attain its profit goal.

Price-Floor Pricing A form of cost-based pricing whereby a firm determines the lowest price at which it is worthwhile to increase the amount of goods or services it makes available for sale.

Price Guarantees Assure resellers that the prices they pay are the lowest available. Any discount given to competitors will also be given to the original purchasers.

Price Leadership A form of competition-based pricing in which one firm is (or a few firms are) usually the first to announce price changes and others in the industry follow.

Price Lining Involves selling products at a range of prices, with each representing a distinct level of quality (or features).

Price Planning Systematic decision making by an organization regarding all aspects of pricing.

Price-Quality Association A concept stating that consumers may believe high prices represent high quality and low prices represent low quality.

Price Wars Situations in which various firms continually try to undercut each other's prices to draw customers.

Primary Data Consist of information gathered to address a specific issue or problem at hand.

Primary Demand Consumer demand for a product category. It is important when a good or service is little known.

Private (Dealer) Brands Use names designated by their resellers, usually wholesalers or retailers, and account for sizable U.S. revenues in many product categories. Resellers have more exclusive rights for these brands, and are more responsible for distribution and larger purchases.

Private Carriers Shippers with their own transportation facilities.

Problem Awareness The stage in the final consumer's decision process during which a consumer recognizes that the good, service, organization, person, place, or idea under consideration may solve a problem of shortage or unfulfilled desire.

Problem Definition *See* Issue Definition.

Process-Related Ethical Issues Involve the unethical use of marketing strategies or tactics.

Product Consists of a bundle of attributes capable of exchange or use, usually a mix of tangible and intangible forms. It may be an idea, a physical entity, or a service, or any combination of the three.

Product Adaptation An international product-planning strategy in which domestic products are modified to meet foreign language needs, taste preferences, climates, electrical requirements, laws, and/or other factors.

Product Development A product/market opportunity matrix strategy in which a firm develops new or modified products to appeal to present markets.

Product Development Stage of New-Product Planning Converts an idea for a new product into a tangible form and identifies a basic marketing strategy.

Product Differentiation Occurs when a product offering is perceived by the consumer to differ from its competition on any physical or nonphysical product characteristic, including price.

Production Era Devotion to the physical distribution of products due to high demand and low competition. Consumer research, product modifications, and adapting to consumer needs are unnecessary.

Product Item A specific model, brand, or size of a product that a company sells.

Product Life Cycle A concept that attempts to describe a product's sales, competitors, profits, customers, and marketing emphasis from its beginning until it is removed from the market. It is divided into introduction, growth, maturity, and decline stages.

Product Line A group of closely related product items.

Product (Brand) Manager System A product management organizational format under which there is a level of middle managers, each of whom is responsible for planning, coordinating, and monitoring the performance of a single product (brand) or a small group of products (brands). The managers handle both new and existing products and are involved with all the marketing activities related to their product or group of products.

Product/Market Opportunity Matrix Identifies four alternative marketing strategies to maintain and/or increase sales of business units and products: market penetration, market development, product development, and diversification.

Product Mix Consists of all the different product lines a firm offers. It can be described in terms of its width, depth, and consistency.

Product Planning Systematic decision making relating to all aspects of the development and management of a firm's products, including branding and packaging.

Product Planning Committee A product management organizational format staffed by high-level executives from various functional areas in a firm, such as marketing, production, engineering, finance, and research and development. It handles product approval, evaluation, and development on a part-time basis.

Product Positioning Enables a firm to map each of its products in terms of consumer perceptions and desires, competition, other company products, and environmental changes.

Product Recall The primary enforcement tool of the Consumer Product Safety Commission, whereby the Commission asks—orders, if need be—firms to recall and modify (or discontinue) unsafe products.

Product-Related Ethical Issues Involve the ethical appropriateness of marketing certain products.

Product Screening The stage in the new-product planning process when poor, unsuitable, or otherwise unattractive ideas are weeded out from further consideration.

Profit-Based Pricing Objectives Those that orient a firm's pricing strategy toward some type of profit goals: profit maximization, satisfactory profit, return on investment, and/or early recovery of cash.

Promotion Any communication used to inform, persuade, and/or remind people about an organization's or individual's goods, services, image, ideas, community involvement, or impact on society.

Promotion Mix A firm's overall and specific communication program, including its involvement with advertising, public relations (publicity), personal selling, and/or sales promotion.

Promotion Planning Systematic decision making relating to all aspects of an organization's or individual's communications efforts.

Prospecting The stage in the selling process which generates a list of customer leads. It is common with outside selling, and can be blind or lead in orientation.

Publicity The form of public relations that entails nonpersonal communication passed on via various media but not paid for by an identified sponsor.

Publicity Types Consist of news publicity, business feature articles, service feature articles, finance releases, product releases, pictorial releases, video news releases, background editorial material, and emergency publicity.

Public Relations Includes any communication to foster a favorable image for goods, services, organizations, people, places, and ideas among various publics—such as consumers, investors, government, channel members, employees, and the general public.

Publics' Demand Refers to the attributes and needs of employees, unions, stockholders, the general public, government agencies, consumer groups, and other internal and external forces that affect company operations.

Pulling Strategy Occurs when a firm first stimulates consumer demand and then gains dealer support.

Purchase Act The stage in the final consumer's decision process in which there is an exchange of money, a promise to pay, or support in return for ownership of a specific good, the performance of a specific service, and so on.

Purchase Terms The provisions of price agreements.

Pure Competition A situation in which many firms sell virtually identical goods or services and they are unable to create differential advantages.

Pushing Strategy Occurs when various firms in a distribution channel cooperate in marketing a product.

Q

QR Inventory System *See* Quick Response Inventory System.

Question Mark A category in the Boston Consulting Group matrix which describes a strategic business unit that has had little impact (low market share) in an expanding industry (high growth). A question mark needs a big marketing investment in the face of strong competition.

Quick Response (QR) Inventory System A cooperative effort between retailers and suppliers to reduce retail inventory while providing a merchandise supply that more closely addresses the actual buying patterns of consumers.

R

Rack Jobbers Full-service merchant wholesalers that furnish the racks or shelves on which products are displayed. They own the products on the racks, selling them on a consignment basis.

Railroads Transporters of heavy, bulky items that are low in value (relative to weight) over long distances.

Raw Materials Unprocessed primary industrial materials from extractive and agricultural industries. They are expense rather than capital items.

Reach Refers to the number of viewers, readers, or listeners in a medium's audience. For TV and radio, it is the total number of people who watch or listen to an ad. For print media, it has two aspects: circulation and passalong rate.

Real Income The amount of income earned in a year adjusted by the rate of inflation.

Rebates A form of price adjustment in which cash refunds are given directly from the manufacturer to the customer to stimulate the purchase of an item or a group of items.

Reciprocity A procedure by which organizational consumers select suppliers that agree to purchase goods and services, as well as sell them.

Reference Group A group that influences a person's thoughts or actions.

Relationship Marketing Exists when marketing activities are performed with the conscious intention of developing and managing long-term, trusting relationships with customers.

Relative Product Failure Occurs if a firm makes a profit on an item but that product does not reach profit goals and/or adversely affects a firm's image.

Rented-Goods Services Involve the leasing of goods for a specified period of time.

Reorder Point Sets an inventory level at which new orders must be placed. It depends on order lead time, the usage rate, and safety stock. The reorder point formula is

Reorder point = (Order lead time × Usage rate) + (Safety stock)

Research Design Outlines the procedures for collecting and analyzing data. It includes decisions relating to the person collecting data, data to be collected, group of people or objects studied, data-collection techniques employed, study costs, method of data collection, length of study period and time, and location of data collection.

Retail Chain Involves common ownership of multiple outlets.

Retail Cooperative A format that allows independent retailers to share purchases, storage and shipping facilities, advertising, planning, and other tasks.

Retailers Buy or handle goods and services for sale (resale) to the final (ultimate) consumer.

Retail Franchising A contractual agreement between a franchisor (a manufacturer, wholesaler, or service sponsor) and a retail franchisee, which allows the latter to run a certain form of business under an established name and according to specific rules.

Retailing Encompasses those business activities involved with the sale of goods and services to the final consumer for personal, family, or household use. It is the final stage in a channel of distribution.

Retail Store Strategy Mix Consists of an integrated combination of hours, location, assortment, service, advertising, prices, and other factors retailers employ.

Revolving Credit Account A credit arrangement in which the buyer agrees to make minimum monthly payments during an extended period of time and pays interest on outstanding balances.

Robinson-Patman Act Prohibits manufacturers and wholesalers from price discrimination in dealing with different channel-member purchasers of products with "like quality" if the effect of such discrimination is to injure competition.

Routine Consumer Decision Making Occurs when a person buys out of habit and skips steps in the decision process. In this category are items with which a person has much experience.

S

Sales Analysis The detailed study of sales data for the purpose of appraising the appropriateness and effectiveness of a marketing strategy.

Sales-Based Pricing Objectives Goals that orient a company's pricing strategy toward high sales volume and/or expanding its share of sales relative to competitors.

Sales Engineer A type of sales support person who accompanies an order getter if a very technical or complex item is being sold. He or she discusses specifications and long-range uses.

Sales Era Involves hiring a sales force and sometimes advertising to sell inventory, after production is maximized. The role of the sales force and advertising is to make consumer desires fit the features of the products offered.

Sales Exception Reporting Highlights situations where sales goals are not met or sales opportunities are present.

Sales-Expense Budget Allots selling costs among salespeople, products, customers, and geographic areas for a given period.

Sales Forecast Outlines expected company sales for a specific good or service to a specific consumer group over a specific period of time under a specific marketing program.

Sales Management Planning, implementing, and controlling the personal sales function. It covers employee selection, training, territory allocation, compensation, and supervision.

Sales Penetration The degree to which a firm is meeting its sales potential:

Sales penetration = Actual sales/Sales potential

Sales Presentation The stage in the selling process that includes a verbal description of a product, its benefits, options and models, price, associated services like delivery and warranty, and a demonstration (if needed).

Sales Promotion Involves paid marketing communication activities (other than advertising, publicity, or personal selling) that are intended to stimulate consumer purchases and dealer effectiveness. Included are trade shows, premiums, incentives, giveaways, demonstrations, and various other efforts not in the ordinary promotion routine.

Sales Promotion Conditions Requirements channel members or consumers must meet to be eligible for a specific sales promotion.

Sales Promotion Orientation Refers to its focus—channel members or consumers—and its theme.

Sales Territory Consists of the geographic area, customers, and/or product lines assigned to a salesperson.

Sampling Requires the analysis of selected people or objects in the designated population, rather than all of them.

SBU *See* Strategic Business Unit.

Scientific Method A philosophy for marketing research that incorporates objectivity, accuracy, and thoroughness.

Scrambled Merchandising Occurs if a retailer adds goods and services that are unrelated to each other and the firm's original business.

Secondary Data Consist of information not collected for the issue or problem at hand but for some other purpose. The two types of secondary data are internal and external.

Selective Demand Consumer demand for a particular brand.

Selective Distribution A policy in which a firm employs a moderate number of resellers.

Self-Fulfilling Prophecy A situation in which a firm predicts falling sales and then ensures this by reducing or removing marketing support.

Selling Against the Brand A practice used by wholesalers and retailers, whereby they stock well-known brands, place high prices on them, and then sell other brands for lower prices.

Selling Agents Agents that are responsible for marketing the entire output of a manufacturer/service provider under a contractual agreement. They perform all wholesale tasks except taking title to products.

Selling Process Consists of prospecting for leads, approaching customers, determining consumer wants, giving a sales presentation, answering questions, closing the sale, and following up.

Semantic Differential A survey technique using rating scales of bipolar (opposite) adjectives. An overall company or product profile is then devised.

Service Blueprint A visual portrayal of the service process by a firm. It is essentially a detailed map or flowchart.

Service Gap The difference between customer expectations and actual service performance.

Service Marketing Encompasses the rental of goods, servicing goods owned by consumers, and personal services.

Service Salesperson A type of sales support person who ordinarily deals with customers after sales. Delivery, installation, and other follow-up tasks are done.

Shopping Products Items for which consumers feel they lack sufficient information about product alternatives and their attributes (or prices), and therefore must acquire further knowledge in order to make a purchase decision. Two major kinds of shopping products are attribute-based and price-based.

SIC *See* Standard Industrial Classification.

Simulation A computer-based method to test the potential effects of various marketing factors via a software program rather than real-world applications.

Single-Source Data Collection A technique that allows research firms to track the activities of individual consumer households from the programs they watch on TV to the products they purchase at stores.

Situational Factors Those that can interrupt the organizational consumer's decision process and the actual selection of a supplier or brand. They include strikes, machine breakdowns, organizational changes, and so on.

Situation Analysis The identification of an organization's internal strengths and weaknesses and external opportunities and threats. It seeks to answer: Where is a firm now? In what direction is it headed?

Skimming Pricing Uses high prices to attract the market segment more concerned with product quality, uniqueness, or status than price.

Social Class A status hierarchy by which groups and individuals are classified on the basis of esteem and prestige. Social classes are based on income, occupation, education, and type of dwelling.

Social Marketing The use of marketing to increase the acceptability of social ideas.

Social Performance Refers to how a person carries out his or her roles as a worker, family member, citizen, and friend.

Social Responsibility Involves a concern for the consequences of a person's or firm's acts as they might affect the interests of others. Corporate social responsibility balances a company's short-term profit needs with long-term societal needs.

Social Styles Model A classification system for segmenting organizational consumers in terms of a broad range of demographic and life-style factors. The model divides the personnel representing those consumers into life-style categories.

Socioecological View of Marketing Considers all the stages in a product's life span in developing, selling, purchasing, using, and disposing of that product. It incorporates the interests of everyone affected by a good's or service's use.

Sorting Process The distribution activities of accumulation, allocation, sorting, and assorting. Through this process, intermediaries can resolve the differences in the goals of manufacturers and consumers.

Source A company, an independent institution, or an opinion leader seeking to present a message to an audience. It is part of the channel of communication.

Specialty-Merchandise (Limited-Line) Wholesalers Full-service merchant wholesalers that concentrate on a rather narrow product range and have an extensive selection in that range.

Specialty Products Particular brands, stores, and persons to which consumers are loyal. People are fully aware of these products and their attributes prior to making a purchase decision. They will make a significant effort to acquire the brand desired and will pay an above-average price.

Specialty Store A retailer that concentrates on one product line.

Standard Industrial Classification (SIC) A coding system compiled by the U.S. Office of Management and Budget which may be used to derive information about most organizational consumers. It assigns organizations to eleven industrial classifications.

Standardized (Global) Marketing Approach An international marketing strategy in which a firm uses a common marketing plan for all nations in which it operates—because the firm assumes that worldwide markets are becoming more homogeneous due to better communications, more open country borders, the move to free-market economies, and other factors.

Standard of Living Refers to the average quantity and quality of goods and services that are owned and consumed in a given nation.

Star A category in the Boston Consulting Group matrix that describes a leading strategic business unit (high market share) in an expanding industry (high growth). A star can generate substantial profits but requires financing for continued growth.

Status Quo-Based Pricing Objectives Sought by a firm interested in continuing a favorable business climate for its operations or in stability.

Stimulus A cue (social, commercial, or noncommercial) or a drive (physical) meant to motivate a person to act.

Stock Turnover The number of times during a stated period (usually one year) that average inventory on hand is sold. Stock turnover is calculated in units or dollars (in selling price or at cost):

$$\text{Annual rate of stock turnover (in units)} = \frac{\text{Number of units sold during year}}{\text{Average inventory on hand (in units)}}$$

or

$$\text{Annual rate of stock turnover (in dollars)} = \frac{\text{Net yearly sales}}{\text{Average inventory on hand (valued in sales dollars)}}$$

or

$$\text{Annual rate of stock turnover (in dollars)} = \frac{\text{Cost of goods sold}}{\text{Average inventory on hand (valued at cost)}}$$

Straight Commission Plan A sales compensation plan in which a salesperson's earnings are directly related to sales, profits, customer satisfaction, or some other type of performance.

Straight Extension An international product-planning strategy in which a firm makes and markets the same products for domestic and foreign sales.

Straight-Rebuy Purchase Process Routine reordering by organizational consumers for the purchase of inexpensive items bought regularly.

Straight Salary Plan A sales compensation plan in which a salesperson is paid a flat amount per time period.

Strategic Alliance *See* Joint Venture.

Strategic Business Plan Describes the overall direction an organization will pursue within its chosen environment and guides the allocation of resources and effort. It integrates the perspectives of functional departments and operating units.

Strategic Business Unit (SBU) A self-contained division, product line, or product department in an organization with a specific market focus and a manager with complete responsibility for integrating all functions into a strategy.

Strategic Marketing Plan Outlines the marketing actions to undertake, why those actions are needed, who is responsible for carrying them out, when and where they will be completed, and how they will be coordinated.

Strategic Planning Process Consists of seven interrelated steps: defining organizational mission, establishing strategic business units, setting marketing objectives, performing situation analysis, developing marketing strategy, implementing tactics, and monitoring results.

Subjective Price A consumer's perception of the price of a good or service as being high, fair, or low.

Subliminal Advertising A highly controversial kind of promotion because it does not enable the audience to consciously decode a message.

Substantiation A consumer-protection legal concept that requires a firm to be able to prove all the claims it makes in promotion messages. This means thorough testing and evidence of performance are needed before making claims.

Supercenter A combination store that integrates an economy supermarket with a discount department store, with at least 40 per cent of sales from nonfood items.

Surcharges A form of price adjustment in which across-the-board price increases are published to supplement list prices. These may be used with catalogs because of their simplicity; an insert is distributed with the catalog.

Survey Gathers information from respondents by communicating with them in person, by phone, or by mail.

Systems Selling A combination of goods and services provided to a buyer by one vendor. This gives the buyer one firm with which to negotiate and an assurance of consistency among various parts and components.

T

Tactical Plan Specifies the short-run actions (tactics) that a firm undertakes in implementing a given market strategy.

Tangible Product A basic physical entity, service, or idea; it has precise specifications and is offered under a given description or model number.

Target Market The particular group(s) of customers a firm proposes to serve, or whose needs it proposes to satisfy, with a particular marketing program.

Target Market Strategy Consists of three general phases: analyzing consumer demand, targeting the market, and developing the marketing strategy.

Target Pricing A form of cost-based pricing in which prices are set to provide a particular rate of return on investment for a standard volume of production—the level of production a firm anticipates achieving. Mathematically, it is

$$\text{Target price} = [(\text{Investment costs} \times \text{Target return on investment \%}) / \text{Standard volume}] + [\text{Average total costs (at standard volume)}]$$

Tariff The most common form of trade restriction, in which a tax is placed on imported products by a foreign government.

Technology Refers to developing and using machinery, products, and processes.

Telemarketing An efficient way of operating, whereby telephone communications are used to sell or solicit business or to set up an appointment for a salesperson to sell or solicit business.

Test Marketing The stage in the new-product planning process which involves placing a fully developed new product (a good or service) in one or more selected areas and observing its actual performance under a proposed marketing plan.

Time Expenditures Refer to the activities in which a person participates and the time allocated to them.

Total-Cost Approach Determines the distribution service level with the lowest total costs—including freight (shipping), warehousing, and lost business. An ideal system seeks a balance between low expenditures on distribution and high opportunities for sales.

Total Quality A process- and output-related philosophy, whereby a firm strives to fully satisfy customers in an effective and efficient manner. It requires a customer focus; top management commitment; an emphasis on continuous improvement; and support from employees, suppliers, and distribution intermediaries.

Trade Character A brand mark that is personified.

Trade Deficit The amount by which the value of imports exceeds the value of exports for a country.

Trademark A brand name, brand mark, or trade character or combination thereof that is given legal protection.

Trade Quota A form of trade restriction which sets limits on the amounts of products that can be imported into a country.

Trade Surplus The amount by which the value of exports exceeds the value of imports for a country.

Traditional Break-Even Analysis Finds the sales quantity, in units or dollars, that is needed for total revenues to equal total costs at a given price:

$$\text{Break-even point (units)} = \frac{\text{Total fixed costs}}{\text{Price} - \text{Variable costs (per unit)}}$$

$$\text{Break-even point (sales dollars)} = \frac{\text{Total fixed costs}}{1 - \dfrac{\text{Variable costs (per unit)}}{\text{Price}}}$$

Traditional Department Store A department store that has a great assortment of goods and services, provides many customer services, is a fashion leader, and often serves as an anchor store in a shopping district or shopping center.

Truck/Wagon Wholesalers Limited-service merchant wholesalers that generally have a regular sales route, offer items from a truck or wagon, and deliver goods while they are sold.

U

Unbundled Pricing A strategy that breaks down prices by individual components and allows the consumer to decide what to purchase.

Uncontrollable Factors The external elements affecting an organization's performance that cannot be fully directed by that organization and its marketers. These include consumers, competition, suppliers and distributors, government, the economy, technology, and independent media.

Undifferentiated Marketing (Mass Marketing) Exists when a company targets the whole market with a single basic marketing strategy intended to have mass appeal.

Unfair-Sales Acts (Minimum Price Laws) Legislation in a number of states that prevents firms from selling products for less than their cost plus a fixed percentage that includes overhead and profit.

Unitary Demand Exists if price changes are exactly offset by changes in the quantity demanded, so total sales revenue remains constant.

Unit Pricing Lets consumers compare price per quantity for competing brands and for various sizes of the same brand. With it, prices are shown per unit of measure, as well as by total price.

Universal Product Code (UPC) A series of thick and thin vertical lines used by manufacturers to pre-mark items. Price and inventory data codes are represented by these lines, which are not readable by employees and customers but are read by scanners.

Unplanned Business District A retail location form that exists where multiple stores are located close to one another without prior planning as to the number and composition of stores. The four unplanned sites are central business district, secondary business district, neighborhood business district, and string.

UPC *See* Universal Product Code.

V

VALS (Values and Life-Styles) Program A classification system for segmenting consumers in terms of a broad range of demographic and life-style factors. The VALS program divides final consumers into life-style categories.

Value Analysis A comparison of the costs and benefits of alternative materials, components, designs, or processes so as to reduce the cost/benefit ratio of purchases.

Values and Life-Styles Program *See* VALS Program.

Variability in Service Quality Differing service performance from one purchase occasion to another. Variations may be due to the service firm's difficulty in problem diagnosis (for repairs), customer inability to verbalize service needs, and the lack of standardization and mass production for many services.

Variable Markup Policy A form of cost-based markup pricing whereby separate categories of goods and services receive different percentage markups. Variable markups recognize that some items require greater personal selling, customer service, alterations, and end-of-season markdowns than others.

Variable Pricing Allows a firm to intentionally alter prices in response to cost fluctuations or differences in consumer demand.

Variety Store A retailer that sells a wide assortment of inexpensive and popularly priced merchandise.

Vending Machine A nonstore retail operation that uses coin- or card-operated machinery to dispense goods or services. It eliminates the need for salespeople, allows 24-hour sales, and can be placed outside rather than inside a store.

Vendor Analysis An assessment of the strengths and weaknesses of current or new suppliers in terms of quality, customer service, reliability, and price.

Venture Team A product management organizational format in which a small, independent department consisting of a broad range of specialists is involved with a specific new product's entire development process. Team members work on a full-time basis and act in a relatively autonomous manner.

Vertical Audit An in-depth analysis of one aspect of a firm's marketing strategy. It is also known as a functional audit.

Vertical Price Fixing Occurs when manufacturers or wholesalers seek to control the final selling prices of their goods or services.

Voluntary Simplicity A consumer life-style in which people have an ecological awareness, seek product durability, strive for self-reliance, and buy simple products.

W

Warehousing Involves the physical facilities used to store, identify, and sort goods in expectation of their sale and transfer within a distribution channel.

Warranty An assurance to consumers that a product meets certain standards.

Waste The part of a medium's audience not in a firm's target market.

Waterways Transporters of goods on barges via inland rivers and on tankers and general-merchandise freighters through the Great Lakes, intercoastal shipping, and the St. Lawrence Seaway.

Wearout Rate The time it takes for a message to lose its effectiveness.

Wheel of Retailing A concept describing how low-end (discount) strategies can evolve into high-end (full service, high price) strategies and thus provide opportunities for new firms to enter as discounters.

Wholesale Cooperatives Full-service merchant wholesalers owned by member firms to economize functions and provide broad support. There are producer-owned and retailer-owned wholesale cooperatives.

Wholesalers Buy or handle merchandise and its subsequent resale to organizational users, retailers, and other wholesalers.

Wholesaling Includes buying and/or handling goods and services, and their subsequent resale to organizational users, retailers, and/or other wholesalers—but not the sale of significant volume to final consumers.

Word-of-Mouth Communication The process by which people express opinions and product-related experiences to one another.

World Trade Organization (WTO) An organization whose mission is to open up international markets even further and promote a cooperative atmosphere around the globe.

WTO *See* World Trade Organization.

Y

Yield Management Pricing A form of demand-based pricing whereby a firm determines the mix of price-quantity combinations that generates the highest level of revenues for a given period.

Company Index

Name Index

Subject Index

Asterisk (*) indicates that term is defined in the glossary.

MARKETING AROUND THE GLOBE

(Continued from front endpapers)

AUSTRALIA
News Corporation Ltd. owns the *New York Post, TV Guide*, and Fox Broadcasting.

BOTSWANA
Debswana is a joint mining venture between De Beers (South Africa) and the government of Botswana.

CHINA
Kraft Foods International markets Philadelphia cream cheese, Oscar Mayer meats, Miracle Whip salad dressing, and Jell-o gelatin.

CZECH REPUBLIC
Budejovicky Budvar is a 100-year-old Czech beer maker with the European rights to the name Budweiser.

EGYPT
Orascom Foods and Mansour Foods (both of Egypt) have joint ventures with McDonald's (United States) to operate fast-food outlets.

FINLAND
Nokia is a leader in mobile telephones.

FRANCE
Club Méditerranée operates vacation villages around the globe.

GERMANY
Hoescht AG is the world's largest chemical manufacturer.

GREAT BRITAIN (UNITED KINGDOM)
The Body Shop International, featuring natural personal-care products, has more than 1,000 stores in 45 nations.

INDIA
Baja Auto is a leading maker of motor scooters.

INDONESIA
Indofood exports noodles to China, Chile, and Poland.

IRELAND
Waterford Wedgwood PLC makes glassware, crystal, and fine china.

ISRAEL
Osem is the largest food producer in the Middle East.

ITALY
Benetton Group SPA produces the United Colors of Benetton clothing.

JAPAN
Matsushita Electric has such brands as JVC and Panasonic, and owns the Spencer Gifts retail chain.

KENYA
Nuave Motor is the nation's first national vehicle manufacturer.

KOREA
Daewoo Group operates 19 member companies, ranging from shipbuilding to international trading.

LATVIA
Kellogg has a factory that produces Corn Flakes.

MOZAMBIQUE
Mozambique Airlines has purchased Boeing (United States) 737 and 767 jets.

NETHERLANDS
KPMG Peat Marwick, the accounting and consulting firm, is headquartered here.

NEW ZEALAND
H.J. Heinz (United States) now owns Watties Industries, Ltd., a leading food processor.

NIGERIA
Elf Nigeria is developing the Ibewa natural gas field.

PHILIPPINES
San Miguel Corporation is a beverage company distributing such brands as Coca-Cola, Sprite, and San Miguel Pale Pilsen.

POLAND
General Motors has a joint venture with Fabryka Samachodow Osobowych.

RUSSIA
Russkoye Bistro is a chain of fast-food restaurants featuring borscht, pirogi (pastries stuffed with vegetables or meat), and vodka.

SAUDI ARABIA
Heineken (Netherlands), Stroh (United States), and others market nonalcoholic beer brands because alcohol is forbidden.

SOUTH AFRICA
Vodacom has "phone shops" in areas where people do not have private phones.

SWEDEN
Electrolux AB makes Electrolux, Frigidaire, Tappan, and Gibson appliances.

SWITZERLAND
Nestlé brands include Nescafé coffee, Perrier water, Baby Ruth candy, Carnation milk, and Alpo dog food.

THAILAND
Nynex (United States) has a joint venture with TelecomAsia to build two million main phone lines.

TURKEY
Koç Holding AS makes Döktas auto parts, Otoyol trucks, and Tofas autos (under license from Italy's Fiat).